IRENÄUS EIBL-EIBESFELDT

Human Ethology

Aldine de Gruyter

New York

Aldine de Gruyter
A Division of Walter de Gruyter, Inc.
200 Saw Mill River Road
Hawthorne, New York 10532

Library of Congress Cataloging-in-Publication Data

Eibl-Eibesfeldt, Irenäus.
    [Biologie des menschlichen Verhaltens. English]
    Human ethology / Irenäus Eibl-Eibesfeldt.
        p.   cm. — (Foundations of human behavior)
    Translation of: Die Biologie des menschlichen Verhaltens.
    Bibliography: p.
    Includes index.
    ISBN 0-202-02030-4
    1. Genetic psychology. 2. Behavior evolution. 3. Psychobiology.
I. Title. II. Series.
    [DNLM: 1. Behavior. 2. Genetics, Behavioral. 3. Psychology,
Social. HM 251 E34b]
BF701.E4313 1989
304.5—dc19
DNLM/DLC/DLC
for Library of Congress   88-38152
                                                                CIP

Printed in the United States of America
10 9 8 7 6 5 4 3 2 1

Contents

Preface

With the discovery of conditioned reflexes by I. P. Pavlov, the possibilities for experimenting, following the example set by the classical, exact sciences, were made available to the behavioral sciences. Many psychologists hoped that the component parts of behavior had also been found from which the entire, multi-faceted cosmos of behavior could then be constructed. An experimentally oriented psychology subsequently developed including the influential school of behaviorism. Motivated by pedagogical idealism, psychologists indulged in the hope that education could achieve every desired result. Among behaviorists, the Lockean conviction that humans come into the world with "clean slates" crystallized into a doctrine. It seems certain that this conceptual approach restricted research interest. Although behaviorists carefully investigated the various aspects of learning behavior, and extracted some fundamental laws of learning, their theoretical fixation prevented their perceiving other possible approaches. The possibility that some aspects of behavior might, through phylogenetic adaptation, be genetically programmed was not even considered. Anyone referring to a possible antecedent innate human nature was, until recently, dismissed as a biological determinist or reductionist. As late as the 1970s, the majority of behaviorists and sociologists viewed humans as primarily passive beings subject to the formative influences of their surroundings. It was believed that through rewards and punishments almost all human behavior could be "conditioned" (B. F. Skinner, 1938, 1971). Such an extreme environmentalist approach would consign all behavior to learning, relegate all power to the educators, and ultimately, legitimize them to establish behavior norms as well. Parallel to the development of behaviorism in psychology there developed in anthropology a pronounced cultural relativism (discussed critically by W. Rudolph, 1968) according to which culture is a construct on which the laws of biology have no influence. This school of thought is traceable to Franz Boas (1911, 1928, 1938) and its tenets must have reflected the spirit of the times since leading anthropologists acknowledged them (A. L. Kroeber, 1915; M. J. Herskovits, 1950, among others). Margaret Mead can be regarded as one of the victims of this doctrinal teaching; she was so convinced of the relativism of cultures that she saw and recorded only that which fit those theories. Her reports on Samoa, so often cited, could not stand the test of critical review (D. Freeman, 1983).

The decisive impetus for revising this extreme environmental approach came from behavioral biology (ethology). The work of Konrad Lorenz (1935, 1937, 1961) and Nikolaas Tinbergen (1948, 1951) clarified the notion of instinct, a concept which, until this time, was a philosophical speculation of the vitalists. There were, of course, exceptions, such as W. James (1890) who defined "instinct" in fairly modern terms, as capacities of organisms based on an innate neuronal organization. Lorenz and Tinbergen demonstrated that phylogenetic adaptations determine behavior in well-defined ways, and also voiced the opinion that comparable phylogenetic adaptations influence human behavior. By introducing the dimension of phylogeny into the science of behavior their work incorporated Charles Darwin's findings; behaviorists had apparently forgotten to consider the evolutionary aspects of behavior in their theories.

About the same time that Lorenz formulated his theories, Erich von Holst (1935, 1939) refuted the classical reflex theory, according to which all behavior is a response to external stimuli.

Ethologists can look back over the last decade with a certain sense of satisfaction, for within a short span of 10 years, six biological researchers have received the Nobel Prize: Konrad Lorenz, Niko Tinbergen, and Karl von Frisch in 1973 (as founders of ethology) and Roger W. Sperry, David Hubel, and Torsten Wiesel in 1981 (as pioneers of neuroethology).[1]

The discovery that even the behavior of higher vertebrates is preprogrammed in well-definable ways through phylogenetic adaptation has initiated a process of reconsideration in the human sciences, to date so heavily influenced by behaviorism. In 1971, R. Sperry wrote that the new discoveries on the self-organization of the nervous system up to the point of functional maturity has hardly been noticed in disciplines beyond the fields of biology and ethology. Currently, however, the biological approach is well acknowledged by most fields of science dealing with humans.

Konrad Lorenz indicated in his earlier works that the findings of animal behavior research could contribute to the understanding of human behavior. He devoted a number of important chapters to human behavior in *Die angeborenen Formen möglicher Erfahrung* (1943) and in 1950 he designated as one of the most important objectives of ethology the testing of the hypotheses derived from the study of animal behavior through the study of human behavior.

Clearly, this objective consists of more than simply applying to humans the findings and models of animal behavior research. Ethological research on man was needed, and it truly began in the mid-1960s. I have been able to contribute to the development of this field, bringing to it a considerable background of practical field and laboratory experience in animal behavior on a broad comparative basis.

As a student, beginning in 1946, I had the opportunity to study the behavior of amphibians and mammals at the Wilhelminenberg Biological Station (Vienna). A badger that I hand-raised helped me learn a great deal about animal play behavior. It occurred to me that during the course of its play behavior the badger freely combined behavior patterns from a number of different functional systems. Indeed, in its play behavior we can observe the first manifestations of that freedom to perform derived from voluntary motor control and the ability to detach behavior patterns from emotions which also lies at the root of man's behavioral freedom (I. Eibl-Eibesfeldt, 1950).

In 1949–1950, I joined Lorenz at the newly established Research Center for Behavioral Physiology of the Max Planck Society. In addition to my interest in behavioral development, questions regarding communication caught my attention. How do signals guide the course of social interactions? How do they originate, and how does the understanding of signals develop? In this area I was particularly concerned with the ritualization of aggressive behavior (I. Eibl-Eibesfeldt, 1955a, 1959).

---

[1]Erich von Holst is only absent from this list since his death took him from us too soon.

On a 10-month expedition led by Hans Hass to the Caribbean Sea and the Galapagos Islands, I had the opportunity to study the cleaning symbiosis of fishes and other interspecific relationships of coral fishes (I. Eibl-Eibesfeldt, 1955b). I also observed the ritualized fights of marine iguanas, and became acquainted with adaptive radiation from first-hand observation of Darwin's finches. On another diving expedition (1957–1958), again with Hans Hass, I spend 1 year in the Maldive and Nicobar Islands. My main interest was the behavior and ecology of coral fishes. I assembled a large collection of these fishes and learned much about systematics and functional morphology. On these two research voyages[2] I sharpened my appreciation for interrelationships, especially those concerning ecological factors.

After returning from this expedition I became increasingly involved in the nature-nurture debate. I experimentally refuted a number of assertions about the ontogeny of certain behavior patterns and showed how innate and acquired elements in mammalian behavior intercalate (I. Eibl-Eibesfeldt, 1963).

In the early 1960s I began to include human behavior in my research. Through investigations with children deaf and blind from birth, I was able to demonstrate phylogenetic adaptations in human behavior (I. Eibl-Eibesfeldt, 1973). Between 1963 and 1965 I began with the documentation of unstaged ("natural") human social interactions. The impulse came from my friend Hans Hass, who provided the technical requisites through the development of a specialized reflex lens (p. 112). We tested this technique in 1964 in Africa and in 1965 on a world-wide expedition (I. Eibl-Eibesfeldt and H. Hass, 1966, 1967). From this experience, we developed a program of cross-cultural documentation of human social interactions and rituals on film and tape.

For the longitudinal studies, I selected a number of cultures with different subsistence strategies and which, within certain limitations, could also serve as models for different stages of cultural evolution–from Paleolithic hunters and gatherers to farming societies. In 1970, I was entrusted with an Institute for Human Ethology within the organization of the Max Planck Society.

Cross-cultural documentation formed a principal part of our efforts.[3] We investigated phylogenetic and cultural adaptations, the development of rituals and their function, and, in general, the behavior patterns of communication. In studying strategies of social interactions, I found that certain verbal and nonverbal interactions are structured according to the same universal rules. The exploration of this universal system of rules that structure social behavior is at present one key aspect of our research efforts. To achieve this goal, we are working in conjunction with linguists. In 1967, I concluded my animal ethological studies with the publication of *Ethology: The Biology of Behavior*.[4]

---

[2]A summary is found in the more recently published books *Galapagos* (7th ed., Piper, 1984) and *Die Maldiven* (Piper, 1982).

[3]I spent over 4 years in the field gathering comparative cultural documentation: 1568 days at the target sites (excluding travel time). During this time I produced approximately 200 km of 16 mm film. Many of my findings are based on this large body of material. My zoological field experience comprises 1488 days—in total over 8 years of expedition experience.

[4]Grundriß der vergleichenden Verhaltensforschung, Piper, Munich. The 6th edition of this work appeared in 1980.

As a supplement to my textbook on animal behavior, this new text on human ethology is based on the latter half of my life's work.[5] The findings on animal ethology are only occasionally cited in this work and then only to the extent that they contribute to the understanding of ethological concepts.

I hope that this first text on human ethology presents itself as a unified work, even though not every area could be treated with equal depth. For example, a branch of ethology has developed in the past decades which places particular emphasis on ecology and population genetics. This field, known as sociobiology, has enriched discussion beyond the boundaries of behavioral biology through its stimulating, and often provocative, theses. I will discuss some of its contributions when appropriate in this volume, but, of course, cannot cover this new field in depth.

After vigorous debates between behaviorists, anthropologists, and sociologists, we have entered a period of exchange of thoughts and a mutual approach, which in many instances has led to cooperative projects of researchers from different disciplines. This work offers a biological point of view for discussion and includes data from my own cross-cultural work and research from the staff of our institute. It confirms, above all else, the astonishing unity of mankind and paints a basically positive picture of how we are moved by the same passions, jealousies, friendliness, and active curiosity. It is hoped that it encourages further discussion and thought across traditional academic boundaries.

Before turning to the text, I would like to add that the need to understand ourselves has never been so great as it is today. An ideologically torn humanity struggles for its survival. Our species, who is in a position to send satellites to Mars and Venus and to broadcast photographs of Saturn and Jupiter from space, is helpless when confronted with its social problems. It does not know how it should compensate its workers, and it experiments with various economic systems, constitutions, and forms of government. It struggles for freedom and stumbles into newer conflicts. Population growth is apparently completely out of hand, and at the same time many resources are being depleted. With the continuation of the present exponential growth of the world population looms the catastrophe of a global breakdown of populations. In his book *Mutations of Mankind,* Pierre Bertaux (1963) writes: "Assessing contemporary human existence as a biological phenomenon is not only permissible but mandatory. Anyone rejecting this approach fails to recognize the significance of our existence and thus the extent of human responsibility. . . ." Our hope is to develop an ethic for human survival through gaining insight into the biological processes governing our lives. We must consider our existence rationally in order to understand it, but certainly not with cold, calculating reason but with the warm feeling of a heart concerned for the welfare of later generations. May this book contribute to such an outlook.

Professor Dr. Irenäus Eibl-Eibesfeldt

---

[5]My prior books on this subject include: *Love and Hate. The Natural History of Elementary Behavioral Patterns* (10th ed., 1982); *The !Ko Bushman Society. Group Formation and Aggression Control in a Hunting and Gathering People* (1973); *Pre-programmed Man* (4th ed., 1982); *New Pathways of Human Research* (2nd ed., 1984).

Acknowledgments

In the past 20 years, I have spent nearly one-fourth of my time in societies whose members still follow traditional living patterns. Few of them will read the lines in this book, but perhaps some of their children will, which would make me happy indeed. It would be one of the ways in which my gratitude to them could be expressed—for their hospitality and for what they taught me.

I am especially indebted to my wife Lorle and my children Bernolf and Roswitha for their courage and good spirits during the extended absences necessitated by my expeditions and field studies.

Konrad Lorenz, whom I have regarded as my fatherly friend for the past 40 years, promoted my work in many ways. We engaged in endless conversations and he was open to my ideas. His openness always remained a model for me. I also express my special thanks to another close friend: Hans Hass, who, 35 years ago, led me through the reefs of the Caribbean Sea, and who developed in the early 1960s the reflex lens, the key to our cross-cultural documentary work. The unforgettable diving expeditions on the "Xarifa" were followed by no less fascinating expeditions to human communities where we tested new methods of documentation. Some of the thoughts in this volume were developed on these shared journeys. We have also worked together as editors of the human ethology film archives of the Max Planck Society.

I thank my expedition companions of many years. Quite aside from their assistance, they have enhanced, with their human presence, the pleasure of conducting field work. Thus, I thank from my heart: Kuno Budack, Volker Heeschen, Hans Joachim Heinz, Harald Herzog, Dieter Heunemann, Wulf Schiefenhövel, and Heide Sbreszny-Klein. I thank my co-workers at the Institute and my many friends in Europe and overseas, especially my colleagues Jürgen Aschoff, Ingrid Bell-Krannhals, Norbert Bischof, William Charlesworth, Mario von Cranach, Derek Freeman, Elke and Karl-Friedrich Fuhrmeister, Inga Goetz, Karl Grammer, Anna Guggenberger, Bernhard Hassenstein, Klaus Helfrich, Eckhardt Hess, Les Hiatt, Barbara Hold, Franz Huber, Hermann Kacher, Erich Klinghammer, Gerd Koch, Otto Koenig, Renate Krell, Cornelia von Laue-Canady, Ernie Reese, Margaret and Wolfgang Schleidt, Reinhard Schropp, Gunter Senft, Christa Sütterlin, Pauline Wiessner-Larsen and Wolfgang Wickler.

Special thanks are due to the governments of Australia, Botswana, Indonesia, Namibia, Papua New Guinea, the Philippines, South Africa, and Venezuela, who fostered our work through granting our work permits and who also supported us to the best of their ability. In the field we had continuous help from the local missions. Individual examples include the help of the Salesian Mission in Venezuela; in the early 1970s, the New Tribes Mission in Serra Parima was also a friendly host. Missions in Irian Jaya and Papua New Guinea also helped with their hospitality, by providing transportation assistance and a well-developed infrastructure.

I would like to mention especially the assistance of the German and Austrian embassies, without whom many plans would not have been realized.

The scientific organizations of the Federal Republic of Germany have consistently fostered our work most generously. The Max Planck Society established an independent research center for human ethology and also made possible the creation of a film documentation program. For this sustained support, I thank the Max Planck Society and its President.

Without the financial assistance of the German Research Society (Deutsche Forschungsgemeinschaft) a number of important interdisciplinary projects would not have been carried out. Individual projects were also supported by the Fritz von Thyssen Fund, the Werner von Reimers Fund, and the Maison de l'Homme. The A. von Gwinner Fund provided me with the decisive initial assistance during the early years of my human ethology field research.

I sincerely appreciate the support of Inter Nationes for subsidizing this translation.

It is, furthermore, my great pleasure to thank the Institute for Scientific Film in Göttingen and its director, Hans Karl Galle, for many years of fruitful cooperation.

My heartfelt thanks to Pauline Wiessner-Larsen and Anette Heunemann for their faithful translation of this book. In addition, I wish to express my deepest appreciation to William Charlesworth, Tom Pitcairn, Anne Rasa, and Wulf Schiefenhövel, for consulting and assisting with specific sections of the text.

Last, but not least, I want to thank Melvin Konner, and the Editors of the *Foundation of Human Behavior* series for their interest in my work. I also wish to thank the publisher, and, in particular, Ms. Sheila Johnston, who invested so much work in the final editing of the book.

Mirror-Image Illustrations

The illustrations listed below appear as mirror images when printed since the film sequences from which they were copied were taken with the mirror lens.

2.10, 2.11, 2.15, 2.17, 3.18, 3.19, 3.20c, 3.21A, 3.21B, 3.21C, 3.22, 3.23, 4.1, 4.2, 4.3, 4.5, 4.24, 4.25, 4.26, 4.27, 4.28, 4.30, 4.31, 4.32, 4.33, 4.34, 4.36b,d,e, 4.37, 4.38, 4.40A, 4.40B, 4.41A, 4.41B, 4.46, 4.48, 4.49, 4.50B, 4.67b, 4.68, 4.69, 4.70, 4.77, 4.78, 4.80, 4.81, 4.82, 4.83, 5.1, 5.3, 5.4, 5.5, 5.6, 5.7, 5.8, 5.9, 5.12, 5.13, 5.15, 5.16, 5.18, 5.23, 5.24, 5.26, 5.29, 6.5, 6.13, 6.19, 6.22, 6.23, 6.24A, 6.33, 6.34, 6.35, 6.36, 6.37, 6.38, 6.39a-c, 6.40, 6.45A, 6.45B, 6.47, 6.48, 6.49, 6.54, 6.55b, 6.56, 6.62, 6.64, 6.65, 6.70, 6.71, 6.72, 6.73, 6.74, 6.76, 7.2, 7.3, 7.4, 7.5, 7.6, 7.8, 7.9, 7.10, 7.11, 7.12, 7.13, 7.14A, 7.14B, 7.15, 7.17b, 7.20, 7.21, 7.22, 7.24B, 7.25, 7.29, 7.30, 7.31, 7.32, 7.33, 7.34.

FOUNDATIONS OF HUMAN BEHAVIOR

An Aldine de Gruyter Series of Texts and Monographs

Series Editors
Sarah Blaffer Hrdy, University of California, Davis
Richard W. Wrangham, University of Michigan

Human Ethology. 1989
Irenäus Eibl-Eibesfeldt

Evolutionary History of the "Robust" Australopithecines. 1988
Frederick E. Grine, Editor

Early Hominid Activities at Olduvai. 1988
Richard Potts

Homicide. 1988
Martin Daly and Margo Wilson

The Biology of Moral Systems. 1987
Richard D. Alexander

Child Abuse and Neglect: Biosocial Dimensions. 1987
Richard J. Gelles and Jane B. Lancaster, Editors

Parenting Across the Life Span: Biosocial Dimensions. 1987
Jane B. Lancaster, Jeanne Altmann, Alice S. Rossi, and Lonnie R. Sherrod, Eds.

Primate Evolution and Human Origins. 1987
Russell L. Ciochon and John G. Fleagle, Editors

Human Birth: An Evolutionary Perspective. 1987
Wenda R. Trevathan

School-Age Pregnancy and Parenthood: Biosocial Dimensions. 1986
Jane B. Lancaster and Beatrix A. Hamburg, Editors

Despotism and Differential Reproduction: A Darwinian View of History. 1986
Laura L. Betzig

Sex and Friendship in Baboons. 1985
Barbara Boardman Smuts

Infanticide: Comparative and Evolutionary Perspectives. 1984
Glenn Hausfater and Sarah Blaffer Hrdy, Editors

Navajo Infancy: An Ethological Study of Child Development. 1983
James S. Chisholm

In Preparation

Inujjuamiut Foraging Strategies
Eric Alden Smith

Human Reproductive Ecology
James W. Wood

Ecology, Evolution, and Human Behavior
Eric A. Smith and Bruce Winterhalder, Editors

To the Memory of

My Beloved Friend and Teacher

KONRAD LORENZ

(1903 - 1989)

1

_____

Objectives and
Theoretical Bases of
Human Ethology

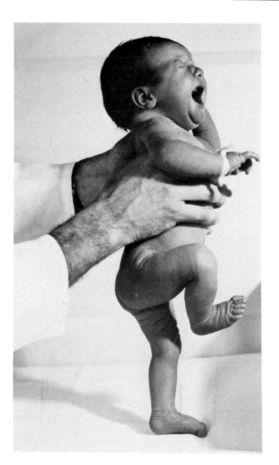

The animal is taught by its organs; man teaches his and controls them.

Johann Wolfgang von Goethe

Whether mankind considers himself the son of God or a successful ape will make a clear difference in his behavior towards actual facts; in both cases he will also hear very different commands from within himself.

Arnold Gehlen (1970, p. 1)

1.1. Inquiry Formulation and Definition

There has never been a shortage of attempts to define man and, by interpretation, attribute meaning to his life. For millennia, priests, artists, and philosophers have considered these questions. Religious revelation has often been contrasted with the efforts to gain insight into human nature through observation and introspection, that is, through experience and with the aid of reason. To this empirical-rational approach, biology gave new impetus with the theory of evolution, a theory that shook our anthropocentric perception of the world. Through evolutionary theory, man became aware not only of his animal heritage, but also of the reality of his incompleteness—man could no longer consider himself as the final "crowning achievement" of creation, but rather, at best, as an intermediate link on the path toward a higher level of humanity.

Of course, this new insight led to a new perspective of man, one of a progressively developing creature, setting ever higher goals and striving toward these objectives. But, at the same time, man became painfully aware that he travels on a narrow ridge, risks toppling off, and is burdened with responsibility, in as much as he accepts his further development as his mission.

If, for some, man was simply one animal species among others, a "naked ape" as Desmond Morris provocatively expressed it, others, in contrast, felt that man had progressed so far above animals in his evolution that he no longer had anything in common with them; that he had gone beyond the biological process of evolution by virtue of his culture. Man, therefore, was considered free to arrange his life in accordance with reason, without any limitations on constraints. These alternate viewpoints became unnecessarily polarized, for both approaches have validity. Biological inheritance determines human behavior, as we will show, in precisely definable parameters. But it is equally true that only man possesses a language, with which he can creatively formulate new statements and thus pass on his cultural heritage by tradition. Only Man can be defined as a cultural being even though some primates show some modest cultural beginnings. Art, reason, and responsible morality, as well as open-mindedness and adaptability, are further distinctive human traits, and no reasonable biologist doubts their special role.[1]

It is important, however, that we are also aware of the more primitive action and reaction patterns that determine our behavior, and to not pretend as if they did not exist. It is especially in the area of social behavior that we are less free to act than we generally assume. This is poignantly demonstrated by the astonishing

---

[1]Konrad Lorenz wrote (1971, p. 509): "Far from underestimating the differences between the previously described behavioral patterns of higher animals and human achievements, molded by reason and morality, I maintain: no one is able to appreciate the uniqueness of these specific human attributes as clearly as those who can perceive them against the background of those much more primitive actions and reactions, which we also share with the higher animals."

discrepancy between our ability to control the external environment and our inability to shape our social life satisfactorily. At the same time that we enthusiastically view the space photographs of Jupiter from the Voyager space probe, we read in our newspapers about executions in Iran, terrorist acts in Ireland, and mass murder in Kampuchea. Of course we should be hopeful for our future based on our potential for responsible morality, but this is possible only when we also recognize the inherited basis of our actions and take them into consideration. In this sense biology can contribute to our enlightenment and emancipation.

Human ethology can be defined as the biology of human behavior. Like its parent discipline ethology, it too is divided into specialties, since the question as to why humans behave one way rather than another can be defined and answered in different ways. If one's interest lies in the function of the underlying physiological mechanisms, then human ethology becomes allied with traditional behavioral physiology. Here we are dealing with an explanation of the proximate cause of a behavior pattern. Inquiry is directed, for example, toward the stimuli that trigger specific responses, how the coordination for muscle action is achieved, what motivates and terminates behavior, as well as other questions. One can also ask how and why specific behavioral patterns evolved. In order to answer these questions, which aim at the ultimate causes, one must first understand in which way the behavior in question contributes to fitness, as measured by the number of surviving offspring. In short, one must establish its function, or in this sense its task. Experimental and ecological designs, including the study of the ontogeny, are used to answer this question.

The observation of behavior in the natural context is an important starting point for such an investigation. Whenever we encounter a structure or a behavioral pattern on a regular basis it is common sense to ask what that pattern's function is, in other words to begin with the presumption that the behavior fulfills some task. It can, of course, be the case that the particular behavior under observation from a selectionistic point of view is either neutral or even a disadvantageous heritage, dragged along as a burden of history, or as a by-product of other adaptations. This is, however, only rarely the case. The various cost–benefit calculations used by sociobiologists constitute a promising new way to study adaptiveness; we shall explore this topic in a special section later in this volume.

Some functions are immediately obvious. If a paleontologist finds a petrified wing impression he needs no experimental procedure to state that this is a flight organ. Should one find the fossil imprint of a structure looking like a camera eye, i.e., with lens, glass body, accommodation structures, and a projection surface like the retina, the investigator can state that he found an eye, an organ used for visual perception. This statement can be made even if the organ was found in a meteorite and it was thus impossible to make any experimental verification of the structure's function.

Questions about function and development can be asked for cultural behavior patterns just as they can for phylogenetically evolved characteristics. We emphasize this because one occasionally comes across the point of view that human ethologists deal only with the basic "animal" heritage in human behavior. This is false. We also investigate man's cultural behavior. Thus questions as to specific adaptiveness can be posed both for phylogenetically and culturally evolved patterns and achievements from the biological point of view mentioned above. O. Koenig (1970) even coined the term "cultural ethology." Excellent examples of the ethological approach to the study of cultural behavior include Koenig's investigations on the biology of uniforms and the ethological analysis of soccer by D. Morris (1981). We must also correct the frequent equating of phylogenetic adaptation with animal heritage. This is unwarranted because there are many phylogenetic adaptations that are specific to *Homo sapiens* alone. Consider, for example, our innate propensity for speech or the expression of crying.

Human ethologists investigate complex behavioral sequences of individuals and of interactions among people and groups of people. They thus work on higher integration levels than physiologists, who are concerned with the elemental life processes such as stimulus perception, muscle contraction, and the conduction of nerve impulses. Although these processes are an important prerequisite to the understanding of behavioral events, one cannot deduce all the laws underlying any given social interaction from these elemental processes. Each higher level of integration has its own laws that cannot be derived from those of the levels below. Special emphasis must therefore be placed on the necessity of formulating questions appropriate to each level of behavioral organization.

Human ethology makes use of experimental and analytical methods of behavioral research developed in related disciplines, including techniques of data sampling developed in anthropology and psychology, such as, the interviewing of informants. From animal ethology we take the methods of nonparticipant observation, techniques of recording and documenting, and the comparative approach. Human ethology also places value in studying behavioral patterns in their natural context (Section 3.3) and thereafter proceeding to experimental analysis.

The theoretical basis of human ethology is critical realism (K. R. Popper, 1973; K. Lorenz, 1973, 1983). Hence, the basic assumption is that every "adaptation" reflects features of a reality outside the subject (p. 8).

In order to make objective statements about the real world, our perception must be capable of reconstructing this world from the sensory data perceived. In order to reconstruct the real world we must be able to recognize constancy, even under changing conditions. Special mechanisms of constancy perception as well as our ability to recognize configurations (Gestalt perception, Section 2.2.2) enable us to do this. Since these are phylogenetic adaptations, we can say that the constancy hypothesis is innate.

The relationships between reality, perception, and knowledge can be demonstrated by using a graphic projection model (G. Vollmer, 1983). If a cube is optically projected onto a screen, we can reconstruct it if we know its structure, the type of the projection, and the characteristics of the screen. In this manner we can accurately reproduce three-dimensional objects from two-dimensional projections on our retina. Even when we look at pictures, we interpret the objects portrayed on them in three dimensions. In the reconstruction of three-dimensional objects, the information lost in the projection process must be recovered. This takes place relatively reliably during the course of the perception process, with the exception of special cases, such as optical illusions.

Cognition can be seen as an effort to reconstruct the real, "true" structures of reality outside the subject from the sensory impressions perceived as projections of these structures. Thus we interpret the cosmic signals perceived by our sensory organs as projections of astronomical objects. That the interpretation of these projections fits the outer world is proved by the success of interplanetary space travel.

The ability to reconstruct a real world from sensory data presupposes a knowledge about this world. This knowledge is based in part on individual experience and, in part, on the achievements of data processing mechanisms, which we inherited as phylogenetic adaptations. Knowledge about the world in the latter instance was acquired during the course of evolution. It is, so to speak, *a priori* knowledge—prior to all individual experience—but certainly not prior to any experience (Section 2.1).

> The process of cognition consists of a step-by-step reconstruction of an hypothetically postulated reality, a stepwise liberation from the limitations of our sensory organs (the "screen" . . .). This reconstruction process works counter to the chain of projections. While each projection effectively reduces information, in the process of cognition we attempt a reconstruction. Naturally, such a reconstruction must remain partial and hypothetical" (G. Vollmer, 1983, p. 64, translation of the German original).

In recent years, promising relationships have developed with other disciplines of human behavior and human culture. In this book we will discuss the work of many researchers who would not regard themselves as ethologists, but whose findings are ethologically relevant. This holds true for psychologists as well as ethnologists, sociologists, political and legal scientists, and art historians.

A particularly close relationship exists with ethnologists and social anthropologists (E. Goffman, 1963, 1967; K. Jettmar, 1973; M. Godelier, 1978; H. Schindler, 1980). Common interests arise from comparative cultural work and from a mutual interest in the general, universal laws of human behavior, as demonstrated, for example, by the structuralism of C. Lévi-Strauss (p. 517). These relationships are so varied that they cannot all be cited here. Our common interests touch on questions of early childhood development and socialization, societal structure, hierarchical organization, aggression, ethical norms, and many more. Ties also exist with psychology and sociology. We will cite specific examples of this in the discussion of these themes. There are further common interests with linguistics, both at the level of concept formation and that of speech itself (p. 523). There have long been mutual relationships with medicine, especially psychiatry and psychoanalysis (D. Ploog, 1964, 1966, 1969; J. Bowlby, 1969, 1973). The growing interest in ethological findings by political scientists is noteworthy. In America, biopolitics has developed as a new discipline (R. D. Alexander, 1979; C. Barner-Bárry, 1983; P. A. Corning, 1981, 1983b; H. Flohr and W. Tönnesmann, 1983; R. D. Masters, 1976, 1981b, c; G. Schubert, 1973, 1975, 1983b; A. Somit, 1976; A. Somit and R. Slagter, 1983). Art history and archeology have also been inspired by findings from ethology (D. Fehling, 1974; G. C. Rump, 1978, 1980; M. Schuster and H. Beisl, 1978).

Summary 1.1

Human ethology can be defined as the biology of human behavior. The research objectives are the elucidation of the physiological mechanisms underlying behavior, the discovery of the functions fulfilled by behavioral patterns and thus the unveiling of the selective pressures to which the behavior in question owes its existence, and, finally, the investigation of behavioral development in ontogeny, phylogeny, and cultural history, with emphasis on the question as to how and to what extent Man became programmed to act through phylogenetically acquired adaptations or by learning during individual ontogeny. Human ethology makes use of the concepts and methods developed in animal ethology, but adapts them to the special requirements associated with the unique position of man within the Animal Kingdom. Methodological techniques are also utilized from the related disciplines of psychology, anthropology, and sociology. Through points of mutual interest human ethology thus endeavors to bridge the gap between the different human sciences. Human ethologists study not only the phylogenetically evolved behavior of man but also its individual and cultural modifiability. Critical realism is the epistemological basis of human ethology.

> *Oh, great star! What would you be, had you not those on which to shine?*
> Friedrich Nietzsche (from Zarathustra's prologue)

1.2. Phylogenetic and Cultural Adaptation

Life is defined today as an energetic process during which organisms, bearers of this process, extract more potential energy from their environment than they must expend in the acquisition of this energy. In other words, organisms are energy-acquiring systems with a positive energy balance. H. Hass (1970), the first to clearly formulate this concept to my knowledge, originated the term "Energon" for such energy-acquiring systems. The life processes are maintained by the multiplicity of organisms and by those energy-acquiring systems developed by them. Although we can trace the development of the process throughout evolution, we have yet to understand its ultimate causes.

The energetic process presupposes structures at its disposal that are "adapted" to the appropriate energy transformations. Each organism must possess structures with which it can extract energy from the environment. These structures are adapted to the appropriate energy sources, that is, they are so constructed that they can tap the specific energy sources and thus aid in the maintenance of the energy-acquiring system.

The environment is not only the source of energy but also the source of a multitude of interfering and even harmful influences against which the organism must protect itself. Organisms must also repair damage and be able to transform their positive energy balance into the procreation of their species. In short, there are a multitude of adaptations that require energy investment, such as reproduction, growth, protection, and similar tasks, which enter the balance as costs (H. Hass, 1970).

Since organisms live in an ever-changing environment, they must be able to modify their adaptations in response to these changes. This may even require changes in their basic construction. Furthermore, there are a variety of changes to which an organism must continually adapt during its lifetime. Thus it must be able to institute short-term, reversible changes in response to temporary environmental changes. The musculature and circulatory systems must be able to adapt to new stresses, and calluses must be able to form on the skin in response to pressure. Finally, an animal must be able to learn from experience in such a way that it modifies its behavior *adaptively*. Adaptive here refers to fitness as measured by reproductive success or, ultimately, the propagation of the genes of the individual in question (see inclusive fitness, p. 92).

Adaptation is thus a central problem for all organisms. Since the entire nature–nurture controversy centers around the question of the source of adaptation, we will add a few basic remarks about this subject here.

Adaptations depict features of the environment relevant to survival. They reflect facets of the external reality, such as, characteristics of the energy source they

7

tap or the environment in which they move. Thus, certain characteristics of water are reflected in the anatomy of fishes and dolphins, by adaptations that are functionally related to the movement of these organisms in this medium. This is what is meant when we say that an adaptation reflects features of the environment. The degree of detail and exactness in which an adaptation depicts the outer world varies from case to case since it is determined by function. The organism only reflects characteristics of the environment relative to fitness and not every detail of the environment. However, the match can be amazingly complete, as for example in the case of mimicry, in which a mimic imitates its model even down to the smallest details. The leaf insects, for example, mimic the leaves of the shrubs on which they live. Interesting examples of mimicry are reviewed in W. Wickler (1968).

K. Lorenz (1941, 1973) has made a significant contribution to the question of what constitutes reality in his biological epistemology. In our adaptations we do not depict the external world—pictorially (iconically), but our thought processes and our perceptual capabilities fit as adaptations in the same way as do our physical characteristics. "Our cognitive and perceptual categories, given to us prior to individual experience, are adapted to the environment for the same reasons that the horse's hoof is suited for the plains before the horse is born, and the fin of a fish is adapted for water before the fish hatches from its egg" (K. Lorenz, 1941, p. 99, translation of the German original).

The adaptations of an organisms, whether these are bodily structures or adaptations in behavior, represent assumptions (hypothesis) about the world in which it is going to live—assumptions which have been tested by selection.

Our perceptual organizations come into disarray when we move into other environments to which we are not phylogenetically adapted, as for example in the atomic or astronomical environments. Our causal thought processes are proof of this. We associate events by means of rigidly determined programs and extrapolate from the coincidence of events: When-then (coincidence) to causes (because—then). We can only think in causal sequences, and this becomes a problem when we use these intellectual tools to inquire into the origin of the universe. David Hume states that causality may not actually exist in nature, but that it is just a "necessity of the soul." The remarkable essay by R. Riedl (1981) contains a chapter on the consequences of causal thought: "The Superstition of Causes." This chapter title is misleading and more appropriately should have been "The Established Faith in Causes," since for the middle level—the "mesocosmos"—causal thinking is an appropriate adaptation. Accurate knowledge based on an iconic depiction of reality cannot be accomplished and is not really necessary for research. We perceive the world with preconceived perceptual and thought processes that strongly influence the postulation of our hypotheses (p. 105). Our perceptive and cognitive mechanisms, nonetheless, fit well enough to an outer world to enable us to send satellites into outer space, which will eventually arrive at their goal even after years of travel. That our cognition is capable of this is a matter of interest and it is more reasonable to assume that our cognition corresponds to external reality than to take the standpoint which disavows the existence of a world independent of a perceiving subject. In P. Watzlawick's (1981) *Die erfundene Wirklichkeit* ("Invented Reality"), these problems are precisely and intelligibly discussed by the various authors. Other notable contributions have been made by R. Riedl (1979), G. Vollmer (1975, 1983), D. Campbell (1974), and G. Radnitzky and W. W. Bartley (1987).

In their organization, organisms mirror facets of the extrasubjective environment. Even though the postulates of critical realism are neither demonstrable nor refutable, as Karl R. Popper states, we can "argue in their favor, and the arguments are convincing" (K. R. Popper, 1973, p. 50, translated from the original German text). This is the position any sensible scientist must take. Whether this is "critical realism" or "hypothetical realism" is, from my point of view, of little significance. G. Vollmer (1983) is of the opinion that one must differentiate between these, since critical realism at least considers the existence of the world as evident, retrospectively unquestioned and intuitively guaranteed, while hypothetical realism differentiates between psychological certainty (hypothesis about the world) and epistemological uncertainty. But critical realists like Popper have a clear understanding of the epistemological uncertainty, and the hypothetical realists proceed from the postulation of an extrasubjective reality, which we reflect incompletely but nevertheless fittingly in our adaptations. This is not surprising, for, using an illustration from Ernst Mayr: the monkey without a realistic perception of the branch on which he wants to jump would soon be a dead monkey—and thus would not be one of our ancestors.

From the above it is evident that every adaptive system must have acquired "information" from its environment at some time relevant to the organism's adaptations, which reflect these environmental features. For this to occur, the organism has had to have interacted with the environment (K. Lorenz, 1961). Such an interaction can occur during phylogeny through the mechanisms of mutation, recombination, and selection. Information relative to survival has thus been collected each generation and became codified genetically, providing the developmental instructions that guide the process of self-differentiation by which the individual organisms or phenotypes develop. This developmental scheme is so strongly controlled by the genes that each individual develops the various species-specific structures during ontogeny. Special feedback mechanisms prevent excessive deviations from the blueprint. This is why sparrows hatch from sparrow eggs and chaffinches from chaffinch eggs and not, accidentally, a duck.

Each characteristic develops within a specified range of variation. This range—the reaction norm—is genetically determined and thus the result of phylogenetical adaptation. The modifications of plants in different habitats illustrate this point. The mountain forms of many plants often have feltlike hairs and are generally shorter-stemmed and more compact than conspecifics growing in valleys. Such variability is clearly adaptive in most cases. However, it can also be an epiphenomenon. There are plants that develop red flowers in acid soil and blue in alkaline soil. The anthocyanins (flower pigments) turn red in acidic cell fluids and blue in weakly alkaline ones. We have not been able to deduce the selective advantage for certain plants to possess both color morphs depending on habitat. Perhaps this characteristic of the range of variation is neutral in terms of selection and may even be an epiphenomenon. The range of variation during development is limited and the environmental pressures cannot force modifications to occur in any arbitrary direction. However, the genetically determined prospective potential is often greater than what is normally observed. Gall wasps possess chemical means of stimulating plant tissue to grow galls, which they would not normally do. Generally the range of modifiability of genetically determined processes of differentiation is rather limited, and the prospective potential decreases with each further step in differentiation.

Phylogenetic development is not directed toward specific goals. The direction taken is dictated more by selection contingencies. In a process analogous to trial-and-error learning, an exploration of possibilities takes place at the level of the species. Many writers have been disturbed by the decisive role of "chance" in the development of the amazing diversity of organisms. Once, however, it is made clear that basically it is a question of species maintaining themselves in an environment of unforeseen changes, then it is understandable that such adaptation only works when a continual testing of all possibilities of constructive change takes place. This is the only way that "promising monsters" (R. B. Goldschmidt, 1940) can be created and open new pathways in evolution.[2] These can be ethological (p. 14) or morphological monsters. Thus in every generation of flies there are wingless mutants that are weeded out from the population as being malformed. However, that even such monsters of evolution have a chance can be seen in the subarctic Kerguelen Islands, where only wingless insects live (beetles, butterflies, and flies). The winged forms are continually blown off the island by storms.

From generation to generation, new genetic variants are thus created and tested by selection. They are, in a way, set into the world to test for new changes that might have come about. Extreme specialization limits the potential for further evolution. Whereas the pentadactylid foreleg of the vertebrate had the potential to evolve into the fin of the whale, the wing of a bat or the hooves of a horse, the potential of these latter specialized structures is greatly limited. A fin cannot become reconstructed into an extremity with five fingers or a wing. Specialists, therefore, run a greater risk of extinction when their environment changes drastically. The future lies with the generalists.

During the daily life of organisms there are numerous situations in which a rapid adaptability is advantageous. An insect seeking flowers would benefit from remembering where a plant had just blossomed. It is also advantageous for animals to remember where predators are or which pathway is a safe escape route. It is useful when an animal can learn from individual experience, i.e., is able to retain information about specific data or experiences, to store this information, and to adapt its behavior accordingly. During the course of phylogeny, structures of the central nervous system evolved that permitted individual experiences to be stored in recallable engrams so that future behavior could be adjusted accordingly on the basis of these experiences. Here, as well, phylogenetic adaptations determine whether what is learned is obligatory or optional. Animals learn what contributes to their fitness and, since this varies from species to species, innate learning dispositions vary accordingly (p. 74).

Even though learning is based on phylogenetic adaptations and channeled by

---

[2]Chance is creative in this way. H. Markl (1980) has provided a pertinent definition: "I have dealt with these problems so exhaustively because chance stands in such poor stead with learned people: chance, it is said, is never creative. It is merely known as the unimaginative shepherd pushing his herd of events toward the gate of average expectation, lacking any originality. Rarely has something been so badly misjudged. For it is only through chance that something new can arise, for novel value only exists in terms of that which does not follow the undeviating path of the standard laws. If we termed it 'spontaneity,' we would recognize the unpredictable character that only freedom of behavior can produce. However, it is important from the molecular level to that of behavior: chance, left to itself, can create nothing lasting, for it destroys as it builds. A mechanism that evaluates chance, retaining the useful and rejecting the unusable, is required to put to use the innovative potential of chance. Chance produces nothing of value without a selection process occurring, but selection has nothing to select without chance" (translated from the German original).

them, new perspectives of evolution were opened with learning, which, among others, is one of the prerequisites for cultural evolution.

In general, each animal learns from experience for itself only. However, some species can also learn by imitation. In a free-living group of Japanese macaques on the Japanese island of Koshima, a female discovered the washing of sweet potatoes before eating them. The others saw this and imitated her. Today this behavior has become established as a group-specific characteristic and is a tradition passed on from one generation to the next. Such behavior is sometimes described as "protocultural," but it was only with the evolution of speech and the subsequent development of writing and other information storage systems that true culture could arise.

In the protocultural stage, one individual has to show another the behavior to be learned. With the development of speech it became possible to carry on a tradition independently of an object by verbal instruction alone. One Japanese macaque must always see another washing potatoes, but one person can instruct another by saying, "We wash potatoes before we eat them." He could also permanently record this information in writing so that it would be available for centuries to literate individuals. Thus, with the introduction of writing, a new, more powerful data bank becomes available to assist the memory enabling knowledge to be passed on without the presence of another society member. Thus accumulative culture develops.

With cultural evolution a new level of existence is achieved, since culturally acquired knowledge can maintain existence, to a large extent, independently of its inventors. If the inventor of the radio or another technical innovation died without heirs, the invention could still be perpetuated. Theoretically it could even be utilized by genetically unrelated inhabitants of another planet. Ideologies can survive in the same way and thus have an existence of their own. K. R. Popper (1973) speaks of a world of objective thought content, which exists even though it is a product of our mental activity. The products of this world (theories, books, and others) can be studied without knowledge of the ways in which they originated, in the same way as we can investigate spider webs and bird nests without having seen the animals that made them. Books can outlive us and be studied by other intelligent beings. Popper categorizes this world of objective ideas as World 3, with the world of states of consciousness and behavioral dispositions (World 2), and the physical world (World 1).[3]

All our "artificial organs" (H. Hass, 1970), from tools to books and from factories to expressways, belong to Popper's World 3. They demonstrate effectively how much and in which ways our accumulating culture dominates human evolution. New ideas, theories, and inventions act like mutations in the biological realm, and they have to stand the test of selection. The problem to be solved is the survival in offspring and this is achieved by the elimination of mistakes. Popper mentions that anatomical and behavioral adaptations of plants and animals are biological analogs of theories: "Theories correspond (like many external objects such as honeycombs . . .) to bodily organs and their functions. Theories and organs alike are experimental adaptations to the world in which we live" (K. Popper, 1973, p. 125).

---

[3]One can also describe World 2 in broader terms as the world of the organic, which differs from World 1 (physical) since its organization is derived from selective pressure (N. Bischof, 1981).

Progress in knowledge is the result of a process quite similar to natural selection but consists of the selection of competing hypotheses. "This interpretation applies to what animals know, prescientific knowledge and also scientific cognition. While the animal and prescientific knowledge grow mainly because those with unsuitable hypotheses are themselves selected out, scientific critics often let our theories die instead of us; they select against our wrong ideas before we ourselves are eliminated because of them (Popper, 1973, p. 289).

Cultural evolution is by no means always a product of rational planning. F. A. von Hayek (1979) pointed out clearly that mankind, with the ability to imitate and to carry on traditions, develops traditions of learned rules of behavior, whose purposes are, in most instances, not understood. Von Hayek continues that in the past, Man has often learned appropriate behavior without understanding why it is correct, and even today many habits usually serve him better than does rational understanding.

The system of traditional rules was tested and developed in a process of screening, which is analogous to selection on at the biological level. Cultural evolution, therefore, is mainly a result of the forces of selection and is, to a lesser extent, the result of conscious rational planning. In a competitive process, the more successful characteristics prevail. Von Hayek is undoubtedly correct when he states that cultural evolution could proceed without any kind of insight and also when he expresses the opinion it has also done so for the majority of mankind's existence.

If we consider culture to be the totality of traditional adaptations, then his statement that we were not even capable of designing culture is also true. Even today we can only understand partial aspects of our own culture.[4] Nonetheless we must come to terms mentally with the problems of our existence, and through reason come up with solutions. Man has had great success with rational planning in many realms of science, economics, and technology. Furthermore, we can set goals for ourselves and thus significantly influence our further cultural development. The developments initiated by founders of states and ideologists testify to such developments.

Ideologies can reverse developmental trends completely by setting new goals and thus by altering contingencies of selection. Whether this is of advantage or not from the point of view of the fitness of the society would not be determined until later. For those Russian sects that forbade their members to engage in sexual intercourse—and who disappeared soon afterward because of so few new recruits—ideology was shown to be deleterious.

The experiments of modern mass societies, whose ideologies stress the equality of all of its members, are fascinating. With few exceptions, in the majority of cultures, successful men, those controlling the natural resources, also produced more descendants. They could afford to have more women, and the women of their subordinates also stood at their disposal. Successful Yanomami chieftains have more wives and children than others in the tribe (N. A. Chagnon, 1979). In

---

[4]Cause and effect are so intertwined here that we cannot usually use our linear causal reasoning to understand all the relationships operating here. D. Dörner and R. Reither (1978) contributed to this concept in their experiment giving twelve intelligent students the task of improving the living conditions on the fictitious developing country "Tana." The conditions in the country were known and could be varied. In almost all cases, the student destroyed the originally stable structure and often produced catastrophic consequences for the country.

China the wealthy not only had supplemental wives and concubines but also access to the wives of their subordinates. The reigning ideology of the Chou Dynasty (1100–222 B.C.) stated that this was their subjects' obligation and fostered among subordinates the wish to comply since they believed that only the ruling class possessed certain magical powers, which they transmitted for the common good through reproduction.

In the above instances the ideology supported those controlling the society's resources and led to growth in the population of the ruling class at the expense of the lower classes (further examples in K. MacDonald, 1983). With Christianity, which interestingly enough spread first among the slaves and the poor of Rome, the ideology of equality—of "leveling" as Nietzsche expressed it—came into existence. It was directed against those controlling the resources and attempted to construct an ethic of sharing and equalization as well as of enforced monogamy. A papal ban against princes was one means of stopping polygamy in the ruling European classes. The ideology of monogamy with its prohibition against birth control was the most decisive step since it removed the privilege of reproduction from the upper classes. Anyone who was capable of providing nourishment for a family could sire offspring.

The division of property was less important, and such differences were eventually tolerated by Christianity. Such an ideology leads to the situation in which there is not a limited number of privileged families reproducing at a higher rate relative to other classes, but one in which all levels of society reproduce. It remains to be established whether the single wife in a monogamous society without birth control has more children than those in polygamous societies. I believe it is possible but cannot cite any figures for this. Perhaps this was a factor responsible for the great success of Europeans throughout the world. The Hutterites of Canada can act as a model as to how a group with a strict monogamy and no birth control achieves a higher birth rate than other groups in the Canadian population. The question here is what sort of effect this pattern of behavior will have in the long term. Populations who obey an ideology of reproductive egalitarity may experience a rapid increase in number over other groups following other prescriptions. At the same time, however, the further evolution of certain traits may be slowed down.[5]

Man is certainly the first being who consciously set goals. Some went as far as to argue that Man, therefore, overpowered nature—that he emancipated himself from the contraints of biology. But whatever man does will be measured by the yardstick of selection. By striving toward a particular goal set by an ideology man directs his future evolution and secures its course within certain limits against the unpredictabilities of chance. However, it will always be selection that will decide whether his choice was correct. Any kind of concept, even the ideas of an insane person, can influence the fate of a people, for better or worse, just as mutations can in the realm of biology.

Today we are experiencing how selection is sifting out the newly established

---

[5]In this context some recent developments are of interest. D. R. Vining (1986) drew attention to the fact that in modern society the less economically successful produce more children than those better endowed. This leads to a decline of the IQ from one generation to the next in modern societies. Presently this does not need to be a matter of grave concern, since such a trend might be temporary. However, it might be useful to observe further developments.

social and economic systems of the world according to their adaptiveness. We cannot know the results of this experiment, but without doubt various goals have selective consequences, and they may ultimately even influence biological evolution.

In the animal world, behavioral changes are the pacemakers of phylogenetic development (E. Mayr, 1950, 1970). If an insect larva shifts to a plant species not yet utilized by the species and becomes imprinted on the new host plant so that the imago henceforth selects this host plant, this new preference will certainly result in other adaptations in the insects' life habits and anatomy. In choosing this new host plant, the insect was placed under new selective conditions. For example, if the epidermis of the new host plant is firmer, the insect may develop stronger mandibles for biting.

K. R. Popper (1973), in his "speartip theory" of behavioral evolution, independently developed the same ideas as Ernst Mayr. He presumes that specific innate tendencies (the avoidance of danger, search for food, etc.) are subject to mutations without organs of the body being simultaneously affected. Any changes affect only the apparatus controlling behavior—in vertebrates it is the central nervous system and not the morphological structures that carry out the actions. These can be independently altered by other mutations. Mutative changes in the mechanism's guiding behavior (Popper speaks of a "central tendency structure"[6]) generally disturb the functions of an organism less than mutations in structures executing behavior. It is easier to correct maladaptive changes in the central tendency structure with compensating behaviors. New behavioral tendencies can determine further development. Popper cites changes in feeding habits as an example and mentions in this context the classic Lamarckian example: the giraffe. He is of the opinion that changes in the eating habits must have preceded the anatomical neck modifications.

A Darwinian explanation can thus be found for the much discussed topic of orthogenesis (goal-directed evolution).

> If a new goal, tendency, disposition, capability or behavior pattern develops in the central tendency structure, this would influence the effects of natural selection in such a way that previously maladaptive (but potentially favorable) mutations now become adaptive ones if they support the newly developed tendency. *This means, however, that the development of the executing organs will be guided by this new tendency or objective and is thus 'goal-directed'* (K. R. Popper, 1973, p. 305).

Popper (1973) speaks of "promising ethological monsters" (see also p. 10), which deviate markedly from their parents in their behavior and thus introduce new developments. Certainly a new development is more likely to be preceded by a new behavior pattern than it is by a change in structure, since a new behavior is less likely to fatally disturb the functioning of an organism as a whole and is also less likely to prove lethal than a monstrous anatomical change. A new behavior pattern that takes advantage of previously existing light-sensitive structures could significantly enhance their selective value. Thus an "interest" in vision could

---

[6]This "central tendency structure" consists of, on the one hand, built-in instructions, for example, to flee from one situation or to attack in another (Popper speaks of goal structures), and, on the other hand, of situations enabling one to interpret external stimuli (ability structures). These two, however, cannot be distinguished from one another, so Popper introduces the concept of "central tendency structure" to unite both structures.

14

become one of the key factors in the orthogenesis of the eye.[7] In this way, according to Popper, changes in the goal structure lead and the development of the anatomical-physiological structures follow. "As the vitalists claim, the direction can actually be determined by a tendency similar to consciousness—by a goal structure or the capability structure of the organism, which can develop a tendency or a 'wish' to use an eye, and an ability to interpret the perceptions which it perceives from it" (K. R. Popper, 1973, p. 307).

I have referred to these concepts in some depth because I feel they are highly significant for Man. What has been stated here does not only apply to genetically controlled behavioral mutations. In the human sphere, new ideas, ideologies, and other mental concepts, as stated earlier, can also become evolutionary pacemakers and determine its future course. Developments like these lead to cultural delineations and thus initiate separate developments, termed aptly "cultural pseudo-speciation" by E. H. Erikson (1966).

To what extent innate values channel the course of evolution will be discussed later. There are indications that our concepts of "differentiated" and "higher" levels are universal goal structures and thus determine our behavior (p. 659). Cultural evolution is also strongly influenced by altruism, which does not appear to be exclusively a product of culture.

With cultural evolution, mankind developed an adaptive mechanism that in historical times has no doubt exceeded the biological ones in importance. It is probable that cultural changes in life style are followed by subsequent genetic modifications and there are sound indications for this. Lactose tolerance is observed in the majority of adults in peoples living on milk products—a trait lacking in hunter/gatherer societies. Presumably with the discovery of agriculture and the growth of the habit of drinking milk as an adult, a corresponding genetic adaptation was selected for (L. L. Cavalli-Sforza, 1981; further citations therein). In general we have not changed much in our anatomy in the last 20,000 years. And from the way we handle our culturally acquired knowledge we may even assume that our basic behavioral outfit has remained the same. People with the motivations and intellectual capacity of late upper paleolithic man are now flying jet bombers and confronted with the task of surviving in anonymous society.

Since phylogenetic and cultural evolution are shaped by similar selection pressures, cultural evolution phenocopies the biological evolution in many ways. Examples of this are found in the comparison of cultural and phylogenetic ritualization (p. 439). The same functional laws apply to both areas. Thus the rate of change or of mutation should in neither case be excessive, for an excessive mutation rate is dangerous. Progress depends on the balance achieved between the preserving "conservative" forces and those promoting change. We stick to the proven, but experiment with change in small doses. This is certainly "adaptive," because it is improbable that the entire store of cultural tradition should have lost its adaptive value from one generation to the next.

Our need for security makes us cling passionately to our "beloved" customs. It is from this secure base that we experiment with new ideas and insights.

---

[7]"Thus an interest in seeing could be fixed and may become a significant factor in the orthogenesis of the eye; even the smallest improvements in its anatomy could have a high survival value if they were utilized by the organism's goal and capability structure" (K. R. Popper, 1973, p. 311).

Summary 1.2

Living systems owe their organization to processes of adaptation through selection. Adaptations are all structures which contribute to the survival of the individual in question and ultimately to its survival in offspring or in short to its fitness. In their adaptations, organisms mirror features of their outer subjective world relevant to fitness. They represent sets of hypotheses about this world which were tested by selection. Thus a fin of a fish, as well as the motor program for its use, both develop prior to hatching within the egg, represent assumptions about the environment in which the fish is going to live. As a prerequisite for adaptation to occur, an interaction between the adapted organismic system and its environment must take place. During phylogeny, variants of the phenotype, brought about by genetic changes, are tested by selection as to their adaptedness and the genotypes for adaptive traits retained. This way the organisms can be said to inform themselves in a process analogous to a trial and error learning about its environment and that information is coded and stored genetically.

Phylogenetic adaptation is supplemented by adaptation via learning and individual experience, and, in humans, also via traditions. It is in the latter case that information transfer occurs. Cultural evolution phenocopies phylogenesis in many respects, since in both cases the shape of the resulting pattern is determined by selection. Customs must prove themselves in order to be retained. We may, however, learn from failures by eliminating customs without sacrificing the life of the individual at the same time. Behavior patterns are often the pacemakers of further development in both cultural and phylogenetic evolution. Cultural evolution has certainly proceeded in an unplanned manner for most of human existence, and we tend to observe certain customs without insight into their rationale since they have proved themselves beneficial.

Culture, because of its complexities, is difficult to plan, but by the setting of goals its development can be directed.

2

Basic Concepts of Ethology

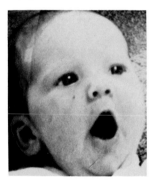

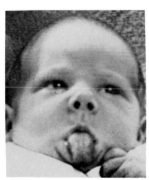

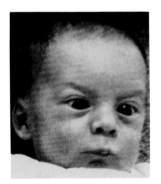

2.1. The Concept of the "Innate"

A blue whale swims with fully coordinated movements immediately after birth. A newborn gnu trots or gallops after its mother when danger threatens, and a freshly hatched duckling waddles into the water, swims with no prior practice, sifts through the mud for food, drinks, and oils its feathers without requiring any model or instructions for these behavior patterns. Hatching the duckling's egg among those of a hen's brood would not alter any of these typical duck behavior patterns. A duckling that hatched with a brood of chicks would, quite contrary to its foster mother's behavior, go straight into the water.

These obviously innate propensities have long been known to behavioral scientists. H. S. Reimarus (1762), Charles Darwin (1872), W. James (1890), and D. A. Spalding (1873) discussed them and distinguished among them and those behavior patterns that an animal acquires during the course of its lifetime through learning processes. They also pointed out that such behavioral patterns do not have to be fully developed at birth. Some behavior patterns mature during the course of ontogeny. Thus, freshly hatched male ducks show no trace of their species-specific courtship patterns. Even if they are raised, however, in complete social isolation, they will nonetheless develop these species-typical courtship behaviors. This simple distinction between innate and learned behavior has proved itself of value in taxonomy. O. Heinroth (1910) employed courtship patterns as distinguishing characteristics in his detailed classification of ducks. He used these patterns in just the same way as morphological characteristics to correctly identify specific systematic categories. He found that homologous movements were modified to a greater or lesser extent according to degree of relatedness in different species and reconstructed the phylogeny of these movements, which he called "arteigene Triebhandlungen," species-specific instinctive behavior patterns. In addition to the species specificity of the movements, the term "Trieb" refers to spontaneity as a characteristic, a quality which we will discuss later. K. Lorenz and N. Tinbergen (1939) spoke of "Erbkoordinationen" (fixed-action patterns) and emphasized that these patterns are passed on through the process of inheritance. More specifically, we may say that fixed-action patterns mature implying that the neuronal networks underlying these behavior patterns grow to functional maturity in a process of self-differentiation, according to the blueprint encoded in the genome of the individual. The processes by means of which a nervous system gets "wired" for its function are basically understood, due to the pioneering work of R. Sperry. Fixed-action patterns are frequently associated with orientation movements (taxes) the combination of which form the more complex "instinctive behavior patterns."

Deprivation experiments have long been used to demonstrate the presence of innate behavioral traits. This methodology has aroused a great deal of criticism. D. S. Lehrman (1953) clearly formulated the argument in a critique directed against Lorenz. Lehrman claimed that the deprivation experiment is meaningless because it is impossible to deprive an animal of all environmental influences. In extreme isolation, an animal is in an environment that influences it, even within the egg or uterus. As a result, it can gain experience and develop the preliminary stages of the behavior pattern in question. He cites the observations of Z. Y. Kuo on the development of precursors to pecking in the chick embryo. I have dealt at length with this and other experiments in *Ethology: The Biology of Behavior* (I. Eibl-Eibesfeldt, 1975, New German edition: 7, 1987).

Lehrman also emphasized that the concept of the innate is defined only from a "negative" point of view by ethologists to mean that "which is not learned." By pointing out a true weakness in the concept of the innate, he made a positive contribution to the discussion of instinct. K. Lorenz (1961) rethought the concept in view of this criticism and defined the concept of the innate positively on the basis of the origin of the adaptation. All adaptations, whether behavioral or morphological represent hypotheses about this world, which have been and which are constantly tested by selection. Some of these hypotheses evolved during phylogeny, others culturally, and, finally, many develop by individual experience, such as by trial and error learning or by insightful discovery. Every adaptation reflects features of a world existing outside the individual, which means, as stated in the previous section, that information concerning these features must have been acquired by the adapted system. To acquire such information, organisms possess three information storage reservoirs: (1) the genetic code; (2) individual memory; and (3) finally, humans have language, the written word, and electronic storing devices, which aid them in creating culture.

The term "innate" refers to phylogenetic adaptiveness. Deprivation experiments are a means to discover whether a behavior pattern owes its adaptiveness to individual learning or to phylogenetic adaptation. By withholding from the developing individual information concerning those features of the environment which the individual reflects in its adaptations, the possibility to adapt by learning is definitely excluded. If adaptive behavior is shown, nevertheless, then we can say that the structure in question owes its adaptedness to phylogeny.

Thus, if a developing bird is prevented from hearing its species-specific song during ontogeny and later still performs the species-typical song, we have irrefutable evidence that the underlying song pattern is based on phylogenetically acquired information, which is genetically coded. The frequently voiced argument that precursors for specific behavior may be found during ontogeny, and that environmental influences could play a role in their development does not invalidate this statement. As I have emphasized repeatedly since 1963, the concept of phylogenetic adaptation always refers only to a specific level of integration. If I assumed the unlikely position that breathing movements of birds were learned, yet the bird developed the species-specific song in isolation, might I then still maintain that this song is phylogenetically adapted? (In this case, the breathing movements would then—so to speak—be the acquired building blocks for the song.) Even if such a learning process as postulated here were fact it would not alter our conclusion about the phylogenetic adaptation of the song, since it refers to a different *level* of integration. The results of this postulated experiment would nonetheless prove that the information concerning the specific patterning of the song (here: melody, rhythm, and syllable formation) did not have to be acquired through individual learning. The necessary information, therefore, which led to the adaptation at this level, must have been acquired during the course of phylogenetic history.

For the same reasons we can state that the food caching behavior of the squirrel is innate (phylogenetically adapted). Every squirrel hides nuts and acorns in the Fall with a sequence of stereotyped behavioral patterns: it digs a hole, places the nut inside, presses it firmly into the ground with rapid snout movements, covers the nut with earth using alternating foreleg strokes, and finally pats the earth firm with its front paws. This adaptive sequence is also carried out by squirrels which grow up in complete social isolation and which are completely deprived of any opportunity to handle solid objects. The first time such squirrels are given nuts and the opportunity to bury them, they will do so. They will still search for a hiding place on the ground, dig a hole, and hide the nut using the behavior sequence described above. The stereotypy of the movement sequence becomes particularly obvious in captivity, where inexperienced animals will try to dig a hole in the solid floor of a room, where no hole can be dug. They perform all the movements already described, covering and patting the nut, even though there is no earth available; the preset program simply runs its course (I. Eibl-Eibesfeldt, 1963).

Now, if someone were to discover that squirrels exercise during their embryonic development some building blocks of this behavior, such as the coordination of antagonistic muscles, we could still, on the basis of our experiments, state that food caching behavior owes its specific adaptiveness to phylogenetic adaptation. We are dealing here with a particular level of adaptation requiring a highly specific prerequisite "knowledge," which in this case could not have been acquired during ontogeny under the conditions of the deprivation experiment.

J. C. Fentress (1976) conducted a very radical deprivation experiment. Mice groom their heads and snouts by stroking their forelegs from the back to the front over the head, eyes, and snout and, thereafter, licking their paws. Newborn mice cannot yet do this. Fentress amputated the arms of newborn mice and thus deprived them of the opportunity to perform grooming behavior. When the developmental stage at which mice clean their heads with their paws was reached, the deprived mice performed grooming movements with the remaining stumps of their arms with the same timing and actions that is characteristic of normal grooming. The mice even closed their eyes when their paws would normally have covered them, and licked in the air, washing paws that were not present. This experiment should certainly prove the existence of innate, phylogenetically adapted motor patterns, although I hope such radical procedures will prove unnecessary in the future.

Surprisingly, these really rather straightforward relationships are even today still misunderstood by many critics of ethological concepts, who monotonously repeat the same old arguments. D. S. Lehrman (1970) is an exception, for he accepted the Lorenz' (1965) arguments, although he emphasized that his interests lay in a different area, namely, the detailed analysis of behavioral development rather than an investigation as to whether a particular behavior pattern was phylogenetically adapted or not. We feel, on the other hand, that it is precisely this question of phylogenetic adaptation that constitutes the first decisive step in the investigation of ontogeny. The conclusion that a behavior pattern is phylogenetically adapted does not mean that ethologists stop here with their analyses and ignore problems of ontogeny. The usual admission by the opponents of ethology that inherited components are important in sorting out behavior patterns, and that both genes and environment contribute to behavioral development, which no one has ever disputed, in general, serves only to obscure the problem. Someone designates himself as an "interactionist" and in the same breath maintains that it is impossible to disentangle the contributions of innate and acquired characteristics.[1]

---

[1] In one target article (I. Eibl-Eibesfeldt, 1979b) I put forth for discussion several themes of human ethology. Typical responses in opposition included the following: "Most researchers have now lost interest in the nature-nurture false dichotomy" (J. H. Barkow, 1979, p. 27); "I find it curious that the nature-nurture question, which is now so widely dismissed by behavioral scientists (because everything is known to depend (*continued*)

It is especially with reference to the origin of specific adaptations that a researcher can make binding statements.

At the turn of the century, biologists were already working on understanding the processes of self-differentiation during embryogeny; H. Spemann received the Nobel Prize for his study on the embryogenesis of organs in the newt. He showed that the various tissues have a prospective potential. Of all possible ways that the tissues could differentiate, the specific developmental pathway taken is selected by means of specific chemical key stimuli called inductors.

If one transplants the eye cup of a newt embryo into the abdominal region, then the epidermis above the eye cup will develop into a lens in the new location. Substances secreted from the rim of the eye cup trigger those processes which, from the various genetically provided options, result in the development of a lens. They activate "prospective potentials," which are available as the result of phylogenetic adaptations.

Modifiability is limited; i.e., development is actually safeguarded against excessive deviation from the norm. Neither the fact of polymorphism, nor the given range of modifiability, nor an occasional uncovering of potentialities, which would normally not be activated (p. 9), change the fact that the process of self-differentiation is based on developmental instructions provided by the genetic code. This holds true for the development of any organ or organ system, such as the nervous system, the liver, the excretory system, and the sensory organs. In order to develop a retina or a kidney glomerulus, a growing organism certainly requires a great deal from the environment such as food, oxygen, humidity, and a certain temperature, but none of these "environmental factors" contain the information for the specific cytoarchitecture of these tissues.

How strict the determination of the development of the nervous system is, can be demonstrated by the investigations of R. W. Sperry (1945a, b, 1965, 1971). If a piece of skin from the back of a frog embryo is transplanted to the abdomen, before the sensory nerves have developed, this piece of skin is sought out by the growing nerve fibers and innervated as if it were at its original site. Thus, if the frog is tickled on this ventrally located back skin, the frog will still scratch its back. This and many other experiments demonstrate a precise and prefunctional growth of neuronal networks and nerves on the basis of genetic instruction. It seems as if selective chemical affinities determine which cells make contact with which others. Likewise, the developing nerve fibers may be matched to their target organs through specific chemical makeup of the organ (C. S. Goodman and M. J. Bastiani, 1986; C. S. Goodman et al., 1984; J. Dodd and T. M. Jessell, 1988; A. L. Harrelson and C. S. Goodman, 1988). Cultured nerve cells form complex networks with fully operational connections between the cells, even though there are no tasks for them to perform. Xylocaine suppresses all electrical functions, yet organized neuronal networks do develop in xylocaine-treated cell cultures (P. G. Model et al., 1971).

(continued) upon both) might be revived just because some behavioral scientists have become interested in human behavior." (R. C. Bolles, 1979, p. 29); "Genetic heritage and instincts are obviously important elements in the organization of cerebral mechanisms of behavior, but the age-old debate of nature versus nurture, its dichotomy of percentages (50-50?) and the possible existence of a unique nature are losing scientific interest" (J. M. R. Delgado, 1979, p. 31). And the usually insightful R. D. Alexander (1979a) writes: "For many years we have asked: Is this behavior learned or genetic? Finally we are coming to realize that the answer is always both."

Summary 2.1

The concept of the "innate" is no longer defined negatively as "that which is not learned," but positively according to the origin of adaptations. We consider behavioral and perceptual faculties as being phylogenetically adapted if their organic-physiological substrate (the nerve cells in their special connections with sensory and executing organs) develops under genetic control in a process of self-differentiation to functional maturity. The objection that such a distinction is theoretically possible but in practical terms unverifiable, because the animal is always under some kind of environmental influence, can be answered with the fact that it is possible to withhold specific information relevant to a specific adaptation. If the animal nonetheless performs the adapted behavior, its phylogenetic adaptiveness is demonstrated. The statement is valid only for a specific level of integration of the adaptation.

2.2. Phylogenetic Adaptations in Behavior

The survival of an animal depends upon many very different capabilities. It must be able to feed, reproduce, and defend itself, for example. All this requires that it be furnished with various programs which coordinate and guide behavior. The animal must move through space and be able to interact with the environment. It must know what to do and what to avoid. It must perceive and process stimuli and be so structured that it can respond to specific stimulus categories with specific actions, for example, to court a sexual partner, but to respond to a predator with flight, playing dead, or defensive behavior. It must behave adaptively at the appropriate time, thus requiring feedback circuits that signal deviations from physiological equilibrium (homeostasis). Motivating mechanisms must ensure that the animal searches actively for prey, social partners, resting sites, or inquisitively seeks new information. Preferences and aversions must be built-in, just as complex regulatory systems that activate or stop behavior at appropriate times are. Animals must be provided with the norms (central reference structures) against which they can match their behavior.

In man, such norms determine what we perceive as "good" or "evil," and these are the basis of what we experience as "good" or "bad" conscience. Furthermore, animals and human beings must be able to adapt their behavior individually to changing environmental conditions. Adaptive modifiability of behavior through learning requires complicated neuronal systems, which, for example, determine what is associated with what and what constitutes a reward. The programs include information regarding whether a species is typically monogamous, and when it should deviate from this pattern, whether it lives in groups and develops hierarchies, follows incest taboos, differentiates sex roles, and much more.

For these kinds of performances, animals and humans require a certain basic endowment of phylogenetic adaptations, even if they are required to learn a great deal in addition. These adaptations may be in the form of movements, like readily available tools, existing as knowledge of specific releasing stimuli, and in the form of activating mechanisms ("drives"). Naturally, movements or "drives" as such are not innate to the animal. We have already stated that this term is used as a "shorthand" description, and that the neuronal networks underlying the previously mentioned characteristics grow by a process of self-differentiation to functional maturity.

How the neuronal network is "wired" for a particular function is, to date, known for only a few behavior patterns (S. Goodman and M. T. Bastiani, 1984). It is only in a few invertebrate species that the generator systems underlying certain motor patterns have been traced back to the neuronal level (G. S. Stent *et al.,* 1978; J. C. Fentress, 1976). Analysis of data-processing mechanisms at the neuronal level have been carried out by D. H. Hubel and T. N. Wiesel (1962, 1963), F. Huber (1974, 1977), and J. P. Ewert (1974), to name only a few. I will not discuss these remarkable findings here but must refer to my detailed presentation in *Ethology: The Biology of Behavior*. We still know very little about the neuronal substrate which controls behavior.

Genes must not only control the differentiation of the neuronal networks underlying instinctive behavior but they also control the development of the specific chemistry by which particular neuronal networks are activated and which facilitate and inhibit the activity of neurons in a specified manner, so that the sequence of behavior patterns progress in the proper order. Studies in egg-laying behavior of the marine snail *Aplysia* were the first to demonstrate how genes are involved. The investigators (R. H. Scheller *et al.,* 1982, 1983; L. B. McAllister *et al.,* 1983; R. H. Scheller and R. Axel, 1984) localized a group of genes responsible for the development of a group of related neuropeptides, whose ordered release controlled the appearance and sequencing of the fixed-action patterns of egg-laying.

The claim that no one would ever be able to determine the genetic contribution to the process of differentiation of behavior does not dishearten biologists. Although we are certainly just at the beginning of such investigations, decisive breakthroughs have already been achieved.

When studying behavior, we generally perceive the events and their dependence upon controllable variables. We depict these changing relationships in systems (cybernetic) diagrams. They represent a level of reality, display the functional organization *("Wirkungsgefüge")* of the system and its appropriateness at this level, and allow predictions to be made that can be tested by experiment. Examples of such systems diagrams can be found in the work of B. Hassenstein (1973a, 1983), E. von Holst and U. von St. Paul (1960) (see also N. Bischof, 1975, p. 210).

When we distinguish between phylogenetic adaptation on the motor side, on the receptor side, motivating mechanisms, learning dispositions, and so on, we must keep in mind that, in doing so, we categorize and isolate parts from the functional whole. To a certain extent, any of these aspects can be studied separately. I can thus investigate the neuronal generator (drive) systems underlying a fixed-action pattern, or the basic feedback circuits for constancy in visual perception, as individual entities.

We must, however, never forget that in categorizing adaptations we are dealing with subsystems that must work with others in a functional whole. Although one can, for example, study innate expressive movements and the innate releasing mechanisms involved as independent entities, one must remember that they both operate within the framework of a communicative system. We must also realize that we are far from understanding the many physiological mechanisms underlying the programs controlling behavior. We recognize specific innate dispositions, such as obedience to norms, but we do not yet know in detail how they are constructed. Learning disposition as well as different "drives" can be based on quite different constructs. We conceive of them on the level of functional categories of behavior even though the mechanisms underlying them may not be unitary at all (p. 162).

2.2.1. Fixed-Action Patterns and Instinctive Actions

In his studies on the taxonomy of ducks, O. Heinroth (1910) found that he could use courtship behavior for minute taxonomic classification, just as one does with morphological structures. These patterns proved to be characteristic for each species, and Heinroth called them species-specific instinctive behavior patterns *("arteigene Triebhandlungen")*. The patterns were characterized by their constancy in form. They consisted of distinct behavioral sequences that could be homologized within closely related species. These motor adaptations have been investigated more closely since then, and their innate character has been verified (for examples, see p. 21). They are known as "fixed-action patterns." Together with orientation movements, they comprise a higher functional unit: instinctive behaviors (K. Lorenz and N. Tinbergen, 1939).

The term *"fixed-action pattern"* may imply a strict rigidity, and this has led to investigations on its variability. Measurements have been made of the time interval between the appearance of two behavioral patterns (R. H. Wiley, 1973) or the duration of a specific pattern (J. A. Stamps and G. W. Barlow, 1973). However, such studies do not deal with the decisive characteristic of the form constancy itself. Because the sequencing and the relative phase interval of the muscle actions involved remain constant, a transposable movement configuration *("Bewegungsgestalt")* is established. Thus the movement pattern is therefore always recognizable, even if the movements are carried out at varying speeds or amplitudes. In this sense, a fixed-action pattern can definitely have variability, but the relative phase interval of the muscle actions involved remains constant. Variability results furthermore from the fact that several simultaneously activated movements can be superimposed upon one another (examples, p. 170; ambivalent behavior).

In this connection it must be especially emphasized that while each fixed-action pattern is form constant not every form constant movement is necessarily a fixed-action pattern. Learned movement sequences can also be of a high degree of stereotypy and thus, by their form constancy, attain the characteristics of a transposable configuration. This is why handwriting patterns are unique for each individual person. Whether the signature is written rapidly or slowly, its configuration remains constant. The criterion of innateness must be met in addition to form constancy before we can speak of a fixed-action pattern. This is often forgotten. Furthermore, fixed-action patterns are also accessible to the modulating influences of feedback and experience.

Since Erich von Holst's studies (1935, 1936, 1937, 1939) we know that fixed-action patterns in vertebrates are activated by spontaneously active motoric cell groups whose neuronal activity is centrally coordinated. Thus even fully deafferentiated nervous systems (those fully isolated from relevant input) can produce well coordinated impulses and transmit them to the musculature. Eels with a completely deafferentiated spinal cord can swim with perfect coordination. Comparable drive systems in invertebrates have been recently investigated more closely. In many species, they have been found to generate the movements of courtship, flight, walking, and swimming. Usually there are feedback systems involved in the control of these movements. The studies by J. C. Fentress (1976) and E. R. Kandel (1976) give good reviews of these questions.

Fixed-action patterns often combine with orienting movements to form higher functional units, which we call instinctive behavior patterns (K. Lorenz and N. Tinbergen, 1939).[2] These building blocks of behavior can, in turn, combine with learning processes to form still more complex functional entities (examples in I. Eibl-Eibesfeldt, 1975b, 1987).

Humans also display phylogenetic adaptations on the motor side. Heartbeat and respiration mature during the embryonic stage. The newborn baby has a broad repertoire of functional movements, including vocalizations.

Premature babies can hold onto a stretched rope with their hands. Newborns make walking movements when they are held upright and moved over a surface (see Figs. 2.1–2.4). These primary walking movements are not under voluntary control. The babies cannot vary the length of their pace. The legs so to speak run with them. If babies are put on their belly into warm water, they move their arms and legs in a typical quadruped movement coordination (diagonal walk). If they are placed on the mother's stomach immediately after birth, they can push themselves upward toward the breast with their legs (Fig. 2.5). They have a special automatic searching movement (search automism; H. F. R. Prechtl and W. M. Schleidt, 1950; Fig. 2.6), and without any guidance they can grasp the nipple with their lips, begin sucking, and coordinate these movements with their breathing so that they do not aspirate any liquid. There are other movements that accompany sucking. For example, they clench their fists during nursing, and use this grip to hold on when they grab something. They indicate their satisfaction or dissatisfaction during nursing by vocalizations. Their vocal repertoire is quite differentiated. A nursing baby has over five different vocalizations (apart from different forms of crying), each with a specific function (M. Morath, 1977; Fig. 2.7):

a. The *contact sound* is an utterance lasting 0.1 second and is given immediately after awakening. If the mother does not respond, the baby begins to cry. This sound has a mixed frequency with an upper limit of 8 kHz.

b. The *displeasure sound* consists of a series of rhythmically repeated short utterances of 14 seconds duration each. Each individual component resembles the contact sound. This sound signals displeasure to the mother during certain specific interactions, such as when she cleans the baby's nose.

c. The *sleep sound* is made at intervals of about 15 minutes during sleep; it signals well-being. Each sleep sound lasts about 0.3 second and shows a mixed frequency with an upper limit of about 0.3 kHz. This pleasant sound is most often heard when the baby changes its position during sleep. If the baby remains quiet for an extended period of time, the mother will check for the cause of this silence, yet she responds without even knowing why.

d. The *drinking sound* is a rather pure tone lasting 0.2 second with overtones as high as 8 kHz. It is uttered rhythmically with drinking, especially when the child nurses. It signals that all is well.

---

[2]How the two components interact was demonstrated in the classical study by Konrad Lorenz and Niko Tinbergen (1939) on the egg-rolling behavior of the graylag goose. If an egg is placed outside the nest, the goose will retrieve it by placing its beak over it and rolling it back, balancing the egg with the underside of its bill. If one removes the egg after the goose has started to roll it, the rolling movements will continue in straight line to the nest without the balancing movements, which depend upon continuous stimulation coming from the egg. These balancing movements are the orientation movements (taxis component) of the instinctive act of egg-rolling. The rolling movement is the fixed-action pattern of this act, which once triggered continues even in the absence of the triggering stimulus.

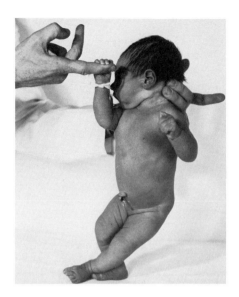

FIGURE 2.1. The handgrasping reflex of
a newborn. From *Sie und
Er,* 1967, p. 36.

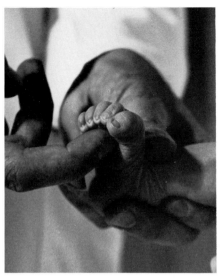

FIGURE 2.2. Footgrasping reflex of a
newborn. From *Sie und Er,*
1967, p. 36.

FIGURE 2.3. Primary stepping movements
in a newborn. From *Sie und
Er,* 1967, p. 36.

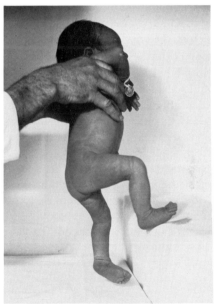

FIGURE 2.4. Diagonal movement coordination of a crawling newborn (after M.B. McGraw,
1943).

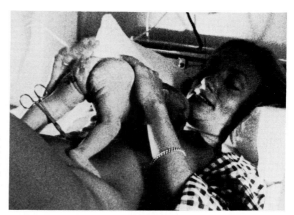

FIGURE 2.5. A newborn baby with the umbilical cord just cut, can crawl forward across its mother under its own power. Photo: S. Austen.

e. The *contentment sound* is a pure tone with overtones up to 5 kHz and a duration of 0.3 second. It is sometimes repeated at 0.5-second intervals. The sound signals well-being and satiation.

There are a large number of highly specific reflex movements, which have been utilized in clinical diagnoses because they are typical for specific maturational levels and health of a baby (H. F. R. Prechtl, 1958; Fig. 2.8).

If a baby is held on its back on one's hands and then dropped for a short distance, the baby spreads its arms out and then pulls them back over the chest (the Moro reaction; Fig. 2.9a, b). The baby will only do this if it is not already holding something. If the baby was holding something before being dropped back, it tightens its grip. The newborn baby exhibits a number of expressive movements, and its responsive behavior will be discussed below.

Babies also rub their eyes in a rather stereotyped fashion, which I have never seen described elsewhere. They rub their closed eyes with the backs of the fingers, especially the index and middle fingers, and the back of the hand, moving them from the outer toward the inner edge of the eye and occasionally rubbing back and forth several times. In this way, the baby avoids scratching its eyes. We retain this eye-rubbing behavior for life. This was observed in babies of every culture we studied (Figs. 2.10, 2.11), and not once did I see a baby accidentally poke itself in the eye with its fingers.

Infants also react to the taste substances that produce "sweet," "sour," and "bitter" sensations with specific facial expressions. This is important since they

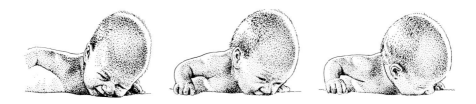

FIGURE 2.6. Rhythmic nipple searching behavior (search automism) (after H.F.R. Prechtl, 1953).

KHz

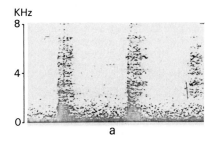

a

KHz

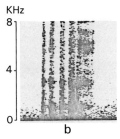

b

KHz

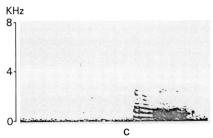

c

KHz

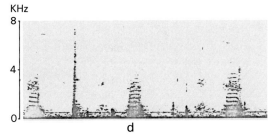

d

KHz

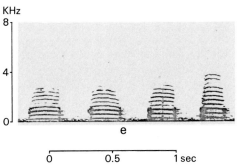

e

0   0.5   1 sec

FIGURE 2.7. Spectrogram of a baby's vocalizations as described in the text. From M. Morath, 1977.

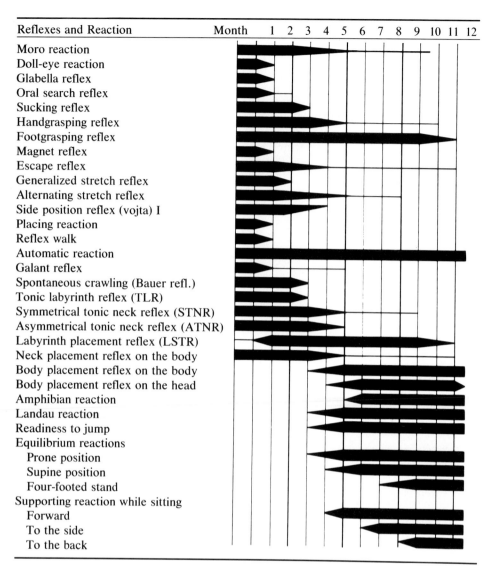

Reflexes and Reaction	Month	1	2	3	4	5	6	7	8	9	10	11	12
Moro reaction													
Doll-eye reaction													
Glabella reflex													
Oral search reflex													
Sucking reflex													
Handgrasping reflex													
Footgrasping reflex													
Magnet reflex													
Escape reflex													
Generalized stretch reflex													
Alternating stretch reflex													
Side position reflex (vojta) I													
Placing reaction													
Reflex walk													
Automatic reaction													
Galant reflex													
Spontaneous crawling (Bauer refl.)													
Tonic labyrinth reflex (TLR)													
Symmetrical tonic neck reflex (STNR)													
Asymmetrical tonic neck reflex (ATNR)													
Labyrinth placement reflex (LSTR)													
Neck placement reflex on the body													
Body placement reflex on the body													
Body placement reflex on the head													
Amphibian reaction													
Landau reaction													
Readiness to jump													
Equilibrium reactions													
Prone position													
Supine position													
Four-footed stand													
Supporting reaction while sitting													
Forward													
To the side													
To the back													

FIGURE 2.8. The diagnostically important reflexes of the newborn. From A. Vossen, 1971.

must be able to signal to the mother whether something tastes good or not and what sort of flavor quality they are perceiving. The fact that even anencephalic babies display these reactions proves that these are not individually acquired facial expressions (J. E. Steiner, 1973, 1974, 1979).

A series of behavioral patterns mature during the course of development. This can be verified by studying humans under specified conditions of sensory deprivation. I have investigated children born deaf and blind. These individuals grow up in eternal darkness and silence. They can never perceive their companions' facial expressions nor hear their voices; yet they develop their facial expressions sufficiently for us to recognize the basic expressions. Deaf and blind children smile when the mother caresses them; they laugh during play, cry when they hurt

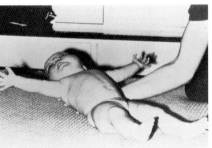

FIGURE 2.9. (A) The Moro reaction in a newborn Eipo baby. Photo: W. Schiefenhövel. (B) The Moro reaction in a newborn European baby. The reaction is elicited when the person holding the baby with the hand lets the baby fall back slightly. From A. Vossen, 1971.

themselves, and emit all the appropriate sounds while doing so. When angry, they frown and clench their teeth. They even stamp their feet in rage, just like any angry person would do (I. Eibl-Eibesfeldt, 1973a, b; Figs. 2.12–2.14).

To the objection that these children could have learned these expressive behaviors by touching their mother's face and thus acquire the necessary information to perform appropriately, I would reply with the observation that even deaf and blind thalidomide children, who could not raise their arm stumps, display these typical facial expressions as well.

The facial expressions of deaf and blind born children are certainly less refined than those of sighted children. But essentially this could be due to the fact that many of the differentiated expressions are activated visually and acoustically during communication with others, and these channels are closed to these deprived children. In support of this contention is the astonishing cross-cultural correspondence of many facial expressions, even in fine detail. The eyebrow flash is an example (p. 118). For many universally occurring expressive behavior patterns we find homologies in anthropoid apes, for instance, the open mouth face (pp. 135 ff.) and pouting (p. 461). When we are frightened we raise the shoulders (Fig. 2.15). This neck-shoulder reaction is an innate protective response with which we protect the vulnerable carotid area of the neck from injury.

There is also a head protective response, in which one or both hands are placed over the head, with the palms down. We observed this in fear situations, particularly when a person was afraid of having his head struck. Crying children often lay one hand over the head as if they want to protect themselves from blows (Figs. 2.16, 2.17). This is practically an automatic reaction, even if there is no threat of blows. Many of the expressive movement patterns are fixed-action patterns. More examples will be given in a later section (6.3.1).

31

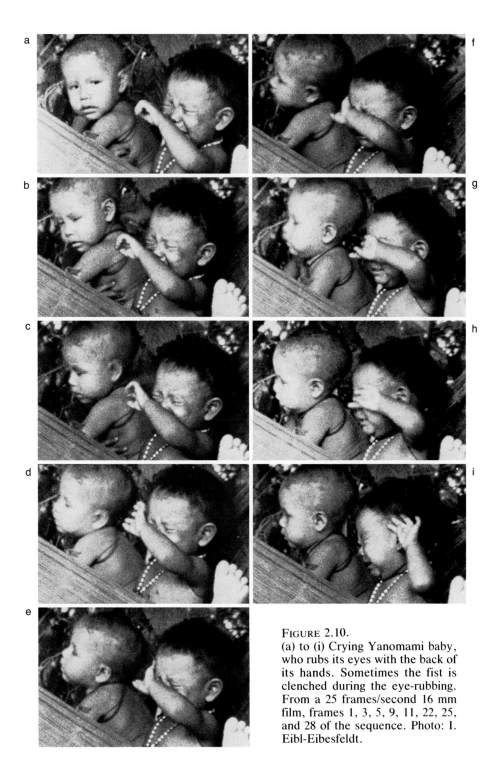

FIGURE 2.10.
(a) to (i) Crying Yanomami baby, who rubs its eyes with the back of its hands. Sometimes the fist is clenched during the eye-rubbing. From a 25 frames/second 16 mm film, frames 1, 3, 5, 9, 11, 22, 25, and 28 of the sequence. Photo: I. Eibl-Eibesfeldt.

FIGURE 2.11. (a) to (f) Sleepy Himba baby rubbing its eyes with the back of the hand. From a 25 frames/second 16 mm film, frames 1, 8, 13, 19, 26, and 38 of the sequence. Photo: I. Eibl-Eibesfeldt.

2.2.2. Phylogenetic Adaptations in Perception: Innate Recognition

Perceptual tasks must satisfy various demands. Animals and humans must move in space and be able to determine which are solid obstacles and which move in relation to themselves. They must not only be able to perceive objects but also react to them adaptively, depending on whether the object is, for example, a predator, prey, or a sexual partner. Furthermore, perceptual skills must take into account different locations, distances, and light conditions, all of which require complex assessment mechanisms. These and a wealth of other data processing mechanisms are at our disposal and many of them are available as phylogenetic adaptations.

Figures 2.18 to 2.20 each show two identical pictures, in which one represents the other rotated 180°. We interpret these "landscapes" differently because our perception operates under the assumption that the light comes from above. That objects are normally illuminated from above and thus cast corresponding shadows is something we experience anew each day.

We might assume that perceptual capability is derived from individual experience, but perhaps this is not the case at all. R. Dawkins (1968) showed that unfed

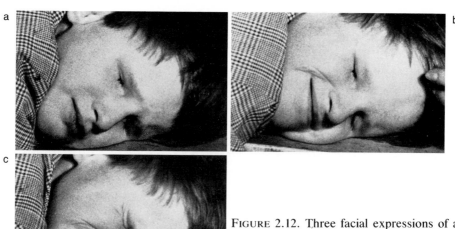

FIGURE 2.12. Three facial expressions of a 10-year-old girl, deaf and blind from birth. (a) Neutral; (b) smiling; (c) crying. From a 16 mm film. Photo: I. Eibl-Eibesfeldt.

FIGURE 2.13. (a) The same girl as seen in Fig. 2.12 expresses anger by biting into her hand. (b) Expression of despair after being left alone. After an angry protest she clasps herself (anger mixed with fear). From a 16 mm film. Photo: I. Eibl-Eibesfeldt.

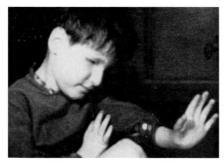

FIGURE 2.14. The warding-off gesture in the previously shown girl. From a 16 mm film. Photo: I. Eibl-Eibesfeldt.

FIGURE 2.15. Neck–shoulder reaction of an Eipo man who is startled and frightened by a rubber spider. From a 50 frames/second 16 mm film, frames 1, 24, and 30 of the sequence. Photo: I. Eibl-Eibesfeldt.

FIGURE 2.16. Head protection reaction of a crying Balinesian boy. From a 16 mm film. Photo: I. Eibl-Eibesfeldt.

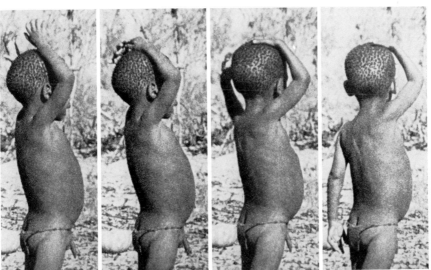

FIGURE 2.17. (a) to (d) Head protection reaction of a crying G/wi Bushman boy. From a 25 frames/second 16 mm film, frames 1, 16, 40, and 56 of the sequence. Photo: I. Eibl-Eibesfeldt.

3-day-old chicks preferred pecking at three-dimensional objects (semispherical nailheads). They also preferred photos of such objects over two-dimensional flat objects if the objects were arranged so that their illuminated side was on top. This preference is not based on the individual experience that objects (feed corn) are illuminated from above. Even chicks that Dawkins raised in cages illuminated from the bottom preferred the pictures of nailheads lit from above, quite contrary to their personal experience with lighting. They obviously responded on the basis of phylogenetically acquired experience that light falls from above and perform on the basis of this assumption; the contrary individual experience did not alter their response at all.

Apparently there is some kind of perceptual bias based on phylogenetic adaptation in the perceptual apparatus. This enables an animal to interpret specific environmental stimuli and respond to them adaptively (that is, so that normally fitness is augmented).

This prior knowledge has been investigated experimentally in many different animals. It guides spatial and object orientation and permits an animal to recognize certain contingencies innately and to respond to them with a preset program. Crickets, for example, recognize their individual species courtship and rival songs; their information processing mechanisms have been minutely analyzed down to the neuronal level (F. Huber, 1977, 1983). Moths react specifically to sex pheromones (D. Schneider, 1962; K. E. Kaissling, 1971) and coral fishes respond to the color patterns and markings of their conspecifics. Most of these fish could not have gained this knowledge in the course of their development, because they mature from the egg far away from their parents among the marine plankton. Only after the larval stage do they reach the coral reef, which is inhabited by a multitude of species. They must already know which fish to court when they are sexually mature and which to fight. In all these cases the animals apparently have data processing mechanisms that act like stimulus filters and are interconnected with

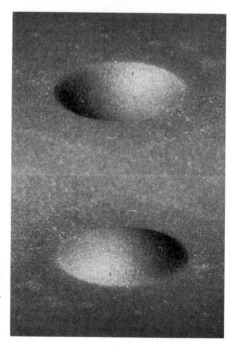

FIGURE 2.18. Both pictures are identical. However, depending on orientation (apparent shadow), we perceive the upper picture as a depression and the lower (which is actually the same picture rotated 180°) as a mound. Drawing: H. Kacher.

36

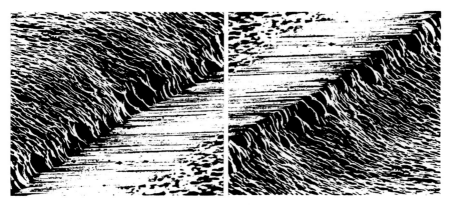

FIGURE 2.19. Depending on the orientation of the picture, we perceive one as a steep slope on the left terminating in a plain on the right, or a plateau on the left meeting a drop-off on the right. From *Umschau in Wissenschaft und Technik* (1972).

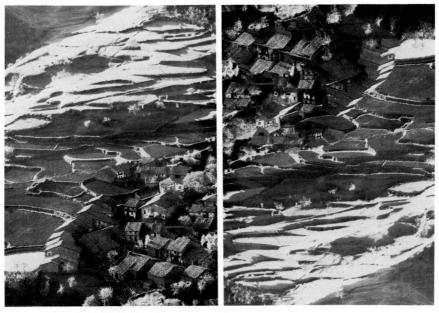

FIGURE 2.20. Spanish landscape, in a normal viewing position and rotated 180°. Again, we interpret the landscape completely differently due to our assumption that light comes from above. Photo: I. Rentschler from H. Schober and I. Rentschler (1979).

the motor systems so that specific behaviors are elicited by specific stimuli. We call these "innate releasing mechanisms" (IRM; Tinbergen, 1951). These mechanisms are specialized unilaterally for specific perception, e.g., enemy or prey objects. The triggering stimuli are called key stimuli. In the case of intraspecific communication and interspecific symbiotic situations it is not only advantageous for the animal perceiving stimuli to react adaptively, but just as important that the partner involved be understood appropriately. Thus, in the service of communication, reciprocal adaptations took place and special signals evolved, such as the color patterns in coral fish. We use the term releasers for such signaling devices. One particular category of releasers are the expressive movements. These are behavior patterns that have been especially differentiated for the sake of communication (see Ritualization).

Key stimuli and releasers generally activate very specific behavior patterns, as for example those of escape, prey catching, courtship, or fighting. Conspecifics are senders of signals, which elicit quite diverse kinds of behavior. Of course, they do not send all their signals simultaneously. However, it does occur that releasers can activate opposing behavior patterns simultaneously, for instance, those patterns for seeking contact and those for defense. This often leads to conflicts.

Releasers can be imitated by models used in experiments. Male European robins react aggressively to the red breast feathers of rivals. The same reactions can be elicited by mounting a tuft of red feathers on a branch in the robin's territory. Models can be used to increase the effects of a natural releaser and thus create a supernormal stimulus. Finally, a behavior pattern can be elicited by a number of separate characteristics of an object. When these key stimuli are presented individually, responses of a certain strength result. But when several such stimuli are presented simultaneously, their releasing effects can be additive (further elaboration on this topic, especially regarding experimental data, is found in *Ethology: The Biology of Behavior*).

What is the situation in humans? Can we also confirm a preset knowledge, a capacity of innate recognition?

Let us begin with the simpler processes of perception. Gestalt psychology has produced a wealth of interesting insights in this area. The experimental investigation of visual perception led to the formulation of various laws of vision, which in principle are universally valid. Various cultural influences, as far as is known, result in only minor changes. Furthermore, it was found that certain phenomena, such as Prägnanz (i.e., our preference for simple but meaningful figures, pp. 42, 46) or categorical perception, are "transmodal" in that they are found in other sensory modalities besides vision.

Experiments conducted by Gestalt psychologists were never done with visually inexperienced individuals. However, the fact that environmental data were in principle processed in identical ways everywhere (so as to result in similar illusions and misjudgments) suggests that innate programs are involved. This assumption is reinforced by the fact that visual illusions persist even in the face of contrary experience. If a moonlit sky is partly cloud-covered, we have the impression that the moon is moving across the clouds. We know, of course, that in reality the clouds are moving across the moon, but we do not perceive it as such. Our perceptual apparatus forces this illusion despite our knowledge to the contrary. Our perceptual mechanisms proceed from the fact that objects normally move across a stationary background, and this assumption has been proved to be accurate on earth. Animals and humans move against a stationary background, and it is essential for survival that moving objects be recognized as such without having to reflect on them, since they could be enemies or prey. In the case of the moon, in contrast, it is now the background (the clouds) that moves and not the object itself, and this leads to our false interpretation. The fact that we continue to be deceived supports our contention that we are dealing with a phylogenetically preprogrammed perceptual process.

If we observe two equally long lines meeting at right angles (one vertically, the other horizontally), we tend to overestimate the length of the vertical one. If we look down from a 2-meter high wall, this distance appears to us longer than the same distance in the horizontal. This is important for a heavy, climbing mammal, because it warns the animal of the danger of falling and reduces the likelihood of it carelessly leaping down from a great height. G. J. von Allesch (1931) referred to the "non-Euclidean" structure of our spatial assessment of phenomena.

In the Müller-Lyer illusion (Fig. 2.21A), the vertical with outward diverging lines appears to be longer than the other one. We persist in this perception despite our knowledge to the contrary. We estimate object size by its relationship to neighboring objects (Figs. 2.21B C, and D), which is probably related to our capacity for perceiving constancy (R. H. Day, 1972). We thus can recognize objects of equal size as such at varying distances.

Size constancy is based on several parameters. Our perception utilizes converging optical axes with binocular vision and accommodation. As we move our head, the apparent motion of an object against its background is used to determine the object's distance from us, even if we use only monocular vision. Closer objects appear to move faster in the opposite direction than do distant ones (movement parallax). Binocular vision has the advantage of stereoscopic perception, enabling the retina to perceive three-dimensional objects in both the right and left eyes. Other criteria for depth perception include air opacity (illumination perspective) or albedo, linear (geometrical) perspective, and texture gradients.

Texture gradients can be used in two-dimensional drawings to give the impression of depth and thus an estimate of relative distances between objects in such pictures. Thus, the two identical human figures in Fig. 2.21C (C and D) appear different in size, because the upper person is perceived as further into the background. In contrast, the people in A and B also look approximately the same size (but are actually different) for the same reasons.

Geometrical illusions are basically distance illusions. The mechanisms which have evolved for the perception of object constancy can be deceived in artificially constructed situations. Other illusions operate in a similar way. Day summarizes this as a general rule as follows: ". . . any stimulus which serves to maintain the perceptual constancy of a property of an object as the visual representation of that property varies will, when independently manipulated with the retinal image not varied, produce an illusion" (R. H. Day, 1972, p. 1340).

It is not known which of these criteria are used as a result of individual experience and to what extent phylogenetic adaptations prepare us to perceive depth. Depth perception has been demonstrated in infants at an early age, and in some animals there is experimental proof that this capacity is innate.

If a table is covered with a thick glass pane projecting far beyond the table's edge and under it lies a cloth with a checkerboard pattern stretching downward and spread out on the floor beneath the glass, freshly hatched chicks and newborn lambs will avoid walking across this visual cliff. E. J. Gibson and R. D. Walk (1960) placed 36 infants (ages 6–14 months) on a small cushion right at the borderline of the table and the visual "cliff" and had their mothers call to them. Nine infants stayed on the cushion. Of the 27 who crawled to their mothers, 24 clearly avoided the drop.

If 8-week-old infants who cannot yet crawl are placed right over the visual cliff, their pulse rate slows; when they are back on the tabletop their pulse accelerates (J. Campos *et al.*, 1977). Clearly, infants at this early age can perceive apparent

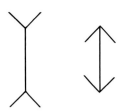

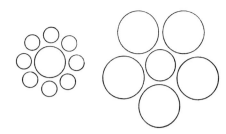

FIGURE 2.21(A). The Müller-Lyer illusion. Both verticals are the same length, but we perceive them as different.

FIGURE 2.21(B). Equality illusion. The central circle enclosed by smaller ones looks larger than an equally sized circle surrounded by the larger ones.

FIGURE 2.21(C). Size illusions created by the size of neighboring objects and their spatial configuration, illustrating their significance for size constancy perception: distance in two-dimensional pictures is suggested by height of an object, size gradient, and frequency of nearby objects. These criteria determine an estimated distance by means of which we judge the height of an object. The human figures in **A** and **B** appear to be approximately equal in size despite their true discrepancy, because the smaller one is seen in its higher position in the picture and in the context of nearby objects. Size illusions arise when key objects of one size do not vary but the signals of distance do (as in **C** and **D**). Thus the higher human figure in **C** (and to some extent in **D**) appears to be much larger than the lower one, although they are identical. From R.H. Day (1972).

FIGURE 2.21(D). The Müller-Lyer illusion is one of perspective. The left-hand figure suggests the far corner of a room and is perceived as having a higher vertical than the right figure, which looks like the near corner of a room. People living in rooms are more susceptible to the Müller-Lyer illusion than those who do not. Appropriate experience thus reinforces a basically universal kind of visual information processing (see Fig. 2.22). From Schober and I. Rentschler (1979).

depth differences. One would expect their pulse rate to increase, however, above the visual cliff, if the babies were afraid of being there. The decrease in pulse rate suggests that the new situation merely elicited heightened awareness by the infants and not fright. On the shallow side the infants were in a familiar situation whereas they had never before been above a visual cliff. These studies demonstrate that depth perception is present early in life and, as other investigations have shown, is probably innate in humans. J. Campos *et al.* (1977), on the other hand, consider that the fear of falling is acquired. Only one-third of the children in his tests, who had reached the crawling stage, avoided the visual cliff. The others crawled right over it when their mothers called to them. But this does not prove that the perceptual process involves individual learning, for a maturational process could have been involved.

The contradicting results of the different experimenters find an explanation in the more recent investigations by N. Rader, M. Bausano, and J. E. Richards (1987) and J. E. Richards and N. Rader (1981). Infants in a walker fail to avoid the visual cliff. Infants who would avoid the visual cliff when crawling, will cross the visual cliff in a walker. When in a walker, the infant seems to act as if held and guided by a caretaker. Cliff avoidance of the infants was dependent on the age when the infants started to crawl. Babies who crawled prior to the age of 6.5 months crossed the cliff. They start with tactile orientation and continue to do so. In contrast, those infants who start to crawl after age 6.5 months are visually oriented from the beginning and respond to the visual cliff even though they have less crawling experience (N. Rader *et al.*, 1987).

If we briefly project a single spot of light against a wall in a dark room and replace it by an identical spot displaced along the horizontal to the right we perceive the illusion of motion. Our built in hypotheses assume that the spot moved to the right. If an object disappears behind a screen, we still know that it is there. According to the classical theory, the baby learns this by manual exploration of what is hidden behind the screen. T. G. Bower (1971) covered objects in front of a baby with a screen for different periods of time. When he removed the screen and the object was still there the babies did not show any signs of unrest. However, if the object had disappeared, the infants appeared restless provided the time interval was not too long. In babies as young as 20 days old, the heart rate increased significantly when the object had disappeared. In further experiments, Bower found that 8-week-old babies anticipate that an object disappearing behind a screen, by its active movement, should appear on the other side. If it fails to appear or if it appears too fast the babies behave in an irritable manner. It does not matter, however, at this age, if the object changes. If a ball disappears behind the screen and a cube reappears, the baby is not disturbed as long as the movement pattern fits. The object identity might be learned.

Two-month-old infants can already recognize identical objects in various spatial positions and distances. If they are offered a cube measuring 30 cm/side at a distance of 1 meter and a cube 90 cm/side at a distance of 3 meters (thus with identical retinal image size), the infants successfully differentiated between the two cubes. The task consisted of working an electric switch in the pillow with their heads when the appropriate reinforcer was seen, for which the subjects were rewarded by the appearance of a person who smiled (T. G. R. Bower, 1966). If one conditioned the children with a 30-cm cube at 1-m distance as the positive stimulus, then they recognized it as the same object at the 3-m distance, even though the retinal image site differed.

Experience no doubt plays a role in depth perception and object constancy. Nonetheless we can assume that infants possess an innate capacity for a rough, approximate orientation.

The finding that similar illusions are experienced in different cultural groups is in favor of this interpretation, although the amplitude of the response varies due to local experience. The Müller-Lyer illusion and the horizontal-vertical illusion have been verified in a number of different cultural groups (Fig. 2.22).

Inhabitants of open terrains are less responsive to the Müller-Lyer illusion and the horizontal-vertical illusion than those of urbanized environments where vertical and horizontal lines are more prevalent (M. Segall *et al.*, 1966). This explains the difference in the graphs for Europeans and non-Europeans in Fig. 2.22. With respect to the horizontal-vertical illusion, the Banyankole are an exception. That perception is influenced by ecological conditions has also been shown by V. M. Stewart (1973). Urban blacks in Zambia were found to be more sensitized to the illusions than those living outside cities. No differences were found between black and white people living in cities in the United States.

Gestalt psychologists formulated a number of laws that operate for non-European as well as European cultures (S. Morinaga, 1933; T. Obonai, 1933, 1935; T. Obonai and H. Hino, 1930). According to the laws pertaining to figure and ground, a picture is organized into two components, a figure (in the foreground and sharply resolved) and a background (more diffuse). The recognition of the figure against the ground is the active process of our perception mechanisms, as illustrated by the Rubin cup. If the cup is white, we initially perceive the profiles, which are resolved as dark against a white background. If the cup is black, then it is the first to be perceived (Fig. 2.23). After a few seconds, however, we perceive the profiles by means of a shift of attention, which will be discussed later. Artist Maurits Escher uses this perceptual principle in many of his works.

Our perception organizes the incoming sensory data in such a way that we perceive wholes rather than isolated parts and that our perception tends toward the simplest form (principle of Prägnanz). Thus, two rectangles which overlap crosswise are perceived as a cross and not as five rectangles. The main laws by which this perceptual organization takes place are similarity, proximity, and closure. Similarity refers to the tendency to group like-stimuli, such as dots, together. According to the law of proximity, neighboring points or lines are joined into a unified figure sooner than distant ones (Fig. 2.24). If the far ends, of what appear to be converging lines, are joined in Fig. 2.24, an entirely new shape is discerned. Enclosed objects are perceived as figures (law of closure; Fig. 2.25). We also combine similar elements into a unified configuration (law of similarity).

The law of experience operates when we recognize known objects in accidental configurations (such as animal shapes in the clouds). I would add that this phenomenon involves more than just individual experience. Our tendency to physiognomize (to perceive specific expressions in random patterns) is probably based on innate releasing mechanisms (IRMs, p. 55). This is an example of a priori knowledge based on phylogenetic experience—the biases of our perception.

One characteristic of Gestalt perception of particular importance is the tendency toward Prägnanz: out of a mass of unordered, irregular formations we can recognize primary configurations because of their regularity and order (law of the good figure). Max Wertheimer (1927) found that if we view slightly asymmetrical or distorted figures, such as a triangle missing one corner, in a tachystoscope for fractions of a second, we tend to perceive the objects without these irregularities. The

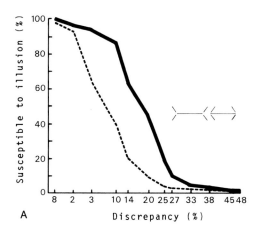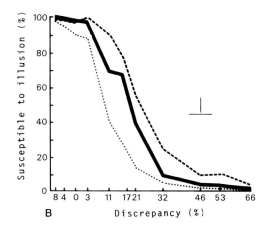

FIGURE 2.22. Frequency distribution curves showing the percentage of subjects susceptible to the Müller-Lyer (a) and horizontal-vertical (b) illusions as line lengths were changed. In the first example, most subjects perceive the line with outward diverging ends as longer. If the other line is lengthened, fewer people are responsive to the illusion. The same process occurs with the horizontal-vertical illusion. Initially the vertical line is perceived as longer (that is, when both are actually equal in length). If the horizontal line is lengthened, the percentage of people identifying the vertical as longer is reduced. The distribution curves in various cultures are similar but not identical. The Banyankole and Bété are African tribes (see text). (A) Solid line, Europeans ($N = 251$); dashed line, non-Europeans ($N = 1103$). (B) Solid line, Evanston ($N = 198$); dashed line, Banyankole ($N = 261$); dotted line, Bété ($N = 79$). From M.H. Segall et al. (1966).

missing corner of the triangle is replaced perceptually, and the asymmetrical shape becomes symmetrical. We not only even out irregularities, we also tend to exaggerate certain key characteristics of configurations. When subjects are asked to recreate from memory shapes seen previously, they tend to exaggerate certain characteristics or to make these more uniform than they were before (Fig. 2.26). A zigzag line becomes steeper when drawn repeatedly. In the reproduction of a given shape, the following tendencies occur: (1) symmetry increases; (2) the figure is simplified; (3) subdivisions are enhanced; (4) incompatible details are isolated; (5) borderlines are joined; (6) similar components are repeated; (7) oblique lines are straightened.

All these modifications increase order, simplicity, and completeness. The tendency for creating order is so strong that it will produce order even where none exists. W. Metzger spoke metaphorically of the "love of order of our senses."

This love of order is reflected in children's behavior, for they will arrange blocks on the basis of color even before they are able to speak; they correctly complete segments cut out of figures (Fig. 2.27), and protest when a missing piece is wrongly completed.

D. Dörner and W. Vehrs (1975) gave subjects the task of arranging red and green squares on a grid board so that they would present either a pleasing or not so pleasing arrangement. The experimental results yielded distinct differences between pleasing and displeasing arrays. The pleasing ones displayed crosses, parallel rows, and other geometrical figures (Fig. 2.28). Apparently we are satisfied esthetically by discovering orderly relationships within originally disordered configurations.

43

FIGURE 2.23. Rubin's cup. The dark cup contrasts against its white background, and the two light profiles are only discovered later. If they were dark, the profiles would be seen first, as figures against a white background.

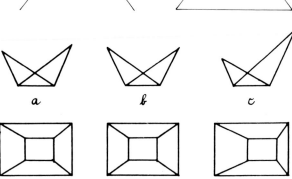

FIGURE 2.24. Law of proximity. The lines closer together are combined perceptually and look like converging beams.

FIGURE 2.25. If we join the far lines together, they appear to be united configurationally (law of closure).

a   *b*   *c*

d   *e*   *f*

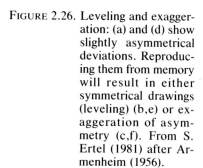

FIGURE 2.26. Leveling and exaggeration: (a) and (d) show slightly asymmetrical deviations. Reproducing them from memory will result in either symmetrical drawings (leveling) (b,e) or exaggeration of asymmetry (c,f). From S. Ertel (1981) after Armenheim (1956).

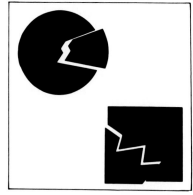

FIGURE 2.27. Tendency toward completion of shapes in the direction of more perfect figures. From S. Ertel (1981).

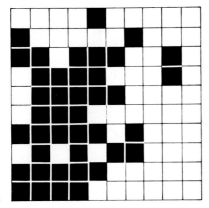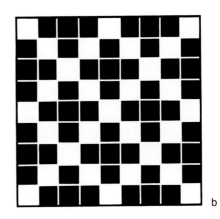

FIGURE 2.28. Displeasing (a) and pleasing (b) grid board configurations. The arrangement of field (b) exhibits various configurations of order. From D. Dörner and W. Vehrs (1975).

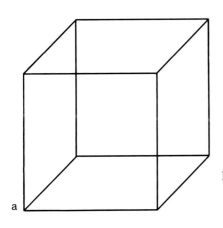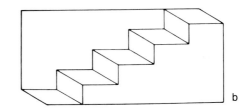

FIGURE 2.29. The Necker cube (a) and the stairway illusion (b) can be seen to oscillate between alternative perspectives.

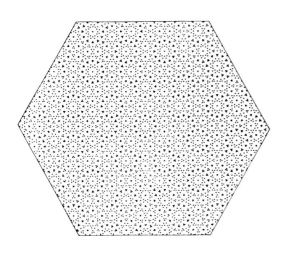

FIGURE 2.30. The automatic structuring processes of our perception. In 2- to 3-second intervals the perceived pattern changes; our perception interprets relations, discards them, and reinterprets, which causes the whole pattern to "simmer" from the competing interpretations. After J. Marroquin from D. Marr, 1982, p. 50.

The active performance of Gestalt perception becomes evident in a phenomenon called "reversible figures." If we look at the Necker cube, we first see one of the squares as the front side of the cube and the other as the rear side. After 2 or 3 seconds, however, the rear square appears to become the front surface. Our perception is constructed in such a way as if we were asking, "What else can be seen here?" (E. Pöppel, 1982; Figs. 2.29a, b). The same phenomenon of autonomic structuring processes of our perception can be observed in Fig. 2.30.

Our ability to abstract configurations is the basis of our capacity to categorize visual objects in the environment. We construct schematic representations, acquired schemata—of trees, houses, people, dogs, etc. Without this organizing ability we would be unable to cope with the environment. Small children utilize this capability when they say "Wow wow" to a dachshund, for example, a type of dog they have never seen before. Repeated perception of similarities permits the recognition of invariant structures and thus the formation of perceptive schemata.

In a remarkable investigation, S. Ertel has shown that this tendency toward Prägnanz also exists in the highest cognitive functions of humans; and it is even reflected in language behavior.

The organism begins with the phylogenetically programmed hypothesis that there are regularities in nature, and that they can be discovered (S. Ertel, 1981):

On all levels the organism expects regularities—permit me the comparison—like a spider waiting for flies in its web. Invariance is the primary hypothesis, which—from the viewpoint of perception in the narrow meaning of the term—is developed to a great extent prior to any previous experience. Perceptual Prägnanz or conciseness operates when there is no information to the contrary preventing the primary hypothesis to be used. Generally the invariance hypothesis is adequate for most experiences. The laws of vision, according to which objects are seen so redundantly under certain circumstances, lead generally to the best representation of reality (pp. 123–124).

This pressure to conform can also lead to errors. The geocentric world view is a classic example. "Disruption of configurations and liberation from the primary perceptual organization does not mean: the abandonment of the perceptual level (as some abstract artists do constantly), but rather: the recognition of disturbed planetary epicycles, small spots on the sun, irregular peaks and deflections in scientists' measuring devices, and the searching out of asymmetries and anomalies, which may lead to the dissolution of some of the good old ideas and thus lead to a better understanding at a higher level" (S. Ertel, 1981, p. 124). K. Lorenz used to say that it belonged to a scientist's virtues to be prepared to throw some pet hypothesis overboard each morning.

S. Ertel illustrates tendencies toward Prägnanz in language behavior with a number of quotations:

1. Mao Tse-tung

The world moves forward and the future is brilliant; no one can alter this general tendency of history.

2. Hitler

They will not conquer us militarily, economically or spiritually. Under no circumstances will they experience a German capitulation.

3. Communist Manifesto

To date, the history of all societies has been the history of class struggle.

4. Mohammed

Are not those who would make a distinction between Allah and his messengers and who say: we believe in some and not in others and want to choose an intermediate path between them: these are the true nonbelievers, and for these nonbelievers we have prepared horrible punishments.

These quotations vary in content but according to Ertel all utilize the same train of thought: world development cannot be stopped; the armies cannot be defeated; historical interpretation is fully valid; and man must heed all prophets without exception. The authors create a strict order in the realm of ideas that excludes everything that does not fit and which delineates the statement clearly and thus polarizes it strongly against the others.

For comparison, Ertel contrasts the above statements with those of weak Prägnanz for each of the same thoughts. They conform more to the real world but are less easily remembered and concise:

1. Mao Tse-Tung

There is a certain progress observable in some parts of the world that will probably continue in the future, even if it is hampered by conflicts between nations.

2. Hitler

They will hardly defeat us militarily, at least initially. We can also withstand them economically for some time, and the German people also appear to have the necessary spiritual strength. As long as current conditions do not substantially change, we could hardly conceive of capitulation.

We are confronted here with two different styles of thinking, which Ertel calls A-style and B-style. They can be recognized lexically, for there are A and B expressions (Table 2.1). One can determine the degree of dogmatism in any body of text by searching out the use of A and B expressions in it.

In word-picture matching experiments Ertel required subjects to match Type A and Type B nonsense words with figures either showing or lacking Prägnanz. Subjects had no difficulty sorting Prägnanz-type words like "must" with Prägnanz-type pictures; and, conversely, they easily matched non-Prägnanz-type pictures with non-Prägnanz-type words like "can."

The Dogmatism Quotient (DQ) reflects the Prägnanz level of cognitive activity that underlies the production of the amount of text being investigated.

A dogmatism index analysis of position papers and programs of German political parties displays a U-shaped curve from the left through liberals to the political right (Fig. 2.31). A remarkable fact is that the DQ is sensitive to certain effects (such as applause; see Figs. 2.32–2.34). It is worth noting that the DQ is sensitive to affective responses. It increases with the level of fear, anger, and aggression, but also with positive emotions (euphoria, being in love, and triumph). Fear limits vision and love makes blind. We will come back to these facts in the discussion of human rationality later on. For now, it will suffice to note that a number of elementary laws of perception transmodally influence the cognitive realm.

Table 2.1. A and B Expressions from Ertel's (1981) DoTA Dictionary

	A Expressions	B Expressions

Category 1
Frequency
    duration and
    distribution
	Lasting, always, every
	    time, never, each time, etc.
		Occasionally, in general, on
		    occasion, usually, often,
		    now and then, normally,
		    mostly, sometimes, etc.

Category 2
Number and
    quantity
	All, without exception, without
	    limits, uniquely, whole, not
	    in the least, every, every-
	    one, etc.
		A number of, a little, some,
		    certain, largely, mostly
		    several, a large number,
		    a pair, partly, etc.

Category 3
Degree and
    extent
	Absolutely, entirely, totally, in
	    principle, etc.
		Especially, a little, to some
		    extent, highly, scarcely,
		    etc.

Category 4
Certainty
	Excluding, unquestionably,
	    certainly, not in the least,
	    naturally, etc.
		Apparently, presumably,
		    scarcely, possibly,
		    hardly, etc.

Category 5
Exclusion,
    inclusion, and
    applicability
	Alone, all else but, exclusively,
	    one and only, either/or,
	    neither/nor, solely, nothing
	    but, etc.
		Among other things, on the
		    other hand, beyond
		    that, furthermore, in-
		    cluding, for one thing,
		    further, etc.

Category 6
Necessity and
    possibility
	Must, have to, have to be, not
	    permitted, cannot, cannot
	    permit ourselves, not able,
	    etc.
		May, can, allow, be in a po-
		    sition to, not needing to,
		    not having to, etc.

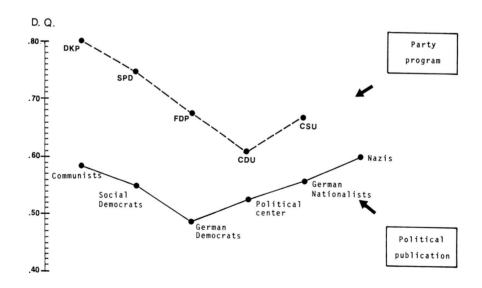

FIGURE 2.31. Top graph: Political programs, including the post-1945 period. Lower graph: Political publications from the Weimer Republic. DKP, Communists; SPD, Social Democrats: FDP, Free Democrats and other liberals; CDU, Christian Democrats; CSU, Christian Socialists. From S. Ertel, 1981.

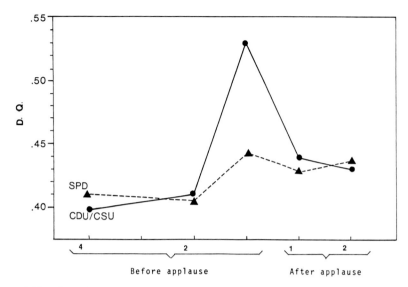

FIGURE 2.32. The DQ in political speakers of the German Bundestag (Parliament) before
and after applause. Numbers (4, 2, 1, 2) are the fourth sentence, second
sentence, first sentence, and second sentence, respectively. SPD, Social
Democratic Party; CDU/CSU, Christian Democrats/Christian Socialists. From
S. Ertel (1981).

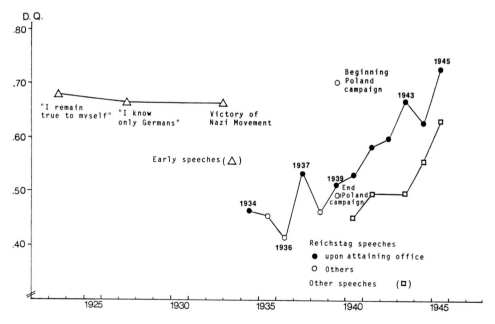

FIGURE 2.33. The DQ curve of Adolf Hitler's speeches. Early speeches, Reichstag addresses,
and "other" speeches after 1933. From S. Ertel (1981).

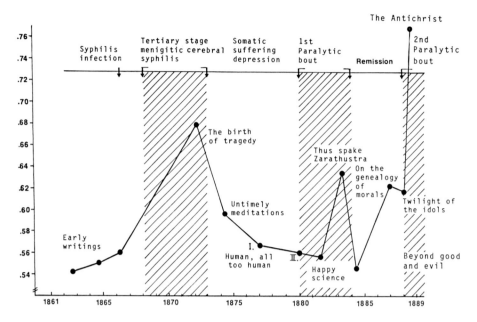

FIGURE 2.34. The DQ curve for the life work of Friedrich Nietzsche. From S. Ertel (1981).

Perceptual constancies of space, size, and color are of particular importance. E. von Holst (1957) investigated their organization. The effect of spatial constancy is such that we perceive objects in space at rest, even when we turn our eyes or head, so that their images, in fact, move across our retina. This is achieved when the instruction for the eye to move is duplicated centrally and stored as an efferent copy. The resulting movement from the instruction is then reported by the eye as a reafferent signal, which, in turn, is compared with the efferent copy, and is canceled when both agree. Passive movement of the eye does not result in an efferent copy, since there is no instruction for the eye to move, therefore the displacement of the retinal image will appear as a movement of the object that in fact has not moved. We can easily convince ourselves of this by pressing a finger against the eyeball: objects in the visual field appear to move, and the passive movement of the eyeball is misinterpreted as a movement of the environment. Another experiment allows us to perceive the efferent copy: If we paralyze the muscles of the eyeball with novocaine and ask the subject to move the eye to the left, then the subject will subjectively experience that the objects in the visual field leap to the left. Since, in fact, neither the environment nor the eye moved in this case, the spatial perception must have a central origin, namely in the efferent copy of the instruction to turn the eye; since the efferent signal is not canceled by reafference, we erroneously perceive the movement (Figs. 2.35 A and B).

Size constancy operates on the same principle in which convergence and accommodation are achieved. Color constancy is based on the "assumption" on the part of the perceptual apparatus that the predominant color in a field of view is the color of the light source. The organism must perceptually extinguish this light in order to see objects in their true colors. Thus the color "white" was invented, which has no color value. The perceptual apparatus also provides each color with a complementary color, which is produced as a perception and with whose help the undesired color can be canceled.

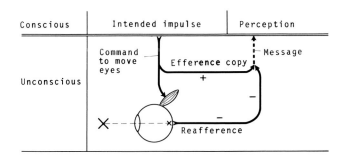

Intended impulse	Objective event	Perceived event
a. Visual direction unchanged	Eye moved passively to left	Cross moves to right
b. Visual direction to left	Eye is stationary	Cross moves to left
c. Visual direction to right	Eye moves left	Cross stands still

Eye movement and perception

Conscious	Intended impulse	Perception
Unconscious	Command to move eyes — Efference copy +	Message
	Reafference	−

FIGURE 2.35. (A) Experiments to determine the functional organization of spatial constancy. From E. von Holst (1955). (B) The functional organization of spatial constancy according to E. von Holst (1955).

This kind of information processing can also lead to erroneous interpretations. If a small grey field is viewed within a predominantly red area surrounding it, we perceive this grey as green, since our perception assumes that the light source is a red one. We create the green to reduce the excess redness, a phenomenon known as simultaneous contrast. Thus our perception has built-in assumptions based on phylogenetic experience and these are reflected in these kinds of perceptual inferences.

It was long believed that color categories were culturally acquired. Subjects from different cultures were presented with colors to name, and it was found that the same number of colors were not named in all cultures; often several colors were combined under one category. However, we also have general color concepts as "bright" or "colorful." If, however, subjects were asked to arrange colors into categories, it was found that this arranging followed the same pattern across cultures. Even if a subject had no name for a particular color, similar colors were placed into the same categories (literature cited in P. Kay and W. Kempton, 1984). Thus color perception is not culturally determined; instead, the same color categories are perceived in all cultures.

Perceptual categories are also found in other sense modalities. Just as we arrange the continuum of lightwaves into classes of primary colors, we categorize acoustic impressions (Fig. 2.36). If a person hears a series of artificially produced sounds that change gradually from *ba* to *pa,* the person will hear only *ba* up to a certain point and thereafter *pa,* but never anything in between. All test subjects experienced the transition at the same point in the experiment, even those with different language backgrounds. Even 1- to 6-month-old infants hear in categories. We will return to this topic in the chapter on "verbal communication."

Like color categories, temporal categories are also a product of the human brain (E. Pöppel, 1983, 1984). The shortest detectable auditory time unit is three thousandths of a second. Events occurring within two thousandths of a second of each other are perceived as a single unit. For the visual system the data are different. Here, intervals from about twenty thousandths of a second on are experienced as distinct. However, when two events are separated by this interval, it is impossible to determine which of the two signals occurred first. At least thirty thousandths of a second must separate events for us to be able to place them in sequence. This holds true for visual, auditory, and tactile stimuli. According to E. Pöppel the event identification system arises from a brain mechanism which functions like an oscillating system with a frequency of 30 Hz.

The experience of sequencing of events requires an additional mechanism that combines sequential events into perceptual configuration that we experience as "now." This "now" has a duration of about 3 seconds. It is a universal, basic phenomenon of human temporal experience, and its length corresponds to the units of speech (p. 696). Thus, in Pöppel's formulation, the brain divides the continuum of speech into 3-second time units. This is also reflected in the duration of musical themes and the length of lines in poetry.

Metronome beats of equal volume are subjectively structured, for the perceived loudness fluctuates in 3-second intervals. Thus our perception in this case is certainly not "objective." It orders, categorizes, and interprets the events.

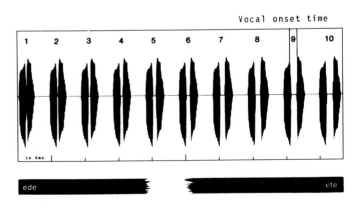

FIGURE 2.36. The categorial shift from ede to ete. The graph shows ten vocal sounds with gradually increasing vocal onset time. At the vocal onset time of approximately 80 msec the utterance is perceived with the new quality ete. From W.J.M. Levelt (1987).

A comparable segmentation was found in movement patterns in four independent cultures (Europeans, Trobriand Islander, Yanomami Indians, and Kalahari Bushmen). The analysis of these documents of unstaged social interactions revealed a time constant of about 3 seconds. In this way, behavior becomes structured into units which fit the perceptive 3-second bias. And this is probably what is "meant" to be, since movements often serve communication (M. Schleidt *et al.*, 1987).

K. R. Popper (1973, p. 165) is therefore correct in asserting that no sensory data or perception can exist that is not processed by some theory. However, he diminishes the significance of sensory data as the basis, and hence induction, when he states that: "The data are therefore no basis or guarantee for theories, and they are no more certain than any theory or 'bias' but are probably less certain. . . . The equivalents of primitive, uncritically accepted theories are contained in the sense organs and these have been less thoroughly tested than scientific theories. . . ."

To this I would counter that the theories which are built into our perception have been more "comprehensively tested" over millions of years of evolution than scientific theories. Popper (1973, p. 108) states that "The natural laws are *our* invention, made by animals and man, genetically a priori, but they are not necessarily a priori valid. We attempt to ascribe them to nature." Popper here follows Kant that human reason established these laws, imposed them on our "sensory swamp," and only thereby created order in nature. This is no doubt true for the process of categorical perception, in which a continuum is arranged into categories by the perceptual apparatus. In general, the way we think and look at the world represents a reality that is valid within the average measuring range of the Mesokosmos toward which we are adapted—as Popper does emphasize elsewhere. K. Lorenz (1959, p. 263) comments follows: "It is as unlikely that the fins of fishes determine the physical properties of water, or that the eye determines the characteristics of light, as that the way we think and view the world has 'invented' space, time and causality."

Perception and the motor apparatus form one functional system in whose development maturational processes play an important part.

Two-week old infants reach for visually presented objects. Hence, the expectation that visual entities can also be touched is already present. The reaction is still little differentiated, resulting in what C. Trevarthen (1975) calls "prereaching."

Children make intentional grabbing movements before they are physically able to grasp objects by bringing their arms and hands together in front of the body. They have a significant tendency to perform these grasping movements more frequently when the object is of an appropriate size for grasping. If in a choice situation a ball of appropriate size and an oversized one are offered, infants make more intention movements toward the appropriate ball rather than the oversized one. This shows that grasping objects is coordinated by visual information about the graspability of the target object, which is already available to the child before it had any experiences with holding objects (J. S. Bruner and B. Koslowski, 1972).

Newborn infants turn their heads in the direction of a sound source and attempt to look at it, as if they "knew" that one could see the source of the sound. They do this according to an inborn central fixation program. Children blind from birth behave in the same way (D. G. Freedman, 1964). We will later consider the social significance of this reaction (p. 195).

Infants also want to focus and learn to bring into focus a blurred slide projected to them by sucking on a pacifier (I. V. Kalnins and J. S. Bruner, quoted in R. C.

Hulsebus, 1973). Hence, children come into the world with the expectation that objects have sharply defined contours, and they need to create this condition when they do not see objects in focus. This can be accomplished by accommodation of the lens, but also by other behavior patterns.

T. G. R. Bower (1971) found that 2-week-old infants only reached for graspable objects and not for pictures of them. D. DiFranco *et al.* (1978) could not confirm Bower's findings. In their studies, children reach for three-dimensional objects as well as for pictures. In principle, this does not alter the conclusion that children at an early age associate visual impressions with tactile expectations, as other studies have verified.

If a symmetrically expanding shadow or dark spot is projected onto a screen in front of a 14- to 20-day-old infant secured in a chair, then the infant interprets this perception as an object on a collision course with itself. The infant lifts an arm protectively before its face, turns away, and blinks. An asymmetrically expanding spot does not elicit this defensive response, since it is interpreted as a passing object (W. Ball and F. Tronick, 1971). Figure 2.37 depicts a variation of a study by J. Dunkeld and T. G. R. Bower (1976), which was repeated with slight modifications by A. Yonas *et al.* (1979). They found that blinking was a good indicator of collision expectation. Their test subjects blinked their eyes when objects moved toward them on collision course. This work, in principle, confirms the results obtained by Ball and Tronick.

Previously, developmental psychologists had maintained that the infant perceived various facets of reality separately but would not know that the tactile impressions, for example, are related to visual or other attributes of the object. It was held that the child learned these relationships primarily in the first two years of life, acquiring, among other things, object constancy and achieving (after

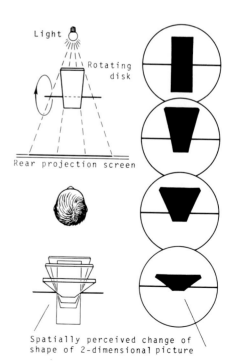

FIGURE 2.37. Procedure of shadow projection used by Dunkeld and Bower, with which the test infants were given the impression of an object moving (rotating) toward them. From J. Dunkeld and T.G.R. Bower (1976).

J. Piaget's theory) a new cognitive organizational level. The studies of T. G. R. Bower, W. Ball, and F. Tronick verify that integration capacity does not have to rest solely upon individual experience.

The interpretation of stimuli apparently proceeds on the basis of phylogenetic experience. It is certainly advantageous to avoid objects approaching rapidly without having to undergo the painful personal experience of a previous collision with them. The necessary "knowledge" for this adaptive response is contained in information-processing mechanisms as a result of phylogenetic adaptation. In this and similar cases, these adaptations are so structured that specific stimuli or stimulus configurations release specific motoric acts, that is, elicit specific behavioral patterns—in our example, defensive and avoidance behavior. These mechanisms are termed innate releasing mechanisms (IRM's; N. Tinbergen, 1951).

They act like a stimulus filter, in that they only effect the release of certain behavior patterns when certain key stimuli are presented but remain impervious to other stimuli. They can be understood using a lock-and-key analogy. IRMs are not only specific to visual stimuli. If a newborn infant is touched at the corner of its mouth with a finger, the baby turns its head from side to side (search automism), and finally grabs the finger with its mouth to suck it. Targeted orientation toward the point of tactile contact can also be elicited (H. F. R. Prechtl, 1958; H. F. R. Prechtl and H. G. Lenard, 1968). Here a tactile stimulus is connected with a particular behavior pattern by means of an innate releasing mechanism.

IRMs have been investigated in animals both in model experiments and neuroethological studies (J. P. Ewert, 1974a, b; F. Huber, 1974; other examples in I. Eibl-Eibesfeldt, 1987). Many social responses of animals are mediated by such IRMs. Reciprocal adaptations between the sender and receiver of signals took place in such contexts. Signals evolved for various sensory systems (visual, auditory, olfactory, tactile, and even electrical). Expressive behavior patterns as well as morphological structures such as color patterns and manes serve this purpose. Signals that evolved to serve the specific function of communication are known as "social releasers."

IRM mechanisms play an important role in human social behavior as well. If newborn infants hear a selection of tape recordings of the same loudness, one of them being of a baby crying, they will start to cry when they hear the recording of crying, but not when they hear recordings of other vocalizations (A. Sagi and M. L. Hoffmann, 1978). The sound of crying releases crying, a process known also as mood induction. The term "imitation" would be a poor choice here, for it suggests trial and gradual practice, but here we are faced with, as it were, preprogrammed response based upon an innate releasing mechanism. Visual perception studies have shown similar results.

A. N. Meltzoff and M. K. Moore (1977) discovered that 12- to 21-day-old infants are capable of imitating such facial movements as mouth opening, tongue extension, and lip protruding, as well as a number of finger movements (Figs. 2.38, 2.39). In a late study (1983a–c) they were even able to demonstrate this ability in the first 72 hours following birth. The investigations of J. Dunkeld (1978), S. W. Jacobson (1979), A. P. Burd and A. E. Milewski (1981), and J. Kugiumutzakis (1985) confirm these results. The latter found that eyebrow movements as well as mouth movements were responded to with similar expressions. T. M. Field *et al.* (1982) demonstrated that such an "imitative" ability is already present in newborns at an average age of 36 hours. They mimed expressions of astonishment (open mouth), pouting (protruding lips), and joy (smiling and wide open lips) and elicited the

55

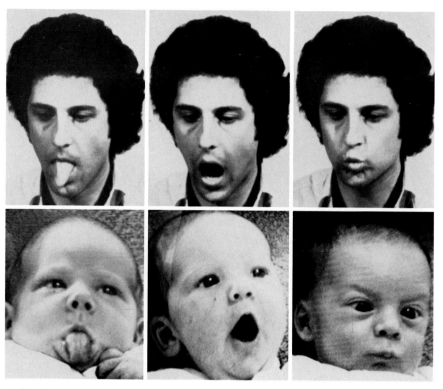

FIGURE 2.38. The model and its imitation in a 2- to 3-week old infant. From A.N. Meltzoff and M.K. Moore (1977).

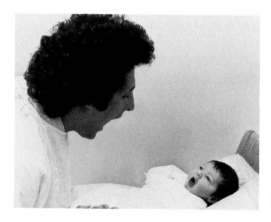

FIGURE 2.39.
A 19-hour-old girl imitates tongue exten-
sion and mouth opening. Photo: A.N.
Meltzoff.

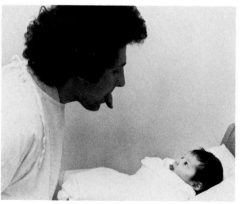

same expressions from the infants (Figs. 2.40, 2.41). M. Kaitz *et al.* (1988) demonstrated that newborns responded to tongue protrusion by reproducing this gesture but failed to imitate the facial expressions of happiness, sadness, and surprise.

Some researchers, however, reported that they had no success at all eliciting such imitation in very young babies (M. Hamm, M. Russell, and J. Koepke, 1979; L. A. Hayes and J. L. Watson, 1981; H. Neuburger *et al.,* 1983; B. McKenzie and R. Over, 1983; O. M. Ewert, 1983). A. N. Meltzoff and M. K. Moore (1983a, b, c) discuss possible reasons for this. In this context, experiments performed by A. Vinter (1985) are of particular interest. She offered the babies static and moving models. Only the moving models were imitated. If a person just stuck out his tongue without moving, the babies seemed to have difficulty in perceiving the stimulus pattern.

These results lead to the conclusion that infants are capable of responding to observed facial and hand movements with corresponding behavior, copying the behavior of the model in their own behavior with no need for prior learning experience. This would require the existence of structures that are, in principle, similar in function to IRMs.

A. N. Meltzoff and M. K. Moore (1983a, b, c) and T. M. Field *et al.* (1982) consider the possibility of this interpretation in their discussion but conclude that the concept of the IRM was not sufficient to explain the undoubtedly inborn capabilities of the babies. They felt that the responses made by the infants were not sufficiently stereotyped to correspond to this ethological concept. Furthermore, they believed that the behavior patterns normally elicited by an IRM should always be different from the behavior patterns eliciting them. This, however, is not always so. Fighting cichlid fish answer tail beats with tail beats and ram-butting with ram-butting. The effect is, as it were, imitation. However, it is actually an IRM-mediated response. If we should find that the ability, i.e., to respond at once to perceived behavior patterns with the same behavior, included any nonspecific behavior patterns, including those which definitely have no signal function, then it would be appropriate to distinguish this inborn ability from responses to specific releasers. However, at this time, there is no need for this. The stimuli responded to are basic facial expressions and thus, in all probability, social signals. In any case, the performance presupposes projections from the sensory to the motor areas of the brain that allow perceived movements to be translated into an individual's own movements.[3] This kind of primary imitation would be distinguished from learning through imitation, which involves trial and error corrections and extensive visual and proprioceptive movement control where one can trace a gradual learning process.

---

[3]A. N. Meltzoff and M. K. Moore speak of "active intermodal matching." "In contrast, we postulate that infants use the equivalence between the act seen and the act done as the fundamental basis for generating the behavioral match. By our account even this early imitation involves active matching to an environmentally provided target or 'model.' Our corollary hypothesis is that this imitation is mediated by a representational system that allows infants to unite within on common framework their own body transformations and those of others. According to this view, both visual and motor transformations of the body can be represented in a common form and thus directly compared. Infants could thereby relate proprioceptive motor informations about their own unseen body movements to their representation of the visually perceived model and create the match required" (A. N. Meltzoff and M. K. Moore, 1983a).

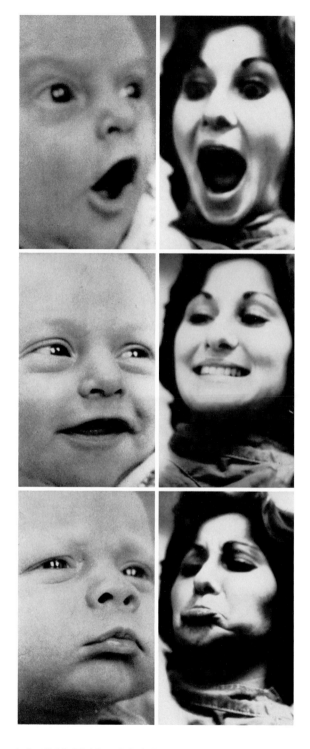

FIGURE 2.40. Facial expressions made by T.M. Field and their imitation. From T.M. Field *et al.* (1982).

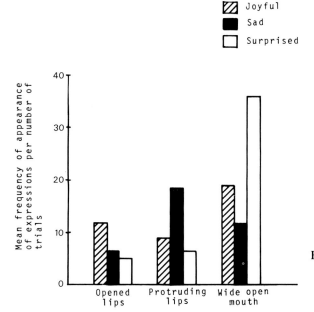

FIGURE 2.41. Frequency with which infants imitated the three displayed lip movements. From T.M. Field *et al.* (1982).

The argument that the responses are too variable to be explained with the IRM concept does not hold true since ethological concepts do not exclude individual and situational variability. Responses are by no means all-or-nothing behaviors, although ethological terminology ("fixed-action pattern") has led to misunderstandings (p. 25). Imitative behavior of infants of the type discussed can be fully explained with the IRM concept. The objection that there are so many facial movements one could scarcely conceive of an IRM for each one of them is untenable. Why should the many innate mimic expressions not have corresponding recipient adaptations?

Be it as it may, our American colleagues have been most successful in demonstrating the existence of highly differentiated innate capabilities. This is a tribute to the experimental skill of the Americans and English, which seems to have its roots in the skillful experimental heritage of American behaviorism.

The surprising ability to respond to facial movements at such an early age contrasts with the findings of several investigators, who report a very slow development of face recognition in babies (R. Ahrens, 1954; F. L. Fantz, 1966; D. Maurer, 1985). In these experiments, however, the babies were shown static presentations of simplified drawings. The length of time the babies looked at these (fixation time) was taken as a measure of preference. Babies only started to look somewhat longer at 2-dimensional models of human faces at an age of 2 months. This led to the conclusion that the recognition of face develops slowly. I doubt, however, that these experiments are conclusive. One would need to work with presentations in which babies could also perceive movements to come to a valid conclusion.

Animal experiments with models performed by ethologists have revealed that some of the visual releasers are configurational, namely, based on very simple

59

relational characteristics. These studies also demonstrated that a specific behavior is often elicited by a number of key stimuli, each operating independently, which when presented together as a whole elicit a summation effect. Finally, artificial "super releasers" could be fabricated (e.g., key stimuli simulating a sexual partner) whose effect was greater than the normal stimulus. This also occurs in humans. K. Lorenz (1943) noted that we respond to specific cues of infant characteristics with affectionate behavior. We perceive them as cute or cuddly, the latter expression referring to the parental care behavior released by those stimuli. Our stimulus "detectors" are adapted to certain anatomical proportions of infants. They have large heads relative to their torsos and relatively short extremities, something the doll industry has cleverly exploited.

More specific childlike features include a large forehead relative to the rest of the head and relatively large eyes compared to the small face. B. Hückstedt (1965) tested 330 male and female subjects in various age groups with schematic profile drawings of children's heads, in which the forehead arch and the height of the top of the head were varied. Cranial emphasis was preferred by female subjects in the 10- to 13-year-old age bracket and by males 18 to 21 years old. Female subjects preferred a supernormal (i.e., exaggerated) upper head even more than male subjects did. Hückstedt's results (see Fig. 2.42) were verified by B. T. Gardner and L. Wallach (1965) and W. Fullard and A. M. Rieling (1976).

All these baby characteristics have been exaggerated by the model experiments of industry. Many dolls and comic book characters utilize these childlike proportions in an exaggerated way (Fig. 2.43A). The child appeal of Mickey Mouse has improved over the last 50 years. The size of the head and eyes and the curvature

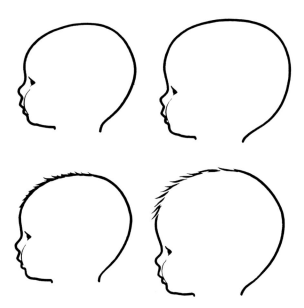

FIGURE 2.42. Infant schema. *Top:* head with normal shape (left) and exaggerated shape (right). The latter drawing was preferred by 10- to 13-year-old girls and 18- to 21-year-old boys. *Bottom:* modifications of the frontal bone curvature (left) and the upper head height (right) in B. Hückstedt's study. Isolated exaggeration of both characteristics resulted in preference for the mean (but not maximum) proportional exaggeration. From B. Hückstedt (1965).

FIGURE 2.43. (A) Infant schema. Walt Disney's familiar creations: Donald Duck's nephews Huey, Dewey, and Louie; Little Eagle Eye; and Tramp. (B) The development of Walt Disney's Mickey Mouse during the 50 years of its existence. The size of the head in relation to the body increased and so did the relative size of the eyes, while the extremities got shorter and thicker. All these changes increased its appeal to the child. Courtesy Walt Disney Productions. (C) Infantilized depiction of women from a magazine, *Picapiedras,* Bogota.

61

of the cranial vault increased (S. J. Gould, 1980). The size of the eyes changed from 27 to 42% of the size of the head and the size of the head from 42.7 to 48.1% of the size of the body. The forehead curvature could not be changed, since the head was conventionally drawn as a circle. But the ears were moved backward, so that the distance nose–ears was increased. The teddy bear underwent similar changes. The extremities became increasingly shortened and the head curvature increased continually from 1900 to 1985 (R. A. Hinde and L. A. Barden, 1985). The stepwise improvement indicates selection by the market (Fig. 2.43B).

Whereas all these proportional characteristics mentioned so far did not arise in the service of communication (since they are one-sided and only effect the recipient), the chubby cheeks of infants and young children are social releasers serving as signals to release parental behaviors. Presumably the *Corpus adiposum buccae* strengthen the cheeks for sucking, but our most closely related primate species do not have this adaptation. Infants elicit friendly (smiling) behavior just by their appearance alone, even from strangers (M. Schleidt *et al.,* 1981; C. L. Robinson *et al.,* 1979). Other appealing child signals include behavior patterns. Thus, we consider their uncoordinated movements cute. Since a friendly mood also inhibits aggressive impulses, small children are often used in appeasement ceremonies (see greeting rituals, p. 493). The female face also exhibits childlike features, predisposed to eliciting caring behavior. This is often emphasized in drawings (Fig. 2.43C).

Courting couples display many childlike behavior patterns; people in sorrow also elicit comfort by this means. Such appeals to the infant schema are blended together in television commercials to make them appealing, not irritating, to viewers.

How strong the bias of our perception is, is shown even in our response to animals that possess some of these characteristics. It is clear that some kind of fundamental reaction is involved, for even very small children already cuddle simple infant-schema models such as teddy bears.

Difficulties arise in attempting to ascribe our highly emotional response to child characteristics by means of typical learning paradigms. The child pays for the care it demands through its charm alone. In all other respects its behavior is rather burdensome and irritating—it cries, is dirty, and needs much care.

As to the role played by IRMs in adults, we have to rely on circumstantial evidence. When adults respond to simple models with the appropriate predicted behavior, this may suggest that their reaction has been activated by IRMs. However this criterion alone is not sufficient to support this hypothesis. The Prägnanz tendency of perceptual mechanisms, the "cognitive love of order," leads us to continuously formulate schemas (templates) and general concepts. When children draw trees, houses, and people, they continually schematicize and select out the generalized invariable elements of their subjects. This is, as mentioned earlier, achieved by innate perceptual mechanisms (p. 42). When we draw a caricature of a person with a few lines we schematize. We then emphasize certain characteristics of the individual in line with the tendency toward Prägnanz, and we simplify the whole. A caricature, however, must contain certain essential elements which cannot be omitted if the Gestalt is to be recognized. This is not strictly the case with the schematic representations to which we respond by means of innate releasing mechanisms. There are cases in which some basic configuration must be presented but, in many cases, components of the complex releasing situation can be presented in isolation. For instance, the chubby cheeks of babies, the head–body proportions, and the face–head proportions each have a releasing quality by themselves, their effects being additive when they are presented together. This also holds true for other social signals where we can observe that the same characteristics are emphasized and exaggerated cross-culturally to indicate maleness or femaleness, and even features which in reality are not very noticeable (Figs. 2.44, 2.45).

Thus, in various cultures men's shoulders are artificially emphasized with clothing or special adornments. This amounts to emphasizing a characteristic that is today no longer anatomically significant. If we analyze the hair growth patterns on a man we find that tufts of hair would develop on the shoulders if hair growth were increased to a significant length (P. Leyhausen, 1983). We can assume that males had more hair in earlier times than they do today and that the hair growth patterns served to enlarge the body outline of our upright ancestors (Fig. 2.44A). Hair growth declined during the course of hominization, but the receptor adaptation may have remained, which resulted in a preference and thus drew particular attention to this region of the body.

E. Jessen (1981) presented German and Tanzanian children of various ages with drawings of simple geometric figures (circles, squares) and placed triangles standing either on their base or apex. The children were asked to designate the figures as either male or female. Children 4 to 6 years old could not differentiate between them, but 7- to 16-year-olds could. The 7- to 12-year-old children interpreted characteristics in the figures that reflect individual, culturally determined experience: for example "skirt" as a female characteristic and "stout belly" as a male feature (for European subjects; Tanzanians chose other features). During puberty, however, there is a pronounced change in the character assessment. Pubertal children characterized soft and round features as females and angular, coarse, and rough ones as males. The most frequently selected choice for male was the triangle standing on its apex, probably an abstract exaggeration of the shoulder emphasis mentioned earlier. This transformation in perception occurred similarly in both European and Tanzanian subjects. Thus, through the development of new perceptual filters in both cultures, identical emphasis appears in the perception of people.

We must expect that some IRMs, such as those responding to attributes of sexual partners, mature functionally during the course of ontogeny. During this time, however, the organism is exposed to so many experiences that it is only possible in exceptional cases to experimentally demonstrate the existence of IRMs. So, in the case of responses to simple key stimuli and releasers that appear later in life, we have to depend mainly on circumstantial evidence. Subjects born blind but whose vision was later restored by cataract operations could offer possibilities for experimentation, however, only positive results of such studies would be significant. We know from animal studies that fully functional visual systems present at birth soon degenerate if they are not used (see *Ethology: The Biology of Behavior*).

The tactile drawings of subjects blind from birth are of particular interest in this regard. The subjects were given ball point pens to use for drawing, which, on a particular writing surface, left relief line traces. The way in which the lines were drawn reflected a number of universal perceptual principles. In drawing outlines of objects, the subjects accounted for the viewer's position. Thus any parts of a structure that were hidden from the viewer's visual field were not shown in the drawing; only the lines of the covering object were included. A table seen

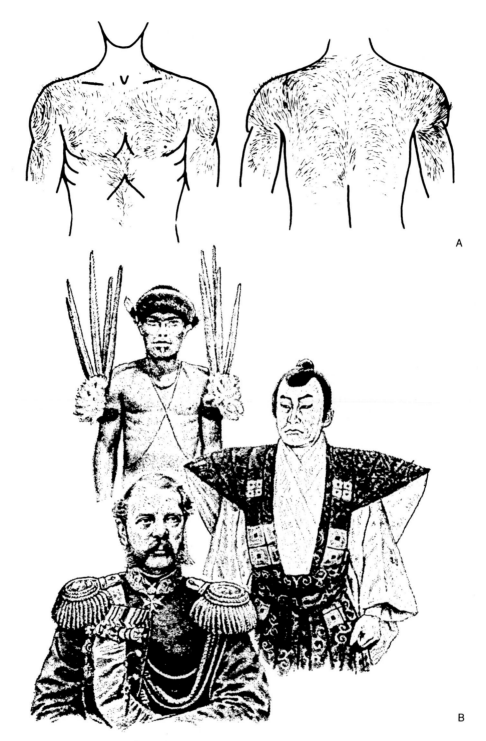

FIGURE 2.44. (A) Hair growth pattern in males: (i) front view; (ii) back view. If man had more hair, tufts would form on the shoulders. From P. Leyhausen (1983). (B) Examples of artificial shoulder emphasis in males: a Yanomami Indian with feather ornaments, a Kabuki actor (Japan), and Tsar Alexander II of Russia after a contemporary portrait. Drawing by H. Kacher from I. Eibl-Eibesfeldt (1970a).

FIGURE 2.45. (A) Women's fashions emphasize the hip region and often the buttocks as well: (a) Marie Antoinette, after an engraving; (b) Pauline Lucca, 1870, photo from M. Von Boehn. (B) Dancers from Kaleuna (Trobriand Islands). Their skirts emphasize the hip region. Photo: I. Eibl-Eibesfeldt.

from the top was drawn as a rectangle (tabletop). From a side view, subjects drew two table legs, which is as the viewer would see them. The view from below showed four legs. The blind subjects also utilized convergence and thickness of lines to depict inclinations, proximity, and distance (J. M. Kennedy, 1980, 1982, 1983).

G. P. Sackett (1966) demonstrated perceptual maturation in rhesus monkeys. He raised the monkeys in social isolation in cages with nontransparent walls, which were built so that the monkeys could not even see their own reflections in the sides of the cages. Each day the monkeys were shown slides of landscapes, fruits, and other rhesus monkeys. After each projection of a slide the monkey could select the picture itself by activating a lever, which caused the slide to show for 15 seconds. Self-initiated projection could be repeated over a 5-minute interval. The monkeys soon learned how to use the lever, and the choices they made during self-projection were a good measure of preference for individual pictures. Initially, the monkeys showed a preference for seeing conspecifics, because the frequency of projecting other monkeys was higher than for other slide subjects. Furthermore, pictures of other monkeys elicited contact sounds, approach, and play invitation behavior. One of the slides showed a monkey in threat posture. This picture, too, was initially preferred along with the other monkey slides. However, after 2½ months there was a drastic change in their responses to this slide. While the subjects continued to prefer other monkey slides, the picture of the threatening monkey produced defensive reactions and fright calls; the rate of viewing for this slide dropped substantially. Apparently the subjects now interpreted the monkey's threat face and threat posture as dangerous, and since they had no prior social experience with conspecifics, this perceptual ability could only arise from the functional maturity of IRMs. The development of fear of strangers in humans is a closely related phenomenon (p. 170).

2.2.3. Templates

Templates are a special category of perceptual adaptations. They permit incoming signals to be compared with some built-in reference pattern and behavior to be adjusted appropriately. Thus chaffinches must learn their species' song, but they know which song pattern is the correct one to imitate. If chaffinches raised in social isolation hear tape recordings of various bird songs, they choose their own species song as a model for learning (W. H. Thorpe, 1958). Their selection process is based on an innate template. Similar relationships hold in the swamp sparrow *Melospiza georgiana,* but here the template is tuned to recognize species-specific syllables. Swamp sparrow syllables can be used to compose a wide variety of songs; these are learned. But songs composed of alien species' syllables were not accepted by the swamp sparrows even if they produced a song corresponding to the pattern of the swamp sparrow song (P. Marler, 1976, 1978). For swamp sparrows then, the template for the recognition of syllables is a phylogenetic adaptation, but the template of the entire song must be acquired through learning. This happens before the sparrows are actually able to sing. If they are isolated after acquiring the template, then they learn their song later on the basis of this acquired pattern. They must hear themselves vocalize; if they are deafened they develop atypical songs.

It is likely that norms for our human behavior are also laid down in comparable

neuronal structures. As templates they determine what is right or wrong, good or bad or, in other words, "expected behaviors." The universality of certain behavioral norms expressed in the widely recurring themes reinforcing the "right" social conduct and manifesting themselves as attitudes even against the strongest teaching attempts to the contrary indicate that some of these templates are innate. Deviation from the norm makes humans feel uneasy, while conformity elicits satisfaction. M. Gruter (1979, 1983) suggests that brain amines (endorphins) are responsible for this.

2.2.4. Motivating Mechanisms, Drives, Biological Rhythms

Man, like every other animal, is subject to changing moods, which are not always induced by corresponding fluctuations in the environment. Motivating mechanisms ensure that we do not wait passively for stimuli in order to respond. They create a specific behavioral preparedness we call "moods" in which we actively seek out stimulus situations that permit the performance of specific behavior patterns. When we are hungry, we search for food; when thirsty, we search for water. If we are bored we are driven by curiosity to seek entertainment. Our senses respond selectively to specific stimuli depending on the mood we are in at the time.

This searching for releasing stimuli has been known as "appetitive behavior" since the time of W. Craig (1918). Once a hungry individual has found food, various behavior patterns run their course, which are concluded by the final consummatory act of feeding. Often, the individual will experience many different behaviors before reaching the final consummatory act. The performance of a behavioral sequence leads to satisfaction of the specific need and in animals and humans a change of mood has taken place as a result. Many disparate mechanisms combine to achieve this change. The individual often causes changes in the environment through its actions, and thus a consummatory situation is achieved. Feedback from internal receptors are another means of inducing a change in appetence—so are hormonal changes. Most interesting of all, but least understood to date, are changes in mood brought about by changes within the central nervous system, in the sense of a discharge of a reaction by performance of a particular consummatory act.

The mechanisms underlying hunger and thirst have been studied in depth. Sensory cells measure the blood sugar level, that is, the osmotic value of tissue fluids. Deviations from the norm release behavior that finally restores physiological equilibrium or homeostasis. But even before this is accomplished the individual ceases eating or drinking. Eating, drinking, and stomach distention are registered and then hunger or thirst are turned off, preventing excessive consumption. Time is required for homeostasis to be restored, since nourishment has to be resorbed. But, if within a certain time, physiological equilibrium has not been restored, the appetitive behavior will be instigated anew. If the glucose receptors of the hypothalamus are destroyed, mammals overeat, their hunger continuing unabated (literature in I. Eibl-Eibesfeldt, 1987).

Not every appetitive behavior is motivated by physiological disequilibrium. The sexual drive, for instance, has an entirely different motivational basis. Hormonal influences produce a lasting readiness for sexual activity. An oscillating sexual motivation determined by external stimuli, internal sensory stimuli, and central nervous contingencies is superimposed on this readiness. In man the decline in the sexual drive after orgasm is in part (but not exclusively) determined by the fullness of the seminal vesicle; but this is certainly not the only factor involved, because there are men who can experience an orgasm without an ejaculation. Women, of course, always experience a nonejaculatory orgasm, but the neuroethology of the female orgasm has not been closely studied.

Many vertebrates exhibit, on occasion, a distinct appetence for fighting, and this has led to the postulation of an "aggressive drive." Internally, readiness for aggressive behavior is linked in the human males, among other things, to the androgen hormone level. Both performance of the behavior as well as achievement of the final consummatory act reduce aggressive appetence (p. 367).

Again different is the physiology of curiosity. We are, without doubt, highly inquisitive beings, actively searching for new information. Entire industries are based on selling us news which we basically do not need at all. Newspapers, magazines, television, and radio ensure that we do not become bored with life. A tourism industry grossing billions is quite successful in luring us to travel to far off lands. This industry is responsive to the human need for new experiences and change. However, we do not know in detail how the curiosity-motivating mechanisms are constructed. However, it is certain that the inquisitive person does not seek physiological equilibrium, but stimulation and excitement, nourishment for the imagination. Once his need is satisfied, he seeks rest. M. Holzapfel (1940) was, to the best of my knowledge, the first to suggest that there is also appetence for rest and quiet.

The discovery of a neurophysiological basis of motivation was of prime significance for the development of ethological theory. Konrad Lorenz saw long ago, that animals have an internal need to carry out specific behavior patterns. In extreme cases the drive can become so strong that it will be released without an adequate releasing stimulus, so that a behavioral sequence can even occur as a vacuum activity. From these observations, Lorenz developed the theory of centrally produced action-specific energy, which would build up and later have to be discharged. Interestingly enough, he initially considered innate behavior patterns as chain reflexes. Only Erich von Holst's work caused him to completely reject the reflex concept. Von Holst showed that fully deafferent eels[4] swim with perfect coordination, demonstrating a neurological basis for spontaneous locomotion. Automatically active groups of motor cells (the so-called automatisms) produced spontaneous impulses and coordinated them centrally so that the appropriate impulse patterns reached the appropriate muscles. Since then such central generator systems have been discovered for a whole series of behavioral patterns (literature cited in J. C. Fentress, 1976; E. R. Kandel, 1976; G. S. Stent *et al.,* 1978; C. R. Gallistel, 1980; E. Delcomyn, 1980; G. Hoyle, 1984).

It is well-founded that even our need for locomotor activity (running, swimming, walking) is based on the spontaneous action of groups of motor neurons in the central nervous system. In other words, this activity is neurogenically motivated. In animals many innate behavior patterns are probably so motivated as well. The classic example suggesting this is provided by the starling that Lorenz kept as a pet. This well-fed bird, lacking any opportunity to hunt, flew up from time to time, snapped at a nonexistent object, flew back to its perch, executed the killing motion, and then swallowed. Because of the lack of opportunity to perform these move-

---

[4]These were spinal preparations. The brain and spinal cord were severed, as were all dorsal spinal roots through which normally messages from the periphery are transmitted to the central nervous system. Thus the preparations could only display behavior that was generated centrally.

ments in their natural context, they occurred as a "vacuum activity." There are many other examples of vacuum activities, and some have been observed in mammals (P. Leyhausen, 1965). These activities are not involved in restoring homeostasis.

Even learned behaviors can develop their own appetence (motivation, e.g., skiing). This is not surprising, since automatic motor cell groups also underlie acquired behavior patterns. What distinguishes them from fixed-action patterns are the new stable phase relationships between the automatisms that have arisen as a result of learning processes.

The phenomenology of excitatory buildup and abreaction (discharge) is well known, but its physiology is not yet fully understood. There are indications that the metabolism of cerebral amines may play a key role. We know that specific transmitter substances collect in submicroscopic vesicles near the synapses (the sites where two nerve cells connect). The transmitter substances created by the presynaptic cell will be released spontaneously or upon stimulation into the gap between the synapses. They occupy receptors on the postsynaptic cell membrane. Each neurotransmitter molecule, according to the lock-and-key model, has a specific equivalent molecule at the synapse of the postsynaptic cell. The electrical characteristics of the postsynaptic cell membrane change when these two molecules join, a change that either raises or lowers the probability of an electric discharge at the postsynaptic cell. Thus neurotransmitters can either inhibit or facilitate cell activity and thus control activity.

Neurotransmitters are not only produced within the nerve cells but also in the dendrites and other sites. Adrenaline is an example of this type of transmitter. It is produced as a transmitter by some nerves but is also transported to the brain by the bloodstream and acts as a neurohormone at this site. The most important neurotransmitters of the brain are the catecholamines (epinephrine, norepinephrine, and dopamine), the endorphins (endorphin, enkephaline), serotonin, and the amino acids γ-aminobutyric acid (GABA), glycine, and glutamic acid. Some 60 neurohormones and neurotransmitters have been identified, and it has been shown that certain of these predominate at specific brain sites. Thus serotonin is concentrated in the Raphe's nucleus in the brain stem, norepinephrine in the blue nucleus of the brain stem, and dopamine in the black substance and the ventral crest of the mesencephalon.

Serotonin has both excitatory and inhibitory functions. It is involved in circuits mediating sleep and emotional arousal and inhibits aggressive behavior in rats. Accordingly, a decrease of the serotonin level leads to increased aggression. This seems also to be the case in man (L. Valzelli and L. Morgese, 1981). High-ranking vervet monkeys are characterized by high blood serotonin levels. If one keeps high-ranking individuals in isolation, the blood serotonin levels decrease to the serotonin levels of low-ranking individuals. If high-ranking isolates are permitted to see a low-ranking individual through a one-way mirror, these monkeys threat-display. However, the lack of response by the low-ranking monkeys will cause the levels of serotonin to decrease further in the high-ranking individuals. Only if he can observe the effects of his display will the level of blood serotonin rise. Thus, social behaviors have their physiological repercussions (M. T. McGuire and M. J. Raleigh, 1986).

The catecholamines are "energizers." They increase arousal (drive induction) and act as incentives for learning. The endorphins, on the other hand, reduce arousal (drive reduction) and seem to act as a satisfier. Both serve rewarding functions (L. Stein, 1980). Endorphins (brain opioids) suppress pain and induce states of comfort and relaxation. Isolation-induced stress of young animals and of adults in gregarious species can be soothed by drugs, which promote endorphin synthesis in the brain. Drugs which inhibit the synthesis, in contrast, cause an increase of stress vocalizations (J. Panksepp *et al.*, 1978).

GABA is the main inhibitory transmitter of the brain and glutamic acid is probably its principal excitatory neurotransmitter.

Advances in the chemistry of the brain lead to the discovery of the receptors for drugs like opium, heroin, and valium, which, in turn, lead to the search for the natural substances that normally activate these receptors. The catecholamines were found to be those for which cocaine and amphetamine act as a drug substitute; endorphins (opioid peptides) were found to be "endogenous morphines"—the body's own "narcotics." Rapid advances are being made in the whole field of brain chemistry. For reviews see M. Angrick, 1983; K.G. Bailey, 1987; R.C. Bolles and M.S. Faneslow, 1982; A. Herz, 1984; M. Konner, 1982; J. Panksepp, 1981, 1986; J. Panksepp *et al.*, 1978; V.P. Poshivalov, 1986; M.R. Rosenzweig and A.L. Leiman, 1982; S.H. Snyder, 1980; K. Vereby, 1982).

Research on biological rhythms has provided excellent examples of endogenous motivation. Many organisms display activity fluctuations within a 24-hour rhythm. A large number of studies established that the regular alternation of periods of wakefulness and rest is determined by endogenous factors, known as internal clocks, which correspond approximately to the 24-hour rhythm. The alternating periods are brought into phase with the normal day by means of external time cues *(Zeitgeber),* for example, light–dark periodicity. Organisms kept under constant conditions will show a periodicity in their activity, whose cycle approximates a 24-hour period. We speak therefore of a "circa diem" or circadian rhythm (see J. Aschoff, 1981, and E. D. Weitzman, 1982 for additional references). The exclusion of external time cues results in a free-running activity period that deviates from the natural circadian cycle, but which can be brought back into phase by reintroducing external time cues. Chicks incubated and maintained after hatching under constant conditions and living without external time cues show circadian rhythms. Their internal clock is already present as a phylogenetic adaptation.

Humans also have circadian rhythms for sleeping and waking, changes in body temperature, potassium excretion, and many other processes (Figs. 2.46, 2.47).

Physicochemical and psychic states change during the course of the day, so that drugs can have differing effects at different times, an important factor for chemotherapy.

People kept under constant conditions show a periodic change between the states of sleep and waking, this period being usually somewhat longer than the natural day. Interestingly enough, various physiological processes have their own circadian rhythms. Body temperature, for example, is regulated by an oscillator with a shorter period than the one controlling the sleep–wake cycle. Therefore, under constant conditions internal desynchronization arises (Fig. 2.48) that is subjectively felt as a sense of discomfort (J. Aschoff and R. Wever, 1980, 1981; R. Wever, 1978).

Newborns are initially polyphasic. P. Stratton (1982a, b) noted a 40-minute cycle of vocalization in a 1-day-old infant. J. N. Mills (1974) raised infants under relatively constant conditions (continuous light). After 8 weeks the subjects developed a circadian rhythm. This started off asynchronously with the natural day and showed a free-running circadian rhythm. Such patterns are also seen under

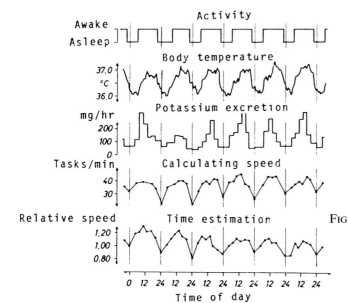

FIGURE 2.46. Circadian rhythms of several variables, measured on a 31-year-old male subject living in standardized conditions under a strict 24-hour routine. After R.A. Wever (1978).

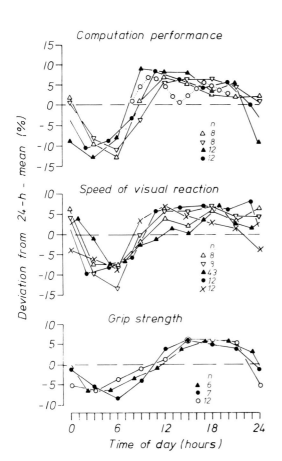

FIGURE 2.47. Circadian rhythms of three variables, measured in several test groups living in identical conditions to the subject in Fig. 2.46. From J. Aschoff and R.A. Wever (1980).

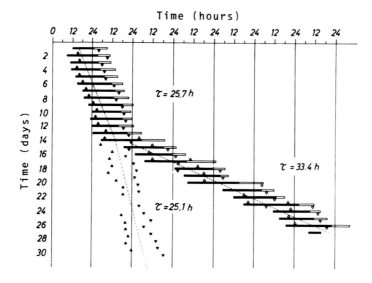

FIGURE 2.48. Example of internal desynchronization. In the test situation, a person living in a bunker under constant conditions without time cues first has a combined free-running rhythm in body temperature and wakefulness of 25.7 hours. From the 14th day onward, the two processes desynchronize and become independent of each other, temperature developing a 25.1 cycle and the sleep–wake cycle 33.4 hours. From R.A. Wever (1975).

normal conditions. The beginning of the sleep period shifted daily, thus indicating the presence of a rhythm of approximately 25 hours (N. Kleitman and T. C. Engelmann, 1953; N. Kleitman, 1963). There are, however, also cases of shorter periods (Figs. 2.49, 2.50).

In addition to circadian and the less studied ultradian rhythms, seasonal periodicity is also present in human behavior, which J. Aschoff (1981) has shown for suicide, mortality, and conception.

2.2.5. Emotions

Behavior and perception are accompanied by subjective experiences we call feelings, mood changes, or emotions. Both behaviorists and ethologists have avoided dealing with such subjective "accessory phenomena." This is reasonable in animal studies, but not in human studies. We can interview people and obtain statistically analyzable data on their experiences. One can discuss feelings or investigate relevant literature on such studies and thus draw appropriate conclusions about human emotional responses. We find, for example, that all cultures identify the same kinds of emotions: anger, hatred, love, jealousy, envy, fear, a bad conscience, to name but a few. This is noteworthy, because we could not have taught each other all these emotions. We cannot learn the subjective correlates to specific behavior or perceptions; what we learn is the object of the hatred or love and not the emotion itself. We can talk to others about our emotions, and the fact that we can communicate about emotions presupposes a shared biological basis.

Emotions may derive their origin in programmed neuronal connections within the visceral-limbic system. We can obtain data on the functional operation of this

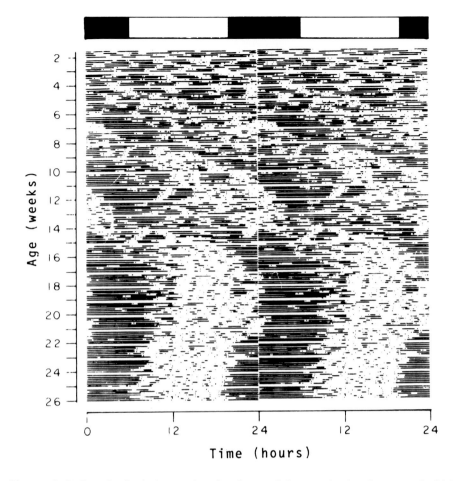

FIGURE 2.49. Longitudinal observations in a human infant on the development of a 24-hour periodicity while sleeping and awake. After a polyphasic start a free-running circadian rhythm develops (between the sixth and sixteenth days), this finally synchronizing with the natural day. From N. Kleitman and T.C. Engelmann (1953).

emotive circuitry from introspection and responses from test subjects (J. Panksepp, 1982), relate them to concrete behavior, and thus infer the relationships between the emotions, which is useful in forming further hypotheses (see also R. Plutchik, 1980; C. E. Izard, 1971).

Subjective experiences correspond to biochemical processes in the brain (see also pp. 69, 79). Social facilitation is basically associated with the activation of cerebral chemical processes underlying emotions. If we perceive someone smiling, cerebrochemical processes are presumably activated, these inducing a friendly mood and smiling in response. The same is true of crying, a process which activates sadness and crying in sympathy. Social signals, such as facial expressions and vocalizations, trigger chemical processes that cause us to reflect the same emotions and expressions as those we perceive from the social partner. M. R. Liebowitz (1983) has published a number of interesting speculations about the brain chemistry of love. The study of the biochemistry of emotions is still in its infancy and it is no doubt a highly promising one (D. M. Warburton, 1975).

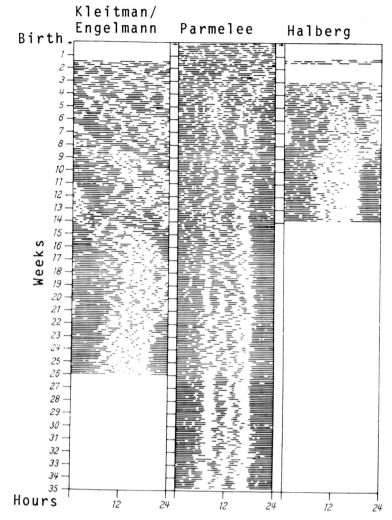

FIGURE 2.50. Longitudinal observations in circadian rhythm development of the sleeping and waking periods of three children with self-selected daily schedules. Note the durations of individual circadian fluctuations. After T. Hellbrügge (1967).

2.2.6. Learning and Learning Dispositions

Most animal organisms can modify their behavior adaptively through individual experience: they learn. The learning capacity of various species is not just based on a general ability to learn but also on what is learned and when learning takes place. Animals learn preferably that which contributes to their fitness, and this varies from species to species, as do their innate learning dispositions. Initially behaviorists were not aware of this fact; only much later did researchers like K. and M. Breland (1966) acknowledge the presence of species-specific learning dispositions.

Classical learning theory distinguishes mainly between two types of learning: "classical conditioning" or "conditioned reflex type I" and trial and error learning ("instrumental" or "operant" conditioning, also known as "conditioned reflex type II"). If a neutral stimulus immediately precedes a stimulus that releases a specific reaction, eventually the previously ineffective stimulus may release the response. Thus if a dog is shown a piece of meat, it salivates (unconditioned stimulus: unconditioned response). If a bell is sounded, however, just before the meat is presented, the dog associates the bell signal with subsequent feeding, and after a number of paired trials starts salivating at the sound of the bell alone. An initial perception is followed by a positive experience, and this leads to the signal activating specified behavioral patterns. I. Pavlov worked with restrained dogs that could not do much more than salivate. He spoke of conditioned reflexes. If he had worked with unrestrained animals, he would have seen that he had actually activated an entire repertoire of appetitive behavior for food searching and intake. B. Hassenstein (1973a) updated the terminology to "conditioned appetence."

Negative experiences evoke specific aversive behavior: if a painful stimulus such as an electric shock is preceded regularly by a previously neutral signal, the latter will subsequently elicit the fear and escape reactions associated with the shock. This is negative conditioning or "conditioned aversion" (B. Hassenstein, 1973a).

The operant conditioning processes which arise from the perceived changes brought about by acting on the environment, must be distinguished from associative learning based on perception coupled with positive or negative experiences. Man and animals actively experiment by trial and error and learn from the success of their performance. In this way, new uses of already existing behavior patterns or even new movement coordinations will arise. An animal conditioned to open its cage by pressing a lever so as to free itself or to obtain a food reward will retain this behavior, and systematic reward parameters can enable the experimenter to link a chain of behavior patterns into a highly complex sequence.

B. F. Skinner developed a high degree of skill at conditioning, e.g., by teaching doves to play ball games. W. Verplanck told me that his students conditioned professors by systematically reinforcing specific behavior patterns. If one of the professors was accustomed to placing a foot on a chair during a lecture, the students increased their apparent attention to his discussion. Female students would inconspicuously raise their skirts just above the knee. If the lecturer left the chair, the students feigned less interest and the skirts were lowered a few inches. Soon the lecturer was standing with one leg on the chair, and finally climbed up on it. Another professor who continually changed his position during lectures was conditioned with similar tactics to prefer a particular part of the room and finally to deliver his talk from one corner of the lecture hall.

When negative experience follows some behavior pattern the behavior is extinguished. This is called "conditioned inhibition." The basic learning processes involved are shown below (Table 2.2) (after B. Hassenstein).

Table 2.2. Elementary Learning Processes from the General Concept "Learning by Experience"

Type of experience	Learned	
	Releasing stimulus situation	Behavior
Reward	Conditioned appetence < 1 >	Conditioned action < 2 >
Punishment	Conditioned aversion < 3 >	Conditioned inhibition < 4 >

According to E. von Holst (1939), new motor coordinations arise through a new arrangement of central automatisms which enter into new stable phase relationships. They form a new, transformable movement configuration. Acquired behavior patterns are form constant; this is the reason that signatures can be used in identification (p. 25). Sensory feedback from the executing organs is not always necessary to form these new phase relationships. Rhesus monkeys confined to a chair learned to reach toward a cylinder at one location with a fully deafferentated arm in order to shut off an electrical shock announced acoustically (E. Taub *et al.*, 1965). They could not see their hands during the training phase or during the test. Von Holst indicated that it is not always advantageous to practice the components of a new motor sequence individually. This would necessitate that, for each learning step, the phase relationships present between the motor cell groups must be interrupted and rearranged. To what extent this rule holds true remains to be tested. It is also conceivable that already learned components can be integrated to form new and more complex behavior patterns.

Not all motor learning involves integration. Through a detachment process, behavior can be reduced to smaller units, this being a prerequisite for their voluntary availability (Section 8.1). The development of directed grasping from reflexive grasping is an example of this kind of "differentiation."

Normally an animal's behavior is modified on the basis of individual experience so as to increase the animal's chances of survival. Such behavioral changes presuppose the presence of special phylogenetically developed, genome-coded programs that prepare the individual for changes in its surroundings.

Generally, in the formation of a conditioned appetence or aversion, an immediately preceding stimulus is associated with the conditioned stimulus. We mentioned the pairing of the stimuli of food and bell, whereby the bell must sound just prior to food presentation in order to be associated with it. If the bell is sounded afterward it is not associated with the presentation of food. The organism is operating with an if—then assumption, associating cause and effect on the basis of phylogenetic experience. When two events occur simultaneously as described above, we tend to assume a causal relationship between them. E. R. Guthrie's (1952) contiguity theory assumes that everything which is linked temporally and spatially becomes associated. This, however, is not always the case. Innate programs provide the basis for other causative linkages. J. Garcia and F. R. Ervin (1968) evoked physical nausea in rats using x-ray radiation. This nausea, however, was not associated with the acoustic and optical signals present at its onset. In fact, the test animals later responded by not eating foodstuffs which they had consumed 1 to 2 hours prior to the test (see also J. Garcia *et al.*, 1968). Humans also associate nausea with prior food intake and develop the appropriate aversions. Once again a predisposed knowledge based on phylogenetic experience determines our concept of causality. There are various programs for causal linkages and thus different forms of the causality concept. What is associated with what for reinforcing or extinguishing behavior is programmed by species-specific learning dispositions.

Originally it was assumed that every stimulus associated with the fulfillment of physiological needs (hunger, thirst, sexual requirements) would act as a positive reinforcer. Later it became evident that there are many other needs whose fulfillment would be reinforcing.

Specific reactions such as digging and standing upright can be reinforced in hamsters using food as a reward, while other responses, such as territorial marking, facial grooming, and body care behavior in contrast, are suppressed by the same experimental procedures (J. S. Shettleworth, 1975).

In humans learning is also induced by curiosity (p. 580) or the challenge of solving a task. This holds true even for babies. If a buzzer is sounded when an infant turns its head to the right, it quickly learns to make this movement, but as soon as it realizes what the task is, it loses interest. When the program is changed, however, and the buzzer sounds when it turns its head to the left, its interest is reawakened until it has recognized the regularity of this process. A change in task will sustain interest (T. G. R. Bower, 1977; H. Papoušek, 1969; E. R. Siqueland and L. P. Lipsitt, 1965). It is rewarding and apparently enjoyable for an infant to cause a reaction or activate something. A child smiles more when it has learned to make a mobile move through the performance of some learned task than if the mobile moves by itself. This has been verified even in 2-month-old infants (J. S. Watson, 1971, 1972, 1979; J. S. Watson and C. T. Ramsey, 1972).

At a very early age, babies recognize smiling and other forms of friendly attention, such as encouragement and praise, as rewards. They can be utilized as positive reinforcers. The expectation of being praised, however, may be innate, because disappointment when such expectation is not fulfilled can be observed even in small children.

Punishment does not always extinguish behavior. Some actions can be inhibited through punishment, while others are enhanced. The effect of punishment varies between and even within a species depending on the motivation involved. If a rooster is punished with an electric shock every time it displays, it will stop displaying; a conditioned extinction has been developed. If the same rooster, however, is punished each time it shows submissive behavior, then this behavior is reinforced, and the rooster becomes more and more submissive. The function of these responses are obvious. Submission is a response to punishing stimuli emanating from conspecifics. Through submission, continued maltreatment is avoided. Similarly, children maltreated by their mothers do not always show avoidance reactions. In contrast, they are, as a rule, strongly bonded to their mothers. Chicks, ducklings, and rhesus monkey young will follow their mothers even when they are punished for doing so (D. W. Rajecki et al., 1978).

This behavior is adaptive under natural conditions, because when in fear or pain it is best to seek the protection of the mother. In animals, it is improbable that the mother herself should be the source of pain, and even in such cases, the seeking out of her protection is useful as a submissive appeal. The youngster would certainly die if abandoned. Adult baboons seek out higher ranking group members when they are frightened, even if they are the cause of their fear. We know from human behavior that fear evokes the desire for a strong, guiding personality. Bonding through fear is used advantageously in dictatorships (I. Eibl-Eibesfeldt, 1970a).

Fear not only induces infantile behavior patterns associated with appeals for sympathy, but also induces a childlike readiness to accept and learn. Thus adults in fear are more amenable to change their beliefs or ideologies. When people are brainwashed, a conversion by means of fear takes place. Timid behavior patterns, however, will hardly be extinguished by punishment.

Dogs punished by their trainers are more strongly bonded to them than those that are handled kindly (A. E. Fisher, 1955). Objects offered to young animals as surrogate mothers are accepted even when they deliver punishing stimuli. Chicks that had been hit and knocked over by an imprinting object followed it particularly closely. Young monkeys even accepted surrogate mothers that punished them for so doing by expelling a draft of cold air (L. A. Rosenblum and H. F. Harlow, 1963). Juveniles of monkey mothers that had been brought up in isolation and that were mishandled by these mothers displayed a stronger preference for them than the young of a control group (B. Seay *et al.*, 1964).

The presence of the mother or surrogate mother provides the young with security. Hen chicks peck at foreign objects or unfamiliar conspecifics more vigorously in the presence of the imprinting object than when this is absent. Young rhesus monkeys are less anxious in strange surroundings when they have some imprinting object with them (even a towel; D. K. Candland and W. A. Mason, 1968). A badger I raised quickly calmed down in unfamiliar surroundings when I held an object with its own scent marks in front of its nose (I. Eibl-Eibesfeldt, 1950).

The human mother is undoubtedly a source of comfort to children and here, as well, it is known that abused children generally have a very powerful bond with their parents and protest, to the amazement of the authorities, when they are removed from their care and placed in a foster home. D. W. Rajecki *et al.* (1978) found this surprising, and felt that the ethological statement that a child is adapted to its mother had to be revised:

> Ethological theory emphasizes that infant behavior systems have been shaped by the ordinary expectable environment and depend on that environment for their functioning, yet infants of many species form bonds to objects not typical in any species environment, or even to sources of maltreatment. (p. 417)

Elsewhere they write:

> In terms of the behavior of social objects, can we possibly view abuse or maltreatment as constituting part of an ordinarily expectable environment? These conditions hardly seem conducive to the survival of the offspring, yet infants do become attached to objects that severely maltreat them (p. 417).

To that we may respond that child abuse is relatively uncommon. Furthermore, throughout the entire course of history, a child has had no other choice than to stay with its biological mother. Certainly, a child that avoids its own mother out of fear would hardly have any chance of survival.

In humans, fear evokes infantilization, which has the fatal tendency of making them attach themselves in blind trust to leaders offering security (p. 184).

M. E. P. Seligman (1971) promoted a preparedness theory of phobia, which postulates that humans are biologically prepared to learn to fear certain objects and situations which are threatening to survival. Rapid acquisition, irrationality, and resistance are the main characteristics of this type of learning. We seem indeed to learn very fast to avoid snakes and to fear spiders, but we seem much less prepared to associate dangers with a car, even though we are exposed on a daily basis to threats from the traffic. Resistance to extinction of electrodermal responses established to fear-relevant stimuli has been demonstrated experimentally. Ease of acquisition, however, has so far received only minimal or equivocal support (R. J. McNally, 1987).

The hedonics of operant learning advanced with the discovery that rats rapidly learn to self-stimulate certain hypothalamic areas electrically, the stimulation being their only reward. Special pleasure centers and pathways were postulated (J. Olds,

1956), that is, natural reward systems that are normally activated by the performance of certain behaviors. Later investigations suggested that the hedonic pathways maintained by intracranial self-stimulation share a common pharmacology, whereby the hedonics of motivation is paralleled by a hedonics of learning. According to the interesting, although still speculative, investigations by L. Stein (1980), neurohormones motivate, steer, and terminate response sequences by providing satisfaction at each step. Dopamine acts as an incentive activating pursuit behavior, noradrenaline acts as a reinforcer guiding response selection via knowledge of response consequences, and enkephalin brings the behavioral sequence to a satisfying conclusion, thus causing gratification. Less is known about the aversion centers, except that there are corresponding areas in the brain mediating displeasure and discomfort, causing aversive responses (for an excellent discussion of the subject of motivation and learning, see K. Bailey, 1988).

Learning can be obligatory at a particular period in ontogeny and within a specific functional system. Thus many animals demonstrate sensitive phases during which they are particularly receptive to specific learning experiences. Examples are acquisition of knowledge concerning the characteristics of a sexual partner or knowledge of the species-typical song. They often cling so firmly to what they have learned during these sensitive periods that the phenomenon has been called "imprinting." In contrast to classical learning theory, primacy of learning experience, in this case, outweighs recency. Imprinting has been investigated in depth (K. Immelmann, 1965, 1970, 1975; E. H. Hess, 1975; P. Marler and S. Peters, 1977; W. H. Thorpe, 1961; St. Green and P. Marler, 1979) ever since Lorenz (1935) discovered sexual imprinting. Song sparrows *(Melospiza melodia)*, zebra finches *(Taeniopygia castanotis)*, and other songbirds memorize their species' song during a sensitive period which occurs before they are able to sing, and the birds later sing from memory. In other birds, inborn templates determine what is learned (p. 66).

Object imprinting is a learning disposition first recognized by Konrad Lorenz. Ducklings and goslings have an innate following response. They walk toward objects larger than themselves, particularly when these objects utter certain attracting sounds—here, an innate preference for the species-specific "attraction" call of the mother could be demonstrated. Surrogate objects such as a ball, a stuffed cube, a hen or even a person can elicit the following response. These then become the surrogate mother for the young. Obviously, no phylogenetic protection preventing such mistakes has evolved, since, in nature, there is such a low probability that a duckling would be raised by a different species. A program which relays the information: "Follow the object you are near when you hatch!" is sufficient to bond mother and offspring. The bond thus established is a powerful one. If the duckling follows a certain object for a while, it becomes "imprinted" on that object and the readiness to follow other objects disappears (K. Lorenz, 1935). If a gosling follows a human for a short period of time, for example, it will no longer even attempt to follow its natural mother. The bond thus formed ranges from merely resistant to change to irreversible, depending on the species. The sensitive period is another important characteristic of imprinting. It is only during this phase that the duckling can be imprinted. What is actually imprinted is the following of a certain object. Behavior patterns from the sexual behavior functional system are also imprinted at the same time with respect to a certain class of objects, although these behavior patterns have not yet matured. In this case, the imprinted animal abstracts the species characteristics of the imprinting object. If the imprinting object is a person, the bird will later court humans. The situation with the program to follow is more complicated. It seems that in some cases, the following response to auditory stimuli can be universally imprinted to a class of objects, whereas the animal will follow only a specific individual mother or mother surrogate if visually stimulated. Lorenz established this in his experiments on graylag geese. Goslings from different broods were mixed and then released as a group. They recognized and followed their mother, or their foster mother, respectively (in this case Lorenz himself). The program to follow is constructed in such a way that the juvenile feels comfortable and self-assured in the presence of its mother; it then explores and behaves aggressively toward other young introduced into the group. The absence of the mother illicits fear. The juvenile then attempts to contact her with distress calls. Pain and fear enhance the search for contact, even when the following response is experimentally punished (J. K. Kovach and E. H. Hess, 1963; J. E. Barrett, 1972; E. A. Salzen, 1967).

Neurobiological studies revealed that the imprinting experience causes a reduction in the number of the spines of the dendrites of the neurons, which process the imprinting stimulus. Since the spines are the contact zones with other neurons, there is a corresponding reduction in interneuronal connections. When domestic chicks got imprinted to follow a pure tone, the spines of particular neurons in the auditory area of the chicks forebrain proved to be reduced by 45% versus the nonimprinted controls. After imprinting to the natural call of the hen, which is characterized by a broader sound spectrum, the reduction in the number of spines in the same neuron type amounted to 27% of the controls (E. Wallhäusser and H. Scheich, 1987). Through the reduction of spines the neurons become irreversibly tuned for the perception of only particular stimuli. A similar narrowing of the perceptive potential of neurons was found to take place during the song learning of the Beo (Gracula religiosa), a bird belonging to the starling family (G. Rausch and H. Scheich, 1982). This reduction of synaptic connections thus distinguishes imprinting from other processes of learning, which are characterized by the increase of interneuronal connections.

Object imprinting can take place at a time well before the behavior patterns targeted for the object have actually matured. This is the case in sexual imprinting. Hand-raised male jackdaws and parakeets are found to be sexually imprinted on humans when mature. Even if they are only kept with conspecifics afterward, as soon as they attain maturity, they prefer humans as sexual partners and court them. Thus sexual imprinting has occurred long before. This shows us that recent experience does not always carry the most weight.

People also develop inhibitions during a particular sensitive period against sexual attraction to a member of the opposite sex with whom they have grown up. Their relationships are fraternal in nature, even if the other person is unrelated (see incest taboo, p. 261).

2.2.7. Cultural Transposition of Innate Dispositions

Phylogenetic adaptations of the kind described in the previous sections affect human cultural behavior in manifold ways. C. G. Jung believed that the artistic creations of mankind were the expression of an archetypical foreknowledge. Although his studies were restricted to psychoanalytic interpretation, which largely dispensed with comparative cultural investigations, his intuition was correct.

If we examine the figures and amulets made by humans in order to banish various kinds of danger we are struck by the fact that these often display an erect penis. This is usually combined with a threatening facial expression and other menacing postures (Fig. 2.51). These are examples of phallic threat, which we can interpret as ritualized threat mounting and for which various homologous behavioral patterns exist in a number of monkey species (I. Eibl-Eibesfeldt, 1970; I. Eibl-Eibesfeldt and W. Wickler, 1968; W. Wickler, 1967a).

When a vervet monkey troop forages on the ground, several males will "stand guard" with their backs to the troop. They spread their legs slightly and display their colorful sexual organs. In these monkeys the scrotum is blue and the penis is bright red; here signal effect appears to have been selected for. The guarding is directed toward conspecifics of other vervet monkey groups, and if they approach too closely, the guards develop erections. Similar display behavior has been observed in a number of other primates (D. Ploog *et al.,* 1963; W. Wickler, 1965, 1967a). This behavior can be interpreted as a ritualized threat mounting. Mounting is used as a sign of dominance in many mammals, and as such, is detached from its original function of copulation; it has become a sociosexual signal.

A comparable phallic threat is found in humans. Various New Guinea tribes emphasize the phallus with phallocrypts (penile sheaths). If the Eipo wish to mock an adversary, they loosen the cord that holds the tip of the penile sheath to the hips and jump up and down in one place, usually on some elevated spot that can be seen far away. The penile sheath thus swings prominently up and down. When they are frightened or surprised, they click their thumbnail against the sheath to ward off the possible danger with this threat gesture (I. Eibl-Eibesfeldt, 1976). Phallic threat occurs indirectly in other cultures through the use of wooden figures to mark boundaries or frighten away evil spirits. Smaller figures of this nature are also used as amulets to drive away misfortune ascribed to evil spirits. Such apotropic figures and amulets are found throughout the world. In the literature they are often misinterpreted as fertility demons, probably because investigators did not know how they were arranged and used. Even the word "demon" indicates the deterrent characteristics of these figures' expressions. The figures from Bali, for example, display their threat function by their bared teeth, protruding eyes, and other characteristics of hands and even buttocks that clearly signify repulsion (Figs. 2.52, 2.53).

In ancient Greece, phallic symbols (Hermes) were placed at crossroads and along borders. They depicted a man's head with a beard and an erect penis. Many Romanesque figures adorning the windows and entrances of churches are phallic and act as guards to repulse evil. In earlier times, mens' clothing often emphasized the genital regions in many parts of Europe. This is especially obvious in the clothing of medieval mercenaries (Lansquenets). It is certainly no accident that phallic display on one's own body was maintained so long among these people, for the mercenaries had to compete for employment by particularly aggressive display. Phallic display has largely regressed in mass society as part of the suppression of provocative stimuli, but there are still figures of speech suggesting male dominance threat. Thus the Arabs have the expression "Phallus in your eye," the English "Fuck you" and the French equivalent is "Allez vous faire foutre." Aggressive verbal contests between Turkish men also refer to the sex act (p. 541). Here, so to speak, instinctive behavior is verbalized, a topic we will discuss in more detail subsequently. Aggressive mounting in humans still occurs, in exceptional cases, with the intention of humiliating and subjugating the other party. Thus the last Algerian consul was ritually raped by the rebels. Until recently,

FIGURE 2.51.
Apotropaic figures from Bali in frontal and lateral view. Each of the crouching figures shows a threatening facial expression and a phallic threat. The lateral view shows that each also pulls its buttocks apart. Offerings are placed on the small tabletop on the upper figure's head, thus combining threat with appeasement. Photo: I. Eibl-Eibesfeldt.

FIGURE 2.52. Japanese phallic amulets. *Upper:* phallic bear. The phallus on the base is normally screwed with the base-plate into the figure. *Lower:* amulet with threatening facial expression and hidden penis on the rear behind a sliding plate. Drawing: H. Kacher after the original from I. Eibl-Eibesfeldt, 1970).

FIGURE 2.53. Eipo with phallocrypt (In, Irian Java/West New Guinea). Photo: I. Eibl-Eibesfeldt.

young Hungarian shepherds suffered a similar fate if they trespassed onto another's grazing territory. The erect phallus often becomes a sign of elevated rank and demands respect. There are many idols shown with an erect penis (old Germanic, Egyptian, Indian, Mexican). D. Fehling noted that the phrase used by some authors in antiquity, "a man with testicles" expressed great respect for the person being described. There are also modern terms with similar significance, such as the Italian "cazzo" and the German negative counterpart "Schlappschwanz." Other examples are cited in I. Eibl-Eibesfeldt and W. Wickler (1968), I. Eibl-Eibesfeldt 1970, D. Fehling (1974) and D. Rancourt-Laferriere (1979).

The above examples should suffice. In the section on art we will concern ourselves further with the theme of cultural transposition of innate dispositions.

2.2.8. Actions, Sequences of Actions, and Goals: The Hierarchy Concept and the Concept of the Pathway Network

Craig's schema—appetitive behavior-releasing stimulus—consummatory act describes the exceptional case. Usually an animal is led by a series of behavioral steps (actions) toward a final goal, of which, in most cases, it is not aware, but which the observer may be able to discern. Since each behavioral step has its own appetite component (appetence), an animal thereby follows a chain of appetences.

Niko Tinbergen (1951) showed that in spring, sticklebacks migrate in schools to their spawning sites in shallow water. Once they arrive, males take up their territories and only then do they undergo color changes, become aggressive, prepare for courtship and nest building, and perform other reproductive behavior patterns. Tinbergen developed the concept of a hierarchical organization of functional centers that are mutually inhibitory on one integrational level and which are stimulated by external and internal motivating factors and are activated by specific releasing stimuli. He designates the organization of functional centers of different integrational levels as instincts of various levels, and speaks of a "hierarchy of instincts." Increasingly interconnecting networks occur at lower level consummatory acts (swimming, biting), since these individual behavior patterns can also be used in different behavioral contexts (fighting, courtship, etc.). Electrical brain stimulation studies on chickens (E. von Holst and U. von St. Paul, 1960) suggest a similar hierarchical organization of behavior. The manifestation of the behavior patterns at a certain level is organized by their individual threshold values and by specific innate releasing mechanisms. Thus, via various appetitive behavior patterns, the animal progresses through this hierarchical system to the consummatory act, of which it need not have concrete knowledge. The almost machine-like functioning of insects is a typical example of this hierarchical organization. In birds and higher mammals, however, we may assume that appetitive behavior is probably guided by a conscious awareness of the consummatory goal. Thus a male dog in a hunting mood will intentionally seek out some distant chicken farm that it obviously remembers from prior experience, and obstacles or detours will not prevent the dog from finding it. All this depends upon the dog's particular motivation created by its "parliament of instincts." If the dog is not only motivated for hunting but also fearful, the appearance of danger may cause it to abandon its search or make a wider detour. If the male encounters a female, her presence may temporarily interrupt his hunt, and depending on his mood he can be diverted from his former goal, but to the observer he will act as if driven by specific goal expectations. Objectively, however, we cannot prove the role of insight in such a situation.

In contrast, human behavior is guided primarily by the awareness of concrete goals. A regulated series of behavioral steps leading to specific goals is always present, but each goal can be attained in various ways. Thus we can describe behavior in the form of a pathway network with several choice points. The decisions made at these points depend upon the person's motivational state, the stimuli, and quite decisively on personal experience. This makes human behavior very variable but not entirely unpredictable. Cultural convention and phylogenetic adaptation drastically restrict the range of possible behavior. Generally, people follow similar strategies to attain the same kinds of objectives. There is a universal grammar structuring our social interactions, which will be explained later section.

Summary 2.2

The fixed-action pattern (inherited movement coordination) is a fundamental ethological concept. Form-constant behavioral sequences arise from central nervous generator systems, these often being already coordinated centrally so that well-ordered impulses are transmitted to the muscles. Feedback can be either inhibitory (negative) or facilitative (positive) depending upon the existing program.

Fixed-action patterns are not rigid but are form constant; that is, the phase relationships of the muscle actions utilized in the movement, like a "musical score," remain constant, enabling the movement to occur as a transposable yet recognizable configuration. Furthermore, fixed-action patterns are not defined by form constancy alone. As the name suggests, its innateness is an essential criterion. Thus in a process of self-differentiation based upon developmental instructions laid down in the genes, the neuronal networks and their connections together with sensory organs and effector organs responsible for a particular behavior pattern, grow to functional maturity. Fixed-action patterns are, in general, integrated with orientation movements to form higher functional units known as instinctive acts. The study of children deaf and blind at birth of infants, comparisons between species, and cross-cultural studies strongly suggest that human beings are equipped with a basic repertoire of fixed-action patterns.

Perception as well, at different levels, is determined in part by phylogenetic programs, and some transmodal capacities can be ascertained in the same way in different sensory realms. This holds true for categorical perception as, for example, in color perception and syllable perception. The ''orderliness of the senses,'' however, also shapes higher cognitive functions. The Prägnanz tendency can also be verified across sense modalities. Our perception emphasizes certain characteristics more distinctly and levels out others. This, in general, acts to simplify or schematize our visual as well as linguistic perception.

The key stimulus-IRM concept is particularly significant for explaining certain human responses. Specific stimulus receptors and information processors have evolved as an adaptation to stimuli which report on contingencies relevant to the organism. They are so constructed that they respond to a few key characteristics of the stimulus situation. They act as stimulus filters and are so integrated with the motor system that specific behavioral sequences, such as avoidance of predators or prey capture, are elicited upon presentation of the appropriate key stimuli. We speak, therefore, of innate releasing mechanisms (IRMs). Reciprocal adaptations between sender and recipient have evolved for social communication, and the signals used in such social communication are known as releasers, for example, facial expressions and some of the ''signals of babyishness.''

The neuronal structures in which an a priori knowledge about expected behavior is preserved are called ''templates.'' Behavior is compared against them and they thus have a normative function.

Behavior is not always just a ''response,'' however, as classical reflex theory has postulated. More often, organisms are constructed so that they are in themselves active creatures, driven by a multitude of differently structured motivating mechanisms. Their effect leads animals and man to search with appetitive behavior for stimulus situations that evoke specific behavior patterns. Neurogenous motivation is of great importance here. Automatic groups of motor cells drive the fixed-action patterns. Emotions are experienced as subjective correlates of behavior and perception. They are universal entities in man.

The individual modifiability of behavior is often determined by phylogenetic adaptations in a very specific way, for there are innate learning dispositions. It is not true that everything can be learned and forgotten equally well at the same time or that the temporal and spatial coincidence of events is always considered as having some causal relationship. The phylogenetically developed hypotheses underlying learning in organisms are often much more highly differentiated. Thus organisms associate relevant events: nausea is associated with something eaten previously and not with events occurring at the time the nausea commences. An organism can react with different learning responses, depending upon functional relationships and motivations, to one and the same stimulus situation. Specific information is often acquired only during a well-defined sensitive period. Phylogenetic preprogramming also plays a role in human cultural expressions, such as in sculptures with an apotropic function.

85

Behavior is organized hierarchically. This ordering becomes less binding with increasing levels of development. The network integrating various behavioral systems increases as does the instrumental availability of the preprogrammed behavioral repertoire.

2.3. Decoupling of Actions from Drives and Conscious Self-Control: The Neuroethology of Human Freedom

Freedom has different meanings. Human beings want to be free from restrictions by others. They want to act upon their own decisions and to express their opinions freely. This social aspect will be dealt with later. Humans furthermore subjectively experience that they can choose to do some things and avoid others; that they have freedom of choice between various alternatives. A person sets goals for himself, mentally contemplates various strategies for their achievement, and finally chooses some strategy that he thinks appropriate. The weighing of alternatives necessitates that he judge things from a distance, even when the goal is the satisfaction of a drive. Humans are able to postpone the fulfillment of a drive and thus to decouple themselves from it so that they can create a relaxed field that permits them to weigh alternatives and respond sensibly. Animals display this ability to a limited extent, and their appetitive behavior is played out in a field without tension[5] (G. Bally, 1945). If, however, the animal perceives releasing stimuli that correspond to its motivational state, its innate mechanisms are fully activated so that a largely predetermined sequence of instinctive behavior patterns are released, leading to some cut-off, consummatory (drive-satisfying) act or situation. Mammalian play is a great step toward the autonomy of behavior, since here is the first time that we find actions actively decoupled from specific drives, i.e., the motivating systems which normally activate them.

A badger can "play fight" without becoming aggressive, and is thus able to use its behavior patterns so "freely" that it can combine those of several different functional systems in a way that could not occur in a "serious" encounter (Section 7.2). In play, actions appear to be decoupled from the higher level of organization that normally activate them. This permits experimentation and active learning, during the course of which even new patterns of movement may be acquired. And this lies at the roots of our ability to distance ourselves from a problem and attain a degree of "rational freedom."

In humans the ability to act freely in terms of selecting between alternatives is particularly pronounced. This we experience subjectively as "freedom of choice." This "freedom" must not be equated with "nondeterminism," for goal perceptions and norms used in making choices structure our decision-making process. "Freedom" in the sense of "nondeterminate" would be a concept devoid of any meaning.

Freedom, according to F. Seitelberger (1981, p. 27), "exists not in real or conceptual objectivity, but in the self-reflection of the acting subject. Therefore freedom does not mean acausality but autonomy. . . ." In this connection, Seitelberger

---

[5]G. Bally explains the concept of field tension with the following example: if one places a piece of meat directly before a dog's nose behind a fence open on both sides, the dog will make futile attempts to reach it through the fence. The field tension is so great that the dog does not realize that it can walk around the fence. If the meat is set down a few meters behind the fence, the dog will hesitate after a futile attempt to reach the food directly and then run around the fence directly toward it.

indicates the significance of cerebral cortex development—the "corticalization" which results in our drives being controlled consciously, this leading to their humanization.

However, corticalization is only the first important step toward behavioral self-control. The second step is lateralization, the division of tasks between the two brain halves. The studies of R. W. Sperry (1964), R. W. Sperry and B. Preilowski (1972), J. Levy (1972), and M. S. Gazzaniga et al. (1963, 1965, 1977) have shown that the two cerebral hemispheres are so specialized for different tasks that, roughly speaking, speech and verbal/mathematical thought processes are localized in the left half while the right half controls the integrative capabilities of perception and emotional and artistic talents.

People whose left hemisphere is damaged have impaired speech but are emotionally intact. They show sympathy and emotionality and are also musically competent. Those with right hemisphere damage, in contrast, are emotionally disturbed; they have shallow emotions or show atypical euphoria, and lose the ability to empathize with others. They have no sense of humor, are not musical, and have extremely limited integrative faculties.

Thus our left hemisphere is to a certain extent the analytical and technical brain, while the right is the emotional and integrative one. The hemispheres are joined at the base by a thick bundle of nerve fibers, the corpus callosum. During orgasm, for example, we can register theta waves from the right hemisphere, these being indicators of activity while alpha waves can be registered from the left hemisphere, these being typical of the brain at rest.

Interestingly, the posterior section of the corpus callosum is thicker in women than in men (C. de Lacoste-Utamsing and R. L. Holloway, 1982). Maybe this difference in the connection between the two halves of the brain could be responsible for differences in the emotionality between men and women. Actions lacking in emotionality appear to occur less frequently in women than in men. This could be due to a woman's role in infant and child care, which requires constant emotional bonding in almost all circumstances and a man's role in defense and aggression, which frequently requires detachment of emotion for effective action. Certainly an excess of love is less harmful than an excess of aggression, which must therefore be particularly well controlled. Men need aggressive emotionality in particular phases of fighting competition, but aggression needs to be controlled to prevent a fight from escalating and becoming overly destructive. In this sense, for men, a more distinct separation of the more rational brain from the more emotional brain could be advantageous.

The left visual field projects into the right hemisphere and the right visual field into the left hemisphere because of a partial crossing over of the optic nerves in the optic chiasm. Auditory nerves also cross in the same way, while olfaction is ipsilateral. If the corpus callosum is severed, the verbal left half of the brain is unaware of what the right half sees, and vice-versa (Fig. 2.54). If, for example, the word "nut" (as in nut and bolt) is projected onto the left visual field, it will be transmitted from there to the right hemisphere and conducted further via various cognitive networks to the motor cortex controlling the left hand. The test subject can select the nut from an assortment of other objects with the left hand without any visual guidance. But if asked, the subject cannot say what the left hand is searching for and finding, because the left hemisphere (representing the verbalizing test subject) is unaware of what has happened. As a representative of the rational brain, the left hemisphere attempts to interpret behavior. As the experiments of J. E. LeDoux et al. (1977) show, such hypotheses need not correspond to the

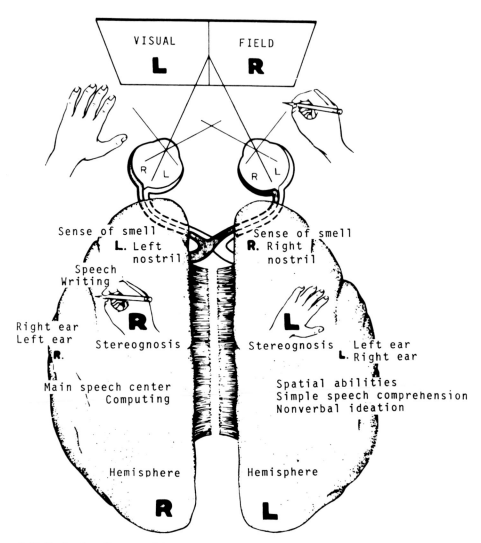

FIGURE 2.54. Projection diagram of the left and right visual fields to the left and right visual cortex, arising from the partial crossing in the *chiasma opticum*. The diagram also shows other sensory inputs from the right extremities to the left hemisphere and from the left extremities to the right hemisphere. Auditory input shows a similar crossing, while olfaction is ipsilateral. The figure depicts writing with the right hand as programmed by the left hemisphere. From R.W. Sperry (1974).

actually perceived reality. They showed a split-brain patient (after separation of the two hemispheres by severing the *corpus callosum*) two different pictures: on the left a winter landscape with snow (for the right hemisphere) and on the right side a hen's foot (for the left hemisphere). The subject then was given a series of other pictures and asked to point out what he had seen before. With his right hand (left hemisphere) he chose the picture of a hen, and with his left hand (right hemisphere) a picture of a shovel! When asked what he had seen, he replied (by means of the verbally competent left hemisphere): "A hen's foot, which is the reason I chose the picture of the hen, and a shovel for removing the hen's droppings" (Fig. 2.55).

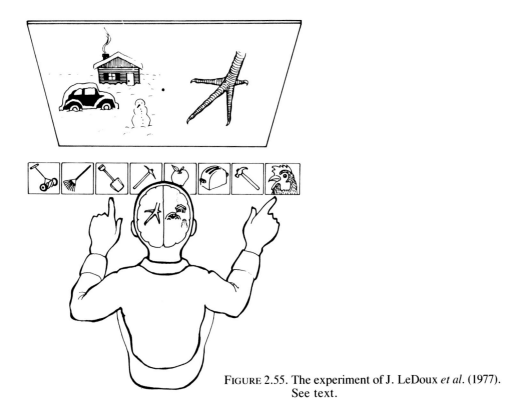

FIGURE 2.55. The experiment of J. LeDoux *et al.* (1977). See text.

The patient behaved as if the left hemisphere formulated a hypothesis based on what it perceived, at the same time rationally integrating the visual impressions of the right hemisphere without being aware of what should have corresponded to the visual information seen on the right.

The differential functional specialization of the hemispheres allows man the freedom to modify the influence of different aspects of his personality by varying their activation. We can consciously switch our thoughts to objectivity and, in doing so, the left hemisphere becomes, so to speak, a mirror in which we reflect our alter ego localized in the right hemisphere. The evolution of speech may have been responsible for this capacity of conscious reflection. Speech translates actions, and this requires a certain capability of self-observation, thus achieving a certain objectivity toward oneself (p. 527).

Introspection shows us that we are indeed able to adapt to different levels of objectivity or emotionality, and it seems to me as if the two hemispheres are like two brothers who at times become rivals and struggle for dominance. The left hemisphere, in its striving for objectivity and sobriety and in art, for abstraction, may attempt to dominate and even intellectually belittle our emotional ego. We sometimes think of such a person with a left brain dominance as a "cold intellectual." Studies with subjects having a severed *corpus callosum* indeed show that two distinct perceiving and feeling personalities actually coexist here. They are normally joined symbiotically, are aware of each other, and act in concert, but man can also deliberately attach more weight to one or the other side of his nature (ego).

P. D. MacLean (1970) categorizes specific behavioral capabilities to hypothetical developmental stages of the brain, speaking of a "triune" (or "tripartite") brain. These three divisions are anatomically distinguishable. The old reptilian brain encompasses the anterior brain stem, the reticular system, and the mesencephalon. The paleomammalian brain grew out of the reptilian cortex and corresponds to the limbic system, which was overgrown by the expanding neomammalian brain. This model explains a number of characteristics of hierarchical neural organization. In simplified terms, the protoreptilian brain controls phylogenetically preprogrammed behavior. The paleomammalian brain improves our ability to adapt through learning, a first step toward the release from the rigid instinct dependency. The neomammalian brain provides the objectivity enabling the organism to detach specific actions from rigidly programmed control. Play only becomes possible at this level of development. In man's social behavior the agonal reptile heritage of a sociality based upon dominance and submission is supplemented by mammalian affiliative sociality characterized by the capacity to act in a friendly manner and by individual bonding which characterizes love (see p. 167).

Lateralization in the form of differential specialization of the two hemispheres enables the tripartite brain to develop into a "fourune" or "quadrupartite" one, following MacLean's terminology.

Summary 2.3

Vertebrate cerebral evolution involved an increase in corticalization enabling the organism to temporarily decouple behavioral patterns from the rigid brain stem control, thus creating a tension-free field providing the opportunity for detached reflection and experimentation on a trial-and-error basis. In humans, through the process of lateralization brain functions have become even further specialized by separating the brain's hemispheres into a rational-analytical left and an emotional right brain with configurational-integrating and creative abilities. This division of labor enables man to detach himself objectively from his emotional ego and thus to exert conscious self-control by means of reflection and introspection. Our capability and tendency to engage in dialectic and polarizing thought processes is probably based on this division of labor specialization. A quadrupartite brain has developed from the tripartite ("triune") brain of higher mammals.

2.4. The Units of Selection—A Critical Evaluation of Sociobiology

With the appearance of E. O. Wilson's *Sociobiology* (1975), a new branch of ethology came into being which included theories and approaches from ecology and population genetics. Sociobiology has evoked a lively discussion, which was sometimes productive while at other times less so. The cost–benefit calculations of this discipline have, however, without doubt contributed to our understanding of evolutionary mechanisms.

Cost–benefit calculations are based on the fact that fitness is ultimately measured by genetic survival. Organisms that do not pass on their genetic material will die out. Everything which reduces reproductive success is therefore considered as a cost. Thus every risk and investment in time and work must be calculated as such. If one individual invests in another, then the balance must not be a negative one if he is to increase his fitness. The benefits factor, measured by success in passing on one's own genes (reproductive success), must outweigh the costs. An organism acts adaptively when it behaves in such a way as to maximize the propagation of its genes through its behavior. It is therefore often stated that organisms are perfect machines for gene propagation, a suitable if highly oversimplified concept. It must be made clear that one can be misled by taking this statement too literally and conceiving of organisms as nothing but accessories which the genes created for their own propagation. This might have been true at the most primitive levels of development, when the first self-replicating molecules formed protective sheaths and other organized structures. In higher organisms, however, a level of existence is achieved where such a description does not apply. One should therefore avoid using the term "selfish genes"[6] (R. Dawkins, 1976), for there are already enough uncritical readers who take this expression literally. To define the problem, it is probably opportune for didactic reasons to state that everything a gene "does" aids in its survival. One must always remember, however, that organisms and genes form a functional unit and that it is of little use to discuss whether a hen is the method by which eggs reproduce themselves or vice versa. Emotional terms or aspirations such as "selfish" can only apply to organisms and not to genes themselves.

There was also a terminological confusion concerning the units of selection. For Dawkins it was the genes. Others spoke of individuals or closely related groups of individuals as the units of selection. Both meant, of course, different things with the same expression. Those who spoke of the genes meant the units that were ultimately selected. Those speaking of individuals meant the units on which selection actually operated. How selection operates and what is ultimately selected by this process were not clearly separated.

The question of how animals and man should behave in order to facilitate the propagation of their genes has evoked numerous mathematical cost–benefit models. Of the many problems tackled by sociobiologists, the question of how altruistic behavior evolved has received most attention and emphasis and this has created a new discipline. Models of individual, kin, and group selection were discussed.[7] Darwin (1859) was the first to recognize the problem of altruistic behavior when he investigated the social insects. The problem appeared to him almost unsolvable and in contradiction to his theory. He presumed that a form of group selection was operating here. The sociobiological calculations were the first to demonstrate that these and other examples of altruism can be explained by individual selection.

Sociobiologists, to begin with, prefer models based on the assumptions of individual rather than group selection for two reasons: (1) mutations appear in the genotypes of single individuals and thus they must first be propagated by individual selection throughout the population. (2) Differential reproduction of individuals throughout the Animal Kingdom is probably more significant than the differential

---

[6]E. Mayr (1976), M. Midgley (1979), and M. A. Kaplan (1979) also warn about such terminology.

[7]R. D. Alexander (1974, 1978, 1979), W. D. Hamilton (1964, 1972), J. Maynard-Smith (1964), E. O. Wilson (1975), R. L. Trivers (1971), B. J. Williams (1974, 1980, 1981), D. S. Wilson (1975, 1977), S. Yokoyama and J. Felsenstein (1978), D. P. Barash (1977), W. Charlesworth (1978), R. Dawkins (1978, 1979a, b), M. K. Uyenoyama and M. W. Feldman (1980), M. J. Wade (1978, 1980), M. J. West-Eberhard (1975), W. Wickler and U. Seibt (1977), G. C. Williams (1966), J. H. Barkow (1978), K. E. Boulding (1978), N. A. Chagnon and W. Irons (1979), D. T. Campbell (1975), D. L. Hull (1978), M. J. Konner (1977), H. Markl (1976), and others.

suppression and disappearance of entire groups of organisms. Individual selection is therefore more significant than group selection in most animals (G. C. Williams, 1966). The latter, however, should not be excluded completely. It should only be considered though when simpler explanations will not suffice.

The development of the concept of inclusive fitness (originated by J. B. S. Haldane, 1955) was perhaps the most significant contribution to the understanding of the evolution of altruistic behavior. With inclusive fitness, the concept of fitness, previously measured by number of surviving offspring of an individual, was extended to not only an individual's own offspring but also those of close genetic relatives who share a high percentage of the individual's genes or alleles. In terms of behavior, this means that investments in offspring of close relatives should be roughly in proportion to degree of relatedness. W. D. Hamilton (1964) developed the concept further after a thorough reconsideration of its tenets to be applied to cost–benefit analysis. It is based on the following arguments.

If an individual who has not reproduced sacrifices itself to save another, then it is obvious that its genes will not survive in any of its own offspring. If we consider the genes alone, it is clear that it is not only the survival of the individual's own offspring that counts but also the survival and reproduction of all individuals which share a certain percentage of the altruist's genes. Sociobiologists base their calculations on the fact that individuals share on the average of 50% of all their rare genes with their offspring and siblings, 25% with their grandchildren, nieces, and nephews, etc. Thus, if one individual sacrifices itself to save two of its offspring or four of its grandchildren, cost and benefit would be in balance. Of course, these are very rough estimates, for a large number of other factors must be included in the calculation, for instance, the age of the altruist. If the altruist is very old and thus has little chance of reproducing, then it would be genetically profitable for it to risk its life for even one grandchild. Furthermore, all these calculations are only valid for those rare genes which characterize the individual or its group. The vast majority of genes are shared with all other group members.

Based on these assumptions, one can construct mathematical models that permit experimentally verifiable predictions.[8] The concept of kin selection maintains that individuals must behave altruistically in such a way as to promote others according to the degree of their genetic relationship in order to increase their inclusive fitness. It is in this sense that we should understand the frequently used term "genetic selfishness."

W. D. Hamilton (1964) used this model of kin selection in a brilliant analysis to explain the evolution of social organization in the social hymenopterans. Sterile workers invest in sisters at the expense of their own reproduction, and they derive a greater genetic profit by investing in the queen and her young than if they produced offspring of their own. The relationship coefficient between siblings is 0.75, because all individuals share the genes of their haploid father and, in addition, another 50% of the genes from their diploid mother. Hamilton thus solved the puzzle that had stumped biologists since Darwin's time.

However the concept of "genetic selfishness" has generated some biological concepts that must be reviewed critically. It is true that there are cases in which individuals of one species place their individual interest above that of the group

---

[8]This can be observed by comparing the variety of survival strategies utilized by different cultures.

or species interest and in conflict situations choose their personal interest in preference to that of the other conspecifics involved. Many sociobiologists, however, maintain that this is a general rule, and this generalization is obviously premature.

In this context we have to distinguish between short- and long-term effects of selection. Changes brought about by individual selection may affect fitness of a closed population in competition with others and what may be selected as fit in the short term by individual selection may, in the long run, lower the fitness of the group. This could, for example, happen to human populations should individuals with criminal or other dispositions which are detrimental to the interests of the group increase in number. Thus far the discussion has focused too narrowly upon short-term effects of selection.

A series of dramatic examples have been used to demonstrate ruthless genetic selfishness, a classic one being that of the Entellus or Hanuman langurs (*Presbytis entellus*). Y. Sugiyama (1964) observed that in some instances after a new male had taken over a harem, the young of the previous harem male were injured or killed, and Sugiyama assumed that this was done by the new male. Later S. M. Mohnot (1971) and S. Hrdy (1977a, b, 1979) reported other instances of infanticide, but only in certain populations of these langurs. This behavior was interpreted as the "reproductive strategy" of the usurper. By killing the predecessor's young, the females would come into estrus again and be mated by the new male. In this way the usurper increases its own reproductive success at the cost of its predecessor's and, of course, that of the females, who have already made substantial investments in their murdered offspring.[9]

This generalization soon led to the statement that this is a reproductive strategy used by many primates, and reports of the disappearance of young in other species proliferated; the presumption that these were all killed by the male was coupled with hints about human history also being filled with reports of infanticide. B. C. R. Bertram (1976) reported that male lions killed their predecessors' young upon taking over a new harem.

An infanticidal male, however, would also be destroying many of his own genes, for within populations every member is related to every other one. Infanticidal genes could only succeed in this manner when they appeared first. The time would soon come for the murderer to loose all he had gained at the onset, if the number of murder mutants would increase so that the next newcomer would then kill the murderer's own offspring. At best, such mutants could manage to be sustained for a small percentage of a population, who, in turn, might be weakened as a long-term consequence of an increase of murderous individuals. One would then be justified to speak of them as "pathologies," that is, of maladaptive deviations since their "strategy" evidently fails in the long run. Some of these deviants may just occur as mutants from generation to generation, just as genetic diseases (such as Down's Syndrome) are sustained due to the fact that counter selection is not sufficiently strong to eliminate the genes completely from the population. Such cases are usually called pathological, for populations with infanticidal individuals in competition with noninfanticidal ones would be at a great disadvantage. It is

---

[9]"Hanuman langurs (are) a species in which adult males routinely resolve their conflicting interests with females by killing the female offspring" (S. Hrdy 1977, p. 2); and: "Infant killing is part of a reproductive strategy whereby (an) usurping male increases his own reproductive success at the expense of the former leader, the mother and her infant" (S. Hrdy, 1977, p. 247).

certainly premature to describe infanticide as a "reproductive strategy" in Hanuman langurs, since a close study of the data reveals that the behavior is not as widespread as the reports make it out to be. This behavior has actually only been seen in a few populations, while in others it has never been noted even after considerable observation periods. C. Vogel (1979), who observed langurs and various male takeovers over many years, originally saw no infanticide. He surveyed the literature critically and found that other investigators had actually observed such killing in just three instances. In all three cases the same male did the killing (S. M. Mohnot, 1971). Two of these infanticides took place immediately after taking over the harem, while a third juvenile was killed 6 months later, a time when the reproductive success of the new male could no longer be impaired. The remainder of the forty instances of supposed infanticide death were based on speculation arising from the disappearance of young or the occurrence of injured young. A juvenile would be noted as missing, and entered in the records as "killed by the usurper;" another juvenile would be found with wounds, and the new male was considered responsible for these.

C. Vogel found that dogs often chased the langurs in the research area, which could explain the observed wounds. Furthermore, nearly one-half of all the cases of supposed infanticide would not fit in with sociobiological theory. Either the juvenile killed was already so old that the female would have come into estrus without this interference or the juvenile was killed so long after the harem takeover that this occurrence could no longer positively influence the new male's reproductive success. In other words, this oft-quoted example for ruthless genetic selfishness is the product of premature conclusions (I. Eibl-Eibesfeldt, 1987; G. Schubert, 1982).

In the meantime, C. Vogel (Vogel and H. Loch, 1984) has observed instances of male infanticide in harem takeovers, raising the number of observed and sociobiologically compatible cases to eight, including those of H. Mohnot. Only three males were responsible for these eight deaths. That is hardly convincing evidence for this behavior's "normality!"

There are many indications that this is a pathological phenomenon. As mentioned earlier, the behavior is not seen in all populations, but only in a few groups. In addition, only a few males were responsible for all the deaths actually observed. Finally, according to sociobiological criteria the killing of juveniles after a harem takeover would only make sense if these were no more than 4 months old at the time they were killed. Up to this point, however, they bear a special infant coat. If infanticide were a male strategy we would expect that the infants would have developed a counter strategy, as for instance a counter selection against a coat signaling infancy. We would also expect the females to defend their young more effectively. But C. Vogel's observations (personal communication) show that many females only defend their young weakly or not at all. Infants occasionally play with other infants. If they approach the other mother too closely, she kicks them. Sometimes strange mothers have kicked an intruding youngster down a precipice, and the infant's own mother did not even intervene, even though she was sitting only a few meters away and although her youngster screamed pitiably. This certainly does not sound like a normal situation.

Many years ago, J. Calhoun's (1962) observed that in a crowding situation the social behavior of a gregarious mammal (rats) disintegrated to the extent that mothers do not retrieve or otherwise care for their young, even if surplus food was available. It was social irritation that caused the pathological "behavioral sink" situation.

At present it is premature to interpret occasional infanticide as an adaptive male reproductive strategy. Evidence that infanticide is adaptive for males by propagating their genes has not been particularly well substantiated. Although such an explanation is worth considering (as in F. S. vom Sal and L. S. Howard, 1982; I. G. McLean, 1983), other hypotheses must be given equal consideration.

I am inclined to interpret behavior patterns such as the infanticide we have just discussed as pathological. I made the observation that baboons and chimpanzees tend toward aggressive escalation, that is, they lose control in encounters characterized by strong emotional arousal. In the Gombe Stream National Park, a female baboon was mauled so badly by a male that one hand was permanently incapacitated. On the same occasion, her baby was killed by him. This, however, did not occur during a takeover and the youngster was very likely his own. Jane Goodall (personal communication) spoke of the event as an accident. The male was aggressively aroused by another male and displaced his aggression toward the female. Chimpanzees have temper tantrums which are sometimes difficult to distinguish from male displays. During these tantrum displays, males occasionally hurt group members. In addition, Jane Goodall described an occurrence of cannibalism between group members. One female learned to prey upon the babies of other females of the same group and she taught this habit to her daughter. This, too, indicates a tendency toward pathology. It is possible that this tendency toward emotional instability and behavioral pathology might be associated with the rapid evolution of group life, which, in part, is characterized by a rapid growth of the brain. It could well be that the fine structuring of the brain, by which critical points in social behavior get controlled did not keep pace with the rapid quantitative growth of the brain and that selection is still in progress. The same might hold true for humans.

All sociobiological models to date have been constructed on the basis of maximizing reproductive success. If we consider strategies that reduce risk, however, these models should be designed quite differently. The basic concept of a cost–benefit calculation is valid and useful for providing research with new impetus. The question of units of selection, however, has yet to be thoroughly investigated. Individual and kin selection undoubtedly play significant roles. In man, the tightly knit social group provides another possible unit of selection. Whether this is also true for other group-living higher vertebrates remains to be tested.

Before discussing group selection, another important sociobiological concept should be mentioned, the model of evolutionary stable strategies (ESS) developed by J. Maynard-Smith and G. R. Price (1973). This model was developed to explain altruistic behavior without accepting the tenets of group selection. To elucidate their concept of evolutionary stable strategies, Maynard-Smith and Price examined ritualized and injury-producing intraspecific fighting in vertebrates. It is well known that many animals engage in ritualized contests with conspecifics. The loser of such a contest is ousted but not killed and can stand the test again on another occasion. If rivals injured each other during such fights, then—according to traditional ethological formulation—this would weaken the species or, strictly speaking, reduce the reproductive community in competition with other groups. Maynard-Smith and Price in constructing their model based their calculations on a number of assumptions:

1. Each contest must reach a decisive conclusion.
2. The one giving up is the loser; the other animal is the winner.
3. Any animal not killed in the contest would be able to engage in other fights.

4. Previous contests have no influence on fighting behavior, as if the rivals had no memory of their last encounter.

The authors also distinguished between two categories of conflict tactics used in ritualized fighting: "conventional" tactics, in which there are only threats and no serious injuries, and those injurious fights, "dangerous" tactics, carried out using every available means. In a population with both ritual ("Doves") and injury-producing fighters ("Hawks"), we obtain the following combinations:

1. Hawk meets Hawk, and the fight ends when one is injured or killed.
2. Dove meets Dove; no one is injured, but the one giving up loses.
3. Dove meets Hawk; Dove runs away and no one is injured.

If the loser receives 0 points, the winner 50 points, an injured animal -100 points, and time and energy expenditure for the struggle was given a value of -10 points, all values corresponding to reproductive success, one can show mathematically that Doves can be sustained in a population even assuming that individual selection occurs, although they would exist in a mixed ratio with Hawks. This can be determined from the following calculation:[10]

When Doves fight each other, they invest a great deal of energy because such fights last a long time. They are thus accorded -10 points for their time/energy expenditures. The victor receives 50 points and thus achieves a net sum of 40 points. The loser receives 0 points for outcome and thus a net of -10 points. Assuming equal winning chances, each rival in a Dove vs. Dove fight can expect the following value as the outcome of a ritual fight:

$$\frac{+40 - 10}{2} = +15 \text{ points } (Dove \ vs. \ Dove)$$

When Hawks fight each other, the winner receives 50 points and the loser -100 points, so that the average expected result of such a fight is:

$$\frac{50 - 100}{2} = -25 \text{ points } (Hawk \ vs. \ Hawk)$$

Thus on the basis of these simple mathematical calculations, we find that damaging fights (hawks) have greater disadvantages than ritualized fights (doves).

Thus if a Dove appears in a population of Hawks, it would initially have a certain mathematical advantage. If a Dove meets a Hawk, the Dove would run away and receive 0 points, while the Hawk would achieve 50 points for its win. But in a pure Hawk population, any Dove would have an advantage because it would end every contest with 0, while the more frequent Hawk vs. Hawk engagements would close with a net -25 point score. Doves would therefore increase in such a population, thereby meeting other Doves more frequently and gaining 15 points. At the same time, however, Hawks would encounter Doves more often, with an advantageous result. Finally an equilibrium between the two would be attained in a mixed population, calculated as follows:

A Hawk expects a -25 point score in a fight with a Hawk. This expectation

---

[10]In essence, the lucid explanation of W. Wickler and U. Seibt (1977) is being followed here.

occurs in a population with the same frequency as the number of Hawks in it, or $-25 \times [H]$.

A Dove receives 0 points for fights with a Hawk and 15 points for fights with other Doves, both cases as frequently as Hawks and Doves are represented in the population. Thus in a mixed population the total point expectancy of Doves is found using the formula $0 \times [H] + 15 \times [D]$.

The stable mixed relationship of Hawks and Doves is calculated from the expectancy equation:

$$-25 \times [H] + 50 \times [D] = 0 \times [H] + 15 \times [D]$$
$$25 \times [H] = 35 \times [D]$$

Thus the ratio of Hawks to Doves is 7:5. The mean point expectancy for Hawks and Doves is equal in this equation, and the advantages and disadvantages of both fighter types balance each other out, and selection finds no basis on which to favor one type over the other.[11]

In these situations one speaks of an evolutionary stable strategy (EES), a somewhat unfortunately finalistic sounding term; "evolutionary stable state" would be more neutral. Strategy implies acting toward a specific goal, somewhat in the sense of species maintenance, as rejected by sociobiologists. But this is certainly not suggested. The term "evolutionary stable state" describes genetic variants enduring in a specific ratio beside each other within a population. G. M. Burghardt (1975) described an interesting example of behavioral polymorphism in the garter snake *(Thamnophis sirtalis)*. Each newly hatched brood of snakes contains individuals with different innate food preferences, providing a population with an extended adaptability. A somewhat different example are the satellite males of certain frogs and fish; they leave the energy expenditures of courtship to others and then fertilize the females attracted to the area (examples in W. Wickler and U. Seibt, 1977). This would be of benefit to both parties, for if the active males were brothers they could improve their fitness through cooperation. If the satellite male, however, should gain an advantage at the expense of the courting male, this would be a clear case of social parasitism.

In the finalistic terminology of sociobiologists, in this latter case one could speak of a "reproductive strategy" of the social parasite to propagate its genome. Such cases must be distinguished from all those in which a specific portion of the population is sustained not because they maintain themselves genetically but because they emerge anew repeatedly as mutative aberrations or by the meeting of

---

[11]Since each member of such a population encounters an average of seven Hawks for each five Doves, the mean point expectancy for both is seven times the point expectancy from an encounter with a Hawk plus five times the point expectancy from a Dove fighter encounter, divided by the sum of both encounter $(7 + 5 = 12)$. Thus the mean expectancy for Hawks in such a population is

$$\frac{7 \times (-25) + 5 \times 50}{12} = 6.25$$

and for Doves

$$\frac{7 \times 0 + 5 \times 15}{12} = 6.25$$

recessive alleles and against which counterselection is not sufficiently strong enough for their complete elimination. In these cases, we can very well speak of aberrations that reduce individual fitness, something that has been underappreciated in the ongoing discussions. To the contrary, one often has the impression that many investigators are attempting to construct some proof of fitness for every aberration. E. O. Wilson (1975) attempts to do this for homosexuality, W. M. and L. M. Shields (1983) and R. Thornhill and N. Wilmsen-Thornhill (1983) for rape, and L. K. Hong (1984) for premature ejaculation.

Sociobiological cost–benefit calculations demonstrate the compatibility between specific findings and models of the individual and kin selection principles. Different models can be developed, and testable predictions can be made from them. Calculations on ritualized fighting have shown that the most successful strategy is that of the retaliator. Thus the individual initiates the fight in a ritualized fashion with threat displays, and continues to fight ritually when the opponent behaves likewise (Dove vs. Dove). The individual changes at once, however, to injurious fighting if the opponent is a Hawk. Therefore, if the Dove in such instances immediately changes to a Hawk upon encountering a Hawk, Hawks can never attain the 15 point advantage, for they will ultimately always encounter a Hawk. This means that a Hawk mutant could not survive in a Dove population.

In my iguana studies (I. Eibl-Eibesfeldt, 1955c), I was struck by the fact that the ritual fighters could also fight injuriously and would do so under circumstances in which the opponent would not continue fighting ritually, as, for example, when penetrating a territory without displaying the appropriate threat ceremony. At that time I mentioned that this seems to be the rule in many other lizards and in fish. If there were only pure Hawks and Doves in a population, the equilibrium described above as ESS could actually be attained. To date, however, I know of no such population.

The cost–benefit analyses of sociobiology have led to stimulating discussion on many aspects of behavior, for example, those of parental investment and sexual selection (R. L. Trivers, 1972), the parent–child conflict (R. L. Trivers, 1974), sex ratios (W. D. Hamilton, 1967), and a series of cultural conventions such as those of the avunculate (R. A. Alexander, 1977; J. A. Kurland, 1979) and cross-cousin marriages (L. Hughes, 1981).

The data base on which many of these theories rest, however, is often insufficient and the arguments thereby unconvincing. Using the Murdock data catalog, Alexander (1977) and S. J. C. Gaulin and A. Schlegel (1980) investigated the relationship between paternal investment and certainty of paternity. They assumed that wherever infidelity was prevalent (and thus paternity was uncertain), fathers would invest more in their sisters' children than their own since these carried with certainty a quarter of their genetic heritage. Gaulin and Schlegel tested this premise by investigating the prevalence of avunculate in cultures with permissive versus those with strict sexual morals. They believed that they had found a correlation between permissiveness (and thus uncertain paternity) and the avunculate. However their table of uncertain paternity groups included the Samoans and others in which marriage bonds are known to be strictly maintained. Here one would be relatively certain of the married man being the biological father of most of his wife's children. In fact, it is rather difficult to find any groups of people in which paternity is uncertain in more than 50% of all cases, and only then would the sociobiological calculations be valid. Because of the wide distribution of marriage-like partner relationships, one would not expect such uncertain paternity, even in permissive societies. It is not only advantageous for the man but also for the woman to have the husband invest in the children and thus not to endanger the relationship through infidelity. Apart from the fact that genetic studies would have to be conducted to verify paternity, one must also ask why such uncertainty should arise anyway, since it benefits neither marriage partner. To account for heavy investment in sister's children, other hypotheses should also be considered, such as the strong intergroup tie maintained by the avunculate, since brothers and sisters most frequently reside in different groups after marriage.

A second example of careless argumentation can be found in C. J. Morgan (1979). He found that the crews of whale hunting Eskimo boats usually consist of close relatives. He takes this to be an example of kin selection speculating that if such a boat got into trouble, the relatives would stand by each other to the last. He forgets that this is a "high-risk" strategy and that one should also calculate the risk involved in placing all one's genes in a single boat. Morgan, however, does not even discuss this. If the relationship coefficient of the whale hunting crew were small, then Morgan might have considered this as a gene survival strategy which consisted of distributing family members across various vessels.[12]

In developing genetic models for the evolution of reciprocal altruism, sociobiologists are confronted with the difficulty of explaining its initial appearance, since the first altruist in a population is a "lonely" one (J. Moore, 1984). Some attempt to show that supposed altruistic behavior is not really altruistic but actually selfish and as such can be explained on the basis of individual or kin selection. Thus N. G. Blurton-Jones (1984) describes food sharing in humans as originating from "tolerated theft." He means that it would not have profited our ancestors to defend food after satiation, so the theft was tolerated. There is not a single word about altruism. J. Moore's view is somewhat similar, using chimpanzees as a model. Moore is of the opinion that after a chimpanzee kills its prey, the owner can easily defend its kill but it is more difficult to eat it undisturbed. It is for this reason that the chimpanzees distribute small portions of meat so they can eat in peace. In these explanations both writers overlook the fact that maternal care encompasses a number of behavior patterns, such as feeding (giving of food). It has been demonstrated that in mammals and birds many behavior patterns of bonding, such as food sharing, are derived from maternal behaviors (p. 167). There is no need to look for a different explanation for food sharing in chimpanzees.

Much of the confusion derives from mixing up selective consequences and individual intention. All behaviors which contribute to fitness can be said to have egotistic consequences, since they promote the actor's genes. But the intention of the individual may very well be called altruistic, if it is spontaneous and motivated by empathy and aids another individual even at high risk.

The great merit of the sociobiological models lies in the integration of ecological and genetic theories. Their weakness lies in the fact that, to date, sociobiologists have been more involved in model building than in practical research and careful observations. In addition, during the period 1966–1978, the significance of indi-

---

[12]Polly Wiessner, with whom I have corresponded about Morgan's work, wrote me the following: "Until we have statistical data showing that the probability of individual accidents requiring great heroism or altruism on the part of crew members to save the individual is much higher than the risk of everybody in the boat being killed, that argument does not hold. Again, putting all of one's genes in one boat strikes me as a potentially maladaptive strategy!"

vidual and kin selection has been certainly overemphasized, even though E. O. Wilson (1975) also considered models of group selection.

Group selection plays an important role in humans. The individually selected traits of personal bonding and several other adaptations in the service of parental care provided mankind with behavioral patterns and strategies for bonding and maintenance of group harmony (aggression inhibitors, sharing, etc.). These allow the formation of firm bonds even between unrelated members of the group, so that groups appear to be units, even though this may counteract the interests of many group members at the level of the individual.

The phylogenetic-emotional basis of man's familial disposition is enhanced by his cultural talent in extending the familial ethos to a group ethos. The war ethos, the indoctrinability of man with group values, his loyalty to authority, and his ethos of sharing could scarcely have arisen as new characteristics on the basis of individual selection alone (Eibl-Eibesfeldt, 1982b). Group selection in humans is not only possible but highly probable, assuming that group members are more closely related to each other than to the members of the other groups they are confronting, and therefore share a common genetic interest. Through most of human history this was actually the case. People lived in relatively small, tightly knit groups. They shielded themselves off against others and thus represented fairly closed reproductive units. Even today, in hunter-gatherer societies, a people speaking one language, number only several hundred (usually about 500) members (J. B. Birdsell, 1968; H. M. Wobst, 1976). These populations are bonded by their own language and customs and are thus distinct from other groups. They form relatively closed reproductive communities in that intragroup marriage occurs with a much greater frequency than intergroup marriage. Even neolithic horticultural societies number only a few thousand in a single population. If they increase to several thousands, they start fragmenting off into internally warring subgroups, which often develop their own dialects (see also cultural pseudospeciation). The people living together in such groups are certainly more closely related to one another than they are to other groups. This holds true even for a number of the modern nation states ((P.L. van den Berghe, 1981). It would therefore be of advantage if each group member were to help every other one; indeed, cultural devices are developed that place group interests above those of the individual. The reproductive success of individuals leads to an enrichment of the gene pool with certain alleles. Excessive inbreeding is avoided by various marriage conventions to ensure a constant mixing of the gene pool, thus acting counter to nepotism. At a higher level, ethnic nepotism replaces familial nepotism.

Some attempts to calculate the profitability of altruistic acts in relation to the degree of relatedness have so far failed. K. Hawkes (1977, 1983) investigated the Binumarians in the highlands of New Guinea to determine who assisted whom in tending gardens and herding pigs, and found that close genetic relatives are in no way preferred over steprelatives or adopted children. The neighbors played an especially important role.

The Ache of Paraguay, who are hunters and gatherers, share meat and honey with all members of the group without kinship preferences. One does not receive larger portions from relatives than from others. The only exception is made with items brought back from the Mission, which the individual shares preferentially with members of the immediate family (H. Kaplan et al., 1984).

Group selection models are now being utilized more often (B. J. Williams, 1981; P. L. van den Berghe, 1981; R. Boyd and P. J. Richerson, 1982), and a new trend is becoming evident. Currently, it is said that the distinction between blood relatives and social kin are not that important, provided that the combination of social and biological relationships have a higher coefficient of relatedness than that found in the groups considered as "non-kin" (S. M. Essock-Vitale and M. T. McGuire, 1980). This was our standpoint from the beginning.

E. O. Wilson (1978) distinguishes between "hardcore" and "soft" altruism, the latter including what R. L. Trivers calls reciprocal altruism. Reciprocal altruism allows support beyond the limits of the group and even beyond species boundaries (e.g., symbiosis) for mutual benefit. Hardcore altruism is the spontaneous sort of self-sacrifice for the good of the family or small group. If the latter were the only kind of altruism possessed by humans, we would recklessly oppose each other in small groups after the model of the social insects. But fortunately humans possess both forms of altruism, permitting them to cooperate with members of strange groups and thus, theoretically, to build a world community. However, this presupposes reciprocity, which is, of course, indirect in most cases (R. Alexander, 1987). Those who act on others' behalf without receiving anything in return and neglect their own reproductive chances while doing so initiate their own genetic demise. R. Alexander aptly remarked in this context "I do not doubt that occasionally individuals led lives that are truly altruistic and self-sacrificing. However, admirable and desirable such a behavior may be from others point of view, it represents an evolutionary mistake for the individual showing it" (R. D. Alexander, 1987, p. 191). In our last chapter on ethics we will discuss this point in more detail.

E. O. Wilson's *Sociobiology* (1975) has been a breakthrough for biological evolutionary thinking in the United States. Certain extreme environmentalists attacked it vigorously (R. C. Lewontin, 1977), and not always in fair discussion. Critics rightly point at certain weaknesses in the argumentation, but they fail to acknowledge adequately the positive aspects of the new approach. This is also evident in many other ways in the remarkable critique by P. Kitcher (1985, 1987). Many of the critics blamed Wilson for expressing a biological determinism which would lead to racism, imperialism, genocide, and other evils. Such accusations are inappropriate. All knowledge can be misused, as can every theory, even that of environmentalism. W. Charlesworth (1981, p. 22) formulated this point clearly:

> Speaking of rhetoric, there should be an editorial rule that sentences associated with sociobiology, with effort to justify slavery, imperialism, racism, genocide, and to oppose equal rights should always appear next to sentences associating environmentalist/ learning theory with effort to justify propaganda, psychological terror, false advertisement, public indoctrination of hatred of foreigners, class enemies, minority groups, and so on and so on. Juxtaposing sociobiology and learning theory in this manner ought to show how unproductive it is to claim through innuendo or otherwise that science will lead to pseudoscience, will lead to man's inhumanity to man: ergo no science. Actually, one could argue that since man is such a cultural/learning animal we should have greater fear of learning theory since learning has far more power over man's behavior than genes. More specifically, if humans were not such learning animals, they would not learn all that Galton trash: ergo stop learning research so that bad guys will not use the data to teach the trash more effectively.

Sociobiology has undoubtedly provided new impetus to our thought. Thus Wilson's integrative accomplishment deserves full acknowledgment. However, in the hope of a new breakthrough many jumped on this bandwagon in a quite uncritical way and a number of minor publications flooded the market. Wilson's own remark that sociobiology would eventually cannibalize the social sciences and ethology contributed to this development. It is still sociobiology's responsibility to verify its hypotheses and give equal time to alternate ones. They are limited primarily to building interesting quantitative models, but often the trivial is quantified as a "strategy." At the International Ethological Congress in Brisbane (1983), for example, it was reported that juvenile fish invest supplementary food in growth and that adult fish, on the other hand, invest it in reproduction. What a surprising result. In fact, there is hardly another reasonable alternative.

Finally, sociobiology is responsible for confusing levels of action by using psychological concepts to explain and interpret genetic phenomena. This confounding has even led sociobiologists to such absurd conclusions as that there is no such thing as altruism. Starting from the fact that only genetic survival counts—which no scientist will gainsay—organisms are considered as acting appropriately only when their behavior increases their inclusive fitness. This has all been put together to form the concept of "selfish behavior" and sympathy, friendship, and charity are considered as illusions not existing in reality. This is a shocking conclusion, because we are, of course, constructed to experience love subjectively and friendship and, spurred on by such feelings, we will even sacrifice ourselves for certain fellow beings. Nor does this contradict the fact that, in so doing, we also act adaptively, that is, propagating our genes. Support and cooperation are strategies in the struggle for existence, and the corresponding emotions have developed to serve these strategies. Thus friendship exists next to competition, and it is wrong to maintain that an organism only seeks advantages at the expense of others. It is a dangerous and misleading simplification to say that everything which we term cooperation is simply a mixture of opportunism and exploitation and that given the opportunity to act in its own interest, only cold calculation restrains an organism from subordinating or even killing its brother, spouse, parents or children.[13]

Summary 2.4

The cost–benefit calculations of sociobiologists demonstrate that altruistic behavior be maintained via individual and kin selection. Mathematical models stimulate hypothesis formation. This promising new development in ethology, however, has exposed itself unnecessarily to criticism because of its uncritical speculations. The statement that no truly altruistic behavior exists because in terms of his own fitness an altruist is always behaving selfishly is a result of a confusion of levels. Even if the altruist contributes to the propagation of his own genes by self-sacrifice

---

[13]"The Evolution of Society fits the Darwinian paradigm in its most individualistic form. Nothing in it cries out to be otherwise explained. The economy of nature is competitive from beginning to end. Understand that economy, and how it works, and the underlying reasons for social phenomena are manifest. They are the means by which one organism gains some advantage to the detriment of another. No hint of genuine charity ameliorates our vision of society, once sentimentalism has been laid aside. What passes for cooperation turns out to be a mixture of opportunism and exploitation. The impulses that lead one animal to sacrifice himself for another turn out to have their ultimate rationale in gaining advantage over a third; and acts 'for the good' of one society turn out to be performed to the detriment of the rest. Where it is in his own interest, every organism may reasonably be expected to aid his fellows. Where he has no alternative, he submits to the yoke of communal servitude. Yet given a full chance to act in his own interest, nothing but expediency will restrain him from brutalizing, from maiming, from murdering—his brother, his mate, his parent or his child. Scratch an 'altruist,' and watch a 'hypocrite' bleed" (M. T. Ghiselin, 1974, p. 2).

for offspring and relatives, on the behaviorally and psychologically experienced level he acts unselfishly or altruistically. Empathy, sympathy, and related emotions are experienced and observed and thus truly exist. That they contribute to evolutionary fitness is quite consistent with the fact that one can behave in a genuinely altruistic manner. Furthermore, the uncritical citing of extreme examples (such as langur infanticide) cannot be used to support the contention that biological evolution proceeds basically as a battle of everyone for himself. Man especially extends his family ethos to the group, and his emotional and behavioral repertoire allows him to join with others in closed groups that behave as a unit and thus act as units in biological selection. The human propensity for indoctrination, war ethos, and the ethos of sharing lead to the fact that individual interests are often subjugated to those of the group. In humans, at least we can discern various levels of selection: individual, kin, and group selection.

3

Methodology

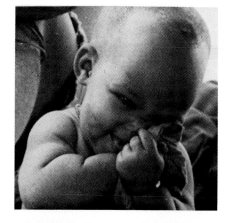
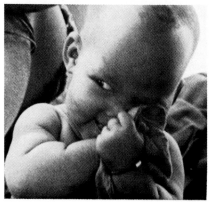

3.1. Gestalt Perception and Cognition

Research proceeds from perceptions. These, without doubt, depict an extra-subjective reality with a more or less refined screen. Because of programs inherent to our cognitive apparatus, our perception interprets and reconstructs the perceived world from the sensory data. We interact, so to speak, with our world on the basis of hypotheses, which evolved since they "fitted" and thus were not weeded out by selection (K. R. Popper, 1973). Such built-in biases can lead our perception astray, as many of the visual illusions demonstrate (p. 5). But since we are able to interact with our environment dialogically and approach a problem from different angles, we can find out about illusions and thus the working of our brain. Thus, by measuring the two lines, which we perceive as different in length in the Müller-Lyer Illusion, we can find out that they are in fact equal in length.

Even though our perceptions are biased and reflect hypotheses about our external world, they do so fairly accurately since they were tested during the course of evolution. Cognition has even been gauged over the course of evolution to recognize regularities, an important predisposition for scientific discovery (K. Lorenz, 1959). Gestalt perception abstracts the incidental and sharply resolves the general elements that characterize not only an individual object but an entire object class. From the many fleeting impressions of our visual perceptions the shared features finally emerge as a mental template of the "ideal" type or "rule" (see Section 9.1). It is evident that there is a strong selection pressure acting upon perceptual performance, for it is vitally important for an animal to recognize objects of relevance under varying conditions. The processes underlying our perception are, as K. Lorenz (1959) stated, analogous to rational operations of reasoning. Therefore, one also speaks of ratiomorphic ability. Gestalt perception allows us to directly grasp the regularity immanent in complex natural events, that is to filter it from the background "noise" information that is simultaneously transmitted by our sensory organs and perceptual apparatus (K. Lorenz, 1959, 257). We grasp such relationships of regularity "intuitively," and this cognitive ability cannot be substituted by the most detailed quantifications. Yet we must not forget that "configurational pressure," "suggestive tendency," may falsely make us perceive a phenomenon as real that other investigational procedures show to be illusory.

Perception is not the only trap awaiting us. Our thought processes also follow specific pathways, leading us to think in contrasts or opposites and thus polarize our thought. This tendency is an ordering process of the brain, using contrast to bring out antitheses and thus foster orientation and clarity while at the same time simplifying our conception of the world.

Our daily life, as our political thinking, is controlled by this polarization. Even scientific work is subject to its effect. We like "clear" positions with sharply delineated opposing arguments, and we will create an opposing view if none exists by setting up "straw men." The nature–nurture controversy (p. 19) provides a good example. Such polarization need not only be seen in negative terms. Opposing views stimulate thought, and for this reason we overstate our position, thereby fostering more controversy. Yet we must be aware that in such cases we tend to artificially exaggerate the opposing position in order to provoke a response.

Monocausal thought is another bias in thinking that often misleads us in daily life as well as in our research. It is certainly important for an organism to determine the immediate cause of some event quickly, and the assumption that something has a cause has stood the test in evolution. Thus in our life and research we tend to elucidate the "cause." This sort of reductionism, into which we get easily trapped by our monocausal thinking, is not to be confused with the legitimate reductionism of any of the natural sciences, which attempt to proceed from the exploration of the special case to the extraction of more general rules and which endeavors to explain events of a higher level of integration by reduction to the more basic laws. Thus, biologists, in an analytical-reductionistic approach, intend to understand phenomena of life, such as the function of a neuron down to the level of biochemistry and finally to elementary chemical processes. We must remain aware, however, that with each level of integration new system characteristics show up that can not be explained by the characteristics of the lower levels. Understanding the function of the neuron helps us to understand many peculiarities of behavior and its pathologies, but certainly it is only of limited value in understanding differentiated social interactions at a higher level. Any "nothing-but-ism" must be avoided.

Assessment biases can profoundly influence our judgment as well. Thus we interpret involutions (evolutionary processes by which differentiations get lost) negatively and always speak of the more differentiated organisms as the higher ones (K. Lorenz, 1983).

Therefore, we certainly cannot speak of observation and research completely free of all bias, since in scientific study we utilize a device whose perception, developed through the course of evolution, already has predisposed judgments based on phylogenetic experience. We can detect the resulting deficiency of interpretation by analyzing reality from different angles. We are also capable of detaching our thought from emotions, thus creating a field without tension which enables the free experimental play of fantasy to occur with a relatively objective orientation. Thanks to differential hemispherical specialization of the cerebral cortex (p. 106), we are finally in a position to observe ourselves, so to speak, by means of a central mirror. Thus when scientists speak of the virtue of unbiased observation, they mean primarily the decoupling of individual prejudices resulting from personal experience.

Another handicap results from our inclination (disposition) to adhere to hypotheses even when we begin to doubt their validity. To understand this tendency one must realize that hypotheses serve as aids in orientation. They present a view of the world that confers security, since they make the world predictable. For example, hunter-gatherers project such a grid of orientation upon their world as can be seen in religious practices of the Kalahari Bushmen. The Bushmen explain disease as caused by invisible arrows that evil forces (demons or enemies) shoot into the bodies of the sick. This hypothesis provides a basis for treatment. The bushmen believe that they can extract these invisible arrows by a curing ritual. To achieve the power to do this, the curers have to put themselves in a state of trance, which they achieve by a dance. The patient is thus helped psychologically—he believes in the ritual and thus is relieved from fear and tension, which, of course, has a positive effect on his state of health. Hypotheses, such as these, may thus be the basis on which religious practices are developed and these practices may later serve as markers of group identity. This function may make them resistent to rational contestation. The unfortunate inclination of man to convert theories from the field of economy and sociology into quasi-religious "Weltanschauungen" is commonly known.

Summary 3.1

Since man perceives and processes sensory data by means of programs which are given as phylogenetic adaptations, there is no such thing as purely objective perception and research. But the hypotheses underlying perceptive ability have been tested over the course of evolution in real situations, so we can state that in general they are valid biases as long as they are compatible with specific environmental conditions relevant for us. Although our perception is not free of distortions, it generally discerns relationships accurately. Those areas in which we are deceived or that are oversimplified by our perception, can be handled by using measurements and observation from other perspectives. Gestalt perception, in particular, remains an important source of cognition, even if we are sometimes misled by some of its features (e.g., the suggestive tendency). A certain proclivity toward getting trapped into dogmatic attitudes stems from our tendency to create order which presses us to categorize and classify in a polarizing fashion, and, in addition, by our inclination for monocausal explanation and our reluctance to discard hypotheses.

3.2. Methods of Data Gathering, Observation, and Description

Data have to be gathered in such a way as to allow other researchers to follow the procedure and thus check the results of others. We often use technical means of data sampling (such as film and sound recordings) in the interest of objectivity. Other means of maintaining objectivity are the use of random sampling with a table of random numbers for subject selection (p. 148) and utilizing technological apparatus to analyze data.

Objectivity is enhanced with distanced observation, a methodology perfected by animal ethologists. H. Hass (1968) said that the observer of human behavior should put himself in the position of someone from another planet. However, participatory observation is also important because we can gain information on peoples' inclinations, desires, and objectives through introspection and as well as through participation with them and subsequent questioning of their behavior. This method is preferred by many researchers and they even discard distanced observation as, in their opinion, it cannot provide any clues on the real intentions of the observed individual. To argue for the use of one or another method alone is inappropriate since both observation methods have their own strengths and weaknesses. I can usually quickly discover via participatory questioning which ideas and objectives guide my subjects' behavior, assuming the subjects are not lying, although formulating the correct questions to elicit the answer is not always easy. However, subjects' initial responses to questions should not necessarily be taken as thoroughly conclusive. For example, the researcher is poorly advised if he is content with a Hopi Indian's explanation that the rain dance exists to make it rain, because he would at best consider the dance to be a ritual without real function since it does not bring forth the longed-for rain. Here distanced observation can help by showing that such rituals serve to bring together the group in times of emergency by reinforcing group bonds and group identity and foster cooperation. In this way, we gain insight into the selective advantage of this ritual.

N. A. Chagnon (1968, 1974) states in a series of studies that territorality or defense of territory would not explain warfare among Yanomami Indians. He argues that wars are not fought to hold competing groups at a distance and to secure hunting grounds, but, as his Yanomami informants told him, to abduct women (Chagnon, 1968). After further research, he reported (1974) that wars are fought to maintain the sovereignty of the Yanomami villages but not to acquire hunting territories or other life necessities. The first reason given by the Yanomami, that wars are fought to abduct women, may be perfectly correct in terms of individual motivation, but the observer must further investigate the selective advantages of warfare. Individual motivation and fitness-sustaining performance are not necessarily congruent. M. Harris (1979) pointed to the fact that availability of animal protein is a limiting factor for the Yanomami. As village size increases, so does the energy expended on hunting (K. Good, 1980). Insufficient hunting success results in a buildup of tension, and we observe that quarrels arise and villages begin to break up when they reach a certain size. Furthermore, intergroup aggression motivates individual groups to maintain a certain living distance between themselves. This effect is what counts regardless of individual motivation. The intergroup tension prevents the exhaustion of the resources of Yanomami territories. Thus there may be multiple motivations and causes for warfare at the individual level (proximate cause) to obtain women and at the group level (the ultimate cause) to space groups in the jungle. In explaining such practices as warfare, we must be careful to avoid the above-mentioned tendency to explain a phenomenon by a single hypothesis.

Each ethological investigation begins with the description and documentation of the behavioral patterns under study. The *ethogram,* as the behavioral inventory is called, thus obtained is the basis of further work. Generally the unprejudiced observer has no difficulty sorting out specific recurring behavioral patterns as units from the flow of behavior observed. We note that the subject smiles or cries, reaches for objects or greets someone. We formulate greeting as a category as well as the simpler behavioral components that comprise the entire greeting ceremony (smiling, rapid brow raising, head nodding, and hand extension). The ethograms of different researchers utilize different principles of organization, and there is an attempt to categorize descriptively according to behavioral pattern (of smiling, rapid brow raising, etc.). Categories are generally named after the appearance of the behavior pattern but occasionally in terms of the muscles used in the action. Often, as in laughing and crying, the pattern is already categorized and named even prior to any scientific description. Categorization is often based on function, a procedure requiring prior knowledge on the part of the researcher. Concerning social behavior, our knowledge of function is often founded on intuition. Functional categories of this kind include greeting, courting, comforting or appeasing. If such category names are used, they must be precisely defined and their function also verified. Furthermore, the researcher must be aware of the fact that range of a category can vary due to the hierarchical organization of behavior. A greeting consists of several behavioral patterns such as head nodding, smiling, rapid raising of the eyebrows, and more.

Behavioral patterns were not always clearly worked out in the early child ethograms, so different authors developed entirely different listings. E. C. Grant (1968, 1969) lists 118 behavioral patterns in his child ethogram. N. G. Blurton-Jones (1972) lists 31, W. C. McGrew (1972) lists 42, and C. R. Brannigan and D. A. Humphries (1972) lists 136.

The choice of categories depends upon the researcher's individual formulation of the problem. In their study of friendship development, M. Lewis *et al.* (1975) listed body contact (touch), nearness, gazing, smiling, offering and taking away toys, sharing, and partner-directed aggression. This inventory sufficed for their analysis of children 1 to 2 years old, but it required expansion for older children. The similar study done by G. Attili, B. Hold, and M. Schleidt (1982) on 3- to 6-year-old children included the additional categories of support, assistance, and the taking of initiatives.

In all cases it is important to define one's categories. This includes a precise, empirical description of the bodily movements within a spatial reference system, which in the case of interaction must naturally include the communicating partner. The distance and orientation between partners must be noted. Further, it must be taken into account that the speed of the occurring pattern can also define a behavior. Thus, a slow turning away from the communicating partner in the sense of a gradual opening of a dyad initiates parting from each other, while rapid turning away oftens signals some sort of offense (insult, irritability). The meaning of contact and pushing are also specified by the speed with which they are carried out against the partner.

Depending upon the context, a light body blow may signify admonition or punishment but also be a friendly gesture. One must examine the social context of the situation and have some knowledge of prior events. Did the children fight with each other before? Have they been friends for a long time? Our predisposition will effect our interpretation of an observed situation. Individual biases can be removed by comparing results with others. For example, films of scenes can be viewed by different observers.

Social environment is not the only reference for assessing behavior. K. Grammer (verbal commun.) found out that the children of a kindergarten group would show quite different attention structure within closed rooms than in the garden outside. A particular problem for the evaluation is the coding of movements (H. M. Rosenfeld, 1982). Fear of perceptual deception (for which cross-observer reliability checks only helps locate individual errors) justified striving for objectivity. It was argued that analytical instruments are not deceived and thus ethologists make use of measuring and calculating devices to best approach reality.

Sometimes this is indeed the only way we can achieve a research goal. So far it has not been possible to develop a satisfactory objective notation of movement patterns by position coding of body and body parts on a body coordinate system (top-bottom, right-left, anterior-posterior; I. Golani, 1969; R. Laban, 1965). Apart from the fact that "descriptions" of organs and body movements using angles, spatial relationships, and positions are difficult to grasp (unless we grossly simplify), such descriptions often fail to capture the essential behavioral components. A person in a lecture hall can greet a friend with a slight turn of the palm without lifting the arm from the desk. The friend, and any neutral observer, would understand this as a greeting. During a lecture intermission, the same person would execute the greeting differently, because he would not have to limit himself to a discreet greeting intention movement. He could raise the entire arm and even wave with the greeting hand. In a spatial/temporal notation system, the two behaviors appear as something completely different, so rejecting our perceptual integrative capacity in favor of supposed objectivity misleads the researcher. However, the physical description of the event in everyday language allows us to describe the facts comprehensibly. A temporary turning of the palm toward someone (one must measure and cite its duration) is used as a greeting gesture in our culture. The movement can be executed intentionally at various intensity levels, and the placement of upper and lower arm can vary considerably.

The turning of the palm toward someone for a particular period of time is the relevant characteristic for this type of communication. Details of the behavioral sequence and context allow us to distinguish a greeting palm turn from a rejecting hand position.

Even such characteristics can be better described by direct verbal account than with one of the so far utilized current notational systems. This also holds for the mimic expressions accompanying greeting and rejection.

R. L. Birdwhistell (1960, 1973) made a microanalysis of the behaviors comprising an expression. He assumed that specific movements are comparable to speech phonemes. His laborious analyses have not led to any further results.

Behavioral patterns are temporal structures characterized by a particular sequence of events (muscle actions). The patterns of nonverbal expressive movements are characterized by form constancy, i.e., constancy of the relative phase interval of the muscle contractions responsible for the underlying movement (see review, p. 25). Thus for the observer a behavior pattern is recognizable as a certain pattern at any time regardless of whether it is simply an intention movement (merely implying what the person intends to do) or a fully executed expressive movement. If I record the temporal sequence of the muscle contractions as a sort of musical score, by assigning each muscle a number, I can describe movements with a terminology that can be understood by another investigator. Such a system has proved useful for facial expressions.

P. Ekman et al. (1971a, b) developed a coding system using C. H. Hjortsjö's (1969) method of describing facial movements according to muscle action. They determined the individual facial muscles causing visible changes of expression and assigned numbers to these muscles. They also grouped various synergistic muscles as "action units" (see p. 447). Mime is particularly well suited for this kind of recording, since the muscle contractions on the face are particularly understandable once one has mastered Ekman's system.

There is no consensus as to what level behavioral analysis should begin. Should one work in increasing order from the most elemental behaviors? J. A. van Hooff (1971), and S. Frey and J. Pool (1976) claim that starting at the bottom is best because the smallest units are easiest to characterize precisely. They can also be used to construct higher behavioral levels. On the other hand, U. Kalbermatten and M. von Cranach (1980) believe there is no synthetic formulation stating which behavioral units should be combined into higher systems. Thus it would be more appropriate to move downward through the behavioral organization. M. von Cranach et al. (1980) start their behavioral analysis from complex goal-directed behavior. They define as behavior every human act characterized by goal orientation, consciousness, planning, and intention (U. Kalbermatten and M. von Cranach, 1980). This behavioral position may seem problematic if we try to apply it to childrens' behavior or in cross-cultural comparisons, wherein the distant observer can at best draw his own conclusions about consciousness, planning, and intention but cannot usually verify them. Yet, I think that their action-theoretical approach is also suitable for objective analysis, since one can determine via observation that there are behaviors extending over longer time periods and which apparently terminate because some recognizable goal was achieved. For example,

110

when a desired object is finally acquired, a request granted, or a consummation permitted.

For the observer it is initially unimportant whether the goal is sought consciously or not. What is essential is to determine a behavioral sequence defined by initiation and termination point. The flow of actions and a terminating goal can be broken down into components, and M. von Cranach *et al.* (1980) speak of behavioral steps. The act of preparing breakfast consists of a series of behavioral steps (such as cooking eggs, preparing coffee) defined by their intermediate goals, and separable into their component behavioral subunits. One grinds the coffee, lights the stove, fills the kettle with water, etc.

Each of these acts consists of a series of complex functional action units within an unmistakable hierarchical organization. Units at upper levels each incorporate several of those at the lower levels, and behavioral diversity decreases at lower levels. Component acts and goals are defined functionally, and some behavior sequences are stereotyped, while others display a great amount of variability. Sometimes they are ordered linearly, and then one act follows another as if keeping to a given track.

There are also behavioral ramifications that permit various pathways to be used to attain a single goal. For example, I can gain a desired object by requesting it, demanding it with threats, or even snatching it from another. When I am driving to a meeting I can take the shortest route or divert my travel if I hear of an accident on the radio. All these possibilities are available to me like behavioral recipes, and the richer my repertoire, the more possibilities I have at my disposal for achieving objectives and the greater my competence. Thus a behavior can be understood as a part of a network.

M. von Cranach *et al.* (1980) use the term "strategy" to indicate the subjective representation of the behavioral pathway network chosen on the basis of preference to attain one final goal. I prefer a somewhat narrower conception of strategy. When we observe that aggression is warded off, we find that various pathways with many different behavioral steps may be effective. Thus I find it more useful to describe alternate behavioral possibilities as strategies of warding off aggression and not just to speak of one strategy. A strategy would then be the attainment of a final objective through choosing one of several possible series of behavioral steps. They could in their entirety be described as the strategic repertoire for the particular individual involved.

The concept of tactics is used for subordinate units composed of several behavioral steps. Whether this concept is useful can only be determined in individual cases. The delineation of behavioral sequences as worked out by M. von Cranach *et al.*, in the form of a series of behavioral steps within a pathway network, is particularly useful in describing human actions. We will cite examples of universal interaction strategies later (p. 493).

The starting point of any behavioral description is the concrete event. If this is a social interaction, let us say between mother and child, then we have to consider this event as an interaction which reflects a relationship which grew in time and not just as an isolated situation. In order to understand the quality of this relation and the variables by which it is determined we need to study more than just one interaction between the individuals concerned. And since we want to learn about the patterning of the mother–child interaction of the culture or species concerned in more general terms, we need, of course, to describe other mothers interacting with their children. Mother and child are also part of a community, whose social structure can be derived from the great variety of interactions between its members. Behavioral description thus involves various levels of abstraction and integration. A conceptual scheme relating interactions, relationships, and group structure was outlined by R. A. Hinde and J. Stevenson Hinde (1976).

Summary 3.2

"Objective" and participatory methods of observation complement each other. Human ethology uses both, but in "natural contexts" it places special emphasis on distanced observation. Individually recognizable units of behavior must be described and named. Interpretive terms are permissible only when the implied function is also verified. Nomenclature and description must also account for the hierarchical organization of behavior. The Hjortsjö-Ekman muscle action coding system can be used to describe human facial expressions. Cranach's pathway network procedure of analysis can be recommended as appropriate for more complex behavioral sequences: a specific behavioral objective can be achieved via various behavioral steps. Several such pathways can be combined into a single network, with each pathway forming a strategy to achieve a goal. The totality of pathways represents the strategic repertoire at the individual's or species' disposal for attaining a behavioral goal.

3.3. Film and Sound Documentation

Film and sound records are important means of collecting data. By following a number of basic rules, we can work out documents of events that can serve as evidence for testing hypotheses.

Technical means permit us to record movements objectively and store them in an archive for later study. This is important for the interpretation of behavioral sequences is always prone to subjective tinge. Even an observer attempting to be completely objective describes only those items that appear to be significant to him, and for someone else essential information could be lost. Animal ethologists, ethnologists, and other social scientists have long recognized the importance of film documentation. However, ethnographic material is primarily aimed at documenting skills, dances, and rituals. Hut construction, bread baking, weaving, pottery, hunting, and dancing has been filmed in numerous cultures.[1] However, little work on documentation of unstaged, daily human interaction has been systematically carried out. Film documents of such behaviors as greeting in various cultures, of affectionate behavior of mothers, flirtatious behavior, and infantile aggression resolution are few. Only pioneer studies, like the one of G. Bateson and M. Mead (1942) who studied everyday life of the Balinese, have been conducted. (See also E. R. Sorenson and D. Gajdusek 1966, and E. R. Sorenson 1967.)

When I began searching for universals in human behavior with Hans Hass in the early 1960s, we initially assumed we could trace what we wanted in film archives, since man is the most frequently filmed creature in the world. But when we found this gap we were alarmed, since we knew that the opportunity to gather

---

[1]Many ethnographic films, often shown in didactically prepared form, are in I. C. Jarvie's (1983) words, "fraught with distortion" and thus at best are "hearsay evidence." This need not be the case!

this documentation on a cross-cultural basis was vanishing quickly because of the rapid change in cultures around due to contact from western societies. This meant that if one missed the opportunity to record daily greeting ceremony in its traditional context, no subsequent reconstruction of it would be possible. Handcrafted artifacts (like mats or pottery) can be analyzed for their construction even if the actual producers' culture disappeared long ago, but this is not possible for social interactions.

A cross-cultural document must fulfill the following requirements:

1. Films should document everyday reality, that is, unstaged social interactions.

Since people alter their behavior under observation, some technical means is needed to record behavior without distorting it. Dances and rituals are usually an exception to this rule, for they often, but not always, are displayed in public in their natural context, and this diminishes disturbance for the performers. The emphasis on documenting spontaneously occurring events does not imply that staged events must be excluded. To the contrary, we film actors and evoke certain behaviors such as facial expressions in standardized testing situations.

2. The data should be processed in such a way that later researchers can use them for subsequent studies.

A particular bias on the part of an observer could be picked up in subsequent studies. This also demands utmost care in collection and storage of data.

A special film recording technique had to be developed to meet these requirements. Telephotography with lenses aimed directly at subjects was not effective due to the human propensity to be on the alert for what is going on around them (H. Hass, 1968). People look up from their activities at regular intervals and scan the horizon, thus perceiving any objects or events that might affect them, including a camera lens directed toward them. H. Hass developed a reflex lens permitting the photographer to film from the side. The principle is simple: a dummy lens containing a side window is placed in front of the real one. A prism built into this assembly permits photography of objects at right angles to the lens barrel. After testing this device, we started a program for the cross-cultural documentation of human behavior (I. Eibl-Eibesfeldt and H. Hass, 1966, 1967; H. Hass, 1968; Figs. 3.1-3.3). More recently, my co-worker D. Heunemann has improved this lens system so that one can even use a zoom lens in conjunction with it.

The use of photographic method is advantageous even in cultures where photography is unknown. A lens aimed directly at a person elicits a fear response even in such cultures. But, if the camera is pointing in a different direction, people do not feel "watched."

We recommend 16 mm film for picture quality. The frame speed should be chosen depending upon the speed of the ongoing behavior. In addition to the standard 25 frames/second speed, we utilize slow motion (50 frames/second) for analyzing rapidly occurring sequences. The signal effect of expressive behavior is also different at a higher speed: we can observe behavior with more objectivity. Longer behavioral events can be recorded with quick motion photography. With 6 pictures/second, we can record a 40-minute event on a single 120 m roll of 16 mm film. This can be used to document the entire sequence of a ritual, dance, or mother–child interaction and to glean regularities such as movement (stereotypes) that would otherwise escape the observer (H. Hass, 1968); one can count how

FIGURE 3.1. (a) Reflex lens showing the window in the dummy lens placed in front of the true lens; (b) reflex lens removed to provide for direct photography.

FIGURE 3.2. Filming with the reflex lens in Tauwema (Trobriand Islands). A mother with an infant is the subject of my attention. A great deal of film documentation of her behavior was gathered using this method. Photo: R. Krell.

FIGURE 3.3. The author films a family at a Bushman hut with the reflex lens. Photo: D. Heunemann.

often a child makes contact with its mother, how far it moves away from the mother in various situations, and other phenomena.

A second camera can be used to record parts of such sequences at the normal speed. Synchronized sound recordings are also important. Since fall 1976 we use the time coding systems developed by NAGRA and ARRIFLEX. A quartz clock records year, month, day, hour, minutes, and seconds within the camera and the tape recorder independently, that is, without any mechanical connection between camera and sound recorder. On the film, the time is coded between film perforations. A computer linked to the editing table can read the coding off the sound track and the film and coordinate both as well as locate any specified time. Thus the computer can search for the sound track matching a particular film frame or vice-versa.

Every photographic record should include a supplementary protocol noting what behavior preceded the sequence and what followed it. Also important is the noting of whom is participating and what their kinship and social relationship is. For children, careful calculation of age is essential. The context of an event, unless obvious from the photography, should also be recorded. These notes are a necessity for subsequent correlational analyses.

How and what is filmed depends on the questions asked. Were we asking how frequently a behavior occurs in the day, we would have to film at randomly chosen intervals. Since our question, however, deals more with the structure, movement patterns, and strategies used particularly in interactions, we place special emphasis on interactions such as those between mother–child, father–child, and siblings. We usually set up where social interactions will be taking place: near children at play, at the village square where men or women have gathered, near a family beside its hut or garden. In addition to concentrating on certain topics, we attempt to film every social interaction, whether we have recorded it before or not. We also film whenever we expect an event to occur, such as when two people meet, without our knowing what will ensue in their interaction. We also do not restrict ourselves to limited themes. Since we use the same procedure in all cultures, errors are leveled out and thus the recorded material becomes comparable and can be evaluated in many ways. We will demonstrate this later with examples.

It is not always easy to determine when to start and stop filming. When two partners separate or turn away from each other, this is generally an indication that an interaction is ending. But often the partners are merely pausing, and when the camera is turned off the partners may promptly resume their interaction. The photography resumes, but one may have lost essential data during the pause. For this reason it is advisable to have a second quick motion camera running to uninterruptedly record the entire sequence.

Our originals are archived unedited so other researchers can have access to them at a later time. We work only with copies and prepare duplicates for publications. Future workers must utilize this same procedure, since much of our data will not be gatherable again due to the rapid cultural changes occurring in many societies!

Our films are published in cooperation with the Göttingen Institute for Scientific Film as a joint production of the Film Archive of Human Ethology of the Max-Planck-Society and the Encyclopaedia Cinematographica of the Institute for Scientific Film. (See list following the Bibliography.)

A number of traditional societies with different subsistence strategies were selected for our documentation to provide us with information on behavior in societies with different kinds of human social organization. They have been selected to represent a wide a geographical selection as possible.

1. The G/wi, !Ko and !Kung Bushmen of the Kalahari (Botswana and Southwest Africa), who during the first years of our investigations (1970–1975) still lived in small groups as hunters and gatherers. They are relatively peaceful people living on what might be considered a paleolithic subsistence strategy with paleolithic technology.
2. The Yanomami (Waika) of the upper Orinoco and the Serra Parima in Venezuela, who are horticulturists and hunters. In contrast to the Bushmen they are rather belligerent.
3. The Eipo and other Mek-speaking tribes of western New Guinea. They were contacted with an interdisciplinary team initiated by Gerd Koch and Klaus Helfrich, with whom we work closely. At the time of contact these were intact neolithic horticulturists entirely free of external influences.
4. The Himba of Southwest Africa, who as nonacculturated Herero-speaking people are traditional belligerent pastoralists.
5. The Trobriand islanders, a culture of horticulturists and fishermen who, despite civilizing influences, maintain many traditional aspects of their culture.
6. The Balinese as a non-western peasant society.

We visit these sample cultures, if feasible, at regular intervals and work together with ethnologists and linguists.[2] So far we have accumulated about 250 km of movie film.

Some of these projects have been running since 1965, and all are continuing when possible. We also make spot checks of other cultures in addition to these long-term studies. Here we concentrate on recording parent–child relationships, sibling interactions, rituals, and such expressions as surprise, agreement, rejection, and others.

For studying western culture we have installed a video recorder in a public kindergarten, with parental consent, permitting us to record the childrens' interactions. These studies provide us with a valuable basis for cross-cultural comparisons (K. Grammer, 1988).[3]

---

[2]Co-workers on the Bushman project include H. J. Heinz and P. Wiessner-Larsen. Among the Yanomami I worked with Kenneth Good (anthropologist) and later with Harald Herzog (linguist). Volker Heeschen (linguist) and Wulf Schiefenhövel (ethnologist and physician) investigated the Mek cultures. Participating on the Trobriands were ethnologist Ingrid Bell-Krannhals and linguist Gunther Senft. With the Himba, I worked with Herero-speaking ethnologist Kuno Budack. Ethological film documentation was largely my responsibility.

[3]The project was set up by my co-worker Barbara Hold. After trial testing in the Munich kindergarten, she installed remote-controlled video observation equipment in the Söcking kindergarten. Three ceiling-mounted cameras, free to move in all directions, and three microphones permitted undisturbed recordings of the children. Each child was recorded over a year on two randomly changing days per week, five minutes per time period, for purposes of multiple analysis. There are a total of 4250 minutes consisting of 850 five-minute videos of twenty children, an average of 42 recordings per child. The data base has been investigated independently by various members of our group (G. Attili, K. Grammer, B. Hold, G. von Oettingen, H. Shibasaka, M. Schleidt, and R. Schropp) for social strategies, social hierarchy phenomena, conflict, object transfer, showing off, friendship development, and others. We will cite this work elsewhere in the text.

Movie film evaluation can be done with different perspectives. Counting the absolute frequency of events, for instance (how often someone laughs in a culture), makes no sense, since our filming is not a random sample. But it is useful to tally frequencies within specific behavioral categories, compare their appearance in individual situations, and to record their effect. Thus, when analyzing our films, Polly Wiessner found remarkable cultural differences in strategies of food requesting and offering in children (p. 503).

Film is the basis for a precise description of behavior for any comparative purpose because it allows the observer to view the interaction again and again and record details of the actions and interrelated actions. (See Fig. 3.4.)

The assessment and statistical analysis of 233 filmed events of rapid brow raising in a contact situation in the Eipo, Yanomami, and Trobriand islanders (using the Hjortsjö and Ekman facial action coding system, p. 447) showed that the pattern of the muscle action were nearly identical in all three cultures.

The phases of onset and offset show little variation both intra- and interculturally. Variation occurs only for the duration of maximum contraction and on an interindividual level. There are no intercultural differences. If eyebrow raising is used as an introduction to interaction, the duration is shortest in all three cultures. Thus, in spite of the great differences between test subjects, the eyebrow raising sequence is a rather rigid program, in the sense of an exclamation mark of the face.

Computer analysis showed further that infants, children, and juveniles display less individual temporal variance in eyebrow raising than adults, which indicates a stronger attachment to the biological program of the behavior. Apparently adults learn to add emphasis to eyebrow raising using a voluntarily prolonged contraction amplitude (K. Grammer *et al.*, 1988).

The contraction of the inner and outer forehead muscles is not arbitrarily combined with other facial expressions. Eyebrow raising and smiling and upward movement of the head appear together most frequently, which confirms my original interpretation of the eyebrow raising as ''yes to social contact'' (eye greeting gesture). This interpretation is even more likely in view of the fact that emotions of rejection, manifested facially by vertical forehead wrinkles above the root of the nose (grim look), are either strongly suppressed (Eipo) or do not appear at all (Yanomami) in some peoples (Fig. 3.5a–c). It is physically feasible for such muscular combinations to occur, since different muscles engage in the action units (p. 456), but great effort is required to do so. Apparently the neuronal connections are different. Vertical forehead wrinkles may occur just before eyebrow raising as a slight expression of skepticism or fear (p. 118).

W. Siegfried's (1983, 1988) work is another example of using film for behavioral analysis. His phenomenological descriptions of dance led to formulating the hypothesis that dancers develop, stabilize, and vary a binding spatial/temporal structure shared by the dancing group. He tested individual elements of his hypothesis with film that I had collected among several cultures. Siegfried used the courtship dance of the Himba (Fig. 3.6) to work out the construction of a spatial configuration. Young men form a semicircle opposite a second semicircle of young women. Individual men or women jump out of their semicircle for a brief display dance. The men execute high leaps, and the women rotate so that their skirts fly up and for a fraction of a second display their backsides. The development of the spatial/temporal structure was studied from films of different Bushman dances. In the girls' ''apron flip dance'' of the !Ko, the dancers stand in a circle oriented toward

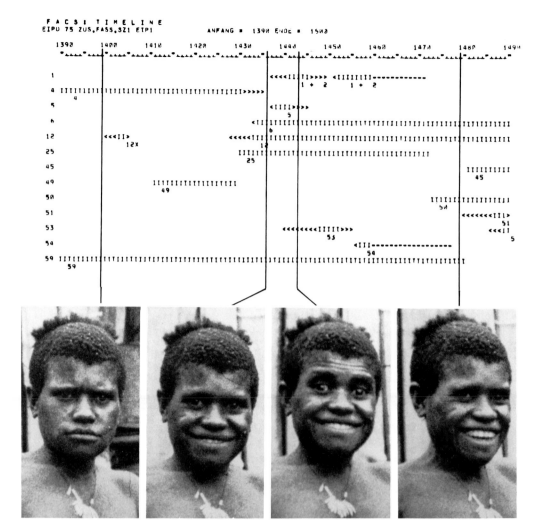

FIGURE 3.4. A greeting with the eyebrow-flash (rapid brow raising) together with smiling and head tossing) of an Eipo woman is illustrated using the facial action coding system (FACS) (P. Ekman and W. V. Friesen, 1978). The frame-by-frame analysis comprises either individual muscle contractions (action units: AU) or muscle groups (action descriptors: AD). In this example, 110 frames were analyzed for the movements of specific muscles. In Frame 1399 the eyebrows are lowered and drawn downward, a motion created by AU4 (brow depressors: depressor glabellae, depressor supercilii, and corrugator supercilii), attaining its apex of contraction shown as the symbol I. We also recorded gazing at the camera (AU59). Thirty-seven frames later (Frame 1436), the eye opening is reduced (AU6 cheek raiser: orbicularis oculi, pars orbitalis) and she smiles (AU12 lip corner puller: zygomaticus major). Furthermore she opens her mouth slightly (AU25 lips part: depressor labii or relaxation of mentalis or orbicularis oris). All motions are shown at their apex. Orientation toward the camera was also recorded (AU59). Seven frames later (1443) the eyebrows are raised (AU1 inner brow raiser: frontalis/pars medialis and AU2 outer brow raisers: frontalis/pars lateralis). The upper lids, formerly raised, are now lowered (AU5 upper lid raiser: levator palpebrae superioris, Offset: symbol >). AU6 and AU12 are still at their apex; she has her mouth open (AU25) and begins lifting the head (AU53 onset of head upward: symbol <). In the last frame (1479), AU1 and AU2 are declining and only the smile and the raised cheeks are sustained (AU 6 + 12). AU50 is also engaged as the woman begins speaking and her gaze is still directed at the camera (AU59). Note the onset of smiling preceding eyebrow raising (AU12) and the termination of AU4. From K. Grammer et al. (1988). Photo: I. Eibl-Eibesfeldt.

the center and they alternate between forward and backward jumps (Fig. 3.7). He recorded the jumps of all the dancers to elucidate the process of their synchronization. Since it is difficult to see in the movie when the foot actually hits the ground (because it sinks into the sand before actually completing a step) and thus seems not to correspond to the dance dynamics, reference frames were those in which the knees were bent at their maximum. This occurs at the dynamic height of the dance, and in most cases it is clearly visible (compare Fig. 3.8). These maximum knee bends were compared for all four dancers in a frame-by-frame study and documented in a sequential record. In Figures 3.9 and 3.10 the initial and terminal phases of the synchronization process are evident. The initially uncoordinated knee bend maximums are synchronized to within 1/25th second in the terminal phase of the dance. Knee bending was recorded in middle, front, or rear positions to account for their spatial relationships. Transposing the points to the spatial relationships will reveal the successive development of the shared space-time structure of the four dancers.

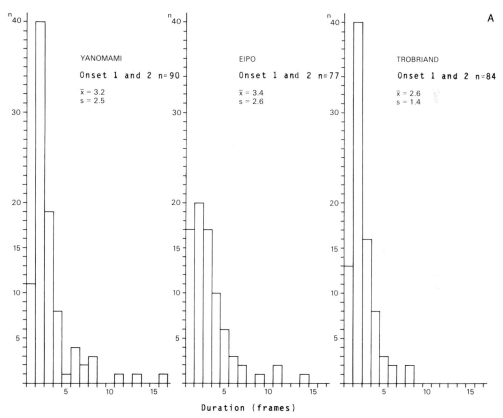

FIGURE 3.5. (A–C) Frequency distribution of the duration of onset, apex, and offset of the contraction of facial muscles, brow raiser (frontalis, pars medialis) and outer brow raiser (frontalis, pars lateralis). Graphs depict the frequencies with which movements of a specific duration occur in movie frames (one frame lasts 0.04 second). No significant differences exist in the mean values of onset and offset in the three cultures. Frequency distributions are nearly identical with the exception of the duration of apex. For the apex, analysis of duration shows a significant difference; in the Trobriand Islanders, the apex of contraction is significantly shorter than in the Yanomami and Eipo. From K. Grammer *et al.* (1988).

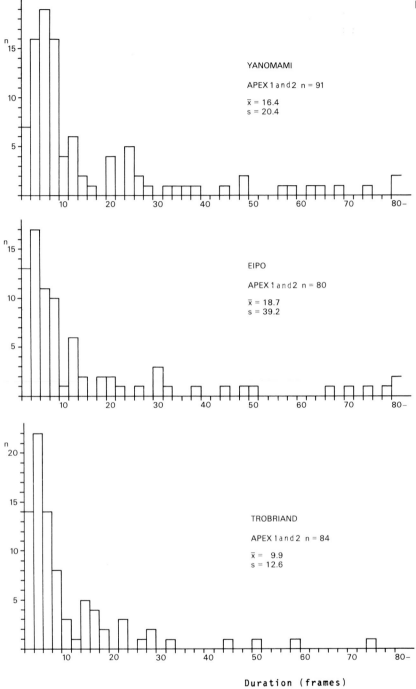

FIGURE 3.5B. See legend on p. 119.

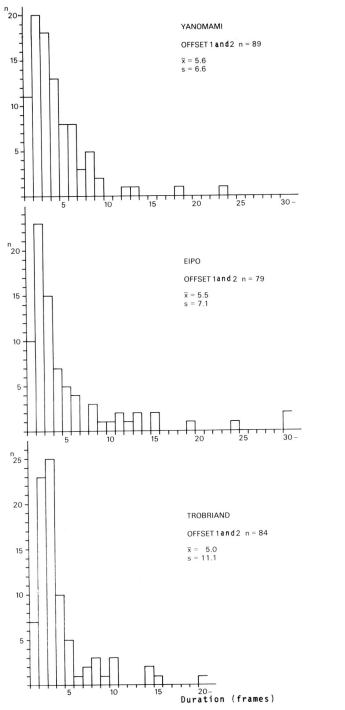

FIGURE 3.5C. See legend on p. 119.

FIGURE 3.6. The dancing area is defined by the spatial relationship of the dancers. Walther Siegfried used R. Deutsch's (1979) symbols to depict the formation and variations in spatial configuration in the Himba courtship dance. Men and women form opposite semi-circles out of which individual men and women jump in display dances into and out of each other's dancing space. Finally, the men dance so close to the young women that the latter jump away (once the last man has approached them) to form a new semicircle at a distance from the men. This spatial development ensues over a period of about 20 minutes. The series of drawings was copied directly from film. From W. Siegfried (1988). Photo: I. Eibl-Eibesfeldt.

3.7

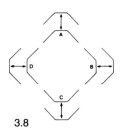

3.8

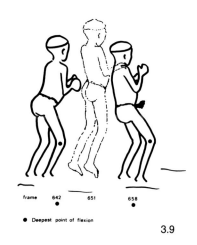

frame   642   651   658
           ●   ●

● Deepest point of flexion

3.9

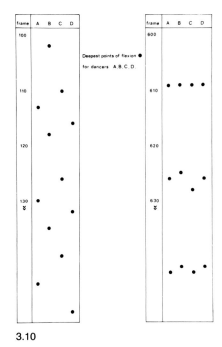

frame	A	B	C	D
100				

Deepest points of flexion ●
for dancers A,B,C,D.

frame	A	B	C	D
600				
610				

3.10

FIGURE 3.7–3.10. Set-up of the spatial/temporal structure in the girls' "apron flip dance" of the !Ko (central Kalahari).

FIGURE 3.7. Sketch of frame 128 of the scene. Dancers are not yet synchronized.

FIGURE 3.8. Spatial/temporal structure during synchronized dancing.

FIGURE 3.9. Knee bend maximum was the reference point for the film analysis.

FIGURE 3.10. Initial and terminal phases of the synchronizing process. Further commentary can be found in the text. After W. Siegfried (1988).

123

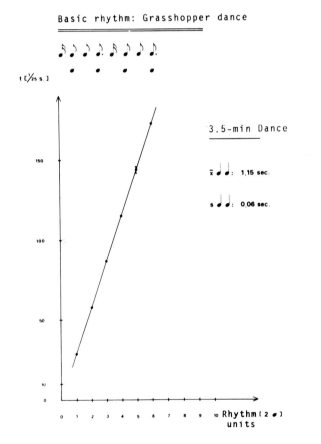

FIGURE 3.11. (a) Tempo stability in the !Ko Bushman grasshopper dance; (b) in a dance group of Munich University medical students (p. 125). The basic rhythm is maintained over a long period with minor deviations. Tempo changes generally took place in stages. The relationships between the various tempos must be studied more closely. According to W. Siegfried there are musical parallels to David Epstein's (1979, 1983) whole-number relationship. From W. Siegfried (1988).

124

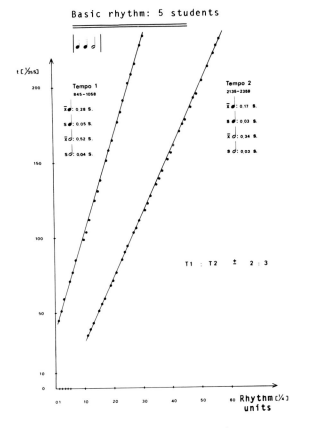

FIGURE 3.11. (b) See legend on opposite page.

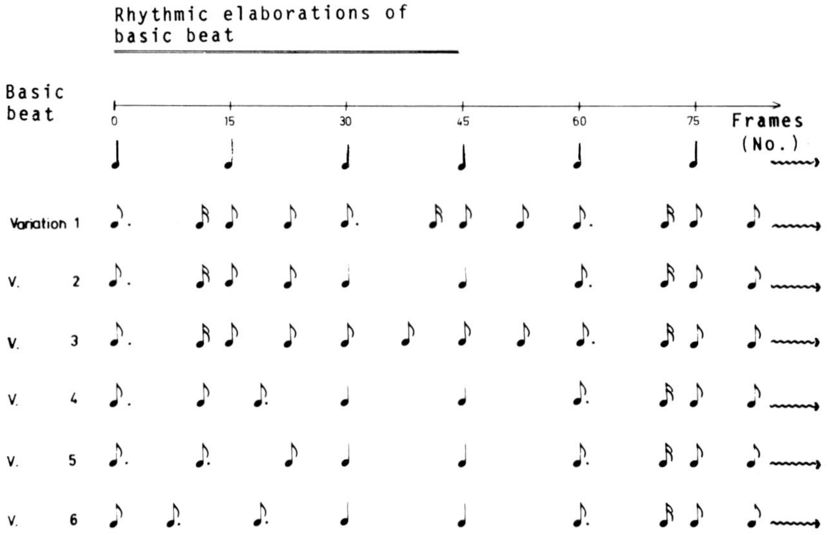

FIGURE 3.12. Temporal variations are based on the commonly stabilized basic rhythm. In the !Ko grasshopper dance depicted here, rich variations are superimposed upon the simple basic rhythm. From W. Siegfried (1988).

   The tempo stability and variations in temporal structure are shown by film analysis of the grasshopper dance of the !Ko Bushman. This is a mens' dance in which two dancers each dance in rhythm in front of the team, creating various figures and leaping away over each other (I. Eibl-Eibesfeldt, 1972). Once the rhythm is established it is maintained over a long time span with astonishing precision. A wealth of variations is superimposed on the basic rhythm (Fig. 3.12). Siegfried formed an experimental dance group comprised of students attending Munich University. They were also able to maintain the basic rhythm over an extended time. Tempo I was followed by an unstable transitional phase which was then followed by another stable one, Tempo II (Fig. 3.11b).
   When dances or other rituals are filmed in their entirety, such longer sequences can be studied for their variability and other characteristics. An example is the comparison of three segments of the Balinese legong dance (I. Eibl-Eibesfeldt and H. Kacher, 1982). It portrays the "Pengipuk" phase of the courtship of the Prince of Lasem for Princess Lankesari (Fig. 3.13).
   This segment begins with a formal greeting of both dance partners, standing opposite each other diagonally, heads swaying tenderly; it ends with a distinct parting ritual, in which the partners are much closer (and the only time they are immediately opposite each other) and swaying their heads. The ambivalence of the princess versus the prince is shown in dance by the princess' turning toward or away from him. With a stylized sorrowful posture she expresses her regret at her own rejecting behavior. She is compelled to reject the prince's advances because she is already promised to another man. Later she reacts to his vigorous courtship with threat expressions, striking him with her fan and elbows, and by avoidance. The tender head swaying executed by both dancers is ritualized nose rubbing, which in Bali is generally an expression of affection. The differentiation of dance, by artistically stylized hand and body movements, is a fine example of

126

man's striving to design behavior according to our own ideas and to master the body.

The graphs shown here (Figs. 3.14, 3.15) enable readers to follow the course of the dance and to note the regularities and temporal variations taking place. Since the temporal structure of the three dances differs and cannot be shown completely in Figure 3.14 at AT, all three dances were brought into conformity at point Z.

Using the accompanying key (Fig. 3.14) one can tell that all the dances can be divided into the phase sequences A through N. Each phase is characterized by a dance segment involving a place change by the female dancer (black fields) and in place dancing (white fields). These phases are also represented at the right margin by lower case letters (mobile dance segment) and upper case letters (stationary dance segment). The orientation of the dance partners, divided into male and female roles, is also keyed. Each phase is marked by the appearance of specific behavioral patterns (1–10 and T). Timing of the events is shown on the left side of the figure. The behavior patterns are indicated solely by their initial appearance with numerals and with the circular symbol, with which their subsequent appearance is noted.

The following behavioral elements were recorded (Fig. 3.13):

1. The first mutual eye contact of the partners with slight swaying (not indicated separately here). We also did not indicate on the right margin this position of the partners only shortly interrupting the flow of the dance segment.

2. "Sorrow" posture following ritualized tear wiping (stationary) S. Stationary dance of the princess with emphasized esthetic body, arm, and hand movements, which portray the feminine attractiveness of the princess.

3. Head swaying as an expression of affection (ritualized nose rubbing). The prince begins with 3 at a distance already in 1 and then again in B. Only suggestions of this movement are indicated by the princess. Prince and princess simultaneously display 3 at a distance during and after E. In H_1 and H_2 there is a mutual head to head 3, with nose rubbing invitation 5 then following head to head 3. At 9, the confrontation, the couple displays I in P_1 and, briefly, 3 in AT, a face to face distinct nose rubbing.

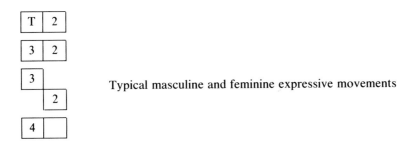

Typical masculine and feminine expressive movements

"Finger trilling" of the prince. The hands are in the initial position with outward turned palms crossing the chest. They are drawn laterally away from the chest as the out-stretched fingers open and close in a scissor-like manner.

FIGURE 3.13. Frames copied from a test dance sequence: (a) Greeting confrontation 1/1 in phase a; (b) display (T-posture) of the prince and regret (2) of the princess in phase A; (c) head swaying of (3) the prince and (2) princess (phase B); (d) S-posture (phase C); (e) W-posture and back-to-back orientation (phase D); (f) mutual rising (hh) in phase D; (g) mutual knee bending (tt) and S-posture (phase D); (h) finger trilling (4) of the prince (phase E); (i) 4 and w (phase E); (k) prince stamping (k) and princess twice indicating sorrowful expression (2); (l) head swaying of prince and princess (3/3) phase H 1; (m) nose rubbing proposition (5) and rejection (6) phase H; (n) pinching attack (7) phase K;

(*continued*)

FIGURE 3.13. *Continued*

(o) Pinching attack (7) and defense (8) phase K; (p) departure confrontation 9 (3/3) phase M; (q) departure: the prince dances behind the princess and attempts to grab her. This frame was copied from another film. All other frames from the sequences taken from HF63 dance (P₁ of Figure 3.14).

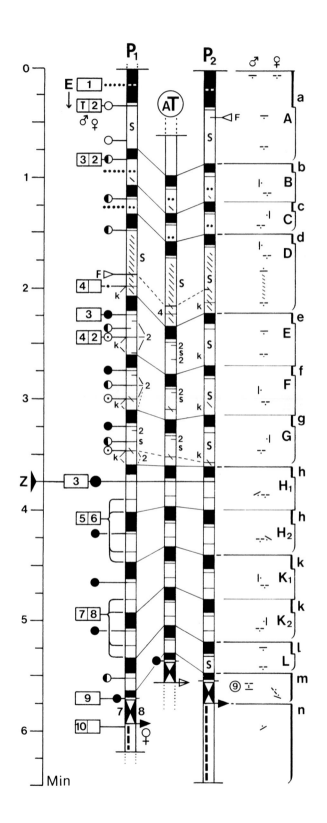

FIGURE 3.14. Key to the dance elements of a legong act (Pengipuk). The graph is based on three complete Pengipuk performances. Abbreviations are as follows: P_1 = First test dance of couple 1; AT = evening performance before the temple (couple 1); P_2 = test performance of couple 2; E = dance elements [1–10]; Z = temporal synchrony at H_{1-3}; a–n, A–L = dance elements. The lower case letters (black areas) designate segments with place changes (stepping dance phases, turns, alternate loops); upper case letters (white areas) are dance phases without place changes. Dance element list: The first clearcut appearance of a behavioral pattern is marked with a numeral and circle symbol. Later, only the circle symbol is shown for the sake of clarity.

[1]		Gazing at each other
[2]	S =	Princess's posture
[T]	T =	Prince's posture
[2]	S =	Princess's posture with closed fan = posture of regret (after wiping tears)
[3]	• =	Head swaying (princess and prince)
	◐ =	Prince sway alone
	○ =	Suggested head swaying
[F]		Fan closing
[4]		Prince's finger trilling
k		Foot stamping
[5]		Prince's nose rubbing
[6]		Turning away with rejecting arm movement of the princess
[7]		Prince's pinching attack
[8]		Rejecting blow with the fan (and evasive step) of the princess
[9]		Prince/princess confrontation: frontal opposition-with head swaying with associated pinching attempt [7] and simultaneous defensive blow [8]
[7+]		Flight and pursuit with various actions [7] and [8], until the prince seizes her about the hips with both hands and she flees over the stairs
[10]		"Angry" foot stamping, after the princess flees.

k[4] is often combined with foot stamping (ritualized stamping) before and after [4] is used for the first time in D after F (fan closing) is used. The prince finger trills toward the princess only in E. In F and G, both stand back to back. [5,6] Nose rubbing with rejecting arm gesture. The princess returns the nose rubbing but always with a rejecting arm gesture. [7,8] Pinching attack with defensive fan strike. [9] Final confrontation. This sole frontal encounter of the entire "Pengipuk" is initiated with a run forward by the prince the start of at segment m. It is presumably a formalized gesture of parting. It ends abruptly at [9], where couple 1 sway heads [3] but couple 2 does not. [7,8] in segment m: After several pinching attempts and corresponding defensive blows during several curved runs in wide arches to the temple stairs, the prince grabs the princess seven times at the hips to hold her back. She escapes nonetheless striking at him in defense and flees up the stairs into the temple. [10] The prince remains behind, watches the fleeing princess and displays the typical foot stamping (left and right series) (expressions of reproach?). (HvG) In segments K_1 and K_2 (both couples) [1,2], the princess once more turns arounds at the head of the stairs, and covers her face with her hands. Further discussion in text. From I. Eibl-Eibesfeldt and H. Kacher (1982).

131

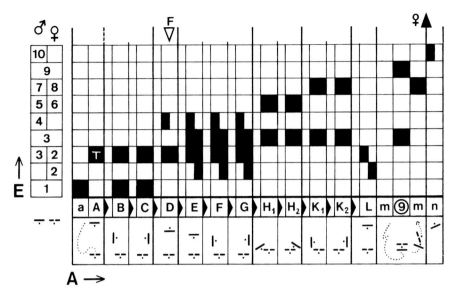

FIGURE 3.15. This graph depicts the three dances in another form. Here movement elements are shown in vertical column E. Phases and posture keys are on the horizontal axis, with mobile dance segments marked with a black triangle. Black squares indicate the appearance of specific behavioral patterns. a–n = dance segments; [1–10] = dance elements; A = total dance sequence and posture key; E = element markings. Further commentary in text. From I. Eibl-Eibesfeldt and H. Kacher (1982).

Summary 3.3

Behavioral descriptions from observations are not sufficient documentation. To accurately record what takes place in an interaction, it must be viewed over and over again. We require film footage and sound track evidence of the processes under study and, in general, this is what is lacking. Methodological problems resulting from shyness at a camera being pointed at the subject are solved using reflex lenses. We presented a program for the cross-cultural documentation of unstaged social interactions. Special care is taken regarding the collection of supplementary data to ensure that these film documents can be used for further studies on the part of future researchers. The original film material is never edited and duplicates are always made from the original film. Fast- and slow-motion filming is done to elucidate patterns that would escape normal observation. The fast-motion procedure is particularly useful for revealing higher order behavioral regularities. Examples of film analyses are given.

3.4. The Comparative Approach

Comparison plays an important role in the biological sciences. After all, it is comparative approach that gave rise to the theory of evolution. It was the comparison of recent species that gave Darwin the idea that all living organisms are related by descent. It was when he studied the Galapagos finches (Geospizidae, now named Darwin's finches) that he noted their graded similarity, which he could not accept as mere accident. On the bases of these similarities, he concluded that there existed a relationship between them derived from common descent.

Naturally, common heritage is only one root of similarity in nature. In addition a similar environment can act upon entirely unrelated organisms shaping them in a similar way. Thus all animals that must move through water are adapted to this environment in their body form. They are subject to the same selective forces and thus adapt in parallel directions quite independently of each other. Deep sea fishes, ichthyosaurs, penguins, and dolphins developed similar body form. In such a case we speak of analogous or convergent developments which gave rise to analogous structures, in contrast to homologous structures which derive their similarity from a shared heritage from a common ancestor.

In the century following Darwin, morphologists have confirmed the value of the comparative approach in countless studies and have developed the criteria for distinguishing between homologies and analogies (A. Remane, 1952; W. Wickler, 1967b; K. Lorenz, 1978).

The criterion of *special quality* refers to the formal similarity between comparable structures. This criterion alone is seldom sufficient to prove homology. But if the compared structures are complex and nonetheless similar in many details and if the species compared differ otherwise in their ecology and life habits, then homology becomes probable.

The second main *criterion of position* refers to the relative position of a characteristic within a larger structural system. Thus vertebrate cranial bones can be identified by their position relative to each other, even if their special form varies from species to species.

The third main criterion is linkage by *intermediate forms*. This enables us to discern a homology even when there are substantial differences between comparable structures as, for example, the third digit of the mammalian limb and the hoof of the horse. The fossil record shows that there exists every transitional form from the vertebrate toe to the final horse's hoof structure.

It is not even necessary to examine the fossil record to document transitional forms, for they can be found comparing present-day species. The vertebrate urogenital, circulatory, and central nervous systems are all examples of such transitional forms. There is no such thing as primitive organisms, of course, but there are primitive, that is, primordial characteristics.

An *auxiliary criterion* is that even simple structures are probably homologous if they appear in a large number of closely related species and that they are probably analogous if they appear in unrelated species.

Analogies occur when particular structures occur frequently among organisms sharing the same life habits (carrion feeding, predatory) or among inhabitants of common biotopes (desert, cliff, forest dwellers), independently of the organisms' systematic position. This is particularly evident when the ancestral forms of the compared species do not have these similarities or had different life habits.

The concepts of homology and analogy are always based upon some point of reference. One and the same organ can be considered homologous from one perspective and analogous from another. Thus if we regard the penguin wing and the whale forefin as fins, they are undoubtedly analogous adaptations. However if we assess them from the viewpoint of vertebrate extremities, they are naturally homologous. Analogies developing from homologous structures are known as *homoiologies*.

As well as being able to make comparisons between organisms one can also compare serially organized organs. If we compare the walking legs with the feeding parts of the crab, we find transitions permitting us to conclude that the feeding parts evolved from modified legs. This is known as serial homology or homonomy.

a

b

FIGURE 3.16. Behavioral analogies: food begging developed in mammals and birds independently into a submissive gesture derived from infantile behavior: (a) a low-ranking wolf approaching a high-ranking pack member in a friendly manner by pushing his snout against the high-ranking member's mouth corner, as if begging for food. After R. Schenkel from I. Eibl-Eibesfeldt (1970); (b) a female black-headed gull approaches a male during courtship like a juvenile begging for food. After N. Tinbergen from I. Eibl-Eibesfeldt (1970).

We can also record behavioral similarities among species, and in quite different realms of behavior. Similar behavioral sequences, social structures, norms, perceptual processes, drives, and others are examples. As with morphological structures, these similarities can arise in various ways.

When a flightless cormorant *(Nannopterum harrisi)* returns from fishing to replace its partner at the nest, it carries a twig, a bundle of seaweed, or some other object and passes it to the partner. The nesting partner takes the material, builds it into the nest, and then changes places with the other bird. If the returning cormorant did not have an "offering," it would be attacked and driven off. Apparently this simple ritual, which ethologists would define in human terms as a "greeting ritual," serves to buffer or inhibit the partner's aggression.

Comparable greeting rituals are not only found in other animals but in humans as well. It would not be difficult for the unbiased reader to find parallels even in the details of such rituals. For example, humans also present gifts in many greeting ceremonies. However, the similarity between the human and avian ceremonies is by no means based on a common phylogenetic origin but rather on parallel adaptations in related contexts. There are no related transitions in species-comparison; we know that the greeting ritual of the cormorant developed from nest-building behavior and thus has a different origin than offering in human behavior (p. 351). There are also clear distinctions in the fine details of the two behavioral sequences. However they share the appeasing bond-enhancing function

FIGURE 3.17. (a) The play-face or relaxed mouth-open face is seen in a playfully wrestling 6-year-old male chimpanzee. He utters no sound and his upper incisors remain covered; (b) a laughing 4-year-old male chimpanzee being tickled by an adult female. He utters soft gasping sounds not unlike human laughter. The upper incisors are often exposed during laughter. The quiet mouth-open face and laughter are related via transitional forms. Photos: F. de Waal, Arnhem Zoo (Netherlands).

of object transfer. In birds and mammals infantile behavior has been molded independently to appeasing gestures. This is different than the similarities observed in the expressive behavior of higher primates and man for whom similar movement patterns with similar function occur in similar contexts. Take, for example, the relaxed open-mouth face (Figs. 3.17–3.20), which is a "play-face" signaling a friendly biting intention. It is seen regularly in small children inviting another child to play or when wrestling together. The mouth is opened so the front of the teeth are displayed. A voiceless rhythmic "h-" "h-h" is often uttered. Pre-speaking infants often make this expression when they playfully strike an adult with a small stick or when they want to wrestle. The above behavior pattern is seen in children throughout various cultures and in similar contexts (Figs. 3.18–3.20).

The formal and contextual similarities suggest that this pattern is homologous and cross-cultural. There is nothing to indicate that the motion might have developed analogously and independently in this form, and nothing speaks in favor of a functional necessity for this particular form of the behavior. This expressive movement is based upon a phylogenetically developed social convention between

135

FIGURE 3.18. A Kosarek girl (Wahaldak, Irian Jaya/western New Guinea) playfully biting and nibbling an infant, occasionally stopping to watch the infant's reaction (with play-face). It is clear here that the play-face is derived from an intention movement of playful biting. From a 25 frames/second 16 mm film, frames 1, 27, 42, 71, 92, 95, 136, and 1021 of the sequence. Photo: I. Eibl-Eibesfeldt.

sender and recipient. The fact that the behavior occurs in various cultures in such a conservatively similar form strongly indicates a phyletic homology.

We can glean other indications of this from human/nonhuman primate comparisons. In old world monkeys a very similar "play-face" appears in the same context. It is called the relaxed open-mouth face, which, according to J. A. van

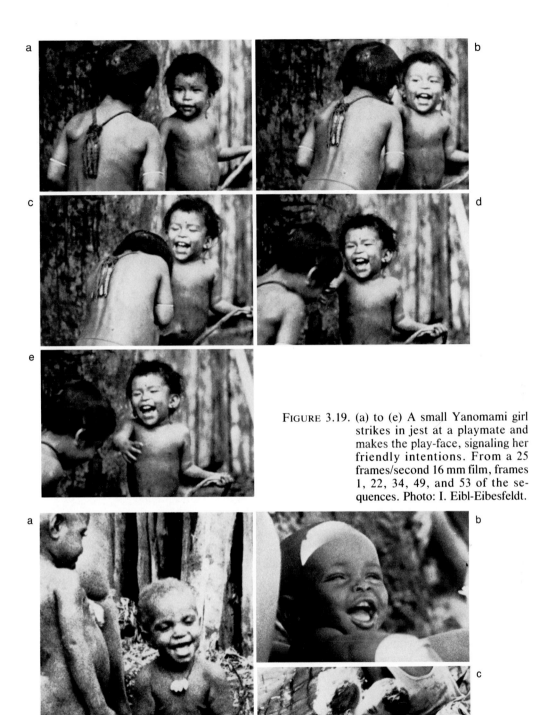

FIGURE 3.19. (a) to (e) A small Yanomami girl strikes in jest at a playmate and makes the play-face, signaling her friendly intentions. From a 25 frames/second 16 mm film, frames 1, 22, 34, 49, and 53 of the sequences. Photo: I. Eibl-Eibesfeldt.

FIGURE 3.20. (a)–(c) "Play-face" (a) Eipo boy (Irian Jaya/western New Guinea); (b) Himba infant; (c) Trobriand Islands boy turning toward a small girl in a friendly manner. From 16 mm films. Photo: I. Eibl-Eibesfeldt.

Hooff (1971), is derived from an intention movement of playful biting and is a phyletic precursor of laughing. In human children laughter often starts with a relaxed open-mouth face (Fig. 3.17).

The open-mouth face bears strong resemblance to smiling. I assume that both are derived from a common root, namely biting intention. The latter can be defensive and in old world monkeys is seen in the form of a silent bared-teeth display. Friendly, submissive smiling is often motivated by fear, unlike laughter which is an extroverted, friendly aggressive behavior (Figs. 3.18–3.20).

The play-face is so similar in chimpanzees and humans that each species recognizes its meaning when it is executed by the other (J. A. van Hooff, 1971; see *Ethology: The Biology of Behavior*). There are also occasional gasping sounds uttered during playful wrestling.

The loud utterance of laughter is derived from an old pattern behavior of mobbing, in which several group members threaten a common enemy. Thus it is a special case of aggressive behavior and this component retains its original significance. If we laugh aloud at someone, this is an aggressive act, bonding those who join in the laughter. Common laughter thus becomes a bonding signal between those who are common aggressors.

The kiss is another simple behavioral pattern whose origin can be elucidated through cross-cultural human/nonhuman primates comparisons. Such studies show us that mothers kiss their children affectionately in all cultures known to us. We also noted what we call "kiss feeding" in all cultures that we studied in which babies are fed supplementary food pre-chewed by the mother. This was also previously practiced in western cultures. But kiss feeding is also exercised as a friendly, calming gesture with no nutritional component. In this case the lips are placed on the child's lips, and the tongue is pushed briefly between the receptively opened lips of the child, without transmitting anything more than saliva. There exists all transitional stages between kiss feeding and kissing, which leads us to presume that kissing was indeed derived from kiss feeding (Figs. 3.21–3.25).

Each partner always behaves in a specific way: the initiator presses his lips against the partner's and, when the behavior is fully executed, pushes his tongue between the partner's lips, while the recipient opens his lips and (in complete execution) begins sucking. All transitional forms exist between the complete behavioral sequence and mere contact with the lips. The kiss also undergoes many culture-specific ritualizations. For example, the hand kiss is a sign of respect when a man greets a woman.

Primate comparisons reinforce the viewpoint that kissing is ritualized kiss feeding. Anthropoid apes (gorillas, orangutans, and chimpanzees) kiss feed their young, and chimpanzee friends embrace and kiss feed or greet each other in fleeting mouth-to-mouth contact (J. van Lawick-Goodall, 1975; R. Bilz, 1944; M. Rothmann and E. Teuber, 1915).

While the motherly kiss may be considered universal, little is known about kissing as an expression of heterosexual affection. It is often said that this form of kissing is absent in certain cultures. This could well be, yet that fact would not contradict our viewpoint that kissing is a universal (i.e., preprogrammed) behavior, for man is capable of suppressing innate behavior patterns.

At any rate, there are few observations of kissing in a sexual context, for man generally hides his intimate behavior from public view. It was often stated that the Japanese learned kissing from Europeans, and I believed that myself until I found an old Japanese quote in a work by F. J. Krauss (1965), in which lovers are warned about pressing the tongue between the lips of their partner during intercourse, since there had been cases of women biting off the tips of their lovers' tongues during orgasm. Thus kissing must have existed in ancient Japan.

My interpretation of kissing as ritualized kiss feeding was dismissed as intuitive speculation by G. Hausfater (1979). He said that he could just as well speculate intuitively that kissing was derived from ritualized grooming, since mammals often lick each other during social grooming. However, I would point out that the formal behavior sequence of kissing and licking is quite distinct, and the existence of all transitional forms between kiss feeding and kissing have been documented. It is true that behaviors derived from body care can be used as affectionate expressions, including licking, tender biting, and nibbling, but their behavior sequence looks quite different from kissing.

The same methods used to distinguish homologies and analogies in animal species can be used in cross-cultural research. Thus individual similarities can be interpreted as related or analogous ones (examples in Chapter 6).

Just as zoologists are often asked to what extent they can "transpose" animal findings to humans, so we are often asked to what extent findings from one culture may apply to others.

As we stated initially, although we only gain working hypotheses from studying one species, which must be tested for its reliability when applied to another species, we do not blindly apply to one culture what we have found in another. We can only detect graduated similarities and differences between cultures which are investigated in any of a number of ways (i.e., from ontogeny or experimental research). Cultures present in themselves an experiment, such as when socialization practices are guided by some specific ideal. In this context the notable investigations of M. E. Spiro (1979) on the development of sex roles in the kibbutz (p. 279) should be mentioned.

For a long time it was thought that behaviors defined as homologous (using the criteria mentioned earlier) were always phylogenetic adaptations (i.e., innate). In the animal world, homology as a rule also indicates that bearers of homologous traits are genetically related. There are however also homologies of tradition, which must be treated distinctly from those that are phyletic (W. Wickler, 1967b).

This distinction between phyletic and traditional homologies is particularly important for humans, but it also applies in some animals. For instance, many songbirds learn their song from their parents and pass it on to their offspring. Their song is homologous to that of the parents according to all standard criteria, for its basic information is handed over by him. This same process is found in human speech. Using homology criteria, linguists established long ago that there are relationships between languages, although they are not genetic in nature. Chinese learned by a European is homologous to native Chinese, but it is learned via tradition. One cannot use homology criteria alone to determine whether a given similarity is homologous by tradition or phylogeny; additional information is required regarding the ontogeny or genetics of the characteristics under consideration. Homology criteria only indicate that a common source of information has been tapped (W. Wickler, 1967b, p. 429).

As a rule, homologies of tradition are restricted in humans to individual groups, for which language is a telling example. One refers to Germanic or Indoeuropean languages and peoples.

But if homologous characteristics occur in all cultures and human races, then there is a high probability that they are phyletic in nature, since traditioned patterns

FIGURE 3.21A. !Ko Bushman woman calming her small half-sister with kiss feeding. The infant opens its mouth upon contact with her lips, and a morsel of melon is pushed into the mouth. From a 50 frames/second 16 mm film, frames 1, 13, 45, and 50 of the sequence. Photo: I. Eibl-Eibesfeldt.

FIGURE 3.21B. A Yanomami mother kiss feeding her 3½-month-old infant with pre-chewed banana. The infant opens its mouth receptively at the mother's approach. From a 50 frames/second 16 mm film, frames 1, 24, 67, and 97 of the sequence. Photo: I. Eibl-Eibesfeldt.

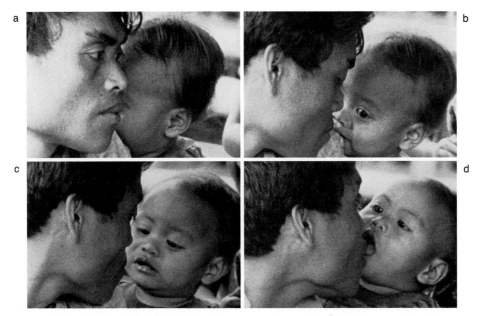

FIGURE 3.21C. Oral affection. A small Blit girl (Mindanao, Philippines) elicits her father's attention by biting him on the shoulder. He kisses her, and she opens her mouth just as in food intake. From a 25 frames/second 16 mm film, 1, 114, 132, and 200 of the sequence. Photo: I. Eibl-Eibesfeldt.

change within a few generations, as the rapid evolution of languages clearly document. Facial expressions are a good example of phyletic homology. Similar expressions occur in all cultures in similar situations and with similar consequences.

One occasionally encounters the objection that cross-cultural similarities might arise solely by chance, as the number of possible expressions are limited by the number of facial muscles activating those expressions.

In fact, the number of possible muscle combinations is much greater than the number of expressions actually observed. If we assume that a facial expression consists of four simultaneously occurring muscle movements and the number of possible combinations is 23, then the total number of combinations would already amount to 8855 different facial expressions.

Clearly, the regular appearance of such simple behavioral patterns as smiling or any other expressive gesture could hardly be attributed to adaptations developed independently in so many cultures. That *this behavior* and not just any movement of the corner of the mouth signals a friendly demeanor is a historical fact based upon phylogenetically evolved "convention."

We argue the topic of homologies similar to the way the archeologist assesses the relics of ancient civilizations. Similarities in the blade of stone axes alone would not suggest cultural relationships between the groups sharing that blade shape, for blade function is not highly variable and it is likely that different cultures would develop a similar blade shape independently. But a definite, nonfunctional form of pottery or a distinctive ceramic ornamentation would suggest the presence of cultural interaction. Verbal similarities also indicate relationships, such as the various words for mother (mater, Mutter, madre, mère) or father (pater, Vater,

141

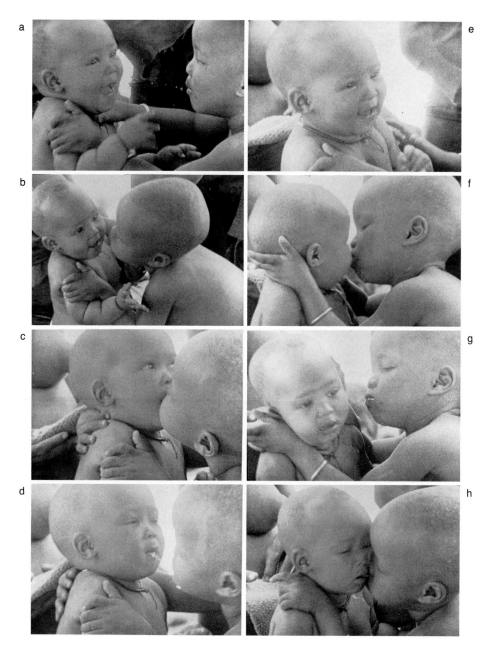

FIGURE 3.22. G/wi girl kiss feeding a baby girl with saliva and water. At first the infant accepts the offer and smiles (frames 817-859), but she rejects the second feeding attempt. From a 25 frames/second 16 mm film frames 1, 734, 817, 831, 859, 970, 979, and 1005 of the sequence. Photo: I. Eibl-Eibesfeldt.

père) and in the numerals for two (dva, zwei, dos); it is unlikely that these are chance similarities.

Human ethology uses the comparative method for various objectives at different comparative levels and with various systematic categories. The discipline compares not only behavioral patterns but also perceptual processes, motivational mechanisms, ethical norms, and more.

FIGURE 3.23. Yanomami girl tenderly kiss feeding her small sibling with saliva. From a 25 frames/
second 16 mm film, frames 1, 54, 124, 127, 129, and 219 of the sequence. Photo:
I. Eibl-Eibesfeldt.

Our comparative studies are not only used to discover homologies. I mention
this because one hears repeatedly that "relevant" data for humans can only be
gleaned from the closest related organisms, and whatever occurs in greylag geese
or cichlid fishes would add to our general edification but not to the understanding
of human behavior. The idea that comparative research be concerned only with
phyletic or cultural relationships can be fallacious. Therefore, I wish to emphasize
that the study of analogies provides insights into general conformities arising from
specific functions which are generally valid for the formulation of the basic laws
that govern them. Thus the flight organs of insects, birds, and mammals reflect
the general laws of aerodynamics to which these organs must conform; we could
even include the manmade artificial "flight organs" (airplane wings) in a comparative study of analogies, and the field of "biotechnology" demonstrates the
usefulness of this type of study.

143

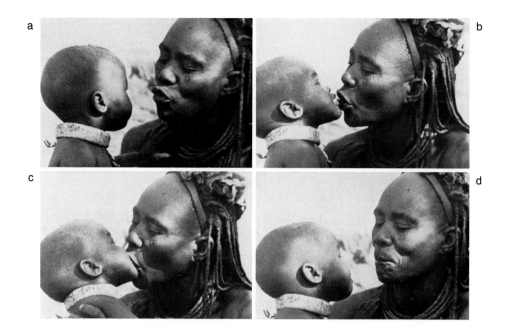

FIGURE 3.24. Kiss feeding in the Himba (Kaokoland, Southwest Africa). Grandmother and granddaughter kiss feeding. The child gives its grandmother a small tidbit, with the child's extended tongue clearly visible. From a 50 frames/second 16 mm film, frames 1, 72, 110, and 147 of the sequence. Photo: I. Eibl-Eibesfeldt.

We also inquire into rituals, social structures, and other features of behavior (W. Wickler, 1967b), using the comparative method. The comparative study of such phenomena particularly in animal groups, which are otherwise not closely related, provides insights into the functional laws underlying these behaviors. This is helpful in understanding, for example, the bond-strengthening rituals as well as social structures.

Melvin and Carol R. Ember (1979) made an excellent study of convergence. They examined the question of why marriage is an institution in all known cultures. However a cross-cultural approach alone would not provide the desired cues, since there are too many other universals that could provide an explanation. Thus the Embers' broadly based study encompassing many species—theirs was a random selection of various birds and mammals—provided the needed answers: heterosexual partnerships develop wherever the need of the mother to obtain her nutrition interferes with the care of the young. The duration of this bond is dependent upon the parental care time. Other examples of this type of study are found in W. Wickler and U. Seibt (1981) and G. E. King (1980).

Apart from the origin of a convergency, we can also gain insights into functional laws. Phylogenetic and culturally developed behavioral patterns may even be compared for this purpose.

If we compare the form and origin of friendly bonding mechanisms within a broader context, we find that affectionate behavior does occur between adults wherever brood care behavior exists. Here those bonding behaviors occur which

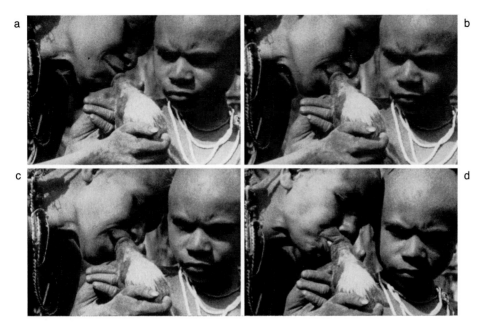

FIGURE 3.25A. Affectionate kiss feeding in animals also occurs. (a–d) An Eipo woman greets a small pig, carried by another person, by kiss feeding with her saliva. From a 16 mm film. Photo: I. Eibl-Eibesfeldt.

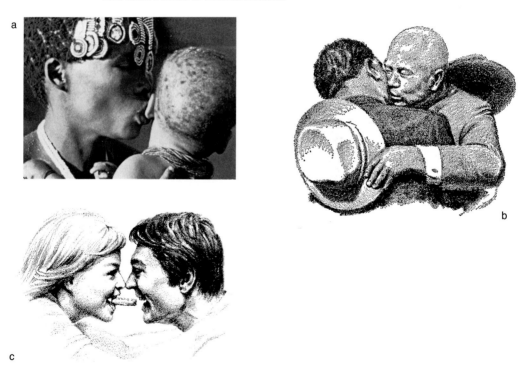

FIGURE 3.25B. The kiss, derived from kiss feeding: (a) !Kung Bushman woman kissing the earlobe of an infant. Photo: I. Eibl-Eibesfeldt; (b) Party chief Nikita Khrushchev greets his American host with a kiss on the cheek. From a UPI photo; (c) Feeding as a friendly courtship behavior. From an advertisement in the German magazine *Bunte Illustrierte* (1968, p. 20). Drawing by H. Kacher from I. Eibl-Eibesfeldt (1970).

developed primarily in the mother–young relationship. Thus behaviors derived from mother–young patterns are preferred in facilitating the bonding between the adults: childlike appeals and care for others. When a male sparrow courts a female, he shakes his wings like a begging juvenile, eliciting feeding. The partners change roles, and the females in turn "begs" and elicits feeding behavior from the male. This courtship feeding is seen in many bird species, often in such purely a symbolic manner as billing.

Courting European male hamsters utter the nestling's contact calls when they pursue a female. There are many more examples of this derived infantile behavior (I. Eibl-Eibesfeldt, 1970, 1987). In human courtship we similarly find infantile-derived behavior (p. 243).

The parallels above are pure analogies. Birds and mammals developed parental care independently. With it, mother–child signals became a preadaptation for a higher form of sociability. Our cooperative life as humans would never have been possible without this fundamental "invention."

The behaviors of bonding and personal care we are disposed to are derived from a repertoire of parental care behavioral patterns and the infantile appeals that release such behavior. Even our group ethos is an extension of family ethics. The extraordinary difference between sociability in birds and mammals versus other, parental caring species, becomes clear when one studies the social inter-actions of the latter. For instance, the Galapagos iguanas are gregarious animals; they lie about by the hundreds, beside and on top of each other on the rocks. But they truly live beside and not with each other, for they have no expression of friendliness toward each other. They do not feed each other, scratch one another, or mutually lick each other. All communication is restricted to display behavior. Males intimidate their rivals and even females with displays; they have no other way to court. Iguanas have no inclination to friendly behavioral patterns. Such behavior did not appear until parental care developed (I. Eibl-Eibesfeldt, 1970).

Our position that brood care behavior led to the development of higher forms of social communication is reinforced by the social insects, where feeding derived from parental care maintains group cohesion.

As the previous examples show, the study of analogies makes clear certain relationships and distinctions. Thus in comparing social insects and the higher vertebrate communities we find that individualized bonding is not the basis of community structure in insects but are significant for birds and mammals. This personal bonding (love, in the narrower sense) developed primarily as an adaptation serving mother–offspring bonding (see p. 167) and is the foundation of friendship and love.

Remarkable analogies are revealed by cultural comparison. Thus I found in the Himba of southwest Africa rituals of discipline maintenance whose special meaning only became clear in comparison with similar rituals in other cultures. The Himba are a Herero-speaking people living as cattle breeders in the most traditional man-ner. Each kraal community has a headmen, and the kraals are joined by a chieftain hierarchy into a tribe, which unites in times of emergency as a warring unit. This is of utmost importance for a pastoralist people widely scattered over an arid region. Cattle are a prized possession that must be defended. The Himba have often been attacked by Hottentots, and only their reprisals afforded them pro-tection. Occasionally they must also conquer new grazing lands, which also re-quires a concerted military effort. But it is not possible to simply call forth military readiness on command at the moment it is required. Military preparedness and obedience must be fostered in daily life, and the Himba practice it on an ongoing basis with their so-called milk ritual "Okumakera." The kraal members are not permitted to consume milk as soon as they have completed milking their cows. They must first appear before the headmen with their milk, for he is officially the owner of all the cows. They offer their milk vessels to the headmen, and he either takes a sip of it or symbolically sticks his finger in the milk, and only thereafter it is free for use. The morning milk ritual reinforces the dependency and thus subordination of kraal members to the headmen's leadership on a daily basis. Each day his rank is thus reaffirmed, and if someone were to rebel against this system (something I never observed), he would be subject to appropriate disciplinary measures. The hat of provincial governor Gessler mounted on a stick which William Tell refused to greet probably fulfilled the same purpose.

Comparable rituals of discipline maintenance are well known in our culture. The military morning and evening roll call with flag saluting and the assemblies in schools and other organizations throughout Europe, the Americas, and Japan are all examples.

The Himba also foster military preparedness and obedience training by cultivating heroic traditions. This is done unobtrusively at social gatherings using tales and praise songs about heroic models. The warring European nations maintained similar heroic sagas and battle songs. Such customs are absent in cultures lacking a warring tradition; in the Bushmen of the Kalahari I never heard heroic praise songs or observed rituals of obedience maintenance.

Linguists and ethnologists often speak of universals when referring to characteristics which occur in all groups of man independently of race and ethnicity. Mostly this is inferred from a broad sampling of the characteristic in question. More precisely it should read "supposed universals" since it is often difficult to really prove universality. Most supposed universals have a few exceptions when traits become culturally suppressed. Nonetheless we may assume universality if a trait appears in all members of a broad sample. Whether it be a shared cultural or biological heritage and whether reoccurring independent development in response to similar conditions gave rise to the universality of the pattern remains open. The comparative method as developed in morphology in most cases will allow conclusions to be drawn concerning origin, particularly if combined with studies on the ontogeny including the evaluation of "experiments of culture" (p. 279).

Summary 3.4

If we compare the behavior of various species, we often find similarities requiring an explanation. If similarities in comparable characteristics of two species arise from a common ancestral form, the resemblance is known as homology. But if the similarity is the result of an independently developed adaptation to similar environmental contingencies, we speak of analogies.

The criteria of homology used by morphologists (the criterion of special quality, special position within a system, and linkage by transitional forms) are applicable for behavioral studies. We speak of phyletic homologies when the homologous characteristics are genetically transmitted and of homologies of tradition if the feature is culturally transmitted. The latter are particularly prominent in humans, for which comparative linguistics provides many examples.

Homologies of tradition often characterize well-defined human groups, such as language groups. Since cultural evolution occurs at a fast pace, cultural diversity results. There are cultural universals which are explained by a shared function. In addition, there are also universals in human behavior, which can be considered phyletic homologies. The relaxed mouth-open face (play-face) is cited as one example. Contrary to general opinion, ethologists are not only interested in phyletic or cultural homologies. We utilize the study of analogies to learn which selective forces shape behavior patterns and customs along similar lines. The laws derived from such studies are independent of the systematics position of the organisms under study and are, therefore, of more general validity.

3.5. Quantifying Ethology

3.5.1. Sampling and Statistical Analysis of Observational Data

In the previous sections we have emphasized that ethologists attribute great importance to the observation of behavior in its natural context. They have developed methods of data sampling and its statistical analysis that permit drawing and testing hypotheses from pure observational data. We shall describe these quantifying techniques, making use primarily of the work of J. Altmann (1974), D. S. Tyler (1979), and P. W. Colgan (1978).

One major problem in data sampling is the observer's personal bias, which might lead to highly selective data gathering. In order to reduce this factor as much as possible, subjects for observation are selected out of a group using a table of random numbers, a process known as "random sampling" which can be "stratified" when the sample base is specified by age and sex classes.

"Event sampling" or "all occurrences sampling" is used when all events of a given category are recorded as they appear within a given observational period of a group.

"Time sampling" may be executed in three ways and depends in a complex way on frequency of the behavior under observation, bout length, and length of sampling intervals (see Tyler, 1979) (Fig. 3.26):

1. In "one-zero sampling" only the appearance (or lack of same) of a behavior of an individual or group is recorded within a predesignated time frame. This method is of limited value in sampling duration and frequency of a behavior.

2. "Instantaneous" or "scan sampling" records subject behavior frequency at predetermined regular time intervals. If the intervals are short and all individuals are observed in random order, this method approaches the simultaneous observation of all group members (example p. 151).

3. In "predominant activity sampling" that behavior executed most of the time in a designated interval is recorded.

"Sequence sampling" occurs when recording begins at the onset of an interaction between two individuals and continues until their interaction is terminated. The interest here is more in the interactions than the individuals themselves. "Focal person sampling" consists of recording all interactions or actions of an individual occurring within a specified (usually extended) time frame. These last two methods are the basis of film documentation. There are numerous descriptions of these methods and the statistical analysis of the data (summarized in P. W. Colgan, 1978).

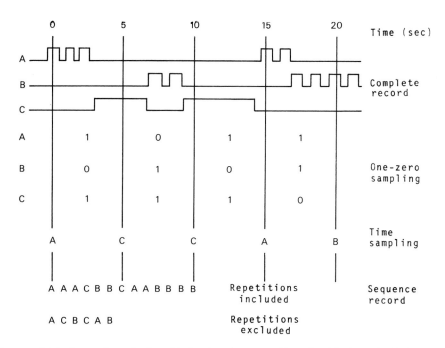

FIGURE 3.26. Several methods of behavior data sampling. In this hypothetical case the individual was observed for 20 seconds and executed three behavior patterns (A, B, C). The complete behavior record is shown at the top as would be indicated by a multiple pen recorder, in which each behavior produces a pen displacement on the recording paper. Below are the results of different sampling techniques. Instantaneous sampling has also been termed "time sampling." We use it as a group concept for the three techniques of one-zero, instantaneous, and predominant activity sampling. Predominant activity sampling (not shown here) differs from the other two multimoment methods in its temporal definition. The primary activity occurring more than half the recorded time is sampled (see text).

Various statistical methods can be used for analyzing the data. Correlation is used to determine relationships between two variables (when such exist). Positive correlations may indicate a common causal factor, while negative correlations indicate inhibiting influences, and the lack of correlation suggests the absence of causal relationships. However, all these are mere clues, and correlation coefficients alone cannot be used to verify a causal relationship.

The time units chosen for such analyses is critical. Two behavioral patterns correlating significantly within a time frame of half hours may not correlate when the interval is reduced 2 minutes!

The Markov analysis is used to determine the probability that a specific act is followed by another specific one. A transition frequency of 1 means that one behavior is invariably followed by another.

Multivariate statistical methods are those that permit the observation and analysis of several variables at once occurring within one subject. These methods will arrange and simplify huge amounts of data and often help discern the relationships between the individual variables. But except for MANOVA and discriminance analysis these methods are inappropriate for testing hypotheses; they are aids for describing data and formulating new hypotheses.

149

Multivariate analysis of variance (MANOVA) is used to test which of the variables under investigation exert a significant influence on the data and from this one can then estimate the relative influence of the individual variables. Friedman's two-way rank variance analysis is a well-known example. It is used to analyze the effects of two variables simultaneously.

Discriminance analysis investigates whether (and via which variables) two or more a priori postulated groups can be distinguished from each other. This is used where the postulated groups cannot be distinguished on the basis of a single variable.

Cluster analysis arranges data, organizing a group of objects (e.g., individuals or behavioral patterns) into subgroups (clusters). This suggests that members of subgroups are more closely related to each other than to those of other subgroups. Many variables or variable combinations can be used as reference points here, and the relationships thus gleaned can be arranged visually in a *dendrogram*. Animal systematics is an example of cluster analysis familiar to every biologist: animal relationships are determined using a large number of characteristics as reference points, from which the phylogenetic tree emerges as the dendrogram.

Multiple regression is the multivariate elaboration of simple regression analysis. It enables the determination of the value of one dependent variable against those of numerous independent variables. Correlations between the dependent and independent variables must exist. When there are two independent variables (e.g., velocity of an automobile and street incline angle), a regression factor can be calculated for the dependent variable (e.g., gasoline consumption).

Chief component and *factor analysis* are closely related. They are used to extract a few "factors" from a large number of variables, which are not directly measurable but that mutually influence several of the measured variables. Ethology also postulates the existence of such factors, as in P. R. Wiepkema's (1961) investigation of bitterling reproductive behavior. He recorded the transition probabilities of twelve typical behavioral patterns, which served as his measurable variables. Wiepkema found that several behavioral patterns were closely correlated and often followed each other, while others were mutually exclusive. From these correlations between the variables he extracted three essential factors acting "from the background" that he interpreted as behavioral tendencies and motivations: he termed them sexual, aggressive, and nonreproductive factors.

Multivariate statistical methods, particularly those involving many variables, require substantial calculating work which only in part can be accomplished with electronic processing.

Moreover, the formal statistical "construction" of several procedures is being debated. Cluster, factor, and chief component analysis can of themselves structure data even if they are applied to disorganized data produced by random generators. J. A. van Hooff (1982) cites several statistical manipulations which can deal with reliability problems.

According to P. Lehner (1979), valid results can only be ascertained when multivariate analysis is carefully planned and executed. Methodical, accurate collection of relevant data is essential to its success. Multivariate methods are no miraculous means of transforming data within the computer to evident results. They must supplement other analytical techniques. Thus Lehner advises his readers: "In short, use the best methods and equipment available to both generate and test hypotheses; however avoid methodological overkill" (1979, p. 294). Other pertinent literature is found in W. P. Aspey and J. E. Blankenship (1977, 1978), B. J. T.

Morgan *et al.* (1976), P. H. Sneath and R. Sokal (1973), D. W. Sparling and J. D. Williams (1978), H. L. Seal (1966), and J. P. van de Geer (1971).

The value of quantifying procedures is illustrated with the work of Karl Grammer (1979, 1982, 1985), who investigated the behaviors of helping and supporting (standing by during conflict) in terms of their dependence on friendship and rank position among children in two kindergartens. He refers to helping when person A helps person B to overcome some obstacle to a particular behavioral goal and to thereby achieve that objective. Support occurs in conflict situations and always involves at least three parties. In its simplest expression, an aggressive encounter occurs between B and C. A appears, takes sides, and through his intervention enables B to resolve the conflict to B's satisfaction.

Grammer had to first ascertain the relationship of help and support to the childrens' rank order and to their friendship relations in order to analyze them. M. R. A. Chance (1967) discovered the phenomenon of "attention structure" in investigating rank relationships in primates. Lower ranking members display clearly ambivalent behavior toward higher ranking members. They find superiors attractive and also fearsome for their aggressiveness. Therefore, they are always aware of a superior's location (M. R. A. Chance and R. R. Larsen, 1976). The alpha animal is the one observed most by the other animals. He enjoys "high standing" and is the focus of attention. B. Hold (1974, 1976, 1977) showed that this criterion can be used to determine rank order in childrens' groups. The child looked at most by other children also displays behavior characteristics of high ranking group members. High ranking children suggest and organize games, support others, settle disputes, represent the group to others, and can protect their preferential status through aggressive acts. Lower ranking children search for, follow, question, and show objects to the higher ranking member. Thus the attention criterion is a reliable rank indicator, and K. Grammer used it in his studies. The criterion was used when one child was watched simultaneously by three or more others (focus of attention).

The friendship criterion was preference for a playmate. All data were collected with "time sampling." This procedure can be used if events ("focus of attention") are short and states ("play with") are long as compared to the respective time intervals. Grammer used a time interval of 8 seconds for recording individual subjects in random order. Every 8 seconds he observed another child and recorded whether it was at the center of attention and who looked at it, whether it played alone or in a group, and if so with whom, and finally whether the child sat alone or stood while others looked on. He made 75 to 100 observations per child over a 4-week period. In a second study the results were replicated in an extended analysis which was made possible by the use of a video focal child sampling method.

The results from two kindergarten groups are summarized in Fig. 3.27. Each diagram shows the distribution of the rank criterion (focus of attention) on the left. Since individual children were not always present, the relative frequency of each was calculated. The child most frequently in the focus of attention was listed as Rank #1. Children were then ordered on the basis of their frequency of standing in the attention focus. Thus 1 designated the top ranking child. If several children were in the focus of attention equally often, their positions were calculated by the sum of their ranking positions divided by the number of those equally ranked children. The right side of the diagram displays relative frequencies with which children looked on and played alone. The graph clearly shows that the frequency   151

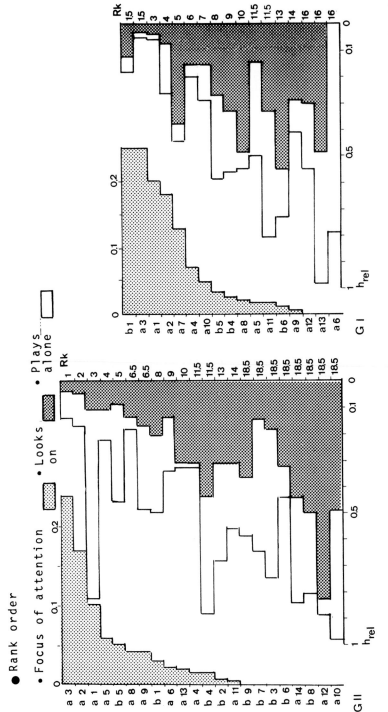

FIGURE 3.27. Rank order: the figures depict the relative frequencies for the rank criteria of "focus of attention," "looking on," and "playing alone." "Looking on" and "playing alone" are shown as sums in the histogram. On the right of each is the rank number (RK) of the children. From K. Grammer (1979).

of playing alone and looking on increases with lower rank position. Using boy A1 of Fig. 3.28A, it is furthermore evident that "Loners" who participate less in group activities, would nonetheless comply with the rank criterion if they are high ranking individuals.

Grammer counted the frequency of play contacts during group play to determine friendship relationships, a measurement recommended by W. W. Hartup (1975). Since group composition changed on various days, the absolute frequency of play contacts had to be compared with the time any two children spent together in a group:

$$\text{Play relation a:b} = \frac{\text{Number of observed play contacts between a and b}}{\text{Time spent in group together (in ``time spacing'' intervals)}}$$

With this formula Grammer describes the relationship between actually observed play contacts between a and b and the number of possible times the two could have been observed playing together. In order to obtain a comparison of play partnerships within a group, the percentage of one play partnership was calculated from the sum of a child's total play partnerships after F. B. Moreno (1942):

$$\text{Play partner index } (PI_{a,b}) = \frac{\text{Play relationship a,b}}{\text{Sum of play relationships}} \times 100$$

Thus the play partner index describes the percentage of a play partnership relative to the total time a child plays with others in a group. Figure 3.28 shows the play structure matrixes that Grammer developed. Playmates are shown beside each other. One can see that each child has a preferred circle of children as playmates, out of which there are one or two "clearly preferred." "Preferences" need not be reciprocal.

An analysis of the relation between rank and friendship showed that rank differences between friends approached zero, and rank neighboring children were usually friends. Grammer observed helping and support over an interval of approximately 80 hours, always between 9:00 and 10:00 A.M. He recorded helping behavior 47 times in Group I and 20 times in Group II. Thus this behavior does not occur that frequently, and can only be ascertained with the technique of event sampling.

Using total frequency distribution of the play partner index, Grammer determined an expected frequency for help interactions in *PI* classes from 0 to 30 (Fig. 3.29, top). In the middle of this graph is the observed frequency distribution of the various *PI* classes and, below, the resulting difference, which shows clearly that Group I *PI* classes are helped more frequently within friendship circles than outside; Group II shows only a tendency in this direction.

In Group I there is no relation between support and play partnership, while in Group II there is significantly more support offered against non-friends than against friends. Girls are supported by boys and girls against attacks by higher ranking boys, while no-one interfered in conflicts occurring between girls.

By calculating the differences in rank between the interacting children, we find a general tendency that higher ranking children support lower ranking ones and usually against children ranking lower than the supporting child (Fig. 3.30). This finding was extended in a second study (Grammer, 1982). Episodes producing the

153

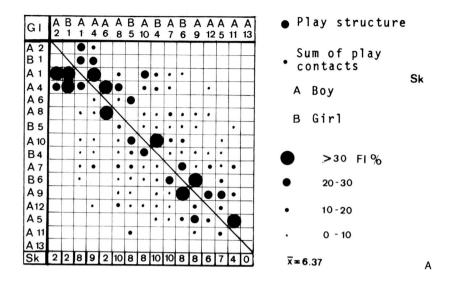

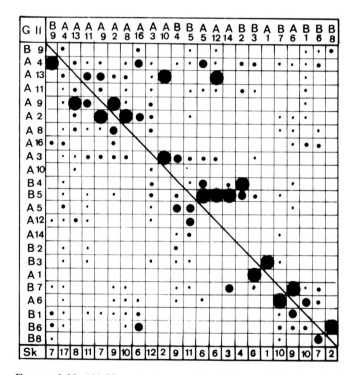

FIGURE 3.28. (A) Play structure matrix. The graph depicts the frequencies of play partner indexes within both groups as a measure of friendship. Mean values produce the magnitude of PI. From the left to right: Identification number of those children whose relationship is observed; from top to bottom to those of their partners. Each matrix shows (bottom, left to right) the sum of play contacts of each individual child (*Sk*) and their mean value (*x*). Horizontal readings show popularity; the vertical axis displays children's frequent play partners. From K. Grammer (1979). (B) Another example of play structure matrix (see A above for explanation).

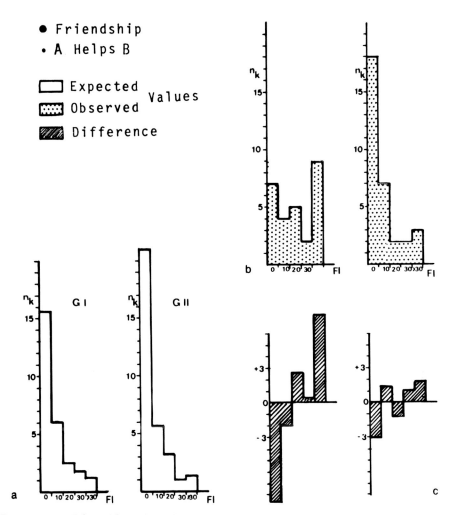

FIGURE 3.29. Friendship and helping (Group I on the left and Group II on the right of each
pair of graphs): (a) expected frequencies of helping in the five classes, calculated from total frequency distribution. If helping varies randomly in play
partner relationships, they display a decrease toward the greater PI. (b) Observed frequency distribution of help within PI classes. Class frequency of
help (n_k) increases as PI increases. (c) Value differences (observed minus
expected) make this particularly clear; they are negative at low PI values and
become positive at higher values, i.e., less help than expected was observed
at low PI values and more than expected at high PI values (Group I: $n = 27$;
Group II: $n = 32$). From K. Grammer (1979).

typical V-structure (in Fig. 3.30) are effective events of aiding and defending.
Whereas the opposite episodes with a Λ-structure in rank are episodes of "gang-
ing," i.e., supporting a winner. Grammer's finds suggest that helping and support
are behavioral strategies serving various functions. Help facilitates the establishment and solidification of friendships, while support during conflicts reinforces
and improves one's own rank order. Those who support someone who is weak
in a conflict gain "respect."

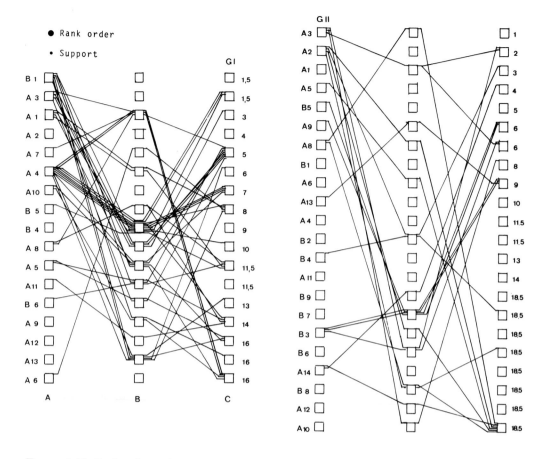

FIGURE 3.30. Rank order and supporting. Children are shown from top to bottom in rank position. Each box from left to right shows the various roles a child can play within the event "supporting": A = supporter, B = supported child, C = child against whom support is oriented. The connecting line between 3 boxes each portrays a "supporting" event. On the right is the rank designation for each child. From K. Grammer (1979).

3.5.2. Questionnaire Analysis

Ethologists also use questionnaires. One example of this is the methodical procedure illustrated here that was used by H. Morishita and W. Siegfried (1983), who investigated the extent to which culturally stylized expressions (in the form of theatrical mime) could be comprehended cross-culturally. They used film material Hans Hass and I collected in Japan, when we photographed scenes from traditional Kabuki performances. Morishita selected sixteen individual frames in which she, as a Japanese, clearly recognized the meaning of the actors' expressions. The frames were shown to 44 Japanese and 36 western European test subjects who were asked to enter their interpretation of the expressions in a questionnaire (Fig. 3.31).

The six listed categories (surprise, fear, anger, disgust, sadness, happiness) were those suggested by P. Ekman (1973). Another category, "other," was offered since certain expressive dimensions appeared to be lacking in the pictures shown to the test subjects. For each emotion the test subject could indicate an intensity

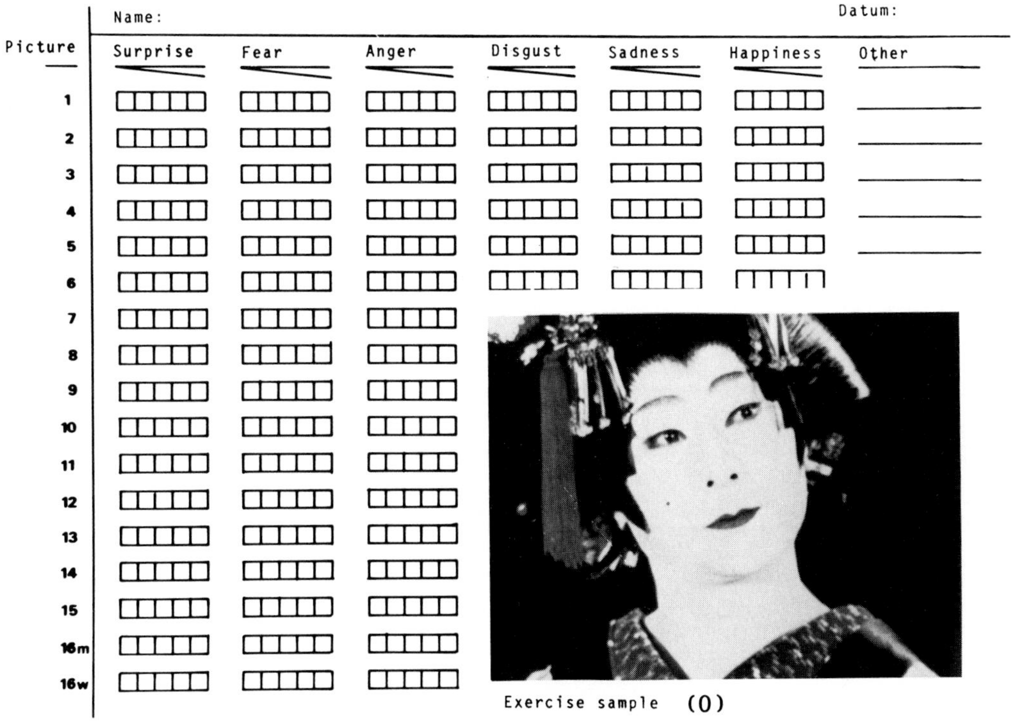

FIGURE 3.31. Questionnaire for the test series with the exercise example (o) (see text for explanation).

level (the five boxes), and five points could be given each frame so that mixtures of emotions could be indicated. For example, one could award three points of happiness and two of surprise. Use of the questionnaire was demonstrated with an exercise frame (o). Each frame was shown to subjects for 10 seconds.

Responses were depicted in a graph, with emotion descriptions on the horizontal axis and intensity on the vertical axis (see Fig. 3.32). If test choices are grouped in a column, subjects demonstrated a high continuity in emotion description, while scattered points indicate varying judgments. Points in the lower part of the graph suggest that the expression was generally perceived as being of low intensity, while a grouping in the upper part of the graph indicates a high emotional level as interpreted by the test subjects. The results of the questionnaires generally confirmed for Europeans and Japanese, with a few exceptions. We shall describe similarities and discrepancies of interpretation with a few examples.

Figures 3.32–3.37 show a number of the test pictures with the answers of the Japanese subjects (top) and Europeans (bottom). Most frames were interpreted alike by Japanese and Europeans: happiness (Fig. 3.32), surprise (Fig. 3.33), and sadness (Fig. 3.34). In three instances the basic emotion described by Europeans conformed to the Japanese opinion, but the Europeans added a supplementary emotion: sadness, but with disgust (Fig. 3.35) and anger, but with fear (Fig. 3.36). Generally the Japanese made clearer distinctions than the Europeans. Marked differences between Japanese and European interpretations occurred in expressions of happiness (especially the man's in Fig. 3.37).

157

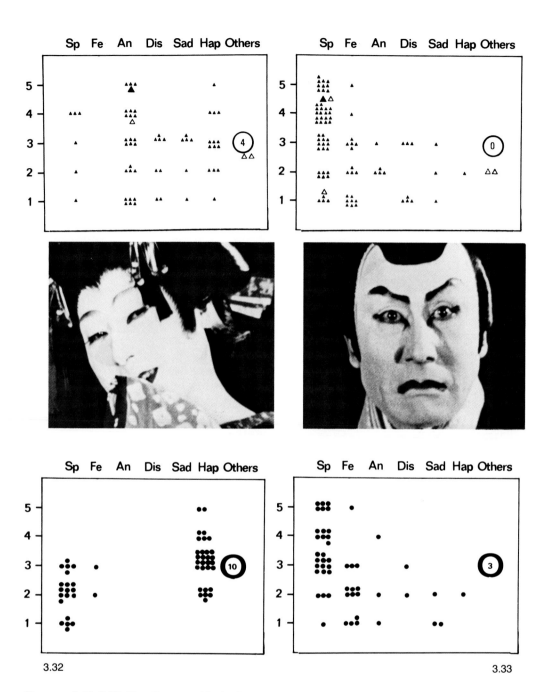

3.32

3.33

FIGURES 3.32–3.37. Test frames with the Japanese (above) and European (below) results shown in comparison. Japanese are divided as follows: 44 test subjects, actors of the male role, Kabuki experts. Key to abbreviations: Sp, surprise; Fe, fear; An, anger; Dis, disgust; Sad, sadness; Hap, happiness (see text). From H. Morishita and W. Siegfried (1983).

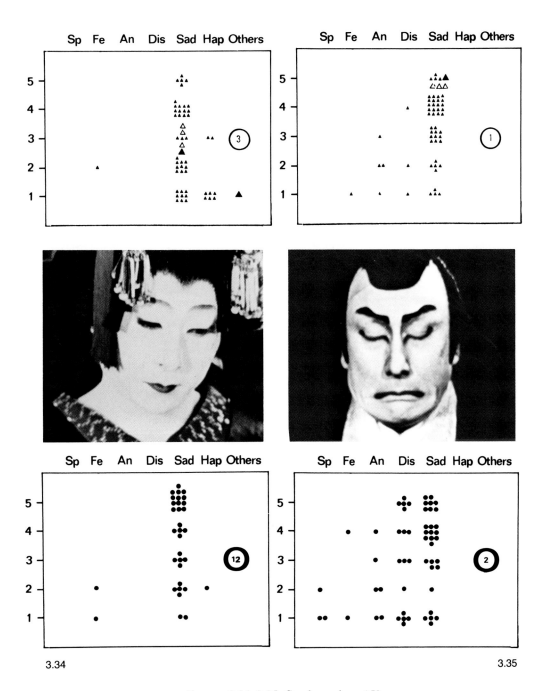

3.34

3.35

FIGURE 3.34–3.35. See legend, p. 158.

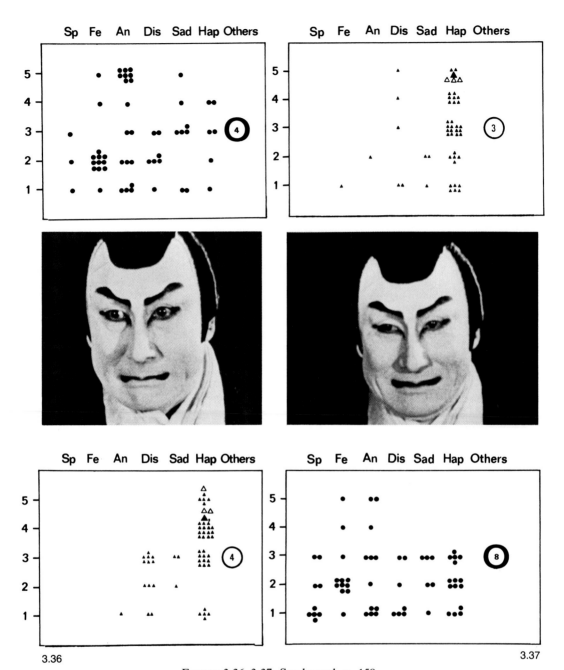

FIGURE 3.36–3.37. See legend, p. 158.

The graphic analysis shows a tendency to interpret the expressions in a similar way among both Europeans and Japanese, the latter being acquainted with Kabuki. Only with happiness was there a substantial divergence, which could be due to the makeup and certainly to the acting in the Kabuki style, which uses antagonistic muscles to restrain the intensity of individual expressions, this restraint being an essential element of Kabuki theater. Kabuki is only *one* of many classical Japanese theatrical styles, each of which has its own intensity of gestures. Thus emotions are much more unrestrained in the "Aragoto" style. This means that the results obtained above should not be considered valid for "Japanese theater" as a whole, but specifically for Kabuki. The fascination in the study of theatrical mime arises from the fact that, unlike spontaneous mime, elements of cultural molding stand out clearly and thus permit the audience to experience the simultaneous manifestation of nature and culture. How is happiness conveyed in various cultures and theatrical styles? How are the various emotions handled? In what directions are the universal expressions stylized and transformed, and to what degree are such stylizations and transformations understood by people of different cultures?

For happiness as expressed by the Kabuki acting out the female role, Europeans added as supplementary emotion, surprise, while the Japanese added disgust. In expressing happiness the actor moves the sleeve toward the face in a movement which we use when coyness is expressed, but such a gesture also occurs in surprise and disgust.

Summary 3.5

Specific techniques of sampling and statistical analysis permit the formulation of hypotheses from observational data. Time sampling, correlation, and multivariate analysis (mainly elaborated in psychological research) are particularly important methodological tools for the human ethologist. Such quantitative techniques are necessary to interpret such (illustrated) findings as rank orders in kindergarten groups, play partnerships, and the effect of such social relationships on behavior as helping or support during conflict. The methodical procedure is illustrated with a kindergarten study and a statistical analysis of a questionnaire.

3.6. Models

Models are the concrete manifestations of hypotheses. They help us understand relations within a functional system and to make predictions, which can be tested experimentally. If the predictions test positively, the model can then be used to describe the substance of the hypothesis.

Models are used extensively in ethology, exemplified by those found in G. P. Baerends and R. H. Drent (1970) and E. von Holst and H. Mittelstaedt (1950). Konrad Lorenz's "psychohydraulic model" is also well known (Fig. 3.38). It is a way of clearly portraying the dependency of the intensity of a behavioral sequence on its endogenous motivating factors and the releasing stimuli. B. Hassenstein (1966, p. 644) describes the model as follows:

> ... it has been much discussed (and—by dilettantes in the assessment of pioneer theoretical scientific achievements—ridiculed as "psychohydraulics"). Many instinctive behaviors and, analogously, this conceptual model, have the following characteristics: two factors influence the intensity of innate behavior and thus the central nervous structures responsible for behavior: the stimulus intensity and an "action-specific potential" (a preparedness to act caused by an endogenous factor); Seitz, the discoverer of this relationship, referred to a "double quantification" of innate behavior via *external*

and *internal* contingencies (18). Less of one can be balanced against more of the other to maintain the same level of external behavior instructions. If action-specific energy is absent, even the optimal stimuli will evoke no response. Often, but not always, the opposite is true: even the greatest level of action specific energy cannot evoke a response in the absence of a stimulus. The *execution* of innate behavior patterns *reduces* action-specific energy, or the appetence to execute the behavior again. But this appetence grows again slowly, independently of external stimuli and thus spontaneously or endogenously. The lack of release of instinctive behavior leads to the damming up of action specific potential and, under certain conditions, to the behavior's execution "in vacuum." Different innate sequences dependent upon the same stimuli and action-specific energy usually require different amplitudes of the releasing causal complex to be activated.

These functional relationships can also be portrayed in a diagram depicting functional relations (Fig. 3.39). The connecting lines represent signal transmitting pathways. The main graphic symbols are listed in Fig. 3.40. Inconsistencies can be more clearly perceived from functional diagrams than from verbal discussions. Furthermore, they are free of all those additional thoughts and suggestions which accompany language. B. Hassenstein exemplifies this by the use of the terms drive, motivation, readiness to act, and mood. If one focuses only upon the function covered by all these different terms and draws a functional diagram, one then becomes aware that their significance can be equated at the functional level.

Hassenstein suggests using the neutral expression "internal status." It is evident from Lorenz's drive model that this device is useful not only for theoretical conceptualization but also for the development of working hypotheses for sensory nerve effector systems and their network of information pathways and data processing mechanisms (Figs. 3.41, 3.42).

N. Bischof (1975) formulated a systems analysis of human social behavior. He investigated the relation between contact seeking and fear in human interactions. As is well-known, the small child seeks its mother's company and avoids strangers, clearly motivated by fear. But later when it comes to making sexual choices the

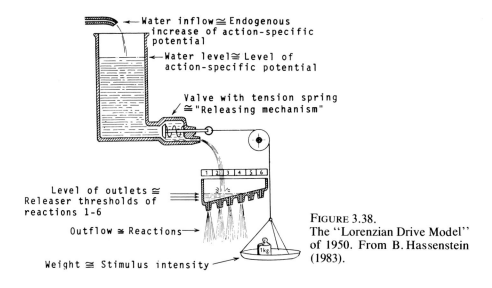

FIGURE 3.38.
The "Lorenzian Drive Model" of 1950. From B. Hassenstein (1983).

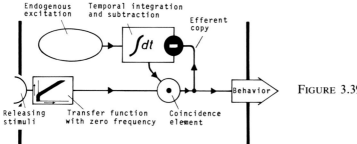

FIGURE 3.39. Functional diagram of a part of the functional relationships modeled in Fig. 3.38. From B. Hassenstein (1983).

opposite sex is selected and blood relatives, with whom one has close family ties, are avoided.

Several variables determine whether and to what extent a child will remove itself from its mother, how close it moves toward strangers, whether it explores, and more. N. Bischof uses a model (Fig. 3.43) to depict the observed causal factor network underlying these processes. His functional circuit array uses two systems, each with its own regulatory mechanisms:

1. An "excitatory" system maturing at 8 months of age; its theoretical value is designated as "enterprise." Normally an excitation deficit elicits exploratory behavior, while a surplus stimulates escape.

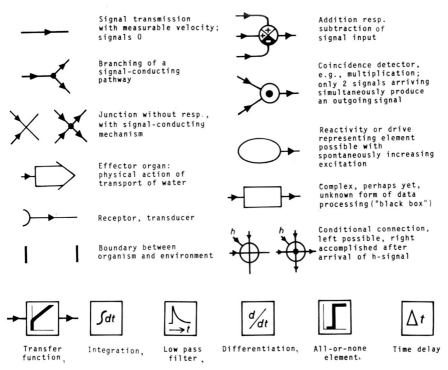

FIGURE 3.40. Graphic symbols for diagrams depicting functional relations. In the case of a signal-conducting pathway both branches conduct the same as (not half of) the arriving message. From Hassenstein (1983).

163

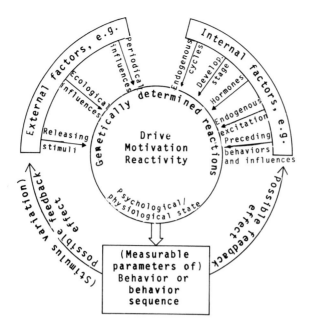

FIGURE 3.41.
Illustrative diagram of the concepts of "drive," "motivation," and "action potential" shows that they are functionally comparable. From C. Becker-Carus and H. Schöne (1972).

2. A "security" system that is mature at birth or at the latest 3 months thereafter. Its theoretical value is termed "dependency." It is high in small children and attains its minimum value at puberty. A dependency deficit arouses increased bonding behavior, while a surplus results in contact avoidance with family members. This behavioral pattern is known as satiety behavior.

N. Bischof's functional array is to my knowledge the first and so far only theoretical systems analysis of human social behavior.

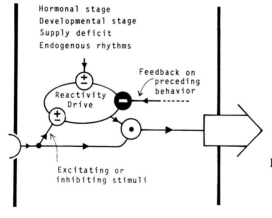

FIGURE 3.42. Functional diagram for the relationships modeled in Fig. 3.41. From B. Hassenstein (1983).

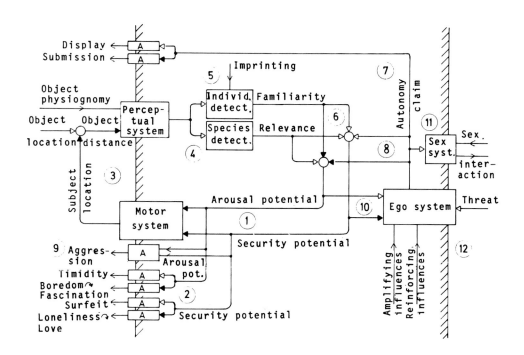

FIGURE 3.43. Hypothetical block diagram of social motivation in higher mammals, including humans. The concepts cited are largely anthropomorphic and must be substituted with more neutral terminology for animal application.

Explanation of symbols: Arrow = variable (not pathways); blocks = systems, subsystems, and pathways. Arrow orientation designates the direction of the causal relationship. Arrows terminating at squares = input; arrows leaving squares = output of the respective subsystem. Arrows originating or terminating in open spaces = variables whose causes or effects are not specified in the model. Branching indicates the influence of a variable on the output value of several subsystems indicated by extra blocks. White triangular arrows = positive correlation with the following dependent variable; black triangular arrows = negative correlation with the following variables. Simple arrowheads = no hypothesis made about input relationships. White circles = operation of addition or multiplication (or, for black arrows, of subtraction or division). Hatched lines = organism boundary. Variables beyond the boundaries are observable, while those within are hypothetical. The latter may presumably be interpretable at some later stage of neurophysiological or endocrinological understanding. A = motor systems controlling expressive behavior (in the broad sense). For paired A-blocks, the upper (or lower, respectively) is activated when the input value exceeds the reference value.

Summary 3.6

Models facilitate the visualization of relationships. The functional diagrams are used to elucidate operational relationships and to make predictions, which can be experimentally tested. They are particularly useful for representing complex systems relationships.

4

Social Behavior

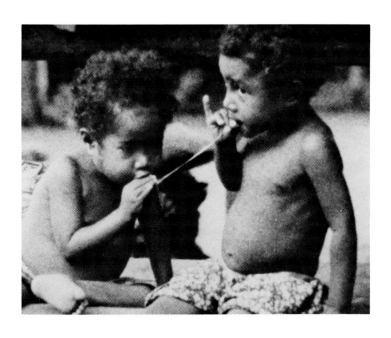

4.1. Origins of Sociability

Animals congregate for different purposes. Fishes of the open sea form schools, for instance, and these congregations are primarily for the sake of protection. An individual in open water is an easily fixated target and has scarcely any chance for escape once seen by the predator, but as part of an entire school the individual can be lost in the masses. Each member of the school is safer than if it were alone, for predator fish must fixate prior to snapping at prey, and the large number of targets confounds the predator's fixating mechanism (I. Eibl-Eibesfeldt, 1962). In such cases signals develop for the sake of maintaining group integrity and also for communicating the presence of danger. Thus many schooling fish emit an alarm substance when they are injured, warning the others (K. von Frisch, 1941). Schools are generally anonymous and individual members do not recognize each other; they are aggregations brought together for predator avoidance.

Another form of social grouping in animals serves pairing with a member of the opposite sex. Physical contact is not necessarily required for fertilization, however. The sperm and eggs must simply be brought into the same vicinity, so generally one partner seeks out another for the sake of fertilization. Close partnership bonds arise only in those instances when partners meet (either rarely or with considerable difficulties), such as in some deep-sea fishes, wherein the males actually adhere to the female when she has been found. Bonding can also occur by behavioral fixation to the sexual partner. The *bonding* characteristic is appetence for *partner proximity*. Proximity could also come about through attachment to a specific location; in this case we would not speak of partner bonding. Bonding is furthermore characterized by *compatibility,* restricted to the partner who is also the selective goal of bonding behavior patterns. Often the partner's presence is a prerequisite for certain behaviors to occur. Duet singing in birds (W. Wickler and D. Uhrig, 1969) provides an example. In this case an appetite for singing, which can only be satiated in the partners presence, is one factor strengthening a bond. Konrad Lorenz (1963), in fact, thought this to be the determining factor in bonding, thus a consummatory act serving to bond. As example he cited the triumph ceremony of greylag geese. Again, without a partner the behavior cannot be performed. But this is certainly not the whole story, since from the work of Monika Meyer-Holzapfel (1940) we know that animals and man demonstrate appetite toward consummatory situations (see also p. 67). An animal may seek a home as a place of rest. In a similar way the proximity of partner can be sought just for proximities sake, the partner being so to speak an individual with home characteristics.

A highly significant event for the development of vertebrate sociability was the evolution of maternal care by which friendliness came into existence. For only with the appearance of parent–offspring signals, infantile appeals, and the corresponding affectionate responses behavior became available that permitted adults to create friendly and affectionate relationships. The "invention" of parental care constitutes a turning point in the behavioral evolution of the higher vertebrates and insects. Parental care occurred independently in insects, birds, and mammals, providing the impetus for analogous rituals of bonding (I. Eibl-Eibesfeldt, 1970, 1987).

The evolution of individual bonding marks a second "propitious event" in vertebrate evolution, and it likewise begins with parental care. Individual bonding is the springboard for *love*. Mother–child relationships developed independently and repeatedly in birds and mammals, wherein parents and young actively seek each other's presence. They are personally acquainted and will defend their bond against all intervention. When individual bonding occurs between mother and young, mothers will reject strange young who seek their proximity (I. Eibl-Eibesfeldt, 1958, 1970). Individualized bonding developed, in particular, in those mammals whose young can move about shortly after birth. Such young are known as "precocial" since they leave the nest at an early age (i.e., geese, field hares). They are distinguished from "altricial young," who are born in a highly undeveloped state and must remain in the nest for some time. H. Schneider (1975) has suggested the more neutral term "mother follower" for precocial young, and he further distinguishes two types: the "hiders," who stay in the place where they are left by their mothers until she returns (e.g., deer), and the "mother clingers," who cling to the mother (e.g., many monkeys). B. Hassenstein (1975) uses the term "parent clinger" ("Elternhocker") for the human infant who can no longer actively hold on to its mother.

In all the above cases, safeguards must exist to allow parents to identify their own young. Mother and child are physiologically perfectly matched and it is only this relationship that guarantees successful rearing. The young must also be sure not to approach strange conspecifics, who in many cases would react aggressively toward their approach. The individualized mother–child bond helps to meet these contingencies. The personalized bond between mother and child often develops immediately after birth or hatching and bears some similarity to an imprinting process.

Those species with personalized mother–offspring bonding also maintain the primary mother–young contact with a repertoire of infantile signals to which the mother reacts innately. The young, in turn, is tuned to respond to corresponding maternal stimuli. Special learning predispositions ensure bonding with the appropriate object.

The mother–offspring relationship is a reciprocal one. Mothers understand the distress calls of their species' young and will immediately rush to their rescue. They also learn to recognize their young on an individual basis, olfactory recognition playing a particularly important role in mammals in this regard.

In some mammals the bond between mother and her young develops during a brief "sensitive" period. Mother goats will accept their kids if they remain together during this period. If the mother and kid together remain for the first 5 minutes following birth and are then separated for 1 hour, the mother will greet and accept the kid upon its return. The mother apparently recognizes her young since she will not accept any other kid. If, however, they are separated immediately following birth for a 1-hour interval, the mother will treat the kid as a stranger and will attack it when it seeks contact with her.

Oxytocin production during the birth process has been implicated as a factor in this brief "sensitive" period. Oxytocin release and the readiness to accept young can be stimulated in goats that have never borne young, by artificially dilating the cervix (P. Klopfer, 1971). Using sheep that had been given estrogen and progesterone, E. B. Keverne et al. (1983) induced complete maternal behavior in nonpregnant sheep by 5-minute mechanical vaginal-cervical stimulation. By means of such stimulation sheep that had just borne young and accepted them could be induced to adopt unfamiliar young which they have previously rejected, since their natural phase of acceptance readiness had already passed. Thus in these animals vaginal-cervical stimulation played a significant role in the release of maternal behavior.

The development of parental care behavior is undoubtedly a propitious event in vertebrate behavioral evolution. With it came about the potential not only to act in a friendly manner, but also individualized bonding and hence love and sympathy, the precursors for the higher forms of sociability that characterize human beings. Our group ethical norms can be understood in terms of extensions of family ethics.

I take a different position than that of Konrad Lorenz (1963), who regards the roots of love to be in aggression. He feels that mutual defense against enemies was the starting point for individual bonding, citing the fact that greylag geese form a defensive entity during pair formation using ritualized threats against a third party and that the threat greeting bonds the pair of geese for life. I know of no terrestrial vertebrate that forms an individualized group solely on the basis of aggression. In all cases in which aggression facilitates bonding there also exists parental care, which likewise plays a substantial role in the life of these animals and, with the signals derived from this behavior, helps to bond adults. Thus the bonding results of common fighting would have been derived from family defense, and only through the defense of the young would the aggressive potential for the group arise.

The invention of parental care is the starting point for the development of higher differentiated social systems. In two decisive steps, it brought into the world (1) the behaviors which allow friendly interaction and (2) the individualized bond or what we call love. Parental care without individualized bonding sufficed to initiate and maintain the organization of the social insects. Mutual feeding (trophallaxis), a behavior derived from parental care, is the most important group-cementing element in insect societies. However the individuals are joined in an anonymous community characterized in bees and ants by a common group scent.

The decisive further developmental stage for humans was the individualized bonding between mother and child (based on recognition of specific individuals), for with it developed love, which is defined here as individualized bonding (I. Eibl-Eibesfeldt, 1970). In modern mass society anonymity endangers love.

It is remarkable that parental care gave the impetus for the development of more complex social organizations. Neither sexuality, aggression nor fear were sufficient preadaptations. Fear is the basis of schooling in fishes, but their social organization does not proceed above this level. Other motivations that play important supplementary roles in human bonding are: sexuality, as in the marital relation (p. 248); fear, in bonding lower ranking members to higher ones (originally children to their parents, p. 184); and aggression, when group members must defend themselves against a common enemy.

Summary 4.1

Sociability can be seen as having developed in several evolutionary steps. Appetence for partner proximity and compatibility occurs in fishes, which seek protection from predators in schools. But the development of parental care was prerequisite for more elaborately differentiated forms of social life. With its development, mother–child signals came into existence. Behavioral patterns of affection and infantile appeals were the preadaptations from which adult bonding behaviors were derived. Friendliness evolved with parental care. In a further decisive evolutionary step, came the capability of forming individualized (personal) bonds. Initially it was used to secure longer lasting mother-offspring bonds in species with an extended parental caring period. But it also gave origin to love, defined personal bonding. The behavioral patterns associated with infant care also permitted the bonding of individuals not closely related by blood, so as to form closed cooperative groups that act as units.

4.2. The Ambivalence of Approach and Withdrawal in Human Interactions

In the higher vertebrates, relationships with conspecifics are marked by a distinct ambivalence. The conspecific is, on one hand, a partner that is sought. On the other hand, the appetence to bond is opposed by aggressive and fearful tendencies that encourage maintaining a distance. The conspecific bears signals releasing both friendly approach and fear-motivated withdrawal or aggression. Blackheaded gulls have great difficulty establishing friendly contact in the first stages of pair formation. Both partners bear a black facial mask, which is an aggression-releasing signal. If the female wants to approach the male, she may not look directly at his face. She approaches him in a stooped posture with intensive begging movements, which inhibit aggressive responses. The head is repeatedly turned away in a ceremony called "head flagging," thereby hiding the blackface mask and displaying the bright rear portion on the head (N. Tinbergen, 1953, 1959). At first they both prefer observing each other from a corner of the eye. Only when the gulls become individually acquainted is the aggressive effect of the facial mask sufficiently diminished (by virtue of their acquaintance) that they can approach and look at each other directly without an appeasement ceremony.

Human relationships are in similar ways characterized by ambivalence. At an age of 5 or 6 months, infants start to show first indications of fear of strangers. Before that time they will smile at anyone who approaches them. Thereafter they make a clear distinction between those individuals they know and others. The infant continues to smile at close acquaintances, but strangers evoke distinct responses of avoidance. The child will smile at them first, but then will turn away and hide its face on its mother, usually to initiate new visual contact with the stranger (Figs. 4.1–4.4). Thus withdrawal and attraction can alternate cyclically. If the stranger respects this sign of shyness and maintains his distance, the child can make friends with him. But if the stranger approaches, the child's behavior often turns to fear, and it begins crying or even panics if the stranger attempts to pick it up against its protests. This reaction is stronger if the stranger deviates significantly from the ethnic appearance of the parents. In S. Feinman's (1980) studies, white children displayed more fear toward black strangers than whites. R. Spitz (1965) interpreted the child's fear of strangers as a fear that its mother is lost to him. The child upon seeing a stranger allegedly believes its mother would not return. However, we can probably dismiss the Spitz hypothesis since children in their mother's arms also display the fear of strangers.

The behavior of the infant indicates that humans bear signals activating contradictory behavioral tendencies toward other humans. Since we know that children display fear toward a stranger even if they have never had a bad experience with an unfamiliar person, we can presume that they react innately with fear response to some specific characteristics of the stranger. The ability to detect these fear-releasing signals mature during the first months of life. This is reminiscent of findings on the recognition of threat signals in rhesus monkeys who had been brought up in social isolation (G. P. Sackett, 1966).

170

FIGURE 4.1. Fear of strangers of an In Infant. A visitor wishes to pick up the infant, but it protests and flees to its father. From a 25 frames/second 16 mm film, frames 1, 16, 30, 41, 96, 125, 215, and 276 of the sequence. Photo: I. Eibl-Eibesfeldt.

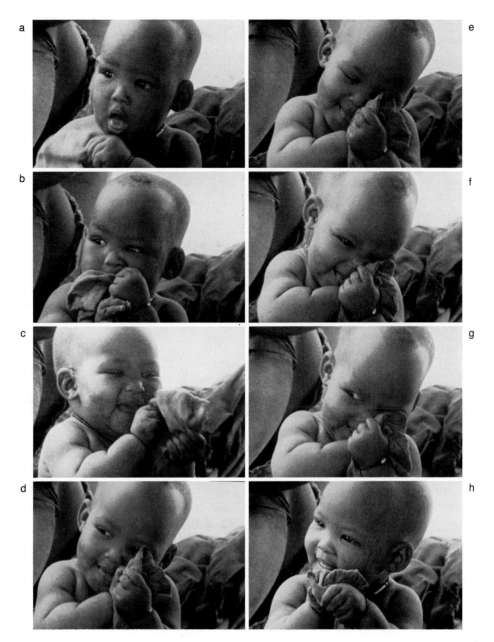

FIGURE 4.2. (a) to (h) The ambivalence between approach and withdrawal expressed in the behavior of a G/wi Bushman (central Kalahari) infant. At visual contact the child places its hand at the lower face as if hiding it, then smiles and turns away before renewing visual contact and turning away again, alternating between attraction and approach and withdrawal tendencies. Note the simultaneous superimposition of withdrawal (body posture) and approach responses (eye contact) in frame g. From a 25 frames/second 16 mm film, frames 1, 40, 199, 244, 247, 275, 287, and 332 of the sequence. Photo: I. Eibl-Eibesfeldt.

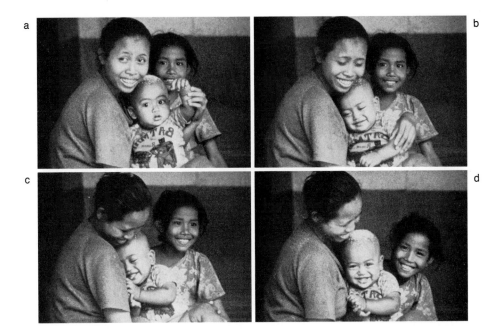

FIGURE 4.3. Ambivalence in the behavior of a mother and her male infant (Bali). The mother waves her baby's hand at the observer and greets him with an eyebrow flash; then both withdraw, huddling together, before turning back toward the observer, again in a friendly manner. From a 50 frames/second 16 mm film, frames 1, 14, 58, and 101 of the sequence. Photo: I. Eibl-Eibesfeldt.

The mother and other reference individuals must also bear these fear-arousing characteristics, but personal acquaintance inhibits their effect. We do not know all the specific characteristics and its correlates that cause fear and will result in withdrawal responses. Eye contact is perceived with ambivalence. On the one hand, we need visual contact to communicate with others, since with eye contact we signal that the channels for communication are open. On the other hand, we must not maintain such contact for too long, for then it becomes staring and thus threatening. In the past, staring was seen as a threat that could lead to a challenge to a duel; at present, staring at strangers is considered to be socially unacceptable, if not rude. A person talking to someone and uninterruptedly fixating on them will make an impression of being aggressive and dominating. In normal speech we note, therefore, that the speaker always interrupts visual contact while the listener may maintain contact uninterruptedly. Though there exists cultural variation, the principle holds true across different cultures. Some tribal people seem particularly sensitive to visual contact, for example, the Tasaday were afraid of what they called our "piercing" eyes (I. Eibl-Eibesfeldt, 1976). Threat stares are part of the normal aggressive repertoire (p. 370).

E. Waters *et al.* (1975) showed that a child's (5 to 10 months old) pulse rate increases dramatically upon the approach of a stranger, even if the stranger approaches with friendly words. The child can break off contact and regulate its own level of excitation by avoiding visual contact. As the child diverts its eyes its pulse rate decreases rapidly.

FIGURE 4.4. An Eipo mother draws her baby's attention to the observer in a friendly way. The infant smiles, then takes shelter by his mother, resumes visual contact, and finally suckles (comfort drinking). From a 25 frames/second 16 mm film, frames 1, 19, 36, 93, 120, and 194 of the sequence. Photo: I. Eibl-Eibesfeldt.

Apart from the eyes, other signals must be significant as well. Children blind from birth, even those born both blind and deaf, display fear of strangers. Children blind from birth recognize strangers by their voices and avoid them, showing all the typical signs of fear (S. Fraiberg, 1975). Children born both blind and deaf investigate people using tactile and olfaction sensations, since body odors are more significant in distinguishing individuals.

Infantile xenophobia was also observed in all cultures we studied (I. Eibl-Eibesfeldt, 1973b), including Bushmen (San), Yanomami, Eipo, Himba, Tasaday, and Pintubi, just to mention a few. Fear was displayed not only toward white visitors but also toward strangers of their same ethnic group. M. J. Konner (1972) investigated fear of strangers in !Kung Bushmen. Apparently xenophobia is an important component of the human behavioral repertoire. It is a phylogenetic adaptation, but one that can be modified strongly through learning. In many cultures it is used by the parents for specific educational purposes and thus is reinforced as a secondary effect: when a Tasaday baby cried, its mother warned the baby that the

174

stranger would take it away if it did not stop whimpering; I heard similar admonishments in the Yanomami.

There is a great deal of literature on infantile xenophobia among European children (summarized in L. A. Sroufe, 1977). According to H. J. Rheingold and C. Eckerman (1973) the concept is of little value because the children displayed fear of strangers in combination with behaviors expressing readiness of contact, an argument also voiced by M. Ferrari (1981). This is precisely what is meant by "ambivalence." The inclination for friendly contact has already been mentioned (p. 170). But we must also accept as fact that a child is phylogenetically programmed to act, so to speak, upon the hypothesis that strangers are potentially dangerous.

Our photographic analysis shows indeed that two antagonistic systems are activated: approach and withdrawal responses alternate, often cyclically. The movement patterns of both systems can also be superimposed upon each other. The bonding system activates contact-seeking behaviors, such as approach, and behaviors signaling contact readiness. The opposed agonal system (p. 363) activates avoidance, flight (escape), and even aggression. The latter may express itself in defensive movements or autoaggression (Figs. 4.5–4.11).

The simultaneous occurrence of such antithetical (opposing) behaviors presents no theoretical difficulties. Naturally there is individual variation according to context and experimental design, but xenophobia cannot be dismissed simply as an artifact of an artificial experimental situation. It is actually an elementary social reaction that can indeed be observed in its natural context.

Studies conducted by M. D. S. Ainsworth (1963, 1969, 1973) and L. Smith and H. Martinsen (1977) confirm that a child selectively seeks its mother's presence. Not only does the child speak and play less exploratively when the mother leaves the room, but crying increases. If the mother returns, the child quiets down and seeks contact. If left alone with a stranger, the child will seek the stranger's company in the mother's absence. "Contrary to attachment theory, stress may induce nonspecific proximity seeking in a young child" (p. 51). However, in what way is this "contrary?" One does not exclude the other. Someone who is terribly frightened will seek a stranger's contact. There is probably selective advantage to seek alternatives according to the following precepts: in the mother's presence, a stranger should be avoided; but in the absence of mother the presence of others should be sought. The chances of survival are limited for a child left abandoned.

K. Kaltenbach et al. (1980) note stranger avoidance reactions are not only typical for children but are even stronger in the mother. Thus they conclude that infantile fear of strangers is not a particularly developmental specific phenomenon. Certainly adults experience ambivalence in their interpersonal relations, for tendencies to approach are in conflict with tendencies to avoid. However, it does not necessarily follow from this that the concept of fear of strangers loses significance for the developmental psychologist.

Fear of others is one of the universals that decidedly influences our social life. It leads to xenophobia, a characteristic that undoubtedly has accelerated human cultural evolution. For most of his history, man has lived in small groups of intimate acquaintances, and as such, trust prevailed. Strangers were encountered only occasionally as visitors, where they were greeted with courtesy, respect, or reserve or as enemies, when they might have been treated aggressively. Today we live in anonymous societies in which most of the people we encounter daily are strangers. Thus, the fear-releasing signals of others are more effective and behavior tends toward mistrust. Studies have shown that people walk faster the larger the city (M. H. and H. G. Bornstein, 1976; M. H. Bornstein, 1979). There is a clear

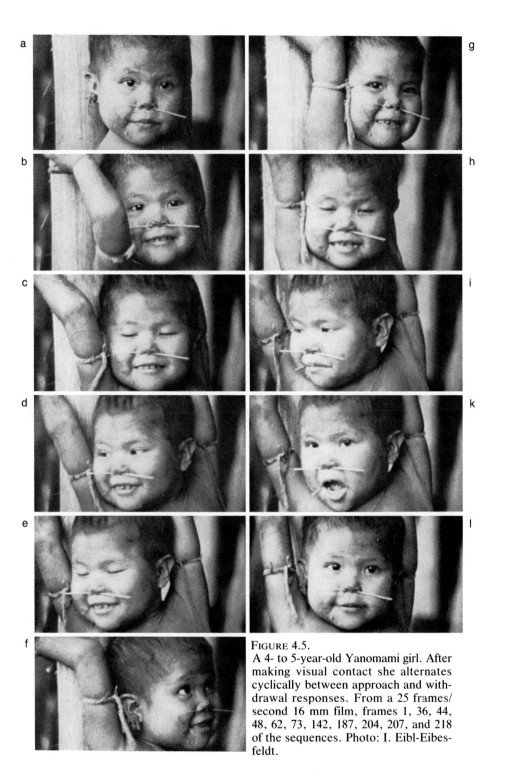

FIGURE 4.5.
A 4- to 5-year-old Yanomami girl. After making visual contact she alternates cyclically between approach and withdrawal responses. From a 25 frames/second 16 mm film, frames 1, 36, 44, 48, 62, 73, 142, 187, 204, 207, and 218 of the sequences. Photo: I. Eibl-Eibesfeldt.

relationship between population density and walking speed (Fig. 4.12). We also avoid visual contact if we have to share a bus or train with strangers, which E. Goffman (1963) called "civil inattention."

J. Newman and C. McCauley (1977) counted how often passersby in three different sized cities established visual contact with a male and female test person stationed at a post office and store. Visual contact was highest in the small country town and least in the large city (Fig. 4.13).

Expression masking is another contact avoidance strategy; one displays no emotional arousal and, in particular, no signs of weakness or else the other person might take advantage of it. One pretends to be neutral or cool to others. Strangers encountered during the day are, in a certain respect, stressors. We are compelled to save face and to exercise self-control in order not to betray emotions of which a stranger might take advantage. This can lead to habitual fixation in which the mask is worn continually, even in the company of friends. This does not mean that we essentially avoid close interpersonal contacts. We search for them but prefer people with whom we are already acquainted. It is not people who stress us in large cities, but strangers. Generally, a large city enhances loneliness, since we are removed from our circle of family and friends. Because of our great mobility, acquaintances in cities are widely scattered (C. McCauley and J. Taylor, 1976; I. Eibl-Eibesfeldt, 1977). Since agonal tendencies are not buffered by personal acquaintance, social life is more under agonal stress than in the individualized community. Women feel threatened by the directness of the "man on the street" (C. Benard and E. Schaffler, 1980). Studies have shown that even in New Guinea, urbanization has changed personal relationships similarly to that described above (P. R. Amato, 1983).

But man is not invariably rejecting toward the stranger; as we have seen, his behavior is ambivalent. We are afraid of strangers, but also seek their company. We need appropriate contact situations to enhance relations. In earlier days these were provided by the city square, the town well, or the village pub. Large cities lack such opportunities as traffic is conveyed on large streets. The opinion that we merely have to build something for people and they will adapt to it has led to city planning insensitive to human needs. Little by little we are realizing that the urban environment must be made to fit man's social as well as his other needs. Designs of large living complexes are now being reformulated (p. 629).

FIGURE 4.6. Himba girl (southwest Africa) who upon eye contact ambivalently protrudes her tongue and intentionally bites her hand. From 16 mm film. Photo: I. Eibl-Eibesfeldt.

FIGURE 4.7. Balinese girl about 10 years old. Visual contact elicits smiling, avoidance of visual contact, often referred to as visual cut off, playful jostling of her nearby friend with subsequent grabbing, and finally turning toward the observer in a friendly way. In each case it is evident that reactions of aggression and flight motivation are activated in addition to attraction. From a 50 frames/second 16 mm film, frames 1, 16, 22, 29, 39, 49, 77, 95, 108, and 126 of the sequence. Photo: I. Eibl-Eibesfeldt.

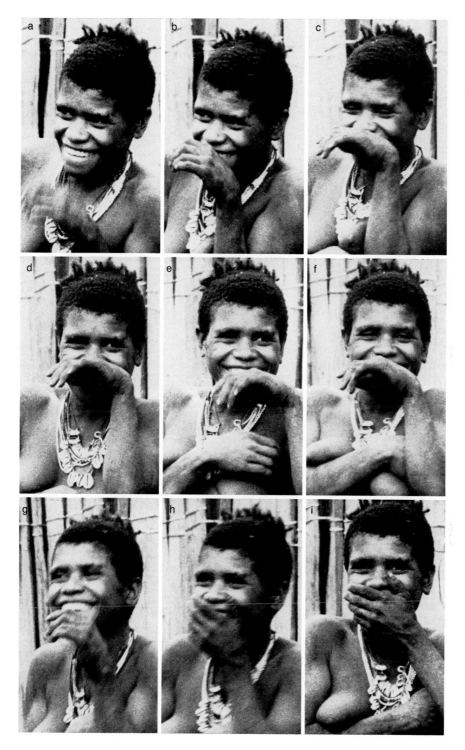

FIGURE 4.8. Reaction of an Eipo woman to friendly verbalization and to nodding as a greeting. From a 25 frames/second 16 mm film, frames 1, 8, 30, 36, 49, 59, 67, 83, and 93 of the sequence. Photo: I. Eibl-Eibesfeldt.

FIGURE 4.9.
Ambivalence of two Tboli girls (Mindanao, Philippines) upon a compliment and visual contact: smiling, burying the face, visual cut off and contact, tongue extrusion. From a 25 frames/second 16 mm film, frames 1, 18, 37, 42, 80, 191, 274, 295, 310, 329, and 345. Photo: I. Eibl-Eibesfeldt.

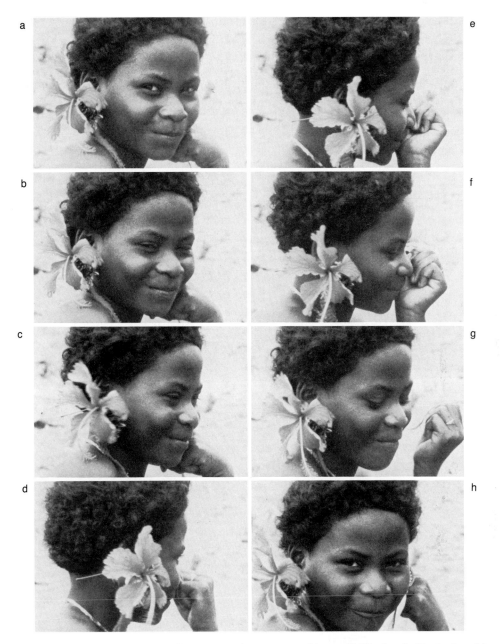

FIGURE 4.10. Ambivalence in a young Agta woman (luzon, Philippines). Contact-seeking behaviors and avoidance characterize interpersonal behavior even into adulthood. From a 50 frames/second 16 mm film, frames 1, 16, 21, 29, 61, 67, 88, and 131 of the sequence. Photo: I. Eibl-Eibesfeldt.

However anonymity continues to grow in many other areas of daily life (p. 625). Some individuals react by protesting with like-minded friends and opposing societal norms; others flee to drugs or the promising arms of secret sects or extreme political groups. In the long run society's financial cost arising from these moves is quite high. How we will live in the year 2000 will depend upon our success in reducing anonymity in interpersonal relationships. Fortunately, we need no laborious training to develop friendly relations. By nature, man is disposed in a friendly manner toward others. The task at hand is to prevent the deterioration

181

of our innate tendency to communicate and form bonds through inhumane socialization.

If interpersonal relations cannot be improved in large cities, we may expect that mistrust and fear will become the determining factors in social relations. This could have harmful consequences for liberal democracy, especially if they are exacerbated by further fears such as anxieties about economic security. During periods of fear, people tend to form attachments with "strong" personalities, or ideologies affording a sense of security. Fearful people are thus susceptible to demagogues and afford them a following.

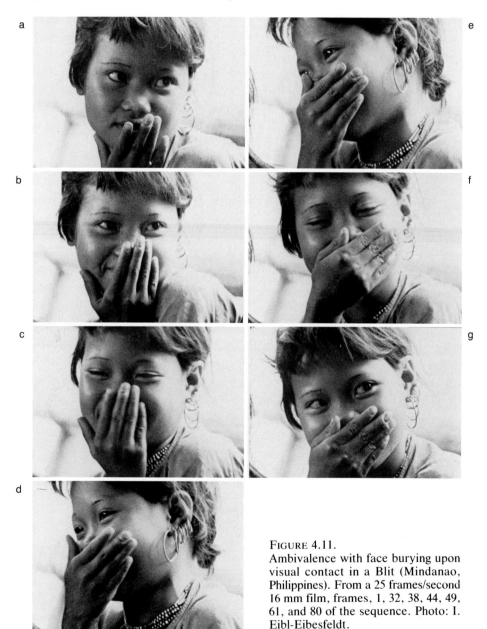

FIGURE 4.11.
Ambivalence with face burying upon visual contact in a Blit (Mindanao, Philippines). From a 25 frames/second 16 mm film, frames, 1, 32, 38, 44, 49, 61, and 80 of the sequence. Photo: I. Eibl-Eibesfeldt.

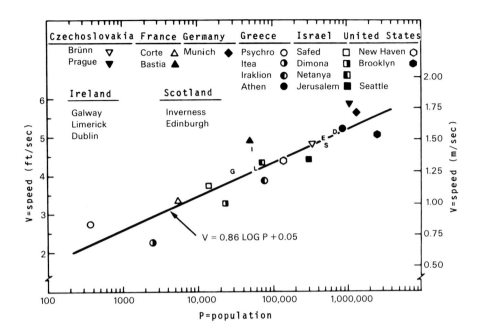

FIGURE 4.12. Walking speed as a function of population size. From M.H. Bornstein (1979).

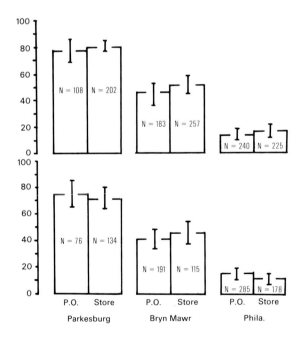

FIGURE 4.13. Percentage of passersby establishing eye contact with a female (upper) and male (lower) experimenter at a post office (P.O.) and a store in cities of different sizes. From J. Newman and C. McCauley (1977).

The roots of this bonding by fear are old and extend back to the early mother–child relationship. In many birds the mother is the goal of flight by the young when danger threatens. This response blindly continues even if the young are punished for such behavior under experimental situations (p. 77). Similar conditions apply for mammals. Young monkeys flee to the mother and typically cling to her for shelter. Punishment of the young likewise reinforces this behavior and we also know that maltreated children are firmly bonded to their mothers and protest against any separation from them. In the hierarchically structured baboon groups, high ranking males are sought by juveniles and low ranking adults, even if the high ranking animals are the cause of anxiety. Likewise, a human seeks escape in times of emergency not only with the mother but with others as well. Desperate people behave much like children: they regress to infantile behavioral patterns. Such infantile action can also seize the masses and make them uncritically ready to be led.

Summary 4.2

Interpersonal relationships are characterized by two antagonistic tendencies. The appetence for friendly contact is in conflict with aversive tendencies of avoidance, an ambivalence manifested even in early infancy. In the first months of life the infant will respond positively to anyone, but after the middle of the first year strangers will also elicit fear and avoidance responses, even if the child has had no bad experiences with strangers. Apparently it is at this time that the capability matures for recognizing those human characteristics that elicit fear, avoidance, and rejection. Thus a human being is the bearer of signals which release in his fellow men approach and avoidance simultaneously, apparently due to an inherited program. Personal acquaintance mitigates the fear-arousing stimuli, so that trust becomes the prevailing characteristic in a circle of close acquaintances. This disposition which developed in connection with maternal behavior fosters the formation of individualized small groups. In modern anonymous society, mankind encounters strangers daily, whose signals release contact avoidance and expressive masking as means of self-protection. Thus, fellow men become stressors, and the constant subliminal fear motivation tends to infantilize the individual in mass society and makes them more susceptible to the slogans of those promising security.

4.3. The Human Family as the Nucleus of Society

4.3.1. The Controversy about Man's Familial Disposition

To what extent are we predisposed for a familial structure? In recent times there have been numerous efforts to depict the family as a purely cultural institution lacking all biological foundations. The motive for these efforts is the wish that we should not prefer family members to others, but be equally friendly and responsible for all others. Familial feelings are thought to present an obstacle in achieving such a goal. Those holding this viewpoint do not give credence to the fact that precisely those characteristics enabling us to see strangers as "brothers and sisters" arise in the family (p. 169). Furthermore there is a feminist faction attempting to demonstrate that familiality is not a primary characteristic of human nature but comes about secondarily as a consequence of cultural shaping. It is maintained in this context that women are not by nature motherly (E. Badinter, 1981; A.

184

Skolnick, 1973; see p. 186). This viewpoint is at the base of the rejection of the traditional gender roles.

Thus we read that the woman's role was only invented some 10,000 years ago when men began breeding animals and learned thereby the meaning of fatherhood (E. Fisher, 1979). This drove men to gain control over the womens' bodies in order to secure their own paternity. Women then became valuable social and economic possessions. The predominance of feminine deities in the upper stone age, which is occasionally interpreted as representing the then esteemed position of women, was in reality, according to this argument, a sign of the social derogation of women as compared with their position in the lower stone age. Women lost control over the number of children they wanted and were reduced to exercising their reproductive function.

Such a position can be easily taken if one disregards the facts and does not expend the effort to thoroughly study the anthropological literature. The role of women in society does indeed change, but not according to the simple formula: Lower Stone Age = Egalitarian and Upper Stone Age to Modern = Male Dominance.

"Creeping familialism," which has recently been noted on the kibbutz (p. 280), has been ascribed by M. Gerson (1978) to the fact that the actual kibbutz is still quite far from the ideals of emancipation; women suffer discrimination and therefore endeavor to regain respect within the family. But this opinion is based upon neither questioning the women involved nor on observation. If these are done, one gains a different insight (p. 281). The less the factual knowledge, the more dogmatically the case is fought against what is called the "ideology" of family and motherhood and the slogan "discrimination" increasingly becomes a meaningless shell. If the concept is applied widely enough it can explain virtually anything, for people invariably draw distinctions between the sexes and thus some sort of discrimination always occurs. People also discriminate when they cultivate friendships.

Since the time of Friedrich Engels many believe that only the working woman is emancipated. According to Engels the "reintroduction of all women into public industry"[1] is prerequisite for womens' liberation. But that would require the dissolution of the single family as an economic unit of society and a collective child care system. Traditional family structure is opposed to such a move, so the attempt is underway to demonstrate there is no obliging reason for such an institution. When Margaret Mead (1935) wrote that the children on Samoa were brought up collectively without any distinctive mother–child bond, her words were accepted, although later it was determined that her assertions were false (D. Freeman, 1983). I still recall vividly when, in 1967 in Samoa Derek Freeman read me that passage of the book, where Mead maintained that there are no strong emotional bonds between mother and child. He then said to me, "Wait and see. Watch that mother going fishing!" And while a mother hurried toward her boat, two children held a third child who was screaming and trying to follow her!

---

[1] "It will be demonstrated that the liberation of the woman first requires the reintroduction of the entire feminine sex into public industry and that this also necessitates the dissolution of the single family as society's economic unit" (1884, p. 213). And further: "The care and upbringing of children becomes a public matter; society will care for all children equally, whether they arise from marital or nonmarital relations" (p. 214).

Biologists and psychologists who attempt to suggest the outstanding significance of a mother–child bond are often chastised for fostering an "ideology of motherhood." The fact that in earlier times in Europe—as well as today in some primitive tribes—infanticide was quite common, serves as an argument that motherly behavior was rather culturally superimposed than a natural behavior. As A. Skolnick (1973, p. 312) states "The fact that infanticide has been widely practiced in Western society and elsewhere is evidence that benevolence toward children is not built into human nature, and is not a societal imperative."

H. Tyrell (1978) takes a similar position. He also interprets the human family as a purely cultural institution. At best the mother–child dyad could be biologically based, but the weak mother–child bond required cultural reinforcement. Tyrell writes: "Such cultural support and specification, whose necessity for the insufficient innate human drive for "parental love" was demonstrated by B. Malinowski (1926, p. 197), may actually have the effect of strengthening the admittedly reduced homicide inhibitions in humans against infants and children" (p. 629). Cross-cultural observations, however, reveal a very different situation. Infanticide is indeed practiced in various parts of the world, but certainly not without any involvement of the conscience (p. 194).

P. Aries (1978) maintains that childhood as such has not always existed. In the Middle Ages, children were treated like small adults, and what we know as a family, the community of parents and children, did not exist until it arose from the kin and tribal groups in the 15th and 16th centuries. Thus the family was not at the roots of tribal communities. A look at the available ethnological literature would have shown otherwise (p. 235).

Margit Eichler (1981) claims that the family is not the site of love and security because it is within the family that the most murders occur and that child maltreatment is the order of the day. Surely there are many crimes of jealousy, and the cramped lifestyle in modern mass society contributes to the many strains on marital relations and attitudes toward children, but these are contemporary pathological developments. When one gleans evidence from those cultures that do not belong to the civilized mass societies, family members are affectionately attached to each other, although this does not mean that family relationships are conflict free.

We must be aware that many mothers are overburdened today, even if they do not work. In former times, families were large and older siblings and other family members were available as baby sitters to relieve a mother of her burden. Today mothers certainly need the support of public institutions like kindergartens. But the needs of the children for personal parental affection must not be sacrificed. Certainly the cultural variety of marital and family relationships demonstrate the adaptability of man in this regard. But we shall demonstrate that there are limits to this adaptability that one should accommodate when the common good is being considered. Man is predisposed through phylogenetic adaptations to marital partnership and family life.

The evolution of the mammalian family started with the mother family where, as we mentioned earlier, mother–offspring signals and individualized bonding evolved (p. 167). In most mammals the mother cares for her young herself and is hormonally prepared for this task. This happens in all known mammals and thus has probably been the case for at least some 200 million years. The male's role in many species is restricted to producing new young, and, less frequently, to their defense, which generally takes the form of territorial defense. However, the males will occasionally defend their own young. The Galapagos sea lion, for example, prevents any young from swimming into the deep water, protecting them from sharks. Occasionally it will even attack sharks (G. W. Barlow, 1972; I. Eibl-Eibesfeldt, 1955a, 1978). In mammals living in small individualized bands (wolves, macaques) or monogamous families (gibbons), the male is even more directly involved in defense of the young. He occasionally brings them food, plays with the young or at least tolerates their social exploratory behavior, and at times carries a juvenile. The details of mammalian parental care behavior will not be discussed here; comprehensive reviews are found in R. F. Ewer (1968) and J. F. Eisenberg (1981). Some higher mammals form groups in which partners of the opposite sex recognize each other and sometimes form quasi-marital lasting partnerships. The long evolutionary history of parental care and specialized division of labor between sexes make it improbable that man has completely abandoned this mammalian heritage.

4.3.2. The Mother–Child Dyad: Bonding Theories and Infantile Monotropy

Man is born in a highly undeveloped state. But he possesses specializations that characterizes him as "Tragling"—a being adapted to be carried. The grasp reflex, for example, is so well developed that an infant can firmly hold on to the mother's clothes or hair. The infant also has relatively well-developed sensory skills that facilitate forming a personal attachment to the mother in the first months after birth. A number of theories have been proposed to explain the mechanism of the development of attachment. Curious, but often quoted is Anna Freud's theory that infantile "love" developed from food intake, which the baby would associate with the wish-fulfilling objects: bottle, milk, breast. These would become beloved objects. Finally, the child would comprehend that the mother is actually responsible for fulfilling these wishes.

The comparative observations described earlier make Anna Freud's interpretation obsolete, since bonding to the mother is not dependent upon her as a food source reference point (E. R. Hilgard and G. H. Bower, 1975; C. T. Morgan and R. A. King, 1975; R. A. Silverman, 1975; R. E. Smith et al., 1978).

Anna Freud's (1946) formulation is paralleled by that of F. Dollard and N. Miller (1950). The child, they state, quickly learns that the mother or other reference person fulfills its physical needs, and it also learns that hunger, wetness, cold, and other unpleasant sensations occur in the person's absence, so the child would eventually actively seek contact with the reference person.

If these secondary reinforcement theories were valid, one would merely have to bond the child to those who provide for its physical well-being. But that is by no means the case. In the kibbutz, the children are cared for by attendants, and parental contact is sometimes limited to an hour of play each evening. Nonetheless the children are strongly emotionally attached to their parents as reference persons, indicating that it is the quality of contact and not physical attendence that determines bonding. H. R. Schaffer and P. Emerson (1964) found that 22% of kibbutz children in their test sample developed a powerful attachment to people who never were involved with their physical care; 17% of the children formed attachments to people who only occasionally attended to their physical needs. We shall not elaborate here on these simple models of the genesis of the mother–child relationship. They have been presented, critically discussed, and rejected by D. W. Rajecki et al. (1978).

The biological attachment theory of J. Bowlby (1958, 1969), further elaborated by M. D. S. Ainsworth (1963, 1967, 1969), based upon ethological findings, has proved useful. In essence, this theoretical position perceives the mother–child bond as a predetermined phylogenetic adaptation permitting a further development into a personalized relationship. The child is not a passive recipient of socializing stimuli; both are active partners. The child, for example, displays a distinct "monotropy" (J. Bowlby, 1958)—the impetus to seek a personalized relationship (normally with the mother). Physical care is not the predominant criterion in establishing this reference person, but rather behavioral patterns of loving attraction, such as cuddling, kissing, speaking to, inciting to dialogue, and, of course, play.

Each child needs a reliable reference person for these interactions, and if left alone by this person the child displays "fear of separation." Initially the response is not linked to a particular person; for the first 3 months an infant left alone will stop protesting and quiet down when anyone picks it up. There are, however, particularly sensitive children who, even in their first month, can only be pacified by the mother. If 4-month-old infants can see their mother (or other reference person), they will protest only when the mother leaves the room; the older infant will try to crawl after her. If that strategy fails, the child will cry as if in great fear. Such distress calls are also known in young mammals.

The mother is the basis of security for the human child, and if she is gone the child experiences "separation fear." It should not be interpreted as meaning that the child fears the permanent loss of the reference person, for it is inaccurate to ascribe predictions of future events to an infant. It is simply the very absence of the reference person that elicits fear—an elemental fear! An abandoned infant would be subject to all sorts of dangers.

Once the child has established a personal bond with its mother, it will protest even when the mother leaves it with other reference people (siblings, aunts). Here it is not being alone that arouses fear, since the other persons could afford security. We must presume, therefore, that it is the departure of a beloved person that is painful. In this context we could speak of "separation grief." Departure of the father can also elicit an infant's protest, even if the child stays with its mother.

Fear of strangers should not be confused with separation anxiety. The latter is the fear to be left alone, whereas the fear of a stranger can even be experienced by a child who sits on its mother's lap. Apparently the child feels threatened by strangers. Thus the contexts of abandonment and threat are clearly distinct. F. R. Renggli (1976, p. 69) summarized the differences between these fears; this summary is presented in Table 4.1.

Table 4.1. Renggli's Summary of Fear Differences

Fear of strangers	Separation fear
1. *Phenomenology*	
At a specific age the child rejects contact with unknown group members in spite of its increasing inclination for friendly and general contact.	In spite of the child's increasing independence, based on motor maturation, it returns repeatedly to the mother to ascertain her presence.
2. *Actual fear sensation occurs in the following situations*	
When the strange group member approaches too closely in any form, i.e., if the stranger wants to carry the child about.	When the mother moves away, or even more powerfully, when the child returns to a point to find the mother and she is no longer there.

continued

Table 4.1. *Continued*

Fear of strangers	Separation fear
3. *Temporal restrictions*	
Begins at the point that it knows the mother, i.e., at the onset of the imprinting phase.	After imprinting is complete, i.e., separation fear readiness operates when child–mother bonding is complete.
4. *Function*	
Lies in imprinting, i.e., an ever stronger preference for the primary contact and care person which we designate as bonding of the child to the mother. Reasons: the child's nourishment and protection are better guaranteed.	Extending that uniquely established relation between mother and child; the child uses the mother as a secure base from which it explores the environment. Reasons: better environmental orientation and an extended learning phase (imitation).
5. *Mother–child relationship*	
The mother orients to the child, not allowing it out of her sight; restricts the child's detachment tendencies and retrieves it when it strays too far.	The child orients to the mother and does not let her out of its sight; it must continually know of her presence. When the mother moves away, the child immediately follows (following response).
6. *Child's primary activities*	
Visual and, above all, manual exploration of the near environs in proximity to the mother, the mother herself, and its own body. The child begins establishing contact with familiar adult partners in addition to the mother.	Exploratory behavior: exploration of the further environs with the mother at its center; also play behavior. The child begins establishing peer relationships and play contacts.
7. *This phase proceeds undisturbed in the following situations*	
If the child can establish body contact anytime by clinging to the mother or by some other contact form.	If the child can return to the mother at any time or otherwise knows of her continual presence.
8. *Upon the mother's absence in this phase*	
If the adequate partner is absent in this early phase, the child will use parts of its own body as a last resort to satisfy its needs.	Either frantic, unplanned running about, or fearful collapse with wild screaming bouts, signifying total drive inhibition, since escape appetence operates continually.

If the child cannot establish an attachment to a reference person for any reason, its further development is seriously disturbed. Hospitalized children display this in a particularly blatant way. If infants who can already distinguish between reference persons and strangers are separated from the reference person by a hospital stay, they undergo a separation shock. First they protest, then become silent, and finally begin to seek a nurse as a new reference person. This is a difficult task since the nurses have little time to spend with individual children; however such contact may be successful. But the nurses rotate in shifts or leave for vacations. Thus a newly established contact is often interrupted and the child must experience a new disappointment after losing this reference person. After protesting there may be a new attempt to establish contact, but the child cannot repeat the process too often. There are then two alternatives: the child can either learn to develop new contacts quickly, without a strong emotional involvement. These children no longer cry when the reference person leaves the area, or even if their mother leaves on visiting day. They are equally friendly to everyone but maintain a certain distance. The child no longer invests in intense relationships. J. Bowlby (1969a, p. 28) portrays this type of adaptation in hospital children:

> Should his stay in hospital or residential nursery be prolonged and should he, as is usual, have the experience of becoming transiently attached to a series of nurses each of whom leaves and so repeats for him the experience of the original loss of his mother, he will in time act as if neither mothering nor contact with humans had much significance for him. After a series of upsets at losing several mother figures to whom in turn he has given some trust and affection, he will gradually commit himself less and less on succeeding figures and in time will stop altogether attaching himself to anyone. He will become increasingly self-centered and, instead of directing his desires and feelings toward people, will become preoccupied with material things such as sweets, toys and food. A child living in an institution or hospital who has reached this state will no longer be upset when nurses change or leave. He will cease to show feelings when his parents come and go on visiting day; and it may cause them pain when they realize that, although he has an avid interest in the presents they bring, he has little interest in them as special people. He will appear cheerful and adapted to his unusual situation and apparently easy and unafraid of anyone. But this sociability is superficial; he appears no longer to care for anyone.

Children that cannot make this adaptation close themselves off from the world. They enter into no more relationships and instead succumb to a type of apathy. They no longer protest, but behave "well" and remain retarded in their development. They are also more susceptible to disease.

R. A. Spitz (1965, 1968) impressively described such children. Although the high mortality rate (one-third) of all children under 2 years old in foster homes was recently shown to be due in part to insufficient nutrition, other pathological manifestations of hospitalism are also seen in well-nourished foster home children. Among other things, their developmental quotient is far behind that of children receiving personalized care. This showed in a comparison Spitz made between foster home children and those in a home for imprisoned mothers. The foster home children were routinely cared for by nurses while minor delinquent mothers (who had been pregnant when sent to the reformatory) cared for their children in the home for delinquent mothers. In the first 4 months, the developmental quotient of the foster home children was higher than that of the others, possibly because the foster children came from a higher social class. In the last one-third of the first year, their developmental quotient had fallen far below the initial level, while that of the children had improved due to the efforts of their delinquent mothers. R. A. Spitz (1968) summarized his findings shown in Table 4.2. In the family division are the developmental quotients for 34 children of various social strata; in the institution division are developmental quotients for institutionalized children (69 in childrens' homes and 61 in foster homes).

A child needs a reliable reference to develop trust in others and himself. Children learn from partner reactions that they can arouse affection and that they are loved for their own sakes (Fig. 4.14).

Table 4.2. Summary of Spitz's Developmental Quotients

Environment	Cultural and social milieu	Average developmental quotient in Year 1	
		First 4 months	Last 4 months
Family	Children of academics	133	131
	Children of villagers	107	108
Institution	Foster home	124	72
	Children's home	101.5	105

There is a trend in some recent publications to downplay the importance of early social deprivation, since compensation to a certain extent can occur at a later date. This is often presented to make it appear as if early deprivation were not so bad after all. This argumentation is inhuman, since we see that the deprived child suffers, regardless of whether the resulting damage is permanent or not. In addition, compensation later does not mean a complete cure, since it has not been determined whether some residual effects remain.

Bowlby's concept of monotropy should not be interpreted too rigidly. Bowlby did not mean that a child could or should be attached to just one reference figure. It is far better for a child's development to also have a bond with a father and other people as well (see also H. R. Schaffer and P. E. Emerson, 1964). We will investigate the significance of a diversified social relationship network for children in more detail. With a wider selection of possible reference figures, the child will

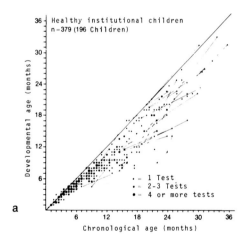
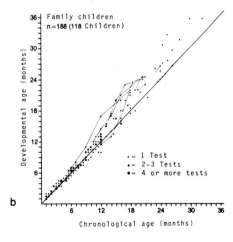

FIGURE 4.14. (a) Behavioral development retardation in institutional children in Munich with no indication of genetic or other health handicap. Body motor ability, hand use, perception, play, speech, comprehension, and contact with others were tested. A "developmental age" for each child was determined per task; it corresponds to the mean age of family children who can execute the test behavior. Mean results were entered in the graphs. Vertical disparity from the 45° line represents developmental retardation in months. Values for repeatedly tested children are joined by lines. (b) Shows the result of a parallel study with family children. Relative to these, the developmental retardation of institutionalized children is even greater. After J. Pechstein from B. Hassenstein (1972).

differentiate distinctly between various persons depending upon the strength of its attachment to them. Thus one often observes children displaying a highly painful separation experience if the father or mother leaves, even if the other parent remains with the child (p. 224). However if an older sibling or a much loved aunt leaves the vicinity, the pangs of separation are not nearly as dramatic. When the parents are absent, an older sibling can assume the parental role and become a secure base for the child in fear arousal contexts (R. B. Stewart, 1983).

In the kibbutz the mother and the attendant are interchangeable in terms of being a secure base. If children are confronted with strangers, they will also seek protection with the attendant. However, the behavior elicited upon reuniting with the reference figure after a separation clearly demonstrates that the emotional ties to the mother are much more powerful (N. Fox, 1977). The mother–child bond is highly significant for the child's healthy development (J. Bowlby, 1969; B. Hassenstein, 1973a; D. N. Stern, 1974, 1977). The mother can indeed be substituted for by another person, but that other reference person must fully engage herself as an adoptive mother. However the social development of a child should not take place solely within the mother-child dyad (B. Stacey, 1980). In kin-based societies many persons care for the child. It grows up, embedded in a multiplicity of social relationships, and actively establishes contacts within the social network. But the mother still plays a more significant role than do others and thus it is incorrect to describe this context a "multiple mothering." The siblings, uncles, aunts, and the many other villagers fondling a child do not play the same role for the child as the mother. The child requires both types of relationships for its healthy development, an intimate mother–child attachment (for which an ersatz mother can substitute) and a differentiated social relationship network. Many discussions of this topic are one-sided elaborations of just one of these two types of relationships.

Extreme supporters of the feminist movements seriously suggest that child care be left to the state. This also suits those who believe that individualized attachments should be avoided since it leads to discrimination against other individuals. Thus this should be countered by raising children collectively. Only then would they feel responsible to the collective society.

Proponents of this viewpoint often also maintain that motherliness does not have a biological basis (E. Badinter, 1981; P. Aries, 1978; A. Skolnik, 1973; and others; p. 186), views that are repeated in otherwise critical books. Thus E. Shorter (1977) writes: "Maternal care for the young is a modern invention. In traditional society mothers were indifferent to the development and welfare of children less than two years of age" (p. 196). Shorter refers to reports from the 18th and early 19th centuries in France, Germany, and England. The fact that at that time children were often given over to wet nurses serves as evidence for his statement. But it does not occur to him that this could simply represent an extreme exercised in particular societal strata. The peasants could not afford wet nurses, and there is no evidence for the claim that peasants did not love their infants. The study of tribal people certainly demonstrates that motherliness is not at all a modern invention and to take such a position indicates a lack of perception and ethnocentricity.

The controversy is strongly influenced by the belief of some proponents of feminism that the acceptance of any biological preparedness for motherhood would pave the way for a reversion to sexism (further references in the review by A. Efron, 1985).

Particularly because certain circles wish to foster humans who are responsible to a collective society, it should be reemphasized that the mother–child bond is the source of that "basic trust" which is the prerequisite of love for others. It is within the individual family that we become able to perceive and trust also unrelated persons as "brothers" and "sisters" and thus transpose the family ethos to the group society. It is also because of this fact that living together in the anonymous mass society is possible. Absence of familial socialization often leads to a brutalization of interpersonal relations, as conditions in many metropolitan areas have shockingly demonstrated.

The consequences of early childhood neglect are alarming. B. Gareis (1978) found that in 1972, 21% of the inmates of the largest Bavarian prison had been love deprived and abused early in childhood. In 1974, the percentage climbed to 24.6, and by 1977 it was 34%. G. Kaiser (1978) found that only 5% of the inmates of a German prison grew up with one consistent reference person, while one-half of the inmates had more than five reference persons by their 14th year. Early childhood social and emotional deprivation produce a socialization deficit that can make such individuals susceptible to criminal behavior later in life. Some of the consequences include insensitivities, which, among others, manifests itself in a lack of guilt feelings.

Since these contexts are now understood, the conditions in childrens' homes have substantially improved in recent years. Early placement with adoptive parents has increased. The SOS (Save Our Souls) childrens' villages of Hermann Gmeiner are proving outstanding, where a specific number of children are assigned an ersatz mother as their constant reference companion. However, the West German laws are filled with deficits in providing for the protection of personal attachments. In divorce cases the child typically resides with one of the parents. Should the custodial parent marry, the child now has a stepfather or stepmother as a reference figure. If, however, the biological parent dies, West German law will place the child with the other parent, even if this parent has never provided care for the child, has no personal bond to it, and even if the child protests against being removed from its familiar household (B. Hassenstein, 1977). If the child has established an emotional attachment to a foster or stepparent, that bond should be respected.

4.3.3. The Significance of Mother–Child Contacts Immediately after Birth

Dramatic evidence exists indicating that the first minutes after birth are probably important for the emotional attachment of the mother to her child and thus for the development of the mother–child relationship. In societies practicing infanticide as a means of birth control, mothers will abandon their children to die or commit infanticide immediately after birth, while avoiding individual contact. Among the Eipo, Grete and Wulf Schiefenhövel (1978) filmed a woman giving birth who had claimed she would abandon her child to die if it were a girl. She bore a girl and prepared everything for the child's death. She packed the child, complete with placenta (without cutting the umbilical cord) in fern leaves and placed the liana (bush-rope) to lace up the package. But the presence of a camera and photographers in one way or other slowed down the entire process. One sees the woman sitting thoughtfully in front of the bundle of fern leaves, with the screaming child hungrily fighting for life, pushing its pink feet and hands through the leaves. The mother leaves the scene without completing her heart-breaking task. After 2 hours she returns, cuts the umbilical cord, and takes the baby, explaining that, almost apologetically, it was a strong child and she could not abandon it (G. and W. Schiefenhövel, 1978).[2]

There are many observations verifying that mothers can only leave their children to die as long as they do not have a personal attachment to them. If an attachment had developed, then the abandoning of an infant is considered to be murder, even if it is an otherwise acceptable practice (I. Eibl-Eibesfeldt, 1975). In many parts of Polynesia such an attachment was once considered to have developed the first time the mother breastfed her infant. In any case, it cannot be claimed that mothers easily leave their own babies to die, as W. Schmidbauer (1971) and others have maintained. Wherever precise observations exist it is found that the adults suffer a great deal of conflict in these situations. H. J. Heinz (1966, p. 36) writes: "I agree with Mrs. Marshall (1960, p. 327) that Bushmen are disturbed about the necessity of losing a child. They denied the practice of parting with children most convincingly until the author witnessed G.'s indecision on the matter of retaining her baby."

N. A. Chagnon asked a young Yanomami mother about her baby's whereabouts—she had just given birth but returned without her baby—the woman burst into tears, and her husband explained that one should not inquire further about the matter:

> "What happened to the baby?" I whispered to Bahimi. We sat huddled under the eaves of the great sloping roof in the circular village . . . Bahimi's cheeks were smeared with black "sadness," a crust of dirt mixed with tears, to signify her mourning. Across the village, women were returning home with firewood. Bahimi gazed at them without seeing. "She exists no more . . . I . . . I . . .," more tears welled up her soft brown eyes, and I knew then that she had killed her daughter at birth. Kaobawa, her husband, the village headman, pressed my arm gently and whispered softly: "Ask no more of this my nephew. Our other baby is still nursing, and he needs the milk" (N. A. Chagnon, 1976, p. 211).

We will leave the matter with this moving document. Anyone making the effort to encounter members of other cultures sensitively will learn that they scarcely deviate from us in their feelings. It is symptomatic of an astonishing degree of ethnocentric presumption, a lack of empathy, and a profound ignorance for someone to maintain that a healthy mother somewhere in the world would commit infanticide "light-heartedly." In most cases it occurs when birth spacing is too narrow. If weaned at an early age, the older child would have no chance for survival. It is thus a choice which child will die, the newborn or its older sibling, to whom bonds are already formed. Another reason, as in the example of the Eipo mother, is population control. Wherever infanticide is necessary, it is done so as a culturally determined imperative, and generally takes place as soon as possible after birth, before the bond between the mother and her child has solidified. Thereafter the inhibitions against infanticide would simply be too strong.

Under normal delivery conditions, bonding takes place relatively quickly. Eipo mothers who delivered sit for a sometime after birth as if deep in thought. They

---

[2]At the time of the filming, the Eipo had just been contacted in the western mountains of New Guinea. Mothers carried out infanticide of their infants out of free will and, as interviews revealed, cognizant of the productivity of their sweet potato fields and, thus, the carrying capacity of the country.

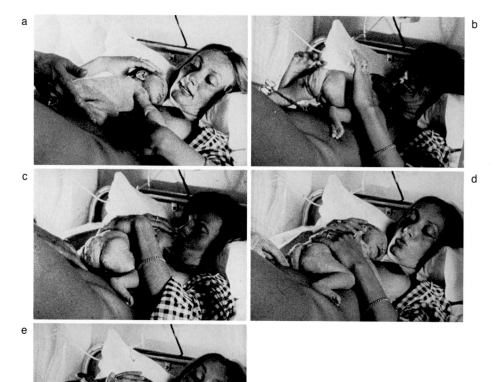

FIGURE 4.15. Example of a mother–child interaction immediately after delivery (in Germany). The umbilical cord has not yet been cut. The mother affectionately touches the child, speaks to it, and pacifies it when it cries. From a 16 mm film. Photo: S. Austen.

watch their child and take it to the breast after cutting the umbilical cord. Mothers in our culture who have not been administered drugs or locally anesthetized during the birth experience a powerful emotional reaction when the newborn baby is placed on their abdomens just after delivery. M. H. Klaus and J. H. Kennell (1976) described their condition as "ecstatic." No doubt there are cultural differences in temperament, but the principle of the mother's active attraction to the baby is constant (M. H. Klaus and J. H. Kennell, 1976; S. Austen, 1979). Mothers speak to their newborns, touch them with their fingertips, stroke them, massage them tenderly with the hands, show them to their husbands or the nurses, and make an effort to establish visual contact with them (Fig. 4.15).

M. H. Klaus and J. H. Kennell (1976) recorded the verbalizations of American mothers during the initial contact period. They found that 70% of their statements regarded the babies' eyes. They said, for example, "Let me see your eyes" or "Open your eyes so I know you love me." They attempted thereby to position their face so they looked directly at the infant's. German mothers behaved similarly. K. Grossmann (1978) demonstrated the great significance of eye contact for the mother's behavior. She recorded the behavior of ten mothers, each during three feedings on three successive days during the time 3–5 seconds before and after the baby opened its eyes. Behavior changed distinctly in 92.5% of all cases. The mothers displayed a livelier miming after their babies opened their eyes; they

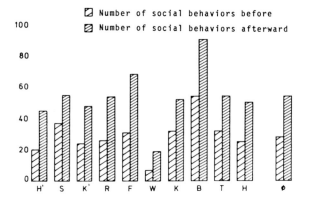

FIGURE 4.16A.
Comparison of the frequencies of "social" behavior of 10 mothers *before* eye opening of their newborn with the frequencies of "social" behavior *after* eye opening. From K. Grossman (1978).

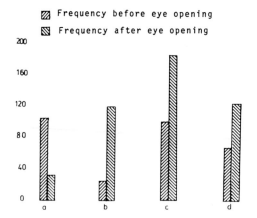

FIGURE 4.16B.
Comparison of the vestibular (a), optic (b), and acoustic (c) stimulation of the newborn by its mother as well as frequencies of approach by the mother to her child (d), both *before* and *after* eye opening of the infant. From K. Grossman (1978).

spoke with greater inflections and approached the child more. Smiling, stroking, and kissing (affectionate behavior) increased 50%, while feeding (care) behavior remained unchanged. Behavioral patterns oriented to others, such as chatting with neighbors, decreased (Figs. 4.16A, 4.16B).

In this context K. S. Robson (1967, p. 15) points to the fact that infants possess only limited means to reward the mother for all her efforts and the unpleasantries precipitated by the demands of child rearing. Within this limited range of expression, the infant's eye contact and smiling play an outstanding role!

> The human mother is subject to an extended, exceedingly trying and often unrewarding period of caring for her infant. Her neonate has a remarkably limited repertoire with which to sustain her. Indeed, his total helplessness, crying, elimination behavior and physical appearance frequently elicits aversive reactions. Thus, in dealing with the human species, nature has been wise in making both eye-to-eye contact and the social smile, that often releases in these early months, behaviors that at this stage of development generally foster positive maternal feelings and a sense of payment for services rendered . . . Hence, though a mother's response to these achievements may be an illusion, from an evolutionary point of view it is an illusion with survival value.

The infant meets its mother's contact initiative by a state of striking alertness during the first hour after birth. This state of wakefulness is induced by the stress of birth, which causes the release of high levels of stress hormones (catecholamines, adrenaline, noradrenaline) which, in turn, prepare the baby for life by causing increased flow of blood to the brain and musculature. The hormones make the baby alert which aids in promoting the process of bonding during the first hours of life (H. Lagercrantz and Th. A. Slotkin, 1986). The baby becomes highly responsive to his mother. He orients to her face, although one cannot know just which maternal characteristics are perceived by the infant at the time, but they are probably few in number. It is known that newborns will orient to a light source (P. Harris and J. A. MacFarlane, 1974) and can follow moving objects with its eyes (S. Barton, B. Birns, and J. Ronch, 1971). At 3 to 5 weeks, their visual responses as a percentage of total fixation time are directed to the contours of the human face (57.4% of fixation), with a preference for the eyes (29.8%) and less attention to nose (7.9%) and mouth (4.9%). Between 9 and 11 weeks of age, the eyes attract more attention (48.9%) than the contours (32.7%; M. M. Haith *et al.*, 1977).

As cited earlier (p. 53), newborns can move their eyes in coordination toward the source of a laterally produced sound, as if they wanted to fixate upon it visually (M. J. Mendelson and M. M. Haith, 1976). But this fixation is initially due to a central fixation process requiring no visual ability and thus no feedback from visual stimuli since children blind from birth will also fixate toward their mothers' voices (D. G. Freedman, 1964). The important fact is that they behave as if they were looking at the mother, and mothers react to this behavior with strong, positive emotions. Not all children blind from birth are capable of this kind of visual "contact," and mothers of such blind children find this lack of attempt at visual contact most disturbing (S. Fraiberg, 1975).

In this relationship it should be mentioned that the use of silver nitrate as a disinfectant after birth inhibits the eye contact process. Silver nitrate-treated babies, as compared to control groups, keep their eyes closed for a long time (Figure 4.17). This routine treatment significantly interferes with mother–child contact at an important period (J. Winberg and P. De Chateau, 1982).

An infant also displays readiness for early contact in that sucking readiness reaches a peak 20 to 30 minutes after birth. The strong motivation for sucking does not occur again until 40 hours (I. A. Archavsky, 1952). Sucking elicits progesterone release and, via oxytocin release, uterine contractions that diminish bleeding. It also fosters a powerful emotional attachment and stimulates nursing.

Mothers who kept their children for 3 hours after birth, nursing them twice, and who were together with their child another 15 hours on the following 3 days, displayed a greater extent of emotional attraction upon retesting 1 month later than mothers lacking such intensive early contact (Figure 4.18; M. H. Klaus and J. H. Kennell, 1976).

Mothers who had early contact are also ready to nurse sooner (M. H. Klaus and J. H. Kennell, 1976), which is of great consequence for the welfare of the child. Early contact facilitates a powerful emotional attraction of the mother to her child. This is evident even 2 years later in that mothers speak with greater inflections to their children if they were together right after birth, which stimulates mental development. They ask twice as many questions as control mothers, use more words for prepositions, less content words, more adjectives, and fewer commands. The latter is symptomatic of a harmonious relationship, since commands are expressions of aggressive dominance (N. M. Ringler *et al.*, 1975, 1978; F. Broad, 1976). M. H. Klaus's and J. H. Kennell's data show that clinically enforced separation of a child from its mother immediately after birth or during the first days of life increases the child's risk of being mistreated later by the mother. The

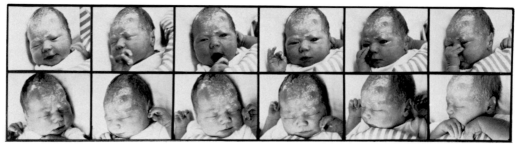

b

● Eyes closed
◑ Eyes partly closed
○ Eyes opened

Child	Min after birth	Prior to treatment (0–14 min)	Silver nitrate	After treatment (0–14 min)	Min after birth	Child
1	37 – 51				102 – 116	1
2	70 – 84				95 – 109	2
3[1]	42 – 56				72 – 86	3
4[1]	50 – 64				75 – 89	4
5	98 – 112				124 – 134	5
6	37 – 51				63 – 77	6
7	50 – 64				70 – 84	7
8[1]	- 60 – 74				- 90 – 114	8
9[1]	- 30 – 44				- 60 – 74	9
10	- 30 – 44				- 60 – 74	10

FIGURE 4.17. (a) A series of photographs showing an infant's eyes before (above) and after silver nitrate treatment (below). A 180-second interval occurs between each photograph. From J. Winberg and P. DeChateau (1982). (b) Visual behavior of ten children before and after silver nitrate prophylaxis. Photographs were taken in 1-minute intervals during a 15-minute period. In subjects 3, 4, 8, and 9 the child turned its head to the side, so only one eye could be photographed. From Y. Andersson et al. (1978).

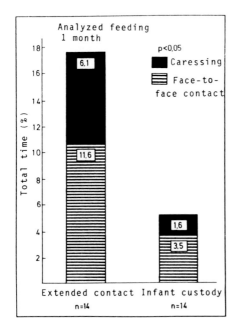

FIGURE 4.18. Mother–child interaction in a control study at the end of the first month. The extend of "caressing" and face-to-face orienting is significantly higher in mothers who had extensive contact with their child immediately after birth. After M.H. Klaus and J.H. Kennell (1976), from H. Schetelig (1979).

percentage of mistreated children, as well as those who fail to thrive for no organic reason, is disproportionately high in newborn children routinely separated from their mothers. Mothers with early child contacts are also more hesitant to place their child in someone else's care during the first months of life. In addition, those mothers who had intensive contact with their children immediately following birth were distinctly more competent with their children than mothers lacking such contact, who were more anxious (A. M. Sostek *et al.*, 1982).

In a study by D. J. Hales *et al.* (1977), twenty normally delivered women in Guatemala were allowed 45 minutes of skin contact with their babies. The first group received their babies immediately after birth, while the others were allowed contact 12 hours afterward. A third control group of twenty women, following the usual hospital routine, were permitted to see their babies shortly after delivery; some 12 hours later the infant was brought to the mothers in the usual wrappings. All mothers were observed 36 hours later. Mothers who had experienced immediate postparturition contact displayed more attraction reactions, such as face-to-face contact, than the other two groups. The delayed contact group had values between those of the early contact group and the control group.

P. DeChateau and B. Wiberg (1977) observed primiparous Swedish mothers, with early birth contact, 3 months later in their homes. These mothers made visual contact with their children more often and kissed them more frequently than control mothers who lacked early child contact and who were also observed in their homes 3 months after delivery. The latter group cleaned their children more frequently. J. Schaller *et al.* (1979) found, however, that increased attraction of mothers with early contact toward their infants could only be verified during the first weeks, and they concluded that one should not overestimate the importance of early mother–child contact. Similarly, B. C. Myers (1984a,b) cautions not to over-interpret the meager positive findings on the effect of early bonding. These are important admonitions especially for those mothers who might develop anxieties because for one reason or another they lacked early contact with their children. We can assure such mothers that during the first months of life an equally powerful mother–child contact can develop. There are multiple mechanisms at work to ensure an intimate mother–child relationship. The sensitive phase immediately after birth probably developed to guarantee that the mother accept the child despite all the hardships of birth, and I would predict that initially the acceptance readiness of women with an extended child contact immediately after delivery is higher than of those with conventional hospital births under drugs and with mother–child separation after birth. If this postulate were true, one would expect that mothers who had decided to give up their children for adoption prior to birth would change their minds more frequently if they had early child contact than those comparable mothers who avoided early contact.

Thus one should not overestimate the significance of early mother–child contact, nor should little value be attached to it. Data on breastfeeding indicate that contact has a positive effect on the mother–child relationship, and data on child neglect and child abuse in relation to early contact interruption likewise point to the importance of early mother–child contact for bonding quality. After all, the fact that mother and child do behave so distinctively and compatibly immediately after birth leads to the conclusion that this interaction is of high significance. A few additional findings follow.

W. S. Condon and L. W. Sander (1974) found that 16-hour-old infants are receptive to language and respond to it with their body movements: "When the infant is already in movement, points of change in the configuration of his moving body parts become coordinated with points of change in the sound patterns characterizing speech. . . ."

When the speaker pauses for air or emphasizes a syllable, the child reacts to that by almost unnoticeably raising a brow or lowering a foot. These speech-coordinated movements are only observed when natural rhythmic speech is presented, not when other non-speech sounds of meaningless syllables are offered rhythmically. English or Chinese sounds will stimulate movement "commentary" by the 16-hour-old infant; the newborn can "comment" with body movements on his mothers words in the first hours after birth, and in this case a synchronizing function facilitating speech acquisition may be operating. W. S. Condon and L. W. Sander (1974) add: "This study reveals a complex interaction system in which the organization of the neonate's motor behavior is entrained by and synchronized with the organized speech behavior of adults in his environment. If the infant, from the beginning, moves in precise shared rhythm with the organization of the speech structure of his culture, then he participates developmentally through complex socio-biological entrainment he later uses in speaking and communicating."

It is astonishing that infants in the first 3 days after birth not only prefer the human voice to other sounds but also their mother's voice to that of strangers. They are already capable of differentiating voices. In one study, infants were given a pacifier as reward if they correctly discriminated between their mother's voice and that of another woman. They quickly learned to recall their mother's voice (A. J. deCasper and W. P. Fifer, 1980; M. Mills and E. Melhuish, 1974). Interestingly, these were children handled in the customary clinical manner in an American hospital who met their mothers only four times daily at feeding times and at most had been in contact with their mothers a total of 12 hours up to the time of the test.

Infants can also discriminate their mothers via olfaction. Newborn infants (mean age 45 hours) furthermore discriminate their mother's face from the face of a stranger (T. M. Field *et al.*, 1984) and their mother's smell from the smell of other individuals. If 6-day-old infants are offered two cloths, one impregnated with their mother's smell and one with the scent of someone else, the infants prefer their mother's cloth significantly more often than the other one (J. A. MacFarlane, 1975, 1977; M. J. Russell, 1976; B. Schaal *et al.*, 1980).

Mothers are also attuned specifically to their own children. Six hours after birth and after just one initial contact, they can distinguish their child from that of a stranger, an ability that fathers could not match (M. J. Russell *et al.*, 1983). Mothers with infants can also differentiate the various cries for hunger, pain, and other utterances better than women without children or even mothers with older children (A. Sagi, 1981). Thirty-six mothers with 1- to 4-month-old infants were tested for this ability. Of these, fourteen already had older children and were experienced in child care, and seventeen were inexperienced in child care. The group of women without infants (non-mothers) were pregnant, and all had one or more older children. Experienced non-mothers tested lower on the ability to distinguish utterances than the inexperienced mothers of young children. "There is apparently some kind of predisposition which either naturally attunes the mother to correctly understand the infant's cries, or makes her differential experience with the crying infant more meaningful and thus increases her skill in identifying his intent . . . The fact that mothers performed better than women who were nine months pregnant, suggests that the changes, whatever they are, occur at parturition and not during pregnancy. However, it is also plausible that the major changes do take place during pregnancy, and establish initial predispositions for an effective mother–infant interaction soon after giving birth. This deserves further investigation" (A. Sagi, 1981, p. 40).

We have already shown that mothers display strong attraction reactions to their children immediately after birth. They also talk a great deal (H. L. Rheingold and J. L. Adams, 1980). We will now consider the mother–child interactions in more detail.

4.3.4. Ethological Aspects of Birth

The typical delivery in a hospital environment does not generally foster the development of early mother–child attachment. This is due primarily to the sterile, hygienic atmosphere, which is unfamiliar and tends to both alienate and produce anxiety for the mother. Security is actually a requisite for a healthy birth, and fear makes the birth process more difficult. Many ungulates hesitate delivering in the presence of an observer, which is probably an adaptation against predators. If an ungulate detected a predator in the vicinity, it would be advantageous to delay parturition. Fear suppresses labor, something that also occurs in humans. There is a psychogenic labor weakness that delays birth and, although it is not adaptive in our case, extends the delivery process. C. Naaktgeboren and E. H. M. Bontekoe (1976) found that epinephrine release is responsible for this change. Transport to the hospital and the strange surroundings can be anxiety producing for a birthing woman. It has long been known that labor pains often cease as a woman is being transported to the hospital after having experienced labor pains at home. We know that moving into unfamiliar surroundings can influence other physiological processes in humans and many other mammals. Defecation, for example, is often inhibited, a phenomenon known as travel constipation. One could speak analogously of a "birth delay" in unfamiliar surroundings.

Practices of peoples who give birth with no western medical care can offer us insights in this matter. Birth among the Eipo and their neighbors in the highlands of West New Guinea has been well documented, to a great extent on film. Grete and Wulf Schievenhövel were able to attend seven births, their observations totaling 16 hours (G. and W. Schievenhövel, 1978; W. Schiefenhövel, 1980, 1982, 1983a). Eipo women deliver in a sitting or squatting position near to the womens' hut, where they also go during menstruation (thus in familiar territory). Experienced relatives and female friends provide loving care to the woman in labor, particularly first-time mothers. Pain and fear are soothed using skin contact, massage, and magic spells. After delivery the mother attends actively to her child, cleans it with leaves, cuts the umbilical cord with a bamboo knife, and often removes the placenta as well. Similar customs can be observed in many other traditional cultures. W. Schiefenhövel and D. Sich (1983) summarize reports on birth behavior in tribal societies.

Cross-cultural comparisons and examples from behavioral biology support giving birth in familiar environs. Mother should become familiar with clinical surroundings prior to delivery. Home births in familiar surroundings take less time on average than hospital deliveries (extensively discussed in C. Naaktgeboren and E. H. M. Bontekoe, 1976). G. and W. Schiefenhövel (1983b) and M. and C. Paciornik (1983) criticize the customary dorsal delivery position. A squatting woman delivers more easily since she is assisted by gravity (Figures 4.19, 4.20). The use of narcotics and strong local anesthetics should also be kept to a minimum. Mothers report

a

b

FIGURE 4.19. (a) and (b). In traditional societies, delivery usually takes place in a squatting posture, which eases birth. Delivering Eipo woman. Photo: W. Schiefenhövel.

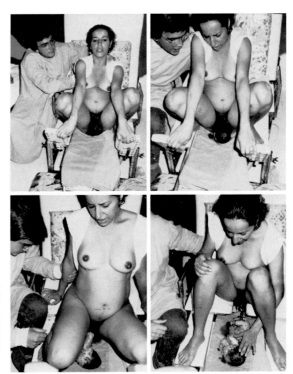

FIGURE 4.20. Modern Brazilian woman delivering in the squatting position with physician assisting nearby. Note the mother's first contact with the child, using her hands. From M. and C. Paciornik (1983).

202

FIGURE 4.21. Eipo women in labor are attended by female relatives or neighbors. They support the laboring woman, cheer her up, activate labor pains by massage, and also use magic. Photo: W. Schiefenhövel.

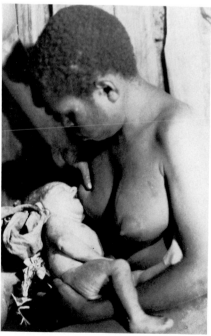

FIGURE 4.22. Breastfeeding begins immediately after or a few hours after delivery. Here another person assists breastfeeding. Photo: W. Schiefenhövel.

203

that post birth relaxation is a highly liberating feeling and is intimately related to the emergence of the child. This coincides with the euphoric, festive mood (previously cited reports) that mothers experience after natural parturition. Narcotized women often feel betrayed by being deprived of their first conscious contact with the child.

Contact with the child immediately after birth is important for both partners. This does not mean that a woman who delivers fully narcotized and does not see her child until several hours later when the narcotic effect has worn off cannot develop just as deep an emotional bond to the child as a normally delivered woman. But extra time is required for that to happen, and one can presume that immediate bonding is less liable to interference.

At present the father's role as a birth assistant and supporter is being debated. In traditional cultures, husbands do not usually participate in birth, these functions being assumed by daughters or other close females (Figures 4.21, 4.22). We do not know why that is so. It might be that the experience of birth could lead some men to develop guilt feelings and that such an effect could impair sexual relations. This is a topic that deserves investigation to help determine the optimal method of birth support. Certainly there is a need for the support of a familiar trusted person, and in many instances today the husband can best fulfill that role. This would suggest the importance of his participation.

4.3.5. Mother–Child Signals, Interaction Strategies

The infant possesses a signal repertory immediately after birth, and is in a position to react adaptively to his mother's advances. We have already discussed his vocal repertory (p. 26).

Crying is used to signal a need for help, while smiling releases friendly attraction. Both expressive behaviors are present at birth and are of great importance. Although smiling is spontaneous and not consciously exercised, it fulfills its function, as does eye contact, of rewarding the mother for her efforts. She interprets the signals as a sign of affection. Mothers of children born blind at birth regret that their children do not smile upon eye contact, and they will attempt to stimulate smiling with strong tactile stimuli. "As observers we were initially puzzled and concerned by the amount of bouncing, jiggling, tickling and muzzling that all of our parents, without exception, engaged in with the babies. In several cases we judged the amount of such stimulation as excessive by any standards. . . . The parents' own need for the response smile, which is normally guaranteed with the sighted child at this age, led them to these alternative routes in which a smile could be evoked with a high degree of reliability" (S. Fraiberg, 1975, p. 231).

Mothers quickly recognize the crying of their own babies, and if they hear their babies cry, the rate of blood flow in the breasts increases (J. Lind et al., 1973). In many women milk flow is so strongly stimulated that milk is actually released from the nipples.

In their evaluation of infant cries, 24 non-parents and 20 parents of both sexes were in basic agreement as to the perceived aversiveness, possible caretaking responses, and semantic differentiation, which indicates that cry perception may be a fundamental species-specific perceptual process that is fine-tuned by the caregiving experience (J. Green et al., 1987).

A newborn infant can also use its facial expressions to communicate whether something tastes good or not, rejecting bitter and sour substances and accepting sweet things with clearly understandable reactions. These facial expressions also appear in anencephalic individuals (J.E. Steiner and R. Horner, 1972). The facial expression repertoire differentiates rapidly; at 2 months infants intentionally smile at their mothers and can pout and otherwise "threaten" their mother's neglect by disengaging from any interaction. L. Murray (1977, quoted in C. Trevarthen, 1979) conducted an experiment in which mothers at first had interacted in a friendly manner with their infants and thereafter only looked at their child for one minute without making any affectionate expressions. After the minute passed they resumed affectionate exchanges with their infants. Initially the children reacted to their mothers' lack of interest with attempts to establish contact and then with cries of protest. When the mothers reinitiated affectionate interaction, the infants turned away, pouting! The child certainly does not cognitively understand the social significance of such a cut off; this strategy must be innate (p. 566).

The visual infantile features that Lorenz (1943) call the "Kindchenschema" (babyschema, p. 60) are not fully developed at birth. They are actually less necessary at this time, since mothers are bonded to newborns with so many other signals. The child always remains close to the mother, unable to move away from her. Contact with non-family individuals increases slowly as the child grows and particularly when it begins to crawl. At this time the infant needs signals protecting itself from others' aggressive reactions, particularly when mischievous behavior is caused by the infant's clumsiness—the "sweet" and cute infant is easily forgiven!

We have already mentioned that infants react to speech immediately after birth. At 3 months, mother and child are known to interact vocally, whereby two structurally and functionally distinct means of communication exist, called co-action and alternation by D.N. Stern et al. (1977).

In co-action mother and child vocalize simultaneously; alternation refers to alternating babbling, which occurs when one of the partners pauses. Co-action dominates in mother–child communication when the infant is 3 to 4 months old, occurring twice as often as alternation. However, this does not mean that co-action is a precursor to alternation. Stern et al. note that both strategies are utilized throughout life. Alternation occurs when the mother teaches her child something, whereas co-action indicates a higher emotional level: "When the two start to really have fun together, they move into a co-action pattern" (D.N. Stern et al., 1977). This trend continues into adulthood. "As the interpersonal situation moves toward intensive anger, sadness, joy, or expressions of love, the alternation dialogue pattern 'breaks down' and co-actional vocalizing again becomes a crucial communicative note. . . ."

The same principle applies to adult's cultural rituals where strong emotional attachment is involved—consider, for example, the vocalization patterns of opera duets, church choral singing, and marching songs (D.N. Stern et al., 1977). We are dealing here with the generalized principle of bonding via shared simultaneous activities, also expressed in dance (I. Eibl-Eibesfeldt, 1973a). Rhythmic synchronization in alternation is another expression of understanding and unity. The bonding function of many synchronized rituals is based on this fact, which is particularly evident in specific dance forms.

Mothers dispose of age-differentiated strategies for interacting with their infants without being aware of it. To some extent such strategies may arise from phylogenetically determined programs. Thus, for example, in face to face interaction they approach their infants up to a distance of 30 cm, a distance infants can best see. Mothers require no special training to establish this distance. H. and M. Papousek indeed recommend that mothers behave spontaneously for then they would generally act appropriately. Maternal behavior must be modified continually so the infant does not become bored. Generally, mothers are well prepared to accommodate their infants' limited capabilities (H. Keller, 1980). H. and M. Papousek (1977) refer to a mirror function of maternal behavior, designating the mother as the "biological mirror" of her child, which accounts for the fact that mothers take up their childs' vocalizations interpreting them as a contribution to a dialogue and carry on "conversation" in response. They state that the mother is responsible for maintaining the interactions until the end of the first year, so these vocal exchanges are in fact "pseudo-dialogues." Mothers undoubtedly effect communication by imitating their infants' last utterances and thus attempt to maintain the communicational flow. But infants also initiate contact and respond to and imitate the mothers' sounds. Contact initiative and thus intentionality have been verified in infants, and is not just based on maternal interpretation.

How important the contribution of the baby for the dialogue with his mother was demonstrated in experiments with 8- to 9-week-old babies whose mother talked to them via a video system designed so that each partner saw a full-face, life-size image of the other on a screen before them. The mothers were presented either with live, real-time video sequences of their infants, where communication was therefore potentially mutually responsive, or else with the same sequence replayed some minutes later. Baby talk of the mother differed consistently between live and replay conditions. In the replay situation more imperatives and declaratives were uttered and mothers claimed that they felt strained (L. Murray and C. Trevarthen, 1986). Three-month-old infants possess a behavioral inventory for establishing contact or maintaining distance with a reference person. Mothers incite, comment, show objects, demonstrate, and, in short, utilize all sorts of techniques adapted to their infants' comprehension level (H. Keller, 1980). Communication is disturbed when the infant is insufficiently stimulated to respond or when it is overstimulated. One method of detecting disturbed parent–child relations is noting the form and quality of reciprocal eye contact. There are infants that can actively avoid the reference person's eye contact at as early as 3 months of age. They use this mechanism when they detect some unpleasant interaction due to the reference person's inappropriate behavior or their own excessively anxious disposition. Often both factors operate which reciprocally enhances withdrawal behavior in a vicious circle. If the reference person does not correctly respond to the infant's contact initiative, for example, by holding the child too far away or orienting it so it cannot establish face to face contact, the child will actively avoid this unpleasant interaction. I believe that infants repeatedly provoked in this manner can fall into a continuous state of sulking that becomes habitual. The strategy of rejecting others by sulking and disengagement in order to elicit a new contact initiative is verified at a very early age.

This syndrome of taking offense, which I have not seen described elsewhere, should be distinguished from autism, as described by E.A. and N. Tinbergen (1972, 1983) which obviously derives from excessive anxiety of a child. Autistic children avoid contact (especially visual) due to pronounced social fear, withdrawing into a capsule shut off from their social environment. These anxious children elicit parental rejection due to the child's inadequate social accessibility. When the children act in an irritating manner they can even provoke aggressive responses from their caretakers. According to A.M. Frodi and M.E. Lamb (1980), children who cry excessively or in a deviant manner (as in "cat cry syndrome" children or premature babies) are more likely to be maltreated. Of course, there are many other factors of the social environment that play a role in child maltreatment besides these abuse-releasing characteristics (J. Belsky, 1980).

The manner in which a mother interacts with her baby differs considerably in a number of ways from adult pathways of communication. Her manner of speech differs from normal speech in rhythm, accentuation, vocabulary, volume, speed, and frequency changes. Speech elements are generally reduced in speed, with certain syllables extended, probably as an adaptation to the child's perceptual skills (S.W. Anderson and J. Jaffe, 1972). Note the frequency difference of about one octave, a difference also found in Eipo, Bushmen, Yanomami, and other cultures (Fig. 4.23). C.A. Ferguson (1964) studied baby talk in seven cultures and found comparable differences in all cultures between baby and adult talk (see also A. Fernald and T. Simon, 1984). D.L. Grieser and P.K. Kuhl (1988) compared maternal speech of Mandarin Chinese, English, and German mothers when addressing babies of 2 months old. Their study confirms that in all three groups a similar upward shift of the fundamental frequency occurs. Closer examination reveals several types of baby talk. The one with the conspicuously raised pitch is used when mothers (or any other person) address a child to get its attention, such as during a greeting episode or when a person wants to animate for active playful interaction. When a mother comforts her child, the fundamental frequency is often low and the child is addressed using slow speech.

"Baby talk" refers to the manner in which men, women, and children talk to infants and others in need of care. When adults speak to other grown-ups with baby talk they do not do so out of superiority but as a genuine expression of affection, and the adult being cared for responds within this context (L.R. Caporael, 1981, 1983). The characteristics of baby talk are as follows:

1. Raising tone frequency relative to normal speech by one octave.
2. Exaggeration of intonation structure, whereby the melodic form conveys specific information (D.N. Stern *et al.*, 1982). Mothers use rising melodies when they elicit their childs' visual contact. Yes–no questions have a similar frequency curve. Why-questions and demands utilize falling melodies. Sinusoidal and bell curves are used when mothers wish to maintain the infant's interest.
3. Emphasis of important elements.
4. Clear, simple speech.
5. Grammatical simplification.

The use of baby talk is sometimes criticized professionally. But as Hannelore Grimm (1983) points out, those critics overlook the positive emotional function of this means of expression: "If it is reduced to a purely academic consideration based theoretically on the linguistics of speech, this argument has a certain validity. But in reference to what actually occurs during the concrete interactional situation, or more correctly what should occur, this argument is untenable. Unless one would wish for speech development without considering the affectivity of words" (p. 591).

In an operant auditory preference procedure 4-month-old infants showed a significant listening preference for the "motherese" speech register (A. Fernald, 1985).

Facial expressions are also modified specifically for children. Mothers exaggerate expressions and change them more slowly. Visual contact is maintained

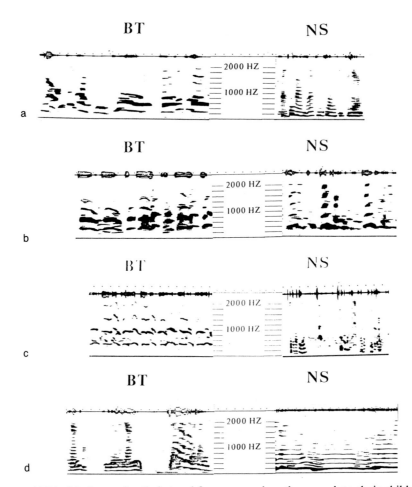

FIGURE 4.23A. Mothers raise their tonal frequency when they speak to their children, and cross-cultural studies suggest the phenomenon is universal. Central European (a) normal speech (NS) falls between 170 and 350 Hz, while baby talk (BT) occurs at 500-850 Hz, approximately one octave higher. The rhythmic structure of BT can clearly be seen in the sonogram. Speech speed reduction (about 50%) is also evident in the amplitude levels shown on the top row of the sonogram. Bushman (b) NS is in the 250-500 Hz range (note their clicking sound patterns). Their BT falls in the 500–1000 Hz range; it is higher pitched than NS, clearer melodically, more simply structured rhythmically, and is half the speed of NS (top spectrograph line). In the Yanomami (c) NS is 180-400 Hz; BT 800–1000 Hz has a more defined melodic character, clear rhythmic structure and overtone pattern, and reduced speed (uppermost spectral line). Eipo (d) speech is highly ritualized, and melodic speech characteristics are barely visible relative to other cultures. Thus NS, song, and BT share a similar melodic structure in which each utterance drops off sharply at its termination, maintaining a single NS frequency of about 200 Hz. BT is elevated (400–500 Hz). Interestingly, BT is rhythmic although its velocity is essentially unchanged. Nonetheless BT displays amplitude variation. From R. Eggebrecht (1983).

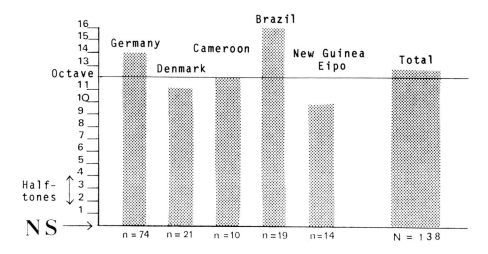

FIGURE 4.23B. Mean frequency difference between baby talk (BT) and normal speech in five cultures. The base line represents mean frequency of normal speech. From R. Eggebrecht (1983).

for a longer time than with adults. The eyebrow movements are accentuated in the eyebrow flash (p. 118), often in conjunction with jesting surprise.[3] We are so accustomed to this behavior that we are no longer even aware of it (Figs. 4.24–4.27). These exaggerated expressions would only be obvious if a woman executed them in all her adult interactions. Stern states that these behavioral patterns are probably species specific, a position that my cross-cultural findings would support.

The basic repertoire of affectionate behavior was identical in all cultures we investigated (p. 136; Section 6.3). We previously cited the kiss, which is not only limited to the mouth region but includes the cheeks and other body parts. Other forms of oral affection, such as licking the sexual organs or blowing with pursed lips, are differentiated on a culture-specific basis. Affectionate nibbling (Figs. 4.28, 4.29) is more widespread and perhaps related to primate behavior. Face to face interactions with head raising, eyebrow raising, and subsequent facial approach or nodding are universal interactional patterns. The mother performing in such a way often speaks in the manner described previously. Mothers fondle their children in all cultures, lift them up or rock them in slumber (Figs. 4.30, 4.31). The rocking, jostling, and lifting of infants, which mothers enjoy doing so much, accommodates the infantile need for vestibular stimulation. An excited infant can be calmed by rocking it. In kin-based societies infants spend most of their time being carried about by the mother or another person. Vestibular stimuli communicate to the infant that he is not alone. Hospitalized children isolated from this stimulus often develop movement stereotypes, like rocking and self-patting, that serves as self-stimulation (E. Thelen, 1980).

---

[3]This reduction in speed of expressive execution also occurs between people who cannot communicate with each other due to cultural differences. Then the eyebrow flash is slowed down and head nodding amplitude is increased.

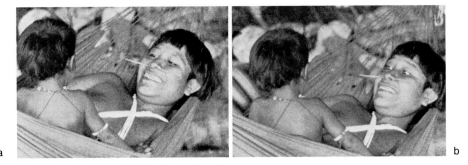

FIGURE 4.24. (a) and (b) Yanomami mother greeting her child with "eyebrow flash." From a 16 mm film. Photo: I. Eibl-Eibesfeldt.

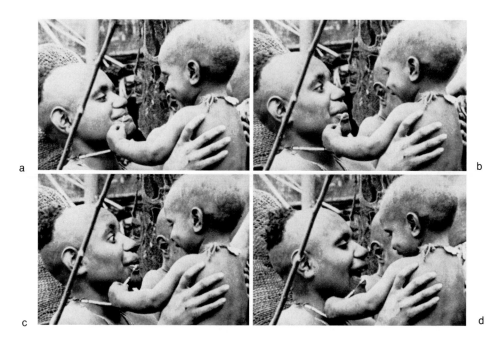

FIGURE 4.25. Eipo woman addressing a child with jesting surprise and eyebrow raising. From a 25 frames/second 16 mm film, frames 1, 10, 14, and 24 of the sequence. Photo: I. Eibl-Eibesfeldt.

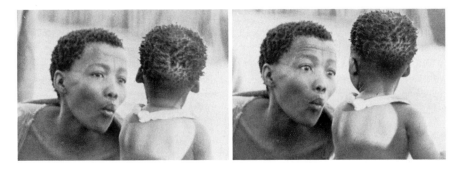

FIGURE 4.26. Bushman woman producing a playful grimace for a child. From a 16 mm film. Photo: I. Eibl-Eibesfeldt.

FIGURE 4.27. Trobriand mother making faces with her child of only a few months of age; she probably tries to attract her child's attention using these striking expressions. From a 25 frames/second 16 mm film, frames 1, 21, and 51 of the sequence. Photo: I. Eibl-Eibesfeldt.

L. Salk (1973) discovered that 80% of all mothers carry their children on the left side. Studies of photographs, paintings, and sculptures indicate that this is a universal phenomenon (O.J. Grüsser, 1983); our photographic results support this as well (see also P. DeChateau et al. 1976, 1978; J.S. Lockard et al., 1979; M.M. Saling and W.L. Cooke, 1984). This phenomenon could be associated with the prevalence of right handedness in all cultures. This frees the mother's right hand for other activities. Adult males show no side preference when they carry infants (J.S. Lockard et al., 1979). L. Salk found that left-handed individuals also carry their infants on the left side. He presumes that the infant becomes conditioned

a

b

c

d

FIGURE 4.28. Nose-rubbing in the Trobriand mother elicits a happy expression on the child's part (play-face), which in turn creates joy for the mother. From a 25 frames/second 16 mm film, frames 1, 9, 26, and 125 of the sequence. Photo: I. Eibl-Eibesfeldt.

FIGURE 4.29. Eipo mother biting her son playfully on the cheek. She observes his reaction and continues oral affection by giving a blow kiss on the child's breast. From a 25 frames/second 16 mm film, frames 1, 13, 70, and 119 of the sequence. Photo: I. Eibl-Eibesfeldt.

to the mother's heartbeat in the uterus and that this sound can have a calming influence on the child after birth. Mothers would learn this fact quickly and thus carry their children on the left side where the heartbeat can be heard more easily. However, H.J. Ginsburg *et al.* (1980) found that infants a few hours old display clear preferences for turning the head. If the infant's head is fixated on the median and then released, it will turn to one side with a clear individual preference. About two-thirds of all infants will turn to the right. Mothers carry these children on the left side. Infants preferring to turn to the left are carried on the right side. Thus in both instances mothers would respond to the infants' preferences, and studies with older children had the same results. It appears that the maternal behavior could reflect the child's head-turning preferences. Although this does not contradict the hypothesis that children are conditioned to the mother's heartbeat while in the uterus, the heartbeat theory seems somewhat farfetched to me. In fact there is a great variety of sounds an infant would hear inside the uterus, and the calming effect of tape recorded heartbeat playback could have an entirely different basis.[4]

A child also perceives its own rhythm. It is also known, for example, that physiological processes in lower vertebrates can be synchronized with rhythmic "Zeitgeber" (time givers). This has been done with goldfish respiration rates using a metronome (J. Kneutgen, 1964). One might also investigate relationships between carrying method and handedness using a larger number of subjects. This

---

[4]According to J.A. Ambrose (1969, verbal communication), the infant is optimally pacified when he is rocked once per second. This corresponds to W. Schiefenhövel's findings of the frequency of normal walking speed. It has yet to be ascertained whether this is a universal frequency of affectionate behavior and whether this effect is derived from the heartbeat or from walking.

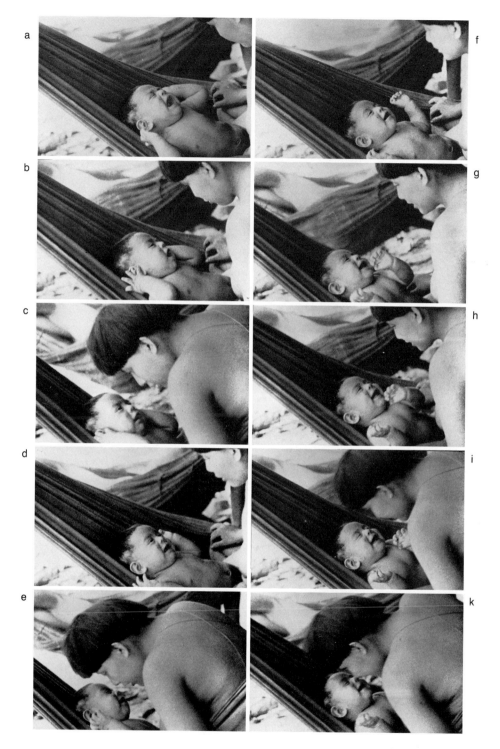

FIGURE 4.30. Comforting via approach, speaking, and contact: a crying Yanomami infant (upper Orinoco). The mother talks to him, bringing her face closer, touching him at the same time on his knee. The infant smiles, and the sequence ends with affectionate nose-rubbing. From a 25 frames/second 16 mm film, frames 1, 42, 63, 99, 118, 141, 174, 182, 190, and 196 of the sequence. Photo: I. Eibl-Eibesfeldt.

FIGURE 4.31. Comforting a crying Eipo infant girl (Irian Jaya/western New Guinea). A woman gives the crying child to another woman sitting on the ground. The mother in the background briefly touches the child on the arm (c) while the sitting woman holds the infant and points toward me as a diversion. The sitting woman then embraces and fondles the child who looks at his slightly injured hand and is quickly calmed. From a 50 frames/second 16 mm film, frames 1, 85, 351, 400, 558, 565, 613, and 711 of the sequence. Photo: I. Eibl-Eibesfeldt.

has always appeared to be a significant factor to me, for it is obviously advantageous for a mother to have her active hand free for domestic duties as she carries her infant about. This is supported by the fact that the children are also preferably carried on the left side when they are borne about on the hips.

In the tribal or kin-based societies children generally have more immediate body contact with the mother than in technological civilized cultures. They are breastfed on demand. Since breastfeeding stimulates prolactin release, it also inhibits follicle budding and thus a premature subsequent pregnancy.

In the Yanomami and the Kalahari Bushmen the author documented mothers and fathers caressing, licking, and otherwise mouthing their babies genitalia, regardless of their sex. This behavior stops, however, as soon as the babies are weaned and is not meant to arouse the babies to orgasm nor is the acting parent working off a sexual arousal. The behavior is an expression of parental affection and also has an hygienic function: Yanomami mothers were observed licking their girls and sucking their little boy's penis in clear intent of cleaning. The behavior should not be mistaken as being sexually motivated. I emphasize this point, since Freud argued that a mother would be shocked if she realized that she was treating her baby as if she or he were a sexual partner. Parents in western society sometimes feel inhibited to express their affection by kissing and mouthing particular parts of their baby's bodies. As previously pointed out, Freud read the direction of the evolution erroneously. Patterns of caressing primarily evolved in the service of parental care and secondarily became incorporated in the repertory of courtship behavior. Affectionate displays are linked with sexual arousal, which is experienced by some mothers during nursing. But it is not a primarily sexual linkage and in most women, according to my inquiries, the quality of the pleasure felt during nursing is said to differ from the sexual arousal felt by nipple manipulation during sexual foreplay. Most important, no incestuous fantasies are experienced during nursing, nor when a father interacts with his baby.

Body contact gives a child trust and security. We can only guess at the effects of the limited body contact occurring in our culture. My impression from working with people in kin-based societies is that the prolonged and intensive degree of body contact results in a strong dependency of infants on their mothers. Weaning often occurs abruptly once the mother knows that she is pregnant again. In Bushmen, a 3- to 4-year period of pronounced affection is followed by a rather dramatic rejection on the part of the mother, who is now fully devoted to the next child. This is often traumatic for the older child and can result in strong sibling rivalry (p. 594; I. Eibl-Eibesfeldt, 1974). In most European countries children become used to independence at a relatively early age. They sleep alone without body contact but tolerate this by using substitute objects for maternal contact while they sleep. Pacifiers, a special blanket, or a doll act as transitional objects offering security. K. Stanjek (1979) found that children in eastern Gabun and southern India do not develop an attachment to substitute objects despite varying weaning times (N'Bono: 13 months; Mottavila and Vizhinyam: 30 months mean time). Thus it is not oral experience but rather the loneliness of a child in bed that is responsible for the need of a substitute maternal object. Randomly sampled children in southern India and eastern Gabun have more social partners than those from a random sample in Munich, Germany, where a smaller number of reference figures exist. Conditions in the United States resemble those in Germany (F. Busch and J. McKnight, 1973). If a child has sufficient affectionate contact, early training

215

Table 4.3. Skin Contact[a]

	Day 1 (21.10.81)	Day 2 (22.10.81)	Day 3 (23.10.81)	Σ	%
Observation time (min.)	633	648	528	1809	100
Skin contact (min.)					
Mother	244	204	119	567	31
Father	98	37	94	229	12
Third party	64	120	117	301	17
Σ (min.)	406	361	330	1097	60
No skin contact (min.)				ca. 712	40

[a] Beres, 18-month-old male infant from highlands of West New Guinea. From W. Schiefenhövel (1984).

for independence has no ill effects for further development. Indeed, this kind of emancipation could foster personality strength.

M. Mead (1965) believed that early childhood contact led to a peaceful disposition, while denial of contact would result in an aggressive, belligerent personality structure. Thus she felt that the Mundugumur were aggressive and warring due to little body contact early in life, while the Arapesh were a peaceful group whose children enjoyed a great deal of body contact.

This generalization is untenable, aside from the fact that the Arapesh are indeed warfaring (R.F. Fortune, 1939). The Masai, Himba, Eipo, and Yanomami, to name just a few examples, offer their children a great deal of contact and affection and yet are warring peoples. Affectionate contact creates a disposition to identify with the reference adult (p. 398), and if they happen to conduct wars the children will also be prepared to do so.

An 18-month-old boy from the aggressive In people (western New Guinea, Wahaldak) experienced an average of 50 individual contacts with various people per sampling day (about 10 hours) on three successive days, and this led W. Schiefenhövel (1984) to speak of a "child-centered interaction turntable" summarized in Table 4.3. They largely confirm our findings in Bushmen (I. Eibl-Eibesfeldt, 1972; see also M. Konner, 1977). The aggressiveness of these adults is not related to any lack of body contact during early childhood.

Three-month-old infants begin to respond to fear-inducing signals of other people. The ambivalence of interpersonal relationships described earlier also occurs in mother–child interactions. After an extended face to face contact with the mother the child will tend to turn away from her momentarily (D.N. Stern, 1971, 1974, p. 208). Stern describes pre-peek-a-boo games beginning at this stage:

> During play a sequence is often observed between mother and infant. In our laboratory we call it the "pre-peek-a-boo-game" with no certainty of its relationship to later peek-a-boo. It consists of the infant looking at the mother, smiling, vocalizing and showing other signs of mounting arousal and positive affects, momentary sobering, and a fleeting grimace interspaced with smiling. The intensity of arousal continues to build up until he suddenly averts gaze sharply with a quick but not extensive head turn which keeps the mother's face in good peripheral view, while his level of "excitement" clearly declines. He then returns gaze bursting into a smile, and the level of arousal and affect build again. He averts gaze, and so on.

Later infants enjoy "now-I'll-get-you" games, in which escape-motivated behavior is acted out. K. Lorenz (1943) described the joy children take in gruesomeness, and B. Bettelheim (1977) adds that this is one reason that children need fairy tales. Many mother–child games are based on acting out this escape motivation. In this connection I wish to add an individual observation from my own close acquaintances. A 3-year-old boy suffered nightmares for some time. With that in mind, his mother invented a game called "The Bad Man Will Get You." The little boy enjoyed this exciting game, and when they repeatedly played this game out just before bedtime the nightmares promptly ended.

The active role of the infant in initiating interactions is significant. Contact initiative occurs quite distinctly at 3 to 4 months of age. The child makes sounds for the mother to come to him, grabbing in the air at her with the arms closing over its chest (Figs. 4.32–4.34). Once the infant can crawl and walk, pointing and reaching objects are incorporated into the repertoire for eliciting contact. In fact this initiation of contact probably even saved the lives of twins in a study of social isolation (W. Dennis, 1941). The experiment dealt with the question of how children develop with a minimum of social contacts. Dennis chose two 5-week-old institutionalized twin girls in this rather dreadful study. During the first 6 months they were kept under rather strict social isolation. The twins were not allowed to see each other, and were cared for by the experimenters without any outward signs of emotion. The experimenters fed, bathed, and put the twins to sleep and conducted their studies but did not respond to their crying and never gave any sign of affection for the twins; they did not smile, cuddle, or fondle the children. Once the subjects were 7 weeks old they began following the experimenters visually, and smiled when the researchers entered the room. The faces of the personnel caring for the children evoked particular attention from the children. Between the ninth and twelfth weeks they began to laugh and flirt, and at 13 to 16 weeks they cried when their attendants left the bedside. At 6 months of age they reacted fearfully to noises and smiled persistently when someone approached them, often babbling as well. In the eighth month one subject was able to touch the hair and face of the chief investigator. After that time the Dennis team submitted to the twins' initiatives for contact. They played with them on a limited basis and permitted the twins to maintain contact with each other while continuing conditions of strict social isolation. Their development was distinctly behind that of other children. One can only hope that this experiment did not have any long-term deleterious effects on the subjects.

4.3.6. Nursing

Human mothers are physiologically adapted to continuous breastfeeding. Their milk has a lower protein and fat content than that of other mammals nursing their young for greater intervals of time. In most kin-based societies infants are breastfed on demand, which, when awake, can be several times an hour (Fig. 4.35). If an infant cries, it is immediately put to the breast; in Bushmen the latency time averages only 6 seconds (M.H. Konner and C. Worthman, 1980). The mechanical stimulation of the nipple releases prolactin; after birth oxytocin is also released, which along with uterine contractions causes the alveolae of the mammary glands to contract and release milk. This is experienced as the "letdown reflex." After a few days, oxytocin production ceases during breastfeeding. Meanwhile the mother has become so conditioned to her child that she no longer requires these

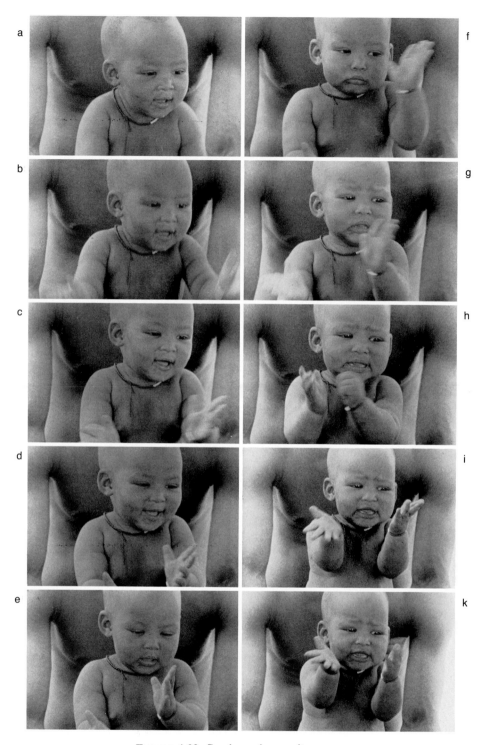

FIGURE 4.32. See legend opposite page.

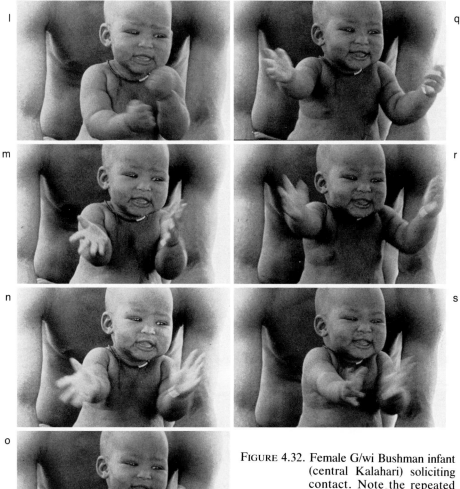

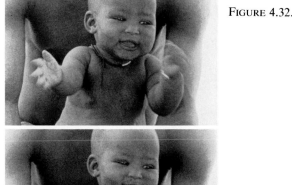

FIGURE 4.32. Female G/wi Bushman infant (central Kalahari) soliciting contact. Note the repeated alternation in expression between affectionate attraction to anger to renewed friendliness and the associated seizing motion of the hands. A child is in control of his expressive repertoire and thus shows communicative competence long before it can walk independently and speak. From a 25 frames/second 16 mm film, frames 1, 12, 24, 34, 60, 148, 162, 166, 177, 180, 183, 186, 192, 196, 199, 202, 206, and 213 of the sequence. Photo: I. Eibl-Eibesfeldt.

FIGURE 4.33. A male Eipo infant (Irian Jaya/western New Guinea) sitting on his mother's shoulder solicits contact from another (in foreground), who likewise signals contact readiness; play-face and embracing intention (spreading the arms). From a 25 frames/second 16 mm film, frames 1, 32, 62, 71, 87, and 1122 of the sequence. Photo: I. Eibl-Eibesfeldt.

FIGURE 4.34. An approximately 1-year-old female infant (Trobriand Islands) soliciting contact with her mother with an embracing intentional movement. From a 16 mm film. Photo: I. Eibl-Eibesfeldt.

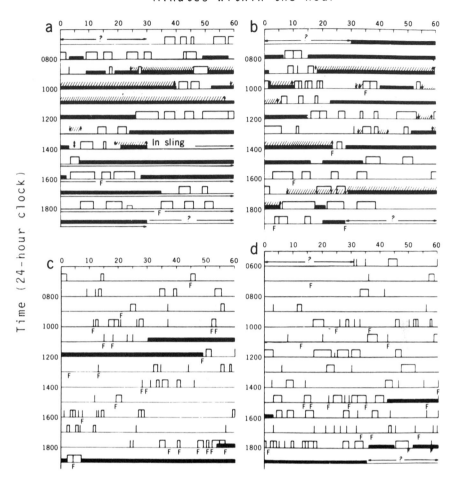

FIGURE 4.35. Four full-day (13-hour) observations of continuous breastfeeding of Kung infants: 3-day (a) and 14-day-old (b) male infant; (c) 52-week-old girl: (d) 79-week-old boy. White blocks with vertical lines, nursing; black thickened lines, sleep. F: angry behavior and crying. Diagonal lines in (a) and (b) indicate the time during which the mother held her child. High vertical lines indicate drinking bouts lasting less than 30 seconds. From M.J. Konner and C. Worthman (1980).

unconditioned reflexes. Prolactin continues to be produced upon any mechanical stimulation of the breast (M.R. Duchen and A.S. McNeilly, 1980; J.E. Tyson *et al.*, 1978). Prolactin production will not occur if the nipples are anesthetized (J.E. Tyson, 1977). However, mechanical stimulation of the breast of nonnursing women will elicit prolactin release (G.L. Noel *et al.*, 1972). During nursing the prolactin level increases up to twenty times, and this elevated level inhibits cyclical hormonal production influencing gonadal functions. This, along with other factors (such as nutrition), explains why the Bushmen women who nurse at short intervals throughout their 3-year nursing period do not become pregnant during this time (R.V. Short, 1984). Frequent nursing *alone* does not seem sufficient to repress ovulation for more than about 20 months.

The sucking rate of the infant has a definite facilitating influence on the mother's

FIGURE 4.36. Playing with the breast. While breastfeeding the infant grabs the free breast of the
mother and manipulates its nipple. This supplementary mechanical stimulation may
enhance prolactin production. (a) Breastfeeding Tasaday (Mindanao/Philippines);
(b) breastfeeding Nursing Himba (southwest Africa); (c) Bushman infant (!Ko, central Kalahari); (d) Balinese; (e) Biami (Papua-New Guinea); (f) !Ko Bushman woman
nursing. Photos I. Eibl-Eibesfeldt.

affectionate behavior. The relationship between the two is linear (D.N. Stern *et al.*, 1977).

Infants with insufficient motivation to suck run the risk of being neglected; breastfeeding mothers are generally more sensitive to their babies. All of this is probably due to hormonal factors related to breastfeeding. However this should not cause anxiety for those mothers whose lactation is disturbed or whose children are not sufficiently motivated to drink enough mother's milk. We have already shown that there are multiple mechanisms ensuring adequate bonding between mother and child, so that mothers who do not breastfeed at all can develop as strong and intense a mother–child relationship as breastfeeding mothers. It is simply important to be aware of all the factors promoting bonding.

Infants when breastfeeding frequently play with the free breast of the mother. The resulting enhanced stimulation may facilitate prolactin production. Furthermore the breast is thereby occupied so that no one else can drink from the mother (Fig. 4.36). The infant regards his mother's breast as a possession to be defended against rivals.

If the periods between breastfeeding are extended the prolactin level can drop so much that gonadal functions are no longer inhibited. Australian aborigines, who breastfeed less frequently than Bushmen, leave their babies with others when they go on gathering excursions. In this group, births occur in shorter intervals than among the Bushmen. Infanticide has been observed among them (F. McCarthy and M. McArthur, 1960; F.G.G. Rose, 1960; J.B. Birdsell, 1968; F. Lancaster-Jones, 1963).

In our culture as a rule we use long intervals between feedings. This leads not only to the physiological consequences for mothers (as stated above) but also can cause digestion problems in the infants, who then consume unnaturally large amounts of milk at one time.

Mothers generally do not distract their infants as they breastfeed. They usually begin talking to them when they finish drinking and release the breast. They listen to the infant's vocalizations and help him when he has difficulties nursing. In traditional societies mothers engage in domestic duties or groom their children while nursing. These activities do not interfere with the infant's drinking, although speaking to the baby often does.

Breastfeeding in traditional societies extends over 3 to 4 years, but infants do receive prechewed supplementary food at an early age (for example, sweet potatoes among the Eipo). Once a sibling is born, nursing may cease abruptly, but the trauma of weaning can be alleviated when the weaned infant enters into a play group of other children (p. 600). The mother remains the basis of security for a long time and children of 6 or 7 years (Bushmen, Himba) will run to seek shelter at the mother's breast when they are frightened or hurt. Children may also suck the breast of other female reference figures for comfort (as from the grandmother in the Eipo).

In traditional societies, mothers treat their children with considerable affection. They stroke, kiss, and delouse them, but will scold when the children do not obey their requests and commands or otherwise fail to live up to their mothers' expectations. To some extent, specific expectations are culturally determined. The Himba, Eipo, and Yanomami expect their boys to grow up to be warriors and thus to be brave and not to cry. Bushmen place less value on these qualities. In general, it appears to irritate mothers when their efforts to comfort their children are in vain. If the baby continues to whine and pout or respond by "cut off" to the comforting efforts of their mothers this will often anger the mother and she

223

Table 4.4. Further Infant Interactions—Some Socialization Strategies

	Day 1 (21.10.81)	Day 2 (22.10.81)	Day 3 (23.10.81)
Crying (ca. 1 sec to 2 min)	16[b]	8	14
Aggressive acts of the child	3	7(1)	10
Request			
Obeyed	11	4	9
Disobeyed	12	9	10
Intervention	18	11	12
Verbal punishment	3(4)[b]	5(4)	6(5)
Corporal punishment	1(1)	3(7)	None(7)
Social grooming	6	3	3
Stroking, kissing, etc.	5	4	3

[a]Beres, 18-month-old male infant from the highlands of New Guinea. From W. Schiefenhövel (1984).

[b]Number indicates number of times an interaction occurred. Number in parenthesis indicates number of times a playful action occurred.

may scold or slap the child. Even in traditional or kin-based societies, the mother will lose her patience if babies nag, misbehave, and dirty themselves continually. Such outbreaks of anger are intense but short-lived, and affectionate interactions are soon reestablished. Aggression is purposefully used for pedagogical means (p. 391), particularly when the child refuses to be obedient in certain situations or behaves in such a way as to endanger himself.

Wulf Schiefenhövel (1984) used a 3-day protocol drawn from the In (western New Guinea) to determine the quantitative distribution of various mother–child interactions. Pedagogical aggression and affection of the mother were about balanced. Scolding predominated in educational aggression, but corporal punishment also occurred. The subject of the study, an approximately 18-month-old boy was somewhat less often obedient than disobedient (Table 4.4).

4.3.7. The Father as Reference Figure, Paternal Behavior

In the cultures we investigated, the father is, next to the mother, an exceptionally significant reference figure. Indeed, although, if given a choice, the child will flee to the mother in fear. However in the Yanomami and Bushmen I have noted repeatedly that children of both sexes protest vigorously when the father leaves in the morning for hunting or for work, even if the mother is staying at home and is thus providing a firm basis of security.

In all cultures I visited I observed that fathers treat their children with tender affection, even in such male-oriented warring cultures as the Eipo, Yanomami, or the Himba. I emphasize this because until recently in our culture it has been considered unmanly to display affection publicly toward an infant. This could be a result of living in anonymous mass society and thus be a fairly recent development, since in rural areas fathers customarily display affection toward their children. In our anonymous society we avoid open displays of our feelings. (p. 177).

In the morning Yanomami fathers play with their children, male and female, for 15 to 30 minutes while their wives tend to domestic tasks. They place their children in the hammock, raise them up, speak to them in the typical high-toned baby talk, kiss, and fondle them. Their repertory of affectionate behavioral patterns is qualitatively identical to that of the mothers. Fathers also feed their children prechewed food. They use social body grooming behavior less frequently than mothers (delousing, cleaning off, removal of pimples, etc.) and engage in more play and athletic activities with the children. The children respond most positively to these play bouts with the father (Figs. 4.37–4.42). They utter cries of joy and babble, giving one the impression that they particularly treasure their moments with their father. These activities also occur when the father returns home toward noon or early in the afternoon, and in the evening before the children are put to

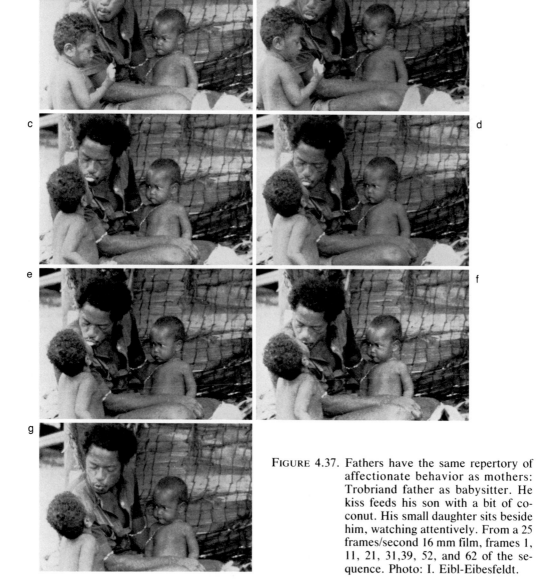

FIGURE 4.37. Fathers have the same repertory of affectionate behavior as mothers: Trobriand father as babysitter. He kiss feeds his son with a bit of coconut. His small daughter sits beside him, watching attentively. From a 25 frames/second 16 mm film, frames 1, 11, 21, 31,39, 52, and 62 of the sequence. Photo: I. Eibl-Eibesfeldt.

FIGURE 4.38. Eipo father (Irian Jaya/western New Guinea) in morning play with his child affectionately air kissing and playing with the ear peg to amuse the small son. From a 16 mm film. Photo: I. Eibl-Eibesfeldt.

bed. Generally a Yanomami youngster has 1–1.5 hours of intensive paternal contact per day. If the father is home he will also pick up an infant for a few minutes to cuddle with him. At night the father often takes a weaned infant into the hammock while the mother cares for the nursing baby. The older child will sleep throughout the night by the father, warmed by his body. This is an important consideration since the Yanomami sleep naked in the hammock and small children could easily become chilled.

M.J. Konner has gathered precise data on contact between !Kung Bushmen and their children. Fathers interacted with their children 13.7% of the total observation time; Table 4.5A (p. 230) provides a detailed summary.

Bushmen supposedly belong to the cultures in which the fathers have the closest contact with their children. It is claimed that fathers have less contact with their children in cultures that practice polygyny, war, and stress paternal obedience. However, I observed equally frequent affectionate father–child behavior among the aggressive Yanomami, Eipo, and Himba. Perhaps some investigators are misled by stereotypes. We recall the descriptions of Margaret Mead, which were dictated by her own bias. In the patrilocal Eipo, a horticulturist people leading a neolithic lifestyle, there is a strong tendency for sex segregation. Men and women gather in the morning before the gardening work begins in separate gathering places in the village. They warm themselves in the sun, play with the children, and chat.

FIGURE 4.39. Eipo (Irian Jaya/western New Guinea) greeting an infant affectionately: repeated contact and for the Eipo typical greeting by waving the raised finger. From a 16 mm film, frames 1, 17, 37, 62, 132, 185, 211, and 304 of the sequence. Photo: I. Eibl-Eibesfeldt.

They occupy themselves with various handicrafts, e.g., the men carving arrows and the women making netbags. Although men and women are spatially separated, they are by no means without contact. They speak to one another, and often a man will come and fetch his infant or young child along to the men's area. For a short time (e.g., one-half hour) the child is the center of a group of men and boys,

FIGURE 4.40A. Even in warlike peoples it is by no means unmanly to spend time with a youngster. Affectionate exchange between a Yanomami (upper Orinoco) and an infant using the "eyebrow flash." From a 16 mm film. Photo: I. Eibl-Eibesfeldt.

FIGURE 4.40B. Yanomami father kissing his small daughter. From a 16 mm film. Photo: I. Eibl-Eibesfeldt.

who all try to please the youngster. The men clearly display their affections, as do the mother's brothers and young boys in the vicinity. The affectionate behavior patterns are equivalent to those of the women. The men cuddle, fondle, and kiss the youngsters, and when they speak to them they do so in an octave higher than normal speech (baby talk, p. 208; Fig. 4.43).

In findings agreeing with those from our own culture, Eipo men feed their infants less often and do not clean them, but they play with them more than the mothers do (R.D. Parke, 1980).

> When the baby coughed, sneezed or spat while feeding . . . fathers were more likely than mothers to simply stop feeding until the baby had settled down and was back under control. The mother was likely to continue feeding and increase touching of the baby, whereas the fathers showed a dramatic drop in this latter area. Despite these differences fathers are sensitive to the baby and respond to the baby in a sensible and competent way. (p. 212)

Mothers feeding their children wipe off their children's hands and face more frequently than fathers in the same situation, and similar differences occur in other routine care behavior (D.B. Sawin, 1981). Fathers in the United States engage in more physical play with their youngsters than the mothers do, whether the children are 3 months or 2 years old. Fathers hold newborns more, shake them more often, and stimulate them more than mothers. Later they engage more in physical games and scuffle with their children (K.A. Clarke-Stewart, 1978, 1980; M.E. Lamb, 1975; M.E. Lamb et al., 1982; D.B. Sawin, 1981; M.W. Yogman, 1981). Mothers,

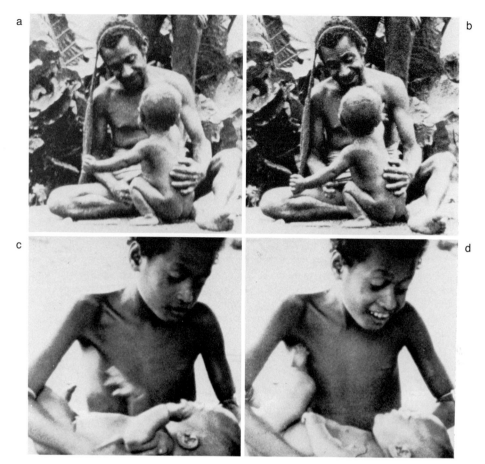

FIGURE 4.41. Eyebrow raising as an affectionate expression is also found in the father–child relationship (a, b) In (Kosarek, Irian Jaya/western New Guinea); (c, d) Trobriand islanders. Brother cuddles with his small sister and addresses her with an eyebrow flash. From a 16 mm film. Photo: I. Eibl-Eibesfeldt.

FIGURE 4.42. Other examples of affectionate behavior in males: (a) Himba (southwestern Africa). (b) !Ko Bushman (central Kalahari). Photo: I. Eibl-Eibesfeldt.

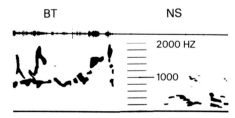

FIGURE 4.43. Males also raise their voice an octave when talking to a baby. Left, baby talk (BT) of a Yanomami male: right, normal speech (NS). From R. Eggebrecht (1983).

Table 4.5A. Frequency of Proximity and Contact[a]

	Father (all observations)	Father (when present)	Mother (always present)
Age: 0–26 weeks			
Body contact	3.80	43.27	123.46
Face/face	0.74	8.46	11.56
Up to 2 ft from reference figure	0.09	1.07	10.54
2–15 ft distance	0.00	0.00	0.11
Age: 27–99 weeks			
Body contact	3.85	32.13	58.41
Face/face	0.25	1.43	3.69
Within 2 ft	2.26	13.00	32.91
2–15 ft distance	0.77	4.41	8.38

[a]Expressed in the mean number of 5-second blocks in which each parent was the primary caretaker for the children during a 15-minute observation period. After M. Maxwell-West and M.J. Konner, 1976.

The number of infant observations with father interaction from which the data of Table 4.5 are derived are presented in Table 4.5B

Table 4.5B. Number of Infant Observations with Father Interaction

	Boys			Girls		
Age (weeks)	Total observations	Father present	%	Total observations	Father present	%
0–26	112	13	11.6	59	2	3.4
27–99	130	29	22.3	94	10	10.6

on the other hand, engage in more verbal play. The children become more aroused by their fathers than their mothers. Although American fathers rock their children more than the mothers do, they smile and kiss them less (R.D. Parke *et al.*, 1975). M.E. Lamb (1976a) observed American fathers and mothers at home and found that mothers played conventional games like goo-goo da-da or with toys. Fathers, on the other hand, played physically active games. Mothers played visual games twice as frequently as fathers, whereby they made motions in front of the children to maintain their attention (46 vs. 20% of all games played with the children; M.W. Yogman, 1982).

In the Kibbutz where child care is the primary task of nonparental caretakers, sex differences in parental behavior were found similar to those in the United States and Sweden. Kibbutz mothers were more likely to vocalize, laugh, display affection, hold, and engage in caretaking than fathers were. This suggests that immediate competing demands on the parents' time do not account for the widely observed sex differences in parental behavior (Sagi *et al.*, 1985).

Parents may play complementary roles in the mother–father–child triad for the child's socialization. "At various stages of development, the father–infant relationship may complement the infant's relationship with the mother and facilitate the development of autonomy by providing a range of novel, arousing and playful experiences for the infant'' (M.W. Yogman, 1982).

Paternal and maternal behavior toward offspring has distinct sexual differences; parents use more affection with the opposite sex and more arousal and play with the same sex. Thus mothers hold their sons more often, and hold them close to the body longer than their daughters, while fathers in contrast display a preference for cuddling their daughters. Women show their daughters toys more often and jostle their daughters more, behavior replicated by fathers with their sons, who play more and use more visual and tactile stimulation than with their daughters. Thus the parents complement each other behaviorally toward their children (R.D. Parke and D.B. Sawin, 1975, 1977).

Parental behavior changes as a child develops insofar as both spend less time with routine care behavior (cleaning the face and hands, etc.) and cuddle less with the infants. But affectionate behavior expressed as kissing and smiling remains unchanged throughout the first 3 months. After the second year, fathers interact twice as frequently with their sons as with their daughters, while mothers display no such differentiation. Boys clearly prefer the father as a play partner once the children are 2 years old; girls prefer the mother (M.E. Lamb, 1977a,b).

In the United States, the father's first contact with a child after birth produces a powerful emotional attachment. Questionnaire responses and interviews show that they develop a strong emotional attachment immediately after first encountering their child, a phenomenon M. Greenberg and N. Morris (1982) call ''engrossment.'' They find their baby beautiful and are attracted to him, experiencing a need to touch the baby, note its individual characteristics, and consider it ''perfect.'' The infant elicits a strong attraction, and fathers immediately after delivery record their feelings as ''elated.'' Feelings of self-worthiness are also improved. The infant's behavior influences paternal reactions, particularly with reference to eye contact. One father reports the following (M. Greenberg and N. Morris, 1974):

> He was sleeping yesterday and his eyes were closed, and as I looked over he opened his eyes, and I moved away and he closed them, and I moved back again—and he opened them. Now I don't know what that is, maybe some kind of telepathy or something, but I just think he knew I was standing over him and he opened his eyes . . . it felt wonderful. This is the closeness that you have with a child knowing that he feels his father is standing over him and he opens his little eyes although he can't see anything. (p. 526)

Other ''responses'' by the infant can elicit affection (M. Greenberg and N. Morris, 1974): ''I put my finger into his little hand and he clasps hold of my finger and squeezes it. That's very encouraging.'' Another father stated: ''You put your finger in its hand and it was holding on . . . and when they just wrapped it up and put it in the cot by the side it immediately took on somebody—somebody that one could look at and touch, and it was moving immediately. I felt suddenly I had a daughter! I didn't just have a baby. This was very satisfying'' (p. 526).

Fathers permitted to touch their child immediately after birth also touch it more often in a play situation 3 months later and fondle it more than fathers lacking such early contact (M. Rödholm, 1981). The initial contact of fathers with their child follows the same pattern as initial maternal contact: after affectionately touching and stroking the extremities with the fingertips the trunk and head are stroked with the fingertips and thereafter with the palm of the hand (M. Rödholm, 1981; L. Abbott, 1975; M. Klaus *et al.*, 1975). M.W. Yogman (1982) made a particularly detailed study of paternal behavior. He also found that fathers' care behavior duplicates maternal patterns. However fathers played with their children for a greater portion of interaction time. W.T. Bailey (1982) speaks of an "evolutionary-based bond" between father and child he terms an "affinity." He distinguishes it from maternal attachment, which also can be reinforced by certain negative stimuli such as the child's crying. While mother–child "attachment" occurs in all mammals, paternal bonding is probably specifically human, excepting only a few New-World monkeys in which the father carries the young and only gives them to the mother for nursing. Bailey notes that 13-month-old children in a room with their mother displayed particularly marked affection upon being reunited with the father after a brief separation. Bailey speaks of a "father-binding strategy."

If we compare the reactions of 3-month-old infants toward unfamiliar fathers and mothers, we find that negative reactions as measured by vertical forehead wrinkles occur in 29.4% of all stranger encounters, but in only 3.9% of all encounters with their mothers and 6.0% with fathers (M.W. Yogman, 1982). Thus there is no doubt that infants can distinguish their parents from other persons at an early stage.

In western culture fathers interact more with their children than the conventional stereotype would have us believe. According to data collected on 231 Toronto families (A. Booth and J.N. Edwards, 1980), when fathers are at home they spend as much time as does the mother with the children. Naturally the total time spent with the children is less since fathers generally work outside of the home for many hours during the day.

Although fathers only devote a small amount of their total time to the children each day, the children are still attached to both parents. In unfamiliar surroundings 12- to 18-month-old infants will initially seek the mother when they encounter strangers. After the end of the second year, mother and father are sought equally (M.E. Lamb, 1967a,b,c). North American children will seek the father when at home if they experience fear of strangers, whereas Eipo, Bushmen, and Yanomami infants consistently prefer the mother in this context. Both parents are important for the emotional development of the child.

Children are aware of parental distinctions at an early age. Thus 15-month-old children asked to select one parent for a game choose the father more frequently than the mother (M.E. Lamb, 1977a), and that even though in the western world the father spends relatively little time with the children. H. Keller (1979) found that paternal time spent with children varies between less than 1 minute per day to 8 hours per week. Paternal behavior undoubtedly has a strong impact on children. Nine-month-old children whose fathers interacted with them a great deal at home could handle the stress of a brief period alone better than children whose fathers did not interact with them much; these children were also more intellectually advanced (R.D. Parke, 1980). The nature of paternal affection varies in our culture with birth order and sex of the child. In Germany, fathers interact with sons more than with daughters, although there now is a tendency to spend time equally with children of both sexes. In the Bushmen, Yanomami, and Eipo, I have the impression that differential attention paid to boys and girls develops over time when the play interests of the children begin differentiating (Section 7.2). Boys often form play groups for hunting and war games, in which adult males occasionally participate. Boys also enjoy participating in adult male activities. Males in all cultures undoubtedly have paternal skills. They display a strong emotional attachment and a need to interact with their children, and are equipped with a repertory of behavioral patterns adapted for this activity and an empathetic understanding for their children. Thus parental behavior is part of the male program. Loving affection imparted by both parents to the child fosters his ability to identify with the culturally determined role of his own sex.

R.N. Adams (1960), M. Mead (1949), and A.S. Rossi (1975) were of the opinion that the father–child relationship arose as a consequence of the marital bond. Thus males assumed their parental role through this route, while women were born mothers. But I have found in all investigated kin-based cultures that boys display a strong emotional attachment to small children, albeit less often than girls. This indicates that we are dealing with a genuine behavior based on an innate disposition.

W.C. Mackey (1979) observed men and women interacting with their children in public squares in nine cultures.[5] He found that although women were together with their children more often men devoted a considerable amount of time to interacting with the children. The sex of the child did not significantly influence paternal behavior (comparing all cultures), but older boys predominated in pure adult male groups, while younger boys were underrepresented. Boys chose mens' company and girls preferred womens' if the adults gathered in sex-distinct groups. In mixed sexual groupings the relationships were more equal. Men and women interacted with children in a similar way and the nature of the interactions was determined more by the age than the sex of the child. W.C. Mackey concludes that there is an autonomous father–child bond independent of the mother–child and husband–wife bond. J. Money and A.A. Ehrhardt (1972) had previously noted that paternal behavior largely resembles maternal and that the only essential difference was that the threshold releasing and maintaining such behavior is higher in men than women. This agrees with our cross-cultural observations.

The fact that paternal behavior belongs to the natural behavioral repertoire in humans does not mean that paternal and maternal roles are interchangeable. Their roles are rather complementary.

However, with the vast diversity of behavior potential in humans, many fathers are fully capable of substituting for mothers even when caring for small children. Yet W.E. Fthenakis (1983) is overzealous with his enthusiasm for fathers when he claims that mothers are by no means better adapted to care for small children than fathers. In support for this he refers to the fact that fathers understand infant signals as well as mothers and respond to them equally well. But this says nothing about motivation and endurance; women, in general, are less aggressive and have more patience than men.

There exists no counterpart to human paternal behavior in Old-World monkeys. Adult males tolerate social exploration and the approach of juveniles, but they do not play with the young, help with feeding, or interact with them in any other caretaking manner. They will, however, defend the young and respond to their alarm cries, which is quite unlike behavior in the canids. Here also the males feed the young and play intensively with them. Perhaps this behavior arose analogously in humans and canids in associating with hunting large prey and sharing the catch (G.E. King, 1980).

---

[5]Ireland, Spain, USA, India, Peru, Karaya Indians (Brazil), Ivory Coast, Morocco, Japan.   233

Summary 4.3

The question of to what extent a family is a natural social unit is a much discussed topic. An ethological investigation discloses phylogenetic adaptations operating at several levels implying that there is an innate disposition for family structure. These adaptations allow for cultural modification within a specific framework.

Mother and child are bonded to each other with a series of signals and behavioral patterns that belong to the innate human repertory. Both partners are disposed to develop a strong personal attachment. In tribal societies the mother is also the distinct reference figure, if not the only one. The fact that a child develops within a differentiated social network and has many contacts with others does not mean that a child is brought up collectively without having an individual reference figure. The claim that motherliness is a recent innovation can be easily refuted with ethnological data. This is an ethnocentric viewpoint reflecting the ideological position of those few who would prefer to see society formed on the basis of their personal perception.

Mothers attempt to establish visual contact with their child immediately after birth, and the infant's reactions facilitate these efforts. Given an opportunity to interact shortly after delivery, the mother will experience a powerful affection and attachment toward her infant. Hormonal mechanisms probably contribute to this phenomenon. If such contact cannot be made, similarly powerful bonds can develop with time, because the attachment process is secured in a number of different ways.

As for giving birth, familiar surroundings ease the delivery process, while fear (as for example in clinical settings) makes delivery more difficult. Support of the mother by intimate reference persons is widespread among tribal people.

The interaction pattern between mother and child, e.g., face to face interaction, speaking to the child in a higher tone, dialogue type, fondling, and kissing is universal as are the child's responses. Fathers possess essentially the same affectionate behavior repertoire as mothers, also speaking to their children with baby talk one octave higher than normal; those in warfaring societies also cuddle and kiss their children of both sexes. Fathers are important reference figures for children, and infants display pain of separation when the fathers leave them alone with their mothers, as for example when they leave for the hunt. Even though father spend relatively little time with their children in traditional and modern societies, their regular play contact with their children is highly significant for the childrens' emotional development.

In kin-based societies, children experience a great deal of body contact; they are breastfed for 3 to 4 years. The often abrupt weaning occurring when a sibling is born can be traumatic. An extended nursing period, which is important for healthy development, in people lacking milk substitutes makes the child dependent on its mother for longer periods than in our culture. In contrast, the western pattern provides early training for independence.

Early childhood body contact and warm relationships with the reference figure have occasionally been associated with a peaceful nature, while a lack of affection and body contact allegedly led to aggression and warfaring tendencies. Such simple relationships do not exist. Even warring peoples like the Eipo or Yanomami offer their children a great deal of love and physical contact. A child learns from parental affection and warmth to identify with his parents' values and his group, whether these be aggressive or peaceful. A lack of warmth and absence of attachment to a reference person inhibits such identification and fosters asocial aggressive traits.

4.4. Family and Marriage

The mother–child–father triad is the nucleus of the human family and society, a family type scarcely found in primates and other higher mammals. Human family triads are generally extended by the grandparent generation, who play an important role in the world of the children. In many cultures their relationship to the children is of quite a different nature than the child–parent relation, namely, less formalized. Parents often carry the burden of education and, therefore, demand respect (p. 294). Grandparents are indulgent with their love and do not see discipline as one of their major roles.

We know of no human group that lives without permanent marital partnerships, and in most instances one man lives with one woman in a marital tie. There are other forms of marriage though: of 849 societies surveyed (P.M. Murdock, 1967), 708 (83.5%) were potentially polygynous. Only 137 (16%) were monogamous by law and 4 were polyandrous. This survey could give the impression that polygyny is the typical marital form for humans. But even within polygynous societies only leaders and wealthy men usually have more than one wife and within polygynous societies monogamous marriages are 2.5 times as frequent as polygynous ones.[6] Polygynous marriages in Bushmen comprise at most, 5% of all marriages (M.M. West and M.J. Konner, 1976), and most of these result from the fact that a man is obligated to marry his brother's widow. The expression "polygyny" is misleading, since in most polygynous societies men are rarely married to more than two wives.

Nonetheless the data indicate a clear tendency toward polygyny. In monogamous societies polygyny is expressed in the form of extramarital relationships, which in some cultures are even permissible. In the western world polygyny is concealed by the pattern of serial monogamy (divorce, remarriage). This strikes me as the least successful solution to creating legal polygyny since the consequence of western divorce is that the children lose a reference figure.

The polygynous inclination can be explained by the fact that males have a higher reproductive potential, a woman being restricted in the number of children she can bear and raise. A man can produce many children, and if he has the means he can provide for them as well. This would foster the propagation of the genes of those who are in a position to control the natural resources, thus leading consequently to the development of polygyny and patriarchal societal structure. The spread of egalitarian ideologies (p. 13), which foster monogamy, counters this trend.

Promiscuous small groups arise only occasionally as alternatives to the traditional family, and none of the groups, to our knowledge, uses this form of group life as a norm. There are sound reasons to believe that promiscuous groupings were never typical for *Homo sapiens*. Man is emotionally and in his sexual physiology adapted to a marital, long-term relationship. In all nonanthropoid apes, sexual behavior is restricted to brief fertile periods. Males do not copulate with females outside of these fertile periods. Occasional exceptions do occur in the anthropoids. Chimpanzee females seeking precedence at feeding sites present themselves sexually by turning their hind ends toward the males and they are mounted (R.M. and A.W. Yerkes, 1929). Here begins a certain emancipation of female sexual behavior from its original purpose of reproduction—it can be used instrumentally.

---

[6]G.P. Murdock and D.R. White found that 1% of all marriages are polyandrous (one woman married to several men), 17% are monogamous, 51% are occasionally polygamous and only 31% are strictly polygamous.

This emancipation of sexual behavior is already well developed in humans, for the sexual act has been extended into the realm of partner bonding, and with that the woman's capacity and emotional disposition for intercourse outside the fertile period has likewise developed. She provides the reward by satisfaction that strengthens the male's bond, while her orgasm strengthens her attachment to her partner. In mammals, female orgasm is known to occur in only a few primates (D.A. Goldfoot *et al.*, 1980).

Continual sexual readiness in males, with minor fluctuations, is also indication that human sexual behavior serves bonding purposes. The "hypersexualization" of humans has occasionally been criticized morally, but those critics overlook the fact that sexuality has transcended reproductive functions and has achieved an additional role in bonding, something that has posed a problem for many church discussions of birth control (I. Eibl-Eibesfeldt, 1970a; D. Morris, 1968; W. Wickler, 1969). The generally reliable church practice of studying nature to determine behavioral norms fails to reach the entire issue since an examination of animal behavior would neglect man's unique role in sexuality. In animals the sexual act is exclusively for procreation; in humans it has a supplemental bonding function. This new function, which is specifically human, is as important as the procreative function of sexuality. Selection forces that have programmed mankind for long-term marriage probably came about from the need of extended care for children, for which the father's role has long been underappreciated in the literature.

Undoubtedly, both human sexes have the capability of caring for children. This fact, plus the adaptations for heterosexual partnerships mentioned earlier, suggest that the lasting familial bonds are typical for *Homo sapiens*. The earlier sociological thesis that primitive cultures practiced group marriages within which sexual freedom prevailed has long been discarded. This form of group partnership does certainly not conform to human disposition and recent attempts to live this kind of lifestyle have repeatedly failed when partners fall in love with other individuals. Thus humans have a distinct monotropic disposition. Nonetheless there are persistent attempts to demonstrate that the patriarchal family is unnatural and repressive and thus should be dissolved. One of the favorite sources for proponents of this view is F. Engels (1884), drawing upon L.H. Morgan (1877) and J.J. Bachofen (1861), who developed the theory that natural matriarchal group marriages developed out of economic necessity into patriarchal monogamous families. He saw this as a victory of private possession, which was then transmitted to one's heirs contrary to the natural order of group ownership. Although Engels regretted that as a result of this development woman's status declined, he considered as positive that modern individualized sexual love had arisen from monogamy which, as he believed, did not exist before.

It is known that marriage exists among hunters and gatherers, although they generally have no possessions to pass down. Close studies of such peoples also indicate that the young people fall in love. The love songs of "savages" are particularly tender. Thus individual sexual love did not just arise in recent times. The great theoretician Engels was unconsciously biased by his own ethnocentrism.

Engels's thoughts about the family are today of historical significance for having provoked new avenues of thought, especially regarding the emancipation of women within industrial society. If a family-less social state ever existed, an institutional *tabula rasa* of the primitive band (H. Tyrell, 1978), such conditions predated mankind.

The nearest approach to such family-less state are found in our closest relatives, the chimpanzees, who live in territorial closed groups comprising several males, females, young, and juveniles (p. 322). Groups are structured according to rank hierarchy relationships and there are no long-term sexual partnerships. Chimpanzees are promiscuous, but there are also strong mother–child attachments lasting until puberty. Juveniles long since weaned visit their mothers for years (J. van Lawick-Goodall, 1968) and demonstrate clear signs of affection and attachment. Chimpanzee bands are patrilocal. Only females, usually during their first estrous, emigrate to other groups (J. Goodall, 1986).

If we were to assume that the forefathers of *Homo sapiens* lived in this manner, it would mean that the family or the familialization of mankind is a recent evolutionary development. But it would not follow that the new adaptations associated with familialization could not be genetically (phylogenetically) fixed. Nonbiologists often commit the error of interpreting human behavioral adaptations, which are not found in nonhuman primates, as solely cultural, an untenable generalization. Just as many morphological and physiological human characteristics are recent phyletic adaptations but nonetheless phylogenetic, so many of the behavioral peculiarities specific for *Homo sapiens* recently acquired phylogenetic adaptations and are thus inborn.

H. Tyrell (1978) formulates an interesting theory to explain the development of the family, which are thoroughly acceptable if we disregard the fact that he postulates purely cultural adaptation stages. Tyrell begins with the premise that the matriarchal family is the initial entity, a special feature being that mothers are bonded even to children who are no longer physiologically dependent upon them. Tyrell states that within this family structure there was an archaic discovery of blood relationship. Mothers discovered that their offspring had their same flesh and blood, and thus arose the idea of relationships. Obviously the development of an attachment to offspring need not originate from a cognitive awareness of genetic relationships. Chimpanzees also have attachments lasting for years beyond physiological dependency (J. van Lawick-Goodall, 1975). Here we may exclude insights into the identity of flesh and blood between mother and children as an origin of bonding. However, the selective advantages of such attachment behavior are evident. The extended period of childhood and adolescence, made possible for parental care, enables the young to absorb complex cultural traditions that humans need to live. Clearly we are, by nature, programmed through phylogenetic adaptations to be cultural creatures. If we disregard Tyrell's speculations about cognition of blood relationships, evidence would be rather strong that the matriarchal family with children of various ages launched the development of the human family. This matrilineal connection is still recognized in our patriarchal culture in that the wife as a rule takes custody of children in divorce proceedings. A lasting marital partnership may have developed out of this protofamily structure. However it is a species-typical characteristic for contemporary mankind and, like adaptations in reproductive physiology and behavior, somewhat phylogenetically programmed.

A number of adaptations determining interpersonal relations are also found in lower primates and will be discussed in the sections on territoriality, rank order, and ownership. C. Vogel (1977) writes:

> On the basis of the latest findings in primate sociology . . . it is increasingly likely that a whole range of cultural norms, traditions and institutions that are essentially universal are not the result of "rational" human invention but rather institutionalized embodiments and differentiations of social behavioral tendencies already phylogenetically existent in the prehuman sphere. That is, they have a precultural crystallization nucleus. This is even more likely for the in principle transcultural (with detail differentiation!) sex role polarization and the "mother-centered" nuclear family. (p. 22)

237

Summary 4.4

Lasting marital partnerships and inclusion of more than one generation characterize the human family, and a family-less society probably never existed in *Homo sapiens*. In chimpanzees mother and young remain bonded even after the children are adults. A similar matrilineal structure may have launched the development of the human family. The familialization of the male is a recent development of the human species but is already genetically based upon a series of adaptations. Cultural variations of marriage exist, with polygynous societies prevailing. But even in polygynous societies, only a relatively small percentage of men have more than one wife. To this extent monogamy appears to be a trend. Societies lacking marital relationships do not exist.

4.5. Pair Formation, Courtship, Sexual Love

bakasirasi vaponu
  We take the wave

bakavamapusi vana
  We exchange the fragrant herbs
  in our bracelets

bakavagonusi buita
  We pluck the wreath

From the Dorai song cycle of
"Milamala," the harvest festival
of the Trobriands (G. Senft,
tape recording T 3A-1982)

Das macht, es hat die Nachtigall
Die ganze Nacht gesungen;
Da sind von ihrem süssen Schall,
Da sind in Hall und Widerhall
Die Rosen aufgesprungen.

Sie war doch sonst ein wildes Kind;
Nun geht sie tief in Sinnen,
Trägt in der Hand den Sommerhut
Und duldet still der Sonne Glut,
Und weiss nicht, was beginnen.

Theodor Storm

Man cultivates all facets of his natural behaviors and thus distinguishes himself from the animals. That the realm of sexuality motivates man to the most subtle expressions of art, may be in part explained by the paramount importance of sexual behavior for bonding. Man belongs to those few species in which a lifelong sexual bond is established, the need for this deriving from the slow development of the human child, necessitating many years of parenting.

Beneath the cultural layer, so characteristic of man, there are two biological strata determining human sexual behavior, the oldest being the archaic layer of agonistic sexuality, characterized by male dominance and female submission. This "reptilian heritage" still determines certain aspects of human sexual behavior. It is controlled, however, by affiliative sexuality, which is mammalian heritage, and by individual bonding. A predominance of the archaic agonistic sexuality gives raise to certain pathologies (p. 258).

Probably unique for man is the phenomenon of falling in love, whose physiology is not yet understood at all. Scientific study of human sexual behavior is all too frequently limited to the sex act (A.C. Kinsey *et al.*, 1948, 1966; W.H. Masters and V.E. Johnson, 1966). The ethologically more interesting phases of heterosexual contact initiative, courtship, and falling in love, have only recently been given

238

attention (D. Morris, 1977; M. Cook, 1981; R.A. Hinde, 1984; M.M. Moore, 1985).

M.R. Liebowitz (1983) developed a number of interesting thoughts on the physiology of falling in love. He states that the euphoric perception of those in love could arise from a chemical change in the brain caused by the production of the cerebral phenylethylamine, a compound closely related to the stimulant amphetamine.

The earliest phases of pair formation indicate that man is disposed toward marital long-term partnerships. Falling in love is often celebrated in poetry due to its astonishing dynamics, which often transcend reason. Love is one of the universals, yet one often hears that it is a modern invention, as in the words of N. Luhmann (1982) when he writes: "It is sociological common knowledge that the communal living conditions of earlier societies had little room for intimate relationships. . . ." (p. 198).

E. Shorter (1977) states this position even more clearly in attempting to demonstrate that the farmers and property owners of 18th century France, England, and Germany had not experienced romantic love. Marriage was based on social position and means. Much of this was undoubtedly accurate, but to generalize broadly that love is a modern invention is a bit premature and grossly ethnocentric. Tribal peoples are well acquainted with romantic love. And even when marriages were not formed from initially loving relationships, they tended to result nonetheless in affectionate relationships between partners.

Ethnological literature occasionally portrays intimate relationships in tribal societies as superficial as well. Margaret Mead (1935, 1949) reported that Samoan love relationships were promiscuously alternating and lacked firm partner attachments, but her statements did not stand up to critical review. Derek Freeman's (1983) carefully sampled data showed that Mead's viewpoint of Samoan love life was incorrect.

The female partner in love with a male typically responds with "coy" resistance. This is probably based on the previously discussed ambivalence occurring in interpersonal relationships but is enhanced in a ritualized manner and forces the man to expend a great deal of effort and time to win his woman.

W. Wickler and U. Seibt (1977) point out that species living in long-term sexual partnerships are not generally bonded until after an extended courtship. The greater the effort the male must expend, the more important it is for him to keep that partner at a later time, otherwise the cost of courtship would outweigh the benefits. The coyer the female partner, the more valuable she becomes in terms of invested courtship efforts, up to an optimal level. The responses of the partner being courted determine the course of courtship. By her coyness a woman also tests the male's readiness (preparedness) to invest into the relation as well as his characteristics as provider and protector. From a sociobiological point of view, her investment by the physiological burden and risk of pregnancy and birthgiving is much higher than that of the male, and this of course reflects itself in gender characteristic behaviors (R.A. Hinde, 1984). There can be little doubt that the sex differences in behavior reflect evolutionary pressures, and that the tactics of self-presentation, criteria for mate choice, and strategies used in the development of relationships correspond to different "ultimate necessities" in both sexes.

In an experiment with German young adults (K. Grammer, in press) found distinct sex differences. The subjects, who did not know each other before the experiment, were left alone in a room and filmed through a one-way mirror. After 10 minutes, a questionnaire was presented, which assessed two main dimensions:

subjective ratings of attractiveness of the partner, the readiness to date the partner, and the probability (risk) of acceptance by the partner. As predicted by socio-biological theories, females are more choosy than males. Males show an overall greater willingness to date a female, which is dependent on the rating of the partner's attractiveness in both sexes: the higher the rating of attractiveness, the higher the risk perception and the greater the willingness to date the partner. But whether the male initiates contact also depends on his self-esteem. If she is too attractive he might consider his chances low and accordingly refrain from courting in order to save face. Only males, who are more overtly competitive than are females, take their own attractiveness into account for risk perception: the more attractive they rated themselves, the lower the risk they perceive. In questionnaires presented to same-sex dyads as controls, this relationship was not observed.

A high rate of laughing signified interest of a woman to join the young man; laughing together signalled communality. But laughter is not the sole criteria. The content of the statements preceding the laughter were remarks about the immediate situation and refer to the speaker himself. Females laugh more than males when they talk about others. A second dimension is the qualification of statements. Males use more qualifying parts of sentences than females, while females use them less or not at all. Males use positive qualifiers in their statements, while females use negative ones. Thus, males laugh about positive self-presentation, and as predicted use self-presentation more often than females. In addition, verbal self-presentation varies with perception of risk. Males are more indirect the higher they perceive the risk of female nonacceptance. When perceived risk is high, they avoid the use of "I did, I will, etc." Instead, they use the inclusive "we," or even no personal pronouns.

Thus, tactics of male self-presentation depend on risk perception, generated by ratings of attractiveness of the partner. Although males take the verbal initiative and present themselves verbally as potential mates, the episodes are structured by the female's nonverbal behavior. Thus females control the structure of the episodes by manipulation of male risk perception and encourage or impede male self-presentation. According to biological theories, females show a great degree of selectivity, whereas males tend to advertise overtly due to the pressures of male–male competition.

There are also important nonverbal signs, which indicate contact readiness during the opening phase. Thus, when males and females folded their raised hands behind the neck thus exposing their acillae this indicated readiness for contact (Fig 4.44). Other signs of contact readiness were all kinds of "open" positions (legs open, arms open), presentation signals by which secondary sex characteristics such as the breasts were visually presented, and orientation toward the partner. Males respond to the signals of the female partner, but pay particular attention to signs of nervousness, such as self-grooming, which betray genuine interest (K. Grammer, in press).

Looking at the universal features of courtship behavior we find that the reticence of females is overcome in stages and by means of a variety of universal strategies. Direct questions are usually avoided.

One must regard with great skepticism the claims that tribal people normally approach each other directly (C.S. Ford and F.A. Beach, 1969). B. Malinowski (1922) ascribed this behavior to the Trobriand islanders, but obviously never questioned female subjects. I. Bell-Krannhals (1984) found that direct questions

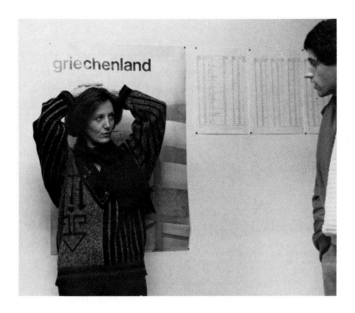

FIGURE 4.44. One position indicating openness for contact. It is also a position of relaxation; this is probably indicated and signalled by the posture. The photograph was a candid snapshot. Photograph by Ch. Doermer. From K. Grammer (in press).

were rarely used. Trobriand men court mainly with songs and by means of persons acting as mediators.

The reason for using the indirect approach is that this strategy leaves open alternatives. In forming any social relationship the partners seek to preserve their own decision-making ability and thus to save face. At the same time, each partner tries to win the other over to his own interests and thus foster common goals, which requires subtlety. If indirect suggestions are rejected, the relationship remains intact. Such is also the case when a man uses a mediator.

It is important that the approach strategies be subtle ones if the partners are not yet well acquainted. Visual contact is important for initiating contact at a distance. One communicates to the partner that he is the focal point of interest. The prominent white eyeball enables us to perceive partners' eye movements quite readily (Fig. 4.45). Eye contact return is a sign of a positive response, but alone is uncommitted. Affection and interest are also indicated by the eyebrow flash.

In the succeeding contact conversations the partners test each other's interest in further contact. The cultural scope of these encounters varies, and approach strategies vary with the degree of existing acquaintance. If the partners are unacquainted, they will attempt to develop a *common reference system*. Common interests are determined and compatibility is expressed. D. Morris (1977) writes that courting individuals nod to one another a great deal. However it is not unusual that the one being courted expresses different opinions and thus tests through exploratory aggression the earnestness of the partner's efforts as well as his self-control.

The partners' next step is to *construct a basis of trust*. One confides in another partner by disclosing one's weaknesses, but always in conjunction with a *positive projection of self*, which I distinguish as *courtship display* from *dominance display*.   241

In the latter one attempts to achieve a dominant position relative to the other interacting party. In courtship display the male attempts to demonstrate that he is in a position to dominate others and thus to protect his partner. This elevates her esteem for him. Konrad Lorenz describes an interesting analogy of greylag ganders attacking other ganders and then "triumphantly" running to their courtship object while continuing to threaten a fictious enemy. Thus, the courtship threat display is meant to impress the partner without being directed at her.

Demonstrating dominance over the social environment, which can occur in a variety of ways, is not the only way to present a positive self-image. One also represents oneself as a competent and reliable provider, for example, by means of displaying material goods (wealth, etc.) and by caregiving expressions. Finally,

FIGURE 4.45.
The large white eyeball permits us to perceive optical signals of others accurately: reaction of a young Indian woman to a compliment—affection and timidity are juxtaposed. From a 50 frames/second 16 mm film, frames 1, 57, 83, 146, 184, 232, and 286 of the sequence. Photo: I. Eibl-Eibesfeldt.

the man (and the woman as well) presents himself through infantile appeals as a suitable object for caregiving which complies with the wish for mutual care.

Love poetry and songs reveal that the verbal cliches of courtship are universal. In Medlpa (New Guinea) love songs, the female partner is addressed by the male as a "young bird," a tender diminutive also used in western culture. Positive self-presentation, appeals for attention, and infantile appeals during courtship are common in all cultures. What is considered a positive projection of self varies culturally. In warlike cultures, for example, it is bravery. In others it may be wisdom and knowledge or skill in hunting.

Body contact is brought about in a noncommital manner. In some cultures custom offers opportunity for contact, as in dance. When contact occurs outside of such a societal context the man generally takes the initiative often by utilizing a quasi-accidental and harmless contact, as for example laying a shawl over the woman's shoulder or otherwise offering assistance that the partner may invite in a subtle way.

The man usually makes the proposition and the woman makes the decisive selection by accepting or rejecting her suitor. This does not exclude her from taking an initiative as they flirt. The role of the woman during courtship varies considerably from culture to culture. Thus statements about "human nature" in this regard are speculative.

The barriers of intimacy are broken when the further behavior of embracing, stroking, and kissing are initiated. Of course, we kiss our children and fondle them out of paternal, maternal, or friendly motivation. But in heterosexual contacts these affectionate expressions introduce sexual foreplay, which leads to sexual union upon touching and stroking the erogenous zones. Thus the standards of modesty, which exist in all cultures, are breached. These behavioral patterns of physical affection are found in various cultures, even in those that were obviously not influenced by Europeans (Fig. 4.46). Thus oral affection with mouth-to-mouth contact (kissing) is found in Peruvian ceramics dating from pre-Columbian times (F. Kauffmann-Doig, 1979).

Affectionate kiss feeding is also observed in diverse cultures. In the Kamasutra lovers are described sipping wine mouth-to-mouth. A. Strathern related to me that Viru lovers (southern highlands of Papua/New Guinea) utilize mouth-to-mouth feeding (and even have an expression for it: "Yangu peku"). We lack a word for this but execute it occasionally. Embracing, stroking erogenous zones, fondling, and social grooming are all universally practiced (I. Eibl-Eibesfeldt, 1970). Many tribal people groom each other during sexual foreplay.

In many cultures these intimate contacts are preceded by formalized courtship rituals, particularly in those cultures that do not permit premarital sex in an effort to prevent illegitimacy. In these situations the society arranges partner contacts. In the Medlpa of New Guinea the parents of marriageable girls invite potential husbands to a *tanim het*. The colorfully decorated partners sit in pairs in a communal room. They sing and after introductory head swaying rub foreheads and noses, always twice. Then they bow deeply twice, rub noses two more times, and continue the courtship dance by alternating bowing and rubbing noses. This "head rolling" is a courtship dance during which course the partners synchronize their movements. The song itself does not impart the rhythm. The partners develop a common rhythm during the dance (T.K. Pitcairn and M. Schleidt, 1976). The easier they obtain movement synchrony, the better the partners seem to adapt to each other, as synchronization serves to express harmony. This also operates in pair dances found in western culture.

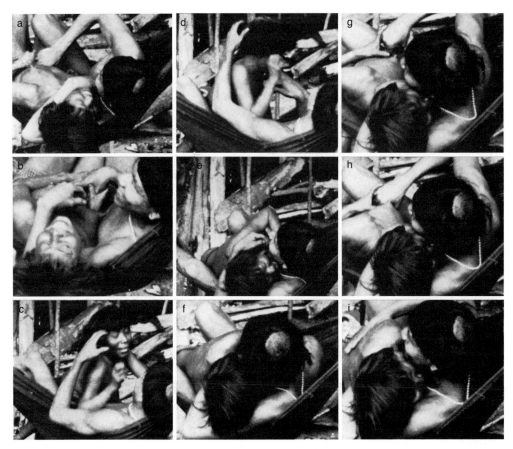

FIGURE 4.46. A flirting Yanomami couple. The playful withdrawal of the woman and her simultaneous attraction can be discerned readily in her expression (play-face). In this series the man makes the initiative first, then the woman. Their playful jostling reflects the conflict between attraction and coyness. I have selected this example from the Yanomami because one occasionally hears that they would not display any mutual attraction in heterosexual relations, which is certainly false. From a 25 frames/second 16 mm film, frames 1, 136, 622, 629, 646, 700, 987, 991, and 1062 of the sequence. Photo: I. Eibl-Eibesfeldt.

Heterosexual pair formation thus takes place in several stages whose course depends on the degree of existing acquaintance. In the phase of contact initiative one partner subtly signals interest to the other; the response leads to further approach. The man particularly maintains a positive projection of himself whereby he also presents himself as trustworthy to overcome personal shyness. R.A. Lewis (1972) states that middle-class Americans utilize various steps of pair formation in which they initially (1) find points in common (values, interests, personality characteristics determined by sociocultural means). Then (2) the pair relationship is established, which is expressed by ease of communication, positive mutual evaluation, and satisfaction with the relationship. Then follows the formation of (3) trust and mutual candor with defined role compatibility (4) and (5) role adaptation (fine tuning of role compatibility, complementarity of roles, needs, similarities, and agreements). Finally, this leads to (6) pair bonding expressed in elaborated interactions, behaving as a dyad, showing mutual responsibility, and pair identity.

L.A. Kirkendall (1961) questioned 200 male subjects in the United States on these events. Self-projection plays a major role in the first phases of contact initiative, but the way it is expressed varies. Importance is attached to the projection of a good impression, and the introduction of the courted partner to one's friends. Another method consists of allowing oneself to be seen by others with a girl. This demonstrates that one is desired and thus challenges other girls. Often a relationship is tested at the start by asking little favors.

The rich cultural elaboration of courtship procedures is based upon an innate repertoire of expressive movements and elemental interaction strategies, as we have shown previously. It has often been discussed whether love is a necessary prerequisite for marital pair formation, and it is often pointed out, quite accurately, that many peoples arrange marriages. In these situations the partners typically become acquainted just a short time prior to their marriage. But it would be incorrect to assume that love does not exist among such peoples. It often develops during the marriage, whereby the sexual relationship may play a significant role.

In all cultures investigated in this respect, human sexual behavior is regulated by specific prohibitions. Initially mutual attraction is comprised of a high level of sexual interest combined with curiosity. Thus sexuality has the potential to disrupt the harmony of the community. Since inborn restraints (controls) seem insufficient, cultural ones come into play. They may also have prevented selection pressures which would have shaped instinctual controls. On one hand, this allows for great flexibility, but, on the other, it must be the source of many problems (including pathologies) since cultural restrictions are easily broken, particularly, if they are very repressive. In this regard, *Homo sapiens* is a culturally molded primate, for which he is well disposed by his genuine friendly nature. However, his biological programs are not sufficient to ensure harmonious family and group life.

Sexual morality usually contains a double standard in that males have more freedom than females. For example, in almost all cultures, adultery by women is more strongly disapproved of than by men and there may be sociobiological grounds for this. The man, as the provider for wife and child, must ensure that he is indeed caring for his own genetic heritage since he is making a substantial investment in the family. If he also deposits his genes elsewhere he is fostering his own genetic survival. The woman, on the other hand, must ensure that her husband maintains the responsibility of a caretaker and keeps her affection for her. The question of whether this selective pressure produces differential dispositions toward fidelity, despite the natural sexual interest of both sexes, has not yet been answered. It appears as if women have a stronger tendency to bond with a single partner, as if they are by nature more monogamous than men, while men are faithful to an individual partner, but not as strictly monogamous. Women certainly also have appetences to enter into extramarital relations, for they too are sexually curious, even if less so than the male. M. Shostak's (1982) brilliantly written autobiography of Bushman women is quite revealing in this respect.

Rules governing sexual behavior vary from culture to culture, and in our western world we often interpret this as a reason for slackening our customary sexual discipline. Some of our cultural restrictions may indeed be passé due to new techniques in birth control and thus the possibility of enjoying the bonding role of sexuality without the reproductive role. But before we casually throw all the restrictions overboard in the name of liberalism, we must clearly understand that cultural regulations are adaptations to the unique requirements of human groups evolving at a specific time and under specific economic, climatic, and social contingencies. These adaptations have survival value! New environmental conditions may make their modification desirable, but we should always consider their adaptive value. Cultural practices concerning sexuality are flexible but only within certain limits if societies are to reproduce themselves, maintain harmony, and thus survive.

Sexual modesty is another cultural universal element of behavior. It is found in all cultures and is expressed in various ways. The sexual organs are often covered by clothing, although there are people who, in our view, walk about completely naked. One example is the Yanomami, whose women wear only a thin cord around their waists (Fig. 4.47). But even this cord is symbolic "clothing." If a Yanomami women is asked to remove the cord she becomes just as embarrassed as a woman in our culture would be if she were asked to remove her clothing.

Yanomami men wear a cord around their foreskin by which they fasten their penis to their abdomen and they become embarrassed if the cord loosens. In their culture "clothing" is adapted to the moist, warm rain forest climate. It is likely that hip (waist) cords are vestigial articles of clothing as the Yanomami ancestors probably did not transverse the cool Bering Strait naked.

Modesty demands that one conceal sexual activity from others. A number of attempts have been made to identify the origin of modesty. B. Hassenstein (1982) states that we would want to cover this unattractive part of the body. But is it not more likely that people cover their sex organs around others with whom they have no sexual contact in order to maintain an undisturbed group life? This would conform to the fact that women, unlike other mammalian females, do not have a visible estrus. While in all other mammals there are prominent estrous signals during ovulation in order to attract males' sexual interest, in humans this type of signal disappears. That certainly facilitates group life through reducing overt sexual competition.

Group disruptions are known to occur, for example, in nonhuman primates and some birds (greylag geese). A sexual union can provoke attacks, especially by higher ranking male group members. They attempt to interrupt copulation with threats and even attacks. This is a form of sexual rivalry through which the higher ranking members maintain multiple options for propagating their genes. It is less developed but also observed in females who primarily defend their bond (C.L. Niemeyer and J.R. Anderson, 1983). In this context an observation made by van de Waal (1982) is noteworthy. A low ranking chimpanzee who became sexually aroused by a female in estrous hid his erection behind one hand when a high ranking male looked toward him.

It is interesting to note that due to conventions of modesty, that revealing oneself before others can express scorn and mockery. Thus !Ko girls jestingly mocked us by lifting their skirts and thus breached rules of conduct (Fig. 4.48). Otherwise, they only do this in dance while flirting.

Another reason for concealing sexual activity is that during the sexual act a person is so involved with the partner that he cannot perceive the environment accurately and thus is vulnerable.

Many of us in the western world believe that modesty should be abandoned for the sake of sexual emancipation. Thus, in the kibbutz, boys and girls were brought up together and used the same sanitary facilities and showers. However, at puberty girls developed feelings of modesty and protested against the lack of sexual separation in these intimate situations (M.E. Spiro, 1979).

There are societies with liberal sexual norms that tolerate partnership changes prior to marriage. The Mangaians of the southern Cook Islands allegedly are highly

FIGURE 4.47. Yanomami women in their everyday clothing, which is limited to a thin cord about the hips. Without this symbolic garment they would feel "naked." Photo: I. Eibl-Eibesfeldt.

promiscuous in youth and frequently have sexual unions with different partners. Copulation supposedly occurs independent of personal acquaintance and it is sexual prowess and not an emotional involvement that is the determining factor in achievement (D.S. Marshall, 1971). However these claims are based on hearsay and thus must be considered with many reservations, especially since the Mangaians do eventually marry. Marshall concludes that the European notion of love is absent in the Mangaians because he found that the they were amazed when he discussed the concept of love with them. This seems to me a highly questionable basis for making such a conclusion. B. Malinowski's (1952) description of unrestricted sexual activity among Trobriand island boys and girls, who supposedly engaged in sex between 6 and 8 years of age, does not hold at all, as W. Schiefenhövel and J. Bell-Krannhals (pers. commun.) recently stated. Malinowski had greatly underestimated their ages! Furthermore, the young people do fall in love. They are indeed sexually liberated but subject to the restraint that one has a single partner at any given time except during the festival period after the yam harvest. Similar relaxation of norms is seen in our culture during festive cycles, for instance, during the carnival in southern Germany.

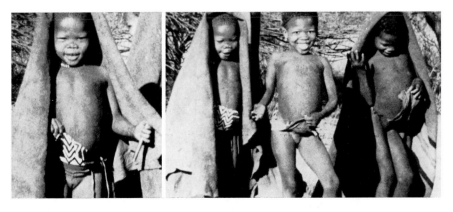

FIGURE 4.48. Mocking !Ko girls (central Kalahari): they raise their aprons. From a 16 mm film. Photo: I. Eibl-Eibesfeldt.

247

So far, no culture is known in which adults live communally and freely change partners. Attempts to form such communities are recent experiments, and they have usually failed because firm family bonds developed between specific individuals within the commune.

The Oneida community in the United States is a notable experiment in extreme collectivism. This religious, communistic movement, founded in 1830 by John Humphrey Noyes, had 500 members at its height. The group settled in Oneida, New York in 1847. All possessions, including clothing and childrens' toys, were common property. The children were raised communally and were taught to love all the adults as if they were their own parents. Adults were expected to respond equally to all others; romantic love was considered to be selfish and monogamy was thought to be detrimental to community life. While the lack of ownership and a classless society were achieved, the group failed to abolish sexual division of labor, dominance of men over women and children, the formation of individual sexual partnerships, and parent–child bonds, and the community was dissolved in 1881 (R.J. Muncy, 1973; W.M. Kephardt, 1976). We will discuss similar developments in the far less radical setting of the kibbutz at a later point.

In discussing adaptations fostering marital ties we cited the bonding power of sexuality and, in particular, the strong sexual interest of the male and the woman's capacity (in contrast with other mammalian females) to receive the man outside her fertile period. Thus she offers both her male partner and herself positive bonding experiences. She is also motivated to seek sexual union due to her capability to experience orgasm.

If there were visible signs of estrus in the human female, the small group would be disturbed and marriages endangered by male–male rivalries. Thus I believe that the maintenance of group harmony and the preservation of heterosexual long-term partnerships developed hand-in-hand with the concealment of estrous signals. The female thus acquired sexual readiness for a longer time span, which fostered continual bonding. There has been a great deal of recent speculation on the origin of the concealed ovulation (summarized in J.P. Gray and L.D. Wolfe, 1983). D. Symons (1980) states that the lack of visible female estrus did not arise in the service of marital bonds but to enable women to offer themselves to men to obtain portions of the booty from the hunt. I find this less plausible since prey is already shared in chimpanzees without any such sexual reward by the partner. Symons also contends that the female orgasm occurs only as a by-phenomenon without function since it is experienced infrequently, which seems an unacceptable hypothesis.

According to data from England, the United States, and Germany between 31 and 50% of all women questioned always experience orgasm and only 2–14% never do (A.C. Kinsey et al., 1953, 1954; E. Chesser, 1957; S. Fisher, 1973; H.J. Eysenck, 1976; S. Hite, 1976). Furthermore these surveys indicate that mainly women in successful partnerships experience orgasm. Only 3% of all women who regularly experience orgasm with their partner are prepared to sleep with other men, versus 10% of all women who do not experience orgasm with their partner (E. Chesser, 1957). Thus the bonding influence of sexual satisfaction is certainly significant. D. Rancourt-Laferriere (1983), who contested Chesser's conclusions, claims that besides the hedonistic function that preserves the woman's general sexual interest and the bonding function there exists a potency-maintaining function for the male. Thus "the delicate male ego" is maintained intact with the knowledge of his partner's satisfaction. Although there may be truth to this argument, his further con-

248

tention that this enhances the male's trust of being the children's father seems farfetched to me.

Female orgasm differs from the male orgasm in a number of ways. While male orgasm reaches a high point after which sexual appetence declines and is not aroused again until after a refractory period, female orgasm can be aroused repeatedly in short intervals. Furthermore there probably exists both clitoral and vaginal orgasms.

In the 1940s, gynecologist E. Grafenberg described a site of particularly sensitive distensible tissue on the ventral side of the vaginal wall directly behind the pubis, and stimulation of the site seems to stimulate vaginal orgasm (E. Grafenberg, 1950; A. Kahn-Ladas *et al.*, 1982; J. Perry and B. Whipple, 1981; F. Addiego *et al.*, 1981; E. Belzer, 1981; D.C. Goldberg *et al.*, 1983). However stimulation of the cervix and uterus are also implicated in vaginal orgasm. L. Clark (1970) reports that several women lost their enjoyment of sexual intercourse following a complete hysterectomy due to the loss of this stimulation.

Many women clearly distinguish the two forms of orgasm. Perhaps the vaginal is the earlier orgasmic form, for clitoral stimulation only occurs when the partners are oriented face to face, which is known to be the phylogenetically more recent pair position.

Sexual intercourse is particularly important in its bonding value for the woman. Perhaps it's related to the birth experience. Vaginal and cervical stimulation in goats and sheep release via hormonal stimulation a powerful readiness for individualized bonding (p. 168). In the human female strong uterine contractions accompany vaginal orgasm. Oxytocin is also released, which likewise occurs during birth. This would conform quite well to the fact that mother–child bonding mechanisms were commonly extended during our evolution to maintain adult attachments and in this case to strengthen the individualized bonds with a male.

It appears to me that falling in love in women is often reinforced and sometimes even triggered by orgasm, as if it is followed by a reflex-like formation of a physiological/psychological condition in which there is a nearly irrational attachment to just this particular sexual partner. However, I express this strictly as an hypothesis. This could be tested with questionnaires and with physiological investigations. If complete vaginal-cervical orgasm was followed by oxytocin release, this would be a strong indication of the validity of my hypothesis.

We know, of course, that people can fall in love—and desperately so—prior to any physical contact. Fantasy and imagination are of paramount importance in sexual bonding. People can fall in love idealistically without sex, but sexual contact may also lead to love.

In paraplegic patients, genitopelvic and cerebro-cognitional eroticism function independently of one another. Even though the lower half of the body is paralyzed and without sensation, paraplegic males and females experience sexual dreams which culminate in orgasm (J. Money, 1960). I assume that neurochemical events (massive release of transmitter substances) are responsible for this phenomenon and that they also play a significant role providing the intense rewarding climax in normal orgasm.

The close relationship between infantile care and sexual behavior is manifested in the woman in many ways. During sexual arousal, as in nursing, the nipples are erect and can lactate (W.H. Masters, 1960; N. Newton, 1958; B. Campell and W.E. Petersen, 1953). In some women stimulation of the nipples suffices to elicit an orgasm (A.C. Kinsey *et al.*, 1954). Finally, uterine contractions occur both during nursing and sexual intercourse (C. Moir, 1934; A.C. Kinsey *et al.*, 1948). This is consistent with the fact that the breast is not only a source of nourishment for the infant but is a sexual releaser for the male (P. Anderson, 1983).

Female sexual libido fluctuates with the menstrual cycle. It is often particularly high during ovulation; sexual fantasies reach their apex during this time (T. Benedeck, 1952). According to M. Shostak (1982), !Kung Bushmen women have more interest in sex at this time and discuss it more. Yet American women react to erotic tape recordings with identical vaginal blood accumulation in all phases of the menstrual cycle (P.W. Hoon *et al.*, 1982). Generally libido is reduced during menstruation, but it does not vanish. Cultural regulations generally prohibit intercourse during menstruation, and this has elicited a great many naive interpretations, often made without any in depth consideration. Thus W.N. Stephens (1962) came to the conclusion that the prohibition was caused by castration fear,[7] an apprehension that the blood could endanger the male's own genitals. Bruno Bettelheim (1954) wrote this prohibition was based on male jealousy of the reproductive capabilities of women; thus menstrual taboos were essentially masculine attempts to minimize the feminine function's importance simply because of the male's incompleteness in procreation. These fantasy-laden theoretical jugglers never take into account that esthetic and hygienic considerations (avoidance of bacterial infection) could have played a role here.

The blood testosterone level of males increases after sexual intercourse with a female. A similar change in the hormone level takes place after success in all competitive situations (p. 304). Masturbation, however, does not lead to an increase of the blood testosterone level (C.A. Fox *et al.*, 1972).

Coital positions vary (S.B.J. and V.A. Sadock, 1976). Japanese woodcuts and pre-Columbian Peruvian ceramics show that these are always variations on a few basic positions. Thus there is a certain variable range of human behavior.

Most mammals, including the anthropoid apes, mate with the male mounting the female posteriorly. The sexual signals of the female are on her bottom and are presented to the male by displaying the rear. During the course of hominization, with the evolution of upright body posture, a new orientation arose with the sexual-releasing signals being transposed to the front of the body. One can readily speak of humanization of the act whereby the mutual orientation toward each partner's face plays an important role. It is, in fact, so important that many people place a greater value on the esthetics of the face than on other secondary sexual characteristics. Upright posture facilitated this orientation and face-to-face contact which already played an important role in mother–child interactions in the pongids certainly served as a preadaptation in this context.

Of female secondary sexual characteristics, not only the aforementioned body contours but also the breast plays a role as a releaser. The form-giving lipid bodies of the breast are not required for nourishment of the child, but instead give the breast display value. D. Morris (1968) maintains that the breast became a display organ in conjunction with the development of the upright posture as sexual orientation changed to the front of the woman. Human ancestors oriented to the posterior of the female, which in nonanthropoid apes is still an important sexual display organ with its prominent swelling during estrus. Morris claims that in humans the breast acts as a mimicry of the posterior, copying the buttocks in form.

---

[7] Once one learns how many phenomena have been explained with this completely unproved castration fear, one understands why many physicians reject this classic psychoanalytical hypothesis.

The preadaptation and thus the point of departure for this selection was the releasing effect of the posterior region on the male. This idea is, of course, speculative but should not be offhandedly rejected since there are interesting parallel adaptations in the nonanthropoid primates. In the gelada (*Theropithecus gelada*), who sits a great deal and does not display its posterior, the female bears an astonishingly accurate copy of her rear on her breast. The closely placed red teats replicate the labia; a white, hourglass-shaped field with white warts on the periphery replicate the rear of the female exactly (W. Wickler, 1967a). One often hears that the human breast would not serve in all cultures as a sexual releaser since in many tribal cultures the men would not react to breasts since they see them continuously. But Bushmen and Yanomami as well as men in many other tribal societies find a young girls' breasts attractive, and a girl with beautiful breasts is esteemed (Fig. 4.49).

A well-formed breast is definitely (a signal of sexual attraction) significant for the early phases of partner formation and marriage. I observed flirting Yanomami men playing with their partner's breast in sexual foreplay.

The ancient releasing function of the female posterior remains. In the Khoisan the female buttocks are emphasized by fatty deposits (steatopygia), and in our culture the posterior is emphasized in various styles of clothing, while certain dance forms (such as the can-can) contain stylized genital displays by baring the

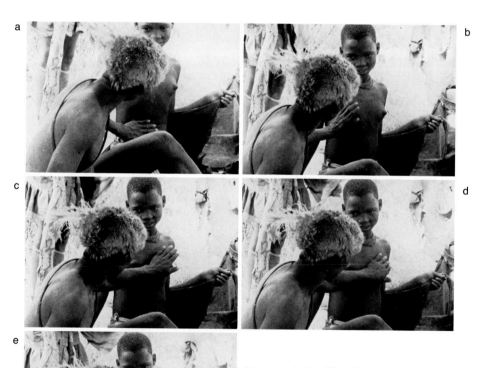

FIGURE 4.49. G/wi Bushman (central Kalahari) playfully approaches and touches the breast of a young girl. Also in traditional societies, the breast of a young woman is an erogenous characteristic. From a 25 frames/second 16 mm film, frames 1, 34, 50, 54, and 57 of the sequence. Photo: I. Eibl-Eibesfeldt.

A

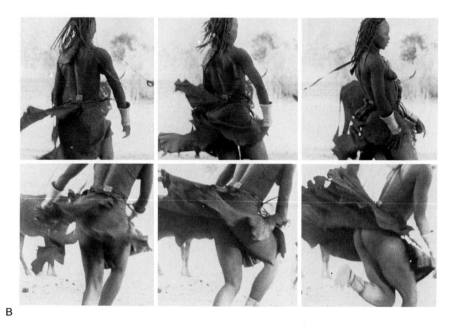

B

FIGURE 4.50. (A) Parisian nightclub dancer. She moves from left to right, presenting her posterior in the center photo. Photo: W. George, Gunpress. (B) Himba woman dancing and raising her skirt with a rapid turn. She jumps in front of the group of clapping, singing women opposite whom stand a group of men (Fig. 3.6). From a 25 frames/second 16 mm film, frames 1, 3, 12, 146, 148, and 150 of the sequence. Photo: I. Eibl-Eibesfeldt.

FIGURE 4.50. (C) Ancient Greek vase decoration.
From L.B. Lawler (1962).

C

posterior or displaying the frontal region (Figs. 4.50A–C). There are comparable dances in the Bushmen and Himba. The elongated labia of the Bushmen women serve as signals in genital display from the rear. Bushmen often copulate from behind (*a tergo*) while lying down on their sides, a position facilitated by the pronounced lordosis of the pelvic spinal column.

In *Ethology: The Biology of Behavior* I stated that the female schema to which men respond is based upon two fundamental ideal types, which can be categorized as the Lower Stone Age ideal of the Venus of Willendorf and the ideal of the Grecian and Roman Venus. Since then I have found that Bushmen, whose adult women correspond closely to the Lower Stone Age ideal, also find as beautiful the young slender women with firm breasts and lacking exaggerated steatopygia as is the case in our western culture. Thus I now theorize that the Lower Stone Age idols do not depict the idealized sexual partner but rather the mature woman and successful mother, not because such idols were considered to be particularly attractive sexually but because they symbolize the fertile mother.

While men respond highly to visual stimuli of their female sexual partners, females also respond to such stimuli in men, albeit not to them alone. We know that narrow hips, a small firm buttocks, broad shoulders, and, in general, a muscular body are perceived as handsome features in men.

The beard is one of the prominent male secondary sexual characteristics in many races. This feature appears to have evolved less as a heterosexual signal and more for its display value for other male group members as a signal of strength and maturity (see p. 482). Hair is a lifelong accessory developing into a white adornment with age that camouflages the body's aging process and elicits respect and thus perhaps is a status-enhancing characteristic associated with wisdom and experience.

E.A. Hess (1977) developed a way to measure preferences using pupillary reactions. The pupils dilate briefly whenever someone sees something interesting and pleasing. Hess constructed an apparatus with which a person's pupil could be filmed while the subject observed slides. The pupillary reaction study showed that normal males and females respond to naked women and muscular men, respectively, even if the female subjects claimed they had no interest in muscle men (Fig. 4.51A). Hess found that male subjects were divided into two groups. One showed a clear preference for large female breast, while others preferred pictures of women with well-developed but not excessively large breasts and in which the women were presented in such a way as to also display the posterior body portion.

Most heterosexual American men conformed to the first type, while Europeans conformed, in general, to the second type. However, each group contained a number of individuals that did not conform to the within-group norms. Thus, some American subjects preferred normal breasts while some Europeans preferred exceptionally large ones. Later Hess found a correlation between these preferences and bottle or breastfeeding. Those Americans and Europeans who preferred large breasts had been bottle fed. One is inclined to speculate that these subjects retained an infantile desire for the maternal breast. Those who had been nursed preferred the young woman's breast but not the unusually large ones. Homosexuals could also be identified with this test, for they reacted positively to partners of the same sex (Fig. 4.51B) and not to those of the opposite sex. We have already discussed the male and female body contour, particularly the significance of shoulder breadth as a male characteristic (see also T. Horvath, 1979, 1981).

K.H. Skrzipek (1978, 1981, 1982, 1983) used model choice tests to investigate the preferences of children, juveniles, and adults of both sexes for schematicized male and female faces and body contours. The drawings did not depict any primary sexual characteristics but in preceding studies other interviewed subjects had categorized the drawings statistically significant as male or female according to impression. Skrzipek found that young boys and girls select faces and silhouettes of their own sex. This probably expresses their appetence for the same sex in terms of social role imprinting (B. Hassenstein, 1973). A dramatic change in preference of body contours occurs at puberty, when the silhouettes of the opposite sex are preferred (Fig. 4.52). The pleasing qualities of body silhouettes are developmentally specific and probably caused by hormonal changes. The responses to faces were more complex, in that boys indeed changed their preference from the male to female prior to puberty around the age of 10, while girls continued to prefer the female face beyond puberty. This may be due to the fact that the female face model corresponds more closely to the baby schema (childlike features).

Flirting behavior and female and male postures are universals that to some extent are programmed by phylogenetic adaptation. Olfactory releasers also are significant, for women react subconsciously to specific substances with male odors. Their olfaction threshold varies with the menstrual cycle. We will discuss this in more detail in the section on olfactory communication (Section 6.1).

Sexual studies show that imprinting-like fixations on specific visual characteristics of one's sexual partner also occur. Thus there are male fetishists that are only aroused when, for example, a woman wears black shoes, gloves, or a fur. Others are stimulated by a handkerchief or some specific part of the body, or only within some individual context (perhaps while on a swing). In many instances, these phenomena are associated with some sexual experience that led to the individual's first orgasm (R. von Krafft-Ebing, 1924) in which the object involved played some role.

At present we can only speculate on the role of imprinting in normal sexual development. It may foster cultural demarcation (pseudospeciation, p. 15) by making the opposite sex of one's own culture particularly attractive and distinguished from members of other cultures by clothing, decoration, and also by his/her demeanor. Certain forms of homosexuality may also be imprinting phenomena. K. Leonhard (1966) described a number of such cases. Here imprinting occurs on a very specific visual image and not generally on the opposite sex.

One of Leonhard's subjects, Knut D., was a 28-year-old who reported to have engaged in sexual games with a male friend that highly aroused him. The genitals of this friend could be clearly outlined beneath his slacks. After this sexually

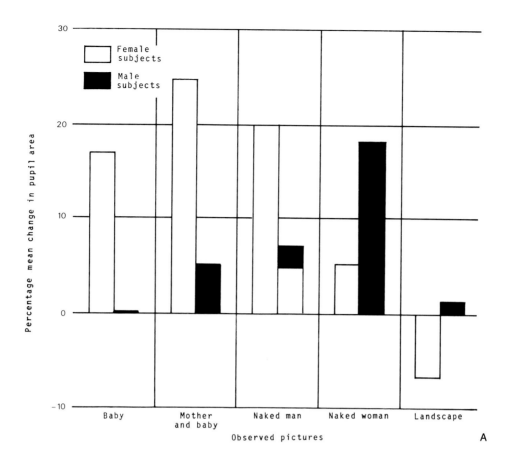

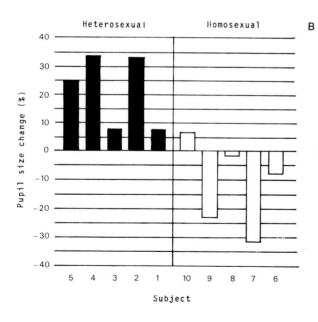

FIGURE 4.51. (A) The pupillary reaction of male and female test subjects in response to various pictures. After E. Hess (1977). (B) The pupillary reaction of heterosexual and homosexual males in response to pictures of naked women. After E. Hess (1977).

arousing experience, D. began masturbating. While he was masturbating, he mentally fantasized about his friend's protuberance, and he developed a proclivity toward homosexuality and only became aroused when the phallus was prominent under tight slacks. The uncovered penis was not arousing. Another of Leonhard's homosexual subjects was fixated on the upper body, while a third was fixated on the face of a male partner. As in heterosexual fetishism, these object imprinting

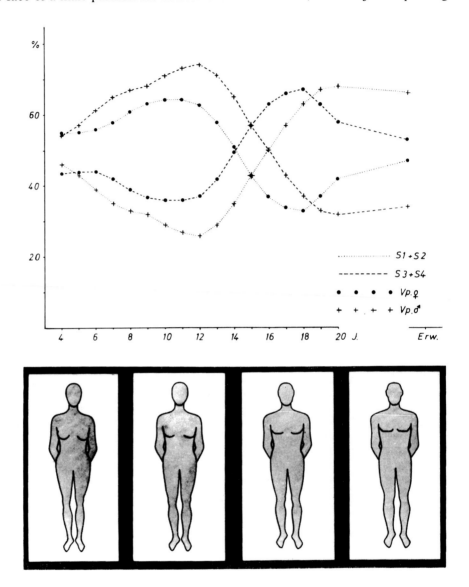

FIGURE 4.52. Model choice study with human silhouettes: selection of female (. . . .) and male (--- --) body contours by female (•) and male (+) test subjects of various age classes. Abscissa: % of choices. Ordinate: age classes (at least 100 subjects per year and sex). Below are shown the female and male silhouette models (S1-4). One sees from the frequency curves that a change in preference occurs at puberty, with the same sex preferred before puberty and the opposite one thereafter. The preference for the same sex in childhood probably fosters identification with one's own sexual role and thus its acceptance. After K.H. Skrzipek (1978).

phenomena are highly resistant to therapy. Women can be imprinted in the same way as men (K. Leonhard, 1966), but their fixation is often less complete since sexual arousal during the imprinting experience is rarely as intense as it is in boys. The fact that the imprinted form of homosexuality is often a consequence of seduction experience obligates lawmakers to protect minors from such acts. Juveniles could become imprinted aberrantly if such behavior is generally accepted.

Homosexuality derived from juvenile seduction is distinguished from another type that is less dependent upon a learned experience as it is from early hormonal factors. Since this is a prebirth condition one refers to such individuals as primary homosexuals.

J. Marmor (1976) summarizes a number of studies demonstrating hormonal differences between homosexual and heterosexual men. M.S. Margolese (1970) investigated the amounts of the breakdown products of testosterone, androsterone (A) and etiocholanolone (E), in urine. In homosexuals E values were higher than A values, while the opposite was found in heterosexuals. Since women also have relatively higher E values in their urine, Margolese concluded that higher A values in men produced a preference for women. R.C. Kolodny et al. (1971) found that homosexual men have a distinctly lower level of plasma testosterone than heterosexuals. Other investigations indicate that some homosexual men possess a type of feminized differentiated brain derived from a lack of androgen during embryonic development (G. Dörner, 1981; G. Dörner et al., 1975). The free plasma testosterone level is lower in homosexuals than heterosexuals, although the total testosterone level is identical in both (G. Dörner, 1980; F. Stahl et al., 1976).

Testosterone deprivation during a critical period of the embryonic development of male rats causes feminization of their brains, and upon reaching sexual maturity the rats become homosexual. This can be induced by putting pregnant rats under stress, causing the mother's adrenal gland to produce substances which lower the testosterone level of the male embryos. The deficiency will then occur in the male young, whereby homosexuality occurs at maturity. Dörner found that human males born during stressful periods during World War II displayed a higher rate of homosexuality. Another indication that the male homosexual brain has been feminized is that the brain of primary homosexuals reacts to estrogen injections by releasing ovulation-inducing hormones, just as the female brain reacts to signals from the ovaries. Heterosexual males do not react similarly (Fig. 4.53). Experiments by B.A. Gladue et al. (1983) confirmed these findings. Brain feminization of some male homosexuals is often correlated with the fact that as children they preferred female rather than masculine activities (E.A. Grellert, 1982).

Studies on homosexuals with twin brothers bear out the possibility of a genetic disposition for homosexuality. All monozygote twins in F.J. Kallmann's (1952) study were similarly homosexual, while there was a lower correlation between heterozygote twins.

Freud assumed that bisexuality is normal and that each person experiences a homoerotic phase during childhood. Homosexuality would arise when the patient remained at an infantile level or regressed to it from castration fear. Modern medicine is rejecting these speculations.

A.P. Bell et al. (1981), using a large body of questionnaires, came to the conclusion that pure homosexuals can scarcely be modified by their environment whereas bisexuals are accessible with social learning. Earlier psychoanalytical theories ascribing homosexuality to particular parental constellations early in life (maternal dominance, weak father, oedipal conflict) are currently being rejected.

Homosexuality does not occur in all cultures. Of 76 cultures surveyed by C.S.

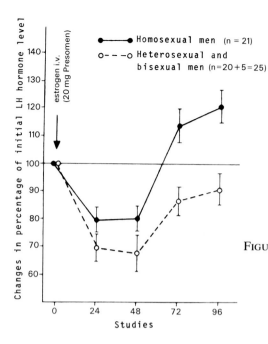

FIGURE 4.53. Changes of the luteinizing hormone levels in the blood serum following intravenous estrogen injection in homosexuals and heterosexual as well as in bisexual males. From G. Dörner (1980).

Ford and F.A. Beach (1969), 28 did not have homosexual members. A.C. Kinsey, using data on 5000 Americans, found that 37% of all males experienced at least transient homosexual experiences. He included all cases of transitory homosexual activity (e.g., mutual masturbation in boys) and chance occurrences in prisons. If such events are excluded, we find that 4% of the subjects in this group were exclusively homosexual, in addition, and about 6% were predominantly homosexual. In Holland 2% of males were found to be exclusively homosexual and 4% bisexual. Similar figures exist for Germany.

In addition to deviations regarding the sex object there are also those deviations in humans that, in my opinion, can be ascribed to the hypertrophy of normal drive components of sexual behavior. Male dominance behavior is closely associated with male sexuality. This is undoubtedly an ancient vertebrate legacy from which we are gradually liberating ourselves.[8] In many fishes and some higher vertebrates, courtship is initiated with mutual display behavior. The female will also display threat in such contexts. The victor, usually the male, assumes the masculine role. Thus pair formation only succeeds when the male is able to dominate his partner. Male sexuality is thus associated with aggressivity but not with fear. Female sexuality is the exact opposite: in lower vertebrates aggressive motivations inhibit sexuality, although flight motivation (fear) does not necessarily suppress it.

In the marine iguana, for example, the courtship of the male consists of a threat display of the same type as demonstrated in agonal encounters with rivals. Receptive females respond by submission—by lying flat on their belly, which invites copulation. The reptile pattern of *agonistic sexuality* is thus characterized by a male dominance and a female submission sexuality. In birds and mammals, this archaic agonistic sexuality is superceded by a phylogenetically new pattern of

---

[8]As we mentioned earlier, display behavior in higher mammalian courtship and some long-term pair-forming birds is not always directed to the partner being courted but toward a third as a demonstration of power for the courted object.

affiliative sexuality which in some of them, including man, gave rise to a love relationship based upon individual bonding. The origin of affiliative sexuality can be traced to the evolution of maternal behavior which gave rise to care-taking behaviors such as grooming, feeding, and protecting and of the infantile behaviors which release them (p. 169). The tools are thus provided for friendly interactions, which could serve for adult bonding. In addition, the mother–child relation gave origin to the individualized bond.

Human sexual behavior is characterized by affiliative responses and love. However, the archaic layers of agonistic sexuality did not disappear. There still exists a connection between male dominance and male sexuality as expressed in certain phallic dominance displays, as well as in hormonal responses such as the increase in levels of blood testosterone after achievement (such as winning in a tennis match, p. 304).

There also seems to still exist a linkage between fear and female sexual arousal, suggestive of the archaic female submission sexuality. Sexual fantasies of women often describe situations as arousing which involve domination by the sexual partner (Kitzinger, 1984). Cleptomaniacs report that they experience sexual arousal and even orgasm during the act of stealing and the subsequent flight (Keupp, 1971; Stoller, 1975). One subject told me that she experienced her first orgasm at 14 years old when she became fearful of a mathematics assignment. Her fear-induced orgasm occurred repeatedly without any mechanical stimulation until her sixteenth year. Both the tendencies to dominate and submit are exploited in western pornographic material.

Some of the pathologies of sexual behavior observed can be explained as phylogenetic regressions to an archaic agonistic sexuality. Among others, there exists one form of male homosexuality which is characterized by the lack of bonding (frequent change of partners) and brutal expressions of dominance. These homosexuals seek partners who allow themselves to be dominated. The components of dominance sexuality are the lust for dominance and the lust for submission. I speculate that sadism, which often accompanies homosexuality, and masochism are two forms of pathological derivations of these desires which are present in what we would call normal human beings, but that they are controlled by affiliative sexuality and love.

Our phylogenetic model contributes to the understanding of sexual pathologies in man, but, of course, should not be taken as the sole explanatory principle. Nonetheless, we can state that sexuality without love and affiliation is a pathological regression to an archaic reptile stage level of sexuality (p. 238).

Under isolated conditions, males in groups often verbally express heterosexual fantasies in a vulgar, joking way. According to H. Schelsky (1955) this is a means of maintaining interest in the opposite sex. Pathological male exhibitionism is less a sexual need than an impulse to frighten someone, representing hypertrophy of the phallic threat (p. 81; Müsch, 1976).

Human sexual behavior has been emancipated in a number a ways from the bonds of our phylogenetic heritage. However, this has increased its susceptibility to imprinting and other environmental influences which, under certain conditions, can lead to deviations. The very lack of innate controls demands that we be particularly aware of the need for cultural controls over this extraordinarily powerful drive. The fact that not only sexual perversions but also other kinds of deviations from the expected norm in sexual behavior are so widespread does not mean that these are normative. According to Kinsey one-half of all white North American males engage in extramarital intercourse at some time. The fact that a behavior persists does not of in itself make it "natural" nor does it imply that it should be legitimized (see the concept of the norm). As I have already emphasized repeatedly, mankind only attains an orderly, harmonious social life when he cultivates his behavior in many respects. This is particularly true regarding the control of sexual behavior, not only because of its strength as a social explosive but also for the sake of our offspring who can claim a moral right to be taken care by their progenitors. The various cultures of the world have all designed controls corresponding to their unique environmental contingencies and economic situation. They are binding for each culture, since as H. Schelsky (1955) convincingly showed, only the cultural standardization of human sexuality ensures the function of procreation, satisfaction, and social integrity in marriage and family, and has a positive effect on the self-confidence of the individual. Thus, a sexuality so integrated brings with it the possibility of developing higher forms of love.

The cultivation of this realm of behavior does not mean repression, for cultivation also means the accentuation of enjoyment. In this sense, the biologist is by no means opposing a liberalization of sexual behavior, but he feels a special obligation for life and is moved to oppose decadent developments that endanger fitness.

Summary 4.5

Human sexual behavior is characterized by love and affiliative responses which superimpose upon an archaic layer of agonistic sexuality characterized by male dominance and female submission. Some of the sexual pathologies observed (e.g., sadism) can be explained as phylogenetic regressions to the archaic "reptilian stage" agonistic sexuality. Man is biologically disposed toward long-lasting sexual partnerships, and romantic love is not a recent discovery. It finds manyfold expression in traditional societies in song and poetry, among others. The basic appeals used in courtship, as far as is known, are identical in all cultures. Display, infantile appeals, and caregiving behavior are employed. The strategies involve seeking a common reference basis. The man must also succeed in developing a basis for trust, since a woman's investment is greater than the man's and winning her requires a greater courtship effort on the man's part. This in turn results in a powerful attachment of the man to his female partner, who he has made a substantial investment to woo her.

Indirect approaches and veiled speech characterize courtship. Thus a direct rejection, loss of face, and the possibility of conflicts is avoided.

Sexual modesty is a universal. No culture is known in which promiscuity prevails. The more promiscuous societies restrict this behavior to specific developmental periods or ritualized events. Man and woman alike are programmed in their sexual physiology for long-lasting relationships; women have the ability to receive and satisfy men sexually without dependence upon the ovulation cycle as well as the ability to experience orgasm, which bonds them emotionally. The cervical-uterine orgasm is of particular interest in this regard and may be related to the birth experience. In some mammals birth induces, via a hormonal reflex, a readiness to accept the young and to form a powerful attachment to it. Whether a similar bonding mechanism operates in humans via the female orgasm remains to be verified. The sexual bonding theory developed herein suggests that such a mechanism indeed could exist. Whether sexual liberalization due to advanced techniques of birth control exerts an influence upon the strength of partner bonding remains to be investigated.

The upright human posture led to a change of the preferred sexual position and, in conjunction, to the development of sexual releasers on the front of the woman (the breast). In his face to face orientation, man distances himself from animals and humanizes the sexual relationship. Preference changes at puberty were tested using simple male and female contour drawings. Such tests suggest that sexual preferences arise from innate programs.

Sexual pathology shows man's sexual vulnerability. Male homosexuality and fetishism can be imprinted. Male homosexuality, in addition, can also arise from a feminization of the brain in individuals who otherwise are phenotypically and genotypically males. Tolerance toward sexual deviants should not lead to considering pathological manifestations as "normal" since individual imprinting plays a role in this area. Juveniles could become imprinted aberrantly if such behaviors were generally accepted.

The strong sexual drive in man is linked with a likewise powerful curiosity, which calls for particular cultural controls over sex.

4.6. Incest Taboos and Incest Avoidance

The nuclear family typically is bonded by powerful affectionate ties. Parents love their children, and they in turn love their parents and siblings irrespective of the minor rivalries of daily life. Thus it is feasible that these attachments could manifest themselves in sexual love, but this occurs very rarely. Using a questionnaire, D. Finkelhor (1980), tested students in social science and sexology classes, and found that 13% of them had engaged in some kind of sibling sexual interaction, which could suggest that incest is not so rare after all. But if we look at Finkelhor's data closely, we find that less than 15% of those positive responses included sexual intercourse or attempted intercourse with a sibling. Thus only 2% of all respondents actually engaged in incest, and the majority of these did so before the age of thirteen. Of the 796 students, only three of them had or attempted having sibling intercourse, after reaching the age of thirteen.

In a population of approximately 18,000 psychiatric patients, K.C. Meiselman (1979) found only eight instances of father–daughter incest and one instance of mother–son incest. Higher figures would result if we define incest in broader terms of any kind of sexual activity without coitus. Meiselmann estimates its prevalence as 1–2% of psychiatric patients. S.K. Weinberg (1955) reported 0.73 cases of incest per year per million inhabitants in Sweden, while figures in the United States were 1.9 cases per million inhabitants in 1930. Further data is found in R.H. Bixler (1981).

Incest is prohibited in all cultures by an incest taboo. It is universally valid, and since the prohibition often appears as a codified one, it was long thought to be a learned cultural adaptation, particularly when Freud (1913) claimed that incestuous desires occur during certain developmental stages of the parent–child relationship. It was also believed that animals have no incest inhibitions. Finally it was thought that since a formal prohibition was necessary, incest taboos must be purely cultural arrangements lacking any biological basis. Thus until quite recently (C. Levi-Strauss, 1969; M. Harris, 1971; L. White, 1959) prevailing thought held that there was no reason to assume a genetic basis for the incest taboo.

In Weston LaBarre (1954, p. 122) we read: "Human incest taboos are not instinctual or biological. They are, rather, the initial (and universal) cultural artifact, deriving immediately from the universal fact of familiar social organization in humans. For secondary incest taboos vary widely in their range and hence can scarcely be instinctual if they can be modified by mere cultural change, even so minimal a change as state legislation." And on p. 216 he continues: "Much as one might wish to believe that incest avoidance rests on the rock of the instinctual, and not on the shifting unsure sands of our indoctrinated psyches (this is what makes philosophical absolutists), no one can pretend that mere genes, bearing the bright banner of instinct, could thread their way through this maze of fickle cultural contingencies."

We will see in the following that there are indeed culturally variable incest taboos but that they arise from a biological basis. The diversity of many cultural taboos is fully compatible with its biological origin.

In the early 1970s it was learned that there is a whole series of animals, included nonhuman primates, that display incest inhibitions. These animals will not copulate with conspecifics with whom they have grown up (N. Bischof, 1972a, b, 1975). Incest taboos develop particularly where strong parent–child and associated sibling ties exist and where the animals remain in the vicinity of each other beyond puberty. Thus parent–child or sibling mating would be likely if such inhibitions did not exist. In some species the young are driven out by the parents and dispersed over a large area upon reaching sexual maturity ensuring that they do not mate with closely related individuals. Thus incest inhibitions are not needed (Eibl-Eibesfeldt, 1970). This occurs, for example, in squirrels and house mice.

Long ago E. Westermarck (1894) and H. Ellis (1906) observed that people growing up with each other experience little mutual sexual attraction and that, in fact, a sexual aversion develops, even between unrelated individuals, who experienced close daily contact during childhood. A.P. Wolf (1966, 1970) confirmed these observations in a comparative study of two kinds of Chinese marriage arrangements on Formosa. These marriage arrangements are distinguished chiefly by the fact that in one the couple meet as adults while in the other so-called *sim-pua* marriage the bride and groom meet in childhood; the bride is adopted by the groom's family and is brought up like a sister. The consequence of this common upbringing period is frequently a pronounced lack of sexual interest. These marriages lack sexual harmony, excitement, and result in fewer children being born. Partners meeting and marrying as adults bear 30% more children. The divorce rate in *sim-pua* marriages is also higher. Of 132 *sim-pua* marriages Wolf investigated, 46.2% resulted in separation and divorce while only 10.5% of the 171 adult marriages were so terminated.

The objection was raised that these differences could have arisen from social class. A.P. Wolf (1974) then investigated a third Chinese marital form, in which the future groom is obligated to serve the bride's father and live with his future father-in-law because he could not afford to pay the dowry. This type of marriage is one of low esteem; nonetheless, these marriages are particularly fertile! Thus status cannot be the cause of lower fertility between partners.

Another theory offered was that the reduced fertility was due to the fact that the *sim-pua* marriage partners are frequently of the same age, and the woman could readily resist her husband on grounds of status equality. However in marriages involving bridal service (the last type discussed) the men are clearly inferior economically in rank to the women and yet such marriages, as stated above, are very fertile. A.P. Wolf (1974) found a linear relation between the age of the groom at the time of adoption of the wife and the separation rate. If the groom was 4 years old or younger, 14.6% of the marriages ended in divorce. If at the time of adoption he was between 5 and 9 years old, 12% of such marriages terminated in divorce. When the future groom was 10 years old or more, the divorce rate sank to 5.4%! This suggests that a common upbringing during a particular developmental stage results in inhibitions against sexual union. These findings have been supported by those of J. McCabe (1983) for the FBD (Fathers Brothers Daughters) marriages of the Sunnites of Bayt al-'asir, Lebanon, where a patrilineal parallel cousin is preferred for marriage partners. Parallel cousins grow up in a family relationship, bound by sibling-like ties. But such marriages produce less children and suffer a higher divorce rate than other marriages.

Further evidence for the existence of incest inhibitions arising from common upbringing is found in J. Shepher (1971, 1983). In the kibbutz children are brought up communally in age classes. Girls and boys use the same showers and toilets, since kibbutz leaders wish to abolish sex discrimination and the discomfort in being seen unclothed by the opposite sex. The children raised in this way experienced no embarrassment with the opposite sex until reaching the age of twelve, but from that time on the girls refused to have contact with the boys. They avoided undressing in front of the boys and taking showers with them, in short, displaying all the signs of modesty that the kibbutz leaders were attempting to suppress. They also became interested in young men who had not grown up with them. After puberty the tensions between boys and girls raised together eased, and they developed friendly sibling-like relationships. But age class members did not marry. J. Shepher (1983) investigated 2769 marriages between individuals raised in the kibbutz, and in no instance did members who were brought up together marry. Group members regard each other as brother and sister, and not because of any external authority but out of their own choice. Since these children were not blood relatives, the adults would have held no objections against such marriages and in fact desired them. But such marriages did not take place because those who grew up together did not experience any mutual sexual attraction. Later, J. Shepher discovered thirteen exceptions in his data, that is of marriages between members brought up together. A close analysis of these showed that in every case an extended interruption of the "sibling" life relationship had occurred before the sixth year. Shepher concludes that there is a sensitive period before the sixth year in which one learns whom one does not desire sexually at a later time in life. This conforms well to the observations of A.P. Wolf. Homosexual male twins likewise avoid incestuous relations with each other. Once again the evidence suggests that growing up together results in reduced mutual sexual interest (R.H. Bixler, 1983).

The biological mechanism underlying this process has not yet been elucidated, but K. Kortmulder (1968) and N. Bischof (1972a, b, 1985) have formulated some theories regarding it. Kortmulder starts from the observation that pair formation in animals is usually accompanied by aggression and fear reactions. Since these reactions are eliminated or inhibited between family members, interrelations become less exciting and thus pair formation is less likely. In this view aggressive and sexual motivation are closely connected, and such a finding has been verified ethologically in male vertebrates. In females, aggression inhibits sexuality whereas fear does not. A. Kortmulder refers to an "agonistic sexual arousal link." N. Bischof observed that goslings do not arouse each other with stimuli that would normally elicit fear and aggression, and he feels that this dampens the curiosity and exploratory drive, and with it sexual excitability. Indeed a large number of studies of both animals and humans demonstrate a positive relationship between aggression and sexual arousal (see summary in S. Parker, 1976, including neurophysiological studies). Since aggression is inhibited in the course of human familial socialization, the accompanying sexual arousal would be thereby reduced.

In my opinion this view touches on the proximate mechanisms but is not the

263

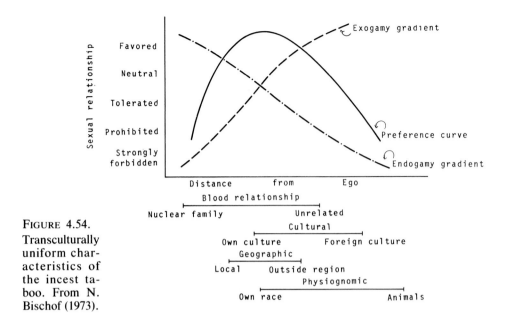

FIGURE 4.54. Transculturally uniform characteristics of the incest taboo. From N. Bischof (1973).

ultimate explanation. The sensitive period must also be considered. Subsequent pacification by no means disposes one asexually, so we must consider innate learning dispositions for incest taboos. Without an incest avoidance mechanism, sexual reproduction, which was developed to accelerate evolution, would occur senselessly since new combinations of genes would not be taking place. The importance of incest avoidance can be seen from the fact that even plants have many kinds of adaptations inhibiting self-fertilization.

In addition to incest taboos, humans have other kinds of sexual restrictions determining that marriages occur only within a specific caste, race, geographic area, or within a particular ethnic group. Distance in all cultures is an important determining factor for marriage regulations, for the marriage partner should be neither too close to oneself nor too distant. N. Bischof (1972a,b) expressed these relationships graphically (Fig. 4.54). The dotted line (endogamy gradient) in the graph represents the distance of positive "we feelings." If this criterion were the only one, then nuclear family members would be preferred as marriage partners. But another factor counteracts this one, the exogamy gradient rising from left to right. The joint effect of both forces, symbolized by the gradients, results in an inverted U-curve of preference. Relation and distance scales can be interpreted differently in different cultures, so the peak of the preference curve can vary culturally based on different tolerances within a given cultural group.

Summary 4.6

The incest taboo can no longer to accepted as a purely cultural invention. During a sensitive period from infancy to about 6 years of age, children learn with whom they should not fall in love. An innate program facilitates developing inhibitions against copulating with those raised together with them during this period. Thus the incest taboo has a biological basis but undergoes numerous cultural transformations.

4.7. Sex Roles and Their Differentiation

Marital partnership is based upon a division of labor. Man and wife fulfill various tasks in virtually all societies. To some extent, role differentiation is physiologically determined. Women nurse and in tribal societies they often nurse an individual child for up to 3 years. Since women usually raise several children, they spend many years closely attached to an infant, carrying it around and providing for its needs. It is easy to see that during this time a woman needs protection and that she should not unnecessarily expose herself or her children to danger. In most tribal cultures women do not participate in warfare or in the hunting of large game. These tasks are left to men who are physically and physiologically better adapted for such activities.

Constitutional differences in anatomy and physiology between man and woman are substantial. However, we often read that these distinctions were of secondary importance for the development of sex roles and that they could be overcome. F. Salzman (1979) even wrote that they were created by physical training alone and that it was not phylogenetic adaptations but culture that defined and created sex roles. Margaret Mead (1935) remarked that man is the rawest of all raw materials: "We may say that many if not all the personality traits which we have called masculine or feminine are as lightly linked to sex as are the clothing, the manners and the form of headdress that a society at a given period assigns to either sex" (p. 280).

Her statement has been quoted repeatedly. The biologist reads these words with a certain skepticism, since the intimate physiological unity of mother and child has existed since mammals first appeared some 200 million years ago. Thus we would expect from the biological perspective that phylogenetic adaptations exist for female and male personality characteristics, determining sex-typical behavior and gender roles. Margaret Mead was aware of them herself. After her initial, perhaps overstated, formulations she stated in a later work (1949) that the "core gender identity" is probably determined biologically and her subsequent commentary indicated that she meant behavioral characteristics.

She speaks of natural male and female dispositions in temperament and remarks that American society rarely permits the role of the male to be emotionally satisfactory since domestic virtues such as patience, perseverance, and stability would prevail which fit more for women. According to Mead, men are placed in a difficult position since they have no means of expressing their biologically disposed aggressive role as protector or their desire for individual bravery. She then suggests that society should structure male tasks so that they offer males the possibility of engaging these masculine dispositions. She felt that any society would experience difficulties if it attempted to influence one sex toward the direction of the other counter to its natural temperament. The Mundugumur would suffer because of masculinizing their women, and the Arapesh would conversely experience difficulties for feminizing their men. These observations cited by M. Mead in *Male and Female* (1949), which substantially expand on her statements in *Sex and Temperament* (1935), are rarely quoted, perhaps because Mead was thinking in biological terms here and such thoughts do not fit the theories of those who deny that biological factors play a role in determining gender roles.

Before we begin a discussion of the biological bases of gender roles, a number of concepts should be clarified. We will use the concept "gender role" to designate that behavior expected or prescribed culturally for males or females.

Within the general area of gender role behavior we can distinguish between sex-typical and sex-specific behavior patterns. Sex-typical behaviors are those appearing in both sexes but differentially. Thus men and women are both aggressive, but men clearly more so. Sex-specific behavior is restricted to a single sex.

Our interest lies in determining behavioral sex differences, testing their universality or cultural specificity, following their development, and thus determining what factors are responsible for the origin of sexual differences. Finally we investigate the adaptive aspects of such differences and thus glean the actual basis of their existence.

Clear distinctions exist cross-culturally in the tasks performed by men and by women. Typical male activities include hunting large game and group defense. There is no tribal culture in which women are warfaring. Only in the current age of technological civilization did mankind "progress" to this stage.

Women are primarily responsible for caring for infants and small children and for maintaining the household and usually bear a substantial proportion of subsistence work load through gathering and gardening. There are spheres in which men and women work together, as in field and gardening work, whereby the heavier physical tasks like clearing the forest are left to the men. In societies in which men and women contribute equally economically by each performing their own tasks one could speak of an economically egalitarian system. Economic equality, however, does not necessarily imply social equality.

In the !Kung Bushmen of the Kalahari, hunter-gatherers who are often described as egalitarian and thus used as a model for the original human conditions, men definitely are dominant although women contribute as much or more economically then the men. Marjorie Shostak (1982) found that men more frequently have internally influential positions (as group spokesmen and healers), and this authority over many aspects of !Kung life is universally accepted. The extreme subordination of the woman, as exists in some modern and tribal cultures, does not occur in Bushmen; rather we observe women's dominance in particular contexts. !Kung women are primary decision makers in situations involving the children. Of course, one could say that the women bear 90% of the "burden" of child care, but one could as easily claim that they provide 90% for the welfare of their children. In addition, Bushmen women contribute the major proportion of the subsistence income through gathering and according to Shostak the woman determines how she will distribute her gathered produce. In reciprocal exchanges (Hxaro) women play as substantial a role as men.

Male activities, however, achieve more general recognition. Shostak (1982, p. 243) writes that most gathered food items, excepting mongongo nuts, are described as "things comparable to nothing," while meat is equated with nourishment. "Squeals of delighted children may greet women as they return from gathering, but when men walk into the village balancing meat on sticks held high on their shoulders, everyone celebrates, young and old alike." In 1949 Margaret Mead wrote that in every known society the male need for success can be verified. A man may cook, sew, clothe dolls, or hunt hummingbirds, and if society considers that to be adequate male activity it is also defined as significant. But when the same activities are carried out by women they are considered less important. The !Kung Bushmen are no exception to this:

> Unfortunately, though, the !Kung are not the exception they first appear to be. !Kung women do have a formidable degree of autonomy, but !Kung men enjoy certain distinct

advantages, in the way the culture values their activities, both economic and spiritual, and in the somewhat greater influence over decisions affecting the life of the group. (M. Shostak, 1982, p. 243)

Perhaps there exists something like an androgen-induced appetence for recognition (and I suspect that there is). We know that success elevates the level of androgen in males. In societies such as the Enga (P. Wiessner, pers. commun.) where competition between males is intense, men gain wealth and status through the ceremonial exchange of pigs raised largely by women.

Outgroup representation is a man's affair, probably derived from territorial defense. Men usually control political relations between groups and in this connection are the main mediators to the higher forces in religious rites. In a certain respect this is also a representation of the group to the outer world. This role, however, is not exclusively male, since women are often engaged in religious rituals as well.

What has been stated thus far holds in principle for the matrilineal cultures as well. In such cultures, the men of the maternal lines are the political decision-makers. The Nayar of Malabar, southern India, are characterized by matrilineality and communal property is inherited through the female line. Although these are a belligerent people, the women have little political influence. Economic leadership and group representation to the outside lies in the hands of elder males, usually the maternal uncles (H. Zinser, 1981). We know of no matrilineal culture in which women assumed these traditional male roles.

Once these role differences are identified one can inquire how they developed as adaptations in the various tribal cultures and whether this adaptation is still valid for modern industrial society. One should furthermore investigate the contribution of phylogenetic and cultural adaptations to shaping these different roles.

It could well be that some of the norms controlling gender roles, whether of cultural or biological origins, are no longer "adaptive" in our contemporary society. The modern feminist movement questions such norms as male dominance (and in my opinion, rightly so). With this in mind the question must be asked for which of the diverse demands of social and economic aspects of life do women or men possess particular predispositions. This does not mean that we simply acquiesce to such biological dispositions, but rather that these dispositions should be taken into consideration.

There are extremists in the womens' movement who advocate an indiscriminate mimicking of male behavior. This is tantamount to the very male dominance they wish to eliminate. For example, some feminists maintain that women should be conscripted into military service, which is neither an "emancipation" nor an improvement in social standing. Rather than mimicking male behavior, women's traditional roles as mothers, educators of their children, and managers of a household could be revalorized in order to present this as an alternative option to the many other alternatives currently open to women.

Most investigations of the behavior differences between the genders have been conducted on white children and juveniles in the United States and Europe (summarized in E.E. MacCoby and C.N. Jacklin, 1974). Newborn girls are quieter than boys (S. Phillips et al., 1978; J. Feldman et al., 1980); beginning in the third year boys are usually more physically active than girls. Newborn girls smile spontaneously with closed eyes more frequently than boys and, later, more often communicatively (intended smiling).

In a quantitative study of altruistic behavior in 279 North American school children, girls were shown to be significantly more altruistic than boys. These behavioral observations confirm independent evaluations made by their teachers (C.C. Shigetomi *et al.*, 1981).

Boys are generally more aggressive than girls, which is most observable at 2 and 2½ years of age. This aggression is both verbal and behavioral (B.B. Whiting and C.P. Edwards, 1973; E.E. MacCoby and C.N. Jacklin, 1974). T. Tieger (1980) criticized the claim that men are biologically more disposed to aggressive behavior than women, but his line of reasoning is untenable. J. MacCoby (1980) responded to T. Tieger and showed additional evidence that differences in aggressive behavior between boys and girls are evident very early in life. This has also been confirmed cross-culturally (T.S. Weisner, 1979).

Older boys display a higher degree of physical activity than girls (J.H. Block, 1976). Boys distance themselves further from their mothers, their playroom, parental home or playground and thus are more independent than girls, who maintain closer physical contact to the mother and do not wander as far from the house. Boys of 12–36 months of age removed themselves from their mothers in a park more often than girls of the same age (R.C. Ley and J.E. Koepke, 1982). The higher level of independence of boys is basically equal in Londoners and !Kung Bushmen (N.G. Blurton-Jones and M.J. Konner, 1973; P. Draper, 1976). This may be due to greater fearfulness or caution on the part of girls. Questionnaire responses indicate that girls are more fearful from the eighth year on (E.E. MacCoby and C.N. Jacklin, 1974). Their highly ambivalent behavior with strangers is another indication of a high motivational level for fear (p. 170).

Kindergarten boys show greater interest in new play objects than girls (A.D. Daldry and P.A. Russell, 1982). Boys of 12–24 months old play more with toy vehicles than girls, climb over chairs more, and investigate furnishings more, despite admonishments by their parents that they could injure themselves (P.K. Smith and L. Daglish, 1977).

Beginning in the fourth year, boys in mixed groups generally assume a higher rank position than girls, and they display more (B. Hold, 1974, 1976, 1977), although there are exceptions since derived rank plays a major role. Thus if one girl in the group is the daughter of the teacher, her relationship elevates her rank position.

Verbal abilities are in general more developed in girls beginning in the eleventh year. Girls are in general more obedient and follow suggestions of adults more often than boys. Spatial orientation is superior in boys beginning in the eleventh year (H.A. Witkin *et al.*, 1967).

Preschool children display a clear preference to form play groups with members of the same sex (E. Goodenough-Pitcher and L. Hickey-Schultz, 1983). This may be due to a shyness of the opposite sex. In the study conducted by G.A. Wasserman and D.N. Stern (1978), children of both sexes maintained a greater distance between themselves and members of the opposite sex, turning away from the other sex more frequently. However, differential play interests may be the primary factor determining this behavior. Similar relationships occur in the Kalahari Bushmen. Children have the opportunity to play in mixed sex groupings, but they gravitate toward members of the same sex.

Data from H. Sbrzesny (1976) on !Ko Bushmen from 126 play groups show that sixty of them (47.6%) were composed of boys only, forty eight (38.1%) were exclusively girls, and just eighteen (14.3%) were mixed. Table 4.6 presents distinct sex differences in Bushmen child play activities.

Other data also indicate that interests of Bushmen children is sex differentiated. Shortly before H. Sbrzesny concluded her work on the Bushmen, the New Zealand teacher Liz Wiley initiated schooling of !Ko children as part of a developmental

Table 4.6. Sex Differences in Child Play Activities

Game activity	n	Distribution (%)
Boys ($n = 93$)		
Playful pursuit, scuffling	17	18.28
Experimental games	40	43.01
Fighting and competitive games	14	15.05
Dance	2	2.15
Other games (movement games, ball games, jumprope, sand games)	20	21.51
	93	
Girls ($n = 76$)		
Melon dance game	39	51.32
Melon rock game (a game of skill played alone)	16	21.05
Playful pursuit	3	3.94
Experimental games	4	5.26
Other games (mother-child games, ball games, sand games, jumprope)	14	18.42
	76	

project. In some of her classes children were permitted to draw whatever they wished. H. Sbrzesny's evaluations of the drawings confirmed significant sex differences regarding subjects drawn and is based on 556 drawings by boys and 610 drawings by girls. Their differential interests are reflected in their drawings. One could explain this series of differences by claiming that the children oriented their interests toward adult role models. Thus the fact that men hunt could be the reason that boys drew animals more frequently. The differential interest in technical apparatus, alien to the Bushman culture, can be seen from the data. No one encouraged the girls to be less occupied with these objects; they were genuinely less interested in them. We will discuss the related significant observations on play in egalitarian-raised kibbutz children (p. 279).

Many sex typical differences are first manifested at puberty. A. Degenhardt and H.M. Trautner (1979) summarized these in tabular form, which we show here in Table 4.8.

The more social interests of girls at this period are manifested in, among other things, a desire for contact with other people and the need for security within the

Table 4.7. Objects of Drawings

Depicted object	Boys (%)	Girls (%)
Domestic and wild animals	29.8	10.2
Flowers	8	23.7
Technical apparatus (wagons, airplanes)	19.5	1.5
Huts	9.5	23.6
Man	15.4	4.9
Woman	3.5	21.8
"Human" (sex not identified)	5	3.7

Table 4.8. Sex Typical Differences at the Time of Adolescence

	Female	Male
Cognitive aspects	Verbal abilities Perceptual speed Perceptual acuity	Quantitative abilities Spatial orientation

Social aspects	Conformity
	Person orientation
	Socially referenced
	    interests
		Self-confidence
		Occupational orientation
		Materially subject-
		    oriented interests

Self-image	Interaction related	Assertion related

group. Young girls cite as their most significant problems those that are personal, interpersonal, and familial. Young boys, on the other hand, cite school and financial problems (J.P. Adams, 1964). In contrast to the socially oriented self-images of juvenile girls and young women, boys and young men are power and strength oriented (E.E. MacCoby and C.N. Jacklin, 1974). Data from American school classes show that girls form more exclusive friendships than boys. Their dyads and triads are closed units (D. Eder and M.T. Hallinan, 1978). Girls also tend to remain in isolated dyads for a longer time. Boys are less exclusive, a characteristic facilitating social interactions in such activities as competitive games. New class members are more readily accepted by the boys. This perhaps reflects what L. Tiger (1969) described as the difference between male and female group formation. Tiger feels that the male tendency to form larger groups derives from a phylo-genetically based disposition adapted to common fighting and hunting. Of course, that should not be interpreted to mean that "female bonding" does not exist. But it could be that females are more small group oriented, which would certainly not exclude girls from forming larger compatible play groups. Sociability and friendship cannot be equated.

Adult males have a stronger skeletal structure, and the pectoral girdle is more developed than in females. This makes males better at throwing, using a bow, and wrestling, and thus "prepares" the male for hunting and fighting. Men's longer

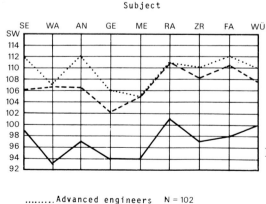

........Advanced engineers   N = 102
‒ ‒ ‒ ‒ Engineers   N = 126
———— Technical craftsmen   N = 627

FIGURE 4.55. Comparison of the intelligence test components (endowment profiles) of persons in technical occupations (commentary and terms in text). After Amthauer (1966).

legs and the nature of articulation between the thigh and the hips enables men to partake in activities which require sustained strength and rapid locomotion. Women have particular difficulty running downhill. On the other hand, women enjoy a certain genetic advantage from their double X chromosome: hemophilia and color blindness occur only in males, and males are more susceptible to infectious diseases. Male mortality is higher than that of females. The conception ratio of male to female fetuses is 125–135:100. This ratio declines to 106:100 at birth. In addition to the higher life expectancy of female, there is a lower accident rate, which may be due to reduced risk-taking in girls. From 1962 to 1966, in the German Democratic Republic, 3905 boys had accidents as compared to 1319 girls.

Central European women are, on the average, 10 cm smaller and 10 kg lighter than men of equal age. Male musculature weighs 35 kg, while in women it only weighs about 23 kg, and the relative muscular performance in women is also reduced, due to differential chemical composition of the muscle fibers. Women possess 30–40% less muscular strength than men. This is one of the reasons for separate competition of men and women in sporting events. Female basal metabolism is lower than that of the male, and there are differences in oxygen intake capability (males have a greater number of red blood corpuscles per cubic centimeter, greater lung capacity, differences in heart volume, blood composition, breathing technique, etc.). All these factors combine to enhance the physical capabilities of the male (H. Dannhauer, 1973; A. Anastasia, 1958). One can thus readily understand the role of these factors in group defense and hunting. Their more easily aroused aggression also makes men more prepared for combat.

R. Amthauer (1966) analyzed the endowment profiles of 1000 men and 1000 women, all adults with differing educational and professional backgrounds. Nine task categories were included: sentence completion (SE) -‘‘judgment formation’’; word selection (WA)- ‘‘linguistic sensibility’’; analogies (AN) -‘‘combination ability’’; commonalities (GE) -‘‘abstraction ability’’; retention tasks (ME) -‘‘retention ability’’; calculating tasks (RA) -‘‘practical quantitive thought’’; number series (ZR) -‘‘inductive thought with numbers’’; figure selection (FA) -‘‘power of imagination’’; cube tasks (WU) -‘‘spatial concept ability.’’

Sharply defined individual functions (appearing in quotation marks) were not tested in this study. However, the general direction is clear. This analysis produced capability profiles that could be studied on the basis of individuals or groups. Thus technical craftsmen, engineers and advanced engineers, despite their different working levels, shared superior performance in the nonverbal areas RA, ZR, FA, and WU (Fig. 4.55). Combination ability (AN) performance was significantly higher than concept formation (GE). These kinds of performance profiles are more helpful for occupational counseling than the typical measurement of intelligent quotients, for individuals with equal intelligent quotients can have entirely different endowments.

Amthauer ascertained the mean standard values for all task groups. He also determined the arithmetic mean of this standard value and developed the mean deviation for each task group. The differences are shown in Fig. 4.56. Results of the test showed sex differences, with women superior in verbal tasks, particularly in abstraction and retention ability, while males excelled in calculating tasks, conceptual ability and, especially, in spatial orientation. If randomly selected female subjects are compared with an equal number of males selected only from technical occupations, the profiles are exactly bilaterally symmetrical. The profile of technical male personnel was found to be opposite the trend found for randomly selected women (Fig. 4.57).

The verbal superiority of women has also been verified in numerous American studies. Females learn to speak faster, rapidly acquire and use a larger vocabulary, and write longer school essays. Speech disorders occur twice as often in boys as in girls. Interestingly, girls grades in mathematics, are not lower than boys (although boys scored higher in Amthauer's tests). On the basis of grades, then, girls score higher in general than boys, and this is probably due to their superior verbal ability in expressing themselves.

The extensive studies of C. P. Benbow and J. Stanley (1980, 1983) also bear out significant differences in mathematical ability. Beginning at puberty, boys are significantly superior in mathematical performance. Benbow and Stanley found no environmental factors responsible for this differential ability (see also M. Wittig and A. Petersen, 1979).

The female brain is somewhat less hemispherically specialized than the male brain (J. Levy, 1972), and the *corpus callosum* that joins the two hemispheres is somewhat thicker in females. This corresponds with the fact that women are superior to men in integrating verbal and nonverbal information and that language loss after traumatic damage of the left hemisphere in women is easier to cure by therapy than comparable traumatic injuries in men. Whereas, in women, language is more a means of social communication, in men it is perhaps more a means of analytical thought.

Male and female language differs correspondingly in syntactic structure. Italian women for instance, utilize a great many terms of doubt, make fewer expressive statements, and use indirect speech a great deal. Many of their sentences are not completed. "Women use a series of non-verbal means of communication which fit in with what we defined as 'natural rhetoric' of their linguistic behavior; we could say that women use pathos, persuasion appealing to the emotions, where men use logos, persuasion based on logical argumentation" (G. Attili and L. Benigni, 1979). J. Durden Smith and D. Desimone (1983, p. 59) state that women have been selected for improved communication ability: "Women are communicators and men are takers of action." Women had greater social sensitivity as peacemakers, welfare workers, and social mediators, whereas the male could be portrayed as the lone hunter and, due to stronger lateralization, had less verbal access to his emotions.

This is, of course, a somewhat rough generalization. It may well be that men communicate in other ways. They maintain intergroup relations and the complex contract songs of the Yanomami, which establish alliances, or their argumentative conversation. Male courtship finds manifold expression in poetry and song.

The more unified organization of the female brain makes it less susceptible to malfunction. The superior spatial orientation with its corresponding right hemisphere specialization of the male probably developed in conjunction with hunting and defense, which requires precise estimates of direction and distance.

If right-handed boys and girls are given the task of identifying objects with their hand without any visual aids, girls can identify equally well with both hands but boys have left hand superiority. This suggests that spatial and visual information is processed in the right hemisphere (S. Wittelson, 1978).

Women are more sensitive to touch and have superior fine motor control (D. McGuinness, 1981; D. McGuinness and K. H. Pribram, 1979). The above researchers also found differences in the means of information intake and problem solving. Men are more bound to rules and less sensitive to environmental distractions. They are more single-minded and have a superior ability to concentrate upon and maintain a task.

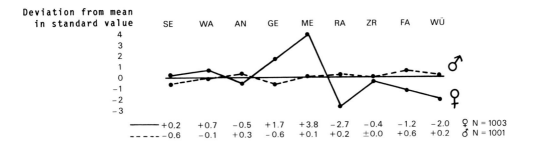

——	+0.2	+0.7	−0.5	+1.7	+3.8	−2.7	−0.4	−1.2	−2.0	♀ N = 1003
- - - -	−0.6	−0.1	+0.3	−0.6	+0.1	+0.2	±0.0	+0.6	+0.2	♂ N = 1001

FIGURE 4.56. Sex differences in intelligence structure from two randomly selected (alphabetically) groups. After R. Amthauer (1966).

Distinct sex differences exist in susceptibility to specific types of behavioral disturbances. Autism, hyperactivity, dyslexia, and stuttering occur more frequently in males than females. Men are also more inclined to commit violent crime. Depression and hysteria are more prevalent among women.

Other distinct differences occur in body postures. Men stand with their legs further apart, spread them when they sit and also tend to spread their arms and to spread their bodies in other ways. Thus they subconsciously occupy more space, a posturing that suggests dominance. Women occupy less space: they neither stand with legs spread, sit with their thighs opened, nor do they spread their arms while sitting. Thus their bearing conveys less dominance (G. H. Hewes, 1957; M. Wex, 1979; E. Goffman, 1976; N. M. Henley, 1977). We regard the thrusting forward of the thigh while standing as specifically feminine, a trait that occurs in many cultures. Many body postures are developed through training, for girls are admonished not to spread their legs and not to loll about indecorously. Older women are frequently more unconstrained and often sit in a masculine manner, which

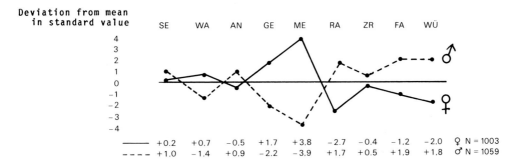

——	+0.2	+0.7	−0.5	+1.7	+3.8	−2.7	−0.4	−1.2	−2.0	♀ N = 1003
- - - -	+1.0	−1.4	+0.9	−2.2	−3.9	+1.7	+0.5	+1.9	+1.8	♂ N = 1059

FIGURE 4.57. Sex differences in intelligence structure from randomly selected females (alphabetically only), and males in technical occupations (selected from a large file). After R. Amthauer (1966).

may be due in part to a hormonal masculinization related to the onset of meno-pause.

According to Marianne Wex (1979), men display more "possessive" behavior than women, more frequently placing the arm over a female partner's shoulder or about the hips. Chimpanzees behave in the same way. The interpretation of this behavior as "possessive" or "possession taking" strikes an emotional chord that is negative and problematic, since one could also interpret the behavior as a "caregiving" gesture. Both are actually correct. Mothers and fathers protectively embrace their children, and they develop attachments, which they jealously defend like possessions. We even say that we have "captured" someone's affections. This does not mean that the relationship is one-sided for the relationship between two individuals is reciprocal—they "possess" each other, so to speak.

A study of 1296 photographs from school and university yearbooks showed that women smiled more frequently and vigorously, than men, often holding the head slightly to the side (J. M. Ragan, 1982). Thus women express subordination through head posture more than men, while men display dominance. Differences in carrying objects, based on anatomical distinctions, have also been verified. Women support books on their hips, while men simply hold them against their body (J. Scheman, J. S. Lockard, and B. S. Mehler, 1977).

The differences discussed up to this point concern sex-typical behavior. The differentiated reproductive behavior patterns are sex-specific, although to a lesser degree in courtship. Both sexes, as stated earlier, possess a similar repertoire of affectionate behavior patterns. The extent to which it is sex typically different remains to be investigated. Copulatory behavior includes a number of sex-specific acts. This is true for the erection and thrusting of the male as well as his orgasm. Female sex-specific behavior includes the contraction of the pelvic musculature, glandular activity facilitating lubrication, and the specific form of the female or-gasm.

There are indications that humans respond to sex-specific sexual stimuli. Women perceive musk odors at lower concentrations than men, whereas men can only perceive them in high concentrations. The female olfactory threshold also varies with the menstrual period, which is reduced during ovulation. Estrogen injections influence the olfactory threshold (P. R. Good et al., 1976; J. LeMagnen, 1952; R. L. Doty, 1976). Recently, a substance (androstenol) was isolated from human male axillary perspiration that smells like musk. This substance is also produced by the male wild pig causing arousal in the female pig (D. R. Melrose et al., 1971; R. L. S. Patterson, 1968; E. B. Keverne, 1978; R. Claus and W. Alsing, 1976). This would indicate that this phenomenon is an older phylogenetic adaptation.

R. P. Michael et al. (1975) found substances in human vaginal secretions called copulines that were already known from rhesus monkeys. In the monkey they have a sexually arousing effect on males. The quantities of copulines produced by women varies cyclically except in women using birth control pills, where co-pulines are found only in trace amounts.

Obviously, men and women react visually to different releasing stimuli. How to elicit these reactions and to present them in a stylized manner is learned. More information has been found on the key stimuli to which men respond. It is oc-casionally stated that women react less readily to visual stimuli then men, although contradictory opinions exist in this regard. Certainly there are differences in the tactile qualities of the erogenous zones. The nipple region in females is easily aroused, while in men this zone has less erogenous function.

If children are shown pictures of small childrens' faces and those of adults, they will prefer the adult faces. But a change in preference occurs in girls at 12 to 14 years of age, for at this time they prefer baby pictures. This preference change may be hormonally induced. Boys display the same trend 2 years later (W. Fullard and A. M. Rieling, 1976). K. H. Skrzipek (1978) found a similar preference change at the onset of puberty with male and female body silhouettes. Before puberty the same sex was preferred, while thereafter the opposite sex was chosen (p. 256).

J. E. Williams and D. L. Best (1982) investigated the sex stereotypes by asking respondents in 25 countries which of 300 adjectives they attributed as masculine or feminine. They found high cross-cultural agreement. The items adventurous, dominant, forceful, independent, masculine, and strong were found to be male-associated in all countries. Sentimental, submissive, and superstitious were female-associated in all countries, whereas affectionate, dreamy feminine, and sensitive were female-associated in all but one.

We can maintain that sex differences occur not only in morphology and physiology but also in human behavior. These consist primarily of differences in the degree to which these characteristics occur in both sexes (sex-typical behavior). Sex-specific patterns have also been verified.

If the same sex-typical behavior patterns, as discussed above, are compared with those of Old-World monkeys, one notes many points in common which suggests a common phylogenetic basis (B. A. Hamburg, 1974; C. Vogel, 1977).

The question of how behavioral differences between men and women arose has been the subject of countless discussions. In extreme cases the psychological differences between men and women are ascribed exclusively to learning processes. Although biologists have always pointed to the significance of phylogenetic heritage in sex role differences, no biologist has gone so far to maintain that differences are entirely innate. It is, in general, presumed that learning processes play a decisive role.

Of the learning theories, the first cited here is the reinforcement theory of sex role development. According to this theory, culturally expected behavior is rewarded and fostered by the social environment, while behavior that does not correspond to the norm is considered to be inappropriate and elicits punishment. In our western culture there are indications that play behavior is differentially reinforced by praise and censure (S. Goldberg and M. Lewis, 1969; B. I. Fagot, 1978). Sex role differentiation is certainly influenced by the way the parents interact with their children. Mothers vocalize more with their daughters (H. Keller, 1979), and fathers play with boys more than with girls (M. A. Tauber, 1979). Generally the parents respond positively when their children behave in their traditional roles (B. I. Fagot 1978). Thus parents expect their boys to achieve, compete with others, and to develop independence and self-control. For example, in our culture crying is considered unmanly. Boys are also punished more, while behavior toward girls tends to be protective and affectionate (I. H. Block, 1976). But that is in part a reaction to differential child behavior; for example, girls call for parental help three times as frequently as boys, and their calls are more frequently answered.

The fact that boys are scolded and punished more often by their fathers as early as 12 months old is due to their tendency to be more daring in play and thus do something "forbidden," including activities that endanger themselves. Fathers rarely offer dolls to their 12-month-old sons, but not because of the children's differential responses, since at this age girls do not prefer dolls (M. E. Snow *et al.*, 1983). Thus parents respond differentially to babies, depending on whether the child is male or female, and this is in all likelihood partially a response to their

Table 4.9. Sex-Typical Behavior Patterns of Catarrhine Nonhuman Primates[a]

Male	Female
Sexual behavior	
More mounting, less presenting	Less mounting, more presenting
Fear suppresses sexual behavior	Fear does not suppress sexual behavior
Juvenile upbringing	
Reduced inclination to care for young (with all essential care components)	Strong tendency to care for young (even before puberty)
Aggressivity	
More violent aggression	Less violent aggression
More juvenile fighting games	Fewer juvenile fighting games
More defense (also territorial)	Less defense
More drive and initiative	Less drive and initiative
More direct social intervention	Less direct social intervention
More display behavior	Less display behavior
More exploration	Less exploratory interest
Higher "arousal" tolerance	Lower "arousal" tolerance
Social behavior and socialization	
Create slowly developing close ties among each other	More rapidly achieve close knit social relationships among each other
Less social contact and care behavior (social "grooming")	More social contact and care behavior
Greater social distance	Lesser social distance
Develops tendency for social peripheralization	Lacks tendency for social peripheralization
Stronger tendency for forming social hierarchies	Lesser tendency for forming social hierarchies
More display behavior	Less display behavior
Less imitation behavior (more "individualistic")	More appropriate imitation behavior (more "opportunistic")
Less concealed and more spontaneous behavior, more "open" social strategy	More concealed behavior, more ramified social strategy

[a]After Vogel, 1977.

sex-typical behavior (H. A. Moss, 1974; M. Lewis and M. Weintraub, 1974; A. F. Korner, 1974). Prevailing differences can thus be strengthened. H. M. Trautner (1979), who tested the effect of differential reinforcement on sex role differentiation using published studies from numerous authors, found that there are significant sex role expectations in our culture but that these are by no means always effective in the form of corresponding differential reinforcement. Sex-typical behavior often manifests itself even when training was precisely to the contrary. Although boys are typically brought up more strictly than girls, they develop the sex-typical male aggressions contrary to this socialization pressure (E. E. Maccoby and C. N. Jacklin, 1974). Further examples will be cited from the observations of M. E. Spiro (1979) on sex role identification in the kibbutz (p. 279).

The imitation and identification theory is another important learning theory used to explain sex role acquisition. According to the imitation theory the child imitates the same sex model, and this selective imitation of the same sex presumes that the child is initially predisposed or biased to do so, even though both small boys and girls spend most of their time with women. This selective interest in their own sex has been verified (J. E. Grusec and D. B. Brinker, 1972; R. G. Slaby and K. S. Frey, 1975). This tendency is reflected in the drawings of Bushmen children (p. 269) and in the behavior of kibbutz children (p. 282). The tendency for spontaneous selective imitation of same sex models is well documented (E. E. Maccoby and C. N. Jacklin, 1974). Innate dispositions account for the fact that girls preferentially choose mothering women as role models (M. E. Spiro, 1979). Learning is channeled in such a way that children identify with and acquire their gender-characteristic behaviors which are the cultural norm, while the more basic dispositions are determined by hormones (H. M. Trautner, 1979).

According to the identification theory, sex role development is based on an emotional attachment to the reference person and the "internalization of a broad pattern of sexually appropriate demeanor, feelings and behavioral patterns, thus one's own sex role, would result" (H. M. Trautner, 1979, p. 66). Once again there is a problem of selective identification with the same sex parent. According to the psychoanalytical hypothesis of defensive identification, the boy identifies himself with the father as an aggressor, but this assumption has not been confirmed empirically. When one observes fathers, affection is observed more frequently than aggressive strictness (p. 224). It appears that admiration and love of the perceived powerful parents could lead to identification with them (P. H. Mussen and M. Rutherford, 1963; R. R. Sears *et al.,* 1965), but this is difficult to verify experimentally.

The identification and imitation concepts are not necessarily mutually exclusive. L. A. Kohlberg (1966) formulated a cognitive theory of sex role development. The developing child acquires knowledge about sex roles during upbringing by observing his environment (parents, siblings). A general concept of sex role develops from this experience as the capability to form judgments progresses. The development occurs in steps. At 2 to 3 years of age, the child normally acquires his own sexual identity ("I am a boy"), and 1 year later he identifies with others ("We boys"). Behavior is organized on the basis of a "need for cognitive consistency" (H. M. Trautner, 1979) toward conforming with one's own sexual identity. It is presumed here that behavior consistent with one's own sex role is self-reinforcing. In other words, innate learning dispositions are postulated here.

Once a child has categorized himself as male or female, this perception is resistant to subsequent external influences. It was thought for sometime that social sex attribution could, to a certain degree, replace chromosomal and hormonal sex attributions. An often cited example concerns a male child who lost his penis at 7 months of age during an attempted circumcision. His parents subsequently raised him like a female and he accepted this identity. Operative corrections (castration) were conducted at the age of 1½, and in a subsequent report (J. Money and A. Ehrhardt, 1972), the experiment was described as successful and quoted as a model example of demonstrating the significance of environmental factors in sex identification. But this conclusion was premature, for in spite of subsequent treatment with estrogens and other surgical procedures (plastic vagina), the experiment did not succeed. This person, who had behaved as a child like an androgenized female, had great difficulties identifying with the assigned sex role (J. Durden-Smith and D. Desimone, 1983).

Social sex assignment has its limitations. An illuminating case in this regard concerns a mutative defect that occurs in males in three villages in the Dominican Republic. This defect causes a deficiency of the particular enzyme that inhibits the transformation of testosterone to dihydrotestosterone in males. Dihydrotestosterone must be present within the fetal tissues of the future gonads to ensure the development of masculine anatomy at the time of birth. Thus, these babies with the genetic make-up of a male come into the world as females. However, at puberty, the clitoris grows into a penis, the testicles migrate into the scrotum, and behavior is masculinized even though these children had been treated as girls throughout their early childhood (since no one knew they were boys). They display distinct masculine sexual interests, seek contact with girls, and can have sexual unions with them. They are sterile since ejaculation occurs through a hole at the base of the penis. Their sexual drive is pronounced. This masculinization is derived from testosterone released by the gonads (dihydrotestosterone is only responsible for developing male characteristics up until the time of birth, while testosterone is effective upon reaching puberty) (J. Imperato-McGinley et al., 1979; R. T. Rubin et al., 1981). In these cases it is clear that the social environment has less influence in sex role determination than was generally assumed.

If we follow the elemental differentiating processes of normal development, we can determine that these are initially under genetic guidance. The sex chromosome mechanism determines whether the gonads will develop into male or female structures. If the zygote has two X chromosomes, female gonads develop; if it has one Y chromosome the gonads will differentiate into male structures. Subsequent development is under hormonal guidance. Under the influence of the androgens produced by the male gonads the initially bisexual organ rudiments develop in a masculine direction. The genital folds coalesce into a scrotum, the penis grows outward, and the gonads descend through the inguinal apertures. In addition, the central nervous system becomes masculinized. If there is no androgen influence, the person develops female characteristics. For example hypothalamic centers guiding the course of the female cyclical sex functions develop. Short-term androgen influence during a sensitive embryonic period will block this development. Androgens can also masculinize genetically female embryos in other ways. Massive androgen influence can substantially alter the appearance of genetic females: the labia majorae coalesce into a scrotum, the clitoris develops into a penis, and body hair patterns take on a masculine character. Smaller androgen doses produce only a masculinization of behavior, so that genetic and phenotypic girls tend to engage more in athletic activities. They enjoy forming play groups with boys, compete with them for rank position, enjoy roughhousing, and later have a more developed urge to maintain a career. They use less makeup and have diminished interest in doll games and maternal-care behavior.

As a result of extreme fetal androgenization genetic females can be born with a penis. Their further gender identity depends on further surgical and hormonal treatment and the social sex assignment. If the patient is to live as a female, clidoridectomy, vaginal exteriorization, and cortisone replacement therapy is required. When the patient is to live as a male, the female internal sex organs must be removed and cortisone and testosterone replacement therapy must be provided. J. Money and J. Dalery (1976) reported on a number of cases of extreme androgenization. Of the seven cases, four were raised as females and took on a female gender identity with ''tomboy-type'' behavior. The other three were reared as males and took on a male gender identity. They were interested in woman as sexual partners and able to engage in sexual intercourse, which ended in ejaculation of a small amount of liquid, probably of prostatic origin. Genetically and gonadally these "males" were females, but androgenized to such an extent that they perceived and functioned as males.

For a long time social scientists attributed all sex differences in human behavior as due to training and sociocultural expectation. The investigations of the last decades made it evident that androgens are a major causative factor. For a review see L. Ellis (1986) and L. Ellis and M. A. Ames (1987).

In addition to these findings, which make clear that the psychological differences between the sexes are by no means only culturally determined, there are the most interesting results of the studies by L. Tiger and J. Shepher (1975) and E. M. Spiro's (1979) work on sex role differentiation on the kibbutz.

The kibbutz is a major social experiment in which, among other things, an attempt is being made to realize the utopian feminism of early socialism. But after one generation this feminist revolution terminated in a feminine counterrevolution with a return of the values of the traditional female gender role, apparently a victory of biology over ideology. What actually happened?

The kibbutz movement pursues the following principle objectives: it is radically egalitarian, both socially and economically. Each member of the community is a worker, and capital and land are under common ownership. The form of government is absolutely democratic so no one has any authority over another. Even children are communally raised so they are liberated from parental dominance. This, in turn, frees women from traditional ties to maternal duties and the household. This emancipation of women is one of the objectives of the kibbutz movement. It is presumed that it is indeed a biological imperative for women to bear children but that there is no corresponding social imperative for them to act as mothers and raise the children, so it is desirable to deindividualize such ties using communal upbringing. Equality of the sexes is conceived as an effective psychic equality in terms of identity. Women in the traditional Kibbutz labored to live up to this ideal. They dressed like men to eradicate the sexual dimorphism considered to be a sign of their inferiority. They believed that femininity had to be suppressed to achieve equality. Lacking makeup and wearing baggy pants, they mounted the tractors and worked overtime to match the higher physical capabilities of men, attempting to exceed male performance whenever possible.

The founders of the kibbutz movement also had as a goal to replace interpersonal ties with attachments to society, and any withdrawal into individualism was considered to be a moral defect. Thus the emotions of love, affection, and cooperation, which would normally be exercised within the family, should be diverted to the collective group, which would serve as the future family, with the nuclear family being dissolved during the course of achieving this new relationship. Marital partnerships were tolerated, and couples had their own living areas, but all celebration of marriage was avoided and everything else that could emphasize the marital relationship was minimized. Divorce was a relatively simple transaction and was not associated with any stigma, in fact the individualization of the sexual bond was perceived as dangerous for group identification. Shortly after birth, children were placed in infant homes and arranged in age categories for collective socialization in order to liberate them from parental authority. They were overseen by specialized child attendants. Mothers visited with the children during appointed playtimes and, initially, to nurse them as well. This occurred communally whenever possible, and an attempt was made to designate the children as "children of the community" so mothers would not address their offspring as "my child." During nursing each mother attempted to give her child as much milk as the other babies received. If a mother had more milk and her infant had already consumed the

279

allotted milk portion (the babies were weighed during feedings), she nursed another child who had received less milk from his mother in an effort to maintain the goal of equality.

The family did not function as a residence unit. The care of the children by specialists freed women for work, making them economically and socially independent of men, and women retained their maiden name to reinforce this independence. Public show of affection between spouses was despised. Kibbutz members ate in communal mess halls, cooked in a communal kitchen, and had a communal laundry.

M. E. Spiro (1979) investigated the kibbutz Kiryat Yedidim (founded in 1920) on two visits (1950 and 1975). At the time of its founding this kibbutz pursued the objective of radical egalitarianism and collectivization. In 1920, 50% of the women were occupied in productive labor. By 1950, 30 years after its founding, only 12% of women were so occupied, the remainder specializing in child care and service professions. By 1975 the percentage of "productively" active women decreased even further. Spiro found very similar results in another kibbutz, Artzi, which was also a highly traditional one. At the time of his study, only 9% of the women were active in agricultural work, and if women employed in industry were included the total of all productively occupied women was only 12%. Artzi men accounted for 87% of the farm workers, 77% of the industrial workers, and 99% of the construction workers. Women, on the other hand, comprised 84% of all the educational and service personnel.

The majority of women born on the kibbutz were not prepared to assume their ideological roles. M. E. Spiro (1979, p. 18) summarized the prevailing attitude when he quoted a sabra (native-born Israeli): "I think that a woman should do the work for which she is suited; not on tractors or in the fields. Women, by nature, cannot be active in agricultural production, particularly if their family life is to be integrated. Of course, some do it, and they do it in Russia. Still, I think it's not natural."

Women often suffered miscarriages during the first phases of intensive physical work as a consequence of their overexertion. Spiro (1979) comments:

> Today this obsessive concern to prove their worth as women, by demonstrating that they are as good as any man in the things that men do—is dead. For the older sabras, it has become a historical memory; for the younger ones it is merely another of those "quaint" ideas that the pioneering generation had dreamed up. This change is especially important relative to the theoretical argument of this book because the sabras' disinterest in agricultural labor persists despite the fact that, as "productive" labor, it is the most prestigeful. Although this would be the avenue to social equality in its "identity" meaning, they are nevertheless not interested in pursuing it. (p. 20)

Women also participate less in administration and thus in political life, for over the long term these areas have not been attractive to them. L. Tiger and J. Shepher (1975) found that men comprised 84% of the public administrators. They occupied up to 71% of the leading positions of the federation and 78% of the political activists.

Of particular significance is the change in the value of family and marriage. When formerly the marital bond was tolerated as an inevitable discomfort and every individual attachment was thought to endanger the collective, they are now evaluated positively. Marriages are celebrated, with the blessings of the community. Bachelors are perceived less positively, and divorce, although permitted, has a more negative value.

280   Women, including those of the pioneer generation and sabras, now value family

more than labor. Of the pioneer generation, 68% of the women consider their role as spouse and mother more important than their role as laborers, and 88% of the sabras share this attitude. In men, the percentage was much lower (pioneer generation 32%, kibbutz-born 27%), which does not mean that men who esteem their work do not experience strong family ties.

Again a quote from Spiro (1979) describes the change in attitude. A highly talented 32-year-old woman working as a bookkeeper was asked whether family or work was more important, and she replied: "What a question! The family is to me more important than anything. Look, my work is extremely important to me. I like my work, but I wouldn't invest one-fourth the thought into my work that I invest in my family, under any circumstances" (p. 31).

The attitude toward children has also changed. From the very beginning, the interest in relinquishing children to the collective was not very strong, but kibbutz members felt they had to yield to this condition. Today although mothers prefer having their children with them, such a change would require a great deal of reconstruction of the facilities, for which funds are lacking. Children are still kept in communal sleeping quarters, but during the first 6 weeks they regularly stay with their mothers, overnight as well, and often for as long as 8 months. Parents visit with their children for longer periods, and children now visit with their parents for 4 or 5 hours without incurring community disapproval. The traditional female roles are acquiring a higher esteem, and radical feminism is being superceded by a femininity movement. Women place a value on feminine appearance, becoming fashion conscious. They enjoy cooking, baking, and embroidery. They recognize sex differences and do not wish to suppress them but to accept them naturally. Equality is viewed as equal esteem and is accepted within the context of role differentiation. This kind of equality has been largely achieved. Inequality still prevails in the assessment of labor in that more is invested technically in male labor than in womens' household work. This turnabout regarding family is all the more astonishing since it is not a refutation by a generation raised in the traditional manner but repudiation by those women born on the kibbutz and raised in an extremely feminist milieu who instituted the counterrevolution of femininity.

M. E. Spiro discusses these events and comes to the conclusion that "precultural" determinants were a factor here. Nature, he states, prevailed against the educational practices on the kibbutz. Most kibbutz objectives have been attained successfully, with the exception of the attempted dissolution of the family by extreme feminists and the elimination of sex-typical division of labor. Thus, to that extent, the kibbutz experiment reflects the boundaries of human ideological manipulation.

It was the women, finding it burdensome to leave their protesting children alone each night, who finally claimed that they experienced more satisfaction bearing and bringing up children than working in the field or in industry. It is noteworthy that Spiro espouses the thesis that there is a precultural basis for sex-typical behavior differences, since initially he assumed there was no such thing as human nature. In his introduction to his book, he states "The roots of this enquiry go back to 1951, when, accepting as axiomatic the widely held social sciences view that human beings have no nature—or, to put it differently, that human nature is culturally constituted and, therefore, culturally relative" (M. E. Spiro, 1979, p. xv).

Spiro's findings are directly opposed to his original expectations and thus are especially significant evidence. He solidified his evidence of precultural determinants by studying childrens' games on the kibbutz. He used his 1951 data as a basis, when children were brought up according to strict egalitarianism. Boys and girls were treated equally in all groups, and the learning experiences for both sexes were equal. One would then expect that no differences should exist during open play if there were no innate dispositions for sex differences, but these expectations were not fulfilled. The analysis of free play activities revealed distinct sex differences. For example, boys played with objects more than girls did (41 vs. 30%), particularly large objects requiring substantial physical strength (17 vs. 9%). If these 17% are added to the 16% of movement games and are categorized in a single class of muscular-physical activities, then play in this category is used by 33% of the boys vs. 21% of the girls. Girls predominated in the categories of verbal and fantasy games (39 vs. 24%). Spiro could not explain these differences in terms of cognitive theory or those of social learning. A study of the fantasy games of the girls revealed that when the girls acted out womens' roles they preferred maternal ones exclusively, and not, of course, as a result of any social reinforcement since none existed. Clearly, the girls did not desire to identify generally with the women around them, since they were occupied in many other roles, such as labor. Therefore one must assume that some need for maternal behavior was manifested in the girls' behavior. M. E. Spiro (1979) summarizes:

> On the assumption that sex preferences in childrens' choice of role models are motivated by differences in precultural needs (whether in degree or in kind), it follows that boys and girls, respectively, should prefer those models whose behavior is viewed as a means for gratifying those needs. By this theory, parenting women may be said to have been the preferred role models of sabra girls because the imitation of their maternal roles served to gratify the girl's own parenting need . . . Now, cognitive theory holds . . . that the choice of role models is motivated by one and the same precultural need. Having established their distinctive gender identities, it is the innate need to value things that are like the self which, according to this theory, motivates children to choose models of their own gender. That in the present case the establishment of a feminine identity was a prior condition for the preference of sabra girls for female models is highly likely—after all, their preferred models were female, not male. But that, of all the female models available to them, the girls chose parenting females exclusively, suggests that this preference was motivated not by a need to value that which the self is likely—femininity—but by a need to value that which the self wishes to be like—a parent . . .
> Contrary, then, to cultural interpretations, this analysis suggests that sex differences in childrens' choices of role models can be determined by precultural needs, and that a preference even for culturally appropriate models need not be culturally determined." (pp. 85–86)

Of course, this does not mean that culture is simply explained away as an epiphenomenon. The girls perceived a whole series of culture-specific behavioral patterns of child care in adult models.

Interestingly, the boys often identified in their symbolic games with animals, such as, horses, dogs, snakes, frogs, and wolves, and not with those surrounding them, like cows, lambs, sheep or chickens. Spiro states that this occurs because these animals are potentially dangerous or wild. At 5 years of age these symbols are gradually replaced by male models.

Other researchers have also confirmed an increasing familialization within the kibbutz (B. Beit-Hallahmi, 1981; S. and H. Parker, 1981). These changes did not occur solely because of the womens' desires but due to the needs of both sexes.

Another reason for the retreat of women from the labor force on the kibbutz is that their work is more routine and is thus perceived as less creative and challenging. Besides, the reality of kibbutz life, even in the founding days, was still far from its ideal of sexual egalitarianism (B. Beit-Hallahmi and A. I. Rabin, 1977). All this led, no doubt, to a return to traditional patterns but still does not explain why the children played in sex-typical manner nor the radical change against the prevailing ideology.

The results of the investigations by M. E. Spiro (1979) and L. Tiger and J. Shepher (1975) on kibbutz sex roles complement perfectly the results of developmental psychology, ethology, and anthropology cited previously. R. P. Rohner (1976) found that in the 101 cultures he investigated, boys aged 2 to 6 years were significantly more aggressive both physically and verbally, than the girls. Observations on the kibbutz children bore similar results. Undoubtedly, such differences are biologically based.

Even if there were only minor differences in behavior of the sexes, differential dispositions or body strength would result in a division of labor that would further reinforce these distinctions. Indeed, such an increasing polarization is occurring. Behavioral differences between partners with children are greater than those between childless partners, and their differences are likewise greater than those between single men and women (G. Allemann-Tschopp, 1979). In general such differences are not insignificant, and in certain areas they are substantial and well differentiated.

The fact that cultures, as Margaret Mead and others have stated, can socialize their members contrary to innate dispositions does not contradict this evidence. Even Margaret Mead (1935, 1949), who described the femininization of Arapesh men and masculinization of Mundugumur women and found a role reversal in the Tchambuli regarding dominance, dependence, care behavior, and aggression, stated that those who were socialized against their natural roles were under stress.

We have already discussed Mead's contention that our society offers the male insufficient roles compatible with is nature. A number of members of the feminist movement belittle women by denigrating their traditional roles as mothers, which can be thoroughly fulfilling. Since they frequently refer to Mead, they should also aware of Mead's comments in 1949 (1968 ed., pp. 168–169):

> The recurrent problem of civilization is to define the male role satisfactory enough . . . so that the male may in the course of his life reach a solid sense of irreversible achievement, of which his childhood knowledge of the satisfactions of childbearing have given him a glimpse. In the case of women, it is only necessary that they be permitted by the given social arrangements to fulfill their biological role, to attain this sense of irreversible achievement. If women are to be restless and questing, even in the face of child-bearing, they must be made so through education. If men are ever to be at peace, ever certain that their lives have been lived as they were meant to be, they must have, in addition to paternity, culturally elaborated forms of expression that are lasting and sure. . . .

She further encourages women to seek political and economic equality as women and not as persons.

In a commentary on the 1965 report by the presidential commission on the status of women, she writes the following on the feminist movement: "But the pendulum must not swing too far, forcing out of the home women whose major creative life is grounded in motherhood and wifehood." Further: "It is known that in societies in which maternal principles are honored, there is greater peace and balance" (quoted by P. R. Sanday, 1980, p. 347).

Simone de Beauvoir (1968) states that the woman is bound to maternity and body like an animal is and thus dependent on a male like a parasite extracting life from another organism. A profession is thus the key to emancipation and through such activities a woman can liberate herself. Marriage ought to consist of a free union terminable at any time, and abortion and birth control should be permitted. Alice Schwarzer (1976) also considers motherhood to be a form of true slavery and states that modern woman should beware of the "trap" of motherhood and marriage. Shulamith Firestone (1970) states that until the discovery of birth control women were dominated by their biological contingencies (menstruation, menopause, birth, nursing, child care). Above all, raising children resulted in a long-term mutual dependency. This natural difference in reproductive functions led to a sex-based division of labor and thus to discrimination based upon biological characteristics. Thus the source of evil should be attacked at its roots. Biological reproduction should be replaced by artificial means (test tube babies) in order that biological sex distinctions no longer determine sex distinctions in social roles. She considers pregnancy to be barbaric, and birth as painful. And the children? Well, the bond within a small group would render the close mother–child attachment superfluous.

The attempt of the kibbutz movement to realize utopian feminism of early socialism, whose goals were closely aligned with those of the cited proponents of the women's movement, failed because of the biologically determined sex differential dispositions. It was the women who increasingly brought their children back from the communal room to the family and who, by choice, retreated continually from land and factory work and from politics and administration. Out of their own free choice and contrary to ideological indoctrination the women of the feminist revolution instituted a feminine counterrevolution. In this regard the large-scale kibbutz experiment has shed light on understanding human behavior. The need of the mother for an individualized bond to her child, distinguished from other attachments, was sustained, reinforced no doubt by the protests of the child against the prolonged absence of the mother, especially at the evening farewell. The child's monotropy played as major a role in this process as the mother's need to care for a child. Before we blindly contest the traditional division of labor of the sexes, we should investigate whether it is not to some extent reasonable, on the one hand, serving the child's welfare and, on the other, corresponding to the constitutional characteristics of men and women.

In a phylogenetic perspective, these differences are quite ancient. W. LaBarre states in his introduction to Spiro's work that one can refer to a trimorphism within the human nuclear family. Childhood, and specialized maleness and femaleness form together a functional unit. Intensive affection and care over an extended period of time for the child by the mother is required to pass on the cultural knowledge required for survival. The woman was capable of performing this tedious but also differentiated and diverse task because she was protected from wild animals and other dangers and was also provided with her needs, and with materials which could only be obtained some distance away from the dwelling. As LaBarre states, the woman is removed from the need of caring for herself like a wild animal by the male. There are numerous criteria of anatomy and physiology (p. 270) that make the male more suitable as hunter and defender of the family. Men can remove themselves more easily from the home site than women. Julia A. Sherman (1978, p. 174) writes,

women in reproductive phases were a danger to themselves, their offspring, and even the group. The smell of blood attracts wild animals. One can imagine how welcome a menstruating women would be in a hunting party. Most of the victims of unprovoked bear attacks in the Yellowstone Park in recent years have been menstruating women. There have been good reasons, then, for the development of male and female cultures as they are, but they are clearly no longer maximally functional.

The reservation in Sherman's remark is appropriate. The extent to which traditional role differentiation is adaptive in industrial society must be investigated. But an uncritical total rejection of the traditional female role is certainly unreasonable. In many respects the woman in the traditional role optimally fulfills her sex-typical tasks even today. The egalitarian movements should place more emphasis on equalizing esteem for typical female activities. In many ways women's culture is richer and seems to me to be superior to man's lot. Consider, for example, achievements in domestic handicrafts. I also doubt that standard occupational work makes more demands on the spirit, imagination, and temperament than raising several children of different ages, when this is done with genuine engagement. The possibility of a working woman should be considered an alternative but certainly not the only worthy role directed at the socialization of girls for feminine roles.

Thus Ramona Frasher *et al.* (1980) oppose the typifying of sex roles through sex-specific toys, and K. and R. Dunn (1977) write:

> If you cannot resist (buying a doll carriage), then do it, but recognize that you are contributing to the stereotypical image of each girl becoming a "mommy," rather than an independent professional woman who may also be a mother. . . . Try to control your inclination to surround her with the traditional restrictive items that suggest domesticity as her central life . . . (If someone gives your daughter a doll and she likes it) permit her to keep it without exhibiting any negative feelings, but do not lapse into cuddling it or encouraging her to do so. Treat it as another object and direct attention to other more beneficial toys (pp. 46–48, quoted by Brian Sutton-Smith).

In other words, one should avoid raising children on the basis of their biological sex roles. I doubt that this is humane counsel. What is so bad about maternal behavior that it should not be a model? The goal of our education should not be to make a person feel insecure or bad if they choose to live according to their traditional gender roles. Certainly, traditional girls' games do not prepare them for career life in the same way as boys' games (B. Sutton-Smith, 1979). Girls are, for example, less competitive. But during the last century girls have greatly broadened their play repertoire. In addition to traditional games, girls now enjoy tennis, ice skating, baseball, and swimming. The question is whether they should imitate all boys' games! "Now that things are beginning to change, we really must ask most seriously . . . whether we want to turn girls into footballers and boxers for the sake of their future in the economic, military and political worlds, or whether there may not be some other alternative" (B. Sutton-Smith, 1979, p. 251).

The dissatisfaction of many modern women must be appreciated. It is, among other factors, founded in the strain (or the humdrum routine) of family tasks and their economic dependence. But that is not the fault of the few men who lead an interesting career life.

The reduction of the family to the nuclear members has probably contributed to the discontent of modern women. Gone are the relatives, aunts, grandparents, and caring neighbors and their older children, who in earlier times (and in rural areas today still) would provide essential relief by attending to smaller children and providing emotional outlets for stimulation and conversation. Contacts with same sex members of the same age bracket are also lacking. In traditional societies, men and women spend many hours of the day with members of the same sex, with obvious enjoyment. Communication is more problem free in such gatherings; I have been impressed with the affability with such groups, with a great deal of joking and laughter. One also gets the impression that within such women's groups the burdens of child rearing are reduced to a level far below that which we observe in technologically civilized society. Such positive conditions still exist in rural Europe. It is in modern society that marriage partners are so limited to each other. This affords the opportunity for deepening relationships but can also lead to difficulties in the form of strain, habituation, or irritation since the spouse cannot fulfill all the social needs of his partner.

The dissatisfaction of modern women is also caused by the denigration of the traditional woman's role, in contrast to gainful occupations. In all tribal societies women have as great or greater economic role than men. It is only with the development of western industrial societies that the man supports the woman economically. Even in the western peasant or farming societies women play a major economic role that is compatible with child rearing. If modern professional activities do not allow for child rearing and since a sexual division of labor is inevitable for survival, child rearing must be become an acceptable salaried profession. In this way women would be liberated from economic dependence on males. But placing all women into the work force is not the solution. Women need the freedom to select between alternatives, and that necessitates elevating the esteem for traditional female roles and motherhood, for children need mothers who have time for them.

The new competition between men and women has created problems for which we seem to be poorly equipped biologically to handle. Women appear to be inhibited in various competitive situations with men. For example, the studies of G. E. Weisfeld et al. (1980) and C. L. Cronin (1980), showed that young girls playing ball with boys were less competitively motivated than when playing among themselves and that they achieved less than their potential (see also S. W. Morgan and B. Mausner, 1973; A. Peplau, 1976; C. C. Weisfeld et al., 1983). Even highly ranking women generally hesitate to dominate their husbands and instead tend to submit to their wishes (E. I. Megargee, 1969). During courtship, women behave toward their suitor as if they needed direction and leadership and often even pretend naivety. This is probably a feminine strategy in recognition of the fact that marital sexual life and partnership would be disturbed by a subdominant male (W. H. Masters and V. E. Johnson, 1970, J. Scanzoni, 1972) and is related to the old infantile appeals for care.

Agnes Heller's (1980, p. 217) remarks are noteworthy in this regard:

> Whenever men do make efforts not to feel and behave in the old "masculine" way and whenever women expect them to change their emotional habits, this happens only within the framework of the family or occasionally in man–woman relationships in general. But no attempt at change is made and no expectations for such a change are developed on the level of sociopolitical activity. Here the traditional male stereotype prevails unchallenged. Wives may require their husbands to be emotional, nonauthoritarian, playful in the family, but they want them to be authoritarian, strong, tough, competitive and earnest in all other areas of social life. They could not even love a man behaving differently that is in an "unmanly" way. . . .

She claims, however, that this is based on cultural traditions which one must overcome over time in favor of an emotional diversity based not on sex but on individuality.

286   Sarah Blaffer-Hrdy (1981) writes that the broadly held view is completely false

that women are not motivated to compete because of their biology, that they are sexually passive, and only interested in child rearing. That is indeed correct. But women originally competed primarily with other women, just as men originally competed with males. As Blaffer-Hrdy correctly notes, they also use men to their advantage, but less in a competitive situation. One female strategy is to submit and in this way effect leadership. It is incorrect to interpret this behavior as passivity and submissive behavior. In fact, this strategy requires much more sensitivity than strategies of so-called male dominance. Furthermore, the woman understands how to put the man into a sexually dependent position, and that is a form of dominance that is specifically female.

The denial of sex differences in dominance behavior will never help to change the situation. It is better to recognize and deal with it. Thus, publications like those of Elanor Burke Leacock (1981) have made significant contributions, not because they have demonstrated that male dominance is a myth, as if males lacked a biological basis for dominance, but rather because they show that there are societies in which dominance apparently plays a smaller role. It confirms that human behavior is malleable and can be modified even contrary to hereditary traits. Leacock's thoughts on the egalitarianism of tribal societies must be interpreted with caution, however, for her data were quite selectively evaluated (E. B. Leacock, 1978 and discussion). We will return to the theme of dominance and rank later (p. 297).

S. and H. Parker (1981, p. 771) add in this connection that womens' liberation has little to do with what an individual woman chooses:

> Ultimately, liberation has little to do with whether a woman chooses to become a professional or a housewife and mother, or both; she can be liberated or traditional in either of these roles. The term liberation . . . can be considered in both psychological and social-structural contexts. In the former, it may be thought of as an attempt to change one's identity—to differentiate oneself, to establish and define one's own boundaries of self—with a concomitant consciousness of new needs, values and goals. In the latter, at a sociological level of conceptualization, it refers to the emergence of a social structure that allows and encourages males and females alike to achieve goals in accordance with their talents and differentiated selves.

Undoubtedly, hereditary predispositions have led to the development of a polarization of the sex roles in various cultures with dominating males and subordinated female roles. In some contemporary Islamic states, women are still dominated by the men in such a way that a modern liberal view cannot be accommodated. Also in our society we ought to refrain from fixed role clichés. As stated earlier, biology does not mean inevitable fate. The great difficulties in understanding the new roles of the sexes and especially new relationships between men and women lie in the fact that for most of their history man and woman have worked cooperatively for the sake of their offspring, something for which we appear to be biologically prepared. Competition was avoided by assigning even the neutral tasks to one sex or another, which is still the case in tribal societies. The economic contribution of woman has always played a major role. Contemporary women face the problem that jobs are incompatible with child rearing, i.e., one can not take one's children to work. Furthermore, jobs are less sex specific with the division of labor breaking down, leading to male–female competition both in jobs within and outside of the home.

In biology, the phenomenon of functional conflict is well known although rarely considered in discussions of humans. For example, armor protects but restricts freedom of movement. A bony skeleton gives the muscles a point of evolved attachment but is heavy. Before the swimming bladder had evolved in fishes a problem existed for those living in the open sea. Skeleton weight had to be reduced, but that meant a loss of power. Signal mechanisms facilitate intraspecies communication but also provide visible cues for enemies. Analogous conflicts determine our interpersonal behavior and especially heterosexual partner relationships. Territorial defense and rivalry fights in primates and many other mammals produced physically more powerful and aggressive male individuals. We also bear this heritage. In a positive sense this means that males can afford protection. But that almost automatically leads to a dominance and a demand for control over the ''weaker sex'' and, correspondingly, to reprehensible abuses. In many cultures the behavior of males toward females is ambivalent—while man honors woman as his beloved and mother and she spurs him on to highest artistic creations, he also represses her. Unfortunately, this repression of females, as K. E. Müller (1984) showed, has been and still is a problem for people of all cultural levels and in all times. We must solve these problems with insight, using our capacity as ''cultural beings.'' However, as in the discussion on problems of aggression, the difficulties are not explained away by denying the existence of sex differences, but by becoming aware of them. We must be ready to accept the positive aspects of sex differences and control those aspects that interfere with our harmonious living together by causing distress. Reason and mind permit us to tame our human nature. Our hereditary disposition allows us to make such changes and if we do not take advantage of it, we are the ones to blame.

Summary 4.7

The claim that human gender roles are as culturally determined as the clothes people wear does not stand up to critical examination. There is a universal pattern of sex division of labor which occurs even in the ''egalitarian'' hunter and gatherer societies. Among their activities, men act as representatives of their group in interactions with others, defend the group in actual combat and ritual, and generally hunt big game. With these tasks, especially those involved with representing the group to outsiders, men have also taken on the leadership roles, even in so-called matriarchal societies, where the men of the matrilineal lines are in authority. In addition to realms of male dominance there are aspects of life where women prevail. This includes the socially important area of child rearing and internal group integrity, that has been researched little to date. In tribal societies, the men and women contribute economically in different but equally significant ways to maintain the household, and they are mutually dependent economically. Thus, for most of history, a partnership of complementarity between man and woman has existed. Only in historically recent times has there been an economic disequilibrium with male economic dominance.

Men and women are biologically predisposed for division of labor anatomically, physiologically, and behaviorally. They differ in action, perception, and motivation. Most differences are quantitative (sex-typical), and a few are qualitative (sex-specific). Differences even develop contrary to upbringing procedures. Thus on the kibbutz there was a concerted effort to raise all members in an ''egalitarian'' manner contrary to the traditional sex roles. But this feminist revolt was followed by a return to traditional family patterns. Studies of childrens' games on the kibbutz have shown that children select their own sex as social models, and girls, in particular, with all the various role models available to them, imitated in play only those women who were mothers caring for young. Phylogenetic adaptations apparently have determined these preferences.

Hormonal factors during embryonic and child development play a major role in realizing male and female dispositions. Girls who are androgenized during embryonic development behave like boys in many respects. In this connection there exists a noteworthy mutant that causes genetically male children to have female phenotypes at birth. They are thus raised as girls and behave like them. Their sex changes with the onset of puberty, not only morphologically but behaviorally into fully functional males. Examples like these show that social sex role determination has its limits. This does not exclude alternative life styles for men and women, but the biological factors should be considered.

The male predisposition to dominate is probably based on his primate heritage. In the past as today this led to domination of woman in many societies, a condition that must change. But this cannot take place by denying inherent sex distinctions. We must be aware of them in order to bring those aspects of our behavior under control. In a positive sense, sex differences are a challenge for the establishment of equality in complementary partnerships.

4.8. The Individualized Group: Family, Kin, and Alliances

Tribal societies are in essence kin based and this organizational principle was probably what characterized human society through most of its history. The families which comprise a group are interconnected by ties of blood relation. The individual thus is embedded in a network of kin who ultimately will support her or him and fill her or his needs when necessary. Likewise, each individual is obligated to these kin. Despite rugged individualism, tribal peoples cannot separate themselves from this community and its obligations. We can neither imagine the good and secure feelings of being enmeshed in such a web nor the incredible burden of the constant obligations. These groups are made up of close genetic relatives. Siblings or cousins account for 80–90% of nonaffinal relationships in a hunter/gatherer group. Kin selection, therefore, undoubtedly was a major reinforcer in the evolution of these groups.

Groups usually demarcate themselves as territorial units distinct from other such groups and are characterized by continuity in membership through time. The members of these local groups in hunter/gatherer societies develop a group feeling that separates them from other groups. At the same time, regular interaction is maintained with other groups. In fact, local groups cultivate relations between themselves. They exchange marriage partners, form alliances, conduct trade, and exchange goods—or consider each other enemies. Thus human groups tend to form relatively stable bounded entities whether they reside in a single area or wander as a unit. The group is characterized by lasting interpersonal relations extending over the family borders. Intergroup mobility is regulated to maintain group identity, so excessive immigration is usually avoided. People who are acquainted with each other are bonded by familiarity, whereas strangers, even if they resemble one another in costume, dialect, and demeanor, are met with reserve. This is even more probable if the stranger deviates more significantly in appearance and behavior from the group norm. Xenophobia is a universal quality (p. 175). A certain demarcation is thus a prerequisite for group formation and maintenance. Groups define their memberships by certain characteristics, such as, costume and dress, dialect, and certain norms to which they adhere. We have observed that individuals who deviate from the group norm in any respect become the targets of aggression of other group members. This norm-maintaining aggression, which we will discuss later in more detail, results in either the adjustment of the deviant individual or his repulsion if he does not conform to the norms of the group. Group exclusivity fosters the development of group-specific behavior, which via dialect and language formation, along with other differentiating mechanisms, can lead to the development of divergent cultures, a process E. H. Erikson (1966) spoke of as "cultural pseudospeciation." The tendency to contrast oneself with one's neighbor and thus segregate one's identity from others, is thus quite strong. Children and adults within an individual group form their own subgroups often also distinguished by some common characteristics, such as speech characteristics or shared a "secret" knowledge.

How do groups form? How do individuals bond within groups? What sets them apart from nongroup members? Groups normally grow by propagation. A child enters a group at birth. As he grows up, he acquires the cultural characteristics of the group, develops personal ties with others, and learns to identify as a group member.

Bonding has been observed to extend beyond the group, even in hunter/gatherers. Local groups develop ties and alliances with other groups. When two allied groups join forces, males from different groups come together to form a new group for a special task. This process of group formation, which plays an important role in the life of the males, has been studied experimentally. M. and C. W. Sherif (1966), in what is now a classical study, investigated the formation of groups in a camp. The 11- and 12-year-old boys were initially unacquainted, but after 2 or 3 days had formed small groups of three or four members each. The boys were given freedom of choice of friends, and when questioned could name their best friends.

The Sherifs then divided the boys into groups, intentionally separating friends. Within the new groups, boys learned to depend upon one another as they worked together to assemble tents, carry canoes, cook, and engage in other activities. The old friendships dissolved and new alliances and group structures developed with a distinct pattern of leader and follower roles. Each group developed specific means of undertaking particular tasks. This became clear in later experiments which caused altercations between groups. The group pursing a tough approach enjoyed having physical encounters with their opponents, while the other group attempted to resolve conflicts without physical aggression. Among other things, they were hopeful that the others might lose. Group-specific jargon developed and each group had its own secrets and jokes.

Once the groups had formed their own identity profiles, group competitive activities, such as baseball games, were held and the winners awarded sought-after prizes. Tensions between groups arose as a consequence. The losers complained and embarked on revenge campaigns whereby both parties threw green apples at each other. As out-group members were repulsed, the members of the in-group grew closer, overestimated their own capabilities and underestimated those of the opponents in an interesting denigration of the opponents. After one contest for collecting the most beans, slides were shown allegedly portraying the beans each group had collected. The same number of beans was shown on each slide, but if the slide was announced as that of their own group, the pile of beans was perceived by the viewers as greater than if it was described as the results of the competing group.

The polarization that arose from competition was later alleviated when the groups were united by common task situations. For example, defects in the plumbing system were repaired jointly. Both groups also collected money to rent a film for the camp. A common enemy, introduced artificially, also elicited this effect.

Most of the elements that bond adults or cause their segregation occurred in these camp groups. The environmental contingencies operating at a given time initiate processes of self-organization of the group. This is found at a much more complex level in the organization of the state and thus suggests a universal rule system—a grammar of human social behavior (p. 493).

Since humans respond to particular situations in predictable ways according to given programs ("if . . . then"), the group acts as an entity. As K. Lorenz noted, common combat unifies a group. We have already discussed the reason this is so (see family defense, p. 169). It is always the individuals who behave on the basis of phylogenetic and cultural programming, coordinated by commonly perceived environmental conditions and objectives. This explains why intragroup relationships often obey the same rules as interpersonal relationships. Even at the diplomatic level, for example, one party may claim that the other has committed an offense and threatens to break off relations, a strategy employed by the individual in an attempt to block aggression (p. 500).

However, there are aspects in which group behavior differs from that of the individual. Thus certain situations have an amplifying effect through mood induction (e.g., panic, group aggression). We will discuss this phenomenon in more detail later. At this time, suffice it to say that there are many points in common between interindividual and intergroup behavior, but that the latter is more than a simple extension of the former.

The awareness of belonging to a social category can suffice to produce group behavior (H. Tajfel, 1978). The assigned membership can even be more important than the external similarities between group members. However, similarities are quickly manifested by using common symbols and rituals. Tajfel states that simple mutual attraction of individuals is insufficient to form groups, which requires some social categorization. Social categorization reinforces social identification and leads to the definition of unifying group characteristics, such as similarities in appearance and demeanor, a shared destiny, proximity, perceived or imagined common threat, and others.

Tajfel thus resolves the question of the necessary conditions that take a group of individuals in an aggregate and convert them into group members using a social identification model, which has a cognitive basis. A social cohesion model can also be offered as an explanation. This theory states that a group develops automatically as the product of reciprocal interactions—the people comprising the group merely must like each other.

Tajfel maintains that the first question a group member asks himself is not whether he likes the others in the group, but who is he in relation to it. This indicates how essential group membership is to human identity formation.

The Sherif studies show that initially groups form of their own accord. However, group leaders were also able to institute new groups experimentally by having them identify with new tasks and objectives.

Groups act as units in particular contexts and require that their members make certain community responses at such times. The group also has certain rights, such as owning a particular hunting or grazing ground or perhaps a water hole. The group also has one or more representatives who act as spokesmen during intergroup contacts, even in societies where there is no concept of "chieftainship" in terms of a superior individual in whom authority is vested. Thus the Kalahari

Bushmen do not have chieftains, but there are individuals who, as owners of water holes, must be addressed and persons to whom a stranger desiring to live in the tribe must speak (p. 324).

Individualized groups can take on various forms. Hunters and gatherers live in band communities and move in an annual cycle through a territory owned by the group. Within this territory they have stable camping sites consisting of aggregations of small huts. They spend a great part of the year in these camp sites. Pastoralists move through a familiar region in which each group has individual rights, such as, to watering places. They also use encampment sites owned by a group. Even the so-called nomads, who spend most of the year in family bands, usually possess defined rights to grazing areas, and the migration routes are strictly determined. Several family bands may also unite to form temporary groups. In this case, affiliation with the group does not constantly change but is regulated by lasting continuity in membership.

Segregation and territorial ties are typical for the individualized human group. We find these conditions in hunter/gatherer groups who are often used as models of the original cultural conditions of mankind. I emphasize this because one occasionally hears the Kalahari Bushman (San) described as nomads, as if they lacked territories. Indeed, the Bushman have territories and defend them if necessary against intruders. Group segregation is also manifested in settlement design. The settlements are arranged so that wherever individual family huts or homes are standing they open into a common central space. Thus, the individual families gravitate toward the community naturally. We find basically the same arrangement in the settlement patterns of Bushmen and of European villages where the village square is used as a communications center. On the outside the settlements are often demarcated with fences, palisades, and hedges, which all help to reinforce village or tribal community identity.

Some rather astonishing conceptions of the "original" human community prevail even into the present. Thus collective thought is imputed to "primitives." F. A. von Hayek (1983, p. 165) writes: "Civilization brought differentiation and individualization." I would reverse this concept, since I observed well-developed individualism among the Kalahari Bushmen, the Yanomami, and the Eipo. By specialization into different professions, a great deal of differentiation does indeed occur in "civilized" society. However, it is precisely in a labor-sharing society that a great deal of the generality ("universality") of the individual is lost. The so-called "primitives" are individualists who are much less dependent on external influences (people and events). The Bushmen of Kalahari decide on a individual basis whether to go hunting or stay by the hut. They show no professional specializations but are more involved in a kin-based society with mutual economic obligations. Individual families are bonded to each other through a system of exchange interactions, which acts as a form of social insurance during a time of emergency, but otherwise they are rather autonomous, each family producing practically everything it needs for survival. Every Bushman male can hunt, build his hut, and produce his implements, whether they be weapons, clothing or adornment.

Even in professional circles many misconceptions have prevailed on the nature of original human communities, as represented today by hunters and gatherers. It is often claimed that these nonterritorial, peacefully coexisting open communities are constantly changing their composition. We will discuss this in section 4.11 on territorial behavior. According to another thesis, Bushmen lack long-term social attachments, as did all other hunters and gatherers. This "fluid organization" is said to result from the necessity of the groups to distribute themselves according to the availability of resources (R. B. Lee, 1976; J. Woodburn, 1968; J. Yellen and H. Harpending, 1972).

The thesis of the "instantaneous hunter-gatherer economy" and the transitory ties of the hunter-and-gatherer has been questioned by P. Wiessner (1980). We will discuss her findings in some detail since she conveys an exemplary impression of the permanence and differentiated nature of extrafamilial social relationships. P. Wiessner (1977) investigated the highly developed reciprocal exchange system known as "hxaro" in !Kung Bushmen. Each member of the group develops a personal relationship network based upon mutual obligations of gift giving, which thus acts as a form of social insurance. The hxaro partnerships are quite durable and hxaro partners are often transmitted by parents to their children. They foster a far-reaching involvement of the individual in a broadly based system of social relationships. P. Wiessner (1981, 1982) later added the following facts about the existence of short-lived bonds in the hunter/gatherer society:

> 1. Although the direct organization for work requires little investment (effort) and produces immediate results, the relationships which structure the redistribution of social and natural resources requires a substantial investment, for which repayments are significantly delayed.
> 2. Because the investment is high and repayment postponed, the !Kung make an effort to maintain relationships over time, which leads to numerous relationships each with a long history.
> 3. This stability and continuity of mutual relationships plays a very significant role in the mobile, kin-based society. Reciprocal obligations remain active even after biological relationships are long forgotten. This ensures that each person has a sufficient number of partners who can and want to fulfill his needs. "In other words, it equalizes the number of productive kin available to a person in the face of a highly variable biological reproduction."

With the hxaro exchange system, in which a roughly balanced long-term gift exchange takes place, individuals maintain access to their resources. Each person has an average of 16 such partnerships, 18% of which bond him to another person in the camp, 24% to persons in neighboring camps (in a 5-20 km radius), and 58% to persons in two or three other camps up to a distance of 30-200 km.

The total network of such alliances with other individuals is known as "my people." Via an exchange partner, one also develops relations with the exchange partner's family without actually entering into a direct relationship with them. The one or two exchange partners in another camp, however, do in turn divide what they received with their group members and thus relations are mediated. Census data by R. B. Lee (1968–1969) and P. Wiessner (1977) on annual visiting trips of more than a week for by 30 adults living in /Xai/xai showed that 80 of these visits (93%) were to regions where exchange partners lived. Only six were undertaken in areas where the traveler had no exchange partners. Wiessner estimated that the average amount of time spent making gifts for hxaro exchange is 5 work days per partner per year.[9] This is a considerable amount of time when we remember that each individual has an average of 16 partners.

The expenses of the partner being visited are substantially high and particularly noteworthy. For the first two or three days the host is obligated to provide for the visitor and his family. Thereafter, the guests provide for themselves (they are permitted to hunt and gather in the host region), but they work less than the others

---

[9]Measured by the number of days one needed to produce the gift or earn the money that a gift (e.g., blanket) costs.

and bring less to the community. The social investment in the form of providing for and integrating the guests into the group remains quite high.

Generally an individual makes 1.5 visits annually with a total mean duration of 2.2 months. Thus an individual spends an average of 3 months per year with a hxaro partner. Due to this substantial investment, the Bushmen are interested in maintaining these relationships. During the partners' lifetimes 55% of the partnerships are created, while the rest are inherited. Of the exchange partners, 45% are not closely related. Thus one cannot speak of transitory social ties within hunter/gatherer society; what we find is a long-term complex of relationships.

The relationships within the local group (averaging 30–50 persons) or "band" are differentiated. While the relationships between parents and small children are intimate and spontaneous, those of the other members of the extended family are regulated by a series of cultural conventions. For example, these "joking relationships" determine toward whom one may act casually and to whom one maintains a formal demeanor. Thus in Bushmen and many other African tribes there is a formalization of parent–child relationships (with the exception of infants and small children). As a rule respect is given to those individuals exercising educational authority. The grandparents in these groups are not authorities, so their grandchildren can behave in a relaxed manner with them, making the grandparents "joking partners" (A. R. Radcliffe-Brown, 1930). The children can use these joking partnerships to release tension through banter and other forms of playful aggression. Joking relationships are also formed with siblings of the same sex and with potential spouses. Relations with siblings of the opposite sex are more formalized, as are those with parents-in-law and their joking partners (H. J. Heinz, 1966).

A. Barnard (1978) demonstrated how differentiated just the rules for determining formalized and nonformalized Bushmen relationships are: *Joking partners* for an individual are grandparents, mother's brothers and their wives, father's sisters and husbands (only in the !Ko), and mother's brother's and father's sister's children ("cross cousins").[10] If the individual is a man, a paternal aunt's daughter is excluded from this group, and if the individual is a woman the same holds for the son of a maternal uncle. In some Bushmen, these persons are known as "respect relatives." Joking partners also include all joking partners of the spouse (only in !Ko and Khoekhoe Bushmen) and their spouses, namesakes of the same sex, siblings of the same sex, and parallel cousins of the same sex, the spouse and spouse's siblings of the same sex, and the spouses of siblings of the same sex. *Respect persons* are parents and their siblings of the same sex, one's children and the children of siblings of the same sex, namesakes of the opposite sex (only in Khoekhoe), siblings of the opposite sex, parallel cousins of the opposite sex, paternal aunts and their spouses, and respect figures of the spouse and their spouses.

In view of the precise definition of these relationships, one could say that the regulating system for social relationships in these kin-based societies is more highly differentiated than those for Americans.

---

[10]Children of mother's brothers and father's sisters are known as *cross* cousins; children of father's brother and mother's sisters as *parallel* cousins. However, in kin-based societies, specific kinship terms rarely conform to biological relatedness but are applied to other relatives who occupy a similar position to ego with respect to age, sex, generation, and other attributes of the relationship. Thus, not only a person's real father's sister's children and mother's brother's children are considered to be cross-cousins, but children of all those who are called father's sister or mother's brother. These may be many or few depending on the kin terminology system.

This is also true for the cultural rules which regulate whom a person may marry or not beyond the limits set by the biological incest inhibitions.[11] One of the simplest ones, used in many tribal societies, is that one may marry all those to whom one applies a cross cousin kin term but not those called parallel cousin terms. In some patrilineal societies, children descended from two sisters may marry because their children are descended from the unrelated husbands of these sisters. But children descended from two brothers may not marry in such a society. Genetically there actually is no difference between these relationships. In matrilineal societies the rules are reversed.

Marriage-regulating conventions can be highly complex, as they are, for example, among desert Australian aboriginal societies. They make it difficult for a man to find a suitable marriage partner in his immediate vicinity. Men therefore, are frequently compelled to search for a partner in distant groups. This phenomenon led to the development of a complex network of relations between widely separated groups resulting in a wide variety of mutual rights and obligations. Since the desert aborigines are hunter/gatherers in an arid region, it is vital for them to have access to other districts during severe periods of extreme drought. Thus the complex marriage regulations are ecological adaptations and a means of maintaining social integrity (H. K. Fry, 1934; A. A. Yengoyan, 1968). The Arunta system is a classic example of the degree of complexity of this regulatory system (A. R. Radcliffe-Brown, 1930). It functions as follows:

Man A can only marry woman alpha. Their children are designated as D's. Each D girl must marry a delta male and their children become betas. Each beta women must marry a B male. Their children are C's, and each girl C must marry a gamma male, and the children of this union are alphas. According to this rule, each alpha woman must correspondingly marry an alpha male, and their children are gammas. Each gamma woman must marry a C male, and their children are Bs. Each B woman marries a beta male, and they produce deltas. Each female delta, finally, marries a D man, and their children are As. The A's, B's, C's, and D's represent the exogamous half of the tribe. They must marry the other tribal half (alphas, betas, etc.) and only within the classes specified above.

		Moiety I		Moiety II		
Section One	{	A	—	α	}	Section Three
		B	—	β		
		C	—	γ		
Section Two	{	D	—	δ	}	Section Four

The marriage rules are idealized and in practice are by no means always strictly followed, but by and large they have an ordering effect and ensure a relatively uniform mixture of a gene pool, whereby the cross cousin rules create a network of descending lines (whether patrilineal or matrilineal). Other regulations determine whether the woman resides in her husband's group (virilocal residence) or the man resides in the wife's group (uxorilocal residence), when spouses are from different groups which they often are.

---

[11]Recall briefly that, in all cases, sexual union is forbidden between parents and children, parents and grandchildren, siblings and parents' siblings, and parent's sibling's children, with just a few exceptions.

With such an extended incest taboo, man imposes new structures beyond his biological nature into society. Levi-Strauss clearly recognized this, but he did not distinguish between the primary taboo (see incest inhibition) and its secondary, cultural elaboration. He claimed that incest taboos were determined only culturally, which is certainly incorrect.

A clan system develops within many cultures. If the members of a clan can trace themselves to a single known ancestor, then one can speak of lineage. Lineage is often fictitious with a totemic ancestor as a mythical figure. This has the potential to integrate distant kin via fictive close blood ties. In the Eipo (West New Guinea), for example, there are 11 clans, and members of individual clans are obligated to help their fellow clan members. Since a clan is distributed across the entire language region of the Eipo, clan members can be found in distant villages, and they are obligated to render assistance due to this supposed relationship. Clan exogamy prevails, for members of an individual clan may only marry someone from another clan.

A clan can extend across many territorial groups, and a territorial group can encompass several clan communities. No less than eight clans were represented in the small village of Dingerkon, which in 1978 had only 64 adult inhabitants. In the Eipo, the clan system is supplemented by male initiation groups which cross-cut clan lines forming an additional network of ties. Male initiation takes place only every few years. Several age classes of boys and young men are selected from various villages (sometimes from an entire valley) and are simultaneously initiated (V. Heeschen, 1984b). These individuals are bonded to each other for life and have mutual lifelong obligations. Cultural adaptations of this kind create structures which integrate the territorial local groups into a larger community forming alliances and thus political interactions.

Summary 4.8

Humans appear to have an innate tendency to form larger social groups and establish group identity. Group commonalities are created as groups develop symbols of identification, and distinguish between in- and out-group members. The dynamics of group formation have been experimentally investigated. The process of self-organization of adolescents follows a dynamic resembling adult interactions. We observe emphasis of contrast and group bonding mechanisms, such as co-operative tasks, definition of a common enemy, development of negative attitudes toward outsiders, and other shared features.

Among hunters and gatherers, the family is integrated into local bands of 30 to 50 persons. These bands most likely characterize the original condition of human social life. Bands preserve their own identity and as a rule are bound to one or more specific areas, maintaining relationships with other groups through marriage ties, exchange partnerships, rituals, clan membership, and other cultural conventions. However, they retain their identity and rights and display notable continuity in membership so that it is incorrect to consider them a transient grouping in a completely open and fluid society.

Mobile existence of this societal structure should not be understood to mean that the people are wandering constantly without any restrictions on their movements. The relations between group members as well as those between members of different groups, are more highly differentiated than is generally assumed and are also relatively permanent, such as the reciprocal exchange system among the

!Kung Bushmen. Rules also determine potential marriage partners and toward whom one acts in a formalized manner or in a casual way. Clan organization, initiation groups, and other cultural structures lead to the formation of interrelationship networks extending beyond the small group. These cultural arrangements maintain order in society well beyond those regulatory mechanisms operating within kin and small group systems and through which man distinguishes himself as a political creature.

4.9. Rank Order, Dominance

We observe in humans a relationship to authority that is incongruous. On one hand, we fight for a society of equals and maintain that we are anti-authoritarian, but, on the other hand, we unabashedly hang pictures of leaders on our walls.

Our disposition to submit to leadership is in striking contrast to our outward rejection of dominance. How is this contradiction explained? I believe that the contradiction is only an apparent one. Our natural tendency to form rank order relationships requires that the individual perceives the impulse to rank himself above others, which requires a rebellious attitude toward the top ranking individuals.

Continual rank struggles, however, would severely disturb group harmony and it is also important for those defeated in the rank competition to be prepared to accept a subordinate position and thus have confidence in the superior ranking figure and recognize his important role. If the individual lacked such a capability, he would either have to leave the group or be in a constant contest with the other members of the group. In addition, he would not be able to profit from the positive leadership qualities of a more gifted person. In this context it would be interesting to learn about the function of ranking and to what extent rank orders establish themselves on the basis of innate dispositions. H. Laborit (1980) claims that rivalries about particular matters automatically lead to tests of strength in which one or the other party prevails. But does that suffice to explain the relatively harmonious group life in a rank-structured organization? And must not obedience also be explained?

The phenomenon of rank order was first investigated in animals. T. Schjelderup-Ebbe (1922a, b) found that chickens kept together as a group initially fought among themselves and created a "pecking order" from their encounters. Each hen knew who was superior and who was inferior to herself. She would avoid victors of previous encounters in the future and would peck at a subordinate if she did not make room for her. Rank order can be linear, with alpha pecking at beta, beta at gamma, and so forth down to the omega individual. Generally, however, rank relationships are more complex. Thus a hen A could defeat hen B and B in turn C. But C could by good luck be victorious over A. In such a case C would be dominant over A but subordinate to B, who is ranking below A.

These dominance relationships based on aggression are distinguished from those rank orders in which superior members do not owe their position to aggression alone but also to other "positive" leadership characteristics, such as in supporting others, resolving conflicts, sharing, or imparting other important knowledge to other individuals. In these cases of leadership designation, superior rank position is based primarily upon achievements and thereby upon subsequent recognition of these leadership qualities. But aggression as a rule always makes some contribution to rank determination. A high ranking individual must be able to defend his position if necessary against challenging subordinates, usually younger ones.

Rank order relationships occur in all groups of living primates, especially in chimpanzees, who achieve and maintain their rank position chiefly with displays (often incorporating noise). One male in Jane Goodall's study area that learned to push around empty tin containers noisily used this strategy to move from the second rank position to the first. Animals achieving a high rank position enjoy a number of advantages. They have priority at feeding sites, superior access to females, and thus enhanced individual reproductive success. However, they also expose themselves more to danger since they protect subordinates in threatening situations.

The group profits from high ranking members in a number of ways. They gather round the superiors when danger threatens, profit from their knowledge and from the fact that high ranking individuals are able to solve conflicts due to their social position. Once a rank order has been established, further aggressive encounters within the group are largely blocked. Thus rank order is a means of neutralizing intragroup aggression.

R. Dawkins (1976) views rank order as merely the sum of individual behaviors with no group factor involved and is thus a manifestation of individual behaviors at the group level that only benefit high ranking members. Rank order as such, according to Dawkins, has no group function at all, especially not one of controlling aggression. In my opinion, one must consider not only individual selection, but also group selective advantages in evaluating the role of rank order. High ranking members are not the only ones benefiting from social hierarchies. When groups compete, it is advantageous for one group if it is less torn by internal conflicts than the other group. This is particularly so for man. Furthermore, wherever leadership hierarchies exist, all group members benefit from the abilities of the top ranking individuals. Thus, while rank order may have originated through individual selection, group selection, in the face of competing groups, could have strongly reinforced it, selecting further for mediating rather than aggressive traits in the high ranking.

In many primates, one can identify top ranking members since they are looked at more frequently by other group members and are thereby the "focus of attention" (M. R. A. Chance and R. R. Larsen, 1976). Other individuals orient to them and turn to them, on the one hand, because they are feared but also because high ranking individuals are sought when danger threatens and thus are a source of protection. The significance of the attention structure as a rank order criterion has been doubted recently with the observation that not every individual who is the center of attention is necessarily of high rank (G. Schubert, 1983). A female in estrus can elicit enhanced attention temporarily, as can a particularly cute juvenile, while another time these individuals are peripheral. But these exceptions are rather easily delineated from other situations (for the use of these criteria see also p. 152).

When people are placed into groups, they form rank orders quickly. R. C. Savin-Williams (1979, 1980) found in an American camp that distinct rank orders developed in a cabin of five or six boys within 1 hour of their arrival. The highest ranking individuals were not the biggest and strongest but the best looking, most athletic, and those with the most advanced physical maturity. A parallel study in a girls' camp showed that rank orders developed less rapidly and were formed on the basis of different criteria. Highest rankings were awarded not to the most attractive and athletic but to those who were most mature and maternal.

Human rank order behavior is closely allied to that of nonhuman primates. Thus, B. Hold (1977) showed that the attention criterion as a measurement of rank position operates in humans, which is reflected in such expressions as describing someone as highly "regarded" (the verb regard can mean to observe something with a firm, steady gaze). Highly ranking individuals command respect not only by being seen but also by being heard. Others orient to a high ranking individual when he speaks.

B. Hold (1976, 1977) used the attention criterion to investigate rank order relationships in European kindergartens with different educational approaches, G/wi Bushmen (central Kalahari) childrens' play groups, and Japanese children's play groups. High ranking children displayed the following attributes:

1. They initiate games and, in general, display more initiative than other children.

2. They organize play activities of others and thus significantly determine their activity.

3. They are less place bound, moving more freely throughout the area.

4. They play with various children.

5. They participate more frequently in role playing.

6. They mediate conflicts, preferably as protectors of weaker members. They preferably support losers except for the times when they compete with another high ranking individual for the top position. Then they seek alliance of other high ranking individuals by supporting them in their fights. They become supporters of winners. Once they have solidified their rank position, they again become "protectors" (K. Grammer, 1982).[12]

7. They initiate physical contact more often. The "protective" movement of resting a hand on someone is a typical dominance gesture that arose from a caregiving gesture (I. Eibl-Eibesfeldt, 1980a and figures, p. 432).

8. If high ranking children are given candy to distribute, they use it to maintain control over the other children. On the other hand, low ranking individuals cannot keep control if put in the same situation.

9. They are more aggressive than average but are not the most aggressive group members.

10. They show off more frequently.

The low ranking members display the following typical behavior patterns:

1. They orient to high ranking members.

2. They obey high rankers.

3. They question more.

4. They seek contact with high ranking individuals.

5. They occasionally avoid high ranking members.

6. They offer gifts and assistance to high rankers.

7. They show high ranking members objects and relate messages to them.

8. They are unobtrusive and submissive.

Naturally, the behavior of high and low ranking children is more differentiated than rank order behavior in nonhuman primates, but their ranking behavior is so closely paralleled that we can presume it has a common origin. Humans and primates share the attention criterion, high rank characteristics 3, 6, 7, 9, and 10,

---

[12]It is remarkable that chimpanzees use the same strategy. They assist other powerful individuals when competing for high ranks. Once a high position has been attained, they again support weaker members (F. DeWaal, 1978).

and the low rank characteristics 2, 4, 5, and 8. Point 6 of low rank characteristics applies to primates insofar as low ranking members delouse higher ranking individuals.

Many other factors from the above studies also determine a child's rank: high ranking children generally had the longest kindergarten experience and were quite familiar with the facilities. Boys generally had higher ranks than girls, and in Germany and among the Bushmen they displayed a stronger impetus to display to others. A good relationship between a child and the kindergarten supervisor, who always had a high rank, had positive effects on the child's rank position. This also has nonhuman primate correlates. In chimpanzees and rhesus monkeys the mother's rank is transmitted to her offspring. D. R. Omark and M. S. Edelman (1976) and R. Abramovitch (1976, 1980) confirm B. Hold's findings, while R. A. Hinde (1974) is somewhat skeptical.

Various attempts have been made to use dominance relationships in place of attention structure to determine rank order relationships, such as in determining who wins a contest over an object. But according to U. Kalbermatten (1979) it is not a good criterion, since object struggles are usually decided on the basis of possession norms (see p. 344). C. L. Cronin (1980, p. 317) investigated the dominance relationships between boys and girls in athletic and scholastic competitions. The girls competed with boys but were not highly motivated to outdo them in competition: "Girls played to win (though less intensively than the boys) when their opponents were girls. Girls performed poorly (in dodgeball) and did not take advantage of opportunities (in spelling) when their opponents were boys."

If girls were to compete in some way other than boys do, then rank would have different meanings for the different gender. "Competition, for females, involves at least two strategies, one for female opponents and another for male opponents. Obviously, these differences will not be erased by requiring coeducational gym classes and athletic teams. It may be that these differences are adaptive for our species and in fact should not be erased" (C. L. Cronin, 1980, p. 318).

Hierarchies developing in all-girl groups are less rigid than those in all-boy groups. Boys often affirm their dominance by physical strength, sometimes aggressively. Physical appearance ("attractiveness") also plays an important role, especially the aspect of an upright posture. Rank orders based upon attractiveness are quite stable, and dominant males have superior access to girls (G. E. Weisfeld, D. R. Omark, and C. L. Cronin, 1980).

Children understand how to draw attention to themselves in various ways, with verbal display (imperative and friendly) playing a predominant role (Fig. 4.58 and 4.62). Next in importance is threat, then (in boys) noise, which in chimpanzees is also an important means of display. Noise is less important in girls. They often display with objects, which in boys is in fourth place in importance. Display does not only aim at dominance, for one can become attractive by behaving in an affectionate manner. During the course of the year the display behavior of the kindergarten children showed distinct fluctuations (Fig. 4.59–4.61). High ranking children were quite active after returning from vacation, which probably indicates that renewed self-assertion was necessary after a long separation in order to confirm one's rank for new group members (B. Hold-Cavell and D. Borsutzky, 1986).

In Rhesus monkeys the plasma testosterone level changes as rank order varies. It increases when males attain a dominant position or successfully defend it and decreases when rank is lost (R. Rose et al., 1975; A. Mazur, 1976). This process also occurs in man. Plasma testosterone levels significantly increase in tennis players winning a match (A. Mazur and T. A. Lamb, 1980 and Fig. 4.63). They

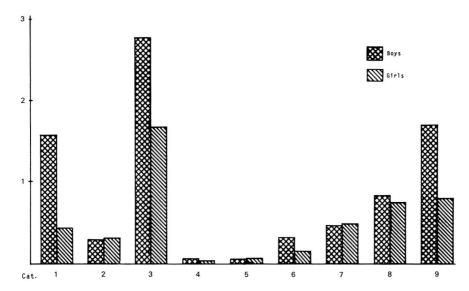

FIGURE 4.58. Method of display and its effect on esteem: the frequency of individual categories of self-presentation in girls and boys in 5-minute intervals. The graphs show that verbal displays (3) predominate, followed by threat behavior (9). In boys, noise making (1) was next in importance, but not in girls. Asserting oneself via objects has much more importance in both sexes (8). The contribution of friendly self-representation is not seen here. Not every verbal display is aggressive, for affectionate behavior occurs as well. *Abscissas:* attention (= frequency with which a child stands in the center of attention) (1) using noise and volume to draw attention to oneself; (2) make oneself larger; (3) impressing verbally (calling names louder, giving orders, demanding etc.); (4) show off; (5) demonstrate personal capabilities with self-made objects; (6) move prominently; (7) use motion to bring attention to oneself; (8) using an object to draw attention to oneself (demonstrating toys, etc.); (9) threat behavior. *Ordinates:* total number of appearances per child, divided by the number of 5-minute samples (per child between 30 and 60). After B. Hold-Cavell and D. Borsutzky, 1986.

experienced an elated mood. Victors dissatisfied with their achievement showed no increase in testosterone levels. In medical students, a rise in plasma testosterone levels was found 1 to 2 days after graduation, these students also experiencing a high positive mood level (Fig. 4.64). Thus biological components play a major role in human rank order behavior. The fact that males differ from females in their rank order behavior may be based on the role of males in dealing with outsiders.

Girls are more prepared to acknowledge another's rank. R. C. Savin-Williams (1979, 1980) states that one advantage of superior rank is access to preferred sites. High ranking individuals occupy the favored place at the table and have the best sleeping spots near the fire in camp cabins. But the most esteemed advantage is the feeling of being the center of attention, which apparently raises one's self-esteem. "Being dominant appears to be its own reward, to be highly satisfying and to be sought" (S. L. Washburn and D. A. Hamburg, 1968, p. 473).

Savin-Williams also points out that high ranking individuals are not the only ones with advantages. Lower ranking individuals enjoy protection and are removed from decision making. M. and C. W. Sherif (1966) found that adults enjoy belonging to a group and becoming subordinate within it in order to obtain security. People are encouraged by success, gaining more self-assurance, and become more ex-

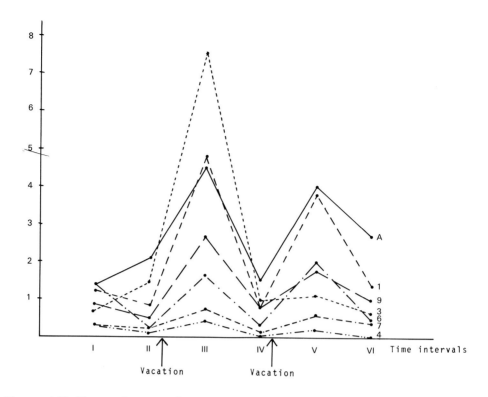

FIGURE 4.59. Temporal course of esteem and the various categories of display in a child enjoying high regard. The year is divided into six segments. Vacations are significant intervals, for thereafter the child's self-presentation increases since the child must renew his rank. Each individual time segment comprises 6 weeks; vacations are marked by arrows. After B. Hold-Cavell and D. Borsutzky, 1986.

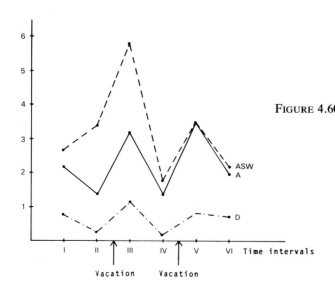

FIGURE 4.60. Course of drawing attention to oneself, of threat, and rank over six time intervals in children enjoying high esteem: ASW, drawing attention to oneself (self-representation); A, rank (frequency with which a child stands in the focus of attention); D, threat. After B. Hold-Cavell and D. Borsutzky, 1986.

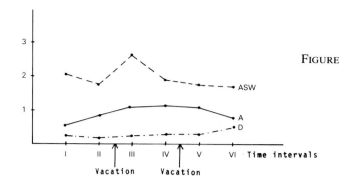

FIGURE 4.61. Course of drawing attention to oneself, threat, and esteem over six time intervals in children with median and lower esteems. After B. Hold-Cavell and D. Borsutzky, 1986.

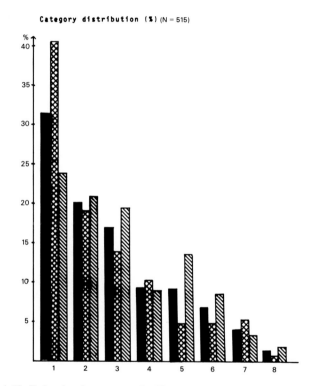

Category distribution (%) (N = 515)

FIGURE 4.62. Behavioral patterns of self-presentation (1) play a major role in kindergartens. Next highly frequent are behaviors of aggression (2) and contact search (3). To counter the impression that agonistic behavior would dominate, it should be recalled that self-presentation includes a great deal of friendly behavior. The graphs show the distribution of categories in percentages. The left column shows the figures for both sexes, while the middle and right columns portray boys and girls, respectively. *Categories:* (1) behavior bringing attention to oneself; (2) aggressive behavior; (3) contact behavior; (4) interactions with the kindergarten teacher; (5) organizing behavior; (6) behavior oriented toward others; (7) behavior after aggression; (8) unclear situations. After B. Hold-Cavell and D. Borsutzky, 1986.

ploratory and take greater risks, which serves their striving for further achievement. Indeed, one can become conditioned to success (G. E. Weisfeld, 1980).

Rank relationships between children and juveniles are dynamic and relative. Small children only initially develop dominance relationships. The strongest members dominate in groups of 3- and 4-year-old children, while leadership qual-

303

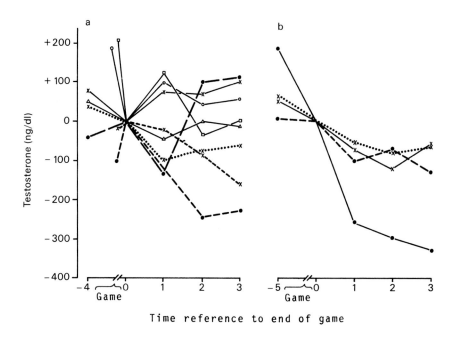

FIGURE 4.63. Change in testosterone level in tennis players: winners (solid lines) and losers (broken lines): (a) in easily won games; (b) in closely won games. After A. Mazur and T.A. Lamb (1980).

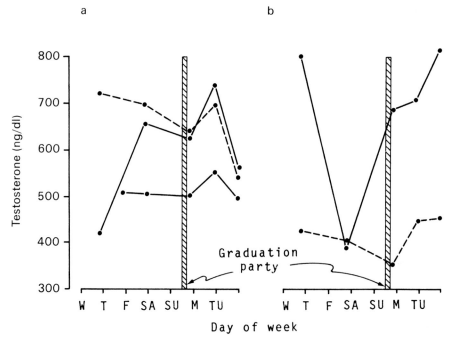

FIGURE 4.64. Testosterone level changes in medical students following graduation: (a) in persons experiencing their mood height the day of graduation; (b) in those experiencing it 1 day later. The testosterone levels corresponded to mood heights with a 1-day delay. After A. Mazur and T.A. Lamb (1980).

ities become significant in 5 and 6 year olds (D. R. Omark and M. S. Edelman, 1976). A child will assume a higher rank with increasing age. In mixed age groups, which are typical for individualized small groupings, each child enjoys some superior position in care and leadership behavior and thus in a specific way a dominance over younger members for whom he provides. Rank order is also determined by specific social contexts. While there are so-called leadership persons within childrens' groups who stand above all the others, within the hierarchy there are a number of children who, because of their individual characteristics, assume a higher rank in particular situations. K. Grammer (1988) found, for example, that some children maintained higher positions outdoors than indoors. These children, so-called "scouts," were more mobile and higher risk takers. They invented movement games more frequently and inspired the others. They could display abilities outdoors that could not be manifested inside the kindergarten.

Corresponding patterns are found in adults. One person can enjoy esteem within a group because of his courage, while another is appreciated for artistic abilities without being particularly courageous, and so on. In the Eipo, a person with a good "garden soul" (one who is industrious and successful at gardening) is esteemed. They even refer to a "sweet potato bigman." Others, who are brave and fight skillfully, are war leaders, while others are unchallenged authorities on construction of houses. H. Marcuse (1967, p. 47) notes in this regard a specialized authority that must be recognized: "What is probably impossible biologically is to make do without some kind of repression. It may be self imposed . . . thus the dominance of a pilot in an airplane is rational domination. It is impossible to conceive of a situation in which the passengers would dictate the pilot's duties to him. The traffic police officer is another example of a typical rational authority. . . ." Marcuse criticizes political dominance, which rests on the basis of suppression and exploitation, i.e., on pure dominance and not on recognized leadership characteristics.

The rank order phenomenon is manifested in the adult world in a highly diverse and differentiated way. In traditional European families it is seen in the seating at the daily table. The father sits at the "head" of the table (at its narrow end). This is the place where he can best be seen by everyone else and also that where he can best survey everything. At conferences, participants are seated in a similar manner according to rank, but with the highest individual at the middle of the long side of the table. In ceremonial contexts the top ranking individual may be specifically delineated, such as judges in a courtroom. He is often enthroned by sitting on a highly adorned chair, as princes and kings did in days past. The word "highness" testifies to this practice. We also speak of a "towering" personality, which manifests a high-low rank relationship (high-ranking, low-ranking; see p. 538).

Large persons more easily assume higher social positions, presumably because size in our society is a positive personal characteristic, so to some extent size is a certain bonus for their success. Beauty is similarly perceived (A. Schumacher, 1982).

In humans there is a clear relationship between age and rank, which also occurs in some nonhuman primates. Older men and women enjoy high esteem in many tribal and civilized societies, valued for their experience and wisdom. In cultures in which knowledge transmission is exclusively verbal, older members are sought for their knowledge and experience, and in our culture elderly individuals play a relatively important role in political life. In many public institutions a "senate" has important decision-making functions. In conjunction with the importance of age in public life, one rarely finds a portrait of a high ranking individual as a young man. Domination by the aged is a questionable practice in politics, since due to medical progress individuals who are senile or whose health is failing oftimes remain in high ranking positions into advanced age. J. D. Frank (1967, pp. 85–86) writes:

> Evident insanity occurs rarely among the leaders of modern democracies, but slowly increasing disability with advancing age and the pressures of office is unfortunately much more widespread than many believe. In this century alone, at least six British prime ministers and a great number of cabinet officers were ill during their term of office. In the United States, Franklin Roosevelt and Woodrow Wilson were examples of presidents who during the latter parts of their terms suffered advanced arteriosclerosis . . . Wilson's inability to lead government was undoubtedly the reason that America lost the opportunity to join the League of Nations. Roosevelt, whose lack of strength was visible in Quebec, was a dying man at Yalta, incapable of comprehending conference proceedings. . . .

Currently, there is less and less dependence on experience in family and economy and, as a result, esteem of the old is rapidly disappearing. We often feel that their knowledge is being quickly overtaken by rapid advances in technology and the natural sciences, which in some respects is no doubt true. But in social contexts the elderly still possess a valuable fund of experience that cannot easily be tapped from libraries and computers. A mother who has raised several children has acquired experiences that do not become outmoded. I should like to add an interesting relationship between age and appearance that demonstrates the significance of older men for society. In spite of age-related deterioration of physical strength, the older man maintains an imposing impression with his wavy white hair, beard and eyebrows. The "display adornment of age" (I. Eibl-Eibesfeldt, 1967, 1987) compensates for physical deterioration and provides the aged with a physical appearance which is impressive. It arouses esteem and permits him to serve the community further. On the other hand, the position of the female is challenged less, since their roles as mothers and grandmothers are well established.

There are societies which strive to achieve equality among their group members. In the !Kung Bushmen equality is enforced with strong social controls. These controls educate members against accumulating private possessions and anyone who does not share with others is punished, pestered, and runs the risk of being ostracized which creates enormous social pressures. Controls are also directed against those who brag about their hunting success to others less fortunate. One's achievement is, of course, recognized, but if someone brags about his success he will endure the mockery of the group (R. B. Lee, 1969; P. Draper, 1978).[13] The necessity for such a system is derived from the dependence on a reciprocal exchange system for social security in societies whose ecology does not permit reliable daily individual provisioning. If this dependence on sharing were to be relaxed, inequalities would develop among the Bushmen. This has been shown by E. A. Cashdan (1980) for the //Gana of the central Kalahari.

Among the Maori there was a distinctive form of norm-maintaining aggression whose objective was leveling out differences in individual wealth. When one person had accumulated possessions, they were open to looting under some pretext. These raids were known as "muru," a term that means to plunder. Any deviation from

---

[13]When R. B. Lee gave his Bushmen an ox for a Christmas present, the Bushmen reacted with disdain and in this way to prevent any boastfulness in the bud.

the norm of daily life, even some misfortune, such as an individual becoming an invalid, a divorce of a wife, a grass fire spreading over a burial site, could be used as an excuse for pillaging. The object of such an attack could only reconcile himself with the fact that some other time he might partake in a similar activity against another person. Chieftains were exempt from this plundering and this could accumulate wealth.

If we investigate modern "egalitarian" societies we find that their egalitarianism is always applied to the masses but not to the leadership hierarchy and that some kind of leadership figure usually stands at the very head of the state (for example, China's Mao Tse-Tung). One can also glean a strategy of authority consolidation on the part of the political leadership espousing egalitarianism, because if all conditions were maintained at an "equal" level, the rise of individuals or groups competing for top leadership positions is prevented. These societies do not have rank pyramids but a well-established cadre. In modern egalitarian states civil egalitarianism is not enforced by pillaging as in the Maori but to varying extents by equalizing taxation.

Rank striving (success striving) is opposed to egalitarianism, so any system that maintains equality as their ideal must of necessity be repressive. In China an attempt was made to counter individualistic tendencies with the Cultural Revolution. There are also human dispositions that conform with egalitarianism. Envy, as investigated in depth by H. Schoeck (1980), is one of them. This basic characteristic occurs in all cultures, and has the benefit of motivating oneself to achieve and also fulfills a regulatory function for norm maintenance by arousing negative reactions to excessive boastfulness and accumulation of property. But if this latter tendency were to result in complete equalization, it would put an end to those that spur cultural progress. By equalization, elites create an easily dominated "mass," and this explains why dictators frequently espouse extreme egalitarianism. They thereby cement the powers of leadership at least until a revolution occurs. Western democracies also increasingly tend to consolidate their leadership by enforcing more equality. With these strategies they might well undermine their own existence, which is founded in the pluralism of personalities and opinions.

The need to win esteem is well developed in humans, and in our society it finds many outlets in substitute activities (D. Morris, 1968). One can achieve status in various ways: as the king of the rabbit breeders, as stamp or beer coaster collector. Indeed, it is satisfying for some to simply imitate high ranking individuals in clothing and behavior. The fashions worn by princesses are rapidly popularized by the masses. The former privileged activities of the ruling classes, for example, hunting and riding, are taken over by the well-to-do citizenry in "rank mimicry." The wealthy in turn continually acquire new status symbols to differentiate themselves from those now used by the masses. They have their own jewelers and fashion designers, whose exorbitant prices guarantee that they and only they will obtain this watch or this dress. The status symbols of British nobility are rapidly abandoned once the common masses acquire them (N. Mitford, 1956). O. Koenig (1969) shows that the uniforms of victorious states are often imitated in a form of rank mimicry. Thus the uniforms of the Hungarian Hussars were imitated in Austria, Germany, Russia, and France. The Hungarians likewise imitated the notorious Turkish guard troops of the Delis, who were the first to attack in battles (after intoxicating themselves with opium). Our culture uses jewelry, attire, office equipment, automobiles, and other devices as status symbols. The objects do not have to be functionally effective, merely expensive enough so that not everyone can acquire them. It is curious that even relatively intelligent people cannot escape 307 the force of status seeking, apparently because not only the cortex governs this behavior.

It would however be incorrect to believe that only our culture is plagued by such excesses. The potlatch festival of the Kwakiutl Indians of Vancouver Island in Canada is well known. These Indians organized festivals in which the host chief sought to impress and even shame his guests with generosity and extravagance (F. Boas, 1895; R. Benedict, 1935). They poured costly oil into the fire, destroyed valuable copper plates, beat boats to pieces, and even killed slaves. The guests, in turn, attempted to maintain their self-esteem the next time by organizing an even more extravagant festival. It was incumbent upon the host chief to demonstrate his superiority, as evidenced in the speeches and songs in which the chiefs praised themselves and mocked their guests as poor fools [Ruth Benedict (13), p. 148ff.]:

I am the great chief who makes people ashamed.
I am the great chief who makes people ashamed.
Our chief brings shame to the faces.
Our chief brings jealousy to the faces.
  Our chief makes people cover their faces by what he is
  continually doing in this world,
Giving again and again oil feasts to all the tribes.

I am the only great tree, I am the chief!
I am the only great tree, I am the chief!
You are my subordinates, tribes.
You sit in the middle of the rear of the house, tribes.
I am the first to give you property, tribes.
I am your eagle, tribes!

Bring your counter of property, tribes, that he may try
  in vain to count the property that is to be given away
  by the great copper maker, the chief. . . .
I search among all the invited chiefs for greatness like
  mine.

I cannot find one chief among the guests.
They never return feasts,
The orphans, poor people, chiefs of the tribes!
They disgrace themselves.
I am he who gives these sea otters to the chiefs, the guests,
  the chiefs of the tribes.
I am he who gives canoes to the chiefs, the guests, the
  chiefs of the tribes.

One facet of the entertainment at the potlatch consists of competition for esteem. However, there is also a bonding element occurring that Benedict did not clearly perceive. The festival is also entertainment for the hosts and guests and is not intended solely for the self-elevation of the host chief. The guests are also offered respect, a point clearly made by W. Rudolph (1968). One offers respect in providing for one's guests, and the opulence of a repast is a reflection of the esteem held for the invited individuals. This is carried beyond optimal levels in the potlatch as the host is engaged in a quest for dominance. Ethnologists refer to these as prestige and "prestige economy" (J. Faublée, 1968). They even play a major role in the political life of democratic governments and are also cultivated quite openly in international gatherings such as the World's Fair.

On the Trobriand Islands there is a most outstanding festival of competition for rank. Each family attempts to harvest as many yams as possible, particularly large ones. The piles of yams are placed on display in the village (Figs. 4.65, 4.66), and the village chieftain judges the result. Whoever collected the largest harvest enjoys the highest esteem. The tubers are then stored in private storage houses, which are constructed so that the tubers can be seen between the beams; the art of storage consists of laying the most beautiful ones, so they are visible. These storage houses are most impressive. Families consume as little of these yams as possible so they remain visible for a long time. Any tubers remaining by the next harvest become refuse, a practice that may seem senseless at first. However when I attended a harvest festival it occurred to me that in this way the people are motivated to produce more domestic crops than they actually require for their annual needs. This encourages a storage economy, which could prove most beneficial during a bad harvest. Thus behind the winning of prestige as the subjective goal is the creation of a reserve stock as, in the selective sense, the "actual" causative factor. This example also shows that a superficial assessment of a practice as having only one function, such as pure display, can be misleading. The striving for rank (esteem, prestige) can indeed degenerate into disorder, but it can also stimulate superior performance that benefits the entire community.

The various cultural manifestations of social hierarchies reflect adaptations to differential environmental conditions. The Herero, Himba, and other cattle herders of Africa must defend their cattle and grazing lands. This requires a chieftain hierarchy for cooperative combat and is fostered by obedience to leaders on a daily basis (p. 147). In times of emergency, similar rigid hierarchies are formed in otherwise liberal democracies. Hierarchical role systems develop within small groups when quick decisions are necessary (R. L. Hamblin, 1958) and when a group has a task to accomplish (M. A. Fisek and R. Ofshe, 1970).

The methods of achieving esteem vary, but from the preceding discussion it is clear that qualities of leadership are involved. Leadership can be manifested in specialized ways so that esteem is limited to highly specific accomplishments. Accumulation of wealth can confer authority and thus engender esteem, but the ability to manipulate social relationships can accomplish the same end. In the Yanomami, I found that young men visiting each other show one another their quivers. They keep a great number of arrows given to them by others, and while showing their arrows they comment on from whom and which village they received this or that arrowhead. Thus they display their social network to others, just as we try to heighten our esteem by "name dropping." This is reminiscent of the visiting card used in many Viennese houses, in which a guest places his card down among the cards already there. Such guest cards not only have a certain sentimental value but also a display function as well.

In the Medlpa (New Guinea) the men wear strips of sticks on their chests, which indicate how the person has performed in the exchange of gold-lipped pearl shells. Each stick stands for a bag of 8 to 12 shells that had been exchanged. Thus, the more shells a person had distributed, the higher his esteem, the number of sticks indicating the individual's rank. These exchange festivals were discontinued in 1970, and from that time, the omak (as these stick arrangements are called), have been frozen into the lengths that had once been attained (A. Strathern, 1983).

Thus rank order, as stated earlier, can only come about when there is not only a striving for rank but also a disposition to accept subordination and obedience. Both tendencies are well developed in humans. Modesty and obedience belong to the virtues, and their high esteem is reflected in the symbolism of Abraham's sacrifice. In this sense, A. Koestler wrote that it is not an excess of aggression

309

FIGURE 4.65.
The competition for es-
teem by harvest success
on the Trobriand Islands
(Kiriwina). The stacks of
yam tubers are displayed
for judging. Photo: I.
Eibl-Eibesfeldt.

a   b

FIGURE 4.66. (a) and (b) After the harvest and judging the yams are stored in the structures
shown. Highly esteemed persons have the right to elaborately decorate their
yam-storage houses. Photo: I. Eibl-Eibesfeldt.

but of loyalty that can ruin us. The danger of excessive loyalty was dramatically
demonstrated by Milgram's (1963, 1966, 1974) studies.

Milgram invited Americans of various occupations as volunteers to take part
in an experiment, for which he provided only modest compensation. He alleged
that he was testing the relationship between punishment stimuli and learning and
that he required assistance for his work. He explained to his subjects that they
would assist by operating the apparatus that delivered punishing stimuli, and an
alleged experimental subject in the other room (actually a colleague of Milgram)
had the task of learning something. If the "subject" erred in answering a question,
the "assistant" would deliver an apparent electrical shock, beginning with a lower
voltage and increasing voltage strength to the next higher increment with each
succeeding "incorrect" response. The apparatus had a keyboard on which the
voltage reading of the shocks was indicated, in 30 increments from 15 to 450 volts.
In addition, the voltage increments were labeled "mild," "strong," and "very
strong." Prior to beginning the study, the assistant was introduced to the "subject,"
310   who was strapped in a seat in the adjacent room. The assistant also received a

mild electrical shock to become acquainted with the negative stimulus. The surprising result of this study was that all assistants carried out Milgram's instructions for punishment despite the fact that they thought they were delivering electrical shocks that could, in reality, have seriously injured the experimental subject.

Milgram ascribed this initial result to a lack of sufficient subject feedback. The assistant could not see the experimental subject in the other room nor could he hear anything from him. In another similarly constructed study, Milgram utilized acoustic feedback: a particular voltage evoked a prerecorded groan, and with increasing voltage the assistant heard sounds of pain, and finally a strong protest to stop because it hurt so much. At the maximum levels, the assistant would hear a painful scream and nothing thereafter. Even under these experimental conditions, 62.5% of the assistants carried out the experiment to its conclusion (maximum voltage). They did so but not without any scruples. Many turned to the chief investigator and said it would be better to stop since the voltage could injure the study subject. But upon the instructions of the investigator to continue in the interests of the experiment, they did so, often verbally making the investigator responsible for any consequences. Others protested against the instruction to continue, stood up as if to leave the room, but returned to the apparatus upon request. The assistants could have left of their own will and would not necessarily have forfeited their compensation by stopping. Yet only 37.5% of the assistants refused to continue the experiment, and most of these only upon activating keys that would have severely injured a test subject. Other variants of this study showed that inhibitions caused by "subject" behavior were stronger when the "subject" was present in the same room; in such cases 60% of the assistants refused to continue the experimental procedure.

The assistants visibly experienced conflicts. They felt sympathy for the subject and stated so, but they could not resist the authority giving instructions. This study also showed that the immediate presence of the authority figure was of decisive importance. Thus, if the investigator gave instructions from a telephone in another room, the number of assistants conducting the study was two-thirds smaller than it was in the investigator's presence. In addition, many of the assistants became devious, claiming they were activating high-voltage punishments but actually activated the keys for lower currents. Apparently they were not sadistically motivated, but rather succumbed to authority, and in this situation authority was more powerful than sympathy.

These studies of Milgram, which are particularly valuable reading for all their interesting details, show that people experience great difficulty resisting an authority figure, especially when they are freely enacting a task that allegedly fosters a higher goal ("for the sake of research"). This was contrary to cultural expectation, for control groups that Milgram questioned regarding the outcome of such a study claimed that at most 0.1% of any assistants would be so insensitive as to carry out such an experiment to its conclusion.

Reality deviated shockingly from prediction. What can be learned from that? Of course, Milgram's work shows that subconscious decision-making processes can play an important role in our social behavior. This suggests that we can, with insight into this phenomenon, become more sensitive to the voice of our conscience than to our tendency to obey authority, and we can also formulate our laws so that they provide more latitude for acts of conscience. In discussing the prevention of war crimes it is easy to say that the individual must disobey certain orders, but in reality this is improbable behavior, for how should the simple soldier stand up against a military authority? He must have the law as a point of support in specific situations regarding how he should and should not behave. Rank striving and obedience are not in and of themselves evil; it is the extreme forms against which we must protect ourselves. If we are so protected, then rank orders would fulfill their function in our society. The disposition for subordination rests upon acknowledging accomplishment and social virtues of the highly esteemed individual as well as on fear and respect of that individual. Popularity, appreciation of knowledge, and respect for the individual must operate together. Domination based entirely on power should be rejected just as inherited leadership or caste systems, since the dominance relationship in such instances is neither rationally founded nor based on public opinion. Leadership figures require consensus of the general public.

Similar characteristics are ascribed to high ranking individuals in various cultures. One example is the song of praise on Sékou Thouré (Guinea) from E. Beuchelt and W. Ziehr (1979). The values as well as the symbolism of the expressions correspond closely to our cultural perspective:

You became good   *And the suppressed*
You became brave   *(The light)*
You became upright   *That lifts itself*
You began to beam   *Is inextinguishable*
You are the protector   *Is immeasurable*
Of the children   *Is glorious*

According to D. Goetze (1977), the enchanting, charismatic personality is characterized by five qualities:

1. *The Mirum:* designates the special, singular, alien, and disconcerting. Ascribed to this quality are the incomprehensible and wondrous and the individual is identified with particular superhuman spiritual or other powers.
2. *The Tremendum:* characteristics of the horrible, dreadful, terrible, and sinister. It is interesting that these qualities are second on the rank order list of characteristics, but indeed there is an element of fear mixed with respect. Rulers who generate fear have often been surnamed "the Great." Terror is not only repulsive, but attractive, writes Goetze, and he adds, disassociating himself, "of course only for those seduced by it." But we can all be led astray, as the fascination for tragedy teaches us (see also bonding using fear, p. 77).
3. *The Fascinans:* this probably has erotic elements and includes enchanting qualities of voice, amiableness, "charm," and an ingratiating nature.
4. *The Majestas:* greatness in this extended meaning signifies the fact that the individual stands in the center of attention.
5. *The Energicum:* vital liveliness, a reflection of many animal displays. Most vertebrate males court with energetic displays of vitality. In this extended sense the magnetic passionate speech in those humans so gifted is an expression of a powerful will and is highly influential.

Love worthiness (amiability), based upon goodness and friendliness and cited in the first line of the above exaltatory song, is missing in this listing of the important characteristics of dominance, which excludes those related to sympathy arousal important for leadership personalities. Of relevance here is the study conducted by R. D. Masters (1981a, b), who evaluated 4356 press photographs of American politicians published in the media during the campaigns between 1960 and 1972. The winners of the elections did not primarily display aggressive dominance expressions in their photographs. They tended to display submissive behavior similar to that observed in children shortly before submitting in a conflict. They behave particularly "obligingly."

The disposition to be led is perhaps one of the most widespread infantile characteristics known in man. A primary rank relationship exists in the mother (parent)–child bond. The mother is a place of security and caregiving, but she is also a restraining authority. Certain concepts of high rank are often coupled with a parental suffix or prefix, such as mother or father of the people or godfather. Also, low ranking submissive behaviors often consist of infantile behaviors and high ranking individuals often refer to their subordinates as children and address them in like manner.

We have shown the difficulties inherent in our ambivalent attitude toward authority and thus to rank problems and to our attempts to formulate a life free from domination. Rank order can contribute to the harmony in group life and that striving for power as well as the readiness to be subordinate and obedient are human characteristics. We can suppress these dispositions but doing so would have doubtful consequences since our striving for "higher" goals, for esteem and power, is the impetus for achievement and thus for productive creativity. On the other hand, life without obedience and loyalty is hardly conceivable. We must only realize that these virtues, like all virtues, can degenerate into nonvirtues. Atrocities have been committed out of loyalty to ideologies. Particularly hazardous is our desire for power since there is no consummatory act nor a consummatory situation that shuts it off. Only the social and environmental conditions place a limit. In the small societies of early human history one could only achieve a limited degree of authority: one could become the chieftain or the medicine man. But technological civilization places means for gaining power at our disposal that far exceed the individual's imagination. Even in liberal democracies the politicians deal with amounts of money far beyond their comprehension. Who is surprised when they have squandered another billion when seeking power, and there is no self-imposed limitation set on this quest, for it is an "open drive."

Thus today a critical perspective toward leadership is more important than ever, and one should not dismiss the "anti-authoritarian" experiments of the late 1960s; rather, they should be analyzed to discern the symptoms of our times. Biological norms, as we already demonstrated are directed toward an optimum, and their excesses are as damaging as insufficiencies. Children deprived of authority and hence guidance are unsettled. J. Rothchild and S. B. Wolf (1976) visited American children who grew up in a very permissive subculture, where freedom was sought against schools, police, opponents to drugs, and even work. The children were not required to do anything—not even brushing teeth was mandatory. These parents wished to give their children freedom in the most literal sense. These children were asocial, bored, and listless individuals. They interpreted their parents' behavior as a lack of interest. They did not feel liberated from parental authority but deserted! Authority in the extreme is certainly destructive, but this does not mean that one can generalize that parental control is "murder of the child" (A. Miller, 1980), nor should the family be dismissed as a "breeding place of hatred," even if such conditions do occur in some family situations. This sort of extreme position, although expressed with good intentions, leads to a polarization and complicates the discussion. It is our misfortune that we tend to follow those authorities blindly who pass themselves off as highly self-confident and who loudly assert their views. We do so out of a fatal infantile disposition that we bear genetically and we must be aware of this tendency in order to restrain it.

Summary 4.9

The human disposition to form rank orders is based on our primate heritage. The focus of attention criterion as an indicator of status already appears in non-human primates in that high ranking individuals are the center of attention of the other group members, i.e., "regarded" by most of the other members present. Obedience and the readiness to become subordinated are as innate in humans as the striving for rank, and both tendencies combine to form a functional system.

Human rank orders are dynamic. They also differ in various spheres of competence so that within a group several individuals can enjoy esteem according to their abilities. Rank orders are based upon recognition of leadership qualities, such as the ability to mediate conflicts, initiate group activities, pull the group together, etc; they are not primarily based upon aggressive dominance. Dominance relationships established solely by aggressive dominance differ from rank order founded on leadership qualities. Leadership hierarchies are even observed in kindergarten groups. In tribal societies the child grows up in mixed age groups and, with increasing age, experiences a change from being guided to being a guide to the younger child. A child thus experiences (and experiments with) all possible roles.

Fear fosters the disposition for subordination, activating infantile behavior. The phylogenetic origin of obedience can be traced back to the mother-child relationship and is a persistent juvenile characteristic maintained into adulthood. Experiments have shown that when obedience conflicts with pity and empathy the tendency to obey prevails under certain conditions. Thus we must be educated to question authority, but not to blindly reject it. Antiauthoritarian indoctrination does not liberate, but unsettles, and children brought up this way are actually more susceptible to the influence of authority figures. Since striving to rise in rank appears to be an innate part of man's behavior that has a phylogenetic basis, societies, which want to abolish rank orders, require continual leveling in order to preserve this ideal. The striving for power (rank) in humans is the impetus for creative performance and thereby a motor of cultural development. The desire is no doubt dangerous, since it is an open-ended drive.

4.10. Group Identity Maintenance

Groups delineate themselves from others. Group members are bonded in a quasi-familial relationship of trust whereas strangers are met with reservation. The bonding effect of familiarity is not only due to personal acquaintance but also the fact that group members behave according to the same norms and thus understand each other. This means that behavior of each group member is fairly predictable for the others. Individuals maintain the roles according to age, sex, status, etc., established by the culture. Group norms are manifested in language, customs, clothing, body adornment, and many other everyday features, with material and spiritual culture tailored to the particular norms. Culture is the determining agent binding us as our "second nature," sometimes in a fairly restrictive way. Of course we can break with tradition when necessary, but unless compelled to do so we tend to prefer to cling to our customs. Custom makes behavior predictable, brings order to the community, and thereby transmits security. Maintenance of group-specific norms is a means of distinguishing the group from others who as strangers do not follow the same customs. The human trait of emphasizing differences led to rapid cultural differentiation (pseudospeciation, p. 15) and allowed humans to fit themselves into highly diverse ecological niches. This tendency is demonstrated by the great diversity of human cultures.

Group norms are defended against those group members who deviate from them. Thus pressure to conform to norms exists in all cultures, first by applying mild sanctions and, if this fails, by escalating into aggression. It culminates in expulsion when the deviating member cannot live up to group standards. Normative aggressive behavior has developed convergently in entire groups of social birds and mammals (G. H. Neumann, 1981).

Outsider reactions in humans have been studied by various investigators (see A. Seywald, 1977, 1980, citing further references as well). Seywald discovered an old poem *"The Land of the Imperfect"* that poignantly describes this phenomenon:

> In ages past there was a land,
>   In which every single man
>   Stuttered when he spoke
>   And limped when he walked,
>   For both were thought to be the way.
>
> A stranger saw this curious sight; and thought
>   "They'll praise me when I show them how,"
>   And so he walked with normal stride.
>   And all who spied him, laughed out loud,
>   And all stood laughing, crying out: "Oh teach
>   the stranger how to walk!"
>
> The stranger felt he was obliged
>   To straighten out this wrong reproach.
>   "You limp!" he called, "I do not:
>   *You* must change, *I* should not."
>
> Their mocking grew and grew and grew,
>   As they heard the stranger speak:
>   "He doesn't even stutter!" They cried,
>   "We'll scoff at him from every side!"
> (From the *Niedersächsisches Wochenblatt für Kinder,* Pt. 3 Bremen 1780)

Those who deviate from the group norm are at first teased and laughed at. This type of laughter may be a phylogenetically ancient form of mobbing. The rhythmic sounds are reminiscent of threat and mobbing sounds made by lower primates, and the baring of teeth may be derived from an intention to bite. This does not contradict the fact that laughter is also bonding. But it only bonds those who laugh together; the person being laughed at rarely laughs along with the others, and he perceives this laughter as an aggressive act. People are laughed at because they are awkward or otherwise behave differently from the norm. The laughter makes the individual aware of his deviating behavior and gives him an opportunity to conform. Laughter is a threat toward the nonconformist but binds together those who join in laughter. When people assemble at social occasions they often joke about others and tell jokes, which allows them to laugh together. The targets of the laughter, either in reality or in the case of a joke in the imagined situation, serve as substitute objects to allow for a bonding and also for cathartic tension-relieving laughter. Laughing at something or someone appears to be highly enjoyable. A good example is the space allotted in our newspapers for comic strips.

FIGURE 4.67. Mocking by showing of the tongue is derived from spitting; it should not to be confused with sexual tongue display which is derived from licking. Mocking (aggressive) tongue display includes prominently protruding the tongue outward or downward and displaying it for a period of time. (a) Yanomami boy mocking by showing the tongue; (b) !Ko Bushman girl derides using the tongue. From 16 mm films. Photo: I. Eibl-Eibesfeldt.

There are also various forms of mockery. The German verb to mock, *spotten,* is derived from the verb to spit *(spucken),* a form of aggression occurring in every culture we have studied (Fig. 4.67). Mockery can be verbal, as in calling others names that stamp them as ridiculous outsiders. Such name calling often plays on awkward traits of the target individual one finds offensive, and those ridiculing the person "ape" the behavior. Finally individuals may respond to the presumed offense against rules of appropriate behavior by behaving badly themselves. !Ko girls mocked me while filming by imitating my filming movements and then flashing their genitals, a distinct offense to proper demeanor (Figs. 4.68–4.70). Last, but not least, the outsider is verbally "adjusted." Gossip plays an extraordinarily powerful role in all cultures as a means of social control. If the person, in spite of all norm-aligning aggression, does not alter his behavior accordingly, he can become an outcast who is segregated from the group and must carry on alone. In serious instances someone like this can even be ostracized from the community. These rejection reactions can become quite harsh if the individual is physically incapable of altering his demeanor, perhaps because of a mental disturbance.

In addition to the disfigured or diseased, there are criminal deviants and those who simply violate custom. Criminal offenses in all cultures are considered to be damaging to society and are dealt with accordingly. In the case of murder and homicide, *lex talionis* (comparable punishment) is a widespread practice. It corresponds to the response of retaliator strategy seen in the animal world. Death due to war and manslaughter are dealt with among tribal people by conventions through which homicide can be compensated using measures other than blood revenge.

In general there is a strong disposition to behave according to societal norms and thus in this sense to conform to majority opinion. This inclination may take unusual forms. For example, individual test subjects were asked to compare lines of various lengths with a standard line, and their estimates were correct. However, if colleagues of the researcher falsely assessed line length when the subjects were tested in a group, only one-fourth of the subjects trusted their own judgment. The others conformed with the majority opinion, sometimes unconsciously and sometimes simply to avoid contradicting the others (S. E. Asch, 1951).

There are numerous characteristics that can make someone an outsider: various abnormalities of behavior and appearance that in each culture would be perceived

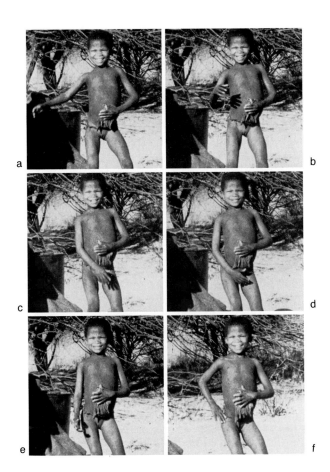

a
b
c
d
e
f

FIGURE 4.68. Frontal genital display as a mocking gesture (see also p. 247). As one hand lifts the apron the other makes a pointing gesture. Finally the girl poses in typical female bearing (!Ko Bushman, central Kalahari). From 16 mm film. Photo: I. Eibl-Eibesfeldt.

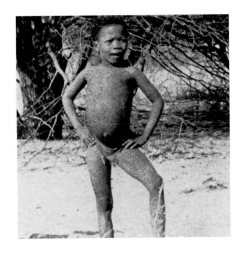

FIGURE 4.69. Challenging posture of a mocking girl (!Ko Bushmen, Central Kalahari). Photo: I. Eibl-Eibesfeldt.

FIGURE 4.70. Female sexual posterior presentation as a mocking gesture (!Ko Bushmen, central Kalahari). From a 16 mm film. Photo: I. Eibl-Eibesfeldt.

317

as deviant or conscious or unconscious violation of conventions and habits of a particular culture. Physical defects can result in stigmatization. Skin diseases can evoke particularly strong repulsion reactions, and it may be that this revulsion elicits an innate reaction that acts to prevent contagious infection (K. Lorenz, 1943b). Disfigured individuals, particularly those with facial deformities, have an especially difficult time in public. Such people sense, even in tolerant surroundings, that they cause discomfort to those in their presence. The aversive reactions of others causes great suffering although close personal relationships can reduce these avoidance responses. Obesity elicits rejection responses in some cultures. J. and A. Wolfgang (1968) investigated this with a spatial placement study. The test subject had to place a figure of himself near figures of other individuals. There was a clear relationship between physical stigma and distance between the subject's figure and that of the afflicted person. Those with broken arms were placed near the subject's figure, while those with amputated limbs and clubfeet were placed at a median distance, and finally figures displaying obesity were placed at the greatest distance.[14] R. E. Kleck *et al.* (1968) found in similar studies that those with non-physical defects (epileptics, the mentally ill) were placed at a greater distance than those with visible ailments. In an interview situation subjects assume a greater distance between themselves and those with physical handicaps than those without handicaps (R. J. Comer and J. A. Piliavin, 1972). In tribal societies people behave quite similarly (K. Schlosser, 1952a, b). Deviant behavior apparently elicits not only rejection but also fear, presumably because the individual's behavior is unpredictable.

People react less vigorously to violations of customs, depending on their perceived severity. Such behavior is disapproved and mocked and leads to isolation within the group but rarely to actual expulsion.

Rejection often occurs without insight and even against better judgment. Could it be that we react innately to norm deviation with rejection? Two mechanisms appear to be operating here. One is via a mental template in which some ideal configuration of the human physical constitution of the particular ethnic group is presumed; a template by means of which a well proportioned human body and a delicate face are regarded as beautiful but as repulsive and alien if modified by disfigurements and disease-related changes. Adults certainly have conceptions of beauty, and a general consensus or beauty of the human body is apparent when we compare the art of highly developed cultures such as Europe and Asia. Naturally there are ethnic variations of the human beauty ideal. There is also the universal inclination toward intolerance of someone who is deviant, which enforces conformity. That phylogenetic adaptation plays a role in these reactions is indicated by the fact that man must be educated to become tolerant, while intolerance is observed in children at an early age without any special instruction. They laugh and deride without being taught to do so and must be restrained to acquire tactful tolerance. One must not overlook the fact, however, that education often reinforces these dispositions especially when the training encourages intolerant attitude toward minorities.

Our interpretation that phylogenetic adaptations contribute to this sphere of behavior is supported by the fact that norm-preserving aggression is observed in

---

[14]Obesity is an expression of being well-to-do and thus occupies a high rank in some cultures (e.g., Polynesia), but even here the obese are considered to be powerful but not beautiful.

chimpanzees and many other vertebrates. J. van Lawick-Goodall (1971) describes high ranking chimpanzees, who after falling ill with poliomyelitis were attacked by their former companions. The healthy animals displayed distinct fear of the partially paralyzed chimpanzees, who moved forward with great effort by dragging themselves along the ground on their posterior. The handicapped chimps sought contact and did not perceive that they themselves were eliciting fear in the others. They looked behind themselves for the cause when they noticed the "fearful grinning" of their healthy cohorts, and searched more intensively for contact, which was not offered to them. Some of the paralyzed chimpanzees were actually attacked. Hugo van Lawick finally had to protect one of them (McGregor). Eventually the group became accustomed to the paralyzed members, although they did not offer them any physical contact, which must have been difficult for the paralyzed ones to endure. Chimpanzees typically delouse each other as a sign of attachment which quite obviously requires physical contact. Jane van Lawick-Goodall (1971, p. 185) poignantly described the situation:

> The most painful moment of the entire ten days from my point of view occurred one afternoon. Eight chimpanzees had collected in a tree about sixty paces from McGregor's sleeping nest, and they deloused themselves mutually. The sick male looked directly at them and now and then uttered a soft grunt. Chimpanzees normally devote much of their time to social skin care, and the old male had to abstain from this important contact since the outbreak of his disease.
>
> Finally McGregor raised himself, with great effort, from his nest, climbed to the ground and made his way, haltingly, along the long path to his conspecifics. When he finally reached the tree, he rested a while in the shadow and finally expended his last strength to climb up until only a short distance separated him from two of the males. With a loud groan of joy he extended his hand in greeting toward them, but before he could touch them they jumped away without looking behind at him and continued their grooming on the other side of the tree. Old McGregor sat motionless there fully two minutes and stared toward them before finally letting himself down to the earth.

In prehistoric times it was no doubt important for each member of small groups to be able to predict the behavior of the others. Furthermore, the maintenance of specific cultural norms allowed for a rapid demarcation against "others," accelerating cultural evolution. In our modern pluralistic society, norm-preserving aggression is more likely to be disruptive and maladaptive. It is precisely the "outsiders" whose artistic and scientific accomplishments can contribute to society's welfare. Thus teaching tolerance is germane, particularly in the sense of a readiness to understand, which does not necessarily imply a general acceptance of every deviation including sexual deviance to criminality. One can be prepared to understand a great deal but at the same time one is permitted to make value judgments.

Teaching tolerance and the acceptance of the handicapped is a necessity that must be fostered. It can be helpful to understand that the tendency to be intolerant is a biological disposition that must be brought under control with insight and appropriate education. G. H. Neumann (1977) suggests that the handicapped be included in regular classes in school, a concept worthy of consideration. This would improve the chances of acceptance for physically handicapped individuals. On the other hand, the prospects to become integrated into a community of normal juveniles are less bright for seriously disfigured and mentally disturbed individuals. Here, a separate schooling may be the lesser of two evils, since the severely handicapped would be confronted with nonacceptance in addition to their handicap on a daily basis, and the nonhandicapped could be severely burdened.

Group identity is defended whenever there is a real or imagined threat. Intergroup relations between different ethnic groups are therefore often strained and dominant cultures often endeavor, either by force or persuasion or a combination of both, to assimilate the weaker groups. Some argue that world peace may finally be achieved when all cultures are merged into one world culture. This Utopia is, however, counter to the evolutionary trend, which constantly creates new variations, giving birth to novel ideas and fostering flexibility.

I am in favor of plurality and feel that a social contract which guarantees each ethnic group survival within their traditional borders could create an atmosphere of tolerance and acceptance, thus taking the sting from ethnocentricity.

As a biologist, I encourage respect for cultural differences.[15] The merging of all cultures corresponds to a huge homogenizing process and with the disappearance of each culture (even if only a tribal "primitive" culture) is the concomitant loss of values. Furthermore, it appears to me that a humanity reduced to a single "world culture" would significantly reduce its adaptive potential, which is based on variation, and that could become highly dangerous. Each culture represents an attempt at mastering the problems of survival, and in the wealth of cultures mankind achieves an adaptation spectrum that could be significant in a crisis. Furthermore, even if a totally unified humanity were produced, "equality" could only be maintained by repressing any new ideas and life styles in favor of conformity. It is fortuitous to perceive a value in maintaining the greatest possible cultural diversity; thus, populations react against threats to their identity and it is highly unlikely that a world sharing a single culture could develop. In this sense those traits that incite us to maintain ethnic identity and territorial integrity are not necessarily only a disruptive, archaic heritage, developed from intergroup competition in the past, and something that is no longer adaptive today. They should also be considered as positive mechanisms of cultural sustenance as long as they do not escalate to ethnocentric domination over and intolerance of other groups. Teaching respect for others and value differences should counter such a possibility.

Summary 4.10

Humans develop "in-group" feelings and delineate themselves from others by emphasizing contrasts and, in turn, by developing unique cultural characteristics. Group-specific norms are defended. Group members deviating from norms become targets of regulating aggression, which are played out in a similar manner in all cultures known to us. Gossiping about and mocking of deviant behavior results in the "realignment" of the deviator. If this norm-enforcing aggression is ineffective, the offending individual runs the risk of being ostracized. The outsider reaction is a norm-maintaining mechanism that also occurs in anthropoid apes (chimpanzees). In the small group it was necessary that all members behaved within a certain range of group norms (i.e., predictably). The tendency for intolerance can be disruptive in a pluralistic society and appropriate education must be instituted to counter it.

---

[15]The organizations Survival International (London) and Gesellschaft für Bedrohte Völker (Göttingen) work for the survival of minorities throughout the world. Both publish periodicals (Survival International, Pogrom).

4.11. Territoriality

4.11.1. Universality and Manifestation of Territorial Behavior

Most higher vertebrates (birds, mammals, reptiles) are territorial. They maintain specific areas known as territories as individuals or in pairs or closed groups, and these territories are defended against intruders. Possession of territory demonstrated by song (birds), scent marking (mammals), or specialized display behavior generally inhibits strangers from encroaching into an occupied territory. It is an open question whether the expectation of defensive retaliation or the existence of a norm of respect for possession (comparable to norms of respect for object and partner possession, p. 340) prevents a conspecific from intruding. There are birds that avoid conspecifics' nests as soon as they have eggs in them, but even in communally brooding birds this is not the rule.

Man is also disposed to take possession of land and to delineate between himself or his group and other individuals and groups. Group members respect the territorial claim of another group member as his possession, as if following some primary norm involving respect of possession. These moral inhibitions against territorial trespassing are less defined if the potential intruder does not know the territory owner. Fear of retaliation then becomes the stronger force to keep the potential intruder from trespassing and conquest.

Territoriality can be expressed by either physical or social boundaries and likewise can be defended by physical aggression or by social and ritual means. For instance, various Australian aboriginal tribes claim their land on the basis of inheritance from totemic ancestors. The spirits of these ancestors guard the territory, particularly sacred sites, against anyone trespassing without permission. Territoriality does not mean that others have absolutely no access to the area in question, but rather that they have to acknowledge ownership by requesting permission to enter the area in a specific way. Territoriality refers to any type of land-bound privileges assuring access to resources. As long as a threat of intrusion is absent, one often does not notice any manifestations of territorial ties to an area. But once such a threat appears, the social relationships of ownership in the group are projected onto the land. As I was told by K. Budack (pers. commun.), the Nama had never demarcated the broad infertile Namib strip which marks off the coastal area where they live from the hinterland as their territory. But once the authorities sought to use this strip as a nature reserve, the subsequent Hottentot protests clearly showed that they indeed regarded it as part of their tribal range.

In most cases, human group territories are protected by the mere knowledge of the possessors' readiness to defend the territory, with force, if necessary.

For a number of reasons, I will explore in detail conventions developed quite early for the mutual respect of territorial rights. Unfortunately, such conventions have not always worked, and fear of revenge remains the greatest constraint against territorial intrusion.

That humans are innately disposed for territorial behavior has been questioned. A rejuvenation in the 1960s and 1970s of the Rousseauian conception of the noble savage led to the image of the peaceful primeval man. Paleolithic man allegedly lacked territorial demarcation and defense but lived in open fluid communities whose composition was constantly changing. Only with the origins of agriculture were the first fences supposedly erected, and only then was land regarded as a possession to be claimed and defended. Thus peace was violated in the world!

V. Reynolds (1966) and R. B. Lee and I. DeVore (1968) point to the apparent peacefulness of most of today's hunter/gatherer societies and to observations that allegedly demonstrate that chimpanzees, our closest relatives, live in open, non-territorial bands. The peacefulness ascribed to chimpanzees, however, has had to be revised substantially in recent years in view of new findings. In her first publications, J. van Lawick-Goodall wrote that chimpanzees indeed lived in open groups, but after many years of field observations she perceived an entirely different picture: "In the early days of my study at Gombe I formed the impression that chimpanzee society was less structured than actually it is. I thought that, within a given area, the chimpanzees formed a chain of interacting units with the extent of an individual's interactions with other chimpanzees limited only by the extent of his wanderings" (J. van Lawick-Goodall, 1968). "Subsequent observations showed that this was not the case" (J. van Lawick-Goodall, 1971).

Now it is known that chimpanzees live in fairly closed groups, of which each possesses a group territory. A group of adult males comprises the center of such communities, the males being more mobile than individual females belonging to the group. The group territory is defended by males controlling the territorial boundaries in troops (J. Goodall *et al.*, 1979):

> Chimpanzees taking part in patrols tended to travel in close compact groups. Travel was silent, with frequent pauses to look and listen. Often an individual stood bipedally, to see over the tall grass or stare down into a valley or ravine ahead. From time to time the party stopped and sat silently, watching and listening: sometimes they climbed into a tree; at other times they sat, often within arms reach on some ridge overlooking a neighboring valley (p. 25).

These animals are clearly on guard in silent watchfulness. If they discover abandoned nests of other chimpanzees, they inspect them olfactorily, often displaying and destroying the nests. Sometimes, although not always, females also participate in such patrols, following the males leading the troop.

If the males see or hear members of other groups they threaten by shaking branches, stomping against tree trunks, and calling loudly. They also throw rocks at the strangers. If the strangers cannot withdraw quickly enough, they will be attacked. Attacks are targeted against unfamiliar females as well as males (J. Goodall *et al.*, 1979).

> Other serious attacks were seen in 1971, prior to the community division by *Bygott* (1972, 1974). In the first instance, five males (Mike, Humphrey, Satan, Jomea, and Figan) suddenly raced forward, there was an outburst of screaming and barking, and when Bygott caught up he found some males attacking, while others displayed around an unhabituated female. Finally she escaped; Humphrey next appeared, holding an infant chimpanzee, between 2 and 3 years old, which he and Mike killed by eating. They tore it on arm and leg, despite the fact that the infant still screamed and kicked . . . . (p. 32)

Females often take part in attacks on strange females. J. Goodall impressively describes how a group gradually wandered apart and finally divided, whereby the stronger group attacked the weaker. In the end the stronger group had killed most of the weaker members. It appears that attacks are particularly brutal when the animals involved had known each other well before. J. D. Bygott (1972) determined that the most violent conflicts occurred between males who had not seen each other for a long period of time.

We can therefore maintain that chimpanzees are indeed territorial, and this is not exceptional primate behavior. This must be emphasized, as V. Reynolds (1966) claims, that the alleged peacefulness of the pongids formed the basis for man's primeval peacefulness.

322

One might then ask about territoriality among hunters and gatherers? H. Helmuth (1967), R. B. Lee (1968), M. D. Sahlins (1960), and J. Woodburn (1968) all claimed that modern hunters and gatherers are peaceful people lacking territories. I. DeVore (1971, p. 310) summarized their viewpoint as follows: "The Bushmen and the hunter-gatherers generally have what in the modern idiom might be called the 'flower child solution.' You put your goods on your back and you go. You do not have to stay and defend any piece of territory or defend fixed assets."

This perspective is based on information from a few selected publications, for in the majority of studies on hunter-gatherers, they are neither described as peaceful nor as peoples without territoriality. W. T. Divale (1972) investigated the warfaring activity of 99 local groups of hunter-gatherers from 37 cultures. Of these, 68 groups distributed across 31 different cultures practiced war at the time the data were obtained. Twenty local groups from five cultures had ceased warfaring 5–25 years before data gathering, and the remainder reported warfare in the more distant past. Not a single group was claimed to have never known war. E. R. Service (1962) clearly showed that hunters and gatherers occupy territories, and of the twelve contemporary hunter-gatherer cultures described by M. G. Bicchieri (1973), nine were distinctly territorial. Details on the others are too inaccurate to make any assessment. But if we examine other literature we also find that they, too, are territorial. There are a great number of references in early ethnological literature demonstrating hunter-gatherer territoriality. Many of them, including the Patagonians, Andamese, and some Australian peoples were distinctly warlike.

Thus a detailed study of the literature disclosed that the peaceful hunter and gatherer or the "flower power" hunter-gatherer of the 1960s is a myth, but one that may be hard to dispell because it corresponds to the idealized conceptions of environmentalism. It is zealously cultivated in secondary and tertiary literature; thus W. Schmidbauer (1973) wrote an entire book on territoriality and aggression in hunter-gatherers without ever having observed a single member of such a culture. Eskimos, Pygmees, Hadza, and Kalahari Bushmen (San) are often taken as model examples of peaceful hunter-gatherers. However, none of them when studied closely, corresponds to the idealized conception. Fridtjof Nansen did describe the Eskimo as peaceful, but H. König (1925) showed that this picture is incorrect and that Nansen drew a positive picture of the Eskimo to elicit sympathy for these people, who at the time were severely oppressed by Europeans. There are indeed ample reports of territorial conflicts in the literature (e.g., H. W. Klutschak, 1881; E. W. Nelson, 1896; K. Rasmussen, 1908). More recently, R. Petersen (1963) cites hunting territories in western Greenland which are each claimed by a group. Those who intrude on such a territory risk their lives. "By no means may you hunt in an eastern direction—a father instructs his son—for Serquilisaq has his camp there. He killed your older brother just as he began to become a good hunter" (R. Petersen, 1963, p. 278). Petersen stresses, however, that it is difficult today to investigate the earlier territorial relationships because declining population and acculturation have led to abandoning previous territorial rights.

Only among polar Eskimo are there no reports of wars, possibly because there are few contiguous borders in their sparsely settled region. At present, their population is only 600 persons, and 50 years ago there were only 254! The small settlements are, on the average, 80 km apart. However, the polar Eskimo had armed conflicts with the Vikings, and conflicts often occur within communities, sometimes leading to homicide and blood revenge as a consequence (C. Adler, 1977).

The Pygmies are frequently cited as examples of peaceful hunters and gatherers;

C. M. Turnbull (1961, 1965) indeed calls them a peaceful people but adds that little is known about the relations between different Pygmy groups. This reservation is cited as rarely as the many express references to Pygmy territoriality. P. Schebesta (1941) describes the forest ranges of the Bambuti as group possessions: "The intrusion of strangers for purposes of hunting and obtaining food is not permitted and leads to dissension and fighting. Neighboring groups with ties of kinship and friendship are granted the right to trespass the boundaries under certain circumstances. My observations show repeatedly that the Bambuti highly dislike traversing foreign zones and would do so only at my insistent urging or the command of the host, and then only for a short time. Pygmies are doubly shy and fearful on strange territory" (P. Schebesta, 1941, p. 274). Other references on Pygmy territoriality are found in M. G. Bicchieri (1969), M. Godelier (1978), and S. Bahuchet (1983).

J. Woodburn (1968) described the Hadza as nonterritorial, living in open groups. He first became acquainted with them after their original 5000 km^2 range had been reduced to 2000 km^2, and under these conditions one would not expect them to display their original pattern of territorial behavior. Earlier reports indicate that the Hadza possessed hunting territories and that they conducted intergroup warfare (L. Kohl-Larsen, 1943, 1958).

M. D. Sahlins (1960), R. B. Lee (1968), and I. DeVore (1971) maintained that the Bushmen of the Kalahari lived without defined territories in open, constantly changing communities. But R. B. Lee (1972, 1973) revised his earlier statements in view of subsequent studies, for he found that in fact specific individual !Kung Bushmen are owners of water holes and that visitors must formally address them when they wish to gain access to the sites.

It is actually puzzling why the Bushmen could be viewed as the prototype nonterritorial hunter-gatherers, since there is so much evidence to the contrary. Bushmen rock paintings from precontact periods depict battles small-scale intergroup warfare (Fig. 4.71) (H. C. Woodhouse, 1987).

There are also numerous earlier ethnological reports on territorial behavior (S. Passarge, 1907; B. Zastrow and H. Vedder, 1930; V. Lebzelter, 1934; F. Brownlee, 1943). All agree that the !Kung Bushmen could only gather and hunt in their own kin group or tribal regions and that trespassing other territories resulted in defensive reactions on the part of the owners. V. Lebzelter (1934, p. 21) writes "Foreign tribal regions may only be traversed by a Bushman without his weapons. Even at the edge of the farming zone the mutual distrust is so great that a Bushman sent as a courier to a farm where another tribe rules does not dare to stray from the roadway which is regarded as a kind of neutral zone: if two armed unacquainted Bushmen approach each other, they lay their weapons down within sight." H. Vedder reports (1937, p. 435): "Each Bushman band possesses a region inherited from their fathers. Some bands even possess two, a summer area and a winter area, which have strictly defined borders. Should a Bushman be hunting or gathering in someone else's range he can be sure that some day he will fall victim to a poisoned arrow. . . ." The existence of defined territories and structured relationships to gain access to other's resources apparently surprised the first observers, for the Bushmen have been envisioned as nomads lacking such territories.

Thus S. Passarge (1907, p. 31) stresses these ordered relationships: "The division of Bushmen in families has long been known. . . . But I never found any report that property is under family ownership. Yet this is a point of tremendous significance, for only taking this into consideration can one win a clear insight into Bushman social organization."

FIGURE 4.71. (a) Depiction of warlike activities in south African rock paintings of Bushmen. From D.F. Bleek (1930). (b) Bushmen rock painting depicting bushmen fighting people of larger stature (left). Farm Godgegeven near Warden, Drakensberge, South Africa. Photo: I. Eibl-Eibesfeldt. (c) Paleolithic cave painting depicting a fight. Morella la Vella, Castellon, Spain. Drawing after E. Hernandez-Pacheco. From H. Kühn (1929).

325

The !Kung of the Nyae-Nyae region are afraid of other !Kung Bushmen (L. Marshall, 1959) and therefore, rarely leave their region. They consider themselves "real people" (Ju/oassi) in contrast to all other !Kung, who are considered to be foreign and potentially dangerous. The Kung Bushmen words for "foreign" and "bad" are one and the same: "dole."

The !Kung do not own the land per se, but rather the strips of land on which produce grows: "It is these patches of 'veldkos' that are clearly and jealously owned and the territories are shaped in a general way around these patches . . . the strange concept of ownership of veldkos by the band operates almost like a taboo. No external force is established to prevent one band from encroaching in another's veldkos or to prevent individuals from raiding veldkos patches to which they have no right. This is just not done" (L. Marshall, 1965, p. 248).

According to R. B. Lee (1972, 1979), the water holes of the various groups are in the possession of individuals designated as owners (K//ausi). A tribal region (n!ore) of 300 to 600 km² surrounds each water hole and is the area that sustains a single group. An individual can inherit a n!ore from father or mother, and relatives from other camps can hunt and gather there if they maintain appropriate relations with the owners and seek their permission. Permission is usually obtained by visiting the owner, living with him, and jointly exploiting his resources. These constraints show that there are privileges that must be respected. The borders between adjacent group territories are not sharply delineated. Water holes of various groups are often far apart, and regions are separated by a strip of no-man's land. Lee claims that the Bushmen purposely maintain indistinct boundaries, but adds that this is merely his own presumption: "Though I cannot prove it, I believe that !Kung consciously strive against to maintain a boundariless universe, because this is the best way to operate as hunter-gatherer in a world where group and resources vary from year to year . . . *Among the !Kung and other hunters-gatherers, good fences do not make good neighbors*" (1979, p. 334).

Note that his last sentence is italicized. Here he attempts to salvage his earlier thesis of Bushman nonterritoriality, and he further contends that despite all of this the Bushmen are nonterritorial. This is quite incomprehensible since he himself notes that visitors can live and gather among their hosts for a period of time but that a strange group passing through an area must formally request permission to doing so. "Visitors join residents in the exploitation of resources, and the day's take is unobtrusively distributed within the camp at the day's end. Later in the year residents will pay reciprocal visits to the visitor's n!ore . . . A different kind of situation arises when a neighboring group wants to make a camp within a n!ore separate from the owner's camp. In this case, the neighboring people must ask permission of the owner group" (R. B. Lee, 1979, p. 336).

A Bushman explained to him the principle of acceptance and exclusion:

> Within the camp people don't fight over food, but between camps people could disagree. For example, if people from /Gam came up to eat the tsin beans of Hxore and one of us /Xai/Xai people happened to find them there, he might report back to us and we would start an argument with them . . . We would go there and seek out our in-laws in the /Gam group and say: Look we have given each other children and today we are (n!umbaakwe) /affines/ and the n!ore is ours (inclusive), but why when we weren't here did you come and bring with you strangers to loot?—My in-law might reply: Oh, when I came here with them, I expected to find you here. How was I to know that you would be over there? But I understand your point and so I'll go home.

If a group arrives from far away and wishes to camp within the n!ore of another group, they must ask for permission with particular care: "Such a group must be especially careful to ask permission because it does not have a joint claim to the resources. By asking to camp, it incurs a reciprocal obligation to play host to the owner group at a later date. Usually if the visiting group is small and its stay is short, permission is freely given; but if the group is large and stays for months, the owner group may take steps to reassert its claim to the food resources" (R. B. Lee, 1979, p. 337).

Lee offers another interesting example of how a group demonstrates its individual possession. In 1968, about 40 /Du/da people penetrated a region under /Xai/Xai ownership. They harvested all the tsin beans and then withdrew. In the following year the /Xai/Xai appeared there 2 months before the main harvest and gathered everything as a demonstration of their ownership rights. They also told others that they would always maintain control over these beans and that the /Du/da should harvest in their own territory.

I have cited Lee extensively because his work is a good example of Bushman territorial behavior. Lee has shown that he is not only an outstanding observer but also an honest reporter; if he maintains that Bushmen are not territorial it can only mean he is using a definition of territoriality that differs from the ethological one. But in what way his definition differs is unclear to me. I presume that in his view territoriality must be expressed as continual defense. This is an opinion I have elsewhere heard and read many times and on which I responded some years ago (I. Eibl-Eibesfeldt, 1975) that such is not the case even with animals. Continuous conflict is prevented by having territories and thus an established order and only in extreme cases does a group owning a territory need to defend it; there are examples of this occurring in !Kung Bushmen. P. Wiessner (1977) reports that a land-owning group took up their bows and arrows and threatened another group when it attempted to dig a water hole on their land. Access to a territory is achieved through birth, marriage, and through the exchange partner (P. Wiessner, 1977).

G. B. Silberbauer (1972, 1973) confirmed territoriality in the G/wi Bushmen. Among the G/wi a group or individual visitor, who was not invited, will ask for permission to visit the region. Thus when in traveling they pass a territory of another band they formally ask permission to stay on the land and "to be allowed to drink water." This is a figure of speech that is also used during arid periods when no water is available. Among the G/wi also, specific individuals are also regarded as owners of the band territory.

The question still remains of how fluid the Bushman groups are. Among the !Kung Bushmen, Wiessner (1977) analyzing her data in coordination with R. Lee's data found that during the period 1964–1974, 22% of the /Xai/Xai population of ca. 150 Bushmen moved away permanently and 15% moved into the research area to live. Lee presumes that at least half of these movements were due to external changing factors, such as population pressure. In any case, a core group would be sustained. "Each n!ore contains a core of people with the longest time association. These people are generally accepted as owners, and it is these who are asked for permission to camp in an area. And the core group is by no means static. The ownership of the land passes from parent to child, but immigrants who come and stay for good are also gradually absorbed into the core" (R. B. Lee, 1979, p. 339).

In the !Ko Bushmen we find three levels of social organization, which are expressed in relation to the land (H. J. Heinz, 1966, 1979): (1) The family and extended family; (2) the local group (band); (3) the nexus. These three units are distinguished by defined patterns of bonding and delineation from others. At the family level, there is a seating arrangement of family members around the fire. It is less strict than in the !Kung (L. Marshall, 1960), but normally a woman sits at the right side of her husband. Parents are expected to set up their hut at least 12 m away from their married children. Entrances should be arranged so that the married children cannot be observed as they sleep.

A !Ko achieves access to a territory through birth, adoption, and marriage, and married couples have access to the territories of both sets of parents. Even though each clan member can, in principle, gather and hunt anywhere within the entire tribal territory, there are zones claimed by families that are respected as such by the community. Thus a hunter working alone is expected to operate on the side of the band territory bordering his hut. Women collecting fruits and wood have similar obligations. This rule is lifted during group activities. During arid periods the band breaks into family groups who move to their own small areas which are respected by others. Although families have no exclusive territorial claim over such areas, they are respected in order that families be provided sufficient resources during times of food shortage. The common band region is clearly bounded and is described as a territory, with a headman exercising authority over this region. Visitors must deal with him personally. Several bands form a "nexus" (often referred to as maximal band) wherein nexus members regard each other as members of a larger alliance. In the !Ko there were no more than seven local bands within a nexus at the time of Heinz's study. No local band contained more than 20 adults (Fig. 4.72). Marriage partners are generally sought from within the nexus and dialect differences also distinguish the unity of these larger groupings. Members of one nexus join for ritualistic occasions, such as for trance dances. The system offers security for local groups belonging to it. During times of emergency the members of various local groups of a nexus can request hunting permission within the territory of another local group, and such requests are never refused to nexus members. One would never expect similar cooperation on the part of a local group of another nexus since the nexus territory is exclusive. Generally nexus territories are separated from each other by a strip of no-man's land. This does not occur in the territories of the local groups.

The social integrity achieved by the !Kung by the reciprocal exchange system (the hxaro system—P. Wiessner) is effected in the !Ko with the nexus system except that hxaro creates ties over a wider spatial area than does the nexus. The different systems may reflect local adaptations to ecological factors. The !Ko live in the central Kalahari, where plants and game are uniformly distributed, while the !Kung live on the edge of the Kalahari where important resources are very irregularly distributed and concentrated in certain areas. For example, the mongongo nut, which is the !Kung's staple, is found in unevenly distributed groves. Thus alliances among the !Ko are more limited in space than those created through hxaro among the !Kung which stretch over a vast region.

Earlier reports from the !Kung and Heikom (R. J. Gordon, 1984) show that there were formerly chieftains who supervised numerous local groups (presumably a single nexus), but today there are no such authorities. Speeches that we recorded at an initiation ceremony indicate that special occasions (such as initiations) were the impetus for inviting members of another nexus for the event; these occasions also probably fostered contacts between quite different language groups (H. J. Heinz, 1979).

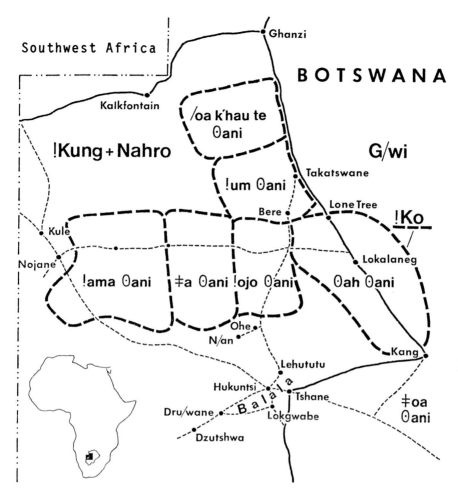

FIGURE 4.72. The !Ko Bushmen nexus territories. Each nexus has its own name. Thus the Takatswane people are called !um Oani (= people who follow the eland antelope). After H.J. Heinz (1979).

I have dealt with the territoriality of Bushmen extensively because in recent years sociologists and environmentalistic psychologists have so often held them up as an example of the open, nonterritorial society, which clearly is incorrect.[16] Such assertions may have unfortunate implications for present-day hunter-gatherers, leading governments to view them as a landless lower class with no historical and thus present rights to land.

The above arguments do not imply that territoriality is a manifestation of a fixed biological imperative, as M. G. Guenther (1981) imputes to H. J. Heinz and myself. Guenther claims without supporting evidence that territoriality is a predominantly cultural mechanism of adaptation. We do not have such a polarized viewpoint. It is an anthropological constant which finds diverse cultural mani-

---

[16]In this connection I also wish to draw attention to a recent study on the territoriality of the Agta living as hunter-gatherers in northeastern Luzon (P. B. Griffin, 1983).

329

festations (see also I. Eibl-Eibesfeldt, 1975). E. A. Cashdan (1983) has placed the various manifestations of territorial behavior for four Bushman groups in relation to their special ecological conditions.

Occasionally the possibilities to express territoriality are lacking. Besides the polar Eskimos, I know of only one hunter-gatherer people with no territorial ties who live in open communities. These are the Batak of the Philippines, who allegedly wander freely throughout their home range, which is rich in food. They have, however, been repeatedly and forcibly resettled in their claims to land and this has probably destroyed their territorial bond. A prior territoriality would account for the otherwise inexplicable fact that three clearly distinguishable dialect groups occur within the Batak. There must have been a period of relative isolation for each of them to develop. Today the Batak wander about freely, but they assume the dialect characteristics of the group which they join probably due to conformity pressure (K. Endicott and K. L. Lampell-Endicott, 1983).

In his detailed investigation, B. J. Williams (1974) shows that in present-day hunter and gatherers the mean size of local groups is about 50 persons. In the European upper paleolithic, the enormous size of many sites indicates groups of 100 to 300. Groups are most frequently patrilocally and patrilineally organized, with territoriality and a rather large marriage pool (connubium) that comprised some 500 individuals. These connubia generally represented the linguistically defined ethnic groups as well.

C. R. Ember (1978) studied contemporary views on hunters and gatherers in cross-cultural comparison and summarizes: "The data presented here suggest that some current views about hunter-gatherers may need to be revised. Specifically the data suggest that, contrary to current opinion, recent hunter-gatherers are typically patrilocal, typically have men contributing relatively more to subsistence than women,[17] and typically have had fairly frequent warfare."

Territoriality is undoubtedly one of the universals, and our territorial disposition probably arises from early primate heritage. Territoriality makes life predictable. A Bushman cannot effectively hunt and gather if he or she does not know who will use which resources. Resource areas are allotted to a large extent to assure predictable and profitable hunting and gathering. Respect of possession is thus to everyone's own benefit. This probably is the main reason why Bushmen respect each other territories. The territorial disposition can find all sorts of culturally modified expressions that can be understood as straightforward ecological adaptations.

The Australian tribes living in central arid regions can control and defend their large hunting and gathering grounds only with difficulty. Yet each local group maintains strict possession of its individual region by means of cultural institutions. Each group derives its territorial claim, as previously cited, from a totemic ancestor who had once lived in the area and whose spirit still watches over it. Particularly prominent local landmarks are interpreted as traces of the totemic ancestor who is usually defined as being half man and half animal. Round rocks are said to represent snake or emu eggs, depending on whether the region belongs to a snake or emu clan; holes in the ground are the caves where the totemic ancestor lived, and so on. The places where such landmarks are situated have been sanctified

---

[17]The claim that men contribute more economically than women only applies to those hunter-gatherers living primarily on wild game. In the Bushmen, women make a greater caloric contribution than men.

a

b

FIGURE 4.73. (a) The sacred site of the totem snake Jarapiri (Ngama, central Australia). This is both a totem site and symbolic territorial marker of the Walbiri. (b) The enlarged rock drawing of the snake totem. Photo: I. Eibl-Eibesfeldt.

and are the ritual center of the group territory (Figs. 4.73–4.75). Only initiated males may traverse these sacred sites. Women and males of other groups are forbidden to visit them and violators are punishable by death. Those individuals from other ranges are discouraged from trespassing because of the watchfulness of these totemic ancestors, who bring misfortune to those who trespass.

The conception of ancestors guarding the region of their descendants is also found in the Melanesian-Papuan area. The Kukukuku tribe of Papua and New Guinea bury their dead on platforms in gardens as guardians. In the Eipo of western New Guinea, skulls and bones are reburied beneath projecting rocks within gardens, where they watch over the region. This discourages intrusion of outsiders, although conflicts over land are still frequent. In another ritualization of territorial rites, the Tsembaga represent ancestral presence by the sacred plant cordyline, which is found throughout New Guinea (R. A. Rappaport, 1968). They believe that their ancestors dwell wherever they plant cordyline. If, in war, a region is conquered by enemies and the residents are driven out, the enemies will not settle in the area until the residents have planted cordyline in their new home region, since with that the ancestral spirits also depart and the acquired zone becomes habitable. Thus protection by ancestors is a powerful means of territorial defense. In central Australian tribes there is yet another cultural institution practiced to discourage intrusion. Each local group carries out rituals on their sacred grounds for the welfare of their totemic animals, who in turn are believed to serve an important function. For example, the honey-ant clan, which is descended from a half honey-ant–half human ancestor, assures that honey-ants flourish; the emu clan does the same for emus. This does not only occur within a single territory but throughout the land. Thus if a clan were to die out, there would be no one

331

FIGURE 4.74. Stone Churinga of the honey-ant clan of the Walbiri of Mt. Allen. The large
central circular figure represents a pan in the northeastern part of the Yuen-
dumu settlement, where ground water is found. This is where the honey-ant
ancestor of the tribe lived. He traveled out from here, creating hills and other
landmarks. These places are designated by additional circular figures, with
lines marking the pathways. Only initiated males possess stone or wooden
churingas. They are a clan crest reminding them of their initiation at which
they received this sign of identification. Churingas become sacred upon the
bearer's death and are then kept at sacred sites. The men can read the history
of their totemic ancestor on these objects; women may not look at them.
This symbol identification ideologically bonds men to their territory and group.
Photo: I. Eibl-Eibesfeldt.

left to care for the propagation of the affected animal, and such a loss would be
damaging to the entire community. Such a practice helps inhibit ventures of land
conquest. We will discuss such rituals again in the section on warfare.

M. J. Meggitt (1962) observed that under these conditions each conquest of a
new region would produce great embarrassment on the part of the conquerors,
and T. G. Strehlow (1970) and N. Peterson (1972) also stress the significance of
this mythical bond with the land. Peterson speaks quite correctly of ritualized
territoriality. "I would suggest that clan totemism is the main territorial spacing
mechanism in aboriginal society. By contrast with animal territoriality, however,
aboriginal territoriality is inward looking, sustained by beliefs and affective bonds

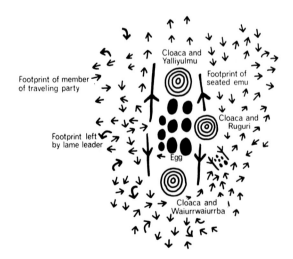

FIGURE 4.75. At male initiations the clan signs and clan history (wanderings of the totemic
ancestor and other events) are painted on the ground and on rocks. This is
a ground drawing of the Emu clan. After N. Peterson (1972).

to focal points of the landscape and the cultural symbols associated with these points'' (1972, p. 23).

In these Australian tribes the young men learn to identify with their region from their extensive initiation travels under the leadership of their elders, and they acquire detailed information about the borders and the productivity of their territory. This ritualization of territorial encounters and the development of the bonding system require time to develop.

The observations of Volker Heeschen (1979–1981) in Irian Jaya (western New Guinea) are related to our discussion. In the In-Valley, which has only recently been settled, each village is at odds with the others. During war engagements there are no distinctions drawn between "archenemies" and those foes with whom reconciliation is possible. War between neighboring villages is not condemned morally. In the Eipomek Valley, which has long been settled by peoples of the same linguistic group, there are in contrast all kinds of alliances, and a valley community is fostered by group initiation of boys of all ages and by other mechanisms. A community ideology is fostered and hamlets are not isolated from each other. Men's houses are made up of men from different clans. In the In, even clansmen from individual village communities separate themselves from others. It is noteworthy that the In utilize an ideological means to express territorial acquisition through sanctifying particular sites within a new region. According to Heeschen, specific trees, springs, streams, caves, and other land features are sanctified. We found similar practices among the Eipo. But the fact that demarcation through sacred objects occurs soon after land acquisition is particularly significant. It is comparable to governments erecting national monuments (quasi sancta) which function as symbols of identification and territorial demarcation.

In New Guinea, the differences between tribes belonging to the same linguistic group and living in the same habitat can be substantial. In those areas where land acquisition recently occurred, these relationships take time to develop. We find a comparable situation in the Yanomami, who recently pressed into the upper Orinoco and its tributaries from the Serra Parima. In this case, however, alliances between individual villages were formed that were particularly fragile. Attempts to avoid war between all parties have not yet been successful.

Ethnologists have often demonstrated the diversity of cultural manifestations of territorial behavior. According to M. Godelier (1978) the WoDaasse Peul, nomadic shepherds in Niger, have no territories. They infiltrate the farming regions of the Hausa, who permit them to use the fallow land and brush in exchange for services and products (sheep). Other shepherds also traverse the land, but custom regulates their temporal rhythms so that conflicts are avoided: the individual groups lay claim to territorial rights purchased from the region owners on a temporal basis only. Alternate use of the same territory by different shepherd peoples is also known in the nomads in southern Iran and Mongolian shepherds (F. Barth, 1959; D. Lattimore, 1951).

Peoples occasionally live in diversified biotopes (those with different vegetation zones) arranged according to altitude. Thus in southern Iran in the upper part of the Zagros Mountains there are Turkish-speaking tribes who live by camel breeding. Iranian-speaking tribes reside on the lower part of the Zagros. They raise horses and small domestic animals. Finally, in the foothills, there are Arabic-speaking tribes who support themselves by breeding dromedaries.

There are also societies in which people utilize different territories in various locations, as the Inca once did (J. Murra, 1958, 1972).

R. Dyson-Hudson and E. A. Smith (1978) have attempted to explain the various forms of territoriality using a cost-benefit model. They argue that territories are only formed when a region is economically defensible. Thus the western Shoshoni, who are sparsely settled in the arid Western Basin, are said to have no known territorial claims. Various families gathered at sites where nuts ripened and where there was a surplus food, without making any property claims. The only possessions were eagles' nests. In contrast, in the neighboring fertile district of the Owens Valley were Paiute territories that were defended. However the more northerly Shoshoni, who cooperatively hunted buffalo on horseback, again were nonterritorial (J. H. Steward, 1938). However, these findings have been contested (E. R. Service, 1971). Furthermore, the example of the Australian aborigines teaches that large, thinly populated regions can indeed be "economically" defended, namely with the help of mythical totemic ancestors guarding the region.

Dyson-Hudson and Smith add that a group can change from nonterritorial to territorial if it modifies its life style. The northern Ojibwa[18] were allegedly nonterritorial big game hunters (although this is poorly documented), but later when they began hunting small game they became territorial. Finally, the two authors stated that a group may be considered territorial or nonterritorial depending on which possessions are used for reference. The Karamojong of Uganda defend their cultivated fields and their cattle but not their grazing areas. However if someone should bring his herds into the region in which another herd was already grazing, he would have to ask permission to stay there. If it is a time of emergency (an arid period), intruding Karamojong would be repulsed. Members of other tribes trespassing Karamojong territory are always attacked (N. Dyson-Hudson, 1966; N. and R. Dyson-Hudson, 1969, 1970). R. Dyson-Hudson and E. A. Smith (1978) wish to demonstrate with these examples that territorial behavior does not depend upon some genetically fixed characteristic:

> Although (as with all behaviors) the capacity to demark and defend territory must have some genetic basis, human territoriality is not a genetically fixed trait, in the sense of being a fixed action pattern, but rather a possible strategy individuals may be expected to choose when it is to their advantage to do so. Analyses arguing that territoriality is an evolutionary imperative or conversely a political aberration of basic human nature, do not seem to us to have explanatory validity (p. 36).

Although we basically agree with their premise, a few corrections are in order here regarding precise terminology. The ethological concept of the fixed-action pattern is a specific one consisting of a motor sequence (see fixed-action pattern, p. 25), and ethology has never equated territoriality and fixed-action patterns! True, R. Ardrey (1966) overshot the mark with his "territorial imperative." K. Lorenz once said jokingly in my presence to an English reporter, "Robert Ardrey stuck out my neck."

It would be worthwhile to investigate which contexts and under which conditions man's territorial disposition develops. This includes observing human behavior in specific contexts such as taking possession of a beach spot on the coast, a place in a park, or a table in a restaurant, and there are a great many studies on these kinds of phenomena.

---

[18]In the northern and western Great Lakes (U.S.A.) region.

4.11.2. The Need to Maintain Distance

In the discussion on ambivalence operating in interpersonal relationships, we stated that humans are both attracted to others and simultaneously fear them, the latter not necessarily on the basis of previous negative experience. We react with shyness to specific characteristics of the other party, and the disposition to behave this way is one of the universals in human behavior (p. 170). Social fear is alleviated with personal acquaintance but remains a principal characteristic of interpersonal human behavior. As a result, we maintain varying degrees of greater distance between ourselves and others depending on the amount of confidence we have in the other. Visual contact invariable elicits arousal.[19] A need for privacy on a family basis (for each family) exists as well as a need to be left in silence or "left alone" amid others. But the need to be completely alone and private is an extension of this need in our society. Privacy in the true sense of being completely alone is by Bushmen only desired for sexual intercourse and defecation.

E. T. Hall (1966) investigated human distance maintenance under a variety of conditions, founding a branch of ethology known as "proxemics." He found that people of different cultures utilize different, culture-specific distances; thus northern Europeans maintain a greater distance between themselves than Mediterraneans and Arabians do, and from this Hall distinguished between "contact" and "distance" cultures. However, other studies have not succeeded in clearly confirming Hall's findings. These somewhat contradictory results may arise from the fact that the investigators did not differentiate between interactions with strangers and those with acquaintances. According to A. Mazur (1977), noninteracting strangers maintain a similar distance when sitting on a bench regardless of whether the culture is a contact or a distance one.

As a rule, distance varies directly with acquaintance, but there are exceptions. In a Tyrolean country inn, one often sits as crammed together as in a Bushman hut. However, even in the closest of families one does not always like to be tightly packed with others. Babies even control their social engagement and thus their arousal level by intermittently looking away from the mother during social play. E. Waters, L. Matas, and L. A. Stroufe (1975) observed that small children interacting with strangers also manipulate their own arousal by looking away. Pulse rate in small children increases with visual contact. If the child's glance is diverted from strangers, their pulse rate slows. Interpersonal interactions, even friendly ones, are often arousing. Each organism requires intermediate phases of rest and recovery, humans most particularly, since we prefer to think and operate in an atmosphere without tension (see play, p. 580). Perhaps the need and the special human capacity of displacing oneself and creating a relaxed, tensionless field, is closely related to man's evolution as a tool user, which requires intense concentration for periods of time and concentration requires freedom from external disturbances. Apparently this need for privacy is fairly strong. For example, in the kibbutz, where collective experience is vigorously propagated, the inhabitants develop diverse strategies for maintaining individual privacy (A. Davis and V. Olesen, 1971).

---

[19] Proximity and skin contact can arouse, but not in every instance. Proximity can calm a child when it approaches its mother, and a fearful adult can seek anxiety reduction in being with others.

S. Bayer-Klimpfinder (pers. commun.) observed in overcrowded Viennese postwar kindergartens that as children engaged in various interactions with each other, some individuals would also sit alone under a table for a while. For the privilege of being away from others and alone for a while, they would waive food and dispense with toys. This need for privacy finds expression in various ways in many cultures. The inclination to avoid contact with other people is greater in mass society where we encounter so many strange faces and thus are subjected to more stressors (p. 177). This gives the impression of a greater degree of unsociability compared with people living in kin-based societies, but we must be careful to make adequate comparisons in order to reach fair conclusions. Thus if we compare interpersonal reactions of kin-based societies where each members knows the other, we do find very similar interaction patterns. One searches both for contact and for time alone. Even among the Bushmen of the central Kalahari, whose small huts stand closely around an open area, the privacy of the family is maintained. The individual can always remove himself from the group if he wishes. This is then a mechanism for reducing dissension. If tensions arise between two families, they can disperse themselves in the field and alleviate difficulties. In the Yanomami (Waika) one can also seek solitude from the group. If one visits a Yanomami village for the first time, one would initially think it inconceivable that privacy could be found here. The large lean-to roofs, often joined to each other, surround a central square, and from his home one can see all the neighbors as well as those opposite his sector. But with the arrangement of the hammocks and specific conventions, each family is allotted its own privacy if so desired. Thus if someone lies in the hammock avoiding visual contact with others, he will be left alone. Thus even here, where everyone lives within view of others all the time, there are subtle shielding mechanisms. This conforms with the cross-cultural findings of A. Westin (1970) that man seeks quiet derived from a need for reducing stress.

Various strategies for displacing ourselves from others and maintaining a distance are at our disposal. We can retreat to a quiet corner and, if necessary, verbally announce that we wish to be alone for a while, to read or do something else, and such wishes are generally respected by adults. If someone disturbs this peace, they do so apologetically, for we are all aware of the increased disposition to defend a private sphere once an individual has withdrawn from the group. Defensive reactions are often manifested in this situation. Disturbances are upsetting, and our verbal reactions vary from the appeal of "Leave me in peace!" to the angry, threat-accompanied "Out!" with all conceivable gestures of rejection of the intruder. N. Felipe and R. Sommer (1966) investigated the behavior of females reading in public libraries. Assistants of the investigators disturbed the readers according to a specifically defined protocol. The readers clearly considered the intruder's behavior obstrusive if the assistant sat at the same table while other tables in the immediate area were unoccupied.

If we occupy a table we feel we have an unwritten right to possess it for the duration of our sitting there. This was confirmed in studies by M. L. Patterson, S. Mullens, and J. Romano (1971). Others also respect this right by politely asking if they may also occupy the extra space. In a train we will look into a compartment and ask if space is still free, a convention used even if the compartment is only half occupied and it is obvious that no one has left temporarily.

If in the above cited study the assistant sat at an already occupied library table, his behavior elicited defense behavior on the part of the reader. If the intruder slid the chair closer, the occupant erected barriers such as a ruler or a stack of books or oriented away from him. Finally, many observed subjects abandoned the spot when the intruder moved too close.

Violation of personal space may occur without approaching another person. One can achieve the same goal by persistently staring strongly at someone, or utilizing various postures and behavior, all of which result in symbolic intimacy that invades the individual's personal space (M. Leibman, 1970). This can consist of verbal intrusion effected over a distance. In many cultures the existence of a personal relationship and thus differential distance relationships is expressed with formal or familiar address forms or simply with the use of specific names (first name, nickname, etc).

Intrusion on personal space causes physiological excitation that can be measured as changes in skin resistance (G. McBride, M. G. King, and J. W. James, 1971). Fear elicited by violation of personal space is manifested in displacement activities (fidgeting, scratching oneself, stroking the chin, etc.). Approaching men elicit more conflict movements and thus greater fear than approaching women, who tend to abandon the field more quickly than men when subject to personal space intrusion. There is a clear relationship between fearfulness and distance maintenance, for the more anxious the person, the less close he permits others to approach (literature cited in I. Altman, 1975). Clothing and body scent can also serve to maintain distance. P. D. Nesbitt and G. Steven (1974) arranged for colorfully dressed men and women to get into admission lines into an amusement park. Someone standing behind a loudly dressed subject maintained a greater distance from them than from someone dressed conservatively. Displaying individuality can thus sometimes be provoking and serves to maintain distance. This is the reason that individuality is hidden in the anonymous mass society (p. 625). Similar phenomena operate in animals. When cichlids swim in schools their display coloration is switched off, but once they occupy an area and become territorial they become quite colorful again (N. Tinbergen, 1951).

Strong odors from perfume or after-shave colognes tended to increase interpersonal distance in Nesbitt's and Steven's studies. Male test persons distinguished male from female undershirts by odor and found male undershirt odors unpleasant, without knowing the sex of the wearer (B. Hold and M. Schleidt, 1977). This may be related to the stronger tendency in males in our culture to maintain distance from other males. The studies of D. A. Booth and M. D. Kirk-Smith (1980, cited on p. 426), found that seats in a dentist's waiting room became less attractive to males after being sprayed with androstenone, while they appeared to become more attractive to females.

People not only protect their individual space but also respect the space of others. They hesitate to break into a conversation (E. S. Knowles, 1973; J. A. Cheyne and M. G. Efran, 1972) and will ask pardon, lower their heads, look at the ground, and briefly behave submissively toward those who are standing in their way if they are forced to pass. These space intrusion inhibitions are particularly strong when two individuals of the opposite sex are involved.

A. H. Esser (1970) and R. J. Palluck and A. H. Esser (1971a, b) observed the behavior of 21 severely retarded children in a richly equipped study room. Each of the children occupied his own part of the room. At the beginning, many conflicts occurred between themselves. However, struggles ceased once a child gained possession of an area. At that point a brief threat sufficed to prevent someone from intruding into their space. This is an interesting documentation of the pacifying effect of a division of space! It is noteworthy that the territorial behavior of these severely mentally handicapped children (IQ below 50) was more developed than in normal children, and less modifiable by educational efforts.

Division of space leads to a social organization that gives the children security in that the possessor has priority and his privileges are respected in that space. This shows that territorial behavior can have an organizing, conflict avoidance function enabling animals as well as man to maintain an intimate relationship with some part of the environment. Such areas are associated with shelter, escape routes, nourishment, and places for hiding; we move with greater security through such areas than we do in unfamiliar terrain.

Groups move in the street as closed units and also make detours as a unit, for instance, when someone on a stairway attempts to press between the group. Body postures convey a number of nonverbal signals indicating to approaching others whether the group is closed and thus intrusion is unwelcome, or whether the group is open to joiners (E. S. Knowles, 1972; R. D. Deutsch, 1977).

For all human interactions there are preferred distances whose trespass is experienced negatively. This distance is smaller among acquaintances than strangers. I. Altman (1975) summarized the relationships graphically; further literature is found in Altman as well. E. T. Hall (1966) distinguished between various interpersonal distance zones: intimate distance is the distance from 0 to 40 cm, the distance at which physical contact occurs. Personal distance varies from 40 cm to 1.20 m (4 ft) and is a transition zone to the social distance (1.20 to about 4 m), which Hall designates as the normal distance. This is the interval maintained between people who are not closely acquainted. The public distance of 4 to 8 m is used by a speaker and his audience.

One might assume that these distances are all learned: "The development of personal space is gradually learned by children" (I. Altman, 1975, p. 101), something that is no doubt correct for culture-specific manifestations of the phenomenon. But the disposition to maintain distance is the result of maturational processes, fear of strangers being just one of its manifestations.

We maintain distance according to the degree of intimacy, and our personal space is carried about with us like an invisible bubble. Territory, on the other hand, is a defended area occupied either permanently or temporarily and which we share, if at all, only with an exclusively selected group of persons. Our homes and yards are examples of such territories. Within the residence each family member has a small zone for himself such as his bed, a place to sit, etc. Outside of the home, the block where one lives is often a secondary territory for the inhabitants. In large American cities, individual neighborhoods are frequently occupied by different ethnic groups. I. Altman (1975) observed that the children of two adjacent neighborhoods in an American city, one Jewish and the other of Irish descent, defended their blocks against intrusion from the other group. Only in the morning, when the children went to school, could they traverse neighborhood boundaries without any qualms, on the basis of a silent agreement.

Territories are often marked, even if they are only temporarily occupied and, as R. Sommer and F. D. Becker (1969) found, are also respected, which increased with personal acquaintance. A jacket draped over a library chair or a pair of glasses on a table are effective means of saving one's place. This may derive from the fact that we respect object possession, a point discussed subsequently (p. 340).

In a study in Connecticut, J. J. Edney (1972) found that persons who used warning signs on their property ("Keep Out," "No Trespassing," etc.) had resided longer in the neighborhood or intended to remain longer than others who did not utilize such signs. They also reacted more sensitively to the presence of strangers in their neighborhood and responded more quickly to the doorbell. Territorial groups also formed on Connecticut beaches (J. J. Edney and N. L. Jordan-Edney, 1974).

Larger groups and mixed sex groups lay claim to a smaller per capita area than smaller ones and same sex groups. Women maintain a smaller personal space than men. These findings have been established in both French and German subjects (H. W. Smith, 1981). Cultural comparisons show that territorial behavior for individual space varies considerably across cultures. The French require much less personal space than the Germans.

Studies of urban graffiti (D. Ley and R. Cybriwsky, 1974) and street symbols in Belfast, northern Ireland show that the symbols are used at the periphery of group territories and are directed toward unfamiliar outsiders, serving as aggressive border delineators. In the territorial center, graffiti functions to transmit information, demonstrate group loyalty, and reinforce group identity (F. Boal, 1969).

Summary 4.11

Human groups occupy territories and demarcate themselves territorially. They claim certain privileges within their territory and are also prepared to defend the territory if necessary. Territoriality does not first appear with agriculture, for it occurs in hunter-gatherers. Since our closest primate relatives are also territorial we may assume that this characteristic is a phylogenetically acquired trait. It is manifested in diverse cultural forms dependent upon specific ecological and historical conditions. They influence the form of group delineation and demarcation and thus the rules according to which territory access is granted (but not the principle itself). Within its own region a group claims privileges above those of others and therefore is dominant there. Within group territories there are subgroups (such as families) and individuals laying claim to their small zones, marking them accordingly on the basis of time or duration. Humans maintain individual distances between themselves. Territoriality is an ordering principle that he!ps prevent continuous conflicts both within and between groups. In general, a territorial claim is respected by other parties.

4.12. Origin and Social Function of Possession

The word possession in the sense of a "claim" or "belongings" originally referred to a location under someone's dominion. Thus a territory can be a possession.

The term property, on the other hand, designates those objects that belong to someone, whether they be physical objects, ideas, or the love of a partner. Today the linguistic distinction between possessions and property is becoming obscured, and both are often used synonymously. But the origin of these two is based upon different forms of ownership. We shall investigate the roots and social aspects of possession. Ownership is often described as an evil, especially the concept of private ownership, and there is no lack of "radical humanists" (E. Fromm, 1976), who associate ownership with egoism and greed without recognizing its positive aspects, for instance, one must own before one can give.

The concept of property can be used for material or nonmaterial entities (M. Godelier, 1978): land, water, objects of various types, rituals, knowledge, and even social ties. Ownership is characterized by the relationship of a person or group of people to that entity and is manifested by the person exercising control over the object and defending it when required to do so. We will show in the following discussion that object and partner possession is respected due to a primary norm of respect of possession. There are many motivations for ownership, not all of which are necessarily related to some drive to possess. The presumption that all these various manifestations were due to an encompassing possession drive would be speculation, at least at the present level of scientific understanding. Animals acquire objects and assume relationships to them when they are required to fulfill particular objectives. These objects may fulfill metabolic or other needs but can be other expressions of possession, such as a mother defending her young. If the possession is threatened, the animals will defend it. E. Beaglehole (1932) wrote that there could be no ''acquisition instinct'' as such, to which we agree. Possession occurs in different functional contexts.

L. Furby (1978) stresses that ownership in children is a means to an end: ''Possessions appear to be seen as a means to an end—they allow one to do what one wants'' (p. 312). Possession enables one to do what one would like to do, so Furby postulates a competence motivation as the chief drive for possessive behavior: ''. . . it is postulated that effectance of competence motivation is a major motivation for possessive behavior: The possibly universal desire to experience causal efficiency leads to attempts to control objects in one's environment. Further, since one's concept of the self is at least partially defined by that which one controls, it is hypothesized that possessions are one constituent of a sense of self—they are experiences as an extension of the self'' (p. 331). The desire to extend one's abilities must be one reason for wishing to possess but certainly not the sole motivation. The motivation to acquire objects for instrumental purposes concerns primarily those that we can use as tools. But attachments to other individuals can also be utilized as ''possessions.''

Humans thus possess in diverse functional contexts, and these forms of possession may be differentially motivated.

4.12.1. Object Possession, Food Sharing

Food is possessed by animals and also shared, especially in connection with infant care. As previously discussed, parental feeding leads to forms of ritualized food offering, such as the courtship feeding of many birds (p. 134) and as kiss feeding in humans. In many cultures infants are fed prechewed food from mouth to mouth, and are offered water in the same manner (p. 141). This kiss feeding can also be an expression of intimacy between adults of different sexes. The kiss is derived from kiss feeding and is found as an affectionate gesture among people of the most diverse cultures and races.

Humans also give food to one another by hand, and such a food transfer requires coordinated action. The disposition to give something must be present as well as the expectation that one is to be given: that one receives when one extends his hand and therefore that the desired object does not have to be snatched from the partner. The one giving offers the gift and releases it at the appropriate moment. Each giving, sharing, and exchange presumes the existence of some norm of respect of possession without which there would be no object transfer. The presence of a norm of respect of possession has highly significant consequences for social object transfer interactions. For example, it determines the strategies of making requests (p. 349).

In our closest relatives, the chimpanzees, possession of food is respected and, in highly specific situations, other objects are respected as well. Chimpanzees hunt small gazelles, colobus monkeys, and young baboons. Once prey has been seized, a great deal of excitement can erupt. But once possession of the prey has been asserted (in the first minutes after its capture, usually by the hunter), fight for the prey discontinues. The high ranking animals sit by and are given some of the food. The owner tears up the prey and hands out small portions to others, who sit around him in expectation with their hands raised as in begging. High ranking members who own prey spend many hours skillfully dividing out small portions to group members, thereby considering each member of the troop (G. Teleki, 1973). This interaction reinforces their positive relation to the others. Usually males hand out morsels from prey. Females share plant food with their young. In the Gombe Reserve, McGrew (1975) recorded 157 instances in which bananas were distributed. In 381 cases (86%), mothers gave bananas to their young, and in 47 cases (10%) adult males gave bananas to unrelated females.

Chimpanzees also extend their hands as if begging when they seek social contact with high ranking members or when they desire some specific object. If a chimpanzee female wants a banana, for instance, she lies before a high ranking animal and extends her open hand to him. Once the dominant animal touches her hand, she may take the banana without fear of repercussions (Jane van Lawick-Goodall, 1968).

Sharing of meat between group members also occurs in human subsistence-based societies with high ranking individuals being responsible for the distribution. Here, too, the esteem of the highly ranked individual is related to his skill in distributing to others. In the Eskimo, Bushmen, and many other hunters and gatherers, prey is divided according to set rules which may be highly specific or very general. The right to divide is granted to the successful hunter who is considered to be the possessor. Skillful distribution confers status while the opposite often incites conflict. Among the !Kung Bushmen, meat distributed to a man's affines (in-laws) is often given in bulk to the father-in-law or somebody who "knows their hearts." This person, in turn, redistributes the meat so as to avoid conflict. In larger groups united by a chieftain, this top ranking person cannot produce everything himself and instead receives tribute for his position as distributor of goods. Since skill is required for effective distribution only socially gifted individuals can attain leadership positions.

Children display a disposition very early in life for sharing with others. They play giving and taking games with their reference person many times throughout the day. Children offer food as a strategy to establish friendly contact before they are able to speak (at 10–12 months of age). They understand the friendly intent of others offering something to them and respond in a friendly way (Figs. 4.76–4.79). Particularly noteworthy is the fact that they understand that rejecting a gift is an insult and use this behavior when they are annoyed.

Third and fourth grade boys were found to be less generous in sharing with good friends apparently because their relation was stable and no particular reinforcement by sharing was needed. They were very sensitive, however, to any signs of discord and responded to any threat to their relationship with increased generosity (E. Staub and H. Noerenberg, 1981). When a boy refused the candy offered to him by a friend, the latter was inhibited to eat the candy and renewed his offers. Investigations of food sharing among boys and girls aged 5–8 revealed that girls were the more active food sharers. Furthermore, they tended to share with every member of their group, generally offering to the entire group ("does anyone want my. . . ."), while boys were more inclined to offer food to specific

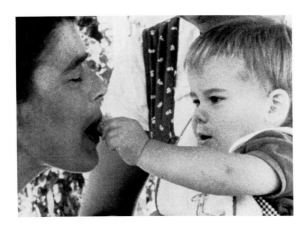

FIGURE 4.76. One-year-old children gladly share objects, usually in a feeding context. Here a 1-year-old girl sitting on her mother's lap feeds another woman well known to her. Note the coordinated movements of the baby's mouth. From a 16 mm film. Photo: I. Eibl-Eibesfeldt.

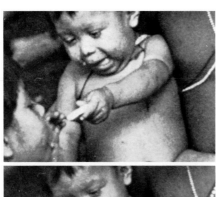

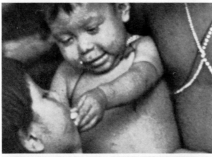

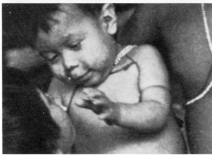

FIGURE 4.77. Yanomami infant feeding its older sister. Note that here the baby also opens its mouth to be fed in return. This feeding, in turn, gives rise to an extended dialogue of giving and receiving, described in *Ethology: The Biology of Behavior*. From a 25 frames/second 16 mm film, frames 1, 40, and 154 of the sequence. Photo: I. Eibl-Eibesfeldt.

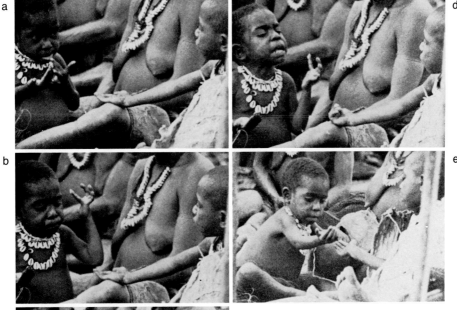

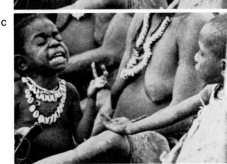

FIGURE 4.78. The disposition to give an object often conflicts with the desire to keep it. A Biami girl (New Guinea) begs to a boy who is eating something. He responds with a threat gesture, whereupon she closes her hand but continues to await a morsel. Shortly after he gives it to her. From a 25 frames/second 16 mm film, frames 1, 21, 51, and 55 of the sequence. Before(e) interruption. Photo: I. Eibl-Eibesfeldt.

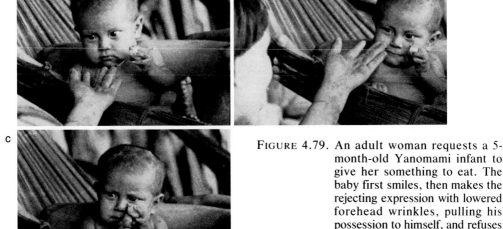

FIGURE 4.79. An adult woman requests a 5-month-old Yanomami infant to give her something to eat. The baby first smiles, then makes the rejecting expression with lowered forehead wrinkles, pulling his possession to himself, and refuses to give it up. From a 50 frames/second 16 mm film, frames 1, 122, and 157 of the sequence. Photo: I. Eibl-Eibesfeldt.

343

individuals. Dominant children tended to be the most active food traders (R. Dyson-Hudson and R. van Dusen, 1972).

With the development of tool cultures it became vital for an undisturbed group life that people respect not only food but also other objects as the possessions of others. It is scarcely possible that an harmonious group could be maintained without an inhibition of theft. For instance, weapons are of the most vital importance for the hunter or warrior, and he must reliably be able to pick them up after having laid them down; no one else may take them in the meantime.

An Eskimo would perish if someone took his boots while he slept. Since we may presume that a norm of respect of possession regarding food developed prior to the origin of tool culture, no new adaptations had to be developed since those already existing served the function.

Since both inhibition against taking something away and the disposition to give objects already existed, these rules would have only to be transferred to other objects. In a National Geographic Society film portraying the field research of Diane Fossey, one sees a gorilla male observing the researcher as she takes notes lying on her abdomen. He approaches her after a while and grabs her pencil. He then moves off a few steps and examines it: sniffs at it, turns it about, and examines it from all sides. Then comes the extraordinary aspect of this event: he goes over to Diane Fossey, gives her the pencil, and takes the notebook! Once again he moves off so he can investigate this object closely, and again he returns and gives her the book after he has satisfied his curiosity. Baboons and macaques would never behave this way! They would simply drop the object once their interest had dissipated.

In addition to this incidental observation we have no knowledge of object possession in gorillas. Since gorillas, unlike chimpanzees, do not hunt and need no tools, only vegetables and fruits could play a role as objects for possession in daily life. But perhaps the ancestors of these anthropoid apes were once on a higher developmental stage than today and needed tools, as A. Kortlandt postulates for chimpanzee ancestors.

In humans, objects are important in social relationships. They are used as means of self-portrayal and are also used to develop and reinforce social contacts.

If we observe small children and infants making friendly contact with family members and strangers, we will see a well-developed tendency for the child to give food or a toy as part of that contact activity. Klaus Stanjek (1979) recorded the manner in which preschool age children made contact with others of their own age. Objects played an important mediating role in this context, as the following data in Table 4.10 from a German kindergarten illustrate.

In another study Stanjek recorded how children in a Munich pediatric ward established contact with adults. Of 275 contacts with strangers, 155 were transitory; the children displayed signs of timidity and avoided further contact. They went away, for example, after initially approaching the adult; they restricted contact to a smile and then looked away, appearing embarrassed. There were 120 instances of friendly, extended contacts with associated interactions, and these contacts included utilizing objects in 76 instances (32 times the child extended an object to the stranger, and 44 times the child showed the stranger an object).

The act of offering is also a strategy of aggression inhibition. The evaluation of film scenes from our cross-cultural documentation from contexts of offering something during an aggressive encounter showed that acceptance of the offered object reduced the level of aggression between the concerned parties (R. Schropp, 1982).

344

Table 4.10. Contact Initiation in Young Children

Object contact initiation		Other forms of contact initiation	
43	Giving	71	Touching, pushing, addressing
39	Showing	82	Following
9	Demonstrating	12	Imitating
7	Sharing	10	Smiling
6	Tossing toward		
104		175	

In a French study, friendly contact and appeasement were the consequences of over 50% of all instances of object offering (H. Montagner, 1978).

Friendly contact initiation by means of an object has been verified in nonhuman primates, albeit in much less differentiated form. In humans objects are also shown by holding them up, pointing at them, or talking about them. In western society it is common to have many types of small items as "conversation pieces" about the house, and they play a role in facilitating social interaction.

In all cultures we investigated, we have observed the giving and extending of objects as a strategy of friendly contact initiation and for purposes of reducing aggression. As stated earlier, the disposition to give and share objects is well developed in children at an early age. Even toddlers will give up objects when requested to do so as long as the request is not understood as a command. If objects are simply taken away from a small child it will protest, usually successfully. H. Müller and K. Kühne (1974) investigated object conflict in kindergarten groups. In most instances, the child originally possessing the object won the dispute. The child who brought the object from home or had received the object in exchange or as a gift or was the first one to take possession of it and play with it (rule of priority) was considered the owner. The authors showed that children without such established rights to specific objects displayed more signs of uncertainty (automanipulation) than the "rightful" owners. The violation of the norm "The Owner has the Right to Use an Object" led to uncertainty in unrightful owners. A thief felt from the beginning that he had no right to an object and acted with uncertainty. Thus even at this age the norm of respect of possession plays a significant role. According to an investigation by R. Bakeman and J. R. Brownlee (1982) even the 2- to 3-year-old obeys a "prior possession rule." And if they played with an object, they were also more successful in defending it. From the second year onward, children start to obey to a shared social rule of possession. Only toddlers are guided by a rule of dominance. During the ontogeny a change takes place from the rules of power to the rules of law. Social learning theory does not explain this shift. The rules emerge quite spontaneously in the context of peer play "not as a result of cultural intervention, but simply as a consequence of a fundamental human propensity to regulate interaction in a ruleful manner" (Bakeman and Brownlee, 1982, p. 99). Learning seems to be channeled by a phylogenetically acquired disposition, so that only moderate encouragement from the environment is needed.

Our cross-cultural documentation demonstrates the universality of these principles. Some key observations may serve as illustration (Fig. 4.80–4.84).[20]

---

[20]See above for the ontogeny of object relationships.

Sharing is governed by a rule: one only gives up something willingly when the partner formulates his request and behaves in such a way that indicates respect for the other's possession. An imperative demand is aggressive and is only tolerated when a substantial rank differential exists between the parties and giving occurs in response to fear. One can also demand something with the intention of challenging or provoking another person. If one wishes to avoid this, one must formulate his request so the partner does not feel compelled to give up the object but can freely decide whether to keep it or not. Thus the question is often veiled with allusion, perhaps initiated with a commentary such as, "You have such a beautiful feather!" (compare V. Heeschen, W. Schiefenhövel, and I. Eibl-Eibesfeldt, 1980). The person being addressed knows then that the partner would like to have the object but is given the chance to explain why he will not give up the feather, perhaps simply because this is his only one. Praise of an item is a very common form of request in many cultures.

In particular ritualized contexts, equally ranked members can make mutual demands. In the contract songs of the Yanomami, demands and counterdemands are carried out in a form of formalized disputes displaying all the transitional stages between friendly bonding rituals to outright conflict.

Metaphor is used for valuable objects. Thus among the Yanomami machetes are called "Wife of the White Man." Another interesting characteristic of gift giving in these Indians is the downplaying of the value of the object in question, which is in effect a self-degradation. This inhibits an escalation in mutual displays of generosity whereby the gift giving would become an aggressive demonstration, as we described in the potlatch ceremony of the Kwakiutl (p. 308). "Take this skinny dog . . . he cannot do much" says a Yanomami giving his dog away (K. Good, 1980). Requesting, demanding, and giving are apparently guided by a universal set of regulations structuring verbal and nonverbal interactions of this kind in the same way, even throughout the various stages of ritualization (V. Heeschen, W. Schiefenhövel, and I. Eibl-Eibesfeldt, 1980). We will return to the theme of giving and gift exchanging when we discuss the cultural differentiation of various gift-giving rituals.

Gifts establish friendly relations, and food gifts play an important role in this context. In Japan it is customary to attach a small artificial fish to gifts as a symbolic gesture. In all cultures, gifts of food and providing one's guests with food is one of the most important acts of hospitality.

Objects can fulfill important functions in interpersonal relationships. Giving is originally a friendly act (Figs. 4.82–4.84). One gives something to create ties with another and to fortify that friendship. Giving is also done spontaneously to block or redirect aggression. All these activities presume the existence of ownership, i.e., the relationship between a person and an object and the readiness to defend that object, and is undoubtedly an ancient disposition.

FIGURE 4.80. Snatching and return of an object. A female Yanomami toddler approaches her playmate with two leaves in her hands. While settling down, her friend snatches one of the leaves, placing it behind her back. Her friend does not notice it, but offers the remaining leaf to her playmate, which she had apparently brought for this purpose. Her playmate accepts the gift and returns the leaf that she had snatched as if aware that it does not belong to her. Frames 1, 109, 166, 193, 283, 372, 402, 421, 504, and 554 from a 16 mm film taken at 50 frames/second. Photo: I. Eibl-Eibesfeldt.

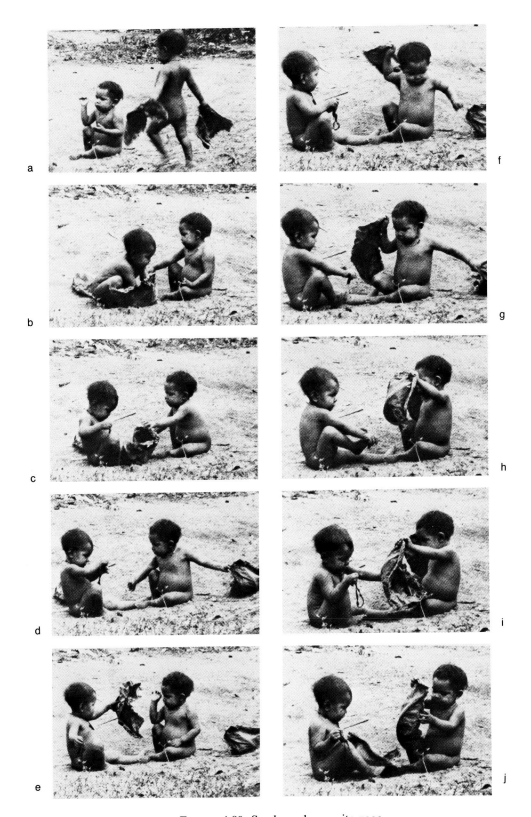

FIGURE 4.80. See legend opposite page.

Norms governing respect of possession of objects are probably of more recent origin than those concerning food (defining them as the disposition to respect another's ownership rights). They arose in social animals to avoid conflicts between group members, with analogous development in several primates and social carnivores (G. E. King, 1980).

The ability to give and receive probably developed with infant care and became incorporated secondarily into adult communication. The diversity in associated cultural rituals represent variations on the theme of the elementary interactional strategy of giving, which infants command before they are able to speak. Objects permit differential social interactions and foster friendship, provided that the objects are regarded as possessions. This fact has been overlooked in some (e.g., Kibbutz) experiments in which it is considered desirable to abolish the sense of private possession.

Experimental attempts to eliminate individual possession in children by instructing them that objects belong to everyone did not lead to the desired objective (M. E. Spiro, pers. commun.). The children in the kibbutz learned that no possessions were privately owned. Nonetheless, these children maintained the tendency to regard specific objects as their own, and since they had to continually defend these beloved objects from the attempts of others to take them, the children became correspondingly more possessive.

In children objects are also a means of self-portrayal used to ascertain recognition by group members and also as weapons in the struggle for rank position. These strategies may be due to phylogenetic disposition since they occur in children and adults belonging to all cultures investigated.

Man also possesses knowledge and "shares" it with others. Privileged information is an important bonding element in many organizations. Children develop secrets spontaneously, and they skillfully use the sharing of secret information to elevate their individual positions.

4.12.2. Social Bonds, Rank

Man displays distinct possessive behavior in his personal relationships. Children zealously defend their bonds to mother and other reference figures, with pronounced rivalries often developing between siblings. Adult relationships are similar, although some authors maintain that one cannot possess love any more than one can possess a partner; E. Fromm maintains that to possess in that way would be "pathological." However these assertions do not conform to observed and subjectively experienced reality. Lovers do indeed possess each other and will defend their possession just as they regret the loss of love as a concrete loss. The decisive characteristic of this situation is the mutual ownership, and this reciprocity distinguishes a loving relationship from object relationships (I. Eibl-Eibesfeldt, 1984).

However, a feeling of reciprocal relations with objects can be attained by projecting human characteristics and emotions onto the objects, as the intense attachments that can be developed to specific beloved objects[21] such as children have for dolls, teddy bears or blankets used as a parental substitute when sleeping (K. Stanjek 1980, M. Mitscherlich, 1984), or which adults in similar fashion use as a talisman or as a partner substitute.

---

348   [21]In psychoanalytical terminology these objects are designated as "transition objects."

FIGURE 4.81. Two Yanomami (Serra Parima/Venezuela) girls eat berries. One shows her
friend her blue tongue. After the girl on the left has eaten her berries, she
impulsively reaches for her friend's berries, who withdraws her food. At this
time the first girl notes her violation of etiquette and waits, holding her hand
out. When she indicates through her behavior that she respects the other girl
as the owner of the food, it is willingly given to her. From a 16 mm film.
Photo: I. Eibl-Eibesfeldt.

FIGURE 4.82. Gifts create a friendly atmosphere. Here a small G/wi boy receives a twig from an adult. The boy's face brightens and he moves off, slightly embarassed. From a 25 frames/second 16 mm film, frames 1, 7, 15, 31, 62, and 98 of the sequence. Photo: I. Eibl-Eibesfeldt.

Partners are also defended as a possession in nonhuman primates. In fact, partner possession is respected. Females defend their young and males will defend their mates in those species that develop long-term bonds. We can also observe in such instances that others respect individual ownership of a partner. Male hamadryas baboons *(Papio hamadryas)* collect small groups of females into harems, and if they see a lone female they will approach it and in a specific manner summon it to join the harem. H. Kummer, W. Götz, and W. Angst (1974) caught a group of female hamadryas baboons in one area and released them in another area. Several males immediately advanced from different directions to the lone female. Once a male reached the female, the others turned away and no fight ensued. Apparently a rule of priority operates by which the first male reaching a female gains possession. Rules like this foster group harmony.

We also consider social rank positions and roles as possessions. We respect the rank positions of others and will defend our own rank if necessary. Humans can allot rank positions to others, or take them away should someone fall from favor.

FIGURE 4.83. Children utilize giving to facilitate friendliness among playmates. Here an approximately 3½-year-old Himba boy greets his friend by giving him a piece of paper he found as a symbolic gift. Photo: I. Eibl-Eibesfeldt.

FIGURE 4.84. In many rituals people give, host, and feed one another, as here in the Balinese tooth filing ceremony. Mutual feeding, in particular, has a bonding effect and is characterized by a powerful quality. At the conclusion of the Balinese initiation ritual ("mapandes") the initiates feed one another. The couples joined by a shawl stick morsels of food in each other's mouth. This prepares them symbolically for marriage, which should be characterized by being good to each other. Reciprocal giving and receiving is considered to be the basis of marriage partnership. Photo: I. Eibl-Eibesfeldt.

4.12.3. On the Ethology of Gift Exchanging

In his monograph on gifts, which has become one of the classic anthropological works, Marcel Mauss poses the question: "What is the basis of right and interest that determines that in a backward, archaic society a gift given compels one to give another in turn?" (M. Mauss, 1968, p. 18). In other words, what is the driving force in the dedicated gift giving that makes the receiver reciprocate? His studies led him to make the following general conclusions: (1) The giving of objects primarily fulfills a social function. (2) There is an obligation of gift giving, receipt of same, and an obligation to give in turn.

This cycle produces a functional entity serving group formation and reinforcement. All objects—women, food, children, goods, talismans, property and soil, labor, services, priestly offices and rank—are objects of giving and regiving.

The many customs of gift giving and primitive trade primarily fulfill social functions in Mauss's view, and these originally had priority over economic functions.

However Mauss strays too far afield when he claims that man developed into an economic being only in recent history in western society. This is an exaggeration, for even at the stone age level useful objects were exchanged. Thus, the Eipo of western New Guinea obtain their blanks[22] for stone axes from a neighboring region since the necessary materials do not exist in their area. They trade net bags and food materials, e.g., *Saccharum edule,*[23] and obtain wood for bows in like manner. Trade also bonds individuals. Thus in western societies it is customary to break off trade negotiations when there are political disagreements. The Eipo foster trade from family to family using specific trade partners, and these partnerships are even inherited. Even where no exchanging of goods is really essential because the necessities of life are abundantly available to all, gift exchanging still takes place. For example, the mutual exchanging of bamboo arrowheads between Yanomami has only the function of establishing and emphasizing social ties.

B. Malinowski (1922) observed that the kula system of the Trobriand islanders should not be considered conventional trade. Kula is a gift exchange restricted to chieftains and is used to unite spatially disparate tribes. Trobriand islanders are well known as superb sailors and traders, and the alliances resulting from chieftain gift exchanges no doubt fostered secure trade relations throughout a wide region. In the kula system, tribes were united from Dobu (d'Entrecasteaux Islands), Kiriwina, Sinaketa, and Vakuta (Trobriands), Kitava (Marshall Bennet Island), Tube-tubé and the Woodlark Islands, and the southern tip of New Guinea. Simply stated, the kula system consists of a kula partner giving specific gifts to another. The gift is kept only a short time before sending it to another individual until finally the gift returns to the original donor. Gifts sent in this circulating manner include a necklace made out of red mother-of-pearl plates from spondylus shells (Soulava) and of mother-of-pearl armbands from conch shells (Mwali). The two prestige objects are sent around the islands in opposite directions, armbands counterclockwise and necklaces clockwise. There are also gifts exchanged that do not make the complete circular route (Figs. 4.85, 4.86).

Gifts are exchanged with utmost modesty. After the donor has ceremoniously brought the gifts to the soundings of a conch shell, he excuses himself for only bringing remnants. He throws the gifts at the recipient's feet or will hand over the necklace with the words: "Here is the rest of my food from today; take it" (B. Malinowski, 1922). We have already described instances of self-deprecating behavior in comparable situations. In ethological terms this is an act of appeasement that should foster acceptance of the gift since with this solicitation should come receipt and the incumbent obligation of mutual exchange.

The figures of speech and magical incantations accompanying the ritual exchange indicate that hatred and war are sworn off and that trade should take place peacefully: "Thy rage ebbs, the dog plays—thy anger ebbs, the dog plays. . . ." The relations between trade partners are characterized by ambivalence.

B. Malinowski's (1922) findings indicate that the people of Kiriwina, for example, fear the people of Dobu. The Dobu man, as those from Kiriwina reported to Malinowski, is not as good as they. He is a cruel cannibal, and the Kiriwinans would be afraid of visiting Dobu. But if they would expectorate the magical ginger

---

[22]Crudely worked stone ax blades.

[23]A kind of sugar cane that does not thrive in their neighbors' lands (W. Schiefenhövel, pers. commun.).

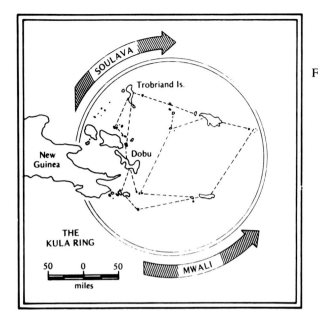

FIGURE 4.85. The kula ring: necklaces (Soulava) are exchanged in clockwise motion from island to island, while armbands (Mwali) are sent in counterclockwise manner. Exchange pathways are indicated by dashed lines. From R.M. Keesing (1981).

FIGURE 4.86. The circulating valuable objects of the kula ring: armband (left) produced from conch shells and the necklace from the pink spondylus shells. From R.M. Keesing (1981).

root[24] the Dobu men would be quite transformed. They would lay down their spears and receive their visitors most courteously.

Besides this kula exchange occurring between different islands there are smaller, local ceremonial trade transactions among the island populace. Food products are the most important trade items; particularly large yams roots are considered prestige objects.

Intra-island kula exchange fosters mutual security for the island inhabitants, since there are occasional harvest failures that would leave entire villages without

---

[24]The chewing and subsequent expectoration of ginger is a magical remedy for disease and evil. Group ginger eating also consolidates friendships in many parts of New Guinea and the surrounding islands. H. Nevermann (1941) relates a delightful anecdote: after he had lived some time with the Makleuga and learned how crazy they were about collecting head trophies, he asked his informant if he would want his head as well. The informant said he would want it very much but once he had eaten of his ginger root they were friends, and his head could not be taken.

food. In such cases they receive food products from those villages with an abundant food supply. Communities are encouraged to overproduce and maintain reserves. Harvests are used competitively and there is status associated with maintaining surpluses. Individual families are awarded for their harvests in intervals of 1 to 3 years, and the harvest is kept on display in yams houses (p. 310). Possession of edibles cultivates esteem but also makes public those that have abundance and can afford to distribute some of their reserves. One keeps as much as possible until the next harvest and then throws away the rest. Particularly large and beautiful roots of other yam varieties are given as gifts. They are not eaten, but are hung up, painted, and often framed in wood along the sides of the homes or the yams storage sheds. Those who produce a large harvest are highly esteemed and maintain their stocks for those who lack food. The stocks, then, are used for distribution to others. Baskets with yams are given as gifts at various occasions. According to W. Schiefenhövel and I. Bell-Krannhals (1986), 83% of the harvest presentations goes to the nearest relatives (Fig. 4.87 and Table 4.11).

In addition to group-bonding functions of gift giving, many forms of exchanges contain an element of competition (as in the kula and the potlatch festivals), the principle being that one attempts to outdo the other in such a way that he is not in a position anymore to reciprocate and therefore in obligation. By such fighting with gifts "dominance relations can get established." The bonding function of giving, however, seems to be the predominant one. M. Harris (1968) in his history of anthropology, downplays the significance of Marcel Mauss's discovery. According to Harris, Mauss discovered some subjective motives of the individuals that would compel an individual to behave in a particular way regarding production, distribution, and consumption, but these "social" reasons had nothing to do with the real causal factors, which were more economic than social. Harris opposes Mauss's attempt to glean a social function from the potlatch festival and the western

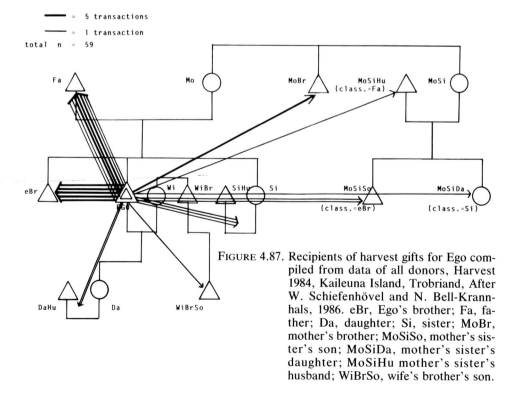

FIGURE 4.87. Recipients of harvest gifts for Ego compiled from data of all donors, Harvest 1984, Kaileuna Island, Trobriand, After W. Schiefenhövel and N. Bell-Krannhals, 1986. eBr, Ego's brother; Fa, father; Da, daughter; Si, sister; MoBr, mother's brother; MoSiSo, mother's sister's son; MoSiDa, mother's sister's daughter; MoSiHu mother's sister's husband; WiBrSo, wife's brother's son.

Table 4.11. Sociobiological View of Harvest Gifts[a]

Kinship degree	Recipient[b]	n	Transactions	%
50%	eBr	25	49	83
	Fa	19		
	Da	2		
	Si	3		
25%	MoBr	5	5	9
12.5%	MoSiSo	2	3	5
	MoSiDa	1		
"0"%	MoSiHu	1	2	3
	WiBrSo	1		

[a]Total transactions at harvest in Kaileuna 1984; $n = 59$. After W. Schiefenhövel and N. Bell-Krannhals, 1986.
[b]eBr, Ego's brother; Fa, father; Da, daughter; Si, sister; MoBr, mother's brother; MoSiSo, mother's sister's son; MoSiDa, mother's sister's daughter; MoSiHu, mother's sister's husband; WiBrSo, wife's brother's son.

celebration of Christmas: "The comparison of course is perfectly apt on the psychological level, but one does not have to be a Marxist to sense that there is another dimension to our Christmas madness. Why is an intelligence so subtle in other respects, unable to penetrate to the not-so-deep function of Christmas purchases in an economy whose productive capacity has reached ahead of the power to buy and consume" (M. Harris, 1968, p. 488). But Harris errs when he sees the economic reason as the sole ultimate cause. Ethological findings support both an economic and social function for giving. As discussed earlier, one cannot give unless one possesses. Possession has its roots in an orderly distribution and respect of possession of economically essential (and nonessential) resources.

Giving, as discussed earlier, most likely has its origins in the mother–child relationship with both an economic and social function.

In the discussion on ritualization we showed that infant care behavior in many birds and mammals led to the development of numerous bonding rituals. They are used during courtship, are the elements of many greeting rituals, and they also function to facilitate social ties in everyday interactions.

Giving is extended to more distant kin in order to create social ties with the function of reducing economic risk, as clearly demonstrated by Wiessner's investigation of the hxaro (p. 293). In his paper on reciprocal altruism, R. L. Trivers (1921) made the intriguing speculation that many human cognitive capacities, particularly abilities to calculate, developed hand in hand with reciprocal altruism, because of the dual social and economic function.

Gift giving as a friendly act is dependent upon reciprocity that is generally delayed over time so that an obligation remains. The !Kung Bushmen thus develop an interrelational network of hxaro exchanges with specific exchange partners and the system serves a security function (P. Wiessner, 1977, p. 380).

For these reasons, giving usually has both economic and social elements, with some transactions being more economic and others more social. In western societies economic and social giving is more clearly delineated than in kin-based societies, making giving relatively conflict free. In kin-based societies, economic and social factors are so intertwined that giving is often conflict-ridden and the constant subject of conversation.

From the mutual aspect of gift exchange relations it follows that there is an optimum for giving. On one hand, to give too much is dominating, but, on the other, to be stingy is frowned upon. Keblob in the village Dingerkon in the Eipomek valley of western New Guinea gave sweet potatoes from his garden to other village inhabitants on a daily basis. He was a diligent gardener and produced a large crop, and the locals said he had a great "garden soul." The distribution of food had provided him with a great deal of joy, for every morning he had come to our hut beaming, placing his sweet potatoes there. And we occasionally overheard him talking to himself in his hut about whom he should give some sweet potatoes the next morning. He was considered to be the "sweet potato bigman" and was afforded high esteem. In 1981, when he suddenly became lame, the entire village in turn cared for him.

When someone gives so much, the recipient cannot reciprocate without difficulties, and thus such lavish giving is only acceptable in stratified societies in which the giver's position authorizes him to do so. Chieftains are also given tribute for distribution and thus for creating bonding in the group. In less hierarchically organized tribal cultures the individual who gives too much is considered to be either stupid or to consider himself a "big shot."

Thus if someone gives more than another can return, he or she assumes a dominance position, and giving can deteriorate into a struggle in which the gifts are the weapons. The potlatch festival of the northwest coast Kwakiutl Indians is the classic example of this form of gift-giving. Chieftains invite others to their festivities and attempt to shame them with their generosity. In boasting songs they praise their might as they distribute blankets and other valuable items, and even go so far as to destroy some of their wealth.

But even where giving is not intended to outdo the other party, objects play a role as a means of display. !Kung Bushmen adorn themselves with beautiful works of beads, which also circulate as gifts. In carrying about these artistic works on their bodies they portray themselves as worthy exchange partners in the hxaro exchange system. A similar function occurs in the decorated warriors of the Mt. Hagen area in Papua, New Guinea, who in dance depict themselves with body adornment as rich, healthy, and thus important and capable (A. Strathern, 1979).

Interesting changes take place in transforming the everyday object to one of value. An object derives its value from the materials, time invested, and skill of the craftsman. The Eipo of western New Guinea produce net bags and trade them for stone blanks coming from another region (see above). Net bags are valued objects, and when the men dance they bear particularly large net bags as decorations on their backs; sometimes the net bags are adorned with feathers. The dance net bags are used only ornamentally, even though they are fully functional. The In, who belong to the same linguistic family and live in an adjacent region, use net bags as pure decoration. The broad, but shallow, net bag is kept spread with a stick and (in the Yali) is covered throughout with feathers. It is merely a substrate for the decorative feathers. These decorative net bags are useless as containers and were never constructed to have any significant capacity.

In other regions one can observe a similar development in axes. Axes are treasured trade articles since their production requires a great deal of labor, and the stone materials for axes are not readily accessible. Once again, more laborious production elevates the value of the object, so the axes are carefully polished by hand (additional investment of labor). Such valued pieces are not used as axes, but are particularly well suited for paying bride wealth. Thus an everyday object changes from a utensil to a form of money.

Trade developed largely from reciprocal exchange systems. If inequalities are intended, trade turns into competition for domination and debtor communities can fall into a position of dependency.

Mauss recognized the social function of gift giving, which Harris at best considers as individual motivation but does not recognize its selective value. Furthermore, Mauss demonstrates the universality of the principle of reciprocity. Its importance in social interaction became clear to me upon observing the worship of a stone symbolizing god Shiva in the vicinity of Katmandu (Nepal). The stone was given gifts, decorated with flowers, sprinkled with milk, given coins, and tinted with colors. This was followed by a simulated reciprocity: one person partook of the dyes previously spread on the stone and adorned his forehead with it, and also took the flowers as if they were a return gift. In short, the participants acted as if Shiva was giving gifts in return.

The willingness to give is balanced by the disposition to defend if someone should attempt to take away something. This would contradict the recently postulated theory of giving as derived from tolerated theft which N. G. Blurton-Jones (1984) proposes because he finds it difficult to imagine the initial mutative appearance of altruism within a population; a lone altruist would therefore be at a disadvantage. He overlooked the fact that with maternal care, which evolved by individual selection, came care-taking behaviors and thus the readiness to give. Thus all members of a population are equally preadapted to give objects and therefore to behave altruistically. Since blood relationship is not directly perceived as such, but in general is inferred from intimacy of living together, the step to extending familial relations to unrelated members of small groups was certainly not particularly difficult.

Certainly one must calculate costs and benefit for each act of sharing and giving. Since within the small group each member is closely related to the next and groups also appear as units in selection, it is advantageous to foster friendliness. Giving to unrelated members must, however, take place on a reciprocal basis.

The individual is generally protected from excessive giving by the disposition to keep items and which together with the readiness to give forms an adaptive system. Education can enhance one or the other inclination, so there is a danger of overstepping the optimal in one direction or the other. Greed and indiscriminate altruism are maladaptive deviations from the norm.

Observations of children show that obligation for reciprocity is felt. Its origin is still unclear, but it is a need that has been found universally. In fact there is such a strong impulse to reciprocate that psychologists speak of a compulsion to reciprocate. In one study, D. T. Regan (1971) had students assess the quality of paintings. They did this together with other students who were assistants to the investigator. During a brief pause, the assistant left the room, only to return after 2 minutes either with two bottles of Coca-Cola (giving one to the other student in the test) or empty handed. In each situation the assistant behaved in an identical manner. After all of the paintings had been evaluated, the assistant asked the fellow student if he would purchase several lottery tickets, because if he sold the most tickets he would win a $50 prize. Those for whom the assistant had done a favor purchased more tickets than those for whom he had not. This obligation to reciprocate is used in sales promotions when free samples are given. Often such gifts are forced upon the potential customer.

Apparent compromises operate according to the same rule. One first requests something unreasonable, then retreats from the original demand and thus obligates the other to make some reciprocal gesture, often eliciting behavior the person would not have done otherwise. In a highly popular and lucid work, R. B. Cialdini (1984) gives a most impressive related example. A Boy Scout approached him on the street and asked him if he would purchase a ticket for a Boy Scout event for 5 dollars. He refused, but the Boy Scout responded by asking him to at least buy some of his chocolate candy bars, which only cost 1 dollar. Even though Cialdini did not like chocolate he purchased some. The boy had made a concession by offering something less expensive as an alternative, and Cialdini incurred a particular obligation as a result. This corresponds to behavior at negotiations for example when unions first make excessive requests. R. B. Cialdini (1975) investigated the phenomenon experimentally. A person asked various zoo visitors to accompany a group of retarded children visiting the zoo; most people refused to do so. In the second part of this experiment a group of young people were asked to volunteer several hours of work per week for the handicapped over a 2-year time period; most of them refused. The investigator then asked as a concession that they simply accompany a group of retarded children on a zoo visit. Three times as many young people agreed to do so versus the number in the first part of the study.

Lévi-Strauss (1969) elaborated on Mauss's ideas into a theory of reciprocity of all social relationships. The universality of this phenomenon led him to postulate a structural unconscious by which all human conceptions become structured in similar ways.

The generalization of the theory of reciprocity to all social phenomena contains an important principle. The social system can be conceived as a reciprocal exchange system in which even women are treated as exchange items. Indeed, marriages are often planned, for purposes of forming specific alliances. Attempts to explain the origin of the incest taboo as a consequence of this, however, do not hold up well. Thus, Lévi-Strauss argues that since it is forbidden to form attachments with one's sister or other women within the incest taboo as sex partners, they become available as objects to establish relations. This is to some extent correct. The incest taboo makes this kind of politics feasible, but did not originate for this purpose. Cultural elaborations and extensions of this taboo, however, clearly serve such functions, such as those operating in the Australian aborigines by which one can find almost no eligible women in the immediate vicinity and thus many are forced to generate ties in some distant area. However, as previously cited (Section 4.6), the inhibition against forming sexual relationships with those with whom one has grown up during a specific sensitive period of development, is an old biological disposition.

Summary 4.12

Objects play an important role as mediators of social relationships. The fact that they are used as gifts in establishing friendly contacts requires that the donor is recognized as the legitimate owner of the object in question and that there is a disposition to give and to accept gifts. A primary norm of respect of object possession is found in the anthropoid apes. Food is not seized from others; it is requested with gestures and then received. With the development of tool culture, object possession became particularly significant for the maintenance of harmonious group life.

In all cultures we investigated, infants utilize the strategy of offering objects prior to learning speech, and enjoy the playful dialogue of give-and-take games,

358

in which the rules of reciprocity are already observed. Rituals of gift exchange play an important role in human societies, and are based upon a mutuality. Trade relations developed from reciprocal gift exchanges. Ethological finds support the position that the social function of object transfer evolved in the context of maternal behavior and was extended to those outside the dyad for social and economic reasons. Attachments to other individuals are respected as possessions and defended as such. Social relationships, however, are reciprocal between partners.

5

Intraspecific Aggression:
Conflict and War

The history of mankind is, among other things, a history of wars. Wars have been used to conquer lands and to disperse populations. What remained of the defeated were often the smoke-blackened ruins unearthed by the spades of archeologists. Wars have spurred human inventiveness to some of its highest levels, particularly in modern times, reaching an expenditure of 455 billion dollars! War has brought unending sorrow to man, destroying irreplaceable cultural values. No modern politician, therefore, openly acknowledges war as a justifiable means to a political end (K. von Clausewitz, 1937). At best, war is accepted as an unavoidable evil, borne out of fear of others.

But if the desire for peace is so strong, why are there still so many wars today? How has this form of human confrontation developed? What functions are fulfilled by war, and wherein lie its roots? These questions must be dealt with if we are to gain control over our lives and our future.

In such a widely occurring phenomenon it is reasonable to postulate initially that it does fulfill certain functions. Once these have been recognized, one can consider by which other means these functions could be fulfilled.

War has plagued mankind since earliest times. Some have claimed that it is the whip that drives human progress (R. S. Bigelow, 1970), while others consider it to be a pathological phenomenon and a debasement of human nature. However one interprets it, war must be considered the most perilous of all dangers currently threatening the human race. We are compelled to prevent nuclear warfare. In order to do so we must first understand the phenomenon of human aggression.

5.1. Concepts

The concept of aggression is derived from the Latin *aggredi* = to go to, in the sense of attack and also as accepting (facing) a challenge. In a broader sense we also attack problems and sink our teeth into our work. Thus, one deals with carrying out desires against some kind of resistance by means of forceful conquest of the opposition, either with fighting or threats. The obstacle can be displaced during the course of the confrontation, e.g., the opponent can be killed, driven off, or subjugated. In all cases the victor achieves dominance over the defeated.

This is true for *inter-* as well as *intra*specific aggressive encounters. The resistance of the prey must be overcome before it can be consumed, and the conspecific rival must be driven off or dominated to gain undisturbed access to a female or to specific resources. During the course of evolution, programs developed that frequently resulted in potential rivals fighting each other.

Intra- and interspecific aggression[1] should be carefully distinguished: the oryx (an African gazelle) fights against a lion quite differently than against another oryx. The oryx attempts to gore the carnivorous predator, while conspecifics are fought in tournament manner according to specific behavioral rules that reduce injuries. A predator likewise behaves quite differently in its struggles with prey than with conspecifics. A cat stalking prey is silent and its attack is specifically targeted toward executing a killing bite at the prey's neck. But in intraspecific fights, the cat's autonomic nervous system is highly activated, as rivals make penetrating threat calls and assume expressive threat postures. They attack each other with their claws. The opponent is injured and driven away but seldom killed.

---

[1] We equate aggression and aggressive behavior, following H. D. Dann (1972).

The encounter often ends at the display stage. Intraspecific aggression is typically under strong hormonal influence and the animal's display fluctuations in readiness to engage in such behavior, which cannot be traced back to corresponding fluctuations of environmental factors (D. J. Reis, 1974).

There are, of course, instances in which no clear distinctions can be drawn between intra- and interspecific aggression, but in most cases these forms of aggression are distinct. If one fails to distinguish between the two forms one can draw the wrong conclusions. Thus R. A. Dart (1949, 1953) ascribes contemporary human aggression to the predatory (carnivorous) life style of his australopithecine ancestors. Australopithecines were "predatory apes," hunting with simple weapons, and the cliché of the "aggressive" predator led to this misconception of a predatory life style as predisposition for aggressive behavior. One failed to notice the fact that a "peaceful" herbivore, like a bull, can fight most aggressively against other bulls and is certainly not activated by blood thirst. The rooster, which feeds on grains and worms, is another example of a noncarnivorous animal that is often used to symbolize aggression.

Psychologists generally define a behavior as aggressive when someone is intentionally injured as a consequence (J. Dollard et al., 1939; S. Feshbach, 1964; F. Merz, 1965; R. A. Baron, 1977). But, only in the case of humans may we, through questioning, find out about intentionality. Yet, even then, we have to draw conclusions from what is observed. Generally observations will reveal whether injuries of people were committed intentionally or not, but this is rarely the case with animals. The observer can usually only determine that a behavioral sequence terminated with the achievement of some particular set of conditions, such as dominance. An iguana will fight another until it leaves the area, and this driving away can be subsequently defined as the behavioral goal in the sense of a consummatory final condition.

Accidental attacks can occur among animals. A group member may, for instance, amidst the vigor of a struggle, such as in a group defense, be attacked by his own kind. Generally attacks like these are broken off immediately, and in higher mammals there are friendly behavioral patterns (e.g., social grooming) that function as appeasement gestures.

The psychological definition characteristic of "injury" requires more precision. When iguanas fight each other, they usually do so in the form of a tournament in which no one is physically injured. The injury sustained consists of a reduction in reproductive success, for the vanquished partner is at least temporarily restrained from mating with a female. This occurs when an animal forces another, by its behavior, to a subordinate rank position or drives it away from the immediate area, regardless of whether the subordinate animal sustained physical injuries or not. The winner gains certain advantages such as access to resources, and ultimately these may culminate in higher reproductive success.

There are also aggressions that are intentional but do not result in injuries but rather benefit the attacked partner. This occurs in educational aggression. A slap constraining a child from performing certain behavior by which it might endanger itself is clearly aggressive, since force was used to compel the child to behave, against its desires, in accord with the parent's will. Thus once again the characteristic of injury as a defining element is only of limited use. However, the establishment of a dominance relationship is a useful criterion. In this sense we can consider territorial bird songs to be aggressive (R. N. Johnson, 1972; H. Markl,

1974) as well as dominance achieved through pheromones in the social insects.[2] Aggression is all behavior that compels a dominance relationship of one individual against another, usually against the other's resistance.

Aggressive behaviors are distinguished from those of defense, subordination, and flight. They form a functional system with aggression known as the agonal[3] system (J. P. Scott, 1960). Fighting and escape systems form a functional unit within this general context. An organism need not always appear as a fighter, since the alternative choices of subordination or flight can also be important for survival. In practice one can see all the transitional stages and combinations of attack and escape intentions. R. W. Hunsperger (1954) located a functional system for attack, defense, and flight behavior in the cat mesencephalon and hypothalamus using electrical stimulation of the brain. Similar results arose from the cerebral stimulation studies of E. von Holst and U. von Saint Paul (1960).

The following listing represents the behaviors of aggression and defense as subsystems of fighting behavior as functionally opposed to a flight (escape) system that activates subordinate and flight behavior. The latter reduces the chances of fighting resulting in self-destruction. These subsystems can be further subdivided as in Tinbergen's hierarchical scheme.

Agonal Behavior (Enemy Behavior)
  Fighting System
    1. Aggressive behavior
       Threat
       Fighting
    2. Defensive behavior
       Threat
       Fighting
  Flight System
    3. Submissive behavior
    4. Flight behavior

Our classification system presents the hypothetical relationships between physiological systems that can be postulated on the basis of current research.

There have been numerous attempts to organize aggression into further subcategories, but such efforts have often resulted in a confusion of highly heterogeneous criteria of organization. Thus, R. Bilz (1965) lists 15 "aggression radicals": frustration, punishment, envy, hunger and sexual aggressions, anarchistic, anal, and urethral aggression, overfatigue, pain, defensive reaction and vengeful motivated aggression, aggression against insect pests, aggression heroism of the mother and alpha partner, etc. The forms of aggression are listed on the basis of manifestation (anal, urethral), presumed motivation (envy, hunger), and finally on the basis of the releasing situation (pain, insects).

---

[2]This is a borderline case since one cannot say that this dominance is being exerted against the resistance of another individual.

[3]From *agon* = competition (in Greek). One often sees the Latinized form "agonistic." I utilize the linguistically preferable *agonal*, which also conforms better to the counter concept of *synagonal* for all bonding behavior.

K. E. Moyer (1971a, b) also fused different categorizing principles of intra-specific aggression into seven classes: (1) aggressive behavior of males toward other males, (2) fear-induced aggression of a fleeing animal when its "critical distance" is transcended (H. Hediger, 1934), (3) "spontaneous irritation aggression," for which animate or inanimate objects must be present to be attacked, (4) territorial aggression released by unfamiliar conspecifics trespassing territorial boundaries, (5) maternal aggression related to brood defense, and (6) sex-related aggression released by stimuli that also activate sexual behavior. His seventh class is used for all other phenomena and is called instrumental aggression.

Moyer's report that the various forms of aggression can be elicited by electrical stimulation of various areas of the brain is interesting. However, it is still an open question whether thereby one system is activated via several different pathways or whether discrete, distinct neural populations are responsible for the various forms of intraspecific aggression.

Erich Fromm's (1974) division of forms of aggression is impregnated with biased terms. He distinguishes between well-intentioned or defensive aggression and "evil" aggression. The well-intentioned forms are those defensive reactions with whose help the individual protects vital interests. According to Fromm, this is the only type of aggression that is phylogenetically programmed. He cites as an example defensive reactions to threats of human liberty, reactions at "injured narcism," the therapeutic attempt to make repressed desires conscious, and the conforming aggression on command and direction. According to Fromm instru-mental aggression is related to defensive forms in that in both cases injury is not the goal of these aggressive acts. Rather, aggression was employed as a tool serving other objective goals. While the previously described forms of aggression serve to maintain life and are thus biologically adaptive (and "well intentioned"), de-structiveness (equated with cruelty by Fromm) is not adaptive and not phyloge-netically programmed. It did not consist of a defense against any particular threat, and its chief manifestations of murder and cruelty were lustful but served no other purpose. Fromm describes specific spontaneous forms of destructive aggressivity including vengeful, ecstatic destructiveness and passionate hatred. He also dis-cusses sadism and necrophilia (love of corpses) and in that connection, necrophiliac personalities. Such individuals are characterized by a compulsive interest in death and decay, a fixation on possessions and the past, tendencies to deify technology, the thought that all living things were objects, the belief that problems can only be resolved with force, and by incestuous relations with the mother.

This does not exhaustively portray the colorful and highly heterogeneous at-tempts to characterize the problem of aggression (further references in G. Pleger, 1976). We will survey the various functions of aggression at a later point in our discussion (Section 5.3).

Summary 5.1

We can define as aggressive those behaviors through which man or animals sustain their interests against the resistance of others, and thus maintain dominance. Aggression, then, is activated in many different functional arrays for the sake of gaining access to resources, defeating rivals, and many other purposes. Obstacles preventing access to a behavioral objective also activate aggression targeted toward removing those obstacles. Intra- and interspecific aggression must be distinguished. Aggression within a species is often ritualized and geared to preventing excessive injuries through displays and tournament-style fights. Agonal behavior is hierarchically organized, and comprises the subsystems of fighting (aggressive and defensive behavior) and flight (flight and submission).

5.2. Aggression Theories

The aggressive behavior of animals is critically but certainly not exclusively determined by phylogenetic adaptations. Motor adaptations in animals include specific behavior patterns of threat and fighting, in which corresponding morphological structures are utilized as weapons (for example, horn structures). Releasers activate aggressive behavior via innate releasing mechanisms, and in some cases endogenous motivation (an aggressive drive) has been demonstrated (for literature see I. Eibl-Eibesfeldt, 1975; K. E. Moyer, 1987). Interaction strategies are, to some extent, programmed by means of phylogenetic adaptation, but a great deal of learning is also involved in aggression, especially in the higher vertebrates. Mammals develop individual skill and individualized attack and defensive tactics during play with conspecifics.

Fighting is often so ritualized that none of the combatants is injured. In tournament fights the animals measure their strength in a bloodless manner according to specific rules until one of them perceives that the other is superior. At that point the animal about to lose either gives up or is forcefully driven out of the area. Specific, likewise innate behavioral patterns of submission and appeasement can terminate a fight and prevent an escalation to a destructive conflict.

The discussion of whether or not human aggressive behavior is determined by phylogenetic adaptations was stimulated by Konrad Lorenz (1963) in his book *On Aggression* (German: *Das sogenannte Böse*). He propounded the viewpoint that human aggression must be understood as an adaptation and, as such, had a long phylogenetic development. He postulates that human aggressive behavior is stimulated by a number of motivational systems.

With this connection to an innate basis, Lorenz does not conceive of aggression as unavoidable and excusable. He writes:

> We have good reasons to consider intraspecific aggression in the present cultural-historical and technological situation of humanity to be the gravest of all dangers. But we will in no way improve our prospects of dealing with it by assuming it is something metaphysical and unpreventable, but rather by pursuing the chain of its natural causal factors. Wherever man has achieved the mastery (skill) necessary to guide a natural force in a certain direction, his ability to do so arises from understanding the causal relationships underlying that tendency. The lessons derived from studying normal, species-preserving life processes, or physiology, are the indispensable basis for teaching its disturbance and its pathology (Lorenz, 1963, p. 47).

Lorenz wanted to contribute to the control of aggression by elucidating its nature. Those who reproach him for belittling and excusing the aggression problem have either read inattentively or have consciously misrepresented the Lorenzian position to set up a "straw man." In doing so they have disqualified themselves as critics.

Thus Erich Fromm writes (1974): "What could be more welcome for those . . . who are afraid and feel incapable of altering the present destructive course of humanity, than Lorenz's theory that violence springs from our animal nature and gives rise to an untameable drive for aggression" (p. 53). This reproach has been repeated with rubber stamplike monotony (A. Schmidt-Mummendey and H. D.

Schmidt, 1971; H. D. Dann, 1972). A. Montagu (1976) went so far as to claim that ethologists are attempting to teach us that we humans were murderers. The introductory chapter of my book *Love and Hate* (1970c) bears the title *"The 'Bestia Humana,' a Modern Caricature of Man"*! The degenerating style of this scientific discussion is shocking and ultimately destructive to a free exchange of ideas. History should have taught us to be more sensitive.

There are many theories on the development of aggression, all based upon accurate observations and experiments and which only then shoot beyond their target when they claim to formulate all-encompassing explanation.

5.2.1. Learning Theories

Success reinforces behavior, and children undoubtedly learn from success to engage aggressive behavior instrumentally in order to achieve certain objectives. Children also learn from social models (A. Bandura, 1973). A. Bandura and R. H. Walters (1963) arranged to have one group of children watch an adult mishandling a rubber doll while another group of children experienced the same event indirectly via a television screen. A third group watched a cartoon in which a cat mishandled a doll and a fourth group watched a presentation without any aggressive acts. After each visual presentation all four groups of children were equally frustrated with some task performance study, and afterward their play with dolls was observed. All children who had watched an aggressive model handled their doll more aggressively than control children who had not observed an aggressive model.

The effect of a model is long lasting. D. J. Hicks (1965) tested the effect of social models on children using methods resembling Bandura's. In a subsequent investigation undertaken 6 months later, he found that those who had experienced an adult as an aggressive model were still influenced by this model! These and other studies (A. Bandura, 1973; R. H. Walters and E. L. Thomas, 1963; S. Feshbach and R. Singer, 1971) clearly confirm the significance of learning from a model for the development of aggressive attitudes.

A child learns from the models of the parents and people in the vicinity. If a child has a good relationship with his parents he will have a strong tendency to emulate the parental model and will be prepared to undertake heroic or pacifistic attitudes, depending on the nature of parental influence. Man also learns to restrain aggression in particular contexts and to target it toward specific individuals regarded by the community as enemies. He learns when to activate aggression within his group and when such activation is illegitimate. The particular techniques of fighting with weapons and other aspects of aggression are acquired. There is no ethological theory in which learning does not play an important role in shaping human aggression. Ethologists only disagree with those who maintain that phylogenetic adaptations (innate characteristics) play no role or an insignificant one in human aggression. We will show that such claims are simply false.

5.2.2. Dollard's Aggression-Frustration Hypothesis

A hindrance to goal-directed behavior (frustration) elicits an aggressive response to help overcome the obstacle, and in this context aggression serves other motivations. According to J. Dollard *et al.* (1939) one need not presume the existence of an independent aggressive drive since such behavior is entirely reactive. The reaction pattern of responding to frustrations (deprivation experiences) with aggression is innate. That frustrations can lead directly to aggression, has been demonstrated experimentally. But whether early frustrating experiences are indeed responsible for the formation of an aggressive adult personality is still open to dispute. Much has been written to that extent but no data confirms the numerous statements. From the early experiences said to account for adult aggressivity, the trauma of birth, early weaning, toilet training, and repression of infant sexuality were considered to be of particular importance. It was argued that only a extremely permissive education would allow for the development of a peaceful personality, which is certainly too simplistic a view.

5.2.3. Drive Concepts

Sigmund Freud postulated an aggressive drive. He conceived it as a mystical death instinct *(thanatos)* counteracting the live instinct *(libido)* and served to drive man toward destructive action. Konrad Lorenz (1963) replaced this concept with a biological theory of an neurogenic drive for intraspecific aggression, the assumption being based upon observations of fluctuations of an animal's aggressive tendencies, which in many species did not coincide with appropriate fluctuations of external factors. He spoke in this context of action-specific excitation produced within the central nervous system.

5.2.4. Ethological Theory of Aggression

The ethological theory of aggression sets a wider framework allowing for the integration of learning theory, the frustration–aggression theory, the drive theory, and the concept of phylogenetic adaptations. Its starting point is the Lorenzian assumption that intraspecific aggression evolved in many species as an adaptation in the service of a variety of functions contributing to fitness. Phylogenetic adaptations preprogram aggressive behavior and are well defined but differ from species to species, the adaptations consisting of motivating systems, innate motor patterns (instinctive action patterns), innate releasing mechanisms, and others. They can change with ambient ecological demands on the species in a species-specific manner and are open to adaptive modification through learning experiences. Individual experience is also responsible for the development of specific aggressive dispositions, as verified in animals, and no ethologist doubts that in humans learning plays an exceptional role in the development of aggressive behavior.

Current research has not determined the extent to which innate adaptations determine agonal behavior in man. But there is no doubt that many sociologists and psychologists underestimate the significance of innate components in aggression. Our knowledge on phylogenetic adaptations in agonal behavior has been taken from ontogenetic work and cross-cultural comparisons. We have already discussed some phenomena, which will be summarized here briefly.

5.2.4.1. Releasing Stimulus Situations. The fact that 6-month-old infants react with fear toward strangers (p. 170) shows that even without prior negative experiences with strangers, certain characteristics of others will stimulate the agonal system. This tendency to react with fear is counteracted by friendly tendencies, which also appear to be innate. The combination of these tendencies leads to a superimposition of movements of approach (orienting movements, expressions of contact readiness, such as smiling) onto movements of rejection (behaviors associated with "flight"—turning away, hiding oneself; and behavior of defense and attack—finger biting, foot stomping; see Fig. 5.1).

The fear of strangers develops independently of the style of upbringing in all cultures known to us. I have observed it among the Bushmen, Australian aborigines (Pintubi, Walbiri, Gidjingali), the Yanomami, Himba, and Tasaday, to name just a few. Mothers occasionally utilize this fear by stating to disobedient children that a stranger will take them away (I. Eibl-Eibesfeldt, 1976). Under certain circumstances this tactic can reinforce the fear of strangers. Initially, however, this response develops independently of the influence of upbringing based on an innate program. We have little information on the signals that activate the agonal system in this interaction, but we have already cited some of the known information, for example, we perceive the eyes ambivalently (p. 173) (R. G. Coss, 1972; M. Argyle and M. Cook, 1976). Still other stimuli must operate as well, for children born deaf and blind react to the scent of strangers with the same fear reactions (I. Eibl-Eibesfeldt, 1973b). One can educate against these reactions, but it is wrong to

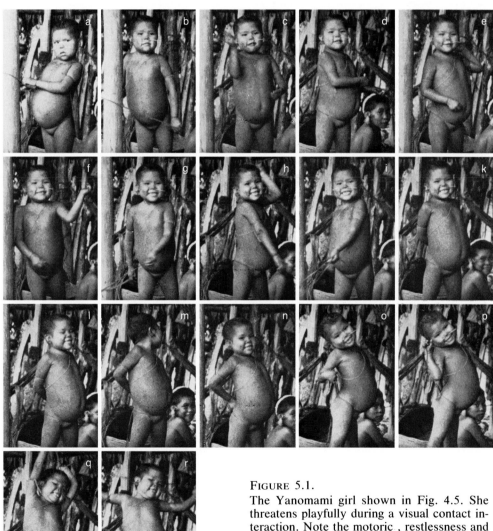

FIGURE 5.1.
The Yanomami girl shown in Fig. 4.5. She threatens playfully during a visual contact interaction. Note the motoric , restlessness and the appeasing head tilt following the threat. From a 25 frames/second 16 mm film, frames 1, 39, 54, 69, 85, 90, 105, 116, 134, 147, 150, 167, 213, 266, 301, 380, and 395 of the sequence. Photo: I. Eibl-Eibesfeldt.

underestimate the importance of this innate disposition. Some of the releasing stimuli activate the agonal system only among individuals of the same sex. Thus the male pheromone androstenol has a repelling effect on males and an attracting one on females (p. 426).

Rejecting signals cause people to maintain a distance between themselves and strangers in everyday encounters (p. 335).

In many primates there are juvenile alarm cries that release protective reactions in adults. Adult group members can also activate support of others by means of emergency calls. Humans possess a specific shrill cry that has the effect of an alarm and activates protective support. This phenomenon, however, has not been investigated systematically.

Human facial expressions and gestures also contain encoded signals that may provoke, intimidate or appease. Many such expressions are developed culturally, but a number of them have a biological basis (see threat stare, p. 370 and aggressive blocking, p. 500).

Physical and psychic pain are other stimuli that universally activate flight, defense, or attack behavior.

Humans react both to simple and complex stimuli situations. We have already discussed that every obstacle to attaining a goal can evoke aggression as a means of overcoming the barrier. This can occur in many kinds of situations. A child whose play is interrupted will protest. Among tribal people I often observed that older babies hit their mothers when they denied them immediate access to the coveted breast. Man reacts according to this schema throughout his lifetime. He will also contest rivals and those superior in rank. In future research it may be possible to identify the key stimuli that activate specific strategies of aggressive and defense behavior. Lorenz (1943) noted in this context that the same motives reappear in all types of literature. Thus aggressive defense reactions are evoked when a scoundrel abducts the heroine or when a helpless child is mistreated. In other situations we identify with those who offer their services for the sake of the community, remain faithful to the heroine, or who maintain their loyality through thick and thin. Lorenz presumes that we respond according to innate value judgments that determine the norms of social behavior—an ethical reference schema. Indeed, particular "situational clichés" reoccur in literature and theater, and are used in similar ways in all cultures using these art forms.

5.2.4.2. Behavioral Patterns. Studies of children born deaf and blind show that they also display many of the expressive movements that normally accompany aggressive acts. When angered these children clamp their teeth and bare them. They develop vertical forehead wrinkles, clench their fists, and stamp with their feet, the latter being a behavior that can be interpreted as a ritualized attack movement toward the opponent. The presumption that these behavior patterns arise from phylogenetic adaptations is supported by results from cross-cultural studies and comparisons with our closest primate relatives.

During moments of great anger the lips are opened and the corners of the mouth are drawn downward. In an expression of bold decision and thus attack readiness the lips are pressed together and the corners of the mouth are "contemptuously" lowered. At the same time, the protracted brows overshadow the eyes as if to shield off the bright light while fixating on a distant object. Vertical wrinkles appear on the forehead. Other expressions of fear, which may run counter to this principle emotion may be superimposed. The superimposition of various expressions at various intensity levels results in a great diversity of expressions. Our perception seems to be tuned to recognizing expressive elements and thus provides and un-

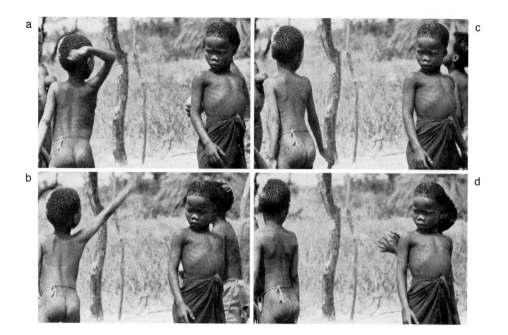

FIGURE 5.2. Examples of individualized aggression. A !Ko girl (central Kalahari) fixates on another with the threat stare. Her adversary swings her hand in the air at her and then turns away as a diversion tactic. From a 50 frames/second 16 mm film, frames 1, 8, 30, and 48 of the sequence. Photo: D. Heunemann from I. Eibl-Eibesfeldt (1972)

FIGURE 5.3. Threat stare. (a) Himba boy (southwestern Africa) fixates on another with a stare. As in Fig. 4.74, his forehead is slightly compressed so that a "vertical frown" ensues. This appears to be typical for static fixation without body movement. (b) A sequence from this conflict. From a 16 mm film. Photo: I. Eibl-Eibesfeldt.

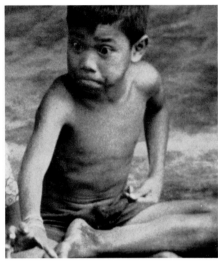

FIGURE 5.4. Balinese boy with threat stare in mimed attack on a playmate. His eyebrows are raised and his mouth is pressed together with corners slightly downward. When people throw stones or other objects they lift their brows in similar fashion, presumably in an attempt to see clearly. They also press their mouths together, something people everywhere do when engaged in physical exertion. From a 16 mm film. Photo: I. Eibl-Eibesfeldt.

derstanding of more complex facial expressions; such comprehension of facial expressions occurs independently of culture.

The threatening stare is a widespread form of display. I have photographed it among Bushmen, Yanomami, Himba, and Eipo. It can be executed as a duel between two partners until one can no longer endure the other's stare and breaks contact (Figs. 5.2–5.6). There are also sex-specific forms of threat and display. Men emphasize their body size and shoulder breadth with artificial means, such as head and shoulder adornments.

Modern man has atavistic traits in his body hair which correspond to agonal behavior. During highly aggressive arousal, especially when emotions of group defense are involved, the muscles at the base of the hair follicles that pull the hair upright (musculi erectores pilorum) contract. This is perceived physically as a slight tingling feeling. The contraction cause "goose bumps" throughout the body. This is actually a behavioral rudiment that is functionless due to our lack of body hair. But it certainly was used by our ancestors to give the impression that the body was visually enlarged. Another related rudiment is postural. When a man is aroused for group defense a particular bearing accompanies piloerection, for the arms are lifted slightly away from the body and rotated outward, which combined with piloerection makes the body appear larger. This can also be observed in chimpanzees, who exhibit the same display behavior.

Phallic threat is another typical display gesture. We find it throughout the world and have also identified homologous behavior patterns in nonhuman primates (p. 81).

Finally, if we compare display behavior of human and chimpanzee males we find a number of similarities. Chimpanzees threaten by stamping with their legs, beating with the palms of their hands against a surface or resonating tree trunks, swinging through branches with their arms, and often making distinct striking threats. They shake branches, small trees, and throw objects.

Man displays a similar behavior that begins early in childhood. I have observed infant boys intentionally strike other people with sticks, using a downward movement (whether playfully or aggressively). They display such behavior even when they have no social model. This use of sticks for display probably evolved as a

371

FIGURE 5.5. Threat gestures and expressive play of a Balinese boy teasing and threatening a girl (foreground) in typical Balinese "theatrical" style. Note the threat posture with outspread elbows (a, f, h), clenched fists (a to d), and the expressive repertoire. He begins with the threat stare, changes to a friendly mocking expression and tilted head, and terminates with a grimace, the vertical frown, and bared teeth display. From a 25 frames/second 16 mm film, frames 1, 20, 30, 40, 141, 161, 183, and 202 of the sequence. Photo: I. Eibl-Eibesfeldt.

FIGURE 5.6. In another form of threat, the "threat gaze," only the eyelids are markedly lifted (with no significant movement of the eyebrows). This displays more of the whites of the eyes and makes the gaze more penetrating. A Balinese mother is shown admonishing her daughter with this stare. The child moves off. The mother subsequently strikes her with her hand and repeats the threat stare. From a 50 frames/second 16 mm film, frames 1, 34, and 52 of the sequence. Photo: I. Eibl-Eibesfeldt.

phylogenetic adaptation. Other fighting behavior patterns (biting, tossing away, beating with the hand or fist, scratching) also appear very early in life and are observed in diverse cultures. Their common features may be functionally conditioned.

In an agonal confrontation there are important social signals in addition to the manifestations of aggressive display. Thus there are various behavioral patterns through which aggression can be blocked. One universal strategy of aggression blocking consists of the threat of breaking off contact. The offended individual demonstratively turns from his adversary by turning the shoulder or refusing to make visual contact. (This sequence is illustrated in Figure 6.69, p. 500). The strategy can also be verbalized. It is only effective when a bond exists, for in anonymous society this gesture loses effectiveness. Infants can be observed to use this strategy (L. Murray, 1977). It consists essentially of a threat. The individual threatening to interrupt contact generally emerges as the victor in such situations.

Aggression blocking also occurs with universal strategies of submission. Subordinates make themselves "smaller," according to the principle of "antithesis," and often also behave in a childlike manner. There are all forms of submission from a slight nodding of the head to prostrating oneself. Subordinate gestures always imply recognition of the victor's dominance. The above examples do not exhaust the number of aggressive blocking strategies. There are various other

appeals to form a friendly bond and thereby inhibit aggression. Crying often elicits sympathy and thus parental behavior, and infantile behavior patterns can defuse aggressive intentions. Film documentation of aggressive interactions confirm the universality of the behavior patterns that appear within this context (Figs. 5.7–5.18). Even small children, including infants, understand how to defend themselves, to attack, to block aggression, to win, and to offer support. These typical patterns of conflict management are present early in life. It is noteworthy that children who are not yet able to talk do not simply submit to attack but instantly retaliate in similar fashion. The *lex talionis* response manifests itself early in life.

When aggression occurs without weapons, a repertoire of behavioral patterns for attack, defense, submission, and retreat are utilized. These patterns are not exclusively culturally determined. They control confrontations so that generally there is no serious injury resulting from the conflict. In fact, conflicts can be resolved with only the use of threat, as in threat stare duels.

Verbal conflict is an extreme example of ritualized fighting. Most likely the possibility to conduct conflict verbally has contributed to harmonizing of interpersonal relationships. It is my feeling that too little attention has been paid to this aspect of the evolution of speech (p. 541). Ritualized duels suggest that a strong selective pressure favors behaviors that prevent damaging fights. Thus, here, cultural evolution phenocopies phylogeny. In this regard the tournament fights of animals are fully comparable to culturally ritualized human duels.

In an excellent investigation of the subject, F. Kiener (1983) dealt with the various aspects of verbal aggression and verbal dueling. Verbal attacks seem to follow universal principles. The patterns of insinuation, accusation, defamation, exposure, inciting, and verbal dehumanization are principally alike in most, if not all, cultures (p. 541, see also W. Schneider, 1976). As a rule verbal challenges aim at our standing or prestige and this is a very effective strategy of provocation, since the fear of losing face is deeply rooted. In fact, it is one key to the understanding of our social conduct (E. Goffman, 1961). We also keep individual distances (p. 335) graded, among others, by familiarity. Again, we also do this verbally. In German, the formal address *"Sie"* is used to keep others at a distance of respect. The familiar address *"Du"* is only used in communication with those close to us, such as friends or family members. If anyone not belonging to this group uses the familiar address, he or she is trespassing the individual distance. Often this is done in a provoking way. Man can act in words, but in doing so, he obeys the same rules of conduct that structure his nonverbal interactions (see strategies of social interaction).

5.2.4.3. Motivating Mechanisms. The question of whether there is a primary aggressive drive or whether aggression secondarily serves other drives (and thus is secondarily motivated) has not yet been answered. The fact that aggression is used instrumentally for a number of different functions means to some researchers

---

◁

FIGURE 5.7. (*See opposite page.*) A Conflict between two Himba boys (southwestern Africa). The boy in the foreground grabs a stick from his playmate (a–d). The owner protests and recovers it. He then threatens the wrongdoer, displaying ambiguous behavior (scratching himself on the head). Finally, in quasi-punishment, he strikes the wrongdoer lightly on the head and pouts thereafter. Generally the owner wins object conflicts. From a 50 frames/second 16 mm film, frames 1, 19, 52, 132, 182, 209, 241, 265, 273, 288, 402, and 512 of the sequence. Photo: I. Eibl-Eibesfeldt.

FIGURE 5.8. Object conflict and conflict resolution via a third party in Himba boys The boy on the right seizes a wooden sword from his friend, who as a result is injured by a splinter. He strikes at the wrongdoer, and then turns to two onlooking boys and shows them what happened (d). The wrongdoer, cognizant of his deed, now approaches the original owner of the wooden sword and wants to return it (e), but the return offer is rejected (f). The wrongdoer then turns to one of the two others, gives him the sword, and he in turn returns it to its rightful owner (g–k). This ends the conflict, and the group continues to play. From a 50 frames/second 16 mm film, frames 1, 89, 181, 344, 1709, 1760, 1877, 1908, 2136, and 2370 of the sequence. Photo: I. Eibl-Eibesfeldt.

FIGURE 5.9. Many confrontations between children are carried out at the level of threat display. A Yanomami boy (foreground, left) approaches a girl, displays his posterior, then threatens with his fist, whereupon the girl returns the threat. From a 25 frames/second 16 mm film, frames 1, 163, 176, 193, and 249 of the sequence. Photo: I. Eibl-Eibesfeldt.

that it could not have its own motivation. But this is not necessarily so. For example we know that locomotor behaviors (swimming, running) in various vertebrates are driven by spontaneously active automatic groups of neurons, even though locomotion is instrumental in the service of many other drives. Locomotion has its own motivations (p. 68) and thus there exists also an appetence for swimming and running. The appetence for locomotion varies from species to species. Carnivores which wait for their prey demonstrate little locomotor appetence and can be seen in the zoo in relaxed rest, whereas active hunters like martens restlessly run around in stereotypic fashion in abreaction of their locomotoric drive. In a similar manner, in some species aggressive behavior is driven. Fighting cocks raised and kept in complete social isolation actively waltz around in their attempt to attack their own tail feathers as a substitute object for their fighting appetence. They also attack their own shadows (J. Kruijt, 1971). Aggression is certainly not only a passive affair, but shows fluctuations of responsiveness, which are not accompanied by corresponding fluctuations of environmental variables.

The argument that a primary aggressive drive would endanger the individual since it would cause it to search for a rival outside of its territory, which would prove to be maladaptive, does not hold. It depends on the strength of the motivation. A moderate drive would not drive an animal out of his territory, but merely produce a readiness to attack that might be adaptive if quick action is called for. It could, so to speak, keep the car running for a fast start. By accepting the idea of motivating mechanisms, we do not postulate a unitary drive mechanism for every endogenously motivated behavior. The drive concept simply refers to internal motivating mechanisms that create a specific readiness to act, of which there are many types (p. 163).

FIGURE 5.10. Hitting threat of an approximately 4-year-old Yanomami boy who thereafter turns away spitefully. From a 25 frames/second 16 mm film, frames 1, 6, 12, 23, 27, and 32 of the sequence. Photo: I. Eibl-Eibesfeldt.

FIGURE 5.11. In aggressive encounters in toddlers and small children, the adversary is often knocked down. A 1½-year-old boy attacks his 2-year-old playmate at the younger child's home, because the older boy had taken one of his toys. The older child is pushed down. The attacker questioningly looks about at his parents. (I requested that the parents not respond to the situation.) A second attack ensued, and the older boy started to cry. The attacker ended his aggression and once again looks questioningly at his parents. The crying boy's sister approaches and comforts him. From a 16 mm film. Photo: I. Eibl-Eibesfeldt.

FIGURE 5.12.
When infants of crawling age meet each other they frequently have aggressive encounters that develop from mutual exploration (see Fig. 7.2, p. 552). Furthermore, as depicted here, aggression can develop from object conflict (for defense of the bond to the reference person, see p. 734). A 10-month-old !Ko infant (central Kalahari) girl tries to take away an object from a boy of the same age. He withdraws the object, then attacks by pushing his adversary over. From 50 frames/second 16 mm film, frames 1, 18, and 67 of the sequence. Photo: I. Eibl-Eibesfeldt.

Individuals show distinct differences in their disposition to behave aggressively, which cannot always be explained by parallel changes in the environment. Hormonal processes, such as androgen release (p. 304) and changes in the serotonin metabolism within the brain (G. L. Brown *et al.*, 1982; P. F. Brain and D. Benton, 1981; B. B. Svaare, 1983), play a role.

The catecholamines dopamine, norepinephrine (noradrenaline), and epinephrine (adrenaline) induce changes in aggressive readiness as well as many other physiological responses. If the norepinephrine level is reduced, rhesus monkeys lose their prior rank position. Norepinephrine causes vasoconstriction and also smooth muscle contraction. The heart rate is accelerated and sugar is released into the bloodstream. Epinephrine has a stronger influence on blood sugar levels and heart rate but a milder effect on skeletal muscle vasoconstriction. Both substances increase metabolic rate and prepare the organism to respond to threat. Epinephrine appears to be more significant for timid defensive responses.

Males are often motivated aggressively without apparent external causes. They experience and report on their aggressive appetence. Some men actually seek aggressive encounters and even peaceful cultures have an array of customs for rechanneling aggression. It has also been demonstrated experimentally that buildup of aggression can be reduced by executing aggressive acts. J. E. Hokanson and

FIGURE 5.13. Pushing one's opponent on his back is the aim of many aggressive confrontations. Here a Himba boy (Southwest Africa) pushes another on his back. From a 25 frames/second 16 mm film, frames 1 and 83 of the sequence. Photo: I. Eibl-Eibesfeldt.

FIGURE 5.14. Two young wrestling !Ko men (central Kalahari). One of the men has forced the other on his back. Photo: I. Eibl-Eibesfeldt.

S. Shetler (1961) irritated students and recorded an increased blood pressure. They then divided the students into two groups and told them that the researcher, who had caused the irritation, would now have to solve some problems. When the researcher made an error, the students could indicate so by pressing a button. One group was led to believe that by pressing the button a blue light would then be turned on, while the other test group thought that the same activity would result in the investigator receiving an electrical shock. In the latter group, blood pressure levels dropped as a result of this means of aggressive release, while blood pressure levels remained elevated in the former group. Further studies showed that verbal aggression and even viewing films of aggressive acts has a tension-reducing effect (S. Feshbach, 1961).

Humor also has a cathartic effect. Angry individuals who watched cartoons with an aggressive content were less aggressive toward the investigator on subsequent verbal testing than persons who did not view such cartoons (D. Landy and D. Mattee, 1969). Other observations on the cathartic effect of aggressive humor are found in E. S. Dworking and J. S. Efran, 1967; D. Singer, 1968; L. Berkowitz, 1970; R. A. Baron and R. L. Ball, 1974; and R. A. Baron, 1977.

Baron claims, however, that irritation reduction was not due to discharge but the result of a change of mood induced by laughing, which he interpreted as friendly. However laughing is primarily aggressive. It bonds those who laugh together but can be directed against those being laughed at (p. 138).

The tension-releasing effect of aggressive behavior has been questioned as well as the cathartic significance of safety-valve customs which discharge aggression (sports, aggressive television presentations). Many claim that these actually rein-

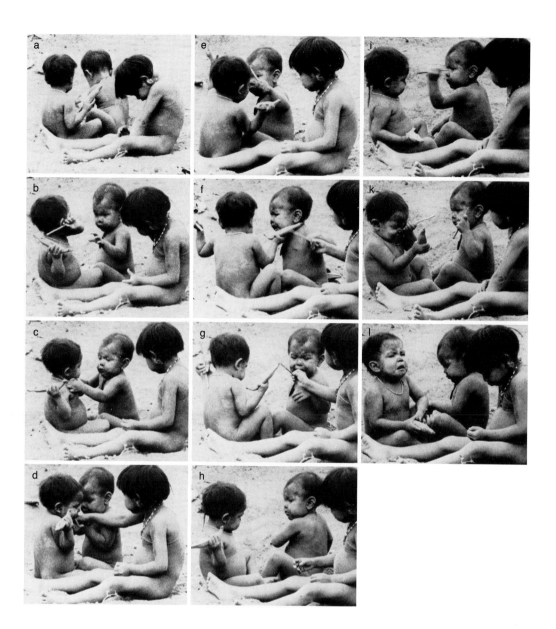

FIGURE 5.15. Example of conflict management in a triad consisting of two Yanomami girls (left, 2½-year-old; right, 1½-year-old) and a 6-year-old. A conflict over an object developed between the younger ones. The toddler on the left takes a little stick away from the other (a, b). She then pulls the stick back and is supported by the older girl (c, d.). The other one does not give up, however; she hits her adversary and retakes the stick (f). During this extended conflict the older girl gives the original owner a piece of wood (g). Third-party intervention is a frequent means of resolving conflict. Note here that the original owner of the stick now strikes the other youngster with her newly obtained piece of wood, injuring her beneath the eye (i–1). The photgraphic sequence ends here, but the film continues to show that the older girl *first struck the crying baby,* then looked at the injury. The injured one calmed down and finally attacked her opponent. From a 50 frames/second 16 mm film, frames 1, 145, 215, 515, 641, 1171, 1218, 1351, 1655, 1707, and 1970 of the sequence. Photo: I. Eibl-Eibesfeldt.

FIGURE 5.16. !Ko girl threatening a boy with a stick. Children hit and threaten one another with objects, but sticks that can cause injury are generally used only for threats. They are thrown in the direction of others but are aimed poorly—no doubt in an attempt to prevent injury. Photo: I. Eibl-Eibesfeldt.

FIGURE 5.17. Chimpanzees threaten and hit with sticks, even in intraspecific confrontations. Drawing: H. Kacher after a photo by J. Van Lawick-Goodall.

a

b

c

d

FIGURE 5.18. Those who are attacked appeal to others for help (a, b). A small boy from Kaleuna (Trobriand Islands) mocks another by sticking out his tongue and pulling the corners of his mouth apart. The boy who is the target of the mocking act, begins to cry, points to the wrongdoer, and looks for support toward a girl. This particular mocking gesture has been used in western medieval paintings and is seen in different cultures. The drawing apart of the corners of the mouth is a universal expression of anger and rage (p. 481). (c) Appeal for support by pointing out the wrongdoer is used by this small Yanomami boy; (d) a Himba boy who hurt his hand during an aggressive encounter appeals for help by displaying his injured hand. From 16 mm films. Photo: I. Eibl-Eibesfeldt.

force aggressiveness (L. Berkowitz, 1970; S. Feshbach and R. Singer, 1971; A. Bandura, 1973, R. G. Sipes, 1973). This is indeed correct in a long-term frame of reference, for the cathartic effect is short term. But every drive system becomes entrained by repeated action. Furthermore, people learn from social models. Thus one should consider the possible consequences of confronting children and young people with aggressive models in television shows. Test subjects whom L. Berkowitz (1962) had angered felt less tense when they were able to deliver punishing stimuli to the individual who had angered them. However, they retained an unfavorable opinion of those they had punished. In contrast, other subjects who were similarly provoked but had no opportunity to exercise revenge judged their provokators less negatively. Although access to aggressive retaliation freed the members of the first group from tensions (a short-term effect), it also reinforced, by virtue of their revenge, the enemy-image (long-term effect). Thus in the short term this phenomenon can have a cathartic effect (V. J. Konecni and A. N. Doob, 1972; V. J. Konecni and E. B. Ebbesen, 1976; R. G. Geen and M. B. Quanty, 1977). However, the requirement for such a catharsis is that the angered individuals can take revenge with affective anger (A. H. Buss, 1961; S. Feshbach, 1961). Furthermore, stress arising from provocation is alleviated if one subsequently claims that the provocation was necessary (S. K. Mallick and B. R. McCandless, 1966) and if this justification is accepted by the provoked party. Angered individuals are also appeased when a third party intervenes and sees to it that the causal insults cease, particularly in instances in which they learn from this mediator that the person causing irritation was punished for his acts (D. Bramel *et al.*, 1968; J. W. Baker and K. W. Schaie, 1969).

It is notable that sex differences exist in these reaction patterns. In both men and women an electrical shock increases blood pressure. If men have the opportunity to retaliate using some form of aggressive revenge their blood pressure falls, but remains high if they have to reward or act in a friendly manner toward their aggressor. In women the reaction is just the opposite—blood pressure decreases when they reward someone but not when they react aggressively (J. E. Hokanson, 1970). If women always receive a punishing shock when they act in a friendly manner and receive a friendly response whenever they deliver a shock, then they, too, will experience a tension reduction after acting aggressively and only minimal tension reduction if they behave in a friendly manner. Men can be similarly conditioned to a certain response pattern which is contrary to their original one. This means that one can learn to react contrary to one's primary disposition. In order to maintain a reaction pattern that deviates from a sex-typical pattern, there must be a continual reinforcement of the deviating response. If this is absent, the test persons return to their former response patterns.

The discussion of catharsis and the concept of drive will suffer when authors resort to heated arguments fueled by ideological motivation not based on factual knowledge. Thus R. G. Sipes (1973) states that aggressive sports could not have any cathartic effect because in warring cultures, where actual fighting engagements can work off aggression, more aggressive games are observed than is found in nonwarring cultures. Indeed, during periods of war there is more aggressive game playing. Sipes failed to realize that warring cultures train for aggressivity and that aggressive games are well suited for that kind of training. He also neglected to note that in the United States, where he did his study, not all members of the armed forces are active on the combat front. His criteria are also inconsistent; for example, he describes the Kalahari Bushmen as peaceful, while in America he describes hunting as an "aggressive sport." If this were true, then the Bushmen and most other peaceful tribal people whose main sustenance depends on hunting should actually be categorized as aggressive. In addition there is a great variety of aggressive and competitive games in these peaceful cultures. Thus Sipes's vociferous arguments against the drive model do not address the central issues.

The appetite for fighting is not only subjectively experienced but its cathartic effects can be measured (p. 384). This indicates endogenous motivation but leaves the question open whether this motivation is a primary or secondary one, as is suggested by the aggression-frustration hypotheses.

The ethological concept of a primary aggressive drive is supported by a number of findings from brain studies. Electrical stimulation of the brain in distinct portions of the brain stem of the domestic rooster evoke not only specific aggressive behavioral patterns but also specific appetences to attack an opponent. Free-moving brain-stimulated roosters will search for objects which allow them to act aggressively (E. von Holst and U. von Saint Paul, 1960). Cats in paradoxical (REM) sleep display vibrissae movements resembling the rapid eye movements found in humans during dreaming. If specific parts of the metencephalon of cats are destroyed, they will display aggressive behavior in up to 80% of their REM sleep phase, which then apparently operates without any inhibitions (M. Jouvet, 1972). This permits us to presume that there are various neuronal networks within the cat metencephalon that inhibit those central nervous factors motivating aggressive behavior.

Central nervous factors for human aggressive behavior have also been discovered. They are located in the temporal lobe, amygdala, and hypothalamus and are closely connected with other brain centers. This is not surprising since this behavior is frequently used for many diverse functions. Neuronal networks responsible for other functions are also located within these same regions. H. Klüver and P. C. Bucy (1937) found that in rhesus monkeys a temporal lobotomy eliminates the animals' aggressivity but that their eating and copulatory behavior were now uninhibited. Nevertheless, many pathologically violent patients have been treated with a temporal lobotomy. Although the procedure did reduce aggression it had side effects resembling those found in rhesus monkeys.

In temporal lobe epilepsy, many patients experience uncontrollable spontaneous bouts of aggression. These kinds of violent attacks could also be activated in these patients by electrical stimulation of those parts of the brain (F. A. Gibbs, 1951; K. E. Moyer, 1968/1969, 1971a, b; W. H. Sweet et al., 1969). This form of spontaneous violence is undoubtedly pathological, but shows that there are neuronal networks that can be spontaneously active, and lead to uncontrollable aggressive bouts. One can, on the basis of general knowledge of nervous system functions, presume that such neuronal networks are probably not completely silent in healthy individuals.

K. E. Moyer (1971, p. 50) agrees with these observations: "The hydraulic model for aggressive behavior of Lorenz (1961) is based upon a number of physiological facts. When the neural systems for aggressive behavior are sensitized by changes in the chemical composition of the blood so that they are more readily stimulated, the 'pressure' toward aggressive behavior can increase. From this follows that the individual is more and more disposed to display antagonistic behavior. But the conception that this 'pressure' for aggression can only be minimized with aggressive acts is slightly oversimplified." We agree with this position, and ethologists have specified other forms of sublimation.

K. E. Moyer (1971, p. 33) writes elsewhere: "In summary one can say that external stimulus conditions for releasing eating and aggressive behavior are important. Aggressive behavior is less stimulus dependent, if at all, than eating behavior. Hungry men will not eat bits of rock, but angry ones will sometimes beat against walls.''

The rejection of the aggressive drive concept is seldom based on concrete findings. It is often believed that accepting the existence of an aggression drive is tantamount to taking a fatalistic position, and the concept is rejected for this reason. Thus J. Rattner (1970, p. 35) writes: ''The teaching of an aggressive drive lends support to an institutionalized concealing technique conforming perfectly to a conservative political position. The reader's viewpoint is diverted . . . from the wants within society and directed solely to a hypothetical instinctive human basis removed from human volition and influence.'' And in H. D. Dann (1971, p. 84) we read: ''Anyone believing in an 'aggressive drive' arising of its own or whoever envisions a frustration-aggression mechanism, which is continually fed by frustrations that can never be completely avoided, must consider it highly unlikely that aggression-free interpersonal relations can ever be feasible.'' But the concrete problem at hand can certainly not be solved by considering ourselves peaceful by nature and simply rejecting anything that contradicts this conception.

Flight and submission are functionally linked to aggression. An animal with only aggressive motivations would not survive. Retreat and flight in man are impelled by the emotions subjectively experienced as fear.

Submission occurs as a rule in intraspecific interactions only and should not be confused with playing possum, which is a last resort in protecting oneself from predators. There are anecdotal reports of people who, although paralyzed by fear, escaped predation or mutilation by attacking animals.

Flight behavior can be pattern-specific depending on the type of predator. Thus in avoiding a bird of prey a hen will run under the cover of a bush. When surprised by a ground predator it will fly up onto a tree. No such predator-specific responses can be found in man.

In some animals the readiness to flee increases if flight behavior is not released for some time. In such a case, some animals show a clear lowering of the release threshold and respond in a sensitized way to stimuli that would not normally suffice to trigger the response. In man, something like an appetence for flight can be deduced from his positive fascination with ''horror stories'' which is exploited by the entertainment industry. Games of flight are also very much enjoyed by children.

Animals and human beings are on the alert, the pattern of which apparently has a biological heritage. People show alertness by looking up and regularly scanning the horizon between other activities such as eating. They do this in a fairly stereotyped fashion, similar to the way other higher vertebrates behave in a similar situation (H. Hass, 1968; B. C. R. Bertram, 1980; C. J. Barnard, 1980; M. A. Elgar and C. P. Catterall, 1981; V. E. Lipetz and M. Bekoff, 1982). Persons eating alone in a dining room look up more often and spend a longer time looking around than people eating with a group (M. Wawra, 1985) presumably because they count on others to warn them of danger (Figs. 5.19 and 5.20).

Summary 5.2

The ethological model of aggression introduces the concept of phylogenetic adaptation into the discussion and integrates the findings of ethological research with those of learning theory and the aggression-frustration hypothesis. It also rejects any claims that the existence of innate elements prepares the way for fatalism, since it can be shown that certain responses can be altered through learning.

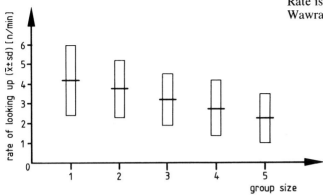

FIGURE 5.19. Rates of looking up (times/minute) of students eating in a communal dining room. Rate is dependent on group size. From M. Wawra, 1985.

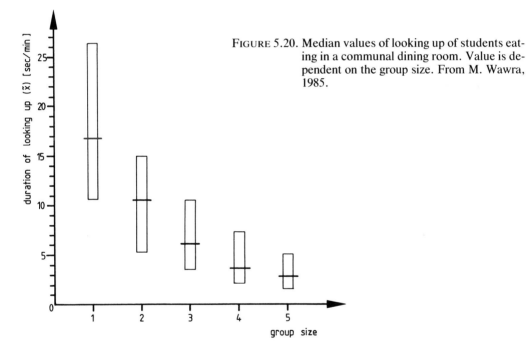

FIGURE 5.20. Median values of looking up of students eating in a communal dining room. Value is dependent on the group size. From M. Wawra, 1985.

Educational factors are thus not only recognized but respected as one of the prerequisites for an effective control of aggression. Knowledge about the phylogenetic programming involved should be an aid in this control.

The extent to which phylogenetic adaptations determine aggressive behavior is still not known, but there are clearly phylogenetic adaptations in both motor and perceptual realms (releasing stimulus situations) and in motivating mechanisms. Humans experience fluctuations in their aggressive disposition, for which internal causal factors must exist since no corresponding environmental fluctuations can be identified. Fighting appetence and catharsis through retaliation can be dem-

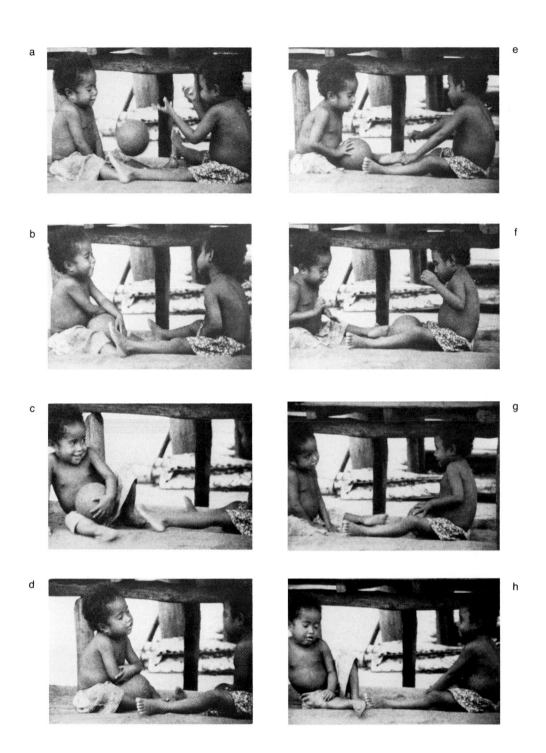

FIGURE 5.21. See opposite page for legend.

FIGURE 5.21. Provoking as a strategy of social exploration. Two Trobriand girls play with a ball. They exchange the ball repeatedly until the girl on the left suddenly decides to keep the ball for herself (b–d). She watches intently for the response of her slightly annoyed playmate. After several provocative attempts at returning the ball—which were not executed—she rolls the ball back to her playmate, who in turn teases her by keeping the ball. After making impressive facial expressions of pouting and cut off-threat, she begs for the ball with open palms (1), but her attempts are in vain. Finally, she decides to take the ball by force (m). This act oversteps the bounds, and her playmate leaves the scene. (Shortly afterward, reconciliation occurs elsewhere, which is initiated by the offender.) From the response of the partners to provoked conflicts, children learn their limits. From a 25 frames/second 16 mm film, frames 1, 78, 148, 285, 646, 665, 732, 793, 801, 863, 943, 1051, and 1100. Photo: I. Eibl-Eibesfeldt.

Figure 5.22. See legend opposite page.

onstrated experimentally, the latter as a short-term effect with a long-term consequence in the form of system training. It is still unclear which factors work together in the endogenous motivation of aggressive behavior. Hormonal (androgens) factors as well as brain amines play a role in the spontaneous activation of those neural substrates that activate aggressive appetence and, in the pathological case, uncontrollable spontaneous aggression.

5.3. Functional Aspects of Aggressive Behavior

We have already shown that aggression fulfills specific functions. We mentioned territorial aggression, the defense of possessions, and social relationships, norm maintenance aggression, the defense of rank position, etc. These by no means exhaust all the functions. We will still show that aggression can be utilized as a "tool" serving quite an array of different tasks and thus is a strategy with whose help a resisting force countering a behavioral objective can be overcome. The behavior can help defeat a rival and thereby win a sexual partner or to conquer an area or maintain possession of it.

We discussed the significance of aggressive behavior in connection with the protection of progeny. Defense of young is an old behavior pattern in mammals and birds that developed independently within both animal groups. While territorial defense is more pronounced in males than females, in many mammals defense of young is performed entirely by the female. In nonhuman primates, males often participate in defense of the young. Male baboons, macaques, and many other primates hurry to the juveniles at the sound of their alarms and offer support. Comparable human behavior may thus have very old roots, although the familialization of the male is a phylogenetically recent development.

One of the most important forms of aggression, the inquisitive or exploratory aggression, is often unrecognized (B. Hassenstein, 1973a). This behavior in effect poses a question to the social environment: "What are the limits of my behavior?" A child discovers the answer through aggression, for example, by taking a stick and hitting another child with it, taking something away from another, or by teasing another and then observing the response of others or the affected individual to this behavior (Figs. 5.21–5.25; further examples are found in chapter 7). If there is no response, the next question then becomes more forceful, for the child utilizes aggression instrumentally to obtain answers about social conventions. It is particularly within this context of exploratory aggression that behavioral escalation occurs if no limits are set (B. Hassenstein, 1973a). This shows that the theory of permissive upbringing makes the erroneous assumption that every prohibition

FIGURE 5.22. (See opposite page.) Playful exploratory aggression between two Eipo girls. The girl to the right playfully provokes an object conflict by taking away a blade of grass with which her friend was playing (a, b). The playmate turns her back on the offender in a staged cut off (c). The other girl, slightly alarmed, looks intently at her friend, to see how earnest she is and relaxes when she sees her smile (d). Both continue to play and once more—this time with the mouth—the girl to the right snatches her friend's blade of grass (f). Again, the playmate behaves as if she were offended (g). The whole interaction is, however, playful and concludes with the two jostling and wrestling. From a 25 frames/second 16 mm film, frames 1, 19, 46, 101, 819, 921, 1186, 1197, and 1281. Photo: I. Eibl-Eibesfeldt.

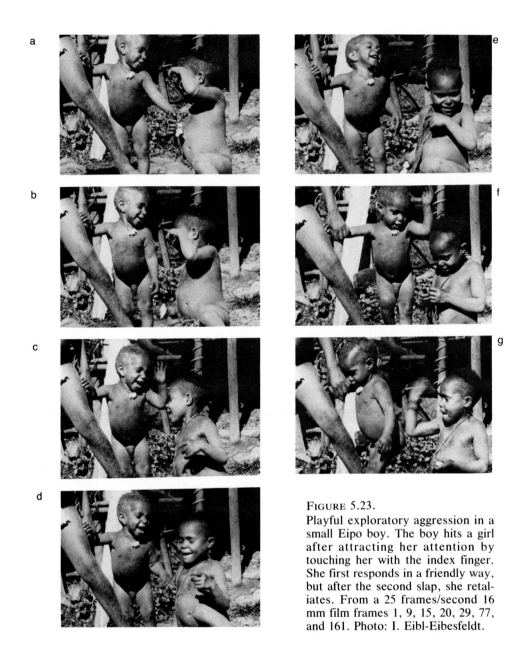

FIGURE 5.23.
Playful exploratory aggression in a small Eipo boy. The boy hits a girl after attracting her attention by touching her with the index finger. She first responds in a friendly way, but after the second slap, she retaliates. From a 25 frames/second 16 mm film frames 1, 9, 15, 20, 29, 77, and 161. Photo: I. Eibl-Eibesfeldt.

fosters aggression because it frustrates the child. Thus, restrictions and rules should be eliminated from child rearing. The products of permissive upbringing are not particularly peaceful individuals but rather children whose aggressions are unrestrained and poorly controlled (J. Rothchild and S. B. Wolf, 1976).

The strategy of exploratory aggression is not only restricted to children. Young people, rulers of new states, and members of subcultures also use them on their social environment. Here, too, lack of a response results in an escalation of the behavior. While in the early stages a distinct but friendly "NO" can eliminate the conflict. However when the behavior begins escalating more repressive measures may be required to quell the aggression. Europe witnessed how a movement critical of the existing society (APO) became criminal because the dynamics of exploratory aggression was not understood in time. Comparable behavior erupted in 1980 and 1981 and finally escalated in Zurich, Vienna, and a number of West German cities in street demonstrations.

In a noteworthy parallel, young states tend to use aggression to test their freedom of behavior, for which Amin's Uganda was an example. Here again the aggressive enquiry escalated since no one countered it at an early stage. In Iran we saw American flags burned and diplomats insulted without meeting serious protest. Is it surprising that finally the situation developed into the taking of hostages[1]?

It would be completely erroneous to assess exploratory aggression negatively because of such occurrences. It also has its positive sides; one must simply accommodate exploratory aggression accordingly. A child is not simply a passive receiver of instructions. Children interact actively with the environment, challenging their partners to react. This can make certain demands on the partner's behavior and result in new adaptations on the partner's part. This is particularly true for dialogues between the generations, in which traditions are generally questioned and discussed.

In discussing norm maintenance aggression, we briefly mentioned educational aggression, which often is a variant of the former. Educational aggression can also include rituals of reprimand, which in European culture can take the form of publicly deriding customs ("Haberfeldtreiben"). This is still occurring in current-day England ("rough music") and France (E. Hoffmann-Krayer and H. Bächtold-Stäubli, 1930, 1933; E. P. Thompson, 1972). "Rough music" consists of a group gathering before a transgressor's home and disciplining him in verse, using cymbals and other instruments and creating a great deal of noise.

E. P. Thompson (1972) quotes as an example a saying used in a village in Surrey, England, before the house of a man who had frequently mistreated his wife:

> There is a man in this house
> Who has beaten his spouse (*forte;* pause)
> Who has beaten his spouse (*fortissimo*)
> It is a great shame and disgrace
> For everyone at this place.
> Yes, so it is, as true as I live.

The people gathered before the home would carry on with a great commotion for a good half an hour.

Figurative reprimand in songs is an important means for social norm control in the Eipo of Irian Jaya. Allusions to concrete events clarify what and who is meant in the songs without disturbing group harmony. Since no individual is directly addressed, he is not required to make a direct response. Thus the censured individual can save face and act as if nothing had happened to him (V. Heeschen, unpublished).

Educational aggression also includes all forms of parental discipline of children, from scolding to corporal punishment as well as diverse forms of reproach, and, finally, the punishment of group members after being judged guilty of wrongdoing.

If among the Walbiri a man has committed adultery, he must present himself to the offended husband, who is permitted to thrust a spear in the transgressor's

---

[1] I use these examples without taking sides. I could have easily chosen others.

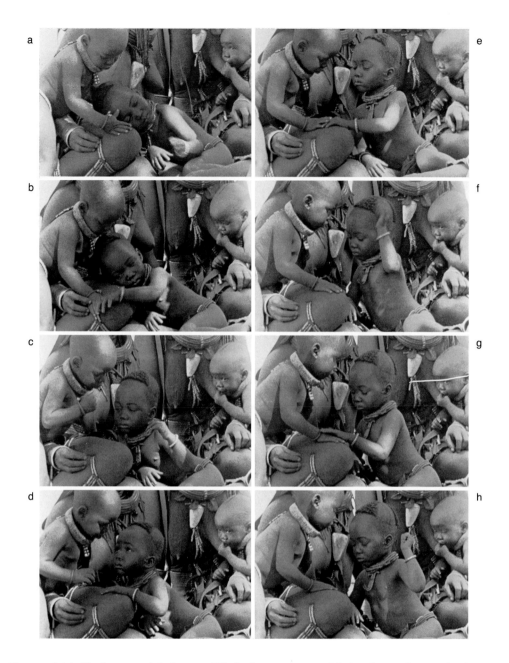

FIGURE 5.24. Challenge and defense: a Himba boy pesters a girl sleeping on her mother's lap by scratching her forehead with his thumb. She pushes his hand away, looks at him with the threat stare, and strikes at him with her hand. Subtle aggressions of this type often have the character of exploratory aggression, with whose help children test reactions of their playmates, exploring their behavioral latitude and provoking rank disputes. From a 25 frames/second 16 mm film, frames 1, 26, 51, 68, 80, 95, 102, and 115 of the sequence. Photo: I. Eibl-Eibesfeldt.

FIGURE 5.25. Example of playful exploratory aggression. A !Ko boy strikes his father with a stick, while making the "play-face". The father responds by laughing, which encourages the child. But older children are admonished if similar behavior becomes too rough. Photo: I. Eibl-Eibesfeldt

thigh or leg but no other part of the body, unless the adulterer attempts to run away from this punishment.

Similar customs are found in the Dsimakani (Fly River, Western Province of Papua New Guinea), where the adulterer is shot with a ceremonial arrow in the thigh. This arrow has many small hooks that break off when they penetrate the body, so that recovery is a long and painful process. If he flees, he can also be shot in the back, which is usually fatal (W. Schiefenhövel, pers. commun.).

In state societies, an executive power is created to administer punishment. Punishment and compensation are of some importance from the viewpoint of natural selection. One often wonders why altruistic individuals are not eventually suppressed by nonaltruistic mutants (like cheaters, etc.; p. 98). In humans, the problem is resolved by recognizing and punishing those who transgress social norms.

In all these cases, aggressive behavior is activated by various releasing stimulus situations and often through differing motivational systems. Thus, B. Hassenstein (1973) distinguishes between aggressivity according to the biological motivation of hunger, fear, sexual desire, territorial ownership drive, rank order rivalry and enmity toward group strangers, inhibited drive satisfaction, and play drive. However it is very likely that the same system is ultimately activated by all these different channels.

Summary 5.3

Aggressive behavior is employed instrumentally in the service of many highly diverse behavioral goals. Exploratory aggression with which children and young people test their social behavioral liberties is of particular significance for society. Newly formed states use the same exploratory strategy in international relations. Aggressive exploration provokes dialogue: if there is no response to the action, it will subsequently escalate. This effective mechanism is not recognized by many educators and politicians, which leads to maladaptive behavior.

5.4. Socialization of Aggressive Behavior

"In brief the ethologists believe that aggressive acts are caused mainly by the build up of aggressive motivation, making aggression both spontaneous and inevitable, even in the absence of any eliciting situation" (R. H. Schuster, 1978, p. 94). Neither Konrad Lorenz nor myself have ever maintained that man cannot control his aggressions and, therefore that they are unavoidable. Such caricatures of ethology are either constructed to set up straw men or are the result of authors repeating second-hand arguments of "What they heard about ethology" and not reading original texts. Quite the contrary, we have consistently emphasized that aggression is subject to restraint through learning. As discussed earlier, most biologists have abandoned simplistic nature–nurture issues. Many physiological structures and probably most behavioral characteristics develop as a result of interaction between genes and environment, which does not mean that behaviors are modifiable with the same ease in all directions. Even learning can be channeled by phylogenetic adaptations and the modifiability of certain behavior patterns, which develop through a process of self-differentiation in same way as bodily structures do, is sometimes quite limited. Aggression, however, is quite complex, composed of innate motivation mechanisms, which are inextricably intertwined with environment and learning. It is senseless, therefore, to speak of one factor without the other. Education and experience, of course, are essential to the channeling and control of aggression, which is also true for other types of drive-activated behavior, for example, sexual behavior. No one would conclude that since the sex drive is clearly innate it must be accepted as unalterable.

Since aggression is the product of genes and environment, it is expressed differently from society to society according to social and ecological factors. A pastoralist in the semiarid zone of Africa has different uses of certain expressions of aggression than a hunter-gatherer Bushman.

A great deal has been written on culture-specific socialization practices. Margaret Mead (1935) ascribed the aggressivity of the Mundugumur (New Guinea) to loveless parental care. She writes that the mothers carried their infants in crude baskets, often leaving the babies alone in them. They provided satisfactory body contact only during nursing. This allegedly creates subsequent aggressive behavior of these warlike people. In contrast, the peaceful Arapesh of New Guinea received warmth and affection as infants.

According to an often expressed viewpoint (R. P. Rohner, 1975), rejecting parents produce aggressive personalities while affectionate ones have friendly, pacifistic children. This assertion is false and although an upbringing of rejection and

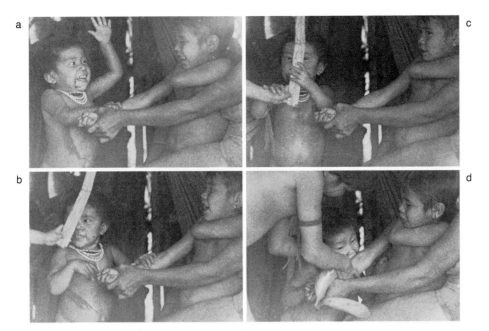

a   c

b   d

FIGURE 5.26. Encouragement for retaliation. A Yanomami boy has struck a girl. He is now held firmly while the girl is encouraged to hit him back, and she is given a piece of wood for this purpose. He takes this as a joke, but his facial expression changes when she bites him. Photo: I. Eibl-Eibesfeldt.

FIGURE 5.27. In the warfaring Yanomami, boys identify with their father as a model. For example, they play war games by forming groups and shooting arrows at one another. From a 16 mm film. Photo: I. Eibl-Eibesfeldt.

397

FIGURE 5.28. The children also imitate other aggressive adult behavior. (a) A young Yanomami man and woman fight with banana bunch stalks; (b) Yanomami children imitate the behavior in their play; (c) children enjoy capturing woman as a form of play. Photo: I. Eibl-Eibesfeldt.

mistrust may foster interpersonal aggression and aggressive personalities, it does so in such a way that the individual is also asocial. Warlike virtues are not cultivated this way, for they require loyalty, a fighting spirit, comraderie, self-discipline, and courage, qualities which are acquired differently. In the warfaring cultures we have studied, the Eipo, Himba, and Yanomami, the children experience affection and body contact beginning early in infancy and are nursed on demand. In short, their lives do not lack for love and affection. Yet male children become warriors, but not because of insufficient love. To the contrary, close bonds of affection actually enhance children's disposition to identify with the parental model, and depending on whether the parents are peaceful or warlike, the children will develop accordingly. Specific socialization practices are also utilized to foster the desired traits. In the Eipo, Yanomami, and Himba, boys are educated early to toughen themselves by learning to bear physical pain and to meet aggression with aggression (I. Eibl-Eibesfeldt, 1976; W. Schiefenhövel, 1980). If a child is struck by another and runs screaming to its mother, the mother or father urge the child get a stick and go after the attacker with it. Among the Yanomami, even girls are brought up this way (Fig. 5.26).

Children also develop fighting skills in their games. Yanomami and Eipo children form two opposing groups and shoot at one another with play arrows (Figs. 5.27,

398

5.28). In all their play activities they imitate the behavior models displayed by the adults. Adults reinforce certain behavior through praise and scolding. If a child cries, it is scolded and is sometimes even struck for behaving like a cry baby. The peaceful Bushmen of the Kalahari manifest other models for their children. Parents do not behave in a belligerent manner, nor do they encourage vengeful behavior when one child is attacked by another. More often they reprimand the attacker and comfort the one who was struck. Mothers whose small infants are quarreling are exceptionally patient. Their primary strategies are ones of diversion and appeasement, and they only rarely use physical force in disciplining their children (I. Eibl-Eibesfeldt, 1976, 1979).

Loving affection toward infants and physical contact alone therefore do not produce peaceful people. Specific upbringing methods are necessary as is the appropriate parental social model. It is equally true that withdrawal of love does not produce warriors, since warfare requires many other dispositions (p. 402). Withdrawal of love may produce individuals who are aggressive both in family and interpersonal relationships.

There is no doubt that love withdrawal is responsible for a number of manifestations of pathological aggression. In judicial proceedings with violent criminals the defense regularly argues that their clients' loveless childhood had an overbearing influence on behavior. An all too frequent change of reference figures is probably a decisive factor in such cases (p. 193).

In some warfaring peoples, militant disciplines are reinforced between adults on a daily basis. We have already cited the rituals of obedience in the Himba and other discipline-fostering customs (p. 147). The Himba also reinforce heroic virtues by singing praise songs which eulogize the deeds of valiant forefathers. A number of parallels to this also exist in European culture.

As can be seen from the above discussion, intergroup aggression in the form of war involves many heroic virtues and feelings of mutual support. Thus, we shall treat it separately from individual aggression.

Summary 5.4

An aggressive disposition can be fostered or suppressed by education directed toward specific aims. Warfaring peoples reinforce the martial virtues in songs and tales, encourage obedience, instruct on battle behavior, and urge retaliation. Children who experience parental affection generally identify with same sex parental role models and assume the values of their culture, whether they are peaceful or militant.

5.5. Duels

Duels are culturally regulated forms of fighting contests, either in earnest or for sport, between two persons. They can assume many different forms and primarily take place between men. Fights between women, apart from verbal battles, are less frequently ritualized.

In Australia, I filmed an example of a rare exception. Among the Walbiri and other aborigines, the women fight with digging sticks. One attempts to hit the other on the head, and the other parries the blow by holding her stick protectively over her head (Fig. 5.29). Girls practice the technique in their games. These confrontations are generally terminated when others separate the fighters. The attacker

FIGURE 5.29. Two quarreling Walbiri women (central Australia). They threaten each other with sticks. The attacker strikes, and her adversary parries with a transversely held stick. Unarmed women intervene and attempt to settle the dispute. From a 25 frames/second 16 mm film, frames 1, 25, 55, and 113 of the sequence. Photo: I. Eibl-Eibesfeldt

continues to insult her adversary verbally for a time, and in one instance she planted a stick between her legs like a phallus and made copulatory movements in the direction of her rival.

In other cultures, too, women fight with each other with digging sticks, but in a less ritualized manner. Women physically fight each other by tearing hair, pulling earrings, and scratching and biting. More frequently, though, women fight verbal battles.

Men more frequently measure their strength in duels, which are conducted according to specialized rules and need not include the use of weaponry. Wrestling and fist fighting are examples. In wrestling the goal is usually to force the opponent onto his back and thus literally make him "subordinate." The rules for wrestling are often geared at avoiding serious injury. R. D. Guthrie (1976) observed that in fist fights the chin is the chief object of the attack. He draws a relationship between this target and human expressive behavior, arguing that a protruding chin indicates decisiveness and an aggressive disposition while a withdrawn chin is a sign of anxious reserve. The boxer's goal is to force the opponent into the latter posture. This kind of psychological interpretation is an interesting one but difficult to verify. What is probably more important is that a blow to the chin can so shake the opponent's brain that he loses consciousness without actually sustaining a serious injury.

Pauline Wiessner (pers. commun.) suggested that one of the reasons that serious injury is avoided in duels, is to restrict the fight to two persons. Otherwise, if one dies, revenge must be taken over by group members, thereby escalating the conflict. It is, in fact, one duty of the duelists to observe that regulations are obeyed.

Duels with weapons are conducted according to precise rules that also reduce the risk of a fatal outcome. There are a number of tournament forms adapted to the use of weapons. Generally weapons utilized are for close combat (sticks, striking and sticking weapons), while those for distant combat (spears, shooting weapons) are less commonly used. There are also levels of escalation varying with the seriousness of the duel. Thus the Yanomami fight in less serious encounters by striking with their fists alternatingly against the opponents chest, and sometimes using the blunt side of their axes as well. Another painful but not life-endangering form of fighting consists of hitting the sides of the body. The opponents stand or sit beside each other and hit the palm of their hands vigorously at each other's sides in the vicinity of the kidneys. In fierce quarrels, the adversaries use hard wooden clubs (N. A. Chagnon, 1968) and hit each other alternatingly on their shaved heads, each offering his head in turn.

In order to partially cushion the blow they sometimes stand on one leg. Once a partner has received a blow, he delivers one to his adversary. The wooden club can penetrate the skin on the skull, create horrible wounds, and occasionally fracture the skull. This exchange of blows can be repeated several times until the opponents, with blood streaming down their faces, finally capitulate. The shaved heads of the men are covered with numerous scars, which they proudly display.

Helena Valero, who spent many years as captive among the Yanomami, has described these duels (E. Biocca, 1970) and narrated how this unloading of anger can foster peaceful relations:

> They began in twos. But when one of them fell, his brother would come along to help him, then the brother-in-law and father-in-law, and when four, or five or six people had collected, the tushua[2] said, 'No, no, the fight is only for two. Stand at the side, for the one who has fallen must seek revenge himself.' They lifted up the fallen man and dashed water on his face, stroked his ears flat against the head, washed his blood off, lifted him again, and gave him the club again. The other man supported himself on his club and awaited the blow, whereby he lowered his head. While they struck each other they said, 'I called you to see if you are really a man. If you are, we will now see whether we can become friends again and let our anger abate . . .' (Valero, according to E. Biocca).

Tournaments can also be sporting events in which the winners gain esteem. These activities can have a ventilating effect that reduces aggressions (for example, see D. F. Draeger and R. W. Smith, 1980). Duel ritualization, in my opinion, may have contributed significantly to right handedness. The partners must be able to react to each other in a fully predictable way (p. 539).

The highest form of ritualized fighting occurs verbally, and we conduct most of our confrontations with others in this way. The tongue can indeed be a sharp as a sword, but it causes different kinds of injuries. One can verbally utilize varying aggressive strategies and resolve an issue without physical assault. We may propose that the necessity of mitigating aggressive encounters was a facilitating selective factor for speech development (p. 541). Verbal conflict can also have a number of ritualized stages. In Tyrol, one challenges another in song, with a specialized

---

[2]Tushua = headman, in this case Helena Valero's husband.

verse and melody form known as "Gstanzln."[3] Its content changes (examples are found in L. von Hörmann, 1877; and F. Luers, 1919) but invariably quick wittedness in finding appropriate answers and rhymes are called for.

In an interesting parallel, the Eskimo have singing duels by which even serious conflicts can be resolved. Thus, even in the case of murder, a person seeking revenge can challenge his adversary in this way and rebuke him before the entire community (texts in H. König, 1925 and E. A. Hoebel, 1967).

Summary 5.5

Armed and unarmed confrontations between men, less often than between women, are often carried out in ritualized form as duels. These are essentially cultural conventions whose function is to permit sporting fights or, in the case of serious duels, to resolve conflict by fighting skill while avoiding excessive injury and by inhibiting continued escalation of the conflict. This would happen if the conflict were not kept as an affair between two people. If one were to die other members of the group would be made party to the conflict by their obligation for revenge. The most extreme ritualization of these duels occurs in verse and song duels.

5.6. Intergroup Aggression—War

5.6.1. Definition

We define war following the definition by Q. Wright (1965)—an armed conflict between groups. While individualized aggression between group members (including man) is regulated by phylogenetic adaptations so that an escalation into destruction is avoided, intergroup aggression may or may not be regulated. Some intergroup fights are highly ritualized, while in others the use of powerful weaponry is aimed intentionally at injuring and even killing the enemy. In the latter cases, the biological inhibitions against aggression have to be deactivated so that combatants no longer respond to signals of submission and various appeals of appeasement, bonding, and the arousal of sympathy.

In tribal societies as well as western civilization this is done through attempts to "dehumanize" the enemy. In addition, in technically advanced societies, it is done by creating deadly weapons that act quickly and at a distance. In both cases, indoctrination transfers the aggressive act to a context of being directed against another species. The opponents are degraded to inferior beings. War is primarily a cultural institution, even though it utilizes some innate dispositions. Insofar that war is a cultural institution, it can be altered to a great degree.

The innate dispositions utilized during war include the following: (1) The tendency to be loyal to group members; (2) the readiness to react aggressively to threats directed against group members; (3) the motivation (especially in men) to fight and dominate; (4) the tendency to occupy territories and defend them; (5) the fear of strangers [i.e., responding to agonal signals of unfamiliar others. Small babies act according to the premise that strangers are potentially dangerous, an assumption evidently proved in the course of evolution]; (6) intolerance against those who deviate from group norms.

---

[3]The Bavarian dialect also has an expression, Schnadahüpfln, which expresses the fact that the verses in exchange rebounds (hüpfln).

All these dispositions play a role in the conflict but not necessarily lead to war, which requires planning and leadership. Even within small groups the members must be stimulated to go out on a war party, usually under the influence of some spokesperson. Small groups, though, may be already incited to do so by some recent threatening event. If larger groups are to go to war, their readiness must be activated through propaganda, and it is often individuals spurred by ambition and striving for power who energize the group. Many modern states have been founded by such leadership.

Group aggression occurs in primates, who even invade territories of other groups. But only man is able to form alliances between different groups to fight a common enemy.

Planning and leadership are supplemented by indoctrination and the destructive use of weapons. The invention of rapidly killing weaponry permits eliminating opponents before they can emit signals inhibiting aggression. Signals inhibiting aggression are further blocked by depicting one's enemies as inferior beings or subhumans lacking human feelings. Members of technological civilizations, as well as of tribal societies, use this strategy. Thus the Eipo deride their enemies as dung flies, lizards or worms, or alluding to physical or psychic defeats as runty people or cowards (I. Eibl-Eibesfeldt, W. Schiefenhövel, and V. Heeschen, in press).

Hand in hand with this dehumanization of the enemy is an elevation of one's own self-estimation, which can grow into an elitist and overestimation of personal ability. Hierarchical structures, furthermore, allow the individual to relieve himself of personal responsibility and become included in the group that shares and thus diffuses feelings of responsibility. (Concerning the power of obedience, see p. 310.) The effects of dehumanization and diffusion of responsibility have been investigated in other recent studies (A. Bandura *et al.*, 1975). Groups of three subjects were given the task of delivering electrical shocks to others who committed errors as part of an alleged learning experiment. Subjects who believed to be individually responsible for delivering shocks, delivered a shock with reduced intensity. But if they were told that a mean value would be determined from the actions of three persons delivering punishment as a group, then the subsequent diffusion of responsibility resulted in individual electrical shocks being of higher intensity. Dehumanizing commentary had an even stronger effect on the results. If the test subjects heard negative remarks about their victim over an "accidentally activated" microphone, they subsequently delivered still stronger shocks, and conversely less powerful shocks when the victim was described as understanding and friendly. The aggressive disposition of test persons increased during the course of a session. The mean shock value increased less with feedback about its results. If there was no feedback, shock strength escalated, but only for the group hearing dehumanizing information (Figs. 5.30–5.32).

5.6.2. Conventions and the Question of Inhibition for Killing

From our knowledge of history and from observations conducted by ethnologists, we know that humans have a tendency to regulate warfare according to conventions of various types, giving the losers the opportunity to submit and thus escape complete annihilation. Various forms of ceasefires developed among tribal people as well as means of making peace. We also observe the development of rules of warfare that help reduce excessive bloodshed and confine warfare to the adult male population. Here cultural evolution strikingly phenocopies those animal ritualizations that lead from damaging fight to ritualized, tournamentlike fighting.

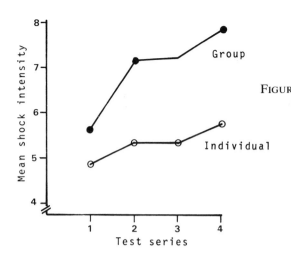

FIGURE 5.30. The effect of diffusion of responsibility on aggression. Persons with the Buss aggression machine can deliver electrical shocks to their victims; those who can share responsibility for the act with an entire group deliver stronger shocks. The apparatus has 10 keys, with increasing intensities from 1 to 10. Figures on the ordinates refer to key numbers. From Y. Jaffe *et al.* (1981).

An analogous development occurs at the individual and group levels in humans—in duels with weapons and by regulating warfare between groups. Similar selective forces may be acting in these cases. Among others, nonritualized fighting may be too risky for all parties involved.

In the cultural mitigation of war, our innate inhibitions against aggression may play a vital role. We have specific signals which inhibit aggression against our fellow man, e.g., when we can perceive certain signs of submission and specific appeals for arousing sympathy in our personal confrontations. Let us recall that crying in newborns evokes crying on the part of nearby babies, thereby awakening sympathy and inducing the same mood. The kindergarten studies of K. Grammer (1982) showed that crying children were always held blameless and those who

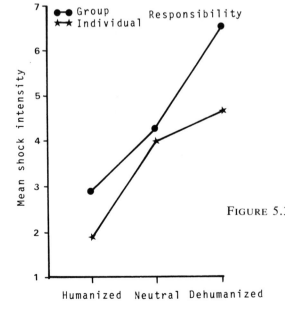

FIGURE 5.31. The mean shock strength as a function of reducing responsibility and dehumanization. After the studies of A. Bandura *et al.* (1975).

were not previously involved in conflict intervened on their behalf. The aggressors who elicited the crying were generally, but not always, inhibited from continuing. Sometimes they continued to tease the crying child.

Appeasement gestures of submission, as the word implies, are the antitheses of threat. One makes oneself small and less conspicuous in a submissive display. This can occur during milder conflicts between children, often by simply lowering the head and then turning it to the side, and also by visual contact avoidance and pouting (p. 500). Extended visual contact arouses negative feelings and correspondingly gaze avoidance and tilting of the head mitigates the situation. The origin of the pouting expression is unclear. It resembles the expression of a baby's mouth who is about to suck. I tend to interpret it as a derived infantile expression. Infantile appeals generally appease and are often combined with submissive displays. Rituals derived from caretaking behaviors have a similar effect. In *Love and Hate* I described examples of the appeasement function of offering food (see prior discussion). Occasionally the appeasing signals of the child are incorporated in appeals for mercy, such as by prisoners of war, who showed photographs of their children to their captors.

Killing a fellow human being is subject to powerful primary inhibitions which, I presume, have a biological basis (p. 194). S. Freud (1913) drew this conclusion upon finding in a survey of ethnological literature that warriors who had killed enemy were initially considered impure. In order to re-enter the society in which they lived they had to undergo a series of purification rites that can be interpreted as rituals of atonement. Freud writes: "We conclude from all these regulations

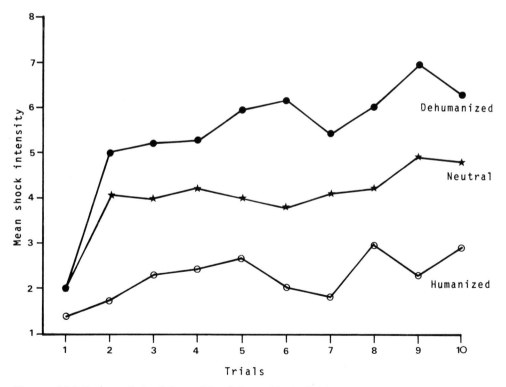

FIGURE 5.32. Increased shock intensities delivered by individual test subjects in sequential sessions to victims represented either as humanized, neutral, or dehumanized. After Bandura *et al.* (1975).

that our behavior toward enemies consists of more than sheer enmity. We also experience regret and a bad conscience in killing others. Thus the commandment comes alive—'Thou shalt not kill' '' (p. 330).

In the (nilotic) tribes of southwestern Ethiopia (Nyangatom), a warrior who has killed is confined to a hut. Women dance about the hut in a specific ceremony and thus help the man experience a rebirth into normal social life. The victorious warrior assumes the name of the vanquished victim, who in this way symbolically lives on. A few weeks later he receives a decorative scar on the chest (S. Tornay, 1979). This is a kind of distinction for the individual but also reassurance on the part of the community that they condone the deed, which helps to resolve guilt feelings. But the procedure of inflicting the scar is painful, so there is also an element of contrition for sins, and perhaps the entire ritual has its origin within this latter context. The feelings experienced by a successful warrior, here as in other cultures, are a mosaic of guilt, pride for the deed reinforced by group recognition, but also fear of the spirit of the dead and revenge on the part of the enemy. A number of practices have developed for dealing with these fears.

When W. Schiefenhövel asked the Eipo of the village where he worked who had killed this or that enemy in the war against the inhabitants of a neighboring valley, they responded with the name Babyal, the war leader. This name was cited repeatedly. Schiefenhövel finally realized that the villagers ascribed all deaths to this Babyal, even those slain by other warriors. With reference to the other group this makes *one* man responsible for their deaths. He assumes responsibility but also the distinction of bravery, with all the consequences of being the target of revenge. The others are thus relieved of blood guilt of their enemies, which makes reconciliation easier (W. Schiefenhövel, 1979).

Volker Heeschen and I discovered another interesting ritual when we questioned the Eipo in Dingerkon in 1979 on cannibalism. During the course of our conversations we learned that the men of the community are essentially obliged to take part in a cannibalistic meal after killing somebody in battle even if they do not particularly enjoy doing so. This implicates everyone in the act of killing, unlike the previous example of individual contrition. But this contradiction is only apparent once we understand that here the moral guilt over the dead person is probably shared and born communally. It represents an outlet or absolution from guilt on the moral level.

Occasionally we are criticized that in assuming the existence of an innate inhibition against killing we were subjects of a romantic illusion, for one can see that in traditional cultures mothers commit infanticide. We have refuted this argument elsewhere and under normal circumstances we can state that the killing of fellow men is experienced with conflicting feelings even when he is an enemy. In my publication *The Biology of War and Peace,* I cite a number of examples of this. Of course, we can superimpose on our biological inhibitions against killing, a cultural norm condoning the killing of enemies, but this does not completely erase the biological inhibitions.

At the beginning of an intergroup conflict, inhibitions are still fairly strong and have to be overcome. This is achieved by the dehumanization of the enemy and by cutting off all communication. Once the Tsembaga (New Guinea) declare war, even people who were formerly friends must henceforth not be contacted if they belong to the enemy group. There are prohibitions against talking to them, looking at them, and eating of food which they have grown (R. A. Rappaport, 1968). Industrialized countries establish nonfraternization laws by which personal contact is impeded, since carefully cultivated hatred deteriorates when such contact occurs.

The use of remotely controlled weapons is preferred, which helps to dilute responsibility for killing. Listening to enemy broadcasts is also forbidden. Thus one builds barriers and places a distance between one's group and the other. Among other factors, group loyalty is significant and obedience is such a powerful disposition that it can block feelings of sympathy. Milgram's experiments, which we cited earlier (p. 310), are most shockingly instructional in this regard.

When personal contact is finally made, however, humans develop their own conventions for such encounters and finally stop shooting at one another. In World War I this was a frequent occurrence on the western front when both sides were entrenched close to one another for months. Naturally, any friendly contacts between enemies would interfere with achieving combat objectives, so the troops are replaced when this begins to happen. These examples instruct us of the ambivalence inherent in human relationships. On the one hand, the fighters storm forth imbued with combat spirit, moved by archaic impulses, and also fired by ideals instilled through indoctrination, and, on the other, are beset by conflicts.

In combat, man can be carried away in an aggressive frenzy, which is contingent on his potential for enormous excitability, based upon his brain chemistry. The brain is often considered the largest gland of a mammal and in man is particularly, if not excessively, large. We mentioned previously man's high arousibility, which makes him prone to emotional escalation. Our cognitive and our emotional capacities are certainly not well balanced, as if the fine structuring of our brain, controlling and balancing out social behavior, lags behind the rapid brain growth experienced during man's evolution. This paves the way for cultural control but also places us at risk. However once the frenzy is over and people calm down, they develop feelings of guilt, even though direct individual responsibility for killing is spread over the group, especially through the use of remotely controlled weapons.

In an important study on peace mechanisms, Thomas Schultze-Westrum (1974) propounds the viewpoint that agonal behavior between conspecifics is the primary human condition and that cessation of agonal relationships is the result of the secondary process of community bonding. Thus war is a normal condition. Conspecifics lacking communal ties with others would continue fighting unceasingly. This thesis is somewhat exaggerated but correctly describes the enormous significance of bonding as an aggression blocker. If people are personally acquainted their behavior shifts from mistrust toward greater trust and the agonal system is less powerfully activated. As we have previously shown (p. 170), infants respond not only agonally toward strangers but also with affectionate behavior. Therefore we cannot simply claim that intraspecific agonal behavior is the primary state that is overcome with communalization but rather that it predominates in relationships between noncommunalized conspecifics. The desire for friendly relationships (one could speak of a bonding or communalization appetence) can also lead to closer relations even between individuals of different communities. This is one reason for erecting communication barriers between warring parties.

For normal individuals, the explosion of aggression in exceptional conditions into uncontrolled frenzy is incomprehensible. Meggitt (1977) reported that in Enga, even subclans fight among themselves which means that people kill their acquaintances. Although in principle, they avoid killing women or children from the other side and multilating bodies of slain warriors, such acts do occasionally occur in the heat of the fight. In this state they seem to loose all inhibitions. With horror we read of massacres of the vanquished and blood-letting orgies that makes the existence of a killing inhibition questionable. In earlier times, groups augmented euphoric, group rage *(dementia pugnax)* through dance and song or drugs such as opium. D. M. Warburton (1975) presumes that the release of hallucinogenic hypothalamic hormones, substances found normally in the body, were triggered during these ceremonies. The sudden loss of inhibitions after the final conquest of an opponent's resistance may be due to a decreased ability to control the liberation of aggressive impulses. We are apparently particularly susceptible to ecstatic conditions of being possessed, of falling into trances, and delirium. Thus it is particularly essential that we use culture as a disciplinary means. This aggressive overkill must be distinguished from pathological forms of aggression causing cold-blooded or sadistic murder, torture, and concentration camp crimes. It is beyond the scope of this work to deal with these.

5.6.3. On the History of War

There are a number of outstanding reviews on the history and manifestations of war (L. Frobenius, 1903; W. E. Mühlmann, 1940; H. H. Turney-High, 1949; Q. Wright, 1965; P. Bohannan, 1967; M. Fried *et al.,* 1968; K. F. Otterbein, 1970; M. A. Nettleship, R. Dalegivens, and A. Nettleship, 1975).

The antiquity of war is contested. Some social scientists firmly cling to the thesis that war did not appear until the onset of agriculture. Paleolithic hunter-gatherers were, according to this view, peaceful and lived in open, nonterritorial bands. This is allegedly true today in hunter-gatherers and thus corresponds to actual human nature. It is claimed that his concept is supported by the peaceful behavior of chimpanzees and gorillas.

But the latest studies in free-living chimpanzees and gorillas show that this presumption is false, but it does not seem to prevent a continuing promulgation of the above view. In chimpanzees even destructive intragroup aggression has been verified (p. 322), and in the section on territoriality we showed that the picture of the aggression-free, nonterritorial primeval society is a myth. A survey of the ethnological literature leaves one surprised that the theory of the peaceful hunter-gatherer was ever seriously entertained, since it is not supported by data. The allegedly peaceful Bushmen of the Kalahari have even portrayed aggressive encounters with other Bushmen and members of alien tribes in their rock paintings (D. F. Bleek, 1930).

Bushmen not only participated in armed conflict, but they also practiced a ritualized form of aggression in their black magic as do most African societies. Thus the Naron and !Kung shot tiny arrows fabricated from the horn of the oryx antelope in the direction of their enemies's dwellings when they wanted to cause them harm. Even today the !Kung Bushmen display a distinct fear of those Bushmen who speak different languages, even for the !Kung of other groups. They distinguish between group members and nongroup members, suggesting an emotional predisposition for war. Melvin Konner (1982, p. 204), a !Kung specialist, writes the following on this theme:

> While the !Kung, like most hunter-gatherers, do not have war or other organized group conflicts, their explicitly stated contempt for non-San people, for San people speaking languages other than !Kung, and even for !Kung in other village-camps, who are not relatives, makes it perfectly clear that if they had the technological opportunity and the ecological necessity to make war, they would probably be capable of the requisite emotions, despite their oft-stated opposition to and fear of war.

Among hunter-gatherer societies, some are relatively pacifistic while others are warlike—this is also true of cultures with other economic bases.

Archeological findings also fail to convey an impression of a particular peaceful stone age man. R. A. Dart (1949, 1953) found that many australopithecines had suffered head injuries that were due to force. M. K. Roper (1969) more recently thoroughly investigated existing australopithecine skull material, material from bone injuries of members of the pithecanthropus group, and skeletal materials found in Europe from the pre-Würm and the Würm glaciation and came to the conclusion that even using very strict standards a great many of the injuries could be derived from effects of fighting. A. Mohr (1971), investigating 158 bone injuries from the palaeolithic and neolithic period reached the same conclusions. Of these, 63% had healed. The injuries were inflicted on the head (47 cases), upper (16) and lower (14) extremities, the vertebral column (16), the sternum (3), and the pelvis (1). She found arrow injuries, some with stone arrowheads embedded in the vertebral bones and those of the lower extremities. Most of the skull injuries had been inflicted with stone axes. This picture is supplemented by the stone age wall paintings portraying scenes of combat (p. 325). In viewing one such scene in the Valtora Ravine in Spain, H. Kühn (1958, p. 105) wrote:

> In one corner I see the picture of a hunter who sinks to the ground, struck with arrows. One leg is moved forward, with his hand placed on his knee. A head ornament like a crown[4] falls from his head, his right hand still holding a bow, but the enemy's arrows have already pierced his body and his life is at an end. We see that people killed each other in earliest times. Where has Paradise fled? A dream of humanity? Is war and fighting its purpose? Is this the eternal way of our life? Here are the archaic pictures of man on this earth, ancient pictures before earliest memories, before all sagas, before all tales, and already the killing of humans by other humans, fighting, and war.

Stone age man competed militarily with others for hunting and gathering grounds, and probably fought for a number of other reasons as well. Q. Wright (1965, p. 22), one of the leading specialists on war, writes: "At no time in human history has there been a golden age of peace." Only if we define war in much more narrow terms, for example, in the sense of Karl von Clausewitz (1937), as a rationally instituted means of foreign policy, can we say that it is an invention of modern civilization. It is then a "continuation of political life with other means." War as an armed conflict between groups is as old as humanity.

5.6.4. Forms of Aggressive Confrontation

Conduct of war in many tribal societies occurs in the form of raids. The adversary is stalked using hunting tactics and is surrounded. Surprise attacks on villages are often conducted in the early morning hours when the enemy is sleeping. H. J. Wilhelm (1953) has described such an attack conducted by the !Kung San for the purpose of revenge. In a quarrel over prey, a member of another group had killed a man, and the group of the deceased attacked the group of the offender by surprise in the early morning hours, using clubs and arrows to kill even women

---

[4]South African Bushmen stick their arrows like head ornaments on a forehead band so they are ready to shoot on short notice. The crownlike head ornament cited by Kühn may very well be this type of forehead band with arrows.

and children. Surprise attacks of this type are known in the Australian aborigines, South American forest Indians, Papuans, African pastoralists, Polynesians, and many others. The acts were executed quickly and without restrictions, killing all. C. Strehlow (1915) described the merciless attacks of the Aranda of Australia. The Maori were known to kill as many enemies as possible and to practice cannabalism (F. E. Maning, 1876).

> . . . when once the enemy broke and commenced to run, the combatants being so close together, a fast runner would knock a dozen on the head in a short time; and the great aim of these fast-running warriors . . . was to chase straight on and never stop, only striking one blow at one man, so as to cripple him, so that those behind should be sure to overtake and finish him. It was not uncommon for one man, strong and swift on foot, when the enemy was fairly routed, to stab with a light spear ten or a dozen men in such a way as to ensure their being overtaken and killed (report of an old Maori from F. E. Maning 1876, p. 14).

However a great number of defeated members survived these kinds of attacks, because weapons were not far-reaching and many would run away. This all changed with the introduction of guns, whereby the Maori practically exterminated themselves. The old style of warfare was no longer adapted to the weaponry introduced by the white man (A. P. Vayda, 1970).

The inhabitants of the New Hebrides had a similar experience, suffering massacres after the introduction of the use of guns. Even the normally formalized conflicts between inhabitants of neighboring villages escalated (J. Layard, 1942, p. 603).

H. Valero (in E. Biocca, 1970) reported bloody surprise attacks in the Yanomami, in which women and children also were killed. However such occurrences were followed by discussions between the warriors in which the headmen reproached his warriors for killing children. Valero reports:

> The Shamatari tushua (chief of the Shamatari) was not a bad man. While we were underway he said, "Why have you killed all these people? You should not have killed so many!" The men responded, "You said we should kill them all!" "I only said so because there were few men there." But the others answered, "There were only a few, because a lot of their men were gone hunting. But they still have their women, who can bear other children and thus become numerous again" (p. 62).

She then describes that those who had killed others were segregated for a period of time, ate only particular food, and were not permitted to talk to others. Later she saw in the Namoeteri (another Waika tribe) that warriors bathed daily, rubbing themselves with coarse leaves, "to cleanse themselves more rapidly of their wrongdoing."

We have cited these examples as comparable to rituals of expiation described repeatedly in our culture. S. Freud has interpreted them as an expression of pangs of conscience.

Behavior toward the enemy in such contexts is ambivalent and the closer one stands to the opponent the more one attempts to mollify the conflict with conventions. This is particularly true for "internal wars" (K. F. Otterbein, 1970) and is understood as armed conflict between people who in some respect are part of a larger group, perhaps because they belong to the same tribe or ethnic group.

In the southern Ethiopian paranilotics there are surprise attacks, with the objective of killing as many opponents as possible, as well as wars in which suffering is reduced through the use of conventions. Thus the Mursi and Hamar are in a

410

constant state of war, with no prospects for peace nor is there any act of pardoning an enemy. Among the Mursi and Bodi war and peace alternate using conventions that limit bloodshed and are utilized especially to protect women and children. Confrontations between local Mursi groups are even more conventionalized. In this case the young unmarried men challenge enemy groups to duels with sticks (D. Turton, 1979). The Dassanetch, also paranilotic, take only a "reasonable" number of cattle when they surprise an adversary (U. Almagor, 1977), enabling the defeated group to maintain their means of sustenance. Everything is taken from any group designated as an arch enemy, however.

The Melanesians of the San Cristobal Islands distinguish between two types of warfare. Traditional warfare between neighboring groups ("heremae") is held on a common combat site, where they meet for battle according to previous agreement. This is distinguished from "surumae," which is the surprise attack undertaken without prior announcement and in which all are killed including women, children, and the aged. This is followed by cannabalism immediately afterward. These two forms of conflict are found throughout Melanesia and New Guinea (C. H. Wedgwood, 1930).

The Eipo differentiate sharply between armed internal group conflict (abala) and war (ise mal), although the former can cause death (W. Schiefenhövel, 1979). I would like to cite the description of one such conflict, an *abala* (fight within a political unit), given by an Eipo to my colleague Wulf Schiefenhövel (Kwengkweng, western New Guinea, 26 April 1980):

The Fight due to Tinteningde's Dog

Tinteningde (T.[5]) thought that his dog, who often ran alone into the mountain forest, was shot by Beteb (B.), a Talim man. T. thereupon took one of B.'s pigs (i.e., stole it) from the vicinity of Talim and said, "Beteb killed my dog, so I will take his pig." The pig was slaughtered and eaten by all the Dingerkon villagers.

B. shouted from the steep shores of the Baknanye stream (near Dingerkon) that he did not kill the dog. T. cried, "Yes you have" The verbal battle grew stronger. T. shot the first arrow and B. answered with shots, for he had Talim warriors with him. The Talim men withdrew and on their way home near the large Ba tree in the Dingerkon gardens, cut the taro plants and destroyed the taro tubers so they could no longer be cultivated. They also pulled out sweet potatoes, sugar cane, bananas, and vegetables, or they destroyed them with their feet and by throwing rocks at them. The Dingerkon men observed this scene and went into the Talim gardens along the shore of the Mabun stream, using two pathways and destroying all taro and sweet potato plants as well as other cultivated plants. T. cried: "Beteb, you pulled out my taro, sweet potatoes, all my bananas, and I will pull yours out!" B. called: "No, you ate my pig, that is what started it!" T. answered: "I did not eat your pig without good reason!" B. called: "I did not kill your dog!" So they fought verbally without end.

The next day they fought again with bows and arrows. They fought for three or four days. Two men were injured on each side. On the fifth day the uninjured dog returned to Dingerkon.

T. called: "The dog came back to me; let us stop fighting!" B. answered: "No, no, you stole my pig, we will continue to fight without stopping!" And they carried on the fight. Men from Londinin, Kolmumdama, and Lyandama were on the side of Dingerkon, while those from Lalekon and Sirabum sided with Talim. Urwo fought especially vigorously. One afternoon he said, "Dusk is coming; let us stop fighting

---

[5]A man from Dingerkon.

and go home!'' Just at this moment Ginyang shot Urwo in the belly with an arrow. The Dingerkon men pulled the arrow out, brought Urwo to the Eglo-aik men's house and conducted the arrow treatment ''kamkamuna'' ceremony. The fight had taken place on the western shore of the Eipo.

After that the Dingerkon people were incensed. When the struggle went on at the east side of the Eipo river, they killed Ebnal as he crossed the Eipo over a tree trunk. Buwungde had hidden on this (eastern) bank behind a rock and shot Ebnal with a single arrow. Ebnal died soon thereafter. Buwundge ran after the other Talim men. He caught Ginyang and held him firmly, but Ginyang tore himself loose. Buwungde shot many arrows into Ginyang's body, but he was still able to run away and recovered (eventually). They fought more. Buwungde had not seen that Ebnal was mortally wounded and thought he had gotten away, so he did not tell the Dingerkon men anything about his arrow shot.

The Dingerkon people came to the place where Buwungde had killed Ebnal, and they saw a great deal of blood there. They looked for and found Ebnal, who lay there as if in deep sleep. T. called to B.: ''I have killed one of yours!'' The Talim men cried a lot about it.

Buwundge's name was not mentioned, and only much later did it become known who had fired the fatal shot at Ebnal.

The Talim people took Ebnal's body, and the Dingerkon warriors withdrew. No fighting occurs during an ''abala'' when a body is being recovered. The Talim people exposed Ebnal's corpse on a tree. Then they fought more and killed Melase right at the bank of the Eipo as he stood alone on the east side. Lingban had fired the arrow that struck Melase on the knee. Melase hid himself but was discovered by the Talim men who stuck him with arrows. The Dingerkon men knew nothing about Melase's wound and could not hear his calls since they were some distance from him and the river rushed past noisily.

The people of Dingerkon got Melase and exposed his corpse when the fight had already lasted about 2 months. The Talim men prepared an ambush with many warriors, supported by Lalekon men and others, where the Dingerkon men went home across the landslip near the Minmin stream. Somson first hit Lekwoleb in the chest, then they stuck him with arrows. Lekwoleb fell down from the rock precipice but was already dead from the arrows. The Dingerkon men brought Lekwoleb into their village and exposed his corpse. Then the fight continued about another 1½ months before peace was concluded.

T. said to B.: ''You have killed two of mine and I have only killed one of yours. We have fought enough and should now make peace.'' They all joined to make peace at the bank of the Eipo, where peace is always made. The same was done after concluding a war with the people from Marikla.

This description is an example of escalation, which leads to overstepping the already low threshold for aggressive acts. The incidents of deaths since 1974 (every fourth person died a violent death!) and reports on intra- and intergroup fighting indicate strongly that a high level of aggressivity is a cultural (and possibly also genetic) Eipo characteristic. It is restrained through ritualization (the tournamentlike nature of fights) so that still greater losses are reduced.

There are also degrees of intensity and rules relating to surprise attack. Thus among all the San Cristobal Melanesians it is forbidden to attack a man who is climbing a tree or someone who is fishing. But on ground one can ambush and kill another person. Night surprise raids were also forbidden as was the killing of the enemy chieftain.

The Murngin of Arnhem Land, Australia, distinguished six types of armed conflict (W. L. Warner, 1930), all of which were regulated by specific warfare rules. One form permitted the punishment of enemy groups without having to expect retaliation. The offended group initiated the punishment proceedings. Men of the opposing group who had incited the warriors to fight, would have to face the spears of their adversaries, but they were allowed to run about in zig-zags and make themselves difficult targets. Furthermore the offended group's friends would run about with the guilty men, inhibiting the punishers from throwing their spears at maximum strength since they could hit someone who was not guilty. In addition, the stone tips of the spears were removed. After all those who felt offended had thrown spears, they could continue to rebuke the guilty ones.

When the "trouble makers" were punished in this way, all those who had contributed to the death had to appear together. They also had to submit themselves to spear tossing, and this time the stone tips were not removed from the spears. But the old men of both groups ran back and forth within this group. One party of old men admonished those seeking revenge not to be overly aggressive and others reminded the guilty ones not to be too angry and to accept their punishment in acknowledgment of their wrongdoing. Once the avenged parties had worked off their feelings of anger the men continued to throw spears, although only sporadically. Finally those who had murdered were hit in the thigh, and were then forgiven for their act. If this did not happen, or if the murderer was only superficially wounded, they were not considered to be forgiven, and the event resulted in only a temporary cease-fire.

In the intratribal wars of northern Australians, the men of opposing groups use their boomerangs like wooden swords in an exchange of blows. Should a man fall during the confrontation, the old women surround him, hold their sticks above him protectively and cry: "Do not kill him, do not kill him!" (C. Lumholtz, 1890). When two groups of the Tsembaga of New Guinea have argued and numerous in-law ties exist between them through various marriages, they make great efforts to prevent an escalation of the conflict. Third parties are used as mediators in their arguments, and if these mediating efforts fail to resolve the differences, the parties both clear off the common traditional fighting area and formally invite each other to a "small" war (R. A. Rappaport, 1968). The groups stand opposite each other on the appointed day, reproaching one another and venting their anger, which can suffice to lead to a peaceful resolution of the conflict. During this phase they may also shoot arrows at one another, but their stabilizing feathers are removed so the arrows cannot be aimed accurately. If this type of confrontation does not produce a resolution, the war escalates to a formally declared "ax war" preceded by a series of ceremonies. Each party calls upon their ancestors for support, and the sacred fighting stones, which are kept in nets on the floors of the huts, are now suspended from the central post. From this time on there is a complete disruption of personal relationships with the enemy, including not looking adversaries in the eye, touching enemies only in fighting, and not eating the fruits they have cultivated. If someone had befriended one of the enemy and called him brother, the relationship is now changed, and former friends are known as "ax men." This is reminiscent of the communication barriers established by civilized countries engaged in war. Once the confrontation has reached this stage, it is not so easily ended.

However, there are a number of conventions limiting an unnecessarily dangerous escalation. The medicine man identifies those enemies who according to the spirits are easy to kill and those of their own group who appear to be particularly vulnerable. This creates a kind of "killing quota" regarding how many should die in the conflict (R. A. Rappaport). Warriors must also obey food taboos. They are compelled to consume highly salted bacon, which induces thirst and thus pauses

413

in the battle. Allies invited to join the fight are not held responsible for the consequences of battle, even if they kill individuals. This convention inhibits a further escalation by involving neighboring groups.

Once a group is beaten, the victor does not immediately take possession of their land. It is guarded by ancestors of the opposing group (a conception that also follows in Australian aborigines). The defeated group must first plant the sacred cordyline plant and slaughter a pig in their newly found territory, actions that call forth their guardian ancestors from the original region and which permits the conquered area to be occupied by the victors. There are also methods of negotiation on the terms of cease-fires, armistice, and finally peace.

In the ethnological literature there are numerous outstanding excellent descriptions of wars, which document the development of conventions to help alleviate confrontations. R. Gardner and K. G. Heider (1968) described them for the aggressive encounters of the Dani, and interesting related notes on the Yalé are found in K. F. Koch (1970, 1974). Other examples are found in: F. L. Bell (1934), R. F. Ferguson (1918), R. F. Fortune (1939), W. W. Hill (1936), R. Karsten (1923), J. Keegan (1976), J. Keegan and J. Darracott (1981), N. Knowles (1940), B. Malinowski (1920), L. Montross (1944), G. S. Snyderman (1948), M. Swadesh (1948), and A. P. Vayda (1960, 1971).

In ancient times in Europe corresponding conventions occurred. There were Roman laws for sparing noncombatants and those fleeing or surrendering and also laws assuring that only those equally armed would fight each other. The use of specific weapons such as lances with hooks and poisoned and flaming arrows was forbidden (W. E. Mühlmann, 1940). The Mohammedan law of war also had listed the requisites of chivalry, forbidding attacks on those praying, the killing of noncombatants, and breaking a promise made to the enemy.

The development of conventions did not always go hand in hand with the development of arms technology; in fact, it always lagged behind. But there is a clear need to ritualize aggressive confrontations so that unnecessary bloodshed could be avoided. Our conscience compels us to establish such ritualizations. They also inherently reduce the risk for both parties engaged in conflict.

In the face of the wars of extermination from antiquity to today, the picture presented here that everyone who participates in war has a bad conscience may seem overly optimistic—nor should one get that impression. But the fact that the Old Testament conquerors had to refer to God's commands verifies the need for justification for their acts and thereby the resolution of a conflict of conscience not unlike the efforts made today to justify the cause when one country attacks another.

5.6.5. Ideological and Psychological War

Man does not only fight with weapons. Psychological warfare is also conducted, and this is becoming an increasingly important way to wage war. It is not difficult to see that one can achieve a victory by creating specific convictions and an appropriate state of mind in the enemy that in the final analysis compels them to behave as one desires. Ideological warfare is constructed along these lines and ranges from flagrant propaganda to subtle forms of persuasion and influence. These methods are generally combined with psychological techniques of flattery, intimidation, and fear arousal.

Ideological and psychological warfare are the techniques of the "Cold War," and their objective is to soften the adversary's resistance, build up receptiveness for one's ideology among one's enemy, and, finally, to assume the propagandized value system, which amounts to submission. For this to occur it is necessary to undermine all those traditions that form the backbone of the opposing society. One can exploit the universally latent conflict between individual freedom and the authority of the state, one of a conflict of individual interest and state interest. One can easily incite people to become disobedient if only some other authority can be proposed. Man seeks authority figures.

Today we can observe how people holding different value systems struggle with each other. They propagate counter values in the first stage of conflict— disobedience instead of obedience, industrial strikes instead of diligence and working, laissez-faire behavior instead of order and self-control—in short, to pursue individual interests. Freedom in all aspects of life are commonly espoused, including liberation from the restrictions of marriage and parental authority. This kind of freedom ideology is appealing, and, indeed, freedom is one of the most common terms used by politicians in soliciting support. Dictatorships and democracies alike use the term similarly; thus the word was utilized and abused again and again by the nazis in their songs. Few appear to have noticed that the appeals to freedom were combined with the demand for blind obedience. Even today, few people realize how the word is abused by leaders in order to present themselves as liberators.

If a group of people succeed in implanting their own ideology and manner of thinking into the minds of their enemy and finally in bringing the opposing group to accept their own value system, they have achieved a bloodless victory. This does not mean that therefore one should close one's eyes to all other thoughts and ideas but rather that they should be studied critically with an appreciation for the context in which new thoughts are propounded. Slogans are weapons in ideological struggle, and ideological conflict is certainly the most humane form of aggressive confrontation, playing a significant role in the conducting of intra-group conflicts in parliamentary democracies. Opposing arguments should be heard and critically tested. This requires independent thinking in combination with loyalty to one's own culture, which does not develop on its own. One must be brought up to be critically sympathetic for one's society, and only then can cultural plurality be maintained and mutually enrich all cultures.

5.6.6. Causes and Consequences of War: The Question of Function

In asking about the causes and motives of aggressive confrontation one must distinguish whether one wants to learn about the subjective motives of the individual participants in war (proximate causes) or whether one wants to inquire about the selective advantages or ultimate causes. Both questions are reasonable ones. When N. A. Chagnon (1968, 1971) determines that the Yanomami conduct wars to rob their enemies of women, he has made an interesting conclusion that is as correct as the position of M. Harris (1979) that the Yanomami carry on war to keep other groups at a distance and thus maintain a region sufficiently large for their hunting needs (p. 108). Thus with increasing population density of individual settlements, men must spend more time hunting, and this leads to irritation, conflict, and a resulting dissension within villages and feuds with one's neighbors. Thus we have two explanations for the same phenomenon. Each is logical but oriented to a different level of behavior. It is difficult to understand why these "differing" viewpoints should lead to academic confrontations, because the investigators have really asked different questions and obtained different answers.

Thus A. N. Chagnon (1971, p. 132) writes: "Territorial acquisitions are neither intended nor achieved during conflicts. This has certain consequences for aggression theories based upon territoriality, especially in the form they have taken in the recent works of Ardrey and Lorenz."

Whatever people may allege as the subjective reasons for their behavior, there are determinable consequences: through warfare there is a pressure on one's neighbors and a territorial disparity. This is the final result of war. Military prowess thus determines the fitness of a group which is quite independent of individual intentions.

In the Tsembaga the damage caused by the ever increasing pig population roaming through neighboring gardens results in increasing unrest and conflict arousal, which can eventually be resolved as aggressions between villages long before there is any overpopulation pressure (R. A. Rappaport, 1968). Headhunting was said to be the reason for conducting war in the Mundurucu, and they kept trophies collected from other tribes. They could not elucidate any other reasons for war except that any non-Mundurucu was considered to be an enemy[6] (R. F. Murphy 1957, 1960). But by headhunting they eliminated competitors for hunting prey, and in this region protein is the limiting factor. W. H. Durham (1976) noted a detail whose significance had escaped Murphy. The successful headhunter received the title "Dajeboisi" (= "Mother of the Peccaries"), and peccaries are important game animals.

The reasons motivating individuals to participate in wars are highly diverse. One important factor is the disposition to obey because of a perceived obligation to the community. It results from an emotionally experienced bond with the group, which is felt to be an extended family. We will return to this point in more detail when we discuss the indoctrinability of people with reference to group values (p. 620). Basically, all the reactions related to family defense can be transposed to the group. Thus contemporary war propaganda typically includes references to family security being threatened by the targeted foe. Thus the highly emotional aggressive group identification associated with highly archaic reactions was pointed out by Lorenz. The "religious fervor" seizing individuals during political mass rallies finds its psychological counterpart in piloerection. We keep bristling, as it were, the fur that is no longer present on our bodies and experience this subjectively as thrill of emotion.

Wherever warriors are esteemed there exists further motivations for the individual to participate in war as a means of winning prestige. Fear of social criticism (fear, cowardice), the motivation to win, hatred, and, finally, pugnacity are further motives. Kelum from the Eipo village Dingerkon took part in a fight between the Talim villagers and the Marikla, even though his village was not even involved in the conflict. Kelum was wounded, and we asked him why he had gotten involved in the fight at all. He said it was due to "fatan" (pugnacity). Anyone watching soccer fans can see that this motivation is not alien to us.

Whatever the individual reasons may be for aggressive motivation, the final result of aggressive group behavior is the dominance of one group over another, which in earlier times often led to the demise of the defeated group and even often today to driving them from their lands. Land acquisition and territorial demarcation

---

[6]They used the term Pariwat for all non-Mundurucu, including peccaries and tapirs within the same term. These means that the people so named were considered to be wild game available for hunting. See also the text on the dehumanization of the enemy (p.).

are historically verifiable consequences of group aggression, for groups use these means to ensure security for their existence. The fighters themselves are often aware of resource acquisition reasons for a war. Thus cattle breeding peoples fight consciously for access to water holes and for grazing lands; they will also steal cattle from each other (K. Fukui and D. Turton, 1979). The territorial function (securing resources) of war has been elucidated in a number of anthropological studies (Q. Wright, 1964; A. P. Vayda, 1960, 1961, 1967, 1971, where further literature is cited).

South American flatland Indian tribes fought for arable land (R. V. Morey and J. P. Marwitt, 1973), as did the Yuma in the region of the Colorado and Gila rivers (United States), wherein the plains surrounding the rivers were the physical objectives. Peoples living in adjacent regions and leading a different life style were not regarded as competitors (E. F. Castetter and W. H. Beli, 1951; E. E. Graham, 1973).

C. R. Hallpike (1973) disagreed with a functional interpretation of war, stating that not everything that exists fulfills functions. In fact he was surprised that one would ask about the function of an institution like warfare. I find it surprising that he would not wonder about a possible functional basis for a phenomenon that is so widespread throughout the world and which has played such a significant role in human history. It is only when we have recognized the functions fulfilled by war that we can pose questions about achieving these functions without bloodshed. There are certainly superior alternatives to be found.

M. J. Meggitt (1962, 1965a), who analyzed 41 Enga wars, found that "encroachment on land" was twice as frequently the cause of warfare as pig stealing or murder. Other examples related to land are found in H. C. Brookfield and P. Brown (1963), and it is well known that land acquisition is a motive for war in contemporary states. But other resources can also be involved. Bedouins commonly fight for camels (L. Sweet, 1965) while the Irokese fight for pelts (G. T. Hunt, 1940). Modern wars have been conducted for oil fields and mineral deposits. Anyone who fails to recognize the instrumental character of warfare will not be able to make constructive contributions to the pacification of the world, because such contributions require acknowledging the functions fulfilled by war in order to propose other means of resolving these issues.

The wars of tribal societies have involved heavy losses. W. L. Warner (1930) reports that of 700 adult male Murngin, 200 (28%) died in wars. J. H. Bennett, F. A. Rhodes, and H. N. Robson (1959) found that 14% of male Fore (New Guinea) died in wars, and W. Schiefenhövel makes similar estimations for the Eipo. It is apparently the groups that stand the test in aggressive encounters with others.

Studies by N. A. Chagnon (1988) on Yanomami warfare revealed that 44% of the males estimated to be 25 years or older have participated in the killing of someone, and nearly 70% of all adults over an estimated 40 years of age have lost a close genetic relative to violence or war. Chagnon's demographic data, collected over a period of 23 years, indicate that men who have killed have more wives and children than those who have not. But to what extent the risk compensates either the individual or the group needs further investigation.[7] War, in the context

---

[7]In the Munducuru the successful warrior capturing a head trophy must abstain from sexual intercourse for 3 years. He is thought to foster the welfare of the peccaries magically, but this practice appears to me to be a disadvantage for the individual's "reproductive fitness."

just mentioned, although not in our genes, has to do with genes, since it aids the propagation of those of the winners.

In view of the high human losses, a number of authors (e.g., W. T. Divale, 1971) have fostered the viewpoint that war may be a population control mechanism. But losses in the male population alone would never suffice as a population control mechanism; the female population must also decrease, and this is not achieved through warfare but by preferential female infanticide. Male newborns are usually only killed when they are deformed. Another population control mechanism is the taboos against intercourse after giving birth, sometimes for as much as 3 years.

Theories that war is a pathological phenomenon bear the character of wishful thinking rather than a scientific assertion: "War is pathological but it is the expression of a sickness in human society itself which arises from the cherishing of ideas hurtful to the general welfare of mankind" is the statement of the Medical Association for the Prevention of War (1963). M. A. Nettleship *et al.* (1975, p. 190) quote this sentence and respond aptly:

> A major criticism of the concept of the pathological nature of war is that it is seldom more than an assumption, and the results of holding the assumption are not explored or integrated with the remainder of an author's work. How, for instance, would it have been possible for war to continue to be passed on to new generations of man for millenia if it was a heritable pathological condition? Would not the mutation or invention of war have been deadly? In most circumstances until recent times it seems instead that war has been positively adaptive and contributory to continued existence and dominance of warlike groups over peaceful groups. Similarly, no matter how unpleasant war is to the losers and the dead, it is difficult to support a conception of war as a social disease of a kind of pathological thinking within or between participating cultures.

In other words: war fulfills functions. It is a cultural invention that unfortunately has been selectively adaptive in intergroup aggression in which the victors achieve clear advantages. This does not mean that we must continue to accept warfare in this function. It is certainly not the best and only solution to problems. But in order to reach a viable solution we must understand that war does indeed fulfill functions, which we must handle in alternative ways if we are to secure peace in this world (I. Eibl-Eibesfeldt, 1975a).

5.6.7. Peacemaking and Coexistence

Some kind of trust for the enemy's thinking must remain in the midst of battle, for without it no peace can be made.

Immanuel Kant: On Eternal Peace

Cultural differentiation of aggressive interactions copy many phylogenetic adaptations which have similar functions. This is not only true for the ritualization of fighting. Animals have developed many techniques of displaying submission and, more rarely, reconciliation so that the fighting parties can resume living together in a group. Functionally comparable conventions exist for human groups, permitting ceasefires, the submission of the defeated groups, and finally for the parties torn by conflict to negotiate peace and resume normal relationships. A rapprochement can only succeed when the parties abide by its terms, and if one violates them, he only hurts himself. The one-sided alignment of the German people under the national socialist banner, praising courage while simultaneously disregarding humane virtues, eliminated any possibility of seeking and arranging meaningful peace during World War II. Thus just as fighting is a functionally adaptive system (p. 363) with an interaction of attack, submission, and flight, in war there must also exist an alternative to attack and victory, such as flight and submission (surrender), and finally a formal peace treaty as a prerequisite for peaceful coexistence. Once we have destroyed these alternatives, the consequences are disastrous. Inhumanity is maladaptive. As Kant wrote, a basis for mutual trust must remain intact so that peace can be restored out of conflict.

Tribal people have developed complex rituals for implementing peace. We refer to the studies of Rappaport on Tsembaga warfare, where battles can extend over a period of weeks. But once a group has killed a member of the enemy group, they break off the fight in order to give the enemy an opportunity to carry out their mourning and burial rites, a notably chivalrous gesture. A cease-fire is usually held for several days as the combatants bring their gardens in order again. A battle pause is also held when a warrior is seriously wounded. Temper are softened and peace talks can eventually begin.

A formal truce is initiated with the planting of cordyline. Each party plants for his own side, and as long as this ritual plant grows, the battle may not be resumed. Sacred stones representing the power of the ancestors, however, still remain hung up in the men's house and a variety of contact taboos are maintained. Such a truce can last for years. The period is used by both parties for raising pigs. A joint pig festival is then held that can last for several months. A number of rituals must be conducted during the festival: a dance area is prepared, the sacred stones are buried (permitting contact with the enemy), and finally a dance takes place. At the high point of this festival, a number of other taboos restricting contact with the enemy are lifted as a first step toward peace. But until that point more pigs must be raised since reserve supplies have been spent and another 2 or 3 years are needed for this second replenishment. At the peacemaking ceremony the parties meet at the border with their wives and children. Pork liver is exchanged and women may also be exchanged (or at least promised) between the former enemies. One woman must be given to the former foe for each fallen warrior, which results in forming marriage ties, which is an effective means of preventing another outbreak of war in the immediate future. The children of these marriages, in a sense, replaces the warriors killed in battle.

Mediators, who do not belong to the warring parties and who watch the battle from a hillside, play an important role in peace-making functions, using moralizing appeals. They observe and call out to the warriors how bad it is for brothers to fight each other.

Men of high esteem are the peacemakers of the tribes of the Mt. Hagen area (Papua New Guinea). They admonish the parties against fighting, since they are all classificatory nephews and nieces, and they distribute gifts (A. Strathern, 1971).

The desire for peace and the negative attitude toward warring in these aggressive Papuan cultures is remarkable and is expressed in many texts. In the Yalémo the party seeking peace sings the following standard verse (K. F. Koch, 1974):

> Fighting is to be abhorred,
> and so is war.
> Like the trees we will stand together
> Like the trees at Fungfung,
> Like the trees at Jelen.

Our natural desire for peace is sincere as are our assertions during peace negotiations. Among the tribes in the Mt. Hagen area the peace vows take the form of a dialogue (C. F. Vicedom and H. Tischner, 1943/1948, quoted in I. Eibl-Eibesfeldt, 1975) and an exchange of gifts, which play an important role as a means of group bonding and during peace talks.

The texts I recorded during a mourning ceremony for killed Medlpa warriors (Papua-New Guinea) were of similar content (translated in I. Eibl-Eibesfeldt 1975a, 1981). War was characterized as evil and associated with guilt, which does not contradict the fact that one can participate in it with enthusiasm and a certain athletic zeal, for guilt and enthusiasm can be activated simultaneously. It is probably for this reason that an attacker, to excuse himself, typically claims that the other parties initiated the hostilities and that he was compelled to protect himself. This is a common position taken by members of traditional societies and the representatives of civilized nations regardless of the type of government.

Enthusiasm and zeal tend to repress guilt and conscience. According to Pauline Wiessner (pers. commun.), the Enga of New Guinea often say that they enter war with sportlike enthusiasm and only when somebody on their side is killed do they ask the question "Why did we get into this?" It is only at this juncture that guilt plays a major role.

Our innate inhibitions against aggression are well developed, and we do not negotiate for peace purely out of fear, as H. Portisch (1970) claims. Our striving for peace reflects a genuine desire for it. A prerequisite for peace is the solution of our ecological problems for population control and those of international competition, which so far were solved by war, by using alternate peaceful strategies.

There is also a psychological prerequisite in that some basis for mutual trust must be found so the contending parties can reach an understanding and thus make peace between themselves. This involves formulating a pact that avoids an excessive loss of face for the opponent. Demands for complete capitulation stand as much in the way of peace as war crimes do. Fear of loss of face drives the opponent to battle and even to his annihilation and unnecessarily increases human suffering.

The growth of fear-inspired mistrust has catastrophic implications today and is reflected in the maddening arms race that continues unceasingly. According to the German periodical *Der Spiegel* (1982, p. 27), between 1945 and the summer of 1982 there were 130 wars, civil wars, uprisings, and terrorist campaigns that affected nearly 100 countries and in which approximately 35 million people died. Military expenditures multiplied fourfold in the developing countries between 1960 and 1978, while in the industrial countries they climbed 44% in the same period. In 1960, 230 billion dollars were spent throughout the world for arms, while in 1980 the figure climbed to 465 billion dollars (Stockholm International Peace Research Institute, SIPRI Yearbook 1981, World Armourments, London 1981). Other statistical sources give even higher figures. The Stockholm Institute figures compensate for inflation so that the figures are directly comparable. The destructive potential has attained unimaginable proportions, and even if we all hope that this will not proceed beyond the threat stage there is a serious danger that the ritual of threat might get on the wrong track. If, during this hectic arms race, still more refined weaponry is developed and the growth of defensive techniques does not keep pace with attack weapons, one side could attempt to utilize its temporary advantage to attack; and, indeed, this is quite likely to happen (C. F. von Weizsäcker, 1977). The balance of fear is unstable and the capacity to destroy has become so great that there is now a danger of civilization self-destructing itself on a worldwide scale. "In the entire world there is now more explosive material, in kilograms per person, than food" (R. L. Sivard, 1980, p. 5).

It would be naive, however, to assume that the mere desire for peace is a sufficient basis to prevent war. The present dangerous world situation has developed from a series of factors whose existence cannot be wished away if we want to pursue peace:

1. The dynamics of arms technology make it increasingly difficult to find appropriate conventions of humanization and thus even slightly defuse the arms race. Although all parties agree that the use of mass destruction weaponry against civilians is contrary to the conventions of civilized nations, such weaponry is being built with the excuse that the enemy also has them and one must be correspondingly armed.
2. Weaponry and counter weaponry are conceived on a vicious pendulum. A behavioral factor contributes to this phenomenon in that in attempting to maintain equality with one's adversary there is the tendency to overshoot a bit, resulting in the unending arms spiral of "equalizing." Since the enemy is feared, his weapons are consistently perceived as being more dangerous than those one is controlling. The dynamics of present day missile development is fed by this type of perception.
3. The trust in the predictability of enemy behavior has been seriously disturbed by the events of World War II. This distrust fosters fear and with it the tendency to disparage the enemy and create communication barriers between states. Their dismantling is one of the most important steps that can be taken to facilitate peace.
4. Mankind has reached the ecological crisis, with mass overpopulation leading to environmental disturbances (resource exhaustion) on a global scale. This could eventually lead to a fight for the last existing resources.

Most well-intentioned writings point out the insanity of endless military expenditures, the potential for self-destruction, and the fact that starvation exists in many parts of the world. Thus Franz Alt (1983) notes that in the 4 short hours it takes to read his book, 500 million DMs are being spent on weapons while approximately 7000 children are starving to death. This shocking information suggests that the same money could be spent feeding the hungry, which would then bring order to the world and peace on earth. But Alt does not consider the fact that it is the overpopulation that is destroying the earth and which fuels the fear-inspired arms race. Peace is possible, but it needs more than the fear of an atomic holocaust and the hopeful tidings of the sermon on the Mount to attain it—it needs immediate and pragmatic action.

Summary 5.6

War, defined, as strategically planned, destructive group aggression, is a product of cultural evolution. Therefore, it can be overcome culturally. It makes use of some universal innate human dispositions, such as man's aggressive emotionality and the preparedness for group defense, dominance striving, territoriality, disposition to react to agonal signals from strangers, etc. But all these traits do not lead to warfare. War requires systematic planning, leadership, destructive weapons, and overcoming sympathy through dehumanizing the enemy in advance of the actual conflict. Man easily falls prey to indoctrination to act in supposed group interest.

421

Some basic norms such as the inhibition against killing and the norm of respect of possession work against conducting war. Superimposed upon them are cultural norms demanding to kill the enemy, but the former cannot be extinguished altogether. A conflict of norms is experienced as pangs of conscience, and conscience is certainly one of the motivating factors for developing conventions that humanize armed conflict and for the establishment and maintenance of peaceful relations. Our motivational structure would allow for peace. But peace requires that one recognize the functions fulfilled by warfare and not simply to dispense with war as a pathological degenerate phenomenon. If we want peace, we must resolve the issues of territorial demarcation and resource security, which until now have been settled with wars, by other, bloodless, means.

6

Communication

Prerequisite for any communication is a tuning in between sender and receiver. The releaser-IRM concept presented earlier can contribute to an understanding of certain aspects of human communicative behavior. Humans possess an innate repertoire of signals as phylogenetic adaptations, and seem capable of understanding a number of these signals prior to individual experience on the basis of innate releasing mechanisms. Due to these biological programs, we are able to communicate across cultural and linguistic barriers.

Our response to a social signal can be an immediate, reflexlike one, such as a response to another's smile. However, this is by no means always the case. We can exercise restraint. Furthermore, our expressive movements are, to a certain extent, under voluntary control, so that we are able to use facial expressions instrumentally to achieve particular objectives. Thus we can feign certain emotions or mask them. In their excellent studies on deceit, P. Ekman (1985, 1981) and P. Ekman and Friesen (1988) revealed subtle differences between felt and feigned expressions. Thus, when a person smiled from actual enjoyment (felt or honest smile) the outer muscles orbiting the eyes were more often contracted than when enjoyment was feigned. When a person smiled in order to mask a negative emotion superposition occurred (p. 463) and traces of the suppressed expressions were visible.

Our communicative interactions are governed by a universal hierarchically organized system of rules, which will be discussed later. They channel our social interactions along phylogenetically established pathways and, at the same time, open up new dimensions of freedom of action (p. 493). Learning enriches our communicative system in many ways. Cultural conventions specify as etiquette our mode of interaction and with language we acquire a particular kind of communication code that permits us to discuss present, past, future or even imagined events (p. 523). With the aid of this signal system we can transmit knowledge to others. We can also act verbally, as in making requests, quarreling, or courting. In such cases our verbal behavior, as we will see, follows the same rules governing our nonverbal social interactions. Thus, in humans, words, sentences, and innate nonverbal cues can supplement each other as functional equivalents within a given system of rules. In this way, man acquired a multiplicity of alternative methods of expression which facilitated his cultural "pseudospeciation" (p. 15). Man can also send contradicting signals via different channels simultaneously and thus, for example, soften a harsh statement by smiling.

Let us start with the discussion of phylogenetic adaptations for communication. Sender and receiver form a functional entity, but this does not mean that phylogenetic adaptations are necessarily present for both the sender and the receiver. It is conceivable that the significance of an innate expressive behavior, such as smiling, would have to be learned individually. In this case, the meaning of an inborn signal would be acquired on the part of the recipient. I know of no such case, but I indicate its theoretical possibility since our response to specific morphological characteristics, such as sexual ones, can arise from associations coupled to these characteristics.

The converse case is also conceivable in which the phylogenetic adaptation rests within the sender's perception and a bias of perception forces him or her to adapt by sending the expected signals. That men in various cultures emphasize the shoulders in their fashions could be due to the existence of an IRM, which was originally adapted to specific male morphological characteristics which later became rudimentary (p. 64).

425

Expressive movements are indicators of emotional states. Ever since Charles Darwin, we distinguish a number of main categories. S. S. Tomkins and R. McCarter (1964) list seven main categories, namely, joy, fear, rage, surprise, anguish, interest, and shame. Others have added disgust and contempt, but the systematics of emotions remains unsatisfactory as long as we fail to understand the neurophysiology underlying these events. Promising steps in this direction were undertaken by J. Panksepp (1982, 1985). His attempts to systematize human moods are structured around several major circuits of the mammalian brain apparently mediating behavioral processes related to (1) interest–desire (expectancies); (2) irritability–anger (rage); (3) trepidation–anxiety (fear); (4) loneliness–sadness (separation distress, panic) and (5) pleasure–lust.

People communicate primarily with acoustic and visual signals. However, tactile and olfactory signals are important in intimate relationships and may play a certain role as tonic (long-acting) signals. Thus caressing, patting, and similar kinds of tactile stimulation contribute to the well-being of some mammalian species. The normal development of baby rats depends, among others, on the tactile stimulation provided by the mother, who licks and grooms them. Isolated babies do not grow well. If gently stroked with a wet brush, however, they grow and develop faster than untreated isolates. Deprivation of tactile stimulation seems stressful and results in a rise of the β-endorphin levels in the brain. This helps to quiet the young, but also causes their retardation. If young who remained with their mother received injections of β-endorphin, they exhibited the same retardation as the noncaressed isolates. Premature-born human babies grew faster when they were gently stroked on their back, arms, and neck three times a day compared to controls without such a treatment. They also increased in weight 1½ times faster. Even after 8 months they showed greater weight gain and were more advanced in their mental and overall motor behavior than the controls (D. M. Barnes, 1988, reporting on the works of S. Schanberg, T. Field, and G. Evonuik).

6.1. Olfactory Communication

Everyday speech is filled with references to olfaction. When we dislike an idea we may say "That stinks!" The enhanced importance of the olfactory sense in interpersonal group life has recently become evident. We have already cited the work of J. LeMagnen (1952), who discovered that women perceive specific musk substances at much lower concentrations than could be perceived by men (p. 274). LeMagnen also found that women become particularly sensitive to musk during ovulation. These studies are still controversial, although they have been confirmed by J. S. Vierling and J. Rock, (1967) and H. S. Koelega and E. P. Köster (1974); they were not confirmed by J. E. Amoore et al., (1975).

We also mentioned that women find the male pheromone androstenone attractive, while men unconsciously avoid seats sprayed with this substance (M. Kirk-Smith and D. A. Booth, 1980). In humans, androstenol and androstenone are found in urine, fatty tissues, and axillary perspiration. However, they are present in high concentration in men (e.g., fatty tissues: males 103 gm/1, females 10–30 gm/1), and only occur in perspiration in females in exceptional cases (D. B. Gower, 1972; B. W. L. Brooksbank et al., 1974). Fresh urine and axillary perspiration contain only androstenol, which does not have an unpleasant odor. To some it smells like musk, while others associate it with sandalwood. Contact with bacteria and air transforms androstenol into androstenone, which smells more like urine (J. E. Amoore et al., 1977). M. Kirk-Smith et al. (1978) found that the

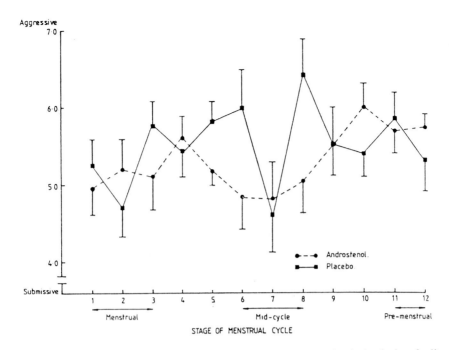

FIGURE 6.1. The influence of androstenol on ratings of aggressive/submissive feelings throughout the menstrual cycle. The ratings (mean ± S.D.) were based on a scale 0–10 where 0 represented extreme submisssive and 10 extreme aggressive feelings. The curve of the control group indicates that during midcycle the aggressivity is normally reduced. This tendency is enhanced by the androstenol treatment. Functionally, this would make sense: if women are less aggressive during their fertile days, their affiliative tendencies would increase. From D. Benton (1982).

moods of test subjects of both sexes change after perceiving androstenol: both sexes responded more positively to photographs of males and females. The opposite sex was considered more sexually attractive by the experimental than the control group. The smell of androstenol caused a more interesting and warmer perception of both sexes. Androstenol thus influences both sexual behavior and the general tendency toward bonding.

Women whose upper lips were dabbed with a solution of androstenol each morning throughout the menstrual cycle experienced a change of mood. During midcycle they rated themselves as less aggressive than did controls who had received a placebo treatment (D. Benton 1982; Fig. 6.1).

The armpits are one of the primary sites for the production of odors. The apocrine sweat glands produce protein-rich perspiration, which impart, with their particular bacterial flora, an individual odor to each person. Genetic factors are obviously in operation here, since identical twins have nearly identical odors when tested with dogs trained to discern such differences (H. Kalmus, 1955; L. Gedda, 1971). The male pheromone supplements this personal odor and axillary hair functions in the propagation of this personal scent; armpits lacking hair have significantly less scent (W. B. Shelley *et al.*, 1953).

People are capable of recognizing one another on the basis of body odor. We have already mentioned that 2-day-old infants recognize their mothers by their odor and mothers similarly recognize their infants (B. Schaal *et al.*, 1980). M. J.

Russell *et al.* (1983) postulated a sensitive phase of the mother immediately after birth; in Russell's study contact during the first half-hour with the newborn infant sufficed for mothers to recognize their infants solely by smell 6 hours later. Children (3–6 years of age) can distinguish their siblings from other children based on scent; parents can similarly distinguish their children (R. H. Porter and J. D. Moore, 1981). Adults of both sexes can distinguish shirts worn by themselves and their sexual partners from strangers by odor (B. Hold and M. Schleidt, 1977); similarly, men and women can be distinguished by scent (M. J. Russell, 1976).

Asked to assess odors, female and male test subjects alike respond more positively to the scent of T-shirts worn by women than to identical T-shirts worn by men, with a single exception: while German women generally found the scent of their male partner to be more pleasant, Italian and Japanese women responded more negatively to their partner's odor. M. Schleidt, B. Hold, and G. Attili (1981) hypothesize that a relationship exists between culturally different forms of marriage preparation and general evaluation of marriage. In Germany, marriage based on love prevails, whereas in Japan many marriages are still arranged by parents. In addition, the importance of married status, especially for the woman, differs in all three countries.

Human odors undoubtedly are tonic signals (W. M. Schleidt, 1973), which act mainly by producing mood shifts. In mass society they are masked with deodorants, such that the olfactory sexual differences disappear (M. Schleidt, 1980). This is probably a strategy of camouflage within anonymous society, and tends to emphasize one's partners' individuality in a less provocative way than the biological smell.

The bonding effect of odors is evident when we consider the long-term memory that most people have for odors (T. Engen, 1982). Other characteristics of olfaction, such as its predominantly unconscious influence on emotionality, suggest that scent perception plays an important role at various levels of bonding in humans, including the mother–child attachment, partner bonding, and home- or geographical bonding (M. Schleidt, 1983).

The pheromonally activated synchronization of female menstrual cycles is still a puzzling mystery (M. K. McClintock, 1971; C. A. Graham and W. C. Grew, 1980). It occurs when women live together over several months. M. J. Russell *et al.* (1977) dabbed axillary perspiration from a woman with a regular menstrual cycle on the upper lips of female volunteers. After 4 months their periods more closely corresponded to the donor's cycle than the control group. G. Preti *et al.* (1986) confirmed, with the same method, that constituents of the axillary sweat from the region of a donor female can shift the time of menstrual onset of another female to conform with the donor's cycle in the absence of social contact. P. W. Turke (1984) assumes that this synchronization developed along with hidden ovulation. This invisible estrus compelled the man to remain faithful to his partner and not to seek other sexual partners since he could potentially miss his partner's fertile period. Once this fertile period was over for the partner, it had also disappeared for the other women due to their synchronization. This may have been the case if our prehuman ancestors lived communally in caves or common huts, but when individual families live within homes, as in the Eipo, and the women are sent to dwell in womens' huts during menstruation, no such synchronization occurs (on the basis of findings from G. Schiefenhövel, pers. commun., in the village of Munggona in the Eipomek valley).

428 Extracts of male axillary secretions placed on the upper lips of woman reduced

FIGURE 6.2. Example of a sweat ritual. As part of a trance ritual, G/wi women (central Kalahari) transmit their axillary sweat to their partners. From a 25 frames/second 16 mm film, frames 1, 9, 18, and 32 of the sequence. Photo: I. Eibl-Eibesfeldt.

the variability and the proportion of aberrant cycle length (W. B. Cutler *et al.*, 1986).

There are all sorts of sweat rituals that support the contention that body odor has a communicative function. In the Gidjingali of Arnhem Land (Australia), I observed a man bidding farewell to another take both hands to his armpits, rubbing sweat onto them, and then rubbing the sides of the body of his friend with them. The trance dances of the G/wi that I filmed depict trance dancers putting axillary and facial sweat on the sick. They also rubbed their heads with their hands, transmitting their hair odor to others. Women also did this to each other in their trances (Fig. 6.2). G. and W. Schiefenhövel (1978) filmed an Eipo woman supporting another in labor whereby she repeatedly pulled a fern frond through her armpit and then stroked the laboring woman with it. In all these cases the partner is thought to gain strength from transmitting one's own scent to the partner; thus there is a strong identification derived from scent. I have described urine and salivary rites in detail in *Love and Hate* (1971). In some parts of Austria and in the Mediterranean countries, young men will wave handkerchiefs they have rubbed in their armpits in front of their female partners during dance.

Summary 6.1

Although human beings are not macrosmates, olfaction plays an important role in interpersonal relations. Mother and child quickly recognize each other by their individual odor, and in experimental situations adults can recognize their spouses to a certain extent and also the sex of other individuals on the basis of the odor borne in their T-shirts. Specific pheromones, such as androstenol, arouse contact readiness in both men and women, while other pheromones (androstenone) stimulate only women. The extent these play a role as sexual pheromones remains to be clarified. The communicative function of body odor is verified by the existence of "sweat" rituals, such as those in which axillary perspiration is transmitted to the partner.

6.2. Tactile Communication

Stroking, fondling, ruffling, touching with the flat palm of the hand, cuddling, and embracing are all among the universal tonic signals stemming from the repertoire of mother–child signals. They have a calming effect and create a friendly mood, not only in the young, but also among adults (I. Eibl-Eibesfeldt, 1970a; Figs. 6.3–6.10) and they contribute to the well-being of the individual (p. 426). Adults can offer comfort by embracing in their arms a desperate fellow-man, who, in turn, clings to him. In general, higher ranking individuals offer subordinates protection and contact. The high ranking individual lays his hand on the subordinate, holding him around the shoulders protectively.

In chimpanzees, physical contact can have a calming effect and is provided by the mother, in the role of a dominant figure. Lower ranking chimpanzees seek hand contact with higher ranking individuals, often as a kind of inquiry. Jane van Lawick-Goodall observed that females who would not dare to take bananas directly in the presence of a dominant male would initially extend their hands to him. If the male responded by making contact, the female had resolved her tension and took the bananas freely. A female, after giving birth, approaches other group members with the baby in her arms. She presents her offspring with outstretched open hands showing all the signs of fear (the youngster is initially foreign to the group and could be attacked by them). Once the partner touches the female, she is calmed (Fig. 6.11).

Physical contact is an expression of both superior rank and affection. Audiences evaluate actors who touch their partners as more self-confident, more dominant, and more affectionate than the one being touched. Female audiences assess actors initiating contact as more attractive than those who do not touch their partners. "Heterosexual contacters" are considered to be more affectionate by audiences than those contacting members of the same sex. Generally, one-sided contact situations create greater esteem for the person initiating the contact than the person being contacted (B. Major and R. Heslin, 1982). This is probably related to the original protective function of contact. Mothers embrace and protect their children by pressing them against their bodies and cuddling with them, the latter actions consisting of ritualized repeated embraces. In chimpanzees, high ranking individuals maintain calming body contact with their subordinates in various ways: they may lay a hand on others or simply touch the extended hand of a partner. Thus contact is both an expression of dominance and affection. Physical contact also expresses a trusting relationship. Thus children seek contact with reference figures (Figs. 6.12–6.14).

The various forms of hand contact have been integrated in humans into bonding rituals, usually in a culture-specific form. Westerners shake hands in greeting, combining friendly contact with an assessment of strength in the handshake (p. 493). Grabbing the lower arm and placing the hand on various parts of the body (hips, shoulders, head) is common in many cultures. Gestures of benediction are derived from this behavior and can be interpreted as a laying on of hands at a distance (Figs. 6.15A, 6.15B).

FIGURE 6.3. (A) Rhesus monkey mother with infant. Young Old-World monkeys seek comfort with their mothers. They clasp them firmly and are protectively embraced by them. Drawing: H. Kacher after a photo from I. Eibl-Eibesfeldt (1970a, 1971c). (B) The need for mother contact is also seen in adolescent Old World monkeys. Here a rhesus monkey mother with nursing young is shown with an older sibling beside her. The need for contact in humans is rooted in this ancient mother-child relationship. Drawing: H. Kacher from a photo in I. Eibl-Eibesfeldt (1970a, 1971c).

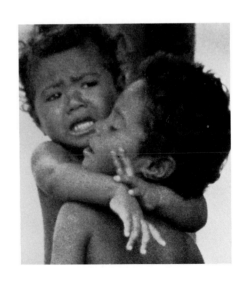

FIGURE 6.4. Sonjo child anxiously clinging to an older child is embraced protectively. Drawing: H. Kacher from a photo in I. Eibl-Eibesfeldt (1970a, 1971c).

FIGURE 6.5. Anxious small girl from Kaleuna (Trobriand Islands) embracing her older sister. From a 16 mm film. Photo: I. Eibl-Eibesfeldt.

FIGURE 6.6. Two young Tboli-blit women (Mindanao) embracing each other as they watch us filming . Photo: I. Eibl-Eibesfeldt.

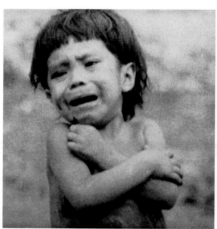

FIGURE 6.7. (A) A despairing Yanomami child embraces itself anxiously. Photo: I. Eibl-Eibesfeldt. (B) Self-embracing in a despairing child, born deaf and blind, who has been left alone (girl, about 8 years old). She grabs one of her feet which she has raised to her chest. From a 16 mm film. Photo: I. Eibl-Eibesfeldt.

FIGURE 6.8. Physical contact with reference figures (friends) transmits a general feeling of security and well-being. Here, two Yanomami girls look at the photographer curiously. Photo: I. Eibl-Eibesfeldt.

432

FIGURE 6.9. In most tribal societies the children receive a great deal of tactile contact by their parents, as is exemplified by a Tasaday father in this photograph. Photo: I. Eibl-Eibesfeldt.

FIGURE 6.10. (A) A 4-year-old chimpanzee female beneath the hand of a chimpanzee male. Drawing: H. Kacher after a photograph by Jane van Lawick-Goodall. (B) A young American protectively embraces his girl friend. Drawing: H. Kacher after a photograph taken in Disneyland (California) by I. Eibl-Eibesfeldt.

FIGURE 6.11. Chimpanzee female soliciting contact with a male by extending her hand. Drawing: H. Kacher after a photo by Jan van Lawick-Goodall.

FIGURE 6.12. Before his first swim in the sea, the grandson seeks comforting contact, soliciting trust and care, with his grandfather. Photo L. Eibl-Eibesfeldt.

We also find that cuddling, stroking, and embracing are behavioral elements of friendly greeting as well as patterns of heterosexual contact initiation. The extent to which the rhythmic aspects of contacts derives its basic frequency from mother–child behavior remains to be determined. In many tribal societies, mothers stroke the genital regions of their children as a gesture of affection. In the Eipo, Daribi, and several other New Guinea tribes men are greeted by older women and partners of the same sex by stroking the scrotum in a movement from bottom to top (I. Eibl-Eibesfeldt, 1977).

A survey of 208 American students showed that contact by a close friend of the opposite sex was invariably experienced as pleasant. Males and females reacted differently to contact by an unacquainted member of the opposite sex. While males

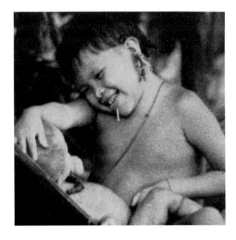

FIGURE 6.13. Affectionate display with hand contact. A small Yanomami girl lovingly lays her hand on her little sister's head. Photo: I. Eibl-Eibesfeldt.

FIGURE 6.14. Yanomami girl friends walking arm around shoulder. Photo: I. Eibl-Eibesfeldt.

434

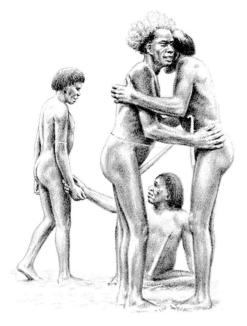

FIGURE 6.15. (A, *top*) Ritualized forms of tactile communication. Dugum Dani (Papua/western New Guinea) greeting one another. Drawing: H. Kacher after films by R. Gardner in I. Eibl-Eibesfeldt (1970a, 1971c). (B *bottom*) Another ritualized form of tactile communication is the priestly laying on of hands. Drawing: H. Kacher after press photos in I. Eibl-Eibesfeldt (1970a, 1971c).

A

B

felt such contact was pleasant, females experienced it as unpleasant and importunate. Thus for them, the significance of contact is primarily determined by the degree of acquaintance with the individual making contact, while in males the sex of the contact initiator is the criterion for the subjective experience (R. Heslin, T. D. Nguyen and M. L. Nguyen, 1983; Fig. 6.16).

The taboo zones are clear from the drawings. Even in the behavior of fathers and mothers toward their children, different taboo zones (varying with the child's sex) are observed. This also varies from culture to culture (K. Sugawara, 1984). In our culture, contact with the genital region of children is only permitted during body care episodes. However, Yanomami mothers and fathers stroke and kiss

435

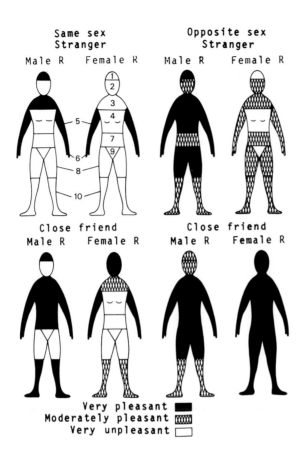

Same sex
Stranger
Male R   Female R

Opposite sex
Stranger
Male R   Female R

Close friend
Male R   Female R

Close friend
Male R   Female R

Very pleasant ■
Moderately pleasant ▨
Very unpleasant ☐

FIGURE 6.16.
Classification of contact on various body parts by acquaintances and strangers of the same and opposite sex, related to the degree of pleasure experienced by the person being touched. Test subjects consisted of 208 American students. From R. Heslin, T. D. Nguyen, and M. L. Nguyen, 1983.

lick the genital region of their children, including that of children of the opposite sex (I. Eibl-Eibesfeldt, 1976).

In certain contexts, touching with the hand also facilitates contact readiness with an unacquainted conversation partner. In a field study by M. Goldman and J. Fordyce (1983), 81 women and 79 men were interviewed by an assistant. One of the interviewer's tasks consisted of determining the effect of frequency of eye and physical contact and a combination of both on the subject's readiness to render aid. After the interview, the interviewer dropped his folder and recorded which subjects assisted picking it up. The study demonstrated that eye contact and physical contact individually increased the subject's readiness to render assistance, but not a combination of the two. Apparently, in this situation the combination was perceived as obtrusive.

Social body care (grooming) is one of the most deeply rooted bonding rituals (Fig. 6.17). A study by Wulf Schiefenhövel (in preparation) showed that females particularly demonstrate a strong inclination to groom their partners' head hair and attend to their faces and bodies for skin blemishes. Social grooming also plays a significant role in the nonhuman primates in terms of bonding members of the group. This can also be found in human groups; for example, the Eipo express particular affection when greeting, by stroking the partner beneath the chin and making some ruffling movements there. Mangat from Malingdam, whom W. Schievenhövel had treated medically greeted him this way. I saw Yanomami and Trobriand Island mothers and fathers affectionately chucking their children's chins (see Fig. 7.33). This kind of scratching has been cited in medieval German literature in the Gudrun epic (cited in L. Röhrig 1967, p. 35).

In kin-based societies, social grooming often precedes sexual foreplay. Social grooming can be done with the hand or with the mouth (biting, tender nibbling, licking), and behavior patterns of affectionate contact grooming are derived from these behaviors.

Social grooming in public is subject to various cultural taboos. In the Eipo only those of the same sex delouse one another in public, while in the Yanomami and San Bushmen, delousing between adults of the opposite sex is also observed, but only when the individuals are intimately acquainted (I. Eibl-Eibesfeldt, 1976). In general, physical contact with group members of the opposite sex is avoided if such individuals are not intimate with each other, e.g., engaged to be married, spouses, children or people in which there is such a great difference in age that no sexual contact would be expected. This contact avoidance probably developed for the sake of maintaining group harmony. Physical contact could too easily entail extramarital sexual relations. Other avoidance taboos may have a similar origin (K. Sugawara, 1984).

Oral forms of affection include kissing and sucking, the former being a maternal caring behavior pattern (kiss-feeding, p. 140) and the latter an infantilism. Both are important in humans in sexual foreplay, where tactile stimuli are among the most powerful bonding signals which finally result in sexual orgasm.

6.3. Visual Communication

Sight and hearing are the main human senses. Visual signals play a significant role in interpersonal communication. We react to physical characteristics of an individual, respond to his demeanor and his gestures, and note his bearing and clothing.

Some physical characteristics probably function as releasers (structures developed for signal purposes), as, for example, chubby cheeks (p. 62). Our perceptions are adapted unilaterally to other infantile characteristics: the bodily proportions of small children were presumably not developed as signals, but they have become significant in the observer's perception and we respond to them in

a   b

FIGURE 6.17. (a) Mutual delousing fosters friendly relationships, but the rules vary in different cultures. In the Eipo (western New Guinea) only those of the same sex delouse one another in public, as seen here in a group of men; (b) in the Tasaday (Mindanao/Philippines), men and women delouse one another publicly. Photo: I. Eibl-Eibesfeldt.

437

a specific way. The same holds true for sexual characteristics. While the female breast is undoubtedly a sexual releaser (p. 251), other characteristics may not have been developed as releasers but still have such an effect on one's sexual partner. If that is the case, sexual selection could emphasize those traits and thus shape them into releasers. Indeed, such a process may have occurred in the distribution of subcutaneous fat in the female body (as it influenced body contours), and for shoulder emphasis in males. We can also presume that the prominent hair distribution pattern in humans has a releaser function.

Man clothes, paints, and decorates himself with tatoos and all kinds of adornments. These artificial displays fulfill a series of functions. Some of them emphasize secondary sexual characteristics (see shoulder emphasis, p. 64). They bond and direct attention with their coloration pattern, braids, buttons, and other attention-seizing and -guiding structures. Adornment (jewelry) and clothes also indicate group and class membership and serve to delineate individual groups from others. Thus clothing fulfills communicative functions in addition to the biological one as a means of protection against the elements; one can speak of the ethology of clothing. Otto Koenig (1970) addressed these issues in his cultural ethology.

6.3.1. Expressive Movements

Expressive movements are behavior patterns that have undergone distinctive differentiation in the service of signaling. In animals they generally have developed during the course of evolution; in humans cultural acquisition also played a role.

Any behavioral pattern can develop into a signal during the course of evolution; it simply needs to accompany some specific arousal condition regularly, so that others can recognize the specific mood and thus behavioral intentions of his partner. These can be purely secondary phenomena of an arousal state (trembling, blushing, going pale, etc.) or behavior patterns fulfilling individual functions. Parental care behavior is primarily friendly. This provided a starting point to develop group bonding through selection and ritualization of feeding behavior (p. 169). Aggressive behavioral patterns (biting, hitting, jumping at) are primarily understood as dangerous and various manifestations of these are well suited to signal, to warn, and to ward off potential enemies. Many expressive motions are derived from intention movements of locomotion (A. Daanje, 1950).

Sticking out the tongue as a gesture of rejection is derived from refusal to take food (Fig. 6.18). Small children and mammals when refusing food do so by making a spitting movement with the mouth, often sticking out the tongue while doing so. But they can also reject food before putting it into the mouth by sticking out the tongue and pushing the food away, sometimes without even touching the offered food at all. Sticking out one's tongue, which is derived from this behavior, should not be confused with tongue flicking, which is a friendly signal of contact readiness. This latter behavior derives from licking and is an important behavior in heterosexual flirtations.

Women utilize tongue flicking at a distance to indicate contact readiness. But most frequently it is a completely unconscious expression of female heterosexual readiness. In this case, the tongue is only slightly protruded and is laid laterally against the upper lip. The tongue is often used to lick the upper lip as well. The behavior may be restricted to a single brief, intentional licking movement, although sometimes the movement of tongue protrusion and licking is emphasized and repeated (Figs. 6.19–6.24).

The distancing function of sticking out one's tongue has been experimentally

438

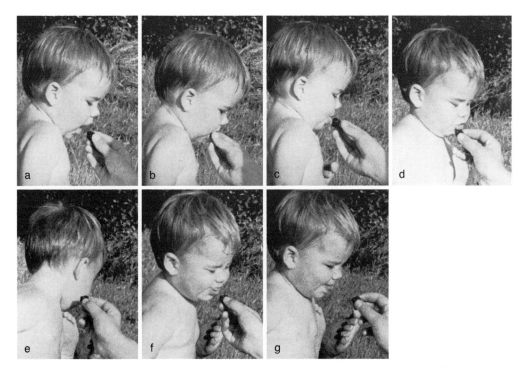

FIGURE 6.18. Tongue movements as signs of rejection. A German girl approximately 1 year old is offered a blackberry. She tastes it but then rejects it and pushes it away with her tongue (a–c). When the blackberry is offered to her a second time, she turns away, and when she sees the blackberry again with her head turned she rejectingly sticks out her tongure. From 16 mm film. Photo: I. Eibl-Eibesfeldt.

verified. Persons who claimed to be deep in concentration performing some task, protruding the tongue slightly, were less likely to be disturbed with a question than those who were also deep in thought but did not extend the tongue (K. G. Dolgin and J. Sabini, 1982).

A puzzling pattern is yawning. It is highly stereotypic, occurs as a universal, and is evidently of old heritage, since all land mammals, birds, and even reptiles yawn. In some nonhuman primates and carnivores, display yawning occurs as a threat. Fish perform a jaw-stretching, which looks similar to yawning and may be its phylogenetic precursor. Surprisingly enough, we do not know the primary function. In man it is contageous. If one person yawns, this pattern is repeated by others. It may well be a signal serving the synchronization of the activity of group members (R. R. Provine, 1986).

In the course of ritualization of behavioral patterns into signals a number of changes typically occur that assist making the signal prominent, unequivocal, and unmistakable (details in I. Eibl-Eibesfeldt, 1987). The most important changes with reference to ritualization are:

1. The movements are simplified and often repeated rhythmically. The amplitude is exaggerated. Orientation components are often modified.

2. In general, ritualized expressive behavior varies in intensity, from intention movements indicating what someone is about to do, to fully executed behavioral sequences. Intermediate stages provide the partner with additional information

439

FIGURE 6.19. The aggressive tongue display is derived from pushing away with the tongue and spitting. The tongue is either protruded as a sharp point and held so for a longer period of time or bent downward, as is shown by this series of photographs (see also Fig. 4.62). A seated Yanomami boy (Serra Parima) on the left threatens a passerby by beating the air with the stick and displays his tongue afterward. From a 25 frames/second 16 mm film, frames 1, 59, 64, and 68 of the sequence. Photo: I. Eibl-Eibesfeldt.

by the intensity of the behavior. There are also cases in ritualized behavior in which the signal is always executed at the same intensity ("typical intensity," D. Morris, 1957), producing an unambiguous signal.

3. Hand in hand with ritualization are changes in the releasing threshold, which is generally lowered making the elicitation of the behavior more likely.

4. As behavioral patterns are differentiated into signals there is often a concomitant development of supporting organic structures. Animals develop manes that can be raised, or highly vascularized parts of the skin that can redden. In humans such functions are also fulfilled by clothing, adornments (jewelry, cosmetics), and other body decorations.

5. The motivation often (but not always) changes. Thus male sexual behavior as dominance display does not only have a new meaning but presumably also a concomitant aggressive motivation.

There are parallels in phylogenetic and cultural ritualization, for in both cases the recipient of the signal must understand with as little ambiguity as possible. This necessitates parallel adaptations through which the expressive behavior is simplified but simultaneously becomes more prominent and unequivocal. Examples of culturally developed expressive behavior include the measured step of a dignitary, the parade pace of marching soldiers, and the choreography of a ballet.

Expressive movements are reliable indicators of one's specific readiness to act. Facial expressions of quarreling children are generally sufficient for an onlooker

440

FIGURE 6.20. The friendly tongue flicking display differs from sticking out the tongue as it has a different orientation. Frequently the tongue is arched upward, touching the upper lip. It may be simply extended, but only for a short period of time, and this may be repeated and is probably derived from licking. A baby girl (Trobriand Island Kaleuna) just over 1 year old displays her tongue in response to friendly visual contact; she also makes intention movements of embrace. From a 25 frames/second 16 mm film, frames 1, 17, 37, 57, and 115 of the sequence. Photo: I. Eibl-Eibesfeldt.

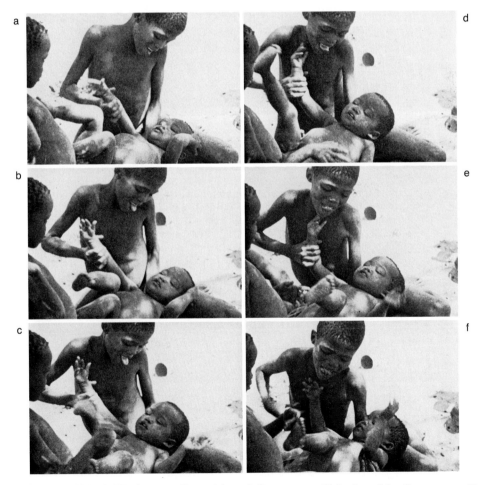

FIGURE 6.21. A !Ko boy tussling with an infant tongue flicks in a friendly manner. From a 25 frames/second 16 mm film, frames, 1, 7, 11, 15, 20, and 24 of the sequence. Photo: I. Eibl-Eibesfeldt.

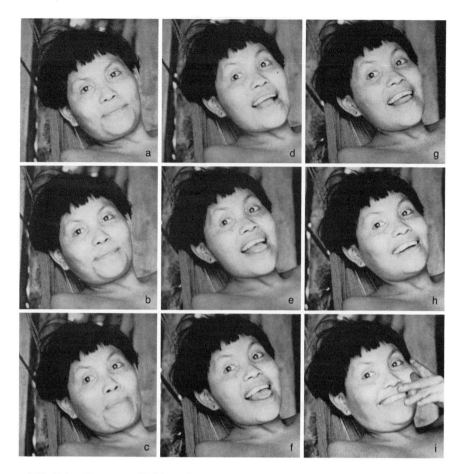

FIGURE 6.22. Friendly tongue flicking of a Yanomami woman, calling the photographer to her. Note also the brow raising. In the last photograph of the sequence she waves at the photographer, requesting glass beads. From a 25 frames/second 16 mm film, frames 1, 3, 9, 15, 18, 25, 27, 29, and 52 of the sequence. Photo: I. Eibl-Eibesfeldt.

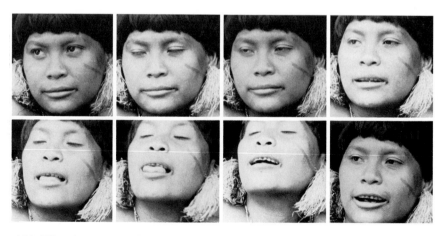

FIGURE 6.23. Flirtatious tongue flicking in a Yanomami woman. From a 50 frames/second 16 mm film. Photo: I. Eibl-Eibesfeldt.

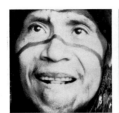

FIGURE 6.24. (A) Flirtatious tongue flicking of a Yanomami man seeking visual contact with a woman. Photo: I. Eibl-Eibesfeldt. (B) Tongue flicking in a central European woman unconsciously establishing visual contact with a man. Photo: I. Eibl-Eibesfeldt.

to determine the winner of the conflict. If one child should hold his head tilted backward with his chin raised, looking at his adversary with the inner parts of the eyebrows raised ("plus face"), he will most likely emerge as the victor in the conflict (G. Zivin, 1977a, b). In preschool children, 67% of the winners demonstrated this expression from the onset. In contrast, losers lowered the chin and eyebrows and avoided visual contact; 52% of the losers had this expression from the outset of the encounter. The "plus face" expression inhibits a rival's further activity, measured by latency periods, by a factor of two to three and is a good indicator of the outcome of a struggle until age 10. It is positively correlated with the child's social rank. Social experience changes this display in that the "plus face" eventually becomes an expression of competence. Older children will display the plus face momentarily, for example, when called upon to read, using this signal to make an appropriate impression on the other pupils. Plus and minus faces tend to disappear with age being replaced by abbreviated forms in which the chin movement alone is sustained. Instead of controlling the outcome of individual conflicts, the expression assumes the role of general competence (Fig. 6.25).

With increasing age man can decouple his expressive behavior from his emotional state, using them more freely. This gives humans more voluntary control over most expressive behavior even though the behaviors are generally activated involuntarily. This capability was one of the prerequisites for the development of verbal language.

6.3.1.1. Facial Expression. The face is one of the most important reference points in interpersonal communication. Face-to-face orientation plays a predominant role in the mother–child relationship (see above). We primarily recognize others by their faces, and one region in the cortical visual segment of the brain is especially adapted to this function (N. Geschwind, 1979). Should this portion of visual cortex be destroyed, a person no longer recognizes their friends faces, a condition called

FIGURE 6.25. The plus and minus faces.
Photo: G. Zivin.

visual physiognomic blindness or "prosopagnosia." Although the contour of a face as such is recognized, as well as other objects in the environment, individual differences cannot be discerned. Instead, others are recognized by voice. Thus, the same person who can no longer recognize their spouses and children from their faces can identify them instantly once they speak. If the brain damage is not too severe, prosopagnosics can still recognize the basic emotional expressions and can also distinguish individual faces using peripheral characteristics such as beard and hair style, but they cannot say whose face they are seeing (H. Hècaen and M. L. Albert, 1978).

In addition, our face is a means of transmitting signals. With our highly differentiated facial musculature we can move individual portions of the face, such as drawing up the corners of the mouth, creating forehead wrinkles and thus convey our concurrence, despondency, irritation, and many other emotions. This development begins in the higher nonanthropoid apes, but in humans the repertoire of facial expressions is much richer and the expressions are far more subtle.

Visual contact is exceptionally important in the early mother–child relationship. The newborn infant maintains visual contact with the mother, interacting at about 30 cm, the distance of the accommodation of the infant's eye. "Eye" language is also emphasized by the contrast between the iris and the whites of the eye. The eyeball permits us to perceive each eye movement of our partner, and we may presume that the white of the eye developed for this signal function. In chimpanzees the eyeball is typically dark, but there are chimpanzees with white eyeballs, which give a peculiarly human touch to their facial expressiveness. I would suggest that the need for signaling during hunting forays and intraspecific group fighting initiated this development.

Besides eye movements, we also perceive changes in pupillary size (E. H. Hess, 1975, 1977; see p. 255). If we perceive something that stimulates our positive interest, our pupils briefly dilate greater than the normal adaptive value corresponding to the ambient illumination. The pupils contract when we see something we reject. We have already mentioned that men react to pictures of nude women with substantial pupil dilation, while pictures of nude men evoke only mild pupil dilation in the same subjects. Women respond in the exact opposite manner. Infants also elicit substantial pupil dilation in women, but only in those male subjects who have children of their own (Fig. 6.26). Hess used identical photographs of a girl to test responses to pupillary size. He retouched the photographs so that only one depicted contracted pupils, while the others showed dilated ones. He found that the photographs with the apparently dilated pupils evoked in male subjects a greater degree of pupillary dilation than those with reduced pupils (Fig. 6.27). If subjects are told to fill in pupils in schematicized facial expressions, smaller pupils are drawn in angry faces than in happy ones (Fig. 6.28). This indicates that one can perceive friendliness or rejection from pupil size.

The region surrounding the eyes is also important in "eye language." We can narrow our eyelid opening or enlarge it and also lift the eyebrows in various ways.

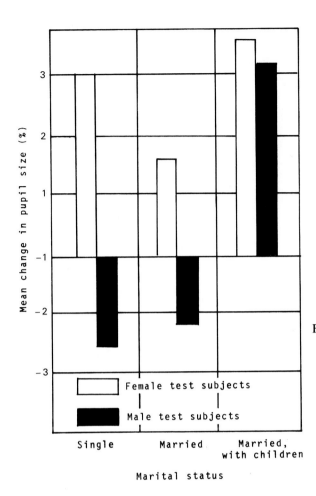

FIGURE 6.26. Changes in pupil size upon seeing a photograph of an infant. Women consistently demonstrate a greater degree of pupillary dilation, which is an indication of positively experienced perception. Men react with pupil dilation when they are married and have children. After E. H. Hess (1975).

We have previously discussed the eyebrow flash (rapid upward movement of the eyebrows) occurring in contexts of friendly encounters.

Over 100 years ago the question was asked of which facial muscles are used to coordinate individual expressions. B. Duchenne, whom Darwin (1872) often cited, painlessly stimulated with electrical pulses individual facial muscles of a test subject who had no sensory innervation in his face and then photographed the expression he obtained. However, his method was not precise enough to stimulate the more deeply lying musculature without influencing the ones above them.

C. H. Hjortsjö (1969) made a breakthrough in the study of human facial movements. He described in precise anatomical terms how the contractions of individual muscles influenced the resulting facial expression and thus laid the foundation for the further elaboration by P. Ekman and W. V. Friesen of the "Facial Action Coding System" (1975, 1976, 1978). Hjortsjö described the changes on the surface of the face (e.g., wrinkle formation, mouth positions) created by the actions of the 23 facial muscles (Fig. 6.29) and then numbered them in detail (see Table 6.1). He depicted the effects of the muscle contractions in simple sketches (Fig. 6.30), and also listed 24 facial expressions, which were organized into eight groups (A–H; see Fig. 6.31). Hjortsjö's categories were developed on the basis of various moods and conditions (angered, friendly, sad, distrustful, surprised, anxious, overbearing, disgusted); but he also uses concepts that refer to behavioral patterns (laughing, smiling). Furthermore, some entities are combined within one category

445

FIGURE 6.27. Two photographs of a woman whose pupils were retouched so that they appeared to be contracted (a) or dilated (b). Men respond with more pupillary dilation (and thus more positively) to the photograph with dilated pupils than the one with contracted pupils. From E. H. Hess (1975).

that may not belong together either on the basis of motivation or in functional terms, such as smiling and hearty laughter.

Smiling, as we will show, is an expression of friendly contact readiness and probably has its origin as a submissive expression, while laughter has an aggressive motivation (laughing at someone, p. 315). It bonds those who laugh together but is targeted toward another party (present or simply imagined). We laugh about something, usually together with others. Hjortsjö's organization should not disturb us, however, since we are not yet in a position to draw up a truly incontestable classification of facial expressions based either on motivation or, alternatively, on the basis of function. We can only do this partially. Thus a functional division

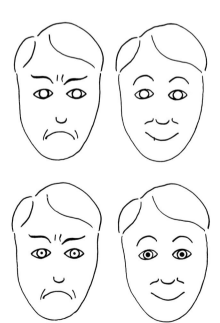

FIGURE 6.28. Test persons were given schematicized facial expressions (top) lacking pupils and asked to fill in the pupils, They completed the angered face with small pupils and the happy one with large ones. From E. H. Hess (1975).

Table 6.1. Muscle and Action Units According to Hjortsjö and Ekman[a]

Hjortsjö (1969)	Ekman[b] (Ekman and Friesen, 1976)
1 M. frontalis,[1] pars medialis	1 M. frontalis,[1] pars medialis
2 M. frontalis,[1] pars lateralis	2 M. frontalis, pars lateralis
3 M. procerus [M. depressor glabellae][2]	3 No designation
4 M. corrugator supercilii	4 M. depressor glabellae; M. depressor supercilii; M. corrugator supercilii
5 M. depressor supercilii	5 M. levator palpebrae superioris[3]
6 M. orbicularis oculi, pars orbitalis	6 M. orbicularis oculi, pars orbitalis
7 M. orbicularis oculi, pars palpebralis	7 M. orbicularis oculi, pars palpebralis
8 M. nasalis	8 For designation see note 4
9 M. levator labii superioris alaeque nasi	9 M. levator labii superioris alaeque nasi
10 M. levator labii superioris (caput infraorbitale)	10 Caput infraorbitale m. levator labii superioris
11 M. zygomaticus minor	11 M. zygomaticus minor
12 M. zygomaticus major	12 M. zygomaticus major
13 M. caninus [M. levator anguli oris]	13 M. caninus [M. levator anguli oris][2]
14 M. risorius	14 M. buccinator
15 M. triangularis [M. depressor anguli oris][2]	15 M. triangularis [M. depressor anguli oris][2]
16 M. depressor labii inferioris	16 M. depressor labii
17 M. mentalis	17 M. mentalis
18 Mm. incisivi labii superioris; Mm. incisivi labii inferioris	18 Mm. incisivi labii superioris; Mm. incisivi labii inferioris
19 Mm. incisivi labii superioris; Mm. incisivi labii inferioris	19 (no designation)
20 M. buccinator[5]	20 M. risorius
21 M. buccinator[6]	21 (no designation)
22 Pars labialis m. orbicularis oris	22 M. orbicularis oris ("Lip funneler")
23 Pars marginalis m. orbicularis oris	23 M. orbicularis oris ("Lip tightener")
	24 M. orbicularis oris ("Lip pressor")

[a][1]Venter frontalis m. occipitofrontalis.

[2]In the tables of P. Ekman and C. H. Hjortsjö and in the illustrations by J. Sobotta and H. Becher (Fig. 6. 29, A–C) the same muscles sometimes bear different names. These are in square brackets.

[3]M. levator palpebrae superioris is not innervated by N. facialis but by N. oculomotorius. Functionally it is also a mimic muscle, but not in a strictly comparative neuro-anatomical sense.

[4]In P. Ekman and W. V. Friesen (1978) designated as action unit (8 + 25, or 8 + 26, or 8 + 27) "Lips toward each other."

[5]Upper muscle fibers merge into the lower lip.

[6]Lower muscle fibers merge into the upper lip.

[b]Ekman organizes muscle actions as "action units." Several muscles may be contributing to an individual action simultaneously. He distinguishes a total of 58 units, including head and eye positions. Included in the list are both those important action units for expressions in the narrower sense and also some that will be discussed in the text later.

Ekman supplements his action units with movements that are not defined according to muscle actions, designating them as "action descriptors." A few that will be discussed subsequently include: 25 lips part; 26 jaw drop; 27 mouth stretch; 54 head down; 64 eye down.

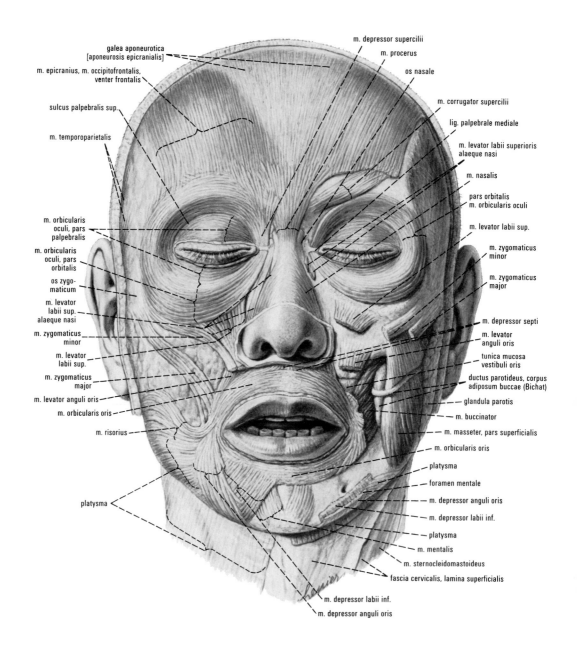

Figure 6.29. (A) The normal musculature of the Europid face, frontal view: left superficial expressive and right deeper expressive musculature (A–C) from J. Sobotta and H. Becher (1972).

448

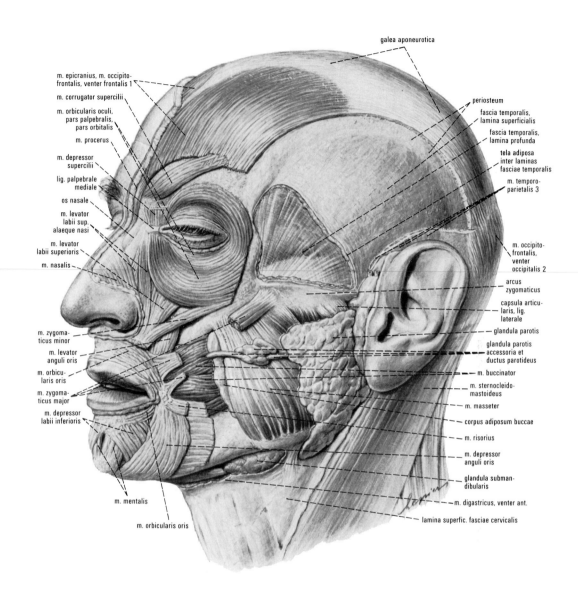

m. epicranius, m. occipitofrontalis, venter frontalis 1

m. corrugator supercilii

m. orbicularis oculi,
pars palpebralis,
pars orbitalis

m. procerus

m. depressor
supercilii

lig. palpebrale
mediale

os nasale

m. levator
labii sup.
alaeque nasi

m. levator
labii superioris

m. nasalis

m. zygoma-
ticus minor

m. levator
anguli oris

m. orbicu-
laris oris

m. zygoma-
ticus major

m. depressor
labii inferioris

m. mentalis

m. orbicularis oris

galea aponeurotica

periosteum

fascia temporalis,
lamina superficialis

fascia temporalis,
lamina profunda

tela adiposa
inter laminas
fasciae temporalis

m. temporo-
parietalis 3

m. occipito-
frontalis,
venter
occipitalis 2

arcus
zygomaticus

capsula articu-
laris, lig.
laterale

glandula parotis

glandula parotis
accessoria et
ductus parotideus

m. buccinator

m. sternocleido-
mastoideus

m. masseter

corpus adiposum buccae

m. risorius

m. depressor
anguli oris

glandula subman-
dibularis

m. digastricus, venter ant.

lamina superfic. fasciae cervicalis

FIGURE 6.29. (B) Europid face, lateral view: superficial musculature.

449

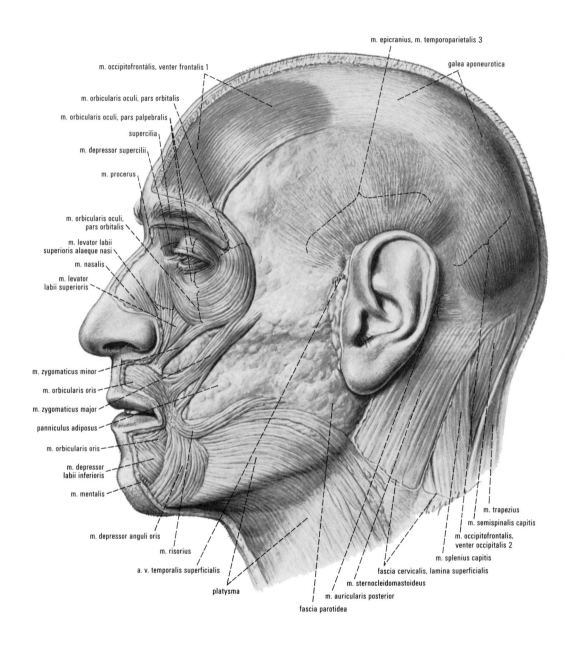

m. epicranius, m. temporoparietalis 3

galea aponeurotica

m. occipitofrontális, venter frontalis 1

m. orbicularis oculi, pars orbitalis

m. orbicularis oculi, pars palpebralis

supercilia

m. depressor supercilii

m. procerus

m. orbicularis oculi,
pars orbitalis

m. levator labii
superioris alaeque nasi

m. nasalis

m. levator
labii superioris

m. zygomaticus minor

m. orbicularis oris

m. zygomaticus major

panniculus adiposus

m. orbicularis oris

m. depressor
labii inferioris

m. mentalis

m. depressor anguli oris

m. risorius

a. v. temporalis superficialis

platysma

fascia parotidea

m. auricularis posterior

m. sternocleidomastoideus

fascia cervicalis, lamina superficialis

m. splenius capitis

m. occipitofrontalis,
venter occipitalis 2

m. semispinalis capitis

m. trapezius

FIGURE 6.29. (C) Europid face, lateral view: deeper musculature.

450

of expressions would include laughter in the repertoire of aggressive (laughing at) as well as bonding behavioral patterns: it unites the aggressions of those laughing together. Thus any categorization on the basis of motivation and function would not always coincide.

The description of the behavior by classifying the specific muscle contractions is a decisive step forward. Hjortsjö asked subjects to produce various expressions after they had read his list of 24 expressions. He photographed the expressions made by his subjects and found a good correlation between their expressions and their assessment of the photographs. He then determined which muscles were responsible for the individual expressions and recorded the information in his sketches, which are reproduced here.

In formulating the "Facial Action Coding System (FACS)" P. Ekman and W. V. Friesen, (1975, 1978) learned to voluntarily contract individual facial muscles, with the sole exception of the Musculus tarsalis, which has the same effect as the M. palpebrae. If they were in doubt as to which muscle they were contracting, they had a neuroanatomist place needles within their facial musculature to monitor muscle activity. After a careful period of training they were able to diagnose muscle movements from facial wrinkles and other superficial changes of the face alone.

Ekman and Friesen described the actions of single or groups of muscles as facial action units, numbering them accordingly. Their figures generally are in agreement with those of Hjortsjö, since most actions are attributable to individual muscles. However, there are deviations wherever several muscles are used to produce a single action and in which their individual contributions cannot be isolated. Thus Ekman and Friesen combine the actions of three individual muscles in their facial action unit No. **4,** while they leave place number 3 in Hjortsjö's list unoccupied in case their facial action unit **4** need be further differentiated.

Ekman's model is useful for describing facial motions, but a number of Ekman's action units are not sufficiently differentiated. The category "tongue out," for example, does not describe a uniform behavior. Here we must distinguish the rapid movement of the tongue in and out in a presumably ritualized licking movement, from an extension of the tongue derived from a spitting motion (p. 438). The temporal course of the movement is also very important (as Ekman recently noted)—it is not enough to simply state that a muscle contracts. Action unit **1 + 2** is both a rapid and a slow eyebrow raising movement, each of which has a different meaning.

We will delve into the expressive movements of the eyebrows in more detail since one can use them to illustrate the various problems of expressive behavior. Eyebrow movements play a major role in interpersonal communication in a variety of contexts. According to Ekman, the following action units contribute to eyebrow movements:

1   The medial portion of the *Frontalis,* whose contraction raises the inner part of the brows. The skin in the middle is drawn upward.
2   The lateral portion of the *Frontalis* raises the outer parts of the eyebrows, whereby both sides of the forehead are also lifted and form wrinkles.
4   *Musculus corrugator, M. depressor glabellae,* and *M. depressor supercilii* pull the eyebrows down as an action unit, toward the middle of the face so that the skin between the brows is compressed and thus wrinkles are formed.

The action units can appear in various combinations, resulting in a total of   451

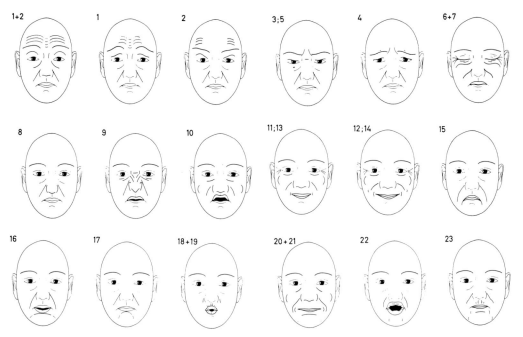

FIGURE 6.30. Schematic of the effect of contractions of various facial muscles, after C. H. Hjortsjö (1969): 1 + 2: m. frontalis; 1: m. frontalis, pars medialis; 2: m. frontalis, pars lateralis; 3: m. procerus or m. depressor glabellae; 5: m. depressor supercilii; 4: m. corrugator supercilii; 6 + 7: m. orbicularis oculi; 6: m.o.o. pars orbitalis; 7: m.o.o. pars palpebralis; 8: m. nasalis; 9: m. levator labii superioris alaeque nasi; 10: m. levator labii superioris; 11: m. zygomaticus minor; 13: m. caninus; 12: m. zygomaticus major; 14: m. risorius; 15: m. triangularis; 16: m. depressor labii inferioris; 17: m. mentalis; 18 + 19: mm. incisivi labii superioris et inferioris; 20 + 21: m. buccinator; 22: m. orbicularis pars labialis; 23: m. orbicularis pars marginalis.

seven different possible expressions (Fig. 6.32). They are elements of specific emotions.[1]

Sadness is expressed by action unit **1** as well as the combination of **1 + 4.**

Surprise and *interest* are expressed by **1 + 2.**

Fear is expressed by the combination **1 + 2 + 4.**

Anger is expressed by **4.**

The combination **2 + 4,** according to Ekman, has no part in emotional expression, but I have observed it as an expression of incensed anger in Kabuki actors. And Ekman states that he is acquainted with this expression as an artistic but not as a natural one.

As the accompanying survey shows, eyebrow raising (**1 + 2**) appears in either a rapid or a slow time sequence. We described the rapid eyebrow movement as the "eyebrow flash" (p. 118 and Figs. 6.33, 6.34), and is an expression of social contact readiness seen in every culture we have observed. It follows visual contact

---

[1]One can realistically speak of emotions or mood-related behavior in humans since we can describe the subjective sides of human experience. These subjective concepts, as in animal ethology, are also correlated with objectively determinable behavioral tendencies, for which expressions act as indicators.

and is embedded within a typical sequence of behavioral patterns. Upon establishing visual contact the head is usually lifted a bit, and the eyebrows are then raised for approximately ⅓ second, while a smile simultaneously spreads; as a concluding gesture the person often nods the head. The accompanying scheme describes the various expressive functions of eyebrow raising:

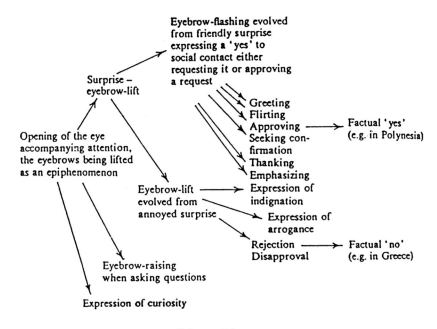

Scheme 6.1

I have observed this behavior in mother–child interactions in every culture I visited; I also saw it throughout the world in situations of friendly contact establishment. However, cultural differences do exist. Samoans and many other Polynesians, many Papuans, and the Yanomami Indians greet strangers in a friendly context with a rapid eyebrow movement, while such behavior between adults in Japan is considered to be unseemly, although children may be greeted in this manner. In Europe and the United States some prior friendly relationship must already exist for this behavior to be used, and it does not generally appear when strangers are greeted. This is probably also the reason that P. Ekman (1979) could not activate this behavior in Americans. I have frequently observed the eyebrow flash in daily American life; Ekman merely needs to watch television shows in his country to see how widespread the eye greeting is in the United States. The eponymous hero of "Magnum" displays this behavior twice during the show's introduction. In our western culture the eyebrow flash is also observed between strangers making heterosexual contact.

The origin of rapid brow raising is probably a ritualized expression of friendly recognition. It occurs in situations of congenial affection, as in thanking, consenting, flirting, greeting, agreeing, surprise, and encouraging, and thus has a broad spectrum of meanings but always within the context of contact readiness and expressing some kind of assent. It occurs also accompanying speech in a figurative

453

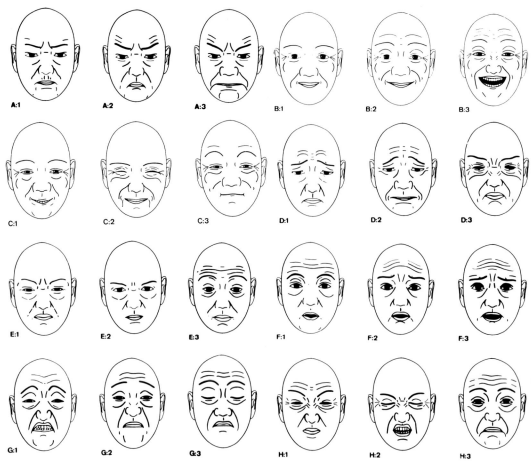

FIGURE 6.31. A-H Schematic representation of important facial expressions after C. H. Hjortsjö (1969): the numbers refer to the contracted muscles (see table). Muscles in parentheses are only indirectly or occasionally involved in creating the expression. A1: precise, resolute, firm, severe (2), 3, 5, (16), (17), (20 + 21), 23; A2: stern, angry: 2, 3, 5, 15, 16, 17, (20 + 21), 23; A3: furious, incensed: 2, 3, 5, 15, 16, 17, (20 + 21), 23; B1: mild, smiling, friendly: (60), 7, 11, 13, (20 + 21); B2: happy: (1), (2), 11, 12, 13, 14, (20 + 21); B3: hearty laughter: 1, 2, 6 + 7, 9, 11, 12, 13, 14, 20 + 21; C1: ingratiating smile: 6 + 7, 11, 12, 13, 14, 16, 23; C2: cunning, craftly, slyly smiling: 6 + 7, 11, 12, 13, (20 + 21), (23); C3: self-satisfied smile: (1 + 2), (6), 7, 11, 12, 13, 14, 20 + 21, 23; D1: sad, worried, grieved: 1, 4, (7), 15, 17; D2: mournful, almost in tears: 1, 4, (7), 15, 17, 20 + 21; D3: physically hurt tormented: 3, 5, 6 + 7, 9, 18 + 19, 22 + 23; E1: suspicious, "Is that really so?": 3, 5, 7, (15), 17: E2: observing, enquiring, examining: 3, 5, (18 + 19), 23: E3: perplexed, "What shall I do?": 1 + 2, 17; F1: surprised: 1 + 2, 18 + 19, 22; F2: frightened: 1 + 2, 4, 18 + 19; F3: panic-stricken, anguished: 1 + 2, 4, (11), 18 + 19, 22; G1: superior scornful, ironic: 1, 7, (9), 10, 15, 17; G2: contemptuous, condescending, supercilious: 1, 7, (9), 10, 15, 17; G3: arrogant, self satisfied, self-sufficient: 1 + 2, 7, 10, 15; H1: disgusted "It smells bad!": 1 + 2, 6 + 7, 8, 9, 17, 18 + 19, 22 + 23; H2: nauseated, "It tastes bad!": 3, 5, 6 + 7, 8, 9, 10, 16, 22 + 23; H3: bitter, woeful, disappointed: 1 + 2, 7, (9), 11, 15, 17.

454

sense as an expressive movement of affirmation. But rapid eyebrow raising as an expression of a factual *"yes"* occurs only in a few cultures, while as a greeting it occurs universally with cultural modifications concerning one's readiness to execute it. In the Japanese, the eyebrow flash seems restricted to interactions with children. Rapid eyebrow raising is distinguished from a slower raising of the eyebrows, which is an expression of rejection and provocation.

The universality, based on the movement pattern and contextual aspects of the eyebrow flash, suggests that it is an innate expressive movement. P. Ekman (1979) contends that if this were so, one would have to observe the signal in other primates as well. However there is no evidence of eyebrow raising as a sign of affection in these animals. Ekman, though, equates "phylogenetic adaptation" with "animal inheritance,"[2] but as we have shown before, that is an erroneous connection, for many innate human characteristics are species specific.

Ekman adds that one can only speak of a phylogenetically evolved communication signal when no other biological function can be demonstrated. But as we have seen earlier, many communication signals are derived from functional movements such as kissing. I hypothesize that the eyebrow flash has its origin in the functional movement of opening one's eyes to see better. It is definitely, though, a derived, ritualized movement, stereotyped in its initiation and cessation and thus marked as a behavioral unit. It is also quite different from opening the eyes as in looking at objects with curiosity. Context, specificity, and uniformity of the behavior across cultures all speak against a purely cultural origin.

There is also an emphatic "opening" of the face as a sign of affection and acceptance, in which all the sensory orifices are extended in an accentuated manner for a longer interval (Figs. 6.35, 6.36). The closing of these orifices, on the other hand, signifies refusal (Fig. 6.37).

A slow eyebrow raising without any further accompanying gestures specifying the expression signifies attention. The visual field is expanded by raising the brows and this probably leads to eyebrow raising in contexts of curiosity, surprise, and inquiry. In all these cases one wishes to improve one's vision, either physically or in a figurative sense of experiencing more. Supplementary cues help to determine the individual significance of the behavior, for example, expectantly fixed visual contact, hesitation, holding the breath and opening the mouth in surprise, and the back and forth movement of the head and eye movements in curiosity.

Finally there is the slow eyebrow raising as an expression of indignation, arrogance, social rejection, and factual "NO." Again, supplementary cues also specify these expressions. Thus the brow movement can be accompanied by a threat stare (indignation) or shutting of the eyes (contact avoidance and thus an expression of rejection, arrogance—No!). In more intense expressions of rejection, the head may be tilted to the rear somewhat (expression of haughtiness or snootiness), and the hand may be lifted up in a rejecting manner as well. Although the slow eyebrow raising is a universal gesture of provocation and social rejection, as a factual "NO" it is restricted to some Mediterranean peoples such as the Greeks (Fig. 6.38).

If somebody behaves badly or outside of expected norms, one says, "That will raise a lot of eyebrows." Slow eyebrow raising is also derived from the expression of surprise. One is surprised and provoked by bad behavior or unreasonable de-

---

[2]"Ritualization presumes that selection of actions for their role as signals occurred through phylogenetic evolution. The implication is that these signals can be traced to other primates."

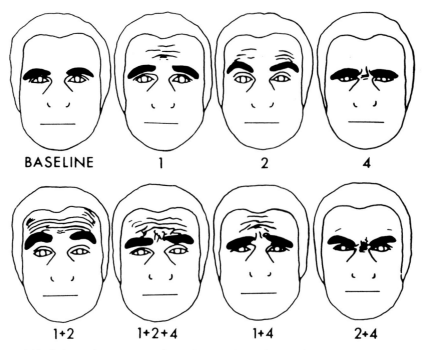

FIGURE 6.32. Schematic representation of the action units for the forehead and eyebrows in their various combinations (after P. Ekman, 1979). See text for details.

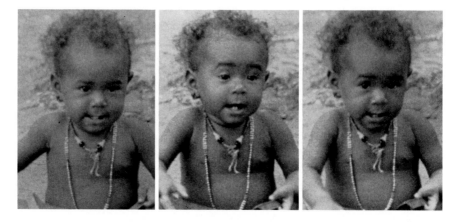

FIGURE 6.33. Female infant (16 months old) from Kaleuna (Trobriand Islands) expressing her contact readiness by raising the eyebrows. From a 25 frames/second 16 mm film, frames 1, 9, and 11 of the sequence. Photo: I. Eibl-Eibesfeldt. A similar sequence of photography documenting eyebrow raising as a friendly signal from a small Bay-aka Pygmie boy was published by A. Heymer (1981).

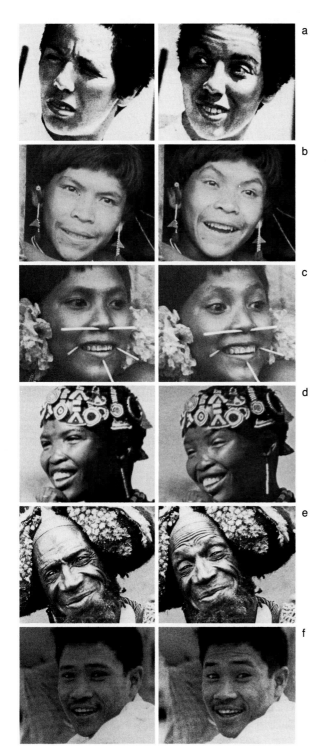

FIGURE 6.34. Examples of the "eyebrow flash": (a) French woman; (b) and (c): Yanomami man (b) and young woman (c); (d) !Kung woman (central Kalahari); (e) Huli (Papua-New Guinea); (f) Balinese. Photos: a, H. Hass; b-f, I. Eibl-Eibesfeldt.

457

FIGURE 6.35. (a) and (b) The "opening" of the face as an expression of affection: an American girl looks happily at the photographer. Photo: I. Eibl-Eibesfeldt.

FIGURE 6.36. The opening of the face as expression of affection. A Yanomami woman waves at the photographer. Photo: I. Eibl-Eibesfeldt.

FIGURE 6.37. (a) and (b) Closing the face as a sign of rejection. Yanomami man rejects visitor. One observes the wrinkling of the nose. Photo: I. Eibl-Eibesfeldt.

mands of another and responds with the threat stare, raising the brows, or refusing visual contact by closing the lids and thereby combining the raised eyebrow in antithesis.

Action unit **4** always occurs in situations characterized by doubt, perplexity or difficulty, and can appear in various contexts of this type, often in combination with other movements. Thus action unit **4** is another nonverbal cue accompanying speech as a mood indicator, and also as a special kind of punctuation mark during pauses. In questioning contexts, action unit **4** expresses doubt, and it also occurs in pauses, when one strains to find the correct word. In the listener it signifies an inquiry for further information.

Action unit **1** + **2** acts functionally to expand the visual field, while **4** protrudes the eyebrows and thus shades the eyes. When someone visually fixates on some distant object, he demonstrates this expression. Thus these are behavioral patterns that primarily also fulfill functions related to visual perception. As such, they could very well be acquired individually by learning, and this could also hold for

458

FIGURE 6.38. Rejection in a Greek man. Photo: I. Eibl-Eibesfeldt

the accompanying expressive movements derived from them. However, those born blind also display action unit **4** when they are confronted with problems and are perplexed. The expression **1** + **2** is more rarely seen in the blind, and then only when emphasizing some verbal statements and occasionally in surprise. Vertical eyebrow movements serve as an "exclamation mark of the face" (G. Grammer *et al.*, 1988) which says "attention—what I am doing is important."

In Table 6.2, taken from P. Ekman and W. V. Friesen (1978), several prototypes and variants of the most important expressive movements are listed according to action units and descriptors.

The FACS has made a significant contribution to the understanding of expressive behavior. It shows a conformity in the most important facial expressions between such disparate groups as the Fore of New Guinea and North Americans. Finally, by testing how the Fore, Japanese, North Americans, Brazilians, Chileans, and Argentinians responded to video recordings of facial expressions of members of other ethnic groups, Ekman and Friesen demonstrated remarkable congruence in their estimates. P. Ekman (1973) also critically reviewed cross-cultural investigations using photographs and often highly schematized drawings of various facial expression to study expressive behavior.

H. C. Triandis and W. W. Lambert (1958) presented photographs of a professional American actress to American and Greek students and villagers from the Greek island of Corfu; all three groups had essentially the same reactions to the photographs, but with some group differences. Thus the results for the student groups were more similar than those of the villagers, which Triandis and Lambert explained was a result of different experiences. The students had seen more television and presumably were more accustomed to the stereotyped expressions of the actress. Certainly, such experience is significant. Ekman debated their findings as well as those of C. E. Izard (1968), D. M. Cüceloglu (1970), E. C. Dickey and F. M. Knower (1941), R. Winkelmayer *et al.* (1971), and W. E. Vinacke (1949). All found evidence of universals, and four also found cultural differences in the evaluation of expressive gestures, but their results did not contradict a universal understanding of expressive behavior and universal expressions, according to Ekman's critical investigation. There was no instance in which a specific expression was ascribed to one emotion by a majority of members of one group, and then ascribed to an entirely different emotion by a majority of another group. Interpretations displayed cultural distinctions, first, in terms of the context in which the specific expressions are observed, second, in the assessment of composite of blended expressions (superimpositions) and, finally, in the accuracy of assessing expressions. Since one's reaction to a releasing stimulus situation depends upon

Table 6.2. FACS Codes for Emotional Expressions[a]

Emotion	Prototype	Possible blends
Surprise	1 + 2 + 5x + 26 1 + 2 + 5x + 27	1 + 2 + 5x 1 + 2 + 26 1 + 2 + 27 5x + 26 5x + 27
Fear	1 + 2 + 4 + 5xyz + 20xyz + 25 or 26 or 27 1 + 2 + 4 + 5xyz + 25 or 26 or 27	1 + 2 + 4 + 5xyz + L or R20xyz + 25 or 26 or 27 1 + 2 + 4 + 5xyz
Joy	6 + 12xyz 12y	
Sadness	1 + 4 + 11 + 15x optional 54 + 64 1 + 4 + 15 optional 54 + 64 6 + 15xyz optional 54 + 64	1 + 4 + 11 optional 54 + 64 1 + 4 + 15 optional 54 + 64 1 + 4 + 15x + 17 optional 54 + 64 11 + 15x optional 54 + 64 11 + 17

25 or 26 can accompany all prototypes

Emotion	Prototype	Possible blends
Disgust	9 9 + 16 + 15 + 26 9 + 17 10xyz 10xyz + 16 + 25 or 26 10 + 17	
Anger	4 + 5xyz + 7 + 10xyz + 22 + 23 + 25 or 26 4 + 5xyz + 7 + 10xyz + 23 + 25 or 26 4 + 5xyz + 7 + 23 + 25 or 26 4 + 5xyz + 7 + 17 + 23 4 + 5xyz + 7 + 17 + 24 4 + 5xyz + 7 + 23 4 + 5xyz + 7 + 24	All prototypes with optional 4,5,7 or 10

[a] x, y, and z designate different stages of the intensity of movements; z designates the maximum contraction of a muscle.

the nature and strength of the releasing stimulus, personal experience, and the prevailing mood of one's partner, it is no wonder that the same response is not always produced following an individual stimulus. The comparison of Japanese and European preschool children showed considerable agreement in response, and expressions scarcely changed between the first and fifth years, which indicates that these are behavioral programs for whose development experience plays a lesser role, quite unlike the situation for body postures and gesticulation, in which cultural differences can be seen (T. Sano, 1983).

We have conducted cross-cultural comparisons in great depth, especially with regard to tribal societies, and congruence exists even in very fine details of facial expression (Figs. 6.39, 6.40).

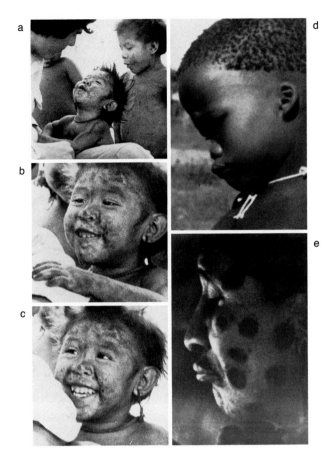

FIGURE 6.39. The lively expressions of man signals specific elemental behavioral tendencies (mood states) and needs, beyond cultural barriers and are thus applicable for all humans. (a to c) Yanomami boy seeking friendly contact with the author's son; (d) pouting !Ko girl and (e) pouting Yanomami. From 16 mm films. Photo: I. Eibl-Eibesfeldt.

It is surprising how much facial movements coincide among the various cultures and races throughout the world, in view of the fact that the differentiation of the facial musculature shows considerable racial variation. In Bantus, Australian Aborigines, Chinese, and Papuans, the muscle bundles are rather coarse and show little differentiation. The Melanesian Papuans lack the risorius muscle. In Europeans, the muscle bundles are less coarse and are clearly differentiated with a distinct zygomaticus and a small independent zygomaticus minor. The skull musculature is reduced and the orbicularis is small (E. Huber, 1931; Figs. 6.41A, 6.41B). And yet the facial expressions of the various human races are so similar that we safely understand them cross-culturally. Most human facial muscles have homologs in the anthropoid apes, with the exception of the risorius and mentalis.

Facial musculature also undergoes considerable individual variation. Figure 6.41C shows variability of the musculus risorius, triangularis, and zygomaticus.

The triangularis varies in the course of its fibers. If the lateral part is closed, the muscle is roughly triangular (a). But in many instances its muscle fibers extend to the platysma, the cheeks, and, in rare cases, all the way to the zygomatic arch (b, d). If fibers separate diagonally from the triangularis, they are called the risorius. That the risorius belongs to the triangularis can be seen from the fact that fibers from both muscles originate together from the corners of the mouth. The risorius is responsible for creating dimples ("amoris digitulo impressum"). Interestingly, fiber tracts extending from the platysma can produce transverse muscles identical in function and location, and this muscle is known as the risorius platysmatis (g,

461

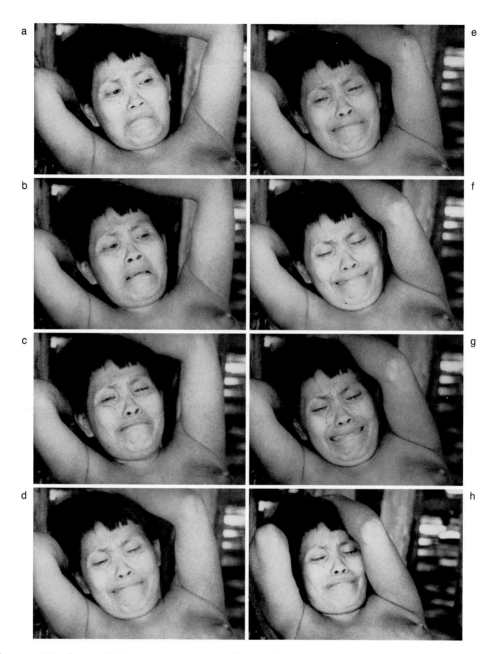

FIGURE 6.40. Sorrowful Yanomami woman. She received the report of the death of an intimate acquaintance. Emotions like joy and sorrow and the corresponding vocalizations induce empathetically a similar mood in the partner. In the case documented here, her approximately 4-month-old daughter began crying with her mother (see next page). From a 25 frames/second 16 mm film, frames 1, 9, 27, 57, 62, 87, 122, 596, 4882, 5388, 5933, and 6499 of the sequence. Photo: I. Eibl-Eibesfeldt.

FIGURE 6.40. See legend, opposite page.

h). It is generally not difficult to determine in specimens whether the muscle fibers at the corners of the mouth are superficial triangularis fibers or those of the more deeply situated platysma. In rare instances, the zygomaticus can also give rise to fibers that can occupy the same sites as the risorius. This presents an unsolved and highly interesting problem that has not yet been explored in the study of expressive behavior, for we have here an instance of a particular expression that can be produced by three different muscles.

If contractions of different facial muscles could arbitrarily be combined, it would result in a great many possible facial expressions (p. 468). But some combinations cannot occur for physical reasons. Thus one cannot open and close the mouth at the same time. This does not mean, of course, that in conflict situations antagonistic muscles cannot be simultaneously and visibly activated. Thus one can smile while at the same time theoretically masking the smile by activating other muscles. Thus, a great number of theoretically possible facial expressions exists. In practice, however, we do not see a great variety of grimaces, but only a few recurrent behavioral patterns.

In representing and investigating expressive behavior, we often conceive of individual, "pure" emotions, but these appear as such only rarely, for there are usually several emotions in operation at any given time. W. Musterle and O. E. Rossler (1986) developed a technique of hypothetically representing superimposed emotions using computer-generated pictures of facial expressions, based upon individual muscle actions to integrate various superimpositions and then to test their prevalence. K. Lorenz (1953) exemplified this in a scheme depicting the superimposition of the expressions of anger and fear in a dog (Fig. 6.42A), and this Lorenzian matrix can be extended to depict human emotional expressions. K. Grammer isolated the individual muscle movements for anger and fear, based

463

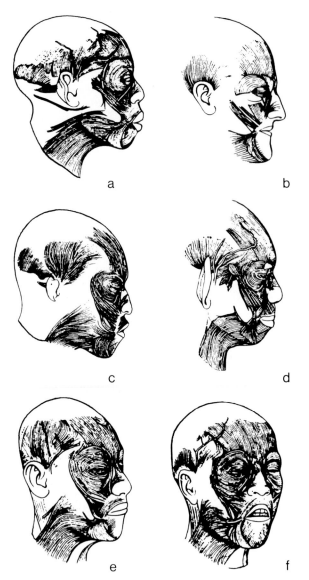

FIGURE 6.41.
(A) Differences in facial musculature arrangement in various human races: (a) Sudan Negroid: broad muscle bundles, little differentiation in face middle, well developed orbicularis; (b) Northern European: fine bundling, highly differentiated, with a distinctly ramified zygomaticus and small independent zygomaticus minor, small orbicularis; (c) Papua: coarse bundling, lack of a risorius; (d) Australid Australian, resembling (a) and (c), with a downward extended zygomaticus; (e) Polynesian (Hawaii): thick but not coarse bundling, well developed orbicularis, and a notch on the frontalis; (f) Northern Chinese: coarse bundling, strong orbitalis with a particularly powerful lower portion. After E. Huber (1931), from E. von Eickstedt (1944–1963).

FIGURE 6.41. (B) Facial musculature of modern man: (a) primitive; (b) progressive differentiation. Note in (a) the coarse and fine bundling patterns as well as the lesser degree of differentiation in the middle portion of the face. After E. Loth (1938) from E. von Eickstedt (1944–1963).

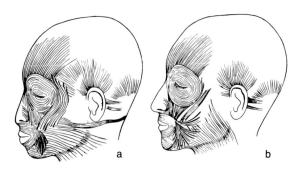

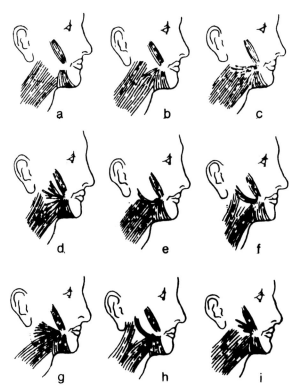

FIGURE 6.41. (C) Individual variations of the musculus risorius, triangularis, and zygomaticus. From H. Braun and C. Elze (1954).

on the work of J. van Hooff (1969, 1973). The tabulation below shows how these components can be incorporated into the FACS system using P. Ekman's numerical nomenclature (p. 447):

	Anger/threat	Fear/submission
Eyelids	Wide open (5)	Upper lid lifted (5) Lower lid tensed (7)
Eyebrows	Lowered (4)	1 + 2 + 4 (Comparable amplitude)
Eye orientation	Fixed	Diverted (slightly left or right, also turned 61 or 62)
Corners of mouth	Forward (23/24) and/or downward (15)	Withdrawn (20) normally or variable
Teeth	Lower teeth visible (possibly 16)	Variable (mouth closed)
Head movement		
Lateral	None	To the side
Vertical	None	Above or (usually) below
Head orientation		
To the body	Forward (57)	Away from the vertical
Held vertically	Below (54)	Below (55)

Thus for anger we find the actions **4 + 5 + 15 + 16 + 23** and/or **24 + 54 + 57** and for fear **1 + 2 + 4 + 5 + 7 + 20 + 55 + 61** or **62**.

If the two facial expressions are blended, without considering head and eye movements, in order of increasing intensity, the matrix shown in Figs. 6.42B and 6.42C arise.

Our perception is adapted to recognize the fixed-action patterns and their combinations and varying degrees of intensity. In addition to simultaneous superimposition, successive alternation of various expressive patterns can occur in motivational conflicts, interchanging, for instance, between movements of approach and those of withdrawal (see Figs. 4.2–4.11).

Most expressive movements vary in intensity, and there exist all the transitional stages from intentional movements to the complete execution of the fixed-action pattern.

The cross-cultural similarities of the expressive motor patterns and of their meaning indicate that many of them are phylogenetic adaptations. Thus cross-cultural studies have confirmed the findings in children deaf and blind from birth. Regarding ontogeny, J. E. Steiner (1973, 1974, 1979) found that newborns respond with typical expressions to flavors of sweet, sour, and bitter, expressions also found in adults. The infant face relaxes at the taste of sweetness, as they smile and make licking and sucking movements. Sour tastes elicit pushing forward of the lips, wrinkling of the nose, closing of the eyes, and often shaking of the head. Adults pull their cheeks between their teeth in a sort of tooth-protective reaction. Bitterness produces a lowering of the corners of the mouth, closing of the eyes, and extending of the flat tongue, a distinct reaction of disgust. The fact that children of different cultures and even acephalic children react in this manner suggest that we are dealing with innate behavior patterns. A cross-culture study of figures of speech reflecting expressions of taste (such as "embittered") would describe these responses as universals.

The oft cited works of W. LaBarre (1947)[3] and R. L. Birdwhistell (1963, 1968, 1970), who claimed there is no universal emotional language have been refuted by the data. I do consider it likely that within a certain range of variation the significance of facial expressive patterns may vary culturally, but at this time there are no quantitative studies of this area.

It was not until the end of the 1970s that even such widespread and relatively simple expressions as smiling were investigated in our culture. R. L. Birdwhistell (1970) and others maintain that smiling appears with both positive and negative emotions, but P. Ekman *et al.* (1980) showed that this kind of claim is much too undifferentiated. Ekman had subjects view one film in which an accident (work injury) was seen and another film in which a gorilla and dog appeared together in

---

[3]Smiling, indeed, I have found may almost be mapped after the fashion of any other culture trait; and laughter is, in some senses, a geographic variable. On a map of the Southwest Pacific one could perhaps even draw lines between areas of "Papuan hilarity" and others where a Dobuan, Melanesian dourness reigned. In Africa, Gorer noted that "laughter is used by the negro to express surprise, wonder, embarrassment and even discomfiture; it is not necessarily, or even often a sign of amusement; the significance given to "black laughter" is due to a mistake of supposing that similar symbols have identical meanings" (G. Gorer, *Africa Dances,* New York, 1935, p. 10). Thus it is that even if the physiological behavior be present, its cultural and emotional functions may differ. Indeed, even within the same culture, the laughter of adolescent girls and the laughter of corporation presidents can be functionally different things. . . .

a friendly context. Both films elicited various forms of smiling. The friendly one of the dog and the gorilla was accompanied by smiling utilizing contraction of the zygomaticus major (action unit **12**), and only this action is apparently a positive signal. In the film with the accident, smiling occurred via contraction of the risorius, buccinator, or zygomaticus minor muscles, although action unit **12** was not entirely lacking. It occurred in the accident film with just one-tenth the frequency of the same action unit in the gorilla film. Ekman *et al.* feel that it may be used to conceal negative feelings. This is also suggested by the fact that this smile is asymmetrical, which is also typical for fake smiling. I would like to add that the accident film also elicited fear, and fear can release appeasement along with other actions. This is shown in a field study conducted by P. Goldenthal *et al.* (1981). In one case, a research assistant stood behind a university shop counter and told those who approached to buy something that this was not his actual job, thus giving the impression that they had committed a social error in assessing his duties. In a second case, persons were placed in a situation in which they were led to feel that they were interrupting a conversation between two other persons. In both instances of social discomfort, the test subjects smiled more frequently than was found in control situations. In such contexts, it appears that smiling plays an appeasement function.

R. E. Kraut and R. E. Johnston (1979) showed that smiling is not just an expression of being in a friendly mood but is, in fact, a social signal. They recorded the behavior of people in a bowling alley. These people only smiled when they were socially engaged, such as by looking at fellow bowlers or at another who had just made a good shot, indicating that smiling is not simply an expression of happiness. Hockey fans smile during social interactions and when their team wins the game. Here a social identification occurs with the team being cheered. Beautiful weather influences our mood but does not significantly increase the prevalence of smiling, as the above workers showed in a different study examining pedestrians.

Homologies are found in chimpanzees and other nonhuman primates for a number of human facial expressions. We have already discussed this for pouting and in laughter and smiling (p. 137); we also discussed the origin of these facial expres-

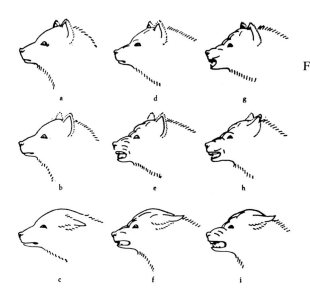

FIGURE 6.42. (A) In higher mammals, as shown here for the dog, different muscle actions corresponding to different emotions can be superimposed to produce, for example, these varying intensity levels of signals of attack and flight. From (a) to (c) increasing escape tendency; from (a) to (g) increasing aggression. (h) and (i) are superpositions—moderate escape tendency + moderate aggression tendency. From K. Lorenz (1953).

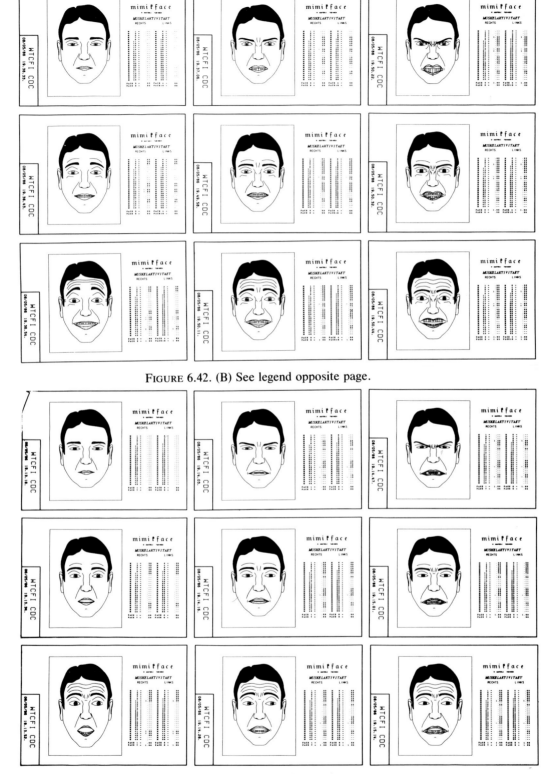

FIGURE 6.42. (B) See legend opposite page.

FIGURE 6.42. (C) See legend opposite page.

sions. S. Chevalier-Skolnikoff (1973) compiled a list of the various chimpanzee expressions which includes a number of additional ones that resemble those found in humans. Of those listed in Fig. 6.43, the following are comparable to those seen in humans:

Chimpanzee expression	Homologous human expression
a	Anger with lips pressed together
c	Anger with bared teeth (threat)
d, e, f	Smiling
g	Pouting and infantile pleading
h	Adult expression of sorrow
i	Infantile crying
k	Laughter

A. Jolly (1972) tabulated a number of important facial expressions of various primates, which are reproduced in *Ethology: The Biology of Behavior* (Eibl-Eibesfeldt 1975). Information on expressions found in nonhuman primates can be found in Redican (1975) and D. Ploog (1980).

We have already discussed a number of examples of the origin of expressive behaviors: tongue flicking from licking, sticking out one's tongue from spitting, laughter arising from the play face (biting intention), and smiling derived from showing the teeth, a defensive biting intention.

The opening and closing of the sensory orifices during pleasant and unpleasant sensory experiences, respectively, became in extended sense expressions of attraction and repulsion (see eyebrow flash, p. 457). If we do not wish to see, we close our eyes or turn away; if we perceive unpleasant odors, we hold our breath, close our nostrils, and wrinkle our nose. We often move the head in an intention movement to the side or rear, and this reaction to unpleasant visual and olfactory stimuli is also used as a gesture of arrogance. We lift the head backward in an intention movement, raising the nose somewhat relative to the eyes (a "snooty" expression). We often wrinkle the nose, close our eyes, and even exhale ("sniff at") in an exaggerated rejection of the reference person transmitting the stimuli.

Figure 6.37 shows the "anti-greeting" of a rejecting Yanomami, who closes up his face as if he wanted to stop all incoming sensory input from the despised individual. Note that he lifts his head backward. We also observe a closing of the sensory orifices when someone perceives a foul odor (Figs. 6.44, 6.45).

◁——————————————————————————————

FIGURE 6.42. (B) Result of computer-generated superimposition of anger-surprise and fear on the basis of the Lorenzian matrix. Increasing fear from (a) to (c); increasing anger from (a) to (g). (e), (f), (h), and (i) represent superimpositions. They result in the expression (i) of terror. We can formulate hypotheses on the composition of a specific expression using computer simulations like these. From W. Musterle and O. E. Rossler (1986). (C) Simple superimpositions of expressions of attraction (upward movements) and rejection (downward movements) using the same methods as in Fig. 6.42B. Increasing attraction from top to bottom, increasing rejection from left to right. The resulting expression (i) occurs in specific situations of social uncertainty (anxiety). One can thus presume that in situations in which this expression is shown, attraction and rejection are being superimposed simultaneously. From W. Musterle and O. E. Rossler (1986).

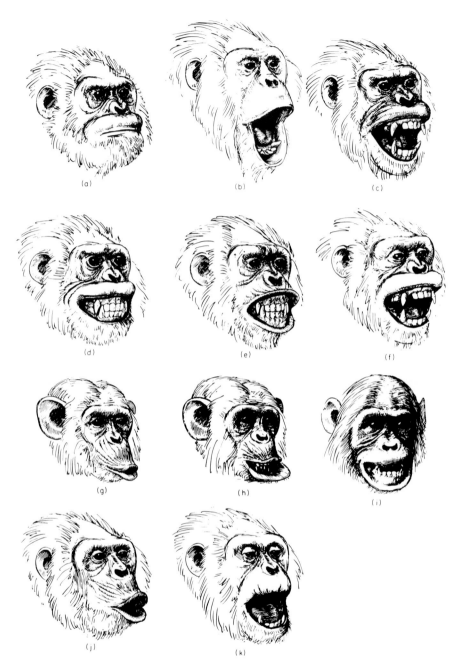

FIGURE 6.43. Chimpanzee facial expressions: (a) "Glare"; anger, type 1; (b) "waa bark": anger, type 2; (c) "scream calls": fear-anger; (d) silent bared-teeth": "type 1, horizontal bared-teeth": submission, (e) "silent bared-teeth": "type 2, vertical bared-teeth": fear-affection (?); (f) "silent bared-teeth": "type 3, open-mouth bared-teeth": affection; (g) "pout face": desiring-frustration (?); (h) "whimper face": frustration-sadness (?), type 1 or type 1-2 transition (infant); (i) "cry face": frustration-sadness, type 2 (infant); (j) "hoot face": excitement-affection (?); (k) "play face": playfulness. From Chevalier-Skolnikoff (1973).

Numerous variants of the gesture of "NO" are observed (Figs. 4.46, 4.47). In the Ayoreo, nose wrinkling accompanies a verbal factual "NO;" it can also stand for a NO without any verbal utterance. Thus the Ayoreo communicate the sense of NO just as we do when we shake our head, an example of culturally differentiated usage of a universal behavioral pattern. As already stated, this rejecting gesture of the Ayoreo occurs all over the world when undesired stimuli are perceived. But it is due to cultural conventions that the gesture explicitly becomes an expression for saying NO. The Greek gesture of NO is also derived from a universal rejecting gesture, but in terms of specifically meaning NO it is used only by Mediterranean peoples and those of Asia Minor. I thought our head-shaking signaling NO to have been derived from the movement of shaking something off. However, film analysis of movements signaling NO in different intensities in the Eipo revealed all gradations from a slow sideways turning of the head to a repeated turning away which changed into a head shake. This conforms more with the interpretation given by Charles Darwin, who thought that our headshake derived from the babies movement of refusing to take the breast after satiation. Since this type of "NO" as such has no negative social connotation, it is more suited as an expression of a factual NO than the Greek gesture. The headshake occurs throughout the world in such diverse peoples as the Bushmen (San), Eipo and other Papuans, Polynesians, Europeans, Japanese, Eskimo, Waika Indians, and many others.

Purely cultural stipulated facial expressions are comparatively rare. One example of this is winking at someone as a gesture of complicity. N. and E. A. Tinbergen (1983) discovered in England that eyelid raising in conjunction with visual contact has the special function of admonishment. The eyelids are opened more than usual and kept in that position for a longer period of time. This makes some of the white of the eye visible and brightens the eye. During this time the face is otherwise nearly expressionless. The movement is listed in Ekman's system as action unit **5,** but not with its own expressive function. I know this expression as a "punitive look" and a "threat glance" from central Europe and Bali, where I photographed the expression in 1973 (see Fig. 5.6, p. 373). I also observed the movement pattern in the Yanomami. It is perhaps more widespread than originally thought.

There are also many similarities, in principle, across the cultures. We already mentioned the phallic displays, which are performed in a variety of ways. Often, innate and culturally molded behaviors combine, such as in the surprise responses. The facial expressions of surprise are universal (Figs. 6.48, 6.49) and so are certain gestures such as the spreading and shaking of the open hands. Culturally derived patterns supplement these behaviors. Thus, surprised Eipo men, as cited earlier, tap their thumbnails against their penis sheath in rapid succession. This behavior is supposed to remove the danger by making reference to the phallus. From whomever the threat may originate, the man counters it with a threat whose roots are anchored in the primate heritage. The Eipo man also calls aloud the words, "Basam Kalye," designating the abdominal fat of a pig, which has a sacred significance. We have similar calls ("invocations") in our culture, calling, for example, Jesus and Mary and thus using sacred words as a form of protective shield. Our profane use of sacred names in swearing is probably a deteriorated form of invocation rituals. Here again, in principle, the same is expressed but in slightly different ways in different cultures. Another example is provided by the way in which the Eipo express that they are *very* happy, *very* sad, or that something tastes *very* good to them, they place both hands on the top sides of the head (Fig.

471

a

b

FIGURE 6.44. (a) and (b) A Yanomami man was given a foul-smelling acifetida sample for smelling on the back of his hand: mouth closure, lid shutting, and wrinkling of the nose follow. Photo: I. Eibl-Eibesfeldt.

6.50). At first glance, the behavior seems inexplicable and is certainly culture specific; I have found the movement in no other culture. I recognized the origin of this pattern only when I saw the same movement as a head-protective gesture in boys shooting at each other with arrows. When I learned that the Eipo verbally express an increased sensation by saying that something is "good to be feared" (it is so good as to cause you fear), its origin was clear: the head-protective movement expresses this "to be feared" notion.

We express similar superlatives related to fear and surprise. The word "terrific," which expresses an intense positive experience, is derived from the word terror. We also use superlatives such as "terribly" or "frightfully" good or sad, etc. Thus fright apparently has a particularly impressive effect by which one can describe very strong feelings (I. Eibl-Eibesfeldt, 1976).

Man can also artificially emphasize existing expressions. For example, the facial expression of anger consists of opening the corners of the mouth and drawing them downward (Fig. 6.51A). The expression can be increased by pulling downward and outward at the corners of the mouth with the fingers. In medieval paintings we find just this gesture as an expression of aggressive mocking, often combined with sticking out the tongue (Fig. 6.51B); we have previously shown a corresponding gesture used by the Trobriand Islanders (p. 383).

An interesting, recently described, expression is the presenting of the beard ("Bartweisen;" I. Eibl-Eibesfeldt and Ch. Sütterlin, 1977). Apotropaic sculptures on old churches often show bearded faces with threatening expressions (exposing

FIGURE 6.45. (A) Eipo woman (Irian Jaya/western New Guinea) rejecting something. She dislikes the odor of the toothpaste. She turns her head and wrinkles her nose. Photo: I. Eibl-Eibesfeldt.

472

FIGURE 6.45. (B) Young Eipo woman showing rejection when asked whether she would like to smell a sample of toothpaste. She turns her head away, wrinkling her nose. From 50 frames/second 16 mm film, frames 1, 12, 28, 33, 39, 43, 47, and 51 of the sequence. Photo: I. Eibl-Eibesfeldt.

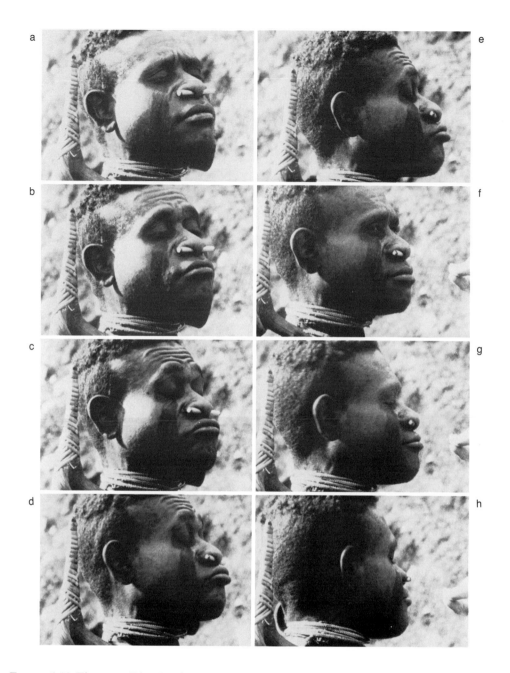

FIGURE 6.46. Eipo man (Irian Jaya/western New Guinea) rejecting a clove of garlic: eyebrow raising together with a forehead frown, closing the eyes and rejecting rearward and sideward movement of the head, and pouting. The example illustrates indignant eyebrow raising. But Yame from Malingdam, the subject of these photos, is not totally put off, for he smiles at the end of the scene. From a 50 frames/second 16 mm film, frames 1, 10, 17, 21, 29, 76, 83, and 90 of the sequence. Photo: I. Eibl-Eibesfeldt.

FIGURE 6.47. Negation by closing the eyes and wrinkling the nose in an Ayoreo man (Paraguay). (See also the verbalized expression, p. 426.) From a 50 frames/second 16 mm film, frames 1, 27, and 42 of the sequence. Photo: I. Eibl-Eibesfeldt.

teeth, showing of the tongue) and presenting the beard by pulling the ends apart with the hands, or holding the beard with one hand in a conspicuous way (Fig. 6.52A and B). Identical displays were discovered in ancestral figures of the Baule (Fig. 6.52C). R. Bilz reminded me in a letter that formerly in our culture a gesture of arrogance consisted of stroking the underside of one's beard with the back of the palms in the direction of the despised person, while the head was slightly tilted back. This gesture is frequently depicted in old cartoons. The Medlpa, when endangered, grasp the tips of the beard and pull them apart in an identical fashion as shown in the Figures 6.52A–C.

Facial expressions convey many types of messages. Most movement patterns underlying them are found universally and, as studies with children born deaf and blind confirm, are to a large extent fixed-action ones.

The extent to which signal recognition is innate remains an open question. The universally uniform recognition of expression could develop independently and could be acquired anew by each individual, since the expressive movements reliably indicate specific mood states of the individual. One argument that our understanding of expressive signals is innate is based on the fact that we also respond clearly to even highly simplified dummylike representations of facial expressions, and, in particular, to exaggerations. Furthermore, we often ascribe human qualities to specific animal facial features. The eagle appears to be "noble" because it has shaded eyes, giving the impression of fixating upon a distant object. The narrow mouth slit, drawn downward at the corners, enhances this effect. Indeed, the eagle's face is a perfect model for an expression of heroic decisiveness, making it particularly suitable as a heraldic symbol, although nothing in the eagle's behavior actually corresponds to behavior we consider to be heroic. The eagle looks the same way when it is frightened. The camel, on the other hand, appears arrogant, because its demeanor causes the nostrils to be held high relative to the eyes, although this "snooty" look has nothing to do with the animal's actual mood state at any given time. But since we reject someone by sticking our nose in air, an intention movement of withdrawing from the other partner whom we dislike, we interpret the camel's disposition as unfriendly. Other animals are responded to more positively, because they appear to be smiling. K. Lorenz has found that we even transpose this expressive scheme to facades of houses, reacting to individual homes as friendly, inviting or arrogant.

475

The studies of A. Öhman and U. Dimberg (1978) are of particular importance in this regard, since they verify in an entirely different way distinctive and apparently deeply rooted readiness to react to facial expressions in specific ways, which is in accordance with the preparedness theory of learning (M. E. T. Seligman, 1970). If facial expressions are used as the conditioned stimulus for a galvanic skin response (GSR), the conditioned response is sustained longer when the punishing stimulus (electrical shock) is delivered in conjunction with a picture of an angry face. If the punishing stimulus is paired with a picture of someone smiling, there is no sustained conditioned response. The orientation of a face is a critical cue when angry faces serve as a conditioned stimuli during aversive electrodermal conditioning. Photographs of angry faces directed toward the subjects showed significant resistance to extinction, whereas responses conditioned to faces directed away extinguished immediately after conditioning. The acquisition speed of the conditioned response did not differ for the two types of presentations. That the learning effect remained only when the face was oriented toward the subject during extinction may be explained by the fact that a person looking away is not perceived as threatening, but may even be interpreted as cut off and appeasement (U. Dimberg and A. Öhman, 1983).

Human facial expressions are controlled by the limbic system and the neocortex. When the cerebral cortex is injured there can be a loss in voluntary control over expressions, while spontaneous brain stem emotional expressions remain intact. The reverse condition can also occur: individuals with Parkinson's disease lack spontaneous emotive movements, but they can voluntarily produce expressive movements. We control our expressions by means of voluntary control over our facial movements. We can prevent others from understanding our true intentions and can even emit false signals with appropriate facial expressions: "Facial cues are faking cues," state B. M. DePaulo et al. (1980). People generally control their expressions relatively well, while body posture and mood state are generally under less voluntary control. The tone of one's voice most frequently betrays our mood (B. M. DePaulo et al., 1980). Voluntary control of expression and thus the possibility of masking expressions undoubtedly facilitates group life. However, the voluntary control of facial expression is imperfect, and it is possible to lie perfectly (P. Ekman, 1987) (p. 425). B. Pentland and T. Pitcairn et al. (1987) have shown that Parkinson's disease patients have problems in self-presentation. They are seen as cold, uncooperative, withdrawn, and unintelligent by medical personnel, despite retaining voluntary control of facial musculature and tone of voice.

The ability to recognize and emotionally respond to expressive behavior is localized in the right cerebral hemisphere. The left hemisphere contains the neuronal networks responsible for naming objects and controlling speech (p. 88).

Emotions are subjective experiences, but a self-examination of one's emotions shows that they are accompanied by specific expressive movements (muscle actions). We can even record physiological reactions typical for individual emotions. One can also collect statements from others on their subjective experiences, and if we compare the statements from members of different cultures we find that there is considerable conformity. Emotions are used metaphorically, and in literary language can be classified into distinct major categories: anger, fear, sadness, joy, surprise, and disgust are generally experienced in the same way throughout the world.

476   As far as is known, the expressive movements associated with the various emo-

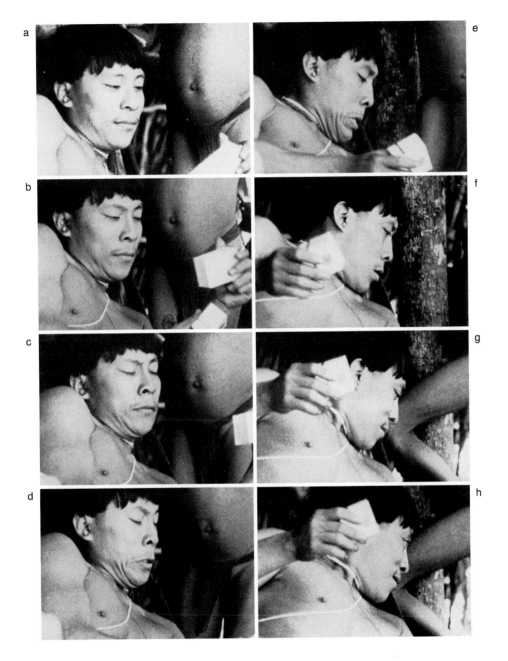

FIGURE 6.48. and 6.49. Fright reactions. Both persons were given a box from which something jumped out unexpectedly when the box was opened—a cloth snake for the girl and a grey cloth mouse for the man.

FIGURE 6.48. The reaction of the Yanomami man. From a 48 frames/second 16 mm film, frames 1, 17, 26, 32, 43, 56, 173, and 189 of the sequence. Photo: I. Eibl-Eibesfeldt.

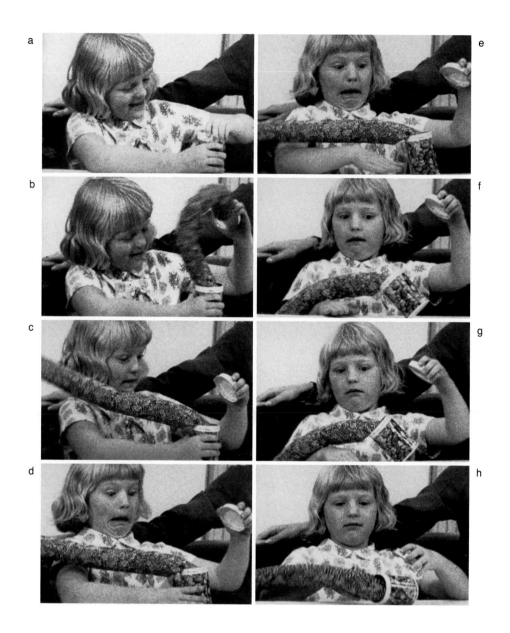

FIGURE 6.49. The fright reaction of the (German) girl. The events are strikingly similar to the episode with Yanomami (Fig. 6.48), but for the girl the sequence lasts longer. Her fright is followed by embarrassment and laughter, reactions that can also be observed in other cultures in similar situations. From a 50 frames/second 16 mm film, frames 1, 17, 34, 47, 51, 60, 68, 88, 101, 116, 136, 160, 180, 214, 223, and 245 of the sequence. Photo: I. Eibl-Eibesfeldt.

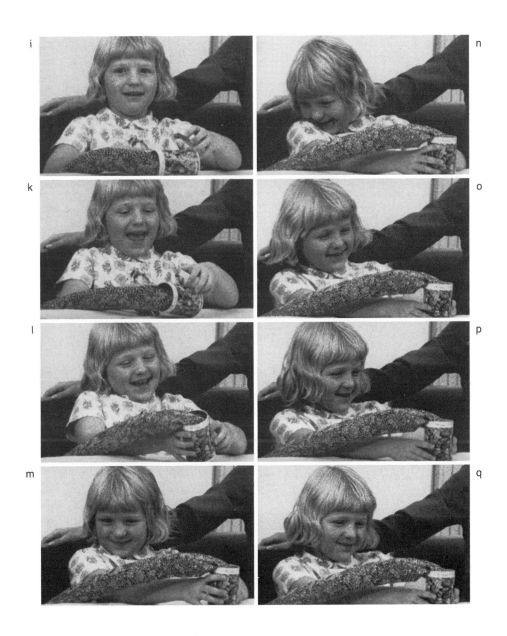

FIGURE 6.49. *Continued.*

tions are essentially identical in all cultures. The various physiological expressions of emotion and thus the emotions themselves are accompanied by emotion-specific changes in skin temperature and pulse rate. The pulse rate increases during fear, while the skin temperature drops. A joyous experience results in a moderate rise of both the pulse rate and skin temperature; both increase strongly in anger but are reduced in disgust, the former being a clear response of the sympathetic nervous system, the latter of its parasympathetic antagonist (P. Ekman *et al.,* 1983) (Fig. 6.53).

The autonomic reactions typical for specific expressions also occur when subjects are asked to stand in front of a mirror and activate their facial muscles to mimic stated emotions. Ekman *et al.* feel this demonstrates that mood changes

479

FIGURE 6.50. When Eipo wish to express that something pleases them "very" much, they lay their hands on the sides of the head as if they wanted to protect it, a notable analogy to our verbal expression of "terrific." From a 16 mm film. Photo: I. Eibl-Eibesfeldt.

occur with the execution of motor patterns. There is a flaw, however, in this particular experiment since the test subjects were able to see the expressions they made, and we know the powerful effect of seeing a smile, for example. It has long been claimed that one can change his mood by modifying behavior,[4] and one can determine from self-observation that a friendly mood can be fostered by assuming a friendly expression. But it is not yet known whether this happens by means of feedback occurring through the muscles.

Viewing happy and angry facial expressions evokes different facial electromyographic activities: zygomatic region activity increased in response to happy stimuli; corrugator region activity increased in response to angry stimuli (U. Dimberg, 1982).

6.3.1.2. Gestures, Body Postures, and Locomotor Patterns with Expressive Character. Most gestures are formed and develop culturally. Pointing with the index finger is one exception, however. We find this pointing gesture throughout the world, even in infants. There is a particular muscle, the musculus extensor indicis

---

[4]Friedrich Nietzsche claimed that one must imitate another person's body movements to understand their feelings. The conjunction of appropriate body gestures and sensitivity for the other person would result in creating a similar feeling in oneself.

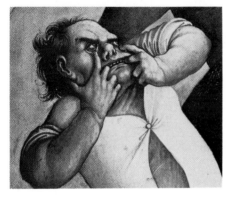

FIGURE 6.51. 1 (A, *top*) A Yanomami mockingly threatening the photographer. Note the typical features of opening the mouth and drawing down of its corners. Photo: I. Eibl-Eibesfeldt. 2 (B, *bottom*) Detail of the "Mocking of Christ" by Jörg Bräu d.Ä. (1544).

longus, used to activate this movement. Pointing gestures fill in the conversation background, depict and indicate subjects, and maintain the flow of conversation (Fig. 6.54).

D. Efron (1941) attempted to classify emotional gestures, using the term *emblem* to designate those symbolic representations for which some gesture has a specific significance. Thus one *emblem* is the outspread hands coupled with a shoulder shrug as an expression of helplessness, akin to saying "I can't help it." Admonition with the pointed index finger also belongs in this category. I have observed it among the Eipo, Bushmen, Himba, Yanomami, and the Australian Pintubi and Gidjingali. It could well be a universal gesture (Fig. 6.55). However its phylogenetic adaptation does not have to be a movement. I suspect that it is actually a phallic threat gesture that arises repeatedly in a new context due to a perceptual bias, using this existing gesture in a novel orientation in the form of finger pointing. This interpretation is supported by the observation that pointing at a person is often perceived as indecent and as an act of aggression, not only in our culture but also, for example, in the Kalahari Bushmen (I. Eibl-Eibesfeldt, 1972). Occasionally we can observe that children engage in pointing duels (Fig. 6.56). Here the gesture is aggressive—accusatively employed. Admonishing with the raised finger is also generally perceived as a threat even though it can occur also as friendly admonishing ("be careful") during a greeting episode (p. 227).

Many emblems are culturally fashioned behavioral patterns, including such behavior as the nose thumb, the vertical horn sign or tapping one's forehead, etc. Desmond Morris *et al.* (1979) summarize numerous examples of these. They show that culturally acquired traditional behavior can become as distinctive for the people in a particular region as dialects can be, often serving to delineate such populations

FIGURE 6.52. (A, *top*) Presenting the beard and tongue showing in a sculpture from the capital of a pillar in the romanesque cathedral of Freising (Bavaria). Photo: I. Eibl-Eibesfeldt.(B, *middle*), Presenting the beard and exposing the teeth in a wood carving on the choir stalls of the gothic cathedral of Ciudad Rodrigo (Spain). Photo: I Eibl-Eibesfeldt.(C, *bottom*) Two ancestral figures from the Baule, Ivory Coast of Africa. Photo: I. Eibl-Eibesfeldt.

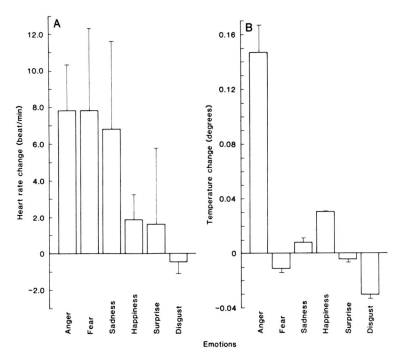

FIGURE 6.53. Changes in heart rate (A) and right finger temperature (B) during the directed facial action task. Values are mean ± standard error. From P. Ekman *et al.*, 1983).

(Fig. 6.57). In Italy the boundary between the negative gesture of head shaking and negative gesture of throwing back the head corresponds to the Greek settlement borders of ancient history, providing evidence of the conservative persistence of such patterns.

P. Ekman and W. V. Friesen (1975, 1976, 1978) and P. Ekman (1979) differentiate between body-related manipulations and illustrators. *Body manipulators* or self-adapters serve as displacement activities (T. Tinbergen, 1940). Thus, in cultures in addition to ours, one also scratches the head or bites the fingernails or lips when perplexed. Body manipulations can become expressive movements with particular functions in highly stylized configurations. For example, the Medlpa express their sympathies in mourning rites by tearing their hair.

Illustrators (gestures accompanying speech) are closely tied to the contents and flow of speech, imparting emphasis by accentuating a particular word or expression. The verbal emphasis afforded by amplitude and frequency changes is synchronized with these nonverbal cues (for example, eyebrow raising, nodding). They help segment the course of the conversation by functioning as a kind of punctuation, steering the interaction between partners by communicating when one wishes to take over the speaking role, turn it over to someone else, or maintain an existing role as speaker. A whole nomenclature was developed to characterize illustrators, such as speaker-state, continuation, and speaker-turn as signals by the speaker (S. D. Duncan, 1974). The auditor sends back-channel signals in response. Efron and Ekman developed the following distinct categories: ''batons'' accentuate words; ''underliners'' lend emphasis to phrases, sentences, or longer

483

FIGURE 6.54. Pointing is a universal gesture: (a) Eipo father and son, pointing; (b) Tboli girl (Mindanao) pointing. Photo: I. Eibl-Eibesfeldt.

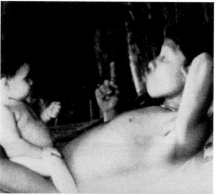

FIGURE 6.55. Threat with raised finger: (a) Australian (Gidjingali, Arnhemland); (b) Yanomami playfully scolding an infant who is sitting on his belly. Photo: Eibl-Eibesfeldt.

statements; "ideographs" point out the direction of thought; "kinetographs" depict actions; "pictographs" depict objects being discussed; "rhythmics" signify rhythmic events; "spatials" depict spatial relationships; and "deitics" indicate reference objects.

No investigations have been made on the use and function of these motions in tribal cultures. We have many photographs of dialogues between Bushmen, Eipo, Yanomami, and others that await study. However, it is possible at the present time to state that the same functional categories of movements accompanying speech in our culture also exist in these others. They seem to be employed in the same way, which may explain why the nonverbal speech accompanying gestures do not have to be learned as an additional effort in speech acquisition. We gain the knowledge of gestures automatically in the process of speech acquisition and it seems that a strong agreement exists among different cultures. The topic of emblems is an area that awaits further study.

Body postures and orientation also have a communication value. One is generally "upright" when the intention is to impress others, and those who "stand

FIGURE 6.56. "Pointing duel" of two male rival !Kung siblings. From a 16 mm film. Photo: I. Eibl-Eibesfeldt. (Film E 2720).

above others" are more "highly esteemed." Body size is equated with strength and power. Thus, men emphasize their body size in various ways: using decorative feathers, fur hats, and other head adornment. We have already discussed the emphasis of the shoulders. In accordance with the Darwinian concept of antithesis, people make themselves smaller in size by not holding the head upright but bowing it, taking off their hat, and letting the shoulders drop, and perhaps even stooping when they display submission. This is seen in all cultures, as far as is known, and these may be universal gestures, although the degree of submission expressed in behavior does vary culturally. One can bow, drop to the knees, or prostrate oneself in submission, but the principle of the behavior remains the same (Fig. 6.58–6.60).

Turning the posterior toward someone while bending is a widely used gesture,

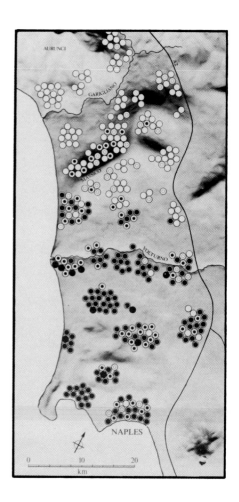

FIGURE 6.57. The map shows how the negative gesture of throwing back the head ("Sicilian No") is distributed in the region north of Naples. The regions are rather clearly delineated and conform to the northern border of the historic Greek distribution within Italy. Key: black circles = relatively frequent occurrence; circles with black centers = relatively rare; white circles = absent. From D. Morris *et al.* (1979).

that can be divided into two different forms. The first is anal presentation, an aggressive mocking gesture and the second genital display which can be an appeasing or warding off movement.

Anal threat is distinguished from female sexual presenting in a number of respects. Whereas Bushmen girls bend forward so far during sexual presenting that their genital cleft is visible, they bend less during the anal display. They often pack sand between their buttocks, releasing it when they bend forward in a clear simulation of defecation. This act has an exclusive aggressive signification (mocking, ridicule, challenge), and it occurs in diverse cultures in this context. The Eipo and the Yanomami pull their buttocks apart, revealing the anus. When possible they also release gas, another indication that this act is a ritualized defecation. Since we react to feces with disgust, the anal threat could have developed independently in various cultures as a repulsive gesture. Female sexual presenting, however, seems to be linked to older phylogenetic origins, since the behavior occurs in many nonhuman primates.

The second form, genital presenting, derived from primate female sexual presenting, has in humans (as in the other primates) an appeasement function. In nonhuman primates, female sexual presentation has been ritualized into an appeasing greeting gesture (W. Wickler, 1967a). In man it occurs as a sexual pre-

486

FIGURE 6.58. Laotian greeting. After C. Bock from I. Eibl-Eibesfeldt (1970).

FIGURE 6.59. Ife people (Yoruba) greeting their ruler. From L. Frobenius in K. Lang 1926, p. 265.

FIGURE 6.60. Fulah women greeting. From a photograph taken by Passarge published in K. Lang, 1926, p. 203.

senting gesture in various dance forms, as a humble greeting gesture (as in the Fulbe), a mocking gesture (a teasing challenge, pp. 247, 252, 317), and, finally, as a frontal genital display used on amulets (Fig. 6.61) to repel evil from the wearer. There are also a number of customs in which women display their genitals in order to ward off bad weather and other misfortunes (examples in I. Eibl-Eibesfeldt, 1970b, 1972; D. Fehling, 1974).

Displaying the breast is a feminine appeasement gesture occurring in many diverse cultures. I filmed a sudden startle reaction of Eipo women. They grasped their breasts, the lactating women squirting their milk (Fig. 6.62). H. Basedow (1906) describes how a patrol group surprised two central Australian Aborigine

487

FIGURE 6.61. Frontal gentital display: (a) sexual presenting dancer (Owa Raha, Solomon Islands). Drawing after a photo by H. Bernatzik. (b) and (c) Genital display on amulets: (b) Japanese automobile key holder. The other side (lower photo) shows a threatening face. This bringer of good fortune combines fright with sexual appeal; (c) Bavarian silver pendant.

women cooking a snake. One of the women ran away, and the other grabbed her breast in her fright, squirting milk. When later asked why she grabbed her breast, the woman said she did it to show that she was a mother and that no one should do her any harm. I have found the depiction of breast display on Balinese figures used to ward off demons, on ancestral figures in New Zealand, and on burial gifts from precolombian Ecuador and Mexico (Fig. 6.63). In addition, several European paintings portray Mary displaying her breasts before God in the role of representing humanity. Cortez reported that Montezuma sent lactating women along with his soldiers, and the women squirted milk at the Spaniards. These are probably all parallel developments based upon a common motivation.

We have already discussed the way people orient to each other with emphasis on the significance of visual contact and face-to-face orientation during conversation. A. Kendon (1977) and R. D. Deutsch (1977) showed that conversation usually occurs with the partners facing each other. When they are standing facing each other the dyad is closed, but it can be opened to a third party. If a third party is welcome, the two persons previously speaking turn away from each other, affording access to the new person. The important point here is that one cannot simply intrude on such dyads and triads—access has to be granted. Furthermore, one cannot simply leave a group, but instead at least must utilize some intention movement of going away by looking away briefly and changing the orientation so the dyad opens up. While doing so, one continues talking by bidding farewell with a few words or excuses oneself for having to leave. This is important, since an abrupt departure signifies breaking off contact or the threat of such action. This

488

FIGURE 6.62. Eipo woman grabbing and pressing her breast in fright. This display of the breast developed independently in various cultures as a protective gesture. Photo: I. Eibl-Eibesfeldt.

FIGURE 6.63. Breast display on various artifacts: (a) female ancestral figure (Maoris, New Zealand) of apotropaic character. The repulsing extended tongue and eye expressions are supplemented with the hands pointing to the breasts; (b) Balinese female guardian figure. A small platform on the head is used to hold small sacrificial offerings; (c) feminine breast display, tongue showing and repulsing eyes: precolombian pottery figure from Ecuador (Jamacoaque). Photo: I. Eibl-Eibesfeldt.

489

FIGURE 6.64. Display strutting in a Yanomami boy, who strikes himself on the chest as he strides. From a 25 frames/second 16 mm film, frames 1, 6, 10, 15, 21, 25, 29, 34, 39, 43, 49, 53, 57, 63, 69, 74, 81, 85, 91, 95, 98, 103, 107, and 166 of the scene. Photo: I. Eibl-Eibesfeldt.

FIGURE 6.65. Playfully aggressive G/wi boy (age about 1½ years) displaying before a man lying on the ground. He strikes himself on the chest with the palm of the hand and then playfully, toward the man on the ground. Anthropoid apes utilize a similar gesture of chest beating. From a 25 frames/second 16 mm film, frames 1, 8, 14, 41, 49, 59, 71, 88, 101, 106, 114, 119, 122, and 149 of the scene. Photo: I. Eibl-Eibesfeldt.

is avoided in the situation of a friendly farewell, and it is expressed clearly by the use of these supplemental parting gestures.

Walking can become ritualized into an expressive movement. High ranking individuals walk with "measured" steps, especially during ceremonial events. Various forms of parade steps demonstrate the strength and discipline of the marching troop. Even small boys will walk imposingly with their arms swinging, distinct steps, and swaying body. In some of my films they also beat their chests

491

while walking in this way, not unlike the pattern seen in anthropoid apes. Perhaps these are the rudiments of archaic display gestures (atavisms) (Figs. 6.64, 6.65).

Women have a slightly swaying gait, due to the way in which the femor joins the hips. This becomes ritualized as a flirting gait: the amplitude of the swing becomes exaggerated. In some cultures, the movement is emphasized by fashion, such as in the Himba where a long apron covers the buttocks, which sways back and forth to the rhythm of the steps. In the presence of men, Japanese women often lapse into an infantile walking style, also enforced by their narrow skirts.

Summary 6.3

Man signals group identity, rank position, and a wealth of other information visually with clothing, body decoration, and behavior. Much of the behavioral/repertoire by which emotional states and intentions to act are communicated has a long phylogenetic history. Most of our facial expressions are therefore found as universals. Basic facial expressions develop even in children who are born deaf and blind and thus deprived of the opportunity to imitate social models. For a number of expressive patterns such as the relaxed open mouth-display (play face), homologous counterparts are found in other primates. The cross-cultural similarity of some of the expressive patterns is sometimes astounding (for example, "eye-brow-flash"). Since different facial expressions can be superimposed in varying degrees of intensity, subtle and varied communication becomes possible. In addition, man's facial muscles are under voluntary control and some expressions can thus be faked. By cultural convention, special meanings can be attributed to innate expressive patterns. Thus several of the universal patterns of refusal and negation have been designated to accompany and express a factual "NO". When signaling NO, the Greek tilt their heads back, close their eyes, and often exhale. The pattern is derived from a universal expression of social rejection (haughtiness). Ayoreo say NO by wrinkling their nose and closing their eyes, a universal expression seen in persons who perceive something offensive, such as a bad smell. Our headshake developed from the movement of turning away the head in rejection. In gesturing and posturing, our cultural and the biological heritage are blended in a variety of ways. Expressive movements arise in a process of ritualization from various types of precursor behaviors, occurring regularly in specific contexts and which are indicators of specific intentions. Thus behavior patterns associated with rejection (closing the sensory openings, spitting, moving away) become ritualized into expressive movements of negation and refusal; analogously, behavior associated with attraction and reception become expressions of affirmation.

Typical changes occur as part of the ritualization of behavioral patterns into signal function. They are simplified, and at the same time exaggerated, often repeated rhythmically and visually marked with the development of supporting structures. In man this occurs in the form of cultural attributes, such as jewelry and clothing. Cultural traditions play an important role along with phylogenetically developed expressive movements. They also change via ritualization, whereby a behavior becomes a signal through a process by which the pattern becomes simplified, conspicuous, and unambiguous. The recipient's perception enforces parallel (analogous) developments for both phylogenetically and culturally evolved signals.

Pointing is a universal gesture as are hand motions that accompany speech as nonverbal cues, even though the gestures themselves are generally more culturally molded than the facial expressions. There are typical masculine and feminine body postures as well as those signaling display or submission.

6.4. Interaction Strategies—The Universal Grammar of Human Social Behavior

6.4.1. The Structure of Complex Rituals

In the chapter on methodology, we showed that human behavior can be described as a network of pathways leading to some specific objective. The same goal, for example, the formation of an alliance, can be attained using different pathways. The flow of actions leading to this goal can be broken down into components or behavioral steps which, in turn, are composed of actions such as smiling, eye closing, head tilting. Each behavioral step is defined by an intermediate goal, such as, establishing the first contact, or starting a conversation. There are intersections at which the individual has the choice between alternative behavioral steps. Thus, if a friendly appeal fails to block a pending aggression, the attacked person may resort to counterthreat, counterattack, to a cut-off, or may even appeal to a third party for help. The preferred sequences of behavioral steps are identified as strategies (p. 111). The behavioral steps which lead to the achievement of a subgoal could be termed substrategies or lower-order strategies, which, in turn, are composed of acts. Lower-order strategies can be instrumental in serving various final goals, such as a display being used to improve one's rank position, but such displays can also be utilized for short-term goals, e.g., to inhibit aggression. Finally, they can be preventative within the framework of a greeting ritual when the partner being greeted attempts to dominate the interaction.

As in the hierarchically organized behavioral sequences of animals, wherein patterns of lower levels of integration (running, swimming) serve as behavioral tools in various functional cycles, so too lower-order strategies can be employed instrumentally in a variety of ways. In the verbal realm, the asking of a question is a good example. Questions are employed in many different functional relationships, for example, in bonding rituals (documenting mutual participation) and in conflicts, in which they act to challenge the adversary.

Human rituals of social interaction are characterized by their richness of variation. This can be exemplified by the behaviors utilized to initiate a friendly interaction, which we call greeting rituals. When a Yanomami (Waika Indian) enters the village of his host who invited him there for a feast, he first performs a war dance, dressed in his finest war attire. Brandishing weapons, often aimed at the host himself, and with an apparently unapproachable demeanor, he executes an impressive display dance. However there is an appeasing ritual associated with this highly aggressive behavior: a child dances with him, waving about green palm fronds. This antithetical conjunction of display and friendly appeals can be arranged in other ways, such as when women dance with the warrior instead of children. The opposed elements of the ritual can also be arranged sequentially, in which children dance initially, followed by the displaying warriors, then by the children again, and so forth. Whatever thematic variations occur, we invariably encounter the conjunction of antithetic elements (Fig. 6.66).

When a state visit takes place in Europe, the guest is greeted with a military display and a salute is fired as part of the ceremony. This aggressive splendor, however, is combined with friendly, bonding rituals: when a child, a girl as a rule, gives the visitor flowers.

When Bavarian villagers get together for their traditional marksmans' festivals, the riflemen march in an almost military manner, but in front of them come small

a

b

FIGURE 6.66. The antithetical combination of display and appeasement in rituals of friendly greetings: (a) and (b) Yanomami warriors invited to a feast dance a round in the "'shabono'" (village) of their host. They combine their aggressive displays with a friendly appeal by means of the child: (a) small boy and (b) young girl. Both children wave green palm fronds in their hands. Photo: I. Eibl-Eibesfeldt.

children or maids of honor, usually positioned near the flag bearers (Fig. 6.67). And when two central Europeans greet each other, they shake their hands mightily as a kind of test of strength. They smile affably at the same time, nod to each other, and exchange pleasantries.

When during the mourning ceremonies of the Medlpa new guests arrive on the ritual site of the mourning community, the men of the mourning group storm at them, swinging their spears, in a kind of mock attack. But they combine this warlike greeting with a symbol of friendliness, for women run behind them waving the green cordyline shoots in their hands. Men and women surround the visitors and lead them to the mourning group (I. Eibl-Eibesfeldt, 1981a). Balinese dances during their temple festivals are introduced with a display dance (Baris) and a flower offering dance (Pendet). The former is derived from a war dance, while

FIGURE 6.67. The combination of display and appeasement is evident in this march of the guests at a Bavarian rifle meeting in which children or young women march in front of the men. Photo: K. H. Leupold.

494

FIGURE 6.68. In the Balinese greeting dance "puspa wresti" male agonal display is combined with the affiliative display of the girls. From a 16 mm Film (E 3027). Photograph: I. Eibl-Eibesfeldt.

the latter developed from a womens' dance in which sacrificial gifts are brought to the temple shrines. After these introductory rituals the legong performances and the other entertaining diversions take place. Sometimes the Pendet and the Baris dance are combined in a special greeting dance ("puspa wresti") (Fig. 6.68) (I. Eibl-Eibesfeldt, 1981b).

Superficially, these rituals may seem rather dissimilar. But the attentive reader will note that in every case display and appeasement are combined in antithesis, and they both appear to be important elements of greeting ceremonies. Their individual form can indeed vary. Behavioral patterns and verbal utterances of diverse origins can thereby appear as functional equivalents.

Naturally, there are variations in which one or the other component is more prominent. If the participants are closely acquainted, display aspects of the ceremonies are muted, and bonding elements are pronounced. However, even good friends will often slap each other firmly on their shoulders in the intense joy of seeing each other again. If high ranking members are greeted, the greeting may occur within a highly submissive context with almost no show of display on the part of the subordinate; among equals though, we generally see this combination of display and appeasement which can be explained by the previously discussed ambivalence existing in interpersonal relationships. Humans have a great propensity to develop dominance relationships. If a weakness is perceived in someone else, this is frequently exploited to establish dominance over that individual. In order to inhibit this tendency, we act in ways that save face and present an appearance of strength, blocking any rank struggles before they even begin.

Via friendly actions like the presentation of gifts, smiling, or words of greeting, we communicate that we wish to initiate or maintain affable relations. What can vary, however, are the ways in which we display individually, how we express appeasement, and the readiness to form bonds, since we have at our disposal behavioral alternatives that can serve one particular function and thus are functionally equivalent. The external form of these events varies, while the underlying rules that structure the events on a deeper level remain constant. Thus, we may

495

speak of a universal strategy for friendly contact initiation when we refer to the rules underlying the surface behavior.

Greeting generally initiates a sequence of further interactions that also display their own typical structure. Once two friends have exchanged greetings, they tend to continue by entering into a brief conversation. One asks the other how he feels and makes small talk about the weather, for example, to which the partner usually agrees. If the partner did not do so, our expectations would be confounded for the deeper meaning of this kind of social intercourse. D. Morris (1968) accurately described this type of conversation as "grooming talk," that is the seeking and obtaining of agreement. For this kind of communication Malinowski (1923) introduced the term "phatic communication." Laver (1975) further noted that this manner of starting a conversation can also be utilized to alter the relationship. There are three forms: neutral, self-oriented, and other-oriented. If, for instance, a dominant, self-oriented person starts talking *("I think the weather is fine")* he lessens the rank difference and forces the other into momentary solidarity. On the other hand, the submissive person uses the other-oriented form, thus trying to modify the rank difference.

If a person is in a friendly mood, the meeting may also be used to make a request and to discuss concerns at hand. The friendly atmosphere created upon first meeting is a prerequisite for continuing in this manner. The person who "jumps straight in" is quickly repulsed. After the meeting is concluded, we do not depart abruptly in an unstructured way but by expressing verbally that we must leave and nonverbally by using cues in the form of changing our orientation to the discussion partner, slowly opening up the dyad. Finally, departure is usually accompanied by the expression of a good wish ("Have a good trip," "Good bye," "Sleep well"), which is a verbal gift.

Public addresses also take place according to this basic pattern. They do not only contain pertinent information, since the speaker typically begins and ends a talk with social rituals, representing himself as competent without being overly dominating.

Thus a speech may begin with some positive self-representation, perhaps by quoting some Latin saying or making some statement of personal credibility. Jokes can imply self-confidence and the sense of being above matters. Some speakers begin with the comment that their hosts convinced them to come despite a busy schedule, but something like this is quickly followed by an appeasing gesture praising the listeners, perhaps by stating that it is a particular honor to speak before such a distinguished audience. Further appeals are used to establish a bond between speaker and audience, perhaps by referring to some point in common that associates the speaker with the society, the location of the talk, the country, or even an anecdote from the speaker's youth. After this brief introduction the speaker comes to the matter at hand, controlling his listeners' pace. The speaker subconsciously perceives the audience's attentiveness and responds to it by inserting comments that incite or appease the group. In the concluding phase the audience is thanked for their attentiveness, and the speaker often briefly excuses himself, behaving submissively as if he were departing from the company of friends.

Earlier, we briefly described the opening of the Yanomami feast (Reaho) with the guests' greeting dance, including the presentation of antithetical elements (display and appeasement).

Here we will take a brief look at all phases of the Yanomami feast in the framework of a ritualized encounter with an opening phase, a bond-reinforcement phase, and a phase of farewell.[5]

The opening phase was described above with the visitors entering the host's village in full war regalia in a mock threat accompanied by children as a symbol of appeasement.

After each visitor individually dances around in greeting, the entire guest group dances together—women, young girls, and children intermingling with the warriors. Gifts that have been brought for the hosts are often displayed at this time. The headman then sends the visitors to individual families who will provide for them during their stay. The guests hang their hammocks up and lie down for a rest, appearing to be indifferent to everything occurring around them. Their apathetic and aloof (cool)[6] manner is necessary because among these highly warlike Yanomami there is something quite dangerous about visiting another village. After some time they appear more relaxed. The host brings them banana soup and they chat and begin sniffing drugs.[7] The men then dance under the influence of the drug, imploring the help of the spirits in their fight against enemies.

This ritual unites the warriors in joint aggression. Another unifying experience in the form of the common mourning for the dead takes place later. Host and guest mourn the most recently deceased and drink some of the ashes of the dead mixed into the banana soup, the ashes having been stored in calabashes for this purpose. Only after these repeated demonstrations of unity do the Yanomami begin singing their contract songs (himou). One host and one guest, in turn, present their demands in a highly formalized manner, requesting gifts and promising some in exchange, but in reality this is simply a reaffirmation of existing contracts. The visitor begins, and partners either sit on the ground during the contract discussion, embracing each other or stand opposite one another. The speech is conducted in a sing-song manner in rapid rhythm. The words are divided to adapt them to the rhythm, and the final syllable of the previous line is always repeated at the beginning of the next line (K. Good, 1988). Thus the opening phrase "Ya ku veiketa" (= "I want to say it") of one of the contact songs is divided into four lines:

```
1   ya ku
  2   ku vei
    3   vei ke
      4   ke ta
```

<hr>

[5] A more complete description is found in I. Eibl-Eibesfeldt, (1971a).

[6] If an individual person or a small group comes to a village without being invited (outside the festival period), they initially settle down on the village square. They stare into space as if their hosts were not even there, displaying "arrogance." They behave haughtily, but display courage by offering themselves, as it were, as targets in the central square. This is indeed taking a risk among the Yanomami, since there are many unresolved blood feuds occurring among them, and one never knows exactly whether some enemy is living in the village they are visiting at the time.

[7] This is composed of a powder from seeds and the rind of a plant containing an intoxicating alkaloid.

At the end of each line the listener responds with a short interjection or by repeating the phrase. This coded speech is almost a secret language that only experienced insiders can understand. Thus the song not only bonds by its content and form but also because it excludes outsiders. Within the Yanomami, as a whole, individual local styles of ceremonial speech have developed.

A great deal of metaphor is also used, for example, a machete being described as the white man's wife, so that it requires extensive knowledge of the culture to understand the dialogue, and even then can only be translated with the help of experienced translators. The contents of the talk and counter talk are gift exchanges, promises, and occasionally, criticism of the partner. Gifts are often belittled by the donor himself: "take this ugly creature!"—when in reality the donor is giving a beautiful dog. One disparages oneself in order not to dominate or embarrass and thus challenge the partner, thereby expressing the desire to avoid any competition.

Introductory words also include references to events that evoke sympathy, perhaps to an accident in which the singer lost another partner or was otherwise injured. The phase of interaction is generally followed on the succeeding day by a phase of formalized farewell. In a kind of summary, a common bond is demonstrated on the following morning by fighting the evil spirits together. With much noise and many threat gestures, the men crawl under the lean-to roofs. Another duet singing bout follows, in which all males form pairs on the open square. They squat together, gesticulate vigorously, and affirm their alliance, often embracing each other while in the squatting position. Here the himou is greatly abbreviated and the performance lasts only a few minutes. It is followed by the exchange of gifts between hosts and guests, who then leave. The festival has basically the same structure as friendly encounters: from the greeting to the "grooming talks" and then to the farewell. The similarities of rituals of friendly encounters (festivals) are summarized below:

a. Opening Phase (Greeting)
   Function: self-presentation, bonding, appeasement. Initiating friendly contact without submission.
   Observed display behavior: display dance, hand shaking, military salute.
   Observed behavior of appeasement and bonding: presenting gifts, smiling, nodding, eye-brow flash, embracing, kissing, friendly appealing via children.

b. Bond-Reinforcement Phase
   Function: reinforcing the relationship; emotional deepening of the bond, often as a preparation for pertinent matters (business, war treaties).
   Observed behavior patterns: assertion of agreement and sympathy in dialogues; testimony of unity through common acts, communal eating, dancing, common fighting against imagined enemies, and common mourning.

c. Phase of Farewell
   Function: maintaining the bond for the future; appeasement.
   Observed behavior: gift exchange or the equivalent exchange of good wishes; mutual assurances of unity.

Our cross-cultural documentation shows that the external manifestation of social manners varies substantially but that these conventions are all subject to essentially the same set of rules everywhere. This is true for simple as well as complex rituals. A friendly meeting (encounter) and a Yanomami feast generally display the same organization, even within individual phases of the entire sequence of events. The strategies of friendly contact initiation, group bonding reinforcement, and of farewell of which the rituals are composed, are likewise structured according to similar rules. Man apparently has a limited set of strategies with which specific objectives can be attained.

In principle the same strategies are found in all cultures. Whether the intention is to gain esteem, obtain something from another person, block some aggressive act, reject or invite another person, these strategies occur in various cultures following essentially the same basic pattern. Some examples of this will follow. Small children generally act out their strategies with body movements, while adults use verbal actions to attain the same goals, but both act in accordance with the same rules. There is thus a universal rule system, a universal grammar of social behavior according to which verbal and nonverbal interactions are similarly structured. An example of this was given previously (Fig. 6.69). It showed two attempts by a Yanomami boy to block the aggressive behavior of a playmate. The first tactic of using a pronounced smile to inhibit aggression failed to have an effect, for the boy attacked and hit him. The boy then modified his behavior, by lowering his head, pulling his eyelids downward so his partner could no longer see his eyes, and displaying an expression of pouting. Even though his partner could strike out at him—in fact by looking away he made himself particularly vulnerable—this behavior had the desired result and the attacker departed.

The behavior of the attacker is initially submissive in nature, as indicated by lowering the head and inclined posture, but it would be incorrect to interpret the boy's behavior as a general strategy of aggression blocking by means of submissive-appeasement behaviors. He does not actually submit himself, and, in fact, he emerges from the encounter as the "victor." He maintains his position, and the decisive behavioral element of his strategy lies in his threat of breaking off contact.

This kind of threat is effective when we oppose someone with whom we are closely acquainted. As social beings, we set great store on personal attachments, and from childhood onward we will defend such bonds against rivals. Mothers know very well how siblings compete for her affections, and it takes time for them to learn that the mother is also a reference figure for others, such as, siblings and fathers. If someone threatens to interrupt this bond, the resulting emotion is one of great alarm. For this is a threat of the loss of a very special possession: without social ties a person is isolated and vulnerable. It is understandable that the individual threatened with exclusion (expulsion) rapidly ceases executing the behavior that led to this threat. The sequence described in the previous paragraph can be observed almost identically in European or Japanese kindergartens. Of course, there are certain variations. A Yanomami can withdraw into his jungle hammock to signify breaking off contact (Fig. 6.70), while others can encapsule this behavior in words. An offended child may say, "I won't play with you any more," or "I'm going home and I won't come back." Adults behave in similar fashion. They use verbal and nonverbal behavior to threaten to disrupt bonds. The figures of speech used in such contexts are similar throughout the world (p. 537). The fact that our repertoire is limited in strategies and that we can express certain ideas in a very limited number of ways can also be seen from the fact that we behave in the same way at the international level as on the interpersonal one. Nations typically threaten each other with a cessation of diplomatic relations.

The threat of cut-off is, however, just one aggression blocking strategy. It is particularly important since it disturbs the relationship with one's partner the least. As we will discuss, it leaves open the greatest number of alternatives. Aggression can also be blocked with counter threats or submission—but these strategies permit

FIGURE 6.69. Interaction strategy of agonal buffering. A Yanomami boy (Serra Parima) is threatened by another boy attempting to push him aside. The attacked boy initially smiles concertedly—an ineffective tactic. After being hit, he diverts his vision (contact avoidance), lowers the head, and pouts. The aggressor then leaves, without disturbing him any more. From a 25 frames/second 16 mm film, frames 1, 18, 46, 52, 63, 140, 151, and 159 of the scene. Photo: I. Eibl-Eibesfeldt.

fewer alternative responses. In these cases, the danger of an escalation in the conflict exists, even though a threat can be highly effective and usually resolves the conflict successfully. All too often, threats followed by counter threats lead to physical strikes and counter strikes. In the case of utilizing submission, the submitting party acknowledges the other's dominance. We have already discussed another form of aggression blocking by means of offering objects (p. 344).

The norm of respect of object possession gives rise to a number of rules concerning social transfer of objects. We showed that a person who wants to obtain something from someone else must express this desire in such a way that the other has the option to refuse with grace. The request must be stated in such a way that the other person is clearly respected as the legitimate owner of the object. If someone simply seizes an object that another person is holding, this is a violation of etiquette, an aggressive act, and if there is no substantial rank difference between the two persons the attempt to seize the object will be rejected. But if the person requesting the object holds his hand out in a proper gesture of request, the object is freely given to him. Corresponding regulations govern imperative demands. If a good relationship is to remain intact, one must proceed with prudence, often with veiled requests. An Eipo who would like to have a particular feather will comment, "That is a nice feather you have." The owner then has the power to decide freely whether to give the feather away or keep it. Direct requests are only made when the partners are intimate acquaintances.

P. Winterhoff-Spurk (1983) investigated the interplay of nonverbal and verbal communication in role playing whose content consisted of direct and indirect requests. Informational deficits in indirect requests were supplemented by nonverbal cues such as extended visual contact. In direct requests, smiling had a pacifying effect, and, in addition an inquiring intonation gave them the characteristic of a question. Verbal and nonverbal elements intermingle in a complementary way and help prevent misunderstanding of the messages being conveyed.

This agrees with the findings of J. S. Lockard (1980), who noted that persons making requests were more successful when they submissively held out their hand for something than those who dominantly demanded objects without any submissive gestures. She assigned two female and male students to approach 500 persons or groups separately and to ask them for 10¢. Submissive approaches included letting the shoulders hang, lowering the head, avoiding visual contact, and extending the hand. Dominant approaches were made by holding oneself upright, raising the head, attempting to make visual contact, and not extending the hand. Women were more successful than the men when requesting, especially when they addressed men who were eating. Those who were eating not only gave the requested 10¢ but offered food as well.

Another verbal strategy which is very important in requesting is explaining of why one wants the object. Among other things, it clarifies that one really has a need not just greed and greatly eases the other's reluctance to give. It also implies to the donor that when he is in need the receiver is likely to reciprocate (P. Wiessner, pers. commun.).

Education generally reinforces the tendencies to give, as shown in one of our film documents of the Eipo. The scene depicts two half siblings. The boy is eating a cooked piece of taro, and his half sister grabs at it, whereupon the boy withdraws the piece. At this point the boy's mother enters the scene. She asks for the piece of taro, which he willingly gives her. He watches tensely as his mother breaks the piece in two and gives both pieces back to him. She thus shows deference for

501

FIGURE 6.70. See legend, opposite page.

the norm of respect of possession, and since the boy now has two pieces and his sister wants one, he gives one to her (Figs. 6.71, 6.72).

Our nervous system is programmed with various built-in expectations. Our fellow man must behave appropriately in order to maintain a harmonious mutual relationship, since deviation from expected behavior results in rejection or withdrawal. Whether expectations are met verbally or nonverbally does not matter. We have closely studied behavior associated with requesting, giving, and taking in the Eipo society, including nonverbal strategies as well as their verbal counterparts (V. Heeschen, W. Schiefenhövel, and I. Eibl-Eibesfeldt, 1980). These findings are summarized in Table 6.3.

Sharing can create bonds and reinforce existing ones, but sharing also contains an aggressive component (p. 308). In giving, one can make the other party obligated, thus gaining status for oneself (p. 351). P. Wiessner investigated one-third of all the film documentation we compiled from the Yanomami, Bushmen, and Trobrianders regarding nonverbal offering and requesting within childrens' groups. In all three cultures, sharing is done with a specific etiquette characterized by respect for rightful possession. Seizing an object elicited rejection and defense. In other regards, there were remarkable differences. Offering occurred in the Yanomami in 22 of 54 cases (41%), while in Bushmen the figure was only 8 in 64 cases (13%). Pleading or begging with an open hand occurred in the Yanomami in only 5 out of 54 interactions (9%), but in the Bushmen in 20 out of 64 interactions (31%). This is not surprising, since Bushmen react to dominance displays with rejection, while such displays are acceptable in Yanomami society, where they regularly show off when giving gifts. Among the Trobrianders, where the display rather than the consumption of food is prized, teasing with food is a prevalent practice. Food teasing occurred 10 times (33%) within 30 events in childrens' groups, while in the Yanomami, teasing occurred once in 54 events (2%) and twice in Bushmen in 64 (3%). Proper requests are also made among the Trobrianders, but asking for food is a rare occurrence since it is embarrassing in this culture to admit that one is hungry. The social strategies of sharing already reflect in children's groups the same social and symbolic rules which operate within adult society. Requesting, offering, and teasing may evoke ambivalent feelings that are often resolved with joking.

P. Brown and S. Levinson (1978) studied verbal politeness (requests) in Tamil

◁————————————————————————

FIGURE 6.70. A variant of a "cut-off" behavior in a conflict between a mother and her son (Yanomami, upper Orinoco). The boy wants to take a piece of banana from the mother. She rejects him (1), whereupon he grabs a cooked banana from a basket hanging over his hammock and throws it on the ground. When his mother fails to react to that he retrieves the banana and throws it further away (2, 3), lies down in the hammock, whimpers, and turns his back to his mother (4). The mother then offers him prechewed bananas in a reconciling manner (5). He refuses the offer and wraps himself up in his hammock (6, 7). The mother then offers the banana again, first in a friendly manner (8), and then admonishingly (9). He knocks the offered piece out of her hand (10, 11), remains completely wrapped up in the hammock, turns his back on her and avoids contact, which angers the mother. She strikes him and he howls. During the further course of this scene the father takes him out of the hammock. He brings the boy to his hammock and delouses him, which quickly calms the boy. From 25 frames/second 16 mm film, frames 1, 1162, 1168, 1581, 1738, 1794, 1930, 2168, 2177, 2191, 2198, 2218, 2224, 2228, 2274, 3184, 3350, and 5441 of the sequence. The last two frames were taken after an interruption. Photo: I. Eibl-Eibesfeldt.

FIGURE 6.71. An Eipo boy (Irian Jaya, western New Guinea) eats a piece of taro. His half sister grabs at it, and he pulls it away from her grasp. His mother intervenes and asks him to give her the piece of taro, which he does. The mother breaks the taro into two pieces and returns them to him. She thus defers to the norm of respect of possession and lets him do the distributing. He gives his half sister a piece, and both eat calmly beside each other. From a 16 mm film. Photo: I. Eibl-Eibesfeldt.

FIGURE 6.72. Two approximately 3-year-old Eipo girls who are playmates. Yoto, the one on the left, eats a piece of taro, of which her friend Metik, on the right, wishes to have a piece. She shows this desire through her facial expression, by alternatingly smiling, pouting, and smiling, but not by grabbing the food. Yoto teases her by holding the morsel out and then, immediately withdrawing her hand. (e, f). Metik reacts to this act by pouting, but she respects Yoto's ownership. From a 25 frames/second 16 mm film, frames 1, 86, 143, 166, 288, 291, 2531, and 2578 of the sequence. The extended scene has many interesting details and is shown here in a greatly edited form. Photo: I. Eibl-Eibesfeldt.

Table 6.3. Behavior in Eipo Requesting, Giving, and Taking

Verbal act	Time of starting	Beginning with . . .	Alternative choices	Typical or possible responses	Preference by age group or participant constellation	Meaning, function, or connotation
Direct request	First speaker	Loud, firm voice, outstretched arm, gaze at potential gift and giver	(All other opening sequences)	Refusing, turning away from addressor, withdrawing the object	All age groups, except old people	Aggressivity
Direct request	After first speaker turns	Short glance into giver's face, normal voice, arm not fully outstretched	—	Giving the object	All age groups, except old people	Bonding act, avoidance of interrupting discourse
Indirect request	Opening sequence or later	*Leklekana*, turning toward the addressee, skin contact, about 2-sec glance at giver	Direct request	Giving the object, but not at once	All age groups	Politeness, request a speaking turn
Indirect request	Opening sequence or later	Prolonged eye contact, outstretched arm, stroking the giver's chin, and pharyneal, nasal, or whimpering intonation	—	Giving the object, but not at once	Children, youth, and adults	Can be repeated; submissive infantile appeals to parental instincts
Humorous remark	After previous contact and introductory silence	Renewed eye contact, shift toward each other	Giving and taking, scene changing	—	All age groups	Initiator of assertion stream
Disputing	After direct request or refusal of direct request	—	Teaching by example without verbal exchange	—	All age groups	Appeal to norms and rules of social behavior
Calling	After direct request or refusal of direct request	Turning away from the requester, withdrawing the object, embarassed smile	Starting a new dyad, continuing the old, sitting apart, singing a song	—	All age groups	Nonbonding marker
Bahai calling	After refusal or direct request	Requesting person turns away with the pharyngeal sound	—	—	All age groups	Deriding the addressor

(southern India), Tzeltal (Mexico), and the English language, with additional linguistic studies of Malagasy and Japanese. They found that small requests are put forward by emphasizing group membership and/or social similarities—and thus stressing elements held in common. This can be called a super strategy of informal politeness.[8] Greater requests require formal courtesy through conventional indirect speech acts and excusing oneself (super strategy of formal courtesy). Requests substantial enough that they may be turned down are formulated in indirect terms, often couched in veiled language (super strategy of indirect suggestion = "off record" in Brown and Levinson).

Selecting one of the three super strategies is not only dependent upon the size of the request but also upon the social distance between the interacting individuals and the relative power exerted in the dyad. The central need existing in all cases is that of saving face. No one wants to degrade himself or endanger his public image, or that of one's partner. This is quite similar to greetings (see previous section), in which we are sensitive to maintain our public esteem. We avoid lowering our own self-esteem, as well as that of our greeting partner, in friendly encounters (p. 493). Thus, esteem is a decisive social factor, a key with far-reaching consequences for the configuration and sequence of interactions. Verbal request strategies vary depending upon the way and the degree in which the speaker assesses the situation in terms of the endangerment of public esteem.

The three super strategies are composed of a series of substrategies. *Informal politeness* contains three of them: (1) claim "common ground"; (2) convey that speaker and partner are cooperators or, if necessary, fabricate an imaginary relationship; and (3) fulfill a number of wants of the one being addressed.

The verbal acts through which these goals are attained are principally the same in all languages. Reference is made to commonality through utilizing intimate everyday terms of endearment ("My dear . . ."); by referring to other's needs and showing an assessment of that person's qualities ("you are a clever fellow . . ., can you do something for me?"); communicating that there is agreement in attitudes and values, adding some points of certain agreement ("Yes, the weather certainly is beautiful today . . ."); avoiding disagreements, making jokes, and if necessary expressing oneself ambiguously or even lying and using in-group identity markers.

Conveying a cooperative relationship means that the actor must indicate that one understands the other's needs, demonstrates understanding for his situation, agrees with him, and cultivates a reciprocal relationship, or offers to do so or to promise one. The partner is incorporated by using the plural pronoun "we" instead of "I" and "you." Partner wishes are fulfilled by giving him gifts (in the form of good wishes, praise, sympathetic remarks).

The *formal politeness* is characterized by distance, respect, and a high degree of conventionalization. It consists of those strategies that fill books on etiquette; Brown and Levinson list five substrategies within this category. The use of conventions permits one to make direct requests with this approach, but these requests are usually formulated in indirect terms so that the partner feels in no way compelled to comply: "Could you perhaps . . .?", "Is there still salt . . .?" (indirect speech acts).

---

[8]Brown and Levinson distinguish between positive politeness and negative politeness. I prefer to avoid these leading terms and instead render the two super strategies as informal politeness (positive) and formal politeness (negative in Brown's and Levinson's usage).

Certain speech acts have direct parallels in other languages, even in cultures that are in no way related to each other. The idea is not to compel the partner, a point we discussed earlier and have found even in small children (p. 379). The person being addressed must always have some means of refusing the request. Cautious questioning, sometimes with a pessimistic undertone, often occurs in such situations ("Could you perhaps give me . . .?"), or one minimizes the threat by delimiting the size of the request ("Could you possibly lend me just one sheet of paper?").

One most interesting example, because it is related to a mistaken interpretation, comes from Gunter Senft (pers. commun.). In the language of the Trobrianders of Kilivila there is a stereotyped request form: "Mesta tobaki," which could initially be translated as a direct, plain request as "Give tobacco!" or "Bring tobacco!" But a deeper study of the language reveals that "mesta" is a slurring of the verb "kumeja" (verb stem: /meja/ combined with the personal pronoun prefix of the second person /ku/) with the noun "sitana." "Mesta tobaki" thus arose from: "kumeja sitana tobaki," meaning literally: "You bring piece tobacco," or more freely translated as "Give me a *little* tobacco!"

Displays of respect operate similarly. Respect is shown by self-deprecation, often regressing to infantilisms, giggling, laughing, and appearing to be helpless.[9] Furthermore, respect can be shown to others by addressing them in the plural or with some title. A further substrategy exists in communicating to the person being addressed that one does not wish to hinder him and bother by excusing oneself, regretting, saying that one is sorry, etc.

The super strategy of figurative language is utilized at a high risk of losing face. The speaker formulates his needs in such a way as to give them multiple meanings. He makes suggestions but leaves the interpretation to the addressee, thus leaving the other person recourse if there is some reason for not granting the request ("What a hot day!" = how about having a drink?); ("It is cold in the room" = Close the window!).

A person can jump from one strategy to another. Thus if there is a disagreement between spouses, for instance, distance is created and with it a formalizing of speech. Likewise, appeals to imagined unity can be used by completely unacquainted individuals, for example, as when a Yanomami boy calls the warrior who wants to kill him "My father" (examples on developing imagined relationships are found in I. Eibl-Eibesfeldt, 1970a, 1971c, 1975).

The studies by Brown and Levinson are extremely rich in material, and reflect the universal basic structure underlying all verbal requests. The mutual needs of the interacting persons for saving face can only be heeded in a particular way by the person making a request, either by veiling the request (indirect expressions), self-deprecation, or other strategies. It is not only the principle that is universal but even the details of such verbal exchanges. Thus formal courtesy is regularly

---

[9]In southern India, if a man belonging to a lower caste is addressed by a higher ranking individual, he begins giggling. "Detailed analyses of tapes from our Tamil Village shows that strategies for this mode of self-humbling are highly developed by low-caste (Harijan) speakers, but only used to high-caste persons of considerable power. For instance, in front of a landlord, a Harijan when reprimanded may giggle like an English child; when given instructions he may appear slow to comprehend; when speaking he may mumble and speak in unfinished sentences as if shy to express foolish thoughts; and when walking he may shuffle along. All this contrasts sharply with the same man bargaining with less powerful but still high-caste persons, and there can be no doubt that this bumbling is a strategically selected style" (P. Brown and S. Levinson, 1978, p. 191).

accompanied by a uniformly high pitch, while intimate courtesy is characterized by a "creaky voice."

Brown and Levinson's findings agree with those of human ethologists researching the underlying structure for verbal and nonverbal interaction strategies. They use the prior findings in universal speech behavior to criticize W. LaBarre's work, which is embedded in cultural relativism with endless catalogs of superficial differences in expressive behavior.[10]

Undoubtedly though, there are also many cultural-specific strategies, as shown in the above example, of differences in patterns of food sharing between cultures. In entering a foreign culture, there are always a number of strategies used that strike the outsider as brash, rude or difficult to understand. It is possible that much of the variation in these strategies is due to different values placed on the events involved. Human ethology seeks to identify similarities between cultures. Undoubtedly analogies of cultural-specific strategies will also yield interesting insights.

Our previous discussions on the universal grammar of human social behavior have already revealed a number of general rules. We will now consider some others: if we observe how children get others to play with them, we can observe a limited number of strategies. Thus we frequently see one child inviting another by running away, waiting with the play-face and, when the other runs up, then runs a bit further off and waits again, continuing in this fashion. Specific play sounds may be uttered during this time, which can be described as "screams of joy." Thus in tireless repetition, a readiness for play can be built up. The child inviting another to play can also touch or embrace him (Fig. 6.73). This is followed by acts demonstrating mutual harmony, through which the initiative established by the one inviting to play can be transferred to the other child, who now does something and thereby expresses his intentions to play together. It now remains for the other child to imitate this behavior and thus express his concurrence.

The Eipo girls shown in the film sequence alternated stepping on tobacco plants. They could just have well have been pivoting in circles, throwing rocks, or hitting a stick against the ground. The point here is that one imitates the other, showing a willingness to play together, an intention that becomes evident through the act of repetition. After this highly stereotyped introductory phase there comes a more flexible, variable period of play. Naturally there are also other strategies used to attract someone to play (Fig. 6.74).

In kindergarten observations, W. A. Corsaro (1979) found that children who wanted to play with others did not usually ask them if they wished to play, although in 80% of the cases they ended up playing together. Instead, the children utilized those strategies that left open the maximum number of alternative choices for the ones being solicited. Thus they would gather along the edges of play groups and gradually work their way into them. It appears that in a general way strategies are used that leave the most options open.

---

[10]"A final goal, perhaps largely unnecessary nowadays, is to rebuff the once-fashionable doctrine of cultural relativity in the field of interaction. Weston LaBarre (1972), for instance, catalogs endless superficial differences in gesture as evidence of relativism in that sphere. We hope to show that superficial diversities can emerge from underlying universal principles and are satisfactorily accounted for only in relation to them" (Brown and Levinson, 1978, p. 61).

FIGURE 6.73. Segments from an extended film sequence during which an almost 3-year-old Eipo girl invites an approximately 3½-year-old boy to play. She oscillates several times between him and her mother, attempting to arouse his interest with the play-face and embracing intentions. Finally both walk off, embracing each other. From a 25 frames/second 16 mm film, frames 1, 88, 251, and 354 of the sequence, showing only the termination of a very long episode. Photo: I. Eibl-Eibesfeldt.

A sequence for effective strategies has the following behavioral steps: the child approaches the goal person and looks at him, referring to the target person without speaking directly to him by using such nonverbal means as repeatedly looking at the person and continuing to approach. Finally, the child executes some variant on the behavior of the target person until he is accepted into the game. Imitation appears to have some kind of bonding effect here, and it can be used to gain familiarity with someone or, as the Eipo children episode illustrates, to solicit another to play.

This study was replicated by K. Grammer and H. Shibasaka (1985), who showed, furthermore, that the actual strategy the children use is dependent upon the relationship (friendship and status difference) between the children, in the sense that access is easier in friendship relationships and if the status of the child trying to gain access is higher than that of the target person.

The strategy described here, inviting the partner to imitative behavior by starting some action oneself or using imitation to express accord and thus a readiness for group play, is a principle of many bonding rituals. Doing things together confirms a sense of unity, and imitation reflects a disposition to follow others (I. Eibl-Eibesfeldt, 1973a). This is also expressed in a great many rituals, for example, in dances and marches. The great diversity of rituals can generally be derived from these kinds of elemental interaction strategies and as such represent the cultural differentiation of such strategies. This means that various kinds of behavioral pat-

FIGURE 6.74. The two Eipo girls Yoto and Metik synchronizing for common play. Once again this is only a small segment of an entire episode. Yoto previously invited her friend to play by running repeatedly to a reed fence. Her friend followed and then both ran back to their mothers. Metik then began kicking at the tobacco plants, an action Yoto imitated. This scene first shows Yoto, inviting Metik to follow her with the play-face, and then the two children imitating each other at the reed fence. Frames 1, 378, 609, and 670 of the 25 frames/second 16 mm film, showing only a small portion of the end of the interaction. Photo: I. Eibl-Eibesfeldt.

terns can be considered to be functional equivalents within the framework of a strategy of rules for behavior.

My co-workers K. Grammer, R. Schropp, and H. Shibasaka (1984) investigated the structure of the following strategies: (1) object offering in aggressive encounters as a strategy of blocking off an attack; (2) seeking incorporation into a play group with the objective of playing together; and (3) supporting a partner by intervening in a conflict with the goal of resolving the conflict in favor of the one being supported.

If a behavioral objective is attained, the strategy would be recorded as effective. They found that effective strategies contain more behavioral steps than ineffective ones which are built up slowly with a definite sequence. The strategist keeps open the possibility of intensifying his behavior. Children who intervene successfully in conflicts begin by making threats, and in this way they leave open the possibility of acting even more vigorously if need be. Successful strategies also take into account the behavioral mobility of their partner by avoiding, if possible, any tactic that forces the partner into making an immediate decision. Thus children seeking contact with groups less often ask directly whether they may join in play.

In the majority of cases, the direct request would be successful. A rejection, however, would be conclusive and no further alternative would remain. It is for

511

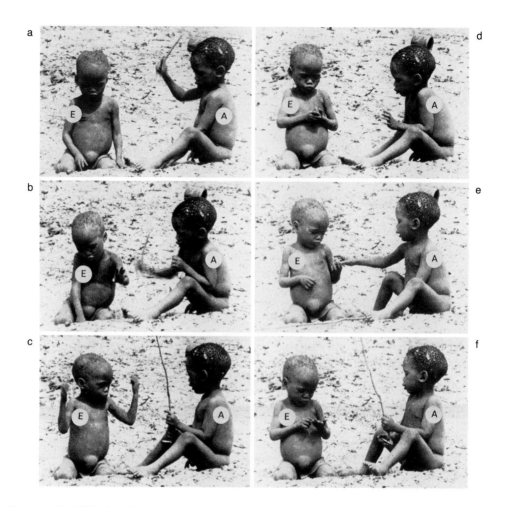

FIGURE 6.75. Effective object offering: (a) two G/wi Bushmen children (offerer A + recipient E) sit on the ground. Child A hits at a bug with a stick, accidentally striking Child E's finger (b); (c) child E stares at child A and threatens to hit back (shortly thereafter E hits A's leg); (d) while child E pouts and feels his fingers, child A picks up the bug from the ground, offering the bug (e) as an act of appeasement, and the gift is accepted; (f) no more aggressive acts are executed; child E investigates the bug and then both play together. From a 25 frames/second 16 mm film, frames 1, 42, 190, 362, 536, and 567 of the sequence. Photo: I. Eibl-Eibesfeldt.

this reason that children in the kindergarten prefer the indirect approach, by playing near the group that they wish to join and by establishing verbal contact by indirectly referring to their goal of playing with others.

Whether unlimited strategies are used depends on the type of interaction and the relationship of the interactants. In every interaction, a person risks failure to achieve his goal, which also implies that he risks his "face" (E. Goffman, 1967) or, as we suggest, his "status." Goffman, who certainly can be said to have pioneered the study of man in everyday life situations, phrased it aptly: "The study of face saving is the study of traffic rules of social interaction" (E. Goffman, 1967, p. 12).

FIGURE 6.76. Ineffective object offering: (a) a Yanomami boy (recipient E) threatens to hit a younger boy (offerer, A); (b) child A sits down and watches child E, who threatens child A with a pole; (c) child A picks up an object from the ground and holds it out in appeasement toward the threatening recipient; (d) child E lowers the pole while child A continues offering the object; (e) immediately thereafter, child E again threatens child A with the pole and does not accept the object; (f) the conflict escalates; child E attacks child A with the pole, and A defends himself with a stick; (g) shortly afterward they break off contact. Child A was unable to appease child E with a gift. From a 25 frames/second 16 mm film. The first frame belongs to a previous scene, so the numbering of frames begins with the second one (b): frames 1, 55, 85, 111, 672, and 859 of the sequence. Photo: I. Eibl-Eibesfeldt.

During aggressive encounters fast actions are required and, therefore, direct strategies are often employed. An example is the offering of an object to an aggressor by the attacked person. Kindergarten studies and the cross-cultural analysis of film documents, taken in the natural context, revealed that this strategy is successful. The objects are either accepted as a token of appeasement or the attack occurs. Thus objects can serve as a sort of "lighting rod" for aggression (Fig. 6.75 and 6.76).

If a person, however, wants a favor or desires an object possessed by another person, than the indirect approach is more appropriate for a number of reasons: the need to demonstrate respect of the norm of object possession (p. 345) as well as the need to protect one's face, which would be endangered by a refusal of the request.

Rank relationships between the interactants influence the selection of the target person in situations such as intervention in conflicts. We already mentioned (p. 153) that dominant (A) children tend to support those (B) who recently lost rank, intervening against those who are ascending in rank (C) which could potentially threaten the rank position of (A). If the intervention is successful the child who received help (B) ascends in rank, while his adversary (C) loses rank. Thus a skilled intervener can manipulate rank relationships within the group. This is seen even in nonhuman primates. Chimpanzees are capable of manipulating social relations by similar interference (F. DeWaal, 1982).

Perceived "risk" varies with the actor's ability to predict the behavior of his interaction partner. If he or she is a close friend whom he or she knows well, the actors will know how to proceed without endangering their face. The higher the desire and the greater the unpredictability and unknowns, the more exploratory communication takes place. Lack of familiarity and status difference create distance and unknown factors and these, in turn, require exploratory communications and thus "detours" for success. Strategies are thus composed of longer chains of action and are only direct when appropriate information about the other has been gathered. The basic rules by which the interactions, depending upon the desired goal and the variables concerning the relationship of the interactants and other characteristics of the situation, are structured seem universally to be similar and so are many of the concrete behaviors employed.

Strategies are generally subject to the rule that one behaves in such a way as to maintain as many possible options as possible while feeling out the situation. We only observe the direct strategy when the actor is highly certain of success without detrimental consequences. Thus if the partners are already in a high state of accord and a request would not be seen as an imposition, he can make his request by asking directly, even using a friendly imperative address without expecting a negative reaction. If one is dominant and places no high priority on the consequences of a particular act, he may also use a direct strategy. In all other cases, the rule is that one use restraint in making requests.

Another general principle was expounded by M. Mauss (p. 351) in his book on gifts as an expression of reciprocity. This principle, as Lévi-Strauss (1969) explained, is effective not only in friendly cooperative interactions but also in conflicts of all types, even those between enemies. The original law of *lex talionis* called for equal compensation, and quarreling children behave according to this rule (W. W. Lambert 1981; W. W. Lambert and A. Tan, 1979).

For each type of interaction used to maintain the ongoing partnership relation, there is also the principle that one should behave in predictable ways. This is also

true for agonistic encounters (war and duels), which also follow certain conventions while permitting the use of stratagems and forbidding deceitful and delusionary practices beyond conventional boundaries. Deception may be permitted over time in confrontations, but beyond that there must also be some framework within which behavior is predictable, and some basis of trust established. In earlier days, pacts were considered to be sacred and might be recalled but not broken. Today we are in the process of discarding this important cultural achievement, which may lead to our downfall.

Lying and deceptive practices are important weapons in intraspecific interactions. A predator will attempt to overcome its prey with every available means, and the prey can make use of any deceptive mechanism (e.g., mimicry) to escape an otherwise certain death. Of course, there is no social relation between predators and prey. But when partnerships develop, whether within small groups or between nations and blocks of countries, some predictability of even the enemies behavior must exist. I stress this point because some sociobiologists propound the viewpoint that it is always advantageous for an animal to give deceptive, false reports: "The classical ethological explanation, that animals exchange information about their 'motivations' or 'intentions' makes little sense from an evolutionary point of view, because honest signaling about motivations would not be evolutionarily stable; it would always pay to misinform, and therefore it would pay to disbelieve" (J. Maynard-Smith, 1984, p. 98).

As G. W. Barlow and T. E. Rowell correctly note in a commentary to this statement, Maynard-Smith fell victim to a frightful oversimplification, perceiving communication only within the context of agonal encounters, where bluffing is indeed adaptive. But some reliable communication must also exist even within the realm of interactions with your enemies, or there would be no tournament fights, submission, and, in humans, no eventual peace (p. 419). Thus, even within the agonistic sphere, excluding interspecific predator behavior, deception is a means that is adaptive only in limited ways. Wherever animals and man are united and are not in an interspecific relationship, there must exist some basis of reliability, otherwise the bond would be destroyed. W. Wickler (1971) noted that in the animal world there are selective forces operating against misunderstanding signals and the development of deceptive behavior, but that a value is placed upon authentic communication.

A relationship is determined on the basis of mutual predictability of behavior, for without such no communicative interaction could even occur. This could be the main adaptative value of relationships (H. Kummer, 1973). Thus, we create certain obligations for ourselves even with our first behavioral step taken in an interaction. We wish to appear as somebody who is relatively constant and also open. Manipulators utilize this by encouraging us to take steps in particular directions for the sake of doing something in common. After certain initial voluntary steps are taken, the next may follow of necessity. J. L. Freedman and S. C. Fraser (1966) asked a group of California homeowners whether they were willing to erect prominent signs in their front yards that read DRIVE CAREFULLY! Most of them refused to place an unsightly billboard in front of their homes. In another part of the same city, the researchers had two weeks earlier asked homeowners to sign a petition, which in flowery terms, asserted the importance of keeping California clean. When these people were then asked the same question about a billboard, they responded affirmatively far more frequently than the first group of homeowners. They had previously declared themselves to be citizens backing socially desirable measures, and they wanted to maintain this self-image.

In addition to all these general rules (maintain restraint, cultivate reciprocity, 515 demonstrate reliability), there are more specialized rules applied to specific categories of interactions. One can roughly distinguish between agonistic and cooperative, bonding strategies. For the latter, the attempt is made not to exert dominance over the partner and prevent similar intentions on the partner's part as well. Thus one behaves in such a way that the partner's self-esteem is preserved while ones' own self-image is maintained. This is a basic principle for every interaction and is observed in courtship, making any requests or demands, and in friendly contact initiation.

We have shown a great many examples of these principles. One should not exert force on the partner, embarrass him or denigrate him. If necessary, one becomes self-deprecating, as described earlier, and gives verbal and nonverbal evidence of modesty. When thanked for something, we respond, "Don't mention it!" Thus we release the other person of any obligation to be thankful, which could have been advantageous for ourselves. Naturally the other individual is not entirely liberated from any obligation, but our response lessens it.

In the ceremonial greeting rituals of the inhabitants of Rennell and Bellona (Polynesia), the greeters state that their homelands are plagued by diseases and demons and that they themselves are so unworthy and therefore content to stay with the host's younger brother, and that they kiss the host's behind, and so on. The greeting partner is similarly humble (S. H. Elbert, 1967). In the contract songs of the Yanomami comparable figures of speech occur, so that when one gives a beautiful dog to another he does it with the remark, "Take this poor creature!"

Some responses to particular stimuli or stimulus configurations are determined by innate releasing mechanisms, and universal motivations enable us to seek or bring about these releasing situations, or to avoid aversive experiences. Norms as reference patterns record any deviations from expected behavior. The existence of a norm of respect of object possession, for example, has far-reaching consequences. It makes object transfer possible as a function of bonding as well as the development of reciprocal exchange systems. Without them there would be no rules for making requests and demands. Without norms regarding killing there could be no conflicts of conscience at death and no atonement rituals. The conflict of fear and simultaneous attraction toward others helps mold greeting and other rituals.

Strategies can be consciously planned and organized. Many of the basic strategies of social interaction, however, follow their course automatically according to phylogenetically evolved programs. Thus a young man will be fully aware of his intentions and goals, when he courts a young woman. And he may fully consciously buy a present for her, knowing that it will please her and make her more obliged. But other behaviors such as the indirectness of approach, which results from his concern about his and her self-esteem, follow its subconscious course. Accordingly his approach will be characterized by indirectness in order not to endanger his face; moved by ambivalent feelings, he may resort to infantile appeals by using a tender intonation or employ caregiving behavior by stroking her, and much of this behavior occurs without conscious planning. Even children not yet able to speak "know" that doing things together fosters unity and that reciprocity facilitates harmonious relations. Thus they solicit play by spontaneously building rituals of group behavior and the basic patterns of coaction and alternation, which play such an important role in adult life (choir singing, duets, p. 511), are seen in the mother–child dyad. The infant masters these techniques at this early stage of life. Alternation requires an ability to wait for something and to postpone behavior until the appropriate moment. A disposition for this, which channels learning, may have developed phylogenetically in connection with giving and taking. D. N. Stern *et al.* (1977) found that the basic interaction pattern of coaction and alternation are already available to babies, and it seems, without the need of prior training. Speech also requires alternation—it is rude to interrupt. We pass the platform of speaking to someone to take over or ask for the permission to talk and excuse ourself, if we feel the need to interrupt.

Although differentiated in various ways, the game hide-and-seek, and games between mother–child are apparently universal. C. Trevarthen (1979, p. 56) adds, "The rules of game are evidently not imparted by the mother although they may be culturated and ritualized as in 'pat-a-cake' or 'peek-a-boo.' They are derived from rules of infants motivation which we are only beginning to discern."

These universal structures, which we can detect by analyzing various events, are probably the expressions of similarly biologically programmed cerebral activities. Certain expectations, perceptions, compulsions, lines of thought, motivations, learning dispositions, and even movement coordinations can be biologically programmed and thus determine how behavior unfolds occurring within some network of pathways. The alternatives are limited in number and with them the number of available strategies that can be engaged to attain specific goals. In this sense we can speak of a universal grammar of human social behavior, a general one covering the rules of all kinds of communicative behavior and a more specific grammar describing the course of specific strategies.

According to Lévi-Strauss, binary contrast and reciprocity are the fundamental structuring principles of cultural forms. He thus generalizes the reciprocity principle of M. Mauss for all types of interactions and the Darwinian concept of antithesis by maintaining that logical categories are invariably developed according to the principle of binary contrast. We have already mentioned the polarizing tendency. Lévi-Strauss claims that this kind of duality underlies most sociocultural phenomena, and this is, in principle, the essence of structuralism. He also speaks of universal structures and functional peculiarities of the human brain, which underlyi all cultural behavior as the "structural unconscious."

Lévi-Strauss is undoubtedly correct in designating these two principles as "fundamental." But as our investigations have shown, they are not the only ones. The ethological perspective permits more precise analysis in terms of in which way phylogenetic adaptations structure our actions on various levels of behavior.

With the discovery of the universal interactional strategies, human ethology achieved a significant breakthrough. One theory now connects the previously separate field of verbal and nonverbal communication. We have recognized the existence of a universal, underlying regulating system governing all interactions and can now begin to explore the grammar of human social behavior. The first steps in this direction have already been taken.

6.4.2. Functional Aspects of Ritualized Behavior

We live in a time in which it is claimed that matter-of-factness has priority over etiquette. With the battle cry "Under the gowns the mould of one thousand years" the student movements of the 1960s turned against certain anachronistic rituals. Many criticized Prince Charles' wedding festivities in 1981, claiming that money had better been spent on the poor instead of pomp and pageantry. Foreign ministries are regularly criticized for receptions and other representative functions.

The Christmas rush is often criticized as devoid of all meaning, and, at first glance, sober reflection does indeed indicate that a great deal of what goes on is truly superfluous. But this does not hold true at a second glance! Indeed, many of our customs have been commercialized, and it could be that some rituals have forfeited their original function, but most fulfill important functions just as they have in the past.

First we should recall that rituals serve communication. This is true for "Good night," "Thank you" as well as saluting at a state visit or the Vienna opera ball. Anyone who wants to communicate cannot avoid using rituals. The question is simply whether the fastest route is best or whether one should use a more costly, elaborate pathway to achieve the desired result. In Salzburg, Austria, college students graduate in a festive ceremony, whereas in Munich they receive a formal handshake for passing their final examinations, and the graduation certificate is simply sent to them in the mail without any ceremony.[11] Which way is better? Certainly one might say that the Salzburgers behave in a more "cultivated" manner. The occasion is truly celebrated, classical music is played, addresses are delivered, with the university deacon and rector on hand to assure the graduates that they continue to feel an association with them even after they depart from the school. The graduates are admonished to be sincere individuals and are held accountable for their status as doctoral students, taking a doctoral oath (this is not done just with the medicine students). Natural scientists are also obliged, according to the oath, to propagate as best they can, only the truth. Are these just pure formalities? Perhaps, but this has not been proved. One thing is certain: the bond that this ceremonious act creates with the university, the academic community, and the country, is a powerful one.

Like an initiation ritual, the celebration marks the entry into a new phase of life, and in it society recognizes the accomplishments of the new graduates. It would have sufficed to receive notification in the mail that the graduate had officially completed his academic course, but all those supplementary messages absorbed during the process of group participation, mutual obligation, and bonding in a society would be absent. Elaborated manners are just what is needed to reinforce these kinds of values.

Rituals also provide security in that they make the behavior of one's partner predictable. The need for this kind of security arises very early in life. Thus, when a mother deviates from her entire sequence of trusted behavioral patterns, even 4-month-old infants react with unrest and contact avoidance.

H. and M. Papoušek (1977) asked mothers to separate themselves from their infants for 15 seconds, just as they would normally do at home. The mothers did this by making their customary farewell ceremony with their children. Separation thus occurred in a stepwise manner with eye contact and repeated verbal explanations and words of departure. When the mothers returned, their children turned to them happily. In a second study group, the mothers left their children alone without these ceremonies. During a 3-second period the light was turned off and the mother left and then returned after 15 seconds. Initially the children greeted their mothers in a friendly manner, but after repeated departures of the mothers without prior notice the children rejected maternal contact in a rather spiteful reaction whose magnitude grew the more the mother attempted to establish contact.

---

[11]The grotesque situation exists in Europe that we regret the passing of custom in other nations while at the same time energetically destroy our own.

These behavioral changes were not elicited solely because of the light, since there were no discernible differences in the childrens' behavior when the light was turned off in the mother's presence without her disappearance. These results fit well with my own observations that children are more easily separated temporarily from their parents (such as when they are left in a kindergarten) when the departure is preceded by the customary farewell ceremonies.

E. B. Greif and J. B. Gleason (1980) claimed that children must learn to request, thank or say "Goodbye," meaning that this behavior is due solely to cultural convention. This is true in terms of the specific behavior under discussion, but it would be false to conclude that these are behavior patterns for which we are completely unprepared. Even in cultures where "please," "thank you," or some departure phrase are not used, there are functional equivalents for thanking and greeting. The critical turning points of an interaction, in which behavior switches to some new pattern, are characterized in such a way that one can recognize what the partner intends to do. This can occur in culturally specific ways, but this change must be marked in some way, and thus even learning the specific ritual conforms to predisposition—it is obligatory.

The human need to put order in daily, yearly, and life cycles by means of ritual is no doubt a very strong one. Even small children invent their own conventions which they maintain during play. Rituals put order into daily life, providing a certain security, and it is not in vain that people are devoted to custom and feel that with shared customs they are part of a community and protected against the unforeseeable.

We have already shown that this need for predictability leads to the production of order in the form of hypotheses about the world, to orient oneself properly in the complexity of the world as, for example, in religious rituals. There have been many historical attempts to do away with ritual. Wherever this happened, however, new rituals arose, with the same functions as those that had been abandoned. This is quite evident in contemporary communist Russia. C. Lane (1979, p. 256) writes "There is a notable tendency in the new Ritual to create its own holy scripture, traditions, ritual attributes, saints and its holy places of pilgrimage. They are holy or sacred in the sense that they are given a timeless importance and are considered as a part of the unalterable order of things. Often Soviet writers will themselves use the word 'holy' to describe them."

Lane notes that no public decision is made without invoking Lenin's name. "Lenin lived, Lenin lives, Lenin will live" is seen on posters and the mass pilgrimages to Lenin's mausoleum are well known. Similar developments occur in other societies as well. A notable work on the rituals of Nazism was done by S. Taylor (1981).

Many of these rituals can be understood as the differentiation of elemental interaction strategies, but probably not all of them. When a central Kalahari Bushman throws his oracle discs before hunting to learn which direction he should head for the hunt, this is not due to any biological program. However we can still pose the biological question about the selective function of this particular task. One might speculate that tossing the oracle discs results in a uniform distribution of hunting patterns in various directions and thus an equalized utilization of the territory.

Strategy and rituals—the latter often being derived from strategies which by convention were shaped and stereotyped in particular ways—can be classified and placed in more general categories such as bonding, aggression, etc. These general categories place behaviors related by their function into groups, such as all behaviors that establish and maintain friendly relations between people. This includes, among others, mother—child bonding rituals and the various strategies of heterosexual courtship or greeting.

We have discussed the hierarchical organization of strategies, as well as the fact that behavioral freedom increases as the integration level decreases. Cultural ritualization is required to establish sequences of behavioral patterns in humans; in some religious ceremonies each step of the sequence is prescribed.

Classification of Interaction Strategies According to Function[12]

1. *Strategies of group maintenance and bonding (affiliative or synagonal strategies).*[13]
   The function of these strategies is to establish, develop, maintain, and repair social relationships, and to maintain group harmony and group unity.
   a. *Strategies of friendly contact initiation*
   Greeting rituals, strategies of ingratiation
   Strategies of heterosexual approach (contact initiation, flirting)
   Strategies of play solicitation, exploration, and development of commonality
   b. *Strategies which reinforce bonds*
   Rituals of unification (rituals of coaction and alternation = mother–child bonding rituals, synchronization rituals, demonstrations of sympathy and other points in common, rituals of group aggression, e.g., against common foes, cultivation of shared values, indoctrination)
   Rituals of reciprocal care (gift giving rituals, hospitality, "grooming talk")
   c. *Strategies maintaining group harmony*
   Strategies to maintain group norms (bringing deviants into line by mocking, censure, or aggression to maintain norms)
   Strategies of pacification (mediation, conflict resolution)
   Strategies of support (support, aid)
   Strategies of making amends (reconciliation, excusing oneself, atonement, mediation)
   Strategies of aggression blocking (threat of breaking off contact, submission, mother–child appeals, strategies of reconciliation)
   Strategies to avoid challenges, appeasement (tactful approach, demonstrative

---

[12]Many strategies in the lower integrational levels are ritualized in whole or in part in behavioral steps. They may also appear in different functional relationships, as, for instance, in friendly contact initiation as well as agonistic confrontations. Rank striving can occur within a context of aggression or as an ordering element for purposes of internal group harmony. Key phrases below suggest broad meanings; see the text for examples.

[13]While hostile behavior is commonly characterized with the word *agonistic* (from the Greek *agon* = competition, but linguistically superior in the form *agonal*), a corresponding term for the various forms of bonding behavior has been lacking. I suggest using the concept of *synagonal* (or Latinized to synagonistic). It is derived from *synago* (from the Greek for bringing together, befriending, bond formation, reconcile, receive with hospitality). (Alternatively the term "affiliative" is used.)

respect of the possession norm, rituals of recognition, such as, admiration, praise, self-deprecation, and other forms of appeasement)

2. *Strategies of social learning and teaching*[14]
   a. Strategies of social exploration (exploratory aggression, p. 391, imitation)
   b. Strategies of instruction (encouragement, educational aggression, demonstration)

3. *Strategies of rank striving*
   a. Strategies of self-presentation (self-presentation as caregiver, powerful person, potlatch, etc., p. 308)
   b. Strategies of rank defense
   c. Rituals of obedience (discipline reinforcement)

4. *Strategies of fighting (agonal strategies)*
   a. Strategies of display and bluffing (demonstration of physical, spiritual, or economic power)
   b. Strategies of challenging
   c. Strategies of attack and fighting (ritualized fights)
   d. Strategies of defense
   e. Strategies of withdrawal
   f. Strategies of reconciliation and peace making
   g. Strategies of submission

6.4.3. Pathologies in Communicative Behavior

In anonymous society, we mask our feelings through certain expressions. We continually save face, motivated by fear, and avoid showing our true feelings. We have discussed the reasons for this in detail (p. 177). We may not want to invite personal contact, but at the same time do not want to betray our feelings, particularly to show any weaknesses, thus preventing others from taking advantage of the situation to achieve dominance. This can become such an ingrained habit that people sometimes become incapable of communicating. They may not even free themselves from this condition within their own families. This type of disturbance in communicative behavior seems to be widespread today, if the increased use of communication therapists is any indication.

Autism is a special instance of a communicative behavior disorder. Autistic individuals often reject human contact at an early age. Social fear, particularly a fear of visual contact, may be a decisive factor in the genesis of this behavior (E. A. and N. Tinbergen, 1972, 1983), but there are also other reasons that can cause someone to avoid contact with others. We have already mentioned the strategy of breaking contact (pouting).

The person whose expectations are continually frustrated also withdraws into himself. Many descriptions of the development of early childhood autism also

---

[14]The strategies listed in categories 2 and 3 use aggression as an instrument, e.g., of education or in rank striving. But this kind of dominance acquired against other's wills is not aimed at driving away the dominated parties but rather serves their own interests, such as in the case of educational aggression. Thus these should be distinguished from aggression aimed at enemies.

point in this direction. Children react with cut off to inappropriate maternal behavior when their expectations are not fulfilled, perhaps also to avoid being hurt and disappointment. This issue is open to debate. If the presumption is correct, then there are two types of essentially distinct early childhood autistic conditions, requiring different therapy: the type generated from within the child manifested as an excessive fear, and another type based on inappropriate maternal behavior. N. and E. A. Tinbergen (1983) have offered important therapeutic suggestions for the treatment of the fear-evoking form of autism. They advise the use of physical, but not visual, contact, even forcefully, until the child has become accustomed to it and overcomes its fears.

Communication disturbances may also arise when one person behaves in a certain way without considering that his behavior may be falsely interpreted. A therapist told me about a man who complained about contact difficulties. He was helped with glasses. This large man actually had a visual defect he corrected by tilting his head to the back slightly, which gave him an impression to others of being arrogant and seemingly unapproachable.

Summary 6.4

The superficial appearance of human interactive behaviors varies enormously from culture to culture, but with closer examination we can recognize that the various strategies of social interactions share a universal pattern, based upon a universal rule system. Within this regulating system, behaviors of different origins but with similar functions can substitute for each other as functional equivalents and even spoken language can replace behavior patterns. Those things that children in all cultures express nonverbally in essentially the same way, adults translate into words, but this verbal behavior follows the same rules underlying the corresponding nonverbal interactions.

The discovery of the interchangeability of verbal and nonverbal behavior opens a new way for the investigation of the universal grammar of human social behavior, which encompasses verbal and nonverbal social interaction while bridging the gap that has previously existed between the two. In addition to general rules resulting from characteristics of human perception, the motivational structure of man, especially his ambivalence toward others, determines the course of social interactions.

One of the basic principles of affiliative strategies arises directly from the human knowledge of the power relationships with one's partner. This means that we behave in such a way as to prevent a loss of face for either the partner or oneself. The combination of positive self-presentation and appeasement, the veiled form of demands, self-deprecation as a friendly act of submission in gift-giving, and other unique aspects of friendly interactions are the immediate results. This also includes the rule that one leaves openings for the other to choose different behaviors by avoiding strategies that act as ultimatums. The directness or indirectness of a strategy will be determined by the relationship of the interacting individuals.

Norms specify the sequential course of strategies, as in the norm of respect of object possession influencing all interactions concerning object transfer. Credibility, reciprocity, and consideration for others are universal principles of human social intercourse.

I will speak daggers to her,
but use none.
Shakespeare
Hamlet, Act 3, Scene 2

6.5. On the Ethology of Verbal Communication

Human verbal language incorporates a sign system that is shared with no other animals. Only man communicates using a traditionally learned vocabulary organized into sentences according to rules of grammar. Within the framework set by these rules and with the given vocabulary, man is free to formulate novel concepts and to relate them to others. Language is without doubt the creative instrument with whose help we pursue entirely new lines of thought. Thus human communication by language can be said to be open. Only man can conduct his affairs using verbal language.

Since we often hear that animals have a language, it is necessary to point out that there is no counterpart to human language in animals. Animal communication generally takes place using innate mechanisms, and only rarely is the code system learned and passed on by tradition. Animals lack the capacity to combine signals in a creative manner. Most animal communication deals with the organism's specific behavioral disposition: they signal their particular motivational state. For example, using their dances, bees can communicate the location of food sources relative to the hive and thus tell others something about the environment, but they do this using a rigidly predetermined communication code, and must always transmit accurate information. They cannot lie, while man occasionally is particularly effective at deception. One of the main advantages of verbal language is to divorce the speaker from the constraints of time and space, to allow him to pass on knowledge about objects and their use even in their absence. Chimpanzees and macaques are now known to transmit knowledge as well, but in these cases one animal must always watch another do something to learn how to do the same thing. Japanese macaques learned to wash sweet potatoes offered to them. One of them accidentally discovered the technique, and others watched it do the washing. In this way, this particular knowledge has now spread throughout the entire macaque colony. Humans, however, can dispense with an actual demonstration by simply telling someone "potatoes are washed before they are eaten." It was only through speech that the explosive cultural evolution of mankind was possible.

6.5.1. Origin, Roots of Speech

A great deal of speculation has taken place on the origin of language. There is no counterpart of verbal language in the anthropoid apes. Thus it is all the more astonishing that under experimental conditions certain communicative functions that closely resemble speech have been developed by these animals. B. T. and R. A. Gardner (1975, 1980) taught a chimpanzee a simplified form of the American system of signs for the deaf (ASL). After a year the chimpanzee was not only able to name objects but also to freely use signs as if they were words, expressing her desires and making statements and commentaries, carrying on simple dialogues, expressing emotions, and even asking questions. A single wish was often expressed by superimposing various symbols. Thus when her trainer, Suzan, set her foot on a doll that the chimpanzee wanted, she could signal: "foot-up,", "Suzan-up," "open-baby," "baby-up," etc., demonstrating that she could use the signals quite freely. The chimpanzee even spontaneously developed novel concepts by simplifying existing patterns and using them in an original way: a radish was a "cry-hurt-food," a watermelon a "drink-fruit," and garden door an "open-flower."

Studies by R. S. Fouts (1975), and D. M. Rumbaugh and T. V. Gill (1977) have added to our knowledge about verbal communication in chimpanzees. Since then, sign language has also been taught to a gorilla, who mastered the signs nearly as well as the chimpanzees (F. G. Patterson, 1978). Thus nonhuman communication with a learned symbol system has been demonstrated, although essential differences between this and human verbal communication exist. Free-roaming chimpanzees and gorillas in the wild scarcely make any use of acquired sets of symbols. A. Kortlandt (1972) described chimpanzees in his research area as placing their young upon the back as a warning gesture when danger threatened, something chimpanzees in other areas did not do. It is not uncommon, however, that certain capacities of animals become evident only under experimental conditions, since complex systems can often do more than the specific functions for which they were initially selected (see also S. T. Parker and K. R. Gibson, 1979).

In the anthropoid apes, however, we should only use the term speech analog communication, since there are still a great many distinctions between the above-mentioned ape communication and human speech. Small children typically communicate in two-word sentences, which are used as individual units of thought. They are the components of a communication structure with sentence boundaries delineated by intonation, frequency changes, and other nonverbal cues. This is also true for the language of the deaf, who bring their hands back to a resting position after expressing a sentence. In asking a question, they momentarily hold their hands in the position of the last expressed sign (W. C. Stokoe et al., 1965).

These kinds of delineation and connecting markers have not been described in chimpanzees. Only when questioned by R. Brown (1970, 1974) did B. T. Gardner (pers. commun.) acknowledge that Washoe uses delineation signs, but Gardner had not noticed them before. Since no further discussion of this interesting point occurs, we should assume that until evidence to the contrary exists there is no significant use of delineation markers by chimpanzees. R. Brown (1970, 1974) adds that children expressing themselves even in two-word sentences quite specifically order the words they use. If they are shown a drawing of a dog biting a cat and a drawing of a cat biting a dog, they will describe the picture of the dog biting the cat as "Dog bites" (agent action) or "Bites cat" (action object) or even "Dog-cat" (agent object) but never "Cat bites." Thus the words are correctly logically ordered. The child would describe the other drawing, respectively, by: "Cat bites," "Bites dog," or "Cat dog." This distinction considering the sequence of elements in the drawings confirms that children recognize structural differences in meaning. This ability, however, is lacking in chimpanzees. Gardner's Washoe did not join words signs in any regular order. Whether chimpanzees can ask questions is still disputed. B. T. and R. A. Gardner (1975) reported that Washoe has asked questions and was also able to answer questions in the negative.

The discussion about animal speech was rejuvenated with the studies of H. S. Terrace et al. (1979), who raised a male chimpanzee (Nim) from the age of 2 weeks and used Gardner's method to teach him signing. A very thorough evaluation of over 19,000 multiple sign expressions showed that the chimpanzee did not combine two words accidentally. Words like "more" usually appeared first in word groupings, while others, like "me," were usually in the second position. It also appeared that Nim comprehended the difference between "me give" and "give me." Combinations using more than two symbols were usually repetitions and did not contain novel information. Similar repetitions are quite rare in the language of small children. Finally, careful analysis of video recordings showed that the few instances of lexical regularities found in two sign combinations given were controlled by unconscious cues by the human conversation partner. In summary: "For the moment, our detailed investigation suggests that an ape's language learning is severely restricted. Apes can learn many isolated symbols (as can dogs, horses, and other nonhuman species), but they show no unequivocal evidence of mastering conversational semantic or syntactic organization of language" (p. 901).

Similar views are held by T. A. Sebeok and J. Umiker-Sebeok (1980) and J. Umiker-Sebeok and T. A. Sebeok (1981). The question of whether Washoe uses syntax in sign language is still open.

E. H. Lenneberg (1974) emphasizes that language is not simply based upon a broad repertoire of associations and that therefore there is no evidence of true verbal communication in chimpanzees. Critically sound evidence of verbal communication between man and animal must involve the successful experimental achievement of the following: (1) A person poses a written question; (2) another person translates it into signs for the chimpanzee; (3) a third person observes the second and writes down what he feels was asked to the chimpanzee; (4) a fourth person observes the chimpanzee and records its answer without seeing the person who placed the question (2). Recently, using these techniques, R. A. Gardner and B. T. Gardner (1984) published a double blind vocabulary test, which indicates that chimpanzees can name natural language categories such as dog for any dog, flower for any flower, etc.

The actual impetus for human speech has been the subject of a great deal of speculation. One of the reasons that has been cited is the need for cooperation in hunting and working. However, hunters do not actually talk a great deal while they are engaged in hunting, so this may have spurred the development of nonverbal communication but certainly not speech. Volker Heeschen spent many hours observing the Eipo at work in their gardens and building huts, recording what they said. They talked a great deal, but none of their comments were directly related to their work! This agrees fully with P. Wiessner's findings (pers. commun.) on the !Kung Bushmen, who never verbally communicated handcraft skills. Such skills were acquired by observation. In ontogeny, verbal cooperation occurs relatively late, namely at the age of 4 years (C. R. Brannigan and D. A. Humphries, 1972). It is certainly an advantage if some skill can be handed down via cultural tradition independently of the object under discussion (p. 11), but apparently this need was not the starting point of verbal development.

Unfortunately there is all too little cross-cultural material on the content of daily conversation. We have interesting samples of specific interactions, but there is a lack of data that could provide a quantitative evaluation of conversation contents. However, quantitative studies on conversation themes exist for the !Kung Bushmen (P. Wiessner, 1981 and pers. commun.) and the Eipo (V. Heeschen, in press). In both cultures, a great deal of talk centered on food, comprising 59% of all !Kung conversations![15] Some discussions concerned where food is found, which products are found in individual gathering areas, and in which gardens one should work. A larger part of the food conversations are concerned with the social aspects of nutrition. Topics include who gives what to whom, and criticisms of those who

---

[15]P. Wiessner recorded these conversations in August, 1977, an exceptional period of time since the mongongo nut harvest was a failure. There was a lack of food, and so conversations about food were more prominent than usual. However, this theme is also important during normal times.

do not share their food. In this connection the findings of V. Heeschen are noteworthy: three-quarters of all words of the Mek-speaking In are based upon giving and taking.

It is self-evident that the people of Kosarek, the In or Yale, explain words like *eat* or *take* with examples taken from social exchange—giving or receiving. However, the predominant significance of these basic types of interaction is that if one is asked to explain the meaning of words which are in no way linked to eating, sharing, or taking, either by origin or semantics, that these types of interactions are referred to in order to describe the meaning of the word. These interactions are fine models for more general interactions:

> *irikildolamla* "He builds (a fence), he wards off (evil spirits)."
> *Explanation:* when you have a lot and do not want to share it and someone comes to you, then you hide your things and "shelter" them (i.e., you build a fence around them).
> *bulolamla* "He sits for himself alone."
> *Explanation:* I come to people who are eating, but I get nothing; I sit here in vain, just for myself.
> *likiblolamla* "He deceives, lies."
> *Explanation:* when you have a lot food and someone comes who wants some of it, then you say, "I only have a little"—you give little away and hide the rest."

In addition to this preoccupation with food and sharing, the coming and going of individuals accounts for a great deal of the conversation. Heeschen found that in the Eipo there is a continual accounting for comings and goings. One comments that someone comes, asks where they are going, and tells others where they are heading.[16] This is due in part to the need for territorial control and for maintaining bonds during spatial and temporal separation. This is the chief function of farewell rituals (p. 540), in which continued attachments are reaffirmed and some return visit is promised, thus bridging the separation by making some future agreement. This bridging across time and space is highly significant for humans, who are the only primates spending many hours away from the group hunting, sometimes even over extended periods of time.

People marry outside of their intimate group, and the bonds established under the conditions of marriage are maintained verbally, whereby the prolonged reciprocal relationships between families in the form of protracted exchanges fulfills extremely important bonding functions. It was with the help of speech that time and space were bridged so that bonds could continue across such barriers. Planning for the future and the building of alliances could scarcely occur without speech. We have already discussed the great significance of verbalized conflict (p. 375). The considerations raised here indicate that the fulfillment of social functions was the decisive impetus for the development of speech. Social themes continue to dominate everyday talk in preindustrial societies. Indeed, a certain amount of

---

[16]V. Heeschen gives an example for the typical course of this kind of commentary conversation in the Eipo: *A:* There he comes. *B:* Fatere comes here, he says. *C:* Fatere comes here, he says. *D:* He is going to Munggona. *A:* Not to Munggona, he was there already. *B:* Not to Munggona, he says. *C:* He is not going to Munggona, he says he was already there. *Several speakers:* Yes, yes, so it is. This also occurs in Enga. "Where are you going," is, in a sense, part of a greeting. More often than not, people lie about their destination. They feel that it is their own business and that if they tell, the information may just be passed on to an enemy (Pauline Wiessner, verbal commun.).

material knowledge is transmitted during such conversations, but this function in tribal societies is much less important than the social ones. A change in thematic content occurred only with the development of technological civilizations. In our technically civilized world the transmission of material and technological matters, both in spoken and written word, has become much more significant, and yet social considerations still predominate in daily conversation. Unfortunately there are, to my knowledge, no studies of this phenomenon.

Since so much of what the Eipo talk about has to do with their orientation, V. Heeschen (in press) assumes that language primarily served this function and was only secondarily adapted for social interaction, where nonverbal communication is still of paramount importance. Nonetheless, I am of the opinion that the need to ritualize social behavior functioned as the most important selection pressure in the evolution of language. In particular, the ritualization of aggression finds its ultimate achievement in verbalization, since a tongue may be sharp as a dagger, but it rarely draws blood.

In order for verbal language to develop at all, certain characteristics had to be already present. They have been discussed as the "roots of language" (A. Gehlen, 1940; O. Koehler, 1954; C. F. Hockett, 1960). These are, so to speak, preadaptations for speech that developed in entirely different contexts. One of these prerequisites for speech is a voluntary control of motor functions.

In animals living in a complex environment, motor functions become independent of rigidly executed programs. They are divided into smaller movement units which connect orientation motions. This permits an improved guidance of movement in adaptation to changing environmental conditions, e.g., consciously aimed stepping with the foot. Horses cannot do this well and so have difficulties traversing mountainous terrain. But as inhabitants of the open steppes they can manage quite well with a relatively rigid locomotion program. On the other hand, a chamois antelope must be able to guide each step precisely, and being liberated from a rigid program the chamois can vary the length of each step voluntarily. In the large nonhuman primates, voluntary motor functions develop in association with braciation and binocular vision (p. 607). They must be able to seize branches accurately to avoid falling, and must also be able to grab at fruits with precision. Furthermore, voluntary motor control is required for social grooming and tool use.

Animals that must learn a great deal also develop a noteworthy behavioral category we call "play." One of its chief characteristics is the liberation of the motor acts from the drives that normally activate them (I. Eibl-Eibesfeldt, 1950, 1951, 1987). For this reason, animals can freely combine acts of different functional categories in play, behaviors that would not appear together in "serious" contexts. It is also possible to change rapidly from one activity to another during play (such as from a play attack to play flight, and vice versa). Such rapid shifts are not possible with full emotional involvement. The liberation of behavior patterns from autochthonous drives enables the animal to experiment freely and exercise a broader spectrum of behavior. This ability to detach oneself emotionally is one of the essential prerequisites for free speech and argument, whose development was discussed previously (p. 86). This allows social confrontations to take place in a detached, sober atmosphere. Although in such contexts one is not entirely removed from an emotional involvement, there is a certain reduction of tension when verbal exchanges can occur (G. Bally, 1945). Note also that when someone is overly emotional, their language loses its usual differentiation. With the loss of

527

self-control there is also a frequent deterioration of verbal coordination. The aroused individual mispronounces words, stutters, and often experiences difficulty finding the correct word. This may have been one reason for a functional separation of the cerebral hemispheres into a more emotional half and a more rationally oriented half guiding verbal motor skills. The cognitive requirements for speech will be discussed in Chapter 7 on ontogeny.

Some neurophysiological findings indicate that selection for improved sound recognition—especially significant for a relatively defenseless inhabitant of the open savannah—changed specific brain structures so much that these centers became predisposed for verbal understanding, while selection for improved communication through expressive movements prepared other neural regions for the later developed ability to read (N. R. Varney and J. A. Vilensky, 1980). The precursors of the more recent cerebral structures responsible for speech and verbal comprehension, such as Broca's center, which mainly controls speech motor functions, and Wernicke's center, which when injured does not impair speech but comprehension, may have developed quite independently of each other to serve different functions.

Certainly the development of tool cultures gave an important impetus for speech, although, as stated earlier, this context was probably not one of the original reasons for speech development. After all, chimpanzees can create and use tools. Actually, the tool cultures of our ancestors utilized a few, very simple and uniform tools (such as the hand axe) over a period of several hundred thousand years, and tools only became much more elaborated some 40,000–50,000 years ago. This may be related to the development of speech, which simplified the passing on of acquired knowledge. The impetus for the development of language came from many sides. J. Hill (1974) pointed out that pioneering bands invading new territories tend to use dialect formation as a means of small group delineation.

I. G. Mattingly (1972) claims that babbling sound sequences like mama, papa, baba, and bubu bring about positive social reactions in the infant via innate releasing mechanisms. Furthermore, the child recognizes individual voice variations of its mother at an early stage, which reinforces its maternal attachment. Later, dialects, in a similar way, would bond group members. Mattingly considers these functions as the most significant for the development of speech, which supposedly became a mechanism fostering cultural evolution through the development of dialect (see cultural pseudospeciation, p. 15). Many other selective advantages have been attributed to speech.

It is not yet known which ancestors of *Homo sapiens* could talk. The mouth cavity did not have the appropriate configuration in the Neanderthal or in *Homo erectus* that is seen in *Homo sapiens*. In particular, the space between the epiglottis and the velum, the so-called extension tube of the throat, had not yet developed. In the nonhuman primates, as in all mammals, the larynx is quite elevated. The free edge of the epiglottis extends across the soft palate or velum into the nasal cavity thereby dividing respiratory and food intake function. This division still exists in infants so they can drink and breathe at the same time without aspirating fluids, but later in ontogenesis the larynx is lowered increasing the danger of breathing in foods or fluids. The secure separation of respiratory and food intake passages was altered in favor of improving the ability to talk. During the course of hominization, the mouth cavity was enlarged through arching of the soft palate, which in anthropoid apes is still flat. This gave the tongue a larger area within which to move, allowing for the production of the palatal sounds of g, k, and kh.

528

This transformation of the mouth and throat cavity also made it possible to form the vowel sounds of a, i, and u.[17] Neanderthals could probably not make these sounds (P. Lieberman, 1977). Another morphologically significant change in the mouth region is the development of closed rows of teeth with vertical incisors, permitting the articulation of the so-called dental sounds of d, t, s, and f.

The building blocks of speech are sound units that themselves have no meaning: phonemes. All languages have a phonological structure with a limited means of combining phonemes to form words, and all languages also have a syllabic structure. That is, consonants are joined with vowels by opening and closing the mouth during speech. Babbling sounds seen in the early mother–child relationships, may be precursors to verbal language (J. H. Scharf, 1981), whereby such sounds as mama and papa are universal releasing signals of positive social contact, defined by linguists as global words. "That these babbling sounds are 'invented' by babies and not adults, since every child makes these sounds on its own, is generally acknowledged: even the Oxford Dictionary uses the term 'instinctive' with some of them" (J. H. Scharf, 1981, p. 488). We have already discussed the fact that some of these sounds may be releasers (see above). True babbling does not occur in pongids. However, newborn deaf children will make babbling sounds, and, Sabine, a girl deaf and blind from birth, whom I studied, also babbled (I. Eibl-Eibesfeldt, 1973b). Thus even without acoustic stimulation and in the absence of acoustic and visual feedback there is an ability, perhaps even an impulse, to articulate babbling sounds. There are, however, significant differences in the time of onset and the frequency of babbling. Babies deaf from birth start much later with the production of mature phonetic sequences (syllables) and their frequency of babbling is very low (D. K. Oller and R. E. Eilers, 1988). The play with syllables, which is practiced by every healthy child, depends on auditory feedback. The studies of W. S. Condon and L. W. Sander (1974) confirm the presence of an innate disposition in infants to react to verbal utterances. Even 12- to 48-hour-old infants react to spoken words but not to artificial sounds of equal volume.

Phonemes are divided into consonants, vowels, and click sounds, which some linguists consider to be very ancient and which today occur solely in the African Hottentot and Bushman languages. But infants throughout the world produce clicking sounds, and according to G. Tembrock (1975) some sounds of infant chimpanzees are difficult to distinguish from the corresponding utterances of human infants.

J. H. Scharf points out three levels of archaic structures in speech. Emotionally toned elements often occur in marginal language that is not a part of formal speech. These, according to Scharf, are common to all anthropoids and are characterized as "relics of the clicking word system used by chimpanzees to express their moods." Scharf refers to the highly speculative work of R. Stopa (1972, 1975), which allegedly demonstrates "that all chimpanzee words"—he means vocal utterances—are maintained with the same meaning in Bushman and that the click groupings of the Bushman language, which according to Stopa, is the oldest existing language, underwent a phonetic change during the course of speech evolution that permitted an elementary vocabulary of African and European cultivated speech to develop from the archaic Bushman vocabulary. Clicking sounds are heard in

---

[17]These, however, are less important than consonants. There is a Papuan language with just one vowel, a.

infants during their babbling stage, but they disappear only to be relearned, for example, in Bushman language. Phonemes and their complexes supposedly also developed from the primate sound inventory. But not all babbling sounds developed from this prehuman sound inventory. Thus, at its deepest "stratigraphic" level, human speech contains a pongid component, most of which has since been discarded. This inheritance supposedly still appears in Bushman language. However, the fact that Bushmen have to acquire their clicking sounds secondarily by relearning them as speech components, leads me to doubt Stopa's interpretation.[18] At another (stratigraphic) level, according to Scharf, human speech contains spontaneously produced babbling sounds, and these belong to the universals of human behavior. Their area of significance encompasses relationship designations, child nutrition, pronouns, elemental verb roots, and deity names. A third level encompasses the so-called elementary parallels, a vocabulary of 300 words in universal distribution. These, however, are not examples of infant talk but rather represent an extremely ancient adult vocabulary.

6.5.2. Biological Programs

The smallest produced speech units are syllables. We cannot say b or p but must verbalize them as be or pe. We do not perceive sound as a continuum, but classify it into categories which we distinguish as voiced (b) or unvoiced (p) sounds. We always perceive either the b or p even when artificially created transition sounds are presented to us. If we measure the interval from the opening of the lips to the onset of vocal cord activity, we find that if this interval is below 20 msec we will perceive all sounds as b and above 20 msec as p. This also occurs in infants and in all languages. Culturally determined fine distinctions are only acquired later in development. For example, the Vietnamese distinguish three hardness grades of the letter b, while the French have other distinctions (Fig. 6.77). The innate normative categories can thus be replaced by ones acquired culturally.

Categorical perception results in an artificial segmentation of sounds that may be responsible for making spoken communication possible. Initially, infants perceive in a categorical way in an identical manner in different cultures. Cultural differentiation occurs later in life. Categorical auditory perception has also been verified in nonhuman primates. This indicates that this perception was not developed solely for the sake of language but is one of the prerequisites for it (A. M. Liberman and D. B. Pisoni, 1977; P. D. Eimas *et al.*, 1973; L. Lisker and A. S. Abramson, 1964; P. Marler, 1979).

Information on emotionality is contained within the melody of speech and presumably also in its rhythm. We apparently possess an innate ability to recognize these emotional states, for we are able to listen to texts in unfamiliar languages and comprehend the mood of the speaker (see above). K. Sedlaček and Y. Sychra (1963, 1969) had the sentence "Tož už mám ustlané" ("The bed is already made") from Leos Janaček's *Diary of One who Vanished* interpreted by 23 different actresses. In this sentence the gypsy Zefka seduces the young village boy Janiček, whereby her courtship is accompanied by sorrow and resignation. Some of the

---

[18]I mention this work mainly to introduce another interesting line of argumentation, which may inspire more critical studies.

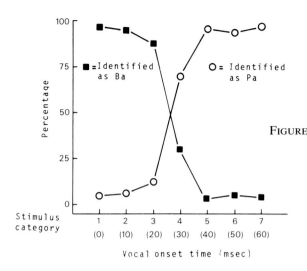

FIGURE 6.77. Categorical perception. Up to 20 msec, we perceive everything as ba and thereafter as pa.

(joy, sorrow, neutral, matter of fact), while others were given a spontaneous choice but were subsequently asked what sort of feeling they meant to convey while reciting the line. The recordings of their readings were played before 70 listeners of various origins and educational levels.

The responses to the recitations were organized into the following categories: (1) simple statement; (2) amorous; (3) joyful; (4) solemn; (5) comical; (6) ironical and angry; (7) sorrowful, resigned; (8) fearful, frightened. If 60% of all responses fell into the same categories, while the others were more or less diffusely scattered in other categories, the example was considered to be distinctly emotionally colored. The subjective evaluation displayed a high degree of conformity of results. Not only the 70 Czech study persons but also students from Asia, Africa, and Latin America, lacking a knowledge of Czech, accurately determined the affective information from the melodic line of the recitations. In order to compare these subjective judgments with objective data, tone frequency, amplitude, and sound spectrography were recorded.

The results of the study are summarized in Fig. 6.78. The tonal range of the neutrally spoken sentence is shown by the hatched lines. Solid lines give examples of melodies interpreted as joyful; dashed lines depict sentences of erotic emotions. The diagram clearly shows that all melodies of a joyful character are above the hatched region. Erotically expressed sentences are lower, but none extends below the hatched zone. Thus joyful emotions are characterized by a distinct elevation of the voice, and joyful and amorous sentences, in contrast to the others, have a doubled lifting of the melodic contour.

The next diagram shows the typical melody lines for resignation, sorrow, and embitteredness, whereby examples without an ironic character are designated by solid lines, those with ironic touch by dashed lines. The negative tone of these sentences is apparent by the sinking of the voice. The melody is monotonic and sinks slightly into the deeper regions. The ironic expression is shown as a livelier melodic course in the deeper frequencies.

The same verbal utterance can thus have different meanings depending on the emotion with which it is spoken (J. Jürgens, 1971; F. Trojan, 1975; J. Jürgens and

531

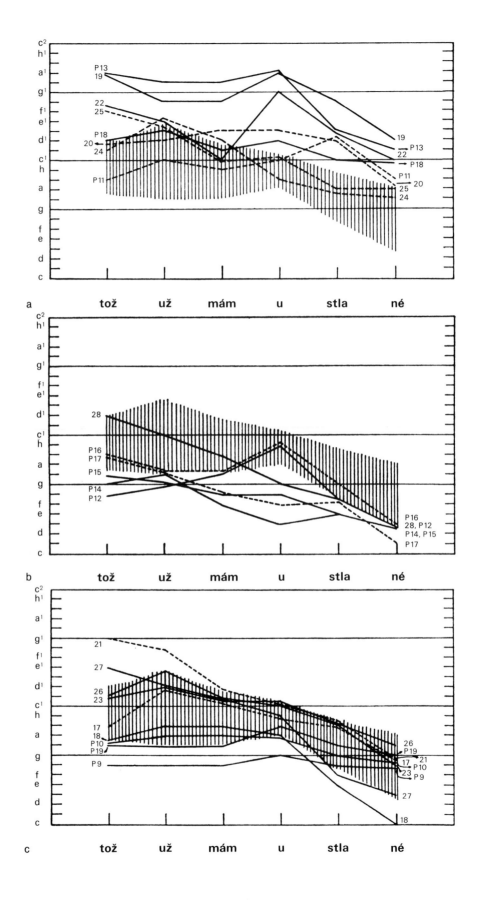

D. Ploog, 1976). Trojan describes three opposing sentence pairs of vocal mood expressions:

1. Compressed and uncompressed voice. They correspond to the emotions of unpleasant and pleasant, respectively. The compressed voice has a greater portion of nonharmonic (noisy) components and is louder as well.

2. Strong and restrained voice, characterized by higher and lower volume levels, respectively.

3. Chest voice and head voice. The chest voice, which expresses self-assuredness, is characterized by deeper frequencies. The higher head voice expresses a feeling of being overwhelmed.

Table 6.4 from Jürgens and Ploog shows the emotions for eight extreme positions.

If someone smiles while speaking, the vocal pitch is simultaneously raised. Persons listening to recording of others speaking while smiling and not smiling will identify the smiling speech as more cheerful (V. C. Tartter, 1980).

The voice can express anger, joy, fear, sadness, boredom, and other emotions. Along with the rhythm of speaking and culture-specific styles of speech, voice also marks social position, sex, personality, and other characteristics (K. R. Scherer and H. Giles, 1979; see also p. 208). Thus confidence is expressed by a strong voice and expressive intonation (greater frequency variation) as well as a relatively rapid and uninterrupted flow of speech (K. R. Scherer and J. J. Wolf, 1973). Higher frequencies and the higher vowel sounds of e and i characterize diminutive style and also immediate proximity. When a person is lying, his vocal pitch is also elevated, and fewer nonverbal accompanying movements are used. Speaking in a lower tone of voice is interpreted by listeners as coming from a relaxed, sociable individual (P. Ekman, W. V. Friesen, and K. R. Scherer, 1976).

Lower and falling tones at the end of the sentences indicates decisiveness, while sentences terminating in higher tones display indecisiveness, uncertainty, and of course questioning. Tone variations like these are apparently universal and follow a uniform pattern. D. Bolinger (1978) claims that speech melodies indicating specific meanings are so widespread that they can be considered an "essentially human trait": ". . . one should look to some still active physiological mechanisms,

◁————————————————————————————————————

FIGURE 6.78. (See opposite page.) (a) to (c) The Czech sentence "tož už mam ustlané" was spoken with different emotions. Tape recordings were played for people unfamiliar with the language for the sake of evaluating the emotion being depicted. They recognized the emotional state of the various readers: (a) The Czech sentence spoken in a joyful tone. The tonal range that a neutrally spoken sentence would display (and thus the central value of the speech patterns) is shown by the hatched lines. Joyful and loving emotions are seen here as sharing higher frequencies and a lively melodic structure (solid lines). The dashed lines designate sentences whose intonation is erotic (courtship), their melodies being somewhat deeper than those of joyfulness. (b) Emotions of sorrow and resignation. Examples of sadness are shown with solid lines, while those of irony are displayed by broken lines. The melodic line is clearly below that of the hatched region of neutral expression. Note the monotonous, sinking melody of the ironic sentences and a particular emphasis of embitteredness displayed in the tendency to begin and terminate in a deeper voice. (c) Examples of simple uniformly expressed "neutral" statements. From K. Sedlaček and A. Sychra (1963).

Table 6.4. Emotions for Eight Extreme Positions[a]

Voice	Head voice	Chest voice	Voice
Compressed	Misery	Chagrin	Low
Compressed	Fear cry	Scolding	Strong
Uncompressed	Tenderness	Enjoyment	Low
Uncompressed	Rejoicing	Impressing	Strong

[a]From Jürgens and Ploog, 1976.

such as expiration and drop in subglottal air pressure or relaxation and untensing of the vocal cords or whether that is past history and we now carry traces in our genetic makeup that compel us to adopt certain definite patterns, the fact is that human speakers everywhere do essentially the same things with fundamental pitch" (D. Bolinger, 1978, p. 518). We previously discussed that tender speech, e.g., to babies, is characterized by a high fundamental frequency. A cross-cultural investigation reveals that high fundamental frequencies generally express submissive, subordinate, nonthreatening, and affiliative intentions. This is derived from the association of high acoustic frequency with the primary meaning of "small vocalizer," since a smaller vocal apparatus produces higher sounds in animals as well as in man. Larger vocalizers produce low acoustic frequency vocalizations and, accordingly, associated with them is the secondary meaning of dominance, aggression, etc. (J. J. Ohala, 1984).

Intonation is the child's first linguistic communication. Babbling infants at the age of 7 to 8 months display intonation patterns similar to adult speech: "So children are either born equipped with innate vocalisations that correspond to intonational patterns, or they are born equipped to learn such patterns with relative ease" (D. Bolinger, 1980, p. 518). It could be, for instance, that infantile whimpering forms the basis for the development of intonation patterns and their association with expressing observable desires. Although the child hears more rising patterns of intonation from its parents, falling tones are more readily acquired. L. Menn (1976) shows that high pitch is associated with weakness and low pitch with strength. He considers it possible that some kind of innate perceptual components are responsible for this association. According to R. Jakobson (1941), u is associated with dark and large, i with bright and small. Artificially synthesized sound sequences in which different acoustic parameters were varied were arranged in high conformity by test persons hearing the sounds. These are summarized in Table 6.5.

The reflexlike interjections, which may initially appear as epiphenomena related to specific arousal states, can become intentional sound symbols utilized with a unique meaning. K. R. Scherer (1977) speaks of vocal emblems and describes and precisely classifies them.

It was linguists who first pointed out that these were innate characteristics in speech. N. Chomsky (1965, 1969, 1970) sharply disputed the studies of B. F. Skinner (1957), who attempted to explain language acquisition as a simple conditioning process. If one observes the way a child acquires language it becomes evident that its language is not just an imitation of what the adults say. Children begin by learning grammatical rules, resulting in certain erroneous words (such as "gooder"

Table 6.5. Emotional Attributions Significantly Associated with Acoustic Parameters[a]

Acoustic parameters of tone sequences	Direction of effect	Emotion rating scale[b]
Amplitude variation	Small	Happiness, pleasantness, activity
	Large	Fear
Pitch variation	Large	Happiness, pleasantness, activity, surprise
	Small	Disgust, anger, fear, boredom
Pitch contour	Down	Fear, surprise, anger, potency
	Up	Boredom, pleasantness, sadness
Pitch level	Low	Boredom, pleasantness, sadness
	High	Surprise, potency, anger, fear, activity
Tempo	Slow	Sadness, boredom, disgust
	Fast	Activity, surprise, happiness, pleasantness, potency, fear, anger
Envelope	Round	Disgust, sadness, fear, boredom, potency
	Sharp	Pleasantness, happiness, surprise, activity
Filtration cut off level (number of harmonics)	Intermediate (few)	Pleasantness, boredom, happiness, sadness
	High (many)	Power, anger, disgust, fear, activity, surprise

[a]From K.R. Scherer and J.S. Oshinsky, 1977.
[b]Scales listed in decreasing order of associative strength.

as the comparative form of "good"). Exceptions to the rules are always learned later. Thus the child brings with it a particular disposition to comprehend the rules of language.

Chomsky postulates an innate "language acquisition device" in humans. J. S. Bruner (1981) adds a corresponding innate teaching disposition, the "language assistance system" of the mother, who has an astonishingly fine sensitivity for teaching the child according to its developmental stages. B. F. Skinner's (1957) viewpoint that language acquisition is solely the result of random associations between some reference person and a verbal utterance is certainly oversimplified. G. A. Miller (1956) opposed this reduction of the complex problems of human language to such a simple process. One can understand only the simplest 1% of all language development with this kind of approach, for reducing speech to conditioning processes alone neglects the most important human ability, namely the arrangement of symbols in meaningful, novel, combinations (G. A. Miller, 1962, 1974). In his criticism of the behaviorist association theory of language acquisition, Miller points out several notable psychological aspects of grammar that indicate that biological programs in the form of specific learning dispositions for language acquisition must exist. The psychological reality of syntactic categories is one example. M. Glanzer (1962) found that we can more easily learn pairs of words when we combine nonsense syllables with words of content (nouns, verbs, adjectives, adverbs) than associating nonsense syllables with functional words (pronouns, prepositions, conjunctions). Thus expressions like YIG-FOOD or MEF-THINK are more readily associated than TAH-OF or LEX-AND. In the context of combinations of three words, functional words are more readily associated with nonsense

535

syllables than content words, and so one more rapidly learns the combinations TAH-OF-ZUM and KEX-AND-WOB than YIG-FOOD-SEB or MEF-THINK-YAT.

Word associations also show that our lexical memory is organized in such a way that facilitates acceptable statements in grammatically correct language (G. A. Miller, 1974). Thus we more readily associate the term animal with the term dog than we associate dog with animal. This is probably due to the fact that we think of all dogs as being animals but not all animals are dogs.

Sentences are always statements than can be true or false, but this is not so with associations. We evaluate sentences. Thus, the sentence "All animals are dogs" is simply wrong. The logical statement, the predicate (subordinating the term to the content of the sentence), is the central problem here.

It is noteworthy that children deaf from birth develop communication systems structured similarly to language, and do so without any parental instruction. Thus they develop their own sign language of gestures when communicating with each other and do not just passively submit to instructional influences (S. Goldin-Meadow and C. Mylander, 1983).

Skinner's attempt to explain language acquisition and verbal behavior solely on the basis of a behaviorist learning theory has been rejected by contemporary linguists. We do not simply maintain a list of memorized words and sentences, but as stated earlier, we are in a position to formulate new sentences that have never been spoken or heard before and therefore to understand statements we have never before experienced. According to N. Chomsky (1965, 1969, 1970) we have a generative grammar whose acquisition is also determined by "innate ideas and principles" among other factors. Chomsky suggests that the child learning a language has a predisposition to assume that the incoming data arise from a specific language of a well-defined type. Thus, the child is equipped with a prior knowledge about the nature of language—a general definition of grammar. Chomsky refers here to an "innate schema" that is specified when the child learns language.

E. H. Lenneberg (1969: 69/70) notes that the capacity for generative grammar can not be verified simply by showing that the study object is linked with various kinds of items. "The word generative in connection with grammar does not refer to the production and composition of sentences. It is used as an abstract metaphor and designates principles from which something is derived."

If a characteristic that we encounter as a universal fullfills its particular function most effectively in the manner encountered, then the characteristic is functionally explained. Thus the word order in the sentence "I came to see you" describes the temporal course of the event being described. It depicts the event iconically, and therefore has an functional explanation. On the other hand, the universal structure-dependent transformation permitting formulation of "YES" and "NO" questions by exchanging positions of subject and predicate, subject or terminal verb, or subject and auxiliary verb, is not functionally explainable. Thus with intonation alone one can transform the sentence "The man who killed the cat had an old gun" into a question, or the grammatical structure can be modified by moving terms around: "Did the man who killed the cat have an old gun?" or "Was the cat killed by a man with an old gun?" However it is not possible to formulate a question by simply reversing the grammatical elements in the sentence, even though there is no reason that simple changes in word position could not be used in a functioning communication system (B. Comrie, 1983). This restriction could be based on general laws of human perception and information processing. It remains to be seen whether speech-specific adaptations exist.

T. G. Bever (1970a, b, c) asks whether most linguistic universals are not ultimately the spoken expression of cognitive universals. The universality of noun–verb distinctions, for example, could be verbal expressions of the general cognitive distinction between objects and the relationships between objects.

This question has been the subject of innumerable discussions. H. Sinclair de Zwart (1974) and D. I. Slobin (1969, 1974), following J. Piaget, state that speech acquisition requires the existence of cognitive structures that developed at an earlier time. Speech acquisition according to this viewpoint requires a cognitive operation developing in the preverbal sensory motor period (p. 549). The development of symbolization is considered to be a highly significant event, for it is maintained that language originally had this symbolic function and has the same roots as symbolic play (see above). "Little will be left of the requirement for postulating specific, innate verbal structures," says Sinclair de Zwart, "when we consider language acquisition in the context of a complete cognitive development, particularly within the framework of its symbolic functions." In contrast, D. McNeill (1974) maintains that while thought processes are dependent upon the development of sensory-motor schemata, speech and thought when closely examined will be seen to be widely independent of each other. Thus, even imbeciles can generally learn to speak quite well.

There is no consensus regarding the question of how much thinking is involved in speaking. T. G. Bever feels that the identification of the cognitive mechanisms serving speech cannot yet explain speech in terms of verbal structures, just as our ability to name abstract concepts does not explain the latter's genesis. "The discovery that certain aspects of language are based on mechanisms of perception, learning, and cognition, presents us with a new problem, namely how these are being integrated in human communicative behavior" (T. G. Bever, 1970c, p. 65).

Naming objects is apparently a universal human propensity. A small child endlessly asks, "What is that?", and is initially satisfied just to hear a name for the object. With the word it has taken possession of something; words also create order. We have annexed objects with concepts, giving us a feeling of security and mastery over the environment and an orientation toward the world.

6.5.3. Concept Formation and Verbal Behavior

Ethologists have contributed to the discussion of phylogenetic adaptations in language acquisition and speech usage by showing that phylogenetic adaptations play an important role both in word formation and on the level of verbal interactions.

Figures of speech, such as, similies and metaphors have always fascinated linguists (R. M. Billow, 1977; S. Asch, 1955, 1958). Metaphors occur in all languages and generally transposes some abstract concept into something graphic or descriptive reflecting the primacy of visual perception discussed earlier. According to Volker Heeschen, the Eipo describe almost all their feelings in graphic, metaphorical terms. Sorrow is conveyed by the image of a footbridge collapsing under one's step. One Eipo expressed joy by saying "the sun shines on my chest."

Similies always express similarities. When a child takes his first glass of soda water and comments that it tastes like his foot is asleep (B. Skinner, 1957), the child is referring to the tingling sensation common to both perceptions. These associations are based upon individual experience. Since similar experiences take place in others as well, similar similies may develop in parallel. Concepts like "hot" are used in various languages to express a powerful emotional arousal. Thus the Eipo describe a powerful feeling as warmth in the liver. Thai and westerners likewise use heat as a metaphorical expression for sexual arousal.

Some metaphorical expressions, however, may be derived from phylogenetic adaptations. One-year-old children perceive nonphysical similarities in sensory modalities, in processes that are not usually associated: thus when a pulsating tone was played, infants fixated upon interrupted lines longer than continuous ones. They also fixated upon an upward pointed arrow longer than one pointed downward when a sound of increasing frequency was played, and looked at a downward arrow longer when the tone frequency decreased (S. Wagner and E. Winner, 1979). These are quasi-metaphorical phenomena.

The universal perception of relating "upright," "towering above," "high standing" elements to particular personal characteristics may refer to specific innate expressive elements of male display of the nonsubmissive upright posturing. H. Werner (1948) and H. Werner and B. Kaplan (1963) point out our tendency to physiognomize.[19] They refer to a dynamic schematization leading to our mental operations that include symbolization.

R. Brown (1968) criticized this argument as circular: dynamic schematization would lead to "physiognomic perception," which would then confirm the existence of dynamic schematization. However in our ethological perspective, Werner's theories are thoroughly reasonable, as are also psychoanalytical theories arising from Jung's concept of the archetype. "A live metaphor reveals a past forgotten experience," wrote E. Sharpe (1968). Today we know that phylogenetic adaptations guide our thinking and our perception in particular ways and that this explains some but not all of the universals in concept formation. Volker Heeschen and I tested the Eipo of western New Guinea on their concept formation. We found, for example, in their self-description, the Eipo metaphor symbolism corresponds very closely to our western language. Thus a man of esteem (and thus of high rank) is one who "is looked at" (Engl: "respected") (dildelamak), thus a headman is someone, as we would say, who "enjoys respect."

Primate studies show that the rank of an individual animal can be determined by observing the behavior of the other group members. The animal that is observed by the greatest number of others at the same time is the highest ranking animal in the group, standing, as M. R. A. Chance wrote, in the "focus of attention." This is also true in humans, as the kindergarten studies of B. Hold (p. 299) within our institute's research program have shown. Verbal formulations express similar rank relationships. In human society, high ranking members place themselves at the center of attention, for instance, by the particular position in which they are seated. Then, since they symbolically tower above the others, we verbally acknowledge this higher rank by our expressions of someone being in "high standing," "eminent," or being "looked up to." Similarly, in contrast, individuals may have "low standing" or a "base" mind. This symbolism of high and low also occurs in the Eipo. People of great esteem are described as "dubnang": "peak people" or "high people." The mythological bringers of culture are said to have descended from the peaks of the mountains.

---

[19]". . . objects are predominantly understood through the motor and affective attitude of the subject . . . Things perceived in this way may appear animate and, even though actually lifeless, seem to express some inner form of life . . . A landscape for instance, may be gay or melancholy or pensive" (H. Werner, 1948, p. 69).

According to the behaviorist interpretation of P. S. Cohen (1980), all people experience as children that adults are powerful, highly esteemed, and enjoy more advantages than the young. They learn this by associating these qualities with the size of adults and, therefore, perceive high objects as being particularly advantageous. But the fact that in vertebrates who have no parental care, in general, size is impressive, suggests that this attitude has a more ancient basis.

In the Eipo there is also a right-left symbolism that corresponds largely with ours. "Sirik" means right and "saboga sirik" is the right (proper) tobacco. Westerners also talk about "right" and "proper" in the same way. I presume that there is some relationship here with our handedness. Our tool culture and many of our rituals are based upon right handedness, which may have developed phylogenetically (p. 401). The selection for this may also have been fostered by the cultural tendency to designate right as good and correct.

Light-dark symbolism is also noteworthy. In English, "fair" means decent, and, in fact, this quality has been interpreted in a racist way. Here I believe that there may be a connection with our living habits as diurnal creatures. We fear the night, leading us to look for home when it becomes dark. However daytime is the period of activity, a time we regard positively. We speak of a "radiant" personality, a "sunny" disposition, and having a "bright" intelligence. This interpretation is supported by the fact that the dark-skinned Eipo say "korunye kanya" ("a bright soul") when they describe someone being open and radiant. They also say "nani korunye" ("you, my bright one") when they address someone affectionately. "Nonge kunmu dognobniil" ("My torso is shaded") is said when something distresses them.

The parallel expressions for "very" (very good or very sad) have been discussed earlier. Eipo usually express this nonverbally by protectively placing the hands on the head like someone who, surprised, covers the head as protection against a blow. If this comparative is verbalized, it is done by saying something is "fearfully good" or "terribly sad," akin to our "terrifically good," etc.

Concepts reflect perceptions, norms, and sensitivities of humans that are apparently universal. The very word concept, derived from the Latin (*concipere* = to take in), is a manifestation of our primacy of haptic-visual entities in concept formation (K. Lorenz, 1973), undoubtedly an ancient primate trait. Lorenz adds that we gain insight into relationships "like a monkey in the tangle of Lianas;" we must "imagine" things, and "grasp" relationships and concepts. Our most abstract conceptualizations are still firmly rooted in the visible and graspable (concept in German: Begriff). Thus we even attempt to depict atomic models visually in order to comprehend certain concepts about the atomic world. We wish to close our discussion of concept formation with this thought.

Turning now to verbal behavior, in the discussion of social interaction strategies we pointed out that basic strategies of social interaction can be carried out both verbally and nonverbally, whereby members of the most diverse cultures follow the same rules of a universal etiquette.

As stated earlier, demanding an object in the imperative is similar to taking it away, and the demand may be rejected. In cultures in which dominance relationships are cultivated and rank striving characterizes everyday life (e.g., on the Trobriand Islands), aggressive demands may become the rule. However, in general, such behavior is considered to be rude, and usually a more indirect request using indirect language is more successful. In the Bushmen and Eipo alike some supplementary comment about the desired object is expressed, such as: "kwelib fotong

539

teleb'' (''beautiful bird of paradise feathers''). The partner then knows that the other person would like to have the objects, and he can either present them or explain why it is not possible to do so in that particular instance. Only in special situations, such as one in which there is a considerable rank discrepancy, can direct requests be made with a high certainty of success.

Parting is another example, for generally there are preparations made for enacting a departure, usually in nonverbal means with one partner making intention movements by turning to the side and thereby opening up the dyad. This has to be done with care, for an abrupt departure signifies a breaking of contact, something one wishes to avoid. The parting should express a continuation of bonds despite the spatial separation of the partners. Gifts are given to the guest in the parting ritual; this can take place verbally by interjecting into the conversation that it is getting late or that one must leave for some other reason (wherein one generally makes some excuse), and then the conversation is closed with a parting wish of ''farewell,'' ''Have a good trip,'' or ''Goodbye.'' These rules are generally observed in most cultures, whether verbally or nonverbally. In the simplest case, as in the Yanomami or Eipo, one simply says, ''I am going.'' It is noteworthy that in the departure context some compelling reason for leaving is frequently given—''I am going to leave, it's getting late,'' ''I'm very tired today,'' ''I am going to warm myself up by the fire''—and other similar expressions are used by the Eipo in this situation.

W. A. Corsaro (1979) claims that very few preschool children he observed said good-bye upon going away, and over 60% of them simply left. He concludes from this that departure ceremonies must be learned. This is illustrated by the following episode from his records, a conversation in which a girl, Barbara (3.8), leaves the girls Susan (3.9) and Linda (4.6).

> B-SL: I want to—I want Charlie Brown.
> S-B: OK-
> L-BS: You're gettin' it [the TV] too close.
> S-BL: OK, we'll turn on Charlie Brown. (Pretends to change channel)
>   (L now gets up and stands on top of TV)
>   (B and S also stand up)
> B-S: I'm tired. Oh—
>   (B suddenly runs off across outside yard to swings. Another child, Rita, is in one of the swings and the other swing is vacant. B runs to vacant swing. B made no verbal marking of her withdrawal and S and L show no awareness of her absence.)
> S-L: Hey, let's jump on the bug, L.
>   (S points to a bug in front of the TV)

This new dyadic episode continued for approximately 10 more minutes until teachers announced ''clean up time'' (W. A. Corsaro, 1979, p. 333).

Corsaro writes ''The child, without comment or remark, merely left the ecological area where the interactive episode was underway.'' What he apparently failed to recognize was that Barbara in explanation stated that she was tired before going away, even though she is not really tired at all, since she goes to the swing. However, what is true is that the others did not respond to her comments verbally. Corsaro's reports do not indicate whether they reacted nonverbally, but even if they did not react at all, Barbara clearly made a parting remark.

540

We give a reason for leaving so that our departure does not create any implication of breaking off contact. Thus V. Heeschen quotes a 3-year-old girl saying "I am going to Grandma because it is beautiful weather." The compelling need for departure is evident here in this obvious contradiction between the alleged reason and any logical consistency with the action undertaken. V. Heeschen, thinking in terms of human territoriality, writes: "Within another's visual field we accompany our actions, especially spatial movements, with appeasement and humbling gestures." He points to the work of J. Piaget (1975a, b), who believes that justification of any action is an essential trait of infantile verbal behavior. Since children lack the concept of the coincidental, they draw the conclusion that all events are related to one another and thus that to give simply any reason for some action is appropriate. However, as Heeschen comments, this does not address the question of the motivations underlying behavior. He notes that a child when exploring new spheres automatically gets into situations in which the child does not know which particular behavior is acceptable or forbidden by this or that activity partner. The invented justifications provide support for his exploratory behavior, and by formulating reasons for his action appease the partner and therefore the child as well. Adult behavior is also marked by rationales and justifications.

Sentences can be used to describe behavior in the course of an interaction, such as a breaking of contact being indicated by the statement "I'm not speaking to you any more." Words can be used as verbal clichés like key stimuli in order to elicit some specific behavior. A comparative study of love songs shows that specific appeals are used again and again, primarily those from mother–child relationships. Thus the beloved is frequently praised as a little bird, as in the love songs of the Medlpa of New Guinea (I. Eibl-Eibesfeldt, 1974; A. Strathern, 1979).

Previously (p. 81), we describe male primate-like phallic display. This can be completely verbalized. The verbal duels of Turkish boys aimed at forcing the adversary into a passive, feminine role (A. Dundes, J. W. Leach, and B. Özkök, 1970). The adversary is described as a submissive anus forced to bear these verbal phallic attacks. Another strategy consists of discrediting one's mother or sister or to threaten them phallically. The one being attacked attempts to parry these verbal blows by putting the agonist into the passive female role.

"Much of the skill in the dueling process consists of parrying phallic thrusts such that the would-be attacker is accused of receiving a penis instead. According to this code, a young boy defends and asserts his virile standing in his peer group by seeing to it that his phallus threatens the anus of any rival who may challenge him" (A. Dundes *et al.*, 1970, p. 135). Besides, the response must rhyme with the opening insult. Most of these verbal encounters traditionally have a fixed structure. It is, therefore, important to know as many of these dueling rhymes as possible. If one is unable to answer in rhyme, he is defeated. It is better to respond with a poorly formulated rhyme than none at all, for in the latter case one has placed himself in the submissive female role.

W. Labov (1966, 1970) describes comparable ritualized forms of insult by young Harlem blacks. Their verbal duels also have a formal structure, and they likewise contain obscene remarks about one's relatives. Originality and conformity of one's statements within the structuring rules are approved of.

Man can fight with words and thus mock, outdo or, in contrast, humble oneself in a friendly manner. The patterns of verbal abasement of one's adversary among the Eipo are, in principle, similar to ours. The opponent is set "down" or made "smaller" by describing him as a fly ("bume") or lizard ("bal"). Thus the con-

541

frontation is transposed to an intraspecific one by dehumanizing the adversary. He can also be scoffed at by characterization as a deficient individual, by claiming he stinks, or is cowardly, incestuous, etc. [See F. Kiener (1983) on the theme of words as weapons.] Children of 3 years old who have learned to speak and come into contact with another language because their parents have moved, first learn terms of abuse from the children speaking the new language.

In the discussion of interaction strategies we mentioned how important it is to maintain one's self-esteem, by showing respect for the other individual without endangering his own. Thus the partner is praised and thereby his rank verbally elevated or reinforced. One often even acts in a submissive manner, obligating the other party to equalize the conversation with countering praise and self-deprecation. Answering praise with the response that anyone else would or could have done the same is a self-humbling gesture to express that one does not intend to dominate the other individual (T. Monberg, 1979). This is particularly well described by Samuel Elbert (1967). On the island of Bellona (of the Solomons) it is common to reduce the significance of a gift one is offering "Take this miserable small fish!" We previously (p. 498) cited the comparable Yanomami example.

High ranking individuals are regularly addressed with verbal submission. Headmen and the supernatural forces are addressed on Bellona with the words "tou noko" or "tou tapungao," which mean "I am worth less than your buttocks" and "I am worth less than the sole of your foot," respectively.

Among the Tikopia, when mourning guests bring food (kai) and request that the mourners join them in a meal, they do not speak of food, but instead invite their partners to drink water ("inu se vai mou;" R. Firth, 1975). They explained to Firth that they would do this so that no one believed they wanted to brag about their food. The gifts given to chieftains are also described indirectly as "vai" (water). The chieftain is not outdone or challenged in this way, nor are the mourners shamed. The Tikopia particularly act submissively toward their deities and spirits. "I eat your excrement" is a typical introduction to their prayers, and there is a similar greeting formula in some parts of New Guinea (I. Eibl-Eibesfeldt, 1977). It is a common practice in many cultures that two persons of equal social rank who are well acquainted with each other use forms of address that would normally be used for subordinate individuals. This is an expression of the more general rule that individuals who want to keep a friendly relationship must avoid anything that could be perceived as a dominance threat. However, in exchanges with unfamiliar equally ranking individuals, one uses the expressions normally reserved for superiors (R. Brown, 1965; R. O. Kroger *et al.*, 1979).

The bonding function of conversing together [D. Morris (1968) aptly spoke of "grooming talk"] was described by B. Malinowski (1923), and it has been cited again many times since (B. C. and T. Luckmann, 1977; D. E. Allen and R. F. Guy, 1974; V. Heeschen, in press). "Grooming talk" includes such things as affirmative responses by one's conversational partner and the listeners expression of attention by the repetition of the speaker's words and sentences. Bushmen do this when they tell stories. We also make affirmative gestures by nodding in response as listeners, and these gestures help maintain the narrative flow.

Speaking always indicates a certain decoupling from one's drives, and this distance is one of the prerequisites for a dialoglike confrontation (see above). This capability can be seen even in the talking games of children. According to V. Heeschen, their rank and aggressive behavior is playfully transformed into verbal expressions. He illustrates this with the example of two girls who pretend they are going on a voyage and during the game seek to outdo each other in a rank dispute. Games and confrontation are in close proximity in this dialogue.

> A: "I am taking everything for my doll."
> B: "I am taking a lot for my doll."
> A: "I am taking still more for my doll."
> B: "I am taking much more for my doll."
> A: "I am taking even more, everything, for my doll."

Speech can replace action, whereby all types of acts can be expressed in words. This is frequently in a less direct, even ritualized manner. Thus aggression can be expressed subtly, often venting such feelings, for instance, in joking partnerships (p. 294). Speech can express social distance through various forms of address, and can be used to define and delineate a group. Local groups are defined by dialect peculiarities, thus delineating them from other groups. Within local groups still smaller subgroups like clans or friendship communities can arise from shared secrets and especially through some kind of "insider-talk." The contract songs of the Yanomami, which contain many figurative and indirect allusions, are a good example of this (K. Good, 1980).

Regardless of whatever special strategy is pursued within a conversation, there are rules regarding the dialogue itself. This includes allowing another to speak without interruption. Such an intrusion is considered to be impolite, even among such people as the Eipo. One gives the opportunity to talk to another by means of intonation and other nonverbal gestures that indicate that the speaker is now ready to listen (K. R. Scherer, 1977; A. J. DeLong, 1977). Naturally, one can use the appropriate excusing phrase to interrupt or otherwise join in a conversation, but this also has its own particular justification and approach. When someone does not want to be interrupted because he has not finished speaking, he indicates this by filling the pauses (K. R. Scherer, 1977).

American children, 4 to 5 years old, indicate that another should take the floor by turning the head to the left and/or down after the second to last or last word. The downward motion can also be executed using other parts of the body, such as the arms (A. J. DeLong, 1977).

Behavior related to speaker change, verbal place maintenance, and displacement is observed in all cultures, but no close cross-cultural analysis of this behavior has been conducted. It has always occurred to me that even when speech ability is impaired one can use nonverbal cues to communicate effectively. And while we must study each word and the rules of grammar thoroughly, we need not be taught how to act nonverbally. These cues always come to us more readily than speech, and we automatically execute the appropriate gesture because, I assume, the basic pattern of accessory movements, as well as intonation (see above), are among the universals of behavior. The special forms of gestures accompanying speech, of course, can demonstrate cultural affiliation (D. Efron, 1941). But when the hands are raised or lowered in specific contexts, when visual contact is sought or interrupted, and many other gestures are seen regularly within similar situations, we may conclude that these gestures are universals.

There are constant functions and forms of speech and thus its expressiveness and formulation are also constant. We also find ethological constants in concept formation, and certainly in language we are dealing with an open system, but its basic tenets are programmed, which channels learning. When and in which ways

543

learned concepts are utilized and how and when they are acquired is undoubtedly prescribed largely through phylogenetic adaptations.

Human ethology attempts to investigate these kinds of relationships, especially at the level of speech and concept formation. Etholinguistics (I. Eibl-Eibesfeldt, 1979a) is characterized by posing the biological question: why do we speak only in a certain way in particular situations? This question can refer to the immediate cause, something that speech physiology deals with, but it can also refer to function and development, and here the comparative observational methodology of ethologists is useful. This provides us with cues about constant functions and forms of speech and thus also of possible phylogenetic programs. We have referred to such universals in speech acts in this section. They conform to semantic constraints but, also on a higher integration level, to the verbal strategies of action.

Verbal interaction strategies obey the same basic rules as nonverbal ones and often are their immediate translation. We act in words and utilize words and sentences as releasers. I have previously discussed verbal cliches in this context (I. Eibl-Eibesfeldt, 1979a). Thus, even instinctive behavior can be verbalized and attenuated by means of this ritualizing process. One of the chief theoretical positions of human ethology is that verbal and nonverbal interactions basically conform to the same rule system, and the research on this universal grammar of human social behavior is one of the major tasks of etholinguistics, as previously discussed (p. 499).

We have presented four theses in the previous sections:

1. The thesis of the potential exchangeability of nonverbal and verbal behavior as functional equivalents.
2. The thesis of the drive decoupling through language.
3. The thesis of the higher ritualization potential of verbal behavior.
4. The thesis of the contribution language makes to the facilitation of harmony in group life, in the sense of defusing confrontations. It results from theses (2) and (3).

S. F. Sager (1983) commented on these points but reiterates them in an oversimplified manner. He interprets my first thesis as meaning that all verbal and nonverbal behaviors are functional equivalents and that all verbal behavior is a direct translation of the nonverbal. His other criticisms, that my equivalence concept contradicts the thesis of ritualization and that the detachment hypothesis cannot be reconciled with the equivalence concept follow from this misunderstanding. When I speak of functional equivalents, I refer to basic strategies of social interactions, and it is in this context that I point to the fact that verbal behavior can be substituted for actions. Thus verbal and nonverbal behaviors serve similar ends in the case of the basic strategies of social interactions, and the same rules of "etiquette" are observed. On the surface the performances may look very different. But in principle, they are the same, that is, an expression of a shared biological heritage. In order to avoid any misunderstanding I want to provide one example. When an Eipo man (New Guinea) is scared he clicks his thumbnail against his phallocrypt; in other cultures, phallic scaredevils are carved as protective devices and in still other cultures, verbal phallic threats may be uttered (p. 81). Although this appears to be very different, all of them are linked to the primate phallic aggressive display associated with striving for rank and to the fact that male dominance and sexuality are physiologically connected (p. 304).

Sager finds that the detachment hypothesis cannot be reconciled with the equivalence concept. But this contradiction is only an apparent one. I am speaking of the *functional* equivalence of concrete verbal and nonverbal acts and not an equivalence in general. Thus, I refer to infantile behavior, rank disputes, self-humbling behavior, or self-praise as being transposable into the verbal realm, and only for the specific functions of appeasement, of display, conflict resolution, self-deprecation, departure, etc., do I claim the existence of a functional equivalence. The functions can be fulfilled in various ways and also with differing efficiency. Language makes the interaction more detached, occurring thus in a less emotionally charged atmosphere. One can talk and is thereby liberated from the compulsion of executing some specific behavioral act. If someone snatches an object from another person, that behavior demands direct physical reaction. In verbal form, a threat or a plea initiates a discussion, which may, without escalation to violence, lead to conflict resolution.

It is in this sense that I speak of ritualization in speech, as follows: a higher ritualization level is achieved in speech versus nonverbal behavior. But this does not mean that an act of speech that is functionally equivalent to a nonverbal behavior is therefore homologous with it. In many instances, it is the set of regulations underlying both behavioral patterns that is probably homologous. And within this regulating system, which maintains for all cultures, the nonverbal behavior is *translated* into the verbal realm, just as we translate one language into another, such as Chinese into German. Then the statements are functionally equivalent, and since the text comes from the same information pool, it can be said to be homologous by tradition. This is not true for the languages in which the statements are being made. We are talking about a translation, in this case from one language to another. If motor behavior is expressed in verbal acts and releasing stimuli in verbal clichés, then translation is occurring within another medium and there is no direct phylogenetic relationship. There is not the slightest evidence that nonverbal and verbal equivalents can be joined by a series of intermediate transitions.

One must not confuse the levels of comparison. There is a concrete, researchable regulating system based upon templates, IRMs and other phylogenetic adaptations, and motivations and strategies in the form of behavioral plans (if-then instructions), which act in such a way as to leave many options open, permitting many different configurations to be shaped upon individual experience.

This innate rule system forms the homologous basis for social behavior in all human beings, and it is only at this level that we can find homologs with nonhuman primate behavior. Functional analogies, on the other hand, occur at many different behavioral levels.

My fourth thesis is described by Sager as one of "appeasement," which is not exactly correct. In my book *Krieg und Frieden aus der Sicht der Verhaltensforschung* [*The Biology of Peace and War* (1975, 1979, Engl. ed., 1984], I speak of the verbalization of aggressive confrontations. This is not simply appeasement but a defusing of confrontation by transferring the struggle into the verbal realm. It is with this technique that the conflict songs of the Eskimo achieve very high ritualization levels.

Thus far, these questions have not been at the forefront of linguistic investigation (see the discussion of V. Heeschen, 1976, on verbal behavior). Sociolinguistics and anthropological linguistics, represented by the works of J. L. Gumperz and D. H. Hymes (1972) and D. H. Hymes (1970) made similar studies of verbal behavior in its natural context, whereby Hymes developed the methodology for analyzing speech patterns. But an integrative theory is still missing. Nevertheless, its merits lie in the methodological approach and in the elaboration of outstanding descriptions. Hymes looked at *who* speaks to *whom,* what speech taboos exist, and which scenarios are used. Conversations do not just take place between two persons. In reprimanding, for instance, one may feign a dialogue, while in fact a third person is actually the one being addressed by the two in conversation. The various forms of class-specific speech, verbal duels, and indirect requests have also been investigated. J. Sherzer (1970) investigated South American Indian speech, including their songs of praise and scolding speech, but without discussing the functional aspect, which is typical of the sociolinguists' theoretical abstinence. New directions have been taken in J. S. Bruner's (1974, 1975a, b) and D. Wunderlich's (1970–1974) work in the investigation of the logic of speech and speech-accompanying behavior.

In the field of psycholinguistics, N. Chomsky's studies on generative grammar caused a sensation. His insights into the existence of an innate "language acquisition device" has provided a valuable stimulus. His concept of the "universal grammar," however, meant something quite different from my concept of a universal grammar of human social behavior. I have in mind those rules according to which verbal interactions are structured, while Chomsky looks at the rules of syntax. Our concept of a "sociogrammar" is also distinguished from E. W. Count's (1970) "biogrammar." Count refers to the social potential characterizing the larger systematic animal categories which is based upon specific key inventions such as brood care. He thus speaks in this sense of a biogrammar of the birds, mammals, and other groups, but he does not refer to a system of rules structuring concrete behavioral sequences. D. I. Slobin (1969) has inspired new directions in language acquisition research by investigating universals in the strategies of speech acquisition. C. E. Snow *et al.* (1976), C. E. Snow and C. A. Ferguson (1977) and J. S. Bruner (1974, 1975a, b) studied the mother–child dialogue. An empirically oriented linguistic discipline is taking the place of a rather more speculative one. The ethological approach was launched by S. F. Sager (1983) and an "etholinguistics" (I. Eibl-Eibesfeldt, 1979b) is on the horizon.

Summary 6.5

With verbal language, man utilizes a system of learned symbols that, within the scope of grammar, can be combined creatively to form unique statements that can still be understood by another individual. Speech gives us the ability to transmit our experiences to others, to hand down knowledge independently of the objects actually involved, and, finally, to interact verbally with each other. In the animal world there is not the slightest counterpart to verbal language. Although chimpanzees can learn the meaning of simple sign language for the deaf and can even form new concepts by innovative combinations of symbols, they never extend beyond forming two-word sentences, and their sentences lack syntactic organization.

The important impetus behind the evolution of speech was probably not so much the need to transmit material knowledge as the continued ritualization of social interactions. Verbal conflict endangers the internal harmony of a small group less than physical fighting. As far as is known, the everyday conversation in tribal societies deals predominantly with social problems.

A number of capabilities required for verbal communication developed in higher mammals in other contexts, for instance, the ability to liberate behaviors from their drives in play, the increase in voluntary motor control in adaptation to climbing by grasping branches, food acquisition, and tool use.

Speech can be more emotionally detached than nonverbal behavior, occurring within a less emotionally charged atmosphere, thus defusing social strife. This mitigating effect is furthermore enhanced by the fact that speech gives more information on present, past, and future conditions, events, and intentions.

Phylogenetic adaptations have been verified on the levels of perception (categorical perception), concept formation, emotional expressivity in voice tone, and finally, verbal behavior. Any intraspecific communication, whether verbal or nonverbal, is based upon the assumption that the partners in an interaction act in a predictable way and share the communicative code and, thus, the basic understanding, and that they communicate sincerely, even though lying can occur.

Ethologists have determined a number of factors which control the course of an interaction. They are rooted in part in our biological heritage and in part are culturally imprinted. They operate at different levels. At the most basic levels are the motivations, whose subjective correlate is experienced as emotion. Thus, our striving for power (dominance, esteem) and with it our fear to lose face, determines which strategies are used in practically all types of interactions, affiliative as well as agonal ones. Accordingly, we find, for example, the universal tendency to combine agonal and affiliative displays in rituals of friendly encounters, be they verbally or nonverbally expressed. As a more general rule, we observe that the fear of losing face causes us to proceed with care. Successful strategies are characterized by detours and indirectness depending on degree of intimacy by veiled or metaphorical expression. Generally, the approach is characterized by more steps of action than would be needed if direct approaches could safely be used. The fear of rebuffs and cut offs that could endanger a friendly relationship controls most of our friendly interactions.

Special motivations determine the goals of actions, prescriptive rules the specific ways of conduct. These, in turn, are determined by a variety of phylogenetic adaptations and cultural norms. A number of rules seem to be encoded in reference patterns, such as the norm of respect of possession which specifies the approach in requesting and giving. At the level of the concrete action, more specific phylogenetic adaptations determine which of the potential pathways to a certain goal might be taken. A smile of the partner may encourage a more direct approach — a pout another step of action. Innate motor patterns and innate releasing mechanisms come directly into play. A persuasive tender voice may be used as appeal, or a verbally expressed phallic threat in an agonal context links, in an interesting way, modern human expression with primate heritage. Thus, we are coping with different levels at which phylogenetic and cultural programs work and interact from the motivational to the receptorical bias. There are hierarchies of motivations and goals and, accordingly, hierarchies of appetitive behaviors, each controlled by special releasing and rewarding situations. In cross-cultural comparisons, cultural context and values may have a marked effect on goals and priorities. Some rules are general in that they govern most types of interactions, for example, the rule of reciprocity and the rule to demonstrate reliability and to act in a self-controlled manner.

7

Behavior Development
(Ontogeny)

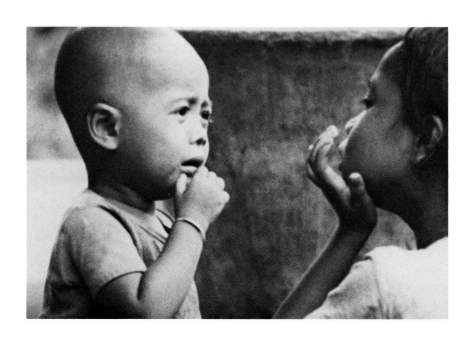

7.1. Developmental Theories

Although the human being is, in many respects, immature at birth, it is time to revise the traditional picture of the baby as a helpless bundle of reflexes. Newborns can suck, breathe, seek out the breast using automatic searching movements, grab with the hands, and crawl with alternating movements. They possess a rich repertoire of body protective movements (reflexes), a series of highly specific vocal utterances with specific functions (p. 29), and a good degree of competence at communicating with the mother (p. 204; C. Trevarthen, 1979; T. G. Bower, 1977; D. N. Stern, 1977; H. F. R. Prechtl, 1981). Furthermore, infants can react adaptively to specific visual, acoustic, and olfactory stimuli as well as localize the sources of such stimuli (p. 53). All these are capabilities which presuppose rather complex structures as products of phylogenetic adaptation. Even such apparently simple movements as sucking can no longer be described simply as a "sucking reflex" on the basis of current knowledge. The act of sucking is actually quite a complex motor program (H. F. R. Prechtl, 1981); with a rhythmic turning motion of the head ("automatic searching mechanism", H. F. R. Prechtl and W. Schleidt, 1950), the infant locates the nipple, which he grabs with his lips, thus terminating the automatic movements. Tactile stimuli then release the likewise rhythmic complex sucking movements of nursing. The act itself requires precise coordination of breathing and sucking motions. While drinking, the neck muscles contract, the arms are bent, the hands are closed into fists, and the legs are extended. Infants possess a biological mechanical clinging mechanism in the ligamentum iliofemorale Bertine, pars medialis within their legs that permits them to be carried about as "parent-clinger." They ride on their mother's hips or press their bellies against their mother's body (Fig. 7.1). In the young baby, the ligament prevents extension of the hip joint and fixes the thigh in an outspread position.

Newborn anthropoid apes have the same adaptation at their disposal (B. Hassenstein, 1981). Furthermore, being carried around in this position facilitates the normal development of the hip bone socket. European children who are not carried about this way often require a spreading binder or spreading pants to prevent subsequent hip joint disease.[1]

Not all infant behavior patterns can be related to some specific function: some, such as uncontrolled spontaneous movements, are probably epiphenomenal expressions of nerve activity. Others, such as the Moro Reflex, are probably a primate characteristic that have largely lost their original function. If an infant is suddenly released, it spreads its arms laterally, seeking a point of support, and then pulls them toward the middle of the body in a seizing movement (p. 31). Reflexive grabbing is probably also a rudimentary pattern, which is suggested by the fact that it is most pronounced in premature infants. Premature babies born in the seventh month can even dangle themselves from a line by their hands (A. Peiper, 1951, 1953); full-term babies are unable to do this.

When drinking, the infants of our human ancestors presumably clung onto the mother's fur. Today clenching of the fists is still executed during nursing. Infants can be aptly described as "parent-clingers" (B. Hassenstein, 1973a), even though they need to be supported by their mother, unlike most primate young who can

---

[1]Wulf Schiefenhövel, pers. commun.

FIGURE 7.1. !Ko infant (central Kalahari) riding in the straddle-posture in a leather carrier on the mother's hips. Photo: I. Eibl-Eibesfeldt.

hold onto their parents using their own strength. Neck musculature is initially not strong enough to hold the head up and make positional corrections. Although the neuronal mechanism of head balance is already fully developed, and the infant attempts holding the head correctly, it can only do so for a short period of time due to the lack of muscular strength. Primary walking movements in the form of alternating placement of the feet can be elicited in newborns by gently leading them in an upright posture with their feet touching any firm surface. This ability disappears, however, during the first few weeks of life. Pressure against the sole of the foot releases counterpressure, and this enables the infant to push itself forward (p. 28). An infant can localize an acoustic source and turn its head in the direction of the sound. We have already mentioned that children blind from birth also fixate visually on an acoustic source. When the source is the mother's voice, this behavior is interpreted by the mother as affectionate behavior, and that may be an important function of this apparently centrally programmed fixation. Infants with normal vision can follow visual stimuli. In their attempt to see clear images, they will perform specific tasks and their execution enables them to see focused rather than unfocused image (p. 53). Thus the human infant has a whole series of behavioral programs we can consider to be phylogenetic adaptations.

Behavior changes after birth by a process of phenotype differentiation based upon a specific sequence of events. We can, in pure descriptive terms, designate this sequence and the individual phases of behavioral development. Thus, on the one hand, development is the result of maturational processes and, on the other, also of individual learning. Child development is summarized in H. Thomae (1954), P. H. Mussen (1970), W. Spiel (1980), and J. D. Osofsky (1979).

Even during the first month we observe a series of interesting behavioral changes arising from restructuring and reorganization of the central nervous functions. Thus some of the behavioral patterns present at birth disappear in the first 14 days (primary walking, primary grasping), only to reappear at a later time. At 4 months an infant again reaches intentionally for objects, and upon close examination one finds that this reaching is unlike that in the newborn a few days old, for it is no longer an automatic grasping. Instead, the older infant reaches for the object, takes it in its hand, or just touches it and releases it once again—in short, he now has voluntary control over grasping, just as later in life walking will utilize voluntary control.

Presumably a "corticalization" takes place, in which in a maturational process the cerebral cortex is activated so that what was originally an automatic reflexive movement now becomes a voluntary movement instrumentally available. The disappearance of the behavioral patterns involved during this restructuring is probably an accompanying phenomenon of this reorganization.[2] The reflexive grasping, however, does not disappear, but exists alongside voluntarily directed grasping. This is also true for other typical infant behavior patterns (such as search automatism and sucking), that disappear during the course of development but may return during old age in individuals suffering from cerebral atrophy (G. Pilleri, 1960a, b; 1961). The fact that maturational processes play an important role, is verified by such facts that Hopi children raised in the traditional manner of being strapped down to a cradle board have no developmental retardation when compared to children raised the modern method of complete freedom of movement (W. Dennis, 1940). No one who has observed children learning to walk would doubt that learning plays a major role in acquiring this skill. From observation alone one can often not determine just what part of an activity is learned and what is maturational, since both processes take place over time, and maturation often resembles a learning process.

The important aspect of walking is that the steps are made intentionally (see also the discussion of the development of voluntary motor skills, p. 527). The central generator for walking is functional at birth,[3] but it requires cortical control of the movements (P. R. Zelazo, 1976, 1983). E. Thelen (1983, 1984) offers a mechanical explanation for the disappearance and reappearance of walking movements during development: the child would not physically be in a position to work against gravity since it acquires substantial fat reserves during the first months of life, gaining weight rapidly during this time. She adds that one does not have to be intelligent to be able to walk, which is certainly correct. If one considers voluntary control of stepping, the situation is different. Voluntary movement coordination is a prerequisite for intelligent behavior, of course, but it cannot be equated with intelligence. Highly intelligent geese cannot accurately step over a simple obstacle standing in their way, although many other birds living in biotopes where such obstacles are common can do this readily.

Albanian children were formerly bound onto carrying boards so firmly that they could hardly move at all, and were only released from the boards at bathing time. These children initially displayed a distinct developmental retardation when they were no longer placed in the carrying board. They did not learn normal crawling until after they were 1 year old, and were also slow to acquire grasping. But once freed from the boards, they quickly made up for lost time. One 10-month-old child studied by L. Danzinger and L. Frankl (1934) could not even hold two objects simultaneously in his hand, and its developmental level corresponded to that of a normally raised 5-month-old child. However, after it played freely for only 3 hours it nearly caught up with the normal level in development

---

[2] Other behavior also disappears temporarily. Newborns can localize sound sources quite efficiently, but after 1 month this ability is gone and does not return until 4 months later.

[3] The coordination is released as a reflexive walking movement when the newborn is lead across a substrate. When an infant stamps his legs while lying on his back he displays the same coordinated movement (E. Thelen, 1984).

FIGURE 7.2. See legend, opposite page.

according to the Bühler baby test. This suggests the existence of a genetically determined maturational process that remains latent even when a child is unable to utilize his capabilities.

A. Gesell (1946) noted that every child is a uniquely developing organism but that individual development is a variation of a general developmental plan determined by the genes. Environmental factors facilitate and modify ontogeny, but they are not the sole determinants of development. The way in which such programs determine in detail the course of ontogeny has yet to be investigated, but some interesting details about these processes have already been identified. Thus D. G. Freedman (1964, 1965) observed that a girl blind from birth at 3 months old "gazed" at her hands at play so intensively it appeared as if she could see them. Apparently this is again due to a central fixation program underlying learning from observation and individual activity.

The question of whether there are developmental differences in the various human races has not been the subject of much investigation. In San Francisco, Chinese and European children born under identical conditions had clearly distinct "temperaments" immediately after birth. Chinese infants were able to be pacified more rapidly when they cried. If their noses were held shut so they had to breathe through their mouths they protested less vigorously than European infants, who in general protested more vigorously to physical insult and uncomfortable positions (D. G. Freedman, 1979).

Ganda children are more mature at birth than European children, in that they can hold their head upright at birth. According to Geber (1958, 1960, 1961; M. Geber and R. Dean, 1957, 1958), Ganda children have a developmental advantage of about 1 to 2 months, and they continue to develop more rapidly throughout the first year. They can crawl on average at 5 or 6 months and walk at 9 months, while European children crawl at 9 months and walk at 14 to 15 months. M. Ainsworth (1967) determined that Ganda children also develop social behavior more rapidly. These developmental advantages are equalized in the third year, and by the fourth year, according to the Gesell test, European children are ahead developmentally.

Infants are subject to educational influences at a very early age. Parents react differently to male and female babies, partly due to responses to given genetic

◁——

FIGURE 7.2. On the social competence of infants. During the crawling stage the haptic (tactile) component dominates exploration but one's partner often defends himself so that interactions may escalate into aggressive ones. Mothers are aware of this and separate the children before any harm is done. Observations of this kind have led to the assumption that infants are socially incompetent, but this is not exactly correct. Babies understand that they can influence other individuals by sending signals to them so that these partners will allow contact with them, will give away things, or will stop fighting with them. Whatever they do depends upon their mood and that of the partner. This series of photos depicts two Himba infants of crawling age. Their mothers placed them together, but intercede (i, k, and u) when the encounter appears to be escalating. The children interact exploratively. They grab at each other's faces as well as defend themselves against this kind of approach. Later in life the children became close playmates (see Fig 4.77). From a 25 frames/second 16 mm film, frames 1, 78, 169, 233, 251, 266, 305, 438, 507, 739, 783, 853, 940, 1059, 1078, 1155, 1185, 1193, and 1224 of the sequence. Photo: I. Eibl-Eibesfeldt.

FIGURE 7.3. See legend on opposite page.

differences, but also in part, no doubt, to parental ideas about future sex roles. The Ashanti teach us how children are trained subconsciously: they name each child after the day on which it is born since it is believed that the name of the day is associated with certain personality traits. Thus a child born on Monday (name Kvadvo) is considered to be peaceable and quiet, while one born on Wednesday (Kvadu) is wild, aggressive, and pugnacious. Juvenile crime studies of the Ashanti reveal that there are far fewer criminals of the Kvadvo group than the Kvaku group (G. Jahoda, 1954). Apparently the expectation of the parents to a certain degree form the childrens' personalities, presumably by selective reinforcement of those behavioral traits corresponding to their expectations.

Siblings and other children are influential in a child's socialization since they react more spontaneously and directly to the child's behavior and distinctly reject inappropriate behavior, while adults are often more tolerant. If a toddler hits another child, the latter will frequently hit back or display some angry threat, while an adult would often laugh off the incident. If an infant pokes another with his finger, he learns from experience based on the response that one does not do this. If a baby pushes another down, he learns from parental reaction that this is not tolerated.

A great deal of learning goes on here regarding the fine tuning of social behavior and the utilization of individual strategies, but it would be a mistake to regard a child as initially socially incompetent. I emphasize this because as recently as the 1970s children were considered to be socially inept until well into their second year. It was believed they could not perceive the needs and feelings of others, treating other children like impersonal objects until the end of the first year. It was thought that this also held for the relationship with the mother until the sixth month. Since then, C. Trevarthen (1981) has shown that 2-month-old infants use facial expressions, verbalization, and gestures to communicate emotions and can have affectionate interactions with the mother using facial and auditory cues. If its expectations are not fulfilled, the infant acts disturbed. It is also untrue that interactions with peers are limited to taking objects away from them, whereby the child causing the disturbance is treated like an obstacle and not like an adversary (see also C. O. Eckermann and J. L. Whatley, 1977; H. Rauh, 1984). Our film documentation depicts empathy and astonishing social competence at the preverbal age (Figs. 7.2–7.16). Preverbal infants show each other objects, give them to each other, and vocalize in agreement, smile, and initiate contact with each other. Of course, they do have difficulties engaging in interactions with others of their own age before the end of their first year without adult assistance. They grab at each other's faces, knock down each other, and take things away from each other. At this age, the confrontations are exploratory, but frequently escalate into aggressive acts and crying. This is not seen in interactions with older children and adults since the more experienced partner guides the baby's behavior. Even in these situations though the baby displays social competence. By pointing to

⊲————————————————————————————————————

FIGURE 7.3. Conflict and its resolution between two approximately 1-year-olds of the opposite sex (Kaleuna, Trobriand Islands). She reaches for a comb he is holding. His protests escalate the situation to an exchange of blows. She runs to her mother and bites her on the shoulder, while the boy offers her the desired object. She smiles, in a change of mood, and breast feeds briefly. The mother then offers the boy and thereafter her daughter her breast. From a 25 frames/second 16 mm film, frames 1, 27, 93, 123, 310, 345, 431, 544, 585, 636, 742, 1302, 1526, and 1655 of the sequence. Photo: I. Eibl-Eibesfeldt.

FIGURE 7.4. Social competence in toddlers. A male Yanomami infant (about 16 months old) sitting by his mother wards off a somewhat younger female baby. He attempts to push her away; she defends herself, and he strikes back (e). The mother then intercedes and protects the girl. He then stands up, runs off, protests, and then sexually mounts the girl (i, k). His mother attempts to restrain him. Then she puts the girl down and takes her son to the breast. From a 25 frames/second 16 mm film, frames 1, 9, 72, 201, 219, 241, 576, 1032, 1213, 1373, 1596, 2029, and 2757 of the sequence. Photo: I. Eibl-Eibesfeldt.

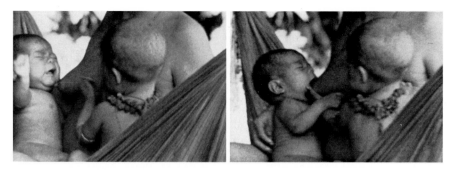

FIGURE 7.5. Infants possess a certain empathy and friendly supportive behavior. Here an approximately 15-month-old female Yanomami infant helps a somewhat younger baby (for whom her mother is babysitting) get to the mother's breast. The boy had been crying. Photo: I. Eibl-Eibesfeldt.

FIGURE 7.6. How a baby behaves depends upon the characteristics of the reference person. Older children and adults are hardly rivals, but partners with whom one seeks contact. They also form the experimental field for the infant. Here a male Eipo infant of crawling age attempts to maintain contact with a 3-year-old girl. He addresses his partner with the play-face, solicits contact with outspread arms and grasping intention movements, and finally holds his partner firmly. From a 50 frames/second 16 mm film, frames 1, 82, 178, 249, 312, 379, 496, 562, and 721 of the sequence. Photo: I. Eibl-Eibesfeldt.

557

FIGURE 7.7. (A)When reference persons cuddle other infants, their behavior often releases aggression in the form of jealousy. The approximately 10-year-old female cousin of the standing, approximately 1-year-old G/wi boy (their mothers are sisters) cuddles a baby girl. He attacks and hits the baby. He follows this later by scratching and pushing her until the cousin and the baby go away. From a 25 frames/second 16 mm film, frames 1, 144, 164, 187, 201, 252, 266, 288, and 325 of the sequence. Photo: I. Eibl-Eibesfeldt.

objects they initiate a "conversation," not unlike the way adults do in conversations about objects. See E. L. Leung and H. L. Rheingold (1981) on the development of communicative pointing.

The play-face and other affectionate signals are social gestures at an infant's disposal, but, in addition, a great deal is undoubtedly learned in the fine tuning of social behavior. In most situations, though, basic rules are observed that apparently are preprogrammed. For instance, preverbal children display a need to save face. They behave shyly toward others in a way that suggests they place a high priority on avoiding a loss of face. One of our films on the Eipo shows two girls 2 to 3 years old starting to play together one morning. Even though they know each other well, they initially are quite shy toward one another, and instead of directly playing together they build up the play activity through numerous intermediate behaviors. One entices the other by running off to a reed fence sur-

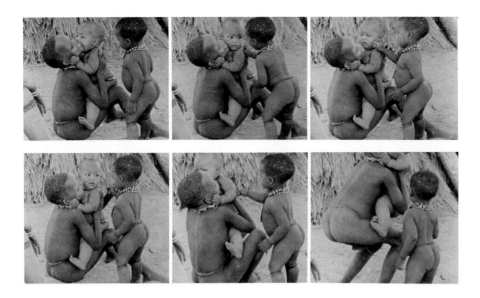

FIGURE 7.7. (B)Continuation of the interaction depicted in Fig. 7.7A. Filming was briefly interrupted between 7.7A and 7.7B so that the frames are counted from the beginning again. Frames 1, 37, 91, 113, 169, and 196 of the 25 frames/second film sequence. Photo: I. Eibl-Eibesfeldt.

rounding a hut, looking at the other invitingly and then, when the partner approaches, running back to her mother, the base of security. Her playmate is enticed to imitate her. This episode was described on p. 511. Finally, they both kick at the tobacco plants, one making some motion and the other imitating it. It is with this common activity that they build up a friendly relationship. In essence, we are observing here a fundamental characteristic of many bonding rituals.

Spontaneous greetings and also marked gestures at parting are observed in children before they can speak and babies also expect that adults behave according to some basic rules of conduct. Generally their behavior is structured in such a way that it cannot simply be interpreted as imitating adult behavior.

We also observe true imitative behavior of adult roles. Culture-specific rituals, like those of greeting, are often acted out quite realistically in play (Fig. 7.17),

FIGURE 7.8. Infants learn from partner reactions which behavior is permitted and which is offensive. The Yanomami boy reacts to an infant's pointing with a threat stare and defensive gestures. Adults generally respond to such behavior in a friendly manner. Photo: I. Eibl-Eibesfeldt.

FIGURE 7.9. A young In woman (Kosarek, Irian Jaya, New Guinea) responds to the contact
initiatives of the boy on the shoulder with friendly affection, inciting him to
continue. From a 25 frames/second 16 mm film, frames 1, 103, 112, 201, 225,
and 264 of the sequence. Photo: I. Eibl-Eibesfeldt.

but even before children acquire these, toddlers initiate contact with elementary
greeting signals which are found in all cultures. Four major variants of social
relationships are observed even in infants:

    friendly–aggressive
    dominant–submissive

Infants are also able to use specific strategies to create or neutralize these relationships. Thus by threatening to break off contact the child can block aggressive
behavior, or use gifts to establish friendly contact. The child can defend himself,
attack, and establish contact by using objects or by smiling and intention movements of embracing. The infant can also use these behavioral patterns to present
himself as being affectionate and caring. Even the use of display postures have
been verified shortly after the first year.

FIGURE 7.10. Infants are also objects for the experiments of older children. Here a Tasaday girl teases a baby boy by holding something out to him and then withdrawing it when the baby tries to grab it. She only offers it to the baby when he begins crying. The baby initially refuses the offer, then accepts it. Again, the girl pulls it back and then returns it once again. From a 25 frames/second 16 mm film, frames 1, 16, 20 74, 149, 233, 254, 287, 298, 314, 324, 358, 445, 475, 600, 633, 659, 753, 758, 918, 950, and 959 of the sequence. Photo: I. Eibl-Eibesfeldt.

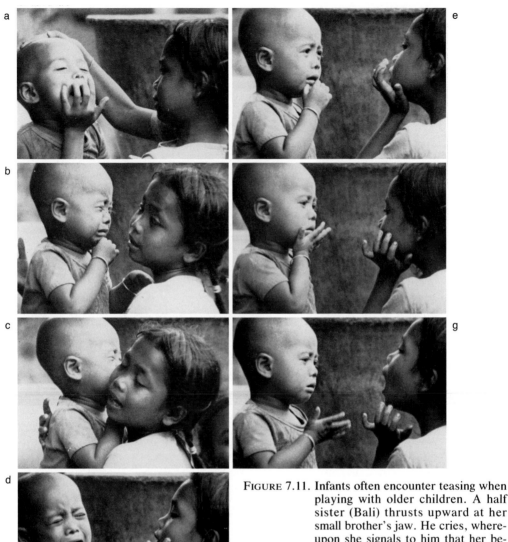

FIGURE 7.11. Infants often encounter teasing when playing with older children. A half sister (Bali) thrusts upward at her small brother's jaw. He cries, whereupon she signals to him that her behavior was not meant aggressively by pressing against her own jaw. He observes her gesture, imitates it, and is then pacified. From a 50 frames/second 16 mm film, frames 1, 169, 193, 301, 506, 574, and 596 of the sequence. Photo: I. Eibl-Eibesfeldt.

The social competence of infants and toddlers is summarized in the listing below.

1. Initiate contact through:
   a. play sounds
   b. expressive movements (mouth-open-face)
   c. embraces
   d. using objects as intermediates by: pointing at an object with the index finger, showing an object by holding it up, offering objects or food to another

a

b

c

d

e

FIGURE 7.12. Experiments with the partner. An Eipo girl not quite 3 years old tests the reaction of an infant by sticking out her tongue. In traditional societies the differentiated social network offers an infant a rich field for social exploration. From a 25 frames/second 16 mm film, frames 1, 73, 273, 296, and 520 of the sequence. Photo: I. Eibl-Eibesfeldt.

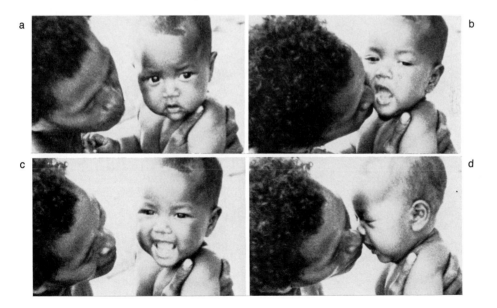

a

b

c

d

FIGURE 7.13. Mothers offer security. Many forms of tender body contact (here nose rubbing) elicit infantile affection. Mother with an approximately 5-month-old infant (Kaleuna, Trobriand Islands). From a 25 frames/second 16 mm film, frames 1, 17, 34, and 133 of the sequence. Photo: I. Eibl-Eibesfeldt.

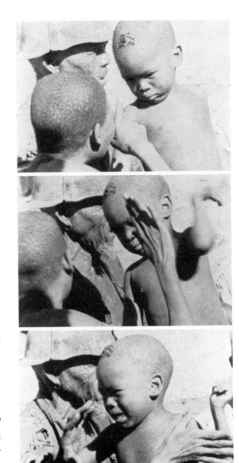

FIGURE 7.14. (A)Mothers are occasionally strict with their young and punish them for the purposes of education. A G/wi mother (central Kalahari) scolds her approximately 3-year-old son (note her finger pointing), who had whined after a conflict with other children. He hits at her, but is finally calmed at her breast. The mother–child relationship in all societies is also burdened with many conflict situations. From a 50 frames/ second 16 mm film, frames 1, 55, and 154 of the sequence. Photo: I. Eibl-Eibesfeldt.

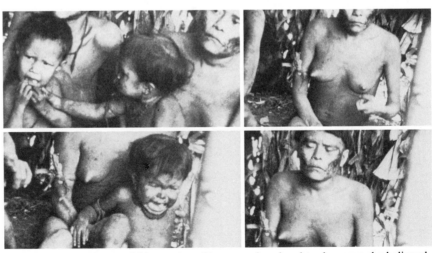

FIGURE 7.14. (B)Yanomami mother punishing and pushing away her daughter because she believed her daughter wanted to take something away from a neighbor who was a guest. She strikes her daughter and pushes her away. Note her expression of rejection in the final frame. From a 16 mm film. Photo: I. Eibl-Eibesfeldt.

FIGURE 7.15. A Himba mother pats her small daughter to the rhythm of her song, but does so too strongly. The child protests and pouts, whereby the mother teases her by repeating the activity, which elicits more protest and pouting by the daughter. Aggressive play interactions of this kind between mother and child occur in all societies. From a 25 frames/second 16 mm film, frames 1, 6, 15, 28, 43, 67, 78, and 146 of the sequence. Photo: I. Eibl-Eibesfeldt.

FIGURE 7.16. Cut off threat (p. 500) is a weapon in confrontations with mothers that infants learn very early. A Yanomami mother (upper Orinoco) ignores her son's contact-seeking. When she turns to the baby again, he then turns away in protest. Only after a brief bout of pouting does he let her pick him up. From a 25 frames/second 16 mm film, frames 1, 234, 531, 574, 602, 839, and 998 of the sequence. Photo: I. Eibl-Eibesfeldt.

2. Initiate play:
    a. from the sidelines (indirect)
    b. by inciting imitative behavior (building commonality) (indirect)
    c. by joining a game or by offering a play object (direct)
3. Acquire objects from others:
    a. by taking an object away as a challenge, calculating that there will be some defense by not only snatching the object away but displaying threat behavior while doing so. Even toddlers who cannot yet speak will react to protests and return objects. However it is common to refuse to take back an object that an aggressor took (pouting, refusing contact instead). The ontogeny of the norm of respect of possession has not yet been elucidated.

FIGURE 7.17. (a) Yanomami in warlike pose; (b) a small Yano-mami imitating the adult pose. Photo: I. Eibl-Ei-besfeldt.

b. indirectly by expressing interest, expectation behavior with pleading gestures (holding out the hand) and smiling, creating a common ground by expressing agreement
4. Terminate contact in a friendly way (departure ceremony)
5. Self-portrayal (to win esteem and favor)
    a. as one seeking care ("childlike appeal")
    b. as one who provides care ("care giving appeal")
    c. displaying to win respect, and/or dominance over others
6. Refuse contact in order to "punish" a partner
    a. by pouting and turning away (visual contact avoidance, "cut off").
    b. by rejecting offered objects
7. Block aggression
    a. through appeasement: smiling, head tilting, lowering the head
    b. through pouting and threatening to break contact, visual avoidance
    c. through offering objects
8. Defense through threat and fighting
    a. for objects
    b. for partners
    c. for one's own individual space
    d. for one's own rank position
9. Attack
    a. as exploratory aggression
    b. as a form of support
    c. to defend oneself and objects (preventative)

Phylogenetic programming prepares the child to interact with others in an adaptive way. During these interactions the child learns to further differentiate behavior, especially culture-specific manifestations, such as manners and daily rituals. Partner reactions teach the child which behavior is permitted and which is unacceptable (see also exploratory aggression, p. 391).

If "expected" responses do not appear, pathological developments can occur. Women who avoid visual contact with their infants can impair their young with this inappropriate behavior. Sensitive children can cease initiating contact after fruitless attempts to do so (H. N. Massie, 1980), and it is quite likely that some cases of autism (but certainly not all) may even arise this way.

In perhaps no other realm than the question of ontogeny is the human trait of polarizing opinions as obvious. Is development a process that is strictly programmed, with, at best, imprinting-like environmental influences operating? Does it consist of processes in which learning experiences, and thus the environment, primarily dictate its course? These questions are often posed as if they were alternatives, and this polarization toward extreme positions has dominated the scene for decades as the "nature-nurture" controversy, even though the question has long been clarified from a biological viewpoint and no longer requires this fruitless argumentation (p. 19).

We explained the concept of phylogenetic adaptation and clarified that ethologists use the term "innate" synonymously with "phylogenetically adapted" and that the concept is always used in reference to a specifically determinable adaptation. In other words, behavioral patterns that owe their specific adaptiveness to a phylogenetic adaptation process are as much or as little innate (genetically preprogrammed) as any organ. Just as an eye develops through a process of self-differentiation as a direct result of developmental instructions encoded in its genes, so many behaviors develop. In this sense, then, development is growth.

In the case of phylogenetically adapted behavior we are speaking of the growth and differentiation of neuronal networks, sensory organs, and executing organs. Environmental factors may have an influence in various ways during this growth period. Among these are some on which the growing organism "counts." The range of modifiability is the result of phylogenetic adaption. Of course, environmental influences with which the organism was not confronted during the course of its evolution also arouse responses, making new, unexpected capabilities evident. Thus various plant parasites make use of the ability of plants to produce nutrient tissues within their leaves in response to specific chemical stimuli; the parasites seeking this nutrient exploit this situation by stimulating gall formation. Gall tissue resembles fruit tissue, but due to the parasite chemical signal the plant forms the tissue on the wrong site. This is actually a case of chemical signal mimicry to which the plant falls victim. The galls are even more than just a fruit (nutrient tissue) growing on the wrong place. They are entirely new organs with delicate mechanisms to open, when the insect is about to hatch. The phenomenon displays entirely new capabilities of plant tissue formation, which would not normally be activated.

Environmental factors include internal and external ones, and there is often some causal relationship between the two. External influences cause internal changes, and these likewise stimulate changes in structure and behavior as well. Some of the "environmental factors" are part of the genetically based developmental programs. The work of H. Spemann and R. W. Sperry (p. 22), should be consulted in this regard.

For the above considerations, our question about the development of behavior is a question about the range of modifiability of the given program. We must not only search for those behavioral programs of man that develop to functional maturity during ontogeny with little environmental contribution, but we also need to learn about those programs that allow for environmental modification (programming) to occur during ontogeny. In the latter case, the system is an open one, taking in information from the environment, and prepared in a special way to be affected by specific "anticipated" external stimuli—an anticipation acquired during phylogeny. Thus, there is an open phase for speech acquisition in which language is acquired with special ease. This period ends with puberty; thereafter, language is much more difficult to absorb. A 13½-year-old girl, found in California, after 12 years of isolation, could no longer fully assimilate a language (S. Curtiss, 1977).

Programs can be open in various ways. There may be switches at particular periods during development which channel the organism's development along certain predetermined lines. Corrective mechanisms may also be present, but in certain instances such mechanisms may no longer operate once a particular pathway has been taken, as in von Driesch's regulative and mosaic embryos. One example is visual disconnection in cross-eyed children. If a child begins to cross his eyes (showing signs of stigmatism) during his first 5 years, one eye is irreversibly centrally disconnected. If cross-eyed vision occurs after the fifth or sixth year, irreversible disconnection does not occur.

The extent to which the environment molds behavior should be discussed. Which types of information are provided for the child and how does he process this information. Is there any selectivity on the part of the child? Is the child actively engaged in the process of information acquisition, or is he, as B. F. Skinner presumes, molded by his upbringing? In other words, do children possess special learning dispositions as phylogenetic adaptations, and are there corresponding innate strategies of instruction? We have already shown that mothers have great skill in responding to the behavior of their child at various stages of development.

Learning is generally defined as process of information acquisition leading to a longer term modification of behavior. We have already discussed the various types of learning (p. 74); they usually lead to adaptive modification of behavior. Under normal conditions an organism's behavior is modified with experiences in such a way that the probability of reproductive success increases. This is achieved by phylogenetic adaptations, which we discussed as learning dispositions. One example of this is imprinting (p. 79).

Studies in sexual pathology teach us that certain sexual experiences early in life fixate sexual preferences. R. von Krafft-Ebing (1924) describes a case of a shoe fetishist, who could only engage in sex with his wife when a woman's shoe was visible to him; a maid had stimulated him sexually with a shoe as a child, and this event was his first conscious sexual experience.

S. Freud and other psychologists recognized early from patients' symptoms that there are sensitive periods in development. If a child is hindered from forming an attachment with a reference figure during the ages of 1 to 2 years, this will lead to depression (among other symptoms). We previously cited the related studies of R. Spitz (p. 190).

Many statements however on the imprinting influence of early childhood experiences are highly speculative.[4] Thus it was concluded from newborn's crying that birth was a traumatic experience, leaving chronic effects behind. Apart from the fact that evidence of trauma has never been verified, we note that Caesarean delivered babies also cry as soon as they begin to breathe. Another fantasy is the belief that the child initially experiences cannibalistic sensations toward the mother, then learns to love the mother as a source of food, and only later establishes a

---

[4]O. G. Brim and J. Kagan (1980) warn against overestimating the impact of early childhood experiences. They are of the opinion that the first 2 to 3 years are so channeled by general maturational processes that interindividual differences are negligible and, should they develop, can be equalized by subsequent experience. This may be true for many, but certainly not all, aspects of behavior.

bond via this feeding training. Freud described an anal or anal-sadistic stage of development between the second and fourth years succeeding an oral stage and followed by a phallic stage. The sexual interest and thus partial sexual drive of the child is directed toward the anal region, since excretion was associated with lustful sensations. Later the child not only associates lust with excretion (= destruction) but also with restraint. Excretion here is equated with possession and is discussed in terms of lustful restraint or retention of a possession. Freud further presumed that a fixation at this anal stage would lead to the development of an anal personality ("anal character"), with excessive cleanliness habits, exaggerated orderliness, stinginess, and pedantry.

Data supporting these hypotheses have not been produced. But quite apart from that, it is astonishing that one would characterize as "anal" that stage of development in which language is acquired and individuality emerges, and instead emphasize the ability to control the rectal muscles. Since the exploratory child can also be destructive and aggressive, "anal" is supplemented with "sadistic." This supposedly characterizes those little children, who meet us with all signs of joy, as sadistic—indeed, a grotesque terminology, as are some of the traditional psychoanalytic concepts. We also hear a great deal about the "oedipal" complex. In the simplistic terminology utilized by psychoanalysts of the second and third generations (Sigmund Freud was more careful in his terminology), one reads statements like this: "The child wishes to form a union with the parent of the opposite sex at the onset of the phallic stage, and at the same time wishes the parent of the same sex were gone" (T. Brocher, 1971). The claim that the child desires a sexual union with the opposite sex parent has many variations.

S. Freud expressed a much more differentiated viewpoint. He said that a partial sexual drive was for the first time directed toward others in this oedipal stage, and in this stage there occurred an identification with the parent of the same sex (or, in improper upbringing, with a rejection of this sex role). The parent of the same sex would be imitated and a relationship with the opposite sex instituted. During this period, boys may very well say they would some day marry their mother, expressing their identification with the paternal model. It is pure speculation that the boy at this age desires sexual relationships with his mother and would prefer to eliminate the father. Such desires have sometimes been described in patients' reminiscences. However, Freud felt that these were concealed memories with which individuals rejected by their parents attempted to obliterate this painful reality by means of this fantasy. Incestuous desires or threats of the same occurred in this fantasy but not in reality (with exceptions). Rather than face the truth of the painful experience of being rejected, they constructed the fantasy of a sexual approach of the father (in the case of a rejected daughter). This exaggeration is for them more acceptable than the rejection. Thus they prefer to assume the role of the victim than that of the abandoned child.

The "oedipal stage" is an important developmental period in which the child identifies with his sexual role, and developmental disturbances will occur if the child is unable to achieve this identity at this time. The use of the word "oedipal" however, is misleading, since the child neither desires to have sexual relations with the parent of the opposite sex (see incest taboo, p. 261), nor wishes to murder the parent of the same sex. Likewise, the images of castration fear in boys and penis envy in girls should not be taken literally. A boy between the ages of 4 and 7 may experience conflicts with his father, who forbids various activities. Dominance disputes begin at this time. The son can rebel against these prohibitions and may also fear the father, who punishes the boy for his misbehavior. The claim that this fear is founded in a conception that the father could punish the boy's incestuous desires with castration is pure speculation. It is also very remote from a girl's nature to develop "penis envy" at this period. In patriarchal societies, girls experience that boys are preferred and generally prevail in rank disputes with sisters due to their physical strength advantage, and it is only in this aspect that they may want to be "like a boy" and not be discriminated against.

In spite of all the reservations described above, psychoanalysis has achieved an uncontested service in pointing out the existence of sensitive periods of development, of which there are many. The sense of basic trust arising early in childhood appears with the formation of personal attachments (p. 190). The identification with the sexual role of those of the same sex occurs between the fourth and sixth years. Imprinting phenomena associated with sexual objects occur probably before and around the time of puberty (p. 254). At this time the young person also is particularly disposed to identify with the values of society and thus with political, religious, tribal or ethnic values which, once absorbed, are apparently firmly entrenched.

There is a great deal of discussion about the extent one can speak of imprinting in such fixations. There is evidence for therapy resistance to these fixations, but since the term imprinting was first used for irreversible learning it is more appropriate to speak of imprinting-like learning processes in human beings.

H. Thomae (1954) discusses social imprinting as a process through which an individual, initially born with many different behavioral possibilities, is led to develop specific behavior defined by group standards.

With the exception of the objections raised earlier, psychoanalysis is certainly correct in stating that early childhood experiences can shape later personality development. The extent of affection or neglect (p. 193) plays a role here, as does the inhibition of infantile desire to show off and efforts to misbehave, which according to Freud influence the development of initiative and self-confidence. Permissive or restrictive rearing, punishment, and other practices in combination with inborn individual characteristics shape specific kinds of personalities.

That aggressive personalities result from the frustrations associated with weaning, early cleanliness routines, and the suppression of sexual activity have not withstood critical tests. Neither has the idea that friendly dispositions toward other humans in the form of generosity, self-giving, and peacefulness were created from rearing systems utilizing later cleanliness training, nursing on demand, and sexual permissivity.

As mentioned many times earlier, Margaret Mead (1930) considered the early and abrupt weaning of the Mundugumur as forming the basis of their aggressivity. The mountain Arapesh, on the other hand, who were nursed on demand and in which the children received a great deal of body contact, were peaceful people because of these experiences. Although this sounds plausible, it is incorrect. For example, the Arapesh do conduct wars (R. Fortune, 1939). We also cited the warlike Yanomami (upper Orinoco), Eipo (western New Guinea), and Himba (western Africa), whose children receive a great deal of body contact and affection and are also nursed on demand but are nonetheless aggressive. Instead of Mead's interpretation we suggest one in which identification occurs with loving parents regardless of whether they happen to be warlike or not. In addition, of course, rearing methods can foster and teach trust and mistrust. Children can be taught to view the world in certain ways.

Explanations from ethnological and psychoanalytical literature (E. H. Erikson, 1950; W. Dennis, 1960; A. Kardiner, 1939, 1945; C. Kluckhohn, 1947; J. W. Whiting, 1941; M. Mead, 1930) may be impressively simple, but this is not sufficient grounds for accepting an explanation (H. Orlansky, 1949). There are also numerous examples in which these simple explanatory models are contradicted by factual evidence. Thus the Pueblo Indians have an anxious demeanor although as children they are brought up permissively and, like the Navajo, receive maximum protection and satisfaction of needs.

The Kaska are allegedly egocentric and introverted, the Hawaiians balanced and extroverted. In both cultures, however, the children experience no pressure and are nursed on demand. The list of such examples is enormous. Certainly there are early childhood influences that can fixate behavior in imprinting-like ways, but so far there is more speculation on this theme than hard evidence. Other examples, taken from H. Thomae (1954), are summarized in Tables 7.1 and 7.2.

Biologists and psychologists have developed various theories regarding the development of cognitive abilities[5] both from observations and experiments, and these theoretical approaches can be characterized as empirical, nativist, and constructivist. According to the empiricists, knowledge is acquired during the course of an individual's life, beginning with a totally "blank page"—knowledge is based solely upon experience. Some behaviorists have been extreme proponents of this *tabula rasa* approach (p. 19). The opposite position is nativism, according to which development is an extreme preformistic sequence of unfolding events wherein knowledge is inherent in the organism's structure and thus is essentially innate. It is perhaps surprising that in spite of our knowledge of the wonderful morphological and physiological structures occurring in the organic world (e.g., the fine structure of insect antennae), no biologist has pursued a totally nativist approach. In spite of a most thorough examination of the literature, I have never encountered such "nativists." J. Piaget (1980) characterized R. W. Sperry as nativist, but I cannot see why. Sperry deals with the processes of neuronal self-differentiation (p. 22), with experimental methodology, and in contrast to many opinions expressed prior to his studies, Sperry found that neuronal organization is variable only to a limited degree. Sperry never maintained that because of this, everything is innate. The "nativist" position, in fact, appears only in the minds of its opponents, who set it up as a strawman. However there have been and still are extreme empiricist positions.

According to a review by M. I. Lisina (1982), most of the Russian psychologists still conceive of the development of the child's social behavior, in particular, as a learning process, through which the child adopts the social historical experience accumulated by previous generations of mankind (A. N. Leontev, 1972; L. S. Vygotsky, 1960). Also the origin of the need to interact is thought to be acquired (M. I. Lisina, 1982; A. N. Leontev, 1977; F. T. Mikhailov, 1976; S. L. Rubinshtein, 1973; A. V. Zaporozhets, 1978). Hospitalized children, it is argued, would not demonstrate any wish to communicate with adults by the age of 2 to 3 years (M. Y. Kistyakovskaya, 1970). But this is not a good argument, since we know that behaviors can wane and deteriorate if not encouraged. Thus, during the first month of life, the smiling response of children who grow up in families and who grow

---

[5]The concept of cognition is a broad one in the scientific literature. In general, it signifies each act of perception and conscious thought, and therefore the ability to recognize. Cognitive psychology investigates perceptual processes and information acquisition, memory storage, problem solving, planning, and goal-directed behavior.

up in institutions develops fairly similarly. But soon, the smiling response of the institutionalized child falls to a very low level, evidently as a result of lack of friendly social stimulation (J. L. Gewirtz, 1961). Ample evidence has already been presented in the previous sections that demonstrates that the newborn is programmed to interact and is by nature a social being. Again, it must be emphasized that there exists no one-sided extreme "nature" point of view that would fail to take into consideration the outstanding importance and contribution of learning.

According to J. Piaget's (1975a,b, 1976, 1980) "constructivist" theory, a child actively constructs knowledge and skills, using innate strategies of knowledge acquisition and interacting with the environment using relatively few predetermined behavioral patterns. The development takes place in various stages, each of which is a precursor for the next one. According to S. T. Parker and K. R. Gibson (1979), this reflects in some respects the phylogenetic development of cognitive abilities within the primate group—a viewpoint that has been disputed.

Piaget distinguishes three developmental stages, divided into various developmental subgroups, which can be further subdivided. The following summary in Table 7.3 may serve as an orientation. Other details are found in G. C. Anderson (1978) and E. D. Neimark (1978). Table 7.4 describes the typical phases in the development of the object concept.

Cross-cultural investigations have shown a basically identical course of development. It can occur at a slower or more rapid pace, but the basic pattern of the sequence does not vary (J. S. Carlson, 1978; P. R. Dasen, 1977).

According to Piaget, two successive processes play a role in this particular course of development: the process of assimilation of new facts, which is an information input stage, followed by the process of accommodation. In the accommodation process the basic concepts or behavioral configurations are modified as a result of the new experiences. Piaget's theory is based on learning theory and can be interpreted as a behaviorist theory of reflex connections. However, Piaget differs from the classic behaviorists by emphasizing the active role of the child, constructing a surrounding world of objects existing in a three-dimensional space, and associated through causal and temporal relationships (P. Watzlawick, 1981). Piaget also emphasizes that the integration of basic elements results in continuously new system characteristics, that determine subsequent steps of development (Table 7.5). Every new achievement builds upon previously acquired skills and requires their prior existence. At first, behavior consists of simple unconditioned responses. The child then constructs behavioral schemata (internal representations of situation-relevant behavior) from concrete perception and action. These schemata are enlarged in the course of development and are linked to each other, causing new cognitive abilities. Piaget is unclear regarding to what extent this internal linking is due to maturational processes. He does state very explicitly, however, that there are no a priori cognitive structures in humans, a statement that is certainly incorrect (p. 33). He acknowledges, however, the child's active contribution in the construction of their schemata for action. And it is in this respect that Piaget's theory differs decisively from the classical behaviorist viewpoint, according to which humans would react passively to their environment during development:

Fifty years of experience have taught us that knowledge does not result from a mere recording of observations without a structuring activity on the part of the subject. Nor do any a priori or innate cognitive structures exist in man; the functioning of intelligence

Table 7.1. Alleged Relationship between Frustration in Early Childhood Development and Personality Formation on the Basis of Ethnological Data[a]

Form of frustration	Very early and abrupt weaning	Very early, strict adherence to cleanliness	Strict suppression of sexual activity or sexual interest
Name of ethnic group	Mundugumur (Melanesian head hunters)	Tanala	Kwoma (Melanesian head-hunting tribe)
Pronounced tribal or national characteristics	Very strong aggression within and without the family; self-certainty and emotional stability maintained solely through head hunting and cannibalism	Unusual personal cleanliness (in terms of obsessional washing); neurotic personality; collection and maintenance of property very pronounced (Kardiner) Japanese and European middle class: Emphasis on sanitation, perfectionism and ritual; strong tendency to conform, accompanied by fear of self-ridicule (Gorer); emphasis on obedience, cleanliness, and acquiring personal property (various authors)	In individual development one observes continuously increasing aggression toward family members and outsiders; strong fear, especially of spirits; later strong tendency to conduct war and head hunt (Whiting)

[a]From H. Thomae, 1954.

Table 7.2. Alleged Relationships between Tolerant Upbringing and Care within One Ethnic Group and Personality Development[a]

Manifestation of tolerant approach	Nursing on the child's need and slow weaning	Late and gradual cleanliness training	Absence of threat and punishment relative to sexual activity
Name of ethnic group	Navajo	Sioux	Comanche
Prominent tribal or national characteristic	Optimistic and friendly disposition to the world and others; predominant feeling of security and reliability in the world (Kluckhohn)	Generosity and open-handedness as behavioral norms; little attachment to possessions (Erickson)	Free, uninhibited, expansive personality development; no symptoms for the existence of an oedipal complex (Kardiner)
Name of ethnic group	Hopi	Mountain Arapesh	Alorese
Prominent tribal or national characteristic	Strong community feeling and group dependency; aggressions expressed at most in the form of gossip and certain forms of rivalry (Dennis)	Generally very friendly and tolerant upbringing; child trust the adult generation; no strong egoism; self-certainty depends on the feeling of being loved by others; almost no infantile tantrums; aggressions are at most directed at objects (Mead)	In the absence of parental care children are anxious, distrustful, without much interest for the world, little effort and initiative expended (Dubois, 1944)

[a]From H. Thomae, 1954.

Table 7.3. Summary of Piaget's Stages with the Defining Characteristics and Mean Ages[a]

Type of stage	Sensory-motor stage	Concrete operations		Formal operations	
		Preoperational stage	Concrete operational stage	Organizational substage	Executive ability substage
Mean	0–1½ or 2 Years	2–7 Years	7–11 Years	11–13 Years	15 Years
Type of usable operation	No operations. nonreversible motor schemata replace operations and are practical but not logical, e.g., sucking, throwing, and looking		Concrete operations, e.g., classification (simple and multiple), ordering, maintenance (invariance)	Formal operations, e.g., deduction, permutation, correlation	
Status of semiotic function	Not represented except in cases in which intensified schemata or imitations of it assume this function, e.g., closing eyes and laying down as symbols of sleep	Development of image concepts and symbols through imitation, play, drawings, concepts, speech	Refinement in forms and function of speech and concepts, e.g., appearance of anticipatory behavior supplementing concepts of reproduction	Further elaborations as well as abstractions and generalizations of concepts and speech in contrast to the concrete operational stage, i.e., formal operational concepts	
Thought elements	No true thinking and thus no distinction of elements is possible	Thought elements are often objects and individuals in context	Thought elements are qualities and relations	Elements of thought are assertions (propositions)	
Organizational structures of the operations			Sight groups: four parallel classes for handling operations of qualities and four for operations of relations	The four groups or INRC-Group and a complete combinational schema	

[a]After J. Piaget, 1970.

alone is hereditary and creates structures only through an organisation of successive actions performed on objects. Consequently, an epistemology conforming to the data of psychogenesis could be neither empiricist nor preformationist, but could consist only of a constructivism, with a continual elaboration of new operations and structures. The central problem, then, is to understand how such operations come about, and why, even though they result from nonpredetermined constructions, they eventually become logically necessary (J. Piaget, 1980, p. 23).

Thus according to Piaget, object offering as a social behavior can only develop when the object is recognized as existing permanently by means of sensory-motor processes and when a corresponding spatial concept also exists. The child must also have learned to relate objects to other objects (i.e., building blocks on top of each other or place them in containers). Only then could an object be offered to another person, by holding it or laying it down in that person's direction, and when that person holds up his hand, to also place the object in his hand. This skill is further practiced, according to Piaget, in dialogues of giving and receiving, stylizing the behavior into social symbolic behavior of contact initiation, since the child learns from the partner's reaction the positive effect of gift giving. From such an experience, the child learns to use objects to establish friendly relations.

Piaget discerns a developmental logic in this sequence. One must first be able to bring two objects into some relationship before one can extend one of these objects intentionally toward another person, and intentional presenting is likewise a prerequisite for the bonding give-and-take dialogue. If the observations are based upon a learning theory interpretation, the developmental logic of Piaget is convincing.

However, from observation alone we cannot deduce that development actually

Table 7.4. Typical Phases in the Development of the Object Concept

State I (0–1 month): when an object disappears, the child displays no particular behavior in response

Stage II (1–4 months): the first searching activity of the child is apparently restricted to staring continuously at the place where the object was last seen

Stage III (4–9 months): the beginnings of object permanence are now possible related to the developing grasping ability of the child. Children now seek fully visible or partially concealed objects

Stage IV (9–12 months): the child now searches actively and successfully for fully concealed objects. But when he sees an object hidden at a second location, he searches at once only at the first place, i.e., the place where the object had been found initially. This is known as a Stage IV error.

Stage V (12–18 months): the child goes directly to sites where objects are obviously concealed without first attending to prior hiding places. But when a child sees an object being placed inside a small box that disappears under a scarf and then reappears, the child will only look for the object in the box.

Stage VI (18–20 months): in the situation above involving invisible concealment the child will now look below the scarf for the object. Finally the child can not only find objects hidden in a box, but also those transferred from one to another hiding place. If the object is not found in the box, the child will initially look in the same and then in the reversed sequence in which the box disappeared.

Table 7.5. The Traditional Description of the Development of the Intercoordination of Configuration[a]

Age and stage	Designation	Configuration development	New skills	Assimilation and accommodation	Summary
I 0–1 month	Reflex activation	Primary, i.e., independent configurations, organized congenitally	Simple modification of primary schemata as a reaction to the environment	Assimilation and accommodation are almost undifferentiated	Attention is directed to expectations and the use of behavioral configurations.
II 1–4 months	The first acquired adaptations and the primary circular reactions	Coordination of primary schemata to secondary schemata	Coordinations lead to new results and their repetition and modification	Coordinations are simple and do not extend beyond the realm of the infant body	Accustomed behavior controls observations; behavior is conservative, directed to repetition and is primarily assimilatory.
III 4–8 months	Secondary circular reactions and the strategies serving to make interesting manifestations last	Coordination of secondary schemata (motor patterns and perceptions) with expectations	Coordinations extend to surrounding objects; early intent investigation of behavior	A new result still due to chance and is only used in the same situation	
IV 8–12 months	Coordination of secondary schemata and their application to new situations	Coordination of secondary schemata for predetermined goals (intentional behavior)	Configurations are reversible, adaptable coordination of means and purpose in each new situation	Methods used are accompanied only by known assimilations	Attention is directed to the intentional differentiation of schemata in reference to objects; new observations control accustomed behavior; behavior is predominantly accommodating
V 12–18 months	Tertiary circular reactions and the discovery of new means through active testing	Elaboration of coordination of secondary schema; primitive induction (conclusive thought)	Search for new means through differentiation of known schema	New means are only found by feeling externally and physically	
VI 18–24 months	Invention of new means through mental combinations	Internalization of behavioral schemata to conceptual schemata; primitive deduction; early representation	New means are found through mental combinations culminating in sudden understanding	All sensory-motor abilities are restricted to directly perceivable objects	

[a]Originally formulated by Piaget (1936, pp. 382–384) and repeated by Flavell (1936, pp. 85–121), Ginsburg and Opper (1969, pp. 20–73), Hunt (1961, pp. 116–169), and Piaget and Inhelder (1966, pp. 4–12). Ages are approximate.

takes place in this manner. A temporal sequence does not imply, by any means, a causal relationship of this nature. Even in maturational processes we observe stepwise integration, for example, bird flight, discussed earlier. The organism constructs its world in interactions with the environment, but it brings a prior knowledge with it, which has been acquired during the course of evolution and is thus innate. The studies of T. G. Bower (1966, 1971, 1977) and W. Ball and E. Tronick (1971) confirm that infants just 14 days old associate visual impressions with tactile expectations (p. 54). The mechanisms of stimulus localization and identification have also been verified in newborns. Blind infants follow their hand movements with their eyes, indicating that the precursors of visual control are innate (see also D. G. Freedman, 1965, p. 76). Blind children of 16 weeks reach for a sound source. This ability disappears, however, even when one attempts to reinforce the behavior through reward, and this auditory manual coordination does not reappear until the age of 10 months, although it is initially present in newborns in the same way as the auditory-visual coordination.

The achievements of object permanence and constancy have also been demonstrated at an even earlier age than one would expect from Piaget's development concept. When an object disappears behind a screen, we still know that it is present. According to classical developmental theories, this is learned when we are children by grabbing behind the screen. In the study by T. G. Bower (1977, p. 35), objects were covered by a screen in front of infants. The screen was drawn away in different intervals. If the object had disappeared and the time interval was not too long, even 20-day old infants reacted by an increase in pulse rate. However, if the object was still present after the screen was drawn, the child displayed no distinct reaction: "It seems that even the very young infants know that an object is still there after it has been hidden, but if the time of occlusion is prolonged, they forget about the object altogether. The early age of the infants and the novelty of the testing situation make it unlikely that such a response has been learned."

At eight weeks, children anticipate an object that disappears behind a screen. They expect its reappearance on the other side and follow it visually. If it does not reappear or stays hidden from view too long, the child becomes excited. But it does not mind if the object changes in form in the meantime, for example, if a ball appears instead of a cube. The movement pattern must conform to the expectation while, in this situation, the object identity appears to be learned.

Thus the world of the infant is by no means so chaotically structured as one might be led to believe from the theories of traditional developmental psychology. A child is born with certain assumptions about the world. These developed as phylogenetic adaptations and portray as such certain facets of reality. However, in the case of object constancy, different rules may at first be utilized depending on whether the object moves or is at rest. Two mutually conflicting rules thus operate (T. G. Bower, 1977):

> To find an object, look for it in its usual place.
> To find an object, follow the path of its movement.

Only later, probably due to experience, are the rules modified:

> To find an object not seen moving, look for it in its usual place.
> To find an object that moved, search by pursuing the path of its movement.

The presumption that in development the initially utilized rules are based on maturational processes rests on the occurrence of behavioral errors which are not caused by corresponding misleading experiences on the part of the child. The child can pursue objects at a very early age, and the objects do not change their configuration. Not only is this ability present in early childhood, but infants are also in a position to recognize persons as well as individual objects and to distinguish them from one another.

Summary 7.1

Biologist and social scientists of today generally recognize that the empiricist/nativist or nature/nurture controversy is obsolete. Attempts of behaviorists to account for all behavior from simple stimulus-response associations via experience (i.e., learning) have fallen short of explaining many aspects of human behavior. Our central nervous system is not a *tabula rasa* at birth to be filled only with input from sensory perception. Nevertheless, in many layperson's eyes, classical behaviorism is still considered to be valid, and its simplistic concepts exercise a continuous influence in some areas of pedagogy, psychology and sociology.

Though Piaget's constructivism is also based on a behaviorist stimulus-response association, it differs from other behaviorist theories in that the child is thought to play an active role in knowledge acquisition. The child constructs his world during a logical sequence of developmental steps. Each new cognitive accomplishment builds on previously developed abilities and skills and requires their presence. New system characteristics appear with the integration of basic abilities. The extent to which maturational and learning processes work together is not clarified in detail. There has never been a pure opposing nativist position to classical behaviorism, and biologists, for the most part, have recognized the great significance of learning. But they have also emphasized the significance of self-differentiation processes on the basis of developmental instructions present in the genes, drawing attention, in particular, to innate learning dispositions.

Piaget studied the cognitive development of the child in terms of object-related behavior. He overlooked the fact that even children just a few months old conceive of others as social partners and are able to interact with a high degree of social competence. Their social abilities precede other cognitive developments considerably.

7.2. Curiosity and Play

The conception that a child is a passive object shaped only by his environment has long been outdated. Piaget's claim that the child itself constructs his environment is, however, correct. We only add that the child comes into the world more richly endowed than Piaget assumes. The child has phylogenetically based a priori knowledge which also includes a series of learning dispositions, and an exploratory drive known as curiosity.

Driven by his curiosity, man actively explores the environment from earliest childhood, looking for new situations from which to learn. He manipulates the objects in his environment in many ways, and his curiosity only terminates when the object or the situation becomes familiar or when the task he was given is accomplished. Man also experiments with his social environment.

Curiosity is undoubtedly an ancient heritage. If a rat is placed in strange surroundings, it first investigates, nibbling and sniffing the objects around until it has oriented itself. Novelty elicits this response, and as long as the environment is still strange most other drives, such as nest building, feeding, and reproduction, are suppressed. In rats, brain sites have been discovered within the lateral hypothalmus and the preoptic region where electrical activities are registered when the rat is exploring, and which rats like to stimulate electrically in self-stimulation experiments (B. R. Komisaruk and J. Olds, 1968). Young mammals are particularly curious, intentionally placing themselves in new situations and exploring new objects. They test the characteristics of the objects with all their senses, even moving the objects around and playing with them in various ways. Predators often handle such objects like prey, and this playful curiosity is a typical juvenile characteristic. Playful experimentation apparently developed in conjunction with the need to collect many experiences. The higher mammals are especially characterized by play, while in birds the only species that play are those like the woodpecker finch *(Cactospiza pallida)* of the Galapagos Islands, which use tools (I. Eibl-Eibesfeldt, 1987).

In man, curiosity remains a prominent part of behavior throughout life. Thus we can be properly called creatures of curiosity, and our curiosity may be interpreted as a persistent juvenile characteristic (K. Lorenz, 1943). Indeed, we seek novelty even into our old age. We read newspaper accounts of events that do not concern us at all, learn about foreign countries and new research findings, visit museums or travel as tourists to find new sights and experiences. Entire areas of our economies are based on our curiosity, and one of the most severe punishments that can be meted out consists of removing or restricting those possibilities for satisfying our curiosity, e.g., by imprisonment.

The assumption that phylogenetic adaptations manifest themselves as learning dispositions from birth is well founded. As early as 1953, Piaget showed that babies will stop nursing when they explore visually. It has also been shown that children seek out new impressions themselves. A baby rapidly learns a behavior, for example, if by sucking on a pacifier he can activate slides to be projected on a screen. The child is not simply stimulated to learn a task out of physiological needs in the sense of maintaining homeostasis. The importance of social reward must be remembered in such situations (J. L. Gewirtz, 1961; H. J. Rheingold, 1961). Babies learn to activate switches in their pillows by head movements, if as a reward, someone appears and talks to them in a friendly manner. Piaget neglected this infantile disposition in his study of cognitive development (C. Trevarthen and P. Hubley, 1978).

If a musical mobile consisting of sounding bars is moved above a 3-month-old infant, although out of reach, this elicits lively interest, but the interest clearly abates after 1 minute, and stops completely after 3. If, however, the mobile is brought within reach so that the baby can create the sounds himself, he will explore the object for a longer period of time with intense attention, and his obvious pleasure is expressed vocally. The infant varies his behavior and can remain with this activity for ½ hour before tiring and turning away (M. Papousek, 1984). Thus, even a baby is highly motivated to investigate his environment actively, although his interest wanes if he is only a casual (passive) observer.

Man does not learn in isolation. His strategies of information acquisition depend upon social partners. The infant expects maternal guidance, actively seeking to communicate (J. S. Bruner, 1979), soliciting dialogues and play, as well as imitating his mother's behavior, who in turn mirrors her child's behavior in a way appropriate to the developmental stage of the infant (H. Papousek, 1969). Later, siblings and other playmates are incorporated into the interaction. The child then tests the strategies of social intercourse (see also exploratory aggression), experiencing further stimulation from the play activities of others. The child imitates others, varying the activity somewhat and making new discoveries in doing so.

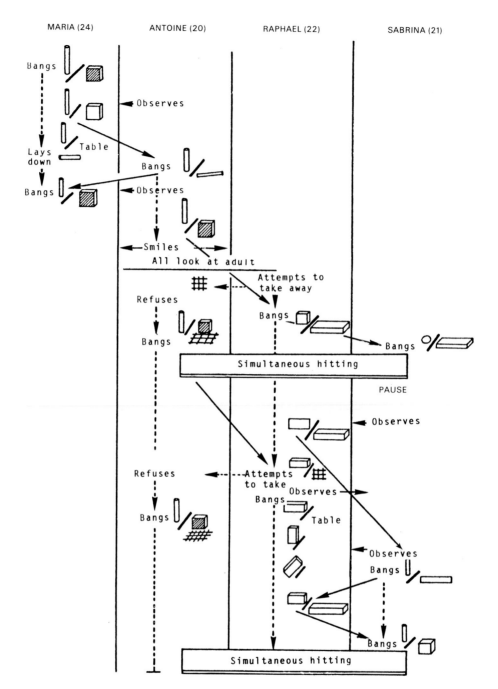

FIGURE 7.18. See legend, opposite page.

M. Verba *et al.* (1982) placed several children, aged 20 to 24 months, by a table on which there was a large selection of objects that could be used for building, striking, rolling, shaping, and so on. The children played with these objects while pausing to watch each other. Although they tended to imitate each other's behavior, they added variations to the activity, thereby encouraging each other to experiment and be creative (Fig. 7.18). Occasionally, the common group activity became a bonding ritual. It was noteworthy that these children observed the possession norm, each child waiting patiently until a partner gave up what they wanted to play with. Without a norm of respect of possession, this kind of group play would not have been possible.

Curiosity drives the child to investigate both the inanimate as well as the animate environment. Once a child is able to pick up objects and place them down again and to place one object onto or into another, he will begin to use these objects instrumentally. Here certain basic patterns of exploration appear to be innate. If a stick is given to an infant who can sit but not yet walk, a number of typical behavioral patterns will ensue. Thus the stick will be used to hit at objects at the floor, or at people, using downward strokes. I have seen this not only in our culture but also in the Yanomami, Eipo, Himba, and others, although I have never seen a mother instruct a child of this age on how to hit with sticks. I have only seen such instruction at a much later time, when the child was asked to strike someone—and such hitting was tolerated as long as it was not done too vigorously, at which time the behavior became irritating and was stopped. At an early age sticks are used to poke things and for digging. Stones are used to hit objects and are thrown, again with the same intention of causing something to happen. The child carefully observes the consequences of his behavior and it is in this respect that the predisposition for tool use becomes quite evident. There are sex differences in the frequency with which sticks and stones are used as tools in specific ways. Table 7.6 presents an example of such usage as observed in the Himba of Namibia.

The extent to which similar differences to those given in Table 7.6 occur in other cultures has yet to be investigated. The exploratory activity of the child has also been characterized as playful exploration, but this continues even into old age with man's curiosity to explore; and certainly this is the root of science. A

◁————————————————————————

FIGURE 7.18. Imitation is frequently the first step to the creative comprehension of ideas, which are then varied and lead to one's own discoveries. Common activity also has a bonding function, and imitation is often used to emphasize points in common. The figure depicts the interactions of four 20- to 24-month-old babies placed by a table where various objects were located. Maria began beating a stick on various blocks and then laid the stick down. Antoine observed her and then beat his stick against the one Maria had laid down, looking at the others and smiling. Maria picked up her stick again and proceeded to beat it against the block. Antoine observed her, then picked up a large block, smiling at Maria and Raphael as they looked at him, and began beating a tube against that block. At first the block just stood in front of him, but then he pulled it to his chest and struck it again. Raphael, who had been an on-looker, then became involved, taking a block and banging it against a board he laid between himself and Sabrina, his neighbor on his left. Sabrina began to bang a bead on this board without hesitation, smiling at the others. At the same time Antoine laid the large block down and continued hitting it with the tube. All three laughed with one another and, at the time continued their banging simultaneously. From M. Verba *et al.* (1982).

Table 7.6. Instrumental Use of Sticks and Stones in Himba Children

Stick use in play	Boys	Girls	Stone throwing	Boys	Girls
Hitting animals (dogs, calves)	13	7	Aggressive throwing		
			At people	2	7
Hitting people	8	2	At dogs	6	3
Striking objects (fences, trees, etc.)	34	13	Playful throwing (often to practice and gain skill in distance throwing)	149	44
Various activities (poking, hitting two sticks against each other, carrying about)	60	17			
	115	39		157	54

byproduct of exploratory curiosity can be found in exploratory aggression, which we have already mentioned, and with which children test their behavioral latitude, using aggression as one of many forms of inquiry (p. 391).

Objects are not only important in instrumental exploration of the nonliving environment. At 10 months of age a child tirelessly plays out dialogues of give and take, an activity we have observed in every culture we studied (p. 342). But this is an ability that develops gradually, since during the first 6 months we observe neither object offering nor a child approaching a partner by means of using an object or pointing out an object. The child enjoys watching someone else play with objects, but the child either occupies himself with an object or with another person—he does not combine the two. The conflict between person and object is most pronounced between 24 and 28 weeks. Thus, if a child plays with an object, he often avoids visual contact with his mother—removing himself from her, so to speak. At this age, a child cannot engage in both activities simultaneously and is not yet able to play with objects cooperatively. Only at 45 to 47 weeks does a child give an object to someone when requested and play cooperatively with others using objects (C. Trevarthen and P. Hubley, 1978). At this age, the child attains a significant level of development that greatly broadens experimentation. Only then can the child develop the ability to play in a group with others.

Thus we observe that initially children orient either to persons or to objects. Toward the end of the first year, objects begin playing an important role in mediating social interactions, especially with other children. Some authors maintain that children are initially interested only in objects and only secondarily in any actions that another child might be performing with those objects, seeking, instead, to influence other children with smiling and other behavioral patterns (E. Mueller, 1979; E. Mueller and J. Brenner, 1977). D. P. Ausubel and E. V. Sullivan (1980) go so far as to say that the beginning of interactions with peers is marked by fighting over play objects. Our cross-cultural observations of infants contradict this interpretation of the origin of peer relationships, as discussed in the section on social competence (p. 562). Other contradictory evidence is seen in D. L. Vandell *et al.* (1980) and J. L. Jacobson (1981), who found that 6-month-old children can initiate social contacts with others without the help of mediating objects.

It has been extremely difficult to articulate the conceptual definition of play. It was frequently maintained that play consisted of activities in which "seriousness" was absent, those with no specific purpose other than just for fun, as an end in itself, and for the reinforcement of success in executing behavior. Although this is all true, it is also an accurate description of many other kinds of behavior that might not necessarily be designated as play. Hardly any young fellow courting a girl associates this activity with the intention of some day becoming the father of a chubby-cheeked baby! The interpretation that play is the execution of immature behavior is also unsatisfactory. It is true that a great deal of undeveloped behavior occurs in play, but adults can play, too, and here play and earnestness are quite distinct entities. Imagine a playful adult dog. If the dog is fighting with conspecifics, his behavior looks entirely different. The fact that everyone knows when a man or a dog is playing and that hardly anyone maintains having seen an insect or a reptile at play, indicates that we perceive a particular type of behavior as play.

The ethological viewpoint has contributed to elucidating this issue, using the observational method along with the question of determining the functions for whose fulfillment a specific behavioral pattern—here play behavior—may have evolved. The comparative study of animal play shows, with a few avian exceptions, that only mammals play, that is, animals characterized by having to acquire many different skills through learning—in particular, by means of self-activated practice. This indicates that play is related to learning. Indeed, predators are particularly playful, for capturing prey requires a high level of skill, and a great deal of learning is involved in a predator developing the techniques for overcoming large prey. Small rodents, on the other hand, play very little (some not at all). Animals at play practice skills that are important for existence. For example, squirrels practice flight games whereby they exercise those behaviors that bring the tree trunk between themselves and their pursuer. In predators there is less emphasis on escape play (I. Eibl-Eibesfeldt, 1951), and more practice in the catching and subduing of prey and, finally, fighting with rivals. The woodpecker finch of the Galapagos Islands, one of the few songbirds that truly plays, will dig up prey with tools when satiated. The bird will hide the prey again, probe, and then dig it out again with the tool, continuing untiringly in playful experimentation. Caged birds will hide mealworms in crevices so they can subsequently twist them out with a digging stick in their beaks (I. Eibl-Eibesfeldt and H. Sielmann, 1962). The role of play in practicing skills has been proved experimentally. This is further supported by the fact that although animals play primarily during their infancy and juvenile periods, some of the higher mammals continue play throughout life, and thus retain this juvenile characteristic.

If we compare serious fighting with play fights in dogs we find that dogs during play may growl, but also produce additional signals like tail wagging to indicate that they mean no harm. Play signals like this are widespread. Polecats exercise exaggerated arched back leaps during play, emitting a soft whimper as a play signal. The play-face of the human is a functionally comparable signal (p. 137). Social inhibitions are particularly prominent in play fighting. The animals never bite so hard that they injure the skin of their partner, and if in the zeal of play one animal bites a little harder than it should, the partner utters specific sounds that immediately inhibit the biting. Certain body parts are bitten gently by dogs: if they interlock their fangs, their bite is gentle. In addition, play fighting animals "freely" change their roles of pursuer and pursued.

This all leads us to conclude that there are differences in the emotional and, therefore, motivational basis underlying play and serious fighting. In serious encounters, the behavioral patterns occur in a specific sequence, from threats to fighting, usually terminating in the loser fleeing or submitting. In play, the behavioral elements intermingle in a varied manner and, in fact, behaviors from different "instincts" (e.g., behavior patterns of prey catching, sexual behavior, and hunting), using the Tinbergen categories, are blended together, while in serious cases they would not be blended together. I interpret this to mean that only part of the "instinct" in its hierarchical organization is activated in play (using Tinbergen's terminology). One must rather postulate a specific play motivation that is able to activate various behavioral patterns without activating their accompanying drives and emotions. In play, these behaviors are liberated from their normal superimposed neuronal "centers"[6] and thus they lack the emotion of an earnest encounter that would be observed in autochthonous activation of an instinct. The play drive activates, so to speak, the various behavioral patterns heterochthonously that is, from a different source than in the nonplay situation and they are, therefore, freely usable just like tools. Normal emotions associated with behaviors are substituted by those of curiosity, interest, and a more general enjoyment. Freed from the constraints of autochthonously motivated drives the animal is able to experiment with its own motor abilities (I. Eibl-Eibesfeldt, 1950, 1951; M. Meyer-Holzapfel, 1956). B. Hassenstein has summarized these relationships functionally (Fig. 7.19). Other literature on play behavior is found in the following sources: O. Aldis (1975), E. M. Avedon and B. Sutton-Smith (1971), J. Chateau (1969), R. Fagen (1981), A. Flitner (1975, 1976), P. Martin and T. M. Caro (1985), M. J. Meaney *et al.* (1985), D. Müller-Schwarze (1978), H. Sbrzesny (1976), and H. B. Schwartzman (1978).

This described ability of liberating behavioral patterns from their drives is obviously the root of what we subjectively experience as freedom, namely the ability to detach ourselves emotionally and therefore to plan and consider within the tension-free field that is created. Only the investigation of animal play permitted this clear understanding of the distinctions between play and non-play. In human beings, everyday behavior (especially when we act verbally) has a less rigid frame; the single behavioral elements are more detached and thus can be more freely deployed. One could also say the even man's serious behavior bears, in this sense, a strain of playful freedom, that may also be interpreted as a persistent juvenile characteristic (p. 607), which allows man to experiment and practice new skills throughout his lifetime.

A prerequisite for play is that the basic motivating systems underlying earnest behavior are not activated by strong physiological needs (hunger) and/or external circumstances (fear), for otherwise the animal or person would be unable to liberate behavior from the normal activating factors. Thus some sort of "relaxed field" (G. Bally, 1945) is required.

We previously cited Bally's example of the dog that can only get at some bait placed some distance behind a fence so that its smell is weaker. If the bait is too close, the dog is unable to make a temporary detachment from the desired object, for the "field tension" is too great (p. 86). Another illustrative example is seen in W. Köhler's experiment with the chimpanzee Sultan. Köhler placed a banana in front of the cage, and provided Sultan with sticks that were too short to reach the banana. Vain attempts to reach the banana caused the chimpanzee to become angry causing him to throw the sticks down. After his anger had subsided, he became playfully occupied with the sticks and, by chance, stuck them together. The then unfulfilled task came to mind and he used the elongated stick to pull the

---

[6]"Center" meant only in functional terms.

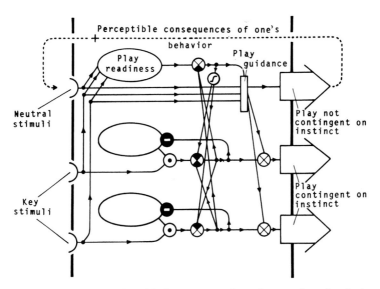

FIGURE 7.19. Idealized, highly simplified representation of some functional elements of play behavior. Many steering functions are combined together in the subsystem "play control" (e.g., the interchange of various play behavior elements). This diagram must be imagined as combined with learning circuits, but how this intertwines has not yet been investigated. From B. Hassenstein (1972).

banana into his cage. Thus, in the "relaxed field" of play, he succeeded in solving the task confronting him (W. Köhler, 1921). Man is aware of creative and flexible behavior that occurs in such tension-free environments. A very common element in social and political strategies is to create such an environment by making people comfortable and relaxed and using humor to break the tension.

Naturally there are transitions between play and earnestness, and occasionally there is an escalation from play fighting to a true struggle. But generally this autochthonous activation of a drive only serves to direct the course of play into specific areas (such as play fighting, play hunting, or play escape behavior). In humans, this is manifested as competitive games and in sporting events, where there is no distinct boundary between play fighting and ritualized fighting. Here, play and ritualized aggression, in which true motivation to fight and win is lived out.

There have been different attempts at categorizing types of play. What might be considered to be "natural" categories do not become apparent since liberation from the normal motivating factors allows a diverse combination of mixed forms of playful behavior. However, in practice, play tends to fall into one functional context or another. K. Groos (1933) distinguished two major play categories: experimental or generalized functional play and specialized functional play.

Experimental play includes the various forms of movement play behavior (running, jumping) in which skill is exercised, such as ball games in which throwing, catching, self-control, and social skills are practiced. The child engaging in this activity acquires knowledge about objects and tests his own movement abilities.

Specialized functional play trains in specialized skills. Thus, in hunting games, hunting skills are learned and in play fights, fighting skills are learned, and so on.

Children practice the sex roles of their individual culture by playing family and imitating one another.

Clearly, according to this categorization we would say that a small child playing with a ball is involved in pure sensory-motor experimental play in which visualization and throwing are the predominantly practiced activities. The same activity in older children, however, becomes a competitive game and therefore a form of play fighting.

F. Queyrat (1905) offers a different categorization. He distinguishes between games determined by predisposition (fighting, hunting, and pursuit play), games of imitation (arrow shooting games, playful hut building), and games of fantasy (transforming objects, giving toys animation). In this division, it is also clear that a single game could, of course, conform to different categories at the same time. Thus, playing at hut building can simultaneously be imitation and fantasy play, since objects or persons could be imagined in the game.

Since neither the content nor the motive, function nor origin, provide clear classification, J. Piaget (1975a) attempted to divide play based on the structures demonstrated. This was attempted earlier by D. N. Stern, who distinguished individual play (games of body or object control, building games, role playing, etc.) from social play (imitation, play fighting, etc.), But here also no distinct delineation exists between the categories.

Piaget (1975a, p. 147) distinguishes three structural types characterizing child play: practice, symbol and rule, and correspondingly differentiates practice play, symbol play, and rule play.

Practice games are all sensory-motor behaviors executed for the pure joy of performing and perfecting movements, such as playful jumping over a ditch. Piaget suggests that this type of play is typical for the behavioral patterns of the animal, since neither symbols, fictions, nor rules play any role in their execution. "When the kitten runs after a dead leaf or a ball of yarn, we have no reason to assume that it takes these objects for symbols for a mouse." Further, he interprets play fighting between a mother and her young as follows: "When a mother cat fights with her kittens by swatting at them and biting them, she knows well that this is not a 'serious' fight, but as explanation it is not necessary that the animal imagines true fighting. It suffices that the totality of all movements that normally function as adaptations in fighting are inhibited by maternal love and therefore function 'à blanc' " (p. 147). This may be, but we do not really know what goes on in the cat's mind.

Symbol games require the use of imaginary objects, which need not be the case in practice games. Thus a child turns a box into an automobile or a rock into a person or an animal.

The *rule games* require social relationships and develop after symbol games as a third category.

A special position is occupied by *construction games* (ship building, house building). According to Piaget they do not define a stage but take a position halfway between play and intelligent work or play and imitation.

Piaget's categories are not satisfactory in all respects. For example, the concept of practice game can lead to the misconception that nothing is practiced in symbol and rule games, which Piaget himself in no way implies. Indeed, training in social roles and discipline occurs during this kind of play. However that should not disturb us, for Piaget is chiefly concerned with the stepwise development in his classification. The various dividing principles can be used simultaneously, de-

588

FIGURE 7.20. (a) and (b): Although still a baby herself, a 2-year-old Yanomami girl, cuddles a banana as if it were a baby infant. Photo: I. Eibl-Eibesfeldt.

scribing various facets of playful activity. If one wishes to avoid any interpretations, one can also use purely descriptive categories (e.g., "dance games").

Boys and girls do not play in the same way; boys playing more aggressively. Furthermore, both sexes have a tendency to selectively imitate their own sex, even if they are not actually encouraged to do so. Girls display a primary interest in their maternal role, imitating this role in playing with dolls (Figs. 7.20–7.23). We already pointed out that girls will play the same kinds of games even if raised in the egalitarian and feminist milieu of the kibbutz. It is particularly noteworthy that out of all possible female roles observed daily on the kibbutz, girls selected out the maternal role as a model. In the cultures we studied, the children also play out sex-typical adult activities, such as in their dances (Fig. 7.24). However, this does not mean that children never assume the role of the opposite sex while playing. When the !Ko children play out the "trance dance," girls will occasionally take the male role (Fig. 7.25). But there is a distinct preference for one's own sex role. Eipo, Himba, Bushmen, Yanomami, and Balinese boys practice mainly fighting, competitive and hunting games, as well as male rituals (Figs. 7.26–7.28). H. Sbrzesny's (1976) outstanding monograph gives details on the !Ko Bushmen in this regard.

We have emphasized the practice value of play and its tension-releasing function as safety valve custom in fighting and competitive games, including athletics. Games[7] and ritual merge into one another with no clear boundaries. This is also true for specific play forms, the basic function of which is the reinforcement and establishment of bonds. Thus in the Bushmen there is a melon ball dance,—a play dance or a bonding ritual, if one wishes—in which the group acts harmoniously as a unit, bonded by the rhythm and the rules of the games. Both women and girls participate in the play dance. They clap out a rhythm with their hands, which

---

[7] Whereas play activities are characterized by fluidity and creativity, games adhere to the rules and are strictly structured. Thus, they are certainly not tension free (fighting games), although the emotions are under control of the rules of the games.

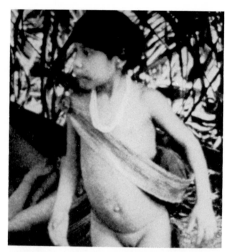

FIGURE 7.21. An approximately 10-year-old Yanomami
girl carries a banana blossom as a doll in
a sling. Photo: I. Eibl-Eibesfeldt.

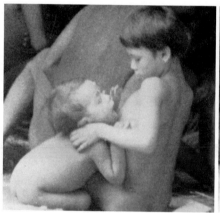 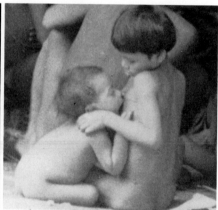

FIGURE 7.22. (a) and (b) Girls play out their future roles as mothers with other infants and small
children. Here a Yanomami girl offers her breast in play to a small child. Photo:
I. Eibl-Eibesfeldt.

FIGURE 7.23. The tsama melon is a substitute for a doll
among the !Ko (central Kalahari). Photo:
I. Eibl-Eibesfeldt.

FIGURE 7.24. (A) and (B) The tendency to imitate the same sex and thus identify with the culture-typical sex role extends across all spheres of life. Thus dances and rituals are acted out with great zeal by children in play, such as the Balinese dance shown here (A) (a flower sacrifice dance, the "pendet"). A 3-year-old girl chooses this dance in play (B). From a 16 mm film. Photo: I. Eibl-Eibesfeldt.

A

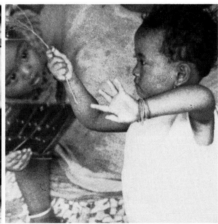

B

FIGURE 7.25. !Ko girls play "trance dance." Two of the girls assume the role of the dancing men. Photo: I. Eibl-Eibesfeldt.

591

FIGURE 7.26. One favorite game of Eipo boys is the grass arrow war, in which they shoot at one another with the stems of hard grasses. They practice the various fighting techniques, including gestures of mockery and triumph. Photo: I. Eibl-Eibesfeldt.

FIGURE 7.27. Even young Eipo boys play the game with ardor. From a 50 frames/second 16 mm film, frames 1, 133, 141, 147, and 149 of the sequence. Photo: I. Eibl-Eibesfeldt.

FIGURE 7.28. Eipo boys play out the ritualized arrival of guests.
Photo: I. Eibl-Eibesfeldt.

consists of a double beat in two successive rhythmic groups. The women stand in a group; one of them dances with a melon in her hand in rhythm in front of the group. She executes several dance steps before tossing the melon to another dancer who has, in the meantime, separated from the rest of the group. This woman catches the melon, dances some more steps, and then gives the melon to the next dancer. In this way the melon makes the entire round of all the dancers. The group is not always stationary, and those in the group often dance as well. The aim of this dance is to pass on the melon gracefully and flawlessly so that the harmonic sequence is undisturbed (H. Sbrzesny, 1976).

The so-called locust dance is a comparable men's cooperative game. Cooperative games like these have very positive effects on the socialization of the children. Canadian kindergarten pupils (age about 5 years), systematically guided in co-operative games over an 18-week period, were more willing to share candies among themselves than control groups without this experience (T. D. Orlick, 1981).

Competitive games also have a bonding effect, including both those who are united in the contest and those who simply identify with them. D. Morris (1981) masterfully made such an ethological analysis of soccer. Soccer has components of play and tension release, and much more. It bears traits of a subculture, its parties struggling for recognition. The motivations of fighting are played out on the soccer field in ritualized form, both in catharsis and in the feeling of success that comes with victory.

As stated earlier, play and serious activity often cannot be separated and this is very typical for humans. Where does the playful experimentation of the child end and true research begin?

Summary 7.2

Higher mammals and birds have a distinct appetence for novelty, which we call "curiosity." The drive develops in learning animals in the service of information acquisition. Curiosity is a juvenile characteristic in animals, sustaining itself in human beings into advanced age.

Play developed to enhance learning. During play, behavior patterns of fighting or flight appear to be freed from the emotions which normally accompany behavior in the serious context. Thus it appears that playful activities are detached from those neuronal mechanisms which motivate them under normal circumstances. Play, therefore, takes place in a relaxed emotional state, free of tension, allowing the individual to playfully experiment, investigate, and learn and create motivated,

593

among others, by curiosity. Intergrades between the playful and serious behavior occurs when autochthonous motivations enter into the picture and escalation, e.g., from playful to serious fighting, occasionally takes place. Even babies actively explore and play. Social exploration is particularly important, for during this time the child builds and practices interaction strategies. Furthermore, in play the child uses objects to incite playmates, imitate others, and vary object manipulations, thereby making discoveries. Thus the origins of research lie in playful experimentation.

7.3. The Development of Interpersonal Relationships[8]

Man learns a great deal in social situations. He acquires the skill to restrain his egoistic impulses and aggressions, taking others into consideration while momentarily postponing the satisfaction of his personal needs. He develops knowledge of human nature and social competence in his interactions with others, learning to differentiate between persons whom he can trust and those with whom he should behave with careful reservations. He learns the rank positions of his society, the value system of his culture, and identifies with his sex role. We have illustrated in the previous chapters of this book how individual experience and phylogenetic adaptation work together here. We have shown, for example, that man develops incest inhibitions in respect to partners of the opposite sex with whom he has grown up in a sibling-type relationship. Thus, this inhibition develops on the basis of a biologically predetermined program, but specifically whom the inhibitions are applied to is learned through experiences. We now wish to discuss some new aspects of child development concerning relationships with siblings and other children.

7.3.1. Sibling Ambivalence

Most mammalian families include only children of a single age class. The female bears a litter and brings up these young together. The litter mates play with one another, practicing specific strategies of intraspecific and interspecific encounters (fighting, flight, prey catching). Special play signals inhibit play behavior from escalating into a serious fight (I. Eibl-Eibesfeldt, 1987). Once the young become independent and scatter, the female bears another litter, and there are no sibling bonds between individuals of different litters. There are only a few mammalian exceptions to this family pattern. J. van Lawick-Goodall (1971a,b) describes a female chimpanzee juvenile infant displaying great interest in a younger sibling, attempting at first to touch the sibling but being prevented from doing so by the mother. Later the young chimpanzee was permitted to hold this new nursing infant and play with it, displaying many caregiving behavior patterns in doing so. Male chimpanzees remain bonded to their mothers and younger siblings even when fully grown. Diane Fossey (1979) found that older gorilla siblings prefer to remain in the vicinity of younger ones, but in this case because the older siblings still seek the company of the mother. Games between gorilla siblings comprise only 10% of all infantile games.

---

[8]Concerning the mother–child and father–child relationships, see Section 4.3. Concerning the ontogeny of special behavioral traits, ethical norms, etc., see special sections throughout the book. For social exploration and the socialization of aggression, in particular, see Sections 5.3 and 5.4.

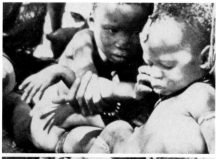

FIGURE 7.29. Sibling rivalry in the !Kung Bushmen. The older brother wants to scratch the younger one, who has driven him away from the mother's breast. The mother holds his arm firmly and pulls him back without punishing him. Photo: I. Eibl-Eibesfeldt.

With humans, siblings of different ages are joined in the family unit in a way that distinguishes this particular bonding arrangement from others; and this particular sibling relationship generally continues for life. It does not begin or continue without its tensions, however. When a sibling is born, the older sibling undergoes emotional stress, for the newborn now requires the mother's affection. The older sibling must learn to share this bond, usually reacting to the newcomer with jealousy. The older one attempts to defend the maternal bond, increasing appeals for care by frequently regressing to an early childhood developmental stage and other strategies, talking like a baby, and even occasionally wetting the bed. Clearly, bonds with other humans are not shared unreservedly, and learning this sharing generally takes place within an often painful process of adaptation. This is quite in contrast to the early disposition of willingly giving up and sharing objects (p. 342).

In our culture, mothers generally prepare their children for the new arrival, conditioning the child for this event, thus lessening the coming shock and drawing out the existing disposition for friendly contact in the form of affection. Usually the older sibling has been weaned for some time and is therefore somewhat less dependent on the mother. In tribal peoples this is somewhat different, since mothers frequently nurse for 3 years and longer, so that the child is living in close dependency on the mother. Although mothers usually wean the moment they know

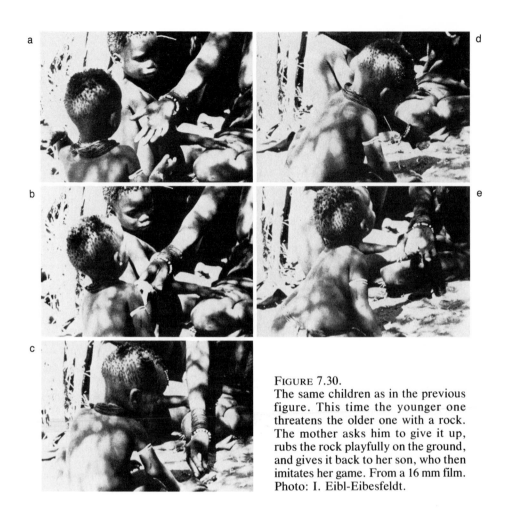

FIGURE 7.30.
The same children as in the previous figure. This time the younger one threatens the older one with a rock. The mother asks him to give it up, rubs the rock playfully on the ground, and gives it back to her son, who then imitates her game. From a 16 mm film. Photo: I. Eibl-Eibesfeldt.

they are pregnant, giving the child some months to adjust, and although relatives assume a great deal of the child care at this time, the mother–child bond remains strong. When a new child is born, mothers turn their full attention to the newborn.

In the !Ko and !Kung Bushmen and the Yanomami, I have observed pronounced sibling rivalry in such cases (I. Eibl-Eibesfeldt, 1972; M. Shostak, 1982), illustrated in Figures 7.29 and 7.30. The rivalry was particularly prominent in the above photographic sequence, since the !Kung group had dissolved into individual families at the time of photography and the older brother could find no outlet in the childrens' play group, where he normally would have been distracted. Confrontations occurred repeatedly between the older and the younger brother. The older one took the younger one's toy away and tried to hit and scratch him, while the no less active younger brother defended his place by the mother by kicking his legs against his brother who sat beside him, even if the older brother was not behaving aggressively at the time. The mother invariably demonstrated great patience during these encounters. She did not punish them, but simply held her hand protectively between them. She also tried to divert the younger boy with games. If a stick was taken from one son, she gave him another, and when he threatened to hit his brother with a rock, she held up her hand and asked him to give it up, which he did immediately. She rubbed the rock on the ground and gave it back

FIGURE 7.31. Sibling ambivalence in the Yanomami (Venezuela). The brother glances grimly at his small rival with whom the father is playing. The father's friendly affection and instruction change the older brother's mood. He imitates his father and embraces his smaller brother. But when he was not watched, he occasionally hit and scratched his brother. From a 16 mm film. Photo: I. Eibl-Eibesfeldt.

to the smaller son, providing him with a model by which the weapon now became a toy, and the son imitated this model, took the rock from his mother, and both boys played together (Fig. 7.30). The mother was also patient with the older son, but she did not encourage him to make body contact with her, acting as if she was "tired" of that. He made various appeals for contact: he offered himself for delousing, pretended something was stuck in his foot, whined, and tried to cuddle with his mother. Phases of aggressive rivalry were interrupted by phases of friendly play together. The siblings also shared food occasionally, so their behavior was ambivalent.

I observed similar cases of sibling rivalry among the Yanomami, where there was likewise a clearly ambivalent relationship. Older siblings embraced and cuddled younger ones and then suddenly, in a flash, they scratched them or squeezed them too tightly (what Mel Konner jokingly calls the "life-threatening" hug). Older girls were also ambivalent in this manner; however, they appeared to me to be less aggressive and more highly motivated for caregiving than boys. Jealousy concerned not only the maternal bond, since siblings also rivaled for the father's attention (Figs. 7.31–7.33).

In spite of this initial rivalry, intimate friendly relationships normally develop between siblings. For older sisters, the newborn brother or sister quickly becomes an object for affectionate care. In tribal cultures, girls are permitted to play out

597

FIGURE 7.32. Sibling ambivalence in the Kaleuna (Trobriand Islands). A father is affectionately occupied with his daughter. The otherwise highly jealous brother mimics his father and looks toward him, no doubt requesting acknowledgment. Fathers provide models to encourage friendly interactions of this type, and rebuke and punish older siblings for misbehaving with the younger ones. From a 25 frames/second 16 mm film, frames 1, 9, 65, 109, 117, 180, and 536 of the sequence. Photo: I. Eibl-Eibesfeldt.

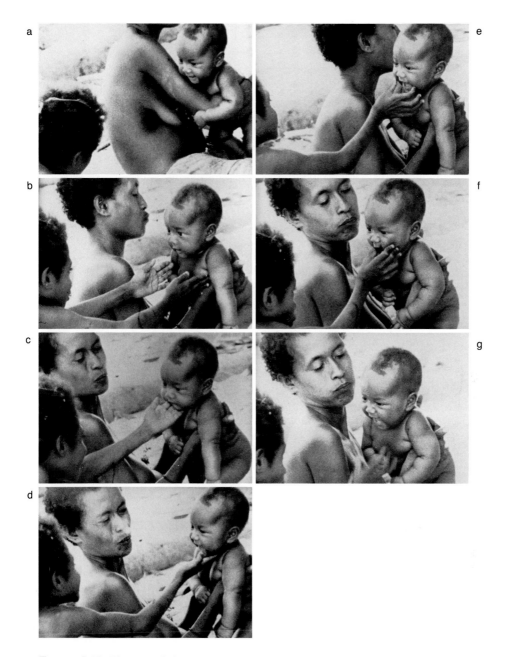

FIGURE 7.33. The same infant as shown in Fig. 7.32, here with the mother in an interaction with the older brother. Here friendliness is not interrupted by any rivalry behavior. The older brother displays affection with embraces, chin scratching, and other forms of loving contact, which have a most positive effect on the infant. From a 25 frames/second 16 mm film, frames, 1, 315, 370, 415, 480, 527, and 534 of the sequence. Photo: I. Eibl-Eibesfeldt.

their need to care for their infant siblings, and therefore rarely need dolls. Girls carry their small siblings about, cuddling, kissing, and feeding them (Fig. 7.22). They also play with them a great deal, only giving the infant up to the mother when the young one begins whining. Older siblings certainly play an important role in the socialization of infants (T. S. Weisner and R. Gallimore, 1977). Boys also join in this activity, but less frequently than girls and for a shorter period of time (H. Barry, M. K. Bacon, and I. L. Child, 1957). Older children learn social responsibility from these experiences. They are scolded if they do not carry the baby about carefully, hit the baby, or otherwise cause injury. When an approximately 19-month-old Bushman baby, accompanied by his sister, stuffed feces in his mouth while the sister was not watching him closely, the sister was scolded by the mother and grandmother and was even slapped (I. Eibl-Eibesfeldt, 1972).

Children are astonishingly tolerant toward their younger siblings while they are still very small, and the sibling bond is generally maintained for life. In many cultures, sibling relationships play an extremely significant role later in life. Since children learn best from those a few years or steps ahead of them, younger siblings are attracted to their older siblings, seeking their attention. This attraction undoubtedly tempers sibling rivalry.

7.4. Child Groups—Child Culture

Children learn at an early stage that they are part of a larger community, particularly in the smaller kin-based societies of village and tribal cultures. The child is initially fixated upon just a few reference persons even in these societies, with the mother and father being far more prominent than others. But children have contact with others from an early age. Relationships are not free of tension, as sibling rivalry indicates (p. 595). Within the family, relationships are subject to various rules of behavior, which the child must respect as he grows older. The stepwise formalization of relationships (see "joking relationship," p. 294), of which the small child has yet to learn, is one example. The child is from an early age in a surrounding of loving affection. In kin-based societies, such as the Bushman, an infant is at the center of attention, particularly when he has reached the age when he can react to affectionate behavior with similar responses. I have repeatedly observed among the !Ko Bushmen (Botswana, Kalahari) how often group members other than the parents have solicited contact with the child, and found that practically no adult or child passed the infant without at least talking to him briefly or touching him. Generally the baby is picked up, cuddled, played with, and then given back to the mother. In a single day, practically every adult made friendly contact with the infant (I. Eibl-Eibesfeldt, 1971). Small girls vie for the privilege of carrying the baby about, even competing with others for this favor.

As soon as a child can walk he will participate in the children's play group. Initially a child cannot play with the others, but participates as an outside player, taking objects offered by a baby sitter. The baby will watch a group at play and imitate the older children, but at this early stage the child lacks the skills to participate directly. Social group play is restricted to simple games with the baby sitter. Three-year-old children are able to join in a play group, and it is in such play groups that children are truly raised. The older ones explain the rules of play and will admonish those who do not adhere to them, such as by taking something away from another or otherwise being aggressive. Thus the child's socialization occurs mainly within the play group. Young children will test their behavioral latitude by social exploration (exploratory aggression, p. 391). Initially the older children behave very tolerantly toward the younger ones, although eventually they place definite limitations on behavior. By playing together in the childrens' group the members learn what aggravates others and which rules they must obey. This occurs in most cultures in which people live in small communities.

The majority of the childrens' games are traditional and passed on by the older children. Bushmen children do not learn the game rules from their parents, who probably forgot a lot of them anyway since they have not been involved with such matters since their childhoods. There is a children's culture, which is transmitted from the older children to the younger ones without adult intervention. Distinct rank order relationships prevail in childrens' groups (p. 299), with the older children generally occupying the center of attention. In Bushmen, older girls were generally the most highly ranked individuals in mixed childrens' groups. They instructed others, mediated conflicts, punished and comforted others, and also organized the games. Older boys were rarely part of these play groups, since boys spend more time away from camp playing in the bush. The girls, on the other hand, ventured less far from their homes and engaged in more contacts with the small children—boys as well as girls. Adults had little influence on the childrens' behavior within play groups. They intervened only if they heard their child crying in protest or if some loud fight began, and then they would merely raise their voices in admonishment.

We have already discussed the remarkable degree of social competence found in small children. Even at preschool age they react in highly differentiated ways to the moods of their playmates. They are readily infected by happy moods, laughing along when others do so. If they perceive a sorrowful context, even the very small children will display sympathy by giving of themselves to comfort someone and by sharing things (see our sequence on the assisting infant, p. 557). Sadness, also, is quite infectious (p. 162). If a child shows signs of pain, the others quiet down and inquire about the cause of his dismay. Children demonstrate these reactions spontaneously and not just in response to some verbal order. Happy children are more reactive than sad ones (J. Strayer, 1980).

While the parent–child relationship is asymmetric due to differences in power and competence, relationships are more uniform among children and are characterized by reciprocity and cooperation (J. Youniss, 1982). A study by R. Hinde *et al.* (1983) conducted over 8 months on 49 English kindergarten children showed that only when interacting with peers did the children utilize neutral conversation, friendly responses, and explanatory behavior, but also refusal, object withdrawal, contradiction, and defense; their behavior toward adults in the kindergarten situation was characterized by dependence. In the family situation, the asymmetry of the adult–child relationships is undoubtedly reduced, particularly in kin-based societies, for certain adults (grandparents in the Bushmen) assume roles as joking partners with whom the child has a carefree relationship (p. 294).

In the childrens' group the child grows into the community, learning social competence through the acquisition of social and technical aptitude, and ascending in rank while doing so. Older members dominate the younger ones in a friendly way. The children can choose their own play partners within the childrens' community, forming groups with members of the same sex, seeking those of the opposite sex, or forming exclusive friendship circles. They may also play alone if they feel like it.

The relationships described here also held for our culture, but have been modified with the development of anonymous mass society and with the progressive destruction of small settlements due to traffic. Children can no longer develop as freely in social and spatial terms as they once could. They are placed in kindergartens at an early age as a substitute for mixed age childrens' groups. In modern kindergartens the children find themselves at best with preschool children of various ages, and older, experienced children are absent from such groups. The kindergarten teacher now assumes the function of ordering and organizing. But the teacher is an adult, and far too removed from the world of children to be a real part of the group. No adult can continually repeat the same and often senseless counting rhymes as effortlessly as children. The adult also lacks the emotional involvement that characterizes children at play. With the disappearance of the older, prepubertal children, the children lose their most stimulating play and socialization partners outside of the nuclear family. Furthermore, children's culture is dying, since it is not maintained by adults. Adults perceive their childrens' activities from the periphery, intervening only rarely, as when a struggle between two children escalates and one of them begins crying. The parents generally then take hold of the one crying and scold the aggressor. Bushmen tend to comfort the crying child, while the Yanomami and Himba, in contrast, just as frequently encourage counter aggression (Fig. 7.34).

7.4.1. Adolescence

Adolescence is a stepchild of developmental psychology, characterized by a number of unique aspects (G. E. Weisfeld and J. M. Berger, 1983). Puberty is a time of rapid physical growth, which is typical for other primates but not for other mammals. In humans, this growth spurt is particularly prominent. Man requires an extended period of education. He must learn more than any other mammal and thus must be guided for a longer time. Initially, it is certainly advantageous that a child is small physically and thus easily led. But at puberty the child must develop both physical and mental maturity, defend and also feed himself, and, therefore, recover this developmental retardation (relative to other primates) within a relatively short period of time. Sexual dimorphism has been verified in all cultures in the form of girls attaining puberty earlier than boys, and with puberty there is a reorientation toward both family and community. This phase is also a time of increased exploratory aggression. This loutish period has its counterpart in the !Kung Bushmen of the Kalahari who call the lazy lounging adolescents "xedi kxao," professionals of the shade (i.e., lying around in the shade). The release from the parents and new orientation toward the community at large is marked in many cultures by so-called initiation rites (A. van Gennep, 1908; G. H. Herdt, 1982). The initiate is segregated from the group and from the everyday routine, and is instructed in and expected to perform a particular behavior. Boys often must endure some kind of abstinence. Instruction is often accompanied by a forcible subjugation, and finally there is a ritual renewed reception by the community, usually in the form of a rebirth. We wish to illustrate these with two examples, thereby posing the question of how distinctions in male and female initiations are to be understood.

At the beginning of the female initiation ceremony among the !Ko Bushmen, a girl is initially isolated for 6 days in a hut near the village. She is attended by her grandmother or another older woman and instructed in her rights and obligations as a woman. She is taught to respect the authority of older persons, to avoid sitting down at stranger's firesides, not to shame her husband, to fulfill her

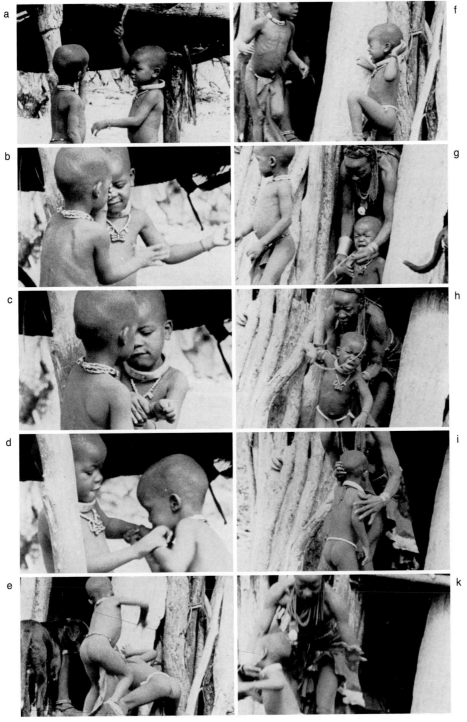

FIGURE 7.34. If child play becomes channeled into fighting, adults will intervene. The Himba boy on the right incites his playmate to play but is then subjugated in a struggle. He runs home, crying. His grandmother presses a stick into his hand, encouraging him to exact revenge. He does not want to, and she hits him. From a 25 frames/second 16 mm film, frames 1, 474, 529, 604, 740, 770, 954, 1026, 1076, and 1092 of the sequence. Photo: I. Eibl-Eibesfeldt.

603

duties as a spouse and to respect specific taboos, such as those of not touching her husband's hunting gear. She is instructed in birth and infant care. H. J. Heinz (1966) states that none of this information is new to them and that the instruction is something of a symbolic summary. During this period of isolation the group dances the eland antelope dance about her hut each morning, a dance distinctly symbolic of fertility.

At the conclusion of the ceremony the girl, beautifully decorated with beads, is led back to the community as a form of rebirth. Her caretaker leads her, as if she were still a child, presenting her to all the group members. Among the G/wi Bushmen she is also shown the land. The girl is given presents and thereby symbolically accepted by every individual.

The initiation of young Bushman boys also includes a rebirth, combined with instruction in adult responsibilities. Initiates are led into the bush by older men, and during their instruction period they must endure a great deal of self-denial. They must bear cold and hunger, and are frightened and intimidated at night. Finally, they receive a scar as an initiation sign, a painful and even hazardous procedure. During this time the initiates are treated like little children. They may not walk alone; they are fed, not permitted to look up, and may not handle anything with their hands. They are placed in an extreme condition of dependency.

This artificial infantilization creates the readiness to be instructed by the adults. The technique is the same one used when adults are brainwashed (I. Eibl-Eibesfeldt, 1970a). For example, in Mao's China, adults were tied up and fed by those who instructed them. Since an extended isolation period was involved, the victims were prepared to listen to their caretakers and their restrictions were reduced in accordance with the degree they were receptive to learning. It is especially in male initiation rites in various cultures that isolation, limitations, and infantilization play a major role as means of creating pliancy. Rebellious boys may often be viciously mistreated under such conditions.

One asks why the men must undergo such a strict procedure. I relate it to the necessity of creating a group spirit, which imprints a group ethic on the initiate extending beyond the sphere of the immediate family.

Polly Wiessner (verbal comm.) asked what the boys were taught during the !Kung male initiation. They replied that they were taught everything they already knew, except that the teacher was a stranger who would slant each teaching with the words: "I am not your father, I am not your mother, but I still tell you this." When Wiessner asked why they said this, they answered "Because young people do not listen to their parents, of course."

During initiation, the man must be emancipated from his family so that he can identify with the group on a new level. He must develop a group loyalty that extends beyond his loyalty to family. Indeed, men must be prepared to sacrifice their lives, if necessary, for the sake of the group, and this requires a particular indoctrination into group values. The various hardships foster one's learning disposition, and the event becomes a powerfully impressive experience that is not forgotten. There is a cost in becoming part of the men's group. Once someone has overcome that cost, a powerful sense of togetherness is engendered. This bond often is reinforced through being privy to the secrets of the entire community.

The woman, on the other hand, does not require as much indoctrination to group values, for she remains very much family centered. Furthermore, since in most cultures she leaves her family when she marries and even settles into another

604

group, there is no great need for an ideological fixation on one specific community group.

In addition, the woman's role is more clear cut from the beginning and thus is not saddled with insecurities. She proves herself to everyone by bearing a child. Thus the woman has a natural position of power, while the man has to establish his authority in confrontation with others, whether that be hunter, warrior, planter, or leader. He is selected for this kind of assertion and requires the continual recognition of others for his achievements. This characteristic is by no means absent in women, but they are less dependent on it than men, whose striving for recognition is much more pronounced. Identity and release from the mother are much greater problems for the growing son than the daughter, who can fully identify with her mother.

Summary 7.4

Each person grows into the community. He (or she) learns where he stands relative to others, whom he may interact with unreservedly and whom he must treat formally and with respect. He finds and adjusts to his rank position and acquires those skills needed for social interactions. All of this requires a great degree of social adaptability and thus high degree of social intelligence.

The infant distinguishes between different persons and establishes individual bonds with reference figures, which he defends like a possession. The readiness to share social bonds is often acquired through painful learning processes. Siblings experience rivalry and a distinct ambivalence between affection and rejection.

In preindustrial society a child joins a childrens' play group after being weaned. This group is composed of children of various ages and of both sexes. The interactions within this group comprise the essential elements of the child's socialization (see also exploratory aggression, p. 391). Older children instruct and lead the others in the childrens' group, carrying on a rich tradition of knowledge of games. There is a true childrens' culture. It is endangered in modern anonymous society.

The transition to adulthood is marked by initiation rites. During this time the initiates are introduced to the values of the group by elders. Isolation, harsh treatment, and infantilization are particularly important means of creating pliant personalities in male rites. This fosters indoctrination into a larger social group and extends loyalty beyond the family.

8

Man and His Habitat:
Ecological Considerations

8.1. Ecotype *Homo sapiens:* Hominization and Behavior

Konrad Lorenz (1943) once characterized man as the specialist in the unspecialized, a reference to human universality. Using the example of the following imaginary athletic competition, he showed how man is superior to all other animals in versatility. If the contest consisted of sprinting 100 m, diving into a pond and retrieving three objects from a depth of 5 m, then swimming 100 m toward a rope at the other bank, climbing 5 m up the rope, and finally walking an additional 10 km, any untrained physically fit adult, even older individuals, could execute the task, where no other vertebrate could perform it. A gazelle could run faster but would fail at the swimming and climbing parts of the contest; concomitantly, a chimpanzee could climb better but would perform the other tasks poorly. In short, while all other vertebrates are specialists, the human being, as a universalist, can master all these different locomotive skills and thus achieve superior results in performance. Humans have the prehensile hand as a generalized tool and an array of sensory organs. Man is also a universalist even in this respect since he has keen senses of sight, hearing, touch, and smell. Finally, a highly developed brain permits the development of a differentiated tool culture, enabling man to adapt to the most diverse environmental conditions. Thus it is by no means surprising that we find humans distributed throughout the world today, and a zoologist would designate the human as a generalist species. Man can become a specialist for a specific subsistence strategy in a particular environment, by specialized cultural adaptations, supplemented to a certain degree by biological ones.

Furthermore, one of the most pronounced basic features of man is his curiosity (p. 580). Indeed, other mammals and the birds display curiosity behavior, but in most of them the phase of active investigation and seeking out new impressions, playful experimentation with the environment, and even investigation of one's own body, is restricted to a relatively short time period occurring during infancy and youth. In man this drive to investigate novelty continues into old age.

In one of his stimulating films, Hans Hass made time-lapse movies in the late 1960s portraying the Acropolis in Athens from a distance (H. Hass, 1968). The tourists are seen to swarm up and down the steps like ants. An observer from another star, Hass commented, would no doubt ask what all the commotion was about. Are the people looking for food or a sex partner? Neither is a correct assessment, for the visitors are simply curious.

In order to appreciate the strength of this drive, one need merely consider the size of the market that has been opened due to this basic human characteristic. All scientific and technological achievements are ultimately due to curiosity, and is undoubtedly a primary motivation in research.

One could say that in man this juvenile characteristic of curiosity is sustained and retained throughout life. The fetalization theory of L. Bolk (1926) may be mentioned in this context; he shows that man has a number of morphological characteristics that can be considered to be long-term juvenile traits.

Because of this disposition, man has also been described as an ''creature of curiosity.'' Of course, there are many other capsule definitions of humanity. The human is the political, speaking, culture-producing, tool-using, thinking, reasonable, playful, foresightful being. He is all of these and more, and because of the interplay of these astonishing capabilities he has not only become a cosmopolitan creature but is on the threshold of conquering space if he does not extinguish himself before that time.

But he has also remained a biological organism, bound to his history and to his biological heritage, and against which a certain distance can be maintained but from which he can, one hopes, never be emancipated as a purely rational being, for to do so would mean to lose that which we call "heart!" Our rational thought, initially developed as an instrument utilized for survival, has attained tremendous dimensions in the intellectual realm, but our archaic emotional side continues to be the center of our being. Our universally shared feelings of longing, pain, love, and hate continue to be the *leitmotiv* of our greatest artistic achievements and the basis of understanding. A very substantial portion of our creative existence is due to the union between thought and feeling.

Undoubtedly mankind is able to accommodate himself to the most diverse habitats due to his culture. He modifies the landscape, irrigating desert wasteland, and building air conditioned cities that protect from the elements. Today he is at home everywhere on the planet. But he does not appear to be equally happy everywhere. It is particularly the high population density of metropolitan areas that cause some discomfort, indicating a limit to man's adaptability to an otherwise, and in many ways, attractive environment (p. 629). This limitation arises from man's biological development. Man originally lived for most of his history as hunter and gatherer. Then in a relatively short period of time, he became transformed into an agriculturalist. Finally, which in evolutionary terms is overnight, he entered the industrial age of the technologically civilized world, and this rapid development has left him breathless. We want to trace this pathway since it appears to me that it would help to understand our current problems of existence.

Some of the australopithecines may have hunted, and there is no doubt that during the lower stone age men hunted wild game and also gathered foods. Thus we know that for 99% of our existence we have been leading the life of hunter-gatherers and thus are in some way biologically molded by this lifestyle. Agriculture and animal husbandry began only some 10–15,000 years ago, and at the time of Christ's birth, two-thirds of the earth was still populated by hunters and gatherers.

It is currently thought that the hominization process began in the savanna habitat of Africa. At the onset of this process there were large, tree-dwelling primates who moved about by brachiating and climbing in trees. This fostered the development of binocular vision, upright posture and differentiation between the fore- and hindlimbs, and the development of the prehensile hand and the pectoral girdle. While the shoulder blades provide support to the barrel-shaped chest cavity in those apes who locomote on all four legs (e.g., macaques and baboons), the shoulder blades in humans, due to the life habits of his ancestors (see below), are in a dorsal position, which pushed the shoulder joint to the side and gave the arm greater freedom of movement. As a relatively large mammal, our apelike tree-dwelling ancestors could not move around in tree branches by leaping and climbing like squirrels and small apes. They had to be able to hold onto the branches and move either by dangling from them or climbing by means of grabbing with the hands, pulling the body forward and at the same time pushing with the hindlimbs ("push and pull climbing"). Since they were less specialized at brachiating than gibbons, we can say that our ancestors were semibrachiators.

This means of locomotion resulted in the development of a number of adaptations. The prehensile hand developed, while the hindlimbs became specialized for bearing weight and pushing the body forward, thus fostering a semi-upright posture. Prehensile hand locomotion led to a number of additional adaptations itself. A heavy brachiator can not afford to grab or step incorrectly, but instead must reach for specific hand holds. This requires an accurate estimation of the distance. Furthermore, and this is not necessarily obvious, the organism must be able to take aim while reaching for objects (see also the discussion on voluntary motor functions, p. 527).

Binocular vision developed for estimating distance. The eyes, which in vertebrates were originally on the sides of the head, moved forward onto approximately the same plane, enabling the organism not only to estimate distance but also to judge spatial relationships and to use the configuration of objects to move efficiently through space. This could include determining alternate routes of getting to some objective. Other vertebrates, who also move about in highly differentiated environments, developed binocular vision analogously, as in the bottom-dwelling fish (e.g., gobies and blennies), which appear to display particular intelligence because of their continual surveying of the surroundings for orientation.

The skills needed for targeted grasping and stepping are not seen in all higher organisms. In many birds and mammals, living on flat terrain, the mechanics of locomotion are so stereotyped that even a low horizontal obstacle is quite difficult to surmount. K. Lorenz (1973) notes that geese will walk right up to a board blocking their path and if their stride is not of such a length that they can step over the board in a single step, they have great difficulty getting past it. They must often retreat and march up to the obstacle again and even then may stumble over it. They are unable to intentionally vary their stride in order to step over the object. In order to execute such movement, the fairly rigid motor program must be subdivided into smaller units that combine with orientation movements in continuous afferent feedback. This enables the organism to constantly control locomotion, which is a prerequisite for voluntary motor control. Our thought and perceptual pathways have thus been significantly influenced by the optical haptic heritage of our tree-climbing ancestors (K. Lorenz, 1943).

The branching off of the hominids from the anthropoid apes (pongids) probably took place in the Miocene as a result of the climatic changes that were occurring— as the great rain forests of Africa and Asia shrank and open forests and savannas arose. This compelled our ancestors to spend more and more time on the ground. Bipedal locomotion, which had already been fostered by push and pull climbing, now developed further. It certainly would have been advantageous if while moving about our ancestors could simultaneously look over the grass cover for predators. Furthermore, this type of locomotion freed the hands, and since they were prehensile they were already capable of seizing objects and holding sticks for tool use. The binocular vision that developed as an adaptation to tree dwelling enabled them to accurately estimate distances.

Sticks could also be used as weapons. In A. Kortlandt's (1972) field experiments using stuffed leopards as potential predators, chimpanzees used sticks to strike leopards with powerful blows. They also aimed and threw bits of wood, rocks, and other objects at them. Savanna chimpanzees were more skillful at these tasks than were the forest dwellers, which suggested to Kortlandt that this was evidence to support the theory that the open savanna fostered hominization. The jumble of branches in the forest habitat hindered this kind of defensive strategy. Kortlandt also propounds the interesting thesis that the ancestors of modern chimpanzees competed unsuccessfully with the first hominids for the occupation of the savanna. They were pressed back into the forests, which were not favorable hominid habitats. Thus, the skills they had developed then deteriorated. Only those still living in savanna habitat knew how to use sticks and stones to ward off enemies. It is probable that these objects were initially used for defensive purposes and

609

perhaps also to chase predators away from their kill so as to secure a portion of the kill for themselves. The original contention that australopithecines hunted big game (R. A. Dart, 1953) has more recently been contested (L. R. Binford, 1981).

Studies of the bone remains of those animals considered to be australopithecine prey revealed distinct marks of bites from large carnivores but without any suggestion of mechanical butchering of the prey using stone tools. Binford also determined that the hollow bones of the big game, which is what most of the prey were, had been split with rocks, probably for the purpose of extracting the marrow. And this was apparently the work of australopithecines. This would mean that we would have to revise our romantic picture of the "predatory ape." It appears that australopithecines were taking left overs from predators, especially the marrow bones, and opening them with stones. The round quarzite rocks found by L. Leakey in Olduvai gorge, and which he thought were bola rocks, were probably used as hammer stones to open the bones. Thus the australopithecines have had certain preadaptations of subsequent significance. Chimpanzees use rocks to break open nuts, and this is accomplished particularly by the females, who are more skilled at the task. Their strokes are more even, indicating superior fine motor control (C. and H. Boesch, 1981). Males often strike too powerfully, smashing both shell and contents. Females also take their hammer rocks into the trees. And, as I see it, the next step toward breaking open hollow bones is not a major one. The female as "gatherer" may have had a decisive impetus on the development of tool use. Females also pass these techniques on to their young. In the Japanese macaques, females were the inventors of new traditions of food processing, the males being too preoccupied with territorial defense and rank displays.

Big game hunting, on the other hand, probably took place after man had developed weapons for use in intraspecific conflicts. Such weapons made feasible the rapid and certain death of large game. The use of sticks for defense against predatory enemies may have been the precursor for this adaptation. Thus, it seems likely that man began as a scavenger rather than as a big game hunter.

Gathering requires differentiated strategies and probably fostered tool use. Besides the previously cited pounding stones for breaking hard-shelled nuts, other early tools may have included the digging stick and simple bags or baskets used to transport gathered items.

Besides pounding stones, chimpanzees use sapling switches and small sticks to poke and extricate termites from their hills (J. van Lawick-Goodall, 1968). The investigation of hollow cavities for their contents, and poking and pounding objects may have all fostered the cognitive development of the early hominids. S. T. Parker and K. R. Gibson (1979) even ascribe primary significance to this process, which they refer to as the "extracting foraging model" of hominization.

The combination of hunting and gathering may have also encouraged a sexual division of labor for food acquisition. The men, preadapted with their greater aggressiveness, their physical constitution, and their role as group defenders may have taken on the often dangerous and wide-ranging hunting expeditions, while the woman, restricted by small children, assumed the responsibility for gathering in the vicinity of the campsite of their local band. In current hunter-gatherer populations, there are just a few exceptions to this rule. Women join in hunting among the Philippine Agta, but they are less successful than the men, who also hunt (P. B. Griffin, 1984).

610   Since food storage would have been kept to a minimum, it was important that

everything be shared with others. This required at least temporary meeting sites, where everyone brought their prey and gathered foods, fostering the development of differentiated forms of social cooperative living. Rules and rites of sharing arose, facilitating group integrity. The object possession norms developed in connection with the rise of the tool culture.

The existence of hunters and gatherers required complex intellectual demands. I refer in this connection to a study of D. F. Lancy (1983), who tested the cognitive abilities of children in two neighboring cultures of New Guinea—the Kilenge and the Mandok. The two cultures engage in trade and share many aspects of each other's cultures: the Mandok are maritime hunters, gatherers, and traders, while the Kilenge live from horticulture.

The children of both groups tested were well nourished and healthy. The Mandok outperformed the Kilenge in tests, which Lancy interprets as a sign that a hunting-gathering lifestyle has greater intellectual demands due to more learning and individual adaptability requirements. This is a thesis that remains to be tested. The fact that the Mandok are also traders could confound these findings, since trading could be the decisive operative variable. The Eipo of western New Guinea, with whom I am closely acquainted, could be the subjects of a comparable study since they are gardeners who also are traders. As traders, they have developed a counting system extending to the number 25! However, there is no doubt that hunting and gathering places great intellectual demands on its adherents.

The growing child has a great deal to learn, which, in turn, requires an extended childhood and long-term care, which fostered the familization of the male. Many bonding and aggression-diverting rituals developed for the sake of harmonizing cooperative life of group members; other developments facilitating harmony probably included hidden ovulation and modesty. A primate living in groups develops a distinct tendency toward long-term attachment to one or a few partners. In addition, sexual competition is reduced.

As a consequence of savanna life, there occurred the further development of the upright posture and the associated pelvic rotation, caused by a lordotic bending of the lower vertebral column. While the vertebral column of apes is structured as a kyphotic arched bridge, as in other four-legged mammals, the human spine is an S-shaped arch modified as a supporting spring system. Pelvis, posterior and leg musculature, and the lower extremities also underwent significant change, the foot being modified for running and standing.

The morphological changes associated with upright posture have by no means attained perfection. There are structural problems associated with this modification that selection has not yet completely resolved. The lower venous system is overburdened, which is occasionally manifested in varicose veins. Problems also exist for the vertebral column and the bony skeleton of the lower extremities, which in advanced age can wear out. The vertebral arch at the lumbar–sacral boundary results in the lumbar vertebrae bearing the weight of the torso and lying transversely on the sacrum, a situation that can result in excessive erosion of the terminal lumbar vertebra. Finally, the fine motor mechanics of walking leaves much to be desired. I have noticed a rather high frequency of injuries to the lower extremities caused by bumping and stubbing (I. Eibl-Eibesfeldt, 1976) in tribal peoples.

The use of tools for killing and butchering prey and processing other food sources, and the tenderizing effect of fire on meat permitted a reduction in the dentition and therefore in the size of the snout region. The canine teeth regressed, and hominids developed their characteristic closed dental arch, an important precursor for the formation of dental sounds and thus the development of a differentiated verbal language.

Since with the regression of the snout region the center of gravity of the skull became more central, there was no longer a need for a powerful neck musculature to support the head. The head became balanced on top of the relatively narrow neck, and this slender, long neck is a species-typical characteristic of *Homo sapiens,* contrasting the ''bullish'' neck of the apes (G. Osche, 1979). Could it be for this reason that we find a long slender neck to be pleasing? Some tribes have emphasized this characteristic to grotesque proportions.

Innate aesthetic ideals could have an effect on sexual selection. During the course of hominization, evolution guiding aesthetic preferences may have developed that led to emphasis of control with the ape-animal traits (see p. 676). Artistic depictions of people from various cultures and racial backgrounds demonstrate a highly similar idealization of the human being. Thus, fine facial features are universally preferred to coarse ones. I am of the opinion that there are aesthetic schemata that influence sexual partner selection as ideals of beauty and which select for the gracile hominid features of modern man. Beauty ideals, even those of cultural origin, certainly influenced the course of human evolution. The positive evaluation of physical beauty leads to appraising beautiful people more positively than those who are ugly, imparting a certain ''beauty bonus'' to attractive individuals (M. Webster and J. E. Driskell, 1983).

One of the most prominent human characteristics is his partial hairlessness. D. Morris (1968) emphasized this taxonomic characteristic provocatively when he described the human being as a ''naked ape.'' The loss of hair and the pronounced development of the sweat glands arose for the purpose of thermoregulation, for they permit the existence of hunters in warm climates to exert themselves physically for extended periods of time.

Notable modifications also occurred in association with the use of tools and their production. The most obvious of these include the long opposable thumb and the elongated terminal phalanges, which permit humans to hold tools in a firm precision grip. This is the grip we utilize when we hold a screwdriver (J. R. Napier, 1962). Furthermore, the development of tool culture may have also fostered handedness, perhaps in conjunction with the development of social conventions including duels or greetings (p. 401) but also because it is advantageous when tools can be used in the same way by different persons.

In the lower stone age, tools were ornamented with simple designs (M. W. Conkey, 1978). Brands and etchings are used to beautify objects, but this kind of simple decoration has another function as well. It can be a distinguishing mark on two different levels: on the one hand, it can be used as an individual sign to mark something as personal property for the purpose of avoiding confusion with similar objects and perhaps to forestall theft. But, as P. Wiessner (1983b) emphasizes, it also can be used for the sake of a positive self-representation. Beauty enhances esteem, in objects as well as individuals. The Mousterian use of red ochre also indicates that this type of image enhancement also occurred during this lower stone age period.

I should also like to cite the related example of the arrowhead exchange among the Yanomami (p. 309). The simple bamboo tips, which are used as implements in war to kill one's enemies, vary individually. Each man collects in his quiver, tips belonging to his friends. Thus, he displays his social network in front of the others as a peacock spreads his tail.

Wiessner found that among hunters and gatherers, producing goods for storage and for trade or gift exchanges, there is a kind of a personal expressive marking. The decoration also has the function of bonding a group with a stylistic identity visible to all (M. W. Conkey, 1978). Here Wiessner refers to an "emblemic style." This type of marking developed rapidly in the beginning of the late paleolithic. It was undoubtedly the earliest combination of communication of group identity via aesthetics, whose marriage has not been dissolved to this day. The great style periods of Europe—Romanesque, Gothic, Renaissance, Baroque, etc., are living expressions for the unity of European culture at a higher level of integration. For this reason, a central European can feel to some extent as at home in Leningrad as in London, Paris, or Florence.

The mass society has created new signs for bonding humanity. Such phenomena as rock music or certain fashions are today's style of technologically civilized society the world over. However, the great numbers and diversity of people bonded by a uniform ideology necessitates simplification of unifying symbols.

It is most probable that hominization occurred in the African savanna, and even today we still have a great preference for the savanna biotope. G. Orians (1980) formulated a "savanna theory" of biotope preference, in which he theorizes that man displays an innate preference for the savanna habitat. He proceeds from the viewpoint that this biotope in which hominization occurred would be particularly favorable for an upright walking hunter and gatherer. In the rain forest, the fruits hidden throughout the leaf cover are not readily accessible, and game is difficult to capture. Furthermore, the cover would make them more susceptible to attacks from hidden predators.

In the savanna, in contrast, productivity takes place on the ground and where a gatherer finds most of the wild foods, including those hidden within the soil in the form of roots, which store fluids and carbohydrates (starch). Such roots provide the necessary staple energy resource. Grazing game also congregates in this habitat. Further, man in this open landscape is less likely to be vulnerable to surprise attack. Trees are good indicators of sufficient precipitation, and also provide protection without limiting visibility since they are distributed either singly or in clusters throughout the otherwise open terrain. Thus, in reality, we can see that for man the forest is not altogether a friendly abode. In the tales and sagas of Europe the forests are inhabited by ghosts and many other dangerous creatures. Also, on the other hand, we perceive the treeless steppe as bleak and deserted. Our idealized concept of a landscape resembles a savanna. The parks we create as ideal landscapes consist of clusters of trees and open grasslands, and this is true not only in our culture. Flowing water, crags, and caverns are other features of beautiful landscapes. There is a certain ambivalence with regard to stagnant water, perhaps because in the tropics water is the breeding place for pathogenic bacteria, parasites, and gnats. Plants and flowers, in particular, have an especially strong aesthetic appeal for us. Even in our city apartments we cultivate green plants and flowers. Foliage, vines, and floral arrangements are found on curtains, hangings, carpets, pottery, and other objects. Flowers are given as gifts and green branches are borne as a sign of peace. Flowers are not really that prevalent in the tropical rain forest, but when the desert blooms we are presented with a sea of blossoms of unusual splendor.

This human preference for plants and water is also expressed in the way we evaluate ambient odors. Questionnaires regarding especially pleasing and displeasing odors show (M. Schleidt, P. Neumann, and Morishita, 1988) that plants, water, and nature are frequently cited as almost especially pleasing, in contrast

613

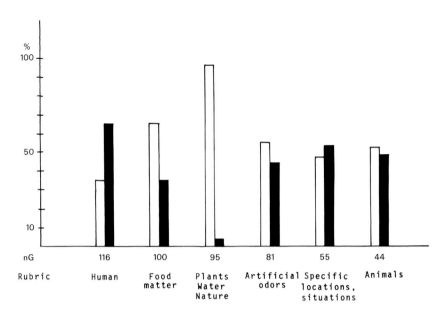

FIGURE 8.1. Man's preference for plants and water is clearly expressed in evaluations of
ambient odors. Test persons ($n = 45$) evaluate odors they recall from memory:
white columns = pleasing classifications; black columns = displeasing classifications; nG = frequency with which a corresponding odor is cited; rubric
= sphere of origin of the odor. After M. Schleidt and P. Neumann (in preparation).

to all other rubrics, where displeasing sensations are quite clear (Fig. 8.1). I consider this "phytophilia" to be an innate preference related to the choice of biotope.
It determines such expressions as the motifs of artistic creations (p. 674).

Man evolved in the African savanna, initially leading the life of a hunter/gatherer.
Homo erectus, who appeared more than 1.5 million years ago, was acquainted
with hunting weapons, housing, clothing, and fire. The earliest fire sites are around
750,000 years old. *Homo erectus* lived until approximately 200,000 years ago.

Excavations at Terra Amata revealed dwelling sites some 300,000 years old.
The oval huts there were 7–17 m long and 4–6 m wide, with walls consisting of
7 cm thick branches with supporting beams 30 cm in diameter bearing the roof.
The settlement was only used at particular times during the year, but it was in
continuous use for an extended period. The resident groups apparently inhabited
a specific region and carried on stable traditions. Group size lay between 20 to
30 persons, and settlement density of this *Homo erectus* group was estimated at
1 person/25 km², which is equivalent to a population density of 0.04 persons/km².
Modern *Homo sapiens* forms appeared some 80,000 years ago. During the Au-
rignacian (some 30,000 years ago), an estimated total of 0.5–1 million people lived
in central and eastern Europe, with approximately 25,000 inhabiting what today
is the Federal Republic of Germany, although such estimates are made on an
extremely speculative basis. This is a density of 0.1–0.2 persons/km², an increase
by a factor of 5 versus the *Homo erectus* population.

Correspondingly low population densities of small local groups occur today in
the modern hunters and gatherers. Local group size of the !Kung is an average
of 25 persons (8–40) (R. B. Lee, 1979; L. Marshall, 1976), in the !Ko 35–45

(H. J. Heinz, 1975), and in the G/wi 22–60 (G. B. Silberbauer, 1972). Each local group is composed of 6 to 15 families.

The territory used by a local group of the !Kung is composed of 300–600 km^2 (R. B. Lee, 1976) and in the G/wi 450–1000 km^2 (G. B. Silberbauer, 1972). !Ko figures resemble those of the G/wi (estimates by P. Wiessner after H. J. Heinz, 1979).

Population density in these above tribes is very small. If the figures are referenced to the utilized land (there is a great deal of unused wilderness), the following estimates are attained: R. B. Lee (1979) assesses the region around the arid period base camp of the !Kung around Dobe at 41 persons/100 km^2. This camp is used 4–9 months out of the year. Population density is considerably higher in areas where water is present throughout the year. In the /xai/xai there is a much higher population density of 150 persons/100 km^2. The !Kung are redistributed during the summertime, when density drops to 20 persons/200–400 km^2. This is approximately the same population density found in other hunters and gatherers. In Alaska, Canada, and Siberia, the density is 0.5–0.005 persons/km^2, with 0.05 being the most frequent density. Archeological evidence leans in this same direction (H. M. Wobst, 1976). On an average, the size of local groups in present day hunters and gatherers is about 25 persons, corresponding to six to seven families.

The basic principles of human society life are fully developed in hunter-gatherer peoples. They live in individualized bands in which each person knows every other and which are composed of families consisting of three generations. Man and woman live in a long-term marital arrangement. Social relationships within the group are differentiated and constant. Local groups are permanent and territorial. We cited the example of the nexus system of the !Ko Bushmen earlier (p. 328). These small societies can only be sustained through mechanisms that maintain reciprocity and bushmen society is indeed ridden by constant hagglings about who did not adequately pay back even though he could have done so.

Several hundred people are joined in a nexus. They form a preferential pool for marriage partners and are ideally economically self-sufficient. According to estimates of L. Livi (1949), a population must contain at least 500 to survive as an endogamous and autonomous entity particularly over the long term (H. M. Wobst, 1976). But according to J. W. MacCluer and B. Dyke (1976), 100–200 persons can also suffice under certain conditions.

In the hunters and gatherers there are headmen who represent the group to outsiders. Sex-based division of labor is developed. In addition to peoples where egalitarianism is enforced by group pressure (Bushmen), there are groups with rigid hierarchically organized communities which, if successful, acquire large amounts of property (Kwakiutl). Group pride, xenophobia, and war do occur in such peoples. We have discussed this at length in previous sections.

The ability to control the environment occurs even at the hunter-gatherer level, enabling man to become cosmopolitan. Although man has no hair covering, he uses clothing in various ways to provide protection from the elements and this thereby allows him to inhabit all types of environments, including rain forest, desert, or Arctic tundra. Indeed, even the hunters-gatherers are able to inhabit diverse geographical areas. Housing and fire are replacements for a home climate. The belief that at this level people have a feeling for nature and are, therefore, particularly considerate of the environment is unfortunately Rousseauian wishful thinking. Hunters and gatherers, too, are exploitative, but their damage is limited since they are so sparsely distributed over the landscape. Nonetheless they still are to blame for extinct species. Furthermore, even paleolithic man contributed to steppe formation by setting fires to create an open terrain, stimulate new grass growth, and lure wild game. Bushmen continue to do this today. There was, in fact, no selection pressure against exploitative behavior, since people were so few. This fact creates a problem today.

Summary 8.1

Hominization occurred in African savannas and this long period of our evolution had a lasting effect on our biological composition. A savanna-like habitat is still aesthetically appealing to us and mimicked in the planned park-scapes. Another expression of our phylogenetically imprinted habitat preference is man's pronounced phytophilia. As arboreal primates, our human ancestors developed binocular vision, the prehensile hand, upright posture, and the ability to carefully place one's steps and seize objects. The savanna, with its reduced tree cover, made it necessary to move across grass-covered terrain, facilitating an upright gait. This freed the hands for carrying tools. Chimpanzees use sticks for defense against enemies, and presumably the australopithecines occasionally hunted with clubs or used sticks instrumentally to drive predators away from their kills.

The life style of the hunter-gatherer fostered the development of local groups with stabilized dwelling sites, where food was brought and distributed. The first tools included simple weapons, carrying bags, and sticks and tools for breaking open hollow bones and hard-shelled fruits; our female ancestors undoubtedly played an important role in their development. At the *Homo erectus* level we find a more developed tool culture, housing, and the use of fire. Thanks to his universality, the lower stone age hunter-gatherer achieved some degree of dominance over his environment. As an open-minded creature of curiosity he was able to spread through the world, settling in deserts, Arctic tundra, and tropical rain forests. Diverse habitat occupation succeeded with culturally acquired subsistence strategies.

At the hunter-gatherer level, man lived in familial manner in small territorial groups bonded by reciprocal altruism.

8.2. From the Individualized Society to Industrial Society

> *No one is in a position to love four billion unacquainted persons, but in spite of that we have every reason to foster a spirit of "cameraderie." Everything responsible for our "human existence" is due to an anonymous multitude of others who lived before us whose achievements have been bestowed upon us as gifts.*
>
> H. Hass (1981, p. 198)

8.2.1. The Neolithic Revolution

With the neolithic period, people in some parts of the world began keeping domesticated animals and cultivating plants, a new subsistence strategy with far-reaching consequences. It reinforced man's ecological dominance and permitted greater population density. Agriculture made man somewhat less dependent on fluctuations in the environment. It increased the productivity of the land and, therefore, its capacity for sustaining people. The effects were so dramatic that we refer to a neolithic revolution.

The central European linear pottery culture, as the earliest tillers in that area, had an estimated population density of 1.45 inhabitants/km^2 in 4500 B.C. They

616

would have numbered some 360,000 in what is now West Germany. This is an increase by a factor of 7 in comparison with the paleolithic Aurignacians and a factor of 35 when compared with *Homo erectus*.

Field tilling and animal husbandry required a number of new cultural adaptations. Familial or individual rights of ownership of land and animals became more important, and with this developed particular rules for the inheritance of these goods. The greater population density resulted in increased competition between groups, which were also less mobile. With improved techniques of fighting came more sophisticated forms of peacemaking and neighborly coexistence. Larger social units developed and with them more complex politics, trade, and specialization of labor. Finally, organizational structures differentiated wherever such leadership hierarchies were needed due to warfare. We previously cited the example of cattle-breeding Himba, who cultivate martial virtues and obedience to the chieftain reinforced by means of special rituals by which discipline is maintained. Cultivated land is often coveted and must be defended. Groups joined with each other, forming tribes and, finally, states.

Man's increasing control over the environment and his sedentism because of an agricultural life style led to a population explosion. While in a more mobile hunting and gathering way of life, abstinence, postpartum taboos on intercourse, and infanticide were necessary to ensure adequate birth spacing; with sedentism, such wide spacing was, in most cases, not necessary. However, new forms of population control were developed. Thus, in Europe, for at least the past 1000 years until this century, marriage was sanctioned only for those who inherited the farmland; in Central Europe, land was not to be partitioned among several heirs. Persons without land had to prove by their trade that they were able to feed a family.

Agricultural man shapes his landscape by caring for the land by preventing erosion and loss of the new growth, at least among advanced gardeners and tillers. The cultivated landscape is attractive, because it is open like the savanna. Through his farming activities man can create a multiplicity of microbiotopes, contributing to differentiation and speciation.

Farming communities in Europe also adapted their strategies of exploitation in such a way that they finally achieved an ecological equilibrium. In parts of Bavaria and Austria, fields have been ploughed for over 1000 years. They are still fertile and show no sign of erosion. This was not always the case however, and with the development of new techniques, new problems arose. For example, heavy tractors now in use compress the ground, inhibiting the microfauna from loosening the soil. The soil remains packed and rainwater is prevented from seeping in. In addition, microfauna are adversely affected by fertilizers and pesticides. Erosion and steppe formation results. We need to readapt. So, too, in the tropics, the shifting agriculturists and pastoralists seriously contribute to desert formation.

Pastoralism, in particular, becomes a problem when grazing lands are common territory, since individuals tend to overstock, which they would not do if it were their own lands. This is a problem of short-term individual interests versus the long-term interests of the group. When the individual sends more animals out to graze than is permissible, he gains an advantage because the costs arising from this practice are borne by the community, a situation described by Garret Hardin (1968). J. L. Gilles and K. Jamtgaard (1981) have noted that this is not the invariable consequence of communal property, but particular controls must be utilized to avoid such damage.

In the biological perspective, agriculture and animal breeding have not yet sig-

617

nificantly altered human beings, for their origin has been too recent. There are a number of physiological adaptations that are perhaps directly related to animal breeding. Pastoralists and dairy farmers have a very high lactose tolerance, and only a small percentage are unable to digest milk as adults, while those peoples lacking a dairy farming have a low lactose tolerance. It is not yet clear to what extent these differences are genetic (p. 15).

The community size of agricultural societies is generally larger than those of hunter-gatherers, but internal organization is basically similar. Kin and family groups remain as the nuclear units of the community. Children grow up in childrens' play groups comprising various age groups, and boys and girls also play together. Occasionally there is separation by gender and age as girls and boys practice different roles, leading to the formation of separate boys' and girls' play groups. Pastoralists, horticulturists, and agriculturalists generally have a higher frequency of warfare than hunters and gatherers, perhaps related to their superior reproductive success. The new subsistence strategy had undoubtedly strengthened man's control over his natural environment leading to a significant population growth as a result.

Agriculture is labor intensive, at least in some parts of the world, particularly where the techniques of agriculture are not yet highly developed. Hunters and gatherers seem, in general, more leisure intensive. The women of the Kalahari bushmen spend 2–3 hours daily collecting food. R. B. Lee (1976) points out that they spend, in addition, considerable time (up to 40 hours a week) for food processing, but this type of work is done in small groups, allowing for social and leisure interaction. Similarly, the men hunt, and although strenuous, it is also a rewarding activity. Certainly, they do not hunt every day. The rest of the daily routine is spent in the community of others performing a variety of manual tasks as well as engaging in games and other social interactions.

Farming is less leisure intensive, although it can be less time demanding through technological advances. In central Europe, work and leisure-intensive phases change with the seasons, permitting a rich cultural life to unfold enhanced by division of labor with people such as the aristocracy specializing in the promotion of the fine arts. With the industrial revolution, man once again entered a work-intensive phase from which he is only now being slowly liberated with the introduction of labor-saving devices (I. Eibl-Eibesfeldt, 1976).

8.2.2. The Development of Mass Society

8.2.2.1. Formation of State and Authority—The Problem of the Relationship between Governing and the Governed. Man lived in small groups for the greatest part of his history. They were structured and capable of forming alliances with other groups but also able to engage in armed conflict. Yet, large-scale organized warfare was limited because of *restrictions imposed by the hunting and gathering way* of life. Once agriculture and animal husbandry were developed, more people were able to live in a specific region and this engendered the growth of competition between groups that led to the development of large-scale organized warfare and finally to growth of states.

The initiation of an armed conflict depended on several factors, including arms technology, the military potential of group strength as measured by the number of recruitable warriors, and their military-political leadership. Selection favored those who could maintain larger political groups and organize their coordinated activation. Group competition fostered the unification of many individuals. This brought various kinds of stress but also advantages. Thus the greatest levels of creativity in the arts and sciences were realized only through the specialization of labor occurring in mass society. Only such societies had the means, in the form of educational institutions, to develop the necessary reservoir of special talents. In addition, in anonymous society the conformity pressure of the small group is released thus allowing for a less restricting use of these talents. On the other hand, individual freedom in large societies is greatly restricted in many other ways. Organizations like administration develop their own dynamics of increasing their perfection, which necessarily restricts some aspects of individual freedom.

The state initially developed during the course of selection in steps that can be followed historically. Often individuals seeking power delivered the impetus for such a development by, for example, uniting various tribes into a state structure using armed force. In competition with others, such groups had to stand the test during selection (R. B. Ferguson, 1984; P. Calvinoux, 1980; J. E. Pfeiffer, 1977; R. Cohen and E. R. Service, 1978; M. Fried, 1961).

The state as a form of organization must offer increased survival potential to its citizens. Thus, if the number of citizens continually decreases from generation to generation or when the society is inferior to others during confrontations, the state and its citizens run the risk of being wiped out.

One of the first tasks of the state and thus of political leadership is the protection of group survival through a defense organization. Consequently, the state had to regulate other activities conducted with different groups, such as alliances and trade.

The assemblage of large numbers of people who do not know each other and whose agonal tendencies are thus not inhibited by personal acquaintance (p. 170) requires additional measures to maintain order and internal harmony. Laws protect possessions and other rights of the citizenry, and such institutions as the military and the police enforce these regulations, with force if necessary. The state is obligated to fight separatist tendencies within the community. This is done through indoctrination but also by using force. As societies develop the state takes on increasing responsibilities: organizing traffic, communication, education, trade, social care, and more. To a point, this is a positive trend, but the optimum level can be overstepped by placing the citizens under excessive restraint or by making excessive demands on the financial resources of individuals to support state efforts.

Every organic system develops its own dynamics. It grows, multiplies, and gains power. This is particularly true for organizations created by people. Behind them stand individuals who are goal oriented and seek to acquire power. This is advantageous for society up to a certain degree. But all biological systems are structured according to the optimality principle, and there is a threshold point at which benefits no longer have a positive effect. If an organization is developed for the sake of draining moors and marshland, such a group is initially beneficial for a region with a great many wet areas. But once activated, the organization invests in costly equipment and hires a staff that wishes to be busily engaged. It grows and will not cease its activity until the very last marsh has been drained, which would then be to the detriment of society. State-organized construction of highways is a highly valued contribution. But even here the optimum can be exceeded, and it becomes difficult to restrain the excessive paving of the landscape, for such an organization wishes to endure and expand.

If I entrust an organization to create hydroelectrical current, it will seriously engage in this activity and will not stop before the very last brook has been tapped. This is not done out of some malicious intent to destroy the environment but simply as a result of an independent dynamics that is not under control.

Education is beneficial, and it is generally assumed that the more schooling the better. But European universities are currently populated by older students (almost 30 years old) who attend school while still being dependents. Rather, students ought to enter university at the age of 17 and complete their studies by 23–25 years of age. But who would enforce a reform like this? The current trend in Europe is to advance the age of graduation. For example, in 1983, the average age in which West German students completed their Diploma examinations was 27.5 years. Their mean graduation age for a doctoral degree was 31.5 years—an untenable situation. Administration and welfare are beneficial, but here there is also a critical point at which (p. 714) developments become maladaptive.

The interests of the state, represented by its organizations (government, administration) and the interests of the citizens must coincide if the system is to have long-term viability. Conflicts of interest between individuals and groups cannot, of course, be avoided and may even serve as an important regulatory mechanism against stagnation. Rank striving on the part of the individual and the organization play substantial roles in this system. If a person is able to use an organization to increase his own power, he has more potential to control others. However, the other individuals experience this restriction of their freedoms as a negative pressure and at least inwardly reject such a process.

In a centrally governed society the competing groups must place the state interest, as an interest for the group, above the priorities of individual interests. In order to achieve this, specialized social techniques are employed by the government, including indoctrination. We recall that in the sagas of old, the hero is extolled who places a greater value on group interests (represented by the princes) than the individual interests of his clan. In Mao's China, children who denounced their parents as traitors were praised and distinguished by the state authorities. This is, of course, an extreme case. But contemporary group ethics are tending to move in this direction which is only adaptive up to a specific optimal level.

From a selective point of view, centrally organized systems function over the long term only when there is a division of labor between the governing and the governed and when the ruling individuals subordinate their interests to those of the governed.

A significant document verifying this position is a letter of Friedrich II, who wrote the following during his first campaign in March 1741 to his minister Heinrich Graf von Podeweils:

> Incidentally: I have twice escaped from the Austrian Husars. If it should be my misfortune to be captured alive, I expressly command you—and your head hangs in the balance—that during my absence you obey none of my orders, that you counsel my brother and that the state undertake no action for my liberation that is below its dignity. . . .

Thus the interest of the state has even, in this case, priority over individual interest, with the prince, who is, in this sense, a servant of the state. It is sufficiently well known that this situation is not always the case and that there are and have been exploitive and thus irresponsible governments; but it is also true that such governments have not been sustained over the long term.

The function of representing the group enhanced display of the rulers, which became, to a certain degree, organs of public display. This led, among other things, to a display of cultural pomp whose artistic manifestations are seen in political architecture (e.g., castles).

Human beings who are biologically adapted to living in small groups are united by the state into an ordered conglomerate of groups consisting of a great many persons. To this degree the state is an artificial (i.e., cultural) construction, as already discerned by Thomas Hobbes and John Locke (H. Catom, 1982).

Integrity is maintained also by culturally developed techniques, and there is a great deal of discussion about the question of whether these and political institutions in general should conform to human nature. Naturally, this problem does not exist for those who deny that there is a human nature in terms of predetermined dispositions, but instead attempt to develop their utopias for a better life without consideration of any of these factors.

History provides us with examples of such societal political experiments, of which Cambodia under the Khmer Rouge would be one of the most recent. After their victory in Spring 1975 they purged the capital city Phnom Penh of its population. The inhabitants had to leave the city within 3 days, and anyone found thereafter would be shot. Nothing was said about where one should turn during this evacuation. The sick, the elderly, and children died by the thousands. Civil and land records were burned, cemeteries were levelled, and most temples were closed. Monks were reeducated in camps, physicians were prohibited from practicing their profession, and silversmiths were executed. All the citizens received new names, and those disobeying this order faced 25 years of forced labor. The world witnessed this mass murder and considered it to be an internal problem of the Cambodians! After the occupation of Cambodia by Viet Nam the world further permitted the Khmer Rouge to be the official representatives of the country.

It is commonly agreed, with the exception of these extremes, that the state should not excessively curtail individual freedom and that the social techniques should rely on persuasion and reward and the feeling of a shared goal rather than force to form a community. In fact they can or must be implemented in order to form a large-scale society in the first place. Force and suppression, however, are often used at the initial stages of state formation. Tribes were often united in war by force. If the conquered ones were closely related to the victors, after a time they usually incorporated themselves into the ideology of the conquerors and prospered under the protection of this now more powerful union. The compelled unification of German tribes under Charlemagne is a good example of this process.

On the question of whether mass society should consider human nature, F. A. von Hayek (1983) states that innate human instincts were not created for the kind of society in which we currently live. Although this is true, it does not mean that we must all overcome all our small group adaptations. They can very well be implemented in the service of a modern society, and indeed must be. As we showed earlier (p. 169), the familial ethic is a precursor for a harmonious group life in a large group. We transfer it to those group members with whom we are unacquainted when we speak of them as our brothers.

If this disposition were not a prerequisite adaptation, the social techniques of the state could actually only be based upon force and suppression by means of a dominating state leadership. Thomas Hobbes took this viewpoint, but was not quite correct. Force is only one of the means used by political leadership, and politicians would be well advised to use force only in emergency situations and for a restricted period of time. We are undoubtedly predisposed to subordinate ourselves, and because of this we can accept dominance, but only temporarily. A leader–obedience relationship is only stable when it exists out of free choice. Rank orders and thus the readiness to obey commands are seen in the individualized small groups. If we look closely, we find that in mass society the same social dispositions are used that enable mankind to live in small bands: loyalty to family and group; the readiness to follow leadership personalities; sharing; identifying with group members; distinguishing one's own group from others; xenophobia; territorial demarcation; banding together; collective aggression when threatened. Modern states also make use of infantilization through fear to induce heightened obedience for bonding masses to a single leadership (p. 78). Group festivals, national holidays, and other events serve this function of unification.

What is new is that the citizens identify with their anonymous society rather than personalized groups by means of common symbols, customs, and language. The more homogeneous the ethnic group, the easier it is to attain this identification. Differences between the groups are emphasized.

Correspondingly, the leadership qualities effective in mass society are, in principle, identical to those in the small society. The chieftain is not only noble, powerful, respected, and, therefore, in this sense dominant. He is also one who can contract for peace, defuse tensions, and who is generous, charitable, etc. (see p. 312).

The state-supporting dispositions are opposed by disruptive tendencies, which must be counteracted by state leadership. Emile Durkheim (1964) states that a person can only identify with a restricted number of individuals. This does not seem true, since people evidently are able to identify with other members of their anonymous society, and frentically so, as the behavior at mass rallies show. But it is also true, that there exists the tendency toward divergent developments (see "cultural pseudospeciation" p. 15) which must be counteracted in order to maintain state functioning. We seem programmed to interpret similarity with genetic relatedness and are prepared to altruistically invest in relatives. Thus, where a physical similarity exists, in addition to shared language and custom, as is the case in most nation-states, it is not particularly difficult to foster a shared feeling of belonging and, accordingly, group loyalty, needed by the state. The less the shared commonness the more emphasis must be placed on a shared ideology and the more important, therefore, political techniques become, to foster unity. In multiethnic states, federalistic structures allow different ethnic groups self-government within certain bounds and in cooperation with the other groups sharing a superordinate interest on the basis of reciprocity. This can work as long as such a social contract implies that differential reproduction at the cost of the other is avoided, since ethnic groups are very sensitive to domination by others.

It seems as if there is an optimal size for a state and if this is exceeded the resulting necessary bureaucratic apparatus makes it too repressive, fostering dissatisfaction and perhaps its demise. Also, this trend would perhaps be countered with a federalistic structure (L. Kohr, 1983).

The acknowledgment of the state as the "union" of interest groups of the many must also be ensured. To do this the group must have a common value system in the form of a state-supporting ideology. In earlier times this existed in the form of recognizing a ruling family in conjunction with a state religion. One could be liberal in many areas of life, but not in terms of permitting religious divisity since this would have inevitably lead to the rupture of the state. This is the reason that the wars between the Protestants and the Catholics in the 16th and 17th Centuries were so violent. Once national states became the base of the supporting ideology, religious plurality could be tolerated.

The rejection of nationalism following World War II led in some European countries to an ideological vacuum. It was thought that the acknowledgment of democracy would suffice. But democracy is a procedural technique to select the government and is based upon very general ideological principles of freedom and equality, which with varying interpretations are used by all states today, even dictatorships, to acknowledge their existence. This is actually a positive minimal consensus. However: "Only to freedom we devote our life" was also sung in the Third Reich. Slogans, indeed, permit a very broad interpretation!

Nevertheless we have generally acknowledged as binding those values listed in the Charters of Human Rights used by most contemporary states, and these must be taken into consideration in constructing state ideologies. In place of the traditional nationalism of this century, which typically fostered excessive national identity and a lack of consideration ("My country, right or wrong"), a liberal patriotism must combine the profession to one's own culture and state, with both an appreciation and recognition of other cultures. This would also be helpful in encouraging worldwide humanitarianism. In practice this is best manifested from the secure basis of ethnic identity. Recognizing worldwide humanitarianism without reinforcement in the form of solidifying membership in a community would facilitate the desired harmony in interpersonal group life less strongly, since it could be easily displaced in favor of anarchy. Just as we first experience from our membership in the family the capability of fraternizing with other group members, we find from the secure membership in the community of a state or a peoples the readiness to perceive all others as brothers. The expansion of the familial ethic to one uniting all humanity is possible in stages and requires a stepwise identification.

H. Tajfel (1982) emphasized that individual and social identity (obtained through membership in one or more social groups) are essential components of human identity. People feel very uncomfortable if either is removed. They have an urge to establish a positive personal and social identity and to present this positively to others. In the introduction to his book on social identity, Tajfel discusses how he previously felt that this tendency was "environmentally induced" but after years of research has come to the realization that the need to establish both is a basic cognitive process.

It also must be pointed out that the concept of mankind is a cultural construct—an ideal based, so to speak, upon a mutation of mind—but certainly not a sociobiological reality. It is a goal set by us and is worthwhile to strive for, since it could indeed operate to unite mankind in a federation of cooperating states. But those who strive to achieve this grand goal must be aware that it can work on the basis of reciprocity only.

Certainly one of the greatest inventions of man is delayed reciprocity ("reciprocal altruism") among distant and non-kin. This is what provided the security network that allowed man to expand into and survive so well in many different environmental zones. For close kin, as sociobiologists have so often argued, it is no problem to explain delayed reciprocal altruism, as the payoff is genetic. For distant kin, this is less the case. With the extension of the familial behaviors of giving to form bonds to distant or non-kin, control mechanisms evolved—that is, people began to calculate economic gain. Relationships of reciprocity then were based not only on social needs to form bonds, but also on economic considerations to ensure that neither party lost out. This problem lies at the core of the struggle in economic anthropology between formalists and substantivists. The former argue that primitive economics can be explained by economic models alone and the substantivists state that social concerns have priority. Of course, both are correct to some extent. This is the real problem of kin-based societies, namely, that social and economic considerations are always intertwined which causes constant calculating and bickering. As Trivers stated in his paper on reciprocal altruism, hand in hand with reciprocal altruism did our capacities to calculate evolve. Thus, we do have the potential to extend family ethics to distant and non-kin, but only do so when reciprocity flourishes. In the absence of reciprocity, bonds dissolve.

The problem of state authority arises from the previously cited power dynamics of the organization, which is also characteristic of the administration apparatus of a government. The state apparatus can become an end in itself. If it overburdens the community, the apparatus will finally be annihilated. This process will not only dissolve the prevailing system, but the weakened society also runs the risk of becoming prey to more efficiently organized states. It is also imaginable that government structures arise that are so rigid that they would leave little or no room for individuality. This does not necessarily mean maladaption. Social insects certainly fare well this way. In this manner, evolution would just continue on the general trend by which higher forms of organization are achieved by subordination and integration of the system parts. However, such developments counter our individualistic values and may even narrow our potential for further evolution (p. 659).

Since the state is historically a very recent development, it is no wonder that man is still in the experimental stage regarding governmental forms. No one could provide a ready-made government recipe, but there are a number of guidelines available. Unless we remain receptive to new ideas and adaptations, we will face serious problems. But openness is a difficult quality to sustain, because in the face of uncertainty and lack of knowledge, we seek security in beliefs and ideologies.

The political sciences have recently attempted to gain an understanding of the phenomena described above by utilizing biological inquiry and methodology, and a summary of many significant contributions is found in H. Flohr and W. Tönnesmann (1983), including, in particular, those of S. M. Hines, S. A. Peterson, R. D. Masters and P. Meyer. Other studies include R. L. Carneiro (1970, 1978), H. Catom (1981, 1982), H. J. M. Claessens and P. Skalnik (1978), P. Clastres (1976), R. Cohen and E. R. Service (1978), P. Colinvaux (1980), P. A. Corning (1981a,b), L. Krader (1968), H. S. Lewis (1981), J. E. Pfeiffer (1977), and E. R. Service (1978).

> *Overpopulation and overorganization have created the modern metropolis, in which a truly human life with diverse, personal relationships has become nearly impossible. Therefore we must, if we wish to avoid the spiritual impoverishment of the individual and entire societies, leave the large cities and repopulate small communities or humanize the great cities by building the municipal equivalents of small rural communities within the networks of mechanical organizations, in which the individuals come together as total personalities and work together, not just as physical embodiments of specialized functions.*
>
> A. Huxley (1981, p. 363)

8.2.2.2. The Togetherness of the Many. Life in mass society is not only troubled by the relationship between the governing and the governed. In addition to the limitations imposed by administrative organs, we also are stressed by the close proximity of others whom we do not know.

The problems of interpersonal relations develop from, among other factors, the fact that fellow persons possess certain characteristics which stimulate approach as well as those which stimulate avoidance. This results in a distinct ambivalence in interpersonal relationships. We mentioned previously that personal acquaintance greatly inhibits the fear-inducing effect of certain characteristics of others, which is the reason we feel secure in our circle of close acquaintances. But in anonymous mass society we are primarily surrounded by strangers. The agonal system is activated, especially its flight components. Thus our behavior is directed more toward feelings of distrust, and other fellow humans thereby become stressors. In order to cope with this situation, city inhabitants have developed a number of strategies of contact avoidance, including avoiding visual contact with strangers (p. 173).

Contact avoidance is not only restricted to visual contact, however. In large cities people behave as if they were unconcerned about the welfare of others to the point where they avoid supporting those individuals in dire need (C. McCauley and J. Taylor, 1976). This is, in part, because responsibility for others is attenuated and each person believes that someone else will come to a person's aid. We also indicated that metropolis residents continuously strive to save face in public encounters and make every effort to avoid displaying some weakness, on the one hand, out of consideration of not burdening others with their private problems, but, on the other, out of fear that others may exploit their weaknesses.

Another strategy consists of discarding provocative characteristics. This is particularly true for the male, who transmits many dominance signals, as opposed to women who more frequently activate bonding behavior of contact initiation. Thus we observe, for example, the dull male uniform, a grey business suit, which disguises any challenging individuality as does shaving. The use of personal deodorants masks our individuality (p. 337). People are more likely to act ruthlessly toward those to whom they are not personally acquainted.

This is one of the reasons that criminality thrives in the anonymous society. People behave less responsibly toward strangers. T. S. Weisner (1979a) compared the behavior of city and rural children in Kenya. City children were less friendly and more dominant and aggressive toward their peers than country children. Similar findings are obtained from New Guinea (M. C. Madsen and D. F. Lancy, 1981). Thus, the increase in aggressivity in the city milieu is not only limited to our culture.

Yet let me also reiterate that life in anonymous society also has its pleasant aspects. In the small-scale community one lives in security, but only as long as he behaves according to the prevailing norms of society. He is under continual observation, and this unending scrutiny can be most disturbing for those who, because of certain unique qualities, occupy an outsider role in the small band. These people rarely have an opportunity to use their skills for the benefit of the community, and remain outsiders if these skills threaten traditional roles. The range of tolerance is generally narrower in traditional societies. The large city, on the other hand, offers such individuals the opportunity of remaining unique without constant pressure of norm conformity. In addition, the large number of people in a relatively small area offers the possibility to develop specific talents, since the larger the surrounding population the greater the chance of finding supportive and interested others.

This is what N. Luhmann (1982, p. 13) means when he states: "It is no doubt an erroneous judgment to characterize modern society as impersonal mass society." Only part of the relations is impersonal, since one can more readily find others with shared interests and can then cultivate and intensify such ties. However, many people in anonymous society have difficulties finding those with similar interests, leading them into the arms of sects and other organizations offering security.

During the last two decades there has been an increasing big city problem of radical youth minorities. The Federal Commission for Youth Questions in Bern investigated youth rioting in Zurich and came to the conclusion that alienation, unkindness, and lack of communication were the prime reasons for the unrest. Slogans such as "Nieder mit dem Packeis" which verbally translates as "Down with the pack-ice" and which means that the encrusting, chilling ice should melt and expressions like "We have nothing to lose but our fear" convey this quite clearly. We find that in the large city the social relationship network (father, mother, children) is simply too small to meet all the social needs of the growing individual.

The anonymity of interpersonal relationships and the lack of bonding in humans are no doubt the major social problems of our society. Unfortunately, they are not sufficiently appreciated, as we can glean from many governmental measures. For example, only recently in Germany, in the course of administrative reform, small community offices were closed in favor of a centralized administration. Although this indeed simplifies administration and makes it more cost-effective, the interpersonal relationships become even more anonymous. Many small village schools have been closed, and in many others there have been recent changes disturbing the class community structure. This has been praised by some ideologists, because they claim that every means of combating group alliances must be fought since group formation leads to discrimination between group members and strangers. They overlook the fact that differentiated social relationships conform to our needs, including the formation of subgroups within groups.

Alliances are also established in a variety of ways in kin-based tribal societies. Thus, among the Eipo of New Guinea, there are always a number of young men of different ages initiated together from an entire valley. They then form a lifelong initiation group. A feeling of group membership both bonds and obligates the individuals. They also have their family ties, clan attachments, bonds to a village community and to trading partners—in short, a complex network of relationships and therefore also perceived responsibilities, which solidify the individuals within the community. Each attachment has its individual importance; they all fulfill, in their various ways, the individual social needs, including the need for esteem, security, support, recreation, discussion, opinion exchange, counsel, and much more. One can readily belong to a number of different groups, cultivating various types of social relationships and thus developing social skills of utmost importance in anonymous society.

Of particular importance is the development of the basis of trust. This cannot be overemphasized. Many politicians are of the opinion that deceit is a socially acceptable political instrument. Eventually, man accepts this himself, and, as a matter of fact, we stop believing in anyone, only taking our closest friends and family members at their word. But how can one be a trustworthy partner in foreign policy if honesty is not accomplished even in domestic policy! In face of the danger of international conflicts, the need for a basis for trust must be recognized again and again. After all, a nuclear war would mean the end of civilization, if not of *all* humanity (R. P. Turco *et al.,* 1983).

A healthy basis of trust would also reduce fears that make many young people susceptible to extreme ideologies. In this connection, it must be mentioned that security is also provided by the attachment to a homeland *(Heimat)*. But today's mobility makes it difficult to form such bonds and people are often uprooted. Of additional importance is the ideological identification with a community (see also Tajfel, p. 291), and one's ethnicity.[2]

This kind of acknowledgment does not exclude religious and political plurality by any means, and it does not have to lead inevitably to an ethnocentrism, and thus rejection of all other groups. On the contrary, the more certain the individual feels in the preservation of his own cultural values, the more open and friendly he will be toward his neighbor. One then learns to esteem cultural diversity as a value, by contributing to this pool with one's own heritage. The negative forms of ethnocentrism develop when groups feel threatened in their ethnicity.

Biologists think in other time frames. They know that by diversity, in the animal world through species and subspecies and among humans by biological subspeciation and cultural diversification, life secures its continuity. We are often disturbed by the often hostile demarcation established by other groups. In order to counteract this, we need to teach each other to esteem cultural diversity. At the same time, every ethnic group should cultivate a consciousness of its own culture or the group will be condemned to disappear. This particularly pertains to the highly vulnerable traditional tribal cultures. This cultivation can best be accomplished in an atmosphere of neighborly coexistence with clearly defined territorial rights, as to avoid domination by others. Each group can then determine its own reproductive rate, environmental protection measures, economic policies, and similar concerns. The desire to help those in need, economic interests, and a lack of foresight by some western countries have led to a situation in which immigration has reached the limits of its assimilatory capabilities. Instead of the expected fraternization, there has instead developed demarcation and tension. Fear of excessive immigration of aliens emerges with all its negative consequences and with it, in my opinion, an ominous susceptibility toward the slogans of extreme political groupings. Immigration and cultural exchange have always existed and this does not necessarily disturb domestic peace—as long as it is done within bounds, it will contribute to mutual cultural exchanges. This is the way it should remain. Yet it is basically important that the various ethnic groups have not only the right but also the obligation to secure their own existence, for only when they survive can they make their positive contribution to the treasure of world cultures.

Arguments that world peace will only be achieved once all differences are leveled out and all borders dissolved, fail to consider that life strives toward diversity,

---

[2]We already stated that the daily rituals help bond people within the community. In a falsely understood rationalism, such rituals are considered to be superfluous, but such an approach leads only to uncertainty, pushing many into the hands of the sects. But unless someone in our immediate family circle is so affected we behave as if this was no concern of ours. Only a major tragedy like that of the supporters of Reverend Jim Jones in Guyana briefly demands our attention. But that was in 1978 and is now long forgotten.

and only highly repressive measures could slow down its pace. I, therefore, favor acknowledging the existence of diversity and enjoying it in mutual respect.

Summary 8.2

With the invention of agriculture and animal husbandry, mankind reinforced his ecological dominance, and the building of a larger population potential introduced developments that enabled the performance of the highest cultural achievements. However, it also threatened the degradation of the environment and resulted in the building of a dangerous power potential in mass societies.

The armed competition of groups led to the formation of organized states; those who, during conflicts, could organize more warriors were at an advantage. As state leadership developed, it organized defense, maintained integrity, and preserved internal peace. State organizations assumed ever more responsibilities, appropriating tasks that until then had normally been the domain of individuals or families.

This resulted, on the one hand, in some benefits but, on the other hand, made it possible to increase restraints on the individual and thereby restricted his freedoms. The problems of the relationship between the governing and the governed have not yet been solved by any means. Mankind has been in an experimental stage with governments since the beginning of history. Of particular significance is the question of how far individual freedom should be restricted for the sake of the community and to what extent social measures should take human nature into consideration. For every such decision it is important that the insight remain that between governing and governed there is a reciprocal dependency and that mistaken measures will eventually lead to corrective ones via group selection or internal revolution.

In practice, social techniques not only follow human nature but make use of dispositions to facilitate group life that evolved among hunter-gatherers during the first 95% of our evolution: the disposition to form closed groups, construct rank orders, maintain territories, the formation of group consciousness with the conscious deprecation of other groups, xenophobia, family ethics, and the many other behavioral mechanisms contributing to bonding. The familial ethic is expanded through indoctrination, placing it above its primary level and extending it to the group. A government could scarcely survive any extended period of time without the consent of its citizens. State ideologies do not necessarily imply the hostile deprecation of other groups, nor do they preclude cultural pluralism. Acknowledgment of one's own culture does not exclude understanding of those of others. Reason must have priority to conviction, since without this corrective there could be a trend toward ideological obduracy.

Organizations developed by people have their own dynamics, which among other factors are driven by the power struggles of their adherents. The optimal level of functional fulfillment in the service of the common welfare, as measured by group fitness, can thereby be overstepped. Just as there can be too much schooling or road construction, there can be too much administration and too much government. This leads to rank struggles between the citizenry, defending their freedoms, and the state bureaucracy, a conflict that endangers the welfare of both parties. It is therefore important to realize that certain structures have an optimal level of functioning beyond which they become detrimental.

Man is motivated by tendencies to bond as well as by fear of strangers. In the anonymous society, the latter prevail. The agonal tendencies tend to isolate strangers from each other and, since fear arouses infantile dependency responses potentially harmful to liberal democracy, all that increases these tendencies should be avoided. If measures are not undertaken then we risk alienation and collapse of democratic society. At the international level, the common use of deceit poses a real threat.

8.3. On the Ethology of Settlement and Residence

"To bad that concrete does not burn" is the banner headline of a story in *Die Zeit* (16 July 1982), a copy of which lies before me. Indeed, the monotonous gray concrete structures of the modern metropolis, whether in row houses or the "brutal style" of such new universities as Bielefeld or Bochum, have an oppressing effect.

Urbanization has increased tremendously in the last 200 years. In Germany the rural population declined between 1800 and 1925 from 75 to 22.8% (Fig. 8.2), and by 1982 it comprised 15.4% of the total population. Similar developments have occurred in other industrialized as well as developing countries. The urban population of the world doubled between 1950 and 1978. If this present trend continues, another doubling will occur by the year 2000, when most of the world's population will be living in cities and, therefore, in a cultural environs removed from nature. This creates problems for human adaptability, problems with which city planners will have to contend.

At present, the large cities offer many attractions indeed. But many citizens are dismayed at their distance from nature. Cities are marked by the prevalence of inanimate structures. Roads are covered with asphalt or concrete, and gray rows of houses with their uniform, starkly styled facades dominate the cityscape. Pedestrians are forced onto the narrow sidewalks due to the high traffic levels. Streets become mere connecting links but are no longer suited for stopping. The danger of this development has been recognized, and attempts are now being made to create pedestrian zones.

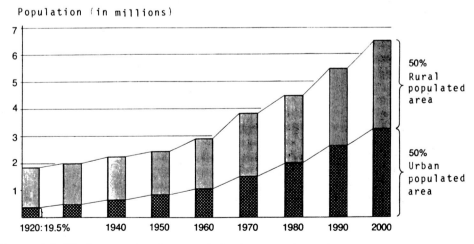

FIGURE 8.2. The increase in urban population in comparison with total population. From W. Engelhardt (1979).

Cities live on the influx of outside energy. Electricity and heat are generally produced by burning fossil fuels (oil and coal) and to some extent through hydro- and atomic energy. Fossil fuels seriously pollute the air (H. Schaefer and W. Flaschar, 1978; H. Schaefer, 1978a). Carbon dioxide and sulfur dioxide, as well as lead compounds, are among the substances of particular detriment to the city environment. In the air soot and smoke filter the sunlight, and cities are polluted by other sources as well. Major efforts have to be undertaken to eliminate refuse and cleanse municipal water, for the self-cleansing forces of the ecosystem are not powerful enough to do the job. The noise levels, particularly of traffic, are also disturbing. Additional irritants result from people living packed together who are unacquainted (p. 75).

If we want to make cities more inhabitable we will have to take into consideration certain social and ecological human needs, which arise from (among other factors) a motivational structure that is not just a product of our present environment but also of a long phylogenetic development and which permeates our personality.

Human environmental needs are quite diverse and have by no means been investigated in depth. But some conclusions about them can be reached by studying human behavior. The mad rush of cars out of the city on the weekend certainly demonstrates that we have a need to be out in "nature." It is evidence that man wishes to move about in fresh air and sunshine, in open land with trees, meadows, and waters. There is even a need to acquire such terrain for oneself and thus develop a territorial attachment. The strength of the city dweller's desire to own real estate in the country has been documented (Udo Hanstein, quoted by K. Buchwald, 1978). It was found that many visitors to the Taunus mountains in Germany would repeatedly return to a particular part of the forested region, as if in possession of that little area for the weekend.

> What does it signify when despite the mobility of the automobile and a rich array of attractive sites the Taunus visitor returns to the same place again and again? Insensitivity or plain habit are not the answers. Do those who perhaps have neither their own home nor garden see in this a certain possession of some plot of land? Have they sought out their campsite, pathway, view, their own bench and made some internal attachment to them? An entire landscape is too large, too unsurveyable, to become closely acquainted with in a short period of time. But one can attain an internal, and for a few dozen hours per year also external, possession of a small segment of this entire terrain. We should heed such questions. If the presumption is correct, then some bit of home will be sought in spite of or perhaps because of the great mobility today" (K. Buchwald, 1978).

Man certainly has a need to seal off a piece of surrounding nature as his territory and to set up a home within this territory. Surveys in Germany showed that 70–80% of the population would prefer to have as their residence a single family home with a garden.

Indeed, a period of high urban concentration is regularly followed by a phase of expansion into outlying areas which leads to the much criticized suburbanization surrounding the city and severe wear on the roads from all the traffic streaming into the metropolis (see also W. Moewes, 1978). The advantages of city life are then lost, and families become isolated without really gleaning the advantages of country living. When they live in a single family home with a garden, their territorial group is reduced to the nuclear family itself. And if a community cannot be built with the surrounding neighbors, only the territorial need will be satisfied and not the need for an individualized group of people.

630   The need for contact and sociability exists together with the need for exclusion

and demarcation, and it is ideal to be able to seek out both according to personal need. Every Bushman and Papuan can do just that. They simply leave their home and find themselves in the middle of their community; they can also withdraw into the hut when there is a need for privacy or quiet. But when the suburbanite steps out of the house, he or she is all alone; and when the urbanite comes outside he or she is in the midst of bustling strangers, hastening past with no time or opportunity to make contact. In both cases the need for privacy is fulfilled but not that for integration into a larger community, and this kind of integration cannot be created by the individual. There is a lack of meeting places in cities, and humane city planning should establish sites for this purpose. Planning must create the possibility for increasing social contact but only when desired. An ideology aimed at compelling social contact by making meeting an unavoidable act would lead to irritation, contact rejection, and conflict. Thus the need for privacy must be considered hand in hand with that for social contact.

These basic needs are met in the settlements of all the tribal peoples known to me. In the G/wi Bushmen of the Kalahari, the small round huts are arranged around a central square, and a similar arrangement is found in the Waika Indians of the upper Orinoco with their lean-to under which individual families hang their hammocks. Among the Eipo, the entire village community meets every morning for a social gathering at the men's and womens' squares before they begin their gardening work. The men also have their own house where those who have been initiated gather during the late afternoon when they feel the need to and where they greet male visitors. In areas where the climate and insects make outdoor activities difficult, there are often communal houses to meet the needs of sociability outside that of family life (Figs. 8.3–8.7).

The home in the simplest case consists of a windscreen, providing protection against the elements. It marks the place of residency and allows for privacy, a need that can be demonstrated universally. Even where several families build a communal house, each family has its own sleeping area and fireplace. It does not require great effort to provide in basic terms for privacy in a community and also to maintain protection from the elements and predators. The small round hut of the Bushmen fulfills this need as does the lean-to shelter of the Yanomami or the windscreen of the Agta. A wall made of thorny twigs and the fireplace protect against predatory animals. Safeguarding against hostile neighbors requires greater efforts. Wherever such enemies exist in larger numbers, the village is arranged so that there is an open visible field making unobserved approach difficult. Thus, typical New Guinea mountain settlements are on ridges that are difficult to attack. Our preference for a home with a view may be derived from this need for security.

Where the climate allows, most of the communal life takes place in front of the family homes. The Bushmen spend many hours of the day in front of their huts, which surround a central place. Here the people sit in groups, chatting, playing with their children or engaging in their diverse handicrafts. Communal life is basically an outdoor activity. This was, to a certain extent, true in our society, especially during summer time. Much of our communal life took place in the village or town square. Villagers also met in the church and the pub for indoor activities. Tribal societies provide similar meeting places, such as women's and men's houses.

Tribal societies are structured in a variety of ways and are composed of groups which are bound together by graded degrees of solidarity, the core units being the nuclear families. The kindred and the local residents comprise additional groupings, which we find universally. Cultural institutions also help to create networks of relationships, uniting people of various residential groups. Clan and ini-

FIGURE 8.3A. (a) A windscreen fulfills primary housing needs. It protects from the sun, rain, and wind and offers privacy. Agta family (Luzon/Philippines) beneath a windscreen. (b) Hut of the !Ko Bushmen (central Kalahari), where primary housing needs are also fulfilled in a straightforward manner. The round hut offers better climatic and predatory protection than the windscreen, but Bushmen do not live in their huts. They serve mainly as a place for sleeping and storage of personal belongings. Photo: I. Eibl-Eibesfeldt.

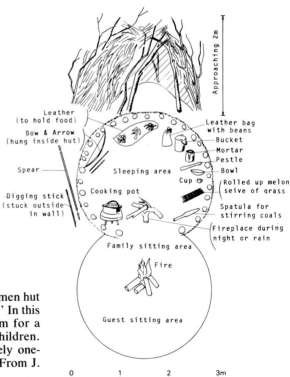

FIGURE 8.3B. The inside of a G/wi Bushmen hut with typical "furnishings." In this kind of hut there is room for a couple and their small children. !Ko huts are approximately one-third smaller than these. From J. Tanaka (1980).

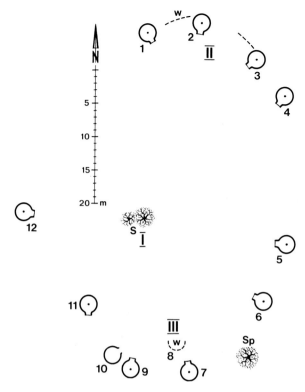

FIGURE 8.3C. A typical G/wi camp. Arabic numerals designate the huts and windscreens (w). Intact huts are marked with dots. Roman numerals depict preferred gathering places outside the huts. s = shade tree under which conversations and daily tasks take place. Young men also sleep here. Sp = play tree, where the children have attached their swing.

The inhibitants and their interrelationships:

1: Ko/aui♂ • Kuzare are the grandparents of Kwekenni and Khru (2). Koa/ui's son of an earlier wife (Ka) live in hut 7.

2: Khosara♂ • Kwekenni: Kwekenni's unmarried sister also lives here.

3: ≠ gon//gukwe♂ • Tshatshva. The old man is considered to be the "owner" of the area. In the same hut is the 15-year-old son of his brother (/rare). They are the parents of Khosara (2) and /gan/gai (6). ≠ gon/gukwe is also the father of Ditaku (4), ≠ oakwa (7), Gukve (9 and 10) and Khrokva (11). A daughter of /gan/gai (//ikwi), married to a man of another local group, often comes visiting with her small son (Daukvi) and her daughter (Hauhivi).

4: Ditaku♂ • Djoutshve; daughters Khaba (4 years) and Kerese (14 years); sons Tatye (9 years) and Semenoa (15 years); Semenoa is from another marriage of Ditaku.

5: Uninhabited.

6: ≠ auge♂ • /gan/gai; daughter: /runkve (10 years); son Aliese (16 years). Brother of /gan/gai in 2, half sisters (same father) are ≠ oakva ♀ (7 and 8) / gukve ♂ (9 and 10) and Khrokva ♀ (11 and 12).

7 and 8: Ka♂ • Oakva; daughter: /noa/noa (4 years); son: Garokha (about 15 years). Also ≠ Oakvas sister ≠ atsa and her granddaughter Batsharelvang (about 11 years); and 10://gukve♂ • Khaukva; daughter: Launa (3 years); sons: Uita (5 years), /eacha (8 years). //gukve is the stepbrother of Ditaku. His stepsiblings are Loakva and Khrokva; and 12: Dyinakve♂ • ≠ ei; daughters: Kvesse (5–6 years) and Weillgei♂ • (8 years); son Krea/khu (16 years). G ≠ ei is the daughter of Keamandu, who usually sleeps beneath the sleeping tree without a hut. Djinakve was divorced shortly before the survey. He moved away, and G ≠ ei formed a common household with the sister of //gukve (Khrokva) and their 2-year-old son Tutu.

633

FIGURE 8.4. The shed roofs of the Yanomami huts (upper Orinoco) have developed from wind screens and are often oriented about in an open communal square, securing the community from enemy surprise attacks. During wars, a palisade fence shields the small community against the outside. Photo: I. Eibl-Eibesfeldt.

a

b

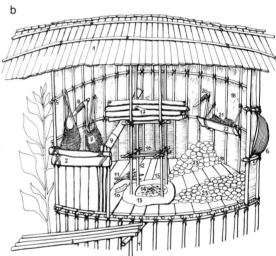

FIGURE 8.5. (a) The Eipo living unit is the family house. These houses have a round circumference with a diameter of 2.5 to 3m. The floor of the house is raised up about 1m from the ground. Even polygamous families live about the central fireplace, often with several domestic animals (pigs and dogs). A village consists of several such houses. There is also a sacred men's house reserved for initiated men and their guests, and a woman's house. Photo: I. Eibl-Eibesfeldt.

(b) Interior of an Eipo family home: *1*. Gable roof made of pandanus leaves; *2*. lower boards of the entrance opening; *3*. entry beams for pigs; *4*. exterior house posts; *5*. ring-shaped struts; *6*. bark container; *7*. net bags with tinder for making fire; the net bags also contain fern leaves for a head cushion and for the matting for small children; *8*. stone ax for men; *9*. bamboo container for drinking water; *10*. grinding stone whose upper surface is covered with crystals on which taro is ground; *11*. flooring made of tree bark; *12*. fire poker for turning food in the fire; *13*. clay around the fireplace; *14*. fireplace; *15*. four posts about the fireplace; *16*. diagonal pieces across the fireplace posts, used for warming feet and hands and as a support for drying objects such as tobacco; *17*. firewood laid over the fire to dry; *18*. planks of the wall of the house; *19*. lower bark covering for protection against drafts; *20*. stone ax for women (smaller and less carefully made than the one used by the men); *21*. old net bags; objects not needed in daily work are kept in these net bags, as are all kinds of things lying about, such as rock knives, pig ropes, jewelry (such as pig teeth necklaces), bird bone hip girdles, plaited sashes from orchid fibers, head decoration, armbands, etc.; *22*. holding board; *23*. stone wall to demarcate the pig quarters; *24*. tobacco planted right beside the house. From T. Michel (1983).

FIGURE 8.6. Most daily activities and social and artistic pastimes take place outdoors among those tribal peoples living in warm climates. Only in societies where weather does not allow for all activities to take place outside are additional demands placed on housing. (a) G/wi women in the melon ball dance; (b) G/wi in the field during the melon seed harvest; (c) two !Ko Bushman half sisters boring holes in ostrich eggshell beads; (d) !Ko Bushmen father and son playing music together with the musical bow. All photographs were taken in the central Kalahari. Photo: I. Eibl-Eibesfeldt.

FIGURE 8.7. The Kaluli of Mt. Bosavi (New Guinea) live in long houses containing some 100 persons. The community consists of nuclear families belonging to different clans. Men and women are separated by a 1.3 m high grass mat wall. There are communal gathering places for men and women as well, and everyone may meet on the veranda. (a) View of the entrance to a long house with the veranda; (b) the central hall with the two men's sleeping compartments on both sides; (c) long house plan; (d) spatial schematic representation of the long house; (e) longitudinal and cross-section view of the long house. Photos and sketches by George Loupis. Description is in G. Loupis (1983). Figure 8.7 (c–e) follow on pp. 636–638.

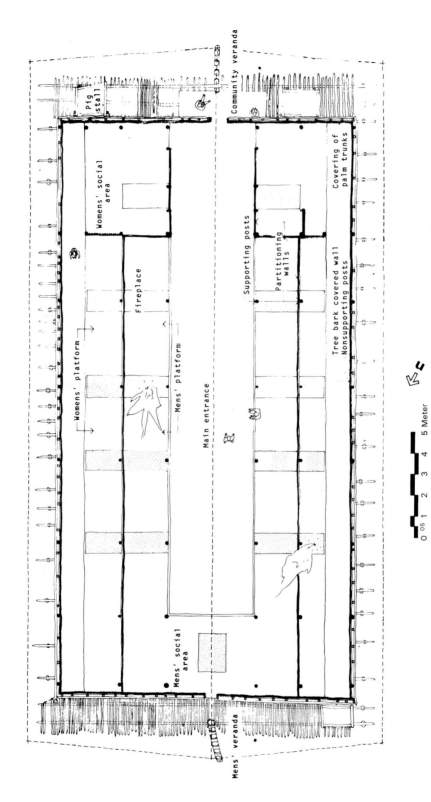

FIGURE 8.7. (c). See legend, p. 635.

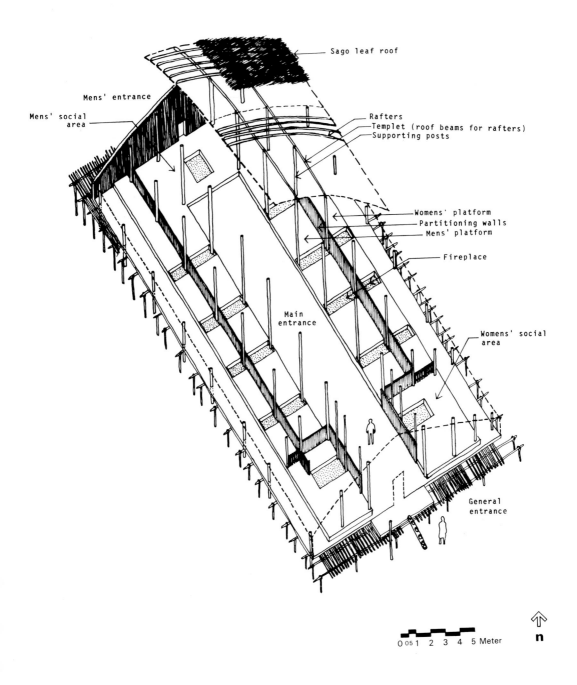

Sago leaf roof

Mens' entrance

Mens' social area

Rafters
Templet (roof beams for rafters)
Supporting posts

Womens' platform
Partitioning walls
Mens' platform

Fireplace

Main entrance

Womens' social area

General entrance

0 05 1 2 3 4 5 Meter

n

FIGURE 8.7. (d). See legend, p. 635.

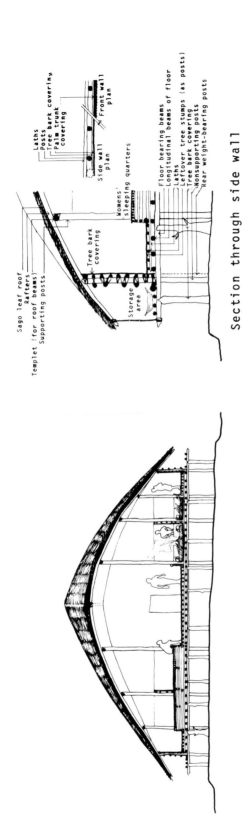

Sago leaf roof
Templet (for roof beams)
Rafters
Supporting posts

Tree bark covering

Storage area

Women's sleeping quarters

Laths
Posts
Tree bark covering
Palm trunk covering

Side wall plan

Front wall plan

Floor bearing beams
Longitudinal beams of floor
Laths
Leftover tree stumps (as posts)
Tree bark covering
Nonsupporting posts
Rear weight-bearing posts

Section through side wall

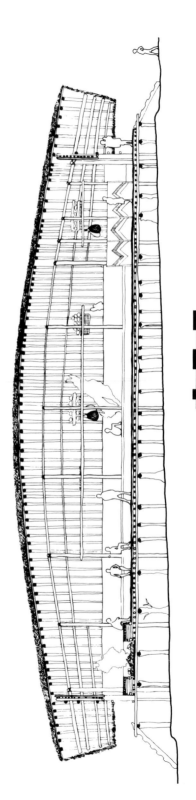

0 0.5 1   2   3   4   5 Meter

FIGURE 8.7. (e). See legend, p. 635.

tiation group membership are just two examples. Such a network of relations provides a system of social security. Clan members, for example, are often obliged to mutually help other members, even if they do not know each other. An Eipo who visits a distant village will find accommodation from a member of the same clan, since all clan members are treated as kin.

Some of this interpersonal network has been lost for the inhabitants of big cities in which the family is essentially restricted to the nuclear family. Here city planners should provide the individual with a means to eliminate some of the isolation created by large cities using appropriate planning techniques thus enabling urbanites to build and maintain a network of differentiated social relationships. This requires not only the previously cited infrastructures, such as locations where informal, noncompulsory encounters can take place, but also possibilities for a neighborly group life involving several generations.

The need for territorial possession can be fulfilled by residential ownership. Interior furnishings provide each home with its individual character. Furthermore, the modern home should also provide space for social gatherings. In earlier times, meetings outside the home took place during the more favorable seasons, but today meetings in urban environments must take place inside the home. Thus a "sitting" room is not only to be considered a luxury, for a home has become a means by which individuals represent themselves to others and present a positive image. This function is particularly significant for the psychological well-being for those in professions without creative outlets. Artists and scientists, who live in a self-contained world and who have other means of portraying themselves can more easily tolerate restricted living conditions than those people lacking such outward representations of self.

The facilities to meet hygenic needs, such as, bath, toilet, and kitchen, and the provision of a certain amount of space does not suffice to quench all human social needs. In some South American cities, it was believed that slum dwellers would be happier being resettled into high-rise apartments with all the necessary hygienic facilities. But these social projects were particularly hard hit by vandalism. The people directed their aggressions toward these public structures even though they were their own dwellings. Both anonymity and criminality rose with the increase in building height (R. Rainer, 1978).

This suggests that the social needs of the people had not been considered here. The poor of the tropic metropolitan areas often live on the edge of the city in apparently crowded conditions with poor hygienic facilities, but each family has its own house, constructed perhaps of cardboard, sheet iron, and boards, and each has neighbors who are usually friends and relatives. The children also have contact with others, playing perhaps in the dirt but with their friends and in the open air. Each tiny house has a little yard in which melons, vegetables, and flowers are grown in rusty cans and in which chickens are free to run about. This is a more stimulating environment for young and old than a cell in a high-rise structure, which may be hygienic but in which one lives in social isolation and where the sun rarely shines.

Slum redevelopment projects in modern Caracas are now undertaken with different measures. Water and electricity are installed and the dwellers are given time to build up and improve their small residences themselves. One can see how the little homes made of cardboard and sheet metal are gradually being replaced by simple brick and wooden structures (as the homeowners gain income), often

639

FIGURE 8.8. (a) Housing on the edge of Caracas. The poor live on the hillside in the background, (b) to (d) scenes from such settlements. The initially poor structures were improved by the motivated house owners. The dwellers here live in more socially hygienic surroundings than those in high rises, which were initially proposed as the means of improving the lot of the disadvantaged. Photo: I. Eibl-Eibesfeldt.

painted brightly as well (Fig. 8.8). Consideration for social factors is as important, if not more so, in home construction than hygienic factors.

City landscapes should be stimulating and should not overly restrict people's mobility. We humans bear the heritage of a great need for locomotor activity, which many of us cannot act out, particularly those who earn their living working in offices.

It is all the more important that the city surroundings invite people to take walks. Grey sides of houses with traffic rushing by right and left are not conducive to this. Light, air, and space for free movement are needed, as well as are parks with foliage and structured, "living" house facades offering the eye variety in color and form. Through these features a community can express its individuality, which, in turn, allows its citizens to identify with it. Post-World War II architects have largely failed to regard this consideration.

While social residential construction after World War I was based on a humanistic concept of architecture, reflected in architectonic expressions, apartments after World War II were barracklike and often called "human silos."

Uniformly anonymous space is multiplied, without spatial structure or stimulating identity. Between the structures is spacing green, with everything arranged as if the buildings were warehouses. One's own home can only be located by finding the right block and reading the address. Evidence of this faulty development are found from Rome via Vienna to the Polar Circle, with only minor variations. For example, in

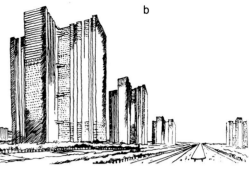

FIGURE 8.9. (a and b) Drawings of the ideal city after Le Corbusier and (c) the city Brasilia. From W. Boesiger and H. Girsberger (1967).

FIGURE 8.10. New city development in East Berlin. Economic systems alone do not explain the deterioration in architecture, for the same high-rise mass dwellings are built in east and west. The roots reside in artistic visions of the 1920s. Technocracy today reigns independent of political ideology. Photo: P. Weish.

Sweden the landscape is more beautiful, and in England they use prefabricated concrete. With the exception of the somewhat poorer construction occurring there, housing construction in the east bloc states is identical. If two such European suburban settlements were exchanged over night, no one would notice the difference in the morning. The desired European unity has been achieved, sadly, in its social residential construction'' (K. Freisitzer and H. Glück, 1979, p. 38).

The house fronts in old established cities are diversely structured and often artistically conceived. We have already shown that they often contain elements of human expression in stylized form. Some house fronts look like friendly faces and are "inviting;" others convey a sense of security in terms of the protection of their study walls, or they transmit a sense of wealth. And above all, they give play to the imagination. A city can be warm, inviting, and beautiful, meeting the needs of its inhabitants.

Artistic visions, technical rationality, and economic considerations without regard for human needs led to the uninhabitability of our cities. There arose those mighty apartment projects that distanced dwellers from nature and created social

FIGURE 8.11. This steel pipe structure, made for the children's playground in Linz, Austria, characterizes the lack of imagination of modern architecture. Photo: B. Lotsch.

a

b

FIGURE 8.12. In many cities, the automobile has forced people off the streets—children can no longer play there and adults can no longer congregate there. Thus, the city often becomes inhumane. (a) A street in Caracas. With the exception of the traffic, the street is void of life. Photo: I. Eibl-Eibesfeldt. (b) Today, traffic routes are still being planned in villages that destroy outdoor life and lead to the disappearance of front yards. The photograph shows the speedway for automobiles which heralded the destruction of the eastern nucleus of the village of Hedeper. Photo: Jürgen Kumlehn.

isolation (Figs. 8.9–8.11). The children were left to play out their curiosity and fantasies in thoughtlessly conceived playgrounds. The street belonged only to traffic (Fig. 8.12).

Today we realize that this kind of city planning was fallacious, and there are attempts to improve the situation with city renovation and new concepts of city architecture. Designs for high-rise buildings compete with those for sprawling street dwellings. I believe that both can stand alongside each other and that both are viable concepts of urban housing whose further development should continue. A number of examples are cited below.

Viennese architect Harry Glück asked himself what needs do people have as a result of their phylogenetic molding with regard to housing and how urban housing

FIGURE 8.13. The concept of the terraced, single family home as a possible solution to attractive mass housing. The lower stories are recommended for mothers with children, since children playing outdoors need visual and vocal contact with the mothers who are busy inside the house (Vienna, district along the Inzersdorfer Street). Photo: I. Eibl-Eibesfeldt.

could best fulfill them. In his survey, he found that most people prefer the single family house with a garden and swimming pool and a good view, an arrangement available only to the more affluent.

Our preferences have been primarily molded by the savanna habitat in which we evolved although culture-specific variations are often imposed on this. In particular, man has an innate love of plants. It is striking how our city apartments, removed from nature, are adorned in the most diverse ways with potted plants and foliage decors. Shoots and blossoms decorate curtains, ceilings, and many other everyday objects. Our "phytophilia" influences our aesthetic preferences (p. 614). Our desire to have an unobstructed view probably has its origins in our need for security from predators and hostile neighbors.

But we also love nature for other reasons. It stimulates us to be active and to move around freely. Fresh air and sunshine stimulate the circulation and activate the homeostatic systems of temperature regulation. As in all biological systems—motor, sensory, etc.—they have their functional appetites which call for exercise to hinder their degeneration. We quite accurately refer to joy of movement, sensation, and more. Thus we occasionally want to experience the fresh wind, and to exercise our bodies to the point of perspiration.

H. Glück summarized the relevant primary human needs for appropriate urban housing in tabular form, whose basis was expanded by workers in sociology, psychology, and ethology.[3] Glück suggested measures for the satisfaction of these needs and actually put them into effect in a number of major construction projects. As an alternative to the prevailing urban housing style, he developed the concept of the "terraced single family home" with small gardens on each terrace (mini-gardens) (Fig. 8.13). The Japanese, who live in extremely dense populations, have highly refined the construction of gardens. They create the illusion of a landscape with water, rocks, and trees within spaces of just a few square meters.

The need for casual social contact stimulated Glück in his Vienna-Alt Erlaa project to design large swimming pools on the roofs of housing developments, which have gained wide acceptance (K. Freisitzer and H. Glück, 1979). He also designed communal hobby rooms to give residents an opportunity to engage in

---

[3]Participants in the work group were I. Eibl-Eibesfeldt, K. Freisitzer, E. Gehmacher, H. Glück, and H. Haas.

communal activities. He found that hobby rooms in comparable developments lacking the swimming pool went unused. He attributed this to the fact that approaching other individuals is a process that must occur in stages without any coercion and that a large swimming pool is an ideal medium for attaining this kind of contact. In another comparable project, in which the pool was small and placed in a separate room, the pool did not entirely fulfill its function. The hobby rooms here were likewise unused. This suggests that spaciousness in proportioning the design of the public facilities that catalyze group integration is necessary to fulfill their objective. This is an example where frugality in construction would be inappropriate. The Viennese administration has proved to be socially responsible in this kind of planning and has made a decisive contribution to the general welfare and thus to the health of its people.

The 6000 persons now residing in this project have identified with their new home. Communal facilities are not vandalized, so their multiple use has proved cost effective. The community has its own newspaper and over a dozen clubs. Within the large community, neighbors within a single building have developed subgroups. In order to acquire the revenues for similar projects as part of municipal

FIGURE 8.14. The 1907 design of H. Tessenow for single-family row houses for workers, combining garden plot, city house, and low-rise high-density concepts with social considerations. The design offers the freedom to work in fresh air, a secure play area for children, and the possibility for social contact. From G. Wangerin and G. Weiss (1976). Translation of terms: Entwurf zu kleinen eingebauten Einfamilien-Wohnhäusern, floor plan for small built-in single family homes; Apfelbaum, apple tree; Gemüse-Garten, vegetable garden; Kellertreppe, basement stairway; Tisch, table; Bank, bench; Küche, kitchen; Spülstein, sink; Herd, stove; Kleider, clothing; Waschtisch, basin; Schlafzimmer, bedroom; Wohnstube, living room; Dachgeschosstreppppe, attic stairway; Flur, hall; Bett, bed; Erdgeschoss, ground floor; Dachgeschoss, attic floor.

644

redevelopment, one could conceivably offer the residents the possibility of eventually acquiring their apartments using long-term payments. This would satisfy the needs for ownership and security and foster the development of roots for family life.

Many city planners have, in the meantime, recognized that spatial related human behavior is strongly influenced by phylogenetic adaptations and one must consider these needs. W. Moewes writes: "Humans are quite probably subject to a number of genetically determined drives of space-related behavior which, if damage is to be avoided, must not be ignored over the long term" (W. Moewes, 1978, p. 181). We discussed the prevailing needs of hunters and gatherers for freedom of mobility, stimulation, physical activity, protection, identification and orientation, privacy, and territorial demarcation, as well as communication and the open community.

The terraced single family home is indeed a concept meeting many human needs. In mass housing it is probably impossible to meet everyone's needs equally by using a single construction design. Thus parents with small children have difficulty using the upper stories of this kind of housing. The child, who plays predominantly in front of the home, should have at least verbal contact with the family, and the family should be able to watch the small child's activities. This possibility is lost

FIGURE 8.15–8.18. Learning from established cultures: intimate inner city yards. The solution to providing free space despite high population density lies in yard construction. House and yard walls enclose a smaller area which is more intimate, private, and protected from the noise and dust than 600–1200 m² large yards in isolated individual homes covering five times the land area and chiefly fulfilling wing and buffer functions (keeping strangers "at a distance")—since only small parts of the yards are intensively used.

FIGURE 8.15. Isfahan, in Iran, is an ancient city composed of single-family atrium yard houses. Despite high population density they provide attractive, climatically adapted housing. Photo: B. Lötsch.

FIGURE 8.16. Yard of a minor official in Isfahan. Photo: B. Lötsch.

FIGURE 8.17. English city home with private yard in York. Photo: R. Stifter.

FIGURE 8.18. Old Viennese yard from the "Gründerzeit," the period of rapid industrial growth in Austria and Germany (1871–1873). Photo: B. Lotsch.

FIGURE 8.19. Yard in the Kolnitzgasse. Vienna (3rd district) 1980 (a) before and (b) after remodeling by the Institute for Environmental Sciences and Nature Preservation, Vienna (Lötsch, Stifter, Weiss and ÖNB Youth) on commission of the ORF for Jörg Mauthe's television play "Familie Merian." Yard revitalization in this pre-World War I district was accomplished with vigorous participation of the inhabitants. Elderly women who had long been unenthused by their dull environment now sunbathe on their "Riviera Square," and children have play space. Renters have become acquainted with each other through the ORF-initiated discussions and thus have formed the "neighborhoods." Since ponds and moist biotopes offer the greatest diversity of species and most varied experiences, they become great adventure spots for astonished children's eyes. The garden pool seen here became a popular attraction for children of the vicinity. Photo: B. Lötsch.

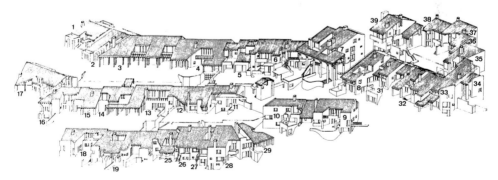

FIGURE 8.20. Seldvyla—example of densely populated single story construction and democratic planning for individualists. Architect Rolf Keller (known from his book "Building as Environmental Disturbance") set an example in Zumikon near Zurich. Housing density is much greater than in the villas of the surrounding area, and the planning process with some 40 families of upper middle class became a successful participation model and created a "village community." Drawing R. Keller from U. Schäufer (1979).

647

when the family lives in one of the upper stories. One could alleviate this problem by building play terraces on upper dwelling levels. Besides, in playground construction one should heed the fact that small children, again because of a need for contact with the reference figure—play primarily around the entrance to the building and the apartment (H. Zinn, 1981; R. Rainer, 1978).

Room for individual variation is also restricted in such dwellings because, although the walls can be adjusted individually, nothing can be added to the structure. Otto Frei considered this kind of possibility in his ecotree house. This consists of concrete plots arranged around a central support structure, on which individual houses can be built and gardens created. Although this is an interesting idea, it is economically unfeasible on a large-scale basis.

The movement of "ecological building" of the Institute for Environmental Sciences of the Austrian Academy of Sciences (B. Lötsch, P. Weish), working toward appropriate city planning, is attempting to depart entirely from high-rise structures. They emphasize the importance of enclosed courtyard-like garden areas which function as microclimatic cells and communication centers (B. Lötsch, 1981), and are attempting to develop a "backyard renovation" movement where closely set smaller structures are arranged in the urban setting around central inner yards. High-rise structures (up to a certain point) require as much space as a densely placed series of dwellings. This is actually a revival of an old tradition of municipal construction, which is found in our and other cultures (Figs. 8.14–8.20). Inner yards are ideal for small children. However, older children feel restricted by the four walls and they move out onto the streets. Currently, there is no single solution for meeting all human needs.

The days of the multistory apartment building may be past. We should accept the fact that there are several solutions for the problem of an appropriate residence, each with its advantages and disadvantages. It appears important to me that we remain open to experimentation for alternatives: whether they be inner-city renovation, densely set lower structures, or the terraced high-rise Glückian structure. This gives us a broad variety of alternatives that can liberate us from the barracklike monotony of the postwar architecture. The greatest obstacle to attractive city planning now, as before, is automobile traffic, which should be reduced within the city and wherever possible placed below street level; this is also true for garage location. Joint work projects by architects, politicians, and biologists will contribute to the development of appropriate urban housing.

For most of his history, man has lived "close to nature," spending a large part of his day hunting, gathering, and interacting socially outside of his "four" walls. His surroundings were stimulating, and their differentiation satisfied his inquisitive drive. Home was primarily a place for sleeping, protection from enemies and the elements, and privacy for the nuclear family and informal social gatherings. With urbanization, the house increasingly takes on other functions, and there develops a "housing culture" with all its problems and possibilities.

Summary 8.3

Human housing is a product of cultural development. There are no biological precursors for the home and, therefore, man has no set program for how to "build his nest." However, there are needs that must be fulfilled by the artificial organ known as the home. The primary living needs are the protection from climatic elements (heat, cold, rain, wind, sun), protection of personal property, and the privacy of an undisturbed resting place secure from an enemy attack. These primary needs are fulfilled by the Eipo house.

In harsh climatic zones, certain functions must take place indoors for at least part of the day or year, such as, the need for social life and for contact with the community at large, which in mild climates occurs in front of the houses. The possibility of receiving guests in one's home and space for hobbies and handicrafts must also be provided. Communal houses are often used among tribal people for these functions. They are also often display instruments of the community, towering above the other huts, frequently magnificently adorned. The small settlements of rural preindustrial societies remain embedded in nature. The needs for proximity to nature, plant growth, sun, climatic stimulation, and water are fulfilled in the immediate surroundings of the house. With the development of the large city, these needs must be considered. Our love of plants (phytophilia) results in city dwellers keeping plants in their homes as ersatz nature, and attaching plant decor to their furnishings.

In ignorance of the ethological needs of the human being, modern mass housing architecture at first fulfilled only the primary living needs (climatic protection, privacy) and the necessary municipal sanitary conditions. It overlooked the fact that psychic hygiene is just as essential for well-being. People were socially isolated, removed from nature, and were deprived of the opportunity to form a community, identify with it, and to acquire a plot of territory. A decisive step toward the humanization of urban housing has been taken with the concept of the single family units in the form of terraced high-rise structures with planned "communal" zones, such as large swimming pools on the roofs which allow for exercise and noncompulsory contact. New concepts of high-density single story structures and backyard renovation are also making important contributions. Cooperation between city planners, architects, politicians, sociologists, and biologists is adding to this effort.

8.4. Social Order and Human Behavior

"Free as a bird" we say, envying the winged creatures for their ability to move in all three dimensions with unrestricted mobility. But unfortunately we forget the dodo bird. Each bird that has learned to create a good living on the ground without being compelled to use its wings will soon cease flying and will remain on the ground forever. This also happens in mankind. When the bread appears three times daily in ample supply, many become quite satisfied to live from bread alone or at least from bread and circus games.

A. Huxley (1981, p. 366)

8.4.1. Objectives of a Survival Ethic

Today, man is in a critical phase of its development. Exhaustion of resources and the population explosion threatens to spark conflicts whose consequences are yet unforeseeable. Minority groups are in danger of annihilation through either peaceful assimilation into other groups or forceful suppression and ultimate extinction. The elimination of cultures by "development" and standardizing influence of the mass media threatens cultural diversity. Mass society has, along with its positive benefits, brought problems with which we must contend. Survival of and quality of life for our descendants must be the unifying goal behind man's efforts. *This must be the first objective of a survival ethic.*

649

Our knowledge of the evolutionary process provides us with perspectives to plan for the future; it also provides us with new responsibilities. One of the most important lessons of evolution is the danger of increasing specialization. We know that the organisms of the Cambrian have only a few descendants still surviving today and that a still smaller percentage of those have further developed in new evolutionary lines. Specialists have tended to become even more specialized, with what I call evolutive potential decreasing. Organisms undoubtedly fall prey to adapting with ever increasing specialization to individual niches from which they can no longer escape. If the environment changes and the niche is lost, they are no longer capable of adapting anew. For example, snakes will scarcely be able to readapt themselves to an herbivorous diet, for their specialization has proceeded too far. For similar reasons, whales can no longer evolve into steppe inhabitants. Development always proceeds from relatively unspecialized forms with potentially many different alternatives. The five-fingered fore extremity of the first land tetrapods developed into the horse's hoof, the paw of the predatory cat, and the wing of the bat.

Further developmental possibilities of these now specialized forelegs are limited, however. The human hand, in contrast, is a universal instrument with a high evolutionary potential. Under the guidance of our brain, these hands can manufacture a great variety of tools to be used as artificial organs.

Universality raises the chances of long-term existence in the stream of life. Thus, it is not the best present adaptation but versatility that is a key to the future. The crustacean Sacculina is perfectly adapted, but during the course of adapting to become a perfect parasite, it lost its universality. Originating from a differentiated crustacean with sensory organs and organs for locomotion, it became a rootlike organism mainly consisting of gonads which was capable of growing in its host's body. The parasite is perfectly adapted to this condition, but should the host species die out, his fate would be the same.

Totalitarian states as those depicted in the utopias of A. Huxley and G. Orwell could also prove to be perfectly adapted. As we shall point out, however, there is a reason for assuming that these kinds of societal forms lead to a reduction in evolutionary potential.

A survival ethic will develop the norms for the previously cited goals, distinguishing between short- and long-term objectives. One long-term objective could be the improvement of our biological construction in the sense of a "higher development" of the unique human characteristics such as rationality, morality, conceptual ability, creative talents, and others, which is, of course, a highly problematic and controversial area of discussion.

While there is no simple consensus on the question of whether and how—if at all—an improvement of our species would be worth seeking, the survival of humanity in descendants would certainly be recognized as a desirable goal. Thus behavior would be considered appropriate when it ensures this kind of survival. In this general conception, such a statement seems trivial. But a survey of the events of the last 50 years shows that humanity and its leadership is by no means always conscious of this straightforward concept. But even if we were all sensitive to this issue, strategies involved in teaching this goal are so complex that suggestions for appropriate behavior are not as easily formulated as one might at first believe. There is no doubt, for example, that we must achieve world peace. But as stated earlier, it does not suffice simply to pose in a peaceful manner.

8.4.2. Maintaining the Ecological Balance: Qualitative Instead of Quantitative Growth

Most people today are aware of the fact that there must be a biological equilibrium between humans and the surrounding nature. But some individuals trust the self-regulating forces operating in nature while others place their hopes on reason and insightful planning. Where is the core of the problem?

The British national economist Thomas Robert Malthus showed in 1798 that uncontrolled population growth generally leads to a situation in which the population exceeds the carrying capacity, with the consequence that there is no longer a sufficient food base to nourish the people in that area. This population theory was formulated even earlier by Giovanni Botero (1559), and criticized as being too simplistic. There are doubtless other variables influencing population growth, but essentially this population theory has been basically confirmed over time. Human growth occurs exponentially and will eventually exhaust natural resources if left unchecked.

Taking the area of Germany in the borders of 1937 as a reference, we find that in 1300 the area contained some 12 million inhabitants; by 1700 the figure rose to 15 million. Thereafter, there occurred a rapid increase (calculations from K. Buchwald, 1978):

Year	Inhabitants
1800	23 million
1825	28 million
1850	35 million
1875	43 million
1900	56 million
1914	67 million

Population density changed as follows:

Year	Density
1780	38 inhabitants/km^2
1914	125 inhabitants/km^2
1973	255 inhabitants/km^2

This population explosion does not only apply to the large industrialized nations of Europe, for exponential population growth is occurring on a global scale. By the year 2000 the earth will be supporting six to seven billion persons. Population growth occurs at different rates in different geographic regions, and by the year 2000 the developing countries will contain 76.5% of the total world population (W. Engelhardt, 1978; Fig. 8.21).

No slowing of this trend is yet visible. On the contrary, in 1982 the number of people worldwide increased by 82 million to 4.7 billion, the greatest population growth ever in a single year, with India the leading country (15.5 million), followed by China (15 million), Indonesia (3.3 million), Brazil (3 million), Bangladesh (2.9 million), the Soviet Union (2.3 million), and the United States (2.1 million). Population decreased in only a few countries, including both West and East Germany. But Germany still ranks as the twelfth most populated country in the world.

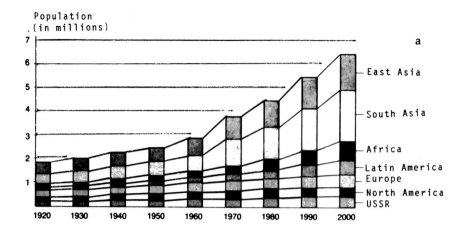

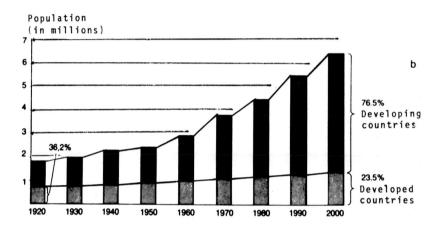

FIGURE 8.21. (a) Differential population growth in various major parts of the world, (b) differential population growth in developing and developed countries. From W. Engelhardt (1978).

The causes for this phenomenon were the vast improvements in hygiene, medicine, and the industrial revolution (using fossil fuels). At the same time, the laws restricting marriage were attenuated and spacing of births as a population control measure decreased. If some 250 million inhabited the earth during the time of Christ, it took about 1600 years (to 1650) to double that figure, while only another 200 years (to 1850) were needed for another doubling, 100 for the third doubling (1950), and a mere 26 years (to 1976) for another doubling, to a figure exceeding four billion! The annual population growth rate, which for many millennia had been 0.2%, was 2% in 1970, which in absolute figures is 70 million persons per year. During the last 10 years this figure has declined somewhat, but in 1975 the world population was still increasing at a rate of 64 million/year. The maximum capacity of the earth has probably been exceeded already by far, for according to the intermediate report of the environmental office of the United Nations (1976), 450 million persons were suffering from hunger, and additional hundreds of millions were living in poverty.

652   Resources of oil and raw materials may scarcely suffice to provide all of these

people the standard of living enjoyed by many in western cultures. Added to this is the problem of population—the destruction of the ozone layer increasing CO_2 levels and air acidification through sulfur dioxide (acid rain)—which are now reaching dangerous proportions even though in Third World countries not everyone drives a car (Fig. 8.22). The gap between the poor and rich nations has doubled since 1960. The annual mean income in 1979 (R. L. Sivard, 1980) in the industrialized countries was equivalent to $5690 and in the developing countries was $530.

Overpopulation is reflected in the increasing insufficiency of food supply. A large part of the population of Africa, India, Pakistan, and other Third World countries suffer from a chronic protein deficiency. Instead of the daily requirement of 75 gm of protein, the average consumption in these countries is 40–60 gm,

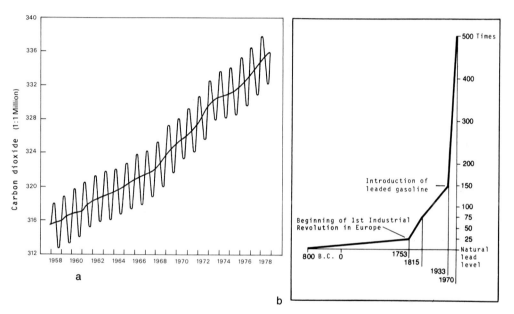

FIGURE 8.22. The exploding human population which relies on fossils fuels, has resulted in environmental disturbances that seriously endanger mankind's future. A great deal has already been documented on the pollution of rivers, lakes, and seas. Pesticides have even been found in the penguins of the Antarctic. The steady increase in carbon dioxide is portrayed here in graph (a). These measurements were made in Mauna Loa, Hawaii, a location far removed from industry. The measurements are so sensitive that they even reflect fluctuations in summer and winter levels in the northern hemisphere. More carbon dioxide is removed from the air in the summer due to photosynthesis. Similar measurements have been made in Antarctica and they are of similar levels. We cannot tell what the consequences of these changes will be, but a climatic catastrophe is possible. The readings clearly show that our "sea of air" is actually only a thin envelope around the planet that cannot be repeatedly disturbed. Deforestation has resulted in higher sulfur dioxide levels that now command a great deal of attention. Yet there have been no measures to significantly restrain harmful factory exhausts or those of the automobile. The increase in atmospheric lead has been measured over the centuries in Greenland ice, and these figures are an alarming document of the poisoning of our environment. (a) from R. Revelle (1982) based on measurements from C. D. Keeling; (b) from K. Buchwald (1980) after M. Murozumi, I. Chow, and C. Patterson (1969).

653

which is particularly injurious to children. According to the UNO report the need for basic foods increases annually at 3.6% due to population growth. The actual production increase between 1966 and 1976, however, was only 2.6%. While world reserves of grain in 1961 sufficed for 105 days, in 1976 the supply dropped to a 30-day level.

World grain production in 1974/75 was 45 million tons below the required minimum level. In addition, for every calorie harvested there are hidden multiple calories in the form of manure and fossil fuels, resources that can no longer be considered as inexhaustible. Thus there are definite limits on the amount of additional production that is possible, and there is even reason to fear that current production levels cannot be sustained. There are already signs of land exhaustion; grain production in many traditionally agricultural parts of the world has shown a yearly decrease during the recent past (L. R. Brown, 1981). If no substitute can be found for the fossil energy sources, a worldwide crisis is imminent.

To some extent, there is still arable land that can be put into production, but the yearly increases of previously cultivated land being turned into desert are quite significant. During the past 50 years, the Sahara desert has increased in size by approximately 250 million acres. Along its 5000 km circumference, it grows southward on average of 10 km each year. The other deserts of the earth are increasing by some 12–17 million acres annually. Attempts to cultivate the South American rain forests on a large scale have not yet succeeded according to the desired plans, since the laterite ground is quickly exhausted, and newly cultivated land is subject to washout and rapid erosion. W. Engelhardt (1978) has summarized these developments, and they do not give us much cause for hope.

Man is already tapping the entire biosphere. He seizes plant, animal, and mineral raw materials from all parts of the world, exploiting in particular coal and oil (fossil fuels) for burning, and these actions have caused global changes in the environment. The increasing carbon dioxide levels in the air and industrially created heat have led to a global warming of the earth (G. M. Woodwell, 1978). The greenhouse effect can become dangerous. There is a possibility of melting the polar ice caps, which would result in flooding of lower lands and coastal cities. There is also the danger of increasing the growth rate of deserts.

However, a much more difficult problem is that mankind is experiencing a rapidly growing population which is dependent on the use of nonregenerating, limited energy sources. The collapse of this population bubble is predestined. Oil and coal supplies are limited. Even at today's limited use levels of about 3 billion tons/year (1973: 2.8 billion), the end of the supply is thought to be in sight, even though we may, with H. Gruhl (1975), estimate that there exists a reserve of 500 billion tons, or, optimistically, three- or fourfold as much.[4] A similar situation exists with other raw materials.

The future of mankind under additional population growth has been described by D. L. Meadows *et al.* (1972) at the suggestion of the Club of Rome. Criticism has been leveled at some of the points made in this description, such as, on the weight put on negative factors. An assumption was made that exploitation and

---

[4]Our generation may find comfort in the thought that oil will be exhausted "only" in 80 or 100 years, aluminum in 260 years, and chromium in 360 years, but these are alarming for biologist, who think in an entirely different time frame and who know from the fossil record that most species that once lived on earth have died out, making survival the less common occurrence.

disturbance of the earth progress exponentially, and some critics claimed that this may be "only" proceeding linearly. But even the more positive estimates of C. Freeman and M. Jahoda (1973) come to the similar conclusion that this process cannot continue unabated. Many other criticisms were raised, but they did not deal with the central issues (W. Wülker, 1976a, b). The studies of H. Gruhl (1975), K. Steinbuch (1973), and F. Vester (1972) are also illuminating as are some of the early warnings (R. Carson, 1962; R. Demoll, 1954, F. Osborn, 1948, and B. and M. Grzimek, 1959). In the light of these publications, the assurances of H. Kahn (1977) are not fully convincing. Suggestions for improving the current condition are found in the book *Das Ende der Verschwendung ("The End of Wastefulness")* by D. Gabor *et al.* (1976), and further suggestions for statesmen are found in J. Tinbergen's (1977) *Wir haben nur eine Zukunft ("We Have Only One Future")*.

We are already witnessing worldwide impoverishment and population crises, despite intensive utilization of fertilizers and in spite of labor-saving energy-intensive agriculture, which are using many calories of fossil fuels to achieve a calorie of grain. This does not bode well for the long term but may help us get through this particularly critical period. Thus there is a basis for optimism, but this should be a critical one and not the naive viewpoint that the solution to all problems lies in quantitative growth.

We must conquer pessimism, the "mental disease of our times" (K. Lorenz, 1983), since it is paralyzing. The common lamenting of today, coupled with reciprocal charges of guilt, is no solution. The nucleus of the problem is in the previously cited competition between groups, which ultimately led to the formation of nations and superpowers, each one putting the other in a series of forced moves (p. 618). In the struggle for international rank position and thus survival, each group seeks to multiply its power base, to increase its industrial productivity and to a certain extent its human potential. This maximizing strategy has proved effective. But according to the optimality principle, we have reached the point at which a pure quantitative growth is detrimental to the common good. This point has been reached in countries like India which does not gain in strength by adding millions of new citizens each year; rather, it becomes weaker by virtue of this growth. Countries such as China have recognized this fact and have instituted state population policies, which, although severe, avoids further, personal and state-endangering suffering.

Similarly, industrial growth, due to power bloc competition, leads to damaging, environmentally disturbing overexploitation that affects the country's own viability, a process whereby important raw materials are being squandered. The existence of competing power blocs has put mankind in a vicious circle economically. Sociologists, economists, and politicians in the past 100 years have unconditionally accepted an unrestrained growth ideology, which today takes increasingly harsher forms. On occasion, we even speak of economic wars.

Competition will not be extinguished, nor should it be, for it is the driving force of evolution. But the question is whether maximizing quantitatively (steel production in tons, increasing the human biomass) is still a desirable objective and a standard of achievement. Qualitative growth could be an alternate goal. Economic policy oriented toward the wish fulfillment of target groups (H. Hass, 1983), competing in service and quality, would be an alternative. Thus the maximizing of achievement by means of quantitative production in the sense of naive growth ideology could be countered by the concept of qualitative growth.

There exists the closely related question of the extent to which economic growth

655

should be controlled by the self-regulating processes of the market as opposed to government planning. I wish to offer a number of remarks on these two questions —quantitative vs. qualitative growth and self-regulation vs. central administration.

In a closed system, growth implies that its achievement is at the cost of others. This fuels competition which is in a sense a positive evolutionary factor. However, over the long term, this creates problems for man because the dynamics of this kind of economic struggle leads to excessive use of nonreplacable resources. Cultural evolution uses the same maximizing strategies that were apparently successful in biological evolution over the course of millions of years. Thus one might have no objection to this principle. I am of another opinion and wish to show the reasons for this.

Admittedly, organisms, as a rule, do not control their propagation by limiting their reproduction. They are opportunistic and utilize the available food supply to maximize their biomass. During favorable years the lemming and field mouse populations increase so much that neither predators nor diseases can restrain their numbers. This eventually leads to exhaustion of the feeding grounds, increasing irritability of individual animals, and, finally, to a mass migration and a collapse of the population induced by density stress. Consequently, the numbers of individuals is reduced drastically, the meadows recover, and the cycle can begin anew. This process is not always this extreme, since disease, predation, and, in some cases, perhaps also autoregulating mechanisms inhibit excessive population growth. Self-regulation does not occur until there is an overpopulation situation and then animals without territories cannot reproduce or become sterile under the influence of population density stress. They are primarily subject to pressure with migration becoming the first alternative.

Organisms are apparently constructed in such a way that they maximize their reproductive success. And this maximizing strategy has been effective. The fact that populations from time to time experience extreme stress when they are too great does not stop the stream of life, for in times of such a "boom" the stream has, so to speak, overflooded its bank; new rivulets are found that provide additional pathways and niches so that some can survive in the wake of mass collapse of the population. This strategy is at the expense of many individuals, but Nature does not care. Even species are only temporary manifestations in the long stream of life, and many of them die out as dead ends of evolution. Of the species alive in the Cambrian, only a very few have survived in the form of modern day descendants.

Proponents of the free market, such as F. A. von Hayek (1979), trust in these self-regulating forces. Using Nature as a model, they encourage a free interplay of forces, meaning that each activity seeks to be maximized through high production numbers and entering new markets. This results in a wealth of ideas and a readiness to undertake risks, since many firms compete for the same markets with similar products, seeking to gain new markets and thus to exceed their competitors' sales.

As H. Hass (1970) has described, these adaptation fronts are basically the same as those confronting organisms. In both cases, a positive energy balance must be achieved, with certain costs associated with growth, maintenance, reserves formation, repair and protection against disturbing influences, defense, protecting and finding new markets, and, finally, the act of acquiring energy—a process by which not only the costs must be covered but a positive economic balance must be achieved which allows for propagation and new adaptations. The determining

656

factors of the acquisition acts are precision and speed. Thus, with so many similarities it is no wonder that free market economic strategies are comparable to those of biological evolution in so many respects and thus phenocopy them to a certain extent. In both cases, survival success is the measurement of fitness, and the selection is a strict one.

Until recently this strategy has been sustained in the economic realm, and if we count the innovations as measured by new patents, then we could conclude that a free market economic system is certainly superior to centrally planned economies that have existed so far in terms of its evolutionistic dynamics. However, a maximizing strategy is always based upon the inconsiderate exploitation of resources. This appears to be advantageous for the short-term competition with others in which the immediate success is the yardstick for determining a standard.

This strategy, however, is loaded with great risks. A "boom" is followed by crises that eliminate many firms and cause people hardship. On the level of biological evolution, the individual is does not count. It is only in humans that evolution became conscious of itself, as Teilhard de Chardin has expressed it, and the individual does count. Thus it is understandable and also correct that we should plan accordingly to avoid crisis and suffering. For man, as a species of reason, rational planning is certainly in order. Even in the free market economy, events are influenced by planned guidance. There are for example antitrust laws, which inhibit groups from becoming monopolies. Furthermore, there are measures to reduce the amplitude of crises through actions to steer cycles.

In the centralized economies, administration has even become a predominant element. Such societies appear to have superior control over unemployment, but centrally planned economies do not fare well in competition with free market economies. Since the individual can improve his economic lot only slightly through his own achievements, there is a lack of individual initiative and thus also of innovation. The system takes few risks. Security is its main maxim and therefore it remains conservative. This reduces creativity. One could say analogously with biological evolution that planned economies are adverse to mutation. They do not fare well in competition with other economic systems.

Planned economies are concerned with social equality and the attenuation of social risk but not with resource-oriented, environmentally conscious economic planning. As collectives, these economic blocs seek to maximize their achievement, measured by net social productivity. And their politicians are likewise also oriented toward growth. Unfortunately, this has happened out of necessity from the competitive position of the people and their economic blocs. Growth and thus increasing power can be used to outdo others. Therefore, one accepts the exhaustion of reserves as part of the process.

How can we promote qualitative growth in this particular economic climate? We have already understood this problem to be one of exploitation of commonly owned resources (p. 713) of the world. On a global basis, air is a common possession. Those who use it with restraint by outfitting productive facilities with costly pollution control devices contribute to the quality of life, although this is of no immediate competitive advantage. And those who do not use such devices can produce at a lower cost and attain a competitive advantage. Thus some international standards need to be established. If guidelines are not attainable in the foreseeable future, each economic bloc should attempt to develop such measures for themselves, even if it means partial economic seclusion. This calls for a certain economic self-sufficiency, which is desirable for the sake of basic security.

However, economic self-sufficiency does not have to be extended to the point where international trade, which creates reciprocal ties, is severly limited. Once again I wish to recall the optimality principle. There is an optimum of involvement and mutual dependency.

We are still quite far from this kind of rational approach to the future, and this can be illustrated with numerous examples, such as, the oil crisis: Only when the oil-producing countries raised the price of oil, did politicians finally become aware of the fact that this is an energy source available only in limited quantities.

The figures cited by the experts prior to the oil crisis about energy use and economic growth through the year 2000 seem extremely naive when reviewed today.[5] However this kind of expertise is used as the basis for population politics and economic planning. Anyone following the fluctuating economic cycles since the end of World War II can see that the growth rates from cycle to cycle become smaller, yet politicians rave about growth and, accordingly, spend more public money than is earned.

It is often the interests of particular lobbies that block reasonable measures. Although the Federal Republic of Germany has 14,000 traffic fatalities annually and a huge number of injuries, no reasonable speed limit law can be instituted. And although ten times as many people, namely 140,000, die each year from smoking, images of masculinity, athletic prowess, and independence are attached to its use. School authorities set up smoking rooms in the schools under a falsely understood liberalism. Thus far, no one has taken legal steps against the school authorities for allowing the seduction of minors by this drug.[6]

In the face of the deplorable number of deaths caused from smoking (140,000 annually), G. P. Ehestorf (1979) writes:

> In order to comprehend the figures they must be compared with others. During the worst years of the French Revolution, 100,000 persons died a violent death. These one hundred thousand victims, after nearly two centuries, still overshadow the aspirations for freedom, equality, fraternity, and similar efforts. But we scarcely take notice of 140,000 smoking deaths. This figure is equivalent to the population of the entire city of Wolfsburg, Bremerhaven or Darmstadt.

---

[5] A graph in the magazine "der Spiegel" (10/1983: 86) portrays the various need prognoses in coal units (= heat content in 1 kg coal). The estimates of the needs for 1985 made in 1973 amounted to 610 million coal unit tons. In 1974 a new estimation of only 510 million tons was made, and this was successively dropped in 1977 and 1981 to 480 million tons and 430 million tons, respectively. Actual use at that time was decreasing and was at 350 million tons. We can only shudder when we consider the fact that long-term planning for power stations and other economic measures is based on such expertise.

[6] In 1981, the 17 million smokers in the Federal Republic of Germany consumed 130 billion cigarettes, spending 20 billion Marks. The government received 11 billion Marks as taxes from this expenditure. The costs for smoking-related disease treatment amounted to 15–20 billion Marks (figures from "*Psychologie heute*," April, 1983). Currently, twice as much is being spent on alcohol, and there are millions in West Germany suffering from alcoholism. In the United States in 1983 there were 350,000 deaths from diseases caused by smoking. Health injuries caused by smoking amounted to a cost of $13.6 billion, and if the indirect costs of work and production losses are included one reaches a sum of $25.8 billion. For these reasons the cigarette industry has been barred from electronic advertising media. Thanks to a massive educational program the number of smokers has dwindled since 1977. In males it decreased from 52 to 35%, in women from 34 to 29%, and in juveniles from 29 to 20%. These significant successes should also be considered.

Ehestorf contrasts the indifference toward deaths from smoking with the hysteria regarding the rabies deaths, which between 1965 and 1979 numbered about one dozen. Although this is less than one case per year, it was enough to inspire medical authorities and hunters to eliminate all the foxes around. "That may have been justified. But when one compares that effort, that brutal intrusion into the environment, with the fact that nothing is done about the 140,000 annual smoking deaths, except that this terrifying figure is merely accepted as published data, then this is indeed more than strange" (G. P. Ehestorf, *"Die Zeit,"* January 6, 1979, p. 63).

Anonymous society has opened many new possibilities for mankind. In addition to achievements in science and technology, there have been major accomplishments in the fine arts, the relief from old sovereign power structures through the establishment of liberal democratic governments, the idea of social justice, attempts at worldwide cooperation, womens' emancipation, the acceptance of diverse value systems, and the formation of a humanitarian consciousness, as expressed in the charter of the United Nations.

But anonymous society has also borne new fears—both ecologically as well as in terms of interpersonal relations—which has led to a distinct deterioration of the quality of life. Inconsiderate exploitation of the planet combined with rapid population increases has led to ecological catastrophes, with even more disastrous ones in the offing. The euphoric age in which one spoke of a "superabundant society," "welfare society" or "throwaway society" lasted barely one decade! A few years have elapsed since then, and we now sense that there are major deficiencies, so much so, that some are now referring to "society of scarcity." Now we must fear that the arms race between the great powers is also a competition for the final resources.

> *Man is something to be overcome. What have you done to conquer him?*
> *All creatures until now created something beyond themselves: and you wish*
> *to be the ebb of this great flood and withdraw to the animal state rather*
> *than surpass mankind?*
>
> Friedrich Nietzsche in: *Thus Spake Zarathustra*

> *The true enemy is neither in the east nor west or in the "developing coun-*
> *tries." It is in neither "good" nor "evil," "poor" or "rich." It is elsewhere.*
> *If we want to determine the chances of our existence—whatever it finally*
> *signifies—we must restrain the development that brought us forth, whose*
> *portion we are and whose stream now threatens to consume us; we must*
> *achieve its control.*
>
> H. Hass (1983, p. 196)

8.4.3. Maintaining Evolutive Potential

Thanks to his universality, man does not only have the capability of adapting to changing conditions, he also has the ability to set goals, planning society according to these objectives. This opens opportunities never before available but also brings dangers. The goals set, determine the future course of cultural development and, finally, also further biological evolution.

Thus it is important to interpret current trends in terms of their effects: their evolutionary potential for mankind, his future prospects, and higher development. Generalists are well known to have superior chances than specialists to maintain themselves in the changing currents of the stream of life. The outlook for our direct descendants to be living one million years from now at some culturally and biologically advanced state of development that would place those humans of today in the position of the "missing link" are by no means bad, presuming that we survive the crises of the present.

However there are cultural developments that could restrict this potential, and they have been described in the utopian novels of G. Orwell (1949) and A. Huxley (1932, 1959), previously cited. In both models people lose their individuality and are absorbed into a communal state identity. Man is administered and his behavior determined by an exterior will. In both societal structures the personal bond that we call love is also dispatched. Marriage, family, and friendship attachments are forbidden. Only loyalty and attachment to the community remain, mediated by representatives of the government administration and by means of symbols. Orwell's model places the dominating party apparatus under the guidance of "Big Brother," a tyrannical father figure demanding love, respect, and obedience. Enemy portraits and continuous warfare solidify the masses and reinforce their obedience, and puritanical ideals control everyday life. Technology controls private life, maintaining the order of future society. And these techniques serve ideological indoctrination, suggesting that people are following all these instructions out of their own free will. Although the two models of Orwell and Huxley diverge in their further details, neither is completely unrealistic. Even though they go against our very individualistic and generalist nature and, therefore, will meet with resistance, we must be alert. Man can set himself goals that even go against his own nature. To date, experiments of this sort, exemplified by the radical egalitarian kibbutz (p. 279) or Mao's China, have not succeeded. But, less radical ones which take advantage of certain hedonistic traits, for example, as Huxley's model, may succeed and selection may finally also create a new human nature in accord with the cultural ideals.

The foundations for such developments have existed and continue to exist. Due to the human trait of behaving in an infantile way when fearful and to become attached to powerful leadership personalities (see bonding through fear, p. 77), these kinds of conditions develop during times of emergency. And it is certainly not accidental that it is precisely the Orwellian systems (but not exclusively these) that maintain fear-motivated behavior through the use of propagandistic suggestion of presumed threats. But it seems difficult to use force and power to subdue people continuously, for history shows that man will eventually rebel against such conditions.

The Huxleyan model of the totalitarian state portrayed in *Brave New World* is much closer to reality and also more dreadful. Here the state leadership utilizes man's striving for happiness, satisfying his greed for this goal so perfectly that man eventually falls under the interdiction of his own hedonism. He sinks to the level of the dependent, satisfied child from whom all cares have been removed. During their artificial upbringing, people are, furthermore, so indoctrinated that they are emotionally programmed for the roles in which they will live. They develop a class pride and joyfully execute the work assigned to them. In addition to the state directly influencing physiological-physical development, there is powerful indoctrination and continuous exposure to phrases, slogans, and songs in stultifying mass rituals glorifying happiness, and all under extremely sophisticated technological control. The life of the individual is a happy one. He is proud of his position and loves his work, which is not excessive since work periods are short. The state

660

attends to diversion during leisure time. There are sports, travel opportunities, and entertainment of the most refined variety, including the use of drugs that are not hazardous to health and that bring about a euphoric state. Sexual freedom is permitted as long as one's partner is continuously changed since love is prohibited. Huxley portrays the picture of a thoroughly hedonistic society, lead by an elite utilizing the hedonistic mechanisms of the individual.

The reader will no doubt be struck by the extent to which we are already headed in this direction. We live in a welfare society, protecting the individual through friendly care in a social network, infantilizing the individual, and making him dependent and leadable.

This trend seems to thrive particularly in Sweden. In ''Der Spiegel'' (43/1983) there is an illuminating article by Wulf Küster, who expresses astonishment at the guardian role of government administration, especially in terms of social welfare. For example, the issue of the rights of women has created a compulsory emancipation so that even women who do not wish to are being forced into the working market since it is old-fashioned and unworthy to live as a housewife and mother. In reality, behind this lies a bureaucratic structure striving to gain control of all social services. What would happen to all the child care centers and everything that pedagogues and social workers have created if mothers took care of their children themselves? This is yet another example of too much of a good thing. It is frightening that the government has closed itself off from the problem and refuses to perceive it, even if it is pointed out, as occurred in the same ''Der Spiegel'' issue in the interview with Olof Palme. This self-righteousness creates a problem of being less open to learning from mistakes.

In organic development, differentiation always means integration and subordination of components; transposed to the development of mass societies it means integration and subordination of the individual to a state apparatus. Perhaps some combination of the dominating strategies portrayed in Huxley and Orwell would be most effective. No matter how this subordination of the individual to the totalitarian state may occur, should it prove to enhance fitness it would have to be accepted as an adaptation. And one may argue: why should we not adapt into a collective being while abandoning our individuality? We can hardly say more than that such developments are repugnant to us because we are still individuals. But when an absolute dissolution of the individual into the larger society leads to a superior human adaptation and serves to promote the harmonizing of interpersonal group life, one could argue that our values would have to, by necessity, change. Evolution, after all, is a continuous process of new adaptation.

This is undoubtedly correct. But it is also true that behavioral patterns and culturally defined goals are evolutionary pacemakers and that we can significantly contribute to determine our future goals. In doing so, we should bear in mind the maintenance of further evolutionary potential. Any excessive specialization, even if it is the best adaptation for the moment, could turn into an evolutionary dead end by restricting the possibility for further species change and thus for new adaptations. The chances for mankind to further evolve reside in our universality, and this is based upon the community of relatively autonomous individuals. Maintaining individuality and thus the creative diversity of individuals should remain a desired objective. Only with its help would an effort succeed to oppose the system-immanent dynamics of mass society which threatens to merge all individuality. Of course, a large primate might, like the social insects, give up his individuality completely, and that might be a perfect adaptation. But we should not want to do that since this kind of change would restrict our evolutive chances. An anonymous society of responsible individuals can certainly function just as well.

One might argue that fears of losing our generality and individuality are unfounded, since it would take a long time to eradicate our innate cognitive capacities and motivations concerning individual identity and individual interest. And, since human nature is individualistic, thus far, anti-individualistic movements tended to reverse. They emerged to recreate balance, when imbalance had gone too far, for example, in communism, but once the corrective is achieved, that is, the balance is corrected, individualism reemerges. A totalitarism exploiting our hedonistic tendencies could, however, persist long enough to counterselect individualistic tendencies and thus select for the docile collective being. Therefore, we should be alert to any form of totalitarism, including the so-called "benevolent."

The anti-individualistic social ethic of anonymous society praises virtues that would become nonvirtues were they to lead to destruction of individuality. According to William Whyte (1958), the catchwords of this new ethic are adaptation, arrangement, socially oriented behavior, teamwork, group loyalty, group dynamics, group thinking, dynamic conformity, and others. They fulfill their community-bonding function in the positive sense if individual values are also sustained. But if individuality is lost through this kind of indoctrination, the situation that then develops becomes dubious.

Summary 8.4

Rapid population growth and resource exhaustion threaten mankind's future, but at the same time new possibilities are being opened for improving the quality of life with the help of energy-saving techniques, enabling us to have the freedom to develop culture creatively.

A shift from quantitative to qualitative growth is needed for this to happen. Closely tied to this is the development of a survival ethic. It should not be oriented solely to adapting to present contingencies since involution, i.e., loss of differentiation, can prove to be adaptive in particular situations. But these kinds of developments might restrict the future evolutive potentiality. Man, as the specialist in the unspecialized, has great chances for maintaining himself in life's stream and to develop further, but there are dangers threatening: system-immanent processes of integration and subordination in the state apparatus are leading increasingly to a loss of universality and the individuality of the person.

These kinds of developments are portrayed in the utopian novels of G. Orwell and A. Huxley, and, in some respects, they have come true. Both outline a supervising state forbidding individual attachments (love). The Huxleyan model is closer to reality since in his model people are manipulated with their pleasure-seeking mechanisms. Welfare states tend to move in this direction because of the previously discussed dynamics of organization. The optimality principle should be considered in this regard.

The suggestion of leaving development to the self-regulating forces of evolution, which in the economic realm means the forces of the market, is a convincing one at first glance. But learning from errors is painful and costly and can lead to developments opposed to our conception of freedom and individuality. Goals, planning, and guidance are necessary. There must be, however, some free space for experiments in all realms of life, or the system will stagnate from lack of innovation.

8.5. Concluding Thoughts

Anonymous society tends to be a society without love. It fights individual relationships in favor of a nondiscriminatory loyalty to the group. It is noteworthy, in this context, that the otherwise quite distinct totalitarian utopias of G. Orwell and A. Huxley agree in one point: long-term heterosexual relationships were prohibited.

Anonymous society burdens people with many problems. Does mankind also have the disposition to overcome them? K. Lorenz states that modern man would recognize as correct the command to love as himself those with whom he is unacquainted, but at the same time he can only love fully those with whom he has an acquaintance.

Does this mean that we would have to wait for the evolution of the new man? This would take long, indeed! Fortunately, we seem preadapted to be able to live in anonymous society, and thus with many others we do not personally know. Certainly, we learn to love and esteem particularly those whom we know personally, but once our capacity to love and trust developed in the individualized group, we were also able to bond emotionally to group members unknown to us by means of identification with them. This ability, together with increasing communication, has led to the development of a new humanitarian awareness. But only those who have developed basic trust in the individualized group through personal ties are capable of loving others beyond their intimate circle. In other words, individualistic values and personal attachments are by no means opposed to loyalty to the greater society. They are actually the prerequisite for this.

9

The Beautiful and True: The Ethological Contribution to Aesthetics

Through science, art, and rationally grounded morals, man stands out above his animal relatives. Culture has become second nature and in humans unfolds with far-reaching consequences for the fate of our species. The various branches of arts and sciences have stated their achievements in many brilliant essays, but a historical survey of these is beyond the scope of this book. Thus, we will limit ourselves to discussing the biological contribution to the understanding of these phenomena.

9.1. Aesthetics and Fine Arts

Aesthetics was originally defined as the study of the beautiful. However, art does not only depict that which is beautiful. Picasso's painting "Guernica," for example, is not beautiful in the classical sense, but is doubtlessly a moving artistic work. In classic drama, the fascination with the horrible is played out and aesthetically perceived. Aesthetics is often understood as the study of sensory perception or recognition through the sensations, the actual translation of the original Greek term *aistanomai*. I believe, however, that this would be too broad a definition to use for aesthetics, since one characteristic of aesthetic perception is that we are somehow "taken with"; that we are fascinated by what we perceive. Sensory enjoyment, interest, satisfaction, and cognitive as well as emotional pleasure are experienced; appetites are aroused and to some extent satisfied. Aesthetic experience intrigues and is self-rewarding. The mechanisms underlying these kinds of experiences are the subject of aesthetic research. Thus aesthetics cannot be called simply the science of perception—it is a perception characterized by the special quality of appeal and captivation. It could be defined as the science of those perceptive and cognitive processes that stimulate us in such a way as to bind interest and attention—in short, as to fascinate.

This fascination is mediated by a variety of mechanisms of perception which evolved to ensure that we are able to orient ourselves in our environment and whose functioning is experienced as rewarding. We need to be able to perceive objects and also to respond to them in an adaptive way, be it an obstacle which causes us to detour or something which we seek and look for. In all such cases an object must be perceived, localized, and also recognized, when reencountered in a variety of positions and at a variety of distances. In case of visual perception the image of the object must be separated in contrast against its background. The basic mechanisms by which this is achieved have already been discussed (p. 33). Once the object is perceived, further data processing mechanisms aid us in deciding what to do.

Knowledge determines or biases our perception. Thus, we see figures and profiles in clouds. This knowledge is based, in part, on individual experience, but in part also by prior knowledge founded on phylogenetic adaptations.

Aesthetic perception is the precondition for art and often the artists play with our aesthetic experience when producing art for arts sake. Often, however, the attention-binding and arousing effect of aesthetic experience is used as a background against which messages are communicated, mostly with normative ethical content. A piece of art then becomes a medium within the framework of a communicative system.

The perceptual biases which determine our aesthetic perception occur at three different levels: first, our basic biases, which we share with the higher vertebrates; next, our species-specific biases; and, finally, our specifically cultural perceptual biases.

At the basic level phylogenetic adaptations determine, for example, our perception of particular objects as three dimensional (see the studies cited on p. 54 of W. Ball and F. Tronick, 1971). Constancy phenomena (object, form, movement, and color constancy) also need not be acquired anew in each individual's life (p. 39). Many of the biases of our visual perception have been revealed by Gestalt psychology. Visual illusions are thus most instructive, showing us that even against better knowledge we can perceive "falsely," such as in thinking that we see objects of different sizes although they are the same length (Müller-Lyer Illusion).

Gestalt psychology has formulated a series of laws of visual perception, of which a number are relevant for other perceptual aspects. We have already discussed these (p. 42). In each case we are dealing with active integrating capabilities of perception. Our perception is based upon innate programs with which we categorize, interpret, and actively seek regularities. This requires, among others, mechanisms that enable us to remove ourselves from an initial perception and take a second look from a new orientation. Necker's cube is an example of this principle (p. 45). Once our perception has seized a particular aspect of some visual object, it seems to release itself from that object, permitting the subsequent question: "What else is there to see here?"

Visual perception also strives to seek order and even creates it. General regularities are initially perceived; details which deviate are noticed afterward. If we are shown a triangle missing a tip for a fraction of a second, we believe we have seen a complete triangle. Asymmetry and other irregularities in simple geometric figures are equalized perceptually. We tend to complete the picture in the direction of regularity and symmetry (see also E. H. Gombrich, 1982).

The fact that we seek to discover regularities visually reduces the mass of information with which we are confronted—we form "super signs" or schematas (H. Frank, 1960; M. Schuster and H. Beisl, 1978). This is of great importance in everyday life. We must be able to reproduce objects in the environment in generalized categories: trees as trees, houses, birds, fishes, etc. This means we must first formulate generalized schemata with which we subsequently recognize categories of events or objects. Otherwise we could not orient ourselves, but would have to learn to know each individual tree anew, since, of course, each tree is slightly different from every other one.

The way in which this categorizing takes place is not known, but a remarkable experiment by H. Daucher (in press) suggests how, by "statistical learning," schemas or ideal types could be formed. Using the eyes as reference points, he superimposed 20 photographs of faces of young woman. Since those parts which were repeatedly exposed became darker the resulting image summarized the shared and thus "typical" or "characteristic" features (Fig. 9.1 A and B). It is interesting to note that the resulting "ideal type" is fairly attractive. The question why we perceive the resulting standard face or type as attractive must remain open. There are strong indications (p. 679) suggesting that reference patterns (templates) evolved which set the standard and against which the perceived is checked and evaluated according to the innate norm.

Daucher's experiment demonstrates in a model how many fleeting experiences could, by superposition, leave memory traces which could result in the creation of acquired schematas or templates. Certainly, our perception is basically typological, that is, categorizing (see Gestalt perception p. 46). Children categorize at a very early age and, in fact, against educational pressures, since when they address a dog, a cat, and a cow according to some shared features as "wau wau" we correct them by insisting that the cat is something different, and must be distin-

A

FIGURE 9.1. Aesthetically appealing image, schematically representing an ideal woman's face (A) is the result of the superimposition of 20 photographs of young women (B). The experiment illustrates in a model the way our typological perception works. Reference points for the superimposition were the eyes of the subjects. Photographs from H. Daucher.

B

B

FIGURE 9.2. Two drawings by a 7-year-old girl who was asked by her mother to draw a picture of her. The girl first drew a schematic representation of a woman's face, which lacked any of the individual characteristics of her mother (A); when her mother insisted that she look at her and paint her as she saw her, she drew a detailed picture depicting individual features of her mother (B). Photograph from A. Nguyen-Clausen.

A

guished from a dog. The tendency for schematic presentation also predominates in children's drawing and only when specifically asked do they reproduce the individual features of a model (Fig. 9.2 A and B), a fact that has to be considered in art education (A. Nguyen-Clausen, 1987).

The discovery of a Gestalt or any other regularity is highly gratifying. The "Aha!" phenomenon (p. 701) is a basic aesthetic experience of the greatest significance and of which we will return to later in our discussion of art. The perception of regularities requires minimal storage costs and is experienced as pleasant and gratifying. This is used in a playful way when an artist conceals signs and communications in some picture to allow others to experience the pleasure of search and discovery. The closure boards of the Trobriand islander boats are decorated with beautiful ornamental carvings inviting visual exploration. But they are not only beautiful; encoded in the ornaments, the observer discovers figures of symbolic significance. In the example shown here (Fig. 9.3) there is a central human figure closely resembling a Polynesian tiki. But on closer examination one sees that the eyes of this figure are the eyes of two laterally opposed birds. The entire board has been outlined as a face. Thus one is challenged to discover different encoded figures. This kind of encoding is rather widespread in aboriginal New Guinea art and has its particular attraction in the joy of discovery.

Order and unity is another characteristic of aesthetic perception (J. Hospers, 1969; E.H. Gombrick, 1982). It permits subsequent recognition and therefore familiarity and orientation. When it is too easy for the observer to discover order, the object lacks aesthetic effectiveness, and the same holds when the object is too complex and no regularity can be detected.

Modern artists like M. C. Escher utilize these basic characteristics of perception and confine themselves to its playful use. Others use them as a means for catching the observer's attention and then conveying other ideas via representations, often allegorical or symbolic, in encoded form. The observer's interest and urge to comprehend the message and, so to speak, discover the super signs plays an important role in this process. The positive aesthetic experience of discovery becomes associated with the message being conveyed. This, then, reinforces the message conveyed by the artistic medium.

The criteria of originality and uniqueness, which since the age of Romanticism have been criteria for an artistic work, are not aesthetic characteristics but were the result of artists competing with each other for recognition. They reflect their creative talents. The desire to create something new, the creative experimental impulse, conforms with the aesthetic wish for innovation and to stimulate the observer's curiosity. Even so-called "primitive art" uses aesthetic perception in this sense.

F. Sander (1931) investigated the principle of the "harmonious configuration" in simple geometric shapes and found that persons respond positively to squares and to rectangles whose sides have the ratio of 1:1.63 (the golden mean). Rectangles deviating somewhat from a square form were considered to be "poor squares," and if they deviated even more they were assessed as "poor rectangles." Finally, if one side of a rectangle was too long relative to the others, the figure was not perceived as a rectangle but as a beam. Sander shows that this principle of the harmonious configuration is used in architecture and can be used to explain the diverse effects of various architectural styles. Proportions found in Renaissance architecture are those of the square and ideal rectangular forms, based on the golden mean. Architects of this period also prefer right angles and arches over other forms, placing windows in rhythmically regular rows. Horizontal structures are arranged symmetrically. This creates a quiet beauty inviting the visitor to remain. In contrast, Baroque architecture is characterized by small imperfections, deviations from the ideal form, which arouse tension, excitement, unrest, and passion in the observer. Baroque architecture is thus dynamic, transmitting the experience of events. The stylistic characteristics mediating these impressions are not quite complete square forms, rectangles with somewhat exaggerated sides (length or width). Arches are elliptical and wide, angles are sharp, and axes of symmetry are not exactly centered. Thus, the architects have moved away from the perfect form of the Renaissance to the nearly perfect forms of the Baroque that excite the observer.

The differential specialization of the two cerebral hemispheres (p. 87) causes everything in the left visual field (left of a central fixation point) to be seen primarily with the right half of the brain, and these images are processed in emotional terms in their entirety, whereas objects in the right visual field (seen with the left hemisphere) first undergo a rational, material analysis. These are expressed in artistic creations. Left-weighted images are generally emotional in character, and the emotional-arousing effect of pictures is altered by reversing the images (E. Pöppel and C. Sütterlin, 1983). Aesthetic preferences in their most basic forms are not restricted to human beings. In choice experiments using monkeys, raccoons, and various birds, B. Rensch (1957, 1958) showed that animals have aesthetic preferences similar to humans. In a free choice situation these animals prefer to handle or pick at cardboards bearing patterns of regular form and symmetry over asymmetry and in learning experiments they associate them faster with the reward. V. Geist (1978) furthermore demonstrated that the color patterns which serve to guide and keep the attention of a viewer to certain body areas of the viewed are in principle the same in fish, birds, and mammals, including man. Prominent marks within a figure (body) attract attention; parallel convergent line or rows of spots direct the attention toward a specific part of the body. Lines framing the body hold the attention in a particular zone. Animals can convey a deceptive impression of their size, etc. in a manner similar to that of the Muller-Lyer illusion (H. B. Cott, 1957; V. Geist, 1978). The same principles of attracting attention are utilized in fashion design (Figs. 9.4–9.7).

In a series of imaginative experiments, Desmond Morris (1968) allowed chimpanzees to paint. Their efforts were aesthetically interesting to human observers. They were characterized by the following regularities: chimpanzees initially painted in a balanced manner, observing the edges of the paper and filling out the field evenly. If Morris gave them a sheet on which one side had a square or circle painted on it, the chimpanzees preferred painting on the free side of the sheet, thus maintaining counter balance. Later they joined both structures with a pair of strokes. The chimps also developed individual styles. One produced various fanlike shapes. If the animals were given different colors to work with, they did not superimpose one color on top of another. Thus if the animal had painted a fanlike structure with one color, it placed brush strokes of another color between those of the first structure. The activity was reminiscent of play and was done for its own sake. Interestingly, the animals knew when they were finished, and avoided destroying a "painting" by painting over it.

When I heard of these studies I took paint brushes, colors, and sheets of paper into the Munich Hellabrunn zoo and had two female chimpanzees paint. They did so right away and with obvious pleasure. The higher ranking individual filled out the entire page evenly, while the other one only painted a small patch on the lower portion of the sheet. If she was given another color, she painted a smaller patch right over the original one, pushing so hard that she eventually tore the paper. She behaved as if she did not trust herself to paint in an open area, reminding me strongly of the projection tests of psychologists. In these tests one can glean personality characteristics from the way a person paints a tree, for example. Mentally healthy individuals will paint trees with the branches freely filling the air space in the picture.

Morris also placed his chimpanzee paintings in a gallery along with work of modern artists, without naming his "artists." No one recognized the animal origin of these paintings, and many praised the work as particularly vital and appealing documentation of abstract motion art.

Of the general principles underlying painting, the following are observed in chimpanzees:

1. The activity is carried out for its own sake.
2. The composition is controlled.
3. The space is filled with a feeling for rhythm and regularity.
4. The activity becomes more skillful with practice.
5. Individual styles, which can be varied, develop over time.
6. A picture is considered complete when a particular optimal condition of order has been achieved.
7. Chimpanzee drawing has characteristic arrangements, and thus a generalized unifying scheme, which is followed in painting.
8. Individual characteristics are expressed.

The chimpanzee, however, does not produce paintings in order to study them afterward, nor is it their intention to appeal by its product to the aesthetic per-

a

b

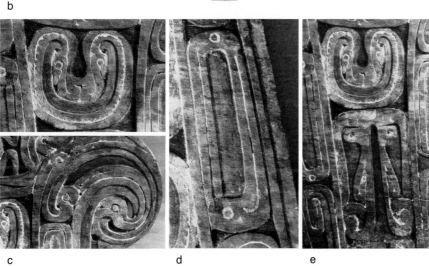

c   d   e

FIGURE 9.3. Lagim (closure board) of a Kaleuna (Trobriand Island) boat. Its function is to protect the boat from danger (a). As a super sign it portrays a face composed essentially of bird heads whose eyes can be seen clearly (b–e). The beaks are extended to form ornamental twirls intertwining with other beaks and bird heads. Birds play an important role in Trobriand mythology. In the middle, four birds are joined into a human figure reminiscent of a Polynesian tiki (e). The figure's eyes are also the eyes of two birds viewed laterally, with beaks pointed downward and outward (c). The mouth, with many small teeth, surrounds the head in an extremely stylized manner. We have seen very similar facial depictions on Hawaiian figures. The body of the figure is also composed of two birds, with their eyes forming the breast. The birds sit laterally (e) along a central, phalluslike upward leading central portion of the figure. Similar avian designs occur in many ornaments, such as on the yams houses. At the very top we see a "heraldic female" with outspread legs in a genital display. Photo: I. Eibl-Eibesfeldt.

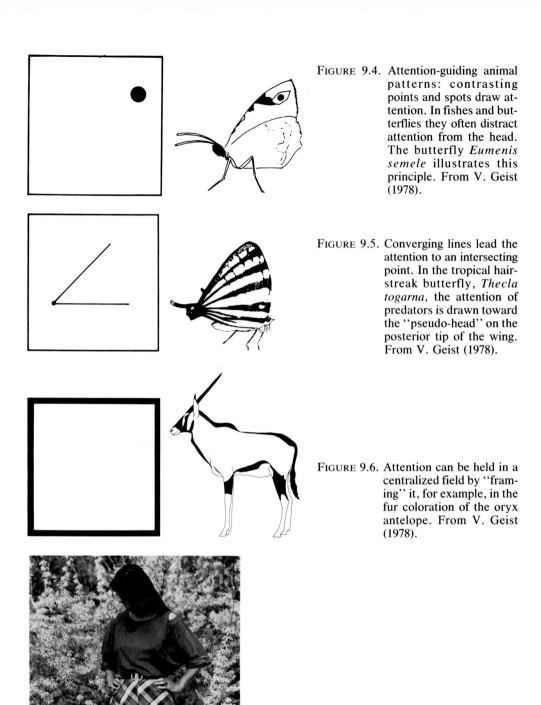

FIGURE 9.4. Attention-guiding animal patterns: contrasting points and spots draw attention. In fishes and butterflies they often distract attention from the head. The butterfly *Eumenis semele* illustrates this principle. From V. Geist (1978).

FIGURE 9.5. Converging lines lead the attention to an intersecting point. In the tropical hairstreak butterfly, *Thecla togarna*, the attention of predators is drawn toward the "pseudo-head" on the posterior tip of the wing. From V. Geist (1978).

FIGURE 9.6. Attention can be held in a centralized field by "framing" it, for example, in the fur coloration of the oryx antelope. From V. Geist (1978).

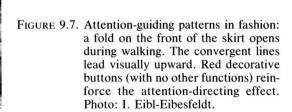

FIGURE 9.7. Attention-guiding patterns in fashion: a fold on the front of the skirt opens during walking. The convergent lines lead visually upward. Red decorative buttons (with no other functions) reinforce the attention-directing effect. Photo: I. Eibl-Eibesfeldt.

ception of others for communicative purposes. The animal also shows no manifestation of aesthetic behavior in the wild. However W. Köhler (1921) reports that in captivity chimpanzees will drape themselves with strips of material and then carry out display dances.

Summary 9.1

Aesthetic perception is appealing. It is based upon the fact that the functioning of the basic mechanisms of perception is experienced as interesting and rewarding and often accompanied by emotional arousal, thus capturing and binding our attention. Perceptual biases specify aesthetic perception. Art exploits these biases either in a playful fashion (''art for arts sake'') or uses aesthetic perception to bind attention in order to effectively convey messages, mostly with normative ethical content. Art then becomes a medium of communication.

Gestalt psychologists studied the primary processes of aesthetic perception in the visual realm including: the search for order and regularity and the search and discovery of super signs, the recognition of which is experienced as highly rewarding. The concealing of super signs in ornamental encoding is widespread, and is even seen in aboriginal art. In jigsaw puzzles this principle is used in a playful manner. Due to basic receptorial biases, symmetrical forms are preferred to asymmetrical ones, rhythmic repetition is experienced as pleasing, and so are certain proportional characteristics of an ideal figure. Our perception is basically typological creating schemata and thus categories of objects. Aesthetic preferences of this basic kind can be found in higher animals; in choice experiments regular patterns are preferred over irregular ones. Chimpanzees do not paint in an attempt to communicate but do so probably playfully for momentary delight. In doing so, they exhibit some of the basic underlying principles of human painting, including individuality.

9.2. Species-Specific Biases of Perception of Aesthetic Relevance

Human behavior is controlled, among other factors, by innate templates and releasing mechanisms (pp. 33, 60). Perception of particular stimuli releases or gratifies specific emotions and appetences. Since the releasing stimuli can be presented experimentally, they can be used to trigger the spectrum of human emotions, thus arousing and calming emotional states. Man strives to attain quiet and security, on one hand, but, at the same time, has an appetence for diversion, excitement, and tension, which must also be acted out.

The species-specific biases of our perception result from adaptations to our natural as well as to our social environment.

Adaptations to our ecological setting are reflected in our preference for certain habitats, reminiscent of the savanna habitat in which man evolved. It constitutes, in essence, the aesthetic appeal of our municipal parks. This preference is the manifestation of phylogenetic environmental imprinting. Jung would probably have referred to it as ''archetypical memory.'' Certain cultural environmental imprinting is secondarily superimposed on these, as illustrated in the romanticized cloud-covered landscapes by Dutch painters, or the mountain landscapes of the southern German local artists.

When we consider the interior furnishings of our homes it becomes evident that flowers and floral decor are of great import. Curtains, carpets, upholstery, and even china are often decorated with floral designs. Picture frames depict patterns of shoots, lamp shades have flowers on them, and so on. Cultivated plants of all types are raised in pots, and balconies are transformed into small gardens. The city person, living in surroundings lacking green plants, will often create aesthetically appealing imitation floral arrangements or will bring flowers or plants into the home. It is evident that here we have a deeply rooted preference for a particular environment. Our ancestors could only prosper as vegetarians in a vegetation-rich region, which explains our "phytophilia" (p. 614).

D. Fehling (1974) investigated which conditions make a home comfortable and secure. First, the home must offer shelter. Thick walls of old buildings transmit this feeling of security (among other impressions) and thus are aesthetically appealing. Castles and other creations of political architecture appeal, among others, to our sense of security. We also find corners comfortable, and we previously mentioned that people in restaurants initially prefer sitting either alongside or with their backs to the walls. A view of open terrain is another of the prerequisites for security. We want to know what is happening around us, probably to be protected from surprises (see also alerting, p. 386). The powerful attraction of homes with a good view is based on this need. These adaptations against predators and enemies is an archaic inheritance that continues to influence the behavior of contemporary man. The adaptations are perceptual and result in our seeking places for relaxation, rest, and residence with particular characteristics. This complex of adaptations also includes our fear of the night and darkness. We are diurnal animals, and it is not surprising that we associate brightness with positive values, such as speaking of a beaming personality or a sunny disposition; in contrast, darkness brings forth negative responses. We talk about someone's gloomy mood, for example. This light-dark symbolism also occurs in other cultures (p. 539).

We now know from color arrangement studies that normal sighted individuals see the same basic color categories everywhere although finer color categories are often culturally determined. (p. 51). Even 4-month-old infants distinguish between the categories of blue, green, yellow, and red (M. H. Bornstein, 1975).

The basis for the similar emotional effects of different colors cross-culturally is not known. There is widespread consensus that yellow and red are considered to be warm colors, red being particularly lively and appealing. A number of speculations have been raised about this. Many fruits are red, and our ancestors were vegetarians and fruit eaters. Furthermore, red is the color of blood. When my 3-year-old grandson Fabian saw two fighting iguanas begin to bleed in a color television presentation, he became highly disturbed and began to cry. The color conveys something alarming. Along with black, it is often used in military uniforms. Elite troops often wear black, the fear-imposing color of the night, while rulers are clothed in purple.

In the Medlpa of New Guinea the black beard is considered to be an intimidating sign of male dominance. When men gather peaceably at festivals they often paint their beards white. Cross-cultural studies have shown that the colors black, white (light), and red are so well recognized that there are individual words for them in almost every language (A. Strathern, 1979, 1983).

Blue and green are considered to be cool, quiet colors. A room painted red-orange were judged to be 3°–4°C warmer than another painted in blue-green, although both rooms were actually the same temperature (J. Itten, 1961). Warm colors also activate the autonomous nervous system, resulting in an increased pulse rate and blood pressure (F. Birren, 1950).

Our aesthetic perception is also significantly influenced by our biases toward others. Thus we tend to imagine seeing faces and facial expressions in inanimate objects. K. Lorenz (1943) pointed to the phenomenon that we tend to interpret house facades as faces. The individual facade elements seem to be renditions of noses, eyes, and mouths, suggesting specific expressions, such as, friendliness, arrogance, or astonishment—windows are eyes, upper moldings the eyebrows, etc. Our living environment is also interpreted physiognomically—heraldic animals stand for symbols of courage and decisiveness according to their physiognomic features. This tendency to physiognomize is only one special case of a general anthropomorphic perceptual disposition. We assess animals with human standards as being either noble or disgusting, brave or cute. This is due to the appeal of innate releasing mechanisms developed for the sake of interpersonal communication.

Mankind's idealizing representation is notable in this regard, and is something that occurs both in deed and in appearances. The ideal model individual is courageous, decent, warm-hearted, and kindly. Key images for the values of loyalty are presented, even when in conflict. We mentioned Abraham's sacrifice, which illustrates the conflict between loyalty to the family and loyalty to the Lord, as a representative of a higher order. Only man in his culturally shaped existence places common good before individual interest and therefore also above family interests. Here, art, especially poetry, becomes a very important value-transmitting medium (p. 698).

Of particular interest is also the ideal representation of the human figure. In various cultures and at various times in history, man is sculptured as slender, muscular, large, and with broad shoulders. Women appear in two different forms, designated as paleolithic and classical Venus, respectively. This may have corresponded to some racial idealized conception, but I feel that it is more likely that the broad-hipped, large bossomed paleolithic figures represent mature motherhood and not young women.

The ideal human face is characterized by regular proportions, with a narrow nasal bridge, a retreat of the prognathy, which in *Praesapiens* forms is still pronounced, and an increasing dominance of the cranium over the facial skull. The art of China, Europe, and the Bantu art of Africa tend to portray the human profile in this direction. Faces with this balanced featuring are considered to be beautiful, even if the ideal does not appear with any frequency within the population. In the Eipo of western New Guinea, W. Schiefenhövel conducted a survey on the relationship of marriage, affection, beauty, and attractiveness. He often received the following answer: "X is a beautiful man, for he has a beautiful nose form (u yal)." In these people the ideal of the finer nasal bridge structure does not commonly occur in reality. In comprehensive experimental studies, B. Rensch (1963) found that the ideal European type is characterized by fine facial features, a delicate and not excessively large nose, and beardlessness, features which do not correspond to the average European face. He states these are juvenile features. I believe this is a universal phenomenon, the basis of which is a preadaptation of the "child schema."[1] We also find certain juvenile features in women particularly attractive. In caricatures these features are frequently exaggerated. If the above thesis is correct, we would have in this preference a guiding factor in our choice of sexual partners which fosters the selection of modern hominid characteristics (Fig. 9.8; see also p. 612). This interpretation finds support in a study on the sexual beauty

---

[1] Not to be confused with the baby schema ("kindchenschema").

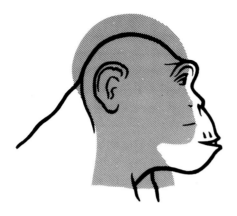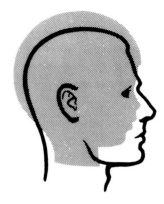

FIGURE 9.8. The childlike face has finer features, even in anthropoid apes, and a facial skull of a smaller proportion to the entire head which is less prominent in relation to the cranium than in the adult. The "child schema" adapted to these proportions may have also effected the further refinement of the human profile in the course of hominization and may continue to promote this development.

ideal by R. Fauss (1988), which shows that both sexes consider those faces of the other sex whose lower parts show features of infantile morphology (e.g., small mouth), as particularly beautiful.

M. R. Cunningham (1986) investigated the relationship between specific adult female facial features and the attraction, attribution, and altruistic responses of adult males. From an international sample of photographs of 50 females, which were rated by males, he obtained precise measurements of the relative size of 24 facial features. Positively correlated with attractiveness ratings were the neonate features of large eyes, small nose, and small chin, the maturity features of prominent cheekbones and narrow cheeks, and the expressive features of high eyebrows, large pupils, and broad smile. These facial features also predicted positive personality attributions, such as higher status. Women characterized by this standard of beauty were also those whom males would preferably select for dating, sexual relations, and child rearing and toward which they would be most inclined to perform altruistic behaviors. This is in accord with other investigations which demonstrate the existence of a "beauty bonus" (S. G. West and T. J. Brown, 1975; G. E. Weisfeld *et al.*, 1984).

In this context it is interesting to note that a study of J. H. Langlois *et al.* (1987) challenges the commonly held assumption that standards of attractiveness are learned through gradual exposure to the cultural standard of beauty. In two studies, 2- to 3-month and 6- to 8-month-old infants were shown slides of faces of adult women which had been previously rated by adults for attractiveness. When presented in contrasting pairs of attractiveness (attractive/unattractive), both groups of children looked longer at the attractive faces.

> The results thus call for a radical reorientation of thinking about the origins of physical attractiveness preferences and stereotypes. Whether intrinsic to the nervous system of the infant or to the spatial characteristics of faces, the tendency to detect and prefer certain faces over others is present very early in life, long before any significant exposure to contemporary cultural standards, definitions, and stereotypes. Our results argue against the common assumption that physical attractiveness is arbitrarily defined, cul-

turally dependent, and only gradually learned. Rather, these findings suggest that the rudimentary beginnings of preferences for attractiveness may be present in infancy and that a universal standard of attractiveness, overlaid with cultural and temporal variation, may exist (H. Langlois *et al.*, 1987, p. 367).

Beauty thus does not solely depend on acquired tastes. Statements to the contrary, as for example, by Jane E. Caputi (1984), are not based on investigations, but express a belief based upon the fear of unjust discrimination. And we agree that the "suggestions of a set of ideal female features" (M. R. Cunningham, 1986) does not legitimize discrimination based on physical appearance alone. Attempts, however, to counteract our aesthetic bias by anti-art and thus destroy or repress our inborn beauty ideals are repressive in itself and thus represent an extreme position, which is rather problematical.

Summary 9.2

Templates and releasing mechanisms cause specific perceptual patterns in our species. They are adapted to characteristics of our environment (example: "phytophilia") as well as those of our fellow humans, who themselves frequently function as releasers. Our perception projects anthropomorphizing characteristics into the environment due to built-in biases. Thus we physiognomize animal faces and house facades and even ascribe human expressions to trees, rocks, and clouds. Some idealized representations of the human body are universal and others culture-specific preferences. Universally preferred features include fine facial lines, a well-developed forehead (and thus a large cranium), and a slender neck over such coarser characteristics more typical of the early stages of human evolution. Here there is perhaps a distinct preference selected for via the "child schema," which in many peoples influences partner selection.

9.3. Art as Communication

The artist, regardless of whether he paints, carves, writes theatrical pieces or poetry, or composes music, is oriented toward other people and, occasionally, toward celestial beings addressed as if they were people. The artist wishes to influence his audience, e.g., by pleasing them or stimulating their fantasy, in short, catching and holding their attention and conveying some message before the background of poignant aesthetic experience. The message could be of a religious or political nature. If the artist's effort does not succeed, the work that he created is considered to be void. The elements represented in the artistic work serve communication and are usually modified from their models in nature, using emphasis and exaggeration of specific characteristics. K. Schlosser (1952a) speaks of "signalism" in art, and she is the first art historian to discuss the ethological concept of key stimulus and releaser in this connection.

Originally, all artistic creativity was tied to specific purposes. Tools were created and marked as individual possessions, decorated with the simplest ornamentation. Music was played for the sake of dance or mourning ceremonies or for singing children to sleep. Traditional knowledge was put into rhyme form in order to be more easily memorized and to be transmitted to others for their aesthetic pleasure; finally, this pleasure effect became an end unto itself. Creativity, for the sheer joy of beauty, was intended to heighten one's own experience and the delight of

677

the companion. But generally art remained tied to other goals, such as display. Aesthetically appealing displays are important even in animal courtship behavior, and sexual selection fosters the development of aesthetically effective features. In *Ethology: The Biology of Behavior* (1975, 1987), I describe a series of examples, of which bowerbirds are perhaps the most impressive. I recall, in particular, the orange-crested gardener bowerbird. The male decorates his tentlike stage by sticking flowers into the green moss wall behind the stage, and placing flowers and fruits in front of the pergola.

Chieftains, nobility, state leaders, and other persons of rank and esteem similarly surround themselves with richness (identical with might). They frequently use artistic objects for such means, since they require an extraordinary amount of work time and skill, which is then reflected in the impression of the finished object.

The group is quite willing to be represented by such leadership. These high ranking individuals are regarded proudly as examples of the group, whose might, wealth, abilities, and values they represent. The magnificent palaces of Islamic princes served this purpose as did the castles and parks of European monarchs. As such, they functioned as display organs and as the adornment of the entire group, and are restored and preserved with sizable investments of love and funds (see M. Warnke, 1984). The need for this kind of group representation is great, and this willingness to support such enormous artistic efforts for those persons symbolizing the group was probably a decisive factor in the development of art. Force alone could scarcely have accomplished this. As stated above, we are proud of these accomplishments, as if they represented our personal talents, and we name the great talents of our country with pride: the poets, thinkers, musicians, and painters. And we are always somewhat disconcerted when these individuals do not fulfill an idealized picture in their actual life (M. Warnke, 1984).

Self-representation by artistic means is an ancient practice. In tribal societies, individuals and groups present themselves in this way. Hand-crafted skill in the fabrication of tools is often the impetus for making some decorative article for the sole purpose of display. The Eipo (Irian, Jaya, in western New Guinea) produce net bags which are used to pay for the raw material they need for stone axes found in quarries outside their home region. Both trade partners invest time in the products and, accordingly they become valuable. The value of an object can be raised by putting more work into making it. Thus the net bags can be decorated by sewing orchid fibers into them, they can be made very large and with a finer mesh, and the net fibers can be painted in patterns, all of which will increase their value. The Eipo make these kinds of modifications, producing particularly beautiful ones, which are borne by the men as a decoration on their backs during festive dances (Fig. 9.9a). They are often decorated with some feathers as well.

Net bags have become "ritualized" from functional objects into purely decorative ones with rich feather decors. This stage has been achieved in the In, who belong to the same linguist family as the Eipo, but speak another language (Fig. 9.7b). Similar developments are known from other parts of New Guinea. Axes are valued objects, since their production requires a great deal of labor. Their value can be increased by highly polishing the blade. This is done by the Yali, for example. Such axes are no longer plain utilitarian tools but are used as currency for dowries and other payments. In the Sentani region, axes are produced with beautifully carved handles and woven haftings, and again such tools are not actually used as axes but function as valued, decorative objects. The same is true for the ceremonial axes of the Mount Hagen people. In his *Biologie der Uniform* ("Biology

678

FIGURE 9.9. During dance festivals, the Eipo (a) bear carefully handmade large net bags as a decoration on their backs (b). The net bags often decorated with colorful feathers, and assume a very decorative rather than functional purpose. (a) Eipomek valley; (b) Kosarek/western New Guinea. Photo: Volker Heeschen.

of the Uniform"), O. Koenig (1968, 1970) shows how the process of functional change works, for example, by transforming cords for tightening into decorative ones and buttons into costly ornaments.

Aesthetic needs are coupled with other functions in body adornment and decoration. Flowers in the hair certainly serve to enhance beauty. Children are adorned with flowers in the Trobriand Islands, probably just for love of beauty, and their faces are painted in an aesthetically appealing manner. But often the floral decoration is combined with some other message. A hibiscus blossom that a young girl sticks behind her left ear signifies on the Trobriand islands that she is still unattached. If it is behind the right ear it means "No longer free!" The disklike glass bead pendants which the !Kung women (Kalahari) and their children use as head decoration, serve also as apotopaic devices. The magnificent head adornment used by Medlpa men (New Guinea) for dancing is used for beauty but also as a display, since the feathers make the wearer look larger and also demonstrate his wealth. Body decoration is also more than an expression of aesthetic needs. Black is the color of aggression and is perceived as threatening. Men color their faces black during festive occasions, but they add the warm, friendly colors of red, white, and yellow. They brush light ashes into their dark beards (A. Strathern, 1983). The Yanomami often put on dark warpaint during festivals, but in antithesis they stick the bright down feathers from raptors in their hair or on their foreheads. In the Yanomami, body color decoration serves as both as clothing and adornment. Both sexes decorate themselves and their children with red or brown rings, wavy

679

lines, and other patterns in an individualized manner. The Himba rub their skin with a pigment made of fat and hematite dust, and here body decoration is used not only for ornamental purposes but also as a shield from the sun. Finally, group identity is broadcast through makeup, tatoo, and jewelry.

Many of the "primitive" artistic creations serve as a means to communicate with spirits and other nonhuman beings, to whom human perceptual patterns are anthropomorphically ascribed. Such beings are frightened with threat gestures and phallic presentation (p. 81), warded off by holding the palm of the hand outward, and appeased by presenting antithetical friendly signals or by using appeasement gestures. These messages often undergo no further encoding. Rather they are presented directly and even in an exaggerated manner, according to the principle of the supernormal model (p. 60). This is true for the warding off, threatening eye patterns, which play such an important role in apotropaic figures and patterns (O. Koenig, 1975) and for representations of bite-threat by baring the abnormally large teeth in exaggerated mouths. Buildings can also serve display function for outstanding families, or a group. They then symbolically dominate surrounding structures. This symbolism of height can be exaggerated, and if several groups compete with each other for sheer height, all sorts of grotesque forms can result (Figs. 9.10–9.16).

The principle of the supernormal releaser is also used in art for our delight. There is a hedonistic art and aesthetic, in which mankind attains a high degree of refinement and cultivation.

The strong appeal of releasers is often used to catch attention and to associate it with a completely different purpose. For example, in advertising pinup girls are often used to promote the sale of automobile tires; the friendly and appeasing appeal of the child is exploited to promote the sale of a product. This technique has the advantage that infantile signals can often be distinct and even exaggerated, since their cuddly qualities do not have an obscene effect. The message being conveyed will be associated with something pleasant and interesting, and this association becomes impregnated in the message. Experimentation with releasers, whether encoded or not, is used in such cases for the purpose of conveying some message to others. The aesthetic effect of the releaser is used instrumentally.

Portraits of rulers depict authority by emphasizing male dominance displays in posture, gesture, and facial expression. They serve as symbols for identification and, in this context, power appeals to man. Furthermore, manly conduct is generally culturally reinforced. Battle scenes and other depictions of history that stimulate interest have been used in the past to justify historical events, and will probably be used for the same purpose in the future (G. C. Rump, 1978, 1980). In this manner, political and religious positions can be formed and impressed on others. Here art serves to instill values. This can even be observed among the hunter-gatherers. In central Australian tribes, for instance, rock paintings serve this function. At the holy sites, the symbolic centers of tribal territories (p. 331), we find depictions of totem ancestors on the rocks. They are revealed during initiation rites and serve as identification symbols. Only men have access to these holy sites.

Initiates experience great deprivation and pain during the initiation rituals. They are also instructed about the history of their totem ancestors (and thereby their group) and other mysteries. They stay away from women during this time. I had often asked myself why male initiation plays such an important role in the life of tribal people. During the course of time it became clear to me that this developed

FIGURE 9.10. Artistically produced objects often display their functional use quite distinctly in tribal peoples. The demon-repelling female figure from the Nikobar Islands (Kondul) shows threatening eyes, a warding off (apotropaic) upraised hand, and a defensive outstretched hand, whose thumb points at the onlooker in a mimicking of a phallic threat. Photograph: I. Eibl-Eibesfeldt.

FIGURE 9.11. To the right and left of the entrance of a house in Katmandu (Nepal) are painted warding off eyes to protect the home; above the door are religious motifs; birds and flowers serve as aesthetic expressions of the need to be close to nature (phytophilia). Photo: I. Eibl-Eibesfeldt.

FIGURE 9.12. Threatening, repelling eyes on the bow of a Balinese outrigger canoe. Photo: I. Eibl-Eibesfeldt.

FIGURE 9.13. (a)Hand marks on the door to a Munda house (in the village Kamre, province Ranchi, India) meant to ward off danger. These expressive gestures are artistically used on ornaments and amulets. Photo: I. Eibl-Eibesfeldt. (b) The repetitive hand mark is almost ornamental. Photo: I. Eibl-Eibesfeldt.

FIGURE 9.14. Turkish amulet in the shape of a hand with a repelling eye. Here the two elements of hand and eye are combined into a single symbol.

9.15

9.16

FIGURES 9.15 and 9.16. Symbol of height as an expression of dominance in architecture (see also A. Rapoport, 1982). Figure 9.15: Steingaden (Bavaria); Figure 9.16: San Gimignano (Italy). Citizens compete with each other for esteem, attempting to outdo one another with the height of their house-towers. From a postcard.

out of necessity for instilling the men with group values. Family values scarcely require reinforcement to become powerful, but since man must be prepared to defend the group and if necessary give his life for the group, special social reinforcement had to be developed to bring this about. The initiation, with all its hardships and techniques of humiliation, creates this readiness to accept the group teachings (p. 604), to accept the symbols of the group, and to place the group ethic above that of family. This function is particularly clearly expressed in poetry.

Art often serves to solidify the group bond and also to set the group apart from others. This occurs in group songs and dances. If a person spends time among the Bushmen of the Kalahari, the simple melodies of the dance games, which girls and women sing continuously, become a familiar keynote of the everyday Bushmen life. In a Balinesian village one continuously hears the melodies of the gamelan orchestra. These are practiced almost daily and are played during temple festivals; small girls hum the major melodies and dance to them in play. The artistic heritage bonds and demarcates the group. We will look more closely at style in the following investigation.

Art is often associated with the concept of beauty, which is no doubt justified. But not all works of art are beautiful; there are also artistic expressions of the horrible, which are ennobled as art since they hold up a mirror to stir our conscience, as Francisco de Goya did with the horrors of war or Käthe Kollwitz did with social suffering. The drama and tension of these works lead to self-reflections, stimulating a conscious awareness of the problems of interpersonal relationships and serving to transmit moral values.

Similarly, the protest against the cold sterility of values of modern city planning makes its expression through forms of art. The aerosol can became the instrument of artistic expression in the struggle against the grey concrete walls of our cities. We speak, quite rightfully, of a graffiti art, as, for example, the humorous and aesthetically appealing creations of Harald Naegeli (Switzerland) (Fig. 9.17).

Art is also an expression of experimental playfulness and curiosity. The artist probes for the way he can achieve his effects, for example by stepwise abstraction, much in the same way a psychologist studies the mechanisms of perception. Abstraction thus signifies a loss of information, but also a vigorous emphasis on the essentials. There are various levels of abstraction. For example, due to their dark backgrounds, Rembrandt's portraits emerge in a fascinating way and maintain the observer's attention to the faces which portray subtle statements about their personalities. The more the abstraction, the less of this latter type of information can be conveyed, and the greater the placard effect of the work. In the spontaneous paintings of the tachists (action painters) only the elementary aesthetic projections are expressed, something we also perceive in the chimpanzee paintings. Indeed, experts in an exhibit in which chimpanzee paintings were included without being so identified discussed the works as if they had been done by humans and engaged in the usual praise jargon of modern experts, behind which the helplessness of modern art critics so often hides (D. Morris, 1963). Robert Ederer (1982) has made a number of appropriate and pointed remarks on this very topic.

One of the prominent features of contemporary life is the rise of anti-art. With the slogan "Everything is art, and everyone is an artist," a group of anti-artists intentionally aimed at leading art into the level of the absurd. The two "Used Corpse Tables" produced by Joseph Beuys illustrate this point. They were purchased with public revenues for 2 million Austrian shillings. When a member of parliament protested ("Are you out of your minds"), he was damned as "reac-

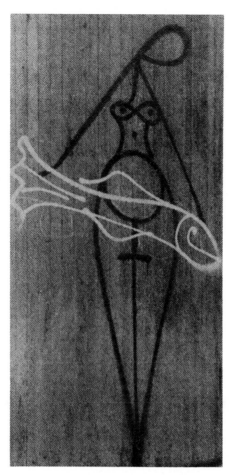

FIGURE 9.17.
Art as protest. The brutal style of modern architects provoked Harald Naegeli to make this artistic attack on a newly built building and thereby to mellow the coolness of concrete. The photo illustrates the female body outline discussed earlier, opposed to that of the man (triangle standing on its tip). From the *Zeit* (30 September, 1983).

tionary-faschistic'' (R. Ederer, 1982). Marcel Duchamp, who sold a urinal as a work of art, made a remarkable self-confession:

> Neo-Dada, New Realism, Pop-Art, Assemblage is cheap amusement and lives on that which Dada does. With my urinal I intended to take the wind out of the aesthetic uproar. Now they are using ready-made items to discover their ''aesthetic value.'' I threw the urinal at their face as a challenge, and now they admire it as aesthetic beauty (quoted by R. Ederer, 1982, p. 147).

Arik Brauer (1983) concludes his critical discussion of objectless painting (he also speaks of modern ''non-arts'') with this statement:

> What is in common in all the described modern efforts is the tendency to turn human values upside down. The subconscious is more interesting than the conscious; accident is superior to human talent; the monkey tail or the dog's paw are better than the masterful human hand. A style is derived from disability and failure. Refuse is a favorite material, while marble and silver are not. Ugliness is good, and beauty is bad. Brutality and horror are favorite themes, while romanticism and poetry are considered to be repugnant kitsch. This all comes to mean the negation of man as an intelligent, civilizing creature. Is that all that remains . . .?

Apparently almost anything can be sold to museums now. Civic revenues purchased ''Garbage Baked into Bread,'' cataloguing it with a number and supplying it with quotations and expert opinion explaining the "fascination of this object." This anti-art is apparently bent on destroying art. R. Ederer has insightfully discussed its means of dehumanizing in a critical report.

If we consider these events, it becomes clear that art is not only used to convey higher values. It can also work to destroy values, to brutalize, and to dehumanize. Its intentions, in other words, can easily become destructive ones.[2]

Summary 9.3

The artist activates and intensifies aesthetic experience through an intuitive combination of sensory stimuli. This can occur for hedonistic ends. But powerful experiences of this kind can also be used for purposes of community bonding and as a means of positive display to others; for artistic creation combines ability with achievement and is thus a mirror of the abilities of a person or group. Messages are conveyed through this medium using an impressive and attention-holding aesthetic experience, to reinforce group norms, group loyalty, and more.

The artist can thereby evoke specific emotions and thus make a person receptive to particular messages: aggressive, if the appeal is for martial activation of the group; humility, if the communication is for identification with the welfare of the larger group, and so on. Thus art serves dual purposes: to communicate and infuse values. It is also used to convey beauty, and where it is not dealing with beauty it is still concerned with the benefit of the good by portraying the grim sides of society and thus instigating critical reactions. There is, however, also a fascination with the horrifying.

9.4. Cultural Manifestations: An Observation on Style and Stylization

We have repeatedly pointed out that there exist cultural aspects of artistic behavior, but in the foreground stood the question of the innate bases of artistic perception and artistic manifestation. We demonstrated our need to recognize order and regularity, to categorize and thus ultimately gain an orientation, which brings the rewarding experience of insight. Some of these fundamental principles of aesthetic perception are shared with higher vertebrates. At another level, we are subject to phylogenetic adaptations more specific to man which cause anthropomorphic biases in our perception.

We now turn to culturally determined perceptual patterns whose function is fostering group identity. Style is of particular significance here, for it expresses common areas of bonding. By stressing similarities in clothing, architecture, and other artistic expressions, it creates a sense of intimacy extending beyond family and kin borders. Thus style can have a group bonding function. Since this can occur at different levels, there are different levels of identity. Europeans have their local and ethnic expressions in dress, architecture, and other characteristics of artistic style. There are also epochs of style (Romanesque, Gothic, Renaissance, Baroque, and so on), characterizing as a cultural entity all of Europe from the Atlantic far into European Russia and from Scandinavia to the Mediterranean. All this is considered to be "western" in style. A comparable situation exists in Islamic art.

---

[2]In terms of harm to the community—whether through the demoralization of individuals, causing value blindness or through perversion, all of which lead to a destruction of interpersonal relationships.

The spontaneity and decisiveness with which groups like punk rockers set themselves apart in their fashions, teaches us that people create new symbols spontaneously and that they can express some things more precisely with material symbols than with words (I. Hodder, 1982).

Interestingly, style fulfills this demarcating and bonding function (one could also say, ideological function) even in hunters and gatherers. P. Wiessner (1984a) investigated the relationship between the style of artifacts and social factors in the !Kung, G/wi, and !Ko Bushmen and found that style fulfilled various functions. At the group level, stylistic features of the arrowhead tips (as markers or emblems) determined linguistic membership. This helps overcome distinctions between local groups, uniting a larger population.

The Bushmen could determine with a glance whether an arrow came from a member of their own linguistic group or an unfamiliar one. Thus they are able to predict whether or not the owner or producer of this arrow holds similar values and behavior norms. If various groups are acquainted with each other, stylistic differences signal the various values and make interactions more predictable. Arrows, on the other hand, from unknown groups evoked spontaneous reactions of fear and discomfort among the !Kung. Conversations recorded when unfamiliar arrowheads were found were noted by Wiessner to deal with horror stories about murder and other gruesome events of the past. Stylistic communications concerning identity also occurred in other artifacts—in body decoration and in clothing. In addition to group styles, there are individual styles designating a person's individuality. The aesthetic appeal, in this case, serves to enhance a positive self-image. Asked why so much effort went into clothing and objects, the !Kung replied that they did this to show they are "one who knows things and does things" and to be more appealing to members of the opposite sex.

The motives for the production and possession of objects of aesthetic value are universal. Aesthetic display plays a major role in courtship and in maintaining sexual relationships. Individual style suggests that a person is industrious. This makes him a valuable partner, as for example in the framework of the reciprocal exchange relationships (P. Wiessner, 1984).

In the investigation of style in beaded headbands among various !Kung groups, P. Wiessner (1984) discovered further important relationships. In the Bushman groups still living in small groups in their traditional home range, most headbands were simple with regular patterns (Fig. 9.18). In Tsumkwe, where Bushmen from many different groups come together, complex patterns appear. These patterns are exaggerated and lack regularity, giving the impression of instability and uncertainty, as if some new order was being sought in this region. The !Kung themselves comment that the bands look like "many people talking at once." When asked about the traditional simple patterns, they responded that these were like somebody "walking softly." This expression refers to the behavior of a hunter who brings in a big kill, and walks quietly to his hut without bragging, a modesty necessary for group harmony.

P. Wiessner found further that headband styles were often chosen to suit the taste of the receiver by executing them in their local style. Thus one avoids imposing a personal signal on somebody from another region. This is the result of the context of exchange. Among the !Kung, headbands are often given to the host upon the giver's arrival for an extended stay. Recognizing the host's preferred style shows respect for him and his rights in his own area. Styles chosen in ex-

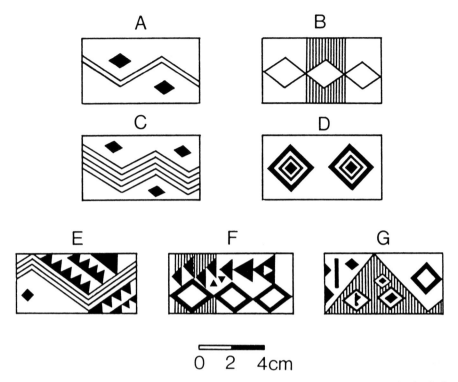

FIGURE 9.18. Patterns found on beaded headbands (!Kung Bushmen). A and B: basic design structure; C and D: further developed designs; E–G: patterns departing from tradition. From P. Wiessner (1984).

change items used in other contexts may function in other ways, such as to document exchange ties. An interesting example of this can be found among the Yanomami who exchange bamboo arrowheads with friends and trade partners and later use them to document this network to visitors to gain esteem without verbal advertisement. Style is also used to encode the cues (messages) presented via aesthetic perception so that only group members can comprehend them.

When pictorial figures are used ornamentally, they typically undergo a process of simplification and schematization (often referred to as stylization). The most distinguishing characteristics are emphasized and become widely schematicized, turning into pure signs whose origin can only be ascertained by reconstructing existing intermediate forms. W. Wickler and U. Seibt (1982) have described the development of precolumbian whorl patterns from their original naturalistic depiction into ornaments (Fig. 9.19). Since the developmental trend proceeds from the naturalistic representation to the abstraction, one can follow the step by step stylization of the pictorial to the symbolic-abstract presentation. The same method was used by A. Lommel (1962) to investigate stylization of human figures on Papuan shields (Figs. 9.20A and 9.20B).

The stylization process is in many respects similar to ritualization, in which,

687

FIGURE 9.19. The development of stylized pelican elements on early Ecuadorian whorl patterns. Note the reduction to a geometric ornament, the origin of which would not be interpreted without examining transition stages. From W. Wickler and U. Seibt (1982).

for purposes of signal functions, prominent features are simplified, and thus become more concise. There is also a distinct repetitive element here. One cannot always determine whether artistic stylization is a conscious process of abstraction or a transformation occurring gradually in many steps as patterns were repeatedly copied. Probably both processes occur. When an artist uses an animal or human figure ornamentally, there is often an attempt made to schematically simplify the form. However, that development is also realized as a result of copying, and this is not a rare occurrence. On the Trobriand Islands we interviewed various people to determine the symbolic significance of the figures carved into the closure boards on their boats. Some elderly people knew their meaning, but many people had already lost the detailed knowledge of these pieces. They were carving on the basis of rote learning "like their fathers," and with the lack of knowledge of underlying symbolism, the figures were further simplified into mere decoration.

Similar trends are seen on Balinese figures developed from guardian figures. Originally these figures depicted a threat face and phallic presentation along with warding off hand gestures and/or posterior presentation. As a new generation of carvers occupied with carving for the tourist emerges, the original significance of these traditional figures is being lost. These craftsmen tend to exaggerate the phallic elements and the threat face, but the other gestures are also being carved without knowledge of their significance. They look like vestigial ornamentation. Japanese amulets depicting the female genitalia (I. Eibl-Eibesfeldt, 1970b) have undergone a similar process, although perhaps consciously.

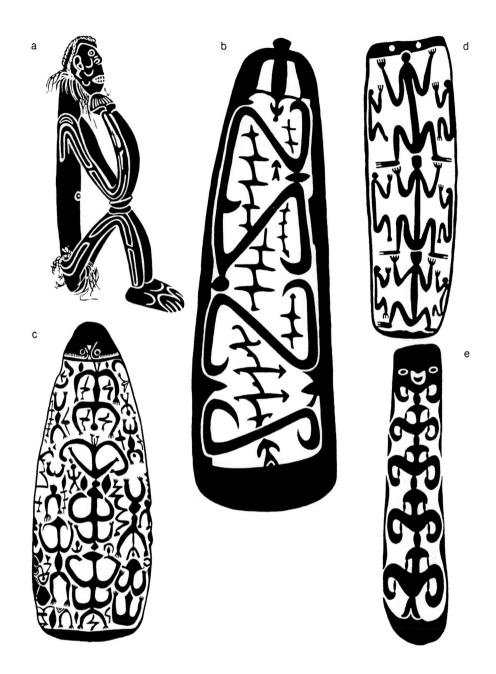

FIGURE 9.20A. Ornamentalization of human figures in Papuan art. The human figures are increasingly abstracted. This process may be due to the perceptual trait of schematization. (a) Profile of an ancestral figure from the Asmat region of western New Guinea (Lorenz River); (b) a shield, also from the Asmat region, with the abstracted profile of a human; (c)–(e) three depictions of stylized human figures on shields from western New Guinea. From A. Lommel (1962).

FIGURE 9.20B. Three representations of highly stylized human figures on shields from western New Guinea. From A. Lommel (1962).

Summary 9.4

Style is a means of signaling membership. It can express individuality or group membership. Both levels of stylistic expression occur in hunters and gatherers. The bonding effect of common aesthetic preferences on specific art styles is particularly evident in the art of Islam and in Christian occidental art. The process of stylization in which figures become transformed into mere ornaments has much in common with the ritualization of behavioral patterns for the sake of signal formation. Simplification and exaggeration occur along with a uniformity, which makes the signal constantly recognizable.

9.5. On the Ethology of Music, Dance, and Poetry

9.5.1. Music

Music has an immediate appeal to our senses. Rhythms synchronize the phases of specific physiological processes, even in lower vertebrates. Thus a metronome can be used to slow or accelerate the rate of gill cover motions of fishes. If persons whose heart rate was accelerated from exercise then hears lullabies, their pulse rate decreases more rapidly than do control groups hearing either nothing or jazz music (H. Kneutgen, 1964, 1970). Lullabies from diverse cultures have a similar effect. They share the feature of melodic and rhythmic elements imitating the slow breathing rhythm of someone falling asleep.

We may presume that there are various basic rhythms that specifically influence human behavior in similar ways and do so cross-culturally. Certain rhythms pacify while others excite. Whether specific rhythmic patterns activate certain emotions like aggression or affection (and thus induce specific moods) is not known. However, the exciting or quieting effect of various rhythms is understood, as is their coordinating effect on groups, who, on the basis of the pattern of coaction or alternation (p. 205), perform either simultaneously or in partnership alternating patterns in time to the music.

Melodies also have primary leitmotifs. People can accurately categorize heroic, hunting, war, mourning, lullaby, and love songs with a high degree of certainty (R. Eggebrecht, 1983; M. Schröder, 1978). We also recall the studies of K. Sedlacek and A. Sychra (1963), who showed that non-Czech speaking persons correctly interpreted the mood in which a Czech sentence was spoken. Emotions of love and joy were characterized by a higher voice frequency and livelier melodic structure (see also baby talk, p. 207). Emotions of sadness and resignation in terms of

690

melodic structure were clearly below the zone of neutrally pronounced sentences. The analysis of several variables in the music of various peoples revealed remarkable similarities, as the Tables (9.1–9.3) from Rainer Eggebrecht studies show (see Fig. 9.21).

David Epstein (1985, 1988) investigated the vocal and instrumental music of seven different non-European cultures. The music was composed of parts (movements) with pauses in between. The analyses revealed that the beat was maintained with utmost precision, even when the pauses lasted several minutes. This indicates the existence of an internal pacemaker for the beat, which continues to operate even during a pause. The second, even more surprising, result was that the tempo changes of different movements or within a piece relate to each other by low-order integral ratios, i.e., ratios of 1:2, 2:3, 3:4 or their reverse. This also holds true for the European classics as well as for music in tribal societies from different parts of the world (D. Epstein, 1988). Leonard Bernstein (1976) pointed out a number of other universal features on the phonetic level, such as, the level of the movements and the level of semantics, the universality of the pentatonal scale, and the playing with overtones which Bernstein considers as the origin of all music. Bernstein's book is one of the most inspiring contributions to the subject. It cannot be reviewed here, but it is imperative reading for all those interested in the subject.

Music is more immediately effective than is visual art. It is directed toward our emotions, with primary leitmotifs presented as releasers in more or less veiled form. Presumably, supernormal sound models are also constructed, for example, as mournful patterns that have a more moving effect than the natural sounds of complaint and crying. The artist can also activate various emotions in sequence by appropriate activation of the key stimuli, arousing the listener's emotions in a way that is not normally experienced. Tensions are built up and are then resolved as a catharsis.

The continuous repetition of a rhythm or melody can act to create a trance-like condition (a state of ecstasy). Presumably neuronal circuits reverberate as a result of the continuously repeated stimulation, whereby more and more neuronal groups are activated in resonance, not unlike an epileptic attack and which consequently causes changes in brain chemistry (p. 696). This then alters the state of consciousness (see M. Winkelman, 1986). The arabesque ornament, in endless repetition, can also induce ecstasy on the part of the audience.

The aesthetic effect of music is determined by the specific encoding determined by particular epochs and cultures. And, as in the visual arts, music is assessed on the basis of originality and uniqueness of the performance. Leitmotifs are created anew and varied, and the listener enjoys the experience of their rediscovery, which also conveys a sense of orientation and familiarity. Music is generally produced for its own sake, which does not mean that it is only produced for hedonistic purposes. Indeed, it is because of its powerful appeal that it is also suited for all those purposes, which were cited earlier in the discussion on visual art. For that means, it frequently combines with words (as in song). Because the textual contents of songs are readily memorized, songs have been used for political indoctrination and also for instruction (H. Elterman, 1983). We will study some texts from songs in the section on poetry.

Music is often used for group bonding, as evident in marches and apparently in choral song as well. As in the style of the visual arts, music can also become a means of facilitating group bonding. During my work on Bali I heard the gamelan orchestra as a continuous background melody, and the children at play hummed

691

the melody of the legong dance. It would not be amiss to maintain that these kinds of leitmotifs exercise a powerful influence on group identity. In the !Ko Bushmen it was the simple melodies of the melon ball dances that we heard again and again, so that they come to mind in a pleasant and familiar association each time I think of Bushmen life in the Kalahari.

R. Jackendorff and F. Lehrdahl (1982) attempted to discover grammatical parallels between music and speech. According to their generative music theory, we not only perceive the surface structure (frequency, volume, timber) but also the underlying deep structure which is responsible for the fact that music can also be recognized in transformations. In perception there occurs a stepwise reduction process, similar to the way the score for individual instruments can be read. But there must remain a conformity with the rhythm of the nonreduced portions. Deviations in rhythm create tension, and are indeed used for this purpose musically, but are always resolved by a return to the rhythmic pattern. The deep structure can be illustrated in a dendrogram. But each transformation grammar requires a "recoverability," which, in this case, cannot be accomplished after a reduction. Thus a decisive criterion for this theory remains unfulfilled. We are left with the statement that we must be able to perceive some basic rhythm. The laws of Gestalt perception cited earlier suffice to explain the re-recognition of transformed melodies.

The sense for musical harmony is based upon the biologically determined ability

Poland

Lullaby

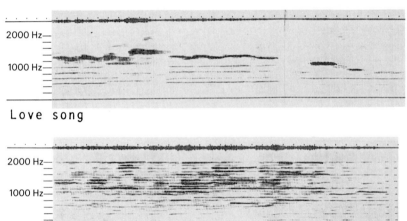

Love song

Mourning song

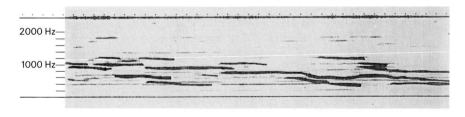

FIGURE 9.21. Sound spectrographs of songs and music of various peoples. After R. Eggebrecht, 1983.

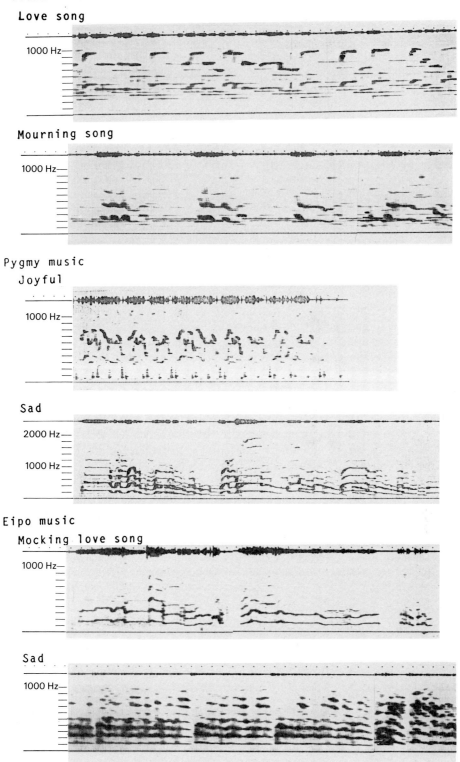

FIGURE 9.21. See legend on opposite page.

Table 9.1. Analysis of Several Variables of San-Bushman Music

	Love song	Mourning song	Normal song
Tempo	= 116 (Moderato)	= 76 (Adagio)	= 92 (Andante)
Volume (level)	Moderate	Low	Moderate
Rhythm	7/8: ♩♪♪♩♪	4/4: ♩♪♪♩♩♩ ♪♪♪♪♩♩	4/4: ♩♩.♪♪♪♪
Overtones	Many harmonics	Few overtones	Average overtones
Tonal range	d² to a sharp³	c sharp¹ to g sharp¹	f sharp to f sharp²
Melody	*[musical notation]*	*[musical notation]*	*[musical notation]*
Melodic contour	*[contour line]*	*[contour line]*	*[contour line]*

to extract a single tone from a chord, the single tone corresponding to the music notion of a "keynote" (apparent tone frequency of psychoacoustics). This perceptual ability is based on a constant calculation of harmonic intervals between the individual partial tones and thus requires a special abstraction ability, since the actual tone frequency does not have to be physically present in the chord itself. Parallels to analogous central information processing strategies in recognition and estimation of human verbal sounds suggest phylogenetically acquired learning programs (E. Terhardt, 1982, 1984).

9.5.2. Dance

Dance is music expressed in movement. Many of the principles and functions we discussed in the section on music are also valid for dance. Dance can be enacted as a performance before an audience, often as a structured ritual. This is exemplified by the dance performances during temple festivals in Bali (I. Eibl-Eibesfeldt,

Table 9.2. Analysis of Several Variables of Pygmy Music

	Daily song	Joyful song	War song	Mourning
Tempo	= 106 (Andante)	= 160 (Allegro)	= 120 (Moderato)	= 66 (Adagio)
Volume	Moderate to broad amplitude	Broad amplitude	Greatly changing amplitude	Low amplitude
Rhythm	Regular binary or uneven	6/8: ♪ ♪ ♩ ♪♪♪	4/4: ♩ ♩ ♩	2/4: ♩ ♩
Overtones	Medium	Many overtones	Few overtones (sharp, forced sounds)	Overtones usually below average (lamenting)
Tonal range	g sharp¹ to g sharp²	g sharp¹ to c sharp³	f sharp¹ to g sharp³	c sharp¹ to b
Melody	*[musical notation]*	*[musical notation]*	*[musical notation]*	*[musical notation]*
Melodic contour	*[contour line]*	*[contour line]*	*[contour line]*	*[contour line]*

Table 9.3. Emotional Attributes in Correlation with Acoustic Parameters

Parameter	Joy	Sadness	Excitement	Balance
Frequency	High	Low	Varied	Medium
Melodic variation	Strong	Slight	Strong	Medium
Tonal course	Moderate, first up, then down	Downward	Strongly up, then down	Moderate
Tonal color	Many overtones	Less overtones	Barely any overtones	More overtones
Tempo	Rapid	Slow	Medium	Medium
Volume	Loud	Soft	Highly varied	Medium
Rhythm	Irregular	Regular	Very irregular	Regular

1976), which begin with a Baris (war dance) followed by a Pendet (offering). The warlike display in the Baris is thus combined with successive symbols of friendly appeasement, which culminates in friendly contact initiation.

Some characteristics of the sex-typical movement patterns of female and male self-portrayal in display dancing are universal. Examples are the abrupt movements and shows of strength in male dance in the form of leaps, frontal orientation to the observer, storming forth, and the outspread position of arms and legs. The body is presented in its entirety as powerful. Women portray their bodies as more gracile and display it in various views, with coquetry playing an important role during their dance. The natural ambivalence between attraction and shy retreat is played out in postures and motions; sexual stimuli are also presented. This occurs through suggestion in encoded form or by means of brief presentations, as in posterior display in the French can-can, by whirling the skirt up briefly during a turn, or in lifting a leg momentarily (see sexual presentation, p. 252).

Dance as an interaction between dancers finds many forms of expression. It is often used in courtship and can thereby be executed either as a couples dance or a group dance. In these dances the partners find out if they are suited to one another, and the ease with which they synchronize their movements may indeed be a direct expression of mutual understanding. We cited the tanim hed of the Medlpa as an example of this (p. 243). In many European folk dances (polonaise, etc.), a person begins with one partner and during the course of the dance makes contact with other partners before returning once more to the primary partner. This form of dance enriches opportunities for contact. Group dances, such as the Austrian landler, are interesting due to the expressive and also highly ritualized form of male and female self-portrayal before one's partner. The essence of dancing interactions remains the establishment of synchrony of the dancing partners.

Group dances are also used to demonstrate unity and thus to consolidate group identity. If this identity is demonstrated to others then patterns of coaction are dominating. When a hundred warriors simultaneously stamp with their feet during a dance, sway together or, as during the pig festivals of the Medlpa, jump in place simultaneously, these patterns convey a sense of unity to the outside observers. These are dances in which the group portrays itself as a unit to others. Dances in which group members move in harmony in a kind of synchronization ritual facilitate internal bonding, such as the melon ball dances of the San women (!Ko,

!Kung and G/wi) of the Kalahari. The success of these dances is achieved when none of the partners are out of sync with the others, so that the group acts as a unit. Of course, this would only take place when each dancer knows the dance rules and has also mastered them, for otherwise they would dance asynchronously and thus become excluded from the group. As in the visual arts styles, dances express group membership.

Finally, dance also induces altered states of consciousness. This is especially evident in the trance dances of the Kalahari Bushmen (I. Eibl-Eibesfeldt, 1972, 1980). The phenomenon has been well documented, but the physiology of the trance has yet to be investigated. Endorphins play an important role (p. 69). Dance can also express the human desire for sovereignty over his biological nature, the wish for self-mastery, and cultivation. Body control in dance is occasionally used to represent this triumph of man over his biological nature, as exemplified in the Balinese legong dance. The movement patterns of this dance are so "artificial" that the dancers cannot learn them just by watching a model. Instead, the dance has to be learned under direct guidance of a teacher. But finally, the dancers achieve a mastery, and these artificial movements are executed with the same grace and suppleness of natural movements (Figs. 9.22 and 9.23).

9.5.3. Poetry

Creative language distinguishes us from all other animals. Therefore, one would expect that it is in the art forms of lyric poetry, prose, and drama that mankind is furthest removed from his biological nature and therefore is freed to develop without the limitations of phylogenetic adaptations, with the exception of pre-programming of a general kind that underlies our ability to acquire verbal language and to speak. Indeed, we can formulate sentences that have never before been written or spoken, but they must obey the grammatical rules of the language in which they are expressed. We have also shown that there is an inner logic of language by which a grammatically correct statement may be perceived as an inconsistency. Finally, we have also pointed out that verbal and nonverbal interactions are controlled by an apparently universal system of rules, which even structure the forms of verbal interactions (p. 544). Universals based on similar perceptions and thought patterns also occur in the formation of metaphors.

The fundamental unit of poetry is the line. It has not only a characteristic time span of $2\frac{1}{2}$–3 seconds but is also a rhythmic, semantic, and syntactic unit. According to F. Turner and E. Pöppel (1983) this is generally true for the poetry of all fourteen cultures investigated so far.[3] Other linguistic rhythms are intertwined in this way with the basic acoustic temporal rhythm. This appears to us as a satisfying combination, which facilitates memorization. Another universal characteristic of poetry is that certain important elements of the line or of line groups remain constant throughout the entire poem, indicating the repetition of some pattern. The universal meter of 3 seconds corresponds to our biological "Now" (p. 52). The length of syllables also corresponds to the minimum period in which a response to an acoustic stimulus can occur (approximately $\frac{1}{3}$ second). The poetic meter thus contains the two low-frequency rhythms of human auditory perception. These rhythms are

---

[3]Latin, Greek, English, Chinese, Japanese, French, Eipo, Ndembu (Zambia), Spanish, Italian, Hungarian, Ural, Slovak, and Celtic.

FIGURE 9.22. In dance, man overcomes his primary nature in several ways. He cultivates his movements, as in the Balinese legong dance, into their most artistic skillfulness, affecting movements into an aesthetically most delightful ritual.

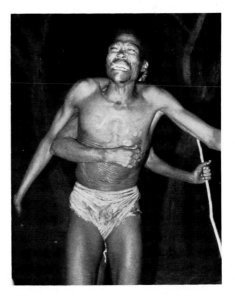

FIGURE 9.23. Man can also alter his state of consciousness, as in the trance dance of the Bushmen. In this condition the dancer becomes a fighter for the group, devoting himself to the group as he is fighting the demons. The photograph shows a !Ko Bushman in trance, with a fellow dancer supporting him from behind. Photos: I. Eibl-Eibesfeldt.

well retained, for even when we forget the words we recall the rhythm. Rhythmic repetition induces an activation of the entire brain, something that also occurs in trances (B. Lex, 1979). Musical and configurational perceptive functions of the right hemisphere of the brain (p. 88) merge with the linguistic capabilities of the left hemisphere through the rhythm of the meter, whereby the auditory drive of the rhythm so affects the deeper levels of the nervous system that they reinforce the cognitive functions of the poem. A similar process occurs in dance, in which a driving rhythm alters the condition of the mood and one's perception. Perhaps the first dance was also the first poem.

The same kinds of principles hold for prose. The art of presentation—even in scientific treatises—exists in the intuitive observance of line rhythm, in which the author presents cognitively comprehendible units. This becomes apparent when one has to reduce some words on a page in order to reduce the total text by one line. Even if this consists of merely striking a number of fill words, the experience of doing so is unpleasant, since in their absence the presentation rhythm is disturbed and the work becomes choppy. A similar difficulty occurs when additions have to be made in a new edition of a work. Here it is helpful to insert not sentences but an entire paragraph, which like the verse of a poem forms a single unit. In poor translations, the rhythm of prose is often lost.

In spite of this constraint, the word is undoubtedly the freest means of communication we have. It permits the communication of material information independent of emotions as well as imbuing emotional appeals with differentiated immediacy. The possibility of encoding statements verbally—thus by using flowery language—is one of the important bases of poetry. The play with metaphors is directly comparable with allegorical representation in the visual arts. In both cases one experiences the joy of discovery of the hidden meaning. Verbal cliches translated into language, words, and phrases can trigger emotions, thereby acting as social releasers. They can represent and reinforce as their subject, themes of social concern, such as loyalty to the family or group and in more differentiated form than is possible in the visual or musical arts. Our innate ethical templates (K. Lorenz, 1943) are involved. But poetry finds even more importance in its transmission of cultural values.

During the course of his cultural evolution, man has placed the group ethic above that of the family. At the same time he developed a war ethic, whereby with cultural indoctrination the killing inhibition against other humans was overcome (p. 405) and a readiness to sacrifice oneself for the group was established. The placement of group values over and above family values required powerful reinforcement, since one's family is initially closer to the individual than is the group and it is not "natural" to prefer group interests over those of family and kin. Lyric poetry, drama, and prose have described the conflict between family and group ethics since the beginnings of prose, and have been used to help build a group ethic. This is easily confirmed by a survey of song lyrics.

The texts appropriate familial values and transpose these to the group. The lyrics of a guard regiment song from the World War I period are as follows:

> We bear the braid of the guard on our coat,
> Fidelity and honor in our hearts,
> The belief in Germany and in God,
> The will to bear arms, to fight . . .

Nothing is stated here about wife and children, since family loyalty hardly requires any special indoctrination. When concepts from the familial realm are used at all, then they are used in a transposed sense, in order to project family values to those of the group ("*Brothers, to the sun, to freedom . . .*").

Ties to one's homeland are also reinforced in song, and interestingly even among hunter-gatherers. The Nama Hottentot living as hunters and gathers in the coastal region of the Walfish Bay (Namibia), praise the sea in exultation songs. The neighboring Nama, adjacent to them but living further inland, greeted their land after an extended absence by spraying water on the ground from their mouths and reciting:

/i //naoxan !hutse	You land of my ancestors,
!gaise !khoi !oa te re	Come to meet me,
eibe mutsi!	I have already viewed you.

(text and translation Kuno Budack, 1983)

Another fine example is a song of the Trobriand islanders that has been translated by Ingrid Bell-Krannhals. It is sung during the evening profane dances and contains the mournful thoughts of a young man who left his homeland for schooling.[4] The song exemplifies the basic similarity of human emotions.

1. Akowana   odaba koya
   I looked up   *on top of the mountain(s)*

2. akululu   u agisi
   I looked down *I saw*

3. kiwaula   ula valu nanugu iomau
   in a haze, cloud *my village my mind was heavy*

4. kapisisi   segwaya
   how sad about   *the friends*

5. oioi   kapisisi   sedayasi
   –   *how sad about*   *all my friends*

6. o pilatala   wolola   tamayaisi
   on the far side *for a long time* *the two of us come here*

7. migisi   itamwau
   their faces   *are lost (hidden)*

8. ginigini   saina   bwoyna
   education   *very*   *good*

9. kala bwoina   davalusi
   very good   *for our village*

10. ilagoki   omapula   iomau   sainela
    goes too high *the price* *it is hard* *very*

The Eipo of western New Guinea praise in song their homeland mountains, from which their ancestors descended, and they call forth their ancestors in battle, pleading for their help (V. Heeschen, 1982).

---

[4]Distant schools attended by Trobrianders include those in Goodenough and Alotau.

The ways used to solidify love of one's native land and group identity are the same in tribal societies as in western culture. The Himba sing songs of praise when they gather, extol the deeds of brave ancestors (p. 146), similar to the way we do in songs and sagas. Mocking songs are used to express reproval and to sustain social norms. Songs and poems are also suitable for courtship, since their veiled expressions permit a cautious approach to the partner, a testing of the other's disposition, and also a separation without crisis if the partner rejects the approach. No direct question was actually posed, so a rejection would not also result in a breakdown of social relationships. Some aspects of courtship rituals, including infantilism (p. 243), are universal.

There is a rich use of metaphors in the contract songs of the Yanomami (K. Good, 1980). At the same time there is an encoding using a regular textual division into small lines composed of few syllables, the terminal syllable being repeated in the subsequent line.

The aesthetic criteria for assessing poetry includes the skillful use of metaphors, whereby, as in pictorial art, the alienation effect stimulates curiosity and thereby attracts attention. The statement made need not be a direct one, but it should also not be too obscure. For Eipo songs as for ours, it holds that they should not be monotonous. Regularity in structure and a division into rhymed verses facilitates the formation of superstructures, thereby enhancing recognition and memorization of the text. A poem becomes, by virtue of its coded nature, a challenge for understanding just like a picture. It seizes the reader's attention, building up a state of expectancy, which is then resolved in a liberating, cathartic understanding ("Aha!") of the message.

Style imprints, builds familiarity, and also bonds. Thus a mocking song, with its playful veiling of an admonishment is not necessarily experienced as negative by the addressee. Instead, he is addressed as a group member, with an encoded message. Metaphors are animating for they stimulate the discovery of new lines of thought. A good part of poetic ability lies in their skillful use.

In tribal societies also, songs are sung for their own sake. The following song, recorded by V. Heeschen (1984a) was sung by an Eipo woman out of sheer joy upon experiencing an earlier event, which is alluded to in the song in encoded fashion.[5]

Wirye wit, cange wit, dikle wit.	Wirye-bird brother, cang-tree brother, dikle-tree brother.
Wirye numdam bongobnil.	The wirye bird is close to my navel.
Na doubne dundam, na wena wendam.	My trap is ready to press, my trap is ready to catch.
Wirye num titinil.	The wirye bird gets caught at my navel.

---

[5]The first line cites a few names in a straightforward manner. But Wirye is also Limne Si, the assumed name of her beloved. The trap is a reference to the vagina. The cang wood mentioned in the first line also appears to be innocuous, but cang also means "long" in reference to penile erection. The frog names refer to women. Here it refers to the grass skirts of the woman.

Cang kim bongobnil.	The cang wood lies on my genitals.
Toktokana ton dobromane-buk,	After I have removed the toktokana frog,
Mokmokana ton dobromane-buk.	After I have removed the mokmokana frog.
Kim bongana num titine titinil.	Lying on my genitals, sticking to my navel, he sticks to me tightly.

Love songs of this type are also sung when a person is completely alone, in a pleasant thoughtful mood. The song thus appears to be freed from social function and be for pure amusement.

9.5.4. Science and Art

We have examined a number of aspects of aesthetic perception and artistic creation. We have attempted to show especially that the same emotions can be evoked by means of different sensory input. Sensations of harmony, order, tension and tension resolution, the need to form super signs, the joy of recognition, and re-recognition of configurations via the orienting "Aha!" experience, are all things we experience by viewing a work of the graphic arts, hearing music, or reading poetry. Apparently the various sensory inputs are brought together and processed by the same interpreting mechanisms.

We have also encountered supernormal releasers in all aspects of artistic creativity, learning that the works of the graphic arts, as well as music and poetry, are produced for their own sake (as joy in the aesthetic experience) and that they can also be used to capture and to hold attention and to convey sensations of pleasure, interest, arousal, or beauty, associating these feelings with other messages. We found that the graphic arts and poetry are used to convey social norms. Other aspects of artistic creation, such as drama, have yet to be discussed.

The actor emphasizes the essential in facial expression and body posture. In the Japanese Kabuki theater a woman's jealousy is conveyed by a very simple, stylized behavior: the actor portraying the woman's role bites a handkerchief, his head nodding slightly to and fro. Thus he enacts the essence of this emotion. Aggression directed against an object and the slight motor unrest describe the feelings of this emotion. The actor portrays the passion and inner strife of the person and encodes it in the form of a veiled message.

Mood induction is but one of the didactic means of involving the audience. Bertolt Brecht used other means in epic theater, appealing, instead, to reason and awakening consciousness of a problem by means of the topic's alienation on the stage. While in earlier times beauty was the object of art, today art presents also "the reality that we do not want to look straight in the eye" (K. E. Logstrup, 1973, p. 319).

We should also discuss what parts of a sequence of movements or behavioral sequences, in general, appeal to us aesthetically. We briefly mentioned in dance that this includes the smooth, well-coordinated movement sequence, and the ability to demonstrate mastery of the body. We mentioned the legong and can add here that for this reason we also enjoy the performances of circus and athletic performers and certainly not the least classical ballet! Control of body and mind is universally appreciated as a virtue, and in general we find cultivated behavior to be beautiful while uncouth demeanor is considered ugly. It insults our aesthetic sensibilities when someone reaches with both hands into a bowl and stuffs his mouth full.

Let us now turn to the relationships between science and art. The most important point they have in common probably is that both savor discovery as an aesthetic experience of perception. The scientist discovers relationships using his gift of gestalt perception. One can also value a scientific approach to a solution of a problem as aesthetically elegant or inelegant on the basis of the originality of underlying thought, on the basis of the expediture relative to the results, etc. These are the same principles that S. Margulies (1977) formulated for the beauty of solving problems in a chess game. Art and science also share the joy of playful experimentation. Clearly, both wish to elucidate "reality"—an ambitious statement. But certainly both disciplines are creative for they transmit new perspectives, depictions, and insights into the world.

Art transmits viewpoints. It describes the world from a new, unaccustomed perspective, pointing out relationships that are not apparent in everyday life. Exactly such new perspectives are also conveyed by science. Thus both fields seek insights into a deeper knowledge about our world. Art probes the depths of man's feelings and is furthermore normative in conveying beliefs and other values. This seems to be a basic difference with science, which attempts to convey objective knowledge. The knowledge conveyed artistically also concerns reality, but this reality is essentially cultural. Nothing real may correspond in the external world to a set of beliefs. But they exist culturally, e.g., as religious concepts and thought patterns and thus are cultural reality. Furthermore, art is not the only normative discipline, for the scientist seeking insights into relationships and using his knowledge about evolutionary processes, also seeks to understand and approve or disapprove norms based on rational considerations. Art *and* science transmit norms and thus share their close relationship to ethics. And both are based on the aesthetic experience of and the transmission of recognition.

Summary 9.5

Perceptual biases determine aesthetic perception at three different levels: basic biases, which we share with the higher vertebrates, species-specific biases, and, finally, culture-specific perceptual biases.

Harmony, order, and the experience of supersign discovery are the basic key experiences of aesthetic perception in the visual arts, as well as in music and poetry. Species-specific key stimuli such as primary auditory signs (primary key motives) are employed to trigger emotions and through their manipulation, tensions are built up and released.

Music has an immediate appeal to the emotions. It is often produced purely for its own sake as an artistically pleasurable experience. But due to its strong emotional appeal it is also effective in combination with verbal instructions in conveying values. Science and art share playful experimentation, joy in supersign discovery, and revelation to others. In the latter respect, art is chiefly concerned with subjective realm, while science seeks an objectively demonstrable description of the world. However the line between the two cannot be sharply drawn.

10

Biology's Contribution to Ethics

That which pleases is permitted (S' ei piace, el lice)
                                  Torquato Tasso, in: "Aminta"

That which is permitted pleases (Piaccia, se lice)
                      Giovanni Battista Guarini, in: "Il Pastor fido"

Many of our actions are guided by a system of values (norms). These can be conceptualized as sets of control systems in which rules for the ideal (expected) conduct are laid down as normative reference patterns (see also templates, p. 66). These systems are activated under certain conditions and our actual conduct is checked with reference to them; they constitute, so to speak, our conscience. The German word "Gewissen" refers to them as a knowledge of what is right or wrong. Deviations from the expected conduct is experienced as a discomforting feeling of guilt (guilty conscience), while acting in accordance with them is highly satisfying and rewarding, probably through the activation of brain endorphins (M. Gruter, 1979, 1982; J. S. Danielli, 1980; B. G. Hoebel, 1983). These normative systems function analogously to those responsible for the maintenance of physiological homeostasis. They set the virtues which guide our lives.

Norms are derived either from experience or are created by reason. Those founded upon experience can be either phylogenetic or cultural. In both cases, selection operated to preserve those that enhanced fitness. We can classify values according to function. Thus, we can distinguish virtues of the agonal system (bravery, chivalry, obedience) and virtues of the affiliative system (charity, generosity, fidelity). The two systems can complement each other in an adaptive way. According to situation and context one may be at times more operative than the other. There are, furthermore, more general virtues such as the universal virtue of self-control. Thus, to control one's greed, in order to be generous, or to control oneself in the face of anger are universally found demands. To behave morally in the word's original meaning (the Latin *mos* = custom) means to act according to custom. But customs have diverse roots, and conflicts between them can occur so that we are frequently forced to make choices. In these situations, it is often considered more virtuous to behave in ways requiring self-control and, in particular, to restrain one's egotistic impulses. But whether agonal or affiliative values are given preference depends upon situation and context.

In animals we can observe behaviors analogous to moral behavior in man (K. Lorenz, 1963). I say analogous because we cannot attribute reflectiveness or lack of it to animals—we just do not know. For instance, animals sacrifice themselves for their young, help conspecifics, respect partner bonds, and spare conspecifics performing submissive displays. The critical points of the social life of animals are safeguarded by phylogenetically evolved norms (W. Wickler, 1971). They involve tradition transmission and authority, respect for older individuals, regulations about the killing of conspecifics, sexual relationships, possession, and reliable ("truthful") communication.

If an animal has conflicting drives, e.g., when a mother is threatened by a predator and thereby stimulated to defend her young, but also to flee, the stronger drive will prevail. K. Lorenz (1963) referred aptly in this connection to a "parliament of instincts." The animal follows the prevailing biological tendency that is activated at a particular moment. It does not base its conduct on insight or reason. The situation in humans is fundamentally different. Man can behave appropriately on the basis of biological drives, but he also has the capacity to behave

705

on the basis of rational, moral principles. Thanks to his ability to foresee events and to temporarily detach (uncouple) behavior from drives (p. 86) and thus to consider situations within a more objective perspective, he can determine which decisions he should make. He can even behave in ways which run contrary to his primary (innate) tendencies.

If man acts according to his preprogrammed values, he does so spontaneously and with little reflection. If a person saves his child, he follows his stronger inborn tendencies which overrule his fears. Would he flee instead, he would be acting against the ranking of norms set by his biological program.

Whether such an act, according to one's inborn tendencies, (i.e., according to the custom of nature) could be valued as moral has been disputed. It has been argued that only behaviors based upon rational decision and directed against our nature would deserve this label. Thus Immanuel Kant was of the opinion that one could only speak of moral behavior when one's dispositions were overcome for more noble purposes. This is a question of definition.

Kant based his ethics entirely upon reason and insight: one must ask whether the rules guiding one's action could be elevated to become a general law, or, in other words, whether one would want others to behave in the same way. Someone thinking in this way is already emotionally engaged, out of feeling responsibility for the community and thus not solely rational.

Morality based upon reason is a very recent product of cultural evolution and may thus be considered a "higher" achievement, but whether it should always be considered as such is uncertain. Friedrich Schiller dealt with this question when he responded to Immanuel Kant's challenge of the categorial imperative: "I like to serve my friends, but alas, I do so with pleasure, and so it rankles me that I am not virtuous. There is no other counsel than you must seek to disdain this and then to accomplish with loathing that for which duty demands" (Friedrich Schiller, epigram from *The Philosophers*). In his treatise "On Grace and Dignity" Schiller describes virtue as nothing more than a "disposition for duty." And as much as behavior due to one's disposition and behavior due to obligation seem opposed to each other in an objective sense, this opposition is not true subjectively, and we should be combining both joy and duty in our actions. "He should obey his reason with joy. Not to discard it like a burden or to strip it away like a coarse shell; no, in order to unite it most internally with his higher self, his pure intellectual nature has its sensual counterpart" (Schiller's Works, edited by O. Güntter and G. Witkowski, Vol. 17, p. 346). When we support a friend in need or sacrifice our life in spontaneous decision out of love for our mate, we are behaving morally, but on an instinctive level. There are certainly cases in which the priority of a rationally based morality must be conceded. We will discuss the reasons why it should always be combined with a feeling of humanitarian engagement.

The relationship between inclination and rational morality was described by Konrad Lorenz (1943) using group defense as an example. The affective experience of enthusiasm with which a person will even sacrifice himself for the sake of the group demonstrates the instinctive basis of this behavior. "But what holds someone in the difficult position of remaining faithful to his decisions that he has implemented in that hour of enthusiasm is the categorical question. When a person has spent many sleepless nights, burdened with lice, dirt, and diarrhea, the innate reaction of enthusiasm . . . is lost, and every other creature would now break off the struggle and run home. That man does not do this but instead stays at his post is a pure achievement of the categorical imperative in which behavior is envisioned in greater time segments than the immediate moment and in which decisions do not just spring out of the mood of that instant" (K. Lorenz, 1943, p. 386). However, what must be added is that the decision springs out of a deeply experienced feeling of obligation, and that is neither the result of rational consideration nor pure entrainment, but rather a biologically inherited trait.

In developmental psychology, the ontogeny of moral behavior and value acquisition are thought to be first instilled by parents through reward and punishment and only later internalized as moral rules and principles. Thus, the external behavioral guidance provided by reward and punishment would later be replaced by inner controls. Furthermore, during development there is a change from "self-centered behavior" to behavior in which there is an increasing consideration for the welfare of others. The final product of this development is rationally based sovereign decision (A. Colby *et al.*, 1983). The attention of psychologists like L. Kohlberg (1969, 1981) focused on the ontogeny of moral reasoning and to a lesser extent on the ontogeny of moral behavior as expressed in the spontaneous altruistic behaviors of empathy already displayed at a very early age. The studies of developmental psychologists dealt mainly with the development of value judgments.

The ontogeny of moral reasoning follows a regular sequence of developmental steps [J. Piaget (1932) and L. Kohlberg (1969, 1981)], whereby experience and maturational processes merge with each other. Social learning undoubtedly plays a great role, as a child assumes the values of its culture, but the infant also displays friendly (and thus "good") behavior such as offering gifts (p. 342) out of his own natural disposition. Furthermore, newborn infants express "sympathy" of the most elementary type by crying when they hear another person crying.

Occasionally the innate aspect of certain norms is challenged with the remark that if this or that inhibition was innate it would not require any regulating laws. This has been the basis for arguing against an innate incest inhibition (p. 261). What is overlooked is that variation also occurs in genetically determined characteristics. Behavioral deviations need to be controlled. Altruistic behaviors can be exploited by nonreciprocal behavior such as, for example, by cheaters, to an extent that could harm the community. Cultural taboos and laws are established as safeguards against this. They function analogously to the retaliator strategy by which in a number of animal species ritualized fighters protect themselves from being displaced by mutants who do not obey the rules of tournament but instead fight in a damaging way.

Occasionally it is maintained that a particular behavior could not be considered to be bad, evil, sick or otherwise negative if it regularly appears in a certain percentage of the population. A. Kinsey *et al.* (1966) used this argument to consider even such deviations as sodomy as "natural."[1] Using similar reasoning, E. O. Wilson (1975) described homosexuality as an adaptation. What is overlooked in these arguments is the distinction between statistical and ideal norms. Even if one

---

[1] Cited in I. Eibl-Eibesfeldt (1970a). *Love and Hate*: "On sodomy, Kinsey writes 'There are reports of individuals raised on farms living in continual fear of the discovery of their past. The physician who can assure these individuals that their activity is biologically and physiologically a component of normal behavioral patterns of mammals and that contact occurs in such a great proportion of the male rural population, can contribute substantially to the resolution of these conflicts'. Apart from the fact that this line of reasoning is unsound, it is also a false statement that comparable behavior in mammals be a normal one. In free living wild animals we know neither interspecific copulation nor homosexuality. We can use imprinting to produce such manifestations artificially."

day 80% of the population were to suffer from a disturbed insulin metabolism, we would scarcely hesitate to acknowledge an increase in diabetes, and we would certainly not characterize the minority not requiring injections as abnormal or sick. The ideal norm is measured with the yardstick of adaptedness. Statistical norms tell us nothing about the way conditions should be.

The fact that mankind in cultural evolution has, to some extent, overcome biological evolution results in biological norms occasionally conflicting with cultural ones. Thus the war ethic conflicts with the innate killing inhibition, and the state ethic can be in conflict with the familial one (p. 621). The case can then arise when biological norms must submit to cultural ones, and self-control must prevail for higher purposes against our deeply rooted biological tendencies.

Thus, self-control is often esteemed as outstanding moral behavior, as when a man sacrifices himself for his people, placing group interests above those of the family. This process can lead to a perversion of morals. Abraham's sacrifice symbolically makes obedience one of the highest values. A new ethic appearing with the rise of states stands in conflict with the archaic small group ethic, a topic to which we shall return.

Value conflicts also occur on another level. State interests and humanitarian values are often in conflict, and crimes against humanity are not infrequently committed under the guise of a good cause, using such slogans as "true belief," "the creation of a new humanity," "new society," "freedom," "equality," or "fraternity." That virtues can be turned into nonvirtues by this process is related to the fact that in our naive standard, good and evil are conceived of as an opposing pair. This contrast creates clearcut categories but also reinforces our tendency to classify values along a one-dimensional scale to extreme values. Charity is a virtue and we are inclined to believe: the more charitable the better. We thereby overlook the fact that biological norms follow an optimality priniciple and adaptiveness decreases on both sides as values move away from the optimal mean (W. Wickler, 1971). Thus every virtue can also be polarized into a vice, whether it be courage, self-sacrifice, or charity.

In World War II the Nazis exaggerated courage and obedience in a one-sided way, to a point in fact in which there was no longer any consideration of other values. This occurred particularly at a loss of charity and humanity, which command us to consider even our enemies as human beings. The simultaneous elitist attitude led to the murder of fellow humans who either thought otherwise or belonged to other ethnic groups. This deplorable exaggeration of agonal virtues led to the holocaust and other crimes against humanity, thus planting the seeds of mistrust from which mankind has yet to recover.

Today the Western world, presumably in counterreaction to one-sided emphasis of elitism and of heroic virtues, is now inclined to polarize affiliative virtues in a similar way. The desired effect of a harmonious coexistence of people is, however, not achieved by such an exaggeration, much to the surprise of the altruist. Thus, foreign aid is often perceived by those receiving help as just another form of colonialism. Why is this so? We have repeatedly demonstrated that sharing and giving are universal strategies of bonding. It is beneficial to give, and all people have an ethic of sharing and giving. The generous individual is esteemed among the Bushmen, Yanomami, and Eipo, but if one is too generous, his act creates the unfavorable impression that he considers himself above others. This occurs in many other cultures as well—overly generous giving is perceived as an attempt to achieve dominance or as an act of stupidity. The bonding effect of giving is based upon reciprocity. If someone receives too much, his partner cannot reciprocate adequately and is then shamed. In this context, giving can become an aggressive act. In the potlatch (p. 308) generous giving and hospitality is geared at humbling the guests in a competition. This is perhaps one of the reasons why, when the rich industrialized states provide aid to Third World nations, they often do not receive appreciation in return, but instead elicit rejection and envy. Assistance that the supported partner cannot return arouses comparable discomfort. No one wants to be indebted to another, and the dominance created by this kind of aid leads to eventual withdrawal from the relationship.

Charity and generosity are virtues, but if an optimum level is exceeded they can become vices—however benevolent the intentions of the giver may be. Only the parent–child relationship is an exception, for it is not based primarily upon reciprocity. However, if this kind of relationship develops among adults, one of the partners falls into a tutelage role. This is also true in principle for excessive social services within a government. There is such a thing as too much of a good thing, of an "excess of virtue," which does not imply ignoble intentions on the part of those rendering the services. The well-meaning social aid organizations within a country can develop to the extent that may restrict individual freedom and personal initiative and replace some of the obligations that people have to one another.

Well meaning does not necessarily imply well doing. Often our fixation upon proximate causes leads to unintended results, as is frequently the case of "do-gooders." Thus it is appropriate to send medicine, foods, and other materials to regions struck by catastrophes. But sending food as relief into countries with chronic starvation due to overpopulation will worsen the problem. Here additional aid as in the form of educational programs to curb overpopulation must be considered.

Failure to inquire into consequences is not only a characteristic of our primary emotionally based ethics. Culturally developed attitudes are also frequently followed in a blind manner under the influence of emotions of loyalty. Max Weber (1919, rev. 1981) thus distinguished between an ethics of intention that does not ask about consequences and an opposing ethics of responsibility. Those ascribing to the former ethical system act out of conviction, and if the consequences of their actions are deleterious, they do not assume any responsibility for this because they acted out of virtuous motives. They feel that the world is responsible for such outcomes, as is the imperfection of fellow humans due to their lack of insight, and perhaps God's will. This does not mean that one would feel absolutely no responsibility, but that feelings of accountability are removed from the practical level of human interaction, such as by those who maintain the flame of protest against social injustice. In contrast, those adhering to an ethic of responsibility consider human weakness and they also accept the responsibilities of the consequences of their own actions.

Which means justify which ends? How can we arrive at a decision when there is a conflict of norms? Are there ends which should always receive priority?

Attempts to deal with these questions extend back to antiquity. Members of ancient cultures invoked the gods and used intuitive knowledge of good and evil, but they also searched for some rational basis of norms. Aspects of expediency were considered as was the concept of reciprocity, whereby social stability, individual happiness, and the general welfare were the primary objectives.

Rationalism and the subsequent constructivism assumed that man has insightfully formulated the structures of society and culture and that mankind can therefore modify these institutions on the basis of new insights and in adaptation to new contingencies. Voltaire wrote: "If you want to have good laws, burn those you have and make new ones" (cited in F.A. von Hayek, 1979b). Only that which we recognize as rationally conceived purpose should be duly recognized. The assertion that our code of morality be a rational invention has been repeated into the present, as in P. Singer (1981), a viewpoint F.A. von Hayek rightfully contests. Many of our cultural habits arose without reflection or conscious insight, simply because they were effective. Culture, according to von Hayek, is neither natural nor artificial, neither genetically transmitted nor planned out rationally. "It is a tradition of learned rules of behavior that was never invented and whose purposes are mainly not understood by the individual" (F.A. von Hayek, 1979, p. 10). And finally he goes so far as to maintain that we are not even in a position to plan culture: "Our brain is an organ that is capable of accepting cultural values but not to formulate them" (p. 15). This is, of course, a provocative position and should not be interpreted to mean that any rational attempts to devise appropriate behavior are in vain. But von Hayek points out that many cultural norms were not formulated out of insight but exist because in competition with others they proved adaptive, and that selection makes the final decision on sifting out cultural practices. Thus culture in its entirety cannot be fully planned rationally. This does not mean that we have to accept blindly what is handed down to us. One can and should test cultural values for their functions. Certainly we must be carrying some cultural excess baggage as a historical burden.

However, an absolute questioning of all values would lead to the destruction of culture (see the discussion on breaking tradition, p. 15). In this connection von Hayek criticizes the destruction of values through "scientific error." He cites Canadian psychiatrist George Brock Chisholm, who acted as general secretary of the World Health Organization for 5 years and then as first president of the World Federation of Mental Health—clearly a figure of international esteem. In his writing, Chisholm indicates his desire to eliminate the concept of right and wrong (1946, p. 9):

> The reinterpretation and eventually eradication of the concept of right and wrong which has been the basis of child training, the substitution of intelligent and rational thinking for faith in the certainties of the old people, these are the belated objectives of practically all effective psychotherapy. . . . The suggestion that we should stop teaching children moralities and rights and wrongs and instead protect their original intellectual integrity has of course to be met by an outcry of heretic or iconoclast, such as was raised against Galileo for finding another planet. . . . If the race is to be freed from its crippling burden of good and evil, it must be psychiatrists who take the original responsibility. This is a challenge which must be met. . . . With the other human sciences psychiatry must now decide what is to be the immediate future of the human race. No one else can. . . .

One cannot exactly say that Chisholm is troubled with modesty. What should be fostered is a critical examination of values, not a blank rejection of them. Biology can offer help in this regard. First, it brings the knowledge of our phylogenetic development, demonstrating the temporal dimensions of specific norms and their firm genetic basis. We have emphasized that mankind need not obey blindly these primary norms which can provide us with a frame of reference, setting limits to attempts to modify human behavior and thus have a positive regulatory effect against excessively cold intellectual planning. We do have sympathy for others, and if we fail to render someone support we experience pangs of conscience. Only upon a superficial examination could one come to the viewpoint of cultural relativism, namely, that everything is relative. True, infanticide is considered to be a crime in our society, while it is necessary in some tribal societies. At this level there are cultural differences. But we have shown that no society is known where mothers kill their own children lightheartedly (p. 194), for an inhibition against killing must be overcome. At this level a universal norm predisposes us to act in certain ways and I am certainly not alone in my feeling when I attach a higher value to this biological norm than on any cultural one indoctrinating us that killing a fellow man is a virtue.

Our innate inhibitions against killing are also dampened in war. A cultural norm making killing a duty is superimposed upon the biological one forbidding murder, and this results in killing actually becoming a virtue. However, a massive indoctrination is required to make this superimposition, during the course of which the enemy is portrayed as a nonhuman. Killing also becomes easier through the use of long-distance weaponry. However, the biological norms are not completely eradicated, for norm conflicts still occur, which we experience in the form of a guilty conscience.

In this sense we can consider ourselves fortunate that not all norms are culturally relative and that by no means only that behavior designated as "good" by the ideologists need be executed. The biological norm of an inhibition against killing is no doubt one of the bases of our yearning for peace. Naturally there is also an emotion of fear of the consequences of war. The desire for peace, however, is older than the atomic bomb (I. Eibl-Eibesfeldt, 1975a). Other important biological norms include the object possession norm, which we discussed previously and which is the basis of the commandment, "Thou shalt not steal," and the partner possession norm commanding us to respect partner attachments. We also mentioned that sincerity, loyalty, and obedience have their biological roots as well as the fact that not all our innate norms are still adaptive today (the intolerance toward outsiders is a particularly apt example). Here we must check "healthy public opinion" by humane reasoning and either suppress our inherited tendencies or vent them in a harmless manner.

But how should a person make a decision in a conflict between two primary norms—such as a conflict between obedience and sympathy (p. 311)? And how does one behave when a cultural norm is contradicted by a biological one?

Ranking between biological norms shift according to mood and external circumstances—at a given time arousing charitable tendencies, and at another time lending more weight to obedience. In the studies of S. Milgram on obedience (p. 311), the presence or absence of an authority proved to be a decisive variable. Education to be critical of authority may help to gain more self-control.

But in order to set the standards, we need to agree first about out *ultimate* goals. The *final* goal, without doubt, is survival. Populations that do not survive genetically remain only as part of the fossil record. Although today we must use rational—but also humane—planning to control our number of descendents we must also assure our survival. No one can reasonably propound an ethic of genetic suicide.

However, we must guard ourselves from ethical relativism when we argue genetically, in the form that some sociobiologists have suggested.[2] If one proceeds from the thesis that the units of selection are the individual and his blood relatives, then each person behaves correctly in representing his own interest exclusively, and this applies to broad spans of evolution. But at that moment when the group becomes the unit of selection, this strategy only holds in a restricted sense. Communities up to the size of modern nation-states form common interest groups without which the individual could not even survive. If someone harms the group to which he belongs, he may achieve a short-term advantage, but if his genome spreads, or if his inconsiderate behavior becomes traditionalized, group fitness will decrease and eventually lead to the extinction even of those few individuals who are loyal to the group. While Tinbergen's herring gulls behave "adaptively," when they kill the young of their neighbors in the same brood colony, displacing competitors for their own young, corresponding human behavior would be expressly maladaptive since group interests are as important as those of the individual, and selection is operating in a two-step process—on the individual as well as on the group level. However, it certainly does not operate on the species level. "Mankind" is not a natural category but an invention of our civilization. It reflects a high ethical standard and it could achieve meaning on the basis of reciprocity and finally culminate in a worldwide federation of otherwise independent ethnic communities. But every one of these communities will have first to look after its own legitimate interests. Were one to sacrifice these in the interest of "mankind" this would certainly not be in correspondence with nature nor with the Kantian imperative; it would have to be labeled maladaptive.

Thus far survival has meant competition on both the individual and group levels which often was fierce, particularly that between groups. This does not necessarily imply that it must continue in this manner. Man can set himself goals and strive toward their achievement. Thus, to survive in harmony with others is one goal which modern man has set for himself. Are we biologically prepared to achieve this goal on a worldwide basis or are there dispositions against it? And, if so, how might they be overcome? Between sacrificing oneself or one's group in an altruistic act and between the ruthless attitude of a "my country right or wrong" there must exist a humane solution.

The problem as well as our hope came into the world with the evolution of the affiliative sociality (p. 167). With the evolution of maternal care, friendliness came into the world as well as love. This new social potential to bond man in groups also introduced new problems, since with love discrimination came into existence. We distinguish between ingroup and outgroup members and thus between two

---

[2]R. D. Masters (1982, p. 284) tends to base ethical norms of humans on an individual selection level: "In the economists model of market behavior, as in the strategists theory of games or the political economists model of collective goods, no single substantive preference or way of life is 'good' in itself. Rather, moral and ethical standards are derived from the interests and advantages of individuals—not vice versa. . . . Again, evolutionary biology follows a similar tradition. For animals, as for humans, the inclusive fitness theorist does not usually argue that there is but one 'natural' way of life (Alexander, 1978). Such concepts as 'species benefit' have been replaced by analysis of costs and benefits to individuals, and since individual organisms vary depending on environment and life experience, there seems to be no single 'way' for all animals—and still all humans—to behave 'properly' (R. D. Masters, 1980a, 1981). In practical terms, neither traditional theology nor any single culture standard of social worth can claim to be the 'natural' basis for moral or political values."

categories of conspecifics. Our relations to ingroup members are characterized by basic trust and affiliation and where competition between group members occurs, it is controlled in such a way that escalation into destructive aggression is avoided. Against outgroup members, agonal behaviors predominate and since no affiliative bonds exist, competition can escalate into destructive group aggression. In our relations to group members we tend to experience a graded loyalty with family and kin coming first. The emotional attachment to nonfamily members of the small group is the result of a long development over time—getting to know somebody and trust them because their behavior became predictable for us and we know what they will and will not do. But even in tribal societies, kindness and reciprocity with group members is and needs to be constantly reinforced, otherwise individual interest takes over. Thus in the !Kung Bushmen a very strong socialization and sanctions help to maintain appropriate reciprocity with others (P. Wiessner, 1977).

The historical development of tribes and states has shown, however, that man's ability to identify sympathetically with other members of the ingroup on the basis of an extended family ethos preadapts him to identify with members of an anonymous society, provided that these are characterized by many features in common, indicating a shared relatedness. Relatedness, is often emphasized culturally by custom and by a shared ideology. Since Man, during his long history, was selected to give priority to both individual and kin interest, the interest of the larger group must be constantly emphasized by indoctrination and nepotism must be counteracted.

The state-ethos tries to reverse the natural hierarchy of graded loyalty, in which the family comes first, by teaching that the larger groups (tribe, state) come first. "Gemeinnutz geht vor Eigennutz" is still a widespread slogan of our times. Thus in Mao's China, children who acused their parents of disobedience to the party direction were officially praised. The dramas of the Greeks and the Germanic sagas are filled with the conflict between loyalty to family (kin) and to the group; they describe the loyalty to the group (represented by the princes) as the higher value (E. R. McDonald, 1981).[3] Furthermore there are legal regulations established for the sake of the protection of the group interests, since we feel less obligated to the group and to our unknown fellow citizens than to our acquaintances and relatives. This is the reason that public property is usually treated more carelessly than personal possessions. A farmer wishes to preserve his private meadow and will not raise too many cattle, but on a collective meadow the farmer will attempt to graze as many cattle as he possibly can. This situation is known as the "tragedy of the commoners" (G. Hardin, 1968). We can observe it in all spheres of mass society, even on a global scale. Think, for example, of the pollution of the biosphere and the reckless exploitation of resources.

The so-called "civic spirit" as a prerequisite for responsible behavior in the anonymous society has to be taught, which is a tedious process, since individual and small group interests normally outweigh these community considerations. The

---

[3]Hegel (cited in A. Gehlen, 1969, p. 123) interprets in this sense the story of the matricide of Orestes. Agamemnon as king sacrifices his daughter in the interest of the Greeks, rupturing the band of familial love that joined him with his daughter and his wife Clytemnestra. Clytemnestra avenges herself on her homeward bound husband. Her son Orestes adores her, but is compelled–we would say for state reasons–to kill his mother as a representative of his father's rights.

problem lies in the right balance between individual and group interests; this balance must be adaptive. One can suppress individual interests in times of emergency, but certainly not easily eradicate them, since selection has worked at the level of the individual and the small group. It is our generalist individuality that constitutes a basic characteristic of man. We could never have appropriate group action if it were not moderated by individual interest.

The balance is often threatened, however. Too much state control can take place in social welfare states, as well as under repressive totalitarian regimes. We discussed the potential dangers involved when individuality is repressed for too long. The welfare state, in particular, has its appeal, since the infantile side in us responds positively to being taken care of. One might reasonably argue that the individuality rooted in our human nature will resist deindividualization in the long run. But we do not know how fast selection operates in Man. We know, however, that our reproductive pattern can change quite dramatically from one generation to another. It is therefore not at all improbable that conditions could obtain that the individualistic members of the society might become depressed to the extent that their willingness to reproduce would decrease dramatically. Such a change in the selective conditions would, of course, have long-term consequences.

If familial values become emphasized one-sidedly, the cohesion of the state may suffer even to the extent of disintegration. In his monograph on "Moral and Hypermoral," A. Gehlen makes the point that the behavior of males and females is determined by the emphasis on different aspects of familial values. Man, as the more expressedly territorial being, draws borders in the cultural and territorial realm, and is prepared to defend them vigorously, in combat if necessary.[4] Female values complement these with opposing priorities: peace, the protection of life, welfare, and the wish for security determine their thinking and conduct. They give priority to the family ethics of peace which conflicts with certain survival needs of the states in an armed world. Gehlen writes:

> Pacifism, the disposition for security and comfort, the immediate interest in sympathetic human detail, government indifference, the readiness to receive objects and people, as they come, are all qualities with their original and legitimate locus in the lap of the family and which are now colored strongly by feminism, since the woman bears instinctively in all her values the interests of her children, the concern for nest warmth, for reduced risks and for welfare. Here the preconditions are set for an endless widening of humanitarianism and eudaimonism if the counter weights of the state ethic are compromised, forbidden or deteriorate (A. Gehlen, 1969, p. 149).

Gehlen refers here to "moral hypertrophy" but also shows that those promoting such viewpoints endorse the state as the preserver of values, and claim that worldwide fraternity can only develop in a pluralistic world with different governments lest a world-dominating dictatorship existed.

The development of ethics of welfare and the ethics of sympathy of the modern western world, which makes all kinds of charity an obligation under the catchword of a worldwide humanitarianism, transforms the state from the guardian of rights to a milk cow. Gehlen points at some interesting historical parallels in this regard. The growth of Greek humanism occurred in their late development period following

---

[4]A study by M. R. Ford and C. R. Lowery (1986) demonstrates that women are indeed more attuned to issues of care and men more attuned to issues of justice, but certainly not in an exclusive way.

horrible wars along their trading routes. In Alexander's era the issues between Barbars and Hellenes were settled; other positive developments took place as well: enemy cities were no longer destroyed, prisoners were released, and women gained increasing influence in politics. Good will toward others became a matter of public discussion. Slaves were offered protection, and social welfare and humane treatment of animals developed. But state interests were pushed into the background, and group loyalty languished as the overburdened state moved toward bankruptcy. Thus, a period of deterioration began. Similar occurrences took place in Rome under Marcus Aurelius, where again a period of prosperity and humanitarian gestures meant the downfall of the state due to their one-sided policies.

Once again we are confronted with the previously cited question of balance. The heroic, inhumane period of history is often followed by a humanitarian phase, but with an excess to the other extreme. This need not happen, for humanitarian and state interests are not necessarily contradictory. Imbalance occurs when the concern for the momentary gains in common welfare lead to neglect of long-term state needs. We thus bear an inheritance that Herbert Spencer cited in his "Principles of Ethics." The conflict results from the fact that all societies are compelled to defend themselves against outsiders while maintaining internal peace.

This necessity results in contrasting feelings arising among group members, an enemy ethic and one of friendship in joint coexistence, which can then lead to contradictions in values.

Is there any chance that we can overcome the agonal intergroup ethics of the closed group? An artificial homogenization and equalization of Mankind would require quite repressive measures of a world dictatorship. It would have to work against our strong urge toward differentiation (see cultural pseudospeciation, p. 15). It seems more promising, therefore, to strive toward peaceful coexistence of different ethnic groups. In order to achieve this we have to counteract our inborn tendencies of interethnic attempts of domination and thus try to take the sting from ethnocentrism. But what are the chances of peaceful pluri-ethnic coexistence?

Since, on the basis of reciprocity, even different animal species can engage in mutualistic relationships, there is no reason why different racial and ethnic groups should not be able to work out mutualistic relations. There is, of course, one major problem to be faced: Mutualistic relations between different animal species exist as a rule only in species that do not compete for the same resources. Interethnic and interracial relations are, at the outset, competitive. History teaches us, however, that different ethnic groups can bond together in alliances. So far they only have done this against a common enemy, but to conclude from that, that a common enemy is a prerequisite for such an alliance is not justified. Common concerns can serve to bond in a similar way, and certainly there are common interests. Thus we share a concern about our future. The degradation of our environment and, in particular, the exploitation and pollution of such common resources as water and air is a problem that demands a solution on a global basis.

The prevailing ethic until now has been oriented to issues of the moment. The future was considered assured by religion in the form of reward or punishment. But until now, the prevailing values have been individual fortune and general welfare. There have been a number of instrumental values derived for the pursuit of these goals on the basis of their usefulness. This includes the previously cited principle of reciprocity, upon which Thomas Hobb's based in *De Cive* a number of "natural laws," including maintaining contracts that have been signed, not

715

breaking one's word, being amiable, and more. They are to some extent "naturally" insightful since they are based, in part, upon innate programs of reciprocity (p. 357). Immanuel Kant's challenge to "behave only according to those maxims that you wish were general laws" is based upon considerations of usefulness and reciprocity. Social contracts based on reciprocity also include sanctions against those who do not reciprocate according to expectations. The family ethos provided the emotional basis for the cultural development of a state ethos. In a similar way, it should be possible to use our concern for our children to develop an ethics for future generations to come. Our long-term survival depends upon responsible planning with personal restriction, if necessary, for the sake of our children and grandchildren. Current discussions are moving in this direction (P. A. Corning, 1976), but we are far from internalizing all these values.

In the *New York Times Magazine* (19 January, 1975), Robert Heilbronner wrote:

> Will mankind survive? . . . Who cares? It is clear that most of us today do not care—or at least do not care enough. How many of us would be willing to give up some minor convenience—say the use of aerosols—in the hope that this might extend the life of man on earth by a hundred years? Suppose we knew with a high degree of certainty that humankind would not survive a thousand years unless we gave up our wasteful diet of meat, abandon all pleasure driving, cut back on every use of energy that was not essential to the maintenance of a bare minimum. Would we care enough for posterity to pay the price of its survival? I doubt it.

However it does not follow from this that we must despair on this point and that there is no chance of developing a survival ethic. There are already a great many individuals engaged in this direction. The calls of Rachel Carson (1962) did not go unheard. I recall in this context the principal human disposition to assume cultural values. While our "indoctrinability" has its problematic aspects, it also has its positive side.

Preserving the biosphere and the securing of world peace (i.e., harmonizing state relations) are prerequisites for assuring the future. A third world war has been avoided so far. But we live in a "peace through fear," as H. Portisch (1970) has expressed it; or in ethological terms through display, a kind of ritualized fighting. Unlike most ritualized fighting though, the weapons of display are deadly. Peace is endangered, since fear often becomes transformed into aggression when it exceeds a certain level. Even a mouse will strike (fear biting) when it is driven into a corner and its critical distance has been exceeded. One must also consider that in the present arms race a distinct military advantage could provoke one side to deliver a preventative strike (C. F. von Weizsäcker, 1977). We must reach peace through trust, for distrust is presently our greatest problem and disturbs international relations. The countless breaches of trust of the last two world wars are the reason for this situation.

Kant demanded that even in war situations opponents must behave in a predictable way, otherwise they would not be able to restore peace. In order to make peace, some trust must exist. The mistrust sown by the numerous violations of the Geneva Convention during World War II overshadows even today the relations between Eastern and Western Europe. Reestablishing trust must have priority. In order to achieve this goal we must again become accustomed to abide by the truth in everyday political life, which must start in one's own country. Most unfortunately, the political lie has become an accepted strategy. Deceit is with us and destroys the vestiges of trust in our anonymous society. How should Man build trust in modern mass society if he learns daily that politicians make one announcement today and reverse this decision tomorrow.

I find several comments by H. Mohr (1979) especially appropriate here; he states that the political lie, intellectual seduction, and primitive manipulation must give way to a politics based upon insightful rationality and intellectual decency. This kind of political ethics ought to be instrumentally conceived after the model of the scientific ethics, which today is the sole cultural universal ethical system. It is based upon the assumption of scientific realism, the notion of freedom of thought and freedom for research, and further on the assumption that insight is good and that reliable knowledge is superior to ignorance. To achieve this goal certain requirements are necessary: one must be honest, undogmatic, precise, fair and without bias, continually attempt to solve a problem, test alternatives, reject no information and make no compromises, use empirical data as the final arbiter, and other requirements such as to be precise in one's statements.

A similar partial ethos could be formulated for political life as well, but Mohr rightfully stresses that the postulate of optimal societal rationality of the human being may not be a reasonable demand. Wherever individual freedom is threatened, there are limits to rationalism. But that does not appear to be compelling to me. An ethical system oriented toward our survival and thus on the maintenance of evolutionary potential can also be the rational basis of individualism and plurality. The challenge for decency in the political sphere must become a primary one. The political lie must be taboo just as the dehumanization of one's political opponent; other standards to be demanded are rational and honest argumentation, the breaking down of communication barriers, for which the guarantee of one's self-esteem via a feeling of membership in the community is a prerequisite (since only from a position of self-certainty is a person friendly without fear). The common desire to survive should be able to bond people above individual concerns, and from this bond a survival ethic could be developed that would lead to peace. We are presented with tasks calling for cooperation, and cooperative efforts have a bonding effect. No single state is in the sole position to resolve the problems of overpopulation, resource exhaustion, and environmental pollution. Our absolute involvement for our children could be the common starting point for our efforts. How would it be if we made symbolic partnerships to guarantee the welfare of the children of other nations. These could lead to personal attachments. This makes use of the human trait of dismantling enmity by means of personal acquaintance. The prerequisite for this is the respect for the diversity of cultures and people in their own way of life, and the recognition of the existence of different value systems. In short, tolerance in the sense of understanding without necessarily instilling one's own values judgmentally is what is required here. In contrast, the cultivation of an ethnic plurality, as repeatedly emphasized herein, is an essential means of assuring our future.

Summary 10

Man behaves morally out of emotional engagement, custom, and, finally, out of thoughtful consideration. Some of the values (norms), which function as sets of control systems in which the rules for ideal conduct are laid down as normative reference patterns, are the result of phylogenetic adaptations.

We can distinguish general virtues, such as self-control, and the more specific virtues such as those belonging to the agonal system (heroic virtues) and those belonging to the affiliative system serving bonding (charity, sharing ethics, etc.). The danger of maladaptive behavior derives from Man's inclination to one-sided exaggeration of virtues which at times becomes a fadlike obsession. This way every virtue can be turned into a vice, asceticism being but one example. In our times, agonal virtues became exaggerated at the cost of humanitarian values. In response, an all-encompassing ideology of charity may endanger the future identity and survival of those who practice it, were it not finally controlled by reason and the insight that survival of one's own offspring is still what counts.

An orientation toward survival value is important for the rational development of norms. By inclination Man shows a graded loyalty according to closeness—loyalty to family and kin is spontaneous and unquestioned. Here a preparedness for unreflected altruism was selected for. This familial ethos is extended to other members of the group. In tribal societies, where the groups are small, emotional attachment, sympathy, and trust grow over time. The extension of the familial ethos to members of our modern anonymous state-societies meets with difficulties. Indoctrination works via emphasis of similarities that bond, common origin (the mystic roots), and, in times of emergency, the state ethos indoctrinates to give priority to the interests of the community before those of the family. Thus the natural order of loyalty becomes reversed. Even at the small group level, rituals of sharing and giving are needed to constantly reinforce the bond between the members and sanctions against those who do not obey the established rules, are invoked.

With the evolution of affiliative behavior and love, discrimination between in-group and outgroup members came into existence. This has spurred human evolution, but also was the source of suffering. Even though Mankind does not exist as a natural entity, but only as competing human populations (local populations, tribes, ethnic groups, nation-states), the idea of humanitarian concern for all people is based on the reciprocal obligation, stemming from the knowledge that everything which characterizes us as human beings was passed on to us from the multitude of people that lived before us. A social contract on the basis of reciprocity could remove fear and unite Mankind on a federal basis of independent groups and nations.

A survival ethic must instill a sense of responsibility for the survival of future generations. Only then will Mankind be prepared to use resources with care and strive toward a cooperative world community of peoples.

Conclusion

Arnold Gehlen described man as the "risked being." This is an apt characterization of the human condition. Our chances of failure are great, but so are our possibilities for further development. The thought that a species that has become so conscious of itself that it can plan its future and might not take advantage of this chance is extremely disturbing. The creature that is sufficiently gifted to reach for the stars is close to extinguishing itself in murderous competition.

Our handicap is, in part, derived from the fact that those phylogenetic adaptations which mold our behavior evolved over a long period during which our ancestors lived in small individualized communities as hunters and gatherers. We have not greatly changed our biological heritage over the past ten thousand years. Through cultural evolution, however, we have radically altered our natural and social environment and in doing so have created a world for which we are not biologically made. This does not mean that we are entirely unfit for the modern anonymous society, but that we have to adapt to it culturally. An awareness of phylogenetic molding that can cause maladaptive behavioral tendencies will help us to achieve these necessary adaptations. I would like to emphasize this point since biologists are often accused of fostering a "biological fatalism." This is a criticism that certainly cannot be aimed at all proponents of the discipline.

In order to avoid the pitfalls of our phylogenetic adaptations, however, we must be aware that men with the emotional baggage of stone age hunter-gatherers today engage in private car races on the highways, and, as leaders of the superpowers, control weapons and armies capable of igniting the world. Man's striving for power is particularly problematical since it is not turned off by biological control mechanisms as are, for example, hunger and thirst when the organism is satiated. The power that one person could acquire in a stone age community was as limited as his technical means. Therefore there was no selection pressure operating to limit his drive. Our striving for power is insatiable. Added to this is the problem that we show less concern for Man in the anonymous society in which individual interest often predominates. People are much more inclined to behave ruthlessly toward those they do not know.

Just as in the past there was no need for biologically based restraints to restrict the drive for power, there was little pressure for limitations on Man's exploitation of the environment. Only recently, with rapid population explosion, has man become aware of the need to treat his environment with more care.

I hope that I have made it clear that most ethologists do not claim that our nature cannot be modified, but to the contrary that our hope rests in our propensities for culture. In addition, we do not claim that our human nature has priority over culture and thus is or should be normative. I have repeatedly pointed out that most adaptive traits can become maladaptive in excess or in certain situations.

In order to cope with our present situation, we have, however, to take our biological heritage into consideration. And when I point to our strong disposition for obedience, I do not do it to justify obedience that leads to crimes, but to point out its dangers in order to find measures to counteract them. In his excellent book, "The Tangled Wing," Melvin Konner wrote "The content of this book can be dangerous" to warn of the possibility that biological knowledge can be used to justify inhumane political measures. I fully accept his warning, but as W. Charlesworth said: "No knowledge is really safe against abuse, and still knowledge is better than ignorance" (p. 101).

We cannot plan evolution, but we can set goals. Life in a society of responsible individuals would be one such goal, and it would correspond to our concept of a higher humanity. We would be in a position emotionally and intellectually to develop a survival ethic opening such perspectives. Processes of self-organization on a supraindividual level may, however, endanger the creative freedom of the individual and thus the evolutionary potential of mankind. The comfort of an extremely regulated life could lead to a state in which every action would be regulated. We would then be integrated into a functional structure of a higher order and lose our generalist individuality.

Bibliography

Abbott, L. (1975). Paternal Touch of the Newborn: Its Role in Paternal Attachment. Thesis, Boston University, Boston, MA.

Abramovitch, R. (1976). The relation of attention and proximity to dominance in pre-school children. *In:* Chance, M. R. A. and Larsen, R. R. (eds.), The Social Structure of Attention. London: Wiley, pp. 153–177.

—— (1980). Attention structures in hierarchically organized groups. *In:* Omark, D. R., Strayer, F. F., and Freedman, D. G. (eds.), Dominance Relations. New York/London: Garland STPM Press, pp. 381–396.

Adams, J. P. (1964). Adolescent personal problems as a function of age and sex. *J. Genet. Psychol.* **104,** 207–214.

Addiego, F., Belzer, E., Comolli, J., Moger, W., Perry, J., and Whipple, B. (1981). Female ejaculation: A case study. *J. Sex. Res.* **17,** 13–21.

Adler, Ch. (1977). Mechanismen der Gruppenbindung. Aggression und Aggressionskontrolle der Eskimos im Thuledistrikt. Diss. München.

Ahrens, R. (1954). Beiträge zur Entwicklung des Physiognomie-und Mimikerkennens. *Z. Exp. Angew. Psychol.* **2,** 412–454.

Ainsworth, M. D. S. (1963). The development of infant-mother interaction among the Ganda. *In:* Foss, B. M. (ed.), Determinants of Infant Behavior, London: Methuen, pp. 67–104.

—— (1967). Infancy in Uganda: Infant Care and the Growth of Love. Baltimore, MD: John Hopkins University Press.

—— (1969). Object relations, dependency and attachment: A theoretical review of the infant–mother relationship. *Child Develop.* **40,** 969–1025.

—— (1973). The development of infant-mother attachment. *In:* Caldwell, B. M. and Ricciuti, H. N. (eds.), Child Development Research. Chicago: The University of Chicago Press, pp. 1–95.

—— (1977). Attachment theory and its utility in cross-cultural research. *In:* Leiderman, P. H., Tulkin, St. R., and Rosenfeld, A. (eds.), Culture and Infancy, Variations in the Human Experience. New York/London: Academic Press, pp. 49–67.

Aldis, O. (1975). Play Fighting. New York: Academic Press.

Alexander, R. D. (1974). The evolution of social behavior. *Ann. Rev. Ecol. Syst.* **5,** 325–383.

—— (1977). Natural selection and the analysis of human sociality. *In:* Goulden, C. E. (ed.), The Changing Scenes in the Natural Sciences, 1776–1976. Philadelphia: Academy of Nat. Sciences (Sp. Publ. 12), pp. 283–337.

—— (1978). Natural selection and social laws. *In:* Engelhardt, T. and Callahan, D. (eds.), Morals, Science, and Society, Vol. 3. Hastings-on-Hudson, NY: Hastings Ctr. Inst. Soc.

—— (1979). Evolution and culture. *In:* Chagnon, N. A. and Irons, W. (eds.), Evolutionary Biology and Human Social Behavior: An Anthropological Perspective. North Scituate, MA: Duxbury Press, pp. 59–79. (a)

—— (1979). Evolution, social behavior, and ethics. *In:* Engelhardt, T. and Callahan, D. (eds.), The Foundations of Ethics and Its Relationship to Science, Vol. 4. Hastings-on-Hudson, NY: The Hastings Center, pp. 124–155. (b)

—— (1979). Darwinism and Human Affairs. Seattle: University of Washington Press. (c)

—— (1987). The Biology of Moral Systems. New York: Aldine de Gruyter.

Alland, A. (1972). Cultural evolution: The Darwinian model. *Social Biol.* **19,** 227–239.

Alland, A. and McCay, B. (1973). The Concept of Adaptation in Biological and Cultural Evolution. *In:* Honigman, J. (ed.), Handbook of Social and Cultural Anthropology. Chicago: Rand McNally, pp. 142–178.

Allemann-Tschopp, G. (1978). Geschlechtsrollen. Bern: Hans Huber.

—— (1979). Geschlechtsrollen. Versuch einer interdisziplinären Synthese. Bern/Stuttgart/Wien: Hans Huber.

Allen, D. E. and Guy, R. F. (1974). Conversion Analysis. The Sociology of Talk. The Hague: Mouton Press.

Allesch, G. J. von (1931). Die nicht-euklidische Struktur des phänomenalen Raumes. Jena.

Almagor, U. (1977). Raiders and Elders: A Confrontation of Generations among the Dassanetch. *In:* Fukui, K. and Turton, D. (eds.), Warfare among East African Herders. Senri Ethnological Studies, No. 3, Museum of Ethnology. Japan: Osaka Press, pp. 119–145.

Als, H. (1977). The newborn communicates. *J. Commun.* **27,** 66–73.

Als, H., Tronick, E. and Brazelton, T. B. (1979). Analysis of face-to-face interaction in infant-adult dyads. *In:* Lamb, M. E., Suomi, S. J., and Stephenson, G. R. (eds.), Social Interaction Analysis: Methodological Issues. Madison: Univ. of Wisconsin Press, pp. 33–76.

Alt, F. (1983). Frieden ist möglich. Die Politik der Bergpredigt. München: Piper.

Altman, I. (1975). The Environmental and Social Behavior. Monterey, CA: Brooks/Cole Publ. Comp.

Altmann, J. (1974). Observational study of behavior: Sampling methods. *Behaviour* **49**, 227–265.

Amato, P. R. (1983). The effects of urbanization on interpersonal behavior. Field studies in Papua New Guinea. *J. Cross-Cultural Psychol.* **14**, 353–367.

Ambrose, J. A. (1960). The Smiling and Related Responses in Early Human Infancy. An Experimental and Theoretical Study of their Course and Significance. University of London, Ph. D. Dissert. Vol. 2.

— (1961). The development of the smiling response in early infancy. *In:* Foss, B. M. (ed.), Determinants of Infant Behaviour, Vol. I. London: Methuen, pp. 179–196.

— (1969). Stimulation in Early Infancy. London: Academic Press.

Amoore, J. E., Pelosi, P., and Forrester, L. J. (1977). Specific anosmias to 5α-Androst-16-en-3-one and w-pentadecalactone: The urinous and musky primary odours. *Chem. Senses Flavour* **2**, 401–425.

Amoore, J. E., Popplewell, J. R., and Whissell-Buechy, D. (1975). Sensitivity of women to musk odor: No menstrual variation. *J. Chem. Ecol.* **1**, 291–297.

Amthauer, R. (1966). Psychologische Grundfragen der Berufswahl. VDI-Nachrichten, 20 (48).

Anastasia, A. (1958). Differential Psychology. New York: Anastasi.

Anderson, G. C. (1978). Der Ursprung der Intelligenz und die sensomotorische Entwicklung des Kindes. *In:* Steiner, G. (ed.), Die Psychologie des 20. Jahrhunderts. 7. Piaget and die Folgen. Zürich: Kindler, pp. 94–120.

Anderson, P. (1983). The reproductive role of the human breast. *Current Anthropol.* **24**, 25–45.

Anderson, S. W. and Jaffe, J. (1972). The Definition, Detection and Timing of Vocalic Syllables in Speech Signals. Scientific Report No. 12 of Communication Sciences, New York State, Psychiatric Institute.

Andersson, Y., Lagercrantz, H., Winberg, J., and Öfverholm, U. (1978). Konjunctivit, mimik och synoeteende hos nyfödda barn före och efter Cre-de-profylax. *Läkartidningen* **75**, 302–304.

Angrick, M. (1983). Endorphine. *Pharmazie Unserer Zeit* **12**, 129–134.

Antonelli, A. (1979). Small Beginnings: The Effects of Social Behavior on Cognitive Development in the First Three Months. Paper presented at the British Psychological Society Developmental Section Annual Conference, University of Southampton.

Archavsky, I. A. (1952). Immediate breastfeeding of newborn infant in the prophylaxis of the so-called physiological loss of weight. *Vopr. Pediat.* **20**, 45–53.

Ardrey, R. (1966). The Territorial Imperative. New York: Atheneum.

Argyle, M. (1969). Social Interaction. London: Methuen.

Argyle, M. and Cook, M. (1976). Gaze and Mutual Gaze. Cambridge: Cambridge Univ. Press.

Argyle, M., Furnham, A., and Graham, J. A. (1981). Social Situations. Cambridge: Cambridge Univ. Press.

Aries, Ph. (1978). Geschichte der Kindheit. München: dtv Wissenschaft.

Asch, S. E. (1951). Effects of group pressure upon the modification and distortion of judgments. *In:* Guetzkow, H. (ed.), Groups, Leadership, and Men. Pittsburgh, PA: Carnegie Press.

— (1955). On the use of metaphor on the description of persons. *In:* Werner, H. (ed.), On Expressive Language. Worcester, MA: Clark University Press.

— (1958). The Metaphor: A Psychological Inquiry. *In:* Taquri, R. and Petrullo, L. (eds.), Person, Perception, and Interpersonal Behavior. Stanford, CA: Stanford University Press.

Aschoff, J. (1981). A survey on biological rhythms. *In:* Aschoff, J. (ed.), Handbook of Behavioral Neurobiology, Vol. 4. London/New York: Plenum, pp. 3–10. (a)

— (1981). Freerunning and Entrained Circadian Rhythms. *In:* Aschoff, J. (ed.), Handbook of Behavioral Neurobiology, Vol. 4. London/New York: Plenum, pp. 81–93. (b)

(1981). Annual rhythms in man. *In:* Aschoff, J. (ed.), Handbook of Behavioral Neurobiology, Vol. 4. London/New York: Plenum, pp. 475–487. (c)

Aschoff, J. and Wever, R. (1980). Über Reproduzierbarkeit circadianer Rhythmen beim Menschen. *Klin. Wochenschr.* **58,** 323–335.

Aschoff, J. and Wever, R. (1981). The circadian system of man. *In:* Aschoff, J. (ed.), Handbook of Behavioral Neurobiology, Vol. 4. London/New York: Plenum, pp. 311–331.

Aspey, W. P. and Blankenship, J. E. (1977). Spiders and snails and statistic tales: Application of multivariate analyses to diverse ethological data. *In:* Hazlett, B. A. (ed.), Quantitative Methods in the Study of Behavior. New York/London: Academic Press, pp. 75–120. (1978). Comparative Ethometrics: Congruency of different multivariate analyses applied to the same ethological data. *Behav. Proc.* **3,** 173–195.

Attili, G. and Benigni, L. (1979). Interazione sociale—ruolo sessuale e comportamento verbale: lo stile retorico naturale del linguaggio femminile nell' interazione faccia a faccia. *In:* Societa di Linguistica Italiana (ed.), Retorica e Scienze. Rom: Bulzoni, pp. 261–280.

Attili, G., Hold, B., and Schleidt, M. (1982). Relationship among Peers in Kindergarten: A Cross-Cultural Study. Paper presented at the IXth Congress of the International Primatological Society, Atlanta, Georgia, USA, 8–13 August, 1982.

Austen, S. (1979). Mutter-Kind-Interaktionen unmittelbar nach der Geburt. Paper presented at 6. Meeting der Int. Studiengemeinschaft für pränatale Psychologie (ISPP), Basel, 4. 9. 1979.

Ausubel, D. P. and Sullivan, E. V. (1980). Das Kindesalter. Fakten—Probleme—Theorie. München: Juventa.

Avedon, E. M. and Sutton-Smith, B. (1971). The Study of Games. New York: Wiley.

Babad, Y. E., Alexander, I. E., and Babad, E. Y. (1983). Returning the smile of the stranger: Developmental patterns and socialization factors. *Monogr. Soc. Res. Child Develop.* **48,** [203], 5.

Bachofen, J. J. (1861). Das Mutterrecht. Stuttgart.

Badinter, E. (1981). Die Mutterliebe. München: Piper.

Baerends. G. P. (1956). Aufbau tierischen Verhaltens. *In:* Kükenthal, W. (ed.), Handbuch der Zoologie, Vol. 8 (10), pp. 1–32.

Baerends, G. P. and Drent, R. H. (1970). The Herring Gull's egg. *Behaviour Suppl.* **17.**

Bahuchet, S. (1983). Territoriality and Values among the Aka Pygmies in the Central African Republic. Paper presented at the 3rd Intern. Conf. on Hunters and Gatherers, Werner-Reimers-Stiftung, Bad Homburg 13–16 June, 1983.

Bailey, K. G. (1987). Human Paleopsychology—Applications to Aggression and Pathological Processes. Hillsdale, NJ: Lawrence Erlbaum.

Bailey, W. T. (1982). Affinity: An ethological perspective of the infant-father relationship in humans. *Infant Behav. Develop.* **5** (special ICIS issue), 12.

Bakeman, R. and Brownlee, J. R. (1982). Social rules governing object conflicts in toddlers and preschoolers. *In:* Rubin, K. H. and Ross, H. S. (eds.), Peer Relations and Social Skills in Childhood. New York: Springer, pp. 99–111.

Baker, J. W. and Schaie, K. W. (1969). Effects of aggression "alone" or with "another" on physiological and psychological arousal. *J. Personality Social Psychol.* **12,** 80–96.

Ball, W. and Tronick, F. (1971). Infant responses to impending collision, optical and real. *Science* **171,** 818–820.

Bally, G. (1945). Vom Ursprung und von den Grenzen der Freiheit, eine Deutung des Spieles bei Tier und Mensch. Basel: Birkhäuser.

Bandura, A. (1973). Aggression: A Social Learning Analysis. Englewood Cliffs, NJ: Prentice Hall.

Bandura, A. and Walters, R. H. (1963). Social Learning and Personality Development. New York: Ronald Press.

Bandura, A., Underwood, B., and Fromson, M. E. (1975). Disinhibition of aggression through diffusion of responsibility and dehumanization of victims. *J. Res. Personality,* **9,** 253–269.

Barash, D. P. (1977). Sociobiology and Behavior. New York/Amsterdam: Elsevier.

Barkow, J. H. (1979). Human ethology: Empirical wealth, theoretical death. *Behav. Brain Sci.* **2,** 27.

Barlow, G. W. (1972). A paternal role for bulls of the Galapagos Islands sea lions. *Evolution* **26**, 307/8.

Barlow, G. W. and Rowell, T. E. (1984). The contribution of game theory to animal behavior. (Open Peer Commentary for J. Maynard-Smith.) *Behav. Brain Sci.* **7**, 101–103.

Barnard, A. (1978). The kin terminology system of the Nharo Bushmen. *Cah. Etud. Afr.* **72**, 607–629.

Barnard, C. J. (1980). Flock feeding and time budgets in the House Sparrow (*Passer domesticus* L.). *Anim. Behav.* **28**, 295–309.

Barner-Bárry C. (1983). Zum Verhältnis zwischen Ethologie und Politik: Macht, Dominanz, Autorität und Aufmerksamkeitsstruktur. *In:* Flohr, H. and Tönnesmann, W. (eds.), Politik und Biologie. Berlin: Paul Parey, pp. 101–110.

Barnes, D. M. (1988). Meeting on the mind. *Science* **239**, 142–144. (Report on the meeting of the American College of Neuropsychopharmacology with reference to the discoveries of Saul Schanberg, Tiffany Field, and Gary Evonuik.)

Baron, R. A. (1977). Human Aggression. New York: Plenum Press.

Baron, R. A. and Ball, R. L. (1974). The aggression inhibiting influence of non-hostile humor. *J. Exp. Social Psychol.* **10**, 23–33.

Barrett, J. E. (1972). Schedules of electric shock presentation in the behavioral control of imprinted ducklings. *J. Exp. Analysis Behav.* **18**, 305–321.

Barry, H., Bacon, M. K., and Child, I. L. (1957). A cross-cultural survey of some sex differences in socialization. *J. Abnormal Social Psychol.* **55**, 327–332.

Barth, F. (1959/1960). The Land Use Patterns of Migratory Tribes of South Persia. *Norsk. Geogr. Tidsk.* **17**, 1–11.

Barton, S., Birns, B., and Ronch, J. (1971). Individual differences in the visual pursuit behavior of neonates. *Child Develop.* **42**, 313–319.

Basedow, H. (1906). Anthropological notes on the western coastal tribes of the northern territory of South Australia. *Trans. Roy. Soc. S. Austr.* **31**, 1–62.

Bateson, G. and Mead, M. (1942). Balinese Character: A Photographic Analysis. Special Publication of the New York Science, II. New York.

Beaglehole, E. (1932). Property: A Study in Social Psychology. New York: Macmillan.

Beauvoir, S. de (1968). Das andere Geschlecht—Sitte und Sexus der Frau. Hamburg: Rowohlt.

Becker-Carus, Ch., Buchholtz, Ch., Etienne, A., Franck, D., Medioni, J., Schöne, H. Sevenster, P., Stamm, R. A., and Tschanz, B. (1972). Motivation, Handlungsbereitschaft, Trieb. *Z. Tierpsychol.* **30**, 321–326.

Beit-Hallahmi, B. (1981). The Kibbutz family. Revival or survival. *J. Family Issues* **2**, 259–274.

Beit-Hallahmi, B. and Rabin, A. I. (1977). The Kibbutz as a social experiment and as a childrearing laboratory. *Amer. Psychol.* **32**, 532–541.

Bell, A. P. and Weinberg, M. S. (1978). Homosexuality: A Study of Diversity among Men and Women. New York: Simon & Schuster.

Bell, A. P., Weinberg, M. S., and Hammersmith, S. K. (1981). Der Kinsey Institut Report über sexuelle Orientierung und Partnerwahl. München: Bertelsmann.

Bell, F. L. (1934). Warfare among the Tanga. *Oceania* **5**, 253–279.

Bell-Krannhals, I. (1984). Was sich liebt, das versteckt sich—Interaktionsmuster zwischen Liebenden auf Kaileuna Island. Paper presented at meeting of the DFG-priority program "Verbale Interaktion," 27 January, 1984, Seewiesen.

Belsky, J. (1980). Child Maltreatment. *Amer. Psychol.* **35**, 320–335.

Belzer, E. (1981). Organic Expulsion of Women: A Review and Heuristic Inquiry. *J. Sex. Res.* **17**, 1–12.

Benard, Ch. and Schlaffer, E. (1980). Der Mann auf der Strasse. Hamburg: Rowohlt.

Benbow, C. P. and Stanley, J. C. (1980). Sex differences in mathematical ability: Fact or artifact? *Science* **210**, 1262–1264.
    (1983). Sex differences in mathematical reasoning ability: More facts. *Science* **222**, 1029–1031.

Benedeck, T. (1952). Psychosexual Functions in Woman. New York: Ronald Press.

Benedict, R. (1935). Patterns of Culture. London: Routledge & Kegan Paul Ltd.

Bennett, J. H., Rhodes, F. A., and Robson, H. N. (1959). A possible genetic base for Kuru. *Amer. J. Hum. Genet.* **II**, 169–187.

Bennett, J. W. (1969). Northern Plainsmen: Adaptive Strategies and Agrarian Life. Chicago: Aldine.

(1976). The Ecological Transition: Cultural Anthropology and Human Adaptation. New York: Pergamon.

Bentley, D. R. (1971). Genetic control of an insect neuronal network. *Science* **174**, 1139–1141.

Bentley, D. R. and Hoy, R. R. (1972). Genetic control of the neuronal network generating cricket song patterns. *Animal Behav.* **20**, 478–492.

Benton, D. (1982). The influence of androstenol—a putative human pheromone—on mood throughout the menstrual cycle. *Biol. Psychol.* **15**, 249–256.

Berger, P. L. and Luckmann, T. (1970). Die gesellschaftliche Konstruktion der Wirklichkeit. Eine Theorie der Wissenssoziologie. Frankfurt/M: S. Fischer.

Berghe, P. L. van den (1979). Human Family Systems. New York: Elsevier.

(1981). The Ethnic Phenomenon. New York: Elsevier.

Bergman, B. A. (1971). The Effects of Groups Size, Personal Space and Success Failure on Physiological Arousal, Test Performance and Questionnaire Responses. Doctoral dissertation, Temple University, Philadelphia, Univ. Microfilm No. 71–31072.

Berkowitz, L. (1962). Aggression: A Social Psychological Analysis. New York/London: McGraw-Hill.

(1970). Aggressive humor as a stimulus to aggressive responses. *J. Personality Social Psychol.* **16**, 710–717.

Bernstein, L. (1976). The Unanswered Question. Cambridge, MA: Harvard Univ. Press.

Bertaux, P. (1963). Mutation der Menschheit. Neuauflage 1983. Frankfurt/M: Suhrkamp.

Bertram, B. C. R. (1976). Kin selection in lions and in evolution. *In:* Bateson, P. P. and Hinde, R. A. (eds.), Growing Points in Ethology. Cambridge: Cambridge University Press.

Bettelheim, B. (1954). Symbolic Wounds. New York: Collier Books.

(1977). Kinder brauchen Märchen. Stuttgart: DVA.

Beuchelt, E. and Ziehr, W. (1979). Schwarze Königreiche. Frankfurt/M: W. Krüger.

Bever, T. G. 1970. The cognitive basis for linguistic structures. *In:* Hayes, J. R. (ed.), Cognition and the Development of Language. New York: Wiley, pp. 279–352. (a)

(1970). The influence of speech performance on linguistic structures. *In:* Flores d'Arcais, G. B., and Levelt, W. J. M. (eds.), Advances in Psycholinguistics. Amsterdam: North Holland Publ. Comp., pp. 4–30. (b)

(1970). The Nature of Cerebral Dominance in Speech Behavior of the Child and Adult. Mechanisms of Language Development. New York/London: Academic Press. (c)

Bicchieri, M. G. (1969). The Differential Use of Identical Features of Physical Habitat in Connection with Exploitative Settlement and Community Patterns: The Bambuti. Contributions to Anthropology: Band Societies. *Proc. Conf. Band Organ. Ottawa, Nat. Museum. Can. Bull.* **230**, 65–72.

(1973). Hunters and Gatherers Today. New York: Holt, Rinehart & Winston.

Bigelow, A. (1977). Infants' Recognition of Mother. Paper presented to the Society for Research in Child Development, New Orleans.

Bigelow, R. S. (1970). The Dawn Warriors: Man's Evolution Toward Peace. London: Hutchinson.

Billow, R. M. (1977). Metaphor: A review of the psychological literature. *Psychol. Bull.* **84**, 81–92.

Bilz, R. (1944). Zur Grundlegung einer Paläopsychologie. I. Paläophysiologie; II. Paläopsychologie. *Schweizerische Z. Psychol.* **3**, 202–212, 272–280.

(1965). Der Subjektzentrismus im Erleben der Angst. *In:* Ditfurth, H. v. (ed.), Aspekte der Angst. Stuttgart.

Binford, L. R. (1981). Bones, Ancient Man, and Modern Myths. New York/London/Toronto: Academic Press.

Biocca, E. (1970). Yanoama: The Narrative of a White Girl Kidnapped by Amazonian Indians. New York: E. P. Dutton.

Birdsell, J. B. (1968). Some predictions for the Pleistocene based on equilibrium systems among recent hunter-gatherers. *In:* Lee, R. B. and DeVore, I. (eds.), Man the Hunter. Chicago: Aldine, pp. 229–240.

Birdwhistell, R. L. (1960). Kinesics and communication. *In:* Carpenter, E. and McLuhan, M. (eds.), Explorations in Communication. Boston: Beacon Press, pp. 54–64.

(1963). The kinesic level in the investigation of the emotions. *In:* Knapp, P. H. (ed.), Expression of the Emotions in Man. New York: International Universities Press, pp. 123–139.

(1968). Communication without words. *In:* Alexandre, P. (ed.), L'Aventure Humaine. Encycl. Sci. de l'Homme, Vol. 5. Paris: Kister, S. A., pp. 157–166.

(1970). Kinesics and Context. Philadelphia: University of Pennsylvania Press.

(1973). Kinesics and Context. Essays on Body-Motion Communication. Harmondsworth, Middlesex: Penguin Books Ltd.

Birren, F. (1950). Color Psychology and Therapy. New York: McGraw-Hill.

Bischof, N. (1972). The biological foundations of the incest taboo. *Social Sci. Inform.* **11**, 7–36. (a)

(1972). Inzuchtbarrieren in Säugetiersozietäten. *Homo* **23**, 330–351. (b)

(1973). Die biologischen Grundlagen des Inzesttabus. *In:* Reinert, G. (ed.), Bericht über den 27. Kongress der Deutschen Gesellschaft für Psychologie, Kiel 1970. Göttingen: C. J. Hogrefe, pp. 115–142.

(1975). A system's approach toward the functional connections of attachment and fear. *Child Develop.* **46**, 801–817.

(1981). Aristoteles, Galilei, Kurt Lewin—und die Folgen. *In:* Michaelis, W. (ed.), Bericht über den 32. Kongress der Deutschen Gesellschaft für Psychologie in Zürich 1980, Bd. 1. Göttingen/Toronto/Zürich: C. J. Hogrefe, pp. 17–39.

Bixler, R. H. (1981). The incest controversy. *Psychol. Rep.* **49**, 267–283.

(1983). Homosexual twin incest avoidance. *J. Sex Res.* **19**, 296–302.

Blaffer-Hrdy, S. (1974). Male-male competition and infanticide among the langurs *(Presbytis entellus)* of Abu, Rajasthan. *Folia Primatol.* **22**, 19–58.

(1976). Care and exploitation of non-human primate infants by conspecifics other than the mother. *In:* Rosenblatt, J. S., Hinde, R. A., Shaw, E., and Beers, C. (eds.), Advances in the Study of Behavior. New York: Academic Press, pp. 101–158.

(1977). Infanticide as a primate reproductive strategy. *Amer. Sci.* **65**, 40–49. (a)

(1977). The langurs of Abu. Cambridge, MA: Harvard University Press. (b)

(1979). Infanticide among animals: A review, classification, and examination of the implications for the reproductive strategies of females. *Ethol. Sociobiol.* **1**, 13–40.

(1981). The Woman That Never Evolved. Cambridge, MA: Harvard University Press.

(1982). Positivist thinking encounters field primatology, resulting in agonistic behavior. *Soc. Sci. Inform.* **21**, 245–250.

Bleek, D. F. (1930). Rock-Paintings in South Africa. London: Methuen.

Blehar, M. C., Lieberman, A. F., and Ainsworth, M. D. S. (1977). Early face-to-face interaction in its relation to later infant-mother attachment. *Child Develop.* **48**, 181–194.

Block, J. H. (1976). Debatable conclusions about sex differences. *Contemp. Psychol.* **21**, 517–522. (a)

(1976). Assessing sex differences: issues, problems and pitfalls. *Merrill-Palmer Quart.* **22**, 283–308. (b)

Block, N. (1979). A Confusion among innateness. (Commentary). *Behav. Brain Sci.* **2**, 27–29.

Blurton-Jones, N. G. (1972). Ethological Studies of Child Behaviour. Cambridge: Cambridge University Press.

(1976). Growing points in human ethology: Another link between ethology and the social sciences? *In:* Bateson, P. P. G. and Hinde, R. A. (eds.), Growing Points in Ethology. London: Cambridge Press, pp. 427–450.

(1984). A selfish origin for human sharing: Tolerated theft. *Ethol. Sociobiol.* **5**, 1–3.

Blurton-Jones, N. G. and Konner, M. J. (1973). Sex differences in behaviour of London and bushman children. *In:* Michael, R. P. and Crook, J. (eds.), Comparative Ecology and Behaviour of Primates. London: Academic Press, pp. 689–750.

Boal, F. (1969). Territoriality on the Shankill-Falls Divide, Belfast. *Irish Geogr.* **6**, 30–35.

Boas, F. (1895, 1970). The Social Organization and the Secret Societies of the Kwakiutl Indians. Report of the U.S. National Museum. New York: Johnson Reprint Corporation.

(1911, rev. 1938). The Mind of Primitive Man. New York: Macmillan.

(1928). Anthropology and Modern Life. New York: Norton.

(1938). General Anthropology. New York: Heath.

Boehn, M. v. (1976, rev. 1982). Die Mode. Eine Kulturgeschichte vom Barock bis zum Jugendstil. Adapted by I. Loschek. München: Bruckmann.

Boesch, Ch. and Boesch, H. (1981). Sex differences in the use of natural hammers by wild chimpanzees. A preliminary report. *J. Hum. Evol.* **10**, 585–593.

Boesiger, W. and Girsberger, H. (1967). Le Corbusier 1910–1965. Zürich: Verlag für Architektur—Artemis.

Bohannan, P. (ed.) (1967). Law and Warfare. Studies in the Anthropology of Conflict. Garden City, NY: Natural History Press.

Boinski-McConnell, H. and Burgess, R. L. (1978). The effect of Physical Attractiveness on Family Interaction Patterns in Problem and Non-Problem Families. The Pennsylvania State University.

Bolinger, D. (1978). Intonation across languages. *In:* Greenberg, J. H., Ferguson, Ch. A., and Maravcsik, E. A. (eds.), Universals of Human Language. Vol. 2: Phonology. Stanford, CA: Stanford University Press, pp. 471–524.

(1980). Intonation and "nature." *In:* Foster, M. L. and Brandes, St. H. (eds.), Symbol as Sense. New York: Academic Press, pp. 9–24.

Bolk, L. (1926). Das Problem der Menschwerdung. Jena.

Bolles, R. C. (1979). The functional significance of behavior. *Behav. Brain Sci.* **2**, 29–30.

Bolles, R. C. and Faneslow, M. S. (1982). Endorphins and behavior. *Annu. Rev. Psychol.* **33**, 87–101.

Bolton, R. (1984). The hypoglycaemia-aggression hypothesis: Debate versus research. *Current Anthropol.* **25**, 1–53.

Booth, A. and Edwards, J. N. (1980). Fathers: The invisible parent. *Sex Roles* **6**, 445–456.

Booth, D. A. and Kirk-Smith, M. D. (1980). Effect of Androstenone on Choice of Location in Other's Presence. Joint Congress on Chemoreception ECRO IV and ISOT VII, Noordwijkerhout, Holland, S. 175.

Borgia, G. (1980). Human aggression as a biological adaptation. *In:* Lockard, J. L. (ed.), The Evolution of Social Behavior. New York: Elsevier, pp. 165–191.

Bornstein, M. H. (1975). Qualities of colour vision in infancy. *J. Exp. Child Psychol.* **19**, 401–419.

(1979). The pace of life: Revisited. *Intern. J. Psychol.* **14**, 83–90.

Bornstein, M. H. and Bornstein, H. G. (1976). The pace of life. *Nature* **259**, 557–558.

Boulding, K. E. (1978). Sociobiology or Biosociology? *Society,* Sept./Oct., pp. 28–34.

Bower, T. G. R. (1966). Slant perception and shape constancy of infants. *Science,* **151**, 832 ff.

(1971). The object in the world of the infant. *Sci. American,* **225**, 30–38.

(1977). A Primer of Infant Development. San Francisco: Freeman.

Bower, T. G. R., Broughton, J. M., and Moore, M. K. (1970). The coordination of vision and touch in infancy. *Perception Psychophys.* **8**, 51–53. (a)

(1970). Infant responses to approaching objects: An indicator of response to distal variables. *Perception Psychophys.* **9**, 193–196. (b)

Bowlby, J. (1958). The nature of the child's tie to his mother. *Intern. J. Psycho-Analysis* **39**, 350–373.

(1969). Attachment and loss. *In:* Masud, M. and Khan, R. (eds.), Attachment 1. London: Hogarth Press, The Int. Psycho-Analytical Library, No. 79. (a)

(1969). Mütterliche Zuwendung und geistige Gesundheit. München: Kindler Taschenbücher "Geist und Psyche." (b)

(1973). Attachment and loss. *In:* Masud, M. and Khan, R. (eds.), Separation and Anger 2. London: Hogarth Press, The Int. Psycho-Analytical Library, No. 95.

Boyd, R. and Richerson, P. J. (1982). Cultural transmission and the evolution of cooperative behavior. *Hum. Ecol.* **10**, 325–351.

Bradley, C. F., Ross, S. E., and Warnyca, J. (1983). A prospective study of mothers' attitudes and feelings following cesarean and vaginal births. *Birth* **10**, 79–83.

Brain, P. F. and Benton, D. (1981). The Biology of Aggression. Alphenaan den Rijn, Netherlands: Sijtoff and Noordhoff.

Bramel, D., Taub, B. and Blum, B. (1968). An observer's reaction to the suffering of his enemy. *J. Personality Social Psychol.* **8**, 384–392.

Brannigan, C. R. and Humphries, D. A. (1972). Human Non-Verbal Behaviour, a Means of Communication. *In:* Burton-Jones, N. G. (ed.), Ethological Studies of Child Behaviour. Cambridge: Cambridge University Press, pp. 37–64.

Brauer, E. (1983). Kunst—Restkunst—Unkunst. München: R. P. Hartmann.

Braun, H. and Elze, C. (1954). Anatomie des Menschen, Bd. 1. Heidelberg: Springer.

Breland, K. and Breland, M. (1966). Animal Behavior. New York: Macmillan.

Brim, O. G. and Kagan, J. (1980). Constancy and Change in Human Development. Cambridge, MA: Harvard University Press.

Brislin, R. W. (1980). Cross-cultural research methods. *In:* Altman, I., Rapoport, A. and Wohlwill, J. F. (eds.), Human Behavior and Environment, Vol. 4. London/New York: Plenum Press, pp. 47–82.

Broad, F. (1976). The Effect of Breast Freeding on Speech Development. J. La Leche League of New Zealand.

Brocher, T. (1971). Psychosexuelle Grundlagen der Entwicklung. *In:* Hassenstein, B. (ed.): Verhaltensbiologie des Kindes. Opladen: Leske Verlag.

Bronner, S. J. (1982). The haptic experience of culture. *Anthropos* **77**, 351–361.

Bronowski, J. and Bellugi, U. (1980). Language, name and concept. *In:* Sebeok, T. A. and Umiker-Sebeok, J. (eds.), Speaking of Apes. New York: Plenum Press, pp. 103–113.

Brookfield, H. C. and Brown, P. (1963). Struggle for Land. London: Oxford University Press.

Brooksbank, B. W. L., Brown, R., and Gustafsson, J.-A. (1974). The Detection of 5α-androst-16-en-3α-ol in human male axillary sweat. *Experientia* **30**, 864–865.

Broude, G. J. (1976). Cross-cultural patterning of some sexual attitudes and practices. *Behav. Sci. Res.* **11**, 227–262.

Brown, G. L., Goodwin, F. K., and Bunney, W. E., Jr. (1982). Human aggression and suicide: Their relationship to neuropsychiatric diagnoses and serotonin metabolism. *In:* Ho, B. T. (ed.), Serotonin in Biological Psychiatry. New York: Raven Press, pp. 287–307.

Brown, L. R. (1981). World population growth, soil erosion, and food security. *Science* **214**, 995–1002.

Brown, P. and Levinson, St. (1978). Universals in language usage: Politeness phenomena. *In:* Goody, E. N. (ed.), Questions and Politeness Strategies in Social Interaction. Cambridge/New York: Cambridge University Press, pp. 56–290.

Brown, R. (1965). Social Psychology. New York: Free Press.
  (1968). Words and Things. New York: Free Press.
  (1974). Die ersten Sätze von Kind und Schimpanse. *In:* Leuninger, H., Miller, M. H., and Müller, F. (eds.), Linguistik und Psychologie, Vol. 2. Frankfurt/M.: Fischer Athenaeum), pp. 30–52.

Brownlee, F. (1943). The social organization of the !Kung Bushmen of the Northwestern Kalahari. *Africa,* **14**, 124–129.

Browntree, L. R. and Conkey, M. W. (1980). Symbolism and the cultural landscape. *Ann. Assoc. Amer. Geographers* **70**, 459–474.

Bruner, J. S. (1974). Nature and uses of immaturity. *In:* Connolly, K. and Bruner, J. S. (eds.), The Growth of Competence. London: Academic Press, pp. 11–48.
  (1975). The ontogenesis of speech-acts. *J. Child Language* **2**, 1–19. (a)
  (1975). From communication to language: A psychological perspective. *Cognition* **3**, 255–287. (b)
  (1981). The social context of language acquisition. *Language Commun.* **1**, 155–178.

Bruner, J. S. and Koslowski, B. (1972). Visually preadapted constituents of manipulatory action. *Perception* **1**, 3–14.

Buchwald, K. (1978). Umwelt, Mensch, Gesellschaft, Die Entstehung der Umweltproblematik. *In:* Buchwald, K. and Engelhardt, W. (eds.), Handbuch für Planung, Gestaltung und Schutz der Umwelt, 1. Die Umwelt des Menschen. München: BLV, pp. 1–46.
  (1980). Umwelt und Gesellschaft zwischen Wachstum und Gleichgewicht. *In:* Buchwald, K. and Engelhardt, W. (eds.), Handbuch für Planung, Gestaltung und Schutz der Umwelt. 4. Umweltpolitik. München/Wien/Zürich: BLV, pp. 1–32.

Buchwald, K. and Engelhardt, W. (eds.) (1978). Handbuch für Planung, Gestaltung und Schutz der Umwelt. 1. Die Umwelt des Menschen. München: BLV.

Buckhalt, J. A., Rutherford, R. B., and Goldberg, K. E. (1978). Verbal and nonverbal interaction of mothers with their Down's Syndrome and non-retarded infants. *Amer. J. Mental Deficiency* **82**, 337–343.

Budack, K. F. R. (1983). A harvesting people on the South Atlantic coast. *S. Afr. J. Ethnol.* **6**, 1–7.

Bullock, T. H. (1961). The origins of patterned nervous discharge. *Behaviour* **17**, 48–59.

Bullock, T. H. and Horridge, G. A. (1965). Structure and Function in the Nervous System of Invertebrates. 2 Vols. San Francisco: Freeman.

Bunge, M. (1979). Some topical problems in biophilosophy. *J. Social Biol. Structures* **2**, 155–172.

Burckhardt, L. (1981). Das Menschenbild des Architekten. *In:* Michaelis, W. (ed.), Bericht über den 32. Kongress der Deutschen Gesellschaft für Psychologie in Zürich 1980, Bd. 1. Göttingen/Toronto/ Zürich: C. J. Hogrefe, pp. 73–80.

Burd, A. P. and Milewski, A. E. (1981). Matching of Facial Gestures by Young Infants: Imitation or Releasers? Vortrag anläßlich der Tagung der Society for Research in Child Development, Boston, April, 1981.

Burgess, R. L. and Conger, R. D. (1978). Family Interaction in Abusive Neglectful and Normal Families. The Pennsylvania State University.

Burghardt, G. M. (1975). Chemical prey preferences polymorphism in newborn garter snakes, *Thamnophis sirtalis*. Behaviour **52**, 202–225.

Busch, F. and McKnight, J. (1973). Parental attitudes and the development of the primary transitional object. *Child Psychiat. Hum. Develop.* **4**, 12–20.

Buss, A. H. (1961). The Psychology of Aggression. New York: Wiley.

Bygott, J. D. (1972). Cannibalism among wild chimpanzees. *Nature* **238**, 410–411.

Calhoun, J. B. (1962). Population density and social pathology. *Sci. Amer.* **206** (2), 139–148.

Calvinoux, P. (1980). The Fates of Nations. A Biological Theory of History. New York: Simon & Schuster.

Campbell, D. T. (1974). Evolutionary epistemology. *In:* Schillp, P. (ed.), The Library of Living Philosophers, Vol. 14, 1 and 2: The Philosophy of Karl Popper, Vol. 1, pp. 413–463. Lasalle, Open Court.

(1975). On the conflicts between biological and social evolution and between psychology and moral tradition. *Amer. Psychol.* **30**, 1103–1126.

Campell, B. and Petersen, W. E. (1953). Milk let-down and orgasm in human female. *Hum. Biol.* **25**, 165–168.

Campos, J. J. Hiatt, S., Ramsay, D., Henderson, C., and Svejda, M. (1977). The emergence of fear on the visual cliff. *In:* Lewis, M. and Rosenblum, L. (eds.), The Origins of Affect. New York: Wiley.

Camras, L. A. (1977). Facial expressions used by children in a conflict situation. *Child Develop.* **48**, 1431–1435.

Candland, D. K. and Mason, W. A. (1968). Infant monkey heartrate: Habituation and effects of social substitutes. *Develop. Psychobiol.* **1**, 254–256.

Caplan, A. L. (1979). Sociobiology, human nature and psychological egoism. *J. Social Biol. Structures* **2**, 27–38.

Caporael, L. R. (1981). The paralanguage of caregiving: Baby talk to the institutionalized aged. *J. Personality Social Psychol.* **40**, 876–884.

Caputi, Jane, E. (1984). Beauty secrets: Tabooing the ugly woman. *In:* R. B. Browne (ed.), Forbidden Fruits: Taboos and Tabooism in Culture. Bowling Green, Ohio: Bowling Green University Popular Press, pp. 36–56.

Carlson, J. S. (1978). Kulturenvergleichende Untersuchungen im Rahmen von Piaget's Theorie. *In:* Steiner, G. (ed.), Die Psychologie des 20. Jahrhunderts. 7. Piaget und die Folgen. Zürich: Kindler, pp. 709–728.

Carneiro, R. L. (1970). A theory of the origin of the state. *Science* **169**, 733–738.

(1978). Political expansion as an expression of the principle of competitive exclusion. *In:* Cohen, R. and Service, E. (eds.), Origins of the State. The Anthropology of Political Evolution. Philadelphia, PA: Institute for the Study of Human Issues, pp. 205–223.

Carson, R. (1962). Silent Spring. Boston: Houghton Mifflin.

Cashdan, E. A. (1980). Egalitarianism among hunters and gatherers. *Amer. Anthropol.* **82**, 116–120.

(1983). Territoriality among human foragers: Ecological models and an application to four Bushman groups. *Current Anthropol.* **24**, 47–55.

Cassidy, J. H. (1979). Half a century on the concepts of innateness and instinct. Survey, synthesis and philosophical implications. *Z. Tierpsychol.* **50**, 364–386.

Castetter, E. F. and Beli, W. H. (1951). Yuman Indian Agriculture. Albuquerque, NM: University of New Mexico Press.

Catom, H. (1981). Domesticating Nature: Thoughts on the Ethology of Modern Politics. *In:* White, E. (ed.), Sociobiology and Politics. Boston: (Heath), pp. 99–134.

(1982). Biosocial Science: Knowledge for Enlightened Political Leadership. Paper presented at Annual Meeting of American Political Science Association, Denver, 11–14 Sept., 1982.

Cavalli-Sforza, L. L. (1981). Human evolution and nutrition. *In:* Kretschmer, N. and Walcher, D. N. (eds.), Food, Nutrition and Evolution. New York: Masson Publ. Inc.

Chagnon, N. A. (1968). Yanomamö, The Fierce People. New York: Holt, Rinehart & Winston.

(1971): Die soziale Organisation und die Kriege der Yanomamö-Indianer. *In:* Fried, M., Harris, M. and Murphy, R. (eds.), Der Krieg. Zur Anthropologie der Aggression und des bewaffneten Konflikts. Stuttgart: Fischer, pp. 131–189.

(1974). Studying the Yanomamö. New York: Holt, Rinehart & Winston.

(1976). Yanomamö, the true people. *National Geog. Magazine* **150,** 211–222.

(1979). Mate competition, favoring close kin, and village fissioning among the Yanomamö Indians. *In:* Chagnon, N. A. and Irons, W. (eds.), Evolutionary Biology and Human Social Behavior: An Anthropological Perspective. North Scituate, MA: Duxbury Press, pp. 86–132.

(1988). Life histories, blood revenge, and warfare in a tribal population. *Science* **239,** 985–992.

Chagnon, N. A. and Irons, W. (1979). Evolutionary Biology and Human Social Behavior: An Anthropological Perspective. North Scituate, MA: Duxbury Press.

Chance, M. R. A. (1967). Attention structures as the basis of primate rank orders. *Man* **2** [NS], 503-518.

Chance, M. R. A. and Larsen, R. R. (eds.) (1976). The Social Structure of Attention. London: Wiley.

Charlesworth, W. (1978). Some models for the evolution of altruistic behavior between siblings. *J. Theoret. Biol.* **72,** 297–319.

(1981). Comments on S. L. Washburn's review of Kenneth Bock's "Human Nature History": A response to sociobiology. *Hum. Ethol. Newsl.* 22–23 Sept., 1981.

Charlesworth, W. R. and Dzur, C. (1987). Gender comparisons of preschoolers behavior and resource utilization in group problem solving. *Child Develop.* **58,** 191–200.

Chateau, J. (1969). Das Spiel des Kindes. Paderborn: Ferdinand Schöningh.

Chesser, E. (1957). The Sexual, Marital, and Family Relationship of the English Woman. New York: Roy.

Chevalier-Skolnikoff, S. (1973). Facial expression of emotion in nonhuman primates. *In:* Ekman, P. (ed.), Darwin and Facial Expression. New York/London: Academic Press, pp. 11–89.

Cheyne, J. A. and Efran, M. G. (1972). The effect of spatial and interpersonal variables on the invasion of group control territories. *Sociometry* **35,** 477–489.

Chisholm, G. B. (1946). The Re-establishment of Peacetime Society. The William Alanson White Memorial Lectures, 2nd series, Psychiatry IX, No. 3. Text citation from: Hayek, F. A. v. (1975). Die Irrtümer des Konstruktivismus. Tübingen: C. B. Mohr Paul Siebeck, p. 30.

Chomsky, N. (1965). Aspects of the Theory of Syntax. Cambridge. MA: MIT Press.

(1969). Language and the mind. *Psychol. Today Magazine* **13,** 424–432.

(1970). Sprache und Geist. Frankfurt/M: Suhrkamp.

Cialdini, R. B. *et al.* (1975). Reciprocal concessions procedure for inducing compliance: The door-in-the-face technique. *J. Personality Social Psychol.* **31,** 206–215.

(1984). Influence. How and Why People Agree to Things. New York: William Morrow.

Claessen, H. J. M. and Skalnik, P. (eds.) (1978). The Early State. The Hague: Mouton.

Clark, L. (1970). Is there a difference between a clitoral and a vaginal orgasm? *J. Sex Res.* **6,** 25–28.

Clarke-Stewart, K. A. (1978). And daddy makes three: The father's impact on mother and child. *Child Develop.* **49,** 466–478.

(1980). The father's contribution to children's cognitive and social development in early childhood. *In:* Pedersen, F. A. (ed.), The Father-Infant Relationship: Observational Studies in a Family Setting. New York: Holt, Rinehart & Winston.

Clastres, P. (1974). Society Against the State. New York: Urizen Books.

Claus, R. and Alsing, W. (1976). Occurrence of 5α-androst-16-en-3-one, a boar pheromone in man and its relationship to testosterone. *J. Endocrinol.* **68,** 483–484.

Clausewitz, K. von (1937, 15th ed.). Vom Kriege. Herausgegeben von K. Linnebach. Berlin.

Clifton, R., Siqueland, E. R. and Lipsitt, L. P. (1972). Conditioned headturning in human newborns as a function of conditioned response requirements and states of wakefulness. *J. Exp. Child Psychol.* **13,** 43–57.

Cohen, P. S. (1980). Psychoanalysis and cultural symbolization. *In:* Foster, M. L. and Brandes, Sr. H. (eds.), Symbol as Sense. New York: Academic Press, pp. 45–70.

Cohen, R. and Service, E. R. (eds.) (1978). Origins of the State. The Anthropology of Political Evolution. Philadelphia, PA: Inst. for the Study of Human Issues.

Colby, A., Kohlberg, L., Gibbs, J. and Lieberman, M. (1983). A longitudinal study of moral judgment. *Monogr. Soc. Res. Child Develop.* **48** [Ser. No. 200], 1–124.

Colgan, P. W. (ed.) (1978). Quantitative Ethology. New York: Wiley.

Colinvaux, P. A. (1980). The Feats of Nations. A Biological Theory of History. New York: Simon & Schuster.

(1982). Towards a theory of history: Fitness, niche and clutch of *Homo sapiens. J. Ecol.* **70**, 393–412.

Collis, G. M. and Schaffer, H. R. (1975). Synchronization of visual attention in mother–infant pairs. *J. Child Psychol. Psychiat.* **16**, 315–320.

Comer, R. J. and Piliavin, J. A. (1972). The effects of physical deviance upon face-to-face interaction. The other side. *J. Personality Social Psychol.* **23**, 33–39.

Comrie, B. (1983). Form and function in explaining language universals. *Linguistics* **21**, 87–103.

Condon, W. S. and Sander, L. W. (1974). Neonate movement is synchronized with adult speech: Interactional participation and language acquisition. *Science* **183**, 99–101.

Conkey, M. W. (1978). Style and information in cultural evolution: Toward a predictive model for the paleolithic. *In:* Redman, Ch. L. *et al.* (eds.), Social Archaeology Beyond Subsistence and Dating. New York: Academic Press, pp. 61–85.

Cook, M. (ed.) (1981). The Bases of Human Sexual Attraction. London/New York: Academic Press. (a)

(1981). Social skill and human sexual attraction. *In:* Cook, M. (ed.), The Bases of Human Sexual Attraction. London/New York: Academic Press, pp. 145–177. (b)

Corning, P. A. (1976). Toward a survival oriented policy science. *In:* Somit, A. (ed.), Biology and Politics. Recent Explorations, The Hague/Paris: Mouton, pp. 127–154.

(1981). Rethinking categories and life. *Behav. Brain Sci.* **4**, 286–288. (a)

(1981). A Synopsis of a General Theory of Politics. Paper presented at the Annual Meeting of the American Political Science Association, Sept., New York. (b)

(1983). Politik und Evolution: Kybernetik und Synergismus in der Entstehung komplexer Gesellschaften. *In:* Flohr, H. and Tönnesmann, W. (eds.), Politik und Biologie. Berlin: Paul Parey, pp. 38–60. (a)

(1983). The Synergism Hypothesis. New York: McGraw-Hill. (b)

Corsaro, W. A. (1979). We're friends, right?: Childrens' use of access rituals in nursery school. *Language Soc.* **8**, 315–336.

Coss, R. G. (1972). Eye-like Schemata: Their Effect on Behaviour. Thesis, University of Reading, PA.

(1973). The cut-off hypothesis: Its relevance to the design of public places. *Man-Environ. Systems* **3**, 417–440.

(1978). Development of face aversion by the jewel fish (*Hemichromis bimaculatus,* Gill. 1862). *Z. Tierpsychol.* **48**, 28–46.

Cott, H. B. (1957). Adaptive Coloration in Animals. London: Methuen.

Count, E. W. (1959). Eine biologische Entwicklungsgeschichte der menschlichen Sozialität. *Homo,* **10**, 1–35.

(1970). Das Biogramm. Anthropologische Studien. Frankfurt/M.: S. Fischer.

Craig, W. (1918). Appetites and aversions as constituents of instincts. *Biol. Bull. Woods. Hole* **34**, 91–107.

Cranach, M. v. (1976). Methods of Inference from Animal to Human Behavior. The Hague/Paris: Mouton.

Cranach, M. v. and Vine, I. (eds.) (1973). Social Communication and Movement. London: Academic Press.

Cranach, M. v., Kalbermatten, U., Indermühle, K., and Gugler, B. (1980). Zielgerichtetes Handeln. Bern/Stuttgart/Wien: Hans Huber.

Creutzfeldt, O. (1979). Repräsentation der visuellen Umwelt im Gehirn (Mustererkennung und Schlüsselreize). *Verhandl. Deut. Zool. Ges.* 5–18.

Cronin, C. L. (1980). Dominance relations and females. *In:* Omark, D. R., Strayer, F. F., and Freeman, D. G. (eds.), Dominance Relations. New York: Garland STPM Press, pp. 299–318.

Crusec, J. E. and Brinker, D. B. (1972). Reinforcement for imitation as a social learning determinant with implications for sex-role development. *J. Personality Social Psychol.* **21,** 149–158.

Cüceloglu, D. M. (1970). Perception of facial expressions in three cultures. *Ergonomics* **13,** 93–100.

Culbertson, G. H. and Caporeal, L. R. (1983). Baby talk speech to the elderly. *Personality Soc. Psychol. Bull.* **9,** 305–312.

Cullen, E. (1960). Experiments on the effects of social isolation on reproductive behaviour in the three-spined stickleback. *Animal Behav.* **8,** 235.

Cunningham, M. R. (1986). Measuring the physical in physical attractiveness: Quasi-experiments on the sociobiology of female facial beauty. *J. Personality Soc. Psychol.* **50,** 925–935.

Curtiss, S. (1977). Genie: A Psycholinguistic Study of a Modern-Day "Wild Child." New York: Academic Press.

Cutler, W. B., Preti, G., Krieger, A., Huggins, G. R., Garcia, C. R., and Lawley, H. J. (1986). Human axillary secretions influence women's menstrual cycles: The role of donor extract from men. *Hormones Behav.* **20,** 463–473.

Cutting, J. E. and Rosner, B. (1974). Categories and boundaries in speech and music. *Perception Psychophy.* **16,** 564–570.

Daanje, A. (1950). On the locomotory movements in birds and the intention movements derived from it. *Behaviour* **3,** 48–98.

Dacy, M., Wilson, M., and Weghorst, S. J. (1982). Male sexual jealousy. *Ethol. Sociobiol.* **3,** 11–27.

Daldry, A. D. and Russell, P. A. (1982). Sex differences in the behavior of preschool children with novel and familiar toys. *J. Genet. Psychol.* **141,** 3–6.

Damas, D. (ed.) (1969). Contributions to Anthropology: Ecological Essays. Natural Museum of Canada. Bull. No. 230, Anthropological Series No. 86.

Damon, F. H. (1982). Calendars and calendrical rites on the northern side of the Kula ring. *Oceania* **52,** 221–239.

Danielli, J. S. (1980). Altruism and the internal reward system. *J. Soc. Biol. Structures* **3,** 87–94.

Dann, H. D. (1972). Aggression und Leistung. Stuttgart: Klett.

Dannhauer, H. (1973). Geschlecht und Persönlichkeit. Berlin: Deutscher Verlag der Wissenschaften.

Danzinger, L. and Frankl, L. (1934). Zum Problem der Funktionsreifung. *Z. Kinderforsch.* **43,** 219–225.

Dart, R. A. (1949). The bone-bludgeon hunting technique of *Australopithecus. S. Afr. Sci.* **2,** 150–152.

——— (1953). The predatory transition from ape to man. *Intern. Anthropol. Linguistic Rev.* **1,** 201–218.

Darwin, Ch. (1859). Origin of Species. New York: Philosophical Library.

——— (1872). The expression of emotion in man and animals. London: Murray.

Dasen, P. R. (1977). Piagetian Psychology: Cross-cultural Contributions. New York: Gardener Press.

Daucher, H. (1967). Künstlerisches und rationalisiertes Sehen. Gesetze des Wahrnehmens und Gestaltens. Schriften der pädagogischen Hochschulen Bayerns. München: Ehrenwirth Verlag.

——— (1979). Psychogenetic Aspects of aesthetics. Report INSIA–Congress in Adelaide (in press).

Davis, A. and Olesen, V. (1971). Communal work and living: Notes on the dynamics of social distance and social space. *Sociol. Social Res.* **55,** 191–202.

Davis, F. C. (1981). Ontogeny of circadian rhythms. *In:* Aschoff, J. (ed.), Handbook of Behavioral Neurobiology, 4. London/New York: Plenum Publ. Corp., pp. 257–274.

Dawkins, R. (1968). The ontogeny of a pecking preference in domestic chicks. *Z. Tierpsychol.* **25,** 170–186.

——— (1976). The Selfish Gene. London: Oxford University Press.

——— (1978). Replicator selection and the extended phenotype . *Z. Tierpsychol.* **47,** 61–76.

——— (1979). Defining sociobiology. *Nature* **280,** 47–428. (a)

——— (1979). Twelve misunderstandings of kin selection. *Z. Tierpsychol.* **47,** 184–200. (b)

Day, R. H. (1972). Visual spatial illusions: A general explanation. *Science* **175,** 1335–1340.

Deag, J. M. and Crook, J. H. (1971). Social behaviour and "agonistic buffering" in the wild barbary macaque *Macaca sylvana* L. *Folia Primatol.* **15**, 183–200.

DeCasper, A. H. and Fifer, W. P. (1980). Of human bonding: Newborns prefer their mother's voice. *Science* **208**, 1174–1176.

DeChateau, P. and Andersson, Y. (1976). Left-side preference for holding and carrying newborn infants. II. Doll-holding and carrying from 2 to 16 years. *Develop. Med. Child Neurol.* **18**, 738–744.

DeChateau, P. and Wiberg, B. (1977). Long-term effect on mother-infant behaviour of extra contact during the first hour postpartum. I. First observations at 36 hours. *Acta Paediatr. Scand.* **66**, 137. (a)

(1977). Long-term effect on mother-infant behaviour of extra contact during the first hour postpartum. II. Follow-up at three months. *Acta Paediatr. Scand.* **66**, 145 ff. (b)

DeChateau, P., Holmberg, H., and Winberg, J. (1978). Left-side preference in holding and carrying. I. Mothers holding during the first week of life. *Acta Paediatr. Scand.* **67**, 169–175.

Degenhardt, A. and Trautner, H. M. (1979). Geschlechtstypisches Verhalten. Mann und Frau in psychologischer Sicht. München: C. H. Beck.

Delcomyn, F. (1980). Neural Basis of Rhythmic Behavior. *Science* **210**. 492–498.

Delgado, J. M. R. (1979). Cerebral building blocks and behavioral mechanisms. *Behav. Brain Sci.* **2**, 31–32.

DeLong, A. J. (1977). Yielding the floor: The kinesic signals. *J. Commun.* **27**, 98–103.

Demoll, R. (1954). Bändigt den Menschen. München: Bruckmann.

Demott, B. (1980). Inzest. Der Angriff auf das letzte Tabu. *Psychol. Heute* **7**, 14–18.

Dennis, W. (1940). The effect of cradling practices upon the onset of walking in Hopi children. *J. Genet. Psychol.* **56**, 77–86.

(1941). Infant development under conditions of restricted practice and of minimal social stimulation. *Genet. Psychol. Monogr.* **23**, 143–189.

(1960). Causes of retardation among institutional children. *Iran. J. Genet. Psychol.* **96**, 47–59.

DePaulo, B. M., Zuckerman, M., and Rosenthal, R. (1980). Modality effects in the detection of deception. *In:* Wheeler, J. (ed.), The Review of Personality and Social Psychology. New York: Sage Publ.

Deutsch, R. D. (1977). Spatial Structurings in Everyday Face-to-Face Behavior. Orangeburg, NY: The Assoc. for the Study of Man-Environment Relations, Inc.

(1979). On the isomorphic structure of endings: An example from everyday face-to-face interaction and Balinese Legong dance. *Ethol. Sociobiol.* **1**, 41–57.

Devereux, G. (1983). Baubo—die personifizierte Vulva. Curare, Sonderband 1/83, Braunschweig: Vieweg, pp. 117–120.

DeVore, I. (1971). The evolution of human society. *In:* Eisenberg, J. F. and Dillon, W. S. (eds.), Man and Beast: Comparative Social Behavior. Smithsonian Annual III. Washington, D. C.: Smithsonian Inst., pp. 297–311.

DeWaal, F. B. M. (1978). Exploitative and familiarity dependent support strategies in chimpanzees. *Behaviour* **17**, 268–312.

Dickey, E. C. and Knower, F. H. (1941). A note on some ethnological differences in recognition of simulated expressions of the emotions. *Amer. J. Sociol.* **47**, 190–193.

DiFranco, D., Muir, D. W., and Dodwell, P. C. (1978). Reaching in very young infants. *Perception* **7**, 385–392.

Dimberg, U. (1982). Facial reactions to facial expressions. *Psychophysiology* **19**, 643–647.

Dimberg, U. and Öhman, A. (1983). The effects of directional facial cues on electrodermal conditioning to facial stimuli. *Psychophysiology* **20**, 160–167.

Dingwall, W. O. (1979). The evolution of human communication systems. *In:* Whitaker, H. and Whitaker, H. A. (eds.), Studies in Neurolinguistics, Vol. 4. New York: Academic Press, pp. 1–95.

Divale, W. T. (1971). An explanation for primitive warfare: Population control and the significance of primitive sex ratios. *New Scholar* **2**, 173–192.

(1972). System population control in the middle and upper Paleolithic: Inferences based on contemporary hunter-gatherers. *World Archaeol.* **4**, 222–243.

Dodd, J. and Jessell, T. M. (1988). Axon guidance and the patterning of neuronal projections in vertebrates. *Science* **242**, 696–699.

Dörner, D. and Reither, F. (1978). Über das Problemlösen in sehr komplexen Realitätsbereichen. *Z. Exp. Angew. Psychol.* **25**, 527–551.

733

Dörner, D. and Vehrs. W. (1975). Ästhetische Befriedigung und Unbestimmtheitsreduktion. *Psychol. Rev.* **37**, 321–334.

Dörner, G. (1980). Sexual differentiation of the brain. *Vitamins Hormones* **38**, 325–381.

——— (1981). Sex hormones and neurotransmitters as mediators for sexual differentiation of the brain. *Endokrinology* **78**, 129–138.

Dörner, G., Rohde, W., Stahl, F., Krell, L., and Masius, W. G. (1975). A neuroendocrine predisposition for homosexuality in men. *Sex. Behav.* **4**, 1–8.

Dolgin, K. G. and Sabini, J. (1982). Experimental manipulation of a human non-verbal display: The tongue show effect and observers' willingness to interact. *Anim. Behav.* **30**, 935–936.

Dollard, J. and Miller, N. E. (1950). Personality and Psychotherapy. New York: McGraw-Hill.

Dollard, J., Doob, L. W., Miller, N. E., Mowrer, O. H., and Sears, R. R. (1939). Frustration and Aggression. New Haven: Yale University Press.

Doty, R. L. (1976). Reproductive endocrine influences upon human nasal chemoreception: A review. *In:* Doty, R. L. (ed.), Mammalian Olfaction, Reproductive Processes and Behavior. New York/London: Academic Press, pp. 295–321.

Draeger, D. F. and Smith, R. W. (1980). Comprehensive Asian Fighting Arts. Tokyo/New York/San Francisco: Kondansha Intern. Ltd.

Draper, P. (1976). Social and economic constraints on child life among the !Kung. *In:* Lee, R. and DeVore, I. (eds.), Kalahari Hunter-Gatherers. Cambridge, MA: Harvard University Press.

——— (1978). The learning environment for aggression and anti-social behavior among the !Kung. *In:* Montagu, A. (ed.), Learning Non-Aggression. New York/Oxford: Oxford University Press, pp. 31–53.

Duchen, M. R. and McNeilly, A. S. (1980). Hyperprolactinaemia and long-term lactational amenorrhoea. *Clin. Endocrinol.* **12**, 621–627.

Duchenne, B. (1862). Mécanisme de la Physionomie Humaine ou Analyse Electrophysiologique de l'Expression des Passions. Paris: Baillière.

Dum, J., Gramsch, Ch., and Herz, A. (1983). Activation of hypothalamic β-endorphin pools by reward induced by highly palatable food. *Pharmacol. Biochem. Behav.* **18**, 443–447.

Duncan, S. D. (1974). On the structure of speaker-auditor interaction during speaking turns. *Language Soc.* **2**, 161–180.

Duncan, S. D. and Fiske, D. W. (1977). Face-to-Face Interaction. Hillsdale, NJ: Lawrence Earlbaum.

Dundes, A., Leach, J. W., and Özkök, B. (1970). The strategy of turkish boys' verbal duelling rhymes. *J. Amer. Folklore* **83**, 325–349.

Dunkeld, J. (1978). The Function of Imitation in Infancy. Dissertation, Univ. of Edinburgh.

Dunkeld, J. and Bower, T. G. R. (1976). Infant Response to Impending Optical Collision. Cited after: Bower, T. G. R. A Primer of Infant Development. San Francisco: Freeman.

Dunn, K. and Dunn, R. (1977). How to Raise Independent and Professionally Successful Daughters. Englewood Cliffs, NJ: Prentice Hall.

Durden-Smith, J. and Desimone, D. (1983). Sex and the Brain. New York: Arbor House.

Durham, W. H. (1976). Resource competition and human aggression, a review of primitive war. *Quart. Rev. Biol.* **51**, 385–415.

——— (1979). Toward a coevolutionary theory of human biology and culture. *In:* Chagnon, N. A. and Irons, W. (eds.), Evolutionary Biology and Human Social Behavior: An Anthropological Perspective. North Scituate, MA: Duxbury Press, pp. 39–59.

Durkheim, E. (1964). The Division of Labor in Society. New York: Free Press.

Dusak Sexton, L. (1982). Wok Meri: A woman's savings and exchange system in Highland Papua New Guinea. *Oceania* **52**, 167–198.

Dworking, E. S. and Efran, J. S. (1967). The angered: Their susceptibility to varieties of humor. *J. Personality Soc. Psychol.* **6**, 233–236.

Dyson-Hudson, N. (1966). Karimojong Politics. London: Oxford University Press.

Dyson-Hudson, N. and Dyson-Hudson, R. (1969). Subsistence herding in Uganda. *Sci. Amer.* **220**, 76–89.

——— (1970). The food production system of a semi-nomadic society. The Karimojong, Uganda. *In:* McLoughlin, P. F. M. (ed.), African Food Production Systems: Cases and Theory. Baltimore, MD: John Hopkins Press, pp. 91–124.

Dyson-Hudson, R. and Smith, E. A. (1978): Human Territoriality: An ecological reassessment. *Amer. Anthropol.* **80**, 21–41.

Dyson-Hudson, R. and Van Dusen, R. (1972). Foodsharing among young children. *Ecol. Food Nutr.* **1**, 319–324.

Eckermann, C. O. and Whatley, J. L. (1977). Toys and social interactions between infant peers. *Child Develop.* **48**, 1645–1656.

Eder, D. and Hallinan, M. T. (1978). Sex differences in children's friendships. *Amer. Soc. Rev.* **43**, 237–249.

Ederer, R. (1982). Die Grenzen der Kunst. Wien/Graz/Köln: Hermann Böhlaus Nachf.

Edney, J. J. (1972). Property, possession and permanence: A field study in human territoriality. *J. Appl. Social Psychol.* **2**, 275–282.

Edney, J. J. and Jordan-Edney, N. L. (1974). Territorial spacing on a beach. *Sociometry,* **37**, 92 ff.

Efron, A. (1985). The sexual body: An interdisciplinary perspective. *J. Mind Behav.* **6**, [Special Issues 1, 2].

Efron, D. (1941). Gesture and Environment. New York: King's Crown Press.

Eggebrecht, R. (1983). Sprachmelodische und musikalische Forschungen im Kulturvergleich. Dissertation, Universität München.

Eibl-Eibesfeldt, I. (1950). Über die Jugendentwicklung des Verhaltens eines männlichen Dachses (*Meles meles* L.) unter besonderer Berücksichtigung des Spieles. *Z. Tierpsychol.* **7**, 327–355. (a)

(1950). Beiträge zur Biologie der Haus-und der Ährenmaus nebst einigen Beobachtungen an anderen Nagern. *Z. Tierpsychol.* **7**, 558–587. (b)

(1951). Zur Fortpflanzungsbiologie und Jugendentwicklung des Eichhörnchens. *Z. Tierpsychol.* **8**, 370–400.

(1955). Ethologische Studien am Galápagos-Seelöwen *Zalophus wollebaeki* Sivertsen. *Z. Tierpsychol.* **12**, 286–303. (a)

(1955). Über Symbiosen, Parasitismus und andere zwischenartliche Beziehungen bei tropischen Meeresfischen. *Z. Tierpsychol.* **12**, 203–219. (b)

(1955). Der Kommentkampf der Meerechse (*Amblyrhynchus cristatus* Bell) nebst einigen Notizen zur Biologie dieser Art. *Z. Tierpsychol.* **12**, 49–62. (c)

(1958). Das Verhalten der Nagetiere. *In:* Kükenthal, W. (ed.), Handbuch der Zoologie, Vol. 8 (10), pp. 1–88.

(1959). Der Fisch *Aspidontus taeniatus* als Nachahmer des Putzers *Labroides dimidiatus*. *Z. Tierpsychol.* **16**, 19–25.

(1962). Freiwasserbeobachtungen zur Deutung des Schwarmverhaltens verschiedener Fische. *Z. Tierpsychol.* **19**, 165–182.

(1963). Angeborenes und Erworbenes im Verhalten einiger Säuger. *Z. Tierpsychol.* **20**, 705–754.

(1967). Concepts of ethology and their significance for the study of human behavior. *In:* Stevenson, H. W. (ed.), Early Behavior, Comparative and Developmental Approaches. New York: Wiley, pp. 127–146.

(1970). Liebe und Haß. Zur Naturgeschichte elementarer Verhaltensweisen. München: Piper; Serie Piper 113, 1976. (a) [English edition: (1971). Love and Hate. The Natural History of Behavior Patterns. New York: Holt, Rinehart & Winston.]

(1970). Männliche und weibliche Schutzamulette im modernen Japan. *Homo* **21**, 175–188. (b)

(1971). Eine ethologische Interpretation des Palmfruchtfestes der Waika (Venezuela) nebst einigen Bemerkungen über die bindende Funktion von Zwiegesprächen. *Anthropos* **66**, 767–778. (a)

(1971). Filmbeiheft: !Ko-Buschleute (Kalahari)—Schamweisen und Spotten. *Homo* **22**, 261–266. (b)

(1972). Die !Ko-Buschmanngesellschaft: Gruppenbindung und Aggressionskontrolle. Monographien zur Humanethologie. München: Piper.

(1973). Der vorprogrammierte Mensch. Das Ererbte als bestimmender Faktor im menschlichen Verhalten. Wien (Molden), München: dtv 4177, 1976. (a)

(1973). The expressive behavior of the deaf-and-blind born. *In:* Cranach, M. v. and Vine, I. (eds.), Social Communication and Movement. London: Academic Press, pp. 163–194. (b)

(1974). Medlpa (Mbowamb)—Neuguinea—Werberitual (Amb Kanant). *Homo* **25**, 274–284.

(1975). Krieg und Frieden aus der Sicht der Verhaltensforschung. München: Piper. [English edition: 1979. The Biology of War and Peace. London: Thames and Hudson; New York: Viking Press.] (a)

(1975 rev. ed.). Ethology, The Biology of Behavior. New York: Holt, Rinehart & Winston. (b)

(1976). Menschenforschung auf neuen Wegen. Wien: Molden.

(1977, 3rd ed., 1984, 7th ed.). Galápagos. Die Arche Noah im Pazifik. München: Piper. (a)

(1977). Ambivalenz von Zuwendung und Abkehr im Begegnungsverhalten des Menschen. *Partner-Beratung* **14**, 113–118. (b)

(1978). Der Mensch und seine Umwelt: Ethologische Perspektiven. *In:* Buchwald, K. and Engelhardt, W. (eds.), Handbuch für Planung, Gestaltung und Schutz der Umwelt. München/Bern/Wien: BLV, pp. 102–115. (a)

(1978). Territorialität und Aggressivität der Jäger-und Sammlervölker. *In:* Stamm, R. A. and Zeier, H. (eds.), Die Psychologie des 20. Jahrhunderts. Band 6: Lorenz und die Folgen. Zürich: Kindler, pp. 477–494. (b)

(1978). Public places in society: Ethological perspectives. *In:* The Public Square, a Space for Culture. Cultures, Vol. V. The Unesco Press and la Baconnière, pp. 105–113. (c)

(1979). Functions of ritual. Ritual and ritualization from a biological perspective. *In:* Cranach, M. v., Foppa, K., Lepenies, W., and Ploog. D. (eds.), Human Ethology: Claims and Limits of a New Discipline. London: Maison des Sciences de l'Homme and Cambridge University Press, pp. 3–93. (a)

(1979). Human ethology: Concepts and implications for the science of man. *Behav. Brain Sci.* **2**, 1–57. (b)

(1979). !Ko-Buschleute (Kalahari)—Grashüpferspiel der Männer. *Homo* **30**, 49–54. (c)

(1980). G/wi-Buschleute (Kalahari)—Krankenheilung und Trance. *Homo* **31**, 67–78.

(1981). Medlpa (Mbowamb)–Neuguinea–Ritual der Totentrauer. *Homo* **32**, 59–70. (a)

(1981). Gesellschaftsordnung und menschliches Verhalten aus dem Blickwinkel der Evolution. *In:* Kaltenbrunner, K.-G. (ed.), Wir sind Evolution. München: Herder Bücherei, pp. 78–93. (b)

(1982). Patterns of parent-child interaction in a cross-cultural perspective. *In:* Oliverio, A. and Zappella, M. (eds.), The Behaviour of Human Infants. London: Plenum Press, pp. 177–217. (a)

(1982). Warfare, Man's indoctrinability and group selection. *Z. Tierpsychol.* **60**, 177–198. (b)

(1982). Interactionism, content, and language in human ethology studies. *Behav. Brain Sci.* **5** [2], 273–274. (c)

(1984). Ursprung und soziale Funktion des Objektbesitzes. *In:* Eggers, Ch. (ed.): Bindungen und Besitzdenken beim Kleinkind. München/Wien/Baltimore: Urban & Schwarzenberg, pp. 29–50.

(1987, 7th ed.). Grundriß der vergleichenden Verhaltensforschung. 7. überarb. und erweiterte Aufl., München: Piper.

Eibl-Eibesfeldt, I. and Hass, H. (1966). Zum Projekt einer ethologisch orientierten Untersuchung menschlichen Verhaltens. *Mitteil. Max-Planck-Ges.* **6**, 383–396.

(1967). Neue Wege der Humanethologie. *Homo* **18**, 13–23.

Eibl-Eibesfeldt, I. and Kacher, H. (1982). Bali (Indonesien)—Legong-Tanz. *Homo*, **33**, 46–56.

Eibl-Eibesfeldt, I. and Sielmann, H. (1962). Beobachtungen am Spechtfinken *Cactospiza pallida*. *J. Ornithol.* **103**, 92–101.

Eibl-Eibesfeldt, I. and Wickler, W. (1968). Die ethologische Deutung einiger Wächterfiguren auf Bali. *Z. Tierpsychol.* **25**, 719–726.

Eichler, M. (1981). The inadequacy of the monolithic model of the family. *Canad. Sociol.* **6**, 367–388.

Eickstedt, E. v (1944, 1963). Die Forschung am Menschen. Stuttgart: F. Enke.

Eimas, P. D., Cooper, W. E., and Corbit, J. D. (1973). Some properties of linguistic detectors. *Perception Psychophys.* **13**, 247–252.

Eimas, P. D., Siqueland, E. R., Jusczyk, P., and Vigorito. J. (1971). Speech perception in infants. *Science* **171**, 303–306.

Eisenberg, J. F. (1981). The Mammalian Radiation. Chicago/London: Univ. Chicago Press.

Eisenberg, L. (1971). Persistent problems in the study of the biopsychology of development. *In:* Tobach, E., Aronson, L., and Shaw, E. (eds.), The Biopsychology of Development. New York: Academic Press, pp. 515–529.

Ekman, P. (ed.) (1973). Darwin and Facial Expression. New York/London: Academic Press. (a)

—— (1973). Cross-cultural studies of facial expression. *In:* Ekman, P. (ed.), Darwin and Facial Expression. New York/London: Academic Press, 169–222. (b)

—— (1979). About brows: Emotional and conversational signals. *In:* Cranach, M. v., Foppa, K., Lepenies, W., and Ploog, D. (eds.), Human Ethology. Cambridge: Cambridge University Press), pp. 169–202.

—— (1981). Mistakes when deceiving. *Ann. NY Acad. Sci.* **364**, 269–278.

—— (1985). Telling Lies. New York: Berkley Books.

Ekman, P. and Friesen, W. V. (1975). Unmasking the Face. Englewood Cliffs, N.J.: Prentice Hall.

—— (1976). Measuring facial movements. *Environ. Psychol. Nonverbal Behav.* **1**, 56–75.

—— (1978). Facial Action Coding System, Palo Alto, CA: Consulting Psychologists Press Inc.

Ekman, P., Friesen, W. V., and Ellsworth, P. (1971). Emotions in the Human Face. New York: Pergamon Press. (a)

Ekman, P., Friesen, W. V., and Tomkins, S. S. (1971). Facial affect scoring technique: A first validity study. *Semiotica* **3**, 37–58. (b)

Ekman, P., Friesen, W. V., and Scherer, K. R. (1976). Body movement and voice pitch in deceptive interaction. *Semiotica* **16**, 23–27.

Ekman, P., Friesen, W. V. and Ancoli, S. (1980). Facial signs of emotional experience. *J. Personality Social Psychol.* **39**, 1125–1134.

Ekman, P., Hager, J. C., and Friesen, W. V. (1981). The symmetry of emotional and deliberate facial actions. *Psychophysiology* **18**, 101–106.

Ekman, P., Levenson, R. W., and Friesen, W. V. (1983). Autonomic nervous system activity distinguishes among emotions. *Science* **221**, 1208–1210.

Ekman, P., Friesen, W. V., and O'Sullivan, M. (1988). Smiles when lying. *J. Personality Social Psychol.* **54**, 414–420.

Elgar, M. A. and Catterall, C. P. (1981). Flocking and predator surveillance in house sparrows: Test of an hypothesis. *Anim. Behav.* **29**, 868–872.

Ellis, H. (1906). Sexual Selection in Man. Philadelphia, PA: F. A. Davis.

Ellis, L. (1985). On the rudiments of possessions and property. *Social Sci. Inform.* **24**, 113–143.

—— (1986). Evidence of neuroandrogenic etiology of sex roles from a combined analysis of human, nonhuman primate and non-primate mammalian studies. *Person. Individ. Diff.* **7**, 519–552.

Ellis, L. and Ames, M. A. (1987). Neurohormonal functioning and sexual orientation: A theory of homosexuality-heterosexuality. *Psychol. Bull.* **101**, 233–258.

Elsner, N. and Huber, F. (1973). Neurale Grundlagen artspezifischer Kommunikation bei Orthopteren. *Fortsch. Zool.* **22**, 1–48.

Elterman, H. (1983). Using popular songs to teach sociology. *Teaching Sociol.* **10**, 519–538.

Elwin, V. (1968). The kingdom of the young. London: Oxford University Press.

Ember, C. R. (1978). Myths about hunter-gatherers. *Ethnology* **17**, 439–448.

Ember, M. and Ember, C. R. (1979). Male-female bonding: A cross-species study of mammals and birds. *Behav. Sci. Res.* **14**, 37–56.

Endicott, K. and Lampell-Endicott, K. (1983). The Sociology of Land Use among the Batek of Malaysia. Paper presented at the 3rd Intern. Conf. on Hunters and Gatherers, Werner-Reimers-Stiftung, Bad Homburg, 13–16 June. 1983.

Engelhardt, W. (1978). Bevölkerungsentwicklung. *In:* Buchwald, K. and Engelhardt, W. (eds.), Handbuch für Planung, Gestaltung und Schutz der Umwelt. 1. Die Umwelt des Menschen. München: BLV, pp. 46–55.

—— (1979). Verstädterung. *In:* Buchwald, K. and Engelhardt, W. (eds.), Handbuch für Planung, Gestaltung und Schutz der Umwelt 1. München: BLV, pp. 55–60.

Engels, Fr. (1884). Der Ursprung der Familie, des Privateigentums und des Staates. Neuabdruck. *In:* Marx, K. and Engels, Fr. (eds.), Ausgewählte Schriften, Bd. 2. Berlin: Dietz Verlag, pp. 155–301.

Engen, T. (1982). The Perception of Odors. New York: Academic Press.

Epstein, D. (1979). Beyond Orpheus. Studies in Musical Structure. Cambridge: MIT Press.

(1985). Tempo relations: A cross-cultural study. *Music Theory Spectrum (J. Soc. Music Theory)* **7**, 34–71.

(1988). Tempo relations in music: A universal? *In:* Rentschler, I. Herzberger, B., and Epstein, D. (eds.), Beauty and the Brain. Basel, Boston, Berlin: Birkhäuser, pp. 91–116.

Erikson, E. H. (1950). Childhood and Society. New York: N. W. Norton.

(1966). Ontogeny of ritualization in man. *Phil. Trans. Roy. Soc. London* **B251**, 337–349.

Ertel, S. (1975). Überzeugung, Dogmatismus, Wahn. IX. Int. Kolloquium der Société Int. de Psychopathologie de l'expression. Hannover.

(1981). Wahrnehmung und Gesellschaft. Prägnanztendenzen in Wahrnehmung und Bewußtsein. *Semiotik* **3**, 107–141.

Escoffier, J., Malyon, A., Morin, Sr., and Raphael, S. (1980). Homophobia: Effects on scientists. *Science* **209**, 340.

Esser, A. H. (1970). Interactional Hierarchy and Power Structure on a Psychiatric Ward. *In:* Hutt, S. J. and Hutt, C. (eds.), Behavior Studies in Psychiatry. Oxford/New York: Pergamon, pp. 25–59.

Essock-Vitale, S. M. and McGuire, M. T. (1980). Predictions derived from the theory of kin selection and reciprocation assessed by anthropological data. *Ethol. Sociobiol.* **1**, 233–243.

Ewer, R. F. (1968). Ethology of Mammals. London: Logos Press.

Ewert, J. P. (1974). Neurobiologie und System-Theorie eines visuellen Mustererkennungs-mechanismus bei Kröten. *Kybernetik* **14**, 167–183. (a)

(1974). The neural basis of visually guided behavior. *Sci. Amer.* **230**, 34–42. (b)

Ewert, O. M. (1983). Eine historische Nachbemerkung zu Neuberger, Merz und Selg: Imitation bei Neugeborenen—eine kontroverse Befundlage (Kurzartikel). Z. f. Entwicklungspsychologie und Pädagog. *Psychologie* **15**, 277–279.

Eysenck, H. J. (1976). Sex and Personality. London: Open Books.

Fagen, R. (1981). Animal Play Behaviour. Oxford: Oxford University Press.

Fagot, B. I. (1978). The influence of sex of child on parental reactions to toddler children. *Child Develop.* **49**, 459–465.

Fantz, R. L. (1966). Pattern discrimination and selective attention as determinants of perceptual development from birth. *In:* Kidd, A. H. and Rivoire, J. L. (eds.), Perceptual Development in Children. New York: Int. Universities Press.

Faublée, J. (1968). Note Sur l'Economie Ostentatoire. *Rev. Tiers-Monde* **9**, 17–23.

Fauss, R. (1988). Zur Bedeutung des Gesichts für die Partnerwahl. *Homo* **37**, 188–201.

Fehling, D. (1974). Ethologische Überlegungen auf dem Gebiet der Altertumskunde. Monographien zur klassischen Altertumskunde, 61. München: C. H. Beck.

Feinman, S. (1980). Infant response to race, size, proximity, and movement of strangers. *Infant Behav. Develop.* **3**, 187–204.

Feldman, J., Brody, N. and Miller, St. (1980). Sex differences in non-elicited neonatal behaviors. *Merrill-Palmer Quart.* **26**, 63–73.

Felipe, N. and Sommer, R. (1966). Invasions of personal space. *Social Problems* **14**, 206–214.

Fentress, J. C. (ed.) (1976). Simpler Networks and Behavior. Sunderland, MA: Sinauer.

Ferguson, C. A. (1964). Baby talk in six languages. *In:* Gumperz, J. L. and Hymes, D. H. (eds.), Directions in Sociolinguistics. The Ethnography of Communication. New York: Holt, Rinehart & Winston, pp. 103–114. (1972).

Ferguson, R. B. (1984). Warfare, Culture and Environment. Studies in Anthropology. New York/London: Academic Press.

Ferguson, R. F. (1918). The Zulus and the Spartans: A comparison of their military systems. *Harvard Afr. Stud.* **2**, 198–227.

Fernald, A. (1985). Four-month-old infants prefer to listen to motherese. *Infant Behav. Develop.* **8**, 181–195.

Fernald, A. and Simon, Th. (1984). Expanded intonation contours in mothers' speech to newborns. *Develop. Psychol.* **20**, 104–113.

Ferrari, M. (1981). An observation of the infant's response to strangers: A test for ecological validity. *J. Genet. Psychol.* **139**, 157–158.

Feshbach, S. (1961). The stimulation vs. cathartic effects of a vicarious aggressive activity. *Abnormal Social Psychol.* **63,** 381–385.

(1964). The function of aggression and the regulation of aggressive drive. *Psychol. Rev.* **71,** 257–272.

Feshbach, S. and Singer, R. (1971). Television and Aggression. San Francisco: Jossey-Bass.

Field, T. M., Woodson, R., Greenberg, R., and Cohen, D. (1982). Discrimination and imitation of facial expressions by neonates. *Science* **218,** 179–181.

Field, T. M., Cohen, D., Garcia, R., and Greenberg, R. (1984). Mother–stranger face discrimination by the newborn. *Infant Behav. Develop.* **7,** 19–25.

Finkelhor, D. (1980). Sex among siblings: A survey of prevalence, variety, and effects *Arch. Sex. Behav.* **9,** 171–194.

Firestone, S. (1970). The Dialect of Sex. The Case for Feminist Revolution. Toronto: Bantam Books.

Firth, R. (1975). Symbols, Public and Private. London: Allen & Unwin.

Fisek, M. A. and Ofshe, R. (1970). The process of status evolution. *Sociometry* **33,** 327–346.

Fisher, A. E. (1955). Thesis, Pennsylvania. Cited in: *In:* Rajecki, D. W., Lamb, M. E., and Obmascher, P. (1978).

Fisher, E. (1979). Woman's Creation: Sexual Evolution and the Shaping of Society. New York: McGraw-Hill.

Fisher, S. (1973). The Female Orgasm: Psychology, Physiology, Fantasy. New York: Basic Books.

Flitner, A. (1975). Spielen-Lernen, München: Piper.

(1976). Das Kinderspiel. München: Piper.

Flohr, H. and Tönnesmann, W. (1983). Selbstverständnis und Grundlagen von Biopolitics. *In:* Flohr, H. and Tönnesmann, W. (eds.), Politik und Biologie. Berlin: Paul Parey, pp. 11–30. (a)

(ed.) (1983). Politik und Biologie. Berlin: Paul Parey. (b)

Ford, C. S. and Beach, F. A. (1969). Formen der Sexualität. Hamburg: Rororo-Sexologie.

Ford, M. R. and Lowery, C. R. (1986). Gender differences in moral reasoning: A comparison of the use of justice and care orientations. *J. Personality Social Psychol.* **50,** 777–783.

Fortune, R. F. (1939). Arapesh warfare. *Amer. Anthropol.* **41,** 22–41.

Fossey, D. (1977). The Behavior of the Free-Ranging Mountain Gorillas of the Virungas. Film shown at the 15th meeting of the Society of Anthropology and Human Genetic, Hamburg.

(1979). Development of the mountain gorilla *(Gorilla gorilla beringei).* The first thirty-six months. *In:* Hamburg, D. A. and McCown, E. R. (eds.), The Great Apes. Menlo Park, CA: Benjamin/Cummings, pp. 138–184.

Fouts, R. S. (1975). Communication with chimpanzees. *In:* Kurth, G. and Eibl-Eibesfeldt, I. (eds.), Hominisation und Verhalten. Stuttgart: Fischer, pp. 137–158.

Fox, C. A. Ismail, A. A. A., Love, D. N., Kirkham, K. E., and Loraine, J. A. (1972). Studies on the relationship between plasma testosterone levels and human sexual activity. *J. Endocrinol.* **52,** 51–58.

Fox, N. (1977). Attachment of kibbutz infants to mother and metapelet. *Child Develop.* **48,** 1228–1239.

Fraiberg, S. (1975). The development of human attachments in infants blind from birth. *Merrill-Palmer Quart.* **21,** 315–334.

Frank, H. (1960). Über grundlegende Sätze der Informationsästhetik. Grundlagenstudien aus *Kybernetik. Geisteswissenschaft* **1,** 25–32.

Frank, J. D. (1967). Muß Krieg sein? Psychologische Aspekte von Krieg und Frieden. Darmstadt: Verlag Darmstädter Blätter, Schwarz & Co.

Frasher, R., Brogan, D. R., and Nurss, J. R. (1980). Effect of model's age and sex upon modification of children's sex-typed toy preferences. *Intern J. Women's Stud.* **3,** 161–172.

Freedman, D. G. (1964). Smiling in blind infants and the issue of innate vs. acquired. *J. Child Psychol. Psychiat.* **5,** 171–184.

(1965). Hereditary control of early social behavior. *In:* Foss, B. M. (ed.), Determinants of Infant Behavior. London: Methuen.

(1979). Human Sociobiology. A Holistic Approach. New York: Free Press, Macmillan.

Freedman, J. L. and Fraser, S. C. (1966). Compliance without pressure: The foot-in-the-door technique. *J. Personality Social Psychol.* **4,** 195–203.

Freeman, C. and Jahoda, M. (1973). Zukunft aus dem Computer? Neuwied: Luchterhand.

Freeman, D. (1966). Social anthropology and the scientific study of human behaviour. *Man* **2,** 330–342.

(1983). Margaret Mead and Samoa. The Making and Unmaking of an Anthropological Myth. Cambridge, MA: Harvard University Press.

(1984). Inductivism and the Test of Truth: A Rejoinder to Lowell D. Holmes and others. *In:* Fact and Context in Ethnography; the Samoa Controversy. Canberra Anthropology Special Volume, The Australian National University, pp. 101–192.

Freisitzer, K. and Glück, H. (1979). Sozialer Wohnbau, Entstehung—Zustand—Alternativen. Wien: Molden.

Freud, A. (1946). The psychoanalytic study of infantile feeding disturbance. *Psychoanal. Study Child* **2,** 119–132.

Freud, S. (1913). Totem und Tabu. Leipzig/Wien (Heller).—Neudruck: S. Freud Studienausgabe, Bd. IX, Frankfurt/M: S. Fischer, pp. 291–444.

(1918). Totem and Taboo. A. A. Brill transl. New York: Moffat, Yard.

Frey, S. and Pool. J. (1976). A New Approach to the Analysis of Visible Behavior. Forschungsberichte aus dem Psychologischen Institut der Universität Bern.

Fried, M. H. (1961). Warfare, military organization, and the evolution of society. *Anthropologica* **3,** 134–147.

Fried, M., Harris, M., and Murphy, R. (eds.) (1968). War: The Anthropology of Armed Conflict and Aggression. Garden City, NY: Natural History Press.

Frisch, K. v. (1941). Über einen Schreckstoff der Fischhaut und seine biologische Bedeutung. *Z. Vergl. Physiol.* **29,** 46–145.

Frobenius, L. (1903). Weltgeschichte des Krieges. Jena: Thüringer Verlagsanstalt.

Frodi, A. M. and Lamb, M. E. (1978). Sex differences in responsiveness to infants: A developmental study of psychological and behavioral responses. *Child Develop.* **49,** 1182–1188.

(1980). Infants at risk for child abuse. *Infant Mental Health J.* **1,** 240–247. (a)

(1980). Child abusers' responses to infant smiles and cries. *Child Develop.* **51,** 238–241. (b)

Frodi, A. M., Lamb, M. E. Leavitt, L. A., Donovan, W. L., Neff, C., and Sherry, D. (1978). Fathers' and mothers' responses to the faces and cries of normal and premature infants. *Develop. Psychol.* **14,** 490–499.

Fromm, E. (1974). Anatomie der menschlichen Destruktivität. Stuttgart: DVA. (a)

(1974). Lieber fliehen als kämpfen. *Bild Wissenschaft* **10,** 52–58. (b)

(1976). Haben und Sein. Stuttgart: DVA.

Fry, H. K. (1934). Kinship and descent among australian aborigines. *Trans. Roy. Soc. S. Australia* **58,** 14–21.

Fthenakis, W. E. (1983). Der Vater als sorge- und umgangsberechtigter Elternteil. *In:* Remschmidt, H. (ed.), Kinderpsychiatrie und Familienrecht. Stuttgart: Ferdinand Enke.

Fukui, K. and Turton, D. (1979). Introduction to warfare among East African herders. *Nat. Mus. Ethnol. (Osaka, Japan)* **3,** 1–13.

Fullard, W. and Rieling, A. M. (1976): An investigation of Lorenz' baby babyness. *Child Develop.* **47,** 1191–1193.

Furby, L. (1978). Possessions: Toward a theory of their meaning and function throughout the life cycle. *Life Span Develop. Behav.* **1,** 297–336.

Gabor, D., Colombu, U., and Galli, R. (1976). Das Ende der Verschwendung. Stuttgart: Deutsche Verlagsanstalt.

Gallistel, C. R. (1980). The Organisation of Action. A New Synthesis. Hillsdale, NJ: Erlbaum.

Garcia, J. and Ervin, F. R. (1968). Gustatory-visceral and telereceptor-cutaneous conditioning—Adaptation in internal and external milieus. *Commun. Behav. Biol.,* **1,** 389–415.

Garcia, J., McGowan, B. K., Ervin, F. R., and Koelling, R. A. (1968). Cues: Their relative effectiveness as a function of the reinforcer. *Science* **160,** 794–795.

Gardner, B. T. and Gardner, R. A. (1975). Evidence for sentence constituents in the early utterances of child and chimpanzee. *J. Exp. Psychol. Gen.* **104,** 244–267.

(1980). Two comparative psychologists look at language acquisition. *In:* Nelson, K. E. (ed.), Children's Language, Vol. 2. New York: Halsted Press.

Gardner, B. T. and Wallach, L. (1965). Shapes of figures identified as a baby's head. *Perceptual Motor Skill* **20**, 135–142.

Gardner, R. and Heider, K. G. (1968). Gardens of War: Life and Death in the New Guinea Stone Age. London: Deutsch.

Gardner, R. A. and Gardner, B. T. (1984). A vocabulary test for chimpanzees (*Pan troglodytes*). *J. Comp. Psychol.* **98**, 381–404.

Gareis, B. (1978). Statistische Zusammenhänge von frühkindlicher Deprivation und späterer Jugendkriminalität. *In:* Nitsch, K. (ed.), Was wird aus unseren Kindern. Heidelberg: Hüthig Verlag, pp. 76–80.

Gaulin, St. J. C. and Schlegei, A. (1980). Paternal confidence and paternal investment: A cross-cultural test of a sociobiological hypothesis: *Ethol. Sociobiol.* **1**, 301–309.

Gazzaniga, M. S., Bogen, J. R., and Sperry, R. W. (1963). Laterality effects in somaesthesis following cerebral commissurotomy in man. *Neuropsychologia* **1**, 209–221.
(1965). Observations in visual perception of the cerebral hemisphere in man. *Brain* **88**, 221–236.

Gazzaniga, M. S., LeDoux, J. E., and Wilson, D. H. (1977). Language, praxis and the right hemisphere: Clues to some mechanisms of consciousness. *Neurology* **24**, 1144–1147.

Geber, M. (1958). The psychomotor development of African children in the first year, and the influence of maternal behavior. *J. Soc. Psychol.* **47**, 185–195.
(1961). Développement psychomoteur des petits Baganda de la naissance à six ans. *Schweiz. Psychol. Anwendungen* **20**, 345–357.

Geber, M. and Dean, R. F. A. (1957). The state of development of newborn African children. *Lancet* **272**, 1216–1219. (a)
(1957). Gesell tests on african children. *Pediatrics* **20**, 1055–1065. (b)
(1958). Psychomotor development in African children: The effects of social class and the need for improved tests. *Bull. WHO* **18**, 471–476.

Gedda, L. (1971). Body odour genetically determined. *J. Amer.* Med. Assoc. **217**, 486.

Geen, R. G. and O'Neal, E. C. (eds.) (1976). Perspectives on Aggression. New York: Academic Press.

Geen, R. G. and Quanty, M. B. (1977). The catharsis of aggression: An evaluation of a hypothesis. *Advan. Exp. Social Psychol.* **10**, 1–37.

Geer, J. P. van de (1971). Introduction to Multivariate Analysis for the Social Sciences. San Francisco: W. H. Freeman.

Gehlen, A. (1940). Der Mensch, seine Natur und seine Stellung in der Welt. Berlin/Frankfurt: Athenaeum.

Geist, V. (ed.) (1978). Life Strategies, Human Evolution, Environmental Design. New York: Springer.

Gennep, A. van (1960). The Rites of Passage. Chicago: The University of Chicago Press; London: Routledge & Kegan Paul Ltd. [Original: (1908). Les rites de passage.]

Gerson, M. (1978). Family, Women and Socialization in the Kibbutz. Lexington, MA: Lexington Books.

Geschwind, N. (1979). Specializations of the human brain. *Sci. Amer.* **241** (3), 158–168.

Gesell, A. (1946). The ontogenesis of infant behavior. *In:* Carmirhael, L. (ed.), Manual of Child Psychology. New York: Wiley.

Gewirtz, J. L. (1961). A learning analysis of the effects of normal stimulation, privation and deprivation on the acquisition of social motivation and attachment in determinants of infant behavior. *In:* Foss, B. M. (ed.), Determinants of Infant Behavior, Vol. 1. London: Methuen, pp. 213–290.

Ghiselin, M. T. (1974). The Economy of Nature and the Evolution of Sex. Berkeley/Los Angeles/London: University of California Press.

Gibbs, F. A. (1951). Ictal and non-ictal psychiatric disorders in temporal lobe epilepsy. *J. Nervous Mental Dis.* **113**, 522–528.

Gibson, E. J. and Walk, R. D. (1960). The visual cliff. *Sci. Amer.* **202**, 64–71.

Gill, T. V. (1977). Conversations with Lana. *In:* Rumbaugh, D. M. (ed.), Language Learning by a Chimpanzee. The Lana Project. New York: Academic Press, pp. 225–246.

Gilles, J. L. and Jamtgaard, K. (1981). Overgrazing in pastoral areas—the commons reconsidered. *Sociol. Ruralis* **21**, 129.

Ginsburg, H. J., Fling, Sh., Hope, M. L., Musgrove, D., and Andrews, Ch. (1980). Maternal holding preferences: A consequence of newborn head-turning response. *Child Develop.* **50**, 280–281.

Gladue, B. A., Green, R., and Hellman, R. E. (1984). Neuroendocrine response to estrogen and sexual orientation. *Science* **225,** 1496–1499.

Glanzer, M. (1962): Grammatical category: A rote learning and word association analysis. *J. Verbal Learning Verbal Behav.* **1,** 31–41.

Godelier, M. (1978). Territory and property in primitive society. *Social Science Inform.* **17,** 399–426.

Goetze, D. (1977). Castro, Nkrumah, Sukarno. Eine vergleichende Untersuchung zur Strukturanalyse charismatischer politischer Führung. Berlin: Dietrich Reimer.

Goffman, E. (1959). The Presentation of Self in Everyday Life. New York: Anchor Books.
(1963). Behavior in Public Places: Notes on the Social Organisation of Gatherings. New York: Free Press (Macmillan).
(1971). Relations in Public. London: Allen Lane, Penguin Press.
(1976). Gender advertisements. *Stud. Anthropol. Visual Commun.* **3,** 2.

Golani, I. (1969). The Golden Jackal. Tel Aviv: The Movement Notation Society.

Goldberg, D. C. Whipple, B., Fishkin, R. E., Waxman, H., Fink, P. J., and Weisberg, M. (1983). The Grafenberg spot and female ejaculation: A review of initial hypotheses. *J. Sex Marital Therapy* **9,** 27–37.

Goldberg, S. and Lewis, M. (1969). Play behavior in the year-old infant: Early sex differences. *Child Develop.* **40,** 21–31.

Goldenthal, P., Johnston, R. E., and Kraut, R. E. (1981). Smiling, appeasement, and the silent bared-teeth display. *Ethol. Sociobiol.* **2,** 127–133.

Goldfoot, D. A., Westerborg-van Loon, H., Groeneveld, W., and Koos Slob, A. (1980). Behavioral and physiological evidence of sexual climax in the female stump-tailed macaque *(Macaca arctoides). Science* **208,** 1477–1479.

Goldin-Meadow, S. and Mylander, C. (1983). Gestural communication in deaf children: Noneffect of parental input on language development. *Science* **221,** 372–374.

Goldman, M. and Fordyce, J. (1983). Prosocial behavior as affected by eye contact, touch, and voice expression. *J. Social Psychol.* **121,** 125–129.

Goldschmidt, R. B. (1940). The Material Basis of Evolution. New Haven: Yale University Press.

Goldstein, A. G. and Jeffords, J. (1981). Status and touching behavior. *Bull. Psychosom. Soc.* **17,** 79–81.

Gombrich, E. H. (1982). Ornament und Kunst. Schmucktrieb und Ordnungssinn in der Psychologie des dekorativen Schaffens. Stuttgart: Klett-Cotta.

Good, K. R. (1982). Limiting Factors in Amazonian Ecology. Paper presented at the 81st Meeting Amer. Anthropol. Assoc., Washington, 4 December, 1982.
(1988). Ritualized Contract-Chants among the Yanomami. *In:* Publikationen des Human-ethologischen Tonarchivs der Max-Planck-Gesellschaft, Nr. 1, Begleitpublikation zum Tondokument Nr. 1 (Andechs: Mimeo).

Good, P. R., Geary, N., and Engen, T. (1976). The effect of estrogen on odor detection. *Chem. Senses Flavour* **2,** 45–50.

Goodall, J. (1986). The Chimpanzees of Gombe, Patterns of Behavior. Cambridge MA/London: Belknap Press of Harvard University Press.

Goodall, J., Bandora, A., Bergmann, E., Busse, C., Matama, H., Mpongo, E., Pierce, A., and Riss, D. (1979). Intercommunity interactions in the chimpanzee population of the Gombe National Park. *In:* Hamburg, D. A. and McCown, E. R. (eds.), The Great Apes. Menlo Park, CA: The Benjamin/Cummings.

Goodenough Pitcher, E. and Hickey Schultz, L. (1983). Boys and Girls at Play: The Development of Sex Roles. New York: Praeger.

Goodman, C. S. and Bastiani, M. J. (1984). How embryonic nerve cells recognize one another. *Sci. Amer.* **251**(6), 50–58.

Goodman, C. S., Bastiani, M. J., Doe, C. Q., Du Lac, S., Helfand, St. L., Kuwada, J. Y., and Thomas, J. B. (1984). Cell recognition during neuronal development. *Science* **225,** 1271–1279.

Goodwin, G. (1971). Western Apache Raiding and Warfare. Tucson: University of Arizona Press.

Gordon, R. J. (1984). The !Kung in the Kalahari exchange: An ethnohistorical perspective. *In:* Schrire, C. (ed.), Past and Present in Hunter-Gatherer Studies. Orlando/New York/London: Academic Press, pp. 195–224.

Gottlieb, G. (1976). Early development of species-specific auditory perception in birds. *In:* Gottlieb, G. (ed.), Neural and Behavioral Specificity. New York: Academic Press.

Gottman, J. M. (1983). How children become friends. *Monogr. Soc. Res. Child Develop.* **48,** Nr. 3.

Gould, S. J. (1980). The Panda's Thumb. New York/London: W. W. Norton.

Gower, D. B. (1972). 16-unsaturated C_{19} steroids. A review of their chemistry, biochemistry and possible physiological role. *J. Steroid Biochem.* **3,** 45–103.

Grafenberg, E. (1950). The role of urethra in female orgasm. *Intern J. Sex.* **3,** 145–148.

Graham, C. A. and McGrew, W. C. (1980). Menstrual synchrony in female undergraduates living on a coeducational campus. *Psychoneurendocrinology* **5,** 245–252.

Graham, E. E. (1973). Yuman Warfare: An Analysis of Ecological Factors from Ethnohistorical Sources. Paper read at the 9th Intern. Congr. of Anthropological and Ethnological Sciences, Chicago.

Grammer, K. (1979). Helfen und Unterstützen in Kindergruppen. Diplomarbeit des Zoologischen Instituts. Universität München.

(1982). Wettbewerb und Kooperation: Strategien des Eingriffs in Konflikte unter Kindern einer Kindergartengruppe. Diss. Univ. München, Fachbereich Biologie.

(1985). Verhaltensforschung am Menschen: Überlegungen zu den biologischen Grundlagen des "Umwegverhaltens." *In:* Svilar, M. (ed.), Mensch und Tier. Bern, pp. 273–318.

(1986). "Social Tool Use" in Human Courtship: The Function of Laughter. Submitted for publication.

(1988). Biologische Grundlagen des Sozialverhaltens. Darmstadt: Wissenschaftliche Buchgesellschaft.

(in press). Human courtship: Biological bases and cognitive processing. *In:* Rasa, A., Vogel, C., Volland, E. (eds.), Sociobiology of Reproductive Strategies in Animals and Men. Beckenham: Croom Helm.

Grammer, K., Schropp, R, and Shibasaka, H. (1984). Contact, conflict and appeasement—children's interaction strategies. The use of photography. *Intern. J. Visual Sociol.* **2,** 59–74.

Grammer, K., Schiefenhovel, W., Schleidt, M., Lorenz, B., and Eibl-Eibesfeldt, I. (1988). Patterns on the face: The eyebrow flash in cross cultural comparison. *Ethology* **77,** 270–299.

Grant, E. C. (1965). The contribution of ethology to child psychiatry. *In:* Howell, J. G. (ed.), Modern Perspectives in Child Psychiatry. Edinburgh: Oliver and Boyd.

(1968). An ethological description of non-verbal behavior during interviews. *Brit. J. Med. Psychol.* **41,** 177–184.

(1969). Human facial expression. *Man* **4**[NS], 525–536.

Gray, J. P. and Wolfe, L. D. (1983). Human female sexual cycles and the concealment of ovulation problem. *J. Soc. Biol. Structures* **6,** 345–352.

Greed, G. W. (1984). Sexual subordination: Institutionalized homosexuality and social control in Melanesia. *Ethnology* **23,** 157–176.

Green, J. A., Jones, L. E., and Gustafson, G. E. (1987). Perception of cries by parents and nonparents: Relation to cry acoustics. *Develop. Psychol.* **23,** 370–382.

Green, St. and Marler, P. (1979). The analysis of animal communication. *In:* King, F. A. (ed.), Handbook of Behavioral Neurobiology. Vol 3: Social Behavior and Communication. New York/London: Plenum Press, pp. 73–158.

Greenberg, M. and Morris, N. (1982). Engrossment—the newborn's impact upon the father. *In:* Cath, S. H., Gurwitt, A. R., and Ross, J. M. (eds.), Father and Child, Developmental and Clinical Perspectives. Boston: Little, Brown. [Reprint from *Amer. J. Orthopsychiat.* **44,** (1974), 520–530.]

Greene, P. J., Morgan, Ch. J., and Barash, D. P. (1980). Hybrid vigor: Evolutionary biology and sociology. *In:* Lockard, J. (ed.), The Evolution of Human Social Behavior. New York: Elsevier.

Greif, E. B. and Gleason, J. B. (1980). Hi, thanks and goodbye: More routine information. *Language Soc.* **9,** 159–166.

Grellert, E. A. (1982). Childhood play behavior of homosexual and heterosexual men. *Psychol. Rep.* **51,** 607–610.

Grellert, E. A., Newcomb, M. D., and Bentler, P. M. (1982). Childhood play activities of male and female homosexuals and heterosexuals. *Arch. Sex. Behav.* **11,** 451–478.

Grieser, D. L. and Kuhl, P. K. (1988). Maternal speech to infants in a tonal language: Support for universal prosodic features in motherese. *Develop. Psychol.* **24**(1), 14–20.

Griffin, P. B. (1984). Forager resource and land use in the humid tropics: The Agta of Northeastern Luzon, the Philippines. *In:* Schrire, C. (ed.), Past and Present in Hunter-Gatherer Studies. New York/London: Academic Press, pp. 95–121.

Grimm, H. (1983). Psycholinguistische Aspekte der frühen Sprachanbahnung. *Sozialpädiatr. Praxis Klinik* 5, 589–593.

Groos, K. (^{3}1933). Die Spiele der Tiere. Jena: Gustav Fischer.

Grossmann, K. (1978). Die Wirkung des Augenöffnens von Neugeborenen auf das Verhalten ihrer Mütter. *Geburtshilfe Frauenheilk.* **38**, 629–635.

Grossmann, K. E. (1977). Frühe Einflüsse auf die soziale und intellektuelle Entwicklung. *Z. Pädagogik* **23**, 847–880.

Grossmann, K. E. and Grossman, K. (1982). Eltern-Kind-Bindung in Bielefeld. *In:* Immelmann, K., Barlow, G., Petrinovich, L., and Maid, M. (ed.), Verhaltensentwicklung bei Mensch und Tier. Berlin: Paul Parey, pp. 794–799.

Grüsser, O. J. (1983). Mother-child holding patterns in western art: A developmental study. *Ethol. Sociobiol.* **4**, 89–94.

Gruhl, H. (1975). Ein Planet wird geplündert. Frankfurt/M.: S. Fischer.

Grusec, J. E. and Brinker, D. B. (1972). Reinforcement for imitation as a social learning determinant with implications for sex-role development. *J. Personality Social Psychol.* **21**, 149–158.

Gruter, M. (1979). Origins of legal behavior. *J. Social Biol. Structures* **2**, 43–51.

(1982). Biologically based behavioral research and the facts of law. *J. Social Biol. Structures* **5**, 315–323.

Grzimek, B. and Grzimek, M. (1959). Serengeti darf nicht sterben. Berlin: Ullstein.

Guenther, M. G. (1981). Bushman and hunter-gatherer territoriality. *Z. Ethnol.* **106**, 109–120.

Gumperz, J. L. and Hymes, D. H. (eds.) (1972). Directions in Sociolinguistics. The Ethnography of Communication. New York: Holt, Rinehart & Winston.

Guthrie, E. R. (1952). The Psychology of Learning. New York: Harper.

Guthrie, R. D. (1976). Body Hot Spots. New York: Van Nostrand-Reinhold.

Habermas, J. (1957). Können Konsumenten spielen? *Frankfurter Allgem. Zeitung, No.* **88**, 13 April, 1957.

Hailman, J. P. (1967). The ontogeny of an instinct. *Behaviour Suppl.* **15**, 1–196.

Haldane, J. B. S. (1955). Population genetics. *New Biol.* **18**, 34–51.

Hales, D. J., Lozoff, B., Sosa, R., and Kennell, J. H. (1977). Defining the limits of the maternal sensitive period. *Develop. Med. Child. Neurol.* **19**, 454–461.

Hall, E. T. (1966). The Hidden Dimension. New York: Doubleday.

Hall, K. R. R. (1966). Social learning in monkeys. *J. Zool.* **148**, 15–87.

Hallowell, A. I. (1940). Aggression in Saulteaux society. *Psychiatry* 3, 395–407.

Hallpike, C. R. (1973). Functionalist interpretations of primitive warfare. *Man* 8, 451–470.

Hamblin, R. L. (1958). Leadership and crisis. *Sociometry* 20, 322–335.

Hamburg, B. A. (1974). The psychobiology of sex differences. An evolutionary perspective. *In:* Friedman, R. C., Richart, R. M., and Van de Wiele, R. L. (eds.), Sex Differences in Behavior. New York/London: John Wiley, pp. 373–392.

Hamilton, W. D. (1964). The genetical evolution of social behavior. *J. Theoret. Biol.* **7**, 1–52.

(1967). Extraordinary sex ratios. *Science* **156**, 477–488.

(1972). Altruism and related phenomena, mainly in social insects. *Ann. Rev. Syst.* **3**, 193–232.

Hamm, M., Russell, M., and Koepke, J. (1979). Neonatal Imitation? Vortrag anläßlich der Tagung der Society for Research in Child Development, San Francisco, March, 1979.

Hardin, G. (1968). The tragedy of the commons. *Science* **162**, 1243–1248.

Harrelson, A. L. and Goodman, C. S. (1988). Growth cone guidance in insects: Fasciclin II is a member of the immunoglobulin superfamily. *Science* **242**, 700–708.

Harris, M. (1968). The Rise of Anthropological Theory. New York: T. Y. Crowell.

(1971). Culture, Man and Nature: An Introduction to General Anthropology. New York: Crowell.

(1974). Cows, Pigs, Wars and Witches: The Riddles of Culture. New York: Random House.

(1975). Culture, People and Nature: An Introduction to General Anthropology. New York: Crowell.

(1977). Cannibals and Kings: The Origins of Cultures. New York: Random House. (a)

(1977). Why men dominate women. *New York Times Magazine* **46**. (b)

(1979). The Yanomamö and the causes of war in band and village societies. *In:* Margolis, M. and Carter, W. (eds.), Brazil: Anthropological Perspectives. Essays in Honor of Charles Wagley. New York: Columbia University Press, pp. 121–132.

Harris, P. and MacFarlane, J. A. (1974). The growth of the effective visual field from birth to seven weeks. *J. Exp. Child Psychol.* **18**, 340–348.

Hartup, W. W. (1975). The origins of friendship. *In:* Lewis, M. and Rosenblum, L. A. (eds.), Friendship and Peer Relations. New York: Wiley, pp. 1–26.

Hass, H. (1968). Wir Menschen. Wien: Molden.

(1970). Das Energon. Wien: Molden.

(1981). Vorteil des Menschen: Er kann sein "Energon" verändern. *In:* Das neue Erfolgs und Karrierehandbuch für Selbständige und Führungskräfte. Geretsried: Verlag Beste Unternehmensführung, pp. 157–198.

Hassenstein, B. (1966). Kybernetik und biologische Forschung. *In:* Gessner, F. (ed.), Handbuch der Biologie, Bd. 1/2: Allgemeine Biologie. Frankfurt/M.: Athenaion, pp. 629–719.

(1972). Bedingungen für Lernprozesse—teleonomisch gesehen. *Nova Acta Leopoldina* [N. F.] **37**, 289–320. (a)

(1972). Verhaltensbiologische Aspekte der frühkindlichen Entwicklung und ihre sozialpolitischen Konsequenzen. Mannheimer Forum 72 (Boehringer), pp. 168–203. (b)

(1973). Verhaltensbiologie des Kindes. München: Piper. (a)

(1973). Kindliche Entwicklung aus der Sicht der Verhaltensbiologie. *Kinderarzt* **21**, 134–136, 191–192, 260–265, 407–410. (b)

(1977). Faktische Elternschaft. Ein neuer Begriff der Familiendynamik und seine Bedeutung. *Familiendynamik* **2**, 104–125.

(1981). Biologisch bedeutsame Vorgänge in den ersten Lebenswochen. *In:* Hövels, O., Halberstadt, E., Laewenich, V. v., and Eckert, I. (ed.), Geburtshilfe und Kinderheilkunde. Stuttgart: Georg Thieme, pp. 56–71.

(1982). Sexualentwicklung des Kindes in verhaltensbiologischer Sicht. *In:* Hellbrügge, Th. (eds.), Entwicklung der kindlichen Sexualität, München: Urban & Schwarzenberg.

(1983). Funktionsschaltbilder als Hilfsmittel zur Darstellung theoretischer Konzepte in der Verhaltensbiologie. *Zool. Jb. Physiol.* **87**, 181–187.

Hausfater, G. (1979). Comments/discussions on Eibl-Eibesfeldt, I. (1979). Human ethology: Concepts and implications for the science of man. *Behav. Brain Sci.* **2**, 36–37.

Hausfater, G. and Vogel, Ch. (1982). Infanticide in langur monkeys (genus *Presbytis*): recent research and a review of hypotheses. *In:* Chiarelli, A. B. and Corruccini, R. S. (eds.), Advanced Views in Primate Biology. Berlin/Heidelberg: Springer, pp. 160–176.

Havemann, R. (1980). Morgen. Die Industriegesellschaft am Scheideweg. München: Piper.

Hawkes, K. (1977). Co-operation in Binumarien: Evidence for Sahlin's model. *Man* **12** [NS] 459–483.

(1983). Kin selection and culture. *Amer. Ethnol.* **10**, 345–363.

(in press): Helping Kin: Is it Nepotism?

Hayduk, L. A. (1978). Personal space: An "evaluation" and orienting overview. *Psychol. Bull.* **85**, 117–133.

(1983). Personal space: Where we now stand. *Psychol. Bull.* **94**, 293–335.

Hayduk, L. A. and Mainprize, St. (1980). Personal space of the blind. *Social Psychol. Quart.* **43**, 216–223.

Hayek, F. A. v. (1975). Die Irrtümer des Konstruktivismus. Walter-Eucken-Institut, Vorträge und Aufsätze 51, Tübingen: J. C. B. Mohr.

(1977). Drei Vorlesungen über Demokratie, Gerechtigkeit und Sozialismus. Walter-Eucken-Institut, Vorträge und Aufsätze 63, Tübingen: J. C. B. Mohr.

(1979). Die drei Quellen der menschlichen Werte. Walter-Eucken-Institut, Vorträge und Aufsätze 70, Tübingen: J. C. B. Mohr. (a)

(1979). Liberalismus. Walter-Eucken-Institut, Vorträge und Aufsätze 72, Tübingen: J. C. B. Mohr. (b)

(1980/1981). Recht, Gesetzgebung und Freiheit. Eine neue Darstellung der liberalen Prinzipien der Gerechtigkeit und der politischen Ökonomie, 3 Bde. Landsberg a. Lech: Verlag Moderne Industrie.

(1983). Die überschätzte Vernunft. *In:* Riedl, R. and Kreuzer, F. (ed.), Evolution und Menschenbild. Hamburg: Hoffmann & Camper, pp. 164–192.

Hayes, L. A. and Watson, J. L. (1981). Neonatal imitation: Fact or artifact? *Develop. Psychol.* **17**, 655–660.

Haynes, H. M., White, B. L. and Held, R. (1965). Visual accommodation in human infants. *Science* **148**, 528–530.

Healey, Ch. (1984). Trade and sociability: Balanced reciprocity as generosity in New Guinea Highlands. *Amer. Ethnol.* **11**, 42–60.

Hecaen, H. and Albert, M. L. (1978). Human Neural Psychology. New York: Wiley.

Hediger, H. (1934). Zur Biologie und Psychologie der Flucht bei Tieren. *Biol. Zentralbl.* **54**, 21–40.

Heeschen, V. (1976). Überlegungen zum Begriff "Sprachliches Handeln." *Z. German. Linguistik* **4**, 273–301.

— (1982). Stil und Inhalt der Lieder und Tanztexte der Eipo. Vortrag auf Einladung der DFG im Rahmen des Symposiums "Mensch, Kultur und Umwelt im zentralen Bergland von Westneuguinea," Berlin.

— (1984). Ästhetische Form und sprachliches Handeln: Sprechen auf der Suche nach einem Partner. Vortrag auf der Jahrestagung der Gesellschaft für Sprachwissenschaft, Bielefeld. (a)

— (1984). Durch Krieg und Brautpreis zur Freundschaft. Vergleichende Verhaltensstudien zu den Eipo und Yalenang. Vortrag gehalten auf dem Kolloquium des Schwerpunktprogramms der DFG "Mensch, Kultur und Areal im zentralen Bergland von Westneuguinea," Seewiesen, 30, 3-1 April, 1984. (b)

— (1984, in press). Singen bei der Arbeit. Publ. zum Film E 2522: Heeschen, V. und Heunemann, D.: Singen bei der Arbeit. Göttingen, IWF.

— (in press). Humanethologische Aspekte der Sprachevolution. *In:* Gessinger, J. and v. Rahden, W. (eds.), Theorien vom Ursprung der Sprache. Berlin: De Gruyter.

Heeschen, V., Schiefenhövel, W., and Eibl-Eibesfeldt, I. (1980). Requesting, giving and taking: The relationship between verbal and nonverbal behavior in the speech community of the Eipo, Irian Jaya (West New Guinea). *In:* Key, R. M. (ed.), The Relationship of Verbal and Nonverbal Behavior. The Hague/Paris/New York: Mouton, pp. 139–166.

Heinroth, O. (1910). Beiträge zur Biologie, insbesondere Psychologie und Ethologie der Anatiden. Verh. 5. Int. Ornith. Kongr. Berlin, pp. 589–702.

Heinz, H. J. (1966). The Social Organization of the !Ko-Bushmen. Masters Thesis. Johannesburg, University of South Africa.

— (1967). Conflicts, Tensions and Release of Tensions in a Bushmen Society. The Institute for the Study of Man in Africa, Isma Papers 23, 2–21.

— (1972). Territoriality among the Bushmen, in general, and the !Ko, in particular. *Anthropos,* **67**, 405–416.

— (1979). The nexus complex among the !Ko-Bushmen of Botswana. *Anthropos* **74**, 465–480.

Heinz, H. J. and Maguire, B. (1974). The Ethno-Biology of the !Ko-Bushmen. Their Ethno-Botanical Knowledge and Plant Lore. Occ. Papers 1, Botswana Soc., Gaborone.

Hellbrügge, Th. (1967). Chronophysiologie des Kindes. *Verhandl. Deut. Ges. Innere Med.* **73**, 895.

Heller, A. (1980). The emotional division of labor between the sexes. *Soc. Prax.* **7**, 205–218.

Helmuth, H. (1967). Zum Verhalten des Menschen: Die Aggression. *Z. Ethnol.* **92**, 265–273.

Henley, N. M. (1977). Body Politics: Power, Sex, and Nonverbal Communication. Englewood Cliffs, NJ: Prentice Hall.

Herdt, G. H. (1982). Rituals of Manhood. Male Initiation in Papua New Guinea. Berkeley: University of California Press.

Herskovits, M. J. (1950). Man and His Works: The Science of Cultural Anthropology. New York: Knopf.

Herz, A. (1984). Biochemie und Pharmakologie des Schmerzgeschehens. *In:* Zimmermann, C. M. and Handwerker, H. O. (eds.), Schmerz, Berlin: Springer, pp. 61–86.

Heslin, R., Nguyen, T. D., and Nguyen, M. L. (1983). Meaning of touch from a stranger or same person. *J. Nonverbal Behav.* **7**, 147–157.

Hess, E. H. (1973). Imprinting: Early Experience and the Developmental Psychology of Attachment. New York: Van Nostrand.

(1975). The Tell-Tale Eye. New York: Van Nostrand Reinhold.

(1977). Das sprechende Auge. München: Kindler.

Hewes, G. H. (1957). The anthropology of posture. *Sci. Amer.* **196**, 123–132.

Hewes, G. W. (1973). An explicit formulation of the relationship between tool-using, tool-making and the emergence of language. *Visible Language* **72**, 101–127.

(1977). Language origin theories. *In:* Rumbaugh, D. M. (ed.), Language Learning by a Chimpanzee. The Lana Project. New York: Academic Press, pp. 3–53.

Heymer, A. (1981). "Schnelles Brauenheben" im Kontext verschiedener sozialer Interaktionen, *Homo* **32** (3, 4), 1981.

Hicks, D. J. (1965). Imitation and retention of film-mediated aggressive peer and adult models. *J. Personality Social Psychol.* **2**, 97–100.

Hilgard, E. R. and Bower, G. H. (1973, 3rd ed.). Theorien des Lernens, 2 Bde. Stuttgart: Klett. Engl. Edition (1975, 4th ed.). Theories of Learning. New York.

Hill, J. H. (1974). Possible continuity theories of language. *Language* **50**, 134–150.

Hill, W. W. (1936). Navaho Warfare. New Haven: Yale Univ. Publications in Anthropology, 5.

Hinde, R. A. (1966). Animal Behaviour: A Synthesis of Ethology and Comparative Psychology. New York/London: McGraw-Hill.

(1974). Biological Basis of Human Social Behaviour. New York: McGraw-Hill.

(1984). Why do sexes behave differently in close relationships? *J. Soc. Personal Relationships* **1**, 471–501.

Hinde, R. A. and Barden, L. A. (1985). The evolution of the teddy bear. *Anim. Behav.* **33**, 1371–1372.

Hinde, R. A. and Stevenson-Hinde, J. (1976). Towards understanding relationships: Dynamic stability. *In:* Bateson, P. P. G. and Hinde, R. A. (eds.), Growing Points in Ethology. Cambridge: Cambridge Univ. Press, pp. 451–479.

Hinde, R. A., Easton, D. F., Meller, R. E., and Tamplin, A. (1983). Nature and determinants of preschoolers' differential behavior to adults and peers. *Brit. J. Develop. Psychol.* **1**, 3–19.

Hines, S. M. Jr. (1983). Die Ursprünge des Staates: Traditionelle Interpretationen, aktueller Forschungsstand und der emergente Charakter des Staates. *In:* Flohr, H. and Tönnesmann, W. (eds.), Politik und Biologie. Berlin: Paul Parey, pp. 68–79.

Hirst, G. (1982). An evaluation of evidence for innate sex differences in linguistic ability. *J. Psycholinguistic Res.* **2**, 95–113.

Hite, S. (1976). The Hite Report: A Nationwide Study of Female Sexuality. New York: Dell.

Hjortsjö, C.-H. (1969). Man's Face and Mimic Language. Malmö: Studentlitteratur.

Hobbes, T. (1968). Leviathan. London: Penguin.

Hockett, C. F. (1960). Logical considerations in the study of animal communication. *Amer. Inst. Sci. Publ.* **7**, 392–430. Dasselbe: *Z. Tierpsychol.* **23**, 250–254.

Hodder, I. (1982). The Present Past. London: Batsford.

Hoebel, B. G. (1983): Neurogene und chemische Grundlagen des Glücksgefühls. *In:* Gruter, M. and Rehbinder, M. (eds.), Der Beitrag der Biologie zu Fragen von Recht und Ethik. *Schrift. Rechtssoziol. Rechtstatsachenforsch.* **54**, 87–109.

Hoebel, E. A. (1967). Song duels among the Eskimo. *In:* Bohannan, P. (ed.), Law and Warfare, New York; Natural History Press, pp. 255–262.

Hörmann, L. v. (1877). Tiroler Volkstypen. Wien.

Hoffmann-Krayer, E. and Bächtold-Stäubli, H. (1930). Haberfeldtreiben. Handwörterbuch des deutschen Aberglaubens, III. Berlin: de Gruyter, p. 1291.

(1933). Katzenmusik. Handwörterbuch des deutschen Aberglaubens, IV. Berlin: de Gruyter, pp. 1125–1132.

Hokanson, J. E. (1970). Psychophysiological evaluation of the catharsis hypothesis. *In:* Megargee, E. I. and Hokanson, J. E. (eds.), The Dynamics of Aggression. New York: Harper & Row, pp. 74–86.

Hokanson, J. E. and Shetler, S. (1961). The effect of overt aggression on physiological tension level. *J. Abnormal Social Psychol.* **63**, 446–448.

Hold, B. (1974). Rangordnungsverhalten bei Vorschulkindern. *Homo* **25**, 252–267.

(1976). Attention structure and rank specific behaviour in pre-school children. *In:* Chance, M. R. A. and Larsen, R. R. (eds.), The Social Structure of Attention. London: Wiley, pp. 177–201.

(1977). Rank and behaviour: An ethological study of pre-school children. *Homo* **28**, 158–188.

Hold, B. and Schleidt, M. (1977). The importance of human odour in non-verbal communication. *Z. Tierpsychol.* **43**, 225–239.

Hold-Cavell, B. (1983). Die Entwicklung und Bedeutung des Ansehens von Kindern im Kindergarten. Universität Regensburg, Institut fur Psychologie.

Hold-Cavell, B. and Stöhr, C. (1986). The significance of attention structure: when do children attend to each other? *Bull. d'Ecol. Ethol. Humaines* **5**, 24–36.

Hold-Cavell, B. C. L. and D. Borsutzky (1986). Strategies to obtain high regard: Longitudinal study of a group of preschool children. *Ethol. Sociobiol.* **7**, 39–56.

Holst, E. v. (1935). Über den Prozeß der zentralen Koordination. *Pflügers Arch.* **236**, 149–158.

(1936). Versuche zur Theorie der relativen Koordination. *Plügers Arch.* **237**, 93–121.

(1937). Baustein zu einer vergleichenden Physiologie der lokomotorischen Reflexe bei Fischen, II. *Z. Vergl. Physiol.* **24**, 532–562.

(1939). Die relative Koordination als Phänomen und als Methode zentralnervöser Funktionsanalyse. *Erg. Physiol.* **42**, 228–306.

(1955). Regelvorgänge der optischen Wahrnehmung. 5th Conf. Soc. Biol. Rhythm. Stockholm, pp. 26–34.

(1957). Aktive Leistungen der menschlichen Gesichtswahrnehmung. *Stud. Generale* **10**, 231–243.

Holst, E. v. and Mittelstaedt, H. (1950). Das Reafferenz-Prinzip. *Naturwissenschaften* **37**, 464–476.

Holst, E. v. and Saint-Paul, U. v. (1960). Vom Wirkungsgefüge der Triebe. *Naturwissenschaften* **18**, 409–422.

Holzapfel, M. (1940). Triebbedingte Ruhezustände als Ziel des Appetenzverhaltens. *Naturwissenschaften* **28**, 273–280.

Hooff, J. A. R. A. van (1969). The facial display of the catarrhine monkeys and apes. *In:* Morris, D. (ed.), Primate Ethology. New York: Garden City, pp. 9–98.

(1971). Aspecten van Het Sociale Gedrag En De Communicatie Bij Humane En Hogere Niet-Humane Primaten (Aspects of the Social Behavior and Communication in Human and Higher Non-Human Primates). Rotterdam: Bonder-Offset (n. v.).

(1973). A structural analysis of the social behavior of a semi-captive group of chimpanzees. *In:* Cranach, M. von and Vine, I. (eds.), Social Communication and Movement. New York: Academic Press, pp. 75–162.

(1976). The comparison of facial expression in man and higher primates. *In:* Cranach, M. v. (ed.), Methods of Inference from Animal to Human Behaviour. Chicago: Aldine; The Hague/Paris: Mouton, pp. 165–196.

(1982). Categories and sequences of behaviour: Methods of description and analysis. *In:* Scherer, K. and Ekman, P. (eds.), Handbook of Methods in Nonverbal Behavior Research. Cambridge/London/New York: Cambridge University Press, pp. 362–439.

Hoon, P. W., Bruce, K., and Kinchloe, B. (1982). Does the menstrual cycle play a role in sexual arousal? *Psychophysiology* **19**, 21–27.

Horvath, Th. (1979). Correlates of physical beauty in men and women. *Soc. Behav. Personality* **7**, 145–151.

(1981). Physical attractiveness: The influence of selected torso parameters. *Arch. Sex. Behav.* **10**, 21–24.

Hospers, J. (1969). Introductory Readings in Aesthetics. New York: The Free Press (Collier).

Hoyle, G. (1984). The Scope of Neuroethology. *Behav. Brain Sci.* **7**, 367–412.

Hrdy, S. B. See Blaffer-Hrdy, S. B.

Hubel, D. H. and Wiesel, T. N. (1962). Receptive fields, binocular interactions and functional architecture in the cat's visual cortex. *J. Physiol.* **160**, 106–154.

(1963). Receptive fields of cells in striate cortex of very young, visually inexperienced kittens. *J. Neurophysiol.* **24**, 994–1002.

Huber, E. (1931). Evolution facial Muscles. *In:* Webster, R. C., Smith, R. C., and Smith, K. F. (1983). Face lift, 2. Etiology of platysma cording and its relationship to treatment. *Head and Neck Surg.* **6**, 590–595.

Huber, F. (1974). Neuronal background of species-specific acoustical communication in orthopteran insects (Gryllidae). *In:* Broughton, W. B. (ed.), The Biology of Brains. Symposia of the Inst. of Biol., No. 21., Chapt. 4, pp. 61–88. Oxford: Blackwell.

(1977). Lautäußerungen und Lauterkennen bei Insekten (Grillen). Rheinisch-Westfälische Akad.Wiss., Vorträge Nr. 265, Opladen: Westdeutscher Verlag.

(1983). Neural correlates of orthopteran and cicada phonotaxis. *In:* Huber, F. and Markl, H. (eds.), Neuroethology and Behavioral Physiology. Berlin: Springer, pp. 108–135.

Hückstedt, B. (1965). Experimentelle Untersuchungen zum "Kindchenschema." *Z. Exp. Angew. Psychol.* **12**, 421–450.

Hughes, A. L. (1981). Female infanticide: Sex ratio manipulation in humans. *Ethol. Sociobiol.* **2**, 109–111.

Hull, D. L. (1978). Scientific bandwagon or travelling medicine show? *Society,* Sept./Oct., pp. 50–59.

Hulsebus, R. C. (1973). Operant conditioning of infant behavior: A review. *Advan. Child Develop. Behav.* **8**, 111–158.

Humphrey, T. (1969). Postnatal repetition of human pre-natal activity sequences with some suggestions of their neuroanatomical basis. *In:* Robinson, R. J. (ed.), Brain and Early Behavior. New York: Academic Press.

Hunsperger, R. W. (1954). Reizversuche im periventrikulären Grau des Mittel- und Zwischenhirns (Film). *Helv. Physiol. Acta* **12**, C4–C6.

Hunt, G. T. (1940). The Wars of the Iroquois: A Study in Intertribal Trade Relations. Madison, WI: University of Wisconsin Press.

Huxley, A. (1932). Brave New World. London: Chatto & Windus.

(1959). Brave New World Revisited. London: Chatto & Windus.

(²1981). Schöne neue Welt, und: Dreißig Jahre danach oder Wiedersehen mit der Schönen Neuen Welt. München; Piper.

Hymes, D. H. (1970). The ethnography of speaking. *In:* Fishman, J. A. (ed.), Readings in the Sociology of Language. Paris/The Hague: Mouton, pp. 94–138.

Ikeda, K. and Kaplan, W. O. (1970). Unilaterally patterned neural activity of a mutant gynandromorph of *Drosophila melanogaster*. *Amer. Zool.* **10**, 311.

Immelmann, K. (1965). Prägungserscheinungen in der Gesangsentwicklung junger Zebrafinken. *Naturwissenschaften* **52**, 169–170.

(1966). Zur Irreversibilität der Prägung. *Naturwissenschaften* **53**, 209.

(1970). Zur ökologischen Bedeutung prägungsbedingter Isolationsmechanismen. *Verhandl. Deut. Zool. Ges.* **64**, 304–314.

(1975). Ecological significance of imprinting and early learning. *Annu. Rev. Ecol. Systematics* **6**, 15–37.

Imperato-McGinley, J., Peterson, R. E., Gautier, T., and Sturla, E. (1979). Androgens and the evolution of the male gender-identity among male pseudohermaphrodites with 5αreductase deficiency. *New Eng. J. Med.* **300**, 1233–1237.

Isaac, G. (1978). The foodsharing behavior of protohuman hominids. *Sci. Amer.* **238**, 90–108.

Itten, J. (1961). Kunst der Farbe. Subjektives Erleben und objektives Erkennen der Wege zur Kunst. Ravensburg: Maier.

Izard, C. E. (1968). The emotions and emotion constructs in personality and culture research. *In:* Cattell, R. B. (ed.), Handbook of Modern Personality Theory. Chicago: Aldine.

(1971). The Face of Emotion. New York: Appleton-Century-Crofts.

(1981). Die Emotionen des Menschen. Weinheim: Beltz.

Jackendorff, R. and Lerdahl, F. (1982). A grammatical parallel between music and language. *In:* Clynes, M. (ed.), Music, Mind and Brain, New York: Plenum, pp. 83–119.

Jacklin, C. N. and Maccoby, E. E. (1978). Social behaviour at thirty-three months in same-sex and mixed-sex dyads. *Child Develop.* **49**, 557–569.

Jacobson, J. L. (1981). The role of inanimate objects in early peer interaction. *Child Develop.* **52**, 618–626.

Jacobson, S. W. (1979). Matching behavior in the young infant. *Child Develop.* **50**, 425–430.

Jaffe, Y., Shapir, N., and Yinon, Y. (1981). Aggression and its escalation. *J. Cross-Cultural Psychol.* **12**, 21–36.

Jahoda, G. (1954). A note on Ashanti names and their relationship to personality. *Brit. J. Psychol.* **45**, 192–195.

Jakobson, R. (1941). Kindersprache, Aphasie und allgemeine Lautgesetze. Språkvetenskapliga Sällskapets i Uppsala, Förhandlingar, pp. 1–83.

James, W. (1890). Principles of Psychology. New York: Holt, Rinehart & Winston.

Jantsch. E. (1979). Sociobiological and sociocultural process: A non-reductionist view. *J. Social Biol. Structures* **2,** 87–92.

Jarvie, I. C. (1983). The problem of the ethnographic real. *Current Anthropol.* **24,** 313–325.

Jensen, A. R. (1980). Bias in Mental Testing. New York: The Free Press. (a)
  (1980). Multiple book review of bias in mental testing. *Behav. Brain Sci.* **3,** 325—371. (b)
  (1983). The definition of intelligence and factor-score indeterminancy. *Behav. Brain Sci.* **6,** 313–315.

Jessen, E. (1981). Untersuchungen zur Geschlechtererkennung—Die Zuordnung einfacher geometrischer Formen zu Mann und Frau in verschiedenen Altersstufen und Kulturen. Dissertation, Ludwig-Maximilian-Universität München.

Jettmar, K. (1973). Die anthropologische Aussage der Ethnologie. *In:* Gadamer, H.-G. and Vogler, P. (eds.), Neue Anthropologie, vol. 4. Kulturanthropologie. Stuttgart: Thieme.

Johnson, R. N. (1972). Aggression in Man and Animals. Philadelphia/London: Saunders.

Johnson, R. S. (1982). Food, other valuables, payment and the relative scale of Ommura ceremonies (New Guinea). *Anthropos* **77,** 509–523.

Jolly, A. (1972). The Evolution of Primate Behavior. New York: Macmillan.

Jouvet, M. (1972). Le discours biologique. *Rev. Med.* **16–17,** 1003–1063.

Jürgens, J. (1971). Soziales Verhalten, Kommunikation und Hirnmechanismen. *Umschau* **71,** 799–802.

Jürgens, J. and Ploog, D. (1976). Zur Evolution der Stimme. *Arch. Psychiatr. Nervenkr.,* **222,** 117–137.

Kagan, J. (1971). Change and Continuity in Infancy. New York: Wiley.

Kahn, H. (1977). Vor uns die guten Jahre. Wien: Molden.

Kahn-Ladas, A., Whipple, B., and Perry, J. D. (1982). The G-Spot and Other Recent Discoveries about Human Sexuality. New York: Holt, Rinehart & Winston.

Kaiser, G. (1978). Comment/discussion. *In:* Nitsch, K. (eds.), Was wird aus unseren Kindern? Heidelberg: Hüthig Verlag, pp. 34–45.

Kaissling, K. E. (1971). Insect olfaction. *In:* Beidler, L. M. (ed.), Handbook of Sensory Physiology, vol. 4. Chemical Senses. Berlin: Springer, pp. 351–431.

Kaissling, K. E. and Priesner, E. (1970). Die Riechschwelle des Seidenspinners. *Naturwissenschaften* **57,** 23–38.

Kaitz, M., Meschulach-Sarfaty, O, Auerbach, J., and Eidelman, A. (1988). A reexamination of newborns' ability to imitate facial expressions. *Develop. Psychol.* **24,**(1), 3–7.

Kalbermatten, U. (1979). Handlung, Theorie, Methode— Ergebnisse. Dissertation, Universität Bern. Zürich: Juris Verlag.

Kalbermatten, U. and Cranach, M. v. (1980). Hierarchisch aufgebaute Beobachtungssysteme zur Handlungsanalyse. *In:* Winkler, P. (ed.), Methoden zur Analyse von Face-to-Face-Situationen. Stuttgart: Metzler.

Kallman, F. J. (1952). A comparative twin study on the genetic aspects of male homosexuality. *J. Nerv. Mental Dis.* **115,** 283.

Kalmus, H. (1955). The discrimination by the nose of the dog of individual human odours and in particular of the odours of twins. *Brit. J. Anim. Behav.* **3,** 25–31.

Kalnins, I. V. and Bruner, J. S. (1973). Infant sucking used to change the clarity of a visual display. *In:* Hulsebus, R. C.: Operant Conditioning of Infant Behaviour, a Review. *Advan. Child Develop. Behav.* **8.**

Kaltenbach, K., Weinraub, M. and Fullard, W. (1980). Infant wariness toward strangers reconsidered: Infants' and mothers' reactions to unfamiliar persons. *Child Develop.* **51,** 1197–1202.

Kandel, E. R. (1976). Cellular Basis of Behavior. An Introduction to Behavioral Neurobiology. San Francisco: W. H. Freeman.

Kaplan, H., Hill, K., Hawkes, K., and Hurtado, A. (1984). Food sharing among Ache hunter-gatherers of Eastern Paraguay. *Current Anthropology.* **25,** 113–115.

Kaplan, M. A. (1979). Is species selfishness a viable concept? *J. Social Biol. Structures.* **2,** 1–7.

Kardiner, A. (1939). The Individual and His Society. New York: Columbia University Press.
  (1945). The Psychological Frontiers of Society. New York: Columbia University Press.

Karsten, R. (1923). Blood revenge, war, and victory feasts among the Jibaro Indians of Eastern Ecuador. *Bur. Amer. Ethnol. Bull.* 79.

Katz, R. J. and Steiner, M. (1979). Dream and motivation: a psychobiological approach. *J. Social Biol. Structures* **2**, 141–154.

Kauffman-Doig, F. (1979). Sexual Behaviour in Ancient Peru. Lima-Surquillo: Kompactos.

Kay, P. and Kempton, W. (1984). What is the Sapir-Whorf hypothesis? *Amer. Anthropol.* **86**, 65–79.

Keegan, J. (1976). The Face of Battle. New York: Viking Press.

Keegan, J. and Darracott, J. (1981). The Nature of War. New York: Holt, Rinehart & Winston.

Keesing, R. M. (1981). Cultural Anthropology. A contemporary Perspective. New York: Holt, Rinehart & Winston.

Keller, H. (1979). Die Entstehung von Geschlechtsunterschieden im ersten Lebensjahr. *In:* Degenhardt, A. and Trautner, H. M. (eds.), Geschlechtstypisches Verhalten. München: C. H. Beck, pp. 122–144.

(1980). Gaze and Gaze Aversion in the First Months of Life. Institut für Psychologie der Technischen Universität Darmstadt, 80/5. (a)

(1980). Beobachtung, Beschreibung und Interpretation von Eltern-Kind-Interaktionen im ersten Lebensjahr. Beobachtungsmanual für die ersten 4 Lebensmonate. Institut für Psychologie der Technischen Universität Darmstadt, 80/8. (b)

Keller, H., Gauda, G., and Miranda, D. (1980). Beobachtung, Beschreibung und Interpretation von Eltern-Kind-Interaktionen im ersten Lebensjahr. Skalen zur Beurteilung "Angemessenes Elternverhalten." Institut für Psychologie der Technischen Universität Darmstadt.

Kendon, A. (1977). Spatial organization in social encounters: The F-formation system. *In:* Kendon, A. (ed.), Studies in Semiotic. Bloomington, IN: Indiana University Press; Lisse: The Peter de Ridder Press.

Kendon, A. and Ferber, A. (1973). A description of some human greetings. *In:* Michael, R. P. and Crook, J. H. (eds.), Comparative Ecology and Behaviour of Primates. London: Academic Press, pp. 591–668.

Kennedy, J. M. (1980). Blind people recognizing and making haptic pictures. *In:* Hagen, M. (ed.), The Perception of Pictures. London/New York: Academic Press, pp. 263–303.

(1982). Haptic Pictures. *In:* Schiff, W. and Foulke, E. (eds.), Tactual Perception. Cambridge/London/New York: Cambridge University Press, pp. 305–331.

(1983). What can we learn about pictures from the blind? *Amer. Sci.* **71**, 19–26.

Kennell, J., Jerauld, R., Wolfe, H., Chesler, D., Kreger, N., McAlpine, W., Steffa, M., and Klaus, M. (1974). Maternal behavior one year after early and extended postpartum contact. *Develop. Med. Child Neurol.* **16**, 172–179.

Kennell, J., Trause, M., and Klaus, M. (1975). Evidence for a sensitive period in the human mother. *In:* Brazelton, T., Tronick, E., Adamson, L., Als, H., and Wise, S. (eds.), Parent-Infant Interaction. New York: Elsevier/Excerpta Media/North Holland, pp. 87–101.

Kephart, W. M. (1976). Extraordinary Groups. New York: St. Martin Press.

Keupp, L. (1971). Aggressivität und Sexualität. München: Goldmann.

Keverne, E. B. (1978). Olfactory cues in mammalian sexual behaviour. *In:* Hutchinson, J. P. (ed.), Biological Determinants of Sexual Behaviour. Chichester/New York: Wiley, pp. 727–763.

Keverne, E. B., Levy, F., Poindron, P., and Lindsay, D. R. (1983). Vaginal stimulation: An important determinant of maternal bonding in sheep. *Science* **219**, 81–83.

Kiener, F. (1986). Das Wort als Waffe. Zur Psychologie der verbalen Aggression. Göttingen: Vandenhoeck & Ruprecht.

King, G. E. (1980). Alternative uses of primates and carnivores in the reconstruction of early hominid behavior. *Ethol. Sociobiol.* **1**, 99–109.

Kinsey, A. C. *et al.* (1966). Das sexuelle Verhalten des Mannes. Frankfurt/M.: Fischer Verlag.—English Edition (1948). Sexual Behavior in the Human Male. Philadelphia: Saunders.

Kinsey, A. C., Pomeroy, W. B., and Martin, C. E. (1954). Das sexuelle Verhalten der Frau. Berlin/Frankfurt/M.: Fischer, Athenaeum. English Edition (1953). Sexual Behavior in the Human Female. Philadelphia: Saunders.

Kirkendall, L. A. (1961). Premarital Intercourse and Interpersonal Relationships. New York: Julian Press.

Kirk-Smith, M. and Booth, D. A. (1980). Effect of androstenone on choice of location in other's presence. *In:* Starre, H. van der (ed.), Olfaction and Taste, VII. London: IRL Press, pp. 397–400.

Kirk-Smith, M., Booth, D. A., Carroll, D., and Davies, P. (1978). Human Social Attitudes Affected by Androstenol. Research Communications in Psychology, *Psychiat. Behav.* **3**, 379–384.

Kistyakovskaya, M.Y. (1970). The Development of Movement in Children during the First Year of Life. Moskau: Pedagogika.

Kitcher, P. (1985). Vaulting Ambition: Sociobiology and the Quest for Human Nature. Cambridge, MA: MIT Press.

(1987). Precis of vaulting ambition. *Behav. Brain Sci.* **10**, 61–100.

Kitzinger, S. (1984). Sexualität im Leben der Frau. München: Biederstein.

Klaus, M. and Kennell, J. (1976). Parent-to-infant attachment. *In:* Hull, D. (ed.), Recent Advances in Pediatrics. Edinburgh/London/New York: Churchill Livingstone, pp. 129–152.

Klaus, M., Kennell, J., Plumb, N., and Zuehlke, S. (1970). Human maternal behavior at the first contact with her young. *Pediatrics* **46**, 187–192.

Klaus, M., Jerauld, R., Kreger, N., McAlpine, W., Steffa, M., and Kennell, J. (1972). Maternal attachment: Importance of the first post-partum days. *New Engl. J. Med.* **286**, 460–463.

Klaus, M., Trause, M., and Kennell, J. (1975). Does human maternal behaviour after delivery show a characteristic pattern? *In:* Brazelton, T., Tronick, E., Adamson, L., Als, H., and Wise, S. (eds.), Parent-Infant Interaction. New York: Elsevier/Excerpta Media/North Holland, pp. 69–95.

Kleck, R. E., Buck, P. L., Goller, W. C., London, R. S., Pfeiffer, J. R., and Vukcevic, D. P. (1968). Effect of stigmatizing conditions on the use of personal space. *Psychol. Rep. 23,* 111–118.

Kleitman, N. (1963). Sleep and Wakefulness. Chicago: University of Chicago Press.

Kleitman, N. and Engelmann, T. C. (1953). Sleep characteristics of infants. *J. Appl. Physiol.* **6**, 269–282.

Klopfer, P. (1971). Mother love: What turns it on? *Amer. Sci.* **59**, 404–407.

Kluckhohn, C. (1947). Some aspects of Navaho infancy and early childhood. *Psychoanal. Soc. Sci.* **1**, 37–86.

Klüver, H. and Bucy, P. C. (1937). "Psychic blindness" and other symptoms following bilateral temporal lobectomy in rhesus monkeys. *Amer. J. Physiol.* **119**, 352–353.

Klutschak, H. W. (1881). Als Eskimo unter Eskimos. Wien: Hartleben.

Kneutgen, J. (1964). Beobachtungen über die Anpassung von Verhaltensweisen an gleichförmige akustische Reize. *Z. Tierpsychol.* **21**, 763–779.

(1970). Eine Musikform und ihre biologische Funktion. Über die Wirkungsweise der Wiegenlieder. *Z. Exp. Angew. Psychol.* **17**, 245–265.

Knowles, E. S. (1972). Boundaries around social space: Dyadic responses to an invader. *Environ. Behav.* **4**, 437–447.

(1973). Boundaries around group interaction: The effect of group size and member status on boundary permeability. *J. Personality Social Psychol.* **26**, 327–332.

Knowles, N. (1940). The torture of captives by the Indians of Eastern North America. *Proc. Amer. Phil. Soc.* 82(2).

Koch, K. F. (1970). Cannibalistic revenge in Jalé society. *Nat. History* 79, 40–51.

(1974). War and Peace in Jalémo: The Management of Conflict in Highland New Guinea. Cambridge, MA: Harvard University Press.

Koehler, O. (1954). Vorbedingungen und Vorstufen unserer Sprache bei Tieren. *Zool. Anz. Suppl.* **18**, 327–341.

Köhler, W. (1921). Intelligenzprüfungen an Menschenaffen. Berlin: Springer; Neudruck 1963.

Koelega, H. S. and Köster, E. P. (1974). Some experiments on sex differences in odor perception. *Ann. NY Acad. Sci.* **237**, 234–246.

König, H. (1925). Der Rechtsbruch und sein Ausgleich bei den Eskimos. *Anthropos* **20**, 276–315.

Koenig, L. (1951). Beiträge zu einem Aktionssystem des Bienenfressers (*Merops apiaster* L.). *Z. Tierpsychol.* **8**, 169–210.

Koenig, O. (1968). Biologie der Uniform. *Naturwiss. Med.* **5,** 3–19, 40–50.

——— (1969). Verhaltensforschung und Kultur. *In:* Altner, G. (ed.), Kreatur Mensch. München: Moos-Verlag, pp. 57–84.

——— (1970). Kultur und Verhaltensforschung. München: Dtv.

——— (1975). Urmotiv Auge, München: Piper.

Koepke, J. E., Hamm, M., Legerstee, M., and Russell, M. (1983). Neonatal imitation: Two failures to replicate. *Infant Behav. Develop.* **6,** 97–102.

Kohlberg, L. A. (1966). A cognitive-developmental analysis of children's sex-role concepts and attitudes. *In:* MacCoby, E. E. (ed.), The Development of Sex Differences. Stanford: Stanford University Press, pp. 82–173.

——— (1969). Stage and Sequence: The cognitive-developmental approach to socialization. *In:* Goslin, D. A. (ed.), Handbook of Socialization Theory and Research. Chicago: Rand McNally, pp. 347–480.

——— (1981). Essays on Moral Development. Vol. 1: The Philosophy of Moral Development: Moral Stages and the Idea of Justice. New York: Harper & Row.

Kohl-Larsen, L. (1943). Auf den Spuren des Vormenschen. Deutsche Afrika-Expedition 1934–36 und 1937–39. Stuttgart: Strecker und Schröder.

——— (1958). Wildbeuter in Ostafrika. Die Tindiga, ein Jäger-und Sammlervolk. Berlin: Reimer.

Kohr, L. (1983). Die überentwickelten Nationen. Salzburg: Alfred Winter.

Kolodny, R. C., *et al.* (1971). Plasma testosterone and semen analysis in male homosexuals. *New Engl. J. Med.* **285,** 1170.

Komisaruk, B. R. and Olds, J. (1968). Neuronal correlates of behavior in freely moving rats. *Science* **161,** 810–812.

Konecni, V. J. and Doob, A. N. (1972). Catharsis through displacement of aggression. *J. Personality Social Psychol.* **23,** 379–387.

Konecni, V. J. and Ebbesen, E. B. (1976). Disinhibition vs. the cathartic effect: Artifact and substance. *J. Personality Social Psychol.* **34,** 352–365.

Konishi, M. (1964). Effects of deafening on song development in two species of juncos. *Condor* **66,** 85–102.

——— (1965). Effects of deafening on song development of American robins and black-headed grosbeaks. *Z. Tierpsychol.* **22,** 584–599. (a)

——— (1965). The role of auditory feedback in the control of vocalization in the white-crowned sparrow. *Z. Tierpsychol.* **22,** 770–783. (b)

Konner, M. J. (1972). Aspects of the development of ethology of a foraging people. *In:* Blurton-Jones, N. G. (ed.), Ethological Studies of Child Behaviour. Cambridge: Cambridge University Press, pp. 285–304.

——— (1975). Relations among infants and juveniles in comparative perspective. *In:* Lewis, M. and Rosenblum, L. A. (eds.), Friendship and Peer Relations. New York: John Wiley, pp. 99–129.

——— (1977). Evolution of human behavior development. *In:* Leiderman, P. H., Tulkin, St. R. and Rosenfeld, A. (eds.), Culture and Infancy, Variations in the Human Experience. New York: Academic Press, pp. 69–109. (a)

——— (1977). Infancy among the Kalahari Desert San. *In:* Leiderman, P. H., Tulkin, St. R. and Rosenfeld, A. (eds.), Culture and Infancy, Variations in the Human Experience. New York: Academic Press, pp. 287–328. (b)

——— (1981). Evolution of human behavior development. *In:* Munroe, R. H., Munroe, R. L., and Whiting, B. B. (eds.), Handbook of Cross-Cultural Human Development. New York/London: Garland STPM Press, pp. 3–51.

——— (1982). The Tangled Wing. Biological Constraints on the Human Spirit. New York: Holt, Rinehart & Winston.

Konner, M. J. and Worthman, C. (1980). Nursing frequencies, gonadal hormones, and birth spacing among !Kung hunter-gatherers. *Science* **207,** 788–791.

Korner, A. F. (1969). Neonatal startles, smiles, erections and reflex sucks as related to state, sex and individuality. *Child Develop.* **40,** 1039–1053.

——— (1971). Individual differences at birth: Implications for early experience and later development. *Amer. J. Orthopsych.* **41,** 608–619.

——— (1974). Methodological considerations in studying sex differences in the behavioral functioning of newborns. *In:* Friedman, R. D., Richart, R. M., and Vande Wiele, R. L. (eds.), Sex Differences in Behavior. New York/London: Wiley, 373–392.

Kortlandt, A. (1972). New Perspectives on Ape and Human Evolution. Stichting voor Psychobiologie, Zoologisch Laboratorium Amsterdam.

Kortmulder, K. (1968). An ethological theory of the incest taboo and exogamy. *Current Anthropol.* **9**, 437–449.

Kovach, J. K. (1970). Critical period or optimal arousal? Early approach behavior as a function of stimulus, age, and breed variables in chicks. *Develop. Psychol.* **3**, 88–97.

Kovach, J. K. and Hess, E. H. (1963). Imprinting: Effects of painful stimulation on the following response. *J. Comp. Physiol. Psychol.* **56**, 461–464.

Krader, L. (1968). Formation of the State. Englewood Cliffs, NJ: Prentice Hall.

Krafft-Ebing, R. v. (1924, 17th ed.). Psychopathia sexualis. Stuttgart.

Krauss, F. J. (1965). Das Geschlechtsleben des japanischen Volkes. Hanau: Schustek.

Krauss, R. M., Curran, N. M., and Ferleger, N. (1983). Expressive conventions and the cross-cultural perception of emotion. *Basic Appl. Soc. Psychol.* **4**, 295–305.

Kraut, R. E. and Johnston, R. E. (1979). Social and emotional messages of smiling: An ethological approach. *J. Personality Social Psychol.* **37**, 1539–1553.

Krieger, D. T. (1983). Brain peptides: What, where, and why? *Science* **222**, 975–985.

Kroeber, A. L. (1915). Eighteen professions. *Amer. Anthropol.* **17**, 283–288.

Kroger, R. O., Cheng, K., and Leong, I. (1979). Are the rules of address universal? A test of Chinese usage. *J. Cross-Cultural Psychol.* **10**, 395–414.

Kruijt, J. (1964). Ontogeny of social behaviour in Burmese red jungle fowl *(Gallus gallus spadiceus)*. *Behaviour Suppl.* 12.

Kühn, H. (1958). Auf den Spuren des Eiszeitmenschen. München: Paul List.

Küster, W. (1983). Ungeborgenheit, Isolierung und Verzweiflung. *Spiegel.* **43**, 185–212.

Kuguimutzakis, J. (1985). Imitation in Newborns 10–45 Minutes Old. Uppsala Psychological Reports No 376, Dept. Psychology Univ. Uppsala, Sweden ISSN 0348–3908.

Kummer, H. (1973). Aggression bei Affen. *In:* Plack, A. (ed.), Der Mythos vom Aggressionstrieb. München: Paul List, pp. 69–91.

Kummer, H., Götz, W., and Angst, W. (1974). Triadic differentiation: An inhibitory process protecting pair bonds in baboons. *Behaviour* **49**, 62–87.

Kuo, Z. Y. (1932). Ontogeny of embryonic behavior. *J. Exp. Biol.* **61**, 395–430, 453–489.
(1967). The Dynamics of Behavior Development. New York: Random House.

Kurland, J. A. (1979). Paternity, mother's brother, and human sociality. *In:* Chagnon, N. A. and Irons, I. (eds.), Evolutionary Biology and Human Social Behavior. North Scituate, MA: Duxbury Press, pp. 145–180.

Laban, R. (1956). Principles of Dance and Movement Notation. New York: Dance Horizons Republication.

LaBarre, W. (1947). The cultural basis of emotions of gestures. *J. Personality* **16**, 49–68.
(1954). The Human Animal. Chicago/London: The University of Chicago Press.

Laborit, H. (1980). L'inhibition de l'action. Paris: Masson.

Labov, W. (1966). The Social Stratification of English in New York City. Washington: Center for Applied Linguistics.
(1970). The study of language in its social context. *Stud. Generale* **23**, 30–87.

Lacoste-Utamsing, Ch. de, and Holloway, R. L. (1982). Sexual dimorphism in the human corpus callosum. *Science* **216**, 1431–1432.

Lagercrantz, H. and Slotkin, Th. A. (1986). The Stress of Being Born. *Sci. Amer.* **254**(4), 92–102.

Lamb, M. E. (1975). Forgotten contributors to child development. *Hum. Develop.* **18**, 245–266.
(1976). The role of the father: An overview. *In:* Lamb, M. E. (ed.), The Role of the Father in Child Development. New York: Wiley, pp. 1–63. (a)
(1976). Effects of stress and cohort on mother-and father-infant interaction. *Develop. Psychol.* **12**, 435–443. (b)
(1976). Twelve-month olds and their parents: Interaction in a laboratory playroom. *Develop. Psychol.* **12**, 237–244. (c)
(1977). The Relationships between Mothers, Fathers, Infants and Siblings in the First Two Years of Life. Paper presented at the Biennial Conference of the Int. Soc. for the Study of Behavioral Development, Pavia: Italien. (a)
(1977). Father-infant and mother-infant interaction in the first year of life. *Child Develop.* **48**, 167–181. (b)

Lamb, M. E. and Hwang, C. Ph. (1982). Maternal attachment and mother neonate bonding: A critical review. *Advan. Develop. Psychol.* **2**, 1–39.

Lamb, M. E., Frodi, A. M., Hwang, C. Ph., Frodi, M., and Steinberg, J. (1982). Mother- and father-infant interaction involving play and holding in traditional and nontraditional swedish families. *Develop. Psychol.* **18,** 215–221.

Lambert, W. W. (1981). Toward an integrative theory of children's aggression. *Ital. J. Psychol.* **8,** 153–164.

Lambert, W. W. and Tan, A. L. (1979). Expressive styles and strategies in the aggressive actions of children of six cultures. *Ethos* **7,** 19–36.

Lancaster-Jones, F. (1963). A Demographic Survey of the Aboriginal Population of the Northern Territory with Special Reference to Buthurst Island Mission. Canberra: Australian Inst. of Aboriginal Studies.

Lancy, D. F. (1983). Cross-cultural studies in cognition and mathematics. *In:* The Co-evolution of Culture, Cognition and Schooling, Vol. 8. New York: Academic Press, pp. 185–211.

Landy, D. and Mattee, D. (1969). Evaluation of an aggressor as a function of exposure to cartoon humor. *J. Personality Social Psychol.* **9,** 237–241.

Lane, C. (1979): Ritual and ceremony in contemporary Soviet society. *Sociol. Rev.* **27,** 253–278.

Langlois, J. H., Roggman, L. A., Casey, R. J., Ritter, J. M., Rieser-Danner, L. A., and Jenkins, V. Y. (1987). Infant preferences for attractive faces: Rudiments of a stereotype? *Develop. Psychol.* **23**(3), 363–369.

Lattimore, D. (1951). The steppes of Mongolia and the characteristics of steppe nomadism. *In*: American Geographic Society (ed.), Inner Asia Frontiers of China. New York: Capital Publ., pp. 53–102.

Lawick-Goodall, J. van (1968): The behavior of free-living chimpanzees in the Gombe Stream Reserve. *Anim. Behav. Monogr.* **1,** 161–311.

(1971). Wilde Schimpansen. Reinbek: Rowohlt. (a)

(1971). In the Shadow of Man. Boston/London: William Collins. (b)

(1975). The behavior of the chimpanzee. *In:* Kurth, G. and Eibl-Eibesfeldt, I. (eds.), Hominisation und Verhalten. Stuttgart: G. Fischer, pp. 74–136.

Lawler, L. B. (1962). Terpischore. The Story of the Dance in Ancient Greece. Dance Perspektives, 13. New York: Johnson's Reprint Corp.

Laver, J. (1975). Communicative function of phatic communion. *In*: Kendon, A., Harris, R., Key, R. M., and Ritchie, M. (eds.), Organisation of Behavior in Face-to Face-Interaction, pp. 215–238 The Hague: Mouton.

Layard, J. (1942). Stone Men of Malekula. London: Chatto & Windus.

Leacock, E. B. (1978). Women's status in egalitarian society: Implications for social evolution. *Current Anthropol.* **19,** 247–275.

(1981). Myths of Male Dominance: Collected Articles on Women Cross-Culturally. New York: Monthly Review Press.

Lebzelter, V. (1934): Eingeborenenkulturen von Süd- und Südwestafrika. Leipzig: Hiersemann.

LeDoux, J. E., Wilson, D. H., and Gazzaniga, M. S. (1977). A divided mind: Observations on the conscious properties of the separated hemisphere. *Ann. Neurol.* **2,** 417–421.

(1979). Beyond commissurotomy: Clues to consciousness. *In:* King, F. A. (ed.), Handbook of Behavioral Neurobiology, vol. 2. New York/London: Plenum Press, pp. 543–554.

Lee, R. B. (1968). What hunters do for a living. *In:* Lee, R. B. and DeVore, I. (eds.), Man the Hunter. Chicago: Aldine, pp. 30–48.

(1969). Eating Christmas in the Kalahari. *Nat. History* **78,** 14–22, 60–63.

(1972). !Kung spatial organization. An ecological and historical perspective. *Hum. Ecol.* **1,** 125–147.

(1973). The !Kung Bushmen of Botswana. *In:* Bicchieri, M. G. (ed.), Hunters and Gatherers Today. New York: Holt, Rinehart & Winston, pp. 327–368.

(1976). !Kung spatial organization: An ecological and historical perspective. *In:* Lee, R. B. and DeVore, I. (eds.), Kalahari Hunter-Gatherers. Cambridge, MA: Harvard University Press, pp. 73–97.

(1979). The !Kung San. Men, Women and Work in a Foraging Society. Cambridge: Cambridge University Press.

Lee, R. B. and DeVore, I. (1968). Man the Hunter. Chicago: Aldine.

Lehner, P. (1979). Handbook of Ethological Methods. New York: Garland STPM Press.

Lehrman, D. S. (1953). A critique of Konrad Lorenz's theory of instinctive behavior. *Quart. Rev. Biol.* **28**, 337–363.

(1970). Semantic and conceptual issues in the nature-nurture problem. *In:* Aronson, L. R., Tobach, E., Lehrman, D. S., and Rosenblatt, J. S. (eds.), Development and Evolution of Behavior. San Francisco: Freeman, pp. 17–52.

Leibman, M. (1970). The effects of sex and race norms on personal space. *Environ. Behav.* **2**, 208–246.

Leifer, A., Leiderman, P., Barnett, C., and Williams, J. (1972). Effects of mother-infant separation on maternal attachment behavior. *Child Develop.* **43**, 1203–1218.

LeMagnen, J. (1952). Les phénomènes olfacto-sexuels chez l'homme. *Arch. Sci. Physiol.* **6**, 125–160.

Lenneberg, E. H. (1964). A biological perspective of language. *In:* Lenneberg, E. H. (ed.), New Directions in the Study of Language. Cambridge, MA: M. I. T. Press, pp. 65–88.

(1967). Biological Foundations of Language. New York/London: John Wiley.

(1974). Ein Wort unter uns. *In:* Leuninger, H., Miller, H. M., and Müller, F. (eds.), Linguistik und Psychologie, Bd. 2. Frankfurt/M.: Fischer Athenaeum, pp. 53–70. English Edition (1969). A Word Between Us. *In:* Roslansky, J. D. (ed.), Communication. Amsterdam/London: Elsevier, pp. 108–131.

Leonhard, K. (1966). Über die Entstehung einer Form von Homosexualität durch ein Prägungserlebnis. *Leopoldina* **12**, 44–152.

Leontev, A. N. (1977). Activity, Consciousness, and Personality. Moskau: Gospolitizdat.

Leung, E. H. L., and Rheingold, H. L. (1981). Development of pointing as a social gesture. *Develop. Psychol.* **17**, 215–220.

Levelt, W. J. M. (1987). Hochleistung in Millisekunden-Sprechen und Sprache verstehen. Max Planck-Gesellschaft, Jahrbuch 1987, pp. 61–77. Ed. Generalverwaltung der Max-Planck-Gesellschaft München: Vandenhoeck & Ruprecht, Göttingen.

Levi-Montalcini, R. (1981). Views on human aggressive behavior and on wars. *In:* Valzelli, I. and Morgese, I. (eds.), Aggression and Violence: A Psycho/Biological and Clinical Approach. Milano: Edizioni Saint Vincent, pp. 21–30.

Levi-Strauss, C. (1949). Les Structures Elémentaires de la Parenté. Paris: Presses Universitaires de France.

(1969). The Elementary Structures of Kinship. Boston: Beacon Press.

Levy, J. (1972). Lateral specialization of the human brain: Behavioral manifestations and possible evolutionary basis. *In:* Kiger, J. A. (ed.), The Biology of Behavior, Corvallis, OR: Oregon State University Press.

(1978). Lateral differences in the human brain in cognition and behavioral control. *In:* Buser, P. (ed.), Cerebral Correlates of Conscious Experience. New York/Amsterdam: North Holland Publ., pp. 285–298.

Lewis, H. S. (1981). Warfare and the origin of the state. *In:* Claessen, H. J. M. and Skalnik, P. (eds.), The Study of the State. The Hague: Mouton.

Lewis, M. (1969). Infants' responses to facial stimuli during the first year of life. *Develop. Psychol.* **1**, 75–86.

Lewis, M. and Weintraub, M. (1974). Sex of parent × sex of child—Socio-emotional development. *In:* Friedman, R. C., Richart, R. M., and Vande Wiele, R. L. (eds.), Sex Differences in Behavior. New York/London: Wiley, pp. 165–189.

Lewis, M., Young, G., Brooks, J., and Michaelson, L. (1975). The beginning of friendships. *In:* Lewis, M. and Rosenblum, L. (eds.), Friendship and Peer Relations. New York: Wiley.

Lewis, R. A. (1972). A developmental framework for the analysis of premarital dyadic formation. *Family Process* **11**, 17–48.

Lewontin, R. C. (1974). The Genetic Basis of Evolutionary Change. New York/London: Columbia University Press.

(1977). Sociobiology—A caricature of Darwinism. *In:* Suppe, F. and Asquath, P. (eds.), PSA 1976, Vol. 2. PSA Lansing, MI.

Lex, B. W. (1979). The neurobiology of ritual trance. *In:* D' Aquili, E. G., Laughlin, C. D., and McManus, J. (eds.), New York: Columbia Univ. Press, pp. 117–151.

Ley D., and Cybriwsky, R. (1974). Urban graffiti as territorial markers. *Ann. Assoc. Amer. Geogr.* **64**, 491–505.

Ley, R. G. and Koepke, J. E. (1982). Attachment behavior outdoors: Naturalistic observations of sex and age differences in the separation behavior of young children. *Infant Behav. Develop.* **5**, 195–201.

Leyhausen, P. (1965). Über die Funktion der relativen Stimmungshierarchie (dargestellt am Beispiel der phylogenetischen und ontogenetischen Entwicklung des Beutefangs von Raubtieren). *Z. Tierpsychol.* **22**, 412–494.

—— (1983). Kleidung: Schutzhülle, Selbstdarstellung, Ausdrucksmittel. *In:* Sitta, B. (ed.), Menschliches Verhalten, seine biologischen und kulturellen Komponenten, untersucht an den Phänomenen Arbeitsteilung und Kleidung. Freiburg/Schweiz: Universitätsverlag.

Liberman, A. M. and Pisoni, D. B. (1977). Evidence for a special speech-perceiving subsystem in the human. *In:* Bullock, T. H. (ed.), Recognition of Complex Acoustic Signals. Life Sciences Research Report, 5, Berlin-Dahlem-Konferenzen. Berlin: Abakon, pp. 59–76.

Lieberman, A. F. (1977). Preschoolers' competence with a peer: Relations with attachment and peer experience. *Child Develop.* **48**, 1277–1287.

Lieberman, PH. (1977). The phylogeny of language. *In:* Sebeok, T. A. (ed.), How Animals Communicate. Bloomington, IN: Indiana University Press, pp. 3–25.

Liebowitz, M. R. (1983). The Chemistry of Love. Boston/Toronto: Little Brown.

Lief, H. (1976). Introduction to sexuality. *In:* Sadock, B. J., Kaplan, H. I., and Freedman, A. M. (eds.), The Sexual Experience. Baltimore: Williams & Wilkins, pp. 1–6.

Liegle, L. (1971). Familie und Kollektiv im Kibbuz. Weinheim: Julius Meltz Verlag.

Limber, J. (1980). Language in child and chimp? *In:* Sebeok, T. A. and Umiker-Sebeok, J. (eds.), Speaking of Apes. New York: Plenum.

Lind, J., Vuorenkoski, V., and Wasz-Hoeckert, O. (1973). The effect of cry stimulus on the temperature of the lactating breast of primiparae: A thermographic study. *In:* Morris, N. (ed.), Psychosomatic Medicine in Obstetrics and Gynaecology. Basel: S. Karger.

Lipetz, V. E. and Bekoff, M. (1982). Group size and vigilance in pronghorns, *Z. Tierpsychol.* **58**, 203–216.

Lipsitt, L. P. and Rovee-Collier, C. K. (eds.) (1983). *Advan. Infancy Res.* **2**.

Lisina, M. I. (1982). The development of interaction in the first seven years of life. *In:* Hartup, W. W. (ed.), Review of Child Development Research, vol. VI. Chicago: The Univ. of Chicago Press, pp. 133–174.

Lisker, L. and Abramson, A. S. (1964). A cross-language study of voicing in initial stops: Accoustical measurements. *Word* **20**, 384–422.

Livi, L. (1949). Considérations théorétiques et pratiques sur le concept de "minimum de population." *Population* **4**, 754–756.

Lockard, J. S. (1980). Evolution of Human Social Behavior. New York: Elsevier. (a)

—— (1980). Studies of human social signals: Theory, method and data. *In:* Lockard, J. S. (ed.), The Evolution of Human Social Behavior. New York: Elsevier. (b)

Lockard, J. S., Daley, P. C., and Gunderson, V. M. (1979). Maternal and paternal differences in infant carry: US and African data. *Amer. Natur.* **113**, 235–246.

Lötsch, B. (1981). Ökologische Überlegungen für Gebiete hoher baulicher Dichte. *Inform. Raumentwick.* **7/8**, 415–433.

—— (1984). Auf der Suche nach dem menschlichen Maß. Teil 1: Habitatsgestaltung für den Homo sapiens. Garten und Landschaft, H. 1, 34–40. (a)

—— (1984). Auf der Suche nach dem menschlichen Maß. Teil 2: Wohnbaualternativen. Menschensilo oder Schrebergarten. Garten und Landschaft, H. 6. (b)

Logstrup, K. E. (1973). Ästhetische Erfahrung in Dichtung und bildender Kunst. *In:* Gadamer, H. G. and Vogler, P. (eds.), Neue Anthropologie 4, Kulturanthropologie. Stuttgart: Georg Thieme, pp. 286–320.

Lommel, A. (1962). Motiv und Variation in der Kunst des zirkumpazifischen Raumes. Publikationen des Staatl. Museums für Völkerkunde, München.

Lorenz, K. (1935). Der Kumpan in der Umwelt des Vogels. *J. Ornithol.* **83**, 137–413.

—— (1937). Über die Bildung des Instinktbegriffes. *Naturwissenschaften* **25**, 289–300, 307–318, 325–331.

—— (1941). Vergleichende Bewegungsstudien an Anatiden. *J. Ornithol.* **89**, 194–294.

—— (1943). Psychologie und Stammesgeschichte. *In:* Heberer, G. (ed.), Die Evolution der Organismen. Jena: Gustav Fischer, pp. 105–127. (a)

—— (1943). Die angeborenen Formen möglicher Erfahrung. *Z. Tierpsychol.* **5**, 235–409. (b)

(1950). Ganzheit und Teil in der tierischen und menschlichen Gemeinschaft. *Stud. Generale* **9**, 555–599.

(1953). Die Entwicklung der vergleichenden Verhaltensforschung in den letzten 12 Jahren. *Zool. Anz. Suppl.* **16**, 36–58.

(1959). Die Gestaltwahrnehmung als Quelle wissenschaftlicher Erkenntnis. *Z. Angew. Exp. Psychol.* **6**, 118–165.

(1961). Phylogenetische Anpassung und adaptive Modifikation des Verhaltens. *Z. Tierpsychol.* **18**, 139–187.

(1963). Das sogenannte Böse. Wien: Borotha Schoeler.

(1965). Evolution and Modification of Behavior. Chicago, IL: Chicago University Press.

(1966). Stammes- und kulturgeschichtliche Ritenbildung. *Mitteil. Max-Planck Ges.* **1**, 3–30; *Naturwiss. Rundschau* **19**, 361–370.

(1971). Der Mensch biologisch gesehen. Eine Antwort an Wolfgang Schmidbauer. *Stud. Generale* **24**, 495–515.

(1973). Die Rückseite des Spiegels. Versuch einer Naturgeschichte menschlichen Erkennens. München: Piper.

(1978). Vergleichende Verhaltensforschung. Wien/New York: Springer.

(1983). Der Abbau des Menschlichen. München/Zürich: Piper.

Lorenz, K. and Tinbergen, N. (1939). Taxis und Instinkthandlung in der Eirollbewegung der Graugans. *Z. Tierpsychol.* **2**, 1–29.

Lorenz, K. and Wuketits, F. M. (eds.) (1983). Die Evolution des Denkens. München/Zürich: Piper.

Loupis, G. (1983). The Kaluli Longhouses. *Oceania* **53**, 358–383.

Luckmann, B. C. and Luckmann, T. (1977). Gespräch und Unterhaltung. *In:* Reden und reden lassen. Stuttgart/Hamburg/München.

Luers, F. (1919). Volkskundliches aus Steinberg beim Achensee in Tirol. Bayr. *Hefte Volksk.* **4**, 106–130.

Luhmann, N. (1982). Liebe als Passion. Zur Codierung der Intimität. Frankfurt/M: Suhrkamp.

Lumholtz, C. (1890). Among Cannibals. An Account of Four Years' Travels in Australia and of Camp Life with the Aborigines of Queensland. London.

McAllister, L. B., Scheller, R. H., Kandel, E. R., and Axel, R. (1983). *In situ* hybridization to study the origin and fate of identified neurons. *Science* **222**, 800–808.

McBride, G., King, M. G., and James, J. W. (1965). Social proximity effects on galvanic skin responses in adult humans. *J. Psychol.* **61**, 153–157.

McBurney, D. H., Levine, J. M., and Cavanaugh, P. H. (1977). Psychophysical and social ratings of human body odour. *Personality Social Psychol. Bull.* **3**, 135–138.

McCabe, J. (1983). FDB marriage: Further support for the Westermarck hypothesis of the incest taboo? *Amer. Anthropol.* **85**, 50–69.

McCarthy, F. and McArthur, M. (1960). The food quest and the time factor in aboriginal economic life. *In:* Mountford, C. P. (ed.), Records of the American-Australian Scientific Expedition to Arnhem Land. Melbourne.

McCauley, C. and Taylor, J. (1976). Is there overload of acquaintances in the city? *Environ. Psychol. Nonverbal Behav.* **1**, 41–55.

McClintock, M. K. (1971). Menstrual synchrony and suppression. *Nature* **229**, 244–245.

MacCluer, J. W. and Dyke, B. (1976). On the minimum size of endogamous populations. *Social Biol.* **23**, 1–12.

MacCoby, E. E. and Jacklin, C. N. (1974). The Psychology of Sex Differences. Stanford, CA: Stanford University Press.

MacCoby, J. (1980). Sex differences in aggression: A rejoinder and reprise. *Child Develop.* **51**, 964–980.

MacDonald, K. (1983). Production, social controls, and ideology: Toward a sociobiology of the phenotype. *J. Soc. Biol. Structures* **6**, 297–317.

McDonald, D. L. (1978). Paternal behaviour at first contact with the newborn in a birth environment without intrusions. *Birth Family J.* **5**, 123–132.

McDonald, E. R. (1981). The cultural roots of ideology: Hagen's concept of honor in the Nibelungenlied. *Mankind Quart.* **21**, 179–204.

MacFarlane, J. A. (1975). The Psychology of Childbirth. Cambridge, MA: Harvard University Press.

(1977). Olfaction in the development of social preferences in the human neonate. *In:* The Human Neonate in Parent-Infant Interaction. *Ciba Found. Symp.* **33,** 103–117.

McGraw, M. B. (1943). Neuromuscular Maturation of the Human Infant. New York: Columbia University Press.

McGrew, W. C. (1972). An Ethological Study of Children's Behavior. London: Academic Press.

(1975). Patterns of plant food sharing by wild chimpanzees. *Proc. Intern. Congr. Primatol.* **5,** 304–309.

McGuinness, D. (1981). Auditory and motor aspects of language development in males and females. *In:* Ansara, A. *et al.* (eds.), The Significance of Sex Differences in Dyslexia. Towson: The Orton Soc., Inc.

McGuinness, D. and Pribram, K. H. (1979). The origins of sensory bias in the development of gender differences in perception and cognition. *In:* Bortner, M., *et al.* (eds.), Cognitive Growth and Development: Essays in Memory of Herbert G. Birch. New York: Brunner/Mazel, pp. 3–56.

McGuire, M. T. and Raleigh, M. J. (1986). Behavioral and physiological correlates of ostracism. *Ecol. Sociobiol.* **7,** 149–156.

McKenzie, B. and Over, R. (1983). Young infants fail to imitate facial and manual gestures. *Infant Behav. Develop.* **6,** 85–95.

Mackey, W. C. (1979). Parameters of the adult-male-child bond. *Ethol. Sociobiol.* **1,** 59–76.

McKnight, D. (1982). Conflict, healing and singing in an Australian aboriginal community. *Anthropos* **77,** 491–508.

McLean, I. G. (1983). Paternal behaviour and killing of young in arctic ground squirrels. *Anim. Behav.* **31,** 32–44.

MacLean, P. D. (1970). The Triune brain, emotion and scientific bias. *In:* Schmitt, F. O., Quarton, G. C., Melnechuk, Th., and Adelman, G. (eds.), The Neurosciences. 2nd study program. New York: The Rockefeller University Press, pp. 336–349.

McNally, R. J. (1987). Preparedness and phobias: A review. *Psychol. Bull.* **101**(2), 283–303.

McNeill, D. (1974). Vorsymbolische Sprache. Anfänge der Grammatikentwicklung. *In:* Leuninger, H., Miller, M. H., and Müller, F. (eds.), Linguistik und Psychologie, Bd. 2. Frankfurt/M.: Fischer Athenäum, pp. 110–121.

(1980). Sentence structure in chimpanzee communication. *In:* Sebeok, T. A. and Umiker-Sebeok, J. (eds.), Speaking of Apes. New York: Plenum, pp. 145–160.

Madsen, M. C. and Lancy, D. F. (1981). Cooperative and competitive behavior: Experiments related to ethnic identity and urbanization in Papua New Guinea. *J. Cross-Cultural Psychol.* **12,** 389–408.

Major, B. and Heslin, R. (1982). Perceptions of cross-sex and same-sex nonreciprocal touch: It is better to give than to receive. *J. Nonverbal Behav.* **6,** 148–162.

Malinowski, B. (1920). War and weapons among the natives of the Trobriand Islands. *Man* **20**(5).

(1922). Argonauts of the Western Pacific. New York: Dutton.

(1923). The problem of meaning in primitive languages. *In:* Ogden, C. K. and Richards, I. A. (eds.), The Meaning of Meaning. London: Routledge & Kegan Paul, pp. 296–336.

(1926). Crime and Custom in Savage Society. New York: Harcourt, Brace & Co., London: Kegan Paul, Trench, Trubner.

(1929). The Sexual Life of Savages in North-Western Melanesia. New York: P. R. Reynolds.

Mallick, S. K. and McCandless, B. R. (1966). A study of catharsis of aggression. *J. Personality Social Psychol.* **4,** 591–596.

Malthus, Th. R. (1978). Essay on the Principle of Population. London: Johnson.

Maning, F. E. (1876). Old New Zealand: A Tale of the Good Old Times; and a History of the War in the North. London.

Marcuse, H. (1967). Das Ende der Utopie. Berlin (V. Maikowski, Kleine revolutionäre Bibliothek 6). (a)

(1967). Der eindimensionale Mensch. Neuwied/Berlin: Luchterhand. (b)

Margolese, M. S. (1970). Homosexuality: A new endocrine correlate. *Horm. Behav.* **1,** 151.

Margulies, S. (1977). Principles of beauty. *Psychol. Rep.* **41,** 3–11.

Markl, H. (1974). Die Evolution des sozialen Denkens der Tiere. *In:* Immelmann, K. (ed.), Verhaltensforchung. München: Kindler. (Supplement of Bernhard Grzimek, Tierleben.)
(1976). Aggression und Altruismus. Coevolution der Gegensätze im Sozialverhalten der Tiere. Konstanzer Universitätsreden. Konstanz: Universitäts-Verlag.
(1980). Ökologische Grenzen und Evolutionsstrategie-Forschung. Festvortrag gehalten am 19. Juni 1980 in der Rheinischen Friedrich-Wilhelms-Universität zu Bonn anläßlich der Jahresversammlung der DFG. Mitteilungen der DFG 3/80.

Marler, P. (1976). Sensory templates in species-specific behavior. *In:* Fentress, J. (ed.), Simpler Networks and Behavior. Sunderland, MA: Sinauer Assoc.
(1978). Perception and Innate Knowledge. *Proc. 13th Nobel Conf. "The Nature of Life,"* pp. 111–139.
(1979). Development of auditory perception in relation to vocal behavior. *In:* Cranach, M. v., Foppa, K., Lepenies, W., and Ploog, D. (eds.), Human Ethology. London/New York: Cambridge University Press, pp. 663–681.

Marler, P., and Peters, S. (1977). Selective vocal learning in a sparrow. *Science* **198,** 519–521.

Marler, P. Zoloth, St., and Dooling, R. (1981). Innate programs for perceptual development: An ethological view. *In:* Gollin, E. S. (ed.), Developmental Plasticity. Behavioral and Biological Aspects of Variations in Development. New York/London: Academic Press, pp. 135–172.

Marmor, J. (1976). Homosexuality and sexual orientation disturbances. *In:* Sadock, B. J., Kaplan, H. J., and Freedman, A. M. (eds.), The Sexual Experience. Baltimore: Williams & Wilkins, pp. 374–391.

Marr, D. (1982). Vision. New York: W. H. Freeman.

Marshall, D. S. (1971). Sexual behavior on Mangaia. *In:* Marshall, D. S. and Suggs, R. C. (eds.), Human Sexual Behavior. New York: Basic Books, pp. 103–162.

Marshall, L. (1959). Marriage Among the !Kung Bushmen. *Africa* **29,** 335–365.
(1960). !Kung Bushmen Bands. *Africa* **30,** 325–355.
(1965). The !Kung Bushmen of the Kalahari Desert. *In:* Gibbs, J. L. (ed.), Peoples of Africa. New York: Holt, Rinehart & Winston, pp. 241–278.
(1976). The !Kung of Nyae Nyae. Cambridge, MA: Harvard University Press.

Martin, P. and Caro, T. M. (1985). On the functions of play and its role in behavioral development. *Advan. Study Behav.* **15,** 59–103.

Massie, H. N. (1980). Pathological interactions in infancy. *In:* Field, T. M. (ed.), High Risk Infants and Children Adult and Peer Interactions. New York/London: Academic Press, pp. 79–97.

Masters, R. D. (1976). The impact of ethology on political science. *In:* Somit, A. (ed.), Biology and Politics. The Hague/Paris: Mouton, pp. 197–233.
(1981). Evolutionary Biology and the Welfare State. Vortrag anläßlich der Jahresversammlung der American Political Science Association, Sept., New York. (a)
(1981). Linking ethology and political science: Photographs, political attention, and presidential elections. *In:* Watts, M. W. (ed.), Biopolitics: Ethological and Physiological Approaches. New Directions for Methodology of Social and Behavioral Science, No. 7. San Francisco: Jossey Bass, pp. 61–80. (b)
(1981). Empirical Analysis of Photographs in Presidential Campaigns. Vortrag auf der Jahresversammlung der American Political Science Association, Sept., New York. (c)
(1982). Is sociobiology reactionary? The political implication of inclusive-fitness theory. *Quart. Rev. Biology,* **57,** 275–292.
(1983). Ethologische Ansätze in der Politikwissenschaft. *In:* Flohr, H. and Tönnesmann, W. (eds.), Politik und Biologie. Berlin: Paul Parey, pp. 80–101.

Masters, W. H. (1960). Sexual response cycle of human female. *West. J. Surg.* **54,** 93–120.

Masters, W. H. and Johnson, V. E. (1966). Human Sexual Response. Boston: Little Brown.
(1970). Human Sexual Inadequacy. Boston: Little Brown.

Matas, L., Arend, R. A., and Sroufe, L. A. (1978). Continuity of adaption in the second year: The relationship between quality and later competence. *Child Develop.* **49,** 547–556.

Mattingly, I. G. (1972). Speech cues and sign stimuli. *Amer. Sci.* **60**, 327.

Maurer, D. (1985). Infants' perception of facedness. *In:* Field, T. and Fox, N. A. (eds.), Social Perception in Infancy. New Jersey: Ablex, pp. 73–100.

Maurer, D. and Salapatek, P. (1976). Developmental changes in the scanning of faces by young infants. *Child Develop.* **47**, 523–527.

Mauss, M. (1968). Die Gabe. Form und Funktion des Austausches in archaischen Gesellschaften. Frankfurt/M: Suhrkamp.

Maxwell-West, M. and Konner, M. J. (1976). The role of the father: An anthropological perspective. *In:* Lamb, M. E. (ed.), The Role of the Father in Child Development. New York: Wiley, pp. 185–217.

Maynard-Smith, J. (1964). Group selection and kin selection. *Nature* **201**, 1145–1147.

(1974). The theory of games and the evolution of animal conflict. *J. Theoret. Biol.* **47**, 209–221.

(1984). Game theory and the evolution of behaviour. *Behav. Brain Sci.* **7**, 95–125.

Maynard-Smith, J. and Price, G. R. (1973). The logic of animal conflicts. *Nature* **246**, 15–18.

Mayr, E. (1950). Ecological factors in speciation. *Evolution* **1**, 263–288.

(1970). Evolution und Verhalten. *Verhandl. Deut. Zool. Ges.*, **64**, 322–336.

(1976). Evolution and the Diversity of Life. Cambridge, MA: Belknap Press, Harvard Univ. Press.

Mazur, A. (1976). Effects of testosterone on status in small groups. *Folia Primatol.* **26**, 214–226.

(1977). Interpersonal spacing on public benches in "contact" vs. "noncontact" cultures. *J. Social Psychol.* **101**, 53–58.

Mazur, A. and Lamb, Th. A. (1980). Testosterone, status, and mood in human males. *Hormones Behav.* **14**, 236–246.

Mazur, A., Rosa, E., Faupel, M., Heller, J., Leen, R., and Thurman, B. (1980). Physiological aspects of communication via mutual gaze. *Amer. J. Sociol.* **86**, 50–74.

Mead, M. (1930). Growing up in New Guinea. New York: William Morrow.

(1935). Sex and Temperament in Three Primitive Societies. New York: William Morrow.

(1949). Male and Female., New York: William Morrow.

(1965). Leben in der Südsee. München: Szczesny.

Meadows, D. L., Meadows, D. H., Zahn, E., and Milling, P. (1972). Grenzen des Wachstums. Stuttgart: Deutsche Verlagsanstalt.

Meaney, M. J., and Stewart, J. (1985). Sex differences in social play: The socialization of sex roles. *Advan. Study Behav.* **15**, 1–58.

Megargee, E. I. (1969). Influence of sex roles on the manifestations of leadership. *J. Appl. Psychol.* **53**, 377–382.

Megitt, M. J. (1962). Desert People. Sydney: Angus & Robertson.

(1965). Desert People. A Study of the Walbiri Aborigines of Central Australia. Chicago/London: University of Chicago Press. (a)

(1965). The Lineage System of the Mae Enga of New Guinea. New York: Barnes & Noble. (b)

Meiselman, K. C. (1979). Incest. San Francisco: Jossey Bass.

Melrose, D. R., Reed, H. C. B., and Patterson, R. L. S. (1971). Androgen steroids associated with boar odour as an aid to the detection of oestrus in pig artificial insemination. *Brit. Vet. J.* **127**, 495–502.

Meltzoff, A. N. (1981). Imitation, intermodal cooperation and representation in early infancy. *In:* Butterworth, G. (ed.), Infancy and Epistomology. Brighton: Harvester Press, pp. 88–114.

Meltzoff, A. N. and Moore, M. K. (1977). Imitation of facial expression and manual gestures by human neonates. *Science* **198**, 75–78.

(1983). The Origins of Imitation in Infancy: Paradigm, Phenomena, and Theories. *In:* Lipsitt, L. P. and Rovee-Collier, C. K. (eds.), Advances in Infancy Research, Vol. 2. Norwood, NJ: Ablex Publ. Corp., pp. 265–301. (a)

(1983). Methodological Issues in Studies of Imitation: Comments on McKenzie and Over and Koepke *et al. Infant Behav. Develop.* **6**, 103–108. (b)

(1983). Newborn infants imitate adult facial gestures. *Child Develop.* **54**, 702–709. (c)

Mendelson, M. J. and Haith, M. M. (1976). The relation between audition and vision in the human newborn. *Monogr. Soc. Res. Child Develop.* **41**, 1–72.

Menn, L. (1976). Pattern, Control, and Contrast in Beginning Speech: A Case Study in the Development of Word Norm and Word Function. Thesis, University of Illinois.

Merz, F. (1965). Aggression und Aggressionstrieb. *In:* Thomae, H. (ed.), Handbuch der Psychologie, Bd. 2: Motivation. Göttingen: C. J. Hogrefe, pp. 569–601.

Metzger, W. (1936). Gesetze des Sehens. Frankfurt/M: Suhrkamp; 2nd ed., 1954.

— (1953). Psychologie. Darmstadt: Steinkopff.

Meyer, P. (1983). Macht und Gewalt im Evolutionsprozeß. Eine biosoziologische Perspektive. *In:* Flohr, H. and Tönnesmann, W. (eds.), Politik und Biologie. Berlin: Paul Parey, pp. 60–68.

Meyer-Holzapfel, M. (1956). Das Spiel bei Säugetieren. *Handb. Zool.* **8** (10), 1–36.

Michael, R. P., Bonsall, R. W., and Warner, P. (1975). Human vaginal secretions: Volatile fatty acid content. *Science* **186**, 1217–1219.

Michel, Th. (1983). Interdependenz von Wirtschaft und Umwelt in der Eipo-Kultur von Moknerkon: Bedingungen für Produktion und Reproduktion bei einer Dorfschaft im zentralen Bergland von Irian Jaya (West-Neuguinea), Indonesien. *In:* Helfrich, K., Jacobshage, V., Koch, G., Krieger, K., Schiefenhövel, W., and Schultz, W. (eds.), Mensch, Kultur und Umwelt im zentralen Bergland von West-Neuguinea, vol. 11. Berlin: Reimer.

Midgley, M. (1979). Gene-Juggling. *Philosophy* **54**, 439–458.

Mikhailov, F. T. (1976). The Riddle of the Human Ego. Moskau: Molodaya gvardiya.

Milgram, St. (1963). Behavioral study of obedience. *J. Abnormal Social Psychol.* **67**, 372–378.

— (1966). Einige Bedingungen von Autoritätsgehorsam und seiner Verweigerung. *Z. Exp. Angew. Psychol.* **13**, 433–463.

— (1974). Obedience to Authority: An Experimental View. New York: Harper & Row.

Miller, A. (1980). Am Anfang war Erziehung. Frankfurt/M: Suhrkamp.

Miller, G. A. (1956). The magical number seven, plus or minus two: Some limits on our capacity for processing information. *Psychol. Rev.* **63**, 81–97.

— (1974). Einige psychologische Aspekte der Grammatik. *In:* Leuninger, H., Miller, M. H., and Müller, F. (eds.), Linguistik und Psychologie, Bd. 1. Frankfurt/M: Fischer Athenäum, pp. 3–31. (a)

— (1974). Vier philosophische Probleme der Psycholinguistik. *In:* Leuninger, H., Miller, M. H. and Müller, F. (eds.), Linguistik und Psychologie, Bd. 2. Frankfurt/M: Fischer Athenäum, pp. 215–238. (b)

Mills, J. N. (1974). Development of circadian rhythms in infancy. *In:* Davis, J. A. and Dobbing, J. (eds.), Scientific Foundations of Pediatrics. London: Heinemann.

Mills, M. and Melhuish, E. (1974). Recognition of mother's voice in early infancy. *Nature,* **252**, 123–124.

Minturn, L. and Lambert, W. W. (1969). Mothers of Six Cultures. New York/London: Wiley.

Mitford, N. (1956). Noblesse Oblige. An Enquiry into the Identifiable Characteristics of the English Aristocracy. New York/London: Harper & Row.

Mitscherlich, M. (1984). Die Bedeutung des Übergangsobjektes für die Entfaltung des Kindes. *In:* Eggers, Ch. (ed.), Bindungen und Besitzdenken beim Kleinkind. München/Wien/Baltimore: Urban & Schwarzenberg, pp. 185–203.

Model, P. G., Bornstein, M. B., Crain, St. M., and Pappas, G. D. (1971). An electron microscopic study of the development of synapsis in cultured fetal mouse cerebrum continuously exposed to xylocaine. *J. Cell Biol.* **49**, 362–371.

Moewes, W. (1978). Stadt-Land-Verbund. Ein neues Leitbild für eine zukünftige Siedlungsstruktur. Schriftenreihe Wissenschaft und Technik, Technische Universität Darmstadt, 175–218.

Mohnot, S. M. (1971). Some aspects of social changes and infant-killing in the hanuman Langur *Presbytis entellus* (Primates: Cercopithecidae) in Western India. *Mammalia* **35**, 175–198.

Mohr, A. (1971). Häufigkeit und Lokalisation von Frakturen und Verletzungen am Skelett vor- und frühgeschichtlicher Menschengruppen. *Ethnogr. Archäol. Z.* **12**, 139–142.

Mohr, H. (1979). Wissenschaft und Ethik. *In:* Hassenstein, B., Mohr, H., Osche, G., Sander, K., and Wülker, W. (eds.), Freiburger Vorlesungen zur Biologie des Menschen. Heidelberg: Quelle & Meyer, pp. 184–221.

Moir, C. (1934). Recording the contradictions of human pregnant and non-pregnant uterus. *Trans. Edinburgh Obst. Soc.* **54,** 93–120.

Monberg, T. (1979/80). Self-abasement as part of a social process. *Folk* 21–22, 125–132.

Money, J. (1960). Phantom orgasm in the dreams of paraplegic men and women. *Arch. General Psychiatry* **3,** 373–382.

Money, J. and Daléry, M. D. (1976). Iatrogenic homosexuality: Gender identity in seven 46,XX chromosomal females with hyperadrenocortical hermaphroditism born with a penis, three reared as boys, four reared as girls. *J. Homosexuality* **1**(4), 357–371.

Money, J. and Ehrhardt, A. A. (1972). Man and Woman, Boy and Girl: The Differentiation and Dimorphism of Gender Identity from Conception to Maturity. Baltimore: Johns Hopkins University Press.

Montagner, H. (1978). L'enfant et la communication. Paris: Pernoud-Stock.

Montagu, A. (1976). The Nature of Human Aggression. New York: Oxford University Press.

—— (1971). Touching: The Human Significance of the Skin. New York/London: Columbia University Press.

Montross, L. (1944). War through the Ages. New York/London: Harper & Brothers.

Moore, J. (1984). The evolution of reciprocal sharing. *Ethol. Sociobiol.* **5,** 5–14.

Moore, M. M. (1985). Nonverbal courtship patterns in women: Context and consequences. *Ethol. Sociobiol.* **6,** 237–247.

Morath, M. (1977). Differences in the non-crying vocalizations of infants in the first four months of life. *Neuropädiatrie* **8,** 543–545.

Moreno, F. B. (1942). Sociometric status of children in a nursery school group. *Sociometry* **4,** 395–411.

Morey, R. V., Jr. and Marwitt, J. P. (1973). Ecology, Economy and Warfare in Lowland South America. Paper read at the 9th Intern. Cong. of Anthropological and Ethnological Sciences, Aug./Sept. 1973, Chicago.

Morgan, B. J. T., Simpson, M. J. A., Hanby, J. P., and Hall-Craggs, J. (1976). Visualizing interaction and sequential data in animal behavior: Theory and application of cluster analysis methods. *Behaviour* **56,** 1–43.

Morgan, Ch. J. (1979). Eskimo hunting groups, social kinship, and the possibility of kin selection in humans. *Ethol. Sociobiol.* **1,** 83–86.

Morgan, L. H. (1877). Ancient Society, or Researches in the Lines of Human Progress from Savagerty, Through Barbarism to Civilisation. London: Macmillan.

Morgan, S. W. and Mausner, B. (1973). Behavioral and fantasied indicators of avoidance of success in men and women. *J. Personality* **41,** 457–470.

Morinaga, S. (1933). Untersuchungen über die Zöllnersche Täuschung. *Jap. J. Psychol.* **8,** 195–242.

Morishita, H and Siegfried, W. (1983). Erkennen von Emotionen in der Mimik von Kabuki-Schauspielern. Vergleich japanischer und europäischer Einstufungen von 17 Bildern. Unveröffentlichtes Manuskript.

Morris, D. (1957). "Typical intensity" and its relation to the problem of ritualization. *Behaviour* **11,** 1–12

—— (1963). Biologie der Kunst. Düsseldorf: Rauch Verlag.

—— (1968). The Naked Ape: A Zoologist's Study of the Human Animal. New York: McGraw-Hill.

—— (1977). Manwatching: A Field Guide to Human Behavior. New York: Abrams; London: Jonathan Cape; Lausanne: Elsevier.

—— (1981). Das Spiel—Faszination und Ritual des Fußballs. München/Zürich: Droemer-Knaur.

Morris, D., Collett, P., Marsh, P., and O'Shaughnessy, M. (1979). Gestures, Their Origins and Distribution. London: Jonathan Cape.

Moss, H. A. (1974). Early sex differences and mother-infant interactions. *In:* Friedman, R. C., Richart, R. M., and Vande Wiele, R. L. (eds.), Sex Differences in Behavior. London/New York: Wiley, pp. 149–163.

Moyer, K. E. (1968/69). Internal impulses to aggression. *Trans. NY Acad. Sci. (2nd Ser)* **31,** 104–114.

—— (1971). Experimentale Grundlagen eines physiologischen Modells aggressiven Verhaltens.*In:* Schmidt-Mummendey, A. and Schmidt, H. D. (eds.), Aggressives Verhalten. München: Juventa. (a)

(1971). The Physiology of Hostility. Chicago: Markham. (b)

(1981). A Physiological model of aggression with implications for control. *In:* Valzelli, I. and Morgese, I. (eds.), Aggression and Violence: A Psycho/Biological and Clinical Approach. Milano: Edizione Saint Vincent, pp. 72–81.

(1987). Violence and Aggression: A Physiological Perspective. New York: Paragon House.

Mühlmann, W. E. (1940). Krieg und Frieden. *In:* Kulturgeschichtliche Bibliothek, Rh. II, Bd. 2. Heidelberg: Winter's Universitäts-Buchhdlg.

Mueller, E. (1979). (Toddlers + toys) = (An autonomous social system). *In:* Lewis, M. and Rosenblum, L. A. (eds.), The Child and Its Family. New York/London: Plenum, pp. 169–194.

Mueller, E. and Brenner, J. (1977). The origins of social skills and interaction among play-group toddlers. *Child Develop.* **48**, 854–861.

Müller, H. and Kühne, K. (1980). Zur Analyse interaktiver Episoden. Unveröffentlichte Lizentiatsarbeit, Universität Bern 1974. *In:* Cranach, M. v., Kalbermatten, U., Indermühle, K., and Gugler, B. (eds.), Zielgerichetes Handeln. Bern/Stuttgart/Wien: Hans Huber, pp. 186 ff.

Müller, K. E. (1984). Die bessere und die schlechtere Hälfte: Ethnologie des Geschlechterkonflikts. Frankfurt/New York: Campus Verlag.

Müller-Schwarze, D. (ed.) (1978). Evolution of Play Behaviour. Stroutsburg, PA: Dowden, Hutchinson & Ross.

Müsch, H. (1976). Exhibitionismus, Phalluskult und Genitalpräsentieren. *Sexualmedizin,* **5**, 358–363.

Muncy, R. J. (1973). Sex and Marriage in Utopian Communities: 19th Century America. Bloomington, IN: University of Indiana Press.

Murdock, G. D. (1949). Social Structure. New York: Macmillan.

Murdock, G. P. and White, D. R. (1969). Standard Cross-Cultural Sample. *Ethnology* **8**, 329–369.

Murdock, P. M. (1967). Ethnographic Atlas. University of Pittsburgh Press, PA.

Murozumi, M., Chow, I., and Patterson, C. (1969). Chemische Konzentration von Bleiteilchen, von Staub und Seesalz in den Schneeschichten von Grönland und dem Südpol. Zitiert nach: Deutsche Zeitung—Christ und Welt vom 29.1.1971.

Murphy, R. F. (1957). Intergroup hostility and social cohesion. *Amer. Anthropol.* **59**, 1018–1035.

(1960). Headhunter's Heritage. Berkeley: University of California Press, CA.

Murra, J. (1958). On Inca political structure. *In:* System of Political Control and Bureaucracy in Human Societies. Seattle: Washington University Press, pp. 30–41.

(1972). El "control vertical" de un maximo de pisos ecologicos en la economia de las sociedades andinas. Visita de Pedro de Leon. Univ. Huanuco (Peru).

Murray, L. (1977). Infants' Capacities for Regulating Interactions with Their Mothers and the Function of Emotions. Thesis, University of Edinburgh.

Murray, L. and Trevarthen, C. (1986). The infant's role in mother–infant communications. *J. Child. Language* **13**, 15–29.

Mussen, P. H. (ed.) (1970). Carmichael's Manual of Child Psychology, Vol. I and II. New York: Wiley.

Mussen, P. H. and Rutherford, M. (1963). Parent-child relations and parental personality in relation to young children's sex role preferences. *Child Develop.* **34**, 589–607.

Musterle, W. A. (1984). Linear-Kombinationen aus stimmungsreinen Computer-Faces. Vortrag am Institutsseminar des Instituts für Theoretische Chemie am 2 Sept. 1984, Universität Tübingen.

Musterle, W. and Rössler, O. E. (1986). Computer faces: The human Lorenz matrix. *BioSystems* **19**, 61–80.

Myers, B. J. (1984). Mother-infant bonding: The status of this critical-period hypothesis. *Develop. Rev.* **4**, 240–274. (a)

(1984). Mother-infant bonding: Rejoinder to Kennell and Klaus. *Develop. Rev.* **4**, 283–288. (b)

Naaktgeboren, C. and Bontekoe, E. H. M. (1976). Vergleichend-geburtskundliche Betrachtungen und experimentelle Untersuchungen über psychosomatische Störungen der Schwangerschaft und des Geburtsablaufes. *Z. Tierzüch. Züchtungsbiol.* **93**, 264–320.

Nance, J. (1975). The Gentle Tasaday: A Stone Age People in the Philippine Rain Forest. New York/London: Harcout, Brace, Jovanovich.

(1977). Tasaday, Steinzeitmenschen im philippinischen Regenwald. München: Paul List.

Nansen, F. (1903). Eskimoleben. Leipzig: Meyer.

Napier, J. R. (1962). The evolution of the hand. *Sci. Amer.* **207**, 56–63.

Neimark, E. D. (1978). Die Entwicklung des Denkens beim Heranwachsenden. *In:* Steiner, G. (ed.), Die Psychologie des 20. Jahrhunderts. 7: Piaget und die Folgen. Zürich: Kindler, pp. 155–171.

Nelson, E. W. (1896/97). The Eskimo About Bering Strait. Annual Report 18, Vol. 1, Washington, D. C.: Bureau of American Ethnology.

Nesbitt, P. D. and Steven, G. (1974). Personal space and stimulus intensity at a southern California amusement park. *Sociometry* **37**, 105–115.

Netting, R. M. C. (1968). Hill farmers of Nigeria: Cultural ecology of the Kofyar of the Jos Plateau. *Amer. Ethnol. Soc. Monogr.* 46.

(1971). The Ecological Approach in Cultural Study. McCaleb Modules in Anthropology. Reading, MA: Addison-Wesley.

Nettleship, M. A., Dalegivens, R. and Nettleship, A. (eds.) (1975). War, Its Causes and Correlates. The Hague: Mouton.

Neuberger, H., Merz, J., and Selg, H. (1983). Imitation bei Neugeborenen—eine kontroverse Befundlage. *Zeitschrift für Entwicklungspsychologie und pädagog. Psychologie* **15**, 267–276.

Neuhaus, H. (1981). Wie antihomosexuell sind Sexualkundebücher? *Sexualpädagogik Familienplanung* **9**, 28–30.

Neumann, G. H. (1977). Vorurteile und Negativeinstellungen Behinderten gegenüber—Entstehung und Möglichkeiten des Abbaues aus der Sicht der Verhaltensbiologie. *Rehabilitation* **16**, 101–106.

(1981). Normatives Verhalten und aggressive Außenseiterreaktionen bei gesellig lebenden Vögeln und Säugern. Forschungsberichte des Landes Nordrhein-Westfalen, Nr. 3014. Opladen: Westdeutscher Verlag.

Nevermann, H. (1941). Ein Besuch bei Steinzeitmenschen. Stuttgart: Franckh'sche Verlagshandlung.

Newcomb, W. W. (1950). A Re-examination of the causes of Plains warfare. *Amer. Anthropol.* **52**, 317–330.

Newman, J. and McCauley, C. (1977). Eye contact with strangers in city, suburb and small town. *Environ. Behav.* **9**, 547–558.

Newton, N. (1958). Influence of let-down reflex in breast feeding on mother-child relationship. *Marriage Family Living* **20**, 18–20.

Nguyen-Clausen, A. (1987). Ausdruck und Beeinflußbarkeit der kindlichen Bildnerei. *In:* Prinz von Hohenzollern, J. G. and Liedtke, M. (eds.), Vom Kritzeln zur Kunst. Bad Heilbrunn: Julius Klinkhardt.

Niemeyer, C. L. and Anderson, J. R. (1983). Primate harassment of matings. *Ethol. Sociobiol.* **4**, 205–220.

Nitsch, K. (ed.) (1978). Was wird aus unseren Kindern? Gesellschaftspolitische Folgen frühkindlicher Vernachlässigung. Heidelberg: Hüthig.

Noel, G. L., Suh, H. K., and Frantz, A. G. (1972). Induction of Prolactin by Breast Stimulation in Humans. *Excer. Med. Internat. Cong. Ser.* 256.

Nottebohm, F. (1970). Ontogeny of bird song. *Science* **167**, 950–966.

Obonai, T. (1935). Contributions to the study of psychophysical induction. VI. Experiments on the Müller-Lyer illusion. *Jap. J. Psychol.* **10**, 37–39.

Obonai, T. and Asano, T. (1937). Contributions to the study of psychophysical induction. IX. The study of the retinal irradiation. *Jap. J. Psychol.* **12**, 1–12.

Obonai, T. and Hino, H. (1930). Experimentelle Untersuchungen über die Wahrnehmung der geteilten Flächenräume. *Jap. J. Psychol.* **5**, 2–5.

O'Connor, S. M., Vietze, P. M., Hopkins, J. B., and Altmeier, W. A. (1977). Postpartum Extended Maternal-Infant Contact: Subsequent Mothering and Child Health. San Francisco: Soc. for Pediatric Research.

Oettingen, G. v. (1985). Erziehungsstil und Sozialordnung. Beobachtungen in zwei englischen Kindergärten. Dissertation des Fachbereichs Biologie der Universität München.

Öhman, A. and Dimberg, U. (1978). Facial expressions as conditioned stimuli for electrodermal responses: A case of preparedness. *J. Personality Social Psychol.* **36**, 1251–1258.

Ohala, J. J. (1984). An ethological perspective on common cross-language utilisation of F_0 of voice. *Phonetica* **41**, 1–16.

Olds, J. (1956). Pleasure centers in the brain. *Sci. Amer.* **193**, 105–116.

Oller, D. K. and Eilers, R. E. (1988). The role of audition in infant babbling. *Child Develop.* **59**, 441–449.

Omark, D. R. and Edelman, M. S. (1976). The development of attention structures in young children. *In:* Chance, M. R. A. and Larsen, R. R. (eds.), The Social Structure of Attention. London: Wiley, pp. 119–153.

Omark, D. R., Strayer, F. F., and Freedman, D. G. (1980). Dominance Relations: An Ethological View of Human Conflict and Social Interactions. New York/London: Garland STPM Press.

Orians, G. H. (1980). Habitat selection: General theory and applications to human behavior. *In:* Lockard, S. J. (ed.), The Evolution of Human Social Behavior. New York: Elsevier, pp. 49–66.

Orlansky, H. (1949). Infant care and personality. *Psychol. Bull.* **46**, 1–48.

Orlick, T. D. (1981). Positive socialization via cooperative games. *Develop. Psychol.* **17**, 426–429.

Orwell, G. (1949). 1984. Harmondsworth: Penguin Books.

Osborn, F. (1948)., Our Plundered Planet. New York: Little Brown.

Osche, G. (1979). Kulturelle Evolution: Biologische Wurzeln, Vergleich ihrer Mechanismen mit denen des biologischen Evolutionsgeschehens. *In:* Hassenstein, B., Mohr, H., Osche, G., Sander, K., and Wülker, W. (eds.), Freiburger Vorlesungen zur Biologie des Menschen. Heidelberg: Quelle & Meyer, pp. 33–50. (a)

(1979). Vom Tier zum Menschen—Schlüsselereignis der morphologischen und verhaltensbiologischen Evolution. *In:* Hassenstein, B., Mohr, H., Osche, G., Sander, K., and Wülker, W. (eds.), Freiburger Vorlesungen zur Biologie des Menschen. Heidelberg: Quelle & Meyer, pp. 7–32. (b)

Osofsky, J. D. (1979). Handbook of Infant Development. New York: Wiley.

Ostermeyer, H. (1979). Ehe, Isolation zu zweit? Frankfurt/M: Fischer Taschenbuch.

Otterbein, K. F. (1970). The Evolution of War. New Haven: HRAF Press.

Paciornik, M. and Paciornik, C. (1983). Birth and rooming-in: Lessons learned from the forest indians of Brazil. *Birth* **10**, 115–130.

Packard, V. (1958). Die geheimen Verführer. Düsseldorf: Econ.

(1963). The Pyramid Climbers. New York/London: McGraw-Hill.

Palluck, R. J. and Esser, A. H. (1971). Controlled experimental modification of aggressive behavior in territories of severely retarded boys. *Amer. J. Mental Deficiency*, **76**, 23–29. (a)

(1971). Territorial behavior as an indicator of changes in clinical behavioral condition of severely retarded boys. *Amer. J. Mental Deficiency* **76**, 284–290. (b)

Panksepp, J. (1981). Brain opioids—A neurochemical substrate for narcotic and social dependence. *In:* Cooper, S. J. (ed.), Theory in Psychopharmacology, vol. 1. London: Academic Press, pp. 149–175.

(1982). Toward a general psychobiological theory of emotions. *Behav. Brain Sci.* **5**, 407–467.

(1985). Mood changes. *In:* Frederiks, J. A. M. (ed.), Handbook of Clinical Neurology, vol. 1 (45): Clinical Neuropsychology. Amsterdam/New York: Elsevier, pp. 271–285.

(1986). The neurochemistry of behavior. *Annu. Rev. Psychol.* **37**, 77–107.

Panksepp, J., Herman, B. H., Wilberg, T., Bishop, P., and DeEskinazi, F. G. (1978). Endogenous opioids and social behavior. *Neurosci. Biobehav. Rev.* **4**, 473–487.

Papouček, H. (1969). Individual variability on learned responses in human infants. *In:* Robinson, R. J. (ed.), Brain and Early Behavior. London: Academic Press.

Papoušek, H. and Papoušek, M. (1977). Die ersten sozialen Beziehungen: Entwicklungschance oder pathogene Situation. *Praxis Psychother.* **3**, 97–108.

Papoušek, M. (1984). Wurzeln der kindlichen Bindung an Personen und Dinge: Die Rolle der integrativen Prozesse. *In:* Eggers, Ch. (eds.), Bindungen und Besitzdenken beim Kleinkind. München/Wien/Baltimore: Urban & Schwarzenberg, pp. 155–184.

Parke, R. D. (1980). The family in early infancy: Social interactional and attitudinal analyses. *In:* Pedersen, F. (ed.), The Father-Infant Relationship: Observational Studies in a Family Context. New York: Praeger, pp. 44–70.

Parke, R. D. and O'Leary, S. E. (1976). Father-mother-infant interaction in the newborn period: Some findings, some observations, and some unresolved issues. *In:* Riegel, K. and Meacham, J. (eds.), The Developing Individual in a Changing World. Vol. II, Social and Environmental Issues. The Hague: Mouton, pp. 653–664.

Parke, R. D. and Sawin, D. B. (1975). Infant characteristics and behavior as elicitors of maternal and paternal responsibility in the newborn period. *Soc. Res. Child Develop. Denver.*

(1977). The family in early infancy: Social interactional and attitudinal analysis. *Soc. Res. Child Develop,,* New Orleans.

Parke, R. D. and Suomi, St. Jr. (1980). Adult male-infant relationships: Human and non-human primate evidence. *In:* Immelmann, K., Barlow, G., Main, M., and Petrinovitch, L. (eds.), Behavioral Development: The Bielefeld Interdisciplinary Project. New York: Cambridge University Press.

Parker, S. (1976). The precultural basis of incest taboo: Toward a biosocial theory. *Amer. Anthropol.* **78,** 285–305.

Parker, S. T. and Gibson, K. R. (1979). A developmental model for the evolution of language and intelligence in early hominids. *Behav. Brain Sci.* **2,** 367–408.

Parmelee, A. H. (1961). A study of one infant from birth to eight months of age. *Acta Paediat.* **50,** 160–170.

Passarge, S. (1907). Die Buschmänner der Kalahari. Berlin: D. Reimer.

Pastor, D. L. (1980). The Quality of Mother-Infant Attachment and Its Relationship to Toddlers' Initial Sociability with Peers. Paper presented at the Intern. Conf. on Infant Studies, New Haven, April, 1980.

Pastore, R. E. (1976). Categorical and perception: A critical re-evaluation . *In:* Hirsch, S. K. *et al.* (eds.), Hearing and Davis: Essays Honoring Hallowell Davis. St. Louis: Washington University Press.

Patterson, F. G. (1978). The gestures of a gorilla: Language acquisition in another pongid. *Brain Language* **5,** 72–97.

Patterson, M. L., Mullens, S., and Romano, J. (1971). Compensatory reactions to spatial intrusion. *Sociometry* **34,** 114–121.

Patterson, R. L. S. (1968). Identification of 3α-hydroxy-5α-androst-16-ene as the musk odour component of boar sub-maxillary salivary gland and its relationship to the sex odour taint in pork meat. *J. Sci. Food Agri.* **19,** 434–438.

Pearson, K. G. (1972). Central programming and reflex control of walking in the cockroach. *J. Exp. Biol.* **56,** 173–193.

Peiper, A. (1951). Instinkt und angeborenes Schema beim Säugling. *Z. Tierpsychol.* **8,** 449–456.

(1953). Schreit- und Steigbewegungen beim Neugeborenen. *Arch. Kinderheilk.* **147,** 135.

Pentland, B., Pitcairn, T. K., Gray, J. M., and Riddle, W. (1987). The effects of reduced expression in Parkinson's disease on impression formation by health professionals. *Clin. Rehab.* **1,** 307–313.

Peplau, A. (1976). Fear of success in dating couples. *Sex Roles* **2,** 249–258.

Perry, J. and Whipple, B. (1981). Pelvic muscle strength of female ejaculators: Evidence in support of a new theory of orgasm. *J. Sex Res.* **17,** 22–39.

Persson-Benbow, C. and Stanley, J. (1980). Sex differences in mathematical ability: Fact or artifact? *Science* **210,** 1262–1264.

Peterson, N. (1963). Family ownership and right of disposition in Sukkertoppen District, West Greenland. *Folk* **5,** 270–281.

(1972). Totemism yesterday: Sentiment and local organization among the Australian aborigines. *Man* **7,** 12–32.

(1975). Hunter-gatherer territoriality: The perspective from Australia. *Amer. Anthropol.* **77,** 53–68.

(1979). Territorial adaptations among desert hunter-gatherers: The !Kung and Australians compared. *In:* Burnham, P. C. and Ellen, R. F. (eds.), Social and Ecological Systems. London/New York: Academic Press, pp. 111–129.

Peterson, St. A. (1983). Biosoziale Korrelate politischen Verhaltens. *In:* Flohr, H. and Tönnesmann, W. (eds.), Politik und Biologie. Berlin: Paul Parey, pp. 127–132.

Pfeiffer, J. E. (1969). The Emergence of Man. New York: Evanston; London: Harper & Row.

(1977). The Emergence of Society: A Prehistory of the Establishment. New York: McGraw-Hill.

Phillips, S., King, S., and Dubois, L. (1978). Spontaneous activities of female versus male newborn. *Child Develop.* **49**, 590–597.

Piaget, J. (1932). The Moral Judgment of the Child. London: Kegan Paul.

(1953). The Origin of Intelligence in the Child. London: Routledge & Kegan Paul.

(1970). Mémoire et Intelligence. *In:* La Mémoire. Symposium de l'Association de Psychologie de langue française. Paris: Presses Universitaires de France, pp. 169–178.

(1975). Nachahmung, Spiel und Traum. Die Entwicklung der Symbolfunktion beim Kinde. Stuttgart: Klett. (a)

(1975). Sprechen und Denken des Kindes. Düsseldorf: Schwann. (b)

(1976). Psychologie der Intelligenz. München: Kindler, Kindler-Taschenbuch 2167.

(1980). The Psychogenesis of Knowledge and Its Epistemological Significance. *In:* Piattelli-Palmarini, M. (ed.), Language and Learning. The Debate between Jean Piaget and Noam Chomsky. Cambridge, MA: Harvard University Press, pp. 23–34.

Pilleri, G. (1960). Über das Auftreten von "Kletterbewegungen" im Endstadium eines Falles von Morbus Alzheimer. *Arch. Psychiatr. Nervenkunde* **200**, 455–461. (a)

(1960). Kopfpendeln ("Leerlaufendes Brutsuchen") bei einem Fall von Pickscher Krankheit. *Arch. Psychiatr. Nervenkunde* **200**, 603–611. (b)

(1961). Orale Einstellung nach Art des Klüver-Bucy-Syndroms bei hirnatophischen Prozessen. *Schweiz. Arch. Neurol. Neurochir. Psychiatr.* **87**, 286–298.

Pitcairn, T. K. and Schleidt, M. (1976). Dance and decision: An analysis of a courtship dance of the Medlpa, New Guinea. *Behaviour* **58**, 298–316.

Pleger, J. (1976). Das Phänomen der Aggression. Dissertation. Erziehungswissenschaft an der Pädagogischen Hochschule Ruhr, Bd. I + II. Dortmund: Herne.

Ploog, D. (1964). Verhaltensforschung und Psychiatrie. *In:* Gruhle, H.-W., Jung, R., Mayer-Gross, W., and Müller, M. (eds.), Psychiatrie der Gegenwart, Bd. 1/1. Berlin/Göttingen/Heidelberg: Springer, pp. 291–443.

(1966). Experimentelle Verhaltensforschung. *Nervenarzt* **37**, 443–447.

(1969). Psychobiologie des Partnerschaftsverhaltens. *Nervenarzt* **40**, 245–255.

(1972). Kommunikation in Affengesellschaften und deren Bedeutung für die Verständigungsweisen des Menschen. *In:* Gadamer, H. G. and Vogler, P. (eds.), Neue Anthropologie, Bd. 2. Stuttgart: Thieme/dtv-Wissenschaftl. Reihe, pp. 98–178.

(1980). Soziologie der Primaten. *In:* Kisker, K. P., Meyer, J.-E, Müller, C., and Strömgren, E. (eds.), Psychiatrie der Gegenwart, Bd. 1/2. Berlin: Springer, 2. Aufl., pp. 379–544.

Ploog, D., Blitz, J., and Ploog, F. (1963). Studies on social and sexual behavior of the squirrel monkey *(Saimiri sciureus). Folia Primatol.* **1**, 29–66.

Ploog, D., Hopf, S, and Winter, P. (1967). Ontogenese des Verhaltens von Totenkopf-Affen *(Saimiri sciureus). Psychol. Forsch.* **31**, 1–41.

Plutchik, R. (1980). A general psychoevolutionary theory of emotion. *In:* Plutchik, R. and Kellerman, H. (eds.), Emotion: Theory, Research, and Experience, Vol. 1. New York: Academic Press.

Pöppel, E. (1978). Time perception. *In:* Held, R., Leibowitz, H. W., and Teuber, H.-L. (eds.), Handbook of Sensory Physiology, vol. III, Heidelberg: Springer, pp. 713–729.

(1982). Lust und Schmerz. Berlin: Severin und Siedler.

(1983). Musikerleben und Zeitstruktur. *In;* Kreuzer, F. (ed.), Auge macht Bild, Ohr Macht Klang, Hirn macht Welt. Salzburger Musikgespräch, Wien: Franz Deutike, pp. 76–87.

(1984). Grenzen des Bewußtseins: Über Wirklichkeit und Welterfahrung. Stuttgart: Deutsche Verlagsanstalt.

Pöppel, E. and Sütterlin, C. (1983). Wahrnehmungs-Asymmetrie und Gestaltung von Links und Rechts in Bildern. Neuropsychologische Aspekte der ästhetischen Wahrnehmung. Symposium "Biology of Esthetics" Reimers-Stiftung, Bad Homburg.

Pöppel, E., Held, R., and Frost, D. (1973). Residual visual function after brain wounds involving the central visual pathways in man. *Nature* **243**, 295–296.

Popp, J. and DeVore, I. (1979). Aggressive competition and social dominance theory. *In:* Hamburg, D., and McCown, E. (eds.), The Great Apes. Menlo Park, CA: Benjamin Cummings, pp. 317–338.

Popper, K. R. (1973). Objektive Erkenntnis. Ein evolutionärer Entwurf. Hamburg: Hoffmann und Campe.

Porter, R. H. and Moore, J. D. (1981). Human kin recognition by olfactory cues. *Physiol. Behav.* **27**, 493–495.

Portisch, H. (1970). Friede durch Angst: Augenzeuge in den Arsenalen des Atomkrieges. Wien: Molden.

Poshivalov, V. P. (1986). Ethological pharmacology as a tool for animal aggression research. *In:* Brain, P. F. and Ramirez, M. (eds.), Cross-Disciplinary Studies on Aggression. Sevilla: Publicaciones de la Universidad de Sevilla, pp. 17–49.

Prechtl, H. F. R. (1953). Stammesgeschichtliche Reste im Verhalten des Säuglings. *Umschau* **21**, 656–658.

— (1958). The directed head turning response and allied movements of the human baby. *Behaviour* **13**, 212–242.

— (1981). The study of neural development as a perspective of clinical problems. *In:* Connolly, K. J. and Prechtl, H. F. R. (eds.), Maturation and Development. London: W. Heinemann Med. Books, pp. 198–215.

Prechtl, H. F. R. and Lenard, H. G. (1968). Verhaltensphysiologie des Neugeborenen. *In:* Linneweh, F. (ed.), Fortschritte der Pädologie, Bd. II. Berlin: Springer, pp. 88–122.

Prechtl, H. F. R. and Schleidt, W. M. (1950). Auslösende und steuernde Mechanismen des Saugaktes, I u. II. *Z. Vergl. Physiol.* **32**, 252–262, **33**, 53–62.

Premack, D. (1971). Language in the chimpanzee? *Science* **172**, 808–822.

Preti, G., Cutler, W. B., Garcia, C. R., Huggins, G. R., and Lawley, H. J. (1986). Human axillary secretions influence women's menstrual cycles: The role of donor extract of females. *Hormones Behav.* **20**, 474–482.

Pribram, K. H. (1979). Behaviourism, phenomenology and holism in psychology: A scientific analysis. *J. Social Biol. Structures* **2**, 65–72.

Prioleau, L., Murdock, M., and Brody, N. (1983). An analysis of psychotherapy versus placebo. *Behav. Brain Sci.* **6**, 275–310.

Proshansky, H. M. (1966). The development of intergroup attitudes. *In:* Hoffman, L. W. and Hoffman, M. L. (eds.), Review of Child Development Research, Vol. 2. New York: Russell Sage Found., pp. 311–371.

Provine, Robert R. (1986). Yawning as a stereotyped action pattern and releasing stimulus. *Ethology* **72**(2), 89–176, 109–122.

Purifoy, F. E. (1981). Endocrine-environment interaction in human variability. *Annu. Rev. Anthropol.* **10**, 141–162.

Quanty, M. (1976). Aggression catharsis: Experimental investigation and implications. *In:* Geen, R. G. and O'Neal, E. C. (eds.), Perspectives on Aggression. New York: Academic Press, pp. 99–132.

Queyrat, Fr. (1905). Les Jeux des Enfants. Paris: Alcan.

Radcliffe-Brown, A. R. (1930). The social organization of Australian tribes. *Oceania* **1**, 34–63.

Rader, N., Bausano, M., and Richards, J. E. (1980). On the nature of the visual-cliff-avoidance response in human infants. *Child Develop.* **51**, 61–68.

Radnitzky, G. and Bartley, W. W. (eds.) (1987). Evolutionary Epistemology, Theory of Rationality, and the Sociology of Knowledge. La Salle, IL: Open Court Publ.

Ragan, J. M. (1982). Gender displays in portrait photographs. *Sex Roles* **8**, 33–43.

Rainer, R. (1978). Kriterien der wohnlichen Stadt. Graz: Akademische Druck- und Verlagsanstalt.

Rajecki, D. W., Lamb, M. E., and Obmascher, P. (1978). Toward a general theory of infantile attachment: A comparative review of aspects of the social bond. *Behav. Brain Sci.* **3**, 417–464. (a)

Rajecki, D. W., Lamb, M. E., and Suomi, S. J. (1978). Effects of multiple peer separation in domestic chicks. *Develop. Psychol.* **14**, 397–387. (b)

Rancourt-Laferriere, D. (1979). Some semiotic aspects of the human penis. *VS (Versus)*, **24**, 37–82.

— (1983). Four adaptive aspects of the female orgasm. *J. Soc. Biol. Structures* **6**, 319–333.

Rapoport, A. (1982). The Meaning of the Built Environment. Beverly Hills: Sage.

Rappaport, R. A. (1968). Pigs for the Ancestors. New Haven/London: Yale University Press.

Rasmussen, K. (1908). People of the Polar North. London: Ed. G. Herring.

Rattner, J. (1970). Aggression und menschliche Natur. Olten: Walter.

Rauh, H. (1984). Soziale Interaktion und Gruppenstruktur bei Krabbelkindern. *In:* Eggers, Ch. (ed.), Bindungen und Besitzdenken beim Kleinkind. München/Wien/Baltimore: Urban & Schwarzenberg, pp. 204–232.

Rausch, G. and Scheich, H. (1982). Dendritic spine loss and enlargement during maturation of the speech control system in the mynah bird (*Gracula religiosa*). *Neurosci. Lett.* **29**, 129–133.

Razran, G. H. S. (1938). Conditioning away social bias by the luncheon technique. *Psychol. Bull.* **35**, 693.

Redican, W. (1975). Facial expressions in nonhuman primates. *In:* Rosenblum, L. A. (ed.), Primate Behavior, Vol. 4. London: Academic Press, pp. 103–194.

Regan, D. T. (1971). Effects of a favor and liking on compliance. *J. Exp. Social Psychol.* **7**, 627–639.

Reich, W. (1949). Die sexuelle Revolution. Frankfurt/M.: Fischer.

Reimarus, H. S. (1762). Allgemeine Betrachtungen über die Triebe der Thiere, hauptsächlich über ihre Kunsttriebe. Hamburg.

Reis, D. J. (1974). Central neurotransmitters in aggression. *In:* Frazier, S. H. (ed.), Aggression. Proceedings (Research Publications) of the Association for Nervous and Mental Diseases. Baltimore: Williams and Wilkins, pp. 119–148.

Remane, A. (1952). Die Grundlagen des natürlichen Systems der vergleichenden Anatomie und der Phylogenetik. Leipzig: Geest & Portig.

Renggli, F. R. (1976). Angst und Geborgenheit. Soziokulturelle Folgen der Mutter-Kind-Beziehung im ersten Lebensjahr. Ergebnisse aus der Verhaltensforschung, Psychoanalyse und Ethnologie. Hamburg: Rowohlt.

Rensch, B. (1957). Ästhetische Faktoren bei Farb- und Formbevorzugungen von Affen. *Z. Tierpsychol.* **14**, 71–99.

(1958). Die Wirksamkeit ästhetischer Faktoren bei Wirbeltieren. *Z. Tierpsychol.* **15**, 447–461.

(1963). Versuche über menschliche "Auslöser-Merkmale" beider Geschlechter. *Z. Morphol. Anthropol.* **53**, 139–164.

Reynolds, P. C. (1982). Affect and instrumentality: An alternative view on Eibl-Eibesfeldt's human ethology. *Behav. Brain Sci.* **5**, 267–273.

Reynolds, V. (1966). Open grounds in human evolution. *Man* **1**, 441–452.

Rheingold, H. J. (1961). The effect of environmental stimulation upon social and exploratory behavior in the human infant. *In:* Foss, B. M. (ed.), Determinants of Infant Behavior, Vol. 1. London: Methuen, pp. 143–177.

Rheingold, H. J. and Eckerman, C. (1973). Fear of the stranger: A critical examination. *In:* Reese, H. (ed.), Advances in Child Development and Behavior, 8. New York: Academic Press.

Rheingold, H. L. and Adams, J. L. (1980). The significance of speech to newborn. *Develop. Psychol.* **16**, 397–403.

Richards, J. E. and Rader, N. (1981). Crawling-onset age predicts visual cliff avoidance in infants. *J. Exp. Psychol. Hum. Perception Performance* **7**(2), 382–387.

Richerson, P. J. (1977). Ecology and human ecology: A comparison of theories in the biological and social sciences. *Amer. Ethnol.* **4**, 1–26.

Riedl, R. (1979). Biologie der Erkenntnis. Die stammesgeschichtlichen Grundlagen der Vernunft. (with cooperation of R. Kaspar.) Berlin/Hamburg: Paul Parey.

(1981). Die Folgen des Ursachendenkens. *In:* Watzlawick, P. (ed.), Die erfundene Wirklichkeit. München/Zürich: Piper, pp. 67–90.

Ringler, N. M., Kennell, J. H., Jarvella, R., Navojosky, B. J., and Klaus, M. H. (1975). Mother-to-child speech at 2 years: Effects of early postnatal contact. *J. Pediatr.* **86**, 141–144.

Ringler, N. M., Trause, M. A., Klaus, M. H., and Kennell, J. (1978). The effects of extra postpartum contact and maternal speech patterns on children's IQs, speech, and language comprehension at five. *Child Develop.* **49**, 862–865.

Robbins, J. H. (1980). Breaking the taboos: Further reflections on mothering. *J. Human Psychol.* **20**, 27–40.

Robinson, Ch. L., Lockard, J. S., and Adams, R. M. (1979). Who looks at a baby in public. *Ethol. Sociobiol.* **1**, 87–91.

Robson, K. S. (1967). The role of eye-to-eye contact in maternal-infant-attachment. *J. Child Psychol. Psychiatry* **8**, 13–35.

Roeder, K. D. (1955). Spontaneous activity and behavior. *Sci. Monthly* **80**, 362–370.

Rödholm, M. (1981). Early Mother-Infant and Father-Infant Interaction. Göteborg.

Röhrig, L. (1967). Gebärde, Metapher, Parodie. Düsseldorf: Pädagogischer Verlag Schwann.

Rohner, R. P. (1975). They Love Me, They Love Me Not: A World-Wide Study of the Effects of Parental Acceptance and Rejection. New Haven: HRAF Press.

——— (1976). Sex differences in aggression: Phylogenetic and enculturation perspective. *Ethos* **4**, 57–72.

Roper, M. K. (1969). A survey of evidence for intrahuman killing in the Pleistocene. *Current Anthropol.* **10**, 427–459.

Rose, F. G. G. (1960). Classification of Kin, Age Structure and Marriage among the Groote Eylandt Aborigines. A Study in Method and a Theory of Australian Kinship. Berlin: Akademischer Verlag.

Rose, R., Bernstein, I., and Gordon, T. (1975). Consequences of social conflict on plasma testosterone levels in rhesus monkeys. *Psychosomat. Med.* **37**, 50–61.

Rosenblum, L. A. (1971). Infant attachment in monkeys. *In:* Schaffer, H. R. (ed.), The Origins of Human Social Relations. New York: Academic Press.

Rosenblum, L. A. and Harlow, H. F. (1963). Approach-avoidance conflict in the mother-surrogate situation. *Psychol. Rep.* **12**, 83–85.

Rosenfeld, H. M. (1982). Measurement of body motion and orientation. *In:* Scherer, K. R. and Ekman, P. (eds.), Handbook of Methods in Nonverbal Behavior Research. Cambridge/London/New York: Cambridge University Press, pp. 199–286.

Rosenzweig, M. R. and Leiman, A. L. (1982). Physiological Psychology. Lexington, MA: C. D. Heath.

Rossi, A. S. (1975). A biosocial perspective on parenting. *Daedalus* **106**, 1–32.

Rothchild, J. and Wolf, S. B. (1976). The Children of the Counterculture. New York: Doubleday.

Rothmann, M. and Teuber, E. (1915). Einzelausgabe der Anthropoidenstation auf Teneriffa: I. Ziele und Aufgaben der Station sowie erste Beobachtungen an den auf ihr gehaltenen Schimpansen. Berlin. 1.–20. Abhandlungen Preußische Akademie der Wissenschaften.

Rubin, R. T., Reinisch, J. M., and Haskett, R. F. (1981). Postnatal gonadal steroid effects on human behavior. *Science* **211**, 1318–1324.

Rubinshtein, S. L. (1973). Fundamentals of General Psychology. Moskau: Uchpedgiz.

Rudolph, W. (1968). Der kulturelle Relativismus. Forschungen zur Ethnologie und Sozialpsychologie, Bd. 6. Berlin: Dunker & Humblot.

Rumbaugh, D. M. and Gill, T. V. (1977). Lana's acquisition of language skills. *In:* Rumbaugh, D. M. (ed.), Language Learning by a Chimpanzee. The Lana Project. New York: Academic Press, pp. 165–192.

Rump, G. Ch. (1978). Bildstruktur—Erkenntnisstruktur. Gegenseitige Bedingungen von Kunst und Verhalten. Kastellaun: A. Henn Verlag.

——— (1980). Verhaltensforschung und Kunstgeschichte. *In:* Hahn, M. and Schuster, M. (eds.), Fortschritte der Kunstpsychologie. Frankfurt/M.: P. A. Lang.

Ruse, M. (1979). Sociobiology: Sense or Nonsense? Dordrecht/Boston/London: D. Reidel.

Russell, M. J. (1976). Human olfactory communication. *Nature* **260**, 520–522.

Russell, M. J., Switz, G. M., and Thompson, K. (1980). Olfactory Influences on the Human Menstrual Cycle. *Pharmacol. Biochem. Behavior* **12**, 737–738.

Russell, M. J., Mendelson, T., and Peeke, H. V. S. (1983). Mother's identification of their infant's odors. *Ethol. Sociobiol.* **4**, 29–31.

Sackett, G. P. (1966). Monkeys reared in isolation with pictures as visual input: Evidence for an innate releasing mechanism. *Science* **154**, 1468–1473.

Sadock, S. B. J. and Sadock, V. A. (1976). Techniques of coitus. *In:* Sadock, S. B. J., Kaplan, H. J., and Freedman, A. M. (eds.), The Sexual Experience. Baltimore, MD: Williams & Wilkins, pp. 206–216.

Sadock, S. B. J., Kaplan, H. J., and Freedman, A. M. (eds.) (1976). The Sexual Experience. Baltimore, MD: Williams & Wilkins.

Sager, S. F. (1981). Sprache und Beziehung. Linguistische Untersuchungen zum Zusammenhang von sprachlicher Kommunikation und zwischenmenschlicher Beziehung. Tübingen: Max Niemeyer Verlag.

(1983). Die Manifestation universaler Verhaltensdispositionen im Verbalverhalten. Zwischenbericht zum DFG-Projekt SA 346/1–2.

Sagi, A. (1981). Mothers' and non-mothers' identification of infant cries. *Infant Behav. Develop.* **4**, 37–40.

Sagi, A. and Hoffmann, M. L. (1978). Emphatic distress in the newborn. *Develop. Psychol.* **12**, 175–176.

Sagi, A., Lamb, M. E., Shoha, R., Dvir, R., and Lewkowicz, K. S. (1985). Parent-infant interaction in families on Israeli kibbutzim. *Intern. J. Behav. Develop.* **8**, 273–284.

Sahlins, M. D. (1960). The origin of society. *Sci. Amer.* **204**, 76–87.

(1976, rev. 1977). The Use and Abuse of Biology. An Anthropological Critique of Sociobiology. Ann Arbor: University of Michigan Press.

Sal, F. S. vom and Howard, L. S. (1982). The regulation of infanticide and parental behavior: Implications for reproductive success in male mice. *Science* **215**, 1270–1272.

Salamone, F. A. (1982). Personal, identity and ethnicity. *Anthropos* **77**, 475–490.

Saling, M. M. and Cooke, W. L. (1984). Cradling and transport of infants by South African mothers: A cross-cultural study. *Current Anthropol.* **25**, 333–335.

Salk, L. (1973). The role of the heartbeat in relations between mother and infant. *Sci. Amer.* **228**, 24–29.

Salzen, E. A. (1967). Imprinting in birds and primates. *Behaviour* **28**, 232–254.

Salzman, F. (1979). Aggression and gender. *In:* Hubbard, R. and Lowe, M. (eds.), Genes and Gender, II: Pitfalls in Research on Sex and Gender. New York: Gordian Press.

Sanday, P. R. (1980). Margaret Mead's view of sex roles in her own and other societies. *Amer. Anthropol.* **82**, 340–348.

Sander, F. (1931). Gestaltpsychologie und Kunsttheorie. Ein Beitrag zur Psychologie der Architektur. *Neue Psychol. Stud.* **8**, 311–334.

Sano, T. (1983). A catalogue of the facial behavior patterns of Japanese preschool children. *J. Anthropol. Soc. Nippon* **91**, 323–336.

Savage-Rumbaugh, E. S. and Rumbaugh, D. M. (1982). Ape-language research is alive and well: A reply. *Anthropos* **77**, 568–573.

Savin-Williams, R. C. (1979). Dominance hierarchies in groups of early adolescents. *Child Develop.* **50**, 923–935.

(1980). Social interactions of adolescent females in natural groups. *In:* Foot, H., Chapman, T., and Smith, J. (eds.), Friendship and Social Relations in Children. Sussex: Wiley.

Sawin, D. B. (1981). Fathers' interactions with infants. *In:* Weiss-Bourd, B. and Musick, J. S. (eds.), Infants: Their Social Environments. Washington: Nat. Assoc. Educat. of Young Children, pp. 147–167.

Sbrzesny, H. (1976). Die Spiele der !Ko-Buschleute. Monographien zur Humanethologie 2. München: Piper.

Scanzoni, J. (1972). Sexual bargaining: Power politics in the American marriage. Englewood Cliffs, NJ: Prentice Hall.

Schaal, B., Montagner, H., Hertling, E., Bolzoni, D., Moyse, A., and Quichon, A. (1980). Les stimulations olfactives dans les relations entre l'enfant et la mère. *Reprod. Nutr. Develop.* **20**, 843–858.

Schaefer, H. (1978). Humanökologisch-anthropologische Grundlagen der Umweltgestaltung. *In:* Buchwald, K. and Engelhardt, W. (eds.), Handbuch für Planung, Gestaltung und Schutz der Umwelt. 1. Die Umwelt des Menschen. München: BLV. (a)

(1978). Schlußbetrachtung. *In:* Nitsch, K. (eds.), Was wird aus unseren Kindern? Gesellschaftspolitische Folgen frühkindlicher Vernachlässigung. Heidelberg: Hüthig, pp. 100–119. (b)

Schaefer, H. and Flaschar, W. (1978). Energiewirtschaft und Umweltbeeinflussung. *In:* Buchwald, K. and Engelhardt, W. (eds.), Handbuch für Planung, Gestaltung und Schutz der Umwelt. 1. Die Umwelt des Menschen. München: BLV.

Schäfer, U. (1979). Herausgefordert—Bewohner und Architekten diskutieren mit Journalisten. *Bauen Wohnen,* **1/2**, 6–10.

Schaffer, H. R. (1966). The onset of fear of strangers and the incongruity hypothesis. *J. Child Psychol. Psychiatry* **7**, 95–106.

(ed.) (1977). Studies in Mother-Infant Interaction. London/New York: Academic Press.

Schaffer, H. R. and Emerson, P. E. (1964). The Development of Social Attachments in Infancy. Monographs of the Society for Research in Child Development 29.

Schaller, J., Carlsson, S. G., and Larsson, K. (1979). Effects of extended post-partum mother-child contact on the mother's behavior during nursing. *Infant Behav. Develop.* **2**, 319–324.

Scharf, J.-H. (1981). Os incae, Blutgruppe 0 und boreische Sprachverwandtschaft. *Anat. Anz.* **150**, 175–211. (a)

(1981). Das erste Wort? Morph. Jahrbuch 127. (b)

Schebesta, P. (1941). Die Bambuti-Pygmäen vom Ituri, II. Inst. Royal Colonial Belge. Bruxelles: Libraire Falk.

Schegloff, E. (1968). Sequencing rules in conversational openings. *Amer. Anthropol.* **70**, 1075–1095.

Scheller, R. H. and Axel, R. (1984). How genes control an innate behavior. *Sci. Amer.* **250**, 44–52.

Scheller, R. H., Jackson, J. F., McAllister, L. B., Rothman, B. S., Mayeri, E., and Axel, R. (1983). A single gene encodes multiple neuropeptides mediating a stereotyped behavior. *Cell* **32**, 7–22.

Scheller, R. H., Jackson, J. F., McAllister, L. B., Schwartz, J. H., Kandel, E. R., and Axel, R. (1982). A family of genes that codes for ELH, a neuropeptide eliciting a stereotyped pattern of behavior in aplysia. *Cell* **28**, 707–719.

Schelsky, H. (1955). Soziologie der Sexualität. Hamburg: Rowohlt.

Scheman, J., Lockard, J. S., and Mehler, B. L. (1977). Anatomical influence on book-carrying behavior. *Bull. Psychonomic Soc.* **93**, 367–370.

Schenkel, R. (1956). Zur Deutung der Phasianidenbalz. *Ornith. Beobacht.* **53**, 182–201.

Scherer, K. R. (1972). Judging personality from voice: A cross-cultural approach to an old issue in interpersonal perception. *J. Personality* **40**, 191–210.

(1977). Affektlaute und vokale Embleme. *In:* Rosner, R. and Reinecke, H. P. (eds.), Zeichenprozesse—Semiotische Forschung in den Einzelwissenschaften. Wiesbaden: Athenaion, pp. 199–214.

(1979). Personality markers in speech. *In:* Scherer, K. R. and Giles, H. (eds.), Social Markers in Speech. Cambridge/London/New York: Cambridge University Press.

Scherer, K. R. and Ekman, P. (eds.) (1982). Handbook of Methods in Nonverbal Behavior Research. Cambridge/London/New York: Cambridge University Press.

Scherer, K. R. and Giles, H. (eds.) (1979). Social Markers in Speech. Cambridge/London/ New York: Cambridge University Press.

Scherer, K. R. and Oshinsky, J. S. (1977). Cue utilization in emotion attribution from auditory stimuli. *Motivation Emotion* **1**, 331–346.

Scherer, K. R. and Wolf, J. J. (1973). The voice of confidence: Paralinguistic cues and audience evaluation. *J. Res. Personality* **17**, 31–44.

Scherer, K. R., Uno, H., and Rosenthal, R. (1972). A cross-cultural analysis of vocal behavior as a determinant of experimenter expectancy effects—A Japanese case. *Intern. J. Psychol.* **7**, 109–117.

Scherer, K. R., Walbott, G., and Scherer, U. (1979). Methoden zur Klassifikation von Bewegungsverhalten. Ein funktionaler Ansatz. *Z. Semiotik* **1**, 177–192.

Schetelig, H. (1979). Die Bedeutung des Stillens in der Ernährung des Säuglings. *Fortschr. Med.* **97**, 349–352.

Schiefenhövel, G. and Schiefenhövel, W. (1978). Eipo, Irian Jaya (West-Neuguinea)—Vorgänge bei der Geburt eines Mädchens und Änderung der Infantizid-Absicht. *Homo* **29**, 121–138.

Schiefenhövel, W. (1979). Aggression and Aggression-Control among the Eipo, Highlands of West-Neuguinea. Poster Paper XVI. International Ethological Conference, Vancouver.

(1980). "Primitive" Childbirth—Anachronism or Challenge to "Modern" Obstetrics? *In:* Ballabriga, A. and Gallart, A. (eds.), Proceedings of the 7th European Congress of Perinatal Medicine, Barcelona, pp. 40–49.

(1982). Die natürliche Geburt—Wie Eipo-Kinder auf die Welt kommen. *Neue Zürcher Zeit.* **113** (19.5.82), 33.

(1983). Geburten bei den Eipo. *In:* Schiefenhövel, W. and Sich, D. (eds.), Die Geburt aus ethnomedizinischer Sicht. Wiesbaden: Vieweg, pp. 41–56. (a)

(1983). Der ethnomedizinische Beitrag zur Diskussion um die optimale Geburtshilfe. *In:* Schiefenhövel, W. and Sich, D. (eds.), Die Geburt aus ethnomedizinischer Sicht. Wiesbaden: Vieweg, pp. 241–246. (b)

(1984). Bindung und Lösung—Sozialisationspraktiken im Hochland von Neuginea. *In:* Eggers, Ch. (ed.), Bindungen und Besitzdenken beim Kleinkind. München/Wien/Baltimore: Urban & Schwarzenberg, pp. 51–80.

Schiefenhövel, W. and Bell-Krannhals, I. (1986). Wer teilt, hat Teil an der Macht: Systeme der Yams-Vergabe auf den Trobriand-Inseln, Papua Neuguinea. *Mitteil. Anthropol. Ges. Wien,* **116,** 19–39.

Schiefenhövel, W. and Sich, D. (eds.) (1983). Die Geburt aus ethnomedizinischer Sicht. Beiträge und Nachträge zur IV. Internationalen Fachtagung der Arbeitsgemeinschaft Ethnomedizin über traditionelle Geburtshilfe und Gynäkologie in Göttingen. Wiesbaden: Vieweg.

Schindler, H. (1980). Humanethologie und Ethnologie. *Z. Ethnol.* **105,** 67–93.

(1982). Language, alliance and descent. *Anthropos* **77,** 524–532.

Schjelderup-Ebbe, Th. (1922). Soziale Verhältnisse bei Vögeln. *Z. Psychol.* **90,** 106–107. (a)

(1922). Beiträge zur Sozialpsychologie des Haushuhns. *Z. Psychol.* **88,** 225–252. (b)

Schleidt, M. (1980). Personal odor and nonverbal communication. *Ethol. Sociobiol.* **1,** 225–231.

(1984). Beziehungen zwischen Riechen, Pheromonen und Abhängigkeit. *In:* Keup, W. (ed.), Biologie der Sucht. 5. wiss. Sympos. der Dtsch. Hauptstelle gegen die Suchtgefahren, Hamm: Arbeitsgemeinsch. der Fachverlage.

(1988). A universal time constant operating in human short-term behaviour repetitions. *Ethology* **77,** 67–75.

Schleidt, M., Neumann, P. and Morishita, H. (1988). Pleasure and disgust: memories and associations of pleasant and unpleasant odours in Germany and Japan. *Chem. Senses* **13,** 279–293.

Schleidt, M., Hold, B., and Attili, G. (1981). A cross-cultural study on the attitude towards personal odors. *J. Chem. Ecol.* **7,** 19–31.

Schleidt, M., Pöppel, E., and Eibl-Eibesfeldt, I. (1987). A universal constant in temporal segmentation of human short-term behaviour. *Naturwissenschaften* **74,** 289–290.

Schleidt, W. M. (1973). Tonic communication; continual effects of discrete signs in animal communication systems. *J. Theoret. Biol.* **42,** 359–386.

Schlosser, K. (1952). Körperliche Anomalien als Ursache sozialer Ausstoßung bei Naturvölkern. *Z. Morphol. Anthropol.* **44,** 220–236. (a)

(1952). Der Signalismus in der Kunst der Naturvölker. (Biologisch-psychologische Gesetzlichkeiten in den Abweichungen von der Norm des Vorbildes.) Arbeiten a. d. Mus. f. Völkerkunder Univ. Kiel, I. Kiel: Mühlau. (b)

(1952). Der Rangkampf biologisch und ethnologisch gesehen. Act. IV. *Congr. Inern. Sci. Anthropol. Ethnol., Wien,* **2,** 43–50. (c)

Schmidbauer, W. (1971). Jäger und Sammler. München: Selecta Verlag.

(1973). Territorialität und Aggression bei Jägern und Sammlern. *Anthropos* **68,** 548–558.

Schmidt-Mummendey, A. and Schmidt, H. D. (eds.) (1971). Aggressives Verhalten. München: Inventa.

Schneider, D. (1962). Electrophysiological investigation on the olfactory specificity of sexual attracting substances in different species of moths. *J. Insect. Physiol.* **8,** 15–30.

Schneider, H. (1975). Entwicklung und Sozialisation der Primaten. München: tuduv Verlagsges.

Schneider, W. (1976). Wörter machen Leute. Magie und Macht der Sprache. München: Piper; 3rd ed. 1983.

Schneirla, T. C. (1966). Behavioral Development and Comparative Psychology. *Quart. Rev. Biol.* **41,** 283–302.

Schober, H. and Rentschler, I. (1979). Das Bild als Schein der Wirklichkeit. München: Moos Verlag.

Schoeck, H. (1980). Der Neid. München/Wien: Herbig.

Schoetzau, A. and Papoušek, H. (1977). Mütterliches Verhalten bei der Aufnahme von Blickkontakt mit Neugeborenen. *Z. Entwicklungs Pädagog. Psychol.* **9,** 231–239.

Schröder, M. (1978). Untersuchungen zur Identifikation von Klageliedern aus verschiedenen Kulturen. Analyse der rhythmischen Struktur der Testlieder. Diplomarbeit, Ludwig-Maximilians-Universität München.

Schropp, R. (1982). Das Anbieten von Objekten als Strategie im Umfeld aggressiver Interaktionen. Diplomarbeit an der Ludwig-Maximilians-Universität München.

Schubert, G. (1973). Biopolitical behavior: The nature of the political animal. *Polity* **6**, 240–275.

(1975).Biopolitical behavioral theory. *Political Sci. Rev.* **4**, 402–428.

(1981). The sociobiology of political behavior. *In:* White, E. (ed.), Sociobiology and Human Politics. Lexington, MA: D. C. Heath & Co., Lexington Books, pp. 193–238.

(1982). Infanticide by usurper hanuman langur males: A sociobiological myth. *Soc. Sci. Inform.* **21**, 199–244.

(1983). The structure of attention: A critical review. *J. Soc. Biol. Struct.* **6**, 65–80. (a)

(1983). Soziobiologie und politisches Verhalten. *In:* Flohr, H. and Tönnesmann, W. (eds.), Politik und Biologie. Berlin: Paul Parey, pp. 111–126. (b)

Schultze-Westrum, Th. (1974). Biologie des Friedens. München: Kindler.

Schumacher, A. (1982). On the significance of stature in human society. *J. Human Evol.* **11**, 697–701.

Schuster, M. and Beisl, H. (1978). Kunst-Psychologie "Wodurch Kunstwerke wirken." Köln: DuMont.

Schuster, R. H. (1978). Ethological theories of aggression. *In:* Kutash, I. L., Kutash, S. B., Schlesinger, L. B. *et al.* (eds.), Violence. Perspectives on Murder and Aggression. San Francisco, CA: Jossey Bass, pp. 74–100.

Schwartzman, H. B. (1978). Transformations. The Anthropology of Children's Play. New York/London: Plenum Press.

Schwarzer, A. (1976). "Das ewig Weibliche ist eine Lüge." Simone de Beauvoir über die Situation der Frauen nach dem Jahr der Frau. Der Spiegel, 15.

Scott, J. P. (1960). Aggression. Chicago: Chicago University Press.

Seal, H. L. (1966). Multivariate Statistical Analysis for Biologists. London: Methuen.

Searle, J. R. (1983). Intentionality. Cambridge: Cambridge Univ. Press.

Sears, R. R., Rau, L., and Alpert, R. (1965). Identification and Child Rearing. Stanford, CA: Stanford University Press.

Seay, B., Alexander, B. K., and Harlow, H. F. (1964): Maternal behavior of socially deprived rhesus monkeys. *J. Abnorm. Soc. Psychol.* **69**, 345–354.

Sebeok, Th. A. and Umiker-Sebeok, J. (eds.) (1980). Speaking of Apes. New York/London: PlenumPress.

Sedlaček, K. and Sychra, A. (1963). Die Melodie als Faktor des emotionellen Ausdrucks. *Folia Phoniatr.* **15**, 89–98.

(1969). The Method of Psychoacoustic Transformation Applied to the Investigation of Expression in Speech and Music. Kybernetika Cislo 1, Rocnik 5.

Segall, M., Campbell, D., and Herskovits, M. (1966). The Influence of Culture on Visual Perception. Indianapolis, IN: Bobbs-Merrill.

Seitelberger, F. (1981). Neurobiologische Grundlagen der menschlichen Freiheit. *In:* Böhme, W. (ed.), Mensch und Kosmos. Herrenalber Texte, 33 Frankfurt: Lembeck, pp. 26–47.

Seitz, A. (1940). Die Paarbildung bei einigen Cichliden. *Z. Tierpsychol.* **4**, 40–84.

Seligman, M. E. P. (1970). On the generality of the laws of learning. *Psychol. Rev.* **77**, 406–418.

(1971). Phobias and preparedness. *Behav. Therapy* **2**, 307–320.

Senft, G. (1982). Tonband T 3A. Mündliche Mitteilung. Tape-transcription.

Service, E. R. (1962). Primitive Social Organization and Evolutionary Perspective. New York: Random House.

(1971). Primitive Social Organization. New York: Random House.

(1978). Classical and modern theories of the origins of government. *In:* Cohen, R. and Service, E. R. (eds.), Origins of the State: The Anthropology of Political Evolution. Philadelphia, PA: Institute for the Study of Human Issues, pp. 21–34.

Seywald, A. (1977). Körperliche Behinderung. Frankfurt a. M./New York: Campus.

(1980). Anstoßnahme an sichtbar Behinderten. Rheinstetten: Schindele.

Shafton, A. (1976). Conditions of Awareness: Subjective Factors in the Social Adaptations of Man and Other Primates. Portland, OR: Riverston Press.

Sharpe, E. (1968). Psycho-physical problems revealed in language: An investigation of metaphor. *In:* Brierlye, M. (ed.), Collected Papers on Psychoanalysis. London: Hogarth, The International Psychoanalytical Library Nr. 36.

Shelley, W. B., Hurley, H. J., and Nichols, A. C. (1953). Axillary odor. *A.M.A. Arch. Dermatol. Syphilol.* **68**, 430–446.

Shepher, J. (1971). Mate selection among second generation kibbutz adolescents and adults: Incest avoidance and negative imprinting. *Arch. Sex. Behav.* **1**, 293–307.

(1983). Incest—A Biosocial View. New York/London: Academic Press.

Sherif, M. and Sherif, C. W. (1966). Groups in Harmony and Tension. New York: Octagon.

Sherman, J. A. (1978). Sex-Related Cognitive Differences. Springfield, IL: Charles C. Thomas.

Sherzer, J. (1970). La parole chez les Abipones. *L'Homme* **10**, 42–76.

Shettleworth, J. S. (1975). Reinforcement and the organisation of behavior in golden hamsters. Hunger, environment and food reinforcement. *J. Exp. Psychol. Anim. Behav. Processes* **104**, 56–87.

Shields, W. M. and Shields, L. M. (1983). Forcible rape: An evolutionary perspective. *Ethol. Sociobiol.* **4**, 115–136.

Shigetomi, C. C., Hartmann, D. P., and Gelfand, D. M. (1981). Sex differences in children's altruistic behavior and reputations for helpfulness. *Develop. Psychol.* **17**, 434–437.

Short, R. V. (1984). Breast feeding. *Sci. Amer.* **250**, 23–29.

Shorter, E. (1977). Die Geburt der modernen Familie. Hamburg: Rowohlt. [English. ed.: The Making of the Modern Family. New York: Basic Books Inc.]

Shostak, M. (1981). Nisa, Life and Words of a !Kung Woman. Cambridge, MA: Harvard University Press.

Siegel, B. (1970). Defensive structuring and environmental stress. *Amer. J. Sociol.* **76**, 11–32.

Siegfried, W. (1983). Development of Space and Time Structures in Opening Phases of Dance Groups. Symposium on Biological Aspects of Aesthetics. Organized by the Werner-von-Reimers-Stiftung, Bad Homburg, 10–13, June.

(1988). Dance, the fugitive form of art—Aesthetics as behavior. *In*: Rentschler, I., Herzberger, B., Epstein, D. (eds.), Beauty and the Brain. Basel, Boston, Berlin: Birkhäuser, pp. 117–148.

Silberbauer, G. B. (1972). The G/wi Bushmen. *In:* Bicchieri, M. G. (ed.), Hunters and Gatherers Today. New York: Holt, Rinehart and Winston, pp. 271–326.

(1973). Socio-Ecology of the G/wi Bushmen. Thesis, Dept. Anthropol. and Sociol., Monash Univeristy.

Simner, M. L. (1971). Newborns' response to the cry of another infant. *Develop. Psychol.* **5**, 136–150.

Sinclair-de-Zwart, H. (1974). Psychologie der Sprachentwicklung. *In:* Leuninger, H., Miller, M. H., and Müller, F. (eds.), Linguistik und Psychologie. Bd. 2, Frankfurt/M: Fischer Athenäum, pp. 73–109.

Singer, D. (1968). Aggression arousal, hostile humor, catharsis. *J. Personality Social Psychol. Monogr. Suppl.* **8** (Vol. 1, Pt. 2).

Singer, P. (1981). The Expanding Circle: Ethics and Sociobiology. Oxford: Clarendon.

Sipes, R. G. (1973). War, sports and aggression: An empirical test of two rival theories. *Amer. Anthropol.* **75**, 64–86.

Siqueland, E. R. and Lipsitt, L. P. (1965). Conditioned headturning in human newborns. *J. Exp. Child Psychol.* **3**, 356–376.

Sivard, R. L. (1980). Entwicklung der Militär- und Sozialausgaben in 140 Ländern der Erde. UN-Texte, 25, WMSE-Report 1979.

Skinner, B. F. (1938). The Behavior of Organisms. New York: Appleton Century Crofts.

(1957). Verbal Behavior. London: Methuen.

(1971). Beyond Freedom and Dignity. New York: Knopf.

Skolnick, A. (1973). The Intimate Environment. Boston: Little Brown.

Skrzipek, K. H. (1978). Menschliche "Auslösermerkmale" beider Geschlechter. I. Attrappenwahluntersuchungen der Verhaltensentwicklung. *Homo* **29**, 75–88.

(1981). Menschliche "Auslösermerkmale" beider Geschlechter. II. Attrappenwahluntersuchungen des geschlechtsspezifischen Erkennes bei Kindern und Erwachsenen. *Homo* **32**, 105–119.

(1982). Menschliche "Auslösermerkmale" beider Geschlechter. III. Untersuchung der Verhaltensentwicklung mit reduzierten Attrappen. *Homo* **33**, 1–12.

(1983). Stammesgeschichtliche Dispositionen der geschlechtsspezifischen Sozialisation des Kindes—eine experimentelle humanethologische Analyse. *Homo* **34**, 227–238.

Slaby, R. G. and Frey, K. S. (1975). Development of gender constancy and selective attention to same-sex models. *Child Develop.* **46**, 849–856.

Slobin, D. I. (1969). Questions of Language Development in Cross-Cultural Perspective. Working Paper No. 14, Language-Behavior Research Laboratory, Berkeley, CA.

(1974). Kognitive Voraussetzungen der Sprachentwicklung. *In:* Leuninger, H., Miller, M. H., and Müller, F. (eds.), Linguistik und Psychologie. Bd. 2, Frankfurt/M: Fischer Athenäum, pp. 122–165.

Smith, H. W. (1981). Territorial spacing on a beach revisited: A cross-national exploration. *Soc. Psychol. Quart.* **44**, 132.

Smith, K. J. (1977). The Behavior of Communicating. Cambridge, MA: Harvard University Press.

Smith, L. and Martinsen, H. (1977). The behavior of young children in a strange situation. *Scand. J. Psychol.* **18**, 43–52.

Smith, P. K., and Daglish, L. (1977). Sex differences in parent and infant behavior in the home. *Child Develop.* **48**, 1250–1254.

Smith, P. K., Eaton, L., and Hindmarch, A. (1982). How one-year-olds respond to strangers: A two-persons situation. *J. Genet. Psychol.* **140**, 147–148.

Smith, P. M. (1979). Sex markers in speech. *In:* Scherer, K. R. and Giles, H. (eds.), Social Markers in Speech. London: Cambridge University Press, pp. 109–146.

Sneath, P. H. and Sokal, R. (1973). Numerical Taxonomy. San Francisco, CA: W. H. Freeman.

Snow, C. E. and Ferguson, C. A. (eds.) (1977). Talking to Children. Input and Acquisition. Cambridge: Cambridge University Press.

Snow, C. E. Arlman-Kupp, A., Hassing, Y., Jobse, J., Joosten, J., and Vorster, J. (1976). Mother's speech in three social classes. *J. Psycholing. Res.* **5**, 1–20.

Snow, M. E., Jacklin, C. N., and Maccoby, E. E. (1983). Sex-of-child differences in father-child interaction at one year of age. *Child Develop.* **54**, 227–232.

Snyder, S. H. (1980). Biological Aspects of Mental Disorder. New York: Oxford Univ. Press.

(1984). Drug and neurotransmitter receptors in the brain. *Science* **224**, 22–31.

Snyderman, G. S. (1948). Behind the tree of peace. A sociological analysis of Iroquois warfare. *Pa. Archeologist* **18**, 3–4.

Sobotta, J. and Becher, H. (1972, 17th ed.). Atlas der Anatomie des Menschen, Bd. 1. München/Berlin/Wien: Urban & Schwarzenberg.

Somit, A. (ed.) (1976). Biology and Politics. Recent Explorations. The Hague/Paris: Mouton.

Somit, A. and Slagter, R. (1983). Biopolitics: Heutiger Stand und weitere Entwicklung, *In:* Flohr, H. and Tönnesmann, W. (eds.), Politik und Biologie. Berlin: Paul Parey, pp. 30–37.

Sommer, R. and Becker, F. D. (1969). Territorial Defense and the Good Neighbor. *J. Personality Social Psychol.* **11**, 85–92.

Sorenson, E. R. (1967). A research film program in the study of changing man: Research filmed material as a foundation for continued study of non-recurring human events. *Current Anthropol.* **8**, 443–469.

(1976). The Edge of the Forest. Land, Childhood and Change in a New Guinea Protoagricultural Society. Washington, D.C.: Smithsonian Inst. Press.

Sorenson, E. R. and Gadjusek, D. C. (1966). The study of child behavior and development in primitive cultures. *Pediatrics Suppl.* **37**, 149–243.

Sostek, A. M., Scanlon, J. W., and Abramson, D. C. (1982). Postpartum contact and maternal confidence and anxiety: A confirmation of short-term effects. *Infant Behav. Develop.* **5**, 323–329.

Soussignan, R. and Koch, P. (1985). Rhythmical stereotypes (Leg-Swinging) associated with reductions in heart-rate in normal school children. *Biol. Psychol.* **21**, 1–7.

Spalding, D. A. (1873). Instinct with original observation on young animals. *MacMillan's Mag.* **27**, 282–283. [Neudruck Brit. J. Anim. Behav. 2, 1–11, 1954.]

Sparling, D. W. and Williams, J. D. (1978). Multivariate analyses of avian vocalizations. *J. Theoret. Biol.* **74**, 83–107.

Spemann, H. (1938). Embryonic Development and Induction. New Haven: Yale University Press.

Sperry, R. W. (1945). The problem of central nervous reorganization after nerve regeneration and muscle transposition. *Quart. Rev. Biol.* **20**, 311–369. (a)

(1945). Restoration of vision after crossing of optic nerves and after contralateral transplantation of eye. *J. Neurophysiol.* **8**, 115–28. (b)

(1964). The great cerebral commissure. *Sci. Amer.* **210**, 42–52.

(1965). Selective communication in nerve nets: Impulse specificity vs. connection specificity. *Neurosci. Res. Program Bull.* **3**, 37–43.

(1971). How a brain gets wired for adaptive function. *In:* Tobach, E., Aronson, L. R., and Shaw, E. (eds.), The Biopsychology of Development. London: Academic Press, pp. 27–44.

(1974). Lateral specialisation in the surgically separated hemispheres. *In:* Schmitt, F.O., and Worden, F. G. (eds.), The Neurosciences-Third Study Program. Cambridge: MIT Press.

Sperry, R. W. and Preilowski, B. (1972). Die beiden Gehirne des Menschen. *Bild Wissenschaft,* pp. 920–928.

Spiel, W. (1980). Die Psychologie des 20. Jahrhunderts, Bd. 12: Konsequenzen für die Pädagogik, 2. Zürich: Kindler.

Spiro, M. E. (1954). Is the family universal? *Amer. Anthropol.* **56**, 839–846.

(1958). Children of the Kibbutz. Cambridge, MA: Harvard University Press.

(1979). Gender and Culture: Kibbutz Women Revisited. Durham, North Carolina: Duke University Press.

Spitz, R. (1965). The First Year of Life. New York: International University Press.

(1968). Die anaklitische Depression. *In:* Bittner, G. and Schmid-Cords, E. (eds.), Erziehung in früher Kindheit. München: Piper.

Sroufe, L. A. (1977). Wariness of stranger and the study of infant development. *Child Develop.* **48**, 731–746.

Stacey, B. (1980). Infant-mother attachment: A social psychological perspective. *Soc. Behav. Personality* **8**, 33–40.

Stahl, F., Doerner, G., Ahrens, L., and Graudenz, W. (1976). Significantly decreased apparently free testosterone levels in plasma of male homosexuals. *Endokrinologie* **68**, 115–117.

Stamps, J. A. and Barlow, G. W. (1973). Variation and stereotypy in the displays of anolis geneus (Sauria: Iguanidae). *Behaviour* **47**, 67–94.

Stanjek, K. (1978). Das Überreichen von Gaben: Funktion und Entwicklung in den ersten Lebensjahren. *Z. Entwicklungspsychol. Pädagog. Psychol.* **10**, 103–113.

(1979). Die Entwicklung des menschlichen Besitzverhaltens. Dissertation der Fak. Biologie der Ludwig-Maximilians-Universität München (Materialien aus der Bildungsforschung, 16, Max-Planck-Institut für Bildungsforschung Berlin).

Staub, E. and Noerenberg, H. (1981). Property rights, deservingness, reciprocity, friendship: The Transactional Character of Children's Sharing Behavior. *J. Personality Social Psychol.* **40**, 271–289.

Stein, L. (1980). The chemistry of reward. *In:* Routtenberg, A. (ed.), Biology of Reinforcement: Facets of Brain-Stimulation Reward. New York: Academic Press, pp. 109–132.

Steinbuch, K. (⁷1973). Kurskorrektur. Stuttgart: Seewald.

Steiner, G. (ed.) (1978). Die Psychologie des 20. Jahrhunderts. 7. Piaget und die Folgen. Zürich: Kindler.

Steiner, J. E. (1973). The gustofacial response: Observation on normal and anencephalic newborn infants. *In:* Bosma, J. F. (ed.), Symposium on Oral Sensation and Perception—IV (Development in the Fetus and Infant). Bethesda, MD: Dhew & Fogarty Int. Center, pp. 254–278.

(1974). Innate discriminative human facial expression to taste and smell stimulation. (Discussion paper). *Ann. NY Acad. Sci.* **237**, 229–233.

(1979). Human facial expressions in response to taste and smell stimulation. *Child Develop. Behav.* **13**.

Steiner, J. E. and Horner, R. (1972). The human gustofacial response. *Israel J. Med. Sci.* **8**, 32.

Steklis, H. D. and Raleigh, M. J. (1979). Behavioral and neurobiological aspects of primate vocalization and facial expression. *In:* Steklis, H. D. and Raleigh, M. J. (eds.), Neurobiology of Social Communication in Primates. New York: Academic Press, pp. 257–282.

Stent, G. S., Kristan, W. B., Friesen, W. O., Ort, C. A., Poon, M., and Calabrese, R. L. (1978). Neuronal generation of the leech swimming movement. *Science* **200**, 1348–1557.

Stephens, W. N. (1962). The Oedipus Complex: Cross-Cultural Evidence. New York: Free Press of Glencoe.

(1963).The Family in Cross-Cultural Perspective. New York: Holt, Rinehart & Winston.

Stern, D. N. (1971). A micro-analysis of mother-infant interaction behavior regulating social contact between a mother and her 3½ months old twins. *J. Amer. Acad. Child Psychiatry* **10**, 501–517.

(1974). Mother and infant at play: The dyadic interaction involving facial, vocal and gaze behaviours. *In:* Lewis, M. and Rosenblum, L. (eds.), The Effect of the Infant on Its Caregiver. London: Wiley, pp. 187–214.

(1977). The First Relationship, Mother and Infant. Cambridge, MA: Harvard University Press.

Stern, D. N., Beebe, B., Jaffe, J., and Bennett, S. L. (1977). The infant's stimulus world during social interaction: A study of caregiver behaviours with particular reference to repetition and timing. *In:* Schaffer, H. R. (ed.), Studies on Interactions in Infancy. London: Academic Press, pp. 177–203.

Stern, D. N., Spieker, S., and MacKain, K. (1982). Intonation contours as signals in maternal speech to prelingusitic infants. *Develop. Psychol.* **18**, 727–735.

Steward, J. H. (1938). Basin-Plateau aboriginal sociopolitical groups. *Bureau Amer. Ethnol. Bull.,* p. 120.

Stewart, R. B. (1983). Sibling attachment relationships: Child-infant interactions in the strange stituation. *Develop. Psychol.* **19**, 192–199.

Stewart, V. M. (1973). Tests of the "Carpentered World" Hypothesis by race and environment in America and Zambia. *Intern. J. Psychol.* **8**, 83–94.

Stokoe, W. C., Croneberg, C. G., and Casterline, D. (1965). A Dictionary of American Sign Language. Washington, D.C.: Gallaudet College Press.

Stoller, R. J. (1975). Perversion: The Erotic Form of Hatred. New York: Pantheon Books. [Perversion: Die erotische Form von Haß. Hamburg, Rowohlt 1979.]

Stopa, R. (1972). Structure of Bushman and Its Traces in Indo-European. Kraków: Polska Akademia Nauk.

(1975). Evolution der Sprache. *Nova Acta Leopoldina* **42** [N. F.] 218, 355–375. Paper presented at the annual meeting of the Deutsche Akademie der Naturforscher Leopoldina, Halle, October 1973.

Strathern, A. (1971). The Rope of Moka: Big-Men and Ceremonial Exchange in Mount Hagen, New Guinea. London/New York: Cambridge University Press.

(1974). Melpa Amb Kenan. Courting Songs of the Melpa people. Institute of Papua New Guinea Studies. The printery Port Moresby.

(1979). Ongka. A Self-Account by a New Guinea Big-Man. London: Duckworth.

(1983). Biology and Aesthetics: Some Thoughts from Papua New Guinea. Paper presented at the 3rd International Conference on Hunters and Gatherers, Reimers-Stiftung, Bad Homburg, June 1983.

Stratton, P. (ed.) (1982). Psychobiology of the Human Newborn. Chichester/New York: Wiley. (a)

(1982). Rhythmic function in the newborn. *In:* Stratton, P. (ed.), Psychobiology of the Human Newborn. Chichester/New York: Wiley, pp. 119–145. (b)

Strayer, J. (1980). A Naturalistic study of empathic behaviors and their relation to affective states and perspective-taking sills in preschool children. *Child Develop.* **51**, 815–822.

Strehlow, C. (1915). Die Aranda- und Loritja-Stämme in Central-Australien. *Veröffentlichungen Städtischen Völkermuseums Frankfurt/M.,* **4**, 1–78.

Strehlow, T. G. (1970). Geography and totemic landscape in Central Australia: A functional study. *In:* Berndt, R. M. (ed.), Australian Aboriginal Anthropology. Nedland, W. Australia: University of W. Australia Press, pp. 92–140.

Studdert-Kennedy, M. (1982). Die Anfänge der Sprache. *In:* Immelmann, K., Barlow, G.,

Petrinovich, L., and Main, M. (eds.), Verhaltensentwicklung bei Mensch und Tier. Das Bielefeld-Projekt. Berlin/Hamburg: Paul Parey, pp. 640–667.

Sugawara, K. (1984). Spatial proximity and bodily contact among the Central Kalahari San. *Af. Study Monogr. Suppl.* **3**, 1–43.

Sugiyama, Y. (1964). Group composition, population density and some sociological observations of Hanuman langurs *(Presbytis entellus)*. *Primates* **5**, 7–37.

Sutton-Smith, B. (1979). The play of girls. *In:* Kopp, C. B. and Kirkpatrick, M. (eds.), Becoming Females: Perspectives and Development. New York: Plenum, pp. 229–257.

Svaare, B. B. (1983). Hormones and Aggressive Behavior. New York: Plenum Press.

Swadesh, M. (1948). Motivations in Nootka warfare. *Southwest. J. Anthropol.* **4**, 76–93.

Sweet, L. (1965). Camel pastoralism in North Arabia and the minimal camping unit. *In:* Vayda, A. P. (ed.), Environment and Cultural Behavior. Garden City, NY: Natural History Press, pp. 155–180.

Sweet, W. H., Ervin, F., and Mark, V. H. (1969). The relationship of violent behaviour to focal cerebral disease. *In:* Garattini, S. and Sigg, E. B. (eds.), Aggressive Behaviour. Amsterdam: Excerpta Media Foundation, pp. 336–352.

Symons, D. (1980). The evolution of human sexuality. (Multiple Book Rev.) *Behav. Brain Sci.* **3**, 171–214.

Tajfel, H. (ed.) (1978). Differentiation between Social Groups. London/New York: Academic Press.

(1982). Social Identity and Intergroup Relations. Cambridge: Cambridge Univ. Press.

Tanaka, J. (1980). The San Hunter-Gatherers of the Kalahari. A Study in Ecological Anthropology. Tokyo: University of Tokyo Press.

Tartter, V. C. (1980). Happy talk: Perceptual and acoustic effects of smiling on speech. *Perception Psychophys.* **27**, 24–27.

Taub, E., Ellman, St. J. and Berman, A. J. (1965). Deafferentiation in monkeys. Effects on conditioned grasp response. *Science* **151**, 593–594.

Tauber, M. A. (1979). Sex Differences in parent-child interaction styles during a free-play session. *Child Develop.* **50**, 981–988.

Taylor, S. (1981). Symbol and ritual under national socialism. *Brit. J. Sociol.* **32**, 504–520.

Teleki, G. (1973). Predatory Behavior of Wild Chimpanzees. Lewisburg: Bucknell University Press.

Tembrock, G. (1975). Phonetische Eigenschaften von Primatenlauten im Evolutions-Aspekt. *Nova Acta Leopoldina* **42** [N. F.] (with record), *218*, 343–353.

Terhardt, E. (1982). Die psychoakustischen Grundlagen der musikalischen Akkordgrundtöne und deren algorithmische Bestimmung. *In:* Dahlhaus C. and Krause, M. (eds.), Tiefenstruktur der Musik. Technische Universität, Berlin, pp. 23–50.

(1984). The concept of musical consonance: A link between music and psychoacoustics. *Music Perception* **1**, 276–295.

Terrace, H. S. (1979). Nim. New York: Alfred A. Knopf.

Terrace, H. S., Petitto, L. A., Sanders, R. J., and Bever, T. G. (1979). Can an ape create a sentence? *Science* **206**, 891–902.

Thelen, E. (1980). Determinants of amounts of stereotyped behavior in normal human infants. *Ethol. Sociobiol.* **1**, 141–150.

Thomae, H. (ed.) (1954). Handbuch der Psychologie 3: Entwicklungspsychologie. Göttingen: C. J. Hogrefe.

(1983). Learning to walk is still an "old" problem: A reply to Zelazo (1983). *J. Motor Behav.* **15**, 139–161.

(1984). Learning to walk: Ecological demands and phylogenetic constraints. *In:* Lipsitt, L. P. and Rovee-Collier, C. (eds.), Advances in Infancy Research, Vol. 3. Norwood, NJ: Ablex, pp. 213–260.

Thompson, E. P. (1972). Rough Music. Le Charivari anglais. *Ann. ESC* **27**, 285–312.

Thornhill, R. and Wilmsen-Thornhill, N. (1983). Human rape: An evolutionary analysis. *Ethol. Sociobiol.* **4**, 137–173.

Thorpe, W. H. (1958). The learning of song patterns by birds, with special reference to the song of the chaffinch, *Fringilla coelebs*. *Ibis* **100**, 535–570.

(1961). Sensitive periods in the learning of animals and men. A study of imprinting with special reference to the introduction of cyclic behavior. *In:* Thorpe, W. H. and Zangwill, O. L. (eds.), Current Problems in Animal Behavior. Cambridge: Cambridge University Press, pp. 194–224.

Tieger, T. (1980). On the biological basis of sex differences in aggression. *Child Develop.* **51**, 943–963.

Tiger, L. (1969). Men in Groups. New York: Random House.

— (1976). Ions of emotion and political behavior: Notes on prototheory. *In:* Somit, A. (ed.), Biology and Politics. Paris: Mouton, pp. 263–267.

Tiger, L. and Fox, R. (1966). The zoological perspective in social science. *Man* **1**, 75–81.

— (1971). The Imperial Animal. New York: Holt, Rinehart & Winston.

Tiger, L. and Shepher, J. (1975). Women in the Kibbutz. New York: Harcourt, Brace Jovanovich, Inc.

Tinbergen, E. A. and Tinbergen, N. (1972). Early Childhood Autism—An Ethological Approach. Fortschritte der Verhaltensforschung 10. Berlin: Parey.

Tinbergen, J. (ed.) (1977). Wir haben nur eine Zukunft. Opladen: Westdeutscher Verlag.

Tinbergen, N. (1940). Die Übersprungbewegung. *Z. Tierpsychol.* **4**, 1–40.

— (1948). Social releasers and the experimental method required for their study. *Wiss. Bull.,* **60**, 6–52.

— (1951). The Study of Instinct. London: Oxford University Press.

— (1955). Tiere untereinander. Berlin: Parey.

— (1959). Einige Gedanken über "Beschwichtigungsgebärden." *Z. Tierpsychol.* **16**, 651–665.

— (^{3}1963). The Herring Gull's World. A Study of the Social Behavior of Birds. London: Collins.

— (1981). On the history of war. *In:* Valzelli, I. and Morgese, I. (eds.), Aggression and Violence: A Psycho/Biological and Clinical Approach. Milano: Edizione Saint Vincent, pp. 31–38.

Tinbergen, N. and Kuenen, D. J. (1939). Über die auslösenden und richtungsgebenden Reizsituationen der Sperrbewegung von jungen Drosseln *(Turdus m. merula* L. and *T. e. ericetorum Turton). Z. Tierpsychol.* **3**, 37–60.

Tinbergen, N. and Tinbergen, E. A. (1983). "Autistic" Children: New Hope for a Cure. London: Allen & Unwin.

Tinbergen, N., Imperkoven, M., and Franck, D. (1967). An experiment on spacing-out as a defense against predation. *Behaviour* **28**, 307–321.

Tinbergen, N., Broekhuysen, G. J., Feekes, F., Houghton, J. C. W. Kruuk, H., and Szulc, E. (1962). Eggshell removal by the blackheaded gull *(Lazarus ribidundus* L.): A behavior component of camouflage. *Behaviour* **19**, 74–117.

Tobach, E. (1976). Evolution of behavior and comparative method. *Intern. J. Psychol.* **11**, 185–201.

Tobach, E., Gianutsos, J., Topoff, H. R., and Gross, C. G. (1974). The Four Horsemen: Racism, Militarism and Social Darwinism. New York: Behavioral Publications.

Tobias, Ph. v. (1964). Bushman-hunter-gatherers. A study in human ecology. *In:* Davis, D. H. S. (ed.), Ecological Studies in Southern Africa. The Hague: W. Junk.

Tomkins, S. S. and McCarter, R. (1964). What and where are the primary affects? Some evidence for a theory. *Percept. Motor Skills* **18**, 119–158.

Tomoda, Z. (1937). The perception of figures as dependent upon their form and size. *Jap. J. Psychol.* **12**, 433–450.

Tornay, S. (1979). Armed conflicts in the lower Oma Valley, 1970–1976. *Senri Ethnol. Stud.* **3**, 97–117.

Trautner, H. M. (1979). Psychologische Theorien der Geschlechtsrollen-Entwicklung. *In:* Degenhardt, A. and Trautner, H. M. (eds.), Geschlechtstypisches Verhalten. München: C. H. Beck, pp. 50–84.

Trevarthen, C. (1975). Growth of visuomotor coordination in infants. *J. Human Movement Stud.* **1**, 57.

— (1979). Instincts for human understanding and for cultural cooperation: Their development in infancy. *In:* Cranach, M. v., Foppa, K., Lepenies, W., and Ploog, D. (eds.), Human Ethology, Claims and Limits of a New Discipline. London/Cambridge: Cambridge University Press, Paris (Maison des Sciences de l'Homme), pp. 530–571.

— (1983). Interpersonal abilities of infants as generators for transmission of language and culture. *In:* Oliverio, A. and Zappella, M. (eds.), The Behavior of Human Infants. New York/London: Plenum, pp. 145–176.

Trevarthen, C. and Hubley, P. (1978). Secondary intersubjectivity: confidence, confiding and acts of meaning in the first year. *In:* Lock, A. (ed.), Action, Gestures and Symbol: The emergence of language. London: Academic Press, pp. 183–229.

Triandis, H. C. and Lambert, W. W. (1958). A restatement and test of Schlosberg's theory of emotion with two kinds of subjects from Greece. *J. Abnormal Social Psychol.* **56,** 321–328.

Tripp, C. A. (1975). The Homosexual Matrix. New York: Signet.

Trivers, R. L. (1971). The evolution of reciprocal altruism *Quart. Rev. Biol.* **46,** 35–37.
    (1972). Parental investment and sexual selection. *In:* Campbell, B. (ed.), Sexual Selection and the Descent of Man, 1871–1971. London: Heinemann, pp. 136–179.
    (1974). Parent offspring conflict. *Amer. Zool.* **14,** 249–264.

Trojan, F. (1975). Biophonetik. Mannheim: Bibliograph. Institut-Wissenschaftsverlag.

Tronick, E., Als, H., Adamson, L., Wise, S., and Brazelton, T. B. (1978). The infant's response to entrapment between contradictory messages in face-to-face interaction. *Amer. Acad. Child Psychiatry,* pp. 1–13.

Turco, R. P., Toon, O. B., Ackerman, T. P., Pollack, J. B., and Sagan, C. (1983). Nuclear winter: Global consequences of multiple nuclear explosions. *Science* **222,** 1283–1292.

Turke, P. W. (1984). Effects of ovulatory concealment and synchrony on protohominid mating systems and parental roles. *Ethol. Sociobiol.* **5,** 33–44.

Turnbull, C. M. (1961). The Forest People. London: Chatto & Windus.
    (1965): The Mbuti Pygmies. An ethnographic survey. *Anthropol. Papers. Amer. Mus. Nat. Hist.* **50,** 282.

Turner, F. and Pöppel, E. (1983). The neural lyre: Poetic meter, the brain and time. *Poetry, August 1983,* pp. 277–309.

Turney-High, H. H. (1949). Primitive War, Its Practices and Concepts. Columbia, SC: University of South Carolina Press.

Turton, D. (1979). War, peace and Mursi identity. *Senri Ethnol. Stud.* **3,** 179–210.

Tyler, D. S. (1979). Time-sampling, a matter of convention. *Anim. Behav.* **27,** 801–810.

Tyrell, H. (1978). Family as the original institution – Recent speculation regarding an old question. *Kölner Z. Sozio. Sozial-Psychol.* **30,** 611–651.

Tyson, J. E. (1977). Nursing and prolactin secretion: Principal determinants in the mediation of puerperal infertility. *In:* Crossignani, P. G. and Robyn C. (eds.), Prolactin and Human Reproduction. New York: Academic Press.

Tyson, J. E., Carter, J. N., Andreasson, B., Huth, J., and Smith, B. (1978). Nursing mediated prolactin and luteinising hormone secretion during puerperal lactation. *Fertility Sterility* **30,** 154–162.

Ultan, R. (1978). Size-sound symbolism. *In:* Greenberg, J. H., Ferguson, C. A., and Maravcsik, E. A. (eds.), Universals of Human Language, 2 Phonology. Stanford, CA: Stanford University Press, pp. 525–568.

Umiker-Sebeok, J. and Sebeok, Th. A. (1981). Clever Hans and smart simians. The self-fulfilling prophecy and kindred methodological pitfalls. *Anthropos* **76,** 89–165.
    (1982). Rejoinder to the Rumbaughs. *Anthropos* **77,** 574–578.

Uyenoyama, M. K. (1979). Evolution of altruism under group selection in large and small populations in fluctuating environments. *Theoret. Popul. Biol.* **15,** 58–85.

Uyenoyama, M. K. and Feldman, M. W. (1980). Theories of kin and group selection: A population genetics perspective. *Theoret. Popul. Biol* **17,** 380–414.

Valzelli, L. and Morgese, L. (eds.) (1981). Aggression and Violence: A Psychobiological and Clinical Approach. Proceedings of the First St. Vincent Special Conference, 14/15 Oct., 1980. Centro Culturale e congressi, Saint Vincent.

Vandell, D. L., Wilson, K. S., and Buchanan, N. R. (1980). Peer interaction in the first year of life: An examination of its structure, content, sensitivity to toys. *Child Develop.* **51,** 481–488.

Varney, N. R. and Vilensky, J. A. (1980). Neuropsychological implications for preadaptation and language evolution. *J. Human Evol.* **9,** 223–226.

Vayda, A. P. (1960). Maori Warfare. Polynesian Society Maori Monographs, 2, Wellington.
    (1961). Expansion and warfare among Swidden agriculturalists. *Amer. Anthropol.* **63,** 346–358.
    (1967). Research on the functions of primitive war. *Peace Res. Soc. Intern. Pap.* Bd. 7
    (1970). Maoris and muskets in New Zealand: Disruption of a war system. *Political Sci. Quart.* **85,** 560–584.

(1971). Phases in the process of war and peace among the marings of New Guinea. *Oceania* 42, 1–24. (a)

(1971). Hypothesen zur Funktion des Krieges. *In:* Fried, M., Harris, M., and Murphy, R. (eds.), Der Krieg. Frankfurt/M.: S. Fischer, pp. 103–110. (b)

Vayda, A. P. and McCay, B. (1975). New directions in ecology and ecological anthropology. *Ann. Rev. Anthropol.* **4**, 293–306.

Vayda, A. P. and Rappaport, R. A. (1968). Ecology, cultural, and non-cultural. *In:* Clifton, J. A. (ed.), Introduction to Cultural Anthropology. Boston: Houghton Mifflin, pp. 477–497.

Vedder, H. (1937). Die Buschmänner Südwestafrikas and ihre Weltanschauung. *South Afr. J. Sci.* **24**, 416–436.

Verba, M., Stambak, M., and Sinclair, H. (1982). Physical knowledge and social interaction in children from 18 to 24 months of age. *In:* Forman, G. (ed.), Action and Thought: Sensory Motor Schemes to Symbolic Operations. London/New York: Academic Press, pp. 267–296.

Verebey, K. (1982). Opioids in mental illness theories, clinical observations and treatment possibilities. *Ann. N.Y. Acad. Sci.,* p. 398.

Vester, F. (1972). Das Überlebensprogramm. München: Kindler.

Vicedom, C. F. and Tischner, H. (1943/48). Die Mbowamb. Band I. Die Kultur der Hagenbergstämme. Monograph. zur Völkerkunde 1. Hamburg.

Vierling, J. S. and Rock, J. (1967). Variations in olfactory sensitivity to exaltolide during the menstrual cycle. *J. Appl. Physiol.* **22**, 311–315.

Vinacke, W. E. (1949). The judgement of facial expressions by three national-racial groups in Hawaii: I. Caucasian faces. *J. Personality* **17**, 407–429.

Vining, D. (1982). On the possibility of reemergence of a dysgenic trend with respect to intelligence in American fertility differentials. *Intelligence* **6**, 241–264. (a)

(1982). Fertility differentials and the status of nations: A speculative essay on Japan and the West. *Mankind Quart.* **22**, 311–353. (b)

(1986). Social versus reproductive success: The central theoretical problem of human sociobiology. *Behav. Brain Sci.* **9**, 167–216.

Vinter, A. (1985). L'Imitation chez le Nouveau Né: imitation, representation et mouvement dans les premiers mois de la vie. Neuchatel/Paris: Delacheaux.

(1986). A developmental perspective on behavioral determinants. *Acta Psychol.* **63**, 337–349.

Vogel, Ch. (1977). Geschlechtstypisches Verhalten bei nichtmenschlichen Primaten – zugleich ein Beitrag zur Evolution geschlechtstypischen Verhaltens beim Menschen. Paper presented at the annual meeting of Anthropology and Humangenetics. Hamburg, 21 Sept. 1977. (a)

(1977). Primatenforschung – Beiträge zum Selbstverständnis des Menschen. Vortragsreihe der Niedersächsischen Landesregierung zur Förderung der wiss. Forschung in Niedersachsen. Göttingen: Vandenhoek & Ruprecht. (b)

(1979). Der Hanuman-Langur *(Presbytis entellus),* ein Paradeexemplar für die theoretischen Konzepte der "Soziobiologie"? Verhandl. *Deut. Zool. Ges.,* pp. 73–89.

Vogel, CH. and Loch, H. (1984). Reproductive parameters. Adult-male replacements, and infanticide among free-ranging langurs *(Presbytis entellus)* at Jodhpur (Rajasthan), India. *In:* Hausfater, G. and Blaffer Hrdy, S. (eds.), Infanticide: Comparative and Evolutionary Perspectives. New York: Aldine, pp. 237–255.

Vogel, Ch., Voland, E., and Winter, M. (1979). Geschlechtstypische Verhaltensentwicklung bei nichtmenschlichen Primaten. *In:* Degenhardt, A. and Thautner, H. M. (eds.), Geschlechtstypisches Verhalten. München: C. H. Beck, pp. 145–181.

Vollmer, G. (1975). Evolutionäre Erkenntnistheorie. Stuttgart: Hirzel.

(1983). Mesokosmos and objektive Erkenntnis – Über Probleme, die von der evolutionären Erkenntnistheorie gelöst werden. *In:* Lorenz, K. and Wuketits, F. M. (eds.), Die Evolution des Denkens. München/Zürich: Piper, pp. 29–91.

Vossen, A. (1971). Die Früherfassung zerebral geschädigter Kinder. *Deut. Ärzteblatt* **68**, 3136–3144.

Vrugt, A. and Kerkstra, A. (1984). Sex differences in nonverbal communication. *Semiotica* **50**, 1–41.

Vygotsky, L. S. (1960). Selected Psychological Research. Moskow: APN RSFSR.

de Waal, F. (1982). Chimpanzee Politics – Power and Sex among Apes. London: Jonathan Cape.

(1986). The integration of dominance and social bonding in primates. *The Quart. Rev. Biol.* **61**, 459–479.

Wade, M. J. (1978). A critical review of the models of group selection. *Quart. Rev. Biol.* **53**, 101–114.

(1980). Kin selection: Its components. *Science* **210**, 665–667.

Wagner, Sh. and Winner, E. (1979/80). Metaphorical Mapping in Human Infants. Paper presented at the Eastern Psychological Association meetings, April, 1979.

Wallhäusser, E. and Scheich, H. (1987). Auditory imprinting leads to differential 2-deoxy-glucose uptake and dendritic spine loss in the chick rostral forebrain. *Develop. Brain Res.* **31**, 29–44.

Walters, R. H. and Thomas, E. L. (1963). Enhancement of punitiveness by visual and audiovisual displays. *Canad. J. Psychol.* **17**, 244–255.

Wangerin, G. and Weiss, G. (1976). Heinrich Tessenow. Essen: Verlag Richard Bacht.

Warburton, D. M. (1975). Brain, Behavior, and Drugs: Introduction to the Neurochemistry of Behaviour. London: Wiley.

Warner, W. L. (1930). Murngin Warfare. *Oceania* **1**, 457–494.

Warnke, M. (1984). Politische Architektur in Europa. Köln: Dumont.

Washburn, S. L. and Hamburg, D. A. (1965). The implications of primate research. *In:* DeVore, I. (ed.), Primate Behavior. New York: Holt, Reinhart & Winston, pp. 607–622.

(1968). Aggressive behavior in old world monkeys and apes. *In:* Jay, P. C. (ed.), Primates: Studies in Adaptation and Variability. New York: Holt, Rinehart & Winston, pp. 458–478.

Wasserman, G. A. and Stern, D. N. (1978). An early manifestation of differential behavior toward children of the same and opposite sex. *J. Genet. Psychol.* **133**, 129–137.

Waters, W., Matas, L., and Sroufe, L. A. (1975). Infants' reactions to an approaching stranger: Description, validation and functional significance of wariness. *Child Develop.* **46**, 348–356.

Waters, E., Wippman, J., and Sroufe, L. A. (1979). Attachment, positive effect and competence in the peer group. *Child Develop.* **50**, 821–829.

Watson, J. S. (1971). Cognitive-perceptual development in infancy: Setting for the seventies. *Merrill-Palmer Quart.* **17**, 139–152.

(1972). Smiling, cooing, and "The Game." *Merrill-Palmer Quart.* **18**, 323–329.

(1977). Depression and the perception of control in early childhood. *In:* Schulterbrandt, J. G. and Raskin, A. (eds.), Depression in Childhood: Diagnosis, Treatment and Conceptual Models. New York: Raven.

(1979). Perception of contingency as a determinant of social responsiveness. *In:* Thoman, E. B. (ed.), Origins of the Infant's Social Responsiveness. Hillsdale, NJ: Lawrence Erlbaum Associates, pp. 33–64.

Watson, J. S. and Ramsey, C. T. (1972). Reactions to response-contingent stimulation in early infancy. *Merrill-Palmer Quart.* **18**, 219–227.

Watzlawick, P. (ed.) (1981): Die erfundene Wirklichkeit. Beiträge zum Konstruktivismus. München/Zürich: Piper.

Wawra, M. (1985). Aufschauverhalten und Gruppengröße beim Menschen. Diplomarbeit, Zoologisches Institut der Universität Freiburg im Breisgau.

Weber, M. (1981). Der Beruf zur Politik. Berlin: Duncker & Humblot.

Webster, M. Jr. and Driskell, J. E. (1983). Beauty as status. *Amer. J. Sociol.* **89**, 140–165.

Wedgwood, C. H. (1930). Some aspects of warfare in Melanesia. *Oceania* **1**, 5–33.

Weinberg, S. K. (1955). Incest Behavior. New York: Citadel.

Weisfeld, C. C., Weisfeld, G. E., and Callaghan, J. W. (1982). Female inhibition in mixed-sex competition among young adolescents. *Ethol. Sociobiol.* **3**, 29–42.

Weisfeld, C. C., Weisfeld, G. E., Warren, R. A., and Freedman, D. G. (1983). The spelling bee: A naturalistic study of female inhibition in mixed-sex competition. *Adolescence* **18**, 695–708.

Weisfeld, G. E. (1980). Social dominance and human motivation. *In:* Omark, D. R., Strayer, F. F., and Freedman, D. G. (eds.), Dominance Relations. An Ethological View of Human Conflict and Social Interactions. New York/London: Garland STPM Press, pp. 273–286.

Weisfeld, G. E. and Berger, J. M. (1983). Some features of human adolescence viewed in evolutionary perspective. *Human Develop.* **26**, 121–133.

Weisfeld, G. E., Omark, D. R., and Cronin, C. L. (1980). A longitudinal and cross-sectional study of dominance in boys. *In:* Omark, D. R., Strayer, F. F., and Freedman, D. G. (eds.), Dominance Relations: An Ethological View of Human Conflict and Social Interactions. New York/London: Garland STPM Press, pp. 205–216.

Weisfeld, G. E., Block S. A., and Ivers, J. W. (1984). Possible determinants of social dominance among adolescent girls. *J. Genet. Psychol.* **144**, 115–129.

Weisner, Th. S. (1979). Urban-rural differences in sociable and disruptive behavior of Kenya children. *Ethnology* **18**, 153–172. (a)

(1979). Some cross-cultural perspectives on becoming female. *In:* Kopp, C. B. and Kirkpatrick, M. (eds.), Becoming Female. New York: Plenum, pp. 313–332. (b)

Weisner, Th. S. and Gallimore, R. (1977). My brother's keeper: Child and sibling caretaking. *Current Anthropol.* **18**, 169–199.

Weitzman, E. D. (1982). Chronobiology of man. Sleep, temperature and neuroendocrine rhythms. *Human Neurobiol.* **1**, 173–183.

Weizäcker, C. Fr. von (1977). Der Garten des Menschlichen. Beiträge zur geschichtlichen Anthropologie. München: Hanser.

Werner, H. (1948). Comparative Psychology of Mental Development. New York: Follett.

Werner, H. and Kaplan, B. (1963). Symbol Formation. New York: Wiley.

Wertheimer, M. (1927). Gestaltpsychologische Forschung. *In*: Saupes Einführung in die neuere Psychologie. Osterwieck/Harz.

West, M. M. and Konner, M. J. (1976). The Role of the Father: An Anthropological Perspective. *In:* Lamb, M. E. (ed.), The Role of the Father in Child Development. New York: Wiley, pp. 185–216.

West, S. G. and Brown, T. J. (1975). Physical attractiveness, the severity of the emergency and helping: A field experiment and interpersonal simulation. *J. Exp. Social Psychol.* **11**, 531–538.

West-Eberhard, M. J. (1975). The evolution of social behavior by kin selection. *Quart. Rev. Biol.* **50**, 1–33.

Westermarck, E. (1894). The History of Human Marriage. London: Macmillan.

Westin, A. (1970). Privacy and Freedom. New York: Atheneum.

Wever, R. (1975). The circadian multi-oscillator system of man. *J. Chronobiol.* **3**, 19–55.

(1978). Grundlagen der Tagesperiodik beim Menschen. *In:* Heimann, H. and Pflug, B. (eds.), Rhythmusprobleme in der Psychiatrie. Stuttgart/New York: Fischer, pp. 1–23.

(1980). Die Tagesperiodik des Menschen. Grundlagen und Probleme *Betriebsärztliches* **1**, 1–32.

Wex, M. (1979). ''Weibliche'' und ''männliche'' Körpersprache als Folge patriarchalischer Machtverhältnisse. Hamburg: Verlag M. Wex.

White, L. (1959). The Evolution of Culture. New York: McGraw-Hill.

Whiting, B. B. and Edwards, C. P. (1973). A cross-cultural anaylsis of sex-differences in the behavior of children aged three through eleven. *J. Social Psychol.* **91**, 171–188.

Whiting, J. W. M. (1941). Becoming a Kwoma. New Haven, CT: Yale University Press.

Whyte, W. (1965). Herr und Opfer der Organisation. Düsseldorf: Econ.

Wickler, W. (1965). Über den taxonomischen Wert homologer Verhaltensmerkmale. *Naturwissenschaften* **52**, 441–444.

(1966). Ursprung und biologische Deutung des Genitalpräsentierens männlicher Primaten. *Z. Tierpsychol.* **23**, 422–437.

(1967). Socio-sexual signals and their intraspecific imitation among primates. *In:* Morris, D. (ed.), Primate Ethology. London: Weidenfeld & Nicolson, pp. 69–147. (a)

(1967). Vergleichende Verhaltensforschung und Phylogenetik. *In:* Heberer, G. (ed.), Die Evolution der Organismen. Stuttgart: Fischer, pp. 420–508. (b)

(1968). Mimikry-Signalfälschung in der Natur. München: Kindler.

(1969). Sind wir Sünder? Naturgesetze der Ehe. München: Droemer.

(1971). Die Biologie der Zehn Gebote. München: Piper, Neuausgabe 1975 (Serie Piper 72).

(1977). Vom Ursprung sozialer Abhängigkeiten. Vortrag der Max-Planck-Gesellschaft, November 1976, Regensburg. Max-Planck-Gesellschaft, Jahrbuch 1977, 86–102

(1978). Die Evolution unsozialen Verhaltens. Berl. Münch. *Tierärztl. Wochschr.* **91**, 486–488. (a)

(1978). Abnormes Sozialverhalten als Strategie des gesunden Individuums. Festvortrag,

Oktober 1978, Regensburg, 61. Fortbildungstagung für Ärzte. (b)

(1979). Pre-Wilsonian Sociobiology. *Z. Tierpsychol.* **49**, 433–434.

Wickler, W. and Seibt, U. (1977). Das Prinzip Eigennutz. Ursachen und Konsequenzen sozialen Verhaltens. Hamburg: Hoffmann und Campe.

(1981). Monogamy in Crustacea and Man. *Z. Tierpsychol.* **57**, 215–234.

(1982). Song Splitting in the Evolution of Dueting. *Z. Tierpsychol.* **59**, 127–140. (a)

(1982). Alt-Ekuadorianische Spinnwirtel und ihre Bildmotive. *Beitr. Allgem. Vergleich. Archäol.* **4**, 315–419. (b)

Wickler, W. and Uhrig, D. (1969). Bettelrufe, Antwortszeit und Rassenunterschiede im Begrüßungsduett des Schmuckbartvogels. *Z. Tierpsychol.* **26**, 651–661.

Wiepkema, P. R. (1961). An ethological analysis of the reproductive behavior of the bitterling (*Rhodeus amarus* Bloch). *Extr. Arch. Néerland. Zool.* **14**, 103–199.

Wiessner, P. (1977). Hxaro: A Regional System of Reciprocity for Reducing Risk among the !Kung San. Ph. D. Diss., University of Michigan, Ann Arbor, University Microfilms.

(1980). History and Continuity in !Kung San Reciprocal Relationships. Paper presented at 2. Int. Conf. on Hunting and Gathering Societies, Quebec, September, 1980.

(1981). Measuring the impact of social ties on nutritional status among the !Kung San. *Soc. Sci. Inform.* **20**, 641–678. (a)

(1982). Risk, reciprocity and social influences on !Kung San economics. *In:* Leacock, E. R. and Lee, R. B. (eds.), Politics and History in Band Societies. London: Cambridge University Press, pp. 62–84.

(1983). Style and social information in Kalahari San projectile points. *Amer. Antiquity* **48**, 253–276.

(1984): Reconsidering the behavioral basis for style: A case study among the Kalahari San. *J. Anthropol. Archaeol.* **3**, 190–234. (a)

(1984): Foodsharing among Children in four Cultures. Paper prepared for a Symposium of the Reimers Foundation on Ritual Aspects of Food. Bad Homburg, December, 1984. (b)

Wiley, R. H. (1973). The strut display of the male sage grouse: A "Fixed" action pattern. *Behavior* **47**, 129–152.

Wilhelm, H. J. (1953). Die !Kung-Buschleute. *Jahr. Museums Völkerkunde (Leipzig)* **12**, 91–189.

Williams, B. J. (1974). A model of band society. *Amer. Antiquity* **39**, 1–138.

(1980). Cognitive Limitation and Hunting Band Size. Vortrag auf der 2. Int. Conf. on Hunting and Gathering Societies, Quebec, 19.–24. Sept. 1980; Proceed., pp. 147–172.

(1981). A critical review of models in sociobiology. *Ann. Rev. Anthropol.* **10**, 163–192.

Williams, G. C. (1966). Adaptation and Natural Selection: A Critique of Some Current Evolutionary Thought. Princeton, NJ: Princeton University Press.

Williams, J. E. and Best, D. L. (1982). Measuring Sex Stereotypes. Beverley Hills, CA: Sage.

Wilson, D. S. (1975). A theory of group selection. *Proc. Natl. Acad. Sci. U.S.* **72**, 143–146.

(1977). Structured demes and the evolution of group-advantageous traits. *Amer. Natur.* **111**, 157–185.

Wilson, E. O. (1963). Pheromones. *Sci. Amer.* **208**, 100–114.

(1975). Sociobiology: The New Synthesis. Cambridge, MA: Belknap Press – Harvard University Press.

(1976). The social instinct. *Bull. Amer. Acad. Arts Sci.* **30**, 11–25.

(1978). Altruism. *Harvard Mag. Nerv. Dev.*, pp. 23–28.

Winberg, J. and DeChateau, P. (1982). Early social development: Studies of infant-mother interaction and relationship. *In:* Hartup, W. W. (ed.), Review of Child Development Research, Vol. VI. Chicago: The University of Chicago Press, pp. 1–44.

Winkelman, M. (1986). Trance states: A theoretical model and cross-cultural analysis. *Ethos* **14**, 174–203.

Winkelmayer, R., Exline, R. V., Gottheil, E., and Paredes, A. (1971). Cross-cultural differences in judging emotions. Unveröffentlicht. *In:* Ekman, P. (ed.) (1973), Darwin and Facial Expression. New York – London: Academic Press, p. 201.

Winterhoff-Spurk, P. (1983). Die Funktionen von Blicken und Lächeln beim Auffordern. Europäische Hochschulschriften, Reihe 6, Psychologie. Frankfurt/Bern/New York: Peter Lang.

Wirtz, P. and Wawra, M. (1986). Vigilance and group size in *Homo sapiens. Ethology (Z. Tierpsychol.),* **71,** 283–286.

Witkin, H. A., Goodenough, D. R., and Karp, S. A. (1967). Stability of cognitive style from childhood to young adulthood. *J. Personality Social Psychol.* **7,** 291–300.

Wittelson, S. (1978). Sex differences in the neurology of cognition: Psychological, social, educational and political implications. *In:* Sullerot, E. (ed.), Le Fait Feminin. Paris: Fayard, pp. 289–303.

Wittig, M. and Petersen, A. (eds.) (1979). Sex-Related Differences in Cognitive Functioning. New York/London: Academic Press.

Wobst, H. M. (1976). Locational relationship in paleolithic society. *J. Human Evol.* **5,** 49–58.

— (1977). Stylistic behavior and information exchange. *In:* Cleland, C. E. (ed.), Papers for the Director: Research Essays in Honor of James B. Griffin. Anthropology Papers. Museum of Anthropology, University of Michigan, 61, 317–342.

Wolf, A. P. (1966). Childhood association, sexual attraction and the incest taboo: A Chinese case. *Amer. Anthropol.* **68,** 883–898.

— (1970). Childhood association and sexual attraction: A further test of the Westermarck hypothesis. *Amer. Anthropol.* **72,** 503–515.

— (1974). More on Childhood Association and Fertility in Taiwan. Unveröffentlichtes Manuskript

Wolfgang, J. and Wolfgang, A. (1968). Personal Space – An Unobtrusive Measure of Attitudes Toward the Physically Handicapped. Proceedings of the 76th Annual Convention of the American Psychological Association, pp. 653–654.

Woodburn, J. (1968): Stability and flexibility in Hadza residential groupings. *In:* Lee, R. B. and DeVore, I. (eds.), Man the Hunter. Chicago: Aldine, pp. 103–110.

Woodhouse, H. C. (1987). Inter- and intragroup aggression illustrated in the rock paintings of South Africa. *S. Afr. J. Ethnol.* 10 (1), 42–48.

Woodwell, G. M. (1978). The carbon dioxide question. *Sci. Amer.* **238,** 34–43.

Wright, Q. (rev. 1965). A Study of War. Chicago: University of Chicago Press.

Wülker, W. (1976). Weltmodelle. *Biologie Unserer Zeit* **6,** 148–155.

— (1976). Die großen Kreisläufe der Natur. *In:* Todt, D. (ed.), Funkkolleg Biologie, Begleittext, Sendg. 23, Weinheim: Beltz.

Wunderlich, D. (1970/71). Pragmatik, Sprechsituation, Deixis. Lili, 1/2, 153–190.

— (1973). Probleme einer linguistischen Pragmatik. Papiere zur Linguistik, **4,** 1–19.

— (1974). Grundlagen der Linguistik. Hamburg: Reinbek. (a)

— (1974). Pragmatik. Einleitung und Referenzsemantik. *In:* Lehrgang Sprache. Einführung in die moderne Linguistik. Basel/Tübingen: Weinheim, pp. 789–811. (b)

Wynne-Edwards, V. C. (1962). Animal Dispersion in Relation to Social Behaviour. London: Oliver & Boyd.

Yellen, J. E. and Harpending, H. (1972). Hunter-gatherer populations and archaeological inference. *World Archaeol.* **4,** 244–253.

Yengoyan, A. A. (1968): Demographic and ecological influences on aboriginal Australian marriage sections. *In:* Lee, R. B. and DeVore, I. (eds.), Man the Hunter. Chicago: Aldine, pp. 185–199.

Yerkes, R. M. and Yerkes, A. W. (1929). The Great Apes. New Haven: CT: Yale Univ. Press.

Yogman, M. W. (1981). Games fathers and mothers play with their infants. *Infant Mental Health J.* **2,** 241–248.

— (1982). Development of the father-infant relationship. *In:* Fitzgerald, H., Lester, B., and Yogman, M. W. (eds.), Theory and Research in Behavioral Pediatrics. Vol. 1. New York: Plenum, pp. 221–279. (a)

— (1982). Observations on the father-infant relationship. *In:* Cath, S. H., Gurwitt, A. R., and Ross, J. M. (eds.), Father and Child: Developmental and Clinical Perspectives. Boston: Little, Brown, pp. 101–122. (b)

Yokoyama, S. and Felsenstein, J. (1978). A model of kin selection for an altruistic trait considered as a quantitative character. *Proc. Natl. Acad. Sci. U.S.* **75,** 420–422.

Yonas, A., Pettersen, L., and Lockman, J. J. (1979). Young infants' sensitivity to optical information for collision. *Canad. J. Psychol.* **33,** 268–276.

Young, M. V. (1971). Fighting with Food. Leadership, Values, and Social Control in a Massim Society. Cambridge: Cambridge University Press.

Youniss, J. (1982). Die Entwicklung und Funktion von Freundschaftsbeziehungen. *In:* Edelstein, W. and Keller, M. (eds.), Perspektivität und Interpretation: Beiträge zur Entwicklung sozialen Verstehens. Frankfurt/M.: Suhrkamp, pp. 78–108.

Zaporozhets, A. V. (1978). The significance of early periods of childhood for formation of children's personality. *In:* Antsyferova, L. I. (ed.), Principles of Development in Psychology. Moskow: Nauka.

Zastrow, B. von and Vedder, H. (1930). Die Buschmänner. *In:* Schulz-Ewerth, E. and Adam, L. (eds.), Das Eingeborenenrecht: Togo, Kamerun, Südwestafrika, die Südseekolonien. Stuttgart: Strecker & Schröder.

Zelazo, P. R. (1976). From reflexive to instrumental behavior. *In:* Lipsitt, L. P. (ed.), Developmental Psychobiology: The Significance of Infancy. Hillsdale, NJ: Lawrence Erlbaum.

(1983). The development of walking: New findings on old assumptions. *J. Motor Behavior* **2**, 99–137.

Zeskind, Ph. S. and Lester, B. M. (1978). Acoustic features and auditory perception of the cries of newborns with prenatal and perinatal complication. *Child Develop.* **49**, 580–589.

Zinn, H. (1981). Sozialisation von Kindern und Jugendlichen unter beengten Wohn- und Wohnumfeldbedingungen. *Inform. Raumentwickl.* **7/8**, 435–444.

Zinser, H. (1981). Der Mythos des Mutterrechts. Frankfurt/M.: Ullstein.

Zivin, G. (1977). Facial gestures predict preschoolers' encounter outcomes. *Soc. Sci. Information* **16**, 715–730. (a)

(1977). On becoming subtle: Age and social rank changes in the use of a facial gesture. *Child Develop.* **48**, 1314–1321. (b)

(1982). Watching the sands shift: Conceptualizing development of nonverbal mastery. *In:* Feldman, R. S. (ed.), The Development of Nonverbal Communication in Children. New York: Springer.

Film Publications of
Human Ethology*

Eibl-Eibesfeldt, I.

Ausdrucksverhalten eines taubblind-geborenen Mädchens (Deutschland)
Expressive Behavior of a Girl Born Deaf and Blind

E2724-HF 49

!Ko-Buschmänner (Botswana, Kalahari) Schamweisen und Spotten
Mocking and Genital Display in Females

E2721-HF 1

!Ko-Buschmänner (Botswana, Kalahari) Sprungspiel der Männer "//oli" (Heuschrecke)
Men's Grasshopper Game

E2955-HF 40

!Ko-Buschmänner (Botswana, Kalahari) Ausschnitte aus einem Trancetanz
Scenes of a Trance Dance

E2954-HF 44

!Ko-Buschmänner (Botswana, Kalahari) Tranceritual "guma"
The Trance Ritual "Guma"

E2953-HF 45

!Kung-Buschmänner (Südwestafrika, Kungveld) Geschwister-Rivalität, Mutter-Kind-Interaktionen
Sibling Rivalry, Mother–Child Interactions

E2720-HF 41

G/wi-Buschmänner (Botswana, Zentralkalahari) Krankenheilung und Trance—Teil I
Curing Ritual and Trance—Part I

E2682-HF 93

---

*Human ethology films are published in cooperation with the Göttingen Institute for Scientific Film as a joint production of the Film Archive of Human Ethology of the Max-Planck-Society (HF) and the Encyclopaedia Cinematographica of the Institute for Scientific Film (E).

G/wi-Buschmänner (Botswana, Zentralkalahari) Krankenheilung und Trance—Teil II
Curing Ritual and Trance—Part II

E2683-HF 94

G/wi-Buschmänner (Botswana, Zentralkalahari) Krankenheilung und Trance—Teil III
Curing Ritual and Trance—Part III

E2684-HF 95

G/wi-Buschmänner (Botswana, Zentralkalahari) Melonenspieltänze der Frauen
Melon Game Dances of Women

E2832-HF 134

G/wi-Buschmänner (Botswana, Zentralkalahari) Verwendung der Tsama-Melone zur
Ernährung
Use of the Tsama Melon as Food

E3059-HF 191

G/wi-Buschmänner (Botswana, Zentralkalahari) Verwendung der Tsama-Melone zur
Körperpflege
Use of the Tsama Melon for Body Care

E3060-HF 200

Himba (Südwestafrika, Kaokoland) Mutter-Kind-Interaktionen
Mother-Child Interactions

E2725-HF 100

Himba (Südwestafrika, Kaokoland) Ritual des "Okumakera"
Ritual of "Okumakera"

E2723-HF 101

Himba (Südwestafrika, Kaokoland) Soziale Kompetenz einer Vierjährigen
Social Competence of a 4-Year-Old Girl

E3075-HF 157

Himba (Südwestafrika, Kaokoland) Mutter mit Säugling
Mother and Baby

E3042-HF 188

Himba (Südwestafrika, Kaokoland) Verhalten von Männern mit Säuglingen
Male Parenting Behavior

E3041-HF 189

Himba (Südwestafrika, Kaokoland) Kindergemeinschaft
Community of Children

E3040-HF 190

Himba (Südwestafrika, Kaokoland) Kußfütterung
Kiss Feeding

E3076-HF 197

793

In (West-Neuguinea, Zentrales Hochland) Interaktionen zweier Knaben im vorsprachlichen Alter
Interaction of Two Boys of Preverbal Age

Fa (West-Neuguinea, Zentrales Hochland) Schlachten und Garen ines Schweines
Slaughtering and Cooking a Pig

Fa (West-Neuguinea, Zentrales Hochland) Erster Kontakt mit weißen Besuchern
First Contact with White Visitors

Trobriander (Ost-Neuguinea, Trobriand-Inseln, Kaile'una) Interaktionen einer 3½ jährigen mit Spielgefährten
Interactions of 3½-Year-Old Girl with Playmates

Yanomami, Ihiramawetheri und Kashorawetheri (Venezuela, Oberer Orinoko) Erstbegegnung mit weißer Besucherin
First Encounter with a White Female Visitor

Yanomami, Patanoetheri (Venezuela, Oberer Orinoko) Mädchen betreuen Säuglinge
Children Baby-Sitting

Yanomami, Patanoetheri (Venezuela, Oberer Orinoko) Interaktionen zweier sechsjähriger Mädchen
Interactions of Two 6-Year-Old Girls

Yanomami, Patanoetheri (Venezuela, Oberer Orinoko) Rasieren einer Tonsur
Shaving of a Tonsure

Yanomami, Patanoetheri (Venezuela, Oberer Orinoko) Geisterbeschwörung im Yopo-Rausch und Abstreifzauber
Exorcism during Yopo Intoxication and Transduction Magic

Eibl-Eibesfeldt, I. and Budack, K.

Himba (Südwestafrika, Kaokoland) Ein vierjähriges Mädchen beim Betreuen eines Kleinkindes und beim Puppenspiel
A 4-Year-Old Girl Baby-Sitting and Playing with a Doll

Himba (Südwestafrika, Kaokoland) Kuhspiel
Playing Cow

Himba (Südwestafrika, Kaokoland) Solitärspiel eines 4-jährigen Mädchens und Bewältigung von Störungen durch ein Kleinkind
Solitary Game of a 4-Year-Old Girl and Dealing with Disturbance by a Toddler

Eibl-Eibesfeldt, I. and Goodall, J.

Pan troglodytes (Pongidae) Termitenfischen
Fishing for Termites

E3012-HF 194

Eibl-Eibesfeldt, I. and Herzog, H.

Yanomami, Patanoetheri (Venezuela, Oberer Orinoko) Yopo-Rausch, Tanz und Geisterbeschwörung (hekuramou) zur Initiation eines Medizinmann-Anwärters—Teil I.
Yopo Intoxication, Dance and Exorcism during the Initiation of a Shaman Applicant—Part I

E2834-HF 136

Yanomami, Patanoetheri (Venezuela, Oberer Orinoko) Yopo-Rausch, Tanz und Geisterbeschwörung (hekuramou) zur Initiation eines Medizinmann-Anwärters—Teil II.
Yopo Intoxication, Dance and Exorcism during the Initiation of a Shaman Applicant—Part II

E2835-HF 137

Yanomami, Patanoetheri (Venezuela, Oberer Orinoko) Yopo-Rausch, Tanz und Geisterbeschwörung (hekuramou) zur Initiation eines Medizinmann-Anwärters—Teil III.
Yopo Intoxication, Dance and Exorcism during the Initiation of a Shaman Applicant—Part III

E2836-HF 138

Yanomami, Patanoetheri (Venezuela, Oberer Orinoko) Interaktionen eines weiblichen Kleinkindes mit Mutter und anderen Bezugspersonen
Interactions of a Female Baby with Her Mother and Others

E2861-HF 144

Yanomami, Patanoetheri (Venezuela, Oberer Orinoko) Männer im Umgang mit Säuglingen
Men's Interactions with Babies

E2862-HF 145

Yanomami, Patanoetheri (Venezuela, Oberer Orinoko) Weinen und Trösten
Crying and Consolation

E2864-HF 146

Yanomami, Patanoetheri (Venezuela, Oberer Orinoko) Mutter-Kind-Interaktionen (männlicher Säugling)
Mother–Child Interactions (Male Baby)

E2860-HF 147

Yanomami, Patanoetheri, (Venezuela, Oberer Orinoko) Bejahung, Verneinung und andere Ausdrucksbewegungen in Gesprächen
Affirmation, Negation, and Other Expressive Behaviors during Conversations

E3073-HF 198

Yanomami, Patanoetheri (Venezuela, Oberer Orinoko) Ausschnitte aus einem Fest (Eintanzen der Gäste, Himou und Abgang)
Scenes from a Feast (Display Dances of the Guests, Himou, and Departure)

E3061-HF 199

Eibl-Eibesfeldt, I. and Senft, G.

Trobriander (Ost-Neuguinea, Trobriand-Inseln, Kaile'una) Fadenspiele "ninikula"
Playing Cats Cradle "Ninikula"

E2958-HF 167

Heeschen, V. and Eibl-Eibesfeldt, I.

Eipo (West-Neuguinea, Zentrales Hochland) Dit-Gesang der Männer
Men's "Dit" Singing

E2833-HF 135

Eipo (West-Neuguinea, Zentrales Hochland) Der Linguist V. Heeschen im Zwiegespräch mit Männern
Linguist V. Heeschen Talking to Eipo Men

E2869-HF 150

Eipo (West-Neuguinea, Zentrales Hochland) Die Frau Danto im Gespräch mit dem Linguisten V. Heeschen
A Woman Named Danto Talking to Linguist V. Heeschen

E2870-HF 151

Heymer, A.

Bayaka-Pygmäen (Zentralafrika) Soziales Lausen bei Frauen und Mädchen
Social Grooming in Women and Girls

E2989-HF 83

Bayaka-Pygmäen (Zentralafrika) Soziales Lausen zwischen Mädchen und einem jungen Mann
Social Grooming between Girls and a Young Man

E2990-HF 84

Bayaka-Pygmäen (Zentralafrika) Reaktionen von Kleinkindern auf einen Fremden
Reaction of Babies to a Stranger

E2991-HF 85

Bayaka-Pygmäen (Zentralafrika) Geben, Nehmen und Teilen
Giving, Taking, and Sharing

E2992-HF 86

Bayaka-Pygmäen (Zentralafrika) Mutter-Kind-Beziehung und allomaternales Verhalten
Mother–Child Relationship and Allomothering Behavior

E2993-HF 87

Bayaka-Pygmäen (Zentralafrika) Schnelles Brauenheben und andere Ausdrucksbewegungen im sozialen Kontext
Rapid Eyebrow Flash and Other Expressive Movements in Social Context

E3082-HF 88

Bayaka-Pygmäen (Zentralafrika) Spielen zweier Geschwister vor den Wohnhütten
Playing of Two Siblings in Front of the Huts

E3083-HF 158

Bayaka-Pygmäen (Zentralafrika) Das Mädchen Molebo und seine soziale Integration in die Gruppe der Erwachsenen
Girl Named Molebo and Her Social Integration into the Group of Adults

E3089-HF 159

Bayaka-Pygmäen (Zentralafrika) Verhalten eines Säuglings in der Gruppe von Frauen und Kindern
Behavior of a Baby Within the Group of Women and Children

E3087-HF 160

Bayaka-Pygmäen (Zentralafrika) Mimik: Junge Personen
Facial Expression: Young Persons

E3084-HF 161/1

Bayaka-Pygmäen (Zentralafrika) Mimik: Alte Personen
Facial Expression: Old Persons

E3085-HF 161/2

Bayaka-Pygmäen (Zentralafrika) Kinderbetreuung im Lager
Care of Children in the Camp

E3086-HF 162

Schiefenhövel, W. and Eibl-Eibesfeldt, I.

Eipo (West-Neuguinea, Zentrales Hochland) Behandlung einer Pfeilwunde
Treating an Arrow Wound

E2800-HF 132

Eipo (West-Neuguinea, Zentrales Hochland) Behandlung eines Panaritiums
Treating a Panaritium

E2923-HF 154

Schiefenhövel, W.

Eipo (West-Neuguinea, Zentrales Hochland) Hochschwangere bei der Gartenarbeit
Woman in Advanced Stages of Pregnancy Working in the Garden

E-HF 91

Eipo (West-Neuguinea, Zentrales Hochland) Baumbestattung und Totenklage
Placing Corpses in Trees and Mourning

E3038-HF 184

In (West-Neuguinea, Zentrales Hochland) Schwierige Erstgeburt
Difficult First Delivery of an Eipo Woman (Primapara)

E2831-HF 118

Schiefenhövel, W. and Schiefenhövel, G.

Eipo (West-Neuguinea, Zentrales Hochland) Geburt eines Mädchens einer Primapara
Birth of a Female Baby (Primapara)

E2681-HF 90

Schiefenhövel, G. and Schiefenhövel, W.

Eipo (West-Neuguinea, Zentrales Hochland) Vorgänge bei der Geburt eines Mädchens und Änderung der Infantizid-Absicht
Events during the Birth of a Female Baby and Change of Plans for Infanticide

E2680-HF 70

Schiefenhövel, W. and Simon, F.

Eipo (West-Neuguinea, Zentrales Hochland) Anfertigen eines Nackenschmucks "Mum"
Making a Back Ornament "Mum"

E2437

Eipo (West-Neuguinea, Zentrales Hochland) Kastrieren eines Schweines
Castrating a Pig

E2456

Eipo (West-Neuguinea, Zentrales Hochland) Vorgänge anläßlich der zeremoniellen Übergabe einer Nassa-Stirnbinde
Practices on the Occasion of the Ceremonial Handing Over of a Nassa Head Band

E2457

Eipo (West-Neuguinea, Zentrales Hochland) Wundbehandlung einer infizierten Wunde
Treatment of an Infected Wound

E2510

Eipo (West-Neuguinea, Zentrales Hochland) Durchbohren der Nasenscheidewand
Perforation of the Nasal Septum

E2511

Eipo (West-Neuguinea, Zentrales Hochland) Durchbohren des Ohrläppchens
Perforation of the Earlobe

E2512

Eipo (West-Neuguinea, Zentrales Hochland) Ab- und Anlegen von Hüftgürtel und Peniskalebasse
Taking Off and Putting On Waist Belt and Penis Gourd

E2513

Eipo (West-Neuguinea, Zentrales Hochland) Schleifen von Steinklingen am Kirimye
Sharpening Stone Blades at the Krimye

E2550

Eipo (West-Neuguinea, Zentrales Hochland) Kinderspiele "taruk linglingana" und "mana"
Children's Games "Taruk Linglingana" and "Mana"

E2551

Eipo (West-Neuguinea, Zentrales Hochland) Körperbemalung der Mädchen
Girls Painting Their Bodies

E2557

Eipo (West-Neuguinea, Zentrales Hochland) Herstellung von Nasenstäben aus Kalzit (Arbeitssituation in der Gruppe)
Making Glate Nose Sticks (Working Situation in the Group)

E2777

Schiefenhövel, W. and Simon, F.

Eipo (West-Neuguinea, Zentrales Hochland) Schäften eines Steinbeils
Shafting a Stone Ax

E2906

Eipo (West-Neuguinea, Zentrales Hochland) Ein Vormittag in Imarin
A Morning in Imarin

E2635

Eipo (West-Neuguinea, Zentrales Hochland) Wundbehandlung mit Schweinefett und Wärmeanwendung
Treatment of Wounds with Pig's Fat and with Heat

E2509

Schiefenhövel, W., Simon, F., and Heunemann, D.

Eipo (West-Neuguinea, Zentrales Hochland) ''mote'' ein Besuchsfest in Munggona
''Mote''—Visiting Feast in Munggona

E2803

Eipo (West-Neuguinea, Zentrales Hochland) Sammeln von Wasserinsekten
Collecting Water Insects

E2538

Heunemann, D., Simon, F., and Blum, P.

Eipo (West-Neuguinea, Zentrales Hochland) Bau einer Schwerkraftfalle
Making a Weight Trap

E2659

Heunemann, D., Simon, F., and Schiefenhövel, W.

Eipo (West-Neuguinea, Zentrales Hochland) Verzehr von Pflanzensalz
Eating of Plant Salt

E2566

Eipo (West-Neuguinea, Zentrales Hochland) Frauen schlachten und garen zwei Schweine
Women Butcher and Steam Two Pigs

E2902

Eipo (West-Neuguinea, Zentrales Hochland) Herstellen einer Maultrommel
Making a Jew's Harp

E2558

Eipo (West-Neuguinea, Zentrales Hochland) Herstellen einer Peniskalebasse ''sanyum''
Making a Penis Gourd (''Sanyum'')

E2654

Heunemann, D., Simon, F., and Simon, A.

Eipo (West-Neuguinea, Zentrales Hochland) Spielen einer Maultrommel
Playing a Jew's Harp

E2559

Heunemann, D., Simon, F., and Walter, S.

Eipo (West-Neuguinea, Zentrales Hochland) Gartenbauarbeiten (Hochbeetbau)
Work in the Garden (Sweet Potato Mounds)

E2660

Heunemann, D. and Schiefenhövel, W.

Eipo (West-Neuguinea, Zentrales Hochland) Aggression gegen eine getötete Zauberin
Aggression Toward a Killed ''Witch''

HF 92

Koch, G., Schiefenhövel, W., and Simon, F.

Eipo (West-Neuguinea, Zentrales Hochland) Neubau des sakralen Männerhauses in
Munggona
Construction of the Sacred Mens' House at Munggona

E2675

Heunemann, D. and Heinz H.-J.*

Feuerbohren und Tabakrauchen
Making Fire and Smoking

E1822

Sprungspiel der Männer (//oli)
The Bushmen Grasshopper Game (//oli)

E1823

Herstellen eines Giftpfeils
Making a Poisoned Arrow

E1824

Jagd auf Springhasen
Hunting Springhares *(Pedetes capensis)*

E1825

Federstabspiel der Männer ''xhana''
The Feather-Reed-Spinner Game of Men ''Xhana''

E1826

Aufheben eines Speise-Verbotes
Releasing a Person from a Food Taboo

E1827

Bau einer Schlingfalle
Setting a Snare

E1828

Herstellen eines Speeres für die Springhasenjagd
Making a Spear for Hunting Springhare *(Pedetes capensis)*

E1829

Festtanz ''guma''
Bushmen Exorcising Dance ''Guma''

E1830

Stockwurfspiel der Männer ''//ebi''
The Stick Game of the Men ''//Ebi''

E1831

---

*All !Ko-Bushmen (Botswana, Kalahari).

Herstellen eines Jagdspeeres
Making of a Hunting Spear

E1847

Herstellen eines Köchers
Making of a Quiver

E1848

Mädchen Initation
!Ko Girls Puberty Ceremony

E1849

Bau einer Hütte
Construction of a Hut

E1850

Herstellen eines Jagdbogens
Making of a Hunting Bow

E1851

Tauschhandel an einer Wasserstation
Trading Objects at a Water Station

E1852

Ballspiel der Frauen "dam"
Ball Game of the Women "Dam"

E2024

Kalahari–Wettstreit "Jäger und Tier" Gestenspiel
Shooting the Animal (A Game of Gesture)

E2105

Spiel Honigdachs mit Zurechtweisung von Spielern wegen Regelverstosses
The Badger Game (!Aloce) and Players Being Reprimanded for Incorrect Performance

E2106

Spiel "Oryx Antilope" mit einer Auseinandersetzung zwischen zwei Spielgruppen
Gemsbok Game, Including an Argument Because of Incorrect Procedure

E2107

Herstellen von Perlen aus Straußeneierschalen
Making of Ostrich Eggshell Beads

E2108

Herstellen eines Kopfschmuckbandes aus Perlen von Straußeneierschalen
Making of a Headband from Ostrich Eggshell Beads

E2109

Anfertigen und Anbringen von Frauenkopfschmuck
Making Bead Decorations and Applying These and Others to Women's Heads

E2110

Tätowieren von Stirn und Schläfen
Tattooing of Forehead and Temple

E2111

Anfertigen einer Tragtasche aus Gazellenleder
Making of a Shoulder Bag from Antelope Skin

E2112

Herstellen von Sandalen
Making of Sandals

E2303

Herstellen eines Giftmörsers
Making of a Poison Mortar

E2302

Heunemann, D. and Sbrzesny, H.*

Herstellen einer Tabakspfeife aus einem Röhrenknochen
Making a Tobacco Pipe from a Tubular Bone

E2304

Anfertigen eines Armreifs aus Grashalmen
Making a Bracelet from Grass Blades

E2305

Anfertigen einer Halskette aus ''Duftstäbchen''
Making a Necklace from ''Aromatic Sticks''

E2306

Herstellen eines Löffels aus einem Schildkrötanpanzer
Making a Spoon from a Tortoise Shell

E2307

Sammeln und Verzehren von ''Veld-Kost''
Collecting and Consuming ''Veld'' Food

E2308

Herstellen und Anlegen eines Männer–Lendenschurzes
Making and Putting on a Men's Loin cloth

E2309

Jagen und Zubereiten eines Springhasan; Krankenbehandlung
Hunting and Preparing a Springhare; Medical Treatment

E2310

Anfertigen eines Frauen-Schurzes
Making a Women's Loin Cloth

E2315

Anfertigen von Zierstäbchen für die Mädchen Initiation
Making Ornamental Sticks for the Girl's Initiation

E2316

Speerjagd auf eine Oryx-Antilope
Hunting a Gemsbok with Spears

E2317

804   *G/wi Bushmen (Botswana, Central Kalahari).

Author Index*

---

*Numbers in italics indicate the page where the complete reference is given.

Chisholm, G. B., 710, *730*

Chomsky, N., 534, 535, 536, 546, *730*

Chow, I., 653, *764*

Cialdini, R. B., 358, *730*

Claessens, H. J. M., 624, *730*

Clark, L., 249, *730*

Clarke-Stewart, K. A., 228, *730*

Clastres, P., 624, *730*

Claus, R., 274, *730*

Clausewitz, K. v., 361, 409, *730*

Clifton, R., *730*

Cohen, D., *739*

Cohen, P. S., 539, *731*

Cohen, R., 619, 624, *731*

Colby, A., 707, *731*

Colgan, P., 148, *731*

Colinvaux, P. A., 624, *731*

Collett, P., *763*

Collis, G. M., *731*

Colombu, U., *740*

Comer, R., 318, *731*

Comolli, J., 249, *721*

Comrie, B., 536, *731*

Condon, W. S., 199, 200, 529, *731*

Conger, R. D., *729*

Conkey, M. W., 612, 613, *728*, *731*

Cook, M., 239, 368, *722*, *731*

Cooke, W. L., 211, *772*

Cooper, W. E., *736*

Corbit, J. D., *736*

Corning, P. A., 6, 624, 716, *731*

Corsaro, W. A., 509, 540, *731*

Coss, R. G., 368, *731*

Cott, H. B., 670, *731*

Count, E. W., 546, *731*

Craig, W., 67, *731*

Crain, St. M., *762*

Cranach, M. v., 110, *731*, *750*

Creutzfeldt, O., *731*

Croneberg, C. G., *779*

Cronin, C. L., 286, *731*, *784*

Crook, J. H., *733*

Crusec, J. E., *732*

Cüceloglu, D. M., 459, *732*

Culbertson, G. H., *732*

Cullen, E., *732*

Cunningham, M. R., 677, *732*

Curran, N. M., *754*

Curtiss, S., 569, *732*

Cutler, W. B., 428, 429, *732*, *769*

Cutting, J. E., *732*

Cybriwsky, R., 339, *756*

Daanje, A., 438, *732*

Dacy, M., *732*

Daglish, L., 268, *777*

Daldry, A. D., 268, *732*

Dalegivens, R., 408, *765*

Daléry, J, 278, *763*

Daley, P. C., *757*

Damas, D., *732*

Damon, F. H., *732*

Danielli, J. S., 705, *732*

Dann, H. D., 361, 366, 386, *732*

Dannhauer, H., 271, *732*

Danzinger, L., 551, *732*

Darracott, J., 414, *751*

Dart, R. A., 362, 409, 610, *732*

Darwin, Ch., 14, 19, 132, 445, 471, *732*

Dasen, P. R., 573, *732*

Daucher, H., 666, 667, *732*

Davies, P., *752*

Davis, A., 335, *732*

Davis, F. C., *732*

Dawkins, R., 33, 36, 91, 298, *732*

Day, R. H., 39, 40, *732*

Deag, J. M., *733*

Dean, R., 553, *741*

DeCasper, A. H., 200, *733*

DeChateau, P., 197, 199, 211, *733*, *786*

DeEskinazi, F. G., *766*

Degenhardt, A., 269, *733*

Delcomyn, F., 68, *733*

Delgado, J. M. R., 22, *733*

DeLong, A. J., 543, *733*

Demoll, R., 655, *733*

Demott, B., *733*

Dennis, W., 217, 551, 571, 575, *733*

DePaulo, B. M., 476, *733*

Desimone, D., 272, 277, *734*

Deutsch, R. D., 122, 338, 488, *733*

Devereux, G., *733*

DeVore, I., 321, 322, 323, 324, *733*, *755*, *769*

DeWaal, F. B. M., 135, 246, 514, *733*, *783*

Dickey, E., 459, *733*

DiFranco, D., 54, *733*

Dimberg, U., 476, 480, *733*, *766*

Dingwall, W. O., *733*

Disney, W., 61

Divale, W. T., 323, 418, *733*

Dodd, J., 22, *733*

Dodwell, P. C., *733*

Doe, C. Q., *742*

Doermer, C., 241

Dörner, D., 12, 43, *733*, *734*

Dörner, G., 257, 258, *734*, *778*

Dolgin, K. G., 439, *734*

Dollard, J., 362, 366, *734*

Donovan, W. L., *740*

Doob, A. N., 384, *753*

811

814

818

821

822

Subject Index

Abraham's sacrifice, as symbol, 309, 708

Abstraction, ability, 46; *see also Categorization; Schemata*

Accommodation, process of, 573

Ache (Paraguay), 100

Actions
co-action, 205
instinctive, 25

Adaptation, 4, 5, 14, 15, 16, 20, 23, 63, 608
arboreal, 608
categorizing of, 24
cultural, 7
horticulture and agriculture, 617
genetic, 15
perceptual, 66
phylogenetic, 7, 9, 16, 20, 23, 33, 36, 80, 107, 139, 174, 237, 265, 425, 581, 718, 719
rapid, 10
responses, 24
of small groups, 621
for speech, 528

Admonition, 481; *see also Gestures*

Adolescence, 602

Adrenaline, 69, 167

Advertising, messages as releasers, 680

Aesthetics, 667–671
bias by anti-art, 677
discovery as experience in, 702
display, role, 686
and fine arts, 665
perception mechanisms, 665, 672
preferences, 669
and sexual selection, 612

Affection, 216, 224
display, 599

Affiliation, 712, 713
behavior, 718
virtues of, 705, 708

Aggregations, role of, 167

Aggression, 87, 169, 216, 361–364, 556, 558
behavior, 362–364, 385, 391, 396
socialization, 396
black magic, as ritualized, 408
blockage, strategies of, 373, 499, 511, 512, 567
characteristics of, 362
demands, 539
drive, 68, 367, 386
encounters, 514
frenzy, 407
–frustration hypothesis, 366
educational, 393
ethological theory of, 367
exploratory function, 391, 393, 567, 602
forms of, 409–414
history, 408, 409
intergroup, 108
interspecific, 361
intraspecific, 361
models of, on television, 384
motivating mechanism for, 375
motor pattern for, 369
neuronal networks of, 385
norm-preserving, 304, 318, 319
pathological, 399, 408
pedagogical, 224
in play, 395
releasing signals, 170
retaliation of, 602
ritualized, 408
sex differences, 268
and sexual arousal, 263
signals for, 368
in small children, 379
spontaneous bouts of, 385
tension-releasing effect of, 381
theories of, 365–386

Agriculture
cultural adaptation for, 617

Dugum Dani (Papua New Guinea), tactile
communication, 435

Ecological building, 648
Economies
centralized, 657
free market, 657
Ecstasy, 408
Ecuador
precolombian figures, 488, 489
whorl patterns, 688
Education, 556, 564, 565, 620
Eels, 25, 68
Egalitarianism, 307
reproductive, 13
Egg-rolling. *See* Behavior
Eipo (New Guinea), 83, 116, 117, 119, 174,
179, 193, 203, 216, 220, 224, 292, 331,
391, 392, 403, 406, 411, 416, 428, 429,
557, 558, 571, 583, 589, 593, 631, 708
anal presentation, 486
birth, 201, 202
conversation, thematic content, 525–527
facial expression
of rejection, 472–474
of surprise, 471
of "very," 480
female display of the breast, 489
giving, 506
greeting, 434
head shaking, 471
housing, 634
infants, 557
baby talk, 207, 208
comforting of, 214
initiation group, 626
metaphor symbolism, 538
mother–child interactions, 210, 212
mother–father, as reference persons,
232
music, 693, 699, 700
net bags, trading value, 356
norm control, 393
paternal behavior, 226–228
play
fighting, 592
invitation to, 509–511
play-face, 137
requesting, 506, 539, 540
respect of possession, 505
sanctification of landmarks, 333
self-representation by art, 678, 679
sharing, 504
social exploration, 563
social grooming, 437

social model learning, 398
startle reaction, 487
strategy of requesting, 501
symbolism
of high and low, 538
of left and right, 539
taking, 506
trade, 352
valued objects, 356
verbalizing of feelings, 537
Eipomek Valley, 333, 356
Emblems, 481
Embracing; *see also Communication*
comforting effect, 430, 431
protective, 433
self-embracing, 432
Embryogenesis, 22
Emotions, 72, 476
expressive movements, 426
Empathy, 707
Empiricists, 572
Endorphins, 69, 70, 426; *see also Enkephalin*
Endowment profiles, 271, 273
Energizers. *See* Catecholamines
Energon, 7
Enga (New Guinea), 267, 407, 417, 420
conversation, 526
English language, 207, 507
Enkephalin, 79
Entities, haptic-visual, in concept formation, 539
Environment
modification, 568
urban, 177, 630
Envy, 307
Epilepsy, temporal lobe, 385
Epinephrine, 380; *see also Catecholamines*
Epistemology, biological, 8
Equality, 12, 306
ethic of, 13
illusion of, 40
Eskimos, 99, 323, 330
conflict songs, 545
head shaking, 471
respect of possession, 344
sharing, 341
singing duels, 402
Esteem
name dropping, 309
need for, 307
Estrogen, 168
Ethic
family, 714
group, 708
norms, 711
political, 717